www.wadsworth.com

wadsworth.com is the World Wide Web site for Wadsworth Publishing Company and is your direct source to dozens of online resources.

At *wadsworth.com* you can find out about supplements, demonstration software, and student resources. You can also send e-mail to many of our authors and preview new publications and exciting new technologies.

wadsworth.com
Changing the way the world learns®

Philosophical Problems in the Law

Fourth Edition

DAVID M. ADAMS

California State Polytechnic University, Pomona

THOMSON

WADSWORTH

Australia • Canada • Denmark • Japan • Mexico • New Zealand • Philippines
Puerto Rico • Singapore • South Africa • Spain • United Kingdom • United States

THOMSON
™
WADSWORTH

Publisher: Holly J. Allen
Philosophy Editor: Steve Wainwright
Assistant Editors: Lee McCracken, Anna Lustig
Editorial Assistant: Barbara Hillaker
Marketing Manager: Worth Hawes
Marketing Assistant: Annabelle Yang
Advertising Project Manager: Bryan Vann
Print/Media Buyer: Doreen Suruki
Permissions Editor: Stephanie Lee

Production Service: Matrix Productions Inc.
Copy Editor: Janet Tilden
Cover Designer: Yuo Riezeboos
Cover Image: Getty Images
Compositor: International Typesetting
    and Composition
Cover and Text Printer: Transcontinental—
    Louiseville

Printed in Canada
1 2 3 4 5 6 7 08 07 06 05 04

For more information about our products, contact us at:
Thomson Learning Academic Resource Center
1-800-423-0563

For permission to use material from this text or product,
submit a request online at www.thomsonrights.com

Library of Congress Control Number: 2003114703

ISBN: 0-534-58428-4

Wadsworth/Thomson Learning
10 Davis Drive
Belmont, CA 94002-3098
USA

Asia
Thomson Learning
5 Shenton Way #01-01
UIC Building
Singapore 068808

Australia/New Zealand
Thomson Learning
102 Dodds Street
Southbank, Victoria 3006
Australia

Canada
Nelson
1120 Birchmount Road
Toronto, Ontario M1K 5G4
Canada

Europe/Middle East/Africa
Thomson Learning
High Holborn House
50/51 Bedford Row
London WC1R 4LR
United Kingdom

Latin America
Thomson Learning
Seneca, 53
Colonia Polanco
11560 Mexico D.F.
Mexico

Spain/Portugal
Paraninfo
Calle Magallanes, 25
28015 Madrid, Spain

Contents

Chapter 2   Constitutional Law: Interpretation and the First Amendment   164

Chapter 3   *Constitutional Law: Equal Protection of the Laws* 276

Chapter 4   Criminal Law   384

Chapter 5   *The Law of Tort*   517

Preface

Challenges and Aims

This latest edition of *Philosophical Problems in the Law* has benefited from the strengths and shortcomings of its predecessors as well as comments and suggestions from many students and numerous helpful colleagues.

The first edition of this text began in frustration. Teaching a course in the philosophy of law to undergraduates at a four-year college or university presents challenges philosophy instructors often do not face in their other courses. These challenges derive from two basic features of a course in the philosophy of law. First, although the course normally draws some philosophy majors, the largest constituency frequently consists of a diverse audience of pre-law students majoring in everything from business administration and criminal justice to history and English literature. For many students, this course is their first exposure to philosophy. Second, the primary source materials for the course—judicial opinions and commentaries upon these opinions—are written in a drab, technical vocabulary for an audience of trained professionals. As such, the materials presuppose substantial specialized knowledge.

The instructor thus faces two challenges: (1) to teach students of varying ability levels and disciplinary backgrounds without presupposing too much sophistication with either philosophy or law and legal institutions, and (2) to motivate students, many of whom most likely are not philosophy majors, to care about the philosophical problems the law raises and to promote philosophical engagement with the law and legal texts. These challenges in turn generate two others: to balance the exploration of contemporary issues

and cases with an examination of broader philosophical problems and to provide enough and the right kind of primary source material.

Philosophical Problems in the Law, both in content and in organization, seeks to address the foregoing challenges and implement their ensuing objectives: to reach a diverse audience and to motivate philosophical inquiry about the law.

Content and Organization

As with the earlier editions, the fourth edition of *Philosophical Problems in the Law* is designed for use in introductory-level courses in philosophy of law or jurisprudence, with selections chosen for overall accessibility and philosophical merit. Where difficult philosophical or legal concepts or arguments are involved, the ideas are first presented and explained in chapter introductions.

The organization of individual chapters and the entire text reflects the aim of making the material more readily "teachable." Instead of being structured around explicitly philosophical theories and debates (with which students are unlikely to be familiar), the text is organized around general areas of law—constitutional, criminal, civil—and within each area more specifically around particular issues and questions. The present edition continues the aim of motivating engagement with abstract topics and problems (for example, the nature of law and legal reasoning, the limits of free expression, the purposes of criminal punishment) by situating them within a concrete context of controversial cases and emerging issues (the legality of "war crimes" tribunals, indecency on the Internet, fairness of the death penalty, and so on).

Most chapters begin with an illustrative case or recent controversy; all chapters include both an introductory overview and two or more sets of Study Questions that test students' knowledge and provoke them to apply and extend insights gained from the readings. Each chapter ends with several Cases for Further Reflection to be used as vehicles for classroom discussion or in connection with assigned written work.

Four other pedagogic aids are included. Appendices explaining legal citations and published law reports and presenting Amendments to the U.S. Constitution continue to appear in this edition. Also continuing is an expanded and updated third appendix providing a review of legal resource information available on the Internet. The glossary of legal terms, also expanded for this edition, continues to provide easy reference to frequently used legal terminology.

Changes in the Fourth Edition

Changes (for the better, it is hoped) continue with this latest edition. Updated selections (both cases and essays) on various theories and issues have been included.

Revisions/Expansions

Every chapter has been revised; Chapters 2 and 3 have been reconfigured and expanded.

Chapter 1, on the nature of law, now includes material from the United Nations war crimes tribunal for the former Yugoslavia (ICTY). The case of Slobodan Milosevic affords a contemporary context within which to situate ongoing debates concerning the meaning of "law" in the international arena. A new selection by Carlos Nino begins the section on classical theories of law. New material on legal positivism, legal realism, and critical race theory also appears, together with an excerpt from Melville's classic novella, *Billy Budd*.

Chapter 2, now entitled "Constitutional Law: Interpretation and the First Amendment," has been restructured both to introduce students to controversies regarding legal reasoning and constitutional interpretation, and to familiarize them with problems of freedom of expression and the "enforcement" of morality

as specific instances of those interpretive debates. Chapter 3 continues the focus upon problems of equality and discrimination in constitutional law. New cases on affirmative action and reparations for slavery are supplemented by a new section of readings dealing with family law. Chapter 4, on criminal law, contains several updated readings, as does Chapter 5 on tort law.

Updated Selections and Cases

As was true in earlier editions, new selections, both cases and essays, have been included in each chapter of the book. New cases in this edition include *Bush v. Gore*, *Ashcroft v. The Free Speech Coalition*, and *Michael H. v. Gerald D.* Recent decisions included in this edition include the "Pledge of Allegiance" case and recent Supreme Court rulings on affirmative action, "three-strikes" laws, the death penalty, and gay sex.

Alternative Paths

As with previous editions, this text comprises five chapters, each as self-contained as possible. This format allows the instructor to pursue alternative paths through the text. Some instructors, for example, may want to begin with Chapter 2 on constitutional interpretation and problems of liberty and morality, move through the chapters on criminal and tort law, and then return to the more heavily theoretical problems dealt with in Chapter 1. This strategy enables students to encounter first a variety of more specific issues and to read a number of judicial opinions, building up to an understanding of what is at stake in debates over the proper methods of legal reasoning or debates between, for example, naturalist and positivist theories of law.

Contributors

Contributors to this edition once again represent a broad spectrum of scholars and practitioners, embracing the work of legal academics, political theorists, and members of the bench and bar in addition to well-known philosophers. New contributors include Brian Bix, Richard Delgado and Jean Stefancic, Gerald Dworkin, Naomi Zack, Cass Sunstein, J. M. Balkin,

Alex Capron, Janet Dolgin, Douglas Husak, Paul Robinson, and David Dolinko.

Acknowledgments

I have accrued many debts throughout the evolution of this text, beginning with my mentors in legal philosophy: Ron Moore, University of Washington; Tom Grey, Stanford Law School; Richard Wasserstrom, University of California, Santa Cruz; and Michael Shapiro, University of Southern California. Among the many others who have kindly contributed their ideas and time over the years, I must thank John Arras, Barnard College; Robert Ashmore, Marquette University; Jeffrey Barker, Converse College; Karen Bell, California State University, Fresno; Raymond Belliotti, State University College, Fredonia; Philip Devine, Providence College; James Drier, Brown University; Gerald Dworkin, University of Illinois, Chicago; Charles Evans, City College, CUNY; Leslie Francis, University of Utah; H. Hamner Hill, Southeast Missouri State University; Lawrence Houlgate, California Polytechnic State University, San Luis Obispo; Douglas Husak, Rutgers University; Jack Green Musselman, St. Edwards University; James Nickel, University of Colorado at Boulder; Don Scheid, Winona State University; Roger Shiner, University of Alberta; Laurie Shrage, California State Polytechnic University, Pomona; Tom Simon, Illinois State University; Larry Solum, Loyola Law School; and Julie Van Camp, California State University, Long Beach. And for their specific comments on the modifications to this edition, I am indebted to Richard Bilsker, College of Southern Maryland; Richard W. Burgh, Rider University; Craig Duncan, Ithaca College; Thomas Huff, University of Montana; and Daniel E. Wueste, Clemson University. My assistant editor, Anna Lustig, was patient but kept me on track; Merrill Peterson and Janet Tilden were of much help regarding production and copyediting. Thanks to all.

Bibliographical Note

David M. Adams is Professor of Philosophy and Director of the Institute for Ethics and Public Policy at the California State Polytechnic University, Pomona. He is also a clinical bioethicist and an adjunct member of the Department of Medicine at Pomona Valley Hospital Medical Center, Pomona, California. He is a graduate of the University of California at Berkeley and the University of Washington (Ph.D.) and holds a master's degree in law from Stanford Law School. His publications include articles in legal theory, ethics, social philosophy, and bioethics. He is the co-author (with Edward L. Maine) of *Business Ethics for the 21st Century*.

Chapter 1

The Nature of Law and Legal Reasoning

The rule of law is something with which we live every day, but which we rarely pause to try to understand. We know that we must pay our taxes, stop at red lights, and refrain from stealing other people's property. We know that if we are threatened with a lawsuit we had better get a lawyer, and that if the suit is filed we may well wind up in court before a judge. We know that the judge's job is to apply something called "the law," as opposed to simply doing as he or she pleases, and we have a vague sense that this requirement is part of what it means to live in a society governed by the "rule of law," as opposed to the "rule of men." But what does living under the rule of law really mean? Why do we think it is better to live in a society in which there are statutes and judges than one in which these are absent?

Most of us are aware of the old theory that a regime of law is necessary to keep us in line, to prevent the "war of all against all" that some warn would immediately follow upon the breakdown of "law and order." Is law then exclusively about power, control over others? If so, who (or what) holds that power? Those who "make" the law? If so, how is the rule of law different from the rule of men? When the Allied nations, at the conclusion of World War II, put on trial the highest-ranking officials of the German government, was this merely (as some critics contended) an arbitrary exercise of naked power, an organized act of revenge? Or was it an attempt to reassert the primacy of law? If, as many people believed, punishing the Nazi leaders was the morally right thing to do, does this fact itself mean that the Nuremberg trials were genuine *legal* proceedings? What is the relationship between that which is morally right and that which is the law? It is obvious to most people that not everything that is morally wrong is also "against the law"; and similarly, not everything that is illegal is "wrong" in a moral sense. Do legality and morality have any more than a coincidental connection? Can a system of immoral rules and principles be a *legal* system? These are the questions and issues explored in Chapter One.

Because this text does not assume any previous study of either philosophy or the law, Section A of this chapter offers an overview of both, beginning with an imaginary case that presents a number of issues both legal and philosophical. Basic features of the law and the legal system are reviewed, followed by an introduction to some theories in the philosophical field of ethics that will have particular relevance to many of the topics covered in this book.

Section B provides a concrete context within which to approach questions about the nature of law and legality: the so-called Nuremberg trials, held at the close of World War II. Robert Jackson and Charles Wyzanski debate the nature of the "law" to which the Nazi leaders were subjected; the documents from the proceedings of the

International Criminal Tribunal for the Former Yugoslavia demonstrate the continuing relevance of the Nuremberg debate for basic questions in international law.

Section C explores two classical theories of law: legal positivism and natural law theory. A fictional case by Carlos Nino introduces the range of arguments commonly made by positivists and naturalists. English legal theorists John Austin and H. L. A. Hart defend versions of legal positivism, and contemporary philosopher of law Brian Bix surveys a few of the latest debates among legal positivists. Lon Fuller responds to Hart with his own conception of legal naturalism. The excerpt from the writings of St. Thomas Aquinas presents the classic formulation of the natural law position. Finally, Martin Luther King, Jr.'s "Letter from Birmingham Jail" illustrates one way in which Aquinas's views on the relationship of natural to human law can be translated into political action moral commitment.

Section D examines three further views of the nature of law, each with roots in the twentieth century: American legal realism, represented here by Oliver Wendell Holmes and Jerome Frank; critical legal studies, outlined by Mark Tushnett and assessed by Andrew Altman; and the interpretive theory of contemporary legal philosopher Ronald Dworkin.

Section E looks at several recently emerging philosophies of law. Federal judge and legal scholar Richard Posner argues on behalf of the law and economics movement; Angela Harris and Margaret Radin articulate and defend forms of feminist jurisprudence; and the excerpt from Richard Delgado and Jean Stefancic outlines the concerns of scholars working in critical race theory.

The readings are followed by several Cases for Further Reflection. The case of *Riggs v. Palmer* famously presents a classic confrontation between legal positivism and natural law in a case involving an heir who murders his grandfather to get rich. This case is followed by an equally famous fictional courtroom drama from the pen of Herman Melville: the trial of the sailor Billy Budd, from Melville's short novel of that name. Another case dealing with the high seas dates from the first half of the nineteenth century. Named after the slave ship *Antelope*, the case chronicles the dilemmas raised when courts were asked to rule on the legality of the slave trade. The "Problem of the Grudge Informer," written by Lon Fuller, nicely portrays the clash of various jurisprudential perspectives in an imaginary state making the transition to democratic rule after years of dictatorial oppression at the hands of the Fascist "Purple Shirts."

A. Philosophy and the Law

The Case of the Overcrowded Lifeboat

In this section, we will cover some basics: the nuts and bolts of the law and the legal system, and the general areas of philosophy most relevant to the study of law. Both to focus our discussion and to illustrate the relevance of philosophy and the law, let's begin with a hypothetical case study, which we can call "The Case of the Overcrowded Lifeboat."

> You are a judge faced with the following case: Several months ago, a 40-foot chartered yacht left Long Beach headed for Hawaii. On board were about forty passengers and crew. The cruise proceeded without incident for two days, but the third saw the yacht confront a terrific storm of unexpected strength and severity. The yacht was badly damaged by smashing waves and eventually began to list and then sink. Because the ship's radio was knocked out soon after the storm hit, the crew were unable to call for help. The captain and some of the passengers were swept away and drowned. The first mate, two crew members, and a number of passengers managed to clamber into a lifeboat and weather the tail end of the storm. (The yacht regularly kept two lifeboats, but during the emergency one was found to be unseaworthy and thus could not be used.)
>
> Adrift in the lifeboat, the remnant of the crew surveyed the situation: the boat could seat twenty people comfortably; twenty-four could ride in the boat without serious danger of causing the craft to founder. Every additional passenger added above twenty-four, however, significantly increased the risk that the boat would capsize or sink (especially in rough seas), yet there was no way of telling precisely how many more people the boat could accommodate while still affording those aboard any real chance of survival. The total number of people now in the boat was twenty-three.
>
> The ship had sunk during the early hours of the morning, and with the first light it immediately became apparent to those in the boat that some survivors still lived and were swimming in the water nearby. When these unfortunates saw that a lifeboat had endured the ordeal, they made for it as quickly as they could. Soon six desperate souls were yelling to those in the boat, asking to be helped aboard. The first mate now had a dilemma: how many, if any, of the swimmers should he try to save? After some moments of seemingly agonizing reflection on his part, the first mate himself reached out and helped aboard the strongest among those in the water. Many of the people already in the boat were older—retirees on their way to lounge in the lazy Hawaiian sun. The mate knew that their only hope was to row toward the main shipping route (from which they had been blown some distance by the storm) in hopes of being spotted. He needed, he felt, a robust man to help row; hence his choice. The mate refused the remaining five permission to enter. At one point, when two swimmers tried to climb aboard anyway, the mate ordered two crew members to push them off. This they did. The bodies of the five were found later by the search-and-rescue team. One of the deceased was a woman three weeks pregnant.
>
> After three days of hard rowing and a narrow escape from a sudden squall, the

lifeboat was spotted by a commercial fishing boat and all aboard were returned safely to shore. After investigating the matter, the Coast Guard took the first mate and the two crew members into custody; they were eventually turned over to civil authorities and indicted in state court on six counts of murder.

Because of the unusual nature of the case, the defendants have waived their right to a jury trial, and the case is brought before you. The relevant law in this case consists of two statutes, one related to the crime charged and one concerning the defense relied upon by the mate and crew:

1. In your state, the penal code defines murder as follows: "Murder is the unlawful killing of a human being with malice aforethought" (that is, with the purpose or intent to kill).

2. Your state defines the defense of "general justification" as follows: "Conduct that the actor believes to be necessary to avoid a harm or evil to himself or to another is justifiable, provided that the harm or evil sought to be avoided by such conduct is greater than that sought to be prevented by the law defining the offense charged."

One further item is relevant to your deliberations. Like many questions of law, that presented here may be affected to one degree or another by prior rulings. Your preliminary investigation turns up one such prior case: *United States v. Holmes* 1 Wall Jr. 1, 226 Fed. Cas. (1842). The case involved a sailing ship, the *William Brown*, which set sail from Liverpool bound for Philadelphia carrying British immigrants to the United States. Off Newfoundland, the ship struck an iceberg and quickly began to sink. The captain, crew, and passengers abandoned ship. Most of the survivors, the ship's mate, and several sailors wound up in a "longboat" (about 22 1/2 feet long). Soon overcrowded, the boat held forty-one, but was meant to carry only a fraction of that number.

On the second day adrift, the sea grew rough, several holes appeared in the overstrained seams, and the mate at last gave the order "men, fall to work, the boat must be lightened or we will all be lost." One robust sailor, Holmes, went to work. Vowing not to throw over any women or children and "not

to part man and wife," Holmes and his fellow crewmen threw overboard close to a dozen men. Subsequently, the survivors were rescued and Holmes charged with murder. Holmes was convicted on the grounds that, although "the law overlooks the taking of life under circumstances of imperious necessity," passengers must be given priority over sailors, and lots must be cast in determining who should be sacrificed. Neither principle had been honored.

Based on these facts, how would you decide the case before you, and on what grounds?

Before we explore this question further, let's look at the law and then at philosophy.

Sources of Law

The law has many sources. For our purposes, we can boil these down to four: *legislative* law; *judicial* law; *constitutional* law; and *administrative* law. Legislative law, or what is sometimes called *statutory* law, consists of the enactments of an elected, legislative body, such as the California State Assembly or the United States Congress. An *ordinance* is another form of written, legislative law, usually referring to the laws passed by a local government body, such as a city council, or county board of supervisors. After being passed, statutes and ordinances remain in force until they are either repealed by the legislative body that created them or ruled unconstitutional by a state or federal court (explained below). Two such statutes are at stake in our lifeboat case: a statute defining "murder" and a statute defining a defense to criminal charges based on "general justification."

Judicial law derives from the process of *adjudication*, that is, the process by which courts apply statutes, ordinances, or constitutional provisions to the facts of a particular case. Courts must apply the language drafted by legislatures to a variety of circumstances, some of which may well not have been fully anticipated by the law's drafters. This means that courts often must interpret what a legislature has said—the rules, of course, cannot apply themselves. As an example, consider the second of the two statutes in our lifeboat case. As the judge in the case, you must decide whether the facts warrant the appeal to "general justification." This may not be an easy matter (we'll look at that in a moment). Just how courts should go about interpreting the written law is a fascinating and contentious issue, which we explore later in this chapter.

The process of adjudication calls upon courts to issue rulings based upon the application of the written law to various circumstances. In this way, courts may develop new legal doctrines that, in turn, also become part of "the law." Lawyers sometimes call judge-made law *case law* or *common law*, to distinguish it from legislative sources. A central element of case law is the principle of *stare decisis*—the process of following the points of law established by other courts in earlier cases. Courts apply *stare decisis* by attempting to use previous decisions as points of reference to guide their decision in a new case. This process is known as following *precedent*, where precedent refers to the authority of a prior ruling in a similar case. By following precedent, courts may actually extend the law to fit unanticipated or new facts. Like the interpretation of written law, however, the process of identifying and following relevant precedent is not necessarily easy. Consider the precedent given in our lifeboat case, which is *U.S. v. Holmes*. In determining whether to follow the guidance afforded by the decision in *Holmes*, you must first decide how closely the facts of our case match the facts of that one. What are the similarities? What are the differences? And are the differences significant legally?

Constitutional law is perhaps best thought of as a kind of hybrid of legislative and judicial law, since it borrows from both. Each state, as well as the federal government, possesses a written constitution, which sets out the basic structure of the state or national government. Consider the federal Constitution. The various "articles" of this document provide for the creation of Congress, of the executive branch of government (the presidency), and for a system of federal courts, topped by the U.S. Supreme Court. The original articles have been supplemented by written "amendments," dealing both with procedural matters (such as the election of senators) and with fundamental rights (such as the right to "equal protection of the laws"). Constitutional law is similar to legislative law in that it exists in the form of a written document; however, much of what lawyers study in law school under the heading of "constitutional law" is really judicial or case law—decisions of courts like the U.S. Supreme Court, wherein one or another provision of the written Constitution has been interpreted and applied. So, for example, cases involving free speech on the Internet, abortion, and discrimination against gays in employment have all been decided under the Constitution and have become part of constitutional law, even though none of these specific topics were included by the framers in the original Constitution of 1789.

One further and very important feature of constitutional law links adjudication and legislation. Courts have the power to invalidate legislative enactments that violate provisions of a state or federal constitution. This power, known as *judicial review*, was not explicitly assigned to the courts by the federal Constitution; nonetheless, the Supreme Court inferred that such a power is implicit in the so-called "supremacy clause" of the Constitution, which declares itself the "supreme law of the land."

A fourth type of law, administrative law, comprises all of the regulations, standards, and decisions that derive from the many administrative agencies created by Congress and the executive branch. These agencies, such as the Federal Communications Commission, the Environmental Protection Agency, and the Food and Drug Administration, were created to regulate certain areas of social life. Such agencies have the authority to issue regulations that have the force of law.

Substantive Law

Regardless of its source, the law can usefully be sorted into one of two types: *substantive* or *procedural*. The principal areas of substantive law are *civil* law and *criminal* law. Civil law is typically defined as law regarding private disputes between parties over property, business transactions, accidents and injuries, and so on. In this sense, "private party" can mean an individual person, a small company, or a huge multinational corporation. "Private," in other words, simply means that the entity involved is not governmental. The category of civil law includes everything from sexual harassment claims to suits for breach of contract to multimillion-dollar legal actions against tobacco companies or breast-implant manufacturers. Personal injury lawsuits, involving the law of *tort*, make up an increasing number of civil cases.

Criminal law is defined as law concerning wrongs against the state, rather than against a private party. When someone commits a robbery or a murder, the perpetrator has wronged us all, violating the rules by which we have all agreed to abide. Criminal law is probably the most visible aspect of the law for most people, endlessly dramatized in movies and on TV. The substantive criminal law is, of course, the law at stake in the lifeboat case with which we began.

Procedural Law

Where substantive law deals with the actual rights and wrongs of life, procedural law is, in effect, the legal referee. Procedural law regulates the process of resolving a civil lawsuit or criminal case. For example, procedural regulations in every state stipulate how an initial complaint in a lawsuit is to be filed, how pretrial motions and fact-finding are to be conducted, how evidence is to be gathered, shared, and then presented at trial, and how appeals are to be handled.

Procedure in civil and criminal cases is largely similar, the differences being attributable in many cases to special rights and protections afforded to criminal defendants under state and federal constitutions. In a typical civil case, the official proceedings begin with the *pleadings*, that is, the documents filed in court by the plaintiff (lodging a complaint) and by the defendant (responding to a complaint). Following the submission of pleadings, the process of *discovery* commences. During this phase, evidence is gathered by both sides, involving, among other things, depositions (sworn testimony) and requests for documents, results of medical examinations, and the like. A *pretrial* hearing is usually conducted by the judge assigned to the case to determine whether the parties are prepared to go to trial. After a jury is selected, a trial is conducted, at the conclusion of which the jury reaches a verdict for the plaintiff or for the defendant.

Procedure in criminal cases is similar, prefaced by the steps necessary to process a crime. When a suspect in a criminal case has been arrested, he or she typically makes an initial appearance in court and is apprised of his or her legal rights, including the right to have an attorney. A *preliminary hearing* is often called to examine the basis for the charges against the defendant, although this step may be waived by the accused. This hearing offers the accused the opportunity to challenge the prosecution's case before the court. If the judge determines that sufficient evidence exists to send the case to trial, the defendant will then face an *indictment*, or formal presentation of the charges against him or her. At an *arraignment*, the defendant must then enter a plea to the charges in the indictment. Criminal defendants have three pleas available to them: (1) A plea of *not guilty* results in a trial.

(2) In a *guilty* plea, the defendant admits having committed the crime and awaits a sentence imposed by the court. As a practical matter, the great majority of guilty pleas are the result of a *plea bargain* or arrangement in which the defendant agrees not to contest the charges if the prosecutor will agree to a lesser sentence. (3) A third plea, less frequently used, is called *nolo contendere* (literally, "I do not contest"). This plea is functionally equivalent to a guilty plea but does not actually admit culpability. A plea of nolo contendere cannot be used in later civil or criminal proceedings as an admission of guilt.

In both civil and criminal cases, the losing party has the right to *appeal* a verdict. An appeal asks another court—an *appellate* court—to examine whether an error occurred in the proceeding in which the losing party lost. Appellate courts do not retry the facts or hear evidence. The role of the appellate court is simply to review the allegation that an error took place at the trial level. Given their place in the system, appellate courts frequently set precedent that then becomes part of the law.

In addition to regulating the trial process, as outlined above, procedural law sets out the roles and functions of the various participants involved in a court proceeding. The job of the judge is to oversee courtroom procedure and to serve as the determiner of the law. The judge is the authority on what the law requires in a given case, and he or she must rule on many different requests from the parties to a civil or criminal proceeding. The parties to a legal case are referred to by standard designations: the *plaintiff* is the person who files a complaint in a civil case; hence the plaintiff could be an individual or a corporation. The *defendant* in a civil case is the person against whom a complaint has been lodged. In criminal law, the defendant is the person charged with an offense.

Whether a proceeding is civil or criminal, the parties involved have lawyers. The basic role of the attorney, according to *Model Rules of Professional Conduct* of the American Bar Association, is one who "zealously asserts the client's position under the rules of the adversary system." What does this mean? Ours is an *adversary* system of law, based on a concept of justice that assumes that the truth is most effectively discovered and justice best obtained by trials in which two opponents vie with each other, clashing before an impartial tribunal, each side testing the other's merits as thoroughly as possible. In this way, it is assumed, all of the facts relevant to an issue will be brought to light and a just verdict thereby rendered. In this light, serving the interests of one's client and serving the "system" are thought to be one and the same.

The final part of the court system consists of the jurors. The jury in a civil or criminal case is composed of citizens who are to serve as the "triers of fact"—the people who sift through the evidence, listen to both sides, and determine what the facts actually are. The jury receives instructions from the judge about the law and must then determine the facts and apply the law to them in order to reach a verdict. Sometimes the roles of the judge and jury are consolidated. In this proceeding, known as a "bench trial," the defendant typically has waived his or her right to a trial by jury, and it falls to the judge to function as both the "finder of fact" and the authority on the law.

The Structure of the Legal System

In the largest sense, the legal system includes everyone who has a role in creating, maintaining, enforcing, changing, or in some way supporting the law. Because most of the issues and questions of philosophical interest in the law have to do with its meaning and interpretation, our primary focus within the legal system will be the courts.

The court system comprises two parallel tracks: federal and state. There are three levels of federal courts in the United States. The first level consists of U.S. District Courts. Currently more than ninety such courts function as the trial courts of the federal system. The U.S. Circuit Courts of Appeal, numbering thirteen, review appeals on all matters of federal law. The U.S. Supreme Court is the final authority on all cases arising under the Constitution, federal statutes, or administrative laws. Most states have a three-tier system of courts that parallels the federal system.

Courts differ also as to their jurisdiction. *Jurisdiction* refers to the power or authority to pass judgment on a given type of case and with respect to certain parties. If a court lacks jurisdiction over persons or issues, it cannot hear the dispute involved. Federal and state courts have differing jurisdictions. In the federal system, cases can be presented when a federal statute, administrative regulation, or provision of the Constitution is involved, or when parties from differing states are embroiled in a controversy. State courts, by contrast, have jurisdiction over the great majority of civil and criminal cases that arise on a daily basis, and over the interpretation and application of their own state constitutions.

Philosophy and Ethics

Suppose you are asked to look at some problem "philosophically." What does that mean? For most people, such a request would be taken as an invitation to get some perspective, to look at the "big picture," to reflect on a variety of factors. In one sense, this reaction captures what it means to have a philosophical attitude. Philosophers try to adopt that frame of mind with regard to a number of fundamental questions. Philosophers wonder what any of us is doing here, about the ultimate purpose of life. Why, philosophers ask, does the universe exist at all? How much, if anything, can we truly know about the world around us? What is truth? Love? Time? Philosophy is concerned with these kinds of fundamental questions and is an attempt to reflect upon them in a sustained and critical way.

Recall now the lifeboat case with which we began this section. It is important to see that several of the legal questions that you, as the judge, must resolve, lead directly into philosophical questions about knowledge, reality, and right and wrong. Consider, for example, the language of the murder statute: "killing a human being with malice aforethought." One obvious problem here is whether the mate and the crew "killed" anyone. Certainly people died, but saying that they were killed seems to ascribe some connection between the mate's actions and the deaths. Did the mate "kill" the swimmers, or did he simply leave them to die? What, exactly, is the difference? And why is the difference important? Trying to puzzle out this problem involves issues in the philosophical field of *metaphysics*—the study of the basic nature of reality. A fundamental part of our picture of the world—which the law assumes—says that persons exist as agents who can act on and cause changes to occur in the world, and for which they can then (at least sometimes) be held responsible. However, this metaphysical picture does not always fit our experience easily. In the lifeboat case, for example, the prosecution will undoubtedly insist that the deceased would not have died but for the neglect of the first mate and crew. But again, for all we know, they would not have died but for the terrible storm that swamped the yacht. The defense attorneys will claim that the swimmers died from exposure; or they might confess that it was an "act of God" for which no person is responsible. But couldn't the mate have intervened by his own agency and saved at least some of the swimmers? Recall also that the crew, at one point, pushed off several swimmers who had tried to climb aboard. Is "pushing someone off" the boat an action for which the crew is responsible? Or should it be viewed merely as failing to rescue the swimmers? This is a crucial question, as it turns out, for as we will learn in Chapter Five, the law traditionally has held people accountable only for their acts, not for their omissions.

A further question is whether the crew acted with "malice aforethought." As we will discover in Chapter Four, this term refers to the state of mind of the crew at the time. Specifically, did the crew, when they refused the swimmers permission to enter the boat, intend for them to die? Or did they intend merely that the swimmers stay out of the boat? The defense will maintain the latter, stating that the crew merely intended that the swimmers remain in the water and out of the boat; maybe they even hoped that the swimmers could miraculously survive. The prosecution, however, will insist that the obvious and easily foreseeable consequence of remaining in the water was death, and that the crew therefore must have intended for the victims to die. After all, if I point a loaded gun to your head and pull the trigger, I can't realistically say that I didn't intend to kill you, but only to pass a bullet through your head, hoping for a miracle. These issues turn, ultimately, on questions that involve metaphysics and *epistemology*—the theory of knowledge. How do we know what the crew really intended? How do we describe their state of mind?

Some of the most profound philosophical questions raised by our lifeboat case fall within the field of *ethics* or moral philosophy—philosophical reflection upon the values and standards that shape our lives and guide our actions. What makes life worthwhile? What are the really important values? Does being moral lead to happiness? Is morality simply a matter of self-interest, obeying the rules and doing what you should simply to avoid hassles or punishment? What rules, principles, or standards should we live by? What validates or justifies the principles I choose to follow? Are those standards relative to my culture or time or place, or are there "objective" moral truths applicable to all cultures and times? Facing up to these questions and trying to think them through as carefully as possible constitute the task of philosophical ethics.

There are many ways of thinking philosophically about moral issues, and to review all of them would transform this into a textbook in ethics. However, at least two general approaches to moral questions have particular relevance to the philosophy of law. It is useful, therefore, to look briefly at each of these approaches.

Utilitarianism and the Greater Good

The first approach to moral issues is illustrated by a common reaction to the lifeboat case: namely, that the mate and crew did the right thing, since they *acted for the greater good*. Think, for example, of the numbers of lives involved. The boat could hold only so many people; with too many aboard, the boat would sink. Assuming that everyone would have died had all five of the swimmers been welcomed into the boat, what reason would there be to prefer twenty-nine deaths to the deaths of five (or six, if we count the fetus)? The underlying appeal here is to the good consequences that would flow from the actions taken by the crew. Philosophically, the idea could be put this way: *The morally right act is that which will produce the best consequences for all affected.* Philosophers call such an outlook *consequentialist* because it makes the consequences of an act the key to understanding its moral status. Philosophers have attempted in several ways to make the basic idea behind consequentialist thinking more precise. For our purposes, however, it suffices to focus on just one of these attempts, and that is the theory called *Utilitarianism*.

The most prominent philosophers to write extensively on utilitarianism were British philosophers in the eighteenth and nineteenth centuries: Jeremy Bentham (1748–1832) and John Stuart Mill (1806–1873). Bentham regarded utilitarianism as an important tool for social and legal reform—a blueprint for legislation. Bentham ridiculed the criminal justice system of England at the time, calling it excessively brutal and outdated. A person's action is criminal, Bentham reasoned, only if it produces genuinely harmful consequences for others. Bentham's cause was taken up by Mill. Mill's book *Utilitarianism*, published in 1863, became a classic statement of the view.

According to utilitarianism, the central moral requirement, sometimes called the "Principle of Utility," can be stated in this way: *Always act so as to bring about the greatest net good for all of those affected by your actions.* Several aspects of this statement must be carefully examined. To begin with, the principle of utility demands that we strive for the greatest *net* good. This reference is meant, of course, to recognize that we may on some occasions be forced to choose between alternatives that each have bad consequences as well as good. In such a case, utilitarianism says, we must choose the course of conduct that has the greatest amount of good or the least amount of bad. Secondly, utilitarianism insists that we do that which will produce the most good. But what do "good" and "bad" mean here? Just what is the "good" that is to be maximized? Plainly, the utilitarian must answer this question, and Bentham, Mill, and later utilitarians have realized this, although not all have agreed on the best response.

Bentham and Mill both believed that the good we must seek to maximize and the bad that we must minimize, reduce, in the final analysis, to pleasure and pain. The theory that explains the good in terms of pleasure and the bad in terms of pain is called *hedonism*. Hedonism holds that pleasure (and the avoidance of pain) is the only thing of intrinsic value or worth—that is, the only thing worth having just for what it is. All of the other things that we humans want—money, cars, fame—are valuable only as a means to obtain pleasure or avoid pain. Imagine, for example, asking someone to explain why she wants a university degree. "To get a good job," she answers. But why do you want that? "So I can make more money." But why do you want more money? "So I can buy things that give me pleasure." Why do you want more pleasure? Most people would find the last question rather strange: everybody wants pleasure just because it is what it is—pleasurable. Here we seem to come to a point at which the thing we desire or seek is sought just for itself, not as a means to get something further. This is the good that Bentham and Mill believed all of us want, ultimately, to get the most of.

Not all utilitarians are hedonists, however, and this is explained by the fact that hedonism itself raises further questions, not all of which have found satisfactory answers. For example, are all pleasures to be regarded as on a par? Is the pleasure derived from donating money to a museum or writing a great novel really no better than the pleasure associated with getting drunk or staring vacantly at the television for hours? Although Bentham seemed willing to accept this consequence, Mill and other utilitarians were less comfortable with it. Mill tried to distinguish between "higher" and "lower" pleasures, insisting that the higher pleasures were more desirable. Philosophers are divided over whether Mill's effort to establish this point is convincing. Others have accused hedonists of placing the cart before the horse. What human beings truly seek, these critics argue, are the things that enable us to lead genuinely and uniquely human lives—for example, friendship, love, and the pursuit of knowledge. These are the good things of life that human beings need, and pleasure usually accompanies them. However, the pleasure such things bring is not what we ultimately seek; in fact, it is often only when we don't specifically aim at getting pleasure that we find it.

If pleasure is not the good that the principle of utility instructs us to maximize, what then is the good to which it refers? Some utilitarians have tried to avoid the problematic implications of hedonism by talking in terms of "happiness" and "unhappiness": the principle of utility entreats us always to act so as to produce the "greatest happiness," leaving it undetermined exactly how happiness is to be cashed out. Other utilitarians have spoken of "satisfying people's preferences" as the good to be maximized in the utilitarian calculus. *Preference utilitarianism*, as it is sometimes called, asks us to take account of the preferences or interests of all of those affected by our conduct; the goal is then to bring about the greatest net satisfaction of preferences.

Two further aspects of the principle of utility are important. Utilitarianism requires that it be possible, at least in principle, to identify and aggregate or add up all of the relevant preferences (or, in the hedonistic version, pleasures and pains) of all of those affected by one's actions. This may strike you as not being terribly realistic, and for several reasons. Are people's preferences really comparable? How can the pleasure I derive from one course of action be compared to the pain you might derive from it? How is the judge or legislator supposed to know whose preference is stronger, or whose pain is greater? Moreover (and this raises a related concern for utilitarians) how can any of us know the precise impact that our actions will have? Wouldn't I need to have the power to see far into the future to know just what consequences my actions might have? To these kinds of questions, utilitarians have responded variously. Some, most notably Bentham, thought it actually possible to quantify episodes of pain and pleasure, and to devise an interpersonal scale or metric against which to compare one person's pleasure with that of another. To many, this view has seemed to require heroic assumptions that just are not realistic. Other utilitarians have responded more circumspectly, claiming only that it is possible to make at least some assumptions allowing for comparisons (for example, that most people prefer the pleasures of friendship or good health over the pleasure of scratching an itch or watching TV). Many utilitarians would insist that omniscience and clairvoyance are not necessary to apply the principle of utility: no one can appreciate in advance all of the consequences of his or her actions, so the best anyone can be expected to do is to judge in light of the best understanding possible at the time. We are all human, after all, and we have to live with our limitations.

One of the most common objections to the moral theory of utilitarianism concerns what the principle of utility might allow—or even require—people to do, under certain circumstances. One complaint is that the principle of utility might, on some occasions, ask too much of us. Suppose for a moment that you are a passenger on the lifeboat. Suppose also that you are a football player weighing 250 pounds and that you notice that two of the swimmers in the water are half your weight. If you were to jump into the water (and thus end your life), two people might be welcomed into the boat in your place without affecting the overall load in the boat. From a purely numerical standpoint, it might seem that it would be better for everyone concerned (although certainly not for you in particular) if you were simply to end your own life. The greater good, in other words, might be best served through the self-sacrifice of your life. Yet, even if the principle of utility appears to demand this course of action, this would seem to many to be asking too much. In fact, some might object that you have a duty to live, and that any principle is just wrong if it seems to suggest otherwise. (We'll return to the subject of duty in a moment.)

The flip side of the complaint that utilitarianism may require too much of us is that it may demand a course of action that seems simply to be wrong. This, of course, is a serious charge for any moral theory— that is, any theory that purports to capture and explain what is most important in moral life. To understand this charge, consider the following case: A rash of violent crimes has plagued a community for some time. Law enforcement officials are baffled as to the perpetrator. Public outrage at the crimes is rising to fever-pitch, and something must be done to calm the public. The police decide to frame an innocent man for the crimes. A trial is held, and the man is convicted on phony evidence. The public anger is quelled and the community and law enforcement are content, but an innocent person's rights have been violated. One could argue, say critics of utilitarianism, that the greater good was best served in this case. However, a grave injustice has been done. Most of us, the critics contend, would insist that to sacrifice an innocent person in this way is wrong, regardless of the benefits to be gained from doing so.

How might a utilitarian respond to these charges? Each of these major arguments against the principle of utility turns on showing that the principle can require that people do something that would otherwise be believed to be wrong. The utilitarian might reply that utilitarianism, properly understood, does not lead to these counterintuitive results. Demanding that people kill themselves or that they be sacrificed in some way to the greater good are not, in fact, actions that would be legitimated or condoned by the principle of utility, despite what the critics say. Utilitarians who make this move often insist that careful attention be paid to the level on which the principle of utility is to be applied. The utilitarian weighing of costs and benefits is not to be undertaken merely on a case-by-case, short-term basis. Any rational person, the utilitarian might claim, must realize the importance of looking at the larger picture. Sacrificing yourself or others to the common good are not actions that have overall positive consequences in the long term. Using people as scapegoats in the name of the greater good does not maximize happiness over time. This is because much unhappiness and distress would be present in a society in which no one could feel safe or secure—in which no one could rely upon others to respect their rights. The utilitarian in this way argues that the principle of utility does not so much apply to individual actions at a particular time and place, but rather to social rules or conventions that are applicable broadly. Rules such as "Do not punish the innocent," which set standards valid in all situations, are justified on utilitarian grounds since the general observance of such rules produces the most good overall in the long run. This version of utilitarianism, often called *rule utilitarianism*, contrasts with *act utilitarianism*, the view that the principle of utility is to be applied to individual actions.

Let's return now to the case of the lifeboat. As we have seen, one way to defend the actions of the crew in refusing to rescue the swimmers is to appeal to a utilitarian calculation: better that five die than everyone perish. How might the prosecution respond? Aside from questioning whether the course of action taken was the one that actually promoted the greater good in the long run, the prosecuting lawyers are likely to ask what right the mate and crew had to decide who would live and who would die. This rhetorical question actually rests on a serious point, for the mate and crew arguably acted in ways that took innocent lives. They, like all of us, the prosecution might argue, had a duty to respect the lives of others. In this they failed. Let's look more closely at the moral outlook reflected in these arguments.

Deontology and Rights

The arguments of the prosecution in the case of the overcrowded lifeboat reflect an underlying approach to moral thinking contrasting sharply with the utilitarian. This view, often called *deontology*, insists that the central fact about moral life is that we all have *duties* or *obligations* to treat others in certain ways, and that these duties are based upon something other than the consequences of our or others' actions. The word "deontology" comes from the Greek root "deon," which means "duty." What makes a decision or an action morally worthwhile or right, according to deontologists, is not the effect it has or the consequences it produces, but rather the fact that it was the right decision to make, the right thing to do. Where consequentialists tend to be forward-looking—estimating the future impact of present actions—deontologists are more likely to look to other ways, examining actions already undertaken or relationships already formed as a basis for obligations in the present. That I have made a promise or a commitment to someone in the past, for example, might be for a deontologist a ground for a moral duty that I must fulfill to that person, regardless of whatever consequences would result from my keeping or breaking the promise.

Deontologism is part of a way of thinking about morality that has a long history, although we cannot examine that history here. It is enough to point out that the writings of contemporary deontologists have been influenced by several sources. One such source is the *natural law* philosophy of the Greek and Roman Stoic philosophers—a school of thought that flourished in the few centuries before and after the birth of Christ and (as we will see later in this chapter) continues to be a significant part of jurisprudential debate. Other sources of deontology are the Hebrew and Christian moral traditions. The common thread running throughout these views is the belief that there exist moral rules or standards of conduct that are universally valid and applicable to all human beings and that can be ascertained by us, at least in principle, through the use of our ability to reason. This universal or common moral code is variously referred to as "moral law" or "natural law." Many Jewish and Christian philosophers explicitly linked this idea of a moral law valid for everyone with their own religious doctrines of God, creation, and human destiny. According to these views, the supreme principle of morality might be "Do whatever God commands." Other deontological philosophers, however, have tried to argue that the

validity of these ultimate principles can be seen independently of more specific religious beliefs. One of the most influential of these philosophers was Immanuel Kant (1724–1804). It is especially instructive to consider Kant's version of deontology because he tried with great care to reconstruct this traditional way of thinking about morality and make explicit what it says and the assumptions upon which it rests. Moreover, Kant's theory has been enormously influential on philosophers of law.

Several concepts are important in understanding the deontological ethic defended by Kant. A review of these will make his theory more understandable and the contrast between deontology and consequentialism sharper. To begin with, Kant disagreed strongly with the hedonism of some of the utilitarians. Pleasure is not, Kant claimed, of intrinsic or inherent value. Nor, he insisted, does the moral value or worth of an action lie in the effects or in the results it produces, whether these are measured by units of pleasure, satisfaction of interests, or what have you. Second, and more fundamentally, Kant disagreed with the basic premises of all consequentialist theories—namely, that the moral value of an action is a function of its results. To understand Kant's reasons for this disagreement, consider another case of possible rescue. John Doe is sitting by the edge of a small lake, enjoying some relaxing sunshine. It is a weekday afternoon; Doe appears to be alone at the lake. He notices a figure down at the shore—a small child who appears to be in trouble in the water. No one else is around. Doe is an excellent swimmer, and the water in the lake is quite shallow. Doe wades into the water and rescues the child. Later we discover that the apparent hero in fact acted only because the child's parents owe him money and he believed that the "good deed" would hasten the repayment. If this is what Doe supposes, he should think twice. Kant would claim that the situation is not one of which Doe can be proud. Outwardly, Kant would say, Doe may have done the "right" thing, but surely he did not do it for the right reason. He acted selfishly, hence his actions really have no moral value. An action is right, Kant claims, only if it is done just because it is the right thing to do, not because doing so will get you something you want, whether that be money, fame, or the pleasure of thinking yourself a hero.

But how, according to the deontologist, can I know that my actions are right? How can I know what my moral duties to others are? To grasp Kant's answers to these questions, we have to explore a further aspect of his view.

Deontology and the Categorical Imperative

Kant assumed that whenever any of us does something deliberately, it is as if we were endorsing a private rule that we are choosing to follow. If I discover that my employer is in violation of state pollution laws and I decide to "blow the whistle" on him by writing to state authorities, I am effectively operating on the basis of a rule that says "When I am convinced that my employer is violating the law, I will alert law enforcement." I may not say this to myself in so many words, of course, but that is the rule I am implicitly endorsing. Kant called all such private rules "maxims," and he believed that those who take morality seriously would never follow a maxim that did not conform to the most basic of all moral principles, which Kant called the *categorical imperative*.

An imperative is a command of the form "You should do this," or "You ought not to do that." Some commands or imperatives, Kant observed, are *hypothetical*, or conditional upon some fact or preference. Examples of hypothetical imperatives include: "If you want to be hired, you should dress professionally"; "If you desire a raise, you ought to increase your productivity"; and "If you want to avoid liability, you should not act negligently." Each of these hypothetical imperatives takes as a given some end or goal already accepted or desired. Moral principles cannot command us in these merely hypothetical ways, Kant thought, since the demands of morality are not dependent upon how we feel or what we want. Feelings and desires are far too flimsy a basis for morality. After all, if the only reason you should act morally is that you feel like doing so or that you desire something in return, what happens when your feelings change (as they often do) or when your desire dissipates? Feelings and preferences are transient and thus too undependable a foundation for genuine moral principles. Hypothetical imperatives can even take the form of immoral demands, followed by people pursing their own ends. An example is an unscrupulous corporate executive who reasons "If we are to stay competitive, we must break any laws that get in our way." For all of these reasons, Kant concluded, a moral imperative must be categorical or absolute: it must be unconditional, providing an enduring incentive to act rightly. It is a mark of a genuine moral command that it tells us what we must do regardless of whether we want to do it.

The moral duties we have, then, as delineated in the deontological theory of Kant, are defined by the categorical imperative. Kant's discussion of the categorical imperative is notoriously complicated, and he himself reformulated the idea in several ways throughout his writings. The essence of his thinking, however, can be stated fairly straightforwardly. According to Kant, the basic and categorical rule behind all moral thinking says that *one ought always to act only on that maxim that one can will to be a universal law*, or, more simply, *act only in ways that you can imagine everyone acting*. This basic principle is one, Kant was convinced, upon which we all rely, whether we are conscious of it or not, in our everyday moral thinking. This is the principle we have in mind when we reprove people who act wrongly with the question "How would you like it if everyone did that?" The moral education of children often proceeds on this basis, getting the child to place herself in the other person's shoes.

To determine whether an action is morally right, I must articulate the maxim upon which it relies and then ask whether I could conceive of this maxim being a "universal law," that is, a rule for everyone. Recall, once more, the case of John Doe, the would-be rescuer. Let's modify the original facts. Suppose that, although he is an excellent swimmer and the water in the lake is quite shallow, Doe decides to leave, telling himself that he doesn't want to get involved. The child survives but is injured. If he were to think deontologically, Doe might pause to consider whether, if the situation were reversed, he would want a potential rescuer to leave him in the water. Kant argued that his deontological concept of morality convincingly explains the judgment that Doe would be acting wrongly in abandoning the struggling child. In the modified case, Doe acts on the basis of a maxim that could be expressed this way: "If it is inconvenient for me, I will refuse to help another, even when doing so would be easy and safe." Remember that Kant's idea is to determine whether someone's action is morally right by asking what it would be like if his maxim were to be universal, that is, if everyone were to act upon it. Kant observed that no one could actually will a maxim of "nonhelpfulness" to be a universal practice, for the world is such that we can be reasonably certain that we shall one day be on the receiving end of such beneficent gestures.

Consider one other example, involving the ethical standards of medical professionals. Imagine that you are a physician and that you have an elderly patient whom you have diagnosed with a terminal illness. You have just told the members of the patient's immediate family the truth about her condition; they now request that you keep the truth from the patient herself. "It will make her final days easier," they plead. Uncertain how to proceed, you delay informing the patient of her status. The patient, however, soon realizes that she is not improving, and one day she confronts you: "What's going to happen to me, doctor? Am I going to die?" What should you say? To act as the family had requested would be tantamount to acting on a maxim that could be expressed this way: "If deceiving my patient will keep him or her from possible suffering and make others happy, I will do so." Could you "will" this maxim to be a universal practice? A Kantian moralist might well respond that you could not, that no rational person would want to live in a world where this practice was the norm. To see why the Kantian would likely give such an answer, we must look at one last aspect of Kant's deontologism.

Deontology and Autonomy

We began our discussion of Kant by noting that acting morally, in his view, means doing what is right just because it is right: this is the only basis for action that has intrinsic worth and unconditional value. Kant tried to connect this idea with the claim that humans are rational beings to explain the value and importance of human life. Kant claimed that each person has an absolute worth, that each rational being exists as an "end in itself," that is, valuable simply by virtue of being what it is. Each of us has an intrinsic value; we do not exist or have importance only because others can use us to suit their purposes. It is for this reason that Kant restates the categorical imperative as follows: *Always act so as to treat others as an end and never as a means alone.* Now, notice that Kant is not saying that we may never use others as a means to something we might want. In fact, we use others all the time: commuters use the bus driver to get them to work; shoppers use manufacturers to supply goods for purchase; workers use their employers as a source of income; and so on. What Kant says is forbidden is treating others *only* as a means: You may use the bus driver as a way to get around, but you must also acknowledge the driver as a person, not just a uniform— as an individual with a life that matters. Kant's point

here is sometimes explained by saying that we must always respect the *autonomy* of others. By "autonomy" Kant means the ability to take charge of one's own life and to live in accordance with valid moral principles, rather than being led around by desires. Kant maintained that only human beings have the capacity intentionally to act in ways that are motivated by an awareness of moral duties. Autonomy is also often expressed in terms of the idea of self-determination: an autonomous person is a determiner of his or her own destiny, and moral relationships depend upon mutual respect for the autonomy of all rational beings. This suggests that respect for others involves, for example, helping them to further their own ends and goals.

The demand that we respect the dignity and worth of each and every person, as autonomous beings, may explain why no rational being could conceive of living in a world where lying to a dying person is a universal practice. To deceive the patient in this way, a deontologist could argue, is an affront to his or her dignity as an autonomous person. We can now fully appreciate the contrast between Kant's deontologism and the consequentialism of the utilitarians. The centerpiece of Kant's ethic is that to act morally is to act on principle—to do the right thing because it is right. This kind of deontological view insists that certain acts simply must not be done, regardless of the consequences that might flow from them. Even if it would make others extremely happy, it might still be wrong to conceal the truth or to break a promise. To lie to or deceive another would be to use that person as a means to the happiness of others— and this one must not do.

This point connects with another that is often made by deontologists. What Kant says about autonomy and treating other persons with dignity and respect is frequently expressed in the language of *rights*: To say that we must respect the lives of other autonomous beings is to say that they are entitled to or have a right to be so treated. A right typically is a claim that others do something for the person who holds the right (or that they refrain from doing something to him), and thus it correlates with a duty or obligation to act accordingly: if X owes money to Y, Y has a right to the money and X has a duty to pay; if I have a duty to rescue you by pulling you into the lifeboat, you have a duty to be so rescued.

The language of rights seems to presuppose a division between the public boundaries limiting your actions—boundaries set by everyone's respective rights—and a private realm of choice within which each of us is free to develop and pursue our own plans and projects in life. To have a right is to occupy a kind of moral space within which one can operate as one pleases, to enjoy a sphere of autonomy or a realm of protected choices and interests. Deontologists sometimes describe this power of right by saying that rights are like trump cards in a game of bridge: they take priority over other factors. (This is not always the case, of course, and few deontologists would declare that any given right is absolute, taking priority over everything else, including other rights.) As we will see, appeals to individual rights and respect for autonomy play a large part in the legal, as well as the moral assessment of many issues and problems covered in this text.

Objections to Deontology

Deontology, like consequentialism, has its critics. One of the most common complaints concerning Kant's deontology centers on what some perceive to be the excessive formality and abstraction of his view. Insisting that moral credit is to be awarded only to those who act solely for the sake of duty is often scorned as an arid and puritanical position, unconnected to any of the particular duties that arise out of the richness and diversity of human relationships; and while Kant may have shown us what morality is like when it is based purely on reason alone, few people actually live their moral lives in this fashion. Defenders of Kant respond that, although one must perform an action from duty to be morally worthy, this is not inconsistent with being a compassionate and loving individual. The happiness and satisfaction that come from doing good for others is not banned from Kant's deontology, as long as they are accompanied by the proper motive for moral action.

More specific criticisms focus on the categorical imperative itself. Critics question, for example, whether the categorical imperative always recommends one best course of action as the "right" one under the circumstances. Isn't it possible that different people, evaluating the same situation (evaluating, that is, the same maxim) might conclude that the categorical imperative demands two or more different actions? Kant seems to have thought that this would not happen, and in this he doubtless shared in the belief of many living during the so-called "Enlightenment" that human reason is universal, with requirements that are the same for everyone. These are overly optimistic assumptions, say the critics, and the categorical imperative is so general and abstract that its requirements can easily be read in differing ways. Nor does it help to invoke the language of rights. Much of contemporary moral and social life is punctuated by appeals to "his right to this" and "her right to that," without any clear sense of how these often conflicting rights are to be weighed or measured against each other, or how conflicts between them are to be resolved. Utilitarians point out that a moral world in which people think only of exercising their rights is not necessarily a better world: a wealthy corporate executive may have the right to donate large amounts of money to the Ku Klux Klan or to groups of neo-Nazis; this fact, of course, is no guarantee that doing so would be the right thing to do. Rights can be exercised in a way that actually increases the unhappiness and disvalue in the world. Utilitarians might question whether the value of individual autonomy and choice is always such as to outweigh the disvalue that exercising rights can create.

Conclusion

We began this section with what seemed to be a straightforward story of a tragedy at sea. We quickly discovered, however, that many aspects of that story raised issues that were deeply philosophical. Just as significantly, we learned that the simple exhortation to solve this case by "applying the law" is deeply problematic as well. What really is "the law," after all? It is to this question that we turn in the next section.

B. *What Is Law?*

The Rule of Law and Military Tribunals

The perplexities embedded in ideals such as the rule of law rarely rise to the level of widespread public debate. But this was not the case in the aftermath of the attacks of September 11, 2001, and the subsequent U.S. military intervention in Afghanistan. In the midst of these events, attention turned to members of the Taliban captured by U.S. forces in Afghanistan, and to the status of "unlawful enemy combatants" arrested within the United States and charged with conspiring to engage in terrorist acts. The administration of President George W. Bush initially proposed that such persons be brought before specially created military tribunals whose proceedings would be closed in an effort to protect national security. The proposed trials were to take place off the U.S. mainland, and the defendants were not to be afforded the standard protections of those subject to criminal prosecution: they would not be informed of their rights upon arrest, would have no right to obtain counsel during interrogation, and would have no right to have evidence that had been illegally seized excluded from their trial.

Though subsequently modified, the procedures for military trials drew heavy criticism both at home and abroad. One basic complaint charged that such proceedings constituted an abrogation of the rule of law, the core of which, it was said, requires impartial and open trials conducted pursuant to previously established procedures and rules designed to ensure fairness. To allow, for example, hearsay testimony or the use of physical evidence lacking a clear chain of custody would be to ignore fundamental aspects of due process, and would constitute a significant break from the rules followed in ordinary criminal proceedings. Supporters of the U.S. administration argued that standard trial proceedings are not appropriate in these cases because the defendants are unlawful, enemy combatants who are not entitled to constitutional protections. Nor, it was contended, are they prisoners of war (POWs) captured while wearing the uniform of an opposing army; thus, they are not owed the protections accorded to POWs under international treaties. These arguments, in turn, raised further questions: If captured Taliban or Al Quaeda personnel are neither prisoners of war nor ordinary criminal defendants, would there be any limits upon what the U.S. government could legally claim to do to them in order (for example) to obtain information? Some in the international community urged that accused terrorists should be handed over by the United States to the International Criminal Court (ICC) at the Hague, formed by treaty in July 2002 with the support of more than one hundred nations. The American government refused to support the ICC, however, and critics accused the United States of seeking to place itself above the law, rather than to operate within it.

The Nuremberg Trial

Many questions regarding the rule of law grew out of the controversy regarding the use of military tribunals for those accused of terrorism in the aftermath of 9/11. Much the same questions also arose decades earlier, during one of the most important military trials of the twentieth century: the Nuremberg trials held at the conclusion of the Second World War. The problems raised and questions posed by the Nuremberg and similar trials provide an illuminating perspective from which to view the fundamental controversy over the nature of law.

At the conclusion of World War II, the Allied powers were faced with the problem of what to do with the senior officials of the Nazi government and with the highest-ranking officers in the Nazi military. It was decided, after some debate, that they should be brought to trial in the first in a series of international legal proceedings. Before the proceedings were over, several series of trials had been held in which German industrialists, judges, lawyers, and businessmen, in addition to military and political leaders, were tried. The first and most dramatic of these trials began in October 1945 and lasted until October of the following year. Twenty-two of the highest-ranking Nazi civilian and military leaders were tried; three were completely exonerated, seven received prison terms, and twelve were handed death sentences and executed.

The Trial of the Major War Criminals proceeded pursuant to an agreement signed by the Allied powers on August 8, 1945: the Treaty of London. This agreement created what became the Charter for the International Military Tribunal at Nuremberg. The Charter specified three categories of criminal activity, for violation of which at least several of the twenty-two defendants were charged:

> *Crimes Against Peace:* Namely, planning, preparation, initiation or waging a war of aggression, or a war in violation of international treaties, agreements, or assurances, or participation in a Common Plan or Conspiracy for the accomplishment of the foregoing . . . ;
> *War Crimes:* Namely, violations of the laws or customs of war. Such violations shall include . . . murder, ill-treatment or deportation to slave labor or for any other purpose of civilian population of or in occupied territory, murder or ill-treatment of prisoners of war . . . wanton destruction of cities, towns, or villages, or devastation not justified by military necessity . . . ;
> *Crimes Against Humanity:* Namely, murder, extermination, enslavement, deportation, and other inhumane acts committed against any civilian population, before or during the war, or persecutions on political, racial, or religious grounds . . . whether or not in violation of domestic law of the country where perpetrated.[1]

Based on these definitions, the Allied prosecutors at the Tribunal indicted the Nazis on four counts: conspiracy to wage aggressive war; waging an aggressive war; commission of war crimes; and perpetration of crimes against humanity.

The evidence presented at the trial overwhelmingly implicated many of the defendants in acts of systematic and deliberate barbarism. It would not have been sufficient for their purposes, however, for the American, British, French, and Soviet prosecutors simply to have condemned the Nazis *morally;* for this was to be a *legal* proceeding, and the Nazis were therefore to be punished (if at all) for having violated the *law,* however much what they did (or instructed others to do) was regarded by everyone involved as grossly immoral. The Nazis were to be sent to prison—or to the hangman—for conduct that was *illegal;* and it is here that serious questions were raised, and continue to be raised, about the Nuremberg trials. These questions, which we will explore throughout this chapter, converge on a core philosophical issue: What was the status of the "law" under which the Nazi leaders were prosecuted? What was the *legal* basis for the categories of criminality and standards of individual liability endorsed by the Charter? Is the Charter itself valid "law"? If so, by virtue of what?

Controversies Regarding Nuremberg

Two opposing responses to these questions—two different conceptions of the trials themselves—are represented in our selections by Robert Jackson, chief American prosecutor of Nuremberg (then on leave from the United States Supreme Court), and Charles Wyzanski, a noted Massachusetts judge.

Wyzanski questions the legality of the Charter's basic provisions with the charge that the Charter created "new law" *ex post facto* (after the fact). As Wyzanski implies, the Charter and the Tribunal were legal novelties in at least two ways: one party to the proceeding became prosecutor, judge, and jury; and the Charter sought to combine elements from both Anglo-American and Continental legal systems. The latter effort proved especially difficult as the two systems differ, both from the standpoint of legal procedure and as regards the content of the (substantive) law. In the English and American systems, as most of us are aware, trials proceed according to a strict division of function. Each of the opposing sides has the responsibility to make the best possible case it can for

---

[1] See *Nazi Conspiracy and Aggression*, Vol. 1, Office of the United States Chief of Counsel for Prosecution of Axis Criminality (Washington, D.C.: U.S. Government Printing Office, 1946), pp. 5–12.

its position by uncovering all of the facts it believes to be relevant and by noting all of the pertinent legal issues and authorities bearing on the dispute. The role of the judge is essentially that of an umpire, reminding each side of what the proper procedures are and penalizing one or the other for violations of the rules. In many European courtrooms, however, this rigid division of labor is not observed; the effort to discover the truth and arrive at a just verdict is conducted in a more collaborative way, with the judge in particular playing a much more active and inquisitorial role than would be permitted in the United States or Britain.

The German defense attorneys at Nuremberg complained bitterly that they were hampered by the Tribunal's decision to rely for the most part upon the Anglo-American procedural system. They also complained that the accusation of participation in a "conspiracy" or "common plan" to start a war had no counterpart in, and was not recognized by, the law of Germany. Wyzanski raises a deeper problem: The Tribunal's "law" effectively permitted it to hold anyone who joined in the Nazi war effort personally liable for anything done by anyone else similarly engaged, and this, Wyzanski insists, was fundamentally unjust.

Behind Wyzanski's specific complaints lies a general concern with the conditions under which an action or decision can be said to be in accord with the rule of law. Wyzanski accuses the Allies of abrogating or negating a principle that is fundamental to the ideas of law and legality: *nullum crimen et nulla poena sine lege* ([there can be] no crime and no penalty without a[n already existing] law). The Charter creates *ex post facto* law, making something punishable after it has been done. Such laws are forbidden by the United States Constitution, and Wyzanski seems to think that the Charter loses in a crucial way its status as "law" by including *ex post facto* provisions.

Wyzanski also questions the wisdom of trials such as those at Nuremberg. If, as seems likely, the Allies never intended that the Nazis go free, are they not reducing a legal proceeding to a propaganda device? This "debases justice" and suggests the same kind of hypocrisy of which the Allies accused the Hitler regime.

In his opening address before the Tribunal, Robert Jackson responds to the objections raised by Wyzanski. Waging an aggressive war was a crime in international law long before the start of World War II, Jackson claims, and the Germans knew this. Jackson notes several international treaties and agreements signed by numerous nations in the early part of this century which, he claims, had the effect of outlawing aggressive warfare. Aggressive warfare was made illegal by these agreements and by international custom; moreover, Jackson adds, the nations of the world have a right to create new customs, to enter into new agreements and understandings that can then serve as a further platform for the development and growth of international law. We cannot allow the defendants to take refuge, Jackson argues, behind the hope that international law will continue to "lag so far behind the moral sense of mankind." To agree with the assertion that the Charter is not law because its core provisions are *ex post facto* would be foolish, Jackson asserts, for the claim is both empty and hypocritical. How could anyone be surprised to discover that genocide and torture are crimes? And how could those guilty of such atrocities have the gall to hide behind the principles of the moral and legal order that their actions sought so completely to repudiate?

Wyzanski believes that Jackson and the Tribunal have sacrificed the principle of *nullum crimen* on the altar of "higher justice." He suggests that international law, as it stood at the time the Nazis began the war, did not unequivocally make aggressive warfare a crime for which individual persons could be held liable. After all, no leading Western nation, in the period from the early 1920s to 1939, condemned any war as an illegal act of aggression. Yet, Wyzanski assumes, someone must have been an aggressor in the confrontations that took place during that time. Shocking and immoral as it was, Wyzanski concludes, the conduct of the Nazis was not for that reason also a contravention of law.

The Continuing Relevance of Nuremberg

The arguments that took place at Nuremberg concerning the nature of law are just as alive today as they were sixty years ago. Questions about the meaning and value of the rule of law continue to inform both scholarly debate and practical decision making in the field of international law.

In June 2001, Slobodan Milosevic, the former president of Yugoslavia, was sent to the Hague to face a 29-count indictment at the International Criminal Tribunal for the Former Yugoslavia (ICTY). The ICTY was created by United Nations Security Council Resolution 808, passed in 1993. The charge of the Tribunal is to seek justice for those victimized by acts of ethnic cleansing, deportation, and summary execution occurring during the bitter wars that raged in the former Yugoslavia throughout the 1990s. These prosecutions for war crimes were the first such international trials since Nuremberg. Under the Tribunal's statute, defendants can be tried for violations of treaties and international conventions, and for crimes against humanity as recognized by the Nuremberg charter. There are differences between the two tribunals and their authority, however. Unlike the Nuremberg Tribunal, the Hague Tribunal lacks direct power to obtain physical custody over the more than seventy persons indicted. Evidence is more difficult to obtain in Bosnia than it was for the Allies after World War II, and the Hague Tribunal cannot try defendants *in absentia*. There is no death penalty for those convicted by the Hague Tribunal, yet the list of war crimes includes rape, which was not included at Nuremberg. Most significantly, the Hague Tribunal is restricted to punishing crimes alleged to have taken place in the former Yugoslavia after 1991. International officials debate whether this means that some incidents in which atrocities are alleged to have occurred are not subject to international law since they may have been internal to Yugoslavia before Bosnia and Croatia were acknowledged as independent nations.[2]

Milosevic faced accusations of having been complicit in acts of genocide, crimes against humanity (including persecution, extermination, torture, and deportation), and violations of the "laws and customs of war" involving, among other events, attacks upon civilians and plunder of property. The first phase of his trial was to focus upon acts for which Milosevic was alleged to be responsible in the province of Kosovo; the second phase was to concentrate upon criminal acts committed during the wars of secession in Croatia and Bosnia, including the siege of Sarajevo and the massacre at Srebrenica. During his first appearance before the Tribunal, on July 3, 2001, Milosevic inveighed against the proceedings in much the way that the Nazis did at Nuremberg: "I consider this Tribunal a false Tribunal and the indictment a false indictment. It is illegal, being not appointed by the UN General Assembly." Milosevic later demanded the right to make a presentation to the court on the "illegality of the Tribunal." The substance of that argument is contained in Milosevic's submission to the court, dated August 30, 2001. In that document, Milosevic argues that the ICTY is illegitimate because it is nothing more than an "ad hoc" political device, conveniently designed to avoid trapping its own creators (the United States and its allies) who, in Milosevic's judgment, are guilty of war crimes themselves. The purpose of the tribunal, he maintains, is to "demonize" the defendants, not to afford them due process. Therefore, Milosevic concludes, the ICTY should be disbanded and its prisoners released. In his decision on Milosevic's request, Judge Richard May examines and rejects each of Milosevic's grounds for impeaching the tribunal, and he invokes the important precedent of Nuremberg to support his position.

The question of how best to respect the value of the rule of law is now being faced by nations from Africa to Latin America to Asia. The overthrow of military juntas and quasi dictatorships frequently exposes a sordid history of torture, political murders, and other human rights violations in many countries. As these oppressive regimes topple and are replaced by elected governments seeking to implement constitutional reforms, these new democracies must determine how best to bring justice to those associated with the wrongs of the prior regime. If those who earlier committed atrocities did so under the cover that such actions were "lawful," according to the statutes and court rulings of that government, how can a democratic administration hold such persons legally accountable for their actions? One example of such a dilemma faced courts in Germany following the reunification of that nation in 1990. That case, the Trial of Border Guards, opens the readings for this section.

---

[2]See Bosnia: The New Nuremberg, *National Law Journal*, 26 Sept. 1994, p. A1.

Natural Law, GDR, Law of United
Germany (retroactive)

Trial of Border Guards

During the time between August 1961 and November 1989, it is estimated that more than two hundred people were shot and killed by border guards of the German Democratic Republic (East Germany) as they sought to flee the communist bloc into West Germany. On February 5, 1989, two East Germans, Chris Gueffroy and Christian Gaudian, attempted to escape the GDR. Although they successfully crossed several barriers constructed by the East German government, they were spotted by members of the East German border guard and shot as they tried to climb the final border fence. Gueffroy was killed; Gaudian was wounded and arrested. Subsequent to the reunification of Germany in 1990, public pressure mounted to punish those responsible for border killings. Four guards involved in the shooting of Gueffroy and Gaudian were placed on trial in 1991. Below are excerpts from the court's ruling.

The 23rd Grand Criminal Court—Court of Assizes—of the Berlin State Court, . . . ruled as follows during the Court Session of 20 January 1992:

The following are hereby sentenced:

Defendant H for homicide to a prison sentence of 3 (three) years and six months,

Defendant K for two crimes, committed as combined act, involving attempted homicide, to a prison sentence of 2 (two) years, whose enforcement is suspended for probation.

Defendants Sch and S are acquitted, Defendant H is also acquitted inasmuch as he was charged with another offense of attempted homicide. . . .

Legal Assessment

. . . The punishability of the defendants is to be judged primarily according to the law of the scene of the act as it applied in the former GDR (Article 2, Paragraph 1, Criminal Code). According to . . . the Unification Treaty of 6 September 1990 . . . —apart from a few exceptions—the Criminal Code of the Federal Republic of Germany took effect on 3 October 1990 in the

Berlin State Court, Docket No. (523) 2 Js 48/90 (9/91).

former territory of the GDR . . . at the same time, the Criminal Code of the GDR—apart from some exceptions that are not significant here—has been invalidated. According to . . . the Unification Treaty, Article 2, Criminal Code, with the measures regulated in Article 315 . . . is applicable to acts committed in the GDR prior to the date of effectiveness of the entry of the GDR in the Federal Republic, in other words, prior to 3 October 1990.

The acts committed by the defendants therefore are to be judged first of all according to GDR criminal law which was applicable at the scene of the action at the time of the action (Article 2, Paragraph 1, Criminal Code) and they are thus to be gauged in favor of the defendants in the light of the criminal law of the Federal Republic which has taken its place since. . . .

In the case at hand . . . the punishment threatened under the Criminal Code [of the Federal Republic] is less and therefore . . . this is to be applicable.

The following applies to the individual defendants:

[Defendant H]

With the aimed round fired, single-shot, from the Kalashnikov submachine gun, from a range of less than 40 m, in the manner described above, at the upper part of the body of Chris Gueffroy, who was standing at the border fence, facing toward him,

Defendant H killed a human being without being a murderer (Article 212, Criminal Code). Chris Gueffroy died on the spot within a few minutes as a consequence of the round which passed through the heart. Even immediate medical assistance could not have prevented the occurrence of death.

Chris Gueffroy's killing was unlawful; the defendant did not have any legally justifying grounds on his side. . . .

According to [the] Border Protection Act, the use of firearms while on Border Guard duty was justified if it served the purpose of preventing the immediately impending execution or continuation of a criminal act which, according to the circumstances, looked like a crime or for the apprehension of persons who were compellingly suspected of a crime. Unlawful border crossing . . . however, was to be classified as a crime only in serious cases. . . . In the case at hand, according to GDR law, there was a serious case of attempted border crossing because the act was committed together with others . . . and because the act was accomplished along with the use of dangerous means or methods, that is to say, with the use of the grappling hook. . . .

. . . In contrast to GDR law, only really grave offenses are qualified as crimes in the Federal Republic. In the then GDR, however, a mere act of "unlawful border crossing" could already become a "crime" if—as in this case—it was committed by at least two persons simultaneously or, to mention another provision that is particularly flexible, "with particular intensity." . . . Firing was permitted in all of these cases; just as to how this was to be done, the law only says: "The life of persons is to be spared to the extent possible." . . .

Within the practice of law, such as it was in effect at the time of the action in what then was the GDR, . . . the soldiers however repeatedly were given the general suggestion during "guard mount"—according to witness Fabian—that no escapee was allowed to slip through and that a "breach of the border" would have to be prevented at all costs. In this way, many soldiers were bound to get the impression and indeed could get the impression that a dead escapee was always better than an escaped escapee with the consequence that their inhibition threshold—when it came to firing their submachine guns at unarmed people—was lowered.

That this is something the superiors wanted in this way is documented particularly clearly by the testimony of witness Fabian according to which soldiers were praised even if they had fired only at a single escapee although, even according to GDR law applicable

at that time, it would not have been permitted to fire on him. In such cases, the soldiers were given to understand from the very beginning that they probably just saw a shadow and that nothing would happen to them as a result of unjustified use of firearms.

The case at hand also confirms that the use of firearms in the final analysis was always considered to be justified; there was no investigation at all as to the legality of firearm use; instead, the defendants were praised and rewarded with special leave and monetary bonuses. But if one wished to accept the reality, which corresponded to the legal situation at that time and to what the law was really like in the GDR, . . . then one would indeed have to note that, in Article 30, the GDR Constitution granted its citizens protection of life, physical integrity, and health. . . . From this, one can deduce that government interference in these assets within the context of a legally permissible use of firearms, was bound to be guided strictly by the principle of proportionality, such as it is also spelled out in the Border Protection Act, although inadequately, at that. . . .

In looking into the question as to whether it may be permissible to threaten with death the person who does not want to abide by the exit prohibition and, disregarding it, wants to cross the border, and whether it may if necessary also be permissible to kill him, we run into the question as to whether everything that is formal and that was considered as a right by virtue of interpretation is indeed rightful.

On this score, it has been recognized in Supreme Court jurisprudence, that there is a certain core area of law which no law and no sovereign act may touch according to the legal consciousness of the general public.

On that point, it says the following in a ruling handed down by the Federal Court in 1952 . . . :

"The freedom of a State to determine, for its area, what is lawful and what is unlawful, no matter how widely it is determined, however, is not unlimited. In the consciousness of all civilized nations, with all of their differences revealed by the various national bodies of law, there is a certain nucleus of the law which, according to general legal concepts, must not be violated by any law and by any other sovereign State measure. It encompasses certain basic principles of human behavior that are considered untouchable and that have taken shape with the passage of time among all cultured nations on the fertile ground of coincident basic moral views and which are considered to be legally binding, regardless of whether individual regulations in national bodies of law seem to allow that they be disregarded" . . .

"Particularly strict requirements must be established when attacks against human life are involved. It is in keeping with jurisprudence such as it prevails among all cultured nations, later on also expressed in the Convention for the Protection of Human Rights, that the individual's right to life must be protected to a greater degree. Killings without a court verdict accordingly are permissible only if they result from an absolutely required use of force."

The Federal Constitutional Court also recognizes the basic principle that laws, which interfere in the described core area of the law, are null and void: . . .

"It was especially the time of the National Socialist regime in Germany that taught us that the legislator can also legislate injustice, in other words, if practical legal usage is not to stand defenseless against such historically thinkable developments, there must be a possibility, in extreme cases, to evaluate the basic principle of material justice more highly than the principle of legal certainty, such as it is expressed in the applicability of positive law for routine cases."

As a criterion for the existence of such a special case, the Federal Constitutional Court points to the formulation by Gustav Radbruch, . . . according to which such a case does exist when the contradiction between positive law and justice has reached such an unbearable degree that the law must yield to justice since it is "incorrect law." The rule of law includes not only certainty and safety under the law but also material justice. . . .

These legal principles, to be sure, were developed on the occasion of the crimes of the National Socialist regime of injustice in Germany which, in the monstrosity of their scope, cannot be compared to the situation under discussion here. Nevertheless, the court has no objection in following this jurisdiction also in the case at hand; this is because the protection of human life applies quite generally and cannot depend on the materialization of a certain number of killings. . . .

. . .

Defendant cannot claim Article 258, Criminal Code/GDR.

According to this regulation, a soldier was not liable under criminal law for an action which he carried out by way of execution of an order given by a superior, unless the execution of the order obviously clashed with recognized standards of international law or if it violated criminal laws.

. . .

[Even] if one were to construe—as "order" within the meaning of Article 258, Criminal Code/GDR—the generally stated requirement that none must be allowed to get through, the results still would not be any different. Such an order would be unlawful and would not have deserved any obedience because this would have been an invitation to commit crimes, that is to say, the unlawful and intentional killing of people, and the execution of the order would have violated criminal laws (Arts. 112, 113, Criminal Code/GDR). . . .

Shooting at people, which may lead to killing, that is to say, people who merely wanted to leave the territory of the then GDR, constitutes such a violation of the standards of ethics and human coexistence that—even considering indoctrination, education, and training in the former GDR—one really cannot visualize that the defendant, considering his origin, his schooling, and his personality, as regards the action against the escapees with which he is charged, was in a state of prohibition misinterpretation that would rule out any guilt on his part. In the case of the defendant, one cannot assume that he was unable to recognize the few basic principles that are indispensable for human coexistence and that belong to the untouchable basic assets and core of the law, such as it lives in the legal consciousness of all cultured nations—perhaps because he had not been educated in a knowledge of these principles. Justice and humanity were explained and pictured as ideals also in the then GDR. To that extent, generally adequate ideas as to the basis of natural justice were indeed disseminated. That this is so is pointed up also by the circumstance that a considerable multitude of inhabitants of the former GDR considered action against so-called border violators along the Berlin Wall and along the inner-German boundary to be unjust. The background of the accused, his schooling, and his comment on the motives and assessments of the conflicts, in which so-called border violators were enmeshed, show that he did have and could have available the fundamentals of a normal legal consciousness. He had every reason to think deeply as to whether it was permitted to happen that people may, if necessary, be shot down along the border only because they wanted to leave the GDR without official permission. He had sufficient references and if he had thought about them carefully, he could have figured out for himself that an event, such as it is to be judged here, was not compatible with the set of values prevailing in his environment. In making this examination, one of course cannot consider as representatives of the environment—as the defense argues—those pillars of the system of justice of the then GDR, such as members of the State Security Ministry, judges, or prosecutors; instead, what is important here is to find out whether the "people of the State" of the GDR did or did not approve the procedures under discussion here.

The realization that deadly shots along the border were a crass injustice and that they were in crying contradiction to the generally recognized basic principles of law and justice should and could have been a matter of general knowledge and usage if the Border Guard soldiers and their superiors had developed the proper conscience.

. . .

Apportionment of Punishment

. . . It follows from the considerations given below that we are dealing here with an "otherwise less grave case" within the meaning of Art. 213, Criminal Code:

The acts carried out by the defendants must be viewed against the background of the inhuman system of compulsion prevailing in the then GDR which educated the defendants, with all means of mass psychology, to blind onesidedness and imparted a restricted image of the world which the defendants, in terms of their personality and education, had little to counter with.

Here again, one had to keep in mind that all those who contributed to the distortion of the legal consciousness of the Border Guard soldiers—be it in school, in the so-called mass organizations, or in political indoctrination sessions in the military—cannot be made liable for this under criminal law because the law does not know any criminal action facts in this context.

. . .

Weighing all of the circumstances that speak for and against the defendants, the administration of the following penalties was quite in keeping with the guilt but it was also required in order impressively to make them aware of the injustice of their actions:

In the case of Defendant H, a prison sentence of 3 years and 6 months.

Opening Address for the United States, Nuremberg Trials

Robert H. Jackson

May it please Your Honors,

The privilege of opening the first trial in history for crimes against the peace of the world imposes a grave responsibility. The wrongs which we seek to condemn and punish have been so calculated, so malignant and so devastating, that civilization cannot tolerate their being ignored because it cannot survive their being repeated. That four great nations, flushed with victory and stung with injury, stay the hand of vengeance and voluntarily submit their captive ene-

From *Trial of the Major War Criminals before the International Military Tribunal* (Nuremberg, 1947–1949), Vol. 2, pp. 98–155.

mies to the judgment of the law is one of the most significant tributes that Power ever has paid to Reason.

This tribunal, while it is novel and experimental, is not the product of abstract speculations nor is it created to vindicate legalistic theories. This inquest represents the practical effort of four of the most mighty of nations, with the support of seventeen more, to utilize International Law to meet the greatest menace of our times—aggressive war. The common sense of mankind demands that law shall not stop with the punishment of petty crimes by little people. It must also reach men who possess themselves of great power and make deliberate and concerted use of it to set in motion evils which leave no home in the world untouched. It is a cause of this magnitude that the United Nations will lay before Your Honors.

In the prisoners' dock sit twenty-odd broken men. Reproached by the humiliation of those they have led almost as bitterly as by the desolation of those they have attacked, their personal capacity for evil is forever past. It is hard now to perceive in these miserable men as captives the power by which as Nazi leaders they once dominated much of the world and terrified most of it. Merely as individuals, their fate is of little consequence to the world.

What makes this inquest significant is that those prisoners represent sinister influence that will lurk in the world long after their bodies have returned to dust. They are living symbols of racial hatreds, or terrorism and violence, and of the arrogance and cruelty of power. They are symbols of fierce nationalisms and militarism, of intrigue and war-making which have embroiled Europe generation after generation, crushing its manhood, destroying its homes, and impoverishing its life. They have so identified themselves with the philosophies they conceived and with the forces they directed that any tenderness to them is a victory and an encouragement to all the evils which are attached to their names. Civilization can afford no compromise with the social forces which would gain renewed strength if we deal ambiguously or indecisively with the men in whom those forces now precariously survive.

What these men stand for we will patiently and temperately disclose. We will give you undeniable proofs of incredible events. The catalogue of crimes will omit nothing that could be conceived by a pathological pride, cruelty, and lust for power. These men created in Germany, under the *Fuehrerprinzip,* a National Socialist despotism equalled only by the dynasties of the ancient East. They took from the German people all those dignities and freedoms that we hold natural and inalienable rights in every human being. The people were compensated by inflaming and gratifying hatreds toward those who were marked as "scape-goats." Against their opponents, including Jews, Catholics, and free labor, the Nazis directed such a campaign of arrogance, brutality, and annihilation as the world has not witnessed since the pre-Christian ages. They excited the German ambition to be a "master race," which of course implies serfdom for others. They led their people on a mad gamble for domination. They diverted social energies and resources to the creation of what they thought to be an invincible war machine. They overran their neighbors.

To sustain the "master race" in its [war-making], they enslaved millions of human beings and brought them into Germany, where these hapless creatures now wander as "displaced persons." At length bestiality and bad faith reached such excess that they aroused the sleeping strength of imperiled civilization. Its united efforts have ground the German war machine to fragments. But the struggle has left Europe a liberated yet prostrate land where a demoralized society struggles to survive. These are the fruits of the sinister forces that sit with these defendants in the prisoners' dock.

In justice to the nations and the men associated in this prosecution, I must remind you of certain difficulties which may leave their mark on this case. Never before in legal history has an effort been made to bring within the scope of a single litigation the developments of a decade, covering a whole Continent, and involving a score of nations, countless individuals, and innumerable events. Despite the magnitude of the task, the world has demanded immediate action. This demand has had to be met, though perhaps at the cost of finished craftsmanship. In my country, established courts, following familiar procedures, applying well thumbed precedents, and dealing with the legal consequences of local and limited events, seldom commence a trial within a year of the event in litigation. Yet less than eight months ago today the courtroom in which you sit was an enemy fortress in the hands of German SS troops. Less than eight months ago nearly all our witnesses and documents were in enemy hands. The law had not been codified, no procedure had been established, no Tribunal was in existence, no usable courthouse stood here, none of the hundreds of tons of official German documents had been examined, no prosecuting staff had been assembled, nearly all the present defendants were at large, and the four prosecuting powers had not yet joined in common cause to try them. I should be the last to deny that the case may well suffer from incomplete researches and quite likely will not be the example of professional work which any of the prosecuting nations would normally wish to sponsor. It is, however, a completely adequate case to the judgment we shall ask you to render, and its full development we shall be obliged to leave to historians.

Before I discuss particulars of evidence, some general considerations which may affect the credit of this trial in the eyes of the world should be candidly faced. There is a dramatic disparity between the circumstances of the accusers and of the accused that might discredit our work if we should falter, in even minor matters, in being fair and temperate.

Unfortunately, the nature of these crimes is such that both prosecution and judgment must be by victor nations over vanquished foes. The worldwide scope of the aggressions carried out by these men has left but few real neutrals. Either the victors must judge the vanquished or we must leave the defeated to judge themselves. After the First World War, we learned the futility of the latter course. The former high station of these defendants, the notoriety of their acts, and the adaptability of their conduct to provoke retaliation make it hard to distinguish between the demand for a just and measured retribution, and the unthinking cry for vengeance which arises from the anguish of war. It is our task, so far as humanly possible, to draw the line between the two. We must never forget that the record on which we judge these defendants today is the record on which history will judge us tomorrow. To pass these defendants a poisoned chalice is to put it to our own lips as well. We must summon such detachment and intellectual integrity to our task that this trial will commend itself to posterity as fulfilling humanity's aspirations to do justice.

At the very outset, let us dispose of the contention that to put these men to trial is to do them an injustice entitling them to some special consideration. These defendants may be hard pressed but they are not ill used. Let us see what alternative they would have to being tried.

More than a majority of these prisoners surrendered to or were tracked down by forces of the United States. Could they expect us to make American custody a shelter for our enemies against the just wrath of our Allies? Did we spend American lives to capture them only to save them from punishment? Under the principles of the Moscow Declaration, those suspected war criminals who are not to be tried internationally must be turned over to individual governments for trial at the scene of their outrages. Many less responsible and less culpable American-held prisoners have been and will be turned over to other United Nations for local trial. If these defendants should succeed, for any reason, in escaping the condemnation of this Tribunal, or if they obstruct or abort this trial, those who are American-held prisoners will be delivered up to our continental Allies. For these defendants, however, we have set up an International Tribunal and have undertaken the burden of participating in a complicated effort to give them fair

and dispassionate hearings. That is the best known protection to any man with a defense worthy of being heard.

If these men are the first war leaders of a defeated nation to be prosecuted in the name of the law, they are also the first to be given a chance to plead for their lives in the name of the law. Realistically, the Charter of this Tribunal, which gives them a hearing, is also the source of their only hope. It may be that these men of troubled conscience, whose only wish is that the world forget them, do not regard a trial as a favor. But they do have a fair opportunity to defend themselves—a favor which these men, when in power, rarely extended to their fellow countrymen. Despite the fact that public opinion already condemns their acts, we agree that here they must be given a presumption of innocence, and we accept the burden of proving criminal acts and the responsibility of these defendants for their commission.

When I say that we do not ask for convictions unless we prove crime, I do not mean mere technical or incidental transgression of international conventions. We charge guilt on planned and intended conduct that involves moral as well as legal wrong. And we do not mean conduct that is a natural and human, even if illegal, cutting of corners, such as many of us might well have committed had we been in the defendants' positions. It is not because they yielded to the normal frailties of human beings that we accuse them. It is their abnormal and inhuman conduct which brings them to this bar.

· · ·

It is my purpose to open the case, particularly under Count One of the Indictment, and to deal with the common plan or conspiracy to achieve ends possible only by resort to crimes against peace, war crimes, and crimes against humanity. My emphasis will not be on individual barbarities and perversions which may have occurred independently of any central plan. One of the dangers ever present is that this trial may be protracted by details of particular wrongs and that we will become lost in a "wilderness of single instances." Nor will I now dwell on the activity of individual defendants except as it may contribute to exposition of the common plan.

The case as presented by the United States will be concerned with the brains and authority back of all the crimes. These defendants were men of a station and rank which does not soil its own hands with blood. They were men who knew how to use lesser folk as tools. We want to reach the planners and designers, the inciters and leaders without whose evil architecture the world would not have been for so long scourged with the violence and lawlessness, and wracked with the agonies and convulsions of this terrible war.

. . .

Even the most warlike of peoples have recognized in the name of humanity some limitations on the savagery of warfare. Rules to that end have been embodied in international conventions to which Germany became a party. This code had prescribed certain restraints as to the treatment of belligerents. The enemy was entitled to surrender and to receive quarter and good treatment as a prisoner of war. We will show by German documents that these rights were denied, that prisoners of war were given brutal treatment and often murdered. This was particularly true in the case of captured airmen, often my countrymen.

. . .

Civilized usage and conventions to which Germany was a party had prescribed certain immunities for civilian populations unfortunate enough to dwell in lands overrun by hostile armies. The German occupation forces, controlled or commanded by men on trial before you, committed a long series of outrages against the inhabitants of occupied territory that would be incredible except for captured orders and the captured reports showing the fidelity with which these orders were executed.

. . .

The end of the war and capture of these prisoners presented the victorious Allies with the question whether there is any legal responsibility on high-ranking men for acts which I have described. Must such wrongs either be ignored or redressed in hot blood? Is there no standard in the law for a deliberate and reasoned judgment on such conduct?

The Charter of this Tribunal evidences a faith that the law is not only to govern the conduct of little men, but that even rulers are, as Lord Chief Justice Coke put it to King James, "under God and the law." The United States believed that the law long has afforded standards by which a juridical hearing could be conducted to make sure that we punish only the right men and for the right reasons. Following the instructions of the late President Roosevelt and the decision of the Yalta conference, President Truman directed representatives of the United States to formulate a proposed International Agreement, which was submitted during the San Francisco Conference to Foreign Ministers of the United Kingdom, the Soviet Union, and the Provisional Government of France. With many modifications, that proposal has become the Charter of this Tribunal.

But the Agreement which sets up the standards by which these prisoners are to be judged does not express the views of the signatory nations alone. Other nations with diverse but highly respected systems of jurisprudence also have signified adherence to it. These are Belgium, The Netherlands, Denmark, Norway, Czechoslovakia, Luxembourg, Poland, Greece, Yugoslavia, Ethiopia, Australia, Haiti, Honduras, Panama, New Zealand, Venezuela, and India. You judge, therefore, under an organic act which represents the wisdom, the sense of justice, and the will of twenty-one governments, representing an overwhelming majority of all civilized people.

The Charter by which this Tribunal has its being embodies certain legal concepts which are inseparable from its jurisdiction and which must govern its decision. These, as I have said, also are conditions attached to the grant of any hearing to defendants. The validity of the provisions of the Charter is conclusive upon us all whether we have accepted the duty of judging or of prosecuting under it, as well as upon the defendants, who can point to no other law which gives them a right to be heard at all. My able and experienced colleagues believe, as do I, that it will contribute to the expedition and clarity of this trial if I expound briefly the application of the legal philosophy of the Charter to the facts I have recited.

While this declaration of the law by the Charter is final, it may be contended that the prisoners on trial are entitled to have it applied to their conduct only most charitably if at all. It may be said that this is new law, not authoritatively declared at the time they did the acts it condemns, and that this declaration of the law has taken them by surprise.

I cannot, of course, deny that these men are surprised that this is the law; they really are surprised that there is any such thing as law. These defendants did not rely on any law at all. Their program ignored and defied all law. That this is so will appear from many acts and statements, of which I cite but a few. In the Fuehrer's speech to all military commanders on November 23, 1939, he reminded them that at the moment Germany had a pact with Russia, but declared, "Agreements are to be kept only as long as they serve a certain purpose." Later on in the same speech he announced, "A violation of the neutrality of Holland and Belgium will be of no importance" (*789-PS*). A Top Secret document, entitled "Warfare as a Problem of Organization," dispatched by the Chief of the High Command to all Commanders on April 19, 1938, declared that "the normal rules of war toward neutrals may be considered to apply on the basis whether operation of rules will create greater advantages or disadvantages for belligerents" (*L-211*). And from the files of the German Navy Staff, we have a "Memorandum on Intensified Naval War," dated October 15, 1939, which begins by stating a desire to comply with International Law. "However," it continues, "if decisive successes are expected from any measure considered as a war necessity, it must be carried through even if it is not in agreement with international law" (*UK-65*). International Law, natural law, German law, any law at all was to these men simply a propaganda device to be invoked when it helped and to be ignored when it would condemn what they wanted to do. That men may be protected in relying upon the law at the time they act is the reason we find laws of retrospective operation unjust. But these men cannot bring themselves within the reason of the rule which in some systems of jurisprudence prohibits *ex post facto* laws. They cannot show that they ever relied upon International Law in any state or paid it the slightest regard.

The Third Count of the Indictment is based on the definition of war crimes contained in the Charter. I have outlined to you the systematic course of conduct toward civilian populations and combat forces which violates international conventions to which Germany was a party. Of the criminal nature of these acts at least, the defendants had, as we shall show, clear knowledge. Accordingly, they took pains to conceal their violations. It will appear that the defendants Keitel and Jodl were informed by official legal advisors that the orders to brand Russian prisoners of war, to shackle British prisoners of war, and to execute commando prisoners were clear violations of International Law. Nevertheless, these orders were put into effect. The same is true of orders issued for the assassination of General Giraud and General Weygand, which failed to be executed only because of a ruse on the part of Admiral Canaris, who was himself later executed for his part in the plot to take Hitler's life on July 20, 1944 (*Affidavit A*).

The Fourth Count of the Indictment is based on crimes against humanity. Chief among these are mass killings of countless human beings in cold blood. Does it take these men by surprise that murder is treated as a crime?

The First and Second Counts of the Indictment add to these crimes the crime of plotting and waging wars of aggression and wars in violation of nine treaties to which Germany was a party. There was a time, in fact I think the time of the [F]irst World War, when it could not have been said that war-inciting or war-making was a crime in law, however reprehensible in morals.

Of course, it was under the law of all civilized peoples a crime for one man with his bare knuckles to assault another. How did it come that multiplying this crime by a million, and adding fire arms to bare knuckles, made a legally innocent act? The doctrine was that one could not be regarded as criminal for committing the usual violent acts in the conduct of legitimate warfare. The age of imperialistic expansion during the Eighteenth and Nineteenth Centuries added the foul doctrine, contrary to the teachings of early Christian and International Law scholars such as Grotius, that all wars are to be regarded as legitimate wars. The sum of these two doctrines was to give [war-making] a complete immunity from accountability to law.

This was intolerable for an age that called itself civilized. Plain people, with their earthly common sense, revolted at such fictions and legalisms so contrary to ethical principles and demanded checks on war immunity. Statesmen and international lawyers at first cautiously responded by adopting rules of warfare designed to make the conduct of war more civilized. The effort was to set legal limits to the violence that could be done to civilian populations and to combatants as well.

The common sense of men after the First World War demanded, however, that the law's condemnation of war reach deeper, and that the law condemn not merely uncivilized ways of waging war, but also the waging in any way of uncivilized wars—wars of aggression. The world's statesmen again went only as far as they were forced to go. Their efforts were timid and cautious and often less explicit than we might have hoped. But the 1920's did outlaw aggressive war.

The reestablishment of the principle that there are unjust wars and that unjust wars are illegal is traceable in many steps. One of the most significant is the Briand-Kellogg Pact of 1928, by which Germany, Italy, and Japan, in common with practically all the nations of the world, renounced war as an instrument of national policy, bound themselves to seek the settlement of disputes only by pacific means, and condemned recourse to war for the solution of international controversies. This pact altered the legal status of a war of aggression. As Mr. Stimson, the United States Secretary of State put it in 1932, such a war "is no longer to be the source and subject of rights. It is no longer to be the principle around which the duties, the conduct, and the rights of nations revolve. It is an illegal thing. . . . By that very act, we have made obsolete many legal precedents and have given the legal profession the task of reexamining many of its codes and treaties."

The Geneva Protocol of 1924 for the Pacific Settlement of International Disputes, signed by the representatives of forty-eight governments, declared that "a war of aggression constitutes . . . an international crime." The Eighth Assembly of the League of Nations in 1927, on unanimous resolution of the representatives of forty-eight member nations, including Germany, declared that a war of aggression constitutes an international crime. At the Sixth Pan-American Conference of 1928, the twenty-one American Republics unanimously adopted a resolution stating that "[a] war of aggression constitutes an international crime against the human species."

A failure of these Nazis to heed or to understand the force and meaning of this evolution in the legal thought of the world is not a defense or a mitigation. If anything, it aggravates their offense and makes it the more mandatory that the law they have flouted be vindicated by juridical application to their lawless conduct. Indeed, by their own law—had they heeded any law—these principles were binding on these defendants. Article 4 of the Weimar Constitution provided that "The generally accepted rules of international law are to be considered as binding integral parts of the law of the German Reich" (*2050-PS*). Can there by any doubt that the outlawry of aggressive war was one of the "generally accepted rules of international law" in 1939?

Any resort to war—to any kind of a war—is a resort to means that are inherently criminal. War inevitably is a course of killings, assaults, deprivations of liberty, and destruction of property. An honestly defensive war is, of course, legal and saves those lawfully conducting it from criminality. But inherently criminal acts cannot be defended by showing that those who committed them were engaged in a war,

when war itself is illegal. The very minimum legal consequence of the treaties making aggressive wars illegal is to strip those who incite or wage them of every defense the law ever gave, and to leave warmakers subject to judgment by the usually accepted principles of the law of crimes.

But if it be thought that the Charter, whose declarations concededly bind us all, does contain new law I still do not shrink from demanding its strict application by this Tribunal. The rule of law in the world, flouted by the lawlessness incited by these defendants, had to be restored at the cost to my country of over a million casualties, not to mention those of other nations. I cannot subscribe to the perverted reasoning that society may advance and strengthen the rule of law by the expenditure of morally innocent lives but that progress in the law may never be made at the price of morally guilty lives.

It is true, of course, that we have no judicial precedent for the Charter. But International Law is more than a scholarly collection of abstract and immutable principles. It is an outgrowth of treaties and agreements between nations and of accepted customs. Yet every custom has its origin in some single act, and every agreement has to be initiated by the action of some state. Unless we are prepared to abandon every principle of growth for International Law, we cannot deny that our own day has the right to institute customs and to conclude agreements that will themselves become sources of a newer and strengthened International Law. International Law is not capable of development by the normal processes of legislative authority. Innovations and revisions in International Law are brought about by the action of governments designed to meet a change in circumstances. It grows, as did the Common Law, through decisions reached from time to time in adapting settled principles to new situations. The fact is that when the law evolves by the case method, as did the Common Law and as International Law must do if it is to advance at all, it advances at the expense of those who wrongly guessed the law and learned too late their error. The law, so far as International Law can be decreed, had been clearly pronounced when these acts took place. Hence, I am not disturbed by the lack of judicial precedent for the inquiry we propose to conduct.

1: Treaty / history of international law

Nuremberg: A Fair Trial?

Charles E. Wyzanski, Jr.

1

The Nuremberg War Trial has a strong claim to be considered the most significant as well as the most debatable event since the conclusion of hostilities. To those who support the trial it promises the first effective recognition of a world law for the punishment of malefactors who start wars or conduct them in bestial fashion. To the adverse critics the trial appears in many aspects a negation of principles which they regard as the heart of any system of justice under law.

This sharp division of opinion has not been fully aired largely because it relates to an issue of foreign policy upon which this nation has already acted and on which debate may seem useless or, worse, merely to impair this country's prestige and power abroad. Moreover, to the casual newspaper reader the long-range implications of the trial are not obvious. He sees most clearly that there are in the dock a score of widely known men who plainly deserve punishment. And he is pleased to note that four victorious nations, who have not been unanimous on all post-war questions, have, by a miracle of administrative skill, united in a proceeding that is overcoming the obstacles of varied languages, professional habits, and legal traditions. But the more profound observer is aware that the foundations of the Nuremberg trial may mark a watershed of modern law.

Before I come to the discussion of the legal and political questions involved, let me make it clear that nothing I may say about the Nuremberg trial should be construed as a suggestion that the individual Nuremberg defendants or others who have done grievous wrongs should be set at liberty. In my opinion there are valid reasons why several thousand Germans, including many defendants at Nuremberg, should

From *The Atlantic Monthly*, Vol. 177 (April 1946), pp. 66–70. Reprinted with permission of *The Atlantic Monthly* and the Wyzanski Estate.

either by death or by imprisonment be permanently removed from civilized society. If prevention, deterrence, retribution, nay even vengeance are ever adequate motives for punitive action, then punitive action is justified against a substantial number of Germans. But the question is: Upon what theory may that action properly be taken?

The starting point is the indictment of October 18, 1945, charging some twenty individuals and various organizations, in four counts, with conspiracy, crimes against peace, war crimes, and crimes against humanity. Let me examine the offenses that are called in Count 3 of the indictment "war crimes," in the strict sense.

It is sometimes said that there is no international law of war crimes. But most jurists would agree that there is at least an abbreviated list of war crimes upon which the nations of the world have agreed. Thus in Articles 46 and 47 of the Hague Convention of 1907, the United States and many other countries accepted the rules that in an occupied territory of a hostile state "family honour and rights, the lives of persons, and private property, as well as religious conviction and practice, must be respected. Private property cannot be confiscated. Pillage is formally forbidden." And consistently the Supreme Court of the United States has recognized that rules of this character are part of our law. In short, there can be no doubt of the legal right of this nation prior to the signing of a peace treaty to use a military tribunal for the purpose of trying and punishing a German if, as Count 3 charges, in occupied territory he murdered a Polish civilian, or tortured a Czech, or raped a Frenchwoman, or robbed a Belgian. Moreover, there is no doubt of the military tribunal's parallel right to try and to punish a German if he has murdered, tortured, or maltreated a prisoner of war.

In connection with war crimes of this sort there is only one question of law worth discussing here: Is it a defense to a soldier or civilian defendant that he acted under the order of a superior?

The defense of superior orders is, upon the authorities, an open question. Without going into details, it may be said that superior orders have never been recognized as a complete defense by German, Russian, or French law, and that they have not been so recognized by civilian courts in the United States or the British Commonwealth of Nations, but they tend to be taken as a complete excuse by Anglo-American military manuals. In this state of the authorities, if the International Military Tribunal in connection with a charge of a war crime refuses to recognize superior orders as a defense, it will not be making a retroactive determination or applying an *ex post facto* law. It will be merely settling an open question of law as every court frequently does.

The refusal to recognize the superior-order defense not only is not repugnant to the *ex post facto* principle, but is consonant with our ideas of justice. Basically, we cannot admit that military efficiency is the paramount consideration. And we cannot even admit that individual self-preservation is the highest value. This is not a new question. Just as it is settled that X is guilty of murder if, in order that he and Y, who are adrift on a raft, may not die of starvation, he kills their companion, Z; so a German soldier is guilty of murder if, in order that he may not be shot for disobedience and his wife tortured in a concentration camp, he shoots a Catholic priest. This is hard doctrine, but the law cannot recognize as an absolute excuse for a killing that the killer was acting under compulsion—for such a recognition not only would leave the structure of society at the mercy of criminals of sufficient ruthlessness, but also would place the cornerstone of justice on the quicksand of self-interest.

Of course, there always remains the fundamental separateness of the problem of guilt and the problem of treatment. And no one would expect a tribunal to mete out its severest penalty to a defendant who yielded to wrongdoing only out of fear of loss of his life or his family's.

2

In addition to "war crimes," the indictment, in Count 4, charges the defendants with "crimes against humanity." This count embraces the murder, torture, and persecution of minority groups, such as Jews, inside Germany both before and after the outbreak of war. It is alleged in paragraph X of the indictment that these wrongs "constituted violations of international conventions, of internal penal laws, of the general principles of criminal law as derived from the criminal law of all civilized nations and were involved in and part of a systematic course of conduct."

I shall pass for the time being the last phrase just quoted, for that is merely a way of saying that the Nazis persecuted the minority German groups to harden the German will for aggression and to develop an issue that would divide other countries. In other words, the legal validity of that phrase rests upon the same considerations as the validity of the charge of "crimes against the peace."

I consider first the legal validity of the other phrases upon which is premised the charge that murdering, torturing, and persecuting German Jews and other non-Nazis from 1933 to 1939 as well as from 1939 to 1945 are crimes. And before I say anything of the legal question, let me make it abundantly clear that as a human being I regard these murders, tortures, and persecutions as being morally quite as repugnant and loathsome as the murders, tortures, and persecutions of the civilian and military personnel of American and Allied nations.

In paragraph X of the indictment, reference is first made to "international conventions." There is no citation of any particular international convention which in explicit words forbids a state or its inhabitants to murder its own citizens, in time either of war or of peace. I know of no such convention. And I, therefore, conclude that when the draftsman of the indictment used the phrase "international conventions" he was using the words loosely and almost analogously with the other phrase, "general principles of criminal law as derived from the criminal law of all civilized nations." He means to say that there exists, to cover the most atrocious conduct, a broad principle of universal international criminal law which is according to the law of most penal codes and public sentiment in most places, and for violations of which an offender may be tried by any new court that one or more of the world powers may create.

If that were the only basis for the trial and punishment of those who murdered or tortured German citizens, it would be a basis that would not satisfy most lawyers. It would resemble the universally condemned Nazi law of June 28, 1935, which provided: "Any person who commits an act which the law declares to be punishable or which is deserving of penalty according to the fundamental conceptions of the penal law and sound popular feeling, shall be punished." It would fly straight in the face of the most fundamental rules of criminal justice—that criminal laws shall not be *ex post facto* and that there shall be *nullum crimen et nulla poena sine lege*—no crime and no penalty without an antecedent law.

The feeling against a law evolved after the commission of an offense is deeply rooted. Demosthenes and Cicero knew the evil of retroactive laws: philosophers as diverse as Hobbes and Locke declared their hostility to it; and virtually every constitutional government has some prohibition of *ex post facto* legislation, often in the very words of Magna Carta, or Article I of the United States Constitution, or Article 8 of the French Declaration of Rights. The antagonism to *ex post facto* laws is not based on a lawyer's prejudice encased in a Latin maxim. It rests on the political truth that if a law can be created after an offense, then power is to that extent absolute and arbitrary. To allow retroactive legislation is to disparage the principle of constitutional limitation. It is to abandon what is usually regarded as one of the essential values at the core of our democratic faith.

But, fortunately, so far as concerns murders of German minorities, the indictment was not required to invent new law. The indictment specifically mentions "internal penal laws." And these laws are enough in view of the way the question would arise in a criminal proceeding.

Under universally accepted principles of law, an occupying belligerent power may and indeed often does establish its own tribunals to administer the domestic law of the occupied country for the inhabitants. Thus if Adolph killed Berthold before the American Army occupied Munich, it would be normal for the United States government to set up a military tribunal to try and to punish Adolph.

But suppose Adolph raised as a defense the contention that he was acting pursuant to orders from superiors which were the law of Germany. If that defense were raised, and if we assume (contrary to what some German jurists tell us) that in Germany there were on the statute books pertinent exculpatory laws, nonetheless under well-known principles of German law, going back to the Middle Ages and differing from current Anglo-American theories, the superior order could be disregarded by a court applying German law, on the ground that it was so repugnant to "natural law" as to be void. That is, perhaps a

German tribunal or one applying German law can disregard an obviously outrageous statute or executive order as offensive to natural law just as the Supreme Court of the United States can disregard a statute or executive order as offensive to the United States Constitution.

But further suppose that Adolph raised as a defense the point that the wrong was so old as to be barred by some statute of limitations. If there is such a statute in Germany, the limitation may be set aside without involving any violation of the *ex post facto* principle. As our own Supreme Court has pointed out, to set aside a statute of limitation is not to create a new offense.

3

I turn now to Count 2 of the indictment, which charges "crimes against peace." This is the count that has attracted greatest interest. It alleges that the defendants participated "in the planning, preparation, initiation and waging of wars of aggression, which were also wars in violation of international treaties, agreements and assurances."

This charge is attacked in many quarters on the ground it rests on *ex post facto* law. The reply has been that in the last generation there has accumulated a mounting body of international sentiment which indicates that wars of aggression are wrong and that a killing by a person acting on behalf of an aggressor power is not an excusable homicide. Reference is made not only to the Briand-Kellogg Pact of August 27, 1928, but to deliberations of the League of Nations in 1924 and subsequent years—all of which are said to show an increasing awareness of a new standard of conduct. Specific treaties outlawing wars of aggression are cited. And, having regard to the manner by which all early criminal law evolves and the manner by which international law grows, it is claimed that now it is unlawful to wage an aggressive war and it is criminal to aid in preparing for such a war, whether by political, military, financial, or industrial means.

One difficulty with that reply is that the body of growing custom to which reference is made is custom directed at sovereign states, not at individuals. There is no convention or treaty which places obligations explicitly upon an individual not to aid in waging an aggressive war. Thus, from the point of view of the individual, the charge of a "crime against peace" appears in one aspect like a retroactive law. At the time he acted, almost all informed jurists would have told him that individuals who engaged in aggressive war were not in the legal sense criminals.

Another difficulty is the possible bias of the Tribunal in connection with Count 2. Unlike the crimes in Counts 3 and 4, Count 2 charges a political crime. The crime which is asserted is tried not before a dispassionate neutral bench, but before the very persons alleged to be victims. There is not even one neutral sitting beside them.

And what is most serious is that there is doubt as to the sincerity of our belief that all wars of aggression are crimes. A question may be raised whether the United Nations are prepared to submit to scrutiny the attack of Russia on Poland, or on Finland, or the American encouragement to the Russians to break their treaty with Japan. Every one of these actions may have been proper, but we hardly admit that they are subject to international judgment.

These considerations make the second count of the Nuremberg indictment look to be of uncertain foundation and uncertain limits. To some the count may appear as nothing more than the ancient rule that the vanquished are at the mercy of the victor. To others it may appear as the mere declaration of an always latent doctrine that the leaders of a nation are subject to outside judgment as to their motives in waging war.

The other feature of the Nuremberg indictment is Count 1, charging a "conspiracy." Paragraph III of the indictment alleges that the "conspiracy embraced the commission of Crimes against Peace; . . . it came to embrace the commission of War Crimes . . . and Crimes against Humanity."

In international as well as in national law there may be for almost any crime what the older lawyers would have called principal offenders and accessories. If Adolph is determined to kill Sam, and talks the matter over with Berthold, Carl, and Dietrich, and Berthold agrees to borrow the money to buy a pistol, and Carl agrees to make a holster for the pistol, and all of them proceed as planned and then Adolph gives the pistol and holster to Dietrich, who goes out alone and actually shoots Sam without excuse, then, of course, Adolph, Berthold, Carl, and Dietrich are all guilty of murder. They should not be allowed to escape with the plea Macbeth offered for Banquo's murder, "Thou canst not say I did it."

If the conspiracy charge in Count 1 meant no more than that those are guilty who plan a murder and with knowledge finance and equip the murderer, no one would quarrel with the count. But it would appear that Count 1 means to establish some additional separate substantive offense of conspiracy. That is, it asserts that there is in international law a wrong which consists in acting together for an unlawful end, and that he who joins in that action is liable not only for what he planned, or participated in, or could reasonably have foreseen would happen, but is liable for what every one of his fellows did in the course of the conspiracy. Almost as broad a doctrine of conspiracy exists in municipal law.

But what is the basis for asserting so broad a substantive crime exists in international law? Where is the treaty, the custom, the academic learning on which it is based? Is this not a type of "crime" which was first described and defined either in London or in Nuremberg sometime in the year 1945?

Aside from the fact that the notion is new, is it not fundamentally unjust? The crime of conspiracy was originally developed by the Court of Star Chamber on the theory that any unlicensed joint action of private persons was a threat to the public, and so if the action was in any part unlawful it was all unlawful. The analogies of the municipal law of conspiracy therefore seem out of place in considering for international purposes the effect of joint political action. After all, in a government or other large social community there exists among the top officials, civilian and military, together with their financial and industrial collaborators, a kind of over-all working arrangement which may always be looked upon, if its invidious connotation be disregarded, as a "conspiracy." That is, government implies "breathing together." And is everyone who, knowing the purposes of the party in power, participates in government or joins with officials to be held for every act of the government?

To take a case which is perhaps not so obvious, is everyone who joins a political party, even one with some illegal purposes, to be held liable to the world for the action that every member takes, even if that action is not declared in the party platform and was not known to or consented to by the person charged as a wrongdoer? To put upon any individual such responsibility for action of the group seems literally to step back in history to a point before the prophet Ezekiel and to reject the more recent religious and democratic teachings that guilt is personal.

4

Turning now from the legal basis of the indictment, I propose briefly to consider whether, quite apart from legal technicalities, the procedure of an international military tribunal on the Nuremberg pattern is a politically acceptable way of dealing with the offenders in the dock and those others whom we may legitimately feel should be punished.

The chief arguments usually given for this quasi-judicial trial are that it gives the culprits a chance to say anything that can be said on their behalf, that it gives both the world today and the world tomorrow a chance to see the justice of the Allied cause and the wickedness of the [Nazis] and that it sets a firm foundation for a future world order wherein individuals will know that if they embark on schemes of aggression or murder or torture or persecution they will be severely dealt with by the world.

The first argument has some merit. The defendants, after hearing and seeing the evidence against them, will have an opportunity without torture and with the aid of counsel to make statements on their own behalf. For us and for them this opportunity will make the proceeding more convincing. Yet the defendants will not have the right to make the type of presentation that at least English-speaking persons have thought the indispensable concomitant of a fair trial. No one expects that Ribbentrop will be allowed to summon Molotov to disprove the charge that in invading Poland Germany started an aggressive war. No one anticipates that the defense, if it has the evidence, will be given as long a time to present its evidence as the prosecution takes. And there is nothing more foreign to those proceedings than either the presumption that the defendants are innocent until proved guilty or the doctrine that any adverse public comment on the defendants before the verdict is prejudicial to their receiving a fair trial. The basic approach is that these men should not have a chance to go free. And that being so, they ought not to be tried in a court of law.

As to the second point, one objection is purely pragmatic. There is a reasonable doubt whether this kind of trial, despite the voluminous and accessible record it makes, persuades anyone. It brings out new evidence, but does it change men's minds? Most reporters say that the Germans are neither interested in nor persuaded by these proceedings, which they regard as partisan. They regard the proceedings not as marking a rebirth of law in Central Europe but as a political judgment on their former leaders. The same

attitude may prevail in future because of the departure from accepted legal standards.

A more profound objection to the second point is that to regard a trial as a propaganda device is to debase justice. To be sure, most trials do and should incidentally educate the public. Yet any judge knows that if he, or counsel, or the parties regard a trial primarily as a public demonstration, or even as a general inquest, then there enter considerations which would otherwise be regarded as improper. In a political inquiry and even more in the spread of propaganda, the appeal is likely to be to the unreflecting thought and the deep-seated emotions of the crowd, untrammeled by any fixed standards. The objective is to create outside the courtroom a desired state of affairs. In a trial the appeal is to the disinterested judgment of reasonable men guided by established precepts. The objective is to make inside the courtroom a sound disposition of a pending case according to settled principles.

The argument that these trials set a firm foundation for a future world legal structure is perhaps debatable. The spectacle of individual liability for a world wrong may lead to future treaties and agreements specifying individual liability. If this were the outcome and if, for example, with respect to wars of aggression, war crimes, and use of atomic energy the nations should agree upon world rules establishing individual liability, then this would be a great gain. But it is by no means clear that this trial will further any such program.

At the moment, the world is most impressed by the undeniable dignity and efficiency of the proceedings and by the horrible events recited in the testimony. But, upon reflection, the informed public may be disturbed by the repudiation of widely accepted concepts of legal justice. It may see too great a resemblance between this proceeding and others which we ourselves have condemned. If in the end there is a generally accepted view that Nuremberg was an example of high politics masquerading as law, then the trial instead of promoting may retard the coming of the day of world law.

Quite apart from the effect of the Nuremberg trial upon the particular defendants involved, there is the disturbing effect of the trial upon domestic justice here and abroad. "We but teach bloody instructions, which, being taught, return to plague the inventor." Our acceptance of the notions of *ex post facto* law and group guilt blunt much of our criticism of Nazi law. Indeed our complaisance may mark the beginning of an age of reaction in constitutionalism in particular and of law in general. Have we forgotten that law is not power, but restraint on power?

If the Nuremberg trial of the leading Nazis should never have been undertaken, it does not follow that we should not have punished these men. It would have been consistent with our philosophy and our law to have disposed of such of the defendants as were in the ordinary sense murderers by individual, routine, undramatic military trials. This was the course proposed in the speeches of the Archbishop of York, Viscount Cecil, Lord Wright, and others in the great debate of March 20, 1945, in the House of Lords. In such trials the evidence and the legal issues would have a stark simplicity and the lesson would be inescapable.

For those who were not chargeable with ordinary crimes but only with political crimes such as planning an aggressive war, would it not have been better to proceed by an executive determination—that is, a proscription directed at certain named individuals? The form of the determination need not have been absolute on its face. It might have been a summary order reciting the offense and allowing the named persons to show cause why they should not be punished, thus giving them a chance to show any mistake of identification or gross mistake of fact.

There are precedents for such executive determination in the cases of Napoleon and of the Boxer rebels. Such a disposition would avoid the inevitably misleading characteristics of the present proceedings, such as a charge presented in the form of an "indictment," the participation of celebrated civil judges and the legal formalities of rulings on evidence and on law. It is these characteristics which may make the Nuremberg trial such a potential danger to law everywhere. Moreover, if it were generally felt that we ought not to take a man's life without the form of a trial, then the executive determination could be limited to imprisonment. The example of Napoleon shows that our consciences would have no reason to be disturbed about the removal from society and the permanent detention of irresponsible men who are a threat to the peace of the world.

To be sure, such an executive determination is *ex post facto*. Indeed, it is a bill of attainder. To be sure, it is also an exhibition of power and not of restraint. But its very merit is its naked and unassumed character. It confesses itself to be not legal justice but political. The truthful facing of the character of our action would make it more certain that the case would not become a precedent in domestic law.

As Lord Digby said in 1641 regarding the Strafford bill of attainder, "There is in Parliament a double Power of Life and Death by Bill, a Judicial Power, and a legislative; the measure of the one, is what is legally just; of the other, what is Prudentially and Politickly fit for the good and preservation of the whole. But these two, under favour, are not to be confounded in Judgment: We must not piece up want of legality with matter of convenience, nor the defailance of prudential fitness with a pretense of Legal Justice."

This emphasis on procedural regularity is not legalistic or, as it is sometimes now said, conceptualistic. If there is one axiom that emerges clearly from the history of constitutionalism and from the study of any bill of rights or any charter of freedom, it is that procedural safeguards are the very substance of the liberties we cherish. Not only the specific guarantees with respect to criminal trials, but the general promise of "due process of law," have always been phrased and interpreted primarily in their procedural aspect. Indeed it hardly lies in the mouth of any supporter of the Nuremberg proceedings to disparage such procedural considerations; for may it not be said that the reason that the authors of those proceedings cast them in the form of a trial was to persuade the public that the customary safeguards and liberties were preserved?

It is against this deceptive appearance, big with evil consequences for law everywhere, that as a matter of civil courage all of us, judges as well as lawyers and laymen, however silent we ordinarily are, ought to speak out. It is for their silence on such matters that we justly criticize the Germans. And it is the test of our sincere belief in justice under law never to allow it to be confused with what are merely our interest, our ingenuity, and our power.

Statement of President Slobodan Milosevic on the Illegitimacy of the Hague "Tribunal"

There are three fatal legal flaws in the so-called International Criminal Tribunal for the Former Yugoslavia. Each has disastrous consequences for the human quest for peace, the rule of law, democracy, truth, and justice.

1. The Charter of the United Nations Does Not Empower the Security Council to Create a Criminal Court.

The U.N. Security Council has seized power it does not possess, corrupting the Charter of the United Nations, placing itself above the law and threatening "We Peoples of the United Nations" with a lawless future in which a superpower employs the scourge of war to have its way. Nothing in the history of the planning, drafting, discussion, approval, or ratifications of the U.N. Charter implies, or is consistent with an intention to empower any body created by, or under, the Charter to establish any criminal tribunal. The words of the Charter and their textual inferences, the structure and allocation of power and duties, including those in the incorporated Statute for the International Court of Justice, all negate the existence of any capacity under the Charter to ordain criminal courts. The Criminal Tribunal for Former Yugoslavia is illegitimate and its creation a corruption of the United Nations.

There would never have been a United Nations if its Charter stated, or implied, that a criminal court could be created under its authority. No one who believes in historical truth or that words have meaning can, after examining the history of its creation and its text, contend that the Charter of the United Nations empowers the Security Council to create a criminal court.

An international criminal court can be created only by a multinational treaty, or amendment to the charter of the United Nations. The national representatives

United Nations Security Council
International Criminal Tribunal for the Former Yugoslavia, The Hague, August 30, 2001. Reprinted by permission.

who have served on the Security Council and in the General Assembly and the scholars, lawyers, and experts who have labored for more than thirty years to bring into being an international criminal court have recognized that the only lawful and binding way such a court can be created is by an agreement among nations through a treaty agreed upon for that purpose, or by amending the Charter of the United Nations under its strict provisions regulating amendments to authorize or establish a court.

When an International Criminal Court was finally agreed upon in July 1998 by 120 nations meeting in Rome, it was by treaty which had been studied, drafted and debated for years. The United States, the most powerful participant in that long process, consistently sought to weaken the treaty to exempt U.S. leaders and military personnel from prosecution before it. Having failed, the U.S. was then the most prominent and powerful of the handful of nations that refused to sign. As of August 1, 2001, 37 nations, the Netherlands the most recent, had ratified the treaty. The United States is vigorously trying to persuade, coerce, or bribe nations not to ratify.

Unless it is limited by the U.N. Charter and international law, the Security Council can do whatever it chooses to do. If it is not restrained by the United Nations Charter, the Security Council can commit any act it desires, disregarding all law. Early proponents of United States world power claimed such unbridled discretion for the Security Council publicly. Thus, in 1950 John Foster Dulles wrote: "The Security Council is not a body that merely enforces agreed law. It is a law unto itself . . . No principles of law are laid down to guide it; it can decide in accordance with what it thinks is expedient." If unchallenged, this concept of Security Council power means that the most powerful international organ created by the Charter of the United Nations "to end the scourge of war" is above all law, domestic and international.

But absolute discretion is the very definition of lawlessness and has been called "more destructive of freedom than any other of man's inventions" by U.S.

Supreme Court Justice William O. Douglas. All rights of all nations, races, religions, cultures, political parties, and individuals are thereby subordinated to the will of the Security Council and the single superpower that too often will dominate it. All but fifteen nations are excluded from Security Council counsels. Each of the five permanent members can veto its actions.

The Security Council is subject to domination by a single nation. The representative of each member votes as instructed by the national government that appoints him and to serve the interests of that government, not as an international statesman serving all peoples and the purposes for which the U.N. was created. The Security Council is inaccessible, anonymous, and less responsive to democratic processes than any other international political institution.

2. A One-Time, One-Episode Court Targeting One Country, Created by International Political Power to Serve Its Geo-Political Interests, Is Incapable of Equality and Conducive to Division and Violence.

The illegitimate Criminal Tribunal for Former Yugoslavia corrupts justice and law because it is incapable of acting equally among nations or within the politically targeted nation. It will increase violence, division and the risk of war with neighboring nations and peoples and within Yugoslavia among the segments of the society the U.S. policy of balkanization of Former Yugoslavia has set against each other and against the new government the United States has installed for its own purposes. If the United Nations Charter had authorized the Security Council to create criminal courts, it could not create a court for one nation, or episode for political purposes, to persecute selected groups or persons, and such a court is incapable of equal justice under law. An ad hoc court violates the most basic principles of all law. Equality is the mother of justice. An international court established to prosecute acts in a single nation and primarily, if not entirely, one limited group is pre-programmed to persecute, incapable of equality.

If the Security Council can create a criminal court to prosecute conduct in a single country like Yugoslavia, it can appoint a court for any country, selecting enemies or political and economic opportunities for targeting one at a time, while never exposing itself, or those

who comply with its wishes, to such selective prosecution. If the United States or any ally or client state it chose to protect was the subject of a serious effort by the Security Council to be honored with a criminal tribunal in its own name, the United States would veto the threatened action.

A Court created only for crimes in one country is by definition discriminatory, incapable of equal justice, a weapon against chosen enemies, or antagonistic interests and war by other means. If there is to be any international criminal court, it must act equally as to all nations, with none above the law. The ad hoc Tribunal for a single nation corrupts international law.

By its very nature, the ad hoc Tribunal can be created only after the conduct the Security Council decides justifies creation of the Court, since there is no other excuse for its creation. It is in every case ex post facto. This violates an ancient principle of law. It also requires the Security Council, if there is to be a rational basis for its action, to make some preliminary claim to finding of facts, a task such a political body is not designed for, that inherently incriminates a country or faction by placing the imprimatur of the Security Council of the United Nations on a political decision of fact necessary to justify creation of the Tribunal. The very charge of the Security Council—genocide, crimes against peace, war crimes, or crimes against humanity—demonizes any person thereafter accused.

Investigators, prosecutors, and administrative personnel who join a temporary Tribunal to pursue allegations of humanity's greatest crimes against a people and leaders already demonized will feel they have failed if there are no convictions. The very psychology of the enterprise is persecutorial. Few judges appointed to serve on a Tribunal created under such circumstances will feel free to acquit any but the most marginal, or clearly mistaken, accused, or to create an appearance of objectivity.

The ad hoc Tribunal which targets a country is incapable of prosecuting what may be greater crimes committed in the same conflict by a power, coalition ally, or political agent that was and remains a much greater source of violence and threat to peace. Most often the power which forced the creation of the target tribunal to further damage and demonize their enemy is shielded from criticism by the avalanche of propaganda against the accused supported by the appearance of United Nations neutrality and peacemaking efforts.

What court will consider the criminality of aerial bombardment by U.S. aircraft of defenseless civilians, their housing, water systems, power plants, factories, office buildings, schools, hospitals, which take thousands of lives directly and causes billions of dollars of property damages in Belgrade, Nis, Novi Sad, and scores of other cities, towns and villages? What threat to peace continues from the U.S. bombing of the Chinese Embassy?

Who will be held accountable for the devastation of Pristina by NATO planes, or the attacks on refugee columns in Kosovo and Metohia? Is the U.S. use of cluster bombs exploding razor-sharp metal fragments over an area as large as a soccer field in the courtyard at the hospital in Nis no crime? Will the Security Council act to prevent and punish the use of depleted uranium by the United States which is as indiscriminate in its radiation as the air, the water, the soil and food chain it touches and contaminates for millions of years?

. . .

3. *The International Criminal Tribunal for Former Yugoslavia Is Incapable of Protecting Fundamental Rights, or Providing Due Process of Law.*

Such an ad hoc Tribunal has a temporary and limited purpose without helpful precedent, common tradition or relevant experience. It lacks power to enforce orders, or compel the disclosure of evidence and presence of witnesses, particularly for the defense. It is not capable of finding facts fairly or defining and applying legal principles equally. It cannot do justice. The statutory mandate for the ICTY makes it hostile to concern for the rights of those accused before it, because it is told the crimes charged have occurred and the accused have been demonized.

The right to assistance of counsel, so firmly established in international law, has been denied and frustrated by the Tribunal even in its most prominent cases. The Registry denied to me the right to consult with lawyers of my choice on legal matters for several weeks after my arraignment.

The Registrar wrote that for the one attorney who visited me during that time and for only two hours, it would have been "inappropriate" to discuss the case because the conversation was monitored and confidences would be violated. Lawyers from Yugoslavia I ask to consult, with one exception, a monitored two-hour visit, were still denied approval and visas to enter the Netherlands seven weeks after my arraignment.

Instead I was held in solitary confinement. I was able to visit my wife only after more than two weeks imprisonment and then only through soundproof glass using monitored telephones. She was prohibited from speaking with the press and kept isolated from all public contacts while in the Netherlands, a virtual prisoner in her hotel room, except as she traveled between the airport, the prison, and the hotel.

. . .

For these reasons, the so-called ICTY should be declared illegal and its prisoners, legally and illegally surrendered, should be released.

The Hague
August 30, 2001

Prosecutor v. Slobodan Milosevic

Decision on Preliminary Motions

Judge Richard May, Presiding

This Trial Chamber of the International Tribunal for the Prosecution of Persons Responsible for Serious

United Nations Security Council
International Criminal Tribunal for the Former Yugoslavia, The Hague, November 8, 2001. Reprinted by permission.

Violations of International Humanitarian Law Committed in the Territory of the Former Yugoslavia since 1991 ("International Tribunal") is seized of two motions filed by the accused on 9 and 30 August 2001 (together "the Motions").

. . .

This Decision deals with all the arguments, written and oral, raised by the accused, the Prosecution, and the *amici curiae*. Although some of the arguments have been dealt with before in the International Tribunal, the Chamber has considered all of them very carefully. Indeed, any judicial body is bound to take seriously a challenge to the legality of its foundation.

· · ·

Illegal Foundation of the International Tribunal

Constitutionality

The accused has argued that the International Tribunal is an illegal entity because the Security Council lacked the power to establish it. . . . The basis of the challenge to the constitutionality of the International Tribunal is that the Security Council is not empowered under Chapter VII of the Charter of the United Nations to establish an international criminal court.

The relevant provision is Article 41 of the Charter, which empowers the Security Council to adopt measures not involving the use of armed force to give effect to its decisions in order to discharge its obligation under Article 39 to maintain or restore international peace and security. Article 41 lists certain measures which may be taken by the Security Council. It is perfectly clear that the list is not exhaustive and that it is open to the Security Council to adopt any measure other than those specifically listed, provided it is a measure to maintain or restore international peace and security.

In the Chamber's view, the establishment of the International Tribunal with power to prosecute persons responsible for serious violations of international humanitarian law in the former Yugoslavia, and with the obligation to guarantee fully the rights of the accused, is, in the context of the conflict in the country at that time, pre-eminently a measure to restore international peace and security. Indeed, the role of the International Tribunal in promoting peace and reconciliation in the former Yugoslavia is highlighted in Security Council resolution 827 which established it. . . . Accordingly, the Chamber dismisses this ground.

The accused argues that the creation of an ad hoc court targeting one country "corrupts justice and law"; that an ad hoc court "violates the most basic principles of all law" and "that an international court established to prosecute acts in a single nation and primarily, if not entirely, one limited group is pre-programmed to persecute, incapable of equality."

Human rights bodies have, on several occasions, pronounced on the legitimacy of ad hoc tribunals. The decisions of these bodies establish that there is nothing inherently illegitimate in the creation of an ad hoc judicial body, and that the important question is whether that body is established by law, in the sense that . . . it "should genuinely afford the accused the full guarantees of fair trial set out in Article 14 of the International Covenant on Civil and Political Rights."

The International Tribunal meets this requirement in that the rights of the accused, comparable to those in the International Covenant on Civil and Political Rights ("ICCPR"), are entrenched in the International Tribunal's Statute, in particular, in Article 21.

Accordingly, this ground is dismissed.

· · ·

Fair Trial and Protection of Human Rights

Allegation of Bias

The *amici curiae* contend that the accused, in arguing that the International Tribunal is either incapable of providing him with a fair trial or of protection of his fundamental human rights, is "implicitly asserting bias." In any event, the accused himself has argued in relation to the International Tribunal that "the very psychology of the enterprise is persecutorial. Few judges appointed to serve on a Tribunal created under such circumstances will feel free to acquit any but the most marginal, or clearly mistaken, accused, or to create an appearance of objectivity."

· · ·

[T]he Appeals Chamber held that there were three ways in which bias on the part of a Judge could be established. First by proof of actual bias. Secondly, if the Judge has some interest, material or otherwise, in the matter being litigated. Thirdly, if a reasonable observer, properly informed, would reasonably apprehend bias.

In the circumstances of this case it is only the third criterion that would be relevant: nothing has been advanced, either by the accused or by the *amici curiae*, on the basis of which a reasonable observer, properly informed, would reasonably apprehend bias on the part of the Chamber. This ground is, therefore, dismissed.

· · ·

The contention that the accused is not amenable to the jurisdiction of the International Tribunal. . . .

The Chamber observes that this argument has not been raised explicitly by the accused. In the passage cited by the *amici curiae*, what is stated is that the International Tribunal "does not have jurisdiction over the person of President Milosevic." The Chamber will, however, deal with the argument, since it has been raised by the *amici curiae*. The Prosecution has argued that Article 7, paragraph 2, of the Statute reflects customary international law and notes, in particular, that the International Criminal Tribunal for Rwanda convicted Jean Kambanda, the former Prime Minister of Rwanda, for his role in the genocide that occurred in that State in 1994.

Article 7, paragraph 2, of the Statute provides that

the official position of any accused person, whether as Head of State or Government or as a responsible Government official, shall not relieve such person of criminal responsibility nor mitigate punishment.

The *amici curiae* say that the accused must be understood to be denying the validity of that Article.

There is absolutely no basis for challenging the validity of Article 7, paragraph 2, which at this time reflects a rule of customary international law. The history of this rule can be traced to the development of the doctrine of individual criminal responsibility after the Second World War, when it was incorporated in Article 7 of the Nuremberg Charter and Article 6 of the Tokyo Tribunal Charter. The customary character of the rule is further supported by its incorporation in a wide number of other instruments, as well as case law.

. . .

[I]n the Nuremberg Judgement, it was said:

The principle of international law, which under certain circumstances, protects the representative of a State, cannot be applied to acts which are condemned as criminal by international law. The authors of these acts cannot shelter themselves behind their official position in order to be freed from punishment in appropriate proceedings . . . the very essence of the Charter is that individuals have international duties which transcend the national obligations of obedience imposed by the individual State. He who violates the laws of war cannot obtain immunity while acting in pursuance of the authority of the State if the State in authorizing action moves outside its competence under international law.

Accordingly, this ground is dismissed.

. . .

Accordingly, all the Motions are dismissed.

Done in English and French, the English text being authoritative.

Richard May
Presiding
Dated this eighth day of November 2001.

Study Questions

1. Jackson claims that the international community has the right to institute new customs that will form the basis for expanding international law. Do you agree?

2. What are some of the specific grounds on which Jackson bases his claim that aggressive warfare was a violation of international law even prior to the formulation of the Nuremberg Charter? Do you find them convincing?

3. In his opening statement at Nuremberg, Jackson asks (rhetorically): "Does it take these men by surprise that murder is treated as a crime?" In what sense is Jackson using "crime" here? Could the force of his remark be trading on an equivocation between crime as a *moral* wrong and crime as a *legal* wrong?

4. In July 2001, the Rome Statute for the International Criminal Court (ICC), took effect. The ICC is to have broad powers to try war criminals and those accused of crimes against humanity. The United States, in a break with virtually all of its allies, refused to support the court. U.S. officials cited primarily political reasons for opposing the treaty, but significant legal obstacles stand in the way of such an undertaking. Which legal system should a world criminal court employ? What procedural rules (covering everything from motions and indictments to introduction of evidence and composition of juries) should be followed? Should trials *in absentia* be allowed? Which crimes would fall within the court's jurisdiction? How should crimes of genocide, for example, be defined? Should other serious crimes, such as drug trafficking, be punishable by the ICC? Should the death penalty be available? Imagine that you are designing an authorizing

statute for a court like the ICC. How would you resolve these issues? Given that no nation currently has laws that can be expected to match completely the rules any such international court would follow, could individuals brought before the ICC claim that they were being subjected to "new" law in violation of the principles of legality and the rule of law?

5. In what ways, according to Wyzanski, did the Nuremberg Charter create "new" law?

6. Why is an appeal to principles of justice or human rights embedded in "the law of civilized nations" necessarily an *ex post facto* appeal? Usually a law is *ex post facto* if what a person did was not a crime at the time he or she did it. But, Jackson might argue, these basic ideals had been around for a long time; they weren't invented in 1945. How would you respond?

7. Some of the Nazi defendants at Nuremberg raised the defense of obedience to superior orders: "I was ordered to kill the civilians." Assuming that such orders were given by Hitler or his top aides, were such orders legal, given a natural law theory? Given a positivist theory?

8. Imagine that you are a judge at Nuremberg on the panel hearing the case against the Nazis. Jackson and Wyzanski have each presented their case before you. Assuming that the evidence in support of Nazi atrocities is strong, would you rule that they have broken "the law"? How would you defend your answer?

9. A classic treatise defined international law as "the body of rules and principles of actions which are binding upon civilized states in their relations with one another" [Brierly, J., *The Law of Nations*, 6th ed. (Oxford: Oxford University Press, 1963)]. How would you go about determining what such "law" contains? Was Robert Jackson's argument before the Nuremberg Tribunal an appeal to some such broad definition?

10. Is international "law" really law at all? Can a legal system exist in the absence of courts with compulsory jurisdiction to resolve disputes and a centralized police authority to enforce the courts' decrees? Is international law based upon the *consent* of various states to be bound by the terms of treaties and customs? If so, what makes such acts of consent legally binding?

11. The drafters of the charter for the International Criminal Tribunal for the Former Yugoslavia were particularly concerned to avoid the charge leveled by Wyzanski and others at Nuremberg: namely, that such trials amount to the imposition of *ex post facto* "victor's justice" in violation of the ideal of the rule of law. For this reason, the ICTY's supporters stressed that the Tribunal would apply standards that are indisputably part of the "customary law of nations." Is it possible to determine with sufficient clarity what such customary laws forbid?

12. In his statement to the ICTY, Slobodan Milosevic insists that "[a]n international court established to prosecute acts in a single nation and primarily, if not entirely, one limited group is pre-programmed to persecute [and is] incapable of equality." Do you agree?

13. Judge May responds in part to Milosevic's denunciation of the ICTY as biased and ad hoc with this rejoinder: "[T]here is nothing inherently illegitimate in the creation of an ad hoc judicial body, and . . . the important question is whether that body is established by law, in the sense that it 'should genuinely afford the accused the full guarantees of fair trial . . .'" Is this an adequate answer to Milosevic?

14. For what purpose does Judge May refer to the Nuremberg trials as precedent? What point does he think Nuremberg established regarding the contention that Milosevic cannot be legally tried by the tribunal?

15. In July 1994, the United Nations Security Council determined that unrest in the island nation of Haiti was a threat to peace and security in the region. A multinational task force was dispatched, including U.S. troops, to end the military dictatorship on the island. Members of the Army's 10th Mountain Division, including Captain Lawrence Rockwood, entered Haiti in September. Rockwood, a Buddhist, was personally concerned about intelligence reports of human rights violations at Haiti's National Penitentiary, in the city of Port au Prince. Rockwood attempted to initiate a task force inspection of prison conditions; he raised the issue with his superiors, the Judge Advocate General's (JAG) office, and the division chaplain. Failing to secure recognition of his concerns, Captain Rockwood, without command authorization, personally went

to the prison to inspect it. Rockwood was subsequently detained and charged with willful disobedience of a superior officer. In his defense, Rockwood claimed that his otherwise criminal acts were justified because he had a personal legal duty as a member of U.S. forces and under international law to prevent human rights violations. Rockwood alleged that he would be liable under the Nuremberg Charter for failing to act. A military Court of

Criminal Appeals rejected Rockwood's arguments. Rockwood, the court maintained, had not been asked to do anything that would be a violation of international law, and the failure of his superiors to act on his concerns, even if illegal under international law, relieved Rockwood of any responsibility for wrongs occurring at the prison. Was Rockwood's case correctly decided? What "law" should take priority in this case?

C. *Classical Theories of Law*

Natural Law Versus Positivism

On trial at Nuremberg, Nazi officials and officers sought to use a variety of defenses. One defense was presented by Professor Hermann Jahrreiss, an associate defense attorney. Jahrreiss argued that the Enabling Act of March 24, 1933, authorized Adolf Hitler to rule by decree: "Now in a state in which the entire power to make final decisions is concentrated in the hands of a single individual, the orders of this one man are absolutely binding on the members of the hierarchy. This individual is their sovereign . . ."[1] Behind Jahrreiss's argument lay a view of law familiar to the average person: A statement or rule becomes a rule of *law* only if it is a *command,* an order backed up by the threat of force and issued by someone in absolute control. Law is erected on a power relationship: the commander issues an order, and the commanded must comply. Hitler's orders were law, Jahrreiss stated, and the Nuremberg defendants were simply obeying their sovereign.

The Nuremberg tribunal rejected the arguments of Jahrreiss: "That a soldier was ordered to kill or torture in violation of the international law of war has never been

recognized as a defense to such acts of brutality. . . ."[2] Although the defense was rejected, the idea of law as an order backed by force has a long history. An opposing view of law has an equally long record. In Sophocles' play *Antigone*, the ancient Greek playwright describes the dilemma confronted by the daughter of the tragic Oedipus. Antigone's brothers have killed each other, and Creon, king of Thebes, has issued an order forbidding the burial of one brother, Polynices. Antigone's sister reminds Antigone that this "law is strong, we must give in to the law."[3] Antigone, who is determined to do what is right and bury her brother properly, rebukes her sister, observing that "apparently the laws of the gods mean nothing to you."[4] Antigone insists that law is what is just, proper, or right—not merely whatever a dictator demands. Antigone sacrifices her life out of fidelity to this ideal.

The history of legal philosophy has been shaped by the conflict between these two opposing general conceptions of law and legality: law as power and law as justice. These general views have, of course, been

---

[1] Quoted in Stanley Paulson, "Classical Legal Positivism at Nuremberg," *Philosophy and Public Affairs*, Vol. 4 (1975), p. 144.

[2] *Ibid.*

[3] Dudley Fitts and Robert Fitzgerald (trans.), *Sophocles: The Oedipus Cycle* (New York: Harcourt, Brace, and Co., 1949), p. 188.

[4] *Ibid.*

much debated and refined. Our discussion begins with two specific forms of these broad approaches: *legal positivism* and *natural law theory*.

Natural law theory, or simply *naturalism*, holds that the phenomenon we call "law" can adequately be understood only in relation to a certain view about the nature of *moral* judgments and standards. What we recognize and venerate as law, according to naturalism, is both essentially connected to and grounded in a "natural moral order"—that is, principles and standards not simply made up by humans but part of an objective moral order present in the universe and accessible to human reason. Naturalism holds that human practices and institutions are to be measured against these "higher" standards, and where they fall short of the mark, specific human arrangements, whether statutes, executive orders, or constitutions, fail fully to have the character of law.

Positivism, by contrast, holds that the phenomenon of law is best understood as a system of orders, commands, or rules enforced by power. For the positivist, law is that which has been "posited"—that is, made, enacted, or laid down in some prescribed fashion. It is as such a purely human product—"artificial" rather than "natural." Moreover, for the positivist, a rule of law need have no connection with what is morally right or correct or true in order to qualify as law: there is no necessary connection between what law is and what it ought to be.

Argentine legal philosopher and human rights activist Carlos Nino vividly depicts the clash between positivism and natural law in his fictional case study, which opens the readings for this section. In a proceeding before a military tribunal in which various human rights violations have been alleged against a group of defendants, Nino's three judges confront the perplexities of determining exactly which definition of "law" to apply in such cases.

Legal Positivism

As H. L. A. Hart points out in his selection, positivism came into its own as a distinct and well-formulated legal theory in the late eighteenth and early nineteenth centuries in the writings of two British philosophers, Jeremy Bentham and John Austin. Central to the legal theory of both was the conviction that law as it is does not necessarily embody law as it ought to be. It does not, they believed, follow from the fact that because a statute or an ordinance is valid law it is also morally good or right. A statute *could,* of course, coincide with what is right, but the fact of its being the "law" does not guarantee its rightness. The morality and legality of a rule are in this way distinct and separate. This "separability thesis," as later positivists have come to call it, led both Bentham and Austin to distinguish sharply between the task of giving an accurate, descriptive account of what law is—"expository" or "analytical" jurisprudence—and the task of evaluating the law morally, or stating what it *ought to be*—"censorial" or "normative" jurisprudence.

As Hart makes clear, in addition to their commitment to positivism, Bentham and Austin shared an allegiance to a general moral and political outlook known as *utilitarianism.* We will have occasion to encounter utilitarianism in more depth later; for now it is enough to note its basic features. Utilitarianism is one of several ethical theories or views of moral life that regard the *consequences* of an act as the sole or exclusive factor to be weighed in determining whether the act is morally right or good. More specifically, utilitarians such as Bentham argue that an action is right or good only if it brings more overall happiness (or at least less unhappiness) into the world than any alternative course of action open to a person at a given time. Bentham appealed to this "Principle of Utility" frequently when it came to evaluating the law from a moral standpoint, and he often found the laws of the England of his time sadly lacking from the perspective of bringing about the greatest happiness.

The work of contemporary positivist H. L. A. Hart is widely regarded as a central statement of modern positivism. Although not all contemporary positivists agree with Hart, all acknowledge that he has largely set the terms in which the contemporary debate about positivism has taken place. Much of what Hart has to say is written against a background of familiarity with the basic outlines of the theories of Bentham and especially Austin. It is therefore useful to acquaint ourselves briefly with the outlines of Austin's account and with the deficiencies that Hart and others have noted in it.

In the selection from his book, *The Province of Jurisprudence Determined*, Austin makes it clear he has little patience for talk of the "natural law," "moral law," or "the law of God." Along with customs and international agreements, these can be called "law" only in an improper sense. What is law? According to Austin, law "properly so called" is something established by a political superior over subjects and takes the form of a command issued by a sovereign. What is a command? It is a signification of desire, backed by a credible threat of punishment, a threat that can in all likelihood be carried out. Is anyone's command a law? No; only the command of the "sovereign" can be certified as law. Who (or what) is the sovereign? Austin makes no attempt to define the sovereign in terms of some normative or value-laden criterion, such as "he who has the right to rule" or "he who legitimately rules." Instead, Austin argues that the sovereign is the person or group of persons that is habitually obeyed by the bulk of a given population but does not habitually obey anyone else; the sovereign is the "unobeying obeyed." If some person, X, is habitually obeyed by the bulk of the population and does not habitually obey anyone else, that person is the sovereign. If X then expresses the desire that certain things be done (or not done) and makes a credible threat that failure to comply will be punished, X has issued a command and his or her command is law. Finally, Austin makes it clear that the existence of a law does not guarantee that the law is fair, just, or right. If a law is morally right or correct, this is merely a contingent `matter, reflecting the particular content of what the sovereign has signified.

Austin's model is elegant in its simplicity, but it is open to seemingly decisive objections, as Hart and others have pointed out. The most fundamental of these objections has to do with the notions of command and sovereign. A command is a desire backed by a threat. Do all laws fit this model? Do all laws have sanctions? Austin's model makes some sense if the paradigm of law is, for example, criminal law. But what about other types of law? What about the law of contracts or of wills? What about American constitutional law? If I enter into a contract with you or write a will leaving you all my money, am I being commanded? By whom? And to do what? Austin tried to deal with these and similar cases by claiming that there *is,* after all, a sanction with which I am being threatened in these cases, what Austin called the "sanction of nullity": the sovereign will "punish" me by not giving effect to my will or my contract in the event that, for example, I don't fill them out properly. But this seems contrived. Isn't the situation better described by saying that the laws of wills and contracts *empower* me to do certain things (for example, sell my house) or bring about certain effects (for example, give all my property to my wife)? The aim here is not to punish but to facilitate.

The laws of our own Constitution do not command us to continue their observance. If the citizens of

what is now the United States were overwhelmingly to decide to repudiate the Constitution in its entirety next Friday at noon, would we all be punished for doing so? It seems not; but that fact does not incline us to say that the Constitution is not "law," at least in some sense. It merely shows that the Constitution is not law as a command (or series of commands) but rather is law as a structure or system of relative powers and competencies designed to facilitate or effect certain aims.

Austin's conception of sovereignty raises further difficulties. Generally, for example, we believe that the framework of our laws persists over time and carries over from one administration to the next (unless repealed or modified). But how would Austin's theory account for such endurance? When one sovereign dies, the habit of obeying him or her dies as well. But the habit of obeying the sovereign's successor will take time to develop, and this seems to mean that, in Austin's view, there will be disruptions or discontinuities in the persistence of the law. According to later positivists, like Hart, the framework of laws must be re-conceived as a set of social rules or practices that do not depend upon the orders of a sovereign to be valid.

Another question for Austin is this: Do all legal systems necessarily have Austinian sovereigns? Consider again our own constitutional democracy. Do we have a sovereign? Who is it? To the extent that we can think in these terms at all, we view *ourselves* ("*we* the people") as those in charge. Austin, it seems, would have us then say that we (the people) in our constitution-enacting-and-maintaining role are sovereign over ourselves in our role as citizens. But does this concept preserve any of the simplicity of Austin's initial model? Furthermore, in our constitutional democracy we have grown accustomed to thinking of ours as a *limited* government. But can Austin's model make sense of limitations upon the power of sovereigns? To do so, Austin would have to argue that sovereigns, in their sovereign capacity, issue commands to themselves in their capacity as citizens. But then, of course, what distinguishes between these two aspects of sovereigns must be some notion of *official* capacity, and this idea cannot be spelled out in terms of Austin's theory.

To illustrate this limitation, consider the following problem. All persons who currently serve as United States senators meet at a football field on a holiday and "vote" to make themselves "kings" of the states from which they come (forget about the problem of having two kings from each state). None of us would be prepared to say that this vote has made "law," because (we would explain) the senators were not acting in their "official" capacity. But Austin has no room for official capacity; his theory sees only these individuals, who are after all the same people (and people habitually obeyed, though not on this occasion) whether inside or outside the Senate chamber.

Hart's Theory

In his central work, *The Concept of Law*[5], Hart attempted to give a fresh start to positivism by resolving the problems implicit in Austin's theory. Austin conceived of law and of a legal system on the analogy of a holdup by an armed robber: orders backed by threats. Law is merely the "gunman situation writ large." Hart argued that this view confuses two quite different states of affairs: being *obliged* to give my money to the robber (to avoid being hurt) and being legally *obligated* to pay my taxes by April 15 (to avoid a penalty). Feeling obliged is just that—a feeling, a psychological state. But being under an obligation is a feature of life that is *social* and that essentially involves the idea of a social rule. Hart argued that a shared activity or practice cannot constitute a social rule unless people manifest a certain attitude toward it, specifically, they accept and use the rule to guide their conduct. In this sense, "Pay your taxes by April 15" is a social rule because most of us use it (however reluctantly!) to guide our conduct and help us plan. "Give me your money or else" is, on the other hand, plainly not such a rule.

Hart summarized his own theory of law as the view that law is a union of primary and secondary rules. *Primary rules* are those social rules that concern themselves directly with the way we live and behave. "No one may drive faster than 55 mph" or "Pay your taxes by April 15" are primary rules. *Secondary rules*, on the other hand, are "secondary" in the sense that their subject matter is not human behavior but rather the primary rules themselves. "The traffic code is exclusively the jurisdiction of the state" and "Proposed changes in the tax code must be approved by Congress" are examples of secondary rules. In order for a body of rules to qualify as *legal* rules, according to Hart, there must be secondary rules to supplement the primary ones. Of particular interest here is Hart's notion of a *rule of recog-*

nition. This is a secondary rule that specifies criteria for what counts as a primary rule. "Whatever the chief utters is law" or "Whatever the legislatures enact consistently with the Constitution is law" are examples of rules of recognition. "Pay your taxes by April 15" is then a valid rule of law because it was created (enacted by a legislature) in the way specified by the ultimate rule of recognition of our legal system.

Much debate has accompanied what Hart says about the existence of rules of recognition. What does it mean for such rules to exist? To say that the rule of recognition exists cannot mean that it is valid because it is enacted in accordance with a procedure laid down in the rule of recognition; plainly, the rule cannot validate itself. The existence of the rule of recognition must be a matter of descriptive fact; it simply *is* the rule acknowledged in the attitudes and behaviors of most legal actors within a given system. The key claim for Hart is that social rules, in order to count as laws, must be regarded, by at least the legal officials, as guides to their own and others' actions—the rules must be accepted from an "internal point of view" such that they provide good reasons for doing what the rules require. Nonetheless, Hart cautioned, the internal point of view does not of itself guarantee that the primary social rules of a given legal system are just or morally right. In this way Hart retains a commitment to the positivist separability thesis.

Debates continue over legal positivism, how best to understand the theory, and its relationship to rival views, particularly those of Ronald Dworkin (whose work is covered in Section D). Philosopher Brian Bix, in his selection, takes up several of these most recent discussions. As Bix explains, one prominent disagreement involves proponents of two forms of the theory: *exclusive legal positivism* and *inclusive legal positivism*. Bix seeks to clarify the distinction between these views by relating them to Hart's notion of a rule of recognition. For the exclusive positivist, no social rule can be part of the law unless it can be traced back to a conventionally recognized source—a legislative enactment or royal edict, for example. As such, the rule of recognition for any given legal system necessarily "excludes" any moral principles or standards from the criteria specifying what is to count as law. In this sense, all genuine laws must have a "pedigree" that is empty of any moral content. For the inclusive legal positivist, by contrast, moral standards may be a part of the criteria of legality. This would happen if, for instance, the officials of the legal system routinely invoked such moral principles when addressing the source of the law in their

---

[5] H. L. A. Hart, *The Concept of Law* (Oxford: Clarendon Press, 1961).

community. Bix explores the extent of the differences between these forms of positivism and shows how each might come close to collapsing into the other.

Hart and Fuller

In his essay "Positivism and the Separation of Law and Morals," included here, Hart notes that critics of positivism sometimes conflate the separability thesis—the claim that legality and morality are separate issues—with Austin's command theory of law, reasoning that since the latter is open to serious objections, so must be the former. Hart believes, however, that it is possible to adhere to the separability thesis (and to a utilitarian moral outlook) and still reject Austin's command model, and this is indeed Hart's position.

Hart considers several objections to the separation of law and morals so important to positivism. Some critics argue that law and morality cannot be separated for the reason that legal rules cannot always say how they are to be applied. For example, the general rule "No vehicles in the park" cannot be applied to the specific situation of my rocket-powered skateboard without the exercise of moral judgment: Should I be allowed to ride through the park on my skateboard? Any positivists who think differently, so these critics say, are guilty of the error of "formalism," the belief that all rules of law can be unambiguously and straightforwardly applied to any situation with complete logical certainty. Hart responds that this criticism relies on a false dilemma. We can, Hart believes, adhere to the separability thesis and yet not fall victim either to a direct appeal to moral values when interpreting a rule such as "No vehicles in the park" nor to the silliness of formalism. Judges can resolve these "penumbral," or "fuzzy," cases by appealing to accepted social policies and purposes.

A further objection to the positivistic insistence that a rule can still be a rule of law even if it is immoral is made by those who have lived under evil legal regimes such as that in effect in Germany during the Nazi period. These critics complain that the positivist separation of law and morals can have (and has had) pernicious effects: by insisting that laws remain valid even if immoral, positivism has been easily exploited by corrupt "law-and-order" regimes eager to exact compliance with their regulations. Hart tries to argue that the proper response to these critics is not to reject the separability thesis but to recognize that some rules or regulations, even though they are the law, are too morally outrageous to obey.

Hart does make one seeming concession to the natural law position. We do have, Hart admits, an obvious need for a system of legal protections and regulations with some minimal moral content. Legal rules prohibiting physical violence are necessary, for example, not because the presence of such values is entailed by the very idea of something's being the law, but simply given the contingent fact that human beings are vulnerable to physical harm and abuse. This, says Hart, is the core of good sense in the naturalist position, but it would be an error to mistake the necessity for such laws for a truth about the nature of law as such.

Hart's essay is followed by one from former Harvard jurist Lon Fuller, a piece written as a response to the essay by Hart. While careful not to endorse the classical natural law theory of Aquinas, Fuller's critique of Hart's positivism nonetheless bears a recognizable "naturalistic" stamp in its insistence that "law" and "what is morally right" are in an important sense inseparable.

Fuller is especially interested in the legal problems that arose in Germany after the Nazi period, such as the case of the housewife-turned-informer. Hart, says Fuller, misunderstands these cases. Hart incorrectly assumes that something deserving the name of "law" persisted throughout the Nazi reign and that it did so in a way that makes meaningful the ideal of *fidelity to law*. Fidelity to law, as Fuller understood it, meant that a statute or an ordinance is deserving of loyalty and respect simply by virtue of its being the law. Fuller maintains that positivism cannot explain or make sense of the ideal of fidelity to law and that positivism is therefore descriptively false or inaccurate.

Fuller concedes that a particular rule of law can still be law even if it is immoral, but he denies that such rules can remain law if they are part of an entire legal system that is itself deeply evil and unjust. Fuller defends the decision of the postwar German courts in the "grudge-informer" cases on the grounds that Nazi "law" was not law at all, as it failed to compose in any meaningful sense a legal *order*. Fuller chronicles a number of features of Nazi law and its operation with the aim of showing that, for any system of legal rules to exist, certain minimum *moral* demands must be satisfied: impartial enforcement, fair notice, promulgation, and so on. Law has its own "internal morality." Law is not merely order, but good order. The positivist insistence on the separation of law and morality does not illuminate the kind of problem raised by the grudge-informer cases. As Fuller sees it, positivism recommends that the German courts acknowledge the validity of Nazi law and then refuse to apply it. But, he responds, how can it further our understanding of fidelity to law to insist that a court should refuse to apply and enforce what it admits is valid law? Positivism, Fuller concludes, fails for the reason that it can give no coherent meaning to the moral obligation of loyalty to law.

Natural Law Theory

Naturalism has a rich and varied history, extending back to the ancient Greeks and Romans. One of the most elaborate and thorough expositions of the naturalist position was given by thirteenth-century Catholic theologian Thomas Aquinas.[6]

St. Thomas Aquinas

In the brief selection included here from his great work, the *Summa Theologica*, Aquinas argues, first, that law necessarily involves rules that (given that they have their source in reason) must have some purpose or goal. Following the Greek philosopher Aristotle, Aquinas insists that this goal must be overall happiness or the "common good." Laws must be "promulgated" or made clear to those who are subject to them, Aquinas continues, and this means that God is the ultimate source of such promulgating authority.

Aquinas sets out his famous typology of four distinct kinds of law: eternal, divine, natural, and human. Eternal law represents God's overall plan for the universe. Divine law was for Aquinas the revealed word of God, the principles revealed by Scripture. Divine law is necessary, Aquinas believed, because human beings have a supernatural destiny to which we must be guided, our native intellect being inadequate to reveal to us the nature of this destiny and how to secure it. Human law, by contrast with eternal and divine law, is created by us for the purpose of carrying out the requirements of natural law.

What, then, is natural law? Aquinas argued that because all things are subject to divine providence and thus are "ruled and measured" by eternal law, all things "partake" in some way of eternal law. Aquinas believed that humans, as rational beings, occupy a special place in God's eternal plan, in that we can under-

stand eternal law as it applies to us and can allow that understanding to guide our conduct. Eternal law, as it applies to human conduct, Aquinas calls "natural law."

What does natural law tell us to do? In answering this question, Aquinas invoked (as he often did) a distinction drawn by Aristotle. Aristotle had distinguished between two kinds of reason: speculative and practical. Speculative reason is our capacity as reasoning beings to apprehend or understand certain truths, such as the truths of mathematics and geometry. Practical reason is not concerned with these abstract matters but rather with human action. Practical reason tells us what things we should value, what goods we should seek in life, and how to obtain them. Aquinas and Aristotle held that, in both speculative and practical reason, certain principles are *per se nota*, known through themselves. These are self-evident propositions, requiring no proof (in the sense of being derivable from something else). As examples of self-evident principles of speculative reason, Aquinas included the principle of non-contradiction ("What is, is, and what is not, is not") and certain truths of mathematics and geometry. Turning to practical reason, Aquinas claimed that the first and most fundamental principle or "precept" of natural law is "Good is to be done and evil avoided." Others include "One should not kill one's father"; and "God's precepts are to be obeyed."

How does natural law relate to human law? Aquinas maintained that human law must be developed to implement and adapt the basic precepts of natural law, which are quite general, to the changing needs and contexts of human societies. The basic precepts are the same for everyone and do not change, but the detailed conclusions drawn from these basic precepts may differ from place to place and time to time, and human law reflects this fact. "Goods held in trust for another should be returned" is, according to Aquinas, a requirement of natural law, but it should not be followed when the good is a gun and the person to whom it should be returned is in a homicidal frenzy. Human law must adjust the principles of natural law to develop regulations that are appropriate for specific situations. Moreover, since human communities need many detailed regulations and ordinances simply to function (for example, tax and traffic laws), natural law requires that they be made, although it does not, of course, dictate their particular content (for example, natural law does not require that we drive on the right side of the road, but only that the community establish rules to meet the fundamental requirement that health and safety be protected).

---

[6] See Anton C. Pegis, ed., *Summa Theologica, The Basic Writings of Saint Thomas Aquinas*, Vol. 2 (New York: Random House, 1945), pp. 742ff.

What about a situation in which human law fails to conform to natural law? It is here that Aquinas's naturalism has potentially far-reaching consequences. As he makes clear in the reading, the force of a human law necessarily depends upon its justice: human enactments or measures that contravene natural law are not laws "but a perversion of law"; they are "acts of violence" and do not bind in conscience. Although it is still debated exactly what Aquinas meant by such statements, these remarks have seemed to many to imply that any human "laws" at odds with natural law have no legal validity. Even entire legal systems, Aquinas suggests, if they are evil "perversions" of natural law (for example, the legal regime of the Nazis) may stand invalidated on that ground.

Martin Luther King, Jr.'s famous "Letter from Birmingham Jail" is included here to illustrate one way in which Aquinas's views on the relationship of natural to human law can be translated into political action and moral commitment. Writing from a jail cell in Alabama in 1963, King responds to criticisms of his disobedience to the segregationist statutes of the South by appealing to a "higher" law—the natural law—and invokes the core naturalist claim that these human enactments, these racist statutes, have forfeited their status as "law" by virtue of their obvious immorality.

Legality and Justice: A Fictional Case

CARLOS NINO

[I]magine we are in the city of Nusquam today and the date is November 25, 1948. The Allied Forces' Military Tribunal for the Far East meets to deliver its judgment against the twenty-eight people accused of crimes against the peace and crimes against humanity. After hearing the arguments of the prosecution and the defense and having received the evidence offered by both parties, the members of the court issue the following opinions:

Justice Sempronius

Distinguished colleagues: We are gathered here to deliver judgment about deeds that were part of what was doubtless the most abhorrent event in the history of humanity. The men sitting here were among those contributing to the suffering of millions of people. Moved by a messianic world view, they conspired to wage an unjust war and committed egregious abuses during that war. They violated fundamental principles of human dignity by causing deaths, inflicting torture, and persecuting people without cause under a totalitarian system of government. Defense counsel does not deny the deeds but questions the legal characteri-

From Carlos Nino, *Radical Evil on Trial* (New Haven: Yale University Press, 1996), pp. 150–154. Reprinted by permission of Yale University Press.

zation which make the deeds punishable. Defense counsel maintains that these people have committed acts which, whatever their moral value, were perfectly legitimate according to the law in force at the time and place in which they were committed. The defendants, according to this thesis, were public officials who acted in observance of legal norms enacted and enforced by the proper bodies of the Japanese empire. The defendants were not only authorized to do what they did but in some cases were obliged to act in that manner. Defense counsel reminds us of an elementary principle of justice which the civilization that we represent has long accepted and which was ignored by the regime for which the defendant worked—*nullum crimen, nulla poena sine lege praevia*, proscribing imposition of a penalty for an act which was not prohibited at the time when the act was performed but was, on the contrary, lawful. We would be contradicting our own philosophy and adopting the one we say we are combating if we ignored this principle and punished the defendants.

These are the arguments of defense counsel. But I believe that one of the greatest services that this court may lend to humanity is to debunk once and for all the absurd and atrocious doctrine enclosed in the thesis of the defense counsel. According to him, a legal system is established each time a human group succeeds in imposing a set of rules on a certain society and gathers enough power to enforce its rules, regardless of the moral content of those rules or the moral legitimacy for enacting them. This has been encapsulated in the obscene slogan "The law is the law," which has served to justify the most abhorrent oppressions. Since ancient times, however, lucid thinkers have demonstrated the fallacy of this proposition with compelling arguments.

They have shown that above the rules enacted by men there is a system of immutable and universal moral principles—sometimes called "natural law"—which establish patterns of justice and rights that belong to men simply because they are men. The positive rules enacted by men are only law insofar as they do not contradict those principles. When we confront rules like the ones which authorized the acts we are judging, calling them "law" denaturalizes this sacred name. What is the difference between these rules and those of a criminal organization except that the former have been more stable because they have ignored in a more radical way elementary principles of justice and morality? Defense counsel's position implies that judges should submit themselves to the internal order of the criminal organization they are judging.

Since the rules of the regime to which the defendants belonged do not constitute a true legal system, they are incapable of legitimizing the acts which were taken in their name. To ignore the rules of the regime, and to apply directly the moral principles blatantly violated by those acts in order to punish the acts in question, does not, thus, violate the principle of legality. . . . I vote, consequently, for the conviction of the defendants.

Justice Caius

I share the moral sentiments that my distinguished friend Sempronius has made of the acts we are here to judge. In formulating and expressing them, however, I am acting not as a judge but as a human being and as a citizen of a civilized nation, and I do not believe we

are allowed as judges to rely on those moral judgments to arrive at a decision in this trial.

Moral judgments are subjective and relative. Historians and anthropologists have shown how they have varied with time and space. What a people at a certain time considers to be morally abominable, another people at another time considers to be perfectly reasonable and legitimate. Can we deny that an authoritarian regime such as the one we are confronting generated a moral conception which was honestly endorsed by most of the society of this country? The idea that an immutable and universal "natural law," which is accessible to human reason, exists is, in the best of cases, an illusion that emerges from projecting our own feelings onto external reality. In the worst case, it is a manifestation of cultural imperialism which may be enforced only by virtue of military victory.

One of the noblest ideals of humanity is that social conflicts should be solved not according to the capricious moral feelings of those who happen to be in power, but according to settled legal rules: This is the ideal of the rule of law. The legal system of a community is a system of rules the content and scope of which may be objectively verified through empirical means, independently of our subjective valuations. Each time we encounter established institutions like courts of justice and a set of norms which are enacted and enforced by a human group that has the monopoly of means of coercion in a defined territory and which exercises force in a stable way, we face a legal system which can perfectly well be identified as such, regardless of our moral assessment of the value of its rules. Moreover, those rules can provide solutions for most if not all conceivable cases, especially if we accept that there is an implicit rule of closure in any legal system that permits those acts which are not explicitly prohibited. There is no doubt that there are relationships between law and morals—law is influenced by moral ideals—and that from the moral point of view the law should reflect the moral values that we happen to endorse. But this is not essential to the identification of law as such. And once we identify a legal system, we must recognize the binding quality of its rules and the legitimacy of the acts done in accordance with them.

The implications of this approach to this case are crystal-clear: We are confronting acts which were authorized by a genuine legal system, which was recognized as such by our own countries before the declaration of war. It is true that we are not judges of that system and thus obliged to apply its norms. But the rules of our own legal system contain the principle of legality and, thus, direct us to take into account what was legal at the time and place of the commission of these acts. Distinguished colleagues: Let us oppose the barbarism of this regime with our deep respect for the rule of law. Consequently, I vote for acquitting the defendants.

Justice Ticius

The opinions of my learned colleagues have perplexed me. I am conscious of our historical responsibility to advance clear and compelling principles which express the response of the civilized world to barbaric deeds such as those judged here. However, I cannot find in the previous opinions elements that allow us to infer those principles. My friend Sempronius has said that there are principles of morality and justice which are universal and accessible to human reason. On the contrary, my friend Caius denies that these principles exist and has asserted that moral principles are subjective and relative. Both positions seem unsatisfactory to me.

The first does not tell us how we know those principles and how we avoid the charge that we are imposing our feelings on others whom we consider, in an elitist way, more ignorant or morally inferior to us, when perhaps they are only weaker. The position of Caius also raises serious doubts: Is it really true that when we morally condemn acts like those we are confronting here, we are only expressing our emotional states or voicing the prejudices of our society? From the fact that societies and men differ in their moral evaluations, can one infer that all of them are equally reasonable and just? Is it reasonable to assume that we cannot judge people according to the principles we deem valid but only according to those they themselves assume, whatever they are? Is it possible to make moral judgments and to assume at the same time that opposite moral judgments may be also valid?

I confess that the two previous opinions leave me in an uncomfortable position. I am not convinced by the arguments so far given to justify principles of justice, yet I am not prepared to accept that they are subjective and relative. But we can leave this difficult matter to the philosophers, since in the end it is not relevant for our task. Even if we adopted a skeptical position about the foundation of ethical judgments, we cannot but formulate them, and if we do so, we are committed to act in accordance with them. We are not here to justify our ultimate ethical principles. What we need to decide is whether, as judges, we must apply those principles in order to decide this case or whether we must exclusively apply the legal norms which in fact authorized the acts committed by the defendants. For Sempronius this disjunctive does not arise, since for him identifying legal norms requires that they pass through the filter of moral principles. I cannot accept this stance and I agree with Caius's rejection of it. The law must be identified on the basis of factual and empirical features. This is the way in which we should proceed in order to adopt a scientific approach to the legal system and prevent mixing law and morality, which only serves to confuse the content of both. When we go to an unknown community and want to know what its legal rules provide, it is absurd that we answer the members of that community by resorting to our moral judgments. Not all who speak of the "imperial law" adhere morally to its content, and Sempronius sometimes has to resort to cumbersome circumlocutions in order to speak of that system without calling it "law."

I am uneasy with my colleague Caius's position. He tells us that the rules of a legal system are binding at the time and place in which they are in force. But what does this mean? If this only implies that these rules prescribe certain behavior, this is true, but the same is true of the orders of a robber. If, instead, Caius means that there is a different obligation to observe the legal rules—one which does not apply to the orders of the robbers—the question is, from where does that obligation emerge? The answer cannot be that it emerges from another legal rule, since this would invite the question of whether we are obliged to obey that legal rule, and at some point we would run out of legal rules. The only response is that the obligation emerges from another set of norms which is intrinsically obligatory and whose bindingness does not need to be supported by other norms. But the only norms that are supposed to have these properties are norms which, if they exist, do not exist on the basis of some enactment and therefore do not provoke the question of how "ought" could be derived from "is." These are norms of an ideal system of morality.

Consequently, for all his moral skepticism, when Caius speaks to us of the bindingness of the legal norms that he recognizes on the basis of pure facts, he is resorting implicitly to a moral principle. He is being inconsistent when he claims that we, as justices, must leave aside our moral convictions, since he is relying on some legal principle. Moreover, the moral principle upon which my friend Caius relies seems dubious. There are some reasons of security, order, and peace which may establish some duty to observe the existing legal order, even when its content is objectionable. But it is entirely implausible to assume this principle is absolute and not to acknowledge that it is overridden when weightier moral values, such as the preservation and promotion of fundamental rights, are at stake. If a judge of the time in which these deeds were committed had ignored the legal system in force in defense of human dignity, we would not have condemned him but would have praised him highly. Could we proceed otherwise with regard to this very court and our own behavior? Certainly not!

Both the principle of effectiveness of international law and the principle *nullum crimen, nulla poena sine lege praevia* of the civilized municipal systems are important principles to be scrupulously observed in normal circumstances, since they express moral ideals of national sovereignty, personal security, and social peace. But no moral value is absolute, and there is an urgent need for the court to affirm the value of human dignity and inviolability of the person. Therefore, the laws permitting these acts should be completely disregarded. I vote for the conviction of the defendants.

Legal Positivism

John Austin

Lecture 1

The matter of jurisprudence is positive law: law, simply and strictly so called: or law set by political superiors to political inferiors. . . .

A law, in the most general and comprehensive acceptation in which the term, in its literal meaning, is employed, may be said to be a rule laid down for the guidance of an intelligent being by an intelligent being having power over him. Under this definition are included, and without impropriety, several species. It is necessary to define accurately the line of demarcation which separates these species from one another, as much mistiness and intricacy has been infused into the science of jurisprudence by their being confounded or not clearly distinguished. In the comprehensive sense above indicated, or in the largest meaning which it has, without extension by metaphor or analogy, the term *law* embraces the following objects: laws set by God to his human creatures, and laws set by men to men.

The whole or a portion of the laws set by God to men is frequently styled the law of nature, or natural law: being, in truth, the only natural law of which it is possible to speak without a metaphor, or without a blending of objects which ought to be distinguished broadly. But, rejecting the appellation Law of Nature as ambiguous and misleading, I name those laws or rules, as considered collectively or in a mass, the *Divine law*, or the *law of God*.

Laws set by men to men are of two leading or principal classes: classes which are often blended, although they differ extremely; and which, for that reason, should be severed precisely, and opposed distinctly and conspicuously.

Of the laws or rules set by men to men, some are established by *political* superiors, sovereign and subject: by persons exercising supreme and subordinate *government*, in independent nations, or independent political societies. The aggregate of the rules thus established, or some aggregate forming a portion of that aggregate, is the appropriate matter of jurisprudence, general or particular. To the aggregate of the rules thus established, or to some aggregate forming a portion of that aggregate, the term *law*, as used simply and strictly, is exclusively applied. . . . As contradistinguished to the rules which I style *positive morality*, and so on which I shall touch immediately, the aggregate

From John Austin, *The Province of Jurisprudence Determined* (London: Weidenfeld & Nicolson, 1954), pp. 9–25, 30–32, 134, 184–186, 193–195. First published in 1832.

of the rules, established by political superiors, may also be marked commodiously with the name of *positive law*. . . .

Though *some* of the laws or rules, which are set by men to men, are established by political superiors, *others* are *not* established by political superiors, or are *not* established by political superiors, in that capacity or character.

Closely analogous to human laws of this second class, are a set of objects frequently but *improperly* termed *laws*, being rules set and enforced by *mere opinion*, that is, by the opinions or sentiments held or felt by an indeterminate body of men in regard to human conduct. Instances of such a use of the term *law* are the expressions—"The law of honour"; "The law set by fashion"; and rules of this species constitute much of what is usually termed "International law."

The aggregate of human laws properly so called belonging to the second of the classes above mentioned, with the aggregate of objects *improperly* but by *close analogy* termed laws, I place together in a common class, and denote them by the term *positive morality*. The name *morality* severs them from *positive law*, while the epithet *positive* disjoins them from the *law of God*. And to the end of obviating confusion, it is necessary or expedient that they *should* be disjoined from the latter by that distinguishing epithet. For the name *morality* (or *morals*), when standing unqualified or alone, denotes indifferently either of the following objects: namely, positive morality *as it is*, or without regard to its merits; and positive morality *as it would be*, if it conformed to the law of God, and were, therefore, deserving of *approbation*.

. . . I shall now state the essentials of *a law* or *rule* (taken with the largest signification which can be given to the term *properly*).

Every *law* or *rule* (taken with the largest signification which can be given to the term *properly*) is a *command*. Or, rather, laws or rules, properly so called, are a *species* of commands.

. . . A command is distinguished from other significations of desire, not by the style in which the desire is signified, but by the power and the purpose of the party commanding to inflict an evil or pain in case the desire be disregarded. If you cannot or will not harm me in case I comply not with your wish, the expression of your wish is not a command, although you utter your wish in imperative phrase. . . .

A command, then, is a signification of desire. But a command is distinguished from other significations

of desire by this peculiarity: that the party to whom it is directed is liable to evil from the other, in case he comply not with the desire.

Being liable to evil from you if I comply not with a wish which you signify, I am *bound* or *obliged* by your command, or I lie under a *duty* to obey it. If, in spite of that evil in prospect, I comply not with the wish which you signify, I am said to disobey your command, or to violate the duty which it imposes.

Command and duty are, therefore, correlative terms: the meaning denoted by each being implied or supposed by the other. Or (changing the expression) wherever a duty lies, a command has been signified; and whenever a command is signified, a duty is imposed.

. . . The greater the eventual evil, and the greater the chance of incurring it, the greater is the efficacy of the command, and the greater is the strength of the obligation. . . .

Rewards are, indisputably, *motives* to comply with the wishes of others. But to talk of commands and duties as *sanctioned* or *enforced* by rewards, or to talk of rewards as *obliging* or *constraining* to obedience, is surely a wide departure from the established meaning of the terms. . . .

It appears, then, from what has been premised, that the ideas or notions comprehended by the term *command* are the following:

1. A wish or desire conceived by a rational being, that another rational being shall do or forbear.

2. An evil to proceed from the former, and to be incurred by the latter, in case the latter comply not with the wish.

3. An expression or intimation of the wish by words or other signs.

It also appears from what has been premised, that *command*, *duty*, and *sanction* are inseparably connected terms: that each embraces the same ideas as the others, though each denotes those ideas in a peculiar order or series. . . .

Now where it obliges *generally* to acts or forbearance of a *class*, a command is a law or rule. But where it obliges to a *specific* act or forbearance, or to acts or forbearance which it determines *specifically* or *individually*, a command is occasional or particular. . . .

If you command your servant to go on a given errand, or *not* to leave your house on a given evening, or to rise at such an hour on such a morning, or to rise at that hour during the next week or month, the command is occasional or particular. For the act or acts enjoined or forbidden are specially determined or assigned.

If you command him *simply* to rise at that hour, or to rise at that hour *always*, or to rise at that hour *till further orders*, it may be said, with propriety, that you lay down a *rule* for the guidance of your servant's conduct. For no specific act is assigned by the command, but the command obliges him generally to acts of a determined class.

If a regiment be ordered to attack or defend a post, or to quell a riot, or to march from their present quarters, the command is occasional or particular. But an order to exercise daily till further orders shall be given would be called a *general* order, and *might* be called a *rule*.

If Parliament prohibited simply the exportation of corn, either for a given period or indefinitely, it would establish a law or rule: a *kind* or *sort* of act being determined by the command, and acts of that kind or sort being *generally* forbidden. But an order issued by Parliament to meet an impending scarcity, and stopping the exportation of corn *then shipped and in port*, would not be a law or rule, though issued by the sovereign legislature. . . .

Now the lawgiver determines a class or description of acts; prohibits acts of the class generally and indefinitely; and commands, with the like generality, that punishment shall follow transgression. The command of the lawgiver is, therefore, a law or rule. But the command of the judge is occasional or particular. For he orders a specific punishment, as the consequence of a specific offence. . . .

It appears, from what has been premised, that a law, properly so called, may be defined in the following manner.

A law is a command which obliges a person or persons.

But, as contradistinguished or opposed to an occasional or particular command, a law is a command which obliges a person or persons, and obliges *generally* to acts or forbearances of a *class*.

In language more popular but less distinct and precise, a law is a command which obliges a person or persons to a *course* of conduct.

Laws and other commands are said to proceed from *superiors*, and to bind or oblige *inferiors*. I will, therefore, analyze the meaning of those correlative expressions; and will try to strip them of a certain

mystery, by which that simple meaning appears to be obscured.

Superiority is often synonymous with *precedence or excellence*. . . .

But, taken with the meaning wherein I here understand it, the term *superiority* signifies *might:* the power of affecting others with evil or pain, and of forcing them, through fear of that evil, to fashion their conduct to one's wishes.

For example, God is emphatically the *superior* of Man. For His power of affecting us with pain, and of forcing us to comply with His will, is unbounded and resistless.

To a limited extent, the sovereign One or Number is the superior of the subject or citizen: the master, of the slave or servant: the father, of the child.

In short, whoever can *oblige* another to comply with his wishes, is the *superior* of that other, so far as the ability reaches: The party who is obnoxious to the impending evil, being, to that same extent, the *inferior.*

The might or superiority of God, is simple or absolute. . . .

A member of a sovereign assembly is the superior of the judge: the judge being bound by the law which proceeds from that sovereign body. But, in his character of citizen or subject, he is the inferior of the judge: the judge being the minister of the law, and armed with the power of enforcing it.

It appears, then, that the term *superiority* (like the terms *duty* and *sanction*) is implied by the term *command.* For superiority is the power of enforcing compliance with a wish: and the expression or intimation of a wish, with the power and the purpose of enforcing, are the constituent elements of a command.

"That *laws* emanate from *superiors*" is, therefore, an identical proposition. For the meaning which it affects to impart is contained in its subject. . . .

According to an opinion which I must notice *incidentally* here, though the subject to which it relates will be treated *directly* hereafter, *customary laws* must be excepted from the proposition "that laws are a series of commands."

By many of the admirers of customary laws . . . they are thought to oblige legally (independently of the sovereign or state), *because* the citizens or subjects have observed or kept them. . . .

At its origin, a custom is a rule of conduct which the governed observe spontaneously, or not in pursuance of a law set by a political superior. The custom is transmitted into positive law, when it is adopted as such by the courts of justice, and when the judicial decisions fashioned upon it are enforced by the power of the state. But before it is adopted by the courts, and clothed with the legal sanction, it is merely a rule of positive morality: a rule generally observed by the citizens or subjects; but deriving the only force, which it can be said to possess, from the general disapprobation falling on those who transgress it.

Now when judges transmute a custom into a legal rule (or make a legal rule not suggested by a custom), the legal rule which they establish is established by the sovereign legislature. A subordinate or subject judge is merely a minister. The portion of the sovereign power which lies at his disposition is merely delegated. The rules which he makes derive their legal force from authority given by the state: an authority which the state may confer expressly, but which it commonly imparts in the way of acquiescence. For, since the state may reverse the rules which he makes, and yet permits him to enforce them by the power of the political community, its sovereign will "that his rules shall obtain as law" is clearly evinced by its conduct, though not by its express declaration. . . .

Lecture 5

. . . Now it follows from these premises, that the laws of God, and positive laws are laws proper, or laws properly so called.

The laws of God are laws proper, inasmuch as they are *commands* express or tacit, and therefore emanate from a *certain* source.

Positive laws, or laws strictly so called, are established directly or immediately by authors of three kinds: by monarchs, or sovereign bodies, as supreme political superiors; by men in a state of subjection, as subordinate political superiors; by subjects, as private persons, in pursuance of legal rights. But every positive law, or every law strictly so called, is a direct or circuitous command of a monarch or sovereign number in the character of political superior; that is to say, a direct or circuitous command of a monarch or sovereign number to a person or persons in a state of subjection to its author. And being a *command* (and therefore flowing from a *determinate* source), every positive law is a law proper, or a law properly so called.

Besides the human laws which I style positive law, there are human laws which I style positive morality, rules of positive morality, or positive moral rules.

The generic character of laws of the class may be stated briefly in the following negative manner: No law belonging to the class is a direct or circuitous command of a monarch or sovereign number in the character of political superior. In other words, no law belonging to the class is a direct or circuitous command of a monarch or sovereign number to a person or persons in a state of subjection to its author. . . .

The existence of law is one thing; its merit or demerit is another. Whether it be or be not is one enquiry; whether it be or be not conformable to an assumed standard, is a different enquiry. A law, which actually exists, is a law, though we happen to dislike it, or though it vary from the text, by which we regulate our approbation and disapprobation. This truth, when formally announced as an abstract proposition, is so simple and glaring that it seems idle to insist upon it. But simple and glaring as it is, when enunciated in abstract expressions the enumeration of the instances in which it has been forgotten would fill a volume.

Sir William Blackstone, for example, says in his "Commentaries" that the laws of God are superior in obligation to all other laws; that no human laws should be suffered to contradict them; that human laws are of no validity if contrary to them; and that all valid laws derive their force from that Divine original.

Now, he *may* mean that all human laws ought to conform to the Divine laws. If this be his meaning, I assent to it without hesitation. The evils which we are exposed to suffer from the hands of God as a consequence of disobeying His commands are the greatest evils to which we are obnoxious; the obligations which they impose are consequently paramount to those imposed by any other laws, and if human commands conflict with the Divine law, we ought to disobey the command which is enforced by the less powerful sanction; this is implied in the term *ought:* the proposition is identical, and therefore perfectly indisputable—it is our interest to choose the smaller and more uncertain evil, in preference to the greater and surer. If this be Blackstone's meaning, I assent to his proposition, and have only to object to it, that it tells us just nothing.

Perhaps, again, he means that human lawgivers are themselves obliged by the Divine laws to fashion the laws which they impose by that ultimate standard, because if they do not, God will punish them. To this also I entirely assent. . . .

But the meaning of this passage of Blackstone, if it has a meaning, seems rather to be this: that no human law which conflicts with the Divine law is obligatory or binding; in other words, that no human law which conflicts with the Divine law *is a law*, for a law without an obligation is a contradiction in terms. I suppose this to be his meaning, because when we say of any transaction that it is invalid or void, we mean that it is not binding: as, for example, if it be a contract, we mean that the political law will not lend its sanction to enforce the contract.

Now, to say that human laws which conflict with the Divine law are not binding, that is to say, are not laws, is to talk stark nonsense. The most pernicious laws, and therefore those which are most opposed to the will of God, have been and are continually enforced as laws by judicial tribunals. Suppose an act innocuous, or positively beneficial, be prohibited by the sovereign under the penalty of death; if I commit this act, I shall be tried and condemned, and if I object to the sentence, that it is contrary to the law of God, who has commanded that human lawgivers shall not prohibit acts which have no evil consequences, the Court of Justice will demonstrate the inconclusiveness of my reasoning by hanging me up, in pursuance of the law of which I have impugned the validity. An exception, demurrer, or plea, founded on the law of God was never heard in a Court of Justice, from the creation of the world down to the present moment.

But this abuse of language is not merely puerile, it is mischievous. When it is said that a law ought to be disobeyed, what is meant is that we are urged to disobey it by motives more cogent and compulsory than those by which it is itself sanctioned. If the laws of God are certain, the motives which they hold out to disobey any human command which is at variance with them are paramount to all others. But the laws of God are not always certain. . . . In quiet times the dictates of utility are fortunately so obvious that the anarchical doctrine sleeps, and men habitually admit the validity of laws which they dislike. To prove by pertinent reasons that a law is pernicious is highly useful, because such process may lead to the abrogation of the pernicious law. To incite the public to resistance by determinate views of *utility* may be useful, for resistance, grounded on clear and definite prospects of good, is sometimes beneficial. But to proclaim generally that all laws which are pernicious or contrary to the will of God are void and not to be tolerated, is to preach anarchy, hostile and perilous as much to wise and benign rule as to stupid and galling tryanny. . . .

Lecture 6

. . . Every positive law, or every law simply and strictly so called, is set by a sovereign person, or a sovereign body of persons, to a member or members of the independent political society wherein that person or body is sovereign or supreme. Or (changing the expression) it is set by a monarch, or sovereign number, to a person or persons in a state of subjection to its author. Even though it sprung directly from another fountain or source, it *is* a positive law, or a law strictly so called, by the institution of that present sovereign in the character of political superior. . . .

The superiority which is styled sovereignty, and the independent political society which sovereignty implies, is distinguished from other superiority, and from other society, by the following marks or characters:

1. The bulk of the given society are in a *habit* of obedience or submission to a *determinate* and *common* superior, let that common superior be a certain individual person, or a certain body or aggregate of individual persons.

2. That certain individual, or that certain body of individuals, is *not* in a habit of obedience to a determinate human superior. Laws (improperly so called) which opinion sets or imposes, may permanently affect the conduct of that certain individual or body. To express or tacit commands of other determinate parties, that certain individual or body may yield occasional submission. But there is no determinate person, determinate aggregate of persons, to whose commands, express or tacit, that certain individual or body renders habitual obedience. . . . By "an independent political society," or "an independent and sovereign nation," we mean a political society consisting of a sovereign and subjects, as opposed to a political society which is merely subordinate: that is to say, which is merely a limb or member of another political society, and which therefore consists entirely of persons in a state of subjection.

In order that a given society may form a society political and independent, the two distinguishing marks which I have mentioned above must unite. The *generality* of the given society must be in the *habit* of obedience to a *determinate* and *common* superior: whilst that determinate person, or determinate body of persons must *not* be habitually obedient to a determinate person or body. It is the union of that positive, with this negative mark, which renders that certain superior sovereign or supreme, and which renders that given society (including that certain superior) a society political and independent.

Inclusive Legal Positivism and the Nature of Jurisprudential Debate

Brian Bix

Legal positivism, like breakfast cereal, seems to come in a wide variety of brands, with modest variations in the ingredients. Each brand offers slightly different promises as to the benefits of choosing it over its competitors. The question of the tired morning consumer is whether anything important is at stake in the choice, or whether he or she should just choose whatever is handy or on sale that month. In this article, I will consider some of the debates within legal positivism, and some of the disputes between legal positivism and its critics, as a means of exploring some more general issues regarding the process of theorizing about law. In discussing the internal debates within legal positivism, I will focus on the debate between inclusive and exclusive forms of positivism, though there are numerous other, if lesser known, intra-group squabbles to be found, which are also of interest and warrant attention.

In the background of most jurisprudential debates, usually but not always unstated, is the question of what kinds of claims the disputants are making, whether the "opponents" are in fact in substantive disagreement or simply talking past one another, and what (if anything) is at stake in the argument. The debates within legal positivism, and between legal positivism and its apparent opponents, have always raised difficult meta-theory questions of the type just described. In this article, I will consider a number of possible concerns, including: (a) that inclusive legal

From Brian Bix, "Patrolling the Boundaries: Inclusive Legal Positivism and the Nature of Jurisprudential Debate," *Canadian Journal of Law and Jurisprudence*, Vol. 12 (1999), pp. 17–33. Reprinted by permission of the *Canadian Journal of Law and Jurisprudence*.

positivism's claims are sometimes presented in ways so general, so vague, or so uncontroversial that there would be no theories in opposition, and no reason to disagree; and, in the alternative, (b) that whatever opposition does appear to (inclusive) legal positivism may be based on inconsistent starting points, such that there would be no basis for adjudicating the argument.

I. Legal Positivism in Five Minutes or Less

Legal positivism is an approach to law and legal theory, with roots in the work of Thomas Hobbes and David Hume, which claims that it is both feasible and valuable to put forward a descriptive theory of law. Unlike the traditional Natural Law theorists, the discussion of law was not merely to be an afterthought or entailment of a larger moral or ethical theory, and the discussion of what the law was, was to be separated from any moral or political prescription of how it *should* be.

Within legal positivism, the theories about the nature of law have varied substantially. For example, while John Austin's theory of law, put forward in the early nineteenth century, offered that legal rules were best understood as general commands from the sovereign, most modern Anglo-American legal positivism derives from the writings of H. L. A. Hart, who constructed a more intricate theory of law based on a rejection of Austin's command theory. Among the significant points of Hart's theory were that modern legal systems can be usefully characterized as the union of both primary rules and secondary rules, that a good legal theory must take into account the attitude of citizens and officials towards the practice ("the internal aspect" of rules and of law), and that every legal system has a rule which sets down the criteria for determining which rules are part of the system ("the Rule of Recognition").

The difference between the inclusive and exclusive legal positivists is a disagreement of what can be or must be in the Rule of Recognition. The disagreement often comes across as a confusing array of modal terms: for the difference between inclusive and exclusive legal positivism is between those who claim that *all* legal systems have certain characteristics, and those that claim that at least *some* legal systems *might not* have those characteristics—or, to put the same point differently, that it is *not* the case that *all* legal systems *must* have the described characteristics. Joseph Raz advocates exclusive positivism: that for *all* (current and possible) legal systems, the content of current legal norms can be ascertained without recourse to moral evaluation (i.e., the criteria of validity given by the "Rule of Recognition" contain no moral terms, only morally-neutral "pedigree" criteria). By contrast, Wilfrid Waluchow and Jules Coleman, among others, advocate inclusive legal positivism: that it is *not* the case that *no* legal systems *could* have moral terms as part of their Rule of Recognition. At the same time, while some legal systems *might* have moral terms in their Rule of Recognition, the presence of moral terms is a *contingent* fact, and there *could* be legal systems that did *not* have moral terms in that role.

The above definition of inclusive positivism is in the modal negative, but it is usually advocated in more positive terms. Professor Waluchow characterizes the approach as a "claim that standards of political morality, that is, the morality we use to evaluate, justify, and criticize social institutions and their activities and products, e.g., laws, can and do in various ways figure in attempts to determine the existence, content, and meaning of valid laws.[1] An inclusive approach allows the consideration of moral principles as part of the law—part of the law *because* so identified by the conventional rule of recognition within the legal system— and this in turn can blunt much of Ronald Dworkin's critique of H. L. A. Hart's version of legal positivism. Professor Dworkin had argued that judges view the application of moral principles (at least in hard cases) as a binding obligation, but that Professor Hart could not account for that aspect of legal practice, because moral principles could not be identified (and their "weight" ascertained) by the content-neutral "pedigree" criteria of Hart's Rule of Recognition. If moral principles *can* be made part of the law by the conventional rules that constitute a legal system's Rule of

Recognition, then much of Dworkin's critique is undermined. Professor Coleman similarly argues that only an inclusive view of the Rule of Recognition "can explain both law's institutional and social basis on the one hand and its connection to abstract moral principles and arguments on the other."[2]

There still seems to be room for further clarifications of or sub-classifications within inclusive positivism. If the key point of inclusive positivism is the (possible) presence of moral standards within the Rule of Recognition, this could mean one (or more) of three things:

1. A rule or standard that would otherwise be part of the legal system would be excluded should it be inconsistent with a moral rule or standard—i.e., consistency with morality is necessary, but not sufficient, for membership in the legal system. This seems to be what is going on (and what needs to be explained) in countries like Canada and the United States, where there is judicial review based on constitutional rights, rights which contain what seem to be moral terms (e.g., "fairness," "justice," "equality").

2. A rule or standard could be law simply because it was part of (either critical or conventional) morality— i.e., the moral content of the rule or standard is sufficient to make it a member of the legal system; another way to put the same point is that a system's Rule of Recognition incorporates into law all of morality or at least whole sections (e.g., all of justice). Unlike the other two versions or aspects of inclusive legal positivism discussed here, which involve morality merely invalidating or modifying laws identified through social sources, this approach would allow morality to be the source of (new or newly recognized) laws. This may seem a radical view, bordering on natural law theory. However, it can also be seen as a fairly traditional view of what occurs (or should occur) in common law reasoning.

3. A rule should be interpreted (i.e., understood and applied) in one way rather another, because moral factors are part of the legal system's approach to interpretation. This arguably occurs in traditional approaches to common law reasoning and statutory interpretation, where an interpretation is disfavored which would lead to an "absurd" result, "absurd results" sometimes being understood to include grossly unfair results. The extent to which this use of morality within law is evidence for inclusive legal positivism against the exclusive approach is not entirely clear: for it is not the use of moral terms in the Rule of Recognition (narrowly understood), but instead the use of such terms in the rules of interpretation and application.

II. *The Boundaries of Law and the Problem of Description*

I want to look briefly at one debate on the border between legal positivism and its competitors, because it shows in a somewhat clearer light a complexity that also occurs in the debates within legal positivism.

In the context of the argument about whether legal positivism is the best (descriptive) theory of law, a key part of Ronald Dworkin's attack on legal positivism was that (the American and English) legal systems contain "principles" as well as rules. For Professor Dworkin, to say that the legal system contains principles is to say that the application of such principles (to determine the outcome of cases where there may not be a clearly applicable rule, or to modify the force of, or to create an exception within, a rule that seems to apply to the facts) fits the criteria of a "social rule" within the legal system. That is, judges will in fact apply such principles; when questioned or challenged, they will refer to a duty to apply the principles as a justification for doing so. Judges who do not apply those principles will be criticized by colleagues and commentators for having failed to follow their duties.

Professor Dworkin asserted that the application and bindingness of principles cannot be adequately captured by a Hartian Rule of Recognition, or an equivalent legal positivist set of criteria (criteria that would offer a pedigree or source-based test of legal validity, distinct from any evaluation of moral worth). Professor Raz, in his elaboration and defense of legal positivism, responded that while judges in some legal systems may have an obligation to apply moral principles to decide cases, those principles are not part of the law. Dworkin's reply was that he could not understand how judges could have an obligation to apply something which is not part of the law. What is the point, Dworkin wondered, descriptively or normatively, for distinguishing the categories "law" and "what judges have an obligation to obey"?

On one hand, Raz was clearly correct that judges sometimes have an obligation to apply norms which could hardly be said to be part of the society's legal system: e.g., when courts resolve disputes which turn on the meaning of the rules for some social organization, or the charter rules for a religious organization; or when the courts resolve disputes which require the

application of laws from other states or other countries; and so on. On the other hand, there may be differences in number that eventually become differences in kind. The argument would go as follows: it is one thing to say that judges occasionally and exceptionally have to apply (and in applying, to interpret) norms from other organizations or other legal systems; it is quite another thing to say that a significant portion of the norms that judges apply must be understood as not properly being part of "law." However, Raz need not be moved by such an argument. He could insist on his basic point: it is the nature of "law" that *legal* rules resolve underlying disputes by giving instructions on how to act, and moral standards, prior to their authoritative application to fact-situations by legal officials, just do not qualify.

It is not surprising that this debate remains at a stand-off, as the disputants have very different starting points: Dworkin's definition of law was tied to how judges should decide cases; Raz's definition of law was tied to the role of law within citizens' practical reasoning. The problem may go even deeper: what makes the debate difficult to comprehend fully, and even more difficult to adjudicate, is that it involves concepts whose ties to empirical facts are loose, and whose borders are deeply contested. The facts with which we have to work include the actual practices of lawyers and judges (e.g., which types of arguments do judges see themselves as bound to apply? What kind of criticisms are leveled at judges, by other judges or by commentators, when they do not apply certain types of arguments?, and so on) and the linguistic practices of the relevant communities regarding certain terms (e.g., whether something is labeled as "law" or "legal" or not).

As to the latter, while many theorists have argued that we should be guided by linguistic practices in our understanding of social institutions, few have argued that our conceptual analyses must always match usage slavishly. Additionally, linguistic usage in these sorts of areas tends itself to be inconsistent and controversial across a community, and therefore far from dispositive. Comparable arguments are raised about actual practices, though the tone here tends to be more deferential and less dismissive. It is not so much that we can ignore how participants in the practice act, or how they refer to their own actions, but that we should approach such self-descriptions and self-understandings with a certain level of skepticism: there are conventions of presentation which may not conform to the actual understandings of the participants; or there is a certain level of deception of the public going on, which most experienced members of the profession admit to in the privacy of their clubs; and the like.

Something comparable to the Dworkin/Raz debate over the "law"/"non-law" borderline can be seen to be going on as well in the inclusive/exclusive debate. Much of Waluchow's criticism of (and defense against) Raz's position turns on the view that legal positivism purports to *describe* the law, not offer a normative view of what law should be. Waluchow writes: "inclusive positivism seems to account better than Raz's exclusive version for certain salient features of legal practice . . . [in particular] the interpretation and application of constitutional documents like the Canadian *Charter of Rights and Freedoms* or the American *Bill of Rights*.[3] Exclusive legal positivism seems contrary to our practices, both in portraying the moral standards incorporated within statutes and constitutional provisions as not being "law" unless and until they are clarified by judicial decisions, and in characterizing those decisions, in turn, as necessarily "creating new law," not just applying existing law.

One problem with having too much of the argument turn on the nature of description is that description assumes agreement on the object being described. As discussed above, if the borderlines of what is being described are themselves up for debate, at the least the argument is substantially more complex; at worst, we can never expect to adjudicate the claims of theorists, who are merely talking past one another. We would now be comparing different ways of seeing the social world, different characterizations which will do better or worse on various aspects of description and explanation. Such evaluations may give enough grounds for individuals to state a preference for one over the other, but may, because of the incommensurable values involved, foreclose definitive statements of one theory being "better than" or "worse than" the other.

III. *What is Left of Legal Positivism?*

Why do people bother to create theories of social practices? (And why do other people bother to read them?) To the extent that the theories are predictive theories, or can be used in that way, one probable purpose of the enterprise is clear. If we know how the institution works, we can try to affect the results by changing the input; at the least, we can see the consequences coming from further away, and brace ourselves accordingly.

Analytical jurisprudence is generally not in the business of predictive social theory, but rather descriptive or explanatory social theory. There is (or, at least, there need be) no point to this process other than knowledge. And if this process is worth doing, it is because we can get pleasure from knowledge, from uncovering certain kinds of insights about a social practice that may not have been clear to us, though the practice has been in front of us all of our lives.

The search for the jarring insight ties into the problem of theory-construction: the more complex and detailed the theory, the more accurate it is likely to be, but the less likely it will be that one will be able to derive grand conclusions from it. Simpler models are more productive of conclusions (just ask the economists), though the distortions introduced by over-simplified assumptions may taint the conclusions (just ask the economists' critics).

John Austin's command theory of law seemed, in its simplicity, to offer certain insights about the core nature of law. However, there was much of law (e.g., power-conferring rules, constitutional rights and disabilities, customary law) that did not fit well within Austin's theory, and so the putative insights of the theory were undermined.

However, once we have Hart's drastic reworking of Austin's theory, and then the reconstruction and recharacterization of Hart's theory by Professors Raz, Coleman, Waluchow, and others to deal with its descriptive and theoretical vulnerabilities, there is a suspicion that what is left is not of great significance. Of no great significance, perhaps, in two different senses: (1) that the claims made are so vague or uncontroversial that we would be hard-pressed to find those who truly disagree; or (2) that even if legal positivism is a position with which people might reasonably disagree, it remains a position of little distinctiveness.

This might be best seen in the context of the ongoing inclusive/exclusive debate. In the course of answering some of Raz's arguments for exclusive legal positivism, Coleman offered clarifications (some might say, modifications) of the legal positivist position regarding the nature and role of the Rule of Recognition within a legal system. The end product may be a more precise theory, and one which arguably offers a more accurate description of our practices, but there are questions about its explanatory force and its distinctiveness.

As Coleman pointed out, the Rule of Recognition can serve a variety of purposes within a legal system. It serves a "metaphysical" function to the extent it determines whether norms are valid members of a legal system or not (whether they are or are not "law"). It serves a "semantic" function to the extent it helps to specify the truth-conditions for general propositions of law ("it is the law that . . ."). Finally, the Rule can serve two different "epistemic" functions: *validation*, through helping *judges* determine whether official actions are valid; and *identification*, through helping *citizens* determine which norms are binding law for them.

Raz's argument for exclusive legal positivism has been based in part on the legal rules being able to be authorities for citizens. From law's necessary claim to authority, it followed, Raz argues, that the Rule of Recognition could not contain moral standards. Coleman maintains that Raz's argument works only if the Rule of Recognition has an identification function; to the extent that the function of identifying law can be performed as well in some other way, Raz's argument from authority seems weakened. Coleman argues that the primary function of the Rule of Recognition is validation, not identification: under Hart's formulation, at least, the Rule is aimed at officials, not citizens, and is used by them to validate, not to identify. While *citizens* do need a pedigree-like means of identification to satisfy the authority function of law, this role need not be (and usually is not) filled by the Rule of Recognition.

In defending inclusive positivism against Dworkin's charge that morality could not be incorporated into the Rule of Recognition without undermining the Rule's epistemic function, Professors Coleman and Leiter distinguish between the epistemic functions of validating and identifying law. As to the former, incorporation does not affect the role of validation, because officials can agree about what the Rule is, even when it includes (controversial) moral standards, and even if the officials may sometimes disagree about how to apply those standards.

Additionally, a certain amount of uncertainty is not precluded by the Rule of Recognition, and may be a cost worth bearing for the other benefits that could be obtained. Finally, Coleman and Leiter point out that the identification function need not be undermined: for it is the officials applying the Rule of Recognition who must deal with the difficulties of application; most citizens seeking to know what the law is do not do so by applying the Rule of Recognition themselves, but by a more indirect method (e.g., speaking to a lawyer, who has looked at the relevant statutes and legal decisions, etc.). Under this last analysis, not only is the validation of law separated from its identification (with the Rule

of Recognition only operating directly in the former), but authority is separated from validity.

In a Razian, exclusivist view of the legal world, it is relatively easy to see the place and purpose of law. Under exclusive legal positivism, the law consists of the decisions already clearly made, which can be pointed out and interpreted through simple methods. In this way, citizens can know what is required of them, and because they can, law can purport to offer authoritative guidance. Where the law runs out, or ambiguous or evaluative language has been used, judges are expressly or implicitly authorized to legislate—to create certainty and predictability where they had not been before. If one rejects exclusive legal positivism, there seems much less to say about the distinctive nature or role of law.

That is the inquiry about distinctiveness. Now as to the problem of controversy (or its absence), we can start again with a definition of inclusive legal positivism. Coleman and Leiter offer its boundaries in the following two claims:

> first, that it is not *necessary* in all legal systems that for a norm to be a legal norm it must possess moral value . . . ; and second, that what norms count as legal norms in any particular society is fundamentally a matter of *social conventions*.[4]

While there does seem to be an active disagreement between advocates of inclusive and exclusive legal positivism, it is important to notice the nature of the contest. Advocates of exclusive legal positivism *do not disagree* with the two tenets of inclusive legal positivism just outlined. Advocates of exclusive legal positivism simply argue that *more* can be said about the nature of law, that there is more that all legal systems share, and *must* share, given the nature of law. The inclusive legal positivist's response is that the additional claims are not warranted (at least at the level of descriptive or conceptual theory, whatever the merits of similar views about law as a normative theory). Thus, the question remains whether there are those who would disagree with the two claims inclusive legal positivists make (rather than simply disagreeing with the implied *third* claim—that there is nothing more of significance to be said about the nature of law).

Regarding the first part of the claim, Stephen Perry reminded us how difficult it would be to argue for a contrary position. Given that the "object" or category "law" has no boundary fixed by nature (it being a human invention), there are doubts about the *meaning* of a claim that "not only *do* all legal systems have certain attributes, but they *necessarily must* have those attributes." Consider an example: someone claims that having some form of an adjudicatory process is a necessary element of a legal system. Another theorist brings as a purported counter-example a community which resolves all disputes through mediation and consensus, and has no processes that even approximate adjudication. The first theorist simply answers that this example is not in fact a counter-example, since that community obviously lacks a legal system. How this argument can go forward without begging the question at issue is far from clear. Similarly in the topic under examination: the claim that legal systems must "necessarily" contain moral tests for legal validity would be an extremely difficult claim to make out.

If inclusive legal positivism can evoke substantial disagreement, it will likely be with the second of Coleman and Leiter's points: that the criteria of legality must be set by social conventions. The only likely competitors to this view are Dworkin's interpretive approach to law, and some variation of natural law theory. The problems with having a version of natural law theory that would *compete* with legal positivism will be discussed in greater detail in the next section. Some commentators have also suggested that Dworkin's theory should not properly be seen as a competitor, because it is not really a descriptive-explanatory theory, but is instead a normative theory; because it is a theory of adjudication, not a theory of law; or because most of the important work is done by the pre-interpretive identification of the law, a stage which seems to correspond with the legal positivist Rule of Recognition. Also, Waluchow at one point states that a legal positivist could adopt or incorporate Dworkin's interpretive approach: that a legal positivist could accept a Rule of Recognition "which prescribes that the system's legal principles include those principles which provide the best interpretive theory of the settled law."[5] To the extent that one accepts that view, the "debate" between legal positivism and Dworkin's approach becomes even harder to make out clearly. Whatever the merits of the above arguments regarding how Dworkin's theory is not inconsistent with legal positivism (either because it is in fact compatible or because it is a different kind of theory), it is worth pointing out that there seem to be a number of commentators who would effectively make of (descriptive) legal theory a one-party state, with all that usually implies for the rigor and interest of ongoing debates.

IV. *Natural Law Theory:* The Missing Opponent

When inclusive legal positivists describe their views, they often describe themselves as being the compromise position between those, like the exclusive legal positivists, who believe that moral standards can never be part of the test for legal validity, and those who believe that moral standards are always (or necessarily) a part of the test of legal validity. As for the first group, there is at least one obvious and prominent proponent, Joseph Raz. The membership of the second group of opponents is a little harder to determine.

One theorist often nominated for this role is Ronald Dworkin, but the fit is, at best, uncomfortable. Dworkin can be seen to be in direct opposition to legal positivism (and a supporter of a modern kind of natural law theory), in the sense that he rejects the notions that law is conceptually separate from morality and that a description of what the law is will be separate from a statement of what the law ought to be. For Dworkin, a statement of "what the law is" or "what the law requires" will require reference not only to past official decisions, but also a determination that one interpretation of those decisions is morally better than other available interpretations.

This makes Dworkin a kind of natural law theorist, but he still does not fit into the above description ("moral standards always (or necessarily) a part of legal validity") very well. There is a sense in which Dworkin's theory does not get involved in "tests of legal validity" at all. From some of his earliest writings on legal theory, he has rejected the notion of a Rule of Recognition, at least as this has been traditionally understood by legal positivists.

What might it mean to say that moral standards were always or necessarily part of the test of legal validity? Though there is some surface similarity between that statement and the "unjust law is no law at all" comments of traditional natural law theorists, important differences are found upon closer inspection. The message of the traditional natural law theorists is that laws which do not meet certain moral standards are not "law in their fullest sense"; in that they do not warrant citizens' obedience. Traditional natural law theory means to tell people what morality ("the natural law," for those for whom the phrase has significance) entails for them, *qua* legislators, or *qua* citizens under a particular legal system. Natural law theorists do not necessarily disagree with legal positivists regarding the nature of the Rule of Recognition.

We should move back a step. What would it mean to say that moral standards are always part of the Rule of Recognition? One possibility we have not considered, which does not quite match the definition, but which does seem to have some connection to some versions of natural law theory, is to claim that certain moral rules *automatically* become *legal* rules. The argument would be, for example, that it would be illegal to commit murder or robbery, even if there were no rules saying as much promulgated by legal officials.

We know what it would mean to say that such actions would be *immoral* regardless of whether there was positive law on the point. What would it mean to say that they were *illegal* regardless of whether there was positive law on point? It might mean that were someone to be prosecuted for such a crime in a society without such promulgated rules, the courts could, legitimately, convict and sentence the person in question (i.e., that no "rule of law" or "retroactive legislation" claim could be successfully raised by the defendant). However, at the moment the court says, "this prohibition is part of our law, even though neither the legislature nor past court decisions have spoken on the matter," at that moment, the court would be recognizing this moral standard as part of the law. It would be an *instance* of an inclusive legal positivist Rule of Recognition in action. How would one go about proving that these moral standards are law *everywhere*, other than through individual moral-legal arguments within the particular legal systems? (Again, one must distinguish arguments for these actions being *morally* prohibited in all societies all the time.)

We again near the conclusion that, to the extent that there are viable natural law alternatives to legal positivism as a descriptive-explanatory theory of law, the borders between the two can be quite difficult, if not impossible, to discern.

V. *Implications of the Inclusive-Exclusive Debate*

I am ambivalent generally regarding the topic of the concrete consequences of abstract theory. On one hand, I certainly do not want to endorse the view that if a theory, or a theoretical debate, does not have an immediate and obvious payoff in real-world events or actual cases, we can and should ignore the discussion. Interesting observations, and insightful descriptions and explanations are of value for their own sake. On the other hand, to the extent that there are implications or consequences for theoretical views, these are at least worth pointing out, without necessarily claiming that they should be dispositive of the underlying theoretical disputes.

1. As Waluchow observes, the preference of judges to be seen as merely applying existing law rather than legislating new law could interact with one's theory of law and have implications for constitutional law. If, as an exclusive legal positivist, one viewed political morality as necessarily extra-legal, the inclination to apply existing law rather than legislate anew would encourage an approach to interpreting constitutions that did not seem to require the interpretation and application of political morality (e.g., a purely textual approach, or one dependent on the intentions of the framers). Alternatively, if one had an inclusive position, where political morality could be considered part of the existing law, a judge might be more willing to interpret the constitution in a way that made use of political morality. Anthony Sebok has similarly shown some interesting connections between various positions in the legal positivism/natural law theory and inclusive/exclusive debates on one hand and views on the proper approach to American constitutional interpretation on the other.

2. Frederick Schauer argues that an important basis for choosing one legal theory over another is the effects each might have regarding other moral ends. He also offers this characterization as the approach which both H. L. A. Hart and Lon Fuller had towards theory in their own debate. For Professor Schauer, the question is: which theories will help us maintain a healthy critical distance from (evil) law? This is a neo-pragmatist view, one that is concerned less with the "truth" of theories and more with their effects. On a similar basis, Schauer himself has rejected both inclusive and exclusive forms of (H. L. A. Hart's) legal positivism, in favor of a John Austin-like, pared-down legal positivism.

Conclusion

This article has explored a number of issues within and around legal positivism, in particular the debates between inclusive legal positivism and exclusive legal positivism. This was done, not in any effort to declare a "winner," but rather as an occasion to explore some meta-theoretical issues: for example, problems regarding the status of claims (e.g., what would it mean to assert that certain elements were "necessary" for "law"?); questions regarding the possible purpose(s) of descriptive theories (e.g., if theories are about showing some basic insight regarding a practice, how can theories be kept simple enough to produce such insights, given the countervailing pressures for detail and descriptive accuracy?); and the constant vigilance necessary to make sure that apparent disputants in analytical theory are not in fact talking past one another.

Endnotes

[1] W. J. Waluchow, *Inclusive Legal Positivism* (Oxford: Clarendon Press, 1994), p. 2.

[2] J. L. Coleman, "Authority and Reason," in R. George (ed.), *The Autonomy of Law: Essays on Legal Positivism* (Oxford: Clarendon Press, 1996), p. 296.

[3] Waluchow, *supra.*, p. 6.

[4] J. L. Coleman and B. Leiter, "Legal Positivism," in D. Patterson (ed.), *A Companion to Philosophy of Law and Legal Theory* (Oxford: Blackwell, 1996), p. 243.

[5] Waluchow, *supra.*, p. 187.

Positivism and the Separation of Law and Morals

H. L. A. HART

In this article I shall discuss and attempt to defend a view which Mr. Justice Holmes, among others, held and for which he and they have been much criticized. . . . Contemporary voices tell us we must recognize something obscured by the legal "positivist" whose day is now over: that there is a "point of intersection between law and morals," or that what *is* and what *ought to be* are somehow indissolubly fused or inseparable, though the positivists denied it. What do these phrases mean? Or rather which of the many things that they *could* mean, *do* they mean? Which of them do "positivists" deny, and why is it wrong to do so?

1

I shall present the subject as part of the history of an idea. At the close of the eighteenth century and the beginning of the nineteenth the most earnest thinkers in England about legal and social problems and the architects of great reforms were the great utilitarians. Two of them, Bentham and Austin, constantly insisted on the need to distinguish, firmly and with the maximum of clarity, law as it is from law as it ought to be. This theme haunts their work, and they condemned the natural-law thinkers precisely because they had blurred this

apparently simple but vital distinction. By contrast, at the present time in this country and to a lesser extent in England, this separation between law and morals is held to be superficial and wrong. Some critics have thought that it blinds men to the true nature of law and its roots in social life. Others have thought it not only intellectually misleading but corrupting in practice, at its worst apt to weaken resistance to state tyranny or absolutism, and at its best apt to bring law into disrepute. The nonpejorative name "legal positivism," like most terms which are used as missiles in intellectual battles, has come to stand for a baffling multitude of different sins. One of them is the sin, real or alleged, of insisting, as Austin and Bentham did, on the separation of law as it is and law as it ought to be.

How then has this reversal of the wheel come about? What are the theoretical errors in this distinction?

Have the practical consequences of stressing the distinction as Bentham and Austin did been bad? Should we now reject it or keep it? In considering these questions we should recall the social philosophy which went along with the utilitarians' insistence on this distinction. They stood firmly but on their own utilitarian ground for all the principles of liberalism in law and government. No one has ever combined, with such even-minded sanity as the utilitarians, the passion for reform with respect for law together with a due recognition of the need to control the abuse of power even when power is in the hands of reformers. . . . Here are liberty of speech, and of press, the right of association, the need that laws should be published and made widely known before they are enforced, the need to control administrative agencies, the insistence that there should be no criminal liability without fault, and the importance of the principle of legality, *nulla poena sine lege* [no punishment without law]. Some, I know, find the political and moral insight of the utilitarians a very simple one, but we should not mistake this simplicity for superficiality nor forget how favorably their simplicities compare with the profundities of other thinkers. Take only one example: Bentham on slavery. He says the question at issue is not whether those who are held as slaves can reason, but simply whether they suffer. Does this not compare well with the discussion of the question in terms of whether or not there are some men whom Nature has fitted only to be the living instruments of others? We owe it to Bentham more than anyone else that we have stopped discussing this and similar questions of social policy in that form.

So Bentham and Austin were not dry analysts fiddling with verbal distinctions while cities burned, but were the vanguard of a movement which laboured with passionate intensity and much success to bring about a better society and better laws. Why then did they insist on the separation of law as it is and law as it ought to be? What did they mean? Let us first see what they said. Austin formulated the doctrine:

> The existence of law is one thing; its merit or demerit is another. Whether it be or be not is one enquiry; whether it be or be not conformable to an assumed standard, is a different enquiry. A law, which actually exists, is a law, though we happen to dislike it, or though it vary from the text, by which we regulate our approbation and disapprobation. This truth, when formally announced as

an abstract proposition, is so simple and glaring that it seems idle to insist upon it. But simple and glaring as it is, when enunciated in abstract expressions the enumeration of the instances in which it has been forgotten would fill a volume.

Sir William Blackstone, for example, says in his "Commentaries," that the laws of God are superior in obligation to all other laws; that no human laws should be suffered to contradict them; that human laws are of no validity if contrary to them; and that all valid laws derive their force from that Divine original.

Now, he *may* mean that all human laws ought to conform to the Divine laws. If this be his meaning, I assent to it without hesitation. . . . Perhaps, again, he means that human lawgivers are themselves obliged by the Divine laws to fashion the laws which they impose by that ultimate standard, because if they do not, God will punish them. To this also I entirely assent. . . .

But the meaning of this passage of Blackstone, if it has a meaning, seems rather to be this: that no human law which conflicts with the Divine law is obligatory or binding; in other words, that no human law which conflicts with the Divine law *is a law.* . . .

Austin's protest against blurring the distinction between what law is and what it ought to be is quite general; it is a mistake, whatever our standard of what ought to be, whatever "the text by which we regulate our approbation or disapprobation." His examples, however, are always a confusion between law as it is and law as morality would require it to be. For him, it must be remembered, the fundamental principles of morality were God's commands, to which utility was an "index": besides this there was the actual accepted morality of a social group or "positive" morality. . . .

In view of later criticisms it is also important to distinguish several things that the utilitarians did not mean by insisting on their separation of law and morals. They certainly accepted many of the things that might be called "the intersection of law and morals." First, they never denied that, as a matter of historical fact, the development of legal systems had been powerfully influenced by moral opinion, and, conversely, that moral standards had been profoundly influenced by law, so that the content of many legal rules mirrored moral rules or principles. . . .

Secondly, neither Bentham nor his followers denied that by explicit legal provisions moral principles might at different points be brought into a legal system and form part of its rules, or that courts might be legally bound to decide in accordance with what they thought just or best. . . .

What both Bentham and Austin were anxious to assert were the following two simple things: first, in the absence of all expressed constitutional or legal provision, it could not follow from the mere fact that a rule violated standards of morality that it was not a rule of law; and, conversely, it could not follow from the mere fact that a rule was morally desirable that it was a rule of law. . . .

2

So much for the doctrine in the heyday of its success. Let us turn now to some of the criticisms.

. . . We must remember that the utilitarians combined with their insistence on the separation of law and morals two other equally famous but distinct doctrines. One was the important truth that a purely analytical study of legal concepts, a study of the meaning of the distinctive vocabulary of the law, was as vital to our understanding of the nature of law as historical or sociological studies, though of course it could not supplant them. The other doctrine was the famous imperative theory of law—that law is essentially a command.

These three doctrines constitute the utilitarian tradition in jurisprudence; yet they are distinct doctrines. It is possible to endorse the separation between law and morals and to value analytical inquiries into the meaning of legal concepts and yet think it wrong to conceive of law as essentially a command. One source of great confusion in the criticism of the separation of law and morals was the belief that the falsity of any one of these three doctrines in the utilitarian tradition showed the other two to be false; what was worse was the failure to see that there were three quite separate doctrines in this tradition. . . . [Some] critics . . . have thought that the inadequacies of the command theory which gradually came to light were sufficient to demonstrate the falsity of the separation of law and morals.

This was a mistake, but a natural one. To see how natural it was we must look a little more closely at the command idea. The famous theory that law is a command was a part of a wider and more ambitious claim. Austin said that the notion of a command was "the *key*

to the sciences of jurisprudence and morals," and contemporary attempts to elucidate moral judgments in terms of "imperative" or "prescriptive" utterances echo this ambitious claim. But the command theory, viewed as an effort to identify even the quintessence of law, let alone the quintessence of morals, seems breathtaking in its simplicity and quite inadequate. There is much, even in the simplest legal system, that is distorted if presented as a command. Yet the utilitarians thought that the essence of a legal system could be conveyed if the notion of a command were supplemented by that of a habit of obedience. The simple scheme was this: What is a command? It is simply an expression by one person of the desire that another person should do or abstain from some action, accompanied by a threat of punishment which is likely to follow disobedience. Commands are laws if two conditions are satisfied: First, they must be general; second, they must be commanded by what (as both Bentham and Austin claimed) exists in every political society whatever its constitutional form, namely, a person or a group of persons who are in receipt of habitual obedience from most of the society but pay no such obedience to others. These persons are its sovereign. Thus law is the command of the uncommanded commanders of society—the creation of the legally untrammeled will of the sovereign who is by definition outside the law.

It is easy to see that this account of a legal system is threadbare. One can also see why it might seem that its inadequacy is due to the omission of some essential connection with morality. The situation which the simple trilogy of command, sanction, and sovereign avails to describe, if you take these notions at all precisely, is like that of a gunman saying to his victim, "Give me your money or your life." The only difference is that in the case of a legal system the gunman says it to a large number of people who are accustomed to the racket and habitually surrender to it. Law surely is not the gunman situation writ large, and legal order is surely not to be thus simply identified with compulsion.

This scheme, despite the points of obvious analogy between a statute and a command, omits some of the most characteristic elements of law. Let me cite a few. It is wrong to think of a legislature (and *a fortiori* an electorate) with a changing membership, as a group of persons habitually obeyed: this simple idea is suited only to a monarch sufficiently long-lived for a "habit" to grow up. Even if we waive this point, nothing which legislators do makes law unless they comply with fundamental accepted rules specifying the essential lawmaking procedures. This is true even in a system having a simple unitary constitution like the British. These fundamental accepted rules specifying what the legislature must do to legislate are not commands habitually obeyed, nor can they be expressed as habits of obedience to persons. They lie at the root of a legal system, and what is most missing in the utilitarian scheme is an analysis of what it is for a social group and its officials to accept such rules. This notion, not that of a command as Austin claimed, is the "key to the science of jurisprudence," or at least one of the keys.

Again, Austin, in the case of a democracy, looked past the legislators to the electorate as "the sovereign" (or in England as part of it). He thought that in the United States the mass of the electors to the state and federal legislatures were the sovereign whose commands, given by their "agents" in the legislatures, were law. But on this footing the whole notion of the sovereign outside the law being "habitually obeyed" by the "bulk" of the population must go: for in this case the "bulk" obeys the bulk, that is, it obeys itself. Plainly the general acceptance of the authority of a lawmaking procedure, irrespective of the changing individuals who operate it from time to time, can be only distorted by an analysis in terms of mass habitual obedience to certain persons who are by definition outside the law, just as the cognate but much simpler phenomenon of the general social acceptance of a rule, say of taking off the hat when entering a church, would be distorted if represented as habitual obedience by the mass to specific persons.

Other critics dimly sensed a further and more important defect in the command theory, yet blurred the edge of an important criticism by assuming that the defect was due to the failure to insist upon some important connection between law and morals. This more radical defect is as follows. The picture that the command theory draws of life under law is essentially a simple relationship of the commander to the commanded, of superior to inferior, of top to bottom; the relationship is vertical between the commanders or authors of the law conceived of as essentially outside the law and those who are commanded and subject to the law. In this picture no place, or only an accidental or subordinate place, is afforded for a distinction between types of legal rules which are in fact radically different. Some laws require men to act in certain ways or to abstain from acting whether they wish to or not. The criminal law consists largely of rules of this sort:

like commands they are simply "obeyed" or "disobeyed." But other legal rules are presented to society in quite different ways and have quite different functions. They provide facilities more or less elaborate for individuals to create structures of rights and duties for the conduct of life within the coercive framework of the law. Such are the rules enabling individuals to make contracts, wills, and trusts, and generally to mould their legal relations with others. Such rules, unlike the criminal law, are not factors designed to obstruct wishes and choices of an antisocial sort. On the contrary, these rules provide facilities for the realization of wishes and choices. They do not say (like commands) "do this whether you wish it or not," but rather "if you wish to do this, here is the way to do it." Under these rules we exercise powers, make claims, and assert rights. These phrases mark off characteristic features of laws that confer rights and powers; they are laws which are, so to speak, put at the disposition of individuals in a way in which the criminal law is not.

. . . Rules that confer rights, though distinct from commands, need not be moral rules or coincide with them. Rights, after all, exist under the rules of ceremonies, games, and in many other spheres regulated by rules which are irrelevant to the question of justice or what the law ought to be. Nor need rules which confer rights be just or morally good rules. The rights of a master over his slaves show us that. "Their merit or demerit," as Austin termed it, depends on how rights are distributed in society and over whom or what they are exercised. These critics indeed revealed the inadequacy of the simple notions of command and habit for the analysis of law; at many points it is apparent that the social acceptance of a rule or standard of authority (even if it is motivated only by fear or superstition or rests on inertia) must be brought into the analysis and cannot itself be reduced to the two simple terms. Yet nothing in this showed the utilitarian insistence on the distinction between the existence of law and its "merits" to be wrong.

3

I now turn to a distinctively American criticism of the separation of the law that is from the law that ought to be. It emerged from the critical study of the judicial process with which American jurisprudence has been on the whole so beneficially occupied. The most skeptical of these critics—the loosely named "Realists" of the 1930s—perhaps too naively accepted the conceptual framework of the natural sciences as adequate for the characterization of law and for the analysis of rule-guided action of which a living system of law at least partly consists. But they opened men's eyes to what actually goes on when courts decide cases, and the contrast they drew between the actual facts of judicial decision and the traditional terminology for describing it as if it were a wholly logical operation was usually illuminating; for in spite of some exaggeration the "Realists" made us acutely conscious of one cardinal feature of human language and human thought, emphasis on which is vital not only for the understanding of law but in areas of philosophy far beyond the confines of jurisprudence. The insight of this school may be presented in the following example. A legal rule forbids you to take a vehicle into the public park. Plainly this forbids an automobile, but what about bicycles, roller skates, toy automobiles? What about airplanes? Are these, as we say, to be called "vehicles" for the purpose of the rule or not? If we are to communicate with each other at all, and if, as in the most elementary form of law, we are to express our intentions that a certain type of behavior be regulated by rules, then the general words we use—like "vehicle" in the case I consider—must have some standard instance in which no doubts are felt about its application. There must be a core of settled meaning, but there will be, as well, a penumbra of debatable cases in which words are neither obviously applicable nor obviously ruled out. These cases will each have some features of common with the standard case; they will lack others or be accompanied by features not present in the standard case. Human invention and natural processes continually throw up such variants on the familiar, and if we are to say that these ranges of facts do or do not fall under existing rules, then the classifier must make a decision which is not dictated to him, for the facts and phenomena to which we fit our words and apply our rules are as it were *dumb*. The toy automobile cannot speak up and say, "I am a vehicle for the purpose of this legal rule," nor can the roller skates chorus, "We are not a vehicle." Fact situations do not await us neatly labeled, creased, and folded, nor is their legal classification written on them to be simply read off by the judge. Instead, in applying legal rules, someone must take the responsibility of deciding that words do or do not cover some case in hand with all the practical consequences involved in this decision.

We may call the problems which arise outside the hard core of standard instances or settled meaning "problems of the penumbra"; they are always with us whether in relation to such trivial things as the regulation of the use of the public park or in relation to the multidimensional generalities of a constitution. If a penumbra of uncertainty must surround all legal rules, then their application to specific cases in the penumbral area cannot be a matter of logical deduction, and so deductive reasoning, which for generations has been cherished as the very perfection of human reasoning, cannot serve as a model for what judges, or indeed anyone, should do in bringing particular cases under general rules. In this area men cannot live by deduction alone. And it follows that if legal arguments and legal decisions of penumbral questions are to be rational, their rationality must lie in something other than a logical relation to premise. So if it is rational or "sound" to argue and to decide that for the purposes of this rule an airplane is not a vehicle, this argument must be sound or rational without being logically conclusive. What is it then that makes such decisions correct or at least better than alternative decisions? Again, it seems true to say that the criterion which makes a decision sound in such cases is some concept of what the law ought to be; it is easy to slide from that into saying that it must be a moral judgment about what law ought to be. So here we touch upon a point of necessary "intersection between law and morals" which demonstrates the falsity or, at any rate, the misleading character of the utilitarians' emphatic insistence on the separation of law as it is and ought to be. Surely, Bentham and Austin could only have written as they did because they misunderstood or neglected this aspect of the judicial process, because they ignored the problems of the penumbra.

The misconception of the judicial process which ignores the problems of the penumbra and which views the process as consisting preeminently in deductive reasoning is often stigmatized as the error of "formalism" or "literalism." My question now is, how and to what extent does the demonstration of this error show the utilitarian distinction to be wrong or misleading? Here there are many issues which have been confused, but I can only disentangle some. The charge of formalism has been leveled both at the "positivist" legal theorist and at the courts, but of course it must be a very different charge in each case. Leveled at the legal theorist, the charge means that he has made a theoretical mistake about the character of legal decision; he has thought of the reasoning involved as consisting in deduction from premises in which the judges' practical choices or decision play no part. It would be easy to show that Austin was guiltless of this error; only an entire misconception of what analytical jurisprudence is and why he thought it important has led to the view that he, or any other analyst, believed that the law was a closed logical system in which judges deduced their decisions from premises. On the contrary, he was very much alive to the character of language, to its vagueness or open character; he thought that in the penumbral situation judges must necessarily legislate, and, in accents that sometimes recall those of the late Judge Jerome Frank, he berated the common-law judges for legislating feebly and timidly and for blindly relying on real or fancied analogies with past cases instead of adapting their decisions to the growing needs of society as revealed by the moral standard of utility. The villains of this piece, responsible for the conception of the judge as an automaton, are not the utilitarian thinkers. The responsibility, if it is to be laid at the door of any theorist, is with . . . Blackstone's "childish fiction" (as Austin termed it) that judges only "find," never "make," law.

But we are concerned with "formalism" as a vice not of jurists but of judges. What precisely is it for a judge to commit this error, to be a "formalist," "automatic," a "slot machine"? . . . It is clear that the essence of his error is to give some general term an interpretation which is blind to social values and consequences (or which is in some other way stupid or perhaps merely disliked by critics). But logic does not prescribe interpretation of terms; it dictates neither the stupid nor intelligent interpretation of any expression. Logic only tells you hypothetically that *if* you give a certain term a certain interpretation then a certain conclusion follows. Logic is silent on how to classify particulars— and this is the heart of a judicial decision. So this reference to logic and to logical extremes is a misnomer for something else, which must be this. A judge has to apply a rule to a concrete case—perhaps the rule that one may not take a stolen "vehicle" across state lines, and in this case an airplane has been taken. He either does not see or pretends not to see that the general terms of this rule are susceptible of different interpretations and that he has a choice left open uncontrolled by linguistic conventions. He ignores, or is blind to, the fact that he is in the area of the penumbra and is not dealing with a standard case. Instead of choosing in the light of social aims, the judge fixes the meaning in a different way. He either takes the meaning that the word most obviously suggests in its ordinary nonlegal

context to ordinary men, or one which the word has been given in some other legal context, or, still worse, he thinks of a standard case and then arbitrarily identifies certain features in it—for example, in the case of a vehicle, (1) normally used on land, (2) capable of carrying a human person, (3) capable of being self propelled—and treats these three as always necessary and always sufficient conditions for the use in all contexts of the word "vehicle," irrespective of the social consequences of giving it this interpretation. This choice, not "logic," would force the judge to include a toy motor car (if electrically propelled) and to exclude bicycles and the airplane. In all this there is possibly great stupidity but not more "logic," and no less, than in cases in which the interpretation given to a general term and the consequent application of some general rule to a particular case is consciously controlled by some identified social aim.

Decisions made in a fashion as blind as this would scarcely deserve the name of decisions; we might as well toss a penny in applying a rule of law. But it is at least doubtful whether any judicial decisions (even in England) have been quite as automatic as this. Rather either the interpretations stigmatized as automatic have resulted from the conviction that it is fairer in a criminal statute to take a meaning which would jump to the mind of the ordinary man at the cost even of defeating other values, and this itself is a social policy (though possibly a bad one); or much more frequently, what is stigmatized as "mechanical" and "automatic" is a determined choice made indeed in the light of a social aim but of a conservative social aim. Certainly many of the Supreme Court decisions at the turn of the century which have been so stigmatized represent clear choices in the penumbral area to give effect to a policy of a conservative type. . . .

But how does the wrongness of deciding cases in an automatic and mechanical way and the rightness of deciding cases by reference to social purposes show that the utilitarian insistence on the distinction between what the law is and what it ought to be is wrong? I take it that no one who wished to use these vices of formalism as proof that the distinction between what is and what ought to be is mistaken would deny that the decisions stigmatized as automatic are law; nor would he deny that the system in which such automatic decisions are made is a legal system. Surely he would say that they are law, but they are bad law, they ought not to be law. But this would be to use the distinction, not to refute it; and of course both Bentham and Austin used it to attack judges for failing to decide penumbral cases in accordance with the growing needs of society.

Clearly, if the demonstration of the errors of formalism is to show the utilitarian distinction to be wrong, the point must be drastically restated. The point must be not merely that a judicial decision to be rational must be made in the light of some conception of what ought to be, but that the aims, the social policies and purposes to which judges should appeal if their decisions are to be rational, are themselves to be considered as part of the law in some suitably wide sense of "law" which is held to be more illuminating than that used by the utilitarians. This restatement of the point would have the following consequence: Instead of saying that the recurrence of penumbral questions shows us that legal rules are essentially incomplete, and that, when they fail to determine decisions, judges must legislate and so exercise a creative choice between alternatives, we shall say that the social policies which guide the judges' choice are in a sense there for them to discover; the judges are only "drawing out" of the rule what, if it is properly understood, is "latent" within it. To call this judicial legislation is to obscure some essential continuity between the clear cases of the rule's application and the penumbral decisions. I shall question later whether this way of talking is salutary, but I wish at this time to point out something obvious, but likely, if not stated, to tangle the issues. It does not follow that, because the opposite of a decision reached blindly in the formalist or literalist manner is a decision intelligently reached by reference to some conception of what ought to be, we have a junction of law and morals. We must, I think, beware of thinking in a too simple-minded fashion about the word "ought." This is not because there is no distinction to be made between law as it is and ought to be. Far from it. It is because the distinction should be between what is and what from many different points of view ought to be. The word "ought" merely reflects the presence of some standard of criticism; one of these standards is a moral standard but not all standards are moral. We say to our neighbour, "You ought not to lie," and that may certainly be a moral judgment, but we should remember that the baffled poisoner may say, "I ought to have given her a second dose." The point here is that intelligent decisions which we oppose to mechanical or formal decisions are not necessarily identical with decisions defensible on moral grounds. We may say of many a decision: "Yes, that is right; that is as it ought to be," and we may mean only that some accepted

purpose or policy has been thereby advanced; we may not mean to endorse the moral propriety of the policy or the decision. So the contrast between the mechanical decision and the intelligent one can be reproduced inside a system dedicated to the pursuit of the most evil aims. It does not exist as a contrast to be found only in legal systems which, like our own, widely recognize principles of justice and moral claims of individuals.

An example may make this point plainer. With us the task of sentencing in criminal cases is the one that seems most obviously to demand from the judge the exercise of moral judgment. Here the factors to be weighed seem clearly to be moral factors: society must not be exposed to wanton attack; too much misery must not be inflicted on either the victim or his dependents; efforts must be made to enable him to lead a better life and regain a position in the society whose laws he has violated. To a judge striking the balance among these claims, with all the discretion and perplexities involved, his task seems as plain an example of the exercise of moral judgment as could be; and it seems to be the polar opposite of some mechanical application of a tariff of penalties fixing a sentence careless of the moral claims which in our system have to be weighed. So here intelligent and rational decision is guided however uncertainly by moral aims. But we have only to vary the example to see that this need not necessarily be so and surely, if it need not necessarily be so, the utilitarian point remains unshaken. Under the Nazi regime men were sentenced by courts for criticism of the regime. Here the choice of sentence might be guided exclusively by consideration of what was needed to maintain the state's tyranny effectively. What sentence would both terrorize the public at large and keep the friends and family of the prisoner in suspense so that both hope and fear would cooperate as factors making for subservience? The prisoner of such a system would be regarded simply as an object to be used in pursuit of these aims. Yet, in contrast with a mechanical decision, decision on these grounds would be intelligent and purposive, and from one point of view the decision would be as it ought to be. Of course, I am not unaware that a whole philosophical tradition has sought to demonstrate the fact that we cannot correctly call decisions or behavior truly rational unless they are in conformity with moral aims and principles. But the example I have used seems to me to serve at least as a warning that we cannot use the errors of formalism as something which per se demonstrates the falsity of the utilitarian insistence on the distinction between law as it is and law as *morally* it ought to be.

We can now return to the main point. If it is true that the intelligent decision of penumbral questions is one made not mechanically but in the light of aims, purposes, and policies, though not necessarily in the light of anything we would call moral principles, is it wise to express this important fact by saying that the firm utilitarian distinction between what the law is and what it ought to be should be dropped? Perhaps the claim that it is wise cannot be theoretically refuted for it is, in effect, an *invitation* to revise our conception of what a legal rule is. We are invited to include in the "rule" the various aims and policies in the light of which its penumbral cases are decided on the ground that these aims have, because of their importance, as much right to be called law as the core of legal rules whose meaning is settled. But though an invitation cannot be refuted, it may be refused, and I would proffer two reasons for refusing this invitation. First, everything we have learned about the judicial process can be expressed in other less mysterious ways. We can say laws are incurably incomplete and we must decide the penumbral cases rationally by reference to social aims. I think Holmes, who had such a vivid appreciation of the fact that "general propositions do not decide concrete cases," would have put it that way. Second, to insist on the utilitarian distinction is to emphasize that the hard core of settled meaning is law in some centrally important sense and that even if there are borderlines, there must first be lines. If this were not so, the notion of rules controlling courts' decisions would be senseless as some of the "Realists"—in their most extreme moods, and, I think, on bad grounds—claimed.

By contrast, to soften the distinction, to assert mysteriously that there is some fused identity between law as it is and as it ought to be, is to suggest that all legal questions are fundamentally like those of the penumbra. It is to assert that there is no central element of actual law to be seen in the core of central meaning which rules have, that there is nothing in the nature of a legal rule inconsistent with *all* questions being open to reconsideration in the light of social policy. Of course, it is good to be occupied with the penumbra. Its problems are rightly the daily diet of the law schools. But to be occupied with the penumbra is one thing, to be preoccupied with it another. And preoccupation with the penumbra is, if I may say so, as rich a source of confusion in the American legal tradition as formalism in the English. Of course we

might abandon the notion that rules have authority; we might cease to attach force or even meaning to an argument that a case falls clearly within a rule and the scope of a precedent. We might call all such reasoning "automatic" or "mechanical," which is already the routine invective of the courts. But until we decide that this is what we want; we should not encourage it by obliterating the utilitarian distinction. . . .

4

The third criticism of the separation of law and morals is of a very different character; it certainly is less an intellectual argument against the utilitarian distinction than a passionate appeal supported not by detailed reasoning but by reminders of a terrible experience. For it consists of the testimony of those who have descended into Hell, and, like Ulysses or Dante, brought back a message for human beings. Only in this case the Hell was not beneath or beyond earth, but on it; it was a Hell created on earth by men for other men.

This appeal comes from those German thinkers who lived through the Nazi regime and reflected upon its evil manifestations in the legal system. One of these thinkers, Gustav Radbruch, had himself shared the "positivist" doctrine until the Nazi tyranny, but he was converted by this experience and so his appeal to other men to discard the doctrine of the separation of law and morals has the special poignancy of a recantation. What is important about this criticism is that it really does confront the particular point which Bentham and Austin had in mind in urging the separation of law as it is and as it ought to be. . . .

. . . Austin, it may be recalled, was emphatic in condemning those who said that if human laws conflicted with the fundamental principles of morality then they cease to be laws, as talking "stark nonsense."

> The most pernicious laws, and therefore those which are most opposed to the will of God, have been and are continually enforced as laws by judicial tribunals. Suppose an act innocuous, or positively beneficial, be prohibited by the sovereign under the penalty of death; if I commit this act, I shall be tried and condemned, and if I object to the sentence, that it is contrary to the law of God . . . the court of justice will demonstrate the inconclusiveness of my reasoning by hanging me

up, in pursuance of the law of which I have impugned the validity. An exception, demurrer, or plea, founded on the law of God was never heard in a Court of Justice, from the creation of the world down to the present moment.

These are strong, indeed brutal words, but we must remember that they went along—in the case of Austin and, of course, Bentham—with the conviction that if laws reached a certain degree of iniquity then there would be a plain moral obligation to resist them and to withhold obedience. We shall see, when we consider the alternatives, that this simple presentation of the human dilemma which may arise has much to be said for it. . . .

It is impossible to read without sympathy [the] passionate demand that the German legal conscience should be open to the demands of morality and [the] complaint that this has been too little the case in the German tradition. On the other hand there is an extraordinary naïveté in the view that insensitiveness to the demands of morality and subservience to state power in a people like the Germans should have arisen from the belief that law might be law though it failed to conform with the minimum requirements of morality. Rather this terrible history prompts inquiry into why emphasis on the slogan "law is law," and the distinction between law and morals, acquired a sinister character in Germany, but elsewhere, as with the utilitarians themselves, went along with the most enlightened liberal attitudes. . . . Let me cite briefly one of these cases.

In 1944 a woman, wishing to be rid of her husband, denounced him to the authorities for insulting remarks he had made about Hitler while home on leave from the German army. The wife was under no legal duty to report his acts, though what he had said was apparently in violation of statutes making it illegal to make statements detrimental to the government of the Third Reich or to impair by any means the military defense of the German people. The husband was arrested and sentenced to death, apparently pursuant to these statutes, though he was not executed but was sent to the front. In 1949 the wife was prosecuted in a West German court for an offense which we would describe as illegally depriving a person of his freedom (*rechtswidrige Freiheitsberaubung*). This was punishable as a crime under the German Criminal Code of 1871 which had remained in force continuously since its enactment. The wife pleaded that her husband's imprisonment was pursuant to the Nazi statutes and

hence that she had committed no crime. The court of appeal to which the case ultimately came held that the wife was guilty of procuring the deprivation of her husband's liberty by denouncing him to the German courts, even though he had been sentenced by a court for having violated a statute, since, to quote the words of the court, the statute "was contrary to the sound conscience and sense of justice of all decent human beings." This reasoning was followed in many cases which have been hailed as a triumph of the doctrines of natural law and as signaling the overthrow of positivism. The unqualified satisfaction with this result seems to me to be hysteria. Many of us might applaud the objective—that of punishing a woman for an outrageously immoral act—but this was secured only by declaring a statute established since 1934 not to have the force of law, and at least the wisdom of this course must be doubted. There were, of course, two other choices. One was to let the woman go unpunished; one can sympathize with and endorse the view that this might have been a bad thing to do. The other was to face the fact that if the woman were to be punished it must be pursuant to the introduction of a frankly retrospective law and with a full consciousness of what was sacrificed in securing her punishment in this way. Odious as retrospective criminal legislation and punishment may be, to have pursued it openly in this case would at least have had the merits of candour. It would have made plain that in punishing the woman a choice had to be made between two evils, that of leaving her unpunished and that of sacrificing a very precious principle of morality endorsed by most legal systems. Surely if we have learned anything from the history of morals it is that the thing to do with a moral quandary is not to hide it. Like nettles, the occasions when life forces us to choose between the lesser of two evils must be grasped with the consciousness that they are what they are. The vice of this use of the principle that, at certain limiting points, what is utterly immoral cannot be law or lawful is that it will serve to cloak the true nature of the problems with which we are faced and will encourage the romantic optimism that all the values we cherish ultimately will fit into a single system, that no one of them has to be sacrificed or compromised to accommodate another.

. . . If with the utilitarians we speak plainly, we say that laws may be law but too evil to be obeyed. This is a moral condemnation which everyone can understand and it makes an immediate and obvious claim to moral attention. If, on the other hand, we formulate our objection as an assertion that these evil things are not law, here is an assertion which many people do not believe, and if they are disposed to consider it at all, it would seem to raise a whole host of philosophical issues before it can be accepted. So perhaps the most important single lesson to be learned from this form of the denial of the utilitarian distinction is the one that the utilitarians were most concerned to teach: when we have the ample resources of plain speech we must not present the moral criticism of institutions as propositions of a disputable philosophy.

Positivism and Fidelity to Law

Lon L. Fuller

Professor Hart emphatically rejects "the command theory of law," according to which law is simply a command backed by a force sufficient to make it effective. He observes that such a command can be given by a man with a loaded gun, and "law surely is not the gunman situation writ large." There is no need to dwell here on the inadequacies of the command theory, since Professor Hart has already revealed its defects more clearly and succinctly than I could. His conclusion is that the foundation of a legal system is not coercive power, but certain "fundamental accepted rules specifying the essential lawmaking procedures."

When I reached this point in his essay, I felt certain that Professor Hart was about to acknowledge an important qualification on his thesis. I confidently expected that he would go on to say something like this: I have insisted throughout on the importance of keeping sharp the distinction between law and morality. The question may now be raised, therefore, as to the nature of these fundamental rules that furnish the framework within which the making of law takes place. On the one hand, they seem to be rules, not of law, but of morality. They derive their efficacy from a general acceptance, which in turn rests ultimately on a perception that they are right and necessary. They can hardly be said to be law in the sense of an authoritative pronouncement, since their function is to state when a pronouncement is authoritative. On the other hand, in the

daily functioning of the legal system they are often treated and applied much as ordinary rules of law are. Here, then, we must confess there is something that can be called a "merger" of law and morality, and to which the term "intersection" is scarcely appropriate.

Instead of pursuing some such course of thought, to my surprise I found Professor Hart leaving completely untouched the nature of the fundamental rules that make law itself possible, and turning his attention instead to what he considers a confusion of thought on the part of the critics of positivism.

. . .

A full exploration of all the problems that result when we recognize that law becomes possible only by virtue of rules that are not law, would require drawing into consideration the effect of the presence or absence of a written constitution. Insofar as a written constitution defines basic lawmaking procedure, it may remove the perplexities that arise when a parliament in effect defines itself. At the same time, a legislature operating under a written constitution may enact statutes that profoundly affect the lawmaking procedure and its predictable outcome. If these statutes are drafted with sufficient cunning, they may remain within the frame of the constitution and yet undermine the institutions it was intended to establish. If the "court-packing" proposal of the 'thirties does not illustrate this danger unequivocally, it at least suggests that the fear of it is not fanciful. No written constitution can be self-executing. To be effective it requires not merely the respectful deference we show for ordinary legal enactments, but that willing convergence of effort we give to moral principles in which we have an active belief. One may properly work to amend a constitution, but so long as it remains unamended one must work with it, not against it or around it. All this amounts to saying that to be effective a written constitution must be accepted, at least provisionally, not just as law, but as good law.

. . .

Most of the issues raised by Professor Hart's essay can be restated in terms of the distinction between order and good order. Law may be said to represent order *simpliciter*. Good order is law that corresponds to the demands of justice, or morality, or men's notions of what ought to be. This rephrasing of the issue is useful in bringing to light the ambitious nature of Professor Hart's undertaking, for surely we would all agree that it is no easy thing to distinguish order from good order. When it is said, for example, that law simply represents that public order which obtains under all governments—democratic, Fascist, or Communist—the order intended is certainly not that of a morgue or cemetery. We must mean a functioning order, and such an order has to be at least good enough to be considered as functioning by some standard or other. A reminder that workable order usually requires some play in the joints, and therefore cannot be too orderly, is enough to suggest some of the complexities that would be involved in any attempt to draw a sharp distinction between order and good order.

For the time being, however, let us suppose we can in fact clearly separate the concept of order from that of good order. Even in this unreal and abstract form the notion of order itself contains what may be called a moral element. Let me illustrate this "morality of order" in its crudest and most elementary form. Let us suppose an absolute monarch, whose word is the only law known to his subjects. We may further suppose him to be utterly selfish and to seek in his relations with his subjects solely his own advantage. This monarch from time to time issues commands, promising rewards for compliance and threatening punishment for disobedience. He is, however, a dissolute and forgetful fellow, who never makes the slightest attempt to ascertain who have in fact followed his directions and who have not. As a result he habitually punishes loyalty and rewards disobedience. It is apparent that this monarch will never achieve even his own selfish aims until he is ready to accept that minimum self-restraint that will create a meaningful connection between his words and his actions.

Let us now suppose that our monarch undergoes a change of heart and begins to pay some attention to what he said yesterday when, today, he has occasion to distribute bounty or to order the chopping off of heads. Under the strain of this new responsibility, however, our monarch relaxes his attention in other directions and becomes hopelessly slothful in the phrasing of his commands. His orders become so ambiguous and are uttered in so inaudible a tone that his subjects never have any clear idea what he wants them to do. Here, again, it is apparent that if our monarch for his own selfish advantage wants to create in his realm anything like a system of law he will have to pull himself together and assume still another responsibility.

Law, considered merely as order, contains, then, its own implicit morality. This morality of order must be respected if we are to create anything that can be called law, even bad law. Law by itself is powerless to bring this morality into existence. Until our monarch is really ready to face the responsibilities of his position, it will do no good for him to issue still another futile command, this time self-addressed and threatening himself with punishment if he does not mend his ways.

There is a twofold sense in which it is true that law cannot be built on law. First of all, the authority to make law must be supported by moral attitudes that accord to it the competency it claims. Here we are dealing with a morality external to law, which makes law possible. But this alone is not enough. We may stipulate that in our monarchy the accepted "basic norm" designates the monarch himself as the only possible source of law. We still cannot have law until our monarch is ready to accept the internal morality of law itself.

In the life of a nation these external and internal moralities of law reciprocally influence one another; a deterioration of the one will almost inevitably produce a deterioration in the other. So closely related are they that when the anthropologist Lowie speaks of "the generally accepted ethical postulates underlying our . . . legal institutions as their ultimate sanction and guaranteeing their smooth functioning," he may be presumed to have both of them in mind.

What I have called "the internal morality of law" seems to be almost completely neglected by Professor Hart. He does make brief mention of "justice in the administration of the law," which consists in the like treatment of like cases, by whatever elevated or perverted standards the word "like" may be defined. But he quickly dismisses this aspect of law as having no special relevance to his main enterprise.

In this I believe he is profoundly mistaken. It is his neglect to analyze the demands of a morality of order that leads him throughout his essay to treat law as a datum projecting itself into human experience and not as an object of human striving. When we realize that order itself is something that must be worked for, it becomes apparent that the existence of a legal system, even a bad or evil legal system, is always a matter of degree. When we recognize this simple fact of everyday legal experience, it becomes impossible to dismiss the problems presented by the Nazi regime with a simple assertion: "Under the Nazis there was law, even if it was bad law." We have instead to inquire how much of a legal system survived the general debasement and perversion of all forms of social order that occurred under the Nazi rule, and what moral implications this mutilated system had for the conscientious citizen forced to live under it.

It is not necessary, however, to dwell on such moral upheavals as the Nazi regime to see how completely incapable the positivistic philosophy is of serving the high moral ideal it professes, that of fidelity to law. Its default in serving this ideal actually becomes most apparent, I believe, in the everyday problems that confront those who are earnestly desirous of meeting the moral demands of a legal order, but who have responsible functions to discharge in the very order toward which loyalty is due.

Let us suppose the case of a trial judge who has had an extensive experience in commercial matters and before whom a great many commercial disputes are tried. As a subordinate in a judicial hierarchy, our judge has of course the duty to follow the law laid down by his supreme court. Our imaginary Scrutton has the misfortune, however, to live under a supreme court which he considers woefully ignorant of the ways and needs of commerce. To his mind, many of this court's decisions in the field of commercial law simply do not make sense. If a conscientious judge caught in this dilemma were to turn to the positivistic philosophy what succor could he expect? It will certainly do no good to remind him that he has an obligation of fidelity to law. He is aware of this already and painfully so, since it is the source of his predicament. Nor will it help to say that if he legislates, it must be "interstitially," or that his contributions must be "confined from molar to molecular motions." This mode of statement may be congenial to those who like to think of law, not as a purposive thing, but as an expression of the dimensions and directions of state power. But I cannot believe that the essentially trite idea behind this advice can be lifted by literary eloquence to the point where it will offer any real help to our judge; for one thing, it may be impossible for him to know whether his supreme court would regard any particular contribution of his as being wide or narrow.

Nor is it likely that a distinction between core and penumbra would be helpful. The predicament of our judge may well derive, not from particular precedents, but from a mistaken conception of the nature of commerce which extends over many decisions and penetrates them in varying degrees. So far as his problem arises from the use of particular words, he may well find that the supreme court often uses the ordinary terms of commerce in senses foreign to actual business dealings. If he interprets those words as a business executive or accountant would, he may well reduce the precedents he is bound to apply to a logical shambles. On the other hand, he may find great difficulty in discerning the exact sense in which the supreme court used those words, since in his mind that sense is itself the product of a confusion.

Is it not clear that it is precisely positivism's insistence on a rigid separation of law as it is from law as it ought to be that renders the positivistic philosophy incapable of aiding our judge? Is it not also clear that our judge can never achieve a satisfactory resolution of his dilemma unless he views his duty of fidelity to law in a context which also embraces his responsibility for making law what it ought to be?

The case I have supposed may seem extreme, but the problem it suggests pervades our whole legal system. If the divergence of views between our judge and his supreme court were less drastic, it would be more difficult to present his predicament graphically, but the perplexity of his position might actually increase. Perplexities of this sort are a normal accompaniment of the discharge of any adjudicative function; they perhaps reach their most poignant intensity in the field of administrative law.

One can imagine a case—surely not likely in Professor Hart's country or mine—where a judge might hold profound moral convictions that were exactly the opposite of those held, with equal attachment, by his supreme court. He might also be convinced that the precedents he was bound to apply were the direct product of a morality he considered abhorrent. If such a judge did not find the solution for his dilemma in surrendering his office, he might well be driven to a wooden and literal application of precedents which he could not otherwise apply because he was incapable of understanding the philosophy that animated them. But I doubt that a judge in this situation would need the help of legal positivism to find these melancholy escapes from his predicament. Nor do I think that such a predicament is likely to arise within a nation where both law and good law are regarded as collaborative human achievements in need of constant renewal, and where lawyers are still at least as interested in asking "What is good law?" as they are in asking "What is law?"

After the collapse of the Nazi regime the German courts were faced with a truly frightful predicament. It was impossible for them to declare the whole dictatorship illegal or to treat as void every decision and legal enactment that had emanated from Hitler's government. Intolerable dislocations would have resulted from any such wholesale outlawing of all that occurred over a span of twelve years. On the other hand, it was equally impossible to carry forward into the new government the effects of every Nazi perversity that had been committed in the name of law; any such course would have tainted an indefinite future with the poisons of Nazism.

This predicament—which was, indeed, a pervasive one, affecting all branches of law—came to a dramatic head in a series of cases involving informers who had taken advantage of the Nazi terror to get rid of personal enemies or unwanted spouses. If all Nazi statutes and judicial decisions were indiscriminately "law," then these despicable creatures were guiltless, since they had turned their victims over to processes which the Nazis themselves knew by the name of law. Yet it was intolerable, especially for the surviving relatives and friends of the victims, that these people should go about unpunished, while the objects of their spite were dead, or were just being released after years of imprisonment, or, more painful still, simply remained unaccounted for.

The urgency of this situation does not by any means escape Professor Hart. Indeed, he is moved to recommend an expedient that is surely not lacking itself in a certain air of desperation. He suggests that a retroactive criminal statute would have been the least objectionable solution to the problem. This statute would have punished the informer, and branded him as a criminal, for an act which Professor Hart regards as having been perfectly legal when he committed it.

On the other hand, Professor Hart condemns without qualification those judicial decisions in which the courts themselves undertook to declare void certain of the Nazi statutes under which the informer's victims had been convicted. One cannot help raising at this point the question whether the issue as presented by Professor Hart himself is truly that of fidelity to law. Surely it would be a necessary implication of a retroactive criminal statute against informers that, for purposes of that statute at least, the Nazi laws as applied to the informers or their victims were to be regarded as void. With this turn the question seems no longer to be whether what was once law can now be declared not to have been law, but rather who should do the dirty work, the courts or the legislature.

But, as Professor Hart himself suggests, the issues at stake are much too serious to risk losing them in a semantic tangle. Even if the whole question were one of words, we should remind ourselves that we are in an area where words have a powerful effect on human attitudes. I should like, therefore, to undertake a defense of the German courts, and to advance reasons why, in my opinion, their decisions do not represent the abandonment of legal principle that Professor Hart sees in them.

. . .

Let us turn at once, then, to the actual case discussed by Professor Hart.

In 1944 a German soldier paid a short visit to his wife while under travel orders on a reassignment. During the single day he was home, he conveyed privately to his wife something of his opinion of the Hitler government. He expressed disapproval of (*sich abfällig geäussert über*) Hitler and leading personalities of the Nazi party. He also said it was too bad Hitler had not met his end in the assassination attempt that had occurred on July 20th of that year. Shortly after his departure, his wife, who during his long absence on military duty "had turned to other men" and who wished to get rid of him, reported his remarks to the local leader of the Nazi party, observing that "a man who would say a thing like that does not deserve to live." The result was a trial of the husband by a military tribunal and a sentence of death. After a short period of imprisonment, instead of being executed, he was sent to the front again. After the collapse of the Nazi regime, the wife was brought to trial for having procured the imprisonment of her husband. Her defense rested on the ground that her husband's statements to her about Hitler and the Nazis constituted a crime under the laws then in force. Accordingly, when she informed on her husband she was simply bringing a criminal to justice.

The defense rested on two statutes, one passed in 1934, the other in 1938. Let us first consider the second of these enactments, which was part of a more comprehensive legislation creating a whole series of special wartime criminal offenses. I reproduce below a translation of the only pertinent section:

> The following persons are guilty of destroying the national power of resistance and shall be punished by death: Whoever publicly solicits or incites a refusal to fulfill the obligations of service in the armed forces of Germany, or in armed forces allied with Germany, or who otherwise publicly seeks to

injure or destroy the will of the German people or an allied people to assert themselves stalwartly against their enemies.

It is almost inconceivable that a court of present-day Germany would hold the husband's remarks to his wife, who was barred from military duty by her sex, to be a violation of the final catchall provision of this statute, particularly when it is recalled that the text reproduced above was part of a more comprehensive enactment dealing with such things as harboring deserters, escaping military duty by self-inflicted injuries, and the like. The question arises, then, as to the extent to which the interpretive principles applied by the courts of Hitler's government should be accepted in determining whether the husband's remarks were indeed unlawful.

This question becomes acute when we note that the act applies only to *public* acts or utterances, whereas the husband's remarks were in the privacy of his own home. Now it appears that the Nazi courts (and it should be noted we are dealing with a special military court) quite generally disregarded this limitation and extended the act to all utterances, private and public. Is Professor Hart prepared to say that the legal meaning of this statute is to be determined in the light of this apparently uniform principle of judicial interpretation?

Let us turn now to the other statute upon which Professor Hart relies in assuming that the husband's utterance was unlawful. This is the act of 1934, the relevant portions of which are translated below:

(1) Whoever publicly makes spiteful or provocative statements directed against, or statements which disclose a base disposition toward, the leading personalities of the nation or of the National Socialist German Workers' Party, or toward measures taken or institutions established by them, and of such a nature as to undermine the people's confidence in their political leadership, shall be punished by imprisonment.

(2) Malicious utterances not made in public shall be treated in the same manner as public utterances when the person making them realized or should have realized they would reach the public.

(3) Prosecution for such utterances shall be only on the order of the National Minister of Justice; in case the utterance was directed against a leading personality of the National

Socialist German Workers' Party, the Minister or Justice shall order prosecution only with the advice and consent of the Representative of the Leader.

(4) The National Minister of Justice shall, with the advice and consent of the Representative of the Leader, determine who shall belong to the class of leading personalities for purposes of Section 1 above.

Extended comment on this legislative monstrosity is scarcely called for, overlarded and undermined as it is by uncontrolled administrative discretion. We may note only: first, that it offers no justification whatever for the death penalty actually imposed on the husband, though never carried out; second, that if the wife's act in informing on her husband made his remarks "public," there is no such thing as a private utterance under this statute. I should like to ask the reader whether he can actually share Professor Hart's indignation that, in the perplexities of the postwar reconstruction, the German courts saw fit to declare this thing not a law. Can it be argued seriously that it would have been more beseeming to the judicial process if the postwar courts had undertaken a study of "the interpretative principles" in force during Hitler's rule and had then solemnly applied those "principles" to ascertain the meaning of this statute? On the other hand, would the courts really have been showing respect for Nazi law if they had construed the Nazi statues by their own, quite different, standards of interpretation?

Professor Hart castigates the German courts and Radbruch, not so much for what they believed had to be done, but because they failed to see that they were confronted by a moral dilemma of a sort that would have been immediately apparent to Bentham and Austin. By the simple dodge of saying, "When a statute is sufficiently evil it ceases to be law," they ran away from the problem they should have faced.

This criticism is, I believe, without justification. So far as the courts are concerned, matters certainly would not have been helped if, instead of saying, "This is not law," they had said, "This is law but it is so evil we will refuse to apply it." Surely moral confusion reaches its height when a court refuses to apply something it admits to be law, and Professor Hart does not recommend any such "facing of the true issue" by the courts themselves. He would have preferred a retroactive statute. Curiously, this was also the preference of Radbruch. But unlike Professor Hart, the German courts and Gustav Radbruch were living participants in a situation of drastic emergency. The informer problem was a pressing one, and if legal institutions were to be rehabilitated in Germany it would not do to allow the people to begin taking the law into their own hands, as might have occurred while the courts were waiting for a statute.

As for Gustav Radbruch, it is, I believe, wholly unjust to say that he did not know he was faced with a moral dilemma. His postwar writings repeatedly stress the antinomies confronted in the effort to rebuild decent and orderly government in Germany. As for the ideal of fidelity to law, I shall let Radbruch's own words state his position:

> We must not conceal from ourselves—
> especially not in the light of our experiences
> during the twelve-year dictatorship—what
> frightful dangers for the rule of law can be
> contained in the notion of "statutory lawless-
> ness" and in refusing the quality of law to
> duly enacted statutes.

The situation is not that legal positivism enables a man to know when he faces a difficult problem of choice, while Radbruch's beliefs deceive him into thinking there is no problem to face. The real issue dividing Professors Hart and Radbruch is: How shall we state the problem? What is the nature of the dilemma in which we are caught?

I hope I am not being unjust to Professor Hart when I say that I can find no way of describing the dilemma as he sees it but to use some such words as the following: On the one hand, we have an amoral datum called law, which has the peculiar quality of creating a moral duty to obey it. On the other hand, we have a moral duty to do what we think is right and decent. When we are confronted by a statute we believe to be thoroughly evil, we have to choose between those two duties.

If this is the positivist position, then I have no hesitancy in rejecting it. The "dilemma" it states has the verbal formulation of a problem, but the problem it states makes no sense. It is like saying I have to choose between giving food to a starving man and being mimsy with the borogoves. I do not think it is unfair to the positivistic philosophy to say that it never gives any coherent meaning to the moral obligation of fidelity to law. This obligation seems to be conceived as *sui generis*, wholly unrelated to any of the ordinary, extralegal ends of human life. The fundamental postulate of positivism—that law must be strictly severed from morality—seems to deny the possibility of any bridge between the obligation to obey law and other moral obligations. No mediating principle can measure their respective demands on conscience, for they exist in wholly separate worlds.

While I would not subscribe to all of Radbruch's postwar views—especially those relating to "higher law"—I think he saw, much more clearly than does Professor Hart, the true nature of the dilemma confronted by Germany in seeking to rebuild her shattered legal institutions. Germany had to restore both respect for law and respect for justice. Though neither of these could be restored without the other, painful antinomies were encountered in attempting to restore both at once, as Radbruch saw all too clearly. Essentially Radbruch saw the dilemma as that of meeting the demands of order, on the one hand, and those of good order, on the other. Of course no pat formula can be derived from this phrasing of the problem. But, unlike legal positivism, it does not present us with opposing demands that have no living contact with one another, that simply shout their contradictions across a vacuum. As we seek order, we can meaningfully remind ourselves that order itself will do us no good unless it is good for something. As we seek to make our order good, we can remind ourselves that justice itself is impossible without order, and that we must not lose order itself in the attempt to make it good.

   . . .

Professor Hart and others have been understandably distressed by references to a "higher law" in some of the decisions concerning informers and in Radbruch's postwar writings. I suggest that if German jurisprudence had concerned itself more with the inner morality of law, it would not have been necessary to invoke any notion of this sort in declaring void the more outrageous Nazi statutes.

To me there is nothing shocking in saying that a dictatorship which clothes itself with a tinsel of legal form can so far depart from the morality of order, from the inner morality of law itself, that it ceases to be a legal system. When a system calling itself law is predicated upon a general disregard by judges of the terms of the laws they purport to enforce, when this system habitually cures its legal irregularities, even the grossest, by retroactive statutes, when it has only to resort to forays of terror in the streets, which no one dares challenge, in order to escape even those scant restraints imposed by the pretence of legality—when all these things have become true of a dictatorship, it is not hard for me, at least, to deny to it the name of law.

I believe that the invalidity of the statutes involved in the informer cases could have been grounded on considerations such as I have just outlined. But if you were raised with a generation that said "law is law" and meant it, you may feel the only way you can escape one law is to set another off against it, and this perforce must be a "higher law." Hence these notions of "higher law," which are a justifiable cause for alarm, may themselves be a belated fruit of German legal positivism.

It should be remarked at this point that it is chiefly in Roman Catholic writings that the theory of natural law is considered, not simply as a search for those principles that will enable men to live together successfully, but as a quest for something that can be called "a higher law." This identification of natural law with a law that is above human laws seems in fact to be demanded by any doctrine that asserts the possibility of an authoritative pronouncement of the demands of natural law. In those areas affected by such pronouncements as have so far been issued, the conflict between Roman Catholic doctrine and opposing views seems to me to be a conflict between two forms of positivism. Fortunately, over most of the area with which lawyers are concerned, no such pronouncements exist. In these areas I think those of us who are not adherents of its faith can be grateful to the Catholic Church for having kept alive the rationalistic tradition in ethics.

I do not assert that the solution I have suggested for the informer cases would not have entailed its own difficulties, particularly the familiar one of knowing where to stop. But I think it demonstrable that the most

serious deterioration in legal morality under Hitler took place in branches of the law like those involved in the informer cases; no comparable deterioration was to be observed in the ordinary branches of private law. It was in those areas where the ends of law were most odious by ordinary standards of decency that the morality of law itself was most flagrantly disregarded. In other words, where one would have been most tempted to say, "This is so evil it cannot be a law," one could usually have said instead, "This thing is the product of a system so oblivious to the morality of law that it is not entitled to be called a law." I think there is something more than accident here, for the overlapping suggests that legal morality cannot live when it is severed from a striving toward justice and decency.

But as an actual solution for the informer cases, I, like Professors Hart and Radbruch, would have preferred a retroactive statute. My reason for this preference is not that this is the most nearly lawful way of making unlawful what was once law. Rather I would see such a statute as a way of symbolizing a sharp break with the past, as a means of isolating a kind of cleanup operation from the normal functioning of the judicial process. By this isolation it would become possible for the judiciary to return more rapidly to a condition in which the demands of legal morality could be given proper respect. In other words, it would make it possible to plan more effectively to regain for the ideal of fidelity to law its normal meaning.

What Is Law? From Summa Theologiae

St. Thomas Aquinas

Question 90

Law is a rule and measure of acts, whereby man is induced to act or is restrained from acting; for *lex [law]*

is derived from *ligare [to bind]*, because it binds one to act. Now the rule and measure of human acts is the reason, which is the first principle of human acts. . . . For it belongs to the reason to direct to the end, which is the first principle in all matters of action, according to [Aristotle]. . . . Reason has its power of moving from the will, . . . for it is due to the fact that one wills the end, that the reason issues its commands as regards things ordained to the end. But in order that the volition of what is commanded may have the nature of law, it needs to be in accord with some rule of reason.

And in this sense is to be understood the saying that the will of the sovereign has the force of law; or otherwise the sovereign's will would savor of lawlessness rather than of law.

[Now] the first principle in practical matters, which are the object of the practical reason, is the last end: and the last end of human life is happiness or beatitude. . . . Consequently, law must . . . concern itself mainly with the order that is in beatitude. Moreover, since every part is ordained to the whole as the imperfect to the perfect, and since one man is a part of the perfect community, law must . . . concern itself properly with the order directed to universal happiness. Therefore Aristotle mentions both happiness and the body politic, since he says that we call those legal matters *just which are adapted to produce and preserve happiness and its parts for the body politic.*

Now in every genus, that which belongs to it chiefly is the principle of the others, and the others belong to that genus according to some order towards that thing. Thus fire, which is chief among hot things, is the cause of heat in mixed bodies, and these are said to be hot insofar as they have a share of fire. Consequently, since law is chiefly ordained to the common good, any other precept in regard to some individual work must . . . be devoid of the nature of law, save insofar as it regards the common good. Therefore every law is ordained to the common good.

Just as nothing stands firm with regard to the speculative reason except that which is traced back to the first indemonstrable principles, so nothing stands firm with regard to the practical reason, unless it be directed to the last end which is the common good. Now whatever stands to reason in this sense has the nature of a law.

[A] private person cannot lead another to virtue efficaciously; for he can only advise, and if his advice be not taken, it has no coercive power, such as the law should have, in order to prove an efficacious inducement to virtue. . . . But this coercive power is vested in the whole people or in some public personage, to whom it belongs to inflict penalties. . . . Therefore the framing of laws belongs to him alone.

[A] law is imposed on others as a rule and measure. Now a rule or measure is imposed by being applied to those who are to be ruled and measured by it. Therefore, in order that a law obtain the binding force which is proper to a law, it must . . . be applied to the men who have to be ruled by it. But such application is made by its being made known to them by promulgation. Therefore promulgation is necessary for law to obtain its force.

Thus, . . . Law is nothing else than an ordinance of reason for the common good, promulgated by him who has the care of the community.

The natural law is promulgated by the very fact that God instilled it into man's mind so as to be known by him naturally. . . . The promulgation that takes place in the present extends to future time by reason of the durability of written characters, by which means it is continually promulgated.

Question 91

Every act of reason and will in us is based on that which is according to nature. . . . For every act of reasoning is based on principles that are known naturally, and every act of appetite in respect of the means is derived from the natural appetite in respect of the last end. Accordingly, the first direction of our acts to their end must . . . be through the natural law.

[Augustine] distinguishes two kinds of law, the one eternal, the other temporal, which he calls human. . . . Just as in the speculative reason, from naturally known indemonstrable principles we draw the conclusions of the various sciences, the knowledge of which is not imparted to us by nature, but acquired by the efforts of reason, so too it is that from the precepts of the natural law, as from common and indemonstrable principles, the human reason needs to proceed to the more particular determination of certain matters. These particular determinations, devised by human reason, are called human laws, provided that the other essential conditions of law be observed.

Question 94

[The] precepts of the natural law are to the practical reason what the first principles of demonstrations are to the speculative reason, because both are self-evident principles. . . . Now as *being* is the first thing that falls under the apprehension absolutely, so *good* is the first thing that falls under the apprehension of the practical reason, which is directed to action (since every agent acts for an end, which has the nature of good). Consequently, the first principle in the practical reason is one founded on the nature of the good, viz., that *good is that which all things seek after.* Hence this is the first precept of law, that *good is to be promoted, and evil is to be avoided.* All other precepts of the natural law are based on this; so that all things which the practical reason naturally apprehends as man's good belong to the precepts of the natural law under the form of things to be done or avoided.

Question 95

[As] Augustine says, *that which is not just seems to be no law at all.* Hence the force of a law depends on the extent of its justice. Now in human affairs a thing is said to be just from being right, according to the rule of reason. But the first rule of reason is the law of nature. . . . Consequently, every human law has just so much of the nature of law as it is derived from the law of nature. But if in any point it departs from the law of nature, it is no longer law but a perversion of law.

[The] common principles of the natural law cannot be applied to all men in the same way because of the great variety of human affairs; and hence arises the diversity of positive laws among various people. . . . In this respect, there are various human laws according to the various forms of government. . . . Tyrannical government, which is altogether corrupt, . . . has no corresponding law.

Question 96

The natural law is a participation in us of the eternal law, while human law falls short of the eternal law. For Augustine says, *The law which is framed for the government of states allows and leaves unpunished many things that are punished by divine providence. Nor, if this law does not attempt to do everything, is this a reason why it should be blamed for what it does.* Therefore, human law likewise does not prohibit everything that is forbidden by the natural law.

[Laws] framed by man are either just or unjust. If they be just, they have the power of binding the conscience from the eternal law whence they are derived. . . . On the other hand, laws may be unjust in two ways: first, by being contrary to human good, . . . as when an authority imposes on his subjects burdensome laws, conducive, not to the common good, but rather to his own cupidity or vainglory. . . . Such are acts of violence rather than laws, because, as Augustine says, *a law that is not just seems to be no law at all.* Therefore, such laws do not bind in conscience. . . .

Secondly, laws may be unjust through being opposed to the divine good. . . . Laws of this kind must in no way be observed, because . . . *we ought to obey God rather than men.*

Letter from Birmingham Jail

MARTIN LUTHER KING, JR.

My dear Fellow Clergymen,

While confined here in the Birmingham city jail, I came across your recent statement calling our present activities "unwise and untimely." Seldom, if ever, do I pause to answer criticism of my work and ideas. If I sought to answer all of the criticisms that cross my

desk, my secretaries would be engaged in little else in the course of the day, and I would have no time for constructive work. But since I feel that you are men of genuine good will and your criticisms are sincerely set forth, I would like to answer your statement in what I hope will be patient and reasonable terms.

I think I should give the reason for my being in Birmingham, since you have been influenced by the argument of "outsiders coming in." I have the honor of serving as president of the Southern Christian Leadership Conference, an organization operating in every southern state, with headquarters in Atlanta, Georgia. We have some eighty-five affiliate organizations all across the South—one being the Alabama Christian Movement for Human Rights. Whenever necessary and possible we share staff, educational and financial resources with our affiliates. Several months ago our local affiliate here in Birmingham invited us to be on call to engage in a nonviolent direct-action program if such were deemed necessary. We readily consented and when the hour came we lived up to our promises. So I am here, along with several members of my staff, because we were invited here. I am here because I have basic organizational ties here.

Beyond this, I am in Birmingham because injustice is here. Just as the eighth century prophets left their little villages and carried their "thus saith the Lord" far beyond the boundaries of their hometowns; and just as the Apostle Paul left his little village of Tarsus and carried the gospel of Jesus Christ to practically every hamlet and city of the Graeco-Roman world, I too am compelled to carry the gospel of freedom beyond my particular hometown. Like Paul, I must constantly respond to the Macedonian call for aid.

Moreover, I am cognizant of the interrelatedness of all communities and states. I cannot sit idly by in Atlanta and not be concerned about what happens in Birmingham. Injustice anywhere is a threat to justice everywhere. We are caught in an inescapable network of mutuality, tied in a single garment of destiny. Whatever affects one directly affects all indirectly. Never again can we afford to live with the narrow, provincial "outside agitator" idea. Anyone who lives in the United States can never be considered an outsider anywhere in this country.

You deplore the demonstrations that are presently taking place in Birmingham. But I am sorry that your statement did not express a similar concern for the conditions that brought the demonstrations into being. I am sure that each of you would want to go beyond the superficial social analyst who looks merely at effects, and does not grapple with underlying causes. I would not hesitate to say that it is unfortunate that so-called demonstrations are taking place in Birmingham at this time, but I would say in more emphatic terms that it is even more unfortunate that the white power structure of this city left the Negro community with no other alternative.

. . .

You may well ask, "Why direct action? Why sit-ins, marches, etc.? Isn't negotiation a better path?" You are exactly right in your call for negotiation. Indeed, this is the purpose of direct action. Nonviolent direct action seeks to create such a crisis and establish such creative tension that a community that has constantly refused to negotiate is forced to confront the issue. It seeks so to dramatize the issue that it can no longer be ignored. I just referred to the creation of tension as a part of the work of the nonviolent resister. This may sound rather shocking. But I must confess that I am not afraid of the word tension. I have earnestly worked and preached against violent tension, but there is a type of constructive nonviolent tension that is necessary for growth. Just as Socrates felt that it was necessary to create a tension in the mind so that individuals could rise from the bondage of myths and half-truths to the unfettered realm of creative analysis and objective appraisal, we must see the need for having nonviolent gadflies to create the kind of tension in society that will help men to rise from the dark depths of prejudice and racism to the majestic heights of understanding and brotherhood. So the purpose of the direct action is to create a situation so crisis-packed that it will inevitably open the door to negotiation. We therefore, concur with you in your call for negotiation. Too long has our beloved Southland been bogged down in the tragic attempt to live in monologue rather than dialogue.

. . .

We know through painful experience that freedom is never voluntarily given by the oppressor; it must be demanded by the oppressed. Frankly, I have never yet engaged in a [direct-action] movement that was "well-timed," according to the timetable of those who have not suffered unduly from the disease of segregation. For years now I have heard the word "Wait!" It rings in the ear of every Negro with a piercing familiarity. This "Wait" has almost always meant "Never." It has been a tranquilizing thalidomide, relieving the emotional stress for a moment, only to give birth to an ill-formed infant of frustration. We must come to see with the distinguished jurist of yesterday that "justice too long delayed is justice denied." We have waited for more than 340 years for our constitutional and God-given rights. The nations of Asia and Africa are moving with jetlike speed toward the goal of political independence, and we still creep at horse and buggy pace toward the gaining of a cup of coffee at a lunch counter. I guess it is easy for those who have never felt the stinging darts of segregation to say, "Wait." But when you have seen vicious mobs lynch your mothers and fathers at will and drown your sisters and brothers at whim; when you have seen hate-filled policemen curse, kick, brutalize and even kill your black brothers and sisters with impunity; when you see the vast majority of your twenty million Negro brothers smothering in an airtight cage of poverty in the midst of an affluent society; when you suddenly find your tongue twisted and your speech stammering as you seek to explain to your six-year-old daughter why she can't go to the public amusement park that has just been advertised on television, and see tears welling up in her little eyes when she is told that Funtown is closed to colored children, and see the depressing clouds of inferiority begin to form in her little mental sky, and see her begin to distort her little personality by unconsciously developing a bitterness toward white people; when you have to concoct an answer for a five-year-old son asking in agonizing pathos: "Daddy, why do white people treat colored people so mean?"; when you take a cross-country drive and find it necessary to sleep night after night in the uncomfortable corners of your automobile because no motel will accept you; when you are humiliated day in and day out by nagging signs reading "white" and "colored"; when your first name becomes "nigger" and your middle name becomes "boy" (however old you are) and your last name becomes "John", and when your wife and mother are never given the respected title "Mrs."; when you are harried by day and haunted by night by the fact that you are a Negro, living constantly at tiptoe stance never quite knowing what to expect next, and plagued with inner fears and outer resentments; when you are forever fighting a degenerating sense of "nobodiness"; then you will understand why we find it difficult to wait. There comes a time when the cup of endurance runs over, and men are no longer willing to be plunged into an abyss of injustice where they experience the blackness of corroding despair. I hope, sirs, you can understand our legitimate and unavoidable impatience.

You express a great deal of anxiety over our willingness to break laws. This is certainly a legitimate concern. Since we so diligently urge people to obey the Supreme Court's decision of 1954 outlawing segregation in the public schools, it is rather strange and paradoxical to find us consciously breaking laws. One may well ask, "How can you advocate breaking some laws and obeying others?" The answer is found in the fact that there are two types of laws: there are *just* and *unjust* laws. I would agree with Saint Augustine that "An unjust law is no law at all."

Now what is the difference between the two? How does one determine when a law is just or unjust? A just law is a man-made code that squares with the moral law or the law of God. An unjust law is a code that is out of harmony with the moral law. To put it in the terms of Saint Thomas Aquinas, an unjust law is a human law that is not rooted in eternal and natural law. Any law that uplifts human personality is just. Any law that degrades human personality is unjust. All segregation statutes are unjust because segregation distorts the soul and damages the personality. It gives the segregator a false sense of superiority, and the segregated a false sense of inferiority. To use the words of Martin Buber, the great Jewish philosopher, segregation substitutes an "I-it" relationship for the "I-thou" relationship, and ends up relegating persons to the status of things. So segregation is not only politically, economically and sociologically unsound, but it is morally wrong and sinful. Paul Tillich has said that sin is separation. Isn't segregation an existential expression of man's tragic separation, an expression of his awful estrangement, his terrible sinfulness? So I can urge men to disobey segregation ordinances because they are morally wrong.

Let us turn to a more concrete example of just and unjust laws. An unjust law is a code that a majority inflicts on a minority that is not binding on itself. This is difference made legal. On the other hand a just law is a code that a majority compels a minority to follow that it is willing to follow itself. This is sameness made legal.

Let me give another explanation. An unjust law is a code inflicted upon a minority which that minority had no part in enacting or creating because they did not have the unhampered right to vote. Who can say that the legislature of Alabama which set up the segregation laws was democratically elected? Throughout the state of Alabama all types of conniving methods are used to prevent Negroes from becoming registered voters and there are some counties without a single Negro registered to vote despite the fact that the Negro constitutes a majority of the population. Can any law set up in such a state be considered democratically structured?

These are just a few examples of unjust and just laws. There are some instances when a law is just on its face and unjust in its application. For instance, I was arrested Friday on a charge of parading without a permit. Now there is nothing wrong with an ordinance which requires a permit for a parade, but when the ordinance is used to preserve segregation and to deny citizens the First Amendment privilege of peaceful assembly and peaceful protest, then it becomes unjust.

I hope you can see the distinction I am trying to point out. In no sense do I advocate evading or defying the law as the rabid segregationist would do. This would lead to anarchy. One who breaks an unjust law must do it *openly*, *lovingly* (not hatefully as the white mothers did in New Orleans when they were seen on television screaming "nigger, nigger, nigger"), and with a willingness to accept the penalty. I submit that an individual who breaks a law that conscience tells him is unjust, and willingly accepts the penalty by staying in jail to arouse the conscience of the community over its injustice, is in reality expressing the very highest respect for law.

Of course, there is nothing new about this kind of civil disobedience. It was seen sublimely in the refusal of Shadrach, Meshach and Abednego to obey the laws of Nebuchadnezzar because a higher moral law was involved. It was practiced superbly by the early Christians who were willing to face hungry lions and the excruciating pain of chopping blocks, before submitting to certain unjust laws of the Roman Empire. To a degree academic freedom is a reality today because Socrates practiced civil disobedience.

We can never forget that everything Hitler did in Germany was "legal" and everything the Hungarian freedom fighters did in Hungary was "illegal." It was "illegal" to aid and comfort a Jew in Hitler's Germany. But I am sure that if I had lived in Germany during that time I would have aided and comforted my Jewish brothers even though it was illegal. If I lived in a Communist country today where certain principles dear to the Christian faith are suppressed, I believe I would openly advocate disobeying these antireligious laws. I must make two honest confessions to you, my Christian and Jewish brothers. First, I must confess that over the last few years I have been gravely disappointed with the white moderate. I have almost reached the regrettable conclusion that the Negro's great stumbling block in the stride toward freedom is not the White Citizen's Counciler or the Ku Klux Klanner, but the white moderate who is more devoted to "order" than to justice; who prefers a negative peace which is the absence of tension to a positive peace which is the presence of justice; who constantly says, "I agree with you in the goal you seek, but I can't agree with your methods of direct action"; who paternalistically feels that he can set the timetable for another man's freedom; who lives by the myth of time and who constantly advised the Negro to wait until a "more convenient season." Shallow understanding from people of good will is more frustrating than absolute misunderstanding from people of ill will. Lukewarm acceptance is much more bewildering than outright rejection.

I had hoped that the white moderate would understand that law and order exist for the purpose of establishing justice, and that when they fail to do this they become dangerously structured dams that block the flow of social progress. I had hoped that the white moderate would understand that the present tension of the South is merely a necessary phase of the transition from an obnoxious negative peace, where the Negro passively accepted his unjust plight, to a substance-filled positive peace, where all men will respect the dignity and worth of human personality. Actually, we who engage in nonviolent direct action are not the creators of tension. We merely bring to the surface the hidden tension that is already alive. We bring it out in the open where it can be seen and dealt with. Like a boil that can never be cured as long as it is covered up but must be opened with all its pus-flowing ugliness to the natural medicines of air and light, injustice must likewise be exposed, with all of the tension its exposing creates, to the light of human conscience and the air of national opinion before it can be cured.

In your statement you asserted that our actions, even though peaceful, must be condemned because they precipitate violence. But can this assertion be logically made? Isn't this like condemning the robbed man because his possession of money precipitated the evil act of robbery? Isn't this like condemning Socrates because his unswerving commitment to truth and his philosophical delvings precipitated the misguided popular mind to make him drink the hemlock? Isn't this like condemning Jesus because His unique God-consciousness and never-ceasing devotion to his will precipitated the evil act of crucifixion? We must come to see, as federal courts have consistently affirmed, that it is immoral to urge an individual to withdraw his efforts to gain his basic constitutional rights because the quest precipitates violence. Society must protect the robbed and punish the robber.

. . .

In spite of my shattered dreams of the past, I came to Birmingham with the hope that the white religious leadership of this community would see the justice of our cause, and with deep moral concern, serve as the channel through which our just grievances would get to the power structure. I had hoped that each of you would understand. But again I have been disappointed. I have heard numerous religious leaders of the South call upon their worshippers to comply with a desegregation decision because it is the *law*, but I have longed to hear white ministers say, "Follow this decree because integration is morally *right* and the Negro is your brother." In the midst of blatant injustices inflicted upon the Negro, I have watched white churches stand on the sideline and merely mouth pious irrelevancies and sanctimonious trivialities. In the midst of a mighty struggle to rid our nation of racial and economic injustice, I have heard so many ministers say, "Those are social issues with which the gospel has no real concern," and I have watched so many churches commit themselves to a completely other-worldly religion which made a strange distinction between body and soul, the sacred and the secular.

. . .

I must close now. But before closing I am impelled to mention one other point in your statement that troubled me profoundly. You warmly commended the Birmingham police force for keeping "order" and "preventing violence." I don't believe you would have so warmly commended the police force if you had seen its angry violent dogs literally biting six unarmed, nonviolent Negroes. I don't believe you would so quickly commend the policemen if you would observe their ugly and inhuman treatment of Negroes here in the city jail; if you would watch them push and curse old Negro women and young Negro girls; if you would see them slap and kick old Negro men and young boys; if you will observe them, as they did on two occasions, refuse to give us food because we wanted to sing our grace together. I'm sorry that I can't join you in your praise for the police department.

It is true that they have been rather disciplined in their public handling of the demonstrators. In this sense they have been rather publicly "nonviolent." But for what purpose? To preserve the evil system of segregation. Over the last few years I have consistently preached that nonviolence demands that the means we use must be as pure as the ends we seek. So I have tried to make it clear that it is wrong to use immoral means to attain moral ends. But now I must affirm that it is just as wrong, or even more so, to use moral means to preserve immoral ends. Maybe Mr. Connor and his policemen have been rather publicly nonviolent, as Chief Pritchett was in Albany, Georgia, but they have used the moral means of nonviolence to maintain the immoral end of flagrant racial injustice. T. S. Eliot has said that there is no greater treason than to do the right deed for the wrong reason.

Study Questions

1. Imagine that you are a judge alongside Justices Sempronius, Caius, and Ticius in Carlos Nino's fictional case. How would you decide the case and on what basis? How would your grounds for decision compare with those of the other judges?

2. In *The Province of Jurisprudence Determined*, Austin insists that "the existence of law is one thing; its merit or demerit is another. Whether it be or be not is one enquiry; whether it be or be not conformable to an assumed standard, is a different enquiry. A law, which actually exists, is a law, though we happen to dislike it, or though it vary from the text, by which we regulate our approbation or disapprobation." Does this statement reflect your understanding of "law"? Given this view, how could Austin explain or account for the idea that there is a moral obligation to obey the law? Does the claim that something is the "law" or is "lawful" carry with it any moral or normative connotation? Does the mere fact that something is the law supply a reason for compliance with it?

3. By 1998, King Bhumibol Adulyadej had served as monarch of Thailand for more than fifty years; he was the world's longest-reigning monarch. Since 1932, Thailand has had seventeen coups, twenty-three prime ministers, and sixteen constitutions. Under the current constitution, the king has few clearly defined powers, but he wields tremendous influence. Disruptive student demonstrations ended when he appeared on television and asked for order; violent clashes between pro-democracy groups and the military stopped when the leaders of the respective groups prostrated themselves before the king to receive a public scolding; governmental turmoil over the appointment of a new prime minister was resolved when rumors were circulated that the king was ill (the illness ceased when the dispute was settled); and during a recent hospitalization, 100,000 Thais came to his hospital to pray for the king's recovery. Is King Bhumibol a "sovereign," as Austin understands that term? Could Thailand have more than one sovereign? How do you think, Austin would respond to these questions?

4. According to Bix's description, *inclusive* legal positivism seems to allow that moral judgments (judgments about what is right or wrong) could be a part of what Hart called the "Rule of Recognition" of a legal community—that is, the ultimate rule or criterion of what is to count as "law" in that community. *Exclusive* legal positivism, by contrast, says that moral standards can never be a part of the test for legal validity. Given these descriptions, which view do you think more accurately captures the overall spirit and aims of legal positivism?

5. Bix maintains that one way to understand the theory opposed to all forms of legal positivism is to say that "certain moral rules *automatically* became *legal* rules." Is this alternative to positivism defensible, in your judgment?

6. In what ways does the positivist separation of law and morals help to clarify the kind of dilemma faced by the postwar German courts in the grudge-informer cases, as Hart claims?

7. Fuller claims that a consistently and thoroughly evil legal *system* is an impossibility, since all legal systems must incorporate his "inner morality of law." Do you agree that such a legal system is impossible? How much actual moral content does Fuller's internal morality have? Could Fuller's principles be satisfied by a legal system that still contained much wickedness? Consider, as an example, the state of South Africa in its racist, apartheid period.

8. What is the difference between human law and the natural law, according to Aquinas?

9. In what ways does Fuller's naturalism differ from that of Aquinas?

10. Give an example of each of Aquinas's four types of laws.

11. According to some natural law theorists, the natural law is grounded in principles that take as their ideal the complete fulfillment of all human persons and their community and that do not depend upon or vary with people's beliefs, wishes, desires, or subjective interests or goals. (See, e.g., Robert P. George, *In Defense of Natural Law* [Oxford: Oxford University Press, 1999]). These principles correspond to the "genuine fulfillment of human persons." In your view, is it sufficiently clear what these aspects of human fulfillment actually are? If so, can you articulate what legal norms you think would flow from such principles?

12. Martin Luther King, Jr. quotes Saint Augustine's famous remark that "an unjust law is no law at all." It has been objected that this claim is plainly false. How can something fail to be "law" simply because it is unjust or in some other way immoral? King, himself, critics point out, was punished and put in jail for, as we would say, "breaking the law." Assuming we believe that King was right and the racially discriminatory statutes and practices of the South were unjust, does the fact that King wound up in jail prove that unjust laws nonetheless remain laws? Does that fact in itself refute Augustine? If not, why not?

13. King rests his justification of civil disobedience on an explicit appeal to natural law. Must disobedience of the positive law be grounded in such an appeal? What other grounds might be offered to justify disobedience? Could those grounds, themselves, be called "legal"?

D. *Modern Theories of Law*

American Legal Realism

The theories of law we have so far examined—positivism and naturalism—are undeniably abstract and seemingly far removed from the day-to-day activities of lawyers, judges, and police officers that most of us would at least initially identify as constituting the "law." During the first several decades of this century, a group of American legal scholars defended an approach to the study of law and legal systems quite unlike that found in Aquinas and Austin. These scholars, who later came to be called *legal realists,* wrote with the explicit aim of understanding the law in its daily operation by focusing on what judges and lawyers (and others) actually *do,* rather than what they, or theorists like Aquinas and Austin, *say* they do. Legal realists were concerned with the "law in action," not with the "law in books." In this section, we encounter the views of two prominent theorists associated with the realist movement.

Holmes and the "Bad Man"

Oliver Wendell Holmes's career spanned a vast period in American history, from before the Civil War to the New Deal. Holmes was a teacher, writer, judge, and justice of the United States Supreme Court, and while he has always defied neat classification into one or another jurisprudential camp, his essay "The Path of the Law," reprinted here, became a classic statement of several key realist themes. To appreciate fully what Holmes has to say, we need a clear sense of the context within which he and other realists wrote, and in particular a clear understanding of the concept of law against which he and they were reacting.

The nineteenth century saw a tremendous growth and expansion of the traditional sciences, as well as the birth of new realms of scientific investigation, such as psychology and biology. The growing social and intellectual prestige of the sciences fueled the desire of legal scholars to make law a "scientific" discipline. In 1870, the new dean of Harvard Law School, Christopher Columbus Langdell, instituted a series of reforms in legal education, with the aim of teaching law as a science. Prominent among these reforms was the introduction of the "case method" of legal study: the student was to confront and analyze the opinions written by judges deciding particular disputes in order to extract from them the fundamental principles of law. Behind Langdell's case method stood a conception of the nature of law that Langdell shared with other influential scholars and teachers, including James Barr Ames, Joseph Beale, and Samuel Williston. According to these men, law is a completely self-contained and thoroughly consistent and systematic body of principles and rules. After a judge or student extracts the rule from the authoritative sources, he or she can logically deduce what conclusion that rule requires in any given case. In this way, every possible legal dispute has a uniquely correct solution that can be rigorously deduced from a coherent set of basic axioms. Law becomes a kind of social geometry.

No sooner was this vision articulated than realists like Holmes began to assail it. They attacked the formalism of the "law-as-science" theorists: "The life of the law has not been logic, it has been experience," as Holmes famously remarked. And the experience that is most relevant here is the experience and perspective of the "bad man," the cynic whose only concern is with the bottom line: How much can I get away with before bringing the power of the state down upon me? Holmes provides several examples of this bad-man perspective in "The Path of the Law" as, for example, in his theory of contract. A contract, says Holmes, is not a moral commitment that the law wants me to keep. This is shown, for example, by the fact that I may be sued for breach of contract even though I intended to make no such commitment. A contract is merely what the bad man would take it to be: a choice to perform as promised or ignore the promise and pay the penalty. In a similar fashion, when I injure another through my negligent behavior, the law of tort requires that I pay damages to the person affected. From the perspective of the bad man, such a penalty is no different from a tax: each is a negative consequence brought on by my conduct. To understand the law, then, is to be able to predict when and under what circumstances one's conduct will trigger society's response. By thus washing the law in "cynical acid," Holmes seeks to boil law down to its bare essentials.

The realists attacked the formalism of the Langdellian legal scholars in another way: by insisting that judges and courts deciding actual disputes do not reason in a logically rigorous fashion from general principles of legal doctrine to particular conclusions in specific situations. As Holmes notes, law and legal doctrine develop only slowly and as a result of judges' decisions; and this development is embedded in history and tradition in a way far deeper than the law-as-science people were willing to admit. Since law develops in this way, the realists claimed, it is futile to seek or expect much "logic" in it. The law is not a rigid body of fixed and unchanging rules but a shifting and flexible social institution, with sufficient play to accommodate the balancing of various and competing interests within a society.

Rationalization and Rule-Skepticism

Holmes and other realists had to admit, of course, that judges and lawyers often write and talk *as if* they were deciding a case, or arguing for a particular position, by deducing conclusions from "rules of law" in a straightforward fashion. But the statements made by judges in their opinions, many realists insisted, are frequently little more than rationalizations for decisions that they had already arrived at on grounds or for reasons other than that the "rules" required them to decide in a particular way. Realists like Jerome Frank, a selection from whose work is included here, proposed that the Langdellian desire for certainty and stability in the law was little more than an expression of unconscious longing for security in a world of uncertainty. As he makes clear in his selection, Frank maintained that legal reasoning characteristically proceeds "backwards," beginning with an intuitive judgment or "gut feeling" that a particular decision is correct or right and proceeding to a rationalization of that decision so cast in legal jargon that it appears to follow from the rules in a logical way. Frank uses as an example a case of vehicular homicide: to justify the charge, must there be a real purpose to cause death on the part of the defendant? The fact that different courts reached opposing results on this point of law is merely a consequence of their antecedent desire to "justify" the answer that seemed to them to be right.

Coupled with their theory of legal reasoning as rationalization stands the realist's *rule-skepticism.* "The law," says Frank, "consists of *decisions,* not of rules."[1] The established way of thinking about the law held that it consists of precepts or rules, formulated in the canonical verbiage of legal doctrine. The trouble with such a view, the realists insisted, is that such rules and doctrines do not relate to society, to the "real" world. Dry legal formulas are mistakenly viewed as having a life of their own, apart from the actions and experiences of prosecutors, magistrates, and appellate judges that create them. But the "rules on paper" exist only insofar as they describe the judgments actually made in particular legal disputes. By denying that the law consists of rules, some realists pushed their doctrine of the flux and flexibility of the law to the limit. Frank, in particular, challenged the concept of *stare decisis* or the doctrine of precedent. This is the idea that a court's decision in one case can serve to guide the decision of future cases that are similar to the original one in relevant ways. (For more on the concept of "following precedent," see Chapter 2.) The realists repeatedly emphasized the indeterminacy or looseness of *stare decisis* by pointing out that a particular ruling in one case never binds a decision maker in any future case, because the future decision maker can always find some aspect of the later

case that can serve as a ground for differentiating or "distinguishing" it from the prior one.

The bottom line for the realists was that law is a matter of *prediction:* "The prophecies of what the courts will do in fact, and nothing more pretentious, are what I mean by the law"[2]; "Law . . . as to any given situation is either (a) actual law, i.e., a specific past decision, as to that situation, or (b) probable law, i.e., a guess as to a specific future decision."[3] Accordingly, many realists advocated the study of judicial behavior, arguing that the patterns of decisions revealed in actual cases are the most reliable guides to, and the most accurate basis for, predicting what future courts will do.

Legal Reasoning and Intuition

Central to the realist criticism of legal reasoning as a rational procedure bound by rules was the conviction, expressed by Holmes, that "general propositions do not decide concrete cases." Cases, not rules, were for the realists the only source of law. A few judges even came openly to express this view. Frank points, for instance, to Judge Joseph Hutcheson, who had famously recounted how his training in a mechanical, "slot-machine" view of the law had given way in the face of his many years in the courtroom to the realization that good judges, like good jurors, "feel" their way to a just decision by waiting for the "hunch" or flash of insight that will light the way, the intuition that will point in the right direction. The rest of what the judge typically does, the lengthy opinion that he or she provides as a preface to the decision, was, according to Hutcheson, mere rhetoric. Supporting the hunch with appropriate legal jargon is necessary, however, to disguise its arbitrary nature. The task of the judge is therefore to reason backward from an intuition of the "desirable" result to a rationalization that will fit it. In these ways, Hutcheson agreed with other realists, many of whom argued that judges deciding particular disputes should be guided by the aim of responding to the real human needs before them, not by the slavish following of inferences from the abstract categories and distinctions embedded in "the rules."

---

[1] Jerome Frank, *Law and the Modern Mind* (New York: Brentano's Publishers, 1930), p. 128.

[2] Oliver Wendell Holmes, "The Path of the Law," *Harvard Law Review,* Vol. 10 (1897), p. 461.

[3] Jerome Frank, *Law and the Modern Mind* (New York: Brentano's Publishers, 1930), p. 33.

If a judge's actual decision or judgment, rather than the verbiage surrounding it, accurately states the law on a given subject, those seeking to predict what the judge will do in the future should look to any and all of those factors likely to influence his or her decision. This conclusion led some legal realists to advocate an empirical or even anthropological study of judges and their decisions, focusing on the collection of data regarding their lifestyle, social status, political affiliation, and even diet, in an effort to account for all factors that could conceivably influence a judge's behavior. "Legal reasoning" for many of the realists, then, was something of a misnomer. What a judge does when faced with a difficult case is much closer to an art or craft than to compliance with a statable, logical procedure.

Critical Legal Studies

Throughout this chapter we have been concerned with the questions: What does it mean to live under the "rule of law" as opposed to the "rule of men"? and What is legality and how does it differ from morality? We have so far examined several theories that try to answer these questions by offering accounts of the nature of law and the value of legality. Many members of the *critical legal studies* (CLS) movement have challenged the very possibility of a society based upon the "rule of law." They perceive a deep inconsistency between the concept of the rule of law and the theory of political liberalism with which that concept has come to be associated. The work of one prominent critical legalist, Roberto Unger, illustrates the CLS position.[1]

The "theory" of CLS is in some ways hard to pin down precisely, for in many ways CLS focuses upon the fragmentary character of the law—the fact that it doesn't really "hang together" very well (if at all). We will see what that means in a moment; for now it is best to try to get our bearings by comparing CLS with legal realism.

CLS scholars share with legal realists the basic conviction that the rules that (when seen as a system) are taken by positivists to form the essence of law are in fact inherently indeterminate; that is, without a clear, fixed meaning. Critical legalists also share the moral skepticism of some of the realists, rejecting the notion of a natural or rational moral order that could serve as the basis for a natural law theory. The critical scholars

similarly reject the formalistic theory of law defended by Langdell. And, like the realists, CLS proponents are deeply skeptical about the doctrine of following precedent, claiming that it provides very little in the way of constraining or challenging legal reasoning. Both legal realists and CLS scholars place more of an emphasis on the role played by factors other than the written law in the shaping of court decisions. CLS theorists have, for example, argued that economic interests have driven many changes in the law: the development of personal injury law in the nineteenth century can be explained, according to one prominent critical scholar, as an effort to further the expansion of large industries.

Proponents of CLS (or "crits") do disagree with the legal realists on some key points. For the crits, the realists did not go far enough in terms of developing a thorough "critique" of the ideological bias concealed within legal doctrines and procedures. The realists were too willing to trust to the social sciences as a way to reform law and legal practice, but even these assumptions, say the realists, must be critiqued.

The central challenge of CLS is directed at the assumption—centrally a part of legal positivism—that the law consists of clear rules that can be applied in an objective and neutral fashion to reach predictable, correct results in a given case. What lawyers and judges call "rules" of law are often vague and indeterminate, in a way that conveniently hides their ultimately political nature. Nor do CLS theorists accept Dworkin's view that an expanded concept of "law"—consisting of rules and principles—can yield right answers in legal cases through Dworkin's process of interpretation. Indeed, many of the crits seem to reject any theory of legal reasoning at all, arguing against any attempt to make sense of adjudication as a rationally defensible process in a way that distinguishes it from a purely political act. Courts do not, as positivists such as Hart would say, legislate only in the restricted "penumbral" zone, but all the time.

The assertion that law is thoroughly political is a direct attack upon the possibility of a society based on the "rule of law," and it is therefore not surprising that much critical literature has focused on this ideal. The most familiar concept of the rule of law, according to CLS scholars such as Roberto Unger, presupposes a society characterized by certain features: a pervasive belief in the "subjectivity" of values; a concomitant pluralism and diversity of moral, religious, and political viewpoints; and the conviction that the government must (given the foregoing facts) remain scrupulously neutral on questions dealing with the "best" way to live. The presence of these conditions,

---

[1]See Roberto Unger, *Knowledge and Politics* (New York: Free Press, 1975); *The Critical Legal Studies Movement* (Cambridge: Harvard University Press, 1983).

some crits believe, gives rise to two problems that the idea of the rule of law is supposed to solve: how to form and sustain a workable social order under conditions of deep moral and political disagreement, and how to do this in a way that will not amount simply to domination of one group through subjugation to the values of another. The attempt to solve these problems gives rise to the ideal of the rule of law, the view that the exercise of collective force should be regulated by general, clear, and authoritative norms that have been set out in advance and are made applicable to all.

The fundamental critical objection to this "liberal legalism" is that the very conditions that give rise to the need for the rule of law also make it impossible. The rule of law requires government neutrality in both the enactment and the interpretation of law, neutrality in both legislation and adjudication. However, statutes and ordinances invariably are colored by the value biases of those with sufficient political power to get them voted into law, and the interpretation of such laws, once established, inevitably relies on the subjective views and values of the interpreter (usually a judge). Since there can be no neutral process either for the enactment or for the interpretation of law, a paradox is concealed in the very idea of legality. As an example of this critique, some CLS writers have pointed to the debate over the proper interpretation of the U.S. Constitution (see the next section for material on that debate). Some crits have argued that no defensible theory of legal reasoning—no interpretive methodology—about the meaning of the Constitution has been or can be produced that would account to or legitimate the "discovery" of fundamental rights in the Constitution, such as the right to privacy.

A further and central preoccupation of the crits lies with the manipulable and indeterminate or vague character of legal doctrine. The critical point here is not simply that the "law on the books" isn't the whole story; the point is rather that it isn't a coherent story at all. Legal doctrines, concepts, and cases can be read and interpreted in almost any way a judge wishes, according to one main CLS argument. The most radical of the crits try to "deconstruct" or "trash" the law by seeking to expose it as a tangled mess; at the very least, most critical legalists believe that the law is a collection of not entirely compatible moral, social, and political perspectives.

Many of the aspects of CLS just outlined can be unified around one theme: an attack upon what has been called "liberal legalism": the view that the concepts and rules of the law are required to be neutral with regard to differing religious, political, and social ideals or views about what is good in life. Law, in this view, is a neutral playing field that secures equal rights and freedoms for everyone. This ideal is fatally flawed, according to the critical legalists, since the law simply cannot be neutral or objective in any meaningful sense.

In the selections included here, CLS scholar Mark Tushnet looks more specifically at the ways in which CLS is an outgrowth of the concerns of the legal realists. Tushnet argues that a core part of the theory of CLS is rejection of the "policy analysis" so prevalent in the law today. An ordinary lawyer or judge, Tushnet maintains, has very likely been taught to argue and decide cases in a way that best balances the competing interests that are always at stake in legal disputes. As Tushnet observes, this approach to law and adjudication is itself one of the long-lasting effects of legal realism—part of the realists' "constructive program." Tushnet then looks at what he calls the "dominant" project within the CLS movement and the ways in which it "deconstructs" and "critiques" the reigning views of the law.

Philosopher Andrew Altman argues that the position of CLS is best conceived as an attack on the ideal of the rule of law—an ideal according to which political power is confined and channeled in a way that promotes the liberal values of liberty, tolerance, and individuality. Altman distinguishes moderate from more radical versions of CLS and sketches some objections to the more radical form.

Law as Interpretation

One of the most widely debated theories of law to have emerged in recent years has been defended and refined by Oxford legal philosopher Ronald Dworkin. Published in a number of essays and books, Dworkin's jurisprudence has undergone several changes, at least some of which are briefly noted here.

Dworkin's Critique of Positivism

In one of his earliest and most influential works, Dworkin summarized what he took to be the essential commitments of Hart's positivism: (1) The law of a community consists of a body of rules identifiable as legal based on their "pedigree," or how they came about. (2) If a given case is not covered by a "pedigreeable" rule, the court must exercise discretion by going beyond the law to reach a decision. (3) Since legal rights can be specified only by rules, in any case that is not covered by rules, the court's resolution of the case cannot involve enforcing anyone's *legal* rights.[2]

One of Dworkin's primary jurisprudential concerns has been to develop and defend a theory of adjudication: an account of how courts can and ought to reason to a conclusion in those "hard" cases in which no settled rule applies. And it is this concern that animated Dworkin's critique of Hart's positivism. Dworkin's core insight was that when courts reason about hard cases, they appeal to standards other than positivistic rules: they appeal to *principles*. Unlike rules, principles have no discernible "pedigree" in Hart's sense. Principles function as a reason in favor of a particular decision but do not compel a result in the way a rule does. Moreover, a principle such as "No one should profit from his own wrongdoing," invoked in the famous *Riggs* case (reprinted at the end of this chapter), can remain a principle of our law despite the fact that it is not always followed. Finally, principles frequently give expression to underlying or background *rights* held by one of the parties to a dispute, and such rights frequently "trump" or take priority over other considerations.

Are principles part of the law? Or do they stand outside it? Hart's theory, says Dworkin, must treat principles as extralegal standards to which judges could appeal when the rules have run out, so that the court is then no longer bound by any standards set by the authority of law. Dworkin regards Hart's picture as both *descriptively* inaccurate and *normatively* (or from a moral point of view) unattractive. It is inaccurate since courts *do*, Dworkin thinks, invoke principles and background rights; it is morally unattractive since the model of the judge enjoying broad discretion after the genuine rules have run out suggests that he or she can and should ignore, or at least significantly downplay, the rights of litigants and focus instead on policy considerations, asking, for example, what decision will be best for society as a whole.

Dworkin's Theory of Law

Dworkin frames his theories of law and adjudication so as to show how the question "What is law?" depends for its solution on correct answers to moral questions. At the same time, Dworkin tries to situate

his theory within the context of recent work by various legal scholars who compare literary texts and the approaches to interpreting and reasoning about them with legal texts and the processes of legal reasoning. A central controversy in both literary and legal theory has turned on the extent to which textual interpretation, whether it be of a novel or a constitution, is merely a "subjective" process in which the interpreter imposes whatever meaning he or she chooses. Is there any sense in which textual interpretation can be said to be "objective"? And what would that mean? Are there meaningful constraints upon interpretive activity? These questions take on particular significance in the law as they intersect with the common assumption that legal reasoning must be conceived as a special form of interpretive activity, distinct from political decision making. Dworkin's discussion of these issues in our selection presents in outline the theory developed at much greater length in his book, *Law's Empire*, from which the selection included in this section is taken.

Adjudication, according to Dworkin, is a form of interpretive activity. Judges are like contributors to a "chain novel": they must take the statutes, prior cases, and other legal materials before them and try to make sense of them in a way that allows them to continue to extend whatever "story" the materials tell in a definite direction. In *Law's Empire*, Dworkin argues that this concept of judicial interpretation follows from a more general view of what it means to *interpret* anything, be it a text, a work of art, or something else. This general view says that in order for me to interpret a theatrical play, for example, I must seek to understand it "from the inside out," trying to grasp what it means to the "society" (actors, audience, critics) whose play it is.

Similarly, the interpretation of a social practice such as law involves the attempt to understand it as a way of life created and sustained by its participants, people who see themselves as part of a larger community ("community of principle," "interpretive community") held together by a commitment to the rule of law. And this means, Dworkin believes, that interpretation cannot simply involve discovering the intent of the author of the play or the drafter of a statute. Instead, interpretation must be *constructive*. Interpreters must try to see the play or the law in its best light, as the coherent embodiment of a unifying theme or point. For judges trying to interpret a series of earlier precedents, the imperative is to seek to state the best constructive interpretation of the legal doctrine of their community as it is expressed in those precedents. And this will require that judges, at some point, rely upon their own

---

[2] See *Taking Rights Seriously* (Cambridge: Harvard University Press, 1977).

opinions and convictions as they attempt to find the best interpretation of the existing law.

Dworkin illustrates these many points in our selection with *McLoughlin v. O'Brian*, a tort case involving a claim of intentional infliction of emotional distress. The question the court must answer is: Must the plaintiff's emotional trauma be induced while she is physically present at the accident scene? Other questions follow in the wake of this one: Was Mrs. McLoughlin a "foreseeable" plaintiff? Would it be bad public policy to allow plaintiffs like Mrs. McLoughlin to recover? Dworkin imagines a judge with vast intellectual powers (and lots of time), aptly named Hercules, before whom the McLoughlin case is presented. Hercules must approach this case as if he were contributing the next in a series of "chapters" in the law dealing with recovery in tort. He must evaluate the several, rival interpretations of past rulings on emotional trauma and determine which is the "best."

Dworkin cautions us not to misunderstand the interpretive task here. Because interpretation is not a mechanical process, the interpreters' own opinions must inevitably shape their interpretations to some degree, but this does not mean that judges can, for example, simply do whatever they please when faced with a hard case. Part of understanding and interpreting the law of their communities requires that judges respect values that are deeply rooted in their society. Values of fairness and democratic rule, for example, require that they must balance their own opinions against public opinion (as expressed, say, by the votes of representatives in Congress), and the value of due process requires that judges protect people's expectation by not allowing the judges'

interpretations of the law to deviate radically or break too decisively with the past.

Judges, then, look for a "reading" or interpretation that will contribute to the legal "story" by portraying the law in its best light. But what if several competing interpretations or readings of that past are possible? Here interpreters must measure and compare these readings along two dimensions. First, the dimension of "fit": How well and to what degree does a particular reading explain all of the fundamental features of our law? Second, the dimension of value: How well does that reading present our law as something coherent and worthwhile? Whichever interpretation succeeds best on both of these scorecards becomes the interpretation judges must choose and enforce. Dworkin sums up his overall theory by calling it "law as integrity": The law is the product of the interpretation that most faithfully sums up the texts, principles, and values of a given community into a coherent and morally attractive whole.

Although he does not object to the label "naturalism" to describe his view, Dworkin makes it clear that this is a naturalism of a very different sort from that defended by Aquinas. Dworkin's judges are not free to follow just any normative or moral principle, nor do the principles to which they do appeal derive their validity from a natural moral order. Dworkin's judges are permitted to recognize only the moral principles and values "present," either explicitly or implicitly, in the legal history and tradition of their communities and to recognize them only for that reason, not because they have some independent moral or religious basis.

The Path of the Law

Oliver Wendell Holmes

When we study law we are not studying a mystery but a well-known profession. We are studying what

From Oliver Wendell Holmes, "The Path of the Law," *Harvard Law Review*, Vol. 10 (1897), pp. 457–468.

we shall want in order to appear before judges, or to advise people in such a way as to keep them out of court. The reason why it is a profession, why people will pay lawyers to argue for them or to advise them, is that in societies like ours the command of the public force is intrusted to the judges in certain cases, and the whole power of the state will be put forth, if necessary, to carry out their judgments and decrees. People want to know under what circumstances and how far they will run the risk of coming against what is so much stronger than themselves, and hence it becomes a business to find out when this danger is to be feared. The object of our study, then, is prediction, the prediction of the incidence of the public force through the instrumentality of the courts.

The means of the study are a body of reports, of treatises, and of statutes, in this country and in England, extending back for six hundred years, and now increasing annually by hundreds. In these sibylline leaves are gathered the scattered prophecies of the past upon the cases in which the axe will fall. These are what properly have been called the oracles of the law. New effort of legal thought is to make these prophecies more precise, and to generalize them into a thoroughly connected system. The process is one, from a lawyer's statement of a case, eliminating as it does all the dramatic elements with which his client's story has clothed it, and retaining only the facts of legal import, up to the final analyses and abstract universals of theoretic jurisprudence. The reason why a lawyer does not mention that his client wore a white hat when he made a contract, while Mrs. Quickly would be sure to dwell upon it along with the parcel gilt goblet and the seacoal fire, is that he foresees that the public force will act in the same way whatever his client had upon his head. It is to make the prophecies easier to be remembered and to be understood that the teachings of the decisions of the past are put into general propositions and gathered into text-books, or that statutes are passed in a general form. The primary rights and duties with which jurisprudence busies itself again are nothing but prophecies. One of the many evil effects of the confusion between legal and moral ideas, about which I shall have something to say in a moment, is that theory is apt to get the cart before the horse, and to consider the right or the duty as something existing apart from and independent of the consequences of its breach, to which certain sanctions are added afterward. But, as I shall try to show, a legal duty so called is nothing but a prediction that if a man does or omits certain things he will be made to suffer in this or that way by judgment of the court; and so of a legal right.

The number of our predictions when generalized and reduced to a system is not unmanageably large. They present themselves as a finite body of dogma which may be mastered within a reasonable time. It is

a great mistake to be frightened by the ever-increasing number of reports. The reports of a given jurisdiction in the course of a generation take up pretty much the whole body of the law, and restate it from the present point of view. We could reconstruct the corpus from them if all that went before were burned. The use of the earlier reports is mainly historical, a use about which I shall have something to say before I have finished.

I wish, if I can, to lay down some first principles for the study of this body of dogma or systematized prediction which we call the law, for men who want to use it as the instrument of their business to enable them to prophesy in their turn, and, as bearing upon the study, I wish to point out an ideal which as yet our law has not attained.

The first thing for a business-like understanding of the matter is to understand its limits, and therefore I think it desirable at once to point out and dispel a confusion between morality and law, which sometimes rises to the height of conscious theory, and more often and indeed constantly is making trouble in detail without reaching the point of consciousness. You can see very plainly that a bad man has as much reason as a good one for wishing to avoid an encounter with the public force, and therefore you can see the practical importance of the distinction between morality and law. A man who cares nothing for an ethical rule which is believed and practised by his neighbors is likely nevertheless to care a good deal to avoid being made to pay money, and will want to keep out of jail if he can.

I take it for granted that no hearer of mine will misinterpret what I have to say as the language of cynicism. The law is the witness and external deposit of our moral life. Its history is the history of the moral development of the race. The practice of it, in spite of popular jests, tends to make good citizens and good men. When I emphasize the difference between law and morals I do so with reference to a single end, that of learning and understanding the law. For that purpose you must definitely master its specific marks, and it is for that I ask you for the moment to imagine yourselves indifferent to other and greater things.

I do not say that there is not a wider point of view from which the distinction between law and morals becomes of secondary or no importance, as all mathematical distinctions vanish in presence of the infinite. But I do say that that distinction is of the first importance for the object which we are here to consider—a right study and mastery of the law as a business with well understood limits, a body of dogma enclosed within definite lines. I have just shown the practical reason for saying so. *If you want to know the law and nothing else, you must look at it as a bad man, who cares only for the material consequences which such knowledge enables him to predict*, not as a good one, who finds his reasons for conduct, whether inside the law or outside of it, in the vaguer sanctions of conscience. The theoretical importance of the distinction is no less, if you would reason on your subject aright. The law is full of phraseology drawn from morals, and by the mere force of language continually invites us to pass from one domain to the other without perceiving it, as we are sure to do unless we have the boundary constantly before our minds. The law talks about rights and duties, and malice, and intent, and negligence, and so forth, and nothing is easier, or, I may say, more common in legal reasoning, than to take these words in their moral sense, at some stage of the argument, and so to drop into fallacy. For instance, when we speak of the rights of man in a moral sense, we mean to mark the limits of interference with individual freedom which we think are prescribed by conscience, or by our ideal, however reached. Yet it is certain that many laws have been enforced in the past, and it is likely that some are enforced now, which are condemned by the most enlightened opinion of the time, or which at all events pass the limit of interference as many consciences would draw it. Manifestly, therefore, nothing but confusion of thought can result from assuming that the rights of man in a moral sense are equally rights in the sense of the Constitution and the law. No doubt simple and extreme cases can be put of imaginable laws which the statute-making power would not dare to enact, even in the absence of written constitutional prohibitions, because the community would rise in rebellion and fight; and this gives some plausibility to the proposition that the law, if not a part of morality, is limited by it. But this limit of power is not coextensive with any system of morals. For the most part it falls far within the lines of any such system, and in some cases may extend beyond them, for reasons drawn from the habits of a particular people at a particular time. I once heard the late Professor Agassiz say that a German population would rise if you added two cents to the price of a glass of beer. A statute in such a case would be empty words, not because it was wrong, but because it could not be enforced. No one will deny that wrong statutes can be and are enforced, and we should not all agree as to which were the wrong ones.

The confusion with which I am dealing besets confessedly legal conceptions. Take the fundamental question, What constitutes the law? You will find some text writers telling you that it is something different from what is decided by the courts of Massachusetts or England, that it is a system of reason, that it is a deduction from principles of ethics or admitted axioms or what not, which may or may not coincide with the decisions. But if we take the view of our friend the bad man we shall find that he does not care two straws for the axioms or deductions, but that he does want to know what the Massachusetts or English courts are likely to do in fact. I am much of his mind. The prophecies of what the courts will do in fact, and nothing more pretentious, are what I mean by the law.

Take again a notion which as popularly understood is the widest conception which the law contains—the notion of legal duty, to which already I have referred. We fill the word with all the content which we draw from morals. But what does it mean to a bad man? Mainly, and in the first place, a prophecy that if he does certain things he will be subjected to disagreeable consequences by way of imprisonment or compulsory payment of money. But from his point of view, what is the difference between being fined and being taxed a certain sum for doing a certain thing? That his point of view is the test of legal principles is shown by the many discussions which have arisen in the courts on the very question whether a given statutory liability is a penalty or a tax. On the answer to this question depends the decision whether conduct is legally wrong or right, and also whether a man is under compulsion or free. Leaving the criminal law on one side, what is the difference between the liability under the mill acts or statutes authorizing a taking by eminent domain and the liability for what we call a wrongful conversion of property where restoration is out of the question. In both cases the party taking another man's property has to pay its fair value as assessed by a jury, and no more. What significance is there in calling one taking right and another wrong from the point of view of the law? It does not matter, so far as the given consequence, the compulsory payment, is concerned, whether the act to which it is attached is described in terms of praise or in terms of blame, or whether the law purports to prohibit it or to allow it. If it matters at all, still speaking from the bad man's point of view, it must be because in one case and not in the other some further disadvantages, or at least some further consequences, are attached to the act by the law. The only other disadvantages thus attached to it which I ever have been able to think of are to be found in two somewhat insignificant legal doctrines, both of which might be abolished without disturbance. One is, that a contract to do a prohibited act is unlawful, and the other, that, if one of two or more joint wrongdoers has to pay all the damages, he cannot recover contribution from his fellows. And that I believe is all. You see how the vague circumference of the notion of duty shrinks and at the same time grows more precise when we wash it with cynical acid and expel everything except the object of our study, the operations of the law.

Nowhere is the confusion between legal and moral ideas more manifest than in the law of contract. Among other things, here again the so called primary rights and duties are invested with a mystic significance beyond what can be assigned and explained. The duty to keep a contract at common law means a prediction that you must pay damages if you do not keep it—and nothing else. If you commit a tort, you are liable to pay a compensatory sum. If you commit a contract, you are liable to pay a compensatory sum unless the promised event comes to pass, and that is all the difference. But such a mode of looking at the matter stinks in the nostrils of those who think it advantageous to get as much ethics into the law as they can. It was good enough for Lord Coke, however, and here, as in many other cases, I am content to abide with him. In *Bromage v. Genning*,[1] a prohibition was sought in the King's Bench against a suit in the marches of Wales for the specific performance of a covenant to grant a lease, and Coke said that it would subvert the intention of the covenantor, since he intends it to be at his election either to lose the damages or to make the lease. Sergeant Harris for the plaintiff confessed that he moved the matter against his conscience, and a prohibition was granted. This goes further than we should go now, but it shows what I venture to say has been the common law point of view from the beginning, although Mr. Harriman, in his very able little book upon Contracts has been misled, as I humbly think, to a different conclusion.

I have spoken only of the common law, because there are some cases in which a logical justification can be found for speaking of civil liabilities as imposing duties in an intelligible sense. These are the relatively few in which equity will grant an injunction, and will enforce it by putting the defendant in prison or otherwise punishing him unless he complies with the order of the court. But I hardly think it advisable to shape general theory from the exception, and I think it

would be better to cease troubling ourselves about primary rights and sanctions altogether, than to describe our prophecies concerning the liabilities commonly imposed by the law in those inappropriate terms.

I mentioned, as other example of the use by the law of words drawn from morals, malice, intent, and negligence. It is enough to take malice as it is used in the law of civil liability for wrongs—what we lawyers call the law of torts—to show that it means something different in law from what it means in morals, and also to show how the difference has been obscured by giving to principles which have little or nothing to do with each other the same name. Three hundred years ago a parson preached a sermon and told a story out of Fox's *Book of Martyrs* of a man who had assisted at the torture of one of the saints, and afterward died, suffering compensatory inward torment. It happened that Fox was wrong. The man was alive and chanced to hear the sermon, and thereupon he sued the parson. Chief Justice Wray instructed the jury that the defendant was not liable, because the story was told innocently, without malice. He took malice in the moral sense, as importing a malevolent motive. But nowadays no one doubts that a man may be liable, without any malevolent motive at all, for false statements manifestly calculated to inflict temporal damage. In stating the case in pleading, we still should call the defendant's conduct malicious; but, in my opinion at least, the word means nothing about motives, or even about the defendant's attitude toward the future, but only signifies that the tendency of his conduct under the known circumstances was very plainly to cause the plaintiff temporal harm.[2]

In the law of contract the use of moral phraseology has led to equal confusion, as I have shown in part already, but only in part. Morals deal with the actual internal state of the individual's mind, what he actually intends. From the time of the Romans down to now, this mode of dealing has affected the language of the law as to contract, and the language used has reacted upon the thought. We talk about a contract as a meeting of the minds of the parties, and thence it is inferred in various cases that there is no contract because their minds have not met; that is, because they have intended different things or because one party has not known of the assent of the other. Yet nothing is more certain than that parties may be bound by a contract to things which neither of them intended, and when one does not know of the other's assent. Suppose a contract is executed in due form and in writing to deliver a lecture, mentioning no time.

One of the parties thinks that the promise will be construed to mean at once, within a week. The other thinks that it means when he is ready. The court says that it means within a reasonable time. The parties are bound by the contract as it is interpreted by the court, yet neither of them meant what the court declares that they have said. In my opinion no one will understand the true theory of contract or be able even to discuss some fundamental questions intelligently until he has understood that all contracts are formal, that the making of a contract depends not on the agreement of two minds in one intention, but on the agreement of two sets of external signs—not on the parties' having *meant* the same thing but on their having *said* the same thing. Furthermore, as the signs may be addressed to one sense or another—to sight or to hearing—on the nature of the sign will depend the moment when the contract is made. If the sign is tangible, for instance, a letter, the contract is made when the letter of acceptance is delivered. If it is necessary that the minds of the parties meet, there will be no contract until the acceptance can be read—not, for example, if the acceptance be snatched from the hand of the offerer by a third person.

This is not the time to work out a theory in detail, or to answer many obvious doubts and questions which are suggested by these general views. I know of none which are not easy to answer, but what I am trying to do now is only by a series of hints to throw some light on the narrow path of legal doctrine, and upon two pitfalls which, as it seems to me, lie perilously near to it. Of the first of these I have said enough. I hope that my illustrations have shown the danger, both to speculation and to practice, of confounding morality with law, and the trap which legal language lays for us on that side of our way. For my own part, I often doubt whether it would not be a gain if every word of moral significance could be banished from the law altogether, and other words adopted which should convey legal ideas uncolored by anything outside the law. We should lose the fossil records of a good deal of history and the majesty got from ethical associations, but by ridding ourselves of an unnecessary confusion we should gain very much in the clearness of our thought.

So much for the limits of the law. The next thing I wish to consider is what are the forces which determine its content and its growth. You may assume, with Hobbes and Bentham and Austin, that all law emanates from the sovereign, even when the first human beings to enunciate it are the judges, or you may think that law is the voice of the Zeitgeist, or what you like. It is all one to my present purpose. Even if every decision required the sanction of an emperor with despotic power and a whimsical turn of mind, we should be interested nonetheless, still with a view to prediction, in discovering some order, some rational explanation, and some principle of growth for the rules which he laid down. In every system there are such explanations and principles to be found. It is with regard to them that a second fallacy comes in, which I think it important to expose.

The fallacy to which I refer is the notion that the only force at work in the development of the law is logic. In the broadest sense, indeed, that notion would be true. The postulate on which we think about the universe is that there is a fixed quantitative relation between every phenomenon and its antecedents and consequents. If there is such a thing as a phenomenon without these fixed quantitative relations, it is a miracle. It is outside the law of cause and effect, and as such transcends our power of thought, or at least is something to or from which we cannot reason. The condition of our thinking about the universe is that it is capable of being thought about rationally, or, in other words, that every part of it is effect and cause in the same sense in which those parts are with which we are most familiar. So in the broadest sense it is true that the law is a logical development, like everything else. The danger of which I speak is not the admission that the principles governing other phenomena also govern the law, but the notion that a given system, ours, for instance, can be worked out like mathematics from some general axioms of conduct. This is the natural error of the schools, but it is not confined to them. I once heard a very eminent judge say that he never let a decision go until he was absolutely sure that it was right. So judicial dissent often is blamed, as if it meant simply that one side or the other were not doing their sums right, and, if they would take more trouble, agreement inevitably would come.

This mode of thinking is entirely natural. The training of lawyers is a training in logic. The processes of analogy, discrimination, and deduction are those in which they are most at home. The language of judicial decision is mainly the language of logic. And the logical method and form flatter that longing for certainty and for repose which is in every human mind. But certainty generally is illusion, and repose is not the destiny of man. Behind the logical form lies a judgment as to the relative worth and importance of competing legislative grounds, often an inarticulate and unconscious judgment, it is true, and yet the very root and nerve of the whole proceeding. You can give any conclusion a logical form. You always can imply a condition in a contract. But why do you imply it? It is because of some belief as to the practice of the community or of a class, or because of some opinion as to policy, or, in short, because of some attitude of yours upon a matter not capable of exact quantitative measurement, and therefore not capable of founding exact logical conclusions. Such matters really are battle grounds where the means do not exist for determinations that shall be good for all time, and where the decision can do no more than embody the preference of a given body in a given time and place. We do not realize how large a part of our law is open to reconsideration upon a slight change in the habit of the public mind. No concrete proposition is self evident, no matter how ready we may be to accept it, not even Mr. Herbert Spencer's "Every man has a right to do what he wills, provided he interferes not with a like right on the part of his neighbors."

Why is a false and injurious statement privileged, if it is made honestly in giving information about a servant? It is because it has been thought more important that information should be given freely, than that a man should be protected from what under other circumstances would be an actionable wrong. Why is a man at liberty to set up a business which he knows will ruin his neighbor? It is because the public good is supposed to be best subserved by free competition. Obviously such judgments of relative importance may vary in different times and places. Why does a judge instruct a jury that an employer is not liable to an employee for an injury received in the course of his employment unless he is negligent, and why do the jury generally find for the plaintiff if the case is allowed to go to them? It is because the traditional policy of our law is to confine liability to cases where a prudent man might have foreseen the injury, or at least the danger, while the inclination of a very large part of the community is to make certain classes of persons insure the safety of those with whom they deal. Since the last words were written, I have seen the requirement of such insurance put forth as part of the programme of one of the best known labor organizations. There is a concealed, half conscious battle on the question of legislative policy, and if anyone thinks that it can be settled deductively, or once for all, I only can say that I think he is theoretically wrong, and that I am certain that his conclusion will not be accepted in practice *semper ubique et ab omnibus.*

Indeed, I think that even now our theory upon this matter is open to reconsideration, although I am not prepared to say how I should decide if a reconsideration were proposed. Our law of torts comes from the old days of isolated, ungeneralized wrongs, assaults, slanders, and the like, where the damages might be taken to lie where they fell by legal judgment. But the torts with which our courts are kept busy today are mainly the incidents of certain well known businesses. They are injuries to person or property by railroads, factories, and the like. The liability for them is estimated, and sooner or later goes into the price paid by the public. The public really pays the damages, and the question of liability, if pressed far enough, is really the question how far it is desirable that the public should insure the safety of those whose work it uses. It might be said that in such cases the chance of a jury finding for the defendant is merely a chance, once in a while rather arbitrarily interrupting the regular course of recovery, most likely in the case of an unusually conscientious plaintiff, and therefore better done away with. On the other hand, the economic value even of a life to the community can be estimated, and no recovery, it may be said, ought to go beyond that amount. It is conceivable that someday in certain cases we may find ourselves imitating, on a higher plane, the tariff for life and limb which we see in the *Leges Barbarorum.*

I think that the judges themselves have failed adequately to recognize their duty of weighing considerations of social advantage. The duty is inevitable, and the result of the often proclaimed judicial aversion to deal with such considerations is simply to leave the very ground and foundation of judgments inarticulate, and often unconscious, as I have said. When socialism first began to be talked about, the comfortable classes of the community were a good deal frightened. I suspect that this fear has influenced judicial action both here and in England, yet it is certain that it is not a conscious factor in the decisions to which I refer. I think that something similar has led people who no longer hope to control the legislatures to look to the courts as expounders of the Constitutions, and that in some courts new principles have been discovered outside the bodies of those instruments, which may be generalized into acceptance of the economic doctrines which prevailed about fifty years ago, and a wholesale prohibition of what a tribunal of lawyers does not think about right. I cannot but believe that if the training of lawyers led them habitually to consider more definitely and explicitly the social advantage on which the rule they lay down must be justified, they sometimes would hesitate where now they are confident, and see that really they were taking sides upon debatable and often burning questions.

. . .

Endnotes

[1] Roll. Rep. 368.

[2] See *Hanson v. Globe Newspaper Co.*, 159 Mass. 293, 302.

A *Realist View of the Law*

JEROME FRANK

. . . Only a limited degree of legal certainty can be attained. The current demand for exactness and predictability in law is incapable of satisfaction because a greater degree of legal finality is sought than is procurable, desirable or necessary. If it be true that greater legal certainty is sought than is practically required or attainable, then the demand for excessive legal stability does not arise from practical needs. It must have its roots not in reality but in a yearning for something unreal. . . . Why do men seek unrealizable certainty in law? Because . . . they have not yet relinquished the childish need for an authoritative father and unconsciously have tried to find in the law a substitute for those attributes of firmness, sureness, certainty and infallibility ascribed in childhood to the father. . . . Most of us are unwilling—and for the most part unable—to concede to what an extent we are controlled by such biases. We cherish the notion that we are grown-up and rational, that we know why we think and act as we do, that our thoughts and deeds have an objective reference, that our beliefs are not biases but are of the other kind—the result of direct observation of objective data. We are able thus to delude ourselves by giving "reasons" for our attitudes. When challenged by ourselves or others to justify our positions or our conduct, we manufacture *ex post facto* a host of "principles" which we induce ourselves to believe are conclusions reasoned out by logi-

cal processes from actual facts in the actual world. So we persuade ourselves that our lives are governed by Reason.

This practice of making ourselves appear, to ourselves and others, more rational than we are, has been termed "rationalization.". . . There are more rationalizations discernible in reasoning about law than in reasoning about many other subjects. Why? Because lawyers, more than most men, are compelled to reconcile incompatibles. Their everyday task is expert practical adjustment. Their life work is based upon a logic of probability. Realistic recognition of novel circumstances, tentativeness, adaptation, are of the very essence of the lawyer's invaluable technique. And yet a powerful bias—an unconscious longing for the re-creation of a child's world stimulated in all men, lawyers and laymen, by the very nature of law—requires the lawyers to seek to achieve certainty, rigidity, security, uniformity. The two aims are contradictory. Seldom can the law serve efficiently its practical function and yet operate definitely, certainly, mechanically. Usually the practical and the "ideal" functions are at cross-purposes. But the conflict between the incompatibles is concealed. In the long run, practicality is served. But by means of rationalizations it is made to appear that there has been little or no sacrifice of the desired rigid certainty.

Viewed thus, lawyers seem to be professional rationalizers, and not, as the layman often charges, professional hypocrites—or worse. It becomes more plain why the practice of law is often referred to as an "art," an art which cannot be taught rationally but must be grasped intuitively. Indeed the practice of law

From Jerome Frank, *Law and the Modern Mind* (New York: Brentano's Publishers, 1930), pp. 11, 21, 29–31, 100–106, 126–128, 130–131.

as now practiced is one of the major arts of rationalization. We can now understand the better why the young lawyer is baffled by the huge gap between what he has learned in school and what he observes in the office and the courtroom. It is clear, too, why older lawyers, regardless of their spoken creeds, often are more daring and creative than recent graduates. Experience has schooled the older men to deal flexibly with changing realities and yet, without hypocrisy, use locutions which enable them to pay tribute to an unconscious childish insistence on the achievement of impossible legal certainty. . . .

We have considered decisions from the point of view of the lawyer and his client. We can now add to our realistic comprehension of the character of law by looking at decisions from the point of view of the judges who render them. As the word indicates, the judge in reaching a decision is making a judgment. And if we would understand what goes into the creating of that judgment, we must observe how ordinary men dealing with ordinary affairs arrive at their judgments.

The process of judging, so the psychologists tell us, seldom begins with a premise from which a conclusion is subsequently worked out. Judging begins rather the other way around—with a conclusion more or less vaguely formed; a man ordinarily starts with such a conclusion and afterwards tries to find premises which will substantiate it. If he cannot, to his satisfaction, find proper arguments to link up his conclusion with premises which he finds acceptable, he will, unless he is arbitrary or mad, reject the conclusion and seek another.

In the case of the lawyer who is to present a case to a court, the dominance in his thinking of the conclusion over the premises is moderately obvious. He is a partisan working on behalf of his client. The conclusion is, therefore, not a matter of choice except within narrow limits. He must, that is if he is to be successful, begin with a conclusion which will insure his client's winning the lawsuit. He then assembles the facts in such a fashion that he can work back from this result he desires to some major premise which he thinks the court will be willing to accept. The precedents, rules, principles and standards to which he will call the court's attention constitute this premise.

While "the dominance of the conclusion" in the case of the lawyer is clear, it is less so in the case of the judge. For the respectable and traditional descriptions of the judicial judging process admit no such backward-working explanation. In theory, the judge begins with some rule or principle of law as his premise, applies this premise to the facts, and thus arrives at his decision.

Now, since the judge is a human being and since no human being in his normal thinking processes arrives at decisions (except in dealing with a limited number of simple situations) by the route of any such syllogistic reasoning, it is fair to assume that the judge, merely by putting on the judicial ermine, will not acquire so artificial a method of reasoning. Judicial judgments, like other judgments, doubtless, in most cases, are worked out backward from conclusions tentatively formulated. . . . Professor Tulin has made a study which prettily illustrates that fact. While driving at a reckless rate of speed, a man runs over another, causing severe injuries. The driver of the car is drunk at the time. He is indicted for the statutory crime of "assault with intent to kill." The question arises whether his act constitutes that crime or merely the lesser statutory crime of "reckless driving." The courts of several states have held one way, and the courts of several other states have held the other.

The first group maintain that a conviction for assault with intent to kill cannot be sustained in the absence of proof of an actual purpose to inflict death. In the second group of states the courts have said that it was sufficient to constitute such a crime if there was a reckless disregard of the lives of others, such recklessness being said to be the equivalent of actual intent.

With what, then, appears to be the same facts before them, these two groups of courts seem to have sharply divided in their reasoning and in the conclusions at which they have arrived. But upon closer examination it has been revealed by Tulin that, in actual effect, the results arrived at in all these states have been more or less the same. In Georgia, which may be taken as representative of the second group of states, the penalty provided by the statute for reckless driving is far less than that provided, for instance, in Iowa, which is in the first group of states. If, then, a man is indicted in Georgia for reckless driving while drunk, the courts can impose on him only a mild penalty; whereas in Iowa the judge, under an identically worded indictment, can give a stiff sentence. In order to make it possible for the Georgia courts to give a reckless driver virtually the same punishment for the same offense as can be given by an Iowa judge, it is necessary in Georgia to construe the statutory crime of assault with intent to kill so that it will include reckless driving while drunk; if, and only if, the Georgia court so construes the statute, can it impose the same penalty under the same facts as could the Iowa courts under the reckless driving statute. On the other hand, if the Iowa court were to construe the Iowa statute as the Georgia court construes the Georgia statute, the punishment of the reckless driver in Iowa would be too severe.

In other words, the courts in these cases began with the results they desired to accomplish: they wanted to give what they considered to be adequate punishment to drunken drivers: their conclusions determined their reasoning.

But the conception that judges work back from conclusions to principles is so heretical that it seldom finds expression. Daily, judges, in connection with their decisions, deliver so-called opinions in which they purport to set forth the bases of their conclusions. Yet you will study these opinions in vain to discover anything remotely resembling a statement of the actual judging process. They are written in conformity with the time-honored theory. They picture the judge applying rules and principles to the facts, that is, taking some rule or principle (usually derived from opinions in earlier cases) as his major premise, employing the facts of the case as the minor premise, and then coming to his judgment by processes of pure reasoning.

Now and again some judge, more clear-witted and outspoken than his fellows, describes (when off the bench) his methods in more homely terms. Recently Judge Hutcheson essayed such an honest report of the judicial process. He tells us that after canvassing all the available material at his command and duly cogitating on it, he gives his imagination play,

> and brooding over the cause, waits for the feeling, the hunch—that intuitive flash of understanding that makes the jump-spark connection between question and decision and at the point where the path is darkest for the judicial feet, sets its light along the way. . . . In feeling or "hunching" out his decisions, the judge acts not differently from but precisely as the lawyers do in working on their cases, with only this exception, that the lawyer, in having a predetermined destination in view—to win the law-suit for his client—looks for and regards only those hunches which keep him in the path that he has chosen, while the judge, being merely on his way with a roving commission to find the just solution, will follow his hunch wherever it leads him. . . .

And Judge Hutcheson adds:

> I must premise that I speak now of the judgment or decision, the solution itself, as opposed to the apologia for that decision; the decree, as opposed to the logomachy, the effusion of the judge by which that decree is explained or excused. . . . The judge really decides by feeling and not by judgment, by hunching and not by ratiocination, such ratiocination appearing only in the opinion. The vital motivating impulse for the decision is an intuitive sense of what is right or wrong in the particular case; and the astute judge, having so decided, enlists his every faculty and belabors his laggard mind, not only to justify that intuition to himself, but to make it pass muster with his critics. Accordingly, he passes in review all of the rules, principles, legal categories, and concepts which he may find useful, directly or by an analogy, so as to select from them those which in his opinion will justify his desired result.

We may accept this as an approximately correct description of how all judges do their thinking. But see the consequences. If the law consists of the decisions of the judges and if those decisions are based on the judge's hunches, then the way in which the judge gets his hunches is the key to the judicial process. Whatever produces the judge's hunches makes the law.

What, then, are the hunch-producers? What are the stimuli which make a judge feel that he should try to justify one conclusion rather than another?

The rules and principles of law are one class of such stimuli. But there are many others, concealed or unrevealed, not frequently considered in discussions of the character or nature of law. To the infrequent extent that these other stimuli have been considered at all, they have been usually referred to as "the political, economic and moral prejudices" of the judge. A moment's reflection would, indeed, induce any open-minded person to admit that factors of such character must be operating in the mind of the judge.

But are not those categories—political, economic and moral biases—too gross, too crude, too wide? Since judges are not a distinct race and since their judging processes must be substantially of like kind with those of other men, an analysis of the way in which judges reach their conclusions will be aided by answering the question, What are the hidden factors in the inferences and opinions of ordinary men? The answer surely is that those factors are multitudinous and complicated, depending often on peculiarly individual traits of the persons whose inferences and opinions are to be explained. These uniquely individual factors often are more important causes of judgments than anything which could be described as political, economic, or moral biases. . . .

What lawyers are engaged in is predicting or procuring determinations of concrete problems. Clients want those concrete determinations rather than generalizations. Judges are called on not to make rules, but to decide which side of some immediate controversy is to win. The rules are incidental, the decisions are the thing.

Whenever a judge decides a case he is making law: the law of that case, not the law of future cases not yet before him. What the judge does and what he says may somewhat influence what other judges will do or say in other cases. But what the other judges decide in those other cases, as a result of whatever influences, will be the law in those other cases. The law of any case is what the judge decides. . . .

The business of the judges is to decide particular cases. They, or some third person viewing their handiwork, may choose to generalize from these decisions, may claim to find common elements in the decisions in the cases of Fox vs. Grapes and Hee vs. Haw and describe the common elements as "rules." But those descriptions of alleged common elements are, at best, some aid to lawyers in guessing or bringing about future judicial conduct or some help to judges in settling other disputes. The rules will not directly decide any other cases in any given way, nor authoritatively compel the judges to decide those other cases in any given way; nor make it possible for lawyers to bring it about that the judges will decide any other cases in any given way, nor infallibly to predict how the judges will decide any other cases. Rules, whether stated by judges or others, whether in statutes, opinions or text-books by learned authors, are not the Law, but are only some among many of the sources to which judges go in making the law of the cases tried before them. . . .

There is no rule by which you can force a judge to follow an old rule or by which you can predict when he will verbalize his conclusion in the form of a new rule, or by which he can determine when to consider a case as an exception to an old rule, or by which he can make up his mind whether to select one or another old rule to explain or guide his judgment. His decision is primary, the rules he may happen to refer to are incidental.

The law, therefore, consists of *decisions*, not of rules. If so, then *whenever a judge decides a case he is making law*. The most conservative or timid judge, deny it though he may, is constantly engaged in law-making; if he were to see himself objectively he would doubtless feel like Molière's M. Jourdain who was astonished to learn that all his life he had been talking prose.

What then is the part played by legal rules and principles? We have seen that one of their chief uses is to enable the judges to give formal justifications—rationalizations—of the conclusions at which they otherwise arrive. From that point of view these formulas are devices for concealing rather than disclosing what the law is. At their worst they hamper the clear thinking of the judges, compelling them to shove their thoughts into traditional forms, thus impeding spontaneity and the quick running of ideas; they often tempt the lazy judge away from the proper task of creative thinking to the easier work of finding platitudes that will serve in the place of robust cerebration.

At their best, when properly employed, they have undeniable value. The conscientious judge, having tentatively arrived at a conclusion, can check up to see whether such a conclusion, without unfair distortion of the facts, can be linked with the generalized points of view theretofore acceptable. If none such are discoverable, he is forced to consider more acutely whether his tentative conclusion is wise, both with respect to the case before him and with respect to possible implications for future cases.

But it is surely mistaken to deem law merely the equivalent of rules and principles. The lawyer who is not moderately alive to the fact of the limited part that rules play is of little service to his clients. The judge who does not learn how to manipulate these abstractions will become like that physician, described by Mill, "who preferred that patients should die by rule rather than live contrary to it." The number of cases which should be disposed of by routine application of rules is limited. To apply rules mechanically usually signifies laziness, or callousness to the peculiar factors presented by the controversy.

Viewed from any angle, the rules and principles do not constitute law. They may be aids to the judge in tentatively testing or formulating conclusions; they may be positive factors in bending his mind towards wise or unwise solutions of the problem before him. They may be the formal clothes in which he dresses up his thoughts. But they do not and cannot completely control his mental operations and it is therefore unfortunate that either he or the lawyers interested in his decision should accept them as the full equivalent of that decision. If the judge so be-lieves, his thinking will be the less effective. If the lawyers so believe, their opinions on questions of law (their guesses as to future decisions) will be unnecessarily inaccurate.

Critical Legal Studies: An Introduction to Its Origins and Underpinnings

Mark Tushnet

These comments take on the task of explaining why Critical Legal Studies (CLS) forms an appropriate part of a jurisprudence course. Additionally, it provides an overview of what might be included in that part of the course. Material from CLS is already infiltrating the materials used in the first-year curriculum, and at least one prominent British text on jurisprudence has included a brief discussion of CLS in its chapter on American Legal Realism. As that discussion suggests, Legal Realism is one of the intellectual origins of CLS; the other is the progressive tradition in American historiography.

In many ways CLS is a direct descendant of American Legal Realism, which flourished in the 1920s and 1930s and left an important legacy to all legal thought. CLS interprets Legal Realism along the following lines. The Realists offered a critical analysis of law as they saw it. At the time the Realists wrote, many lawyers, judges, and scholars seemed to think that they could draw on a relatively small collection of fairly abstract concepts—CLS has focused on "liberty of contract" and "property rights"—as the basis for decisions in particular cases. Results could either be deduced from the necessary meanings of the concepts or intuited from the social understanding of their meanings. The critical dimensions of Legal Realism established that these assumptions were unfounded. The concepts were so abstract that they led to contradictory conclusions, and because of social divisions—between employers and organized labor, for example—there could be no broadly shared social understandings on which intuitions could properly be based.

The second intellectual source of CLS is the progressive tradition in American historiography. Like Legal Realism, progressive historiography flourished in the 1920s and 1930s. The progressive historians, including Charles Beard and Vernon Parrington, argued that the best way to understand the course of American history was to pay attention to the play of interest groups in American society. Much of their work was devoted to debunking the claims of filiopietistic writers that the best way to understand the course of American history was as the working out of the idea of progress within a generally liberal political framework. The progressive historians looked at American policies and politics and saw much more of economic interest at work; for that they were, rather like CLS people today, called Marxists.

. . .

The Realists made another important point, which was constructive rather than critical. They argued that deduction and intuition had to be replaced by explicit and fairly systematic policy analysis. This constructive program had three elements. First, decision makers, whether judges, legislators, or lawyers advising clients, had to identify those social interests actually at issue in a particular controversy, and had to think about how those interests might be affected by the various courses of action that might be pursued.

From Mark Tushnet, "Critical Legal Studies: An Introduction to Its Origins and Underpinnings," *Journal of Legal Education*, Vol. 36 (1986), pp. 505–517. Reprinted by permission of the Journal of Legal Education.

Understanding the consequences of legal decisions required studying the actual operation of the legal system, drawing on sociology and political science for organizing concepts. This study came to be called policy analysis, and it is now so widely accepted a way of thinking about law that the forms for student evaluation of teaching routinely ask whether the teacher adequately explored policy issues in the course.

Second, according to the Realists, although lawyers should abandon abstract legal concepts as the basis for decision, they should still pay attention to some important but nonetheless abstract social interests, such as promoting human freedom and material well-being. For while people might disagree about *how* those interests should be advanced and *whether* other particular values ought to be promoted, no one would disagree *that* these most fundamental values are important. Thus policy analysis could be grounded on these newly identified and broadly shared social understandings.

The third element in the Realists' constructive program was a method of legal analysis, the method of balancing. Once the precise interests at stake have been identified and their relation to the broad social values understood, decision-makers should balance the interests to arrive at an appropriate decision.

The Realists' constructive program provides the framework for most legal thought today. One need only read a randomly selected law review article or—perhaps a better indicator of what we teach our students—a randomly selected student note of comment to find that the right answer to the question at issue can be found by balancing the interests identified in the appropriate three-part test.

CLS accepts the critical aspect of Legal Realism but challenges its constructive program. Because it does so by using the critical techniques developed by the Realists, CLS is in this sense a true descendant of Realism. The way in which CLS is concerned with the political dimensions of law and domination can be explored by examining the CLS attack on policy analysis, balancing, and shared social values—that is, on the constructive program of Legal Realism.

The CLS attack on policy analysis has focused on what is at present the most popular systematic form of policy analysis, law-and-economics. Law-and-economics attempts to identify what the most efficient solution to a legal problem is. That is, suppose we know how wealth is distributed in a particular society and the preferences of its members. Law-and-economics attempts to determine what rule will allow that society to achieve the most of what its members want, given the existing distribution of wealth. Everyone knows that many interesting questions are assumed away when law-and-economics takes the distribution of wealth as a given. But its proponents claim that answers to many questions are insensitive to the distribution of wealth—there could be large changes in that distribution and no changes in the efficient rules—and that, in any event, if you care about wealth distribution, it is pretty silly to worry about tort or contract law rather than, for example, the tax system.

CLS has attacked law-and-economics in a number of ways. I am not competent to evaluate the technical attack, but I can describe it: The legal system, through its rules of property, contract, and tort, creates a set of entitlements. These entitlements consitute the pattern of wealth-holding in the society. If you are trying to figure out what the efficient rule of contract law is, you cannot take the distribution of wealth as given, because the rule you come up with defines the distribution of wealth. A second line of attack is that economic analysis—and by extension policy analysis more generally—necessarily proceeds by making simplifying assumptions about the world. Law-and-economics has increasingly relaxed those assumptions to make the economic models more realistic. But as the realism of the models increases, the conclusions that we draw become weaker and weaker.

· · ·

The most sophisticated economic analyses end up where the Legal Realists began, with a list of things we ought to think about. The third attack on policy analysis is still more general. Legal rules, and the distribution of wealth, do not merely *reflect* individual preferences. To some degree the rules shape those preferences. Decision-makers must therefore ask not only "What can we do to provide what people want?" but "How will what we do affect what people want?"

The Legal Realists' constructive program answered this question by offering its method of balancing. Sensible decision-makers, brought up in their society and sensitive to its present desires and its aspirations, would be able to take into account everything that policy analysis identified and could come up with the right answers. Here CLS makes a simple point. In our society the class of decision-makers is not representative enough to provide the assurance the Realists wanted. Decision-makers are an elite, demographically unrepresentative and socialized into a set of beliefs about society and technology that skew the balance that they reach. The CLS challenge to balancing, then, is the claim that balancing is a social process that needs to be examined sociologically. The concern for sociological analysis of the actual exercise of power is one part of the legacy of progressive historiography. Sociological analysis inevitably raises political questions. For example, CLS argues that the Realists did not go far enough in demanding a democratization of law and, notably, that neither the New Deal nor the present Democratic Party does so either.

Concern for the politics of legal thought is even more evident in the most fundamental part of the CLS challenge to the Legal Realists' constructive program. The Realists wanted lawyers to worry about how the legal system promoted broadly shared social values. Parts of the CLS argument here are simple applications of the Realists' critical arguments: The social values are described so abstractly that they could justify any decision, and there is some disagreement even about these abstract values—consider the environmentalists' challenge to arguments for increasing a society's material wealth. But the more important part of the CLS argument goes deeper. CLS insists that the social values, on which there may well be agreement, are not valuable in some abstract and timeless sense. They are values because our society is structured to produce in its members just that set of values. But if that is so, the entire constructive enterprise collapses on itself, because you cannot think about altering legal rules to conform to a society's values when those values are constructed partly on the basis of the legal rules themselves.

Taken together, the CLS arguments are bound to be unsettling. If the argument about the social construction of values is correct, people who talk about radical changes in social organization are likely to seem at least weird and off-the-wall. CLS tries to put into question the deepest values of a society: Because there is nothing timeless about those values, we might simply decide to abandon them. CLS might not be able to make much headway with these arguments were it not aided by developments in other disciplines such as philosophy and sociology, whose important thinkers have also argued that social reality is itself socially constructed.

. . .

I turn now to a description of the current state of CLS. First, however, I must interject a number of qual-

ifications. CLS is a developing body of thought, and it would be unsound to attempt to freeze it with an absolutely precise description. Further, different participants in the effort to push CLS ahead have different opinions, and as one of the participants, I have my own views on matters in controversy.

One issue should be mentioned, only to be put aside. It seems to be a standard line in statements by critics of CLS that CLS has no constructive program. As I will indicate at the conclusion of these remarks, there is a deep sense in which that is correct. But in the superficial sense that these critics appear to intend, their comments are simply wrong. CLS offers many proposals for alternative programs. These proposals run from the mundane, such as William Simon's suggestion that a random selection of welfare determinations be automatically subjected to review on appeal,[1] to the grandiose, such as Roberto Unger's description of various forms of public control over investment.[2] I suppose that the critics' point is that, though they can *read* these statements about what ought to be done, they cannot quite understand how those practical proposals are related to the critical or theoretical dimensions of CLS.

Here I will give the short answer to this criticism and will devote the rest of my paper to explaining that answer. The short answer is that the point of the proposals is to continue the critique of existing society, not to get these particular proposals adopted in the short run. This position is, as I will now try to argue, related to ongoing discussions within CLS.

To illustrate this relation, I will describe what is, or at least what was, probably the central debate within CLS. The early position in CLS was that one could say something systematic about the relation between legal rules and power—for example, we can say, though with many qualifications, that the legal system is tilted in favor of capitalism. So long as it is not bound by too many qualifications, that statement or some variant has a fairly obvious intuitive appeal.

The dominant position responds by identifying—or perhaps more precisely by stressing more strongly than the early position—the difficulties inherent even in heavily qualified versions of the early formulations. Three of its arguments have been particularly effective. The first emphasizes the Legal Realists' skepticism about rules, which made it impossible to say that "the legal system" is tilted in any direction at all: If decision-makers can in principle reach any conclusion they wish within the legal system, "the system" cannot be tilted, though of course the decision-makers might be biased. The second argument is that no one has shown that any particular aspect of the legal system, or even the legal system as a whole, serves the interests of capitalism better than do obvious alternatives, including wholesale rejection of vast bodies of law. For any particular rule in the law of contracts in some state in the United States which might be thought to support capitalism, there is a precisely contrary rule, within an equally capitalist system, that is, in another state. International comparisons demonstrated that capitalist economic systems could be found in countries with widely divergent legal systems. The final argument against tilt is that the legal system in fact has little direct impact on the maintenance of capitalism. It provides a framework within which bargains can be struck, and its rules are a sort of disaster insurance against unforseen calamities. But it is difficult to see how an institution whose purposes are so limited could have much of systemic impact.

These arguments have forced a reformulation of the early position. Agreeing that tilt could not be found systematically in the rules of the legal system, the reformulation argued that it is located in the construction of the categories used to organize legal thought and in the construction of the operations used to relate those categories. This seems to me the present state of the position: It claims an analytic program, but has not yet made much progress in demonstrating the program's power.

The renunciation of the theoretical dimension of the initial project of CLS helps explain an otherwise curious characteristic of recent critical legal scholarship. Although it devotes a great deal of attention to phenomena that occurred in the past, much of the work is relentlessly ahistorical. It focuses synchronically on particular moments in the past or offers a sort of comparative statics, but never gives a diachronic account of transformation over time. I believe that this ahistoricism is linked to the critique of social theory, because diachronic accounts explicitly or implicitly rely on social theory to give them coherence. One tradition in the philosophy of history holds that narratives must draw on covering laws—the generalizations of social theory—of which sequences of particular events are specific instances based on identified initial conditions. Another tradition is less explicitly theoretical and claims only that historians provide narratives of past events. But the selection of the events that are placed in the narrative's sequence, out of all the possible events that

could be used, seems to require some (usually implicit) theoretical account, if only the common-sense theories held by well-socialized readers of historical narratives. Having renounced social theory, CLS is barred/precluded from using these standard traditions of historical writing—thus its characteristic ahistoricism.

Alternatively, one could provide a multitude of competing stories about how things changed, while insisting that none of the stories has the sort of epistemological priority that social theories give to the narratives of the standard traditions. Or one could rely on the critique of social theory as a background against which only one account was offered, demanding that readers abjure the usual expectations they might hold about the epistemological claims implicit in such narratives. Either of these courses—the many stories or the one told with a raised eyebrow—could force readers to consider what might be the basis for the critical legal scholar's choice of stories to tell. And that would bring the politics of CLS directly into the discussion.

The view of historical analysis that I have just sketched is implicit in much recent critical legal scholarship, but I believe that the body of work would be strengthened by explicit discussions of these issues. More often the issues have been taken up in the use of structuralist and deconstructionist methods. These methods lie behind much of the currently dominant practice. As soon as an analyst offers a systematic explanation of something, the dominant strain in CLS decenters the explanation, rearranging the terms and categories used in the explanation to demonstrate that the reorganized explanation is just as good as the original one. This decentering project has no termination.

The use of deconstruction has developed its insistence that general social-theoretical explanations are unavailable into the position that all one can do is provide minutely detailed maps or descriptions of phenomena. At this point the open question for the dominant view arises. In general, though it has abandoned the search for social theory, it has not abandoned the view that social power (illegitimate hierarchy) exists. Somehow the detailed descriptions are to reveal how power actually operates. They do so not by invoking social theory of covering laws, but by educing, in an essentially intuitive way, understanding out of the reader's immersion in details. But we need to ask, how is this understanding supposed to emerge?

One possible answer is that the dominant program does not really aim at understanding in the usual sense. Rather, this view maintains, proponents of the dominant program have made a strategic judgment that in the present circumstances their political goals are more likely to be reached by using deconstructive methods. This view breaks the connection between the analytic program and the politics of critical legal studies.

A second possibility is that understanding emerges because of the essentially literary techniques used by those presenting the detailed descriptions. It might be that these techniques operate in a sphere epistemologically distinct from that in which social theory is thought to operate. If so, the emptiness of social theory need not imply that we cannot gain knowledge via deconstruction.

A third possibility, and the one that I believe many critical legal scholars would prefer to pursue, is that we can analyze the ways in which intuitive understanding emerges from detailed descriptions. The anthropologist Clifford Geertz has argued that all knowledge is this sort of "local knowledge."[3] But neither Geertz nor anyone who has appropriated his terminology has done much to explain the sense in which "local knowledge" is knowledge. The effort to do so seems sensible for two reasons. First, we know that people sometimes have different intuitions about a particular problem, and we ought to be curious about how and why intuitive understandings are sometimes shared and sometimes divergent. Second, the analytic effort may be required by the CLS emphasis on domination and illegitimate hierarchy. These terms have normative connotations that suggest that any accurate understanding of hierarchal situations would refer to domination. But that judgment plainly needs some sort of defense.

One line of defense, which appears in some works, is to rely on an essentially romantic view of human nature. Joseph Singer, for example, counters hard-nosed views that "what people *really* like is doing horrible things to each other" with the sensible response that they "do not want just to be beastly to each other. . . . [T]hey also want not to harm others."[4] The difficulty is that as Singer pursues his analysis, he forgets the implication of the "not just" and "also"; in other words, he forgets that people do indeed sometimes want to be beastly. What to those on the bottom is an illegitimate hierarchy is to those on the top a perfectly sensible one. The romantic view of human nature denies that anyone could hold the latter belief in good faith, but, in the absence of a fairly elaborate late Sartrean exposition of the concept of bad faith, the denial is unpersuasive.

A second line of defense for judgments about domination can be called strategic silence. Gary Peller's analysis of the reification of consent in the law of rape provides a useful example.[5] In a standard deconstructive analysis, Peller argues that the concept of consent can be applied in particular settings only by "construct[ing] the context which is supposed to provide the ground for representing the event," a course that "promises total circularity."[6] Peller's aim is to demonstrate that the use of consent as a defense in the law of rape projects "the ideological message . . . that consensual sexuality is consistent with male domination in society.[7] But it should be clear that the same analysis could be used to explain what might be called the Maileresque assessment that female domination requires men to engage in sexual behavior that society creates to be coercive. The technique of deconstruction, that is, cannot in itself support the political conclusions implicit in the use of the term "domination" as applied to particular arrangements. Because the political open-endedness of the deconstructive technique is so obvious, the silence about it in the CLS literature should be understood as strategic, designed to place on the table the political judgments implied by any use of language.

But strategic silence only raises the political issues; it does not explain why one ought to adopt the feminist interpretation of consent and reject the Maileresque interpretation of coercion. This fact suggests that the idea of strategic silence could be extended. The extension would hold that there is nothing beyond that silence, that the process of decentering our understandings is indeed interminable. One offers the feminist interpretation of rape because one has made a political judgment that in our society congealed forms of domination are more likely to be broken up by that interpretation than by the Maileresque alternative. But that is an ungrounded political judgment, open to discussion and alteration as times, circumstances, and understandings change.

The critique of social theory thus replaces one form of political analysis with another. Instead of having political positions flow from social theory, the dominant CLS project simply takes political positions. But not just any political positions. The politics of the dominant position is the politics of decentering, disrupting whatever understandings happen to be settled, criticizing the existing order whatever that order is. Some CLS proponents are attracted to small-scale decentralized socialism. But that attraction must be understood as the embodiment of a critique of large-scale centralized capitalism. It cannot set forth a permanent program, the realization of which would be the end of politics. In fact, in a socialist society, the critical legal scholar would criticize socialism as denying the importance of individual achievement, and decentralization as an impediment to material and spiritual achievement. Roberto Unger captured this dimension of the irrationalist project in his description of destabilization rights, "claims to the disruption of established institutions . . . that have . . . contributed to the very kind of crystallized plan of social hierarchy and division that the entire constitution wants to avoid."[8]

With all this in hand, we can in conclusion turn to the implications of the critique of social theory for the future of CLS. Of course the Legal Realist analysis of rules will continue to be used; the legal academy's commitment to the coherence of rules is strong enough to require repeated assaults. It might be useful as well to develop detailed analyses of how law and beliefs about law are implicated in practices of domination and liberation, but the institutional impediments to sustained empirical research by legal academics are so substantial that it is unlikely that critical legal scholars will produce much along these lines.

I should mention too that one part of the future of CLS is continued institutionalization as part of the pluralist intellectual world of the legal academy. It now seems to be a more or less standard practice in symposia and workshops to include someone from CLS, or at least to feel bad if you do not manage to round one up (or if you willfully ignore them).

But the most important implication of the dominant CLS analysis is that any critique of the existing order is consistent with the project of CLS. Statistical studies, casual empiricism, classical social theory, the most old-fashioned doctrinal analysis—all might be critical legal studies so long as three conditions are met. First, the work should not be defended on grounds that suggest that something more enduring than interminable critique might result from following it through. Second, it must be designed as a critique rather than as a defense of the existing order—or of a slightly modified version of the existing order that, once modified, would be the end of politics. Finally, the work should actually operate as a critique.

Perhaps the program of interminable critique swallows itself. If it is widely accepted, people may at first resign themselves to their inability to transcend critique. But they may come to see that inability is itself transcendent, creating a new form of life in which the terms on which critique must proceed today have become unintelligible.

I would like to close by elaborating this point about interminable critique. I will do so by describing one of the more controversial CLS arguments, which has been called the critique of rights. According to this argument, it would seem that we could abandon such valued rights as the constitutional protections our society gives to free speech and to the antidiscrimination principle. The CLS argument has two parts. The first applies the critique of legal concepts to the concepts embodied in these ideas about rights. Here the critique argues that the rights are defined on too abstract a level to be helpful in resolving the claims presented in particular cases. Nor will recourse to underlying values or to a balancing process help, for reasons I have already reviewed. This aspect of the argument is not unusual or, in itself, particularly bothersome, because it relies on positions for which the Realists were thought to have adequate answers.

One person to whom the critique of rights was described reacted by calling the world that it depicted "Kafkaesque." According to the critique of rights, people cannot know what rights they have, and there are no political methods that guarantee those rights. The term "Kafkaesque" is perfectly appropriate and provides a clue to the justification for the constructive program—or for the program of interminable critique. For by invoking Kafka's vision, the term allows CLS to say that it, like Kafka, is describing the condition of the modern world. Those reared in, or attracted to, premodernist traditions may well find the world so described quite distasteful. But the point of modernism is precisely that that is just the way things are these days.

CLS is thus the form that modernism takes in legal thought. Like modernism in philosophy and sociology, it displaces settled understandings, insisting that whatever we have is something we create and re-create daily. As a form of modernism, CLS argues that our lives are structured by institutions that we create and sustain, and that our lives have no meaning outside those institutions and the processes by which we create them—and create ourselves. So, in part, the CLS program is justified in the way all modernist programs are: The program consists of shattering congealed forms of life by showing that they have no particular integrity. And whatever makes that demonstration effective—utopian yearnings, close analysis of legal texts, concrete proposals—is part of the program.

Perhaps this analysis could be continued indefinitely. But if the CLS critique is interminable, this article is not.

Endnotes

[1] William Simon, Legality, Bureaucracy, and Class in the Welfare System, 92 *Yale L. J.* 1198, 1267–68 (1983).

[2] Roberto Unger, The Critical Legal Studies Movement, 96 *Harv. L. Rev.* 561, 596–97 (1983).

[3] Clifford Geertz, *Local Knowledge* (New York, 1983).

[4] Joseph Singer, The Player and the Cards: Nihilism and Legal Theory, 94 *Yale L. J.* 1, 54 (1984).

[5] Peller, *supra* note 22, at 1187–91.

[6] *Id.* at 1189–90.

[7] *Id.* at 1191.

[8] Unger, *supra* note 12, at 600, 611–15.

Critical Legal Studies and Liberalism

ANDREW ALTMAN

The Rule of Law

The CLS movement is a trend in legal scholarship that has developed over the last decade or so in a large number of law-review articles and in a few key books. Its ideas have proved to be unusually controversial, leading the dean at a major American law school to declare that adherents to CLS are not fit to teach in law schools.[1] The controversy stems in large part from the movement's challenge to some of the most cherished ideals of modern liberal thought. In particular, CLS represents a challenge to a principle central to liberal legal thought—the rule of law. The central contention of CLS is that the rule of law is a myth.

Undoubtedly, I have put this contention in a form that is too crude and calls for clarification and qualification. Yet it is an appropriate first approximation of the heart of the CLS view and serves to draw the main battle line along which CLS has chosen to wage its campaign against liberal legal philosophy. Its critique of liberal legal thought largely stands or falls with the success of its attack on the idea of the rule of law as it is understood by liberal thought.

There can be no doubt that a vital element of liberal legal philosophy is the principle that a society ought to operate under the rule of law. Its commitment to the rule of law originates with the birth of modern liberalism in the seventeenth century and remains as strong as ever in contemporary liberal theory. And the terms in which the rule of law is endorsed by liberals have remained remarkably constant throughout rather substantial changes in certain aspects of liberal theory and some rather deep disagreements among liberals themselves. In his *Second Treatise of Government*, Locke expressed his commitment in these words:

> [F]reedom of men under government is to have a standing rule to live by, common to every one of that society and made by the legislative power erected in it, a liberty to follow my own will in all things where the rule prescribes not, and not to be subject to the inconstant, uncertain, unknown, arbitrary will of another man.[2]

Locke went on to argue that

> the legislative or supreme authority cannot assume to itself a power to rule by extemporary, arbitrary decrees, but is bound to dispense justice and to decide the rights of the subject by promulgated, standing laws, and known authorized judges.[3]

And the importance of the rule of law to Locke's thinking is concisely formulated in his *Letter Concerning Toleration*: "There are two sorts of contests amongst men; the one managed by law, the other by force: and these are of that nature, that where the one ends, the other always begins."[4]

Several centuries later, Hobhouse argued for the reconstruction of liberal theory, implicitly and explicitly rejecting significant elements of Locke's early version. Hobhouse argued that the state should adopt economic policies calculated to reduce the vast inequalities generated by the operation of the market. He called for social control over basic economic resources and rejected what he regarded as traditional liberalism's excessive reliance on private ownership and the market mechanism. Yet the ringing endorsement of the rule of law remains the same:

> [T]he first condition of free government is government not by the arbitrary determination of the ruler, but by fixed rules of law, to which the ruler himself is subject.[5]

A few decades after Hobhouse's classic reformulation of liberalism, Hayek repudiated the tendency toward socialism and state economic planning that Hobhouse's liberalism embodied, which was gaining wide acceptance in Western liberal democracies. Yet Hayek too endorsed the principle of the rule of law and even proceeded to claim that socialist economic policies were to be rejected because they were necessarily inconsistent with it:

> Nothing distinguishes more clearly conditions in a free country from those in a country under arbitrary government than the observance in the former of the great principles known as the Rule of Law. Stripped of all technicalities, this means that government in all its actions is bound by rules fixed and announced beforehand—rules which make it possible to foresee with fair certainty how the authority will use its coercive powers in given circumstances and to plan one's individual affairs on the basis of this knowledge.[6]

In recent years, Joseph Raz has rejected Hayek's argument against socialistic economic policies, suggesting that Hayek exaggerated the importance of punctiliously observing the rule of law. But it is manifest that Raz himself places great value on its observance and stands squarely in the liberal tradition when he declares that "it is clear that deliberate disregard for the rule of law violates human dignity."[7]

Finally, we may cite the two most influential American legal philosophers of the last half century, Lon Fuller and Ronald Dworkin. The work of these important liberal thinkers embodies a strong commitment to the rule of law. Fuller writes:

> Surely the very essence of the Rule of Law is that in acting upon the citizen (by putting him in jail, for example, or declaring invalid a deed under which he claims title to property) a government will faithfully apply rules previously declared as those to be followed by the citizen and determinative of his rights and duties. . . . Applying rules faithfully implies, in turn, that rules will take the form of general declarations. . . . [T]he basic principle of the Rule of Law [is] that the acts of a legal authority toward the citizen must be legitimated by being brought within the terms of a previous declaration of general rules.[8]

And Dworkin describes the rule of law in its most general form in this way:

> [T]he most abstract and fundamental point of legal practice is to guide and constrain the power of government. . . . Law insists that force not be used or withheld, no matter how useful that would be to ends in view, no matter how beneficial or noble these ends, except as licensed or required by individual rights and responsibilities flowing from past political decisions about when collective force is justified.
>
> The law of a community on this account is the scheme of rights and responsibilities that meet that complex standard: they license coercion because they flow from past decisions of the right sort.[9]

In citing this line of liberal thinkers from Locke through Dworkin, I do not mean to suggest that they all have precisely the same conception of the rule of law. There are important differences. . . . Yet there is a remarkable similarity of conceptions and commitments, given the immense span of years and the wide divergence on issues in political philosophy that otherwise divide these thinkers.

The rule of law plays such a central and abiding role in the theories of liberal thinkers because they judge it to be an indispensable institutional mechanism for securing the dominant value cherished by their tradition—individual liberty—and those values that are intertwined with it, such as toleration, individuality, privacy, and private property. The liberal believes that in the absence of the rule of law, there would be no way to secure in practice the individual liberty that he cherishes in theory. The law is an indispensable mechanism for regulating public and private power in a way that effectively helps to prevent the oppression and domination of the individual by other individuals and by institutions. Law as such is not sufficient to accomplish this purpose, and every liberal will also concede that oppressive laws are not only a logical possibility but a historical reality as well. But liberal legal thought holds that the rule of law is, in the world of the modern nation-state at least, a necessary condition for securing a sufficiently wide zone of individual liberty. Moreover, it is a necessary condition that in practice, takes us a significant way toward the goal of preventing the oppression or domination of the individual. The rule of law can do this, according to liberal thought, because the law has the power to constrain, confine, and regulate the exercise of social and political power.

The CLS Attack

There are three main prongs to the CLS attack on the liberal embrace of the rule of law, three main elements to the CLS charge that the rule of law, as liberal theory conceptualizes it, is a myth. . . .

The first prong hinges on the claim that the rule of law is not possible in a social situation where the kind of individual freedom endorsed by the liberal view reigns. Such a situation would be characterized by a pluralism of fundamentally incompatible moral and political viewpoints. The establishment of the rule of law under the conditions of pluralism would require some mode of legal reasoning that could be sharply distinguished from moral and political deliberation and choice. There would have to be a sharp distinction, so the argument goes, between law, on one side, and both morals and politics, on the other. Without such a distinction, judges and other individuals who wield public power could impose their own views of the moral or political good on others under the cover of law. Such impositions, however, would destroy the rule of law and the liberal freedom it is meant to protect.

Thus, the liberal view requires that legal reasoning—that is, reasoning about what rights persons have under the law and why—be clearly distinguished from reasoning about political or ethical values. Legal reasoning is not to be confused with deciding which party to a case has the best moral or political argument. Yet it is precisely this kind of legal reasoning that is impossible in a setting of moral and political pluralism, according to CLS. The law-politics distinction collapses, and legal reasoning becomes tantamount to deciding which party has the best moral or political argument. Karl Klare puts the CLS position concisely: "This [liberal] claim about legal reasoning—that it is autonomous from political and ethical choice—is a falsehood."[10]

Duncan Kennedy is even more blunt, but the essential point is the same:

> Teachers teach nonsense when they persuade students that legal reasoning is distinct, *as a method for reaching correct results*, from ethical or political discourse in general. . . . There is never a "correct legal solution" that is other than the correct ethical or political solution to that legal problem.[11]

The second prong of the CLS attack on the rule of law revolves around the claim that the legal doctrines of contemporary liberal states are riddled by contradictions. The contradictions consist of the presence of pairs of fundamentally incompatible norms serving as authoritative elements of legal doctrine in virtually all departments of law. These contradictions are thought to defeat the notion that the rule of law actually reigns in those societies that most contemporary liberal philosophers regard as leading examples of political societies operating under the rule of law. Kennedy contends that the contradictions are tied to the fact that legal doctrine does not give us a coherent way to talk about the rights of individuals under the law: "Rights discourse is internally inconsistent, vacuous, or circular. Legal thought can generate plausible rights justifications for almost any result."[12] Klare echoes Kennedy's claim: "Legal reasoning is a texture of openness, indeterminacy, and contradiction."[13]

As Klare and Kennedy suggest, the CLS view is that the consequence of these doctrinal contradictions is pervasive legal indeterminacy—that is, the widespread inability of the authoritative rules and doctrines to dictate a determinate outcome to legal cases. The contradictions enable lawyers and judges to argue equally well for either side of most legal cases, depending on which of two contradictory legal norms they choose to rely upon. Moreover, the existence of indeterminacy is tied to the collapse of the distinction between law and politics. Judges can and do covertly rely on moral and political considerations in deciding which of two incompatible legal norms they will base their decisions upon. In existing liberal states, we have not the rule of law but the rule of politics. Joseph Singer sums up this phase of the CLS attack on the rule of law nicely:

> While traditional legal theorists acknowledge the inevitability and desirability of some indeterminacy, traditional legal theory requires a relatively large amount of determinacy as a fundamental premise of the rule of law. Our legal system, however, has never satisfied this goal.[14]

Closely associated with the first two prongs of the CLS attack on the rule of law is the thesis that the very idea of the rule of law serves as an instrument of oppression and domination. David Kairys expresses the general idea in a manner characteristic of much CLS writing:

> The law is a major vehicle for the maintenance of existing social and power relations. . . . The law's perceived legitimacy confers a broader legitimacy on a social system . . . characterized by domination. This perceived legitimacy of the law is primarily based . . . on the distorted notion of government by law, not people.[15]

In the CLS view, then, the idea that our political society operates under the rule of law serves to perpetuate illegitimate relations of power. Exposing the rule of law as a myth is thought of in the CLS movement as an essential part of a strategy designed to undermine those relations of power. . . .

The third prong of the CLS attack focuses on the idea that law is capable of constraining the exercise of social and political power. The contention is made that to think of law as capable of such constraint is to adopt a form of fetishism—to be guilty of regarding a human creation as though it were an independent power capable of controlling those who in fact have created and sustained it. This form of fetishism disempowers human beings; it places them in thrall to forces over which they can and should be the masters. In this CLS view, then, the idea of the rule of law must be criticized as part of a general attack on ideas that disempower humans.

The Totalitarian Charge

In light of the CLS attack on the rule of law, it should not be surprising that the movement has generated an unusual degree of controversy and opposition among legal theorists. There is, however, another source of controversy. The CLS literature is often construed by its opponents as strongly inclined toward a total rejection of liberal values. The attack on law is seen as one phase of a more general totalitarian tilt against the individual freedoms associated with the tradition of liberal political philosophy. I do not believe that a fair examination of the CLS literature can support such an interpretation. It is, at best, a gross caricature. Many CLS authors often do argue that liberal values present only one side of the human story, that there are things people do and should cherish that are either omitted or distorted in the liberal picture. Solidarity and community are the values most often invoked in this regard. However, it is a mistake to infer some sort of totalitarian tilt in CLS from its talk of solidarity, community, and so forth; its thinkers are strongly committed to the essential individual freedoms that liberals have fought to secure against their absolutist, fascist, and totalitarian foes. The words of three prominent CLS authors testify to this conclusion.

First, consider the single most important text in the CLS literature, Roberto Unger's *Knowledge and Politics*. This work has been interpreted as a total rejection of liberal values. It is true that Unger repeatedly insists that what is needed is a "total criticism" of liberalism rather than the "partial criticisms" which many thinkers have offered hitherto.[16] However, Unger does not equate "total criticism" with "total rejection."[17] As Unger uses the term, a *total criticism* of liberalism is one that sees liberalism as a whole, as a single, interconnected system of principles and postulates about human psychology, morality, law, and politics. Unger explicitly states that the liberal value of individual freedom is a part of the liberal system that must be cherished and preserved. And in allusion to the great English liberals—including Locke, Bentham, and Mill—Unger declares:

> Many of the liberal thinkers were devoted to freedom. . . . If for no other reason than for this devotion, they will rank forever as heroes and teachers of the human race, and all the sins of England will be forgiven because of her services to liberty.[18]

Unger's purpose is not to reject the liberal devotion to individual liberty but to claim that there are other aspects of human life that ought to be cherished for which liberal theory does not adequately account. It may be wrong that liberalism cannot adequately account for community, solidarity and the like. But it is instructive that liberal philosophers do not reject the importance of those values; rather, they argue that liberal theory can adequately account for them. The propensity of liberal theorists to make such arguments testifies to the fallacy of inferring that CLS is guilty of a totalitarian tilt against individual freedoms because it insists on acknowledging the central importance of community and solidarity in human life.

Another CLS author, Mark Tushnet, echoes Unger's view that liberal values are not to be rejected but are to be seen as part of a fuller account of what humans do and should cherish. For Tushnet, it is the civic republican tradition in modern political thought that provides the needed supplement. He claims that "just as the republican tradition correctly emphasizes our mutual dependence, the liberal tradition correctly emphasizes our individuality and the threats we pose to one another."[19] And Duncan Kennedy is also not hesitant to embrace liberal freedom. In a discussion of the liberal conception of individual rights, Kennedy claims, "Embedded in the rights notion is a liberating accomplishment of our culture: the affirmation of free human subjectivity against the constraints of group life, along with the paradoxical countervision of a group life that creates and nurtures individuals capable of freedom."[20]

These statements by three of the leading critics hardly evidence a commitment to the totalitarian repudiation of individual liberty. To be sure, liberal theorists will see a threat to liberty in the CLS effort to brand the rule of law a myth. But that view hinges on a particular answer to one of the points of contention between the two groups. CLS does not deny the importance of individual liberty, contrary to the claims of those who intimate that the movement is tainted by totalitarianism. Rather, CLS denies that the rule of law does, or could, protect such liberty and so asserts that other social mechanisms must be invented for such protection. I will argue that the CLS position is unsound, but my argument is wholly consistent with recognizing that individual liberty holds a key place in CLS thinking.

Conflict within CLS

It would be a mistake to complete this overview of the CLS–liberalism debate without introducing some of the disagreements that divide the CLS movement. The movement is by no means monolithic, and there are fundamental differences that divide it into various wings. I am especially concerned with two incompatible strands of thinking that run through the CLS literature, one of which may be characterized as *radical*, the other as *moderate*. The radical strand combines a position on the meanings of legal terms and norms that can loosely be described as *deconstructionist* with the idea that there is no objective structure to the law or any social institution. The position on meaning holds that the words that constitute legal norms and doctrines have no stable or fixed meanings, but are rather "empty vessels" into which the individual may pour whatever meaning he or she chooses. This view is conjoined to the position that it is an illusion to see the law, or any other element of social reality, as having a structure independent of any individual's perception of it. Tushnet expresses the radical position on the structure of legal doctrine in the course of endorsing a certain strand of thinking in the American legal realist movement:

> The materials of legal doctrine are almost measureless, and the acceptable techniques of legal reasoning—distinguishing on the basis of the facts, analogizing to other areas of law where cognate problems arise, and the like—are so flexible that they allow us to assemble diverse precedents into whatever pattern we choose.[21]

The moderate strand of CLS rejects the deconstructionist position on meaning and the view that law and social reality have no objective structure. It holds instead that words do have a settled core of meaning but that the interpretations required to render legal decisions are inescapably responsive to the individual's moral and political beliefs. It holds that our law does have an objective structure but that this structure is a function of a certain controversial and inadequate ethical perspective. Unger gives the most consistent and systematic expression to the moderate strand in CLS. He has never even flirted with deconstructionism, and the social theory that he has recently developed involves a clear rejection of the view that social reality and law are not constituted by objective structures. Unger describes the kinds of explanations offered by his social theory by claiming that they

> assign central importance to the distinction between routine deals or quarrels and the recalcitrant institutional and imaginative

frameworks in which they ordinarily occur. . . . In the contemporary Western democracies the social framework includes legal rules that use property rights as the instrument of economic decentralization [and] constitutional arrangements that provide for representation while discouraging militancy.[22]

Unger's idea of a social and legal framework that shapes and guides routine activities and is resistant to change rests on a rejection of the radical premise that social reality and law do not consist of structures independent of the way any particular individual chooses to think about them.

These important differences between the radical and moderate wings of CLS lead to differences in argument when it comes to the three main elements of the attack on the rule of law as the liberal conceptualizes it. The radical wing attacks on the basis of its deconstructionism and its view that law has no objective structure. The moderate wing attacks on the basis of its claims about legal interpretation and the relation of the existing structure of law to a certain (allegedly) deficient ethical viewpoint.

My strategy in defending liberal legal philosophy can now be concisely stated, albeit in a slightly oversimplified form. On the one hand, the strategy aims to show that the radical arguments of CLS rest on flawed theoretical premises regarding language and law: The deconstructionist position on meaning and the idea that law and social reality have no objective structure are both indefensible. On the other hand, my strategy aims to show that the theoretical premises of the moderate wing are basically sound but do not entail any serious deficiency in the liberal conception of the rule of law. There are indeed certain forms of liberal theory whose conceptions of the rule of law are arguably inconsistent with the ideas of the moderate wing, but that is only to say that certain forms of liberal theory are weaker and more vulnerable to criticism than others. The basic ideas of the moderate wing, to the extent that they are sound, are fully consistent with stronger liberal conceptions of the rule of law. . . .

Endnotes

[1] Paul Carrington, "Of Law and the River," *Journal of Legal Education*, Vol. 34 (1984): 227.

[2] John Locke, *Second Treatise of Government* (Indianapolis: Bobbs-Merrill, 1952), p. 15.

[3] *Ibid.*, p. 77.

[4] John Locke, *A Letter Concerning Toleration* (Indianapolis: Hackett, 1983), p. 49.

[5] L. T. Hobhouse, *Liberalism* (New York: Oxford University Press, 1964), p. 17.

[6] Friedrich Hayek, *The Road to Serfdom* (Chicago: University of Chicago Press, 1944), p. 72.

[7] Joseph Raz, *The Authority of Law* (New York: Oxford University Press, 1979), p. 221.

[8] Lon Fuller, *The Morality of Law*, rev. ed. (New Haven: Yale University Press, 1964), pp. 209–10, 214.

[9] Dworkin, *Law's Empire*, p. 93.

[10] Karl Klare, "The Law School Curriculum in the 1980s: What's Left? *Journal of Legal Education*, Vol. 32 (1982): 340.

[11] Duncan Kennedy, "Legal Education as Training for Hierarchy," in Kairys, *Politics of Law*, p. 47.

[12] *Ibid.*, p. 48.

[13] Klare, "Law School Curriculum," p. 340.

[14] Joseph Singer, "The Player and the Cards: Nihilism and Legal Theory," *Yale Law Journal*, Vol. 94 (1984): 13.

[15] David Kairys, "Introduction," in *Politics of Law*, pp. 5–6.

[16] Roberto Unger, *Knowledge and Politics* (New York: Free Press, 1975), pp. 1–3, 10, 15, 17–18.

[17] Karsten Harries appears to misinterpret Unger on this point. See Harries, "The Contradictions of Liberal Thought," *Yale Law Journal*, Vol. 85 (1975–1976): 842.

[18] Unger, *Knowledge and Politics*, p. 277

[19] Tushnet, *Red, White, and Blue*, p. 23.

[20] Duncan Kennedy, "Critical Labor Law Theory: A Comment," *Industrial Relations Law Journal*, Vol. 4 (1981): 506.

[21] Tushnet, *Red, White, and Blue*, pp. 191–92.

[22] Roberto Unger, *Social Theory: Its Situation and Its Task* (New York: Cambridge University Press, 1987), p. 3.

Law As Integrity

Ronald A. Dworkin

Mrs. McLoughlin's husband and four children were injured in an automobile accident in England at about 4 P.M. on October 19, 1973. She heard about the accident at home from a neighbor at about 6 P.M. and went immediately to the hospital, where she learned that her daughter was dead and saw the serious condition of her husband and other children. She suffered nervous shock and later sued the defendant driver, whose negligence had caused the accident, as well as other parties who were in different ways involved, for compensation for her emotional injuries. Her lawyer pointed to several earlier decisions of English courts awarding compensation to people who had suffered emotional injury on seeing serious injury to a close relative. But in all these cases the plaintiff had either been at the scene of the accident or had arrived within minutes. In a 1972 case, for example, a wife recovered—won compensation—for emotional injury; she had come upon the body of her husband immediately after his fatal accident. In 1967 a man who was not related to any of the victims of a train crash worked for hours trying to rescue victims and suffered nervous shock from the experience. He was allowed to recover. Mrs. McLoughlin's lawyer relied on these cases as precedents, decisions which had made it part of the law that people in her position are entitled to compensation. . . .

The judge before whom Mrs. McLoughlin first brought her suit, the trial judge, decided that the precedents her lawyer cited, about others who had recovered compensation for emotional injury suffered when they saw accident victims, were distinguishable because in all those cases the shock had occurred at the scene of the accident while she was shocked some two hours later and in a different place. Of course not every difference in the facts of two cases makes the

Reprinted by permission of the publisher from *Law's Empire* by Ronald Dworkin, pp. 24, 26–29, 225–242, 245–247, 410–413 (Cambridge, Mass.: The Belknap Press of Harvard University Press), Copyright © 1986 by Ronald Dworkin.

earlier one distinguishable: no one could think it mattered if Mrs. McLoughlin was younger than the plaintiffs in the earlier cases.

The trial judge thought that suffering injury away from the scene was an important difference because it meant that Mrs. McLoughlin's injury was not "foreseeable" in the way that the injury to the other plaintiffs had been. Judges in both Britain and America follow the common law principle that people who act carelessly are liable only for reasonably foreseeable injuries to others, injuries a reasonable person would anticipate if he reflected on the matter. The trial judge was bound by the doctrine of precedent to recognize that emotional injury to close relatives at the scene of an accident is reasonably foreseeable, but he said that injury to a mother who saw the results of the accident later is not. So he thought he could distinguish the putative precedents in that way and decided against Mrs. McLoughlin's claim.

She appealed his decision to the next highest court in the British hierarchy, the Court of Appeals. That court affirmed the trial judge's decision—it refused her appeal and let his decision stand—but not on the argument he had used. The Court of Appeals said it *was* reasonably foreseeable that a mother would rush to the hospital to see her injured family and that she would suffer emotional shock from seeing them in the condition Mrs. McLoughlin found. That court distinguished the precedents not on that ground but for the very different reason that what it called "policy" justified a distinction. The precedents had established liability for emotional injury in certain restricted circumstances, but the Court of Appeals said that recognizing a larger area of liability, embracing injuries to relatives not at the scene, would have a variety of adverse consequences for the community as a whole. It would encourage many more lawsuits for emotional injuries, and this would exacerbate the problem of congestion in the courts. It would open new opportunities for fraudulent claims by people who had not really suffered serious emotional damage but could find doctors to testify that they had. It would increase the cost of liability insurance, making it more expensive to drive and perhaps preventing some poor people from driving at all. The claims of those who had suffered genuine emotional injury away from the scene would be harder to prove, and the uncertainties of litigation might complicate their condition and delay their recovery.

Mrs. McLoughlin appealed the decision once more, to the House of Lords, which reversed the Court of Appeals and ordered a new trial. The decision was unanimous, but their lordships disagreed about what they called the true state of the law. Several of them said that policy reasons, of the sort described by the Court of Appeals, might in some circumstances be sufficient to distinguish a line of precedents and so justify a judge's refusal to extend the principle of those cases to a larger area of liability. But they did not think these policy reasons were of sufficient plausibility or merit in Mrs. McLoughlin's case. They did not believe that the risk of a "flood" of litigation was sufficiently grave, and they said the courts should be able to distinguish genuine from fraudulent claims even among those whose putative injury was suffered several hours after the accident. They did not undertake to say when good policy arguments might be available to limit recovery for emotional injury; they left it an open question, for example, whether Mrs. McLoughlin's sister in Australia (if she had one) could recover for the shock she might have in reading about the accident weeks or months later in a letter.

Two of their lordships took a very different view of the law. They said it would be wrong for courts to deny recovery to an otherwise meritorious plaintiff for the *kinds* of reasons the Court of Appeals had mentioned and which the other law lords had said might be sufficient in some circumstances. The precedents should be regarded as distinguishable, they said, only if the moral *principles* assumed in the earlier cases for some reason did not apply to the plaintiff in the same way. And once it is conceded that the damage to a mother in the hospital hours after an accident is reasonably foreseeable to a careless driver, then no difference in moral principle can be found between the two cases. Congestion in the courts or a rise in the price of automobile liability insurance, they said, however inconvenient these might be to the community as a whole, cannot justify refusing to enforce individual rights and duties that have been recognized and enforced before. They said these were the wrong sorts of arguments to make to judges as arguments of law,

however cogent they might be if addressed to legislators as arguments for a change in the law. (Lord Scarman's opinion was particularly clear and strong on this point.) The argument among their lordships revealed an important difference of opinion about the proper role of considerations of policy in deciding what result parties to a lawsuit are entitled to have.

Integrity and Interpretation

The adjudicative principle of integrity instructs judges to identify legal rights and duties, so far as possible, on the assumption that they were all created by a single author—the community personified—expressing a coherent conception of justice and fairness. We form our third conception of law, our third view of what rights and duties flow from past political decisions, by restating this instruction as a thesis about the grounds of law. According to law as integrity, propositions of law are true if they figure in or follow from the principles of justice, fairness, and procedural due process that provide the best constructive interpretation of the community's legal practice. Deciding whether the law grants Mrs. McLoughlin compensation for her injury, for example, means deciding whether legal practice is seen in a better light if we assume the community has accepted the principle that people in her position are entitled to compensation.

Integrity and History

History matters in law as integrity: very much but only in a certain way. Integrity does not require consistency in principle over all historical stages of a community's law; it does not require that judges try to understand the law they enforce as continuous in principle with the abandoned law of a previous century or even a previous generation. It commands a horizontal rather than vertical consistency of principle across the range of the legal standards the community now enforces. It insists that the law—the rights and duties that flow from past collective decisions and for that reason license or require coercion—contains not only the narrow explicit content of these decisions but also, more broadly, the scheme of principles necessary to justify them. History matters because that scheme of principle must justify the standing as well as the content of these past decisions. Our justification for treating the Endangered Species Act as law, unless and until it is repealed, crucially includes the fact that Congress enacted it, and any justification we supply for treating that fact as crucial must itself accommodate the way we treat other events in our political past.

Law as integrity, then, begins in the present and pursues the past only so far as and in the way its contemporary focus dictates. It does not aim to recapture, even for present law, the ideals or practical purposes of the politicians who first created it. It aims rather to justify what they did (sometimes including, as we shall see, what they said) in an overall story worth telling now, a story with a complex claim: that present practice can be organized by and justified in principles sufficiently attractive to provide an honorable future. Law as integrity deplores the mechanism of the older "law is law" view as well as the cynicism of the newer "realism." It sees both views as rooted in the same false dichotomy of finding and inventing law. When a judge declares that a particular principle is instinct in law, he reports not a simple-minded claim about the motives of past statesmen, a claim a wise cynic can easily refute, but an interpretive proposal: that the principle both fits and justifies some complex part of legal practice, that it provides an attractive way to see, in the structure of that practice, the consistency of principle integrity requires. Law's optimism is in that way conceptual; claims of law are endemically constructive, just in virtue of the kind of claims they are. This optimism may be misplaced: legal practice may in the end yield to nothing but a deeply skeptical interpretation. But that is not inevitable just because a community's history is one of great change and conflict. An imaginative interpretation can be constructed on morally complicated, even ambiguous terrain. . . .

The Chain Novel

[We] can usefully compare the judge deciding what the law is on some issue [with] the literary critic teasing out the various dimensions of value in a complex play or poem.

Judges, however, are authors as well as critics. A judge deciding *McLoughlin* adds to the tradition he interprets; future judges confront a new tradition that includes what he has done. Of course literary criticism contributes to the traditions of art in which authors work; the character and importance of that contribution are themselves issues in critical theory. But the contribution of judges is more direct, and the distinction between author and interpreter more a matter of

different aspects of the same process. We can find an even more fruitful comparison between literature and law, therefore, by constructing an artificial genre of literature that we might call the chain novel.

In this enterprise a group of novelists writes a novel *seriatum;* each novelist in the chain interprets the chapters he has been given in order to write a new chapter, which is then added to what the next novelist receives, and so on. Each has the job of writing his chapter so as to make the novel being constructed the best it can be, and the complexity of this task models the complexity of deciding a hard case under law as integrity. The imaginary literary enterprise is fantastic but not unrecognizable. Some novels have actually been written in this way, though mainly for a debunking purpose, and certain parlor games for rainy weekends in English country houses have something of the same structure. Television soap operas span decades with the same characters and some minimal continuity of personality and plot, though they are written by different teams of authors even in different weeks. In our example, however, the novelists are expected to take their responsibilities of continuity more seriously; they aim jointly to create, so far as they can, a single unified novel that is the best it can be.

Each novelist aims to make a single novel of the material he has been given, what he adds to it, and (so far as he can control this) what his successors will want to be able to add. He must try to make this the best novel it can be, construed as the work of a single author rather than, as is the fact, the product of many different hands. That calls for an overall judgment on his part, or a series of overall judgments as he writes and rewrites. He must take up some view about the novel in progress, some working theory about its characters, plot, genre, theme, and point, in order to decide what counts as continuing it and not as beginning anew. If he is a good critic, his view of these matters will be complicated and multifaceted, because the value of a decent novel cannot be captured from a single perspective. He will aim to find layers and currents of meaning rather than a single, exhaustive theme. We can, however, in our now familiar way give some structure to any interpretation he adopts, by distinguishing two dimensions on which it must be tested. The first is what we have been calling the dimension of fit. He cannot adopt any interpretation, however complex, if he believes that no single author who set out to write a novel with the various readings of character, plot, theme, and point that interpretation describes could have written substantially the text he has been given. That does not mean his interpretation must fit every bit of the text. It is not disqualified simply because he claims that some lines or tropes are accidental, or even that some events of plot are mistakes because they work against the literary ambitions the interpretation states. But the interpretation he takes up must nevertheless flow throughout the text; it must have general explanatory power, and it is flawed if it leaves unexplained some major structural aspect of the text, a subplot treated as having great dramatic importance or a dominant and repeated metaphor. If no interpretation can be found that is not flawed in that way, then the chain novelist will not be able fully to meet his assignment; he will have to settle for an interpretation that captures most of the text, conceding that it is not wholly successful. Perhaps even that partial success is unavailable; perhaps every interpretation he considers is inconsistent with the bulk of the material supplied to him. In that case he must abandon the enterprise, for the consequence of taking the interpretive attitude toward the text in question is then a piece of internal skepticism: that nothing can count as continuing the novel rather than beginning anew.

He may find, not that no single interpretation fits the bulk of the text, but that more than one does. The second dimension of interpretation then requires him to judge which of these eligible readings makes the work in progress best, all things considered. At this point his more substantive aesthetic judgments, about the importance or insight or realism or beauty of different ideas the novel might be taken to express, come into play. But the formal and structural considerations that dominate on the first dimension figure on the second as well, for even when neither of two interpretations is disqualified out of hand as explaining too little, one may show the text in a better light because it fits more of the text or provides a more interesting integration of style and content. . . .

Scrooge

We can expand this abstract description of the chain novelist's judgment through an example. Suppose you are a novelist well down the chain. Suppose Dickens never wrote *A Christmas Carol*, and the text you are furnished, though written by several people, happens to be the first part of that short novel. You consider these two interpretations of the central character: Scrooge is inherently and irredeemably evil, an embodiment of the untarnished wickedness of human nature freed

from the disguises of convention he rejects; or Scrooge is inherently good but progressively corrupted by the false values and perverse demands of high capitalist society. Obviously it will make an enormous difference to the way you continue the story which of these interpretations you adopt. If you have been given almost all of *A Christmas Carol* with only the very end to be written—Scrooge has already had his dreams, repented, and sent his turkey—it is too late for you to make him irredeemably wicked, assuming you think, as most interpreters would, that the text will not bear that interpretation without too much strain. I do not mean that no interpreter could possibly think Scrooge inherently evil after his supposed redemption. Someone might take that putative redemption to be a final act of hypocrisy, though only at the cost of taking much else in the text not at face value. This would be a poor interpretation, not because no one could think it a good one, but because it is, in fact, on all the criteria so far described, a poor one.

But now suppose you have been given only the first few sections of *A Christmas Carol*. You find that neither of the two interpretations you are considering is decisively ruled out by anything in the text so far; perhaps one would better explain some minor incidents of plot that must be left unconnected on the other, but each interpretation can be seen generally to flow through the abbreviated text as a whole. A competent novelist who set out to write a novel along either of the lines suggested could well have written what you find on the pages. In that case you have a further decision to make. Your assignment is to make of the text the best it can be, and you will therefore choose the interpretation you believe makes the work more significant or otherwise better. That decision will probably (though not inevitably) depend on whether you think that real people somewhat like Scrooge are born bad or are corrupted by capitalism. But it will depend on much else as well, because your aesthetic convictions are not so simple as to make only this aspect of a novel relevant to its overall success. Suppose you think that one interpretation integrates not only plot but image and setting as well; the social interpretation accounts, for example, for the sharp contrast between the individualistic fittings and partitions of Scrooge's countinghouse and the communitarian formlessness of Bob Cratchit's household. Now your aesthetic judgment— about which reading makes the continuing novel better as a novel—is itself more complex because it must identify and trade off different dimensions of value in a novel. Suppose you believe that the original sin reading is much the more accurate depiction of human nature, but that the sociorealist reading provides a deeper and more interesting formal structure for the novel. You must then ask yourself which interpretation makes the work of art better on the whole. You may never have reflected on that sort of question before—perhaps the tradition of criticism in which you have been trained takes it for granted that one or the other of these dimensions is the more important—but that is no reason why you may not do so now. Once you make up your mind, you will believe that the correct interpretation of Scrooge's character is the interpretation that makes the novel better on the whole, so judged.

This contrived example is complex enough to provoke the following apparently important question. Is your judgment about the best way to interpret and continue the sections you have been given of *A Christmas Carol* a free or a constrained judgment? Are you free to give effect to your own assumptions and attitudes about what novels should be like? Or are you bound to ignore these because you are enslaved by a text you cannot alter? The answer is plain enough: neither of these two crude descriptions—of total creative freedom or mechanical textual constraint—captures your situation, because each must in some way be qualified by the other. You will sense creative freedom when you compare your task with some relatively more mechanical one, like direct translation of a text into a foreign language. But you will sense constraint when you compare it with some relatively less guided one, like beginning a new novel of your own. . . .

Law as integrity asks a judge deciding a common-law case like *McLoughlin* to think of himself as an author in the chain of common law. He knows that other judges have decided cases that, although not exactly like his case, deal with related problems; he must think of their decisions as part of a long story he must interpret and then continue, according to his own judgment of how to make the developing story as good as it can be. (Of course the best story for him means best from the standpoint of political morality, not aesthetics.) We can make a rough distinction once again between two main dimensions of this interpretive judgment. The judge's decision—his postinterpretive conclusions—must be drawn from an interpretation that both fits and justifies what has gone before, so far as that is possible. But in law as in literature the interplay between fit and justification is complex. Just as interpretation within a chain novel is for each interpreter a delicate balance among different types of literary and artistic attitudes, so in law it is a delicate

balance among political convictions of different sorts; in law as in literature these must be sufficiently related yet disjoint to allow an overall judgment that trades off an interpretation's success on one type of standard against its failure on another. I must try to exhibit that complex structure of legal interpretation, and I shall use for that purpose an imaginary judge [Hercules] of superhuman intellectual power and patience who accepts law as integrity. . . .

Six Interpretations

Hercules must decide *McLoughlin*. Both sides in that case cited precedents; each argued that a decision in its favor would count as going on as before, as continuing the story begun by the judges who decided those precedent cases. Hercules must form his own view about that issue. Just as a chain novelist must find, if he can, some coherent view of character and theme such that a hypothetical single author with that view could have written at least the bulk of the novel so far, Hercules must find, if he can, some coherent theory about legal rights to compensation for emotional injury such that a single political official with that theory could have reached most of the results the precedents report.

He is a careful judge, a judge of method. He begins by setting out various candidates for the best interpretation of the precedent cases even before he reads them. Suppose he makes the following short list: (1) No one has a moral right to compensation except for physical injury. (2) People have a moral right to compensation for emotional injury suffered at the scene of an accident against anyone whose carelessness caused the accident but have no right to compensation for emotional injury suffered later. (3) People should recover compensation for emotional injury when a practice of requiring compensation in their circumstances would diminish the overall costs of accidents or otherwise make the community richer in the long run. (4) People have a moral right to compensation for any injury, emotional or physical, that is the direct consequence of careless conduct, no matter how unlikely or unforeseeable it is that that conduct would result in that injury. (5) People have a moral right to compensation for emotional or physical injury that is the consequence of careless conduct, but only if that injury was reasonably foreseeable by the person who acted carelessly. (6) People have a moral right to compensation for reasonably foreseeable injury but not in circumstances when recognizing such a right would impose massive and destructive financial burdens on people who have been careless out of proportion to their moral fault.

These are all relatively concrete statements about rights and, allowing for a complexity in (3) we explore just below, they contradict one another. No more than one can figure in a single interpretation of the emotional injury cases. (I postpone the more complex case in which Hercules constructs an interpretation from competitive rather than contradictory principles, that is, from principles that can live together in an overall moral or political theory though they sometimes pull in different directions.) Even so, this is only a partial list of the contradictory interpretations someone might wish to consider; Hercules chooses it as his initial short list because he knows that the principles captured in these interpretations have actually been discussed in the legal literature. It will obviously make a great difference which of these principles he believes provides the best interpretation of the precedents and so the nerve of his postinterpretive judgment. If he settles on (1) or (2), he must decide for Mr. O'Brian; if on (4), for Mrs. McLoughlin. Each of the others requires further thought, but the line of reasoning each suggests is different. (3) invites an economic calculation. Would it reduce the cost of accidents to extend liability to emotional injury away from the scene? Or is there some reason to think that the most efficient line is drawn just between emotional injuries at and those away from the scene? (5) requires a judgment about foreseeability of injury, which seems to be very different, and (6) a judgment both about foreseeability and the cumulative risk of financial responsibility if certain injuries away from the scene are included.

Hercules begins testing each interpretation on his short list by asking whether a single political official could have given the verdicts of the precedent cases if that official were consciously and coherently enforcing the principles that form the interpretation. He will therefore dismiss interpretation (1) at once. No one who believed that people never have rights to compensation for emotional injury could have reached the results of those past decisions cited in *McLoughlin* that allowed compensation. Hercules will also dismiss interpretation (2), though for a different reason. Unlike (1), (2) fits the past decisions; someone who accepted (2) as a standard would have reached these decisions, because they all allowed recovery for emotional injury at the scene and none allowed recovery for injury away from it. But (2) fails as an interpretation of the required

kind because it does not state a principle of justice at all. It draws a line that it leaves arbitrary and unconnected to any more general moral or political consideration.

What about (3)? It might fit the past decisions, but only in the following way. Hercules might discover through economic analysis that someone who accepted the economic theory expressed by (3) and who wished to reduce the community's accident costs would have made just those decisions. But it is far from obvious that (3) states any principle of justice or fairness. . . .

Interpretations (4), (5), and (6) do, however, seem to pass these initial tests. The principles of each fit the past emotional injury decisions, at least on first glance, if only because none of these precedents presented facts that would discriminate among them. Hercules must now ask, as the next stage of his investigation, whether any one of the three must be ruled out because it is incompatible with the bulk of legal practice more generally. He must test each interpretation against other past judicial decisions, beyond those involving emotional injury, that might be thought to engage them. Suppose he discovers, for example, that past decisions provide compensation for physical injury caused by careless driving only if the injury was reasonably foreseeable. That would rule out interpretation (4) unless he can find some principled distinction between physical and emotional injury that explains why the conditions for compensation should be more restrictive for the former than the latter, which seems extremely unlikely.

Law as integrity, then, requires a judge to test his interpretation of any part of the great network of political structures and decisions of his community by asking whether it could form part of a coherent theory justifying the network as a whole. No actual judge could compose anything approaching a full interpretation of all of his community's law at once. That is why we are imagining a Herculean judge of superhuman talents and endless time. But an actual judge can imitate Hercules in a limited way. He can allow the scope of his interpretation to fan out from the cases immediately in point to cases in the same general area or department of law, and then still farther, so far as this seems promising. In practice even this limited process will be largely unconscious: an experienced judge will have a sufficient sense of the terrain surrounding his immediate problem to know instinctively which interpretation of a small set of cases would survive if the range it must fit were expanded.

Suppose a modest expansion of Hercules' range of inquiry does show that plaintiffs are denied compensation if their physical injury was not reasonably foreseeable at the time the careless defendant acted, thus ruling out interpretation (4). But this does not eliminate either (5) or (6). He must expand his survey further. He must look also to cases involving economic rather than physical or emotional injury, where damages are potentially very great: for example, he must look to cases in which professional advisers like surveyors or accountants are sued for losses others suffer through their negligence. Interpretation (5) suggests that such liability might be unlimited in amount, no matter how ruinous in total, provided that the damage is foreseeable, and (6) suggests, on the contrary, that liability is limited just because of the frightening sums it might otherwise reach. If one interpretation is uniformly contradicted by cases of that sort and finds no support in any other area of doctrine Hercules might later inspect, and the other is confirmed by the expansion, he will regard the former as ineligible, and the latter alone will have survived. But suppose he finds, when he expands his study in this way, a mixed pattern. Past decisions permit extended liability for members of some professions but not for those of others, and this mixed pattern holds for other areas of doctrine that Hercules, in the exercise of his imaginative skill, finds pertinent.

The contradiction he has discovered, though genuine, is not in itself so deep or pervasive as to justify a skeptical interpretation of legal practice as a whole, for the problem of unlimited damages, while important, is not so fundamental that contradiction within it destroys the integrity of the larger system. So Hercules turns to the second main dimension, but here, as in the chain-novel example, questions of fit surface again, because an interpretation is *pro tanto* more satisfactory if it shows less damage to integrity than its rival. He will therefore consider whether interpretation (5) fits the expanded legal record better than (6). But this cannot be a merely mechanical decision; he cannot simply count the number of past decisions that must be conceded to be "mistakes" on each interpretation. For these numbers may reflect only accidents like the number of cases that happen to have come to court and not been settled before verdict. He must take into account not only the numbers of decisions counting for each interpretation, but whether the decisions expressing one principle seem more important or fundamental or wide-ranging than the decisions expressing the other. Suppose interpretation (6) fits only those past judicial decisions involving charges of negligence against one particular profession—say, lawyers—and

interpretation (5) justifies all other cases, involving all other professions, and also fits other kinds of economic damage cases as well. Interpretation (5) then fits the legal record better on the whole, even if the number of cases involving lawyers is for some reason numerically greater, unless the argument shifts again, as it well might, when the field of study expands even more.

Epilogue: What Is Law?

Law is an interpretive concept. Judges should decide what the law is by interpreting the practice of other judges deciding what the law is. General theories of law, for us, are general interpretations of our own judicial practice. We rejected conventionalism [positivism], which finds the best interpretation in the idea that judges discover and enforce special legal conventions, and pragmatism [realism], which finds it in the different story of judges as independent architects of the best future, free from the inhibiting demand that they must act consistently in principle with one another. I urged the third conception, law as integrity, which unites jurisprudence and adjudication. It makes the content of law depend not on special conventions or independent crusades but on more refined and concrete interpretations of the same legal practice it has begun to interpret.

These more concrete interpretations are distinctly legal because they are dominated by the adjudicative principle of inclusive integrity. Adjudication is different from legislation, not in some single, univocal way, but as the complicated consequence of the dominance of that principle. We tracked its impact by acknowledging the stronger force of integrity in adjudication that makes it sovereign over judgments of law, though not inevitably over the verdicts of courts, by noticing how legislation invites judgments of policy that adjudication does not, by observing how inclusive integrity enforces distinct judicial constraints of role. Integrity does not enforce itself: judgment is required. That judgment is structured by different dimensions of interpretation and different aspects of these. We noticed how convictions about fit contest with and constrain judgments of substance, and how convictions about fairness and justice and procedural due process contest with one another. The interpretive judgment must notice and take account of these several dimensions; if it does not, it is incompetent or in bad faith, ordinary politics in disguise. But it must also meld these dimensions into an overall opinion: about which interpretation, all things considered, makes the community's legal record the best it can be from the point of view of political morality. So legal judgments are pervasively contestable.

That is the story told by law as integrity. I believe it provides a better account of our law than conventionalism or pragmatism on each of the two main dimensions of interpretation, so no trade-off between these dimensions is necessary at the level at which integrity competes with other conceptions. Law as integrity, that is, provides both a better fit with and a better justification of our legal practice as a whole. I argued the claim of justification by identifying and studying integrity as a distinct virtue of ordinary politics, standing beside and sometimes conflicting with the more familiar virtues of justice and fairness. We should accept integrity as a virtue of ordinary politics because we should try to conceive our political community as an association of principle; we should aim at this because, among other reasons, that conception of community offers an attractive basis for claims of political legitimacy in a community of free and independent people who disagree about political morality and wisdom.

. . .

I argued the first claim—that law as integrity provides an illuminating fit with our legal practice—by showing how an ideal judge committed to law as integrity would decide three types of hard cases: at common law, under statutes, and, in the United States, under the Constitution. I made Hercules decide several cases I offered as working examples, and my claims of fit can be checked by comparing his reasoning with the kind of arguments that seemed appropriate to lawyers and judges on both sides of those cases. But this is too limited a test to be decisive; law students and lawyers will be able to test the illuminating power of law as integrity against a much wider and more varied experience of law at work.

Have I said what law is? The best reply is: up to a point. I have not devised an algorithm for the courtroom. No electronic magician could design from my arguments a computer program that would supply a verdict everyone would accept once the facts of the case and the text of all past statutes and judicial decisions were put at the computer's disposal. But I have not drawn the conclusion many readers think sensible. I have not said that there is never one right way, only different ways, to decide a hard case. On the contrary, I said that this apparently worldly and sophisticated conclusion is either a serious philosophical mistake, if we read it as a piece of external skepticism, or itself a

contentious political position resting on dubious political convictions if we treat it, as I am disposed to do, as an adventure in global internal skepticism.

I described the nested interpretive questions a judge should put to himself and also the answers I now believe he should give to the more abstract and basic of these. I carried the process further in some cases, into the capillaries as well as the arteries of decision, but only as example and not in more detail than was needed to illustrate the character of the decisions judges must make. Our main concern has been to identify the branching points of legal argument, the points where opinion divides in the way law as integrity promises. For every route Hercules took from that general conception to a particular verdict, another lawyer or judge who began in the same conception would find a different route and end in a different place, as several of the judges in our sample cases did. He would end differently because he would take leave of Hercules, following his own lights, at some branching point sooner or later in the argument.

The question how far I have succeeded in showing what law is is therefore a distinct question for each reader. He must ask how far he would follow me along the tree of argument, given the various interpretive and political and moral convictions he finds he has after the reflection I have tried to provoke. If he leaves my argument early, at some crucial abstract stage, then I have largely failed for him. If he leaves it late, in some matter of relative detail, then I have largely succeeded. I have failed entirely, however, if he never leaves my argument at all.

What is law? Now I offer a different kind of answer. Law is not exhausted by any catalogue of rules or principles, each with its own dominion over some discrete theater of behavior. Nor by any roster of officials and their powers each over part of our lives. Law's empire is defined by attitude, not territory or power or process. We studied that attitude mainly in appellate courts, where it is dressed for inspection, but it must be pervasive in our ordinary lives if it is to serve us well even in court. It is an interpretive, self-reflective attitude addressed to politics in the broadest sense. It is a protestant attitude that makes each citizen responsible for imagining what his society's public commitments to principle are, and what these commitments require in new circumstances. The protestant character of law is confirmed, and the creative role of private decisions acknowledged, by the backward-looking, judgmental nature of judicial decisions, and also by the regulative assumption that though judges must have the last word, their word is not for that reason the best word. Law's attitude is constructive: it aims, in the interpretive spirit, to lay principle over practice to show the best route to a better future, keeping the right faith with the past. It is, finally, a fraternal attitude, an expression of how we are united in community though divided in project, interest, and conviction. That is, anyway, what law is for us: for the people we want to be and the community we aim to have.

Study Questions

1. Holmes attempts to show that concepts such as law, contract, and malice (as in "malice aforethought"), even though they appear at first to contain or imply moral or value judgments, can be explained without reference to moral notions from the perspective of the bad man (or woman). Do you find his attempt successful?

2. Holmes claims that "the prophecies of what the courts will do in fact, and nothing more pretentious, are what I mean by the law." Suppose that you are a judge on the highest court in the land. How would Holmes's claim guide your understanding of what you should do in deciding a legal question?

3. Realists such as Jerome Frank and Joseph Hutcheson insist that (in Hutcheson's words) "the judge does not decide causes by the abstract application of rule of just . . . but having heard the cause and determined that the decision ought to go this way or that way" he looks for "some category of the law into which the case will fit" in order to "support his desired result" ("The Judgment Intuitive"). Frank implies that same point: Lawyers must seek an understanding of the law, not in the *ratio decidendi* (the reasoning) of a case, but in patterns of results or actual judgments, all the while making the results *look* inevitable. If the realists are correct and the process of trying to reason within the concepts of the law is a fake, why should lawyers or judges continue to do it? Can the realist explain what value might attach to continuing such a pretense?

4. The legal realists emphasize the role of "intuition," or "insight"—a hunch—in the process of resolving legal cases. Is there a danger in allowing judges to follow their feelings and hunches openly and candidly in this way? If not, why not? What if their feelings lead to evil decisions? Do Frank and Hutcheson assume that the judges' hunches will guide them to just and "right" results? If so, is the assumption likely to be correct?

5. It has been suggested that the realists' insistence on the almost complete indeterminacy of the law resulted from a distorted or skewed perspective, one explained by the so-called *selection hypothesis:* Cases that reach the appellate court level, and upon which legal scholars (like the realists) tend to focus, are just the cases in which the law is uncertain and in which the opposing arguments are fairly equally balanced. However, the great bulk of the law, the argument continues, is far more stable and determinate than the realists would admit. Does this explanation undermine legal realism?

6. Does the realist indeterminacy thesis express a necessary feature of law or legality? Or is it simply a contingent claim about a specific legal system or legal culture, namely our own?

7. Dworkin argues that the "law" as it applies to any given case is more than simply the positive rules, encompassing as it does all of the principles and ideals that are part of the best or soundest overall justification or interpretation of the existing rules. Could there be such a "best" theory? And if so, could any of us come to know it?

8. In what ways, according to Mark Tushnet, does Critical Legal Studies (CLS) differ from legal realism?

9. How, according to Tushnet, have CLS scholars attacked the premises of the law and economics movement?

10. How does Tushnet respond to the criticism that CLS has no positive or constructive agenda or outlook? Do you find his response convincing?

11. In light of your understanding of CLS from this chapter, recall Dworkin's critique of various forms of "skepticism" about law. Are Dworkin's responses to the crits convincing in your view?

12. According to Andrew Altman, one central contention made by adherents to CLS is that the ideal of the rule of law is unworkable in a pluralistic society, in which numerous and conflicting views of what is right or good contend. The kind of reasoning undertaken by courts in resolving such disputes, therefore, simply collapses into political

argument, with the "winner" being the one whose politics is shared by the most judges. Do you agree with this overall assessment of the prospects of legal reasoning? Why or why not?

13. Based on your reading of Tushnet's article, do you think that Tushnet foresees further development for critical legal studies? Or does he think that CLS has run its course, with nothing further to contribute?

14. CLS scholar Roberto Unger argues that the resolution of cases through the neutral application of the "rules" cannot work, even in simple cases. Suppose that the law forbids "spilling of blood in the streets." Would this law prohibit a medic from performing emergency surgery at an accident scene? Because the rule itself cannot answer this question, its solution must be sought by appealing to the purposes and values that lie behind it. Yet, Unger insists, ours is a society in which shared values and beliefs are not sufficiently apparent to settle such disputes. (See Unger, *Knowledge and Politics*, pp. 63–103.) How would a legal positivist respond to this argument? How would Dworkin respond?

15. According to Dworkin, the task of a court is always to search for the interpretation of the existing state of the law that depicts it in the best moral light. How would this procedure apply to a judge in Nazi Germany who rejects the Nazi laws as immoral?

16. In *Law's Empire*, Dworkin argues that legal theory must be interpretive because useful theories of law must try to understand the "argumentative character" of legal practice—that is, the fact that people debate about what their law means. Taking up this "internal" perspective on law means that the interpretation of law must be "constructive": it must try to see the law as if it expressed a unifying vision or ideal. What could Dworkin say to a legal realist or other skeptic who challenges the assumption that such an "internal" perspective is the best one from which to understand what law is?

17. Does Frank accept the positivist claim that the law as it "ought to be" is distinct (or should be viewed as distinct) from the law "as it is"?

18. Read the case of *The Antelope* (included in the "Cases for Further Reflection" at the end of this chapter). Imagine that you are a judge faced with deciding this case and that you also subscribe to Dworkin's concept of law as interpretation. Would you decide the case in the way that Justice Marshall does? Why or why not?

E. *Contemporary Perspectives*

Contemporary legal scholarship covers a broad array of fascinating perspectives upon and activism with regard to the law. In addition to the work of theorists such as Ronald Dworkin, positivist Joseph Raz, and natural law scholar John Finnis, several newly emerging "schools" of legal thought have captured much attention in the last two decades.[1] Included within this

category are the law and economics movement, feminist jurisprudence, and critical race theory. This section provides a brief overview of these philosophies of the law.

Law and Economics

One characteristic of many new fields of jurisprudence is the effort to look at the law from a different perspective, whether it be the "outsider" perspective of a

---

[1] See Ronald Dworkin, *Law's Empire* (Cambridge: Harvard University Press, 1986); Joseph Raz, *The Authority of Law* (Oxford: Oxford University Press, 1979); John Finnis, *Natural Law and Natural Rights* (Oxford: Clarendon Press, 1982).

person of color victimized by discriminatory laws, or the perspective of a different academic discipline, such as women's studies. One of the most successful of such recent interdisciplinary efforts is the *law and economics* movement. Diverse perspectives among the many writers who have contributed to this view of the law make it somewhat difficult to generalize; nonetheless, the theory of law and economics has at least two basic dimensions: *descriptive* and *prescriptive* (or *normative*). In its descriptive form, law and economics theory says that an economic analysis of the formation and function of legal rules and doctrines provides the best explanation for the law as it exists. "The logic of the law is economics," as economics scholar and federal judge Richard Posner has claimed. In its normative dimension, the theory of law and economics says that an economic analysis of the law is the one that should be used by lawyers and judges to work out the meaning and application of legal doctrine.

A concept basic to the law and economics perspective is that of *economic efficiency.* In a very rough sense, we can say that a legal rule or arrangement is economically efficient when no one can be made better off except at another's expense. The efficiency of a law is to be measured, according to Posner, by first assuming (as economists do) that people act rationally when they strive to increase their own wealth. Wealth here is not simply to be equated to money; rather, it has to do with the satisfaction of one's interests or preferences: wealth is increased to the extent that one's preferences are fulfilled. A further assumption is then made: that when each individual acts to maximize his or her own welfare or wealth, the wealth of society as a whole is thereby also maximized. Thus, where laws are concerned, an economically efficient situation is one in which wealth is optimized or maximized.

The work of law and economics scholars has largely tracked these basic assumptions. Under the descriptive heading, law and economics proponents ask: What behavioral incentives will a particular rule of law produce? And would those incentives push society in the direction of greater efficiency? So, for example, a law and economics scholar might ask whether allowing consumers to sue manufacturers over inadequate warning labels on consumer goods would promote overall efficiency. On the normative or prescriptive side, law and economics theorists want the law, whether it be the law of personal injury, commercial contracts, or antitrust, to ensure that goods and services end up in the control of those who value them the most.

As an example of how the law and economics theory is supposed to work, consider the law of personal injury—what lawyers call the law of *tort* (see also Chapter 5). According to economic analyses of tort law, the purpose of tort is to bring about an efficient allocation of resources with regard to absorbing the cost of accidents that result in injury. In this view, tort law treats the occurrence of accidents as a problem of *social cost.* Suppose O is the owner of a steel mill. The mill produces a useful commodity (steel) and an undesirable by-product (pollution). One effect of the process—steel—is positive; the other—pollution—is negative, representing a cost (social cost) borne by everyone. H is a homeowner living adjacent to the mill. H sues O for failure to abate the nuisance of filthy smoke and other pollutants drifting across his (H's) property. Should O be held liable? It is of course true that the nuisance to H would not have occurred but for the conduct of O; yet it is equally true that H's decision to live where he does is also a necessary condition of the injury. And it will get us nowhere, the economic theorists reason, to ask whether O caused H's loss, as this is just a disguised way of re-asking the basic question of whether O should be made to pay. The idea of holding liable the one who *caused* the injury is therefore of little help. What the courts must do instead is view the problem as one of *social cost:* to adjust the law's response to suits like H's by attempting to strike a cost-efficient balance between the amount of benefit conferred by the factory's total product—steel-plus-pollution—against the amount of costs generated, the most efficient allocation of the joint resources of O and H.

A simple example illustrates how the economic theory is supposed to work. Suppose that O receives $5,000 per ton for the first 100 tons of steel manufactured; and suppose that 100 tons of steel impose a total cost upon H and his neighbors of $550 per ton. Clearly the net result for society as a whole is a benefit of $4,500. Under these circumstances, the economic theory says the courts should find that O has not been negligent and should not be liable for damage to H. Suppose, on the other hand, that the manufacture of ten thousand tons of steel brings only $1,500 per ton for O (given the marginal decline in the value of every extra lot of 200 tons produced), but that, because the factory's pollution-control equipment becomes less efficient at higher volume, it imposes a cost upon residents of the surrounding community of $1,800 per ton. Here the production of so much polluting steel is not cost-justified on an overall basis, so the law must find O liable as a way of forcing him to absorb the excess cost imposed on the community and thereby return the overall level of social expenditures to an efficient point. The question of whether the defendant caused the plaintiff's injury drops out of the picture altogether.

In the economic view, the question is not so much whom to blame for pollution, but rather, how overall social wealth can be maximized.

In our selection, judge and scholar Richard Posner defends the economic approach to law. The actions of legislators and the decisions of judges do, Posner thinks, facilitate wealth-maximizing transactions; and many common-law doctrines can be explained on the assumption that they maximize wealth. Posner examines the objection that, even if the idea of wealth maximization accurately describes what many courts and legislators have done in fashioning the law, the criterion of wealth maximization is not one that *should* serve in this capacity. One important criticism of law and economics insists that the goal of wealth maximization is totalistic, looking only to the attainment of prosperity for the society as a whole, and thus seemingly unconcerned with the welfare, rights, or entitlements of individuals. Posner responds to this objection and argues for a pragmatic response to it.

Feminist Jurisprudence

According to one of its principal spokespersons, feminist legal theory is defined by two central tasks: the exposure ("unmasking") and critique of patriarchal assumptions underlying purportedly neutral and ungendered legal doctrine and legal theory—revealing the "male tilt" in existing law; and the attempt to reconceive law on the basis of categories and concepts distinctively rooted in "women's voice."[2] According to advocates of a feminist jurisprudence, the job of the philosopher of law is to uncover the myriad of ways in which the law wrongly assumes, reflects, and builds upon the experiences of men.

Much early work in feminist legal theory owed its inspiration to the path-breaking work of psychologist Carol Gilligan.[3] Gilligan sought to describe, in broad outline, two distinct moral outlooks or perspectives that, she argued, corresponded roughly to the perspectives of men and of women.

The typically "male" outlook, according to Gilligan, tends to regard the moral and social worlds legalistically and to be preoccupied with rules and rule following and with appeals to basic principles of justice and rights. The male social world is hierarchical and competitive, formal and abstract. Women's voice, according to Gilligan, speaks differently. Women tend to emphasize nurturance and care over competition, and networks of relationships with others over hierarchy. Women generally approach moral and social problems contextually, seeking to embed the dilemma within a larger story or narrative that may then point to some kind of resolution that will preserve the ties and relationships already intact. Where men frequently appeal to "universalizable" principles and rules, women look to more context-relative moral and political considerations. Although Gilligan's work has been enormously influential, some recent feminist lawyers have taken issue with her assumptions: scholars such as Catherine MacKinnon have argued that Gilligan's analysis is flawed because it tends to associate "women's voice" with a concept of "the feminine" that is itself a gender stereotype sustained by a patriarchal society.

MacKinnon was noted for expressing the implicit male bias in the law in strong terms:

> Virtually every quality that distinguishes men from women is . . . compensated in this society. Men's physiology defines most sports, their needs define auto and health insurance coverage, their socially designed biographies define workplace expectations and successful career patterns, their perspectives and concerns define quality in scholarship, their objectification of life defines art, their military service defines citizenship, their presence defines family, their inability to get along with each other—their wars and rulership—defines history, their image defines god, and their genitals define sex. For each of their differences from women, what amounts to an affirmative action plan is in effect, otherwise known as the structure and values of American society.[4]

Other feminist writers have questioned whether there even can be one "woman's voice."

---

[2] Robin West, "Jurisprudence and Gender," *University of Chicago Law Review* 55 (1988), pp. 1–72.

[3] See Carol Gilligan, *In A Different Voice* (Cambridge: Harvard University Press, 1982).

[4] From Catherine A. MacKinnon, *Feminism Unmodified: Discourses on Life and Law* (Cambridge: Harvard University Press, 1987), p. 36.

It is not news, of course, that the opportunities, goals, and hopes women could enjoy and entertain were long restricted by the law openly and blatantly (see Chapter 3 for examples). However, the subordination and devaluation of women, feminist legal theorists argue, is still very much apparent in the laws of sexual harassment and rape, spousal abuse, and discrimination in the workplace. To reveal the erroneous and "gendered" assumptions upon which many of these mistaken legal doctrines are based, feminist legal theorists have urged an appeal to the individual experiences of particular women, and to the traits with which women (according to Gilligan and others) are especially endowed—empathy, sensitivity, and a disdain for abstract and formal solutions to legal disputes.

Not all feminist legal scholars agree, of course. One principal source of disagreement turns on how radically the law must be reformed in order to eliminate the patriarchy implicit in the law. One view argues for the elimination of specific instances of obvious gender bias in, for example, the law of rape. A different, and more radical, critique of patriarchy insists that feminist legal theory must reconceive whole areas of law with an understanding of how existing doctrines silence and subordinate women, trivialize their abuse, and elevate male dominance to appear natural or inevitable. (See, for example, MacKinnon's critique of pornography law in Chapter 2).

Another debate that separates adherents to feminist legal theory is sometimes referred to as the "special" treatment versus "equal" treatment debate, or the "asymmetrical" versus the "symmetrical" approaches to feminism in the law. According to one writer:

> [T]he asymmetrical approach contends that it is crucial to recognize women's unique needs and to value their special contributions. It contends that the best way to do this is by means of sex-specific laws and policies that treat women differently than men. The . . . symmetrical approach argues that women are best served by making sex irrelevant to all decisions governing opportunities available to women and men. It contends that the best way to secure this is by sex neutral statutes and regulations that stress the analogies between the life-situations of women and men.[5]

The symmetrical approach was apparent in the 1960s and 70s in arguments for equal pay, equal work, and the proposed Equal Rights Amendment to the Constitution. The asymmetrical model has been urged more recently by those concerned that women have special needs involving, for example, pregnancy, child care, and work hours, that cannot be assimilated to parallel needs of men. The law must, therefore, make special accommodation for the "real difference" between men and women.

Theorists of the symmetrical approach argue that the moral (and constitutional) ideal of sexual equality is best understood as one of complete gender neutrality or "assimilationism," in which sex-based biological differences are assimilated to that of (say) eye color, so that they become insignificant with regard to the distribution of social goods. As Martha Chamallas has argued, the emphasis here is upon women's similarity to men: "Because women [are] the same as men in all relevant respects, they deserve access to all public institutions, benefits and opportunities on the same terms as men."[6] Advocates of the asymmetrical approach—sometimes called "difference" theorists—on the other hand, argue that an ideal of gender neutrality cannot bring about a condition of substantive equality when the allegedly "neutral" state of affairs against which moral and social progress is to be judged itself conceals a bias against women. Difference theorists argue that assimilationism ignores real differences between men and women, such as the unique needs of women arising out of pregnancy and childbirth. A specific issue in labor law can be used to help students see the relevance of the "sameness/difference" controversy: How should employers respond to the needs of female workers regarding pregnancy and childbirth? Should women be allowed only as much of a "disability" leave as would a man with, say, a hernia, with the consequence that pregnant women and new mothers may, upon returning to work, face hardships (loss of benefits, demotion) not encountered by men? Or should pregnancy be treated as a special "condition" for which employers should be required to give leaves of a certain length, whether or not leaves with similar conditions are given to men with disabilities? (Is pregnancy a "disability"?) What do "equal protection" or "equal treatment" in this context amount to?

---

[5] J. Ralph Lindgren, "Strategic Themes in Recent Feminist Legal Literature," *American Philosophical Association Newsletter on Feminism and Law* 94 (1995), p. 55.

[6] Martha Chamallas, *Introduction to Feminist Legal Theory* (Gaithersburg, MD: Aspen Publishers, 1999).

Two selections included here explore aspects of feminist legal theory. Margaret Radin argues that the philosophical tradition of pragmatism can illuminate and clarify the aims of feminist jurisprudence. Radin sees the primary problem of women and the law as one of a "double bind": an impasse created when one way of using the law to improve the condition of women has a "backlash" effect, worsening women's prospects in other ways. Following American pragmatist philosophers such as William James and John Dewey, Radin claims that such doublebinds must be dealt with by "dissolving" or side-stepping the legal and conceptual frameworks that give rise to them. Radin goes on to claim that pragmatism in philosophy and feminism in legal theory hold several methodological views in common: a commitment to seeking knowledge in the situated particulars of actual experience; a concept of truth as provisional; a rejection of sharp dichotomies (reason versus feeling; theory versus practice, and so on). Radin explores the pragmatist notion of truth as coherence among beliefs and questions whether such a view is compatible with the activist and progressive dimension of a feminist jurisprudential outlook.

Angela Harris takes a different point of view, looking at the nature and limits of feminist jurisprudence from the standpoint of critical race theory (see below). Harris attacks what she calls "essentialism": the assumption, quite apparent in feminist theory, that there is one and only one "women's voice," one and only one set of experiences that qualify as "women's experience." Harris shows how such gender essentialism is presupposed by the work of other feminist scholars, and she explains the connection between gender essentialism and "racial essentialism," the idea that the experience of white women stands for that of all women. For Harris, racial essentialism wrongly excludes the experience of people of color.

Critical Race Theory

The last of the jurisprudential movements to be covered in this chapter is *critical race theory* (CRT). One of the forces contributing to the emergence of CRT was the growing dissatisfaction of women of color and lesbians with the feminist analyses of law developed in the 1970s and 1980s. No one set of experiences, these critics insisted, could claim to speak in a single voice for all women. These criticisms coincided with the development of so-called "positional" critiques of law,

assessing legal doctrine from the perspective of persons from ethnic and economic backgrounds outside the mainstream.

While sharing some of the same convictions about law and its manipulability as CLS lawyers and scholars, critical race theorists agree that CLS does not acknowledge a crucial fact of American law and culture: its racial stratification. Critical race theorists seek to focus attention on the extent to which racial categories deeply affect not only the way that the law is realized in the streets, but also how the law itself is structured and administered. Just as feminist legal scholars have tried to call attention to the gendered nature of many legal statutes and doctrines, critical race scholars have worked to show the various ways in which the law supports racial hierarchies that subordinate people of color, while concealing this fact under the guise of allegedly "neutral" laws. Such laws—the backbone of traditional civil rights doctrine—are not equipped, critical race theorists argue, fully to expose the ways in which people can be discriminated against, or the manner in which a person's race can be used as a weapon to harm him or her.

In a groundbreaking CRT essay, law professor Derrick Bell advocated the need for a "racial realism" in legal thought, paralleling that of legal realism.[7] The realists, as we have seen, attacked the idea of law as a set of neutrally defined rights, adjudicated through an apolitical and objective form of legal reasoning. Realism exposed ways in which this myth of formalism was used to perpetuate the economic status quo in the early part of the twentieth century. In the same way, Bell suggested, racial realism can expose how law is used to preserve a status quo regarding the oppression of Blacks and other people of color. Contemporary civil rights law, Bell contended, has been co-opted to perpetuate racism in less overt forms than the outright segregation prevalent in many parts of the nation in the past. It is these forms that racial realism seeks to unmask.

How deeply rooted in the fabric of our society and culture are forms of racism and discrimination? Are they merely, as political liberalism would hold, expressions of wrongful or false beliefs about those deemed inferior—beliefs which are easily modified without deep structural changes in American society? Or are they more systematically embedded in our daily practices

_____

[7] Derrick Bell, "Racial Realism," 27 *Connecticut Law Review* (1992), pp. 363–378.

and legal institutions? As Richard Delgado and Jean Stefancic argue in their selection, many critical race theorists, including Bell, believe that the marginal gains for Blacks resulting from civil-rights-era legislation were actually rooted in institutional changes that served the interests of middle-class whites. As Delgado and Stefancic explain, revising our accepted understanding of what the civil rights movement really meant is a central theme of CRT, as is the view that some wrongs are "structurally determined" by the very words and concepts we use to frame laws

intended to address those wrongs. As an example, Delgado and Stefancic point to legal efforts to deal with episodes of racist speech and invective directed at members of ethnic minorities. Though well-intentioned, the CRT advocate concedes, the courts are simply not equipped fully to appreciate the gravity of such wrongs, instead relegating plaintiffs to the remedy of "speaking up themselves," asserting their First Amendment rights through "counterspeech." Delgado and Stefancic use several imaginary case studies to illustrate this and other basic CRT claims.

The Economic Approach to Law

RICHARD A. POSNER

The most ambitious and probably the most influential effort in recent years to elaborate an overarching concept of justice that will both explain judicial decision making and place it on an objective basis is that of scholars working in the interdisciplinary field of "law and economics," as economic analysis of law is usually called. I am first going to describe the most ambitious version of this ambitious effort and then use philosophy to chip away at it and see what if anything is left standing.

The Approach

The basic assumption of economics that guides the version of economic analysis of law that I shall be presenting is that people are rational maximizers of their satisfactions—*all* people (with the exception of small children and the profoundly retarded) in *all* of their activities (except when under the influence of psychosis or similarly deranged through drug or alcohol abuse) that involve choice. Because this definition embraces the criminal deciding whether to commit

another crime, the litigant deciding whether to settle or litigate a case, the legislator deciding whether to vote for or against a bill, the judge deciding how to cast his vote in a case, the party to a contract deciding whether to break it, the driver deciding how fast to drive, and the pedestrian deciding how boldly to cross the street, as well as the usual economic actors, such as businessmen and consumers, it is apparent that most activities either regulated by or occurring within the legal system are grist for the economic analyst's mill. It should go without saying that nonmonetary as well as monetary satisfactions enter into the individual's calculus of maximizing (indeed, money for most people is a means rather than an end) and that decisions, to be rational, need not be well thought out at the conscious level—indeed, need not be conscious at all. Recall that "rational" denotes suiting means to ends, rather than mulling things over, and that much of our knowledge is tacit.

Since my interest is in legal doctrines and institutions, it will be best to begin at the legislative (including the constitutional) level. I assume that legislators are rational maximizers of their satisfactions just like everyone else. Thus nothing they do is motivated by the public interest as such. But they want to be elected and reelected, and they need money to wage an effective campaign. This money is more likely to be forthcoming from well-organized groups than

Reprinted by permission of the publisher from *The Problems of Jurisprudence* by Richard Posner, Cambridge, MA: Harvard University Press, © 1990 by the President and Fellows of Harvard College.

from unorganized individuals. The rational individual knows that his contribution is unlikely to make a difference; for this reason and also because voters in most elections are voting for candidates rather than policies, which further weakens the link between casting one's vote and obtaining one's preferred policy, the rational individual will have little incentive to invest time and effort in deciding whom to vote for. Only an organized group of individuals (or firms or other organizations—but these are just conduits for individuals) will be able to overcome the informational and free-rider problems that plague collective action. But such a group will not organize and act effectively unless its members have much to gain or much to lose from specific policies, as tobacco farmers, for example, have much to gain from federal subsidies for growing tobacco and much to lose from the withdrawal of those subsidies. The basic tactic of an interest group is to trade the votes of its members and its financial support to candidates in exchange for an implied promise of favorable legislation. Such legislation will normally take the form of a statute transferring wealth from unorganized taxpayers (for example, consumers) to the interest group. If the target were another interest group, the legislative transfer might be effectively opposed. The unorganized are unlikely to mount effective opposition, and it is their wealth, therefore, that typically is transferred to interest groups.

On this view, a statute is a deal. . . . But because of the costs of transactions within a multi-headed legislative body, and the costs of effective communication through time, legislation does not spring full-grown from the head of the legislature; it needs interpretation and application, and this is the role of the courts. They are agents of the legislature. But to impart credibility and durability to the deals the legislature strikes with interest groups, courts must be able to resist the wishes of current legislators who want to undo their predecessors' deals yet cannot do so through repeal because the costs of passing legislation (whether original or amended) are so high, and who might therefore look to the courts for a repealing "interpretation." The impediments to legislation actually facilitate rather than retard the striking of deals, by giving interest groups some assurance that a deal struck with the legislature will not promptly be undone by repeal. An independent judiciary is one of the impediments.

Judicial independence makes the judges imperfect agents of the legislature. This is tolerable not only for the reason just mentioned but also because an independent judiciary is necessary for the resolution of ordinary disputes in a way that will encourage trade, travel, freedom of action, and other highly valued activities or conditions and will minimize the expenditure of resources on influencing governmental action. Legislators might appear to have little to gain from these widely diffused rule-of-law virtues. But if the aggregate benefits from a particular social policy are very large and no interest group's ox is gored, legislators may find it in their own interest to support the policy. Voters understand in a rough way the benefits to them of national defense, crime control, dispute settlement, and the other elements of the night watchman state, and they will not vote for legislators who refuse to provide these basic public services. It is only when those services are in place, and when (usually later) effective means of taxation and redistribution develop, that the formation of narrow interest groups and the extraction by them of transfers from unorganized groups become feasible.

The judges thus have a dual role: to interpret the interest-group deals embodied in legislation and to provide the basic public service of authoritative dispute resolution. They perform the latter function not only by deciding cases in accordance with preexisting norms, but also—especially in the Anglo-American legal system—by elaborating those norms. They fashioned the common law out of customary practices, out of ideas borrowed from statutes and from other legal systems (for example, Roman law), and out of their own conceptions of public policy. The law they created exhibits, according to the economic theory that I am expounding, a remarkable (although not total—remember the extension of the rule of capture to oil and gas) substantive consistency. It is as if the judges *wanted* to adopt the rules, procedures, and case outcomes that would maximize society's wealth.

I must pause to define "wealth maximization," a term often misunderstood. The "wealth" in "wealth maximization" refers to the sum of all tangible and intangible goods and services, weighted by prices of two sorts: offer prices (what people are willing to pay for goods they do not already own); and asking prices (what people demand to sell what they do own). If A would be willing to pay up to $100 for B's stamp collection, it is worth $100 to A. If B would be willing to sell the stamp collection for any price above $90, it is worth $90 to B. So if B sells the stamp collection to A (say for $100, but the analysis is qualitatively unaffected at any price between $90 and $100—and it is only in that range that a transaction will occur), the wealth of society will rise by $10. Before the transaction

A had $100 in cash and B had a stamp collection worth $90 (a total of $190); after the transaction A has a stamp collection worth $100 and B has $100 in cash (a total of $200). The transaction will not raise measured wealth—gross national product, national income, or whatever—by $10; it will not raise it at all unless the transaction is recorded, and if it is recorded it is likely to raise measured wealth by the full $100 purchase price. But the real addition to social wealth consists of the $10 increment in *nonpecuniary* satisfaction that A derives from the purchase, compared with that of B. This shows that "wealth" in the economist's sense is not a simple monetary measure. . . .

[I]f I am given a choice between remaining in a job in which I work forty hours a week for $1,000 and switching to a job in which I would work thirty hours for $500, and I decide to make the switch, the extra ten hours of leisure must be worth at least $500 to me, yet GNP will fall when I reduce my hours of work. Suppose the extra hours of leisure are worth $600 to me, so that my full income rises from $1,000 to $1,100 when I reduce my hours. My former employer presumably is made worse off by my leaving (else why did he employ me?), but not more than $100 worse off; for if he were, he would offer to pay me a shade over $1,100 a week to stay—and I would stay. (The example abstracts from income tax.)

Wealth is *related* to money, in that a desire not backed by ability to pay has no standing—such a desire is neither an offer price nor an asking price. I may desperately desire a BMW, but if I am unwilling or unable to pay its purchase price, society's wealth would not be increased by transferring the BMW from its present owner to me. Abandon this essential constraint (an important distinction, also, between wealth maximization and utilitarianism—for I might derive greater utility from the BMW than its present owner or anyone else to whom he might sell the car), and the way is open to tolerating the crimes committed by the passionate and the avaricious against the cold and the frugal.

The common law facilitates wealth-maximizing transactions in a variety of ways. It recognizes property rights, and these facilitate exchange. It also protects property rights, through tort and criminal law. (Although today criminal law is almost entirely statutory, the basic criminal protections—for example, those against murder, assault, rape, and theft—have, as one might expect, common law origins.) Through contract law it protects the process of exchange. And it establishes procedural rules for resolving disputes in these various fields as efficiently as possible.

The illustrations given thus far of wealth-maximizing transactions have been of transactions that are voluntary in the strict sense of making everyone affected by them better off, or at least no worse off. Every transaction has been assumed to affect just two parties, each of whom has been made better off by it. Such a transaction is said to be Pareto superior [i.e., at least one person is better off, and nobody is worse off], but Pareto superiority is not a necessary condition for a transaction to be wealth maximizing. Consider an accident that inflicts a cost of $100 with a probability of .01 and that would have cost $3 to avoid. The accident is a wealth-maximizing "transaction" . . . because the expected accident cost ($1) is less than the cost of avoidance. (I am assuming risk neutrality. Risk aversion would complicate the analysis but not change it fundamentally.) It is wealth maximizing even if the victim is not compensated. The result is consistent with Learned Hand's formula, which defines negligence as the failure to take cost-justified precautions. If the only precaution that would have averted the accident is not cost-justified, the failure to take it is not negligent and the injurer will not have to compensate the victim for the costs of the accident.

If it seems artificial to speak of the accident as the transaction, consider instead the potential transaction that consists of purchasing the safety measure that would have avoided the accident. Since a potential victim would not pay $3 to avoid an expected accident cost of $1, his offer price will be less than the potential injurer's asking price and the transaction will not be wealth maximizing. But if these figures were reversed—if an expected accident cost of $3 could be averted at a cost of $1—the transaction would be wealth maximizing, and a liability rule administered in accordance with the Hand formula would give potential injurers an incentive to take the measures that potential victims would pay them to take if voluntary transactions were feasible. The law would be overcoming transaction-cost obstacles to wealth-maximizing transactions—a frequent office of liability rules.

The wealth-maximizing properties of common law rules have been elucidated at considerable length in the literature of the economic analysis of law. Such doctrines as conspiracy, general average (admiralty), contributory negligence, equitable servitude, employment at will, the standard for granting preliminary injunctions, entrapment, the contract defense of impossibility, the collateral-benefits rule, the expectation measure of damages, assumption of risk, attempt, invasion of privacy, wrongful interference with contract rights, the availability of punitive damages in some cases but not others, privilege in the law of evidence, official immunity, and the doctrine of moral consideration have been found—at least by some contributors to this literature—to conform to the dictates of wealth maximization. . . . It has even been argued that the system of precedent itself has an economic equilibrium. Precedents are created as a by-product of litigation. The greater the number of recent precedents in an area, the lower the rate of litigation will be. In particular, cases involving disputes over legal as distinct from purely factual issues will be settled. The existence of abundant, highly informative (in part because recent) precedents will enable the parties to legal disputes to form more convergent estimates of the likely outcome of a trial, and . . . if both parties agree on the outcome of trial they will settle beforehand because a trial is more costly than a settlement. But with less litigation, fewer new precedents will be produced, and the existing precedents will obsolesce as changing circumstances render them less apt and informative. So the rate of litigation will rise, producing more precedents and thereby causing the rate of litigation again to fall.

This analysis does not explain what drives judges to decide common law cases in accordance with the dictates of wealth maximization. Prosperity, however, which wealth maximization measures more sensitively than purely monetary measures such as GNP, is a relatively uncontroversial policy, and most judges try to steer clear of controversy: their age, method of compensation, and relative weakness vis-à-vis the other branches of government make the avoidance of controversy attractive. It probably is no accident, therefore, that many common law doctrines assumed their modern form in the nineteenth century, when laissez-faire ideology, which resembles wealth maximization, had a strong hold on the Anglo-American judicial imagination. . . .

It may be objected that in assigning ideology as a cause of judicial behavior, the economist strays outside the boundaries of his discipline; but he need not rest on ideology. The economic analysis of legislation implies that fields of law left to the judges to elaborate, such as the common law fields, must be the ones in which interest-group pressures are too weak to deflect the legislature from pursuing goals that are in the general interest. Prosperity is one of these goals, and one that judges are especially well equipped to promote. The rules of the common law that they promulgate attach prices to socially undesirable conduct, whether free riding or imposing social costs without corre-

sponding benefits. By doing this the rules create incentives to avoid such conduct, and these incentives foster prosperity. In contrast, judges can, despite appearances, do little to redistribute wealth. A rule that makes it easy for poor tenants to break leases with rich landlords, for example, will induce landlords to raise rents in order to offset the costs that such a rule imposes, and tenants will bear the brunt of these higher costs. Indeed, the principal redistribution accomplished by such a rule may be from the prudent, responsible tenant, who may derive little or no benefit from having additional legal rights to use against landlords—rights that enable a tenant to avoid or postpone eviction for nonpayment of rental—to the feckless tenant. That is a capricious redistribution. Legislatures, however, have by virtue of their taxing and spending powers powerful tools for redistributing wealth. So an efficient division of labor between the legislative and judicial branches has the legislative branch concentrate on catering to interest-group demands for wealth distribution and the judicial branch on meeting the broad-based social demand for efficient rules governing safety, property, and transactions. Although there are other possible goals of judicial action besides efficiency and redistribution, many of these (various conceptions of "fairness" and "justice") are labels for wealth maximization, or for redistribution in favor of powerful interest groups; or else they are too controversial in a heterogeneous society, too ad hoc, or insufficiently developed to provide judges who desire a reputation for objectivity and disinterest with adequate grounds for their decisions.

Finally, even if judges have little commitment to efficiency, their inefficient decisions will, by definition, impose greater social costs than their efficient ones will. As a result, losers of cases decided mistakenly from an economic standpoint will have a greater incentive, on average, to press for correction through appeal, new litigation, or legislative action than losers of cases decided soundly from an economic standpoint—so there will be a steady pressure for efficient results. Moreover, cases litigated under inefficient rules tend to involve larger stakes than cases litigated under efficient rules (for the inefficient rules, by definition, generate social waste), and the larger the stakes in a dispute the likelier it is to be litigated rather than settled; so judges will have a chance to reconsider the inefficient rule.

Thus we should not be surprised to see the common law tending to become efficient, although since the incentives of judges to perform well along any dimension are weak (this is a by-product of judicial independence), we cannot expect the law ever to achieve perfect efficiency. Since wealth maximization is not only a guide in fact to common law judging but also a genuine social value and the only one judges are in a good position to promote, it provides not only the key to an accurate description of what the judges are up to but also the right benchmark for criticism and reform. If judges are failing to maximize wealth, the economic analyst of law will urge them to alter practice or doctrine accordingly. In addition, the analyst will urge—on any legislator sufficiently free of interest-group pressures to be able to legislate in the public interest—a program of enacting only legislation that conforms to the dictates of wealth maximization.

Besides generating both predictions and prescriptions, the economic approach enables the common law to be reconceived in simple, coherent terms and to be applied more objectively than traditional lawyers would think possible. From the premise that the common law does and should seek to maximize society's wealth, the economic analyst can deduce in logical—if you will, formalist—fashion (economic theory is formulated nowadays largely in mathematical terms) the set of legal doctrines that will express and perfect the inner nature of the common law, and can compare these doctrines with the actual doctrines of common law. After translating from the economic vocabulary back into the legal one, the analyst will find that most of the actual doctrines are tolerable approximations to the implications of economic theory and so far formalistically valid. Where there are discrepancies, the path to reform is clear—yet the judge who takes the path cannot be accused of making rather than finding law, for he is merely contributing to the program of realizing the essential nature of the common law.

The project of reducing the common law—with its many separate fields, its thousands of separate doctrines, its hundreds of thousands of reported decisions—to a handful of mathematical formulas may seem quixotic, but the economic analyst can give reasons for doubting this assessment. Much of the doctrinal luxuriance of common law is seen to be superficial once the essentially economic nature of the common law is understood. A few principles, such as cost-benefit analysis, the prevention of free riding, decision under uncertainty, risk aversion, and the promotion of mutually beneficial exchanges, can explain most doctrines and decisions. Tort cases can be translated into contract cases by recharacterizing the tort issue as finding the implied pre-accident contract that the par-

ties would have chosen had transaction costs not been prohibitive, and contract cases can be translated into tort cases by asking what remedy if any would maximize the expected benefits of the contractual undertaking considered ex ante. The criminal's decision whether to commit a crime is no different in principle from the prosecutor's decision whether to prosecute; a plea bargain is a contract; crimes are in effect torts by insolvent defendants because if all criminals could pay the full social costs of their crimes, the task of deterring antisocial behavior could be left to tort law. Such examples suggest not only that the logic of the common law really is economics but also that the teaching of law could be simplified by exposing students to the clean and simple economic structure beneath the particolored garb of legal doctrine.

If all this seems reminiscent of Langdell, it differs fundamentally in being empirically verifiable. The ultimate test of a rule derived from economic theory is not the elegance or logicality of the derivation but the rule's effect on social wealth. The extension of the rule of capture to oil and gas was subjected to such a test, flunked, and was replaced (albeit through legislative rather than judicial action) by efficient rules. The other rules of the common law can and should be tested likewise. . . .

Criticisms of the Normative Theory

The question whether wealth maximization *should* guide legal policy, either in general or just in common law fields (plus those statutory fields where the legislative intent is to promote efficiency—antitrust law being a possible example), is ordinarily treated as separate from the question whether it *has* guided legal policy, except insofar as the positive theory may be undermined by the inadequacies of the normative theory. Actually the two theories are not as separable as this, illustrating again the lack of a clear boundary between "is" and "ought" propositions. One of the things judges ought to do is follow precedent, although not inflexibly; so if efficiency is the animating principal of much common law doctrine, judges have some obligation to make decisions that will be consistent with efficiency. This is one reason why the positive economic theory of the common law is so contentious.

The normative theory has been highly contentious in its own right. Most contributors to the debate over it conclude that it is a bad theory, and although many of the criticisms can be answered, several cannot be, and it is those I shall focus on.

The first is that wealth maximization is inherently incomplete as a guide to social action because it has nothing to say about the distribution of rights—or at least nothing we want to hear. Given the distribution of rights (whatever it is), wealth maximization can be used to derive the policies that will maximize the value of those rights. But this does not go far enough, because naturally we are curious about whether it would be just to start off with a society in which, say, one member owned all the others. If wealth maximization is indifferent to the initial distribution of rights, it is a truncated concept of justice.

Since the initial distribution may dissipate rapidly, this point may have little practical significance. Nor is wealth maximization completely silent on the initial distribution. If we could compare two otherwise identical nascent societies, in one of which one person owned all the others and in the other of which slavery was forbidden, and could repeat the comparison a century later, almost certainly we would find that the second society was wealthier and the first had abolished slavery (if so, this would further illustrate the limited effect of the initial distribution on the current distribution). Although it has not always and everywhere been true, under modern conditions of production slavery is an inefficient method of organizing production. The extensive use of slave labor by Nazis during World War II may seem an exception—but only if we disregard the welfare of the slave laborers.

This response to the demand that wealth maximization tell us something about the justice of the initial distribution of rights is incomplete. Suppose it were the case—it almost surely *is* the case—that some people in modern American society would be more productive as slaves than as free persons. These are not antisocial people whom we want to punish by imprisoning (a form of slavery that is tolerated); they are not psychotic or profoundly retarded; they just are lazy, feckless, poorly organized, undisciplined people— people incompetent to manage their own lives in a way that will maximize their output, even though the relevant output is not market output alone but also leisure, family associations, and any other sources of satisfaction to these people as well as to others. Wealth would be maximized by enslaving these people, provided the costs of supervision were not too high—but the assumption that they would not be too high is built into the proposition that their output would be greater as slaves than as free persons, for it is net output that we are interested in. Yet no one thinks it would be right to enslave such people, even if there

were no evidentiary problems in identifying them, the slave masters could be trusted to be benign, and so on; and these conditions, too, may be implicit in the proposition that the net social output of some people would be greater if they were slaves.

It is no answer that it would be inefficient to enslave such people unless they consented to be enslaved, that is, unless the would-be slave master met the asking price for their freedom. The term *"their freedom"* assumes they have the property right in their persons, and the assumption is arbitrary. We can imagine assigning the property rights in persons (perhaps only persons who appeared likely to be unproductive) to the state to auction them to the highest bidder. The putative slave could bid against the putative master, but would lose. His expected earnings, net of consumption, would be smaller than the expected profits to the master; otherwise enslavement would not be efficient. Therefore he could not borrow enough—even if capital markets worked without any friction (in the present setting, even if the lender could enslave the borrower if the latter defaulted!)—to outbid his master-to-be.

This example points to a deeper criticism of wealth maximization as a norm or value: like utilitarianism, which it closely resembles, or nationalism, or Social Darwinism, or racialism, or organic theories of the state, it treats people as if they were the cells of a single organism; the welfare of the cell is important only insofar as it promotes the welfare of the organism. Wealth maximization implies that if the prosperity of the society can be promoted by enslaving its least productive citizens, the sacrifice of their freedom is worthwhile. But this implication is contrary to the unshakable moral intuitions of Americans, and . . . conformity to intuition is the ultimate test of a moral (indeed of any) theory.

[We can] provide illustrations of collisions between, on the one hand, moral intuitions that have been influential in law and, on the other hand, wealth maximization. Recall, first, that the idea of corrective justice may well include the proposition that people who are wronged are entitled to some form of redress, even in cases when from an aggregate social standpoint it might be best to let bygones be bygones. Such an idea has no standing in a system powered by wealth maximization. Second, the . . . lawfulness of confessions in a system single-mindedly devoted to wealth maximization would depend entirely on the costs and benefits of the various forms of coercion, which range from outright torture to the relatively mild psychological pressures that our legal system tolerates. Cost-benefit analysis might show that torture was rarely cost-effective under modern conditions, being a costly method of interrogation (especially for the victim, but perhaps also for the torturer) that is apt to produce a lot of false leads and unreliable confessions. Nevertheless, even the most degrading forms of torture would not *necessarily* be ruled out, even in the investigation of ordinary crimes. . . . [C]ost-benefit thinking has made inroads into coerced-confession law, but at some point these inroads would collide with, and be stopped by, strong moral intuitions that seem incompatible with economic thinking.

Or suppose it were the case—it may be the case—that some religious faiths are particularly effective in producing law-abiding, productive, healthy citizens. Mormonism is a plausible example. Would it not make sense on purely secular grounds, indeed on purely wealth-maximizing grounds, for government to subsidize these faiths? Practitioners of other religious faiths would be greatly offended, but from the standpoint of wealth maximization the only question would be whether the cost to them was greater than the benefits to the country as a whole.

Consider now a faith that both has few adherents in the United States and is feared or despised by the rest of the population. (The Rastafarian faith is a plausible example.) Such a faith will by assumption be imposing costs on the rest of the community, and given the fewness of its adherents, the benefits conferred by the faith may, even when aggregated across all its adherents, be smaller than the costs. It could then be argued that wealth maximization warranted or even required the suppression of the faith. This example suggests another objection to wealth maximization, one alluded to in the discussion of slavery: its results are sensitive to assumptions about the initial distribution of rights—a distribution that is distinct from the initial distribution of wealth (which is unlikely to remain stable over time), but about which wealth maximization may again have relatively little to say. If Rastafarians are conceived to have a property right in their religion, so that the state or anyone else who wants to acquire that right and suppress the religion must meet their asking-price, probably the right will not be sold. Asking prices can be very high—in principle, infinite: how much would the average person sell his life for, if the sale had to be completed immediately? But if rights over religious practices are given to the part of the populace that is not Rastafarian, the Rastafarians may find it impossible to buy the

right back; their offer price will be limited to their net wealth, which may be slight.

No doubt in this country, in this day and age, religious liberty is the cost-justified policy. The broader point is that a system of rights—perhaps the system we have—may well be required by a *realistic* conception of utilitarianism, that is, one that understands that given the realities of human nature a society dedicated to utilitarianism requires rules and institutions that place checks on utility-maximizing behavior in particular cases. For example, although one can imagine specific cases in which deliberately punishing an innocent person as a criminal would increase aggregate utility, one has trouble imagining a system in which government officials could be trusted to make such decisions. "Wealth maximizing" can be substituted for "utilitarian" without affecting the analysis. Religious liberty may well be both utility maximizing and wealth maximization, and this may even be why we have it. And if it became *too* costly, probably it would be abandoned; and so with the prohibition of torture, and the other civilized political amenities of a wealthy society. If our crime rate were much lower than it is, we probably would not have capital punishment— and if it gets much higher, we surely will have fewer civil liberties.

But at least in the present relatively comfortable conditions of our society, the regard for individual freedom appears to transcend instrumental considerations; freedom appears to be valued for itself rather than just for its contribution to prosperity—or at least to be valued for reasons that escape the economic calculus. Is society really better off in a utilitarian or wealth-maximizing sense as a result of the extraordinarily elaborate procedural safeguards that the Bill of Rights gives criminal defendants? This is by no means clear. Are minority rights welfare maximizing—when the minority in question is a small one? That is not clear either, as the Rastafarian example showed. The main reasons these institutions are valued seem not to be utilitarian or even instrumental in character. *What* those reasons are is far from clear; indeed, "noninstrumental reason" is almost an oxymoron. And as I have suggested, we surely are not willing to pay an infinite price, perhaps not even a very high price, for freedom. While reprobating slavery we condone similar (but more efficient) practices under different names— imprisonment as punishment for crime, preventive detention, the authority of parents and school authorities over children, conscription, the institutionalization of the insane and the retarded. The Thirteenth

Amendment has been read narrowly. Although the only stated exception is for punishment for crime ("neither slavery nor involuntary servitude, except as a punishment for crime whereof the party shall have been duly convicted, shall exist within the United States, or any place subject to their jurisdiction"), laws requiring jury service, military service, and even working on the public roads have been upheld. We reprobate the infliction of physical pain as a method of extracting confessions or imposing punishment but, perhaps in unconscious tribute to the outmoded dualism of mind and body, condone the infliction of mental pain for the same purposes.

Still, hypocritical and incoherent as our political ethics may frequently be, we do not permit degrading invasions of individual autonomy merely on a judgment that, on balance, the invasion would make a net addition to the social wealth. And whatever the philosophical grounding of this sentiment, it is too deeply entrenched in our society at present for wealth maximization to be given a free rein. The same may be true of the residue of corrective-justice sentiment.

I have said nothing about the conflict between wealth maximization and equality of wealth, because I am less sure of the extent of egalitarian sentiment in our society than that of individualistic sentiment (by "individualism" I mean simply the rivals to aggregative philosophies, such as utilitarianism and wealth maximization). Conflict there is, however, and it points to another important criticism of wealth maximization even if the critic is not an egalitarian. Imagine that a limited supply of growth hormone, privately manufactured and sold, must be allocated. A wealthy parent wants the hormone so that his child of average height will grow tall; a poor parent wants the hormone so that his child of dwarfish height can grow to normal height. In a system of wealth maximization the wealthy parent might outbid the poor parent and get the hormone. This is not certain. Amount of wealth is only one factor in willingness to pay. The poor parent might offer his entire wealth for the hormone, and that wealth, although meager, might exceed the amount of money the wealthy parent was willing to pay, given alternative uses to which he could put his money. Also, altruists might help the poor parent bid more than he could with only his own resources. The poor might actually be better off in a system in which the distribution of the hormone were left to the private market, even if there were no altruism. Such a system would create incentives to produce and sell the hormone sooner, and perhaps at a lower price, than if the government controlled its distribution; for the costs of production would probably be lower under private rather than public production, and even a monopolist will charge less when his costs fall.

But what seems impossible to maintain convincingly in the present ethical climate is that the wealthy parent has the *right* to the hormone by virtue of being willing to pay the supplier more than the poor parent can; more broadly, that consumers have a right to purchase in free markets. These propositions cannot be derived from wealth maximization. Indeed, they look like propositions about transactional freedom rather than about distribution only because I have assumed that the growth hormone is produced and distributed exclusively through the free market. An alternative possibility would be for the state to own the property right in the hormone and to allocate it on the basis of need rather than willingness to pay. To argue against this alternative (socialist medicine writ small) would require an appeal either to the deeply controversial idea of a natural right to private property, or to purely instrumental considerations, such as the possibility that in the long run the poor will be better off with a free market in growth hormone—but to put the question *this* way is to assume that the poor have some sort of social claim by virtue of being poor, and thus to admit the relevance of egalitarian considerations and thereby break out of the limits of wealth maximization.

A stronger-seeming argument for the free-enterprise solution is that the inventor of the hormone should have a right to use it as he wishes, which includes the right to sell it to the highest bidder. But this argument seems stronger only because we are inclined to suppose that what has happened is that *after* the inventor invented it the government decided to rob him of the reward for which he had labored. If instead we assume that Congress passes a law in 1989 which provides that after the year 2000 the right to patent new drugs will be conditioned on the patentee's agreeing to limit the price he charges, we shall have difficulty objecting to the law on ethical, as distinct from practical, grounds. It would be just one more restriction on free markets.

. . . [A] quest for a natural-rights theory of justice is unlikely to succeed. Although the advocate of wealth maximization can argue that to the productive should belong the fruits of their labor, the argument can be countered along the lines . . . that . . . production is really a social rather than individual effort—to which it can be added that wealth may often be due more to luck (and not the luck of the genetic lottery, either) than to skill or effort. Furthermore, if altruism is so greatly admired, as it is by conservatives as well as by liberals, why should not its spirit inform legislation? Why should government protect only our selfish instincts? To this it can be replied that the spirit of altruism is voluntary giving. But the reply is weak. The biggest reason we value altruism is that we *desire* some redistribution—we may admire the altruist for his self-sacrifice but we would not admire him as much if he destroyed his wealth rather than giving it to others—and we think that voluntary redistribution is less costly than involuntary. If redistribution is desirable, some involuntary redistribution may be justifiable, depending on the costs, of course, but not on the principle of the thing.

There is a still deeper problem with founding wealth maximization on a notion of natural rights. The economic perspective is thoroughly (and fruitfully) behaviorist. "Economic man" is not, as vulgarly supposed, a person driven by purely pecuniary incentives, but he is a person whose behavior is completely determined by incentives; his rationality is no different from that of a pigeon or a rat. The economic task from the perspective of wealth maximization is to influence his incentives so as to maximize his output. How a person so conceived could be thought to have a *moral* entitlement to a particular distribution of the world's goods—an entitlement, say, to the share proportional to his contribution to the world's wealth—is unclear. Have marmots moral entitlements? Two levels of discourse are being mixed.

By questioning anti-egalitarian arguments I do not mean to be endorsing egalitarian ones. . . . The egalitarian is apt to say that differences in intelligence, which often translate into differences in productivity, are the result of a natural lottery and therefore ought not guide entitlements. But if differences in intelligence are indeed genetic, as the argument assumes, then liberal and radical arguments about the exploitiveness of capitalist society are undermined. A genetic basis for intellectual differences and resulting differences in productivity implies that inequality in the distribution of income and wealth is to a substantial degree natural (which is not to say that it is morally good), rather than a product of unjust social and political institutions. It also implies that such inequality is apt to be strongly resistant to social and political efforts to change it.

The strongest argument for wealth maximization is not moral, but pragmatic. Such classic defenses of the free market as chapter 4 of Mill's *On Liberty* can easily be given a pragmatic reading. We look around the world and see that in general people who live in societies in which markets are allowed to function more or less freely not only are wealthier than people in other societies but have more political rights, more liberty and dignity, are more content (as evidenced, for example, by their being less prone to emigrate)—so that wealth maximization may be the most direct route to a variety of moral ends. The recent history of England, France, and Turkey, of Japan and Southeast Asia, of East versus West Germany and North versus South Korea, of China and Taiwan, of Chile, of the Soviet Union, Poland, and Hungary, and of Cuba and Argentina provides striking support for this thesis.

Writing in the early 1970s, the English political philosopher Brian Barry doubted the importance of incentives. "My own guess," he said, "is that enough people with professional and managerial jobs really like them (and enough others who would enjoy them and have sufficient ability to do them are waiting to replace those who do not) to enable the pay of these jobs to be brought down considerably. . . . I would suggest that the pay levels in Britain of schoolteachers and social workers seem to offer net rewards which recruit and maintain just enough people, and that this provides a guideline to the pay levels that could be sustained generally among professionals and managers." He rejected the "assumption that a sufficient supply of highly educated people will be forthcoming only if lured by the anticipation of a higher income afterwards as a result," adding that "it would also be rash to assume that it would be an economic loss if fewer sought higher education." He discussed with approval the Swedish experiment at redistributing income and wealth but thought it hampered by the fact that "Sweden still has a privately owned economy." He worried about "brain drain" but concluded that it was a serious problem only with regard to airline pilots and physicians; and a nation can do without airlines and may be able to replace general practitioners "with people having a lower (and less marketable) qualification." (Yet Barry himself was soon to join the brain drain, and he is neither a physician nor an airline pilot.) He proposed "to spread the nastiest jobs around by requiring everyone, before entering higher education or entering a profession, to do, say, three years of work wherever he or she was directed. (This would also have educational advantages.) To supplement this there could be a call-up of say a month every year, as with the Swiss and Israeli armed forces but directed towards peaceful occupations."

At least with the benefit of hindsight we can see that Barry wrote a prescription for economic disaster. It may be impossible to lay solid philosophical foundations under wealth maximization, just as it may be impossible to lay solid philosophical foundations under the natural sciences, but this would be a poor reason for abandoning wealth maximization, just as the existence of intractable problems in the philosophy of science would be a poor reason for abandoning science. We have reason to believe that markets work— that capitalism delivers the goods, if not the Good—and

it would be a mistake to allow philosophy to deflect us from the implications. . . .

A sensible pragmatism does not ignore theory. The mounting evidence that capitalism is more efficient than socialism gives us an additional reason for believing economic theory (not every application of it, to be sure). The theory in turn gives us greater confidence in the evidence. Theory and evidence are mutually supporting. From the perspective of economic theory, brain drain is not the mysterious disease that Barry supposes it to be; it is the rational response to leveling policies by those whose incomes are being leveled downward.

The Pragmatist and the Feminist

Margaret Jane Radin

I want to discuss pragmatism and feminism. I undertake this project not because I have read everything considered feminist or pragmatist by its writers or readers, although I wish I had, but rather because I have discovered that in my own work I am speaking both of pragmatism and feminism. I desire to explore how pragmatism and feminism cohere, if they do, in my own thought, and I write with the hope that what I find useful will be useful for others as well. . . .

I. The Double Bind

I begin at the point it became clear to me that I was combining pragmatism and feminism. That point was in my thinking about the transition problem of the double bind in the context of contested commodification of sexuality and reproductive capacity. If the social regime permits buying and selling of sexual and reproductive activities, thereby treating them as fungible market commodities given the current capi-

From Margaret Jane Radin, "The Pragmatist and the Feminist," *Southern California Law Review*, Vol. 63 (1990), pp. 1699–1711. Reprinted with the permission of the *Southern California Law Review*.

talistic understandings of monetary exchange, there is a threat to the personhood of women, who are the "owners" of these "commodities." The threat to personhood from commodification arises because essential attributes are treated as severable fungible objects, and this denies the integrity and uniqueness of the self. But if the social regime prohibits this kind of commodification, it denies women the choice to market their sexual or reproductive services, and given the current feminization of poverty and lack of avenues for free choice for women, this also poses a threat to the personhood of women. The threat from enforced noncommodification arises because narrowing women's choices is a threat to liberation, and because their choices to market sexual or reproductive services, even if nonideal, may represent the best alternatives available to those who would choose them.

Thus the double bind: both commodification and noncommodification may be harmful. Harmful, that is, under our current social conditions. Neither one need be harmful in an ideal world. The fact that money changes hands need not necessarily contaminate human interactions of sharing, nor must the fact that a social order makes nonmonetary sharing its norm necessarily deprive or subordinate anyone. That commodification now tends toward fungibility of women and noncommodification now tends toward their domination and continued subordination are artifacts of the current social hierarchy. In other words, the fact of oppression is what gives rise to the double bind.

Thus, it appears that the solution to the double bind is not to solve but to dissolve it: remove the oppressive circumstances. But in the meantime, if we are practically limited to those two choices, which are we to choose? I think that the answer must be pragmatic. We must look carefully at the nonideal circumstances in each case and decide which horn of the dilemma is better (or less bad), and we must keep redeciding as time goes on.

To generalize a bit, it seems that there are two ways to think about justice. One is to think about justice in an ideal world, the best world that we can now conceive. The other is to think about nonideal justice: given where we now find ourselves, what is the better decision? In making this decision, we think about what actions can bring us closer to ideal justice. For example, if we allow commodification, we may push further away any ideal of a less commodified future. But if we enforce noncommodification, we may push further away any ideal of a less dominated future. In making our decisions of nonideal justice, we must also realize that these decisions will help to reconstitute our ideals. For example, if we commodify all attributes of personhood, the ideal of personhood we now know will evolve into another one that does not conceive fungibility as bad. The double bind, then, is a problem involving nonideal justice, and I think its only solution can be pragmatic. There is no general solution; there are only piecemeal, temporary solutions.

I also think of the double bind as a problem of transition, because I think of nonideal justice as the process by which we try to make progress (effect a transition) toward our vision of the good world. I think we should recognize that all decisions about justice, as opposed to theories about it, are pragmatic decisions in the transition. At the same time we should also recognize that ideal theory is also necessary, because we need to know what we are trying to achieve. In other words, our visions and nonideal decisions, our theory and practice, paradoxically constitute each other.

Having discovered the double bind in true pragmatic fashion, by working on a specific problem, I now see it everywhere. The double bind is pervasive in the issues we have thought of as "women's issues." The reason it is pervasive is to be sought in the perspective of oppression. For a group subject to structures of domination, all roads thought to be progressive can pack a backlash. I shall mention here a few other examples of the double bind: the special treatment/equal treatment debate, affirmative action, the understanding of rape, and the idea of marriage as a contract.

When we single out pregnancy, for example, for "special treatment," we fear that employers will not hire women. But if we do not accord special treatment to pregnancy, women will lose their jobs. If we grant special treatment, we bring back the bad old conception of women as weaker creatures; if we do not, we prevent women from becoming stronger in the practical world. Feminist theory that tends toward the ideal, the visionary side of our thought about justice, has grasped the point that the dilemma must be dissolved because its framework is the conceptual framework of the oppressors (who define what is "special" and what is "equal"). But feminist theory that tends toward the nonideal practical side of our thought about justice has also realized that if the dominant conceptions are too deeply held at this time, trying to implement an alternative vision could be counterproductive. My personal view is that in the case of pregnancy, the time has come to convince everyone that both men and women should have the opportunity to be parents in a fulfilling sense, and that the old conceptions of the workplace now can begin to give way. But I think that each women's issue situation, such as pregnancy, workplace regulation to protect fetuses, and height and weight restrictions, will have to be evaluated separately, and continually reevaluated.

If there is a social commitment to affirmative action, in this nonideal time and place, then a woman or person of color who holds a job formerly closed to women and people of color is likely to be presumed to be underqualified. More women and people of color will hold jobs, but few will be allowed to feel good about it. The dominant group will probably be able to make women and people of color meet higher standards than those applicable to white males, and yet at the same time convince everyone, including, often, the beneficiaries of affirmative action themselves, that as beneficiaries they are inferior. But what is our alternative? If there is no affirmative action commitment in place, far fewer women and people of color will hold these jobs; yet those who do, whatever vicissitudes they endure, will not endure this particular backlash. The pragmatic answer in most cases, I believe, is that backlash is better than complete exclusion, as long as the backlash is temporary. But if backlash can keep alive the bad old conceptions of women and people of color, how will we evolve toward better conceptions of the abilities of those who have been excluded?

Our struggle with how to understand rape seems to be another instance of the double bind. MacKinnon's view—or perhaps an oversimplified version of her view—is that under current conditions of gender hierarchy there is no clear dividing line between the sort of heterosexual intercourse that is genuinely desired by women and the sort that is unwelcome. There can be no clear line because our very conception of sexuality is so deeply intertwined with male dominance that our desires as we experience them are problematic. Our own desires are socially constituted to reinforce patterns of male dominance against our own interest.[1] "Just say no" as the standard for determining whether rape has occurred is both under- and overinclusive. It is under-inclusive because women who haven't found their voices mean "no" and are unable to say it; and it is over-inclusive because, like it or not, the way sexuality has been constituted in a culture of male dominance, the male understanding that "no" means "yes" was often, and may still sometimes be, correct. MacKinnon's view is painful. If there is no space for women to experience heterosexuality that is not suspect, what does that do to our self-esteem and personhood in a social setting in which sex is important to selfhood?

The other prong of the double bind—roughly represented by the views of Robin West—is that we should greet all of women's subjective experience with acceptance and respect.[2] That view is less threatening to personhood in one way but more so in another. How can we progress toward a social conception of sexuality that is less male-dominated if we do not regard with critical suspicion some of the male-dominated experiences we now take pleasure in?

The last example of the double bind I want to mention is the conceptualization of marriage. Is marriage to be considered a contract in which certain distributions of goods are agreed to between autonomous bargaining agents? Upon divorce, such a conception of marriage makes it difficult for oppressed women who have not bargained effectively to obtain much. Or is marriage to be considered a noncontractual sharing status in which the partners' contributions are not to be monetized? Upon divorce, such a conception makes it difficult for oppressed women who have contributed unmonetized services to their husbands' advantage to obtain much. The idea of contractual autonomy may be more attractive in our nonideal world if the alternative is to be submerged in a status that gives all power to men. Yet the autonomy may be

illusory because oppression makes equal bargaining power impossible. At the same time, the reinforcement of individualist bargaining models of human interaction is contrary to our vision of a better world and may alter that vision in a way we do not wish.

Perhaps it is obvious that the reason the double bind recurs throughout feminist struggles is that it is an artifact of the dominant social conception of the meaning of gender. The double bind is a series of two-pronged dilemmas in which both prongs are, or can be, losers for the oppressed. Once we realize this, we may say it is equally obvious that the way out of the double bind is to dissolve these dilemmas by changing the framework that creates them. That is, we must dissolve the prevalent conception of gender.

Calling for dissolution of the prevalent conception of gender is the visionary half of the problem: we must create a new vision of the meaning of male and female in order to change the dominant social conception of gender and change the double bind. In order to do that, however, we need the social empowerment that the dominant social conception of gender keeps us from achieving.

Then how can we make progress? The other half of the problem is the nonideal problem of transition from the present situation toward our ideal. Here is where the pragmatist feminist comes into her own. The pragmatist solution is to confront each dilemma separately and choose the alternative that will hinder empowerment the least and further it the most. The pragmatist feminist need not seek a general solution that will dictate how to resolve all double bind issues. Appropriate solutions may all differ, depending on the current stage of women's empowerment, and how the proposed solution might move the current social conception of gender and our vision of how gender should be reconceived for the future. Indeed, the "same" double bind may demand a different solution tomorrow from the one we find best today.

II. The Perspective of Domination and the Problem of Bad Coherence

. . .

Over the past few years I have been continually struck with some points of resonance between the methodology and commitments of many who call themselves feminists and those of certain important figures in the new wave of pragmatism. It now seems to me that the points of resonance between feminism and pragmatism are worthy of some exploration.

I begin with an awareness that there is something problematic about my ambition to talk theoretically about pragmatism and feminism together. I want to avoid the type of exercise that tries to define two "isms" and then compare and contrast them. Insomuch as they are lively, these "isms" resist definition. There are a number of pragmatisms. At least there are distinctive strains stemming from Charles Sanders Peirce, William James, and John Dewey, and the new wave may be considered a fourth pragmatism. There are also a number of feminisms. One recent survey of feminist thought lists them as liberal, Marxist, radical, socialist, psychoanalytic, existentialist, and postmodern.[3]

One way to frame the investigation I have in mind would be to start with the question, Is feminism "really" pragmatism? (Or, is pragmatism "really" feminism?) If this is the question, one way to respond to it—a way I think would be both unpragmatic and unfeminist—is to ask what commitments or characteristics are common to all the pragmatisms we are certain are pragmatisms, and ask what commitments or characteristics are common to all the feminisms we are certain are feminisms. We would then see whether the feminist list includes both the necessary criteria for being pragmatist and enough or important enough criteria to be sufficient for being pragmatist, or whether the pragmatist list includes the necessary and sufficient criteria for being feminist. This definitional response is a blueprint of conceptualist methodology, an abstract exercise in reification that promises little of interest to a pragmatist or a feminist.

In a more pragmatic and feminist spirit of inquiry, we might ask instead another question. Of what use might it be to think of feminism and pragmatism as allied, as interpenetrating each other? In this . . . essay I will pursue this question in various ways. In order to do so I still have to engage in some problematic cataloguing, but at least it will be easier to deal with the inescapable incompleteness of that way of seeing matters. I can explore how in some ways it might be useful to consider pragmatism and feminism together, without having to have a definite answer to the (to a pragmatist inapposite) question of what pragmatism and feminism "really are." Feminism and pragmatism are not things; they are ways of proceeding. The pragmatists were famous for their theory of truth without the capital T—their theory that truth is inevitably plural, concrete, and provisional. John Dewey wrote, "Truth is a collection of truths; and these constituent truths are in the keeping of the best available methods of inquiry and testing as to matters of fact."[4] Similarly, William James wrote:

Truth for us is simply a collective name for verification processes, just as health, wealth, strength, etc., are names for other processes connected with life, and also pursued because it pays to pursue them. Truth is *made*, just as health, wealth and strength are made, in the course of experience.[5]

Pragmatism and feminism largely share, I think, the commitment to finding knowledge in the particulars of experience. It is a commitment against abstract idealism, transcendence, foundationalism, and a temporal universality; and in favor of immanence, historicity, concreteness, situatedness, contextuality, embeddedness, narrativity of meaning.

If feminists largely share the pragmatist commitment that truth is hammered out piecemeal in the crucible of life and our situatedness, they also share the pragmatist understanding that truth is provisional and ever-changing. Too, they also share the pragmatist commitment to concrete particulars. Since the details of our life are connected with what we know, those details matter. Thus, the pragmatist and the feminist both arrive at an embodied perspectivist view of knowledge.

It is not surprising that pragmatists have stressed embodiment more than other philosophers, nor that feminists have stressed it even more. Once we understand that the details of our embodiment matter for what the world is for us (which in some pragmatist views is all the world is), then it must indeed be important that only one half of humans directly experience menstruation, pregnancy, birth, and lactation. So it is no wonder that feminists write about prostitution, contract motherhood, rape, child care, and the PMS defense. It is not just the fact that these are women's issues that makes these writings feminist—they are after all human issues—but specifically the instantiation of the perspective of female embodiment.

Another pragmatist commitment that is largely shared by feminists is the dissolution of traditional dichotomies. Pragmatists and feminists have rejected the dichotomy between thought and action, or between theory and practice. John Dewey especially made this his theme; and he also rejected the dichotomies of reason and feeling, mind and body, nature and nurture, connection and separation, and means and ends. In a commitment that is not, at least not yet, shared by modern pragmatists, feminists have also largely rejected the traditional dichotomy of public (man) and private (woman). For these feminists, the personal is political.

One more strong resonance between the pragmatist and the feminist is in concrete methodology. The feminist commitment to learning through consciousness raising in groups can be regarded as the culmination of the pragmatist understanding that, for consciousness to exist at all, there must be shared meaning arising out of shared interactions with the world. A particularly clear statement of this pragmatist position is found in Dewey's *Experience and Nature.* Dewey's treatment is suffused with the interrelationship of communication, meaning, and shared group experience. In one representative passage, Dewey says:

> The heart of language is not "expression" of something antecedent, much less expression of antecedent thought. It is communication; the establishment of cooperation in an activity in which there are partners, and in which the activity of each is modified and regulated by that partnership.[6]

The modern pragmatists' stress on conversation or dialogue stems from the same kind of understanding.

The special contribution of the methodology of consciousness raising is that it makes new meaning out of a specific type of experience, the experience of domination and oppression. In order to do so, it must make communication possible where before there was silence. In general, rootedness in the experiences of oppression makes possible the distinctive critical contribution that feminism can make to pragmatism. Feminist methodology and perspective make it possible to confront the problem of bad coherence, as I will now try to explain.

Pragmatists have tended toward coherence theories of truth and goodness. Coherence theories tend toward conservativism, in the sense that when we are faced with new experiences and new beliefs, we fit them into our web with as little alteration of what is already there as possible. James said that "in this matter of belief we are all extreme conservatives."[7] According to James, we will count a new idea as true if we can use it to assimilate a new experience to our old beliefs without disturbing them too much.

> That new idea is truest which performs most felicitously its function of satisfying our double urgency. It makes itself true, gets itself classed as true, by the way it works; grafting itself then upon the ancient body of truth, which thus grows much as a tree grows by the activity of a new layer of cambium.[8]

James also said that truth is what is good in the way of belief, meaning that we should, and do, believe those things that work best in our lives.

To those whose standpoint or perspective—whose embodied contextuality—is the narrative of domination and oppression, these coherence theories raise a question that is very hard for the pragmatist to answer. Is it possible to have a coherent system of belief, and have that system be coherently bad? Those who have lived under sexism and racism know from experience that the answer must be yes. We know we cannot argue that any given sexist decision is wrong simply because it does not fit well with all our history and institutions, for the problem is more likely that it fits only too well. Bad coherence creates the double bind. Everywhere we look we find a dominant conception of gender undermining us.

But how can the pragmatist find a standpoint from which to argue that a system is coherent but bad, if pragmatism defines truth and good as coherence? Inattention to this problem is what makes pragmatism seem complacent, when it does. One answer to the problem of bad coherence, which the pragmatist will reject, is to bring back transcendence, natural law, or abstract idealism. Another answer, which the pragmatist can accept, is to take the commitment to embodied perspective very seriously indeed, and especially the commitment to the perspective of those who directly experience domination and oppression.

What this leads to, first, is either an expansive view of coherence that leaves room for broad critique of the dominant understandings and the status quo, or else, perhaps, to denial that pragmatism espouses coherence theory. Its other consequences need exploring. It seems that a primary concomitant of the commitment to perspectivism might be a serious pluralism. "We" are looking for coherence in "our" commitments, but the most important question might be, Who is "we"? A serious pluralism might begin by understanding that there can be more than one "we." One "we" can have very different conceptions of the world, selves, communities, than another. Perhaps, at least practically speaking, each "we" can have its own coherence. Dominant groups have tended to understand themselves without question as the only "we," whereas oppressed groups, simply by virtue of recognizing themselves as an oppressed group, have understood that there can be plural "we's." Perhaps, then, we should understand the perspective of the oppressed as making possible an understanding that coherence can be plural.

A serious pluralism must also find a way to understand the problem of transition, as the "we" of an oppressed group seeks to change dominant conceptions in order to make possible its own empowerment. One important problem of transition is false consciousness. If the perspective of the oppressed includes significant portions of the dominant conception of the world, and of the role of the oppressed group in it, then the oppressed perspective may well be incoherent, rather than a separate coherence to be recognized as a separate "reality." If this is a useful way to view the matter, then we can say that the perspective of the oppressed struggles to make itself coherent in order to make itself real.

What leads some pragmatists into complacency and over-respect for the status quo is partly the failure to ask, Who is "we"? And what are "our" material interests? Why does it "work" for "us" to believe this? It is not necessary for pragmatists to make this mistake. Dewey, especially, understood the connection between truth, goodness, and liberation. He argued cogently that many of philosophy's earlier errors, such as belief in eternal abstract forms, were expressions of the social position of philosophers as an elite leisure class. But the mistake is tempting for a pragmatist whose perspective is that of a member of the dominant group, because from that perspective it seems that one has "the" perspective. I suggest that feminism, in its pragmatic aspect, can correct this complacent tendency. The perspective of domination, and the critical ramifications it must produce once it is taken seriously, seem to be feminism's important contribution to pragmatism.

. . .

Endnotes

[1] MacKinnon, "Feminism, Marxism, Method, and the State," 533–542; MacKinnon, *Feminism Unmodified*, 85–92.

[2] See Robin West, "The Difference in Women's Hedonic Lives," *Wisconsin Women's Law Journal*, Vol. 3 (1987): 81–145.

[3] Rosemarie Tong, *Feminist Thought: A Comprehensive Introduction* (Boulder, Colo: Westview Press, 1989).

[4] John Dewey, *Experience and Nature*, 2nd ed. (New York: Dover, 1929), 410.

[5] William James, *Pragmatism*, ed. Fredson Bowers (Cambridge, Mass.: Harvard University Press, 1975), 104.

[6] Dewey, *Experience and Nature*, 179.

[7] William James, *Pragmatism*, 35.

[8] *Ibid.*, 36 and 104 (where James elaborates on how we choose what theories to class as true).

Race and Essentialism *in Feminist Legal Theory*

Angela P. Harris

In *Funes the Memorious*, Borges tells of Ireneo Funes, who was a rather ordinary young man (notable only for his precise sense of time) until the age of nineteen, when he was thrown by a half-tamed horse and left paralyzed but possessed of perfect perception and a perfect memory. . . .

From Angela Harris, "Race and Essentialism in Feminist Legal Theory," *Stanford Law Review*, vol. 42 (1990), pp. 581–584, 586–589, 591–592, 601–605, 608–616. Reprinted with permission of the *Stanford Law Review*.

Funes tells the narrator that after his transformation he invented his own numbering system. "In place of seven thousand thirteen, he would say (for example) Maximo Perez; in place of seven thousand fourteen, The Railroad; other numbers were Luis Melian Lafinur, Olimar, sulphur, the reins, the whale, the gas, the caldron, Napoleon, Agustin de Vedia." The narrator tries to explain to Funes "that this rhapsody of incoherent terms was precisely the opposite of a system of numbers. I told him that saying 365 meant saying three hundreds, six tens, five ones, an analysis which is not found in the 'numbers,' The Negro Timoteo or meat blanket. Funes did not understand me or refused to understand me."

In his conversation with Funes, the narrator realizes that Funes' life of infinite unique experiences leaves Funes no ability to categorize: "With no effort, he had learned English, French, Portuguese and Latin. I suspect, however, that he was not very capable of thought. To think is to forget differences, generalize, make abstractions. In the teeming world of Funes, there were only details, almost immediate in their presence." For Funes, language is only a unique and private system of classification, elegant and solipsistic. The notion that language, made abstract, can serve to create and reinforce a community is incomprehensible to him. . . .

Describing the voice that speaks the first sentence of the Declaration of Independence, James Boyd White remarks:

> It is not a person's voice, not even that of a committee, but the "unanimous" voice of "thirteen united States" and of their "people." It addresses a universal audience—nothing less than "mankind" itself, located neither in space nor in time—and the voice is universal too, for it purports to know about the "Course of human events" (all human events?) and to be able to discern what "becomes necessary" as a result of changing circumstances.

The Preamble of the United States Constitution, White argues, can also be heard to speak in this unified and universal voice. This voice claims to speak

> for an entire and united nation and to do so directly and personally, not in the third person or by merely delegated authority. . . . The instrument thus appears to issue from a single imaginary author, consisting of all the people of the United States, including the reader, merged into a single identity in this act of self-constitution. "The People" are at once the author and the audience of this instrument.

Despite its claims, however, this voice does not speak for everyone, but for a political faction trying to constitute itself as a unit of many disparate voices; its power lasts only as long as the contradictory voices remain silenced.

. . .

The metaphor of "voice" implies a speaker. I want to suggest, however, that both the voices I have described come from the same source, a source I term

"multiple consciousness." It is a premise of this article that we are not born with a "self," but rather are composed of a welter of partial, sometimes contradictory, or even antithetical "selves." A unified identity, if such can ever exist, is a product of will, not a common destiny or natural birthright. Thus, consciousness is "never fixed, never attained once and for all"; it is not a final outcome or a biological given, but a process, a constant contradictory state of becoming, in which both social institutions and individual wills are deeply implicated. A multiple consciousness is home both to the first and the second voices, and all the voices in between.

As I use the phrase, "multiple consciousness" as reflected in legal or literary discourse is not a golden mean or static equilibrium between two extremes, but rather a process in which propositions are constantly put forth, challenged, and subverted.

. . .

The need for multiple consciousness in feminist movement—a social movement encompassing law, literature, and everything in between—has long been apparent. Since the beginning of the feminist movement in the United States, black women have been arguing that their experience calls into question the notion of a unitary "women's experience." In the first wave of the feminist movement, black women's realization that the white leaders of the suffrage movement intended to take neither issues of racial oppression nor black women themselves seriously was instrumental in destroying or preventing political alliances between black and white women within the movement. In the second wave, black women are again speaking loudly and persistently, and at many levels our voices have begun to be heard. Feminists have adopted the notion of multiple consciousness as appropriate to describe a world in which people are not oppressed only or primarily on the basis of gender, but on the bases of race, class, sexual orientation, and other categories in inextricable webs. Moreover, multiple consciousness is implicit in the precepts of feminism itself. . . .

In feminist legal theory, however, the move away from univocal toward multivocal theories of women's experience and feminism has been slower than in other areas. In feminist legal theory, the pull of the second voice, the voice of abstract categorization, is still powerfully strong: "We the People" seems in danger of being replaced by "We the Women." And in feminist legal theory, as in the dominant culture, it is mostly white, straight, and socioeconomically privileged people who claim to speak for all of us. Not surprisingly, the story they tell about "women," despite its claim to universality, seems to black women to be peculiar to women who are white, straight, and socioeconomically privileged—a phenomenon Adrienne Rich terms "white solipsism."

. . .

The notion that there is a monolithic "women's experience" that can be described independent of other facets of experience like race, class, and sexual orientation is one I refer to in this essay as "gender essentialism." A corollary to gender essentialism is "racial essentialism"—the belief that there is a monolithic "Black Experience," or "Chicano Experience." The source of gender and racial essentialism (and all other essentialisms, for the list of categories could be infinitely multiplied) is the second voice, the voice that claims to speak for all. The result of essentialism is to reduce the lives of people who experience multiple forms of oppression to addition problems: "racism + sexism = straight black women's experience," or "racism + sexism + homophobia = black lesbian experience." Thus, in an essentialist world, black women's experience will always be forcibly fragmented before being subjected to analysis, as those who are "only interested in race" and those who are "only interested in gender" take their separate slices of our lives.

Moreover, feminist essentialism paves the way for unconscious racism.

In a racist society like this one, the storytellers are usually white, and so "woman" turns out to be "white woman."

Why, in the face of challenges from "different" women and from feminist method itself, is feminist essentialism so persistent and pervasive? I think the reasons are several. Essentialism is intellectually convenient, and to a certain extent cognitively ingrained. Essentialism also carries with it important emotional and political payoffs. Finally, essentialism often appears (especially to white women) as the only alternative to chaos, mindless pluralism (the Funes trap), and the end of the feminist movement. In my view, however, as long as feminists, like theorists in the dominant culture, continue to search for gender and racial essences, black women will never be anything more than a crossroads between two kinds of domination, or at the bottom of a hierarchy of oppressions; we will always be required to choose pieces of ourselves to present as wholeness.

Essentialism in feminist theory has two characteristics that ensure that black women's voices will be ignored. First, in the pursuit of the essential feminine, Woman leached of all color and irrelevant social circumstance, issues of race are bracketed as belonging to a separate and distinct discourse—a process which leaves black women's selves fragmented beyond recognition. Second, feminist essentialists find that in removing issues of "race" they have actually only managed to remove black women—meaning that white women now stand as the epitome of Woman. Both processes can be seen at work in dominance theory.

[The] essentialist approach recreates the paradigmatic woman in the image of the white woman, in the name of "unmodified feminism." As in the dominant discourse, black women are relegated to the margins, ignored or extolled as "just like us, only more so." But "Black women are not white women with color." Moreover, feminist essentialism represents not just an insult to black women, but a broken promise—the promise to listen to women's stories, the promise of feminist method.

. . .

[Robin] West argues that the biological and social implications of motherhood shape the selfhood of all, or at least most, women. This claim involves at least two assumptions. First, West assumes (as does the liberal social theory she criticizes) that everyone has a deep, unitary "self" that is relatively stable and unchanging. Second, West assumes that this "self" differs significantly between men and women but is the same for all women and for all men despite differences of class, race, and sexual orientation: that is, that this self is deeply and primarily gendered.

. . .

In this society, it is only white people who have the luxury of "having no color"; only white people have been able to imagine that sexism and racism are separate experiences. Far more for black women than for white women, the experience of self is precisely that of being unable to disentangle the web of race and gender—of being enmeshed always in multiple, often contradictory, discourses of sexuality and color. The challenge to black women has been the need to weave the fragments, our many selves, into an integral, though always changing and shifting, whole: a self that is neither "female" nor "black," but both-and. West's insistence that every self is deeply and primarily gendered, then, with its corollary that gender is more important to personal identity than race, is finally another example of white solipsism. By suggesting that gender is more deeply embedded in self than race, her theory privileges the experience of white people over all others, and thus serves to reproduce relations of domination in the larger culture.

. . .

In my view, there are at least three major contributions that black women have to offer post-essentialist feminist theory: the recognition of a self that is multiplicitous, not unitary; the recognition that differences are always relational rather than inherent; and the recognition that wholeness and commonality are acts of will and creativity, rather than passive discovery.

Black women experience not a single inner self (much less one that is essentially gendered), but many selves. This sense of a multiplicitous self is not unique to black women, but black women have expressed this sense in ways that are striking, poignant, and potentially useful to feminist theory.

A post-essentialist feminism can benefit not only from the abandonment of the quest for a unitary self, but also from Martha Minow's realization that difference—and therefore identity—is always relational, not inherent. Zora Neale Hurston's work is a good illustration of this notion.

In an essay written for a white audience, *How It Feels to Be Colored Me*, Hurston argues that her color is not an inherent part of her being, but a response to her surroundings. She recalls the day she "became colored"—the day she left her home in an all-black community to go to school: "I left Eatonville, the town of the oleanders, as Zora. When I disembarked from the river-boat at Jacksonville, she was no more. It seemed that I had suffered a sea change. I was not Zora of Orange County any more, I was now a little colored girl." But even as an adult, Hurston insists, her colored self is always situational: "I do not always feel colored. Even now I often achieve the unconscious Zora of Eatonville before the Hegira. I feel most colored when I am thrown against a sharp white background."

. . .

Thus, "how it feels to be colored Zora" depends on the answer to these questions: "Compared to what? As of when? Who is asking? In what context? For what purpose? With what interests and presuppositions?" What Hurston rigorously shows is that questions of difference and identity are always functions of a specific interlocutionary situation—and the answers, matters of strategy rather than truth." Any "essential self" is always an invention; the evil is in denying its artificiality.

To be compatible with this conception of the self, feminist theorizing about "women" must similarly be strategic and contingent, focusing on relationships, not essences. One result will be that men will cease to be a faceless Other and reappear as potential allies in political struggle. Another will be that women will be able to acknowledge their differences without threatening feminism itself. In the process, as feminists begin to attack racism and classism and homophobia, feminism will change from being only about "women as women" (modified women need not apply), to being about all kinds of oppression based on seemingly inherent and unalterable characteristics. We need not wait for a unified theory of oppression; that theory can be feminism.

. . .

Finally, black women can help feminist movement move beyond its fascination with essentialism through the recognition that wholeness of the self and commonality with others are asserted (if never completely achieved) through creative action, not realized in shared victimization.

. . .

[T]he recognition of the role of creativity and will in shaping our lives is liberating, for it allows us to acknowledge and celebrate the creativity and joy with which many women have survived and turned existing relations of domination to their own ends. Works of black literature like *Beloved*, *The Color Purple*, and *Song of Solomon*, among others, do not linger on black women's victimization and misery; though they recognize our pain, they ultimately celebrate our transcendence.

Finally, on a collective level this emphasis on will and creativity reminds us that bridges between women are built, not found. The discovery of shared suffering is a connection more illusory than real; what will truly bring and keep us together is the use of effort and imagination to root out and examine our differences, for only the recognition of women's differences can ultimately bring feminist movement to strength. This is hard work, and painful work; but it is also radical work, real work.

. . .

I have argued in this article that gender essentialism is dangerous to feminist legal theory because in the attempt to extract an essential female self and voice from the diversity of women's experience, the experiences of women perceived as "different" are ignored or treated as variations on the (white) norm. Now I want to return to an earlier point: that legal theory, including feminist legal theory, has been entranced for too long and to too great an extent by the voice of "We the People." In order to energize legal theory, we need to subvert it with narratives and stories, accounts of the particular, the different, and the hitherto silenced.

Whether by chance or not, many of the legal theorists telling stories these days are women of color. Mari Matsuda calls for "multiple consciousness as jurisprudential method"; Patricia Williams shows the way with her multilayered stories and meditations. These writings are healthy for feminist legal theory as well as legal theory more generally. In acknowledging "the complexity of messages implied in our being," they begin the task of energizing legal theory with the creative struggle between Funes and We the People: the creative struggle that reflects a multiple consciousness.

Hallmark Critical Race Theory Themes

Richard Delgado and Jean Stefancic

Imagine that a pair of businessmen pass a beggar on a busy downtown street. One says something disparaging about "those bums always sticking their hands out—I wish they would get a job." His friend takes him to task for his display of classism. He explains that the street person may have overheard the remark and had his feelings hurt. He points out that we must all strive to purge ourselves of racism, classism, and sexism, that thoughts have consequences, and that how you speak makes a difference. The first businessman mutters something about political correctness and makes a mental note not to let his true feelings show in front of his friend again.

Or, imagine that a task force of highly advanced extraterrestrials lands on earth and approaches the nearest human being they can find, who happens to be a street person relaxing on a park bench. They offer him any one of three magic potions. The first is a pill that will rid the world of sexism—demeaning, misogynist attitudes toward women. The second is a pill that will cure racism; the third, one that will cure classism—negative attitudes toward those of lower socioeconomic station than oneself. Introduced into the planet's water system, each pill will cure one of the three scourges effectively and permanently. The street person, of course, chooses classism and throws pill number three into a nearby water department reservoir.

Will the lives of poor people like him improve very much the next day? No. Passersby may be somewhat kinder, may smile at them more often, but if something inherent in the nature of our capitalist system ineluctably produces poverty and class segregation, that system will continue to create and chew up victims. Individual street people may feel better, but they will still be street people. And the free enterprise system, which is built on the idea of winners and losers, will continue to produce new ones every day.

What about racism? Suppose a magic pill were invented, or perhaps an enterprising entrepreneur developed The Ultimate Diversity Seminar, one so effective that it would completely eliminate unkind thoughts, stereotypes, and misimpressions harbored by its participants toward persons of other races. The president's civil rights advisor prevails on all the nation's teachers to introduce it into every K–12 classroom, and on the major television networks and cable network news to show it on prime time.

Would life improve very much for people of color?

A. *Interest Convergence, Material Determinism, and Racial Realism*

This hypothetical question poses an issue that squarely divides critical race theory thinkers—indeed, civil rights activists in general. One camp, which we may call "idealists," holds that racism and discrimination are matters of thinking, mental categorization, attitude, and discourse. Race is a social construction, not a biological reality. Hence we may unmake it and deprive it of much of its sting by changing the system of images, words, attitudes, unconscious feelings, scripts, and social teachings by which we convey to one another that certain people are less intelligent, reliable, hardworking, virtuous, and American than others.

A contrasting school—the realists or economic determinists—holds that though attitudes and words are important, racism is much more than having an unfavorable impression of members of other groups. For realists, racism is a means by which society allocates privilege and status. Racial hierarchies determine who gets tangible benefits, including the best jobs, the best schools, and invitations to parties in people's homes. Members of this group point out that prejudice sprang up with slavery. Before then, educated Europeans held a generally positive attitude toward Africans, recognizing that African civilization was highly advanced with vast libraries and centers of learning. Africans pioneered mathematics, medicine, and astronomy long before Europeans had much knowledge of them.

Materialists point out that conquered nations generally demonize their subjects to feel better about exploiting them, so that, for example, planters and ranchers in Texas and the Southwest circulated notions of Mexican inferiority at roughly the same period that they found it necessary to take over Mexican lands or, later, to import Mexican people for back-breaking labor. For materialists, understanding the ebb and flow of racial progress and retrenchment requires a careful look at conditions prevailing at different times in history. Circumstances change so that one group finds it possible to seize advantage, or to

exploit another. They do so and then form appropriate collective attitudes to rationalize what was done. Moreover, what is true for subordination of minorities is also true for the relief of it: civil rights *gains* for communities of color coincide with the dictates of white self-interest. Little happens out of altruism alone.

In the early years of critical race theory, the realists were in a large majority. For example, scholars questioned whether the much-vaunted system of civil rights remedies ended up doing people of color much good. In a classic article in the *Harvard Law Review*, Derrick Bell argued that civil rights advances for blacks always coincided with changing economic conditions and the self-interest of elite whites. Sympathy, mercy, and evolving standards of social decency and conscience amounted to little, if anything. Audaciously, Bell selected *Brown v. Board of Education*, the crown jewel of U.S. Supreme Court jurisprudence, and invited his readers to ask themselves why the American legal system suddenly, in 1954, opened up as it did. The NAACP Legal Defense Fund had been courageously and tenaciously litigating school desegregation cases for years, usually losing or, at best, winning narrow victories.

In 1954, however, the Supreme Court unexpectedly gave them everything they wanted. Why just then? Bell hypothesized that world and domestic considerations—not moral qualms over blacks' plight—precipitated the pathbreaking decision. By 1954 the country had ended the Korean War; the Second World War was not long past. In both wars, African American servicemen had performed gallantly in the service of democracy. Many of them returned to the United States, having experienced for the first time in their lives a setting in which cooperation and survival took precedence over racism. They were unlikely to return willingly to regimes of menial labor and social vilification. For the first time in decades, the possibility of mass domestic unrest loomed.

During that period, as well, the United States was locked in the Cold War, a titanic struggle with the forces of international communism for the loyalties of the uncommitted Third World, much of which was black, brown, or Asian. It would ill serve the U.S. interest if the world press continued to carry stories of lynchings, racist sheriffs, or murders like that of Emmett Till. It was time for the United States to soften its stance toward domestic minorities. The interests of whites and blacks, for a brief moment, converged.

Bell's article was greeted with outrage and accusations of cynicism. Yet, ten years later, the legal

From Richard Delgado and Jean Stefancic, *Critical Race Theory* (New York: New York University Press, 2001), pp. 15–32. Reprinted by permission of New York University Press and the authors.

historian Mary Dudziak carried out extensive archival research in the files of the U.S. Department of State and the U.S. Department of Justice. She analyzed foreign press reports, as well as letters from U.S. ambassadors abroad, all showing that Bell's intuition was correct. When the Justice Department intervened on the side of the NAACP for the first time in a school desegregation case, it was responding to a flood of secret cables and memos outlining the United States' interest in improving its image in the eyes of the Third World.

B. *Revisionist History*

Derrick Bell's analysis of *Brown* illustrates a second signature CRT theme, revisionist history. Revisionist history reexamines America's historical record, replacing comforting majoritarian interpretations of events with ones that square more accurately with minorities' experiences. It also offers evidence, sometimes suppressed, in that very record, to support those new interpretations. Revisionism is often materialist in thrust, holding that to understand the zigs and zags of black, Latino, and Asian fortunes, one must look to things like profit, labor supply, international relations, and the interest of elite whites. For the realists, attitudes follow, explain, and rationalize what is taking place in the material sector.

The difference between the materialists and the idealists is no minor matter. It shapes strategy on decisions of how and where to invest one's energies. If the materialists are right, one needs to change the physical circumstances of minorities' lives before racism will abate. One takes seriously matters like unions, immigration quotas, and the loss of industrial jobs to globalization. If one is an idealist, campus speech codes, tort remedies for racist speech, diversity seminars, and increasing the representation of black, brown, and Asian actors on television shows will be high on one's list of priorities. A middle ground would see both forces, material and cultural, operating together and synergizing each other, so that race reformers working in either area contribute to a holistic project of racial redemption.

C. *Critique of Liberalism*

[C]ritical race scholars are discontent with liberalism as a framework for addressing America's racial problems.

Many liberals believe in color blindness and neutral principles of constitutional law.

An even more extreme version of color blindness, seen in certain Supreme Court opinions today, holds that it is wrong for the law to take any note of race, even to remedy a historical wrong. Critical race theorists (or "crits," as they are sometimes called) hold that color blindness will allow us to redress only extremely egregious racial harms, ones that everyone would notice and condemn. But if racism is embedded in our thought processes and social structures as deeply as many crits believe, then the "ordinary business" of society—the routines, practices, and institutions that we rely on to effect the world's work—will keep minorities in subordinate positions. Only aggressive, color-conscious efforts to change the way things are will do much to ameliorate misery. As an example of one such strategy, one critical race scholar proposed that society "look to the bottom" in judging new laws. If they would not relieve the distress of the poorest group—or, worse, if they compound it—we should reject them. Although color blindness seems firmly entrenched in the judiciary, a few judges have made exceptions in unusual circumstances.

Crits are also highly suspicious of another liberal mainstay, namely, rights. Particularly some of the older, more radical CRT scholars with roots in racial realism and an economic view of history believe that moral and legal rights are apt to do the right holder much less good than many would like to think. Rights are almost always procedural (for example, to a fair process) rather than substantive (for example, to food, housing, or education). Think how our system applauds affording everyone equality of opportunity, but resists programs that assure equality of results. Moreover, rights are almost always cut back when they conflict with the interests of the powerful. For example, hate speech, which targets mainly minorities, gays, lesbians, and other outsiders, is almost always tolerated, while speech that offends the interests of empowered groups finds a ready exception in First Amendment law. Think, for example, of speech that insults a judge or other authority figure, that defames a wealthy and well-regarded person, that disseminates a government secret, or deceptively advertises products, thus cheating a large class of middle-income consumers.

Moreover, rights are said to be alienating. They separate people from each other—"stay away, I've got my rights"—rather than encouraging them to form close, respectful communities. And with civil rights, lower courts have found it easy to narrow or distinguish the broad, ringing landmark decision like *Brown v. Board of Education*. The group whom they supposedly benefit always greets cases like *Brown* with great celebration. But after the celebration dies down, the great victory is quietly cut back by narrow interpretation, administrative obstruction, or delay. In the end, the minority group is left little better than it was before, if not worse. Its friends, the liberals, believing the problem has been solved, go on to something else, such as saving the whales, while its adversaries, the conservatives, furious that the Supreme Court has given way once again to undeserving minorities, step up their resistance.

Lest the reader think that the crits are too hard on well-meaning liberals, bear in mind that in recent years the movement has softened somewhat. When the movement started in the mid-1970s, complacent, backsliding liberalism represented the principal impediment to racial progress. Today that obstacle has been replaced by rampant, in-your-face conservatism that co-opts Martin Luther King, Jr.'s language, has little use for welfare, affirmative action, or other programs vital to the poor and minorities, and wants to militarize the border and make everyone speak English when businesses are crying for workers with foreign-language proficiency. Some critical race theorists, accordingly, have stopped focusing on liberalism and its ills and begun to address the conservative tide. And a determined group of "idealists" maintain that rights are not a snare and a delusion, rather they can bring genuine gains, while the struggle to obtain them unifies the group.

D. *Structural Determinism*

Everyone has heard the story about Eskimos who have twenty-six words for different kinds of snow. Imagine the opposite predicament—a society that has only one word (say, racism) for a phenomenon that is much more complex than that. For example: intentional racism; unintentional racism; unconscious racism; institutional racism; racism tinged with homophobia or sexism; racism that takes the form of indifference or coldness; and white privilege—reserving favors, smiles, kindness, the best stories, one's most charming side, and invitations to real intimacy for one's own kind or class.

Or imagine a painter raised by parents and preschool teachers who teach him that the world con-

tains only three colors: red, blue, and yellow; or a would-be writer who is raised with an artificially low vocabulary of three hundred words. Children raised in smoggy Mexico City are said to paint pictures with a brownish-yellow, never blue, sky. These examples point out the concept that lies at the heart of structural determinism, the idea that our system, by reason of its structure and vocabulary, cannot redress certain types of wrong. Structural determinism, a powerful notion that engages both the idealistic and the materialistic strands of critical race theory, takes a number of forms. Consider the following three.

1. Tools of Thought and the Dilemma of Law Reform

Traditional legal research tools, found in standard law libraries, rely on a series of headnotes, index numbers, and other categories that lawyers use to find precedent. (With computerization, this reliance is somewhat less acute than it was formerly, but the problem still persists.) Suppose that no case is on point because the lawyer faces a problem of first impression, requiring legal innovation. In such situations, legal categories will lead the lawyer to dead ends—to solutions that have not worked. What is required is innovation, not the application of some preexisting rule or principle. Even when a new idea, such as jury nullification, is beginning to catch on, the legal indexers who compile the reference books and indexing tools may fail to realize its significance. When Sir William Blackstone's *Commentaries on the Laws of England* laid down the basic structure of liberal/capitalist thought, this served as a template for future generations of lawyers, so that legal change thereafter came slowly. Once the structure of law and legal categories is set, it replicates itself much as, in the world of biology, DNA enables organisms to replicate. In some respects, the predicament is the old one about the chicken and the egg. It is hard to think about something that has no name, and it is hard to name something unless one's interpretive community has begun talking and thinking about it.

As a thought exercise, the reader is invited to consider how many of the following terms and ideas, . . . highly relevant to the work of progressive lawyers and activists, are apt to be found in standard legal reference works: intersectionality, interest convergence, anti-essentialism, hegemony, language rights, black-white binary, jury nullification. How long will it take before these concepts enter the official vocabulary of law?

2. The Empathic Fallacy

Consider, next, how in certain controversies, for example, the one over hate speech, a particular type of tough-minded participant is apt to urge a free-market response: if a minority finds himself or herself on the receiving end of a stinging remark, the solution, it is said, is not to punish the speaker or enact some kind of campus hate speech rule, but to urge the victim to speak back to the offender. "The cure for bad speech is more speech."

One difficulty with this approach is that it may be physically dangerous to talk back. Much hate speech is uttered in several-on-one situations where talking back would be foolhardy. At other times, it is delivered in anonymous or cowardly fashion, such as graffiti scrawled on the bulletin board of a minority association, or an unsigned note left in the box of a student of color. In these instances, more speech is, of course, impossible.

But a more basic problem is that much hate speech is *not perceived as such* at the time. The history of racial depiction shows that our society has blithely consumed a shocking parade of Sambos, coons, sneaky Japanese, and indolent, napping Mexicans—images that were perceived at the time as amusing, cute or, worse yet, true. How can one talk back to messages, scripts, and stereotypes that are embedded in the minds of one's fellow citizens, and, indeed, the national psyche? The idea that one can use words to undo the meanings that others attach to these very same words is to commit the empathic fallacy—the belief that one can change a narrative by merely offering another, better one—that the reader's or listener's empathy will quickly and reliably take over.

Unfortunately, however, empathy is in shorter supply than we think. Most people in their daily lives do not come into contact with many persons of radically different race or social station. We converse with, and read materials written by, persons in our own cultures. Yet in some sense, we are all our stock of narratives—the terms, preconceptions, scripts, and understandings that we use to make sense of the world. They constitute who we are, the basis on which we judge new narratives—such as one about an African American who is a genius, or a hardworking Chicano who holds three jobs. The idea that a better, fairer script can readily substitute for the older, prejudiced one is attractive, but falsified by history. Change comes slowly. Try explaining to someone who has never seen a Mexican, except for cartoon figures wearing sombreros and serapes, that most Mexicans wear business suits.

. . .

3. Serving Two Masters

Derrick Bell has pointed out a third structure that impedes reform, this time in law. To litigate a law reform case, the lawyer needs a flesh and blood client. One might wish to establish rights of poor consumers or unmask the legal principle that a school district is not truly integrated if the makeup of certain schools is half black and half Chicano.

Suppose, however, that the client and his or her community do not want the very same remedy that the lawyer does. The lawyer, who may represent a civil rights or public interest organization, may want a sweeping remedy that names a new evil and declares it contrary to American ideals. He or she may be willing to gamble and risk all. The client, however, may want something different—better schools or more money for existing ones. He or she may want bilingual education or more black teachers, instead of classes taught by prizewinning white teachers with Ph.D.'s. A lawyer representing a poor client may want to litigate constitutional due process and welfare hearings, while the client may be more interested in a new pair of Sunday shoes for her child. These conflicts, which are ubiquitous in law reform situations, haunt the lawyer pursuing social change and seem inherent in our system of legal remedies. Which master should the lawyer serve?

4. Race Remedies Law as a Homeostatic Device

Some critics (such as Alan Freeman) even argue that our system of civil rights law and enforcement ensures that racial progress occurs at just the right slow pace. Too slow would make minorities impatient and risk destabilization; too fast could jeopardize important material and psychic benefits for elite groups. When the gap between our ideals and practices becomes too great, the system produces a "contradiction-closing case," so that everyone may see that it is truly fair and just. When social conditions call for a genuine concession, such as affirmative action, the costs of that concession are always placed on minorities—in the form of stigma—or on working-class whites, like Alan Bakke, who sought admission to the University of California at Davis Medical School, least able to incur them.

Study Questions

1. How does Posner use the example of the stamp collection to illustrate the concept of wealth maximization?

2. In what way does Posner think that the model of wealth maximization can be given a "pragmatic" justification?

3. Some critics of law and economics have argued that Posner and others have placed the cart before the horse: the fact that certain legal decisions or doctrines can be shown to promote wealth maximization does not establish that such rulings or parts of the law are best explained by appeal to economic ideas. Moral concepts such as justice and fairness, the critics argue, may provide a better overall explanation of how the law developed and a better justification for its authority. How do you think Posner would respond to this criticism? What makes one explanation of the law better or worse than another?

4. One assumption underlying much work in the field of law and economics says that people are fundamentally rational maximizers of their own self-interest. Does this assumption accurately model the nature of persons, in your view? Do people always act rationally in the way that Posner understands that notion? What would the legal economist say of individuals who (seemingly) act selflessly or with altruistic motives? Why is it rational to pursue one's own self-interest to the exclusion of any other value or concern?

5. According to Angela Harris, what are the characteristics of the "essential woman"? How have those characteristics been identified? Feminist legal scholar Robin West once described women as "people who value intimacy, fear separation, dread invasions, and crave individuation" [Robin West, "The Difference in Women's Hedonic Lives: A Phenomenological Critique of Feminist Legal Theory," *Wisconsin Women's Law Journal* 3 (1987), p. 82]. To what extent are these uniquely feminine attributes? To the degree that the law fails adequately to account for or respond to these attributes, is that failure felt more harshly by biological females?

6. In what ways does Harris argue that the use of stories of "multiple consciousness" will improve legal theory?

7. What legal effects do you think differences between the sexes should have? Are the differences between men and women such that different legal treatment is required? Which differences ought the law to recognize as significant? Should sex-based generalizations ever be used to set policy or to define legal doctrines? If so, under what circumstances?

8. The debate between "equal treatment" feminists, on the one hand, and "special treatment" feminists, on the other, turns on the legal effect that differences between the sexes ought to have. Do those advocating equal treatment deny that there are such relevant differences, or do they hold that sex-related differences are not the most significant differences between the sexes?

9. The federal Family Leave Act, passed in the early 1990s, permits most workers to take up to twelve weeks of unpaid leave subsequent to the birth or adoption of a child, or to care for a sick relative. Does this law call for "equal" or for "special" treatment? How would you tell?

10. According to Margaret Radin, what are the similarities between pragmatism and feminism? Is the emphasis Radin places upon "lived experiences and practical solutions, as opposed to abstract theory, the principal commonality?

11. What does Radin mean by the problem of "bad coherence"? Does she adequately explain how "bad" coherence is to be identified and distinguished from "good" coherence? How does she propose to overcome bad coherence using a pragmatic approach?

12. According to Delgado and Stefancic, the very nature of race and racism is an issue that deeply divides CRT scholars. "Idealists" hold that race and racism are merely beliefs that can be changed through education and modifications to our social and political discourse. For "materialists," however, racial categories are structural features of society, similar to social class, and much more difficult to change. In your opinion, which of these views best explains the nature of race and racial categorization?

13. Why, according to Delgado and Stefancic, do proponents of CRT reject the liberal notion that equality will result from "color-blind" laws and legal institutions?

14. Suppose that legal doctrine and institutions were changed in such a way that they incorporated "women's voices" on a par with that of men. In what ways would the legal system change?

15. CRT theorist Mari Matsuda states a theme echoed by many CRT proponents:

> [T]hose who have experienced discrimination speak with a special voice to which we should listen. Looking to the bottom—adopting the perspective of those who have seen and felt the falsity of the liberal promise—can assist critical scholars in the task of fathoming the phenomenology of law and defining the elements of justice. [Mari Matsuda, "Looking to the Bottom: Critical Legal Studies and Reparations," *Harvard Civil Rights–Civil Liberties Law Review* 22 (1987), p. 324].

In what sense does the experience of being a victim of injustice give rise to a unique perspective on such issues as racial discrimination?

Cases for Further Reflection

Riggs et al. v. Palmer

The confrontation between naturalism and positivism is well joined in this case. As you read through the case, consider these questions: Are the precedents cited by Earl convincing? What is the source of the authoritativeness of the "fundamental maxims" of "universal law" invoked by Earl to support the judgment that Elmer Palmer must not be allowed to collect under his grandfather's will?

Earl [Judge].

On the 13th day of August, 1880, Francis B. Palmer made his last will and testament, in which he gave small legacies to his two daughters, Mrs. Riggs and Mrs. Preston, the plaintiffs in this action, and the remainder of his estate to his grandson, the defendant Elmer E. Palmer, subject to the support of Susan Palmer, his mother, with a gift over to the two daughters, subject to the support of Mrs. Palmer in case Elmer should survive him and die under age, unmarried, and without any issue. The testator, at the date of his will, owned a farm, and considerable personal property. He was a widower, and thereafter, in March, 1882, he was married to Mrs. Bresee, with whom, before his marriage, he entered into an antenuptial

contract, in which it was agreed that in lieu of dower and all other claims upon his estate in case she survived him she should have her support upon his farm during her life, and such support was expressly charged upon the farm. At the date of the will, and subsequently to the death of the testator, Elmer lived with him as a member of his family, and at his death was 16 years old. He knew of the provisions made in his favor in the will, and, that he might prevent his grandfather from revoking such provisions, which he had manifested some intention to do, and to obtain the speedy enjoyment and immediate possession of his property, he willfully murdered him by poisoning him. He now claims the property, and the sole question for our determination is, can he have it?

The defendants say that the testator is dead; that his will was made in due form, and has been admitted to probate; and that therefore it must have effect

---

22 N.E. 188 (1889), Court of Appeals of New York.

according to the letter of the law. It is quite true that statutes regulating the making, proof, and effects of wills and devolution of property if literally construed, and if their force and effect can in no way and under no circumstances be controlled or modified, give this property to the murderer. The purpose of those statutes was to enable testators to dispose of their estates to the objects of their bounty at death, and to carry into effect their final wishes legally expressed; and in considering and giving effect to them this purpose must be kept in view. It was the intention of the lawmakers that the donees in a will should have the property given to them. But it never could have been their intention that a donee who murdered the testator to make the will operative should have any benefit under it. If such a case had been present in their minds, and it had been supposed necessary to make some provision of law to meet it, it cannot be doubted that they would have provided for it. It is a familiar canon of construction that a thing which is within the intention of the makers of a statute is as much within the statute as if it were within the letter; and a thing which is within the letter of the statute is not within the statute unless it be within the intention of the makers. The writers of laws do not always express their intention perfectly, but either exceed it or fall short of it, so that judges are to collect it from probable or rational conjectures only, and this is called "rational interpretation"; and Rutherford, in his Institutes (page 420), says: "Where we make use of rational interpretation, sometimes we restrain the meaning of the writer so as to take in less, and sometimes we extend or enlarge his meaning so as to take in more, than his words express." Such a construction ought to put upon a statute as will best answer the intention which the makers had in view. . . . [M]any cases are mentioned where it was held that matters embraced in the general words of statutes nevertheless were not within the statutes, because it could not have been the intention of the law-makers that they should be included. They were taken out of the statutes by an equitable construction; and it is said in Bacon: "By an equitable construction a case not within the letter of a statute is sometimes holden to be within the meaning, because it is within the mischief for which a remedy is provided. The reason for such construction is that the law-makers could not set down every case in express terms. In order to form a right judgment whether a case be within the equity of a statute, it is a good way to suppose the law-maker present, and that you have asked him this question. Did you intend to compre-

hend this case? Then you must give yourself such answer as you imagine he, being an upright and reasonable man, would have given. If this be that he did mean to comprehend it, you may safely hold the case to be within the equity of the statute; for while you do no more than he would have done, you do not act contrary to the statute, but in conformity thereto." In some cases the letter of a legislative act is restrained by an equitable construction; in others, it is enlarged; in others, the construction is contrary to the letter. The equitable construction which restrains the letter of a statute is defined by Aristotle as frequently quoted in this manner: *Æquitas est correctio legis generaliter latæ qua parte deficit.* If the [law-makers] could, as to this case, be consulted, would they say that they intended by their general language that the property of a testator or of an ancestor should pass to one who had taken his life for the express purpose of getting his property? In 1 Bl. Comm. 91, the learned author, speaking of the construction of statutes, says: "If there arise out of them collaterally any absurd consequences manifestly contradictory to common reason, they are with regard to those collateral consequences void. [. . .] Where some collateral matter arises out of the general words, and happens to be unreasonable, there the judges are in decency to conclude that this consequence was not foreseen by the parliament, and therefore they are at liberty to expound the statute by equity, and only *quoad hoc* disregard it"; and he gives as an illustration, if an act of parliament gives a man power to try all causes that arise within his manor of Dale, yet, if a cause should arise in which he himself is party, the act is construed not to extend to that, because it is unreasonable that any man should determine his own quarrel. There was a statute in Bologna that whoever drew blood in the streets should be severely punished, and yet it was held not to apply to the case of a barber who opened a vein in the street. It is commanded in the decalogue that no work shall be done on the Sabbath, and yet giving the command a rational interpretation founded upon its design the Infallible Judge held that it did not prohibit works of necessity, charity, or benevolence on that day.

What could be more unreasonable than to suppose that it was the legislative intention in the general laws passed for the orderly, peaceable, and just devolution of property that they should have operation in favor of one who murdered his ancestor that he might speedily come into the possession of his estate? Such an intention is inconceivable. We need not, therefore, be much troubled by the general language contained in the laws. Besides, all laws, as well as all contracts, may be controlled in their operation and effect by general, fundamental maxims of the common law. No one shall be permitted to profit by his own fraud, or to take advantage of his own wrong, or to found any claim upon his own iniquity, or to acquire property by his own crime. These maxims are dictated by public policy, have their foundation in universal law administered in all civilized countries, and have nowhere been superseded by statutes. They were applied in the decision of the case of *Insurance Co. v. Armstrong,* 117 U.S. 599, 6 Sup. Ct. Rep. 877. There it was held that the person who procured a policy upon the life of another, payable at his death, and then murdered the assured to make the policy payable, could not recover thereon. Mr. Justice FIELD, writing the opinion, said: "Independently of any proof of the motives of Hunter in obtaining the policy, and even assuming that they were just and proper, he forfeited all rights under it when, to secure its immediate payment, he murdered the assured. It would be a reproach to the jurisprudence of the country if one could recover insurance money payable on the death of a party whose life he had feloniously taken. As well might he recover insurance money upon a building he had wilfully fired." These maxims, without any statute giving them force or operation, frequently control the effect and nullify the language of wills. A will procured by fraud and deception, like any other instrument, may be decreed void, and set aside; and so a particular portion of a will may be excluded from probate, or held inoperative, if induced by the fraud or undue influence of the person in whose favor it is. *Allen v. McPherson,* 1 H. L. Cas. 191; *Harrison's Appeal,* 48 Conn. 202. So a will may contain provisions which are immoral, irreligious, or against public policy, and they will be held void.

Here there was no certainty that this murderer would survive the testator, or that the testator would not change his will, and there was no certainty that he would get his property if nature was allowed to take its course. He therefore murdered the testator expressly to vest himself with an estate. Under such circumstances, what law, human or divine, will allow him to take the estate and enjoy the fruits of his crime? The will spoke and became operative at the death of the testator. He caused that death, and thus by his crime made it speak and have operation. Shall it speak and operate in his favor? If he had met the testator, and taken his property by force, he would have had no title to it. Shall he acquire title by murdering him? If he had gone to the testator's house, and by force com-

pelled him, or by fraud or undue influence had induced him, to will him his property, the law would not allow him to hold it. But can he give effect and operation to a will by murder, and yet take the property? To answer these questions in the affirmative it seems to me would be a reproach to the jurisprudence of our state, and an offense against public policy. Under the civil law, evolved from the general principles of natural law and justice by many generations of jurisconsults, philosophers, and statesmen, one cannot take property by inheritance or will from an ancestor or benefactor whom he has murdered. . . . In the Civil Code of Lower Canada the provisions on the subject in the Code Napoleon have been substantially copied. But, so far as I can find, in no country where the common law prevails has it been deemed important to enact a law to provide for such a case. Our revisers and law-makers were familiar with the civil law, and they did not deem it important to incorporate into our statutes its provisions upon [this] subject. This is not a *casus omissus*. It was evidently supposed that the maxims of the common law were sufficient to regulate such a case, and that a specific enactment for that purpose was not needed. For the same reasons the defendant Palmer cannot take any of this property as heir. Just before the murder he was not an heir, and it was not certain that he ever would be. He might have died before his grandfather, or might have been disinherited by him. He made himself an heir by the murder, and he seeks to take property as the fruit of his crime. What has before been said as to him as legatee applies to him with equal force as an heir. He cannot vest himself with title by crime. My view of this case does not inflict upon Elmer any greater or other punishment for his crime than the law specifies. It takes from him no property, but simply holds that he shall not acquire property by his crime, and thus be rewarded for its commission.

Our attention is called to *Owens v. Owens,* 100 N.C. 240, 6 S.E. Rep. 794, as a case quite like this. There a wife had been convicted of being an accessory before the fact to the murder of her husband, and it was held that she was nevertheless entitled to dower. I am unwilling to assent to the doctrine of that case. The [statutes] provide dower for a wife who has the misfortune to survive her husband, and thus lose his support and protection. It is clear beyond their purpose to make provision for a wife who by her own crime makes herself a widow, and willfully and intentionally deprives herself of the support and protection of her husband. As she might have died before him, and "though" never have been his widow, she cannot by her crime vest herself with an estate. The principle which lies at the bottom of the maxim *volenti non fit injuria* should be applied to such a case, and a widow should not, for the purpose of acquiring, as such, property rights, be permitted to allege a widowhood which she has wickedly and intentionally created.

Gray, [Judge] (dissenting).

The appellants' argument for a reversal of the judgment, which dismissed their complaint, is that the respondent unlawfully prevented a revocation of the existing will, or a new will from being made, by his crime; and that he terminated the enjoyment of the testator of his property, and effected his own succession to it, by the same crime. They say that to permit the respondent to take the property willed to him would be to permit him to take advantage of his own wrong. To sustain their position that the appellants' counsel has submitted an able and elaborate brief, and, if I believed that the decision of the question could be effected by considerations of an equitable nature, I should not hesitate to assent to views which commend themselves to the conscience. But the matter does not lie within the domain of conscience. We are bound by the rigid rules of law, which have been established by the legislature, and within the limits of which the determination of this question is confined. The question we are dealing with is whether a testamentary disposition can be altered, or a will revoked, after the testator's death, through an appeal to the courts, when the legislature has by its enactments prescribed exactly when and how wills may be made, altered, and revoked, and apparently, as it seems to me, when they have been fully complied with, has left no room for the exercise of an equitable jurisdiction by courts over such matters. Modern jurisprudence, in recognizing the right of the individual, under more or less restrictions, to dispose of his property after his death, subjects it to legislative control, both as to extent and as to mode of exercise. Complete freedom of testamentory disposition of one's property has not been and is not the universal rule, as we see from the provisions of the Napoleonic Code, from the systems of jurisprudence in countries which are modeled upon the Roman law, and from the statutes of many of our states. To the statutory restraints which are imposed upon the disposition of one's property by will are added strict and systematic statutory rules for the execution, alteration, and revocation of the will, which must be, at least substan-

tially, if not exactly, followed to insure validity and performance. The reason for the establishment of such rules, we may naturally assume, consists in the purpose to create those safeguards about these grave and important acts which experience has demonstrated to be the wisest and surest. That freedom which is permitted to be exercised in the testamentary disposition of one's estate by the laws of the state is subject to its being exercised in conformity with the regulations of the statutes. The capacity and the power of the individual to dispose of his property after death, and the mode by which that power can be exercised, are matters of which the legislature has assumed the entire control, and has undertaken to regulate with comprehensive particularity. . . .

I cannot find any support for the argument that the respondent's succession to the property should be avoided because of his criminal act, when the laws are silent. Public policy does not demand it; for the demands of public policy are satisfied by the proper execution of the laws and the punishment of the crime. There has been no convention between the testator and his legatee. The appellants' argument practically amounts to this: that, as the legatee has been guilty of a crime, by the commission of which he is placed in a position to sooner receive the benefits of the testamentary provision, his rights to the property should be forfeited, and he should be divested of his estate. To allow their argument to prevail would involve the diversion by the court of the testator's estate into the hands of persons whom, possibly enough, for all we know, the testator might not have chosen or desired as its recipients. Practically the court is asked to make another will for the testator. The laws do not warrant this judicial action, and mere presumption would not be strong enough to sustain it. But, more than this, to concede the appellants' views would involve the imposition of an additional punishment or penalty upon the respondent. What power or warrant have the courts to add to the respondent's penalties by depriving him of property? The law has punished him for his crime, and we may not say that it was an insufficient punishment. In the trial and punishment of the respondent the law has vindicated itself for the outrage which he committed, and further judicial utterance upon the subject of punishment or deprivation of rights is barred. We may not, in the language of the court in *People v. Thornton*, 25 Hun, 456, "enhance the pains, penalties, and forfeitures provided by law for the punishment of crime." The judgment should be affirmed, with costs.

Billy Budd

HERMAN MELVILLE

The following excerpt is taken from Melville's novella about evil, law, and justice. The central figure, Billy Budd, is a simple, well-liked sailor on the British warship Bellipotent, during the Napoleonic wars. Claggart, the ship's master-at-arms, is despised among the crew for his cruelty and wrath. Billy's naiveté and friendly manner set Claggart against him. Claggart, discovering Billy's weakness of stuttering to the point of speechlessness when angry or excited, contrives to exploit this flaw by falsely accusing Billy of plotting mutiny. Claggart confronts Billy in the presence of the ship's commander, Captain Vere. Shocked into silence and indignation by Claggart's lies, Billy is unable to defend himself; instead, he lashes out blindly with his fist. As fate would have it, the blow, which would not normally kill another, knocks the susceptible Claggart dead. Captain Vere convenes a shipboard court-martial and argues that, under military law, Billy must die, despite Vere's belief that the unfortunate youth is morally innocent. How did Vere know that the Mutiny Act required the immediate sanction of death? Is Billy completely innocent, in your opinion? Was there no option but to convict Billy? For example, would it have been possible to delay the trial or the execution until the ship reached a home port? What arguments are suggested in defense of Billy? Does Vere refuse to allow his feelings of compassion for Billy to affect his legal judgment on the case? And, if so, is this the mark of a good judge, or a bad one?

The court was held in the same cabin where the unfortunate affair had taken place. This cabin, the commander's, embraced the entire area under the poop deck. Aft, and on either side, was a small stateroom, the one now temporarily a jail and the other a deadhouse, and a yet smaller compartment, leaving a space between expanding forward into a goodly oblong of length coinciding with the ship's beam. A skylight of moderate dimension was overhead, and at each end of the oblong space were two sashed porthole windows easily convertible back into embrasures for short carronades.

All being quickly in readiness, Billy Budd was arraigned, Captain Vere necessarily appearing as the sole witness in the case, and as such temporarily sinking his rank, though singularly maintaining it in a matter apparently trivial, namely, that he testified from the ship's weather side, with that object having caused the court to sit on the lee side. Concisely he narrated all that had led up to the catastrophe, omitting nothing in Claggart's accusation and deposing as to the manner in which the prisoner had received it. At this testimony the three officers glanced with no little surprise at Billy Budd, the last man they would have suspected either of the mutinous design alleged by Claggart or the undeniable deed he himself had done. The first lieutenant, taking judicial primacy and turning toward the prisoner, said, "Captain Vere has spoken. Is it or is it not as Captain Vere says?"

In response came syllables not so much impeded in the utterance as might have been anticipated. They were these: "Captain Vere tells the truth. It is just as Captain Vere says, but it is not as the master-at-arms said. I have eaten the King's bread and I am true to the King."

"I believe you, my man," said the witness, his voice indicating a suppressed emotion not otherwise betrayed.

From Herman Melville, *Billy Budd and Other Tales* (New York: Penguin Putnam, 1961), pp. 63–71. First published in 1924.

"God will bless you for that, your honor!" not without stammering said Billy, and all but broke down. But immediately he was recalled to self-control by another question, to which with the same emotional difficulty of utterance he said, "No, there was no malice between us. I never bore malice against the master-at-arms. I am sorry that he is dead. I did not mean to kill him. Could I have used my tongue I would not have struck him. But he foully lied to my face and in presence of my captain, and I had to say something, and I could only say it with a blow, God help me!"

In the impulsive aboveboard manner of the frank one the court saw confirmed all that was implied in words that just previously had perplexed them, coming as they did from the testifier to the tragedy and promptly following Billy's impassioned disclaimer of mutinous intent—Captain Vere's words, "I believe you, my man."

Next it was asked of him whether he knew of or suspected aught savoring of incipient trouble (meaning mutiny, though the explicit term was avoided) going on in any section of the ship's company.

The reply lingered. This was naturally imputed by the court to the same vocal embarrassment which had retarded or obstructed previous answers. But in main it was otherwise here, the question immediately recalling to Billy's mind the interview with the afterguardsman in the forechains. But an innate repugnance to playing a part at all approaching that of an informer against one's own shipmates—the same erring sense of uninstructed honor which had stood in the way of his reporting the matter at the time, though as a loyal man-of-war's man it was incumbent on him, and failure so to do, if charged against him and proven, would have subjected him to the heaviest of penalties; this, with the blind feeling now his that nothing really was being hatched, prevailed with him. When the answer came it was a negative.

"One question more," said the officer of marines, now first speaking and with a troubled earnestness. "You tell us that what the master-at-arms said against you was a lie. Now why should he have so lied, so maliciously lied, since you declare there was no malice between you?"

At that question, unintentionally touching on a spiritual sphere wholly obscure to Billy's thoughts, he was nonplussed, evincing a confusion indeed that some observers, such as can readily be imagined, would have construed into involuntary evidence of hidden guilt. Nevertheless, he strove some way to answer, but all at once relinquished the vain endeavor,

at the same time turning an appealing glance towards Captain Vere as deeming him his best helper and friend. Captain Vere, who had been seated for a time, rose to his feet, addressing the interrogator. "The question you put to him comes naturally enough. But how can he rightly answer it?—or anybody else, unless indeed it be he who lies within there," designating the compartment where lay the corpse. "But the prone one there will not rise to our summons. In effect, though, as it seems to me, the point you make is hardly material. Quite aside from any conceivable motive actuating the master-at-arms, and irrespective of the provocation to the blow, a martial court must needs in the present case confine its attention to the blow's consequence, which consequence justly is to be deemed not otherwise than as the striker's deed."

This utterance, the full significance of which it was not at all likely that Billy took in, nevertheless caused him to turn a wistful interrogative look toward the speaker, a look in its dumb expressiveness not unlike that which a dog of generous breed might turn upon his master, seeking in his face some elucidation of a previous gesture ambiguous to the canine intelligence. Nor was the same utterance without marked effect upon the three officers, more especially the soldier. Couched in it seemed to them a meaning unanticipated, involving a prejudgment on the speaker's part. It served to augment a mental disturbance previously evident enough.

The soldier once more spoke, in a tone of suggestive dubiety addressing at once his associates and Captain Vere: "Nobody is present—none of the ship's company, I mean—who might shed lateral light, if any is to be had, upon what remains mysterious in this matter."

"That is thoughtfully put," said Captain Vere; "I see your drift. Ay, there is a mystery; but, to use a scriptural phrase, it is a 'mystery of iniquity,'" a matter for psychologic theologians to discuss. But what has a military court to do with it? Not to add that for us any possible investigation of it is cut off by the lasting tongue-tie of—him—in yonder,' again designating the mortuary stateroom. "The prisoner's deed—with that alone we have to do."

To this, and particularly the closing reiteration, the marine soldier, knowing not how aptly to reply, sadly abstained from saying aught. The first lieutenant, who at the outset had not unnaturally assumed primacy in the court, now overrulingly instructed by a glance from Captain Vere, a glance more effective than words, resumed that primacy. Turning to the prisoner,

"Budd," he said, and scarce in equable tones, "Budd, if you have aught further to say for yourself, say it now."

Upon this the young sailor turned another quick glance toward Captain Vere; then, as taking a hint from that aspect, a hint confirming his own instinct that silence was now best, replied to the lieutenant, "I have said all, sir."

The marine—the same who had been the sentinel without the cabin door at the time that the foretop-man, followed by the master-at-arms, entered it—he, standing by the sailor throughout these judicial proceedings, was now directed to take him back to the after compartment originally assigned to the prisoner and his custodian. As the twain disappeared from view, the three officers, as partially liberated from some inward constraint associated with Billy's mere presence, simultaneously stirred in their seats. They exchanged looks of troubled indecision, yet feeling that decide they must and without long delay. For Captain Vere, he for the time stood—unconsciously with his back toward them, apparently in one of his absent fits—gazing out from a sashed porthole to windward upon the monotonous blank of the twilight sea. But the court's silence continuing, broken only at moments by brief consultations, in low earnest tones, this served to arouse him and energize him. Turning, he to-and-fro paced the cabin athwart; in the returning ascent to windward climbing the slant deck in the ship's lee roll, without knowing it symbolizing thus in his action a mind resolute to surmount difficulties even if against primitive instincts strong as the wind and the sea. Presently he came to a stand before the three. After scanning their faces he stood less as mustering his thoughts for expression than as one inly deliberating how best to put them to well-meaning men not intellectually mature, men with whom it was necessary to demonstrate certain principles that were axioms to himself. Similar impatience as to talking is perhaps one reason that deters some minds from addressing any popular assemblies.

When speak he did, something, both in the substance of what he said and his manner of saying it, showed the influence of unshared studies modifying and tempering the practical training of an active career. This, along with his phraseology, now and then was suggestive of the grounds whereon rested that imputation of a certain pedantry socially alleged against him by certain naval men of wholly practical cast, captains who nevertheless would frankly concede that His Majesty's navy mustered no more efficient officer of their grade than Starry Vere

What he said was to this effect: "Hitherto I have been but the witness, little more; and I should hardly think now to take another tone, that of your coadjutor for the time, did I not perceive in you—at the crisis too—a troubled hesitancy, proceeding, I doubt not, from the clash of military duty with moral scruple—scruple vitalized by compassion. For the compassion, how can I otherwise than share it? But, mindful of paramount obligations, I strive against scruples that may tend to enervate decision. Not, gentlemen, that I hide from myself that the case is an exceptional one. Speculatively regarded, it well might be referred to a jury of casuists. But for us here, acting not as casuists or moralists, it is a case practical, and under martial law practically to be dealt with.

"But your scruples: do they more as in a dusk? Challenge them. Make them advance and declare themselves. Come now; do they import something like this: If, mindless of palliating circumstances, we are bound to regard the death of the master-at-arms as the prisoner's deed, then does that deed constitute a capital crime whereof the penalty is a mortal one. But in natural justice is nothing but the prisoner's overt act to be considered? How can we adjudge to summary and shameful death a fellow creature innocent before God, and whom we feel to be so?—Does that state it aright? You sign sad assent. Well, I too feel that, the full force of that. It is Nature. But do these buttons that we wear attest that our allegiance is to Nature? No, to the King. Though the ocean, which is inviolate Nature primeval, though this be the element where we move and have our being as sailors, yet as the King's officers lies our duty in a sphere correspondingly natural? So little is that true, that in receiving our commissions we in the most important regards ceased to be natural free agents. When war is declared are we the commissioned fighters previously consulted? We fight at command. If our judgments approve the war, that is but coincidence. So in other particulars. So now. For suppose condemnation to follow these present proceedings. Would it be so much we ourselves that would condemn as it would be martial law operating through us? For that law and the rigor of it, we are not responsible. Our vowed responsibility is in this: That however pitilessly that law may operate in any instances, we nevertheless adhere to it and administer it.

"But the exceptional in the matter moves the hearts within you. Even so too is mine moved. But let not warm hearts betray heads that should be cool. Ashore in a criminal case, will an upright judge allow himself off the bench to be waylaid by some tender kinswoman of the accused seeking to touch him with her tearful plea? Well, the heart here, sometimes the feminine in man, is as that piteous woman, and hard though it be, she must here be ruled out."

He paused, earnestly studying them for a moment; then resumed.

"But something in your aspect seems to urge that it is not solely the heart that moves in you, but also the conscience, the private conscience. But tell me whether or not, occupying the position we do, private conscience should not yield to that imperial one formulated in the code under which alone we officially proceed?"

Here the three men moved in their seats, less convinced than agitated by the course of an argument troubling but the more the spontaneous conflict within.

Perceiving which, the speaker paused for a moment; then abruptly changing his tone, went on.

"To steady us a bit, let us recur to the facts.—In wartime at sea a man-of-war's man strikes his superior in grade, and the blow kills. Apart from its effect the blow itself is, according to the Articles of War, a capital crime. Furthermore—"

"Ay, sir," emotionally broke in the officer of marines, "in one sense it was. But surely Budd proposed neither mutiny nor homicide."

"Surely not, my good man. And before a court less arbitrary and more merciful than a martial one, that plea would largely extenuate. At the Last Assizes it shall acquit. But how here? We proceed under the law of the Mutiny Act. In feature no child can resemble his father more than that Act resembles in spirit the thing from which it derives—War. In His Majesty's service—in this ship, indeed—there are Englishmen forced to fight for the King against their will. Against their conscience, for aught we know. Though as their fellow creatures some of us may appreciate their position, yet as navy officers what reck we of it? Still less recks the enemy. Our impressed men he would fain cut down in the same swath with our volunteers. As regards the enemy's naval conscripts, some of whom may even share our own abhorrence of the regicidal French Directory, it is the same on our side. War looks but to the frontage, the appearance. And the Mutiny Act, War's child, takes after the father. Budd's intent or non-intent is nothing to the purpose.

"But while, put to it by those anxieties in you which I cannot but respect, I only repeat myself—while thus strangely we prolong proceedings that should be summary—the enemy may be sighted and an engagement result. We must do; and one of two things must we do—condemn or let go."

"Can we not convict and yet mitigate the penalty?" asked the sailing master, here speaking, and falteringly, for the first.

"Gentlemen, were that clearly lawful for us under the circumstances, consider the consequences of such clemency. The people" (meaning the ship's company) "have native sense; most of them are familiar with our naval usage and tradition; and how would they take it? Even could you explain to them—which our official position forbids—they, long molded by arbitrary discipline, have not that kind of intelligent responsiveness that might qualify them to comprehend and discriminate. No, to the people the foretopman's deed, however it be worded in the announcement, will be plain homicide committed in a flagrant act of mutiny. What penalty for that should follow, they know. But it does not follow. *Why?* they will ruminate. You know what sailors are. Will they not revert to the recent outbreak at the Nore? Ay. They know the well-founded alarm—the panic it struck throughout England. Your clement sentence they would account pusillanimous. They would think that we flinch, that we are afraid of them—afraid of practicing a lawful rigor singularly demanded at this juncture, lest it should provoke new troubles. What shame to use such a conjecture on their part, and how deadly to discipline. You see then, whither, prompted by duty and the law, I steadfastly drive. But I beseech you, my friends, do not take me amiss. I feel as you do for this unfortunate boy. But did he know our hearts, I take him to be of that generous nature that he would feel even for us on whom in this military necessity so heavy a compulsion is laid."

With that, crossing the deck he resumed his place by the sashed porthole, tacitly leaving the three to come to a decision. On the cabin's opposite side the troubled court sat silent. Loyal lieges, plain and practical, though at bottom they dissented from some points Captain Vere had put to them, they were without the faculty, hardly had the inclination, to gainsay one whom they felt to be an earnest man, one too not less their superior in mind than in naval rank. But it is not improbable that even such of his words as were not without influence over them, less came home than his closing appeal to their instinct as sea officers: in the forethought he threw out as to the practical consequences to discipline, considering the unconfirmed tone of the fleet at the time, should a man-of-war's man's violent killing at sea of a superior in grade be allowed to pass for aught else than a capital crime demanding prompt infliction of the penalty.

. . .

In brief, Billy Budd was formally convicted and sentenced to be hung at the yardarm in the early morning watch, it being now night. Otherwise, as is customary in such cases, the sentence would forthwith have been carried out. In wartime on the field or in the fleet, a mortal punishment decreed by a drumhead court—on the field sometimes decreed by but a nod from the general—follows without delay on the heel of conviction, without appeal.

The Antelope

An opinion by legendary Chief Justice John Marshall, this early case represents yet another clash between positive and natural law, set here in the context of the law of nations. Can you explain why, if both the (positive) statutes of the United States and the principles of the "law of nature" condemn the slave trade, Marshall nonetheless orders the return of the slaves to their "owners"? Why does Marshall hold that the positive laws of nations "trumps" the positive law of the United States?

[In 1808 the congress prohibited the importation of slaves into the United States. Subsequent federal laws punished persons who engaged in the slave trade, requiring that their ships be forfeited and that the Negroes be returned to Africa. The slave ship *Antelope*, carrying over two hundred African slaves, was intercepted off the coast of Florida by a United States vessel for suspected violation of the slave-trade laws. The governments of Spain and Portugal insisted that the ship and its cargo be released, maintaining that the Africans were the property of Spanish and Portuguese citizens. The U.S. government resisted and presented the Supreme Court with the question of whether the U.S. federal laws applied to forfeit slaves owned by foreign nationals.]

Marshall, Chief Justice.

In prosecuting this appeal, the United States assert no property in themselves. They appear in the character of guardians, or next friends, of these Africans, who are brought, without any act of their own, into the bosom of our country, insist on their right to freedom, and submit their claim to the laws of the land, and to the tribunals of the nation. The consuls of Spain and Portugal, respectively, demand these Africans as slaves, who have, in the regular cause of legitimate commerce, been acquired as property, by the subjects of their respective sovereigns, and claim their restitution under the laws of the United States.

In examining claims of this momentous importance—claims in which the sacred rights of liberty and of property come in conflict with each other—which have drawn from the bar a degree of talent and of eloquence, worthy of the questions that have been discussed, their court must not yield to feelings which might seduce it from the path of duty, and must obey the mandate of the law.

That the course of opinion on the slave-trade should be unsettled, ought to excite no surprise. The Christian and civilized nations of the world with whom we have most intercourse, have all been engaged in it. However abhorrent this traffic may be to a mind whose original feelings are not blunted by familiarity with the practice, it has been sanctioned, in modern times, by the laws of all nations who possess

23 U.S. (19 Wheat.) 66 (1825) United States Supreme Court.

distant colonies, each of whom has engaged in it as a common commercial business, which no other could rightfully interrupt. It has claimed all the sanction which could be derived from long usage and general acquiescence. That trade could not be considered as contrary to the law of nations which was authorized and protected by the laws of all commercial nations; the right to carry on which was claimed by each, and allowed by each.

The course of unexamined opinion, which was founded on this inveterate usage, received its first check in America; and, as soon as these states acquired the right of self-government, the traffic was forbidden by most of them. In the beginning of this century, several humane and enlightened individuals of Great Britain devoted themselves to the cause of the Africans; and by frequent appeals to the nation, in which the enormity of this commerce was unveiled and exposed to the public eye, the general sentiment was at length roused against it, and the feelings of justice and humanity, regaining their long-lost ascendency, prevailed so far in the British parliament, as to obtain an act for its abolition. The utmost efforts of the British government, as well as of that of the United States, have since been assiduously employed in its suppression. It has been denounced by both, in terms of great severity, and those concerned in it are subjected to the heaviest penalties which law can inflict. In addition to these measures, operating on their own people, they have used all their influence to bring other nations into the same system, and to interdict this trade by the consent of all. Public sentiment has, in both countries, kept pace with the measures of government; and the opinion is extensively, if not universally, entertained, that this unnatural traffic ought to be suppressed. While its illegality is asserted by some governments, but not admitted by all; while the detestation in which it is held, is growing daily, and even those nations who tolerate it, in fact, almost disavow their own conduct, and rather connive at, than legalize, the acts of their subjects, it is not wonderful, that public feeling should march somewhat in advance of strict law, and that opposite opinions should be entertained on the precise cases in which our own laws may control and limit the practice of others. Indeed, we ought not to be surprised, if, in this novel series of cases, even courts of justice should, in some instances, have carried the principle of suppression further than a more deliberate consideration of the subject would justify. . . .

The question, whether the slave-trade is prohibited by the law of nations has been seriously propounded, and both the affirmative and negative of the proposition have been maintained with equal earnestness. That it is contrary to the law of nature, will scarcely be denied. That every man has a natural right to the fruits of his own labor, is generally admitted; and that no other person can rightfully deprive him of those fruits, and appropriate them against his will, seems to be the necessary result of this admission. But from the earliest times, war has existed, and war confers rights in which all have acquiesced. Among the most enlightened nations of antiquity, one of these was, that the victor might enslave the vanquished. This, which was the usage of all, could not be pronounced repugnant to the law of nations, which is certainly to be tried by the test of general usage. That which has received the assent of all, must be the law of all. Slavery, then, has its origin in force; but as the world has agreed, that it is a legitimate result of force, the state of things which is thus produced by general consent, cannot be pronounced unlawful.

Throughout Christendom, this harsh rule has been exploded, and war is no longer considered, as giving a right to enslave captives. But this triumph of humanity has not been universal. The parties to the modern law of nations do not propagate their principles by force, and Africa has not yet adopted them. Throughout the whole extent of that immense continent, so far as we know its history, it is still the law of nations, that prisoners are slaves. Can those who have themselves renounced this law, be permitted to participate in its effects, by purchasing the beings who are its victims? Whatever might be the answer of a moralist to this question, a jurist must search for its legal solution, in those principles of action which are sanctioned by the usages, the national acts, and the general assent, of that portion of the world of which he considers himself as a part, and to whose law the appeal is made. If we resort to this standard, as the test of international law, the question, as has already been observed, is decided in favor of the legality of the trade. Both Europe and America embarked in it; and for nearly two centuries, it was carried on, without opposition, and without censure. A jurist could not say that a practice, thus supported, was illegal, and that those engaged in it might be punished, either personally or by deprivation of property. In this commerce thus sanctioned by universal assent, every nation had an equal right to engage. How is their right to be lost? Each may renounce it for its own people; but can this renunciation affect others?

No principle of general law is more universally acknowledged, than the perfect equality of nations.

Russia and Geneva have equal rights. It results from this equality, that no one can rightfully impose a rule on another. Each legislates for itself, but its legislation can operate on itself alone. A right, then, which is vested in all, by the consent of all, can be divested only by consent; and this trade, in which all have participated, must remain lawful to those who cannot be induced to relinquish it. As no nation can prescribe a rule for others, none can make a law of nations; and this traffic remains lawful to those whose governments have not forbidden it. If it be consistent with the law of nations, it cannot in itself be piracy. It can be made so only by statute; and the obligation of the statute cannot transcend the legislative power of the state which may enact it.

If it be neither repugnant to the law of nations, nor piracy, it is almost superfluous to say, in this court, that the right of bringing in for adjudication, in time of peace, even where the vessel belongs to a nation which has prohibited the trade, cannot exist. The courts of no country execute the penal laws of another; and the course of the American government, on the subject of visitation and search, would decide any case in which that right had been exercised by an American cruiser, on the vessel of a foreign nation, not violating our municipal laws, against the captors. It follows, that a foreign vessel engaged in the African slave-trade, captured on the high seas, in time of peace, by an American cruiser, and brought in for adjudication, would be restored. . . .

The general question being disposed of, it remains to examine the circumstances of the particular case. [The Court denied the Portuguese claims, taking judicial notice of the fact that] Americans, and others who cannot use the flag of their own nations, carry on this criminal and inhuman traffic, under the flags of other countries. . . . [The real owner of the Africans claimed by Portugal] belongs to some other nation, and feels the necessity of concealment. [Because the Court was evenly divided over the legitimacy of the Spanish claim, it affirmed the lower court's decree, though it reduced the number of Africans to be restored to the Spanish owners.]

The Problem of the Grudge Informer

LON L. FULLER

Fuller's imaginary case presents you with a difficult choice: What will you do as the newly elected Minister of Justice? As you read the recommendations of the various deputies, try to detect appeals to one or another of the theories about the nature of law covered in this chapter. Do any of the deputies come close to your solution?

By a narrow margin you have been elected Minister of Justice of your country, a nation of some twenty million inhabitants. At the outset of your term of office you are confronted by a serious problem that will be described below. But first the background of this problem must be presented.

From Lon Fuller, *The Morality of Law* (New Haven: Yale University Press, 1969), pp. 245–253. Reprinted with permission of Yale University Press.

For many decades your country enjoyed a peaceful, constitutional and democratic government. However, some time ago it came upon bad times. Normal relations were disrupted by a deepening economic depression and by an increasing antagonism among various factional groups, formed along economic, political, and religious lines. The proverbial man on horseback appeared in the form of the Headman of a political party or society that called itself the Purple Shirts.

In a national election attended by much disorder the Headman was elected President of the Republic and his party obtained a majority of the seats in the

General Assembly. The success of the party at the polls was partly brought about by a campaign of reckless promises and ingenious falsifications, and partly by the physical intimidation of night-riding Purple Shirts who frightened many people away from the polls who would have voted against the party.

When the Purple Shirts arrived in power they took no steps to repeal the ancient Constitution or any of its provisions. They also left intact the Civil and Criminal Codes and the Code of Procedure. No official action was taken to dismiss any government official or remove any judge from the bench. Elections continued to be held at intervals and ballots were counted with apparent honesty. Nevertheless, the country lived under a reign of terror.

Judges who rendered decisions contrary to the wishes of the party were beaten and murdered. The accepted meaning of the Criminal Code was perverted to place political opponents in jail. Secret statutes were passed, the contents of which were known only to the upper levels of the party hierarchy. Retroactive statutes were enacted which made acts criminal that were legally innocent when committed. No attention was paid by the government to the restraints of the Constitution, of antecedent laws, or even of its own laws. All opposing political parties were disbanded. Thousands of political opponents were put to death, either methodically in prisons or in sporadic night forays of terror. A general amnesty was declared in favor of persons under sentence for acts "committed in defending the fatherland against subversion." Under this amnesty a general liberation of all prisoners who were members of the Purple Shirt party was effected. No one not a member of the party was released under the amnesty.

The Purple Shirts as a matter of deliberate policy preserved an element of flexibility in their operations by acting at times through the apparatus of the state which they controlled. Choice between the two methods of proceeding was purely a matter of expediency. For example, when the inner circle of the party decided to ruin all the former Socialist-Republicans (whose party put up a last-ditch resistance to the new regime), a dispute arose as to the best way of confiscating their property. One faction, perhaps still influenced by pre-revolutionary conceptions, wanted to accomplish this by a statute declaring their goods forfeited for criminal acts. Another wanted to do it by compelling the owners to deed their property over at the point of a bayonet. This group argued against the proposed statute on the ground that it would attract unfavorable comment abroad. The Headman decided in favor of direct action through the party to be followed by a secret statute ratifying the party's action and confirming the titles obtained by threats of physical violence.

The Purple Shirts have now been overthrown and a democratic and constitutional government restored. Some difficult problems have, however, been left behind by the deposed regime. These you and your associates in the new government must find some way of solving. One of these problems is that of the "grudge informer."

During the Purple Shirt regime a great many people worked off grudges by reporting their enemies to the party or to the government authorities. The activities reported were such things as the private expression of views critical of the government, listening to foreign radio broadcasts, associating with known wreckers and hooligans, hoarding more than the permitted amount of dried eggs, failing to report a loss of identification papers within five days, etc. As things then stood with the administration of justice, any of these acts, if proved, could lead to a sentence of death. In some cases this sentence was authorized by "emergency" statutes; in others it was imposed without statutory warrant, though by judges duly appointed to their offices.

After the overthrow of the Purple Shirts, a strong public demand grew up that these grudge informers be punished. The interim government, which preceded that with which you are associated, temporized on this matter. Meanwhile it has become a burning issue and a decision concerning it can no longer be postponed. Accordingly, your first act as Minister of Justice has been to address yourself to it. You have asked your five Deputies to give thought to the matter and to bring their recommendations to conference. At the conference the five Deputies speak in turn as follows:

FIRST DEPUTY: "It is perfectly clear to me that we can do nothing about these so-called grudge informers. The acts they reported were unlawful according to the rules of the government then in actual control of the nation's affairs. The sentences imposed on their victims were rendered in accordance with principles of law then obtaining. These principles differed from those familiar to us in ways that we consider detestable. Nevertheless they were then the law of the land. One of the principal differences between that law and our own lies in the much wider discretion it accorded to the judge in criminal matters. This rule and its consequences are as much entitled to respect by us as the reform which the Purple Shirts introduced into the law of wills, whereby only two witnesses were required instead of three. It is immaterial that the rule granting the judge a more or less uncontrolled discretion in criminal cases was never formally enacted but was a matter of tacit acceptance. Exactly the same thing can be said of the opposite rule which we accept that restricts the judge's discretion narrowly. The difference between ourselves and the Purple Shirts is not that theirs was an unlawful government—a contradiction in terms—but lies rather in the field of ideology. No one has a greater abhorrence than I for Purple Shirtism. Yet the fundamental difference between our philosophy and theirs is that we permit and tolerate differences in viewpoint, while they attempted to impose their monolithic code on everyone. Our whole system of government assumes that law is a flexible thing, capable of expressing and effectuating many different aims. The cardinal point of our creed is that when an objective has been duly incorporated into a law or judicial decree it must be provisionally accepted even by those that hate it, who must await their chance at the polls, or in another litigation, to secure a legal recognition of their own aims. The Purple Shirts, on the other hand, simply disregarded laws that incorporated objectives of which they did not approve, not even considering it worth the effort involved to repeal them. If we now seek to unscramble the acts of the Purple Shirt regime, declaring this judgment invalid, that statute void, this sentence excessive, we shall be doing exactly the thing we most condemn in them. I recognize that it will take courage to carry through with the program I recommend and we shall have to resist strong pressures of public opinion. We shall also have to be prepared to prevent the people from taking the law into their own hands. In the long run, however, I believe the course I recommend is the only one that will insure the triumph of the conceptions of law and government in which we believe."

SECOND DEPUTY: "Curiously, I arrive at the same conclusion as my colleague, by an exactly opposite route. To me it seems absurd to call the Purple Shirt regime a lawful government. A legal system does not exist simply because policemen continue to patrol the streets and wear uniforms or because a constitution and code are left on the shelf unrepealed. A legal system presupposes laws that are known, or can be known, by those subject to them. It presupposes some uniformity of action and that like cases will be given like treatment. It presupposes the absence of some lawless power, like the Purple Shirt Party, standing above the government and able at any time to interfere with the administration of justice whenever it does not function according to the whims of that power. All of these presuppositions enter into the very conception of an order of law and have nothing to do with political and economic ideologies. In my opinion law in any ordinary sense of the word ceased to exist when the Purple Shirts came to power. During their regime we had, in effect, an interregnum in the rule of law. Instead of a government of laws we had a war of all against all conducted behind barred doors, in dark alleyways, in palace intrigues, and prison-yard conspiracies. The acts of these so-called grudge informers were just one phase of that war. For us to condemn these acts as criminal would involve as much incongruity as if we were to attempt to apply juristic conceptions to the struggle for existence that goes on in the jungle or beneath the surface of the sea. We must put this whole dark, lawless chapter of our history behind us like a bad dream. If we stir among its hatreds, we shall bring upon ourselves something of its evil spirit and risk infection from its miasmas. I therefore say with my colleague, let bygones be bygones. Let us do nothing about the so-called grudge informers. What they did do was neither lawful nor contrary to law, for they lived, not under a regime of law, but under one of anarchy and terror."

THIRD DEPUTY: "I have a profound suspicion of any kind of reasoning that proceeds by an 'either-or' alternative. I do not think we need to assume either, on the one hand, that in some manner the whole of the Purple Shirt regime was outside the realm of law, or, on the other, that all of its doings are entitled to full credence as the acts of a lawful government. My two colleagues have unwittingly delivered powerful arguments against these extreme assumptions by demonstrating that both of them lead to the same absurd conclusion, a conclusion that is ethically and politically impossible. If one reflects about the matter without emotion it becomes clear that we did not have during the Purple Shirt regime a 'war of all against all.' Under the surface much of what we call normal human life went on— marriages were contracted, goods were sold, wills were drafted and executed. This life was attended by the usual dislocations—automobile accidents, bankruptcies, unwitnessed wills, defamatory misprints in the newspapers. Much of this normal life and most of these equally normal dislocations of it were unaffected by the Purple Shirt ideology. The legal questions that arose in this area were handled by the courts much as they had been formerly and much as they are being handled today. It would invite an intolerable chaos if we were to declare everything that happened under the Purple Shirts to be without legal basis. On the other hand, we certainly cannot say that the murders committed in the streets by members of the party acting under orders from the Headman were lawful simply because the party had achieved control of the government and its chief had become President of the Republic. If we must condemn the criminal acts of the party and its members, it would seem absurd to uphold every act which happened to be canalized through the apparatus of the government that had become, in effect, the alter ego of the Purple Shirt Party. We must therefore, in this situation, as in most human affairs, discriminate. Where the Purple Shirt philosophy intruded itself and perverted the administration of justice from its normal aims and uses, there we must interfere. Among these perversions of justice I would count, for example, the case of a man who was in love with another man's wife and brought about the death of the husband by informing against him for a wholly trivial offense, that is, for not reporting a loss of his identification papers within five days. This informer was a murderer under the Criminal Code which was in effect at the time of his act and which the Purple Shirts had not repealed. He encompassed the death of one who stood in the way of his illicit passions and utilized the courts for the realization of his murderous intent. He knew that the courts were themselves the pliant instruments of whatever policy the Purple Shirts might for the moment consider expedient. There are other cases that are equally clear. I admit that there are also some that are less clear. We shall be embarrassed, for example, by the cases of mere busybodies who reported to the authorities everything that looked suspect. Some of these persons acted not from desire to get rid of those they accused, but with a desire to curry favor with the party, to divert suspicions (perhaps ill-founded) raised against themselves, or through sheer officiousness. I don't know how these cases should be handled, and make no recommendation with regard to them. But the fact that these troublesome cases exist should not deter us from acting at once in the cases that are clear, of which there are far too many to permit us to disregard them."

FOURTH DEPUTY: "Like my colleague I too distrust 'either-or' reasoning, but I think we need to reflect more than he has about where we are headed. This proposal to pick and choose among the acts of the deposed regime is thoroughly objectionable. It is, in fact, Purple Shirtism itself, pure and simple. We like this law, so let us enforce it. We like this judgment, let it stand. This law we don't like, therefore it never was a law at all. This governmental act we disapprove, let it be deemed a nullity. If we proceed this way, we take toward the laws and acts of the Purple Shirt government precisely the unprincipled attitude they took toward the laws and acts of the government they supplanted. We shall have chaos, with every judge and every prosecuting attorney a law unto himself. Instead of ending the abuses of the Purple Shirt regime, my colleague's proposal would perpetuate them. There is only one way of dealing with this problem that is compatible with our philosophy of law and government and that is to deal with it by duly enacted law, I mean, by a special statute directed toward it. Let us study this whole problem of the grudge informer, get all the relevant facts, and draft a comprehensive law dealing with it. We shall not then be twisting old laws to purposes for which they were never intended. We shall furthermore provide penalties appropriate to the offense and not treat every informer as a murderer simply because the one he informed against was ultimately executed. I admit that we shall encounter some difficult problems of draftsmanship. Among other things, we shall have to assign a definite legal meaning to 'grudge' and that will not be easy. We should not be deterred by these difficulties, however, from adopting the only course that will lead us out of a condition of lawless, personal rule."

FIFTH DEPUTY: "I find a considerable irony in the last proposal. It speaks of putting a definite end to the abuses of the Purple Shirtism, yet it proposes to do this by resorting to one of the most hated devices of the Purple Shirt regime, the *ex post facto* criminal statute. My colleague dreads the conclusion that will result if we attempt without a statute to undo and redress 'wrong' acts of the departed order, while we uphold and enforce its 'right' acts. Yet he seems not to realize that his proposed statute is a wholly specious cure for this uncertainty. It is easy to make a plausible argument for an undrafted statute; we all agree it would be nice to have things down in black and white on paper. But just what would this statute provide? One of my colleagues speaks of someone who had failed for five days to report a loss of his identification papers. My colleague implies that the judicial sentence imposed for that offense, namely death, was so utterly disproportionate as to be clearly wrong. But we must remember that at that time the underground movement against the Purple Shirts was mounting in intensity and that the Purple Shirts were being harassed constantly by people with false identification papers. From their point of view they had a real problem, and the only objection we can make to their solution of it (other than the fact that we didn't want them to solve it) was that they acted with somewhat more rigor than the occasion seemed to demand. How will my colleague deal with this case in his statute, and with all of its cousins and second cousins? Will he deny the existence of any need for law and order under the Purple Shirt regime? I will not go further into the difficulties involved in drafting this proposed statute, since they are evident enough to anyone who reflects. I shall instead turn to my own solution. It has been said on very respectable authority that the main purpose of the criminal law is to give an outlet to the human instinct for revenge. There are times, and I believe this

is one of them, when we should allow that instinct to express itself directly without the intervention of forms of law. This matter of the grudge informers is already in process of straightening itself out. One reads almost every day that a former lackey of the Purple Shirt regime has met his just reward in some unguarded spot. The people are quietly handling this thing in their own way and if we leave them alone, and instruct our public prosecutors to do the same, there will soon be no problem left for us to solve. There will be some disorders, of course, and a few innocent heads will be broken. But our government and our legal system will not be involved in the affair and we shall not find ourselves hopelessly bogged down in an attempt to unscramble all the deeds and misdeeds of the Purple Shirts."

As Minister of Justice, which of these recommendations would you adopt?

Chapter 2

Constitutional Law: Interpretation and the First Amendment

In 2001, the Ninth Circuit Court of Appeals handed down a ruling on a lawsuit brought by several physicians whose practices involved performing abortion procedures. The physicians had sued the American Coalition of Life Activists, a group coordinating the efforts of anti-abortion protesters. The ACLS had posted on a Web site the names and addresses of physicians whom it claimed were guilty of "crimes against humanity." Dubbed the "Nuremberg Files," the posted information included pictures of the doctors, condemned as "baby butchers" and "murderers," together with automobile license plate numbers, and even names of the physicians' children and spouses. The Web site offered rewards to anyone providing information that led to the "arrest and conviction" of abortion providers at Nuremberg-type "war crimes" trials, as well as to those who were able to "persuade" specific physicians to refrain from killing children. The Web site marked the names of those doctors already victimized by anti-abortionists, putting a line through the names of those who had been murdered and graying out the names of those wounded. The doctors sued for what they considered threatening acts of intimidation. The ACLS defended its actions by invoking the constitutional guarantee of freedom of expression.[1]

---

[1] *Planned Parenthood of the Columbia/Willamette Inc. v. American Coalition of Life Activists*, 244 F.3d 1007 (9th Cir. 2001).

Constitutional law consists of many doctrines, principles, and distinctions developed by courts called upon, as was the circuit court in this instance, to adjudicate deeply antagonistic claims. These doctrines touch on many of the most contentious arenas of social life: property rights, religious belief, race, freedom of expression, equality, and criminal punishment. But the decisions rendered by courts in cases presenting fundamental controversies, and the processes by which these decisions are reached, raise perplexing questions. The court in the ACLS case, for example, argued that the organization neither threatened specific physicians nor advocated violence directly, even though its language, and the context of its presentation, made violence against the named physicians more likely. Were these veiled threats? Or merely "political advocacy"? What, after all, is the "law" of the Constitution on this point? How do we know? And should the liberty to express oneself include conduct of this sort?

This chapter focuses upon two of these most difficult parts of constitutional law: the limits of the freedoms of speech and expression, and the process of interpreting and applying the law of the Constitution. The readings in Section A explore the complexities of constitutional interpretation as a vehicle for understanding the nature and process of one important dimension of legal reasoning. The selections by Antonin

Scalia, Ronald Dworkin, and Robert Bork constitute a colloquy on how the abstract language of the Constitution is to be understood and its often-elusive meaning discerned. Parallel problems in statutory interpretation are also canvassed.

The second set of readings examine perennial concerns related to several of the most cherished freedoms guaranteed by the Constitution: How free can I be to put into practice my religious beliefs? How free should I be to express myself in cyberspace? Or in public? Does the idea of freedom of expression protect all forms of expression? Should activities that offend others be legally prohibited? What if others view my conduct as immoral? Can the law fairly be used to impose the moral or religious views of the majority upon the minority? What would this

mean? Shouldn't the law always try to enforce moral standards of behavior? The classic essay by philosopher John Stuart Mill is included, followed with selections by Patrick Devlin, H. L. A. Hart, Gerald Dworkin, and Joel Feinberg evaluating and responding to aspects of Mill's views.

The cases in Section C, together with readings by Joel Feinberg and Catherine MacKinnon, examine the recurrent and divisive issues of obscene and pornographic speech. The Cases for Further Reflection at the end of this chapter involve various claims, among them: that gay sex is a form of intimate conduct shielded from legal scrutiny by constitutional protection; that burning the American flag is a protected form of expression; and that a man may not utter profanities in the presence of a woman or child.

A. *Legal Reasoning and Constitutional Interpretation*

Interpreting the Law: The Presidential Election Case

The 2000 presidential election pitted then-Governor George W. Bush against Vice President Al Gore. The day following the election, it was clear that, although the Vice President had won the nationwide popular vote, the electoral vote—which actually decides the race—was in doubt. It quickly became apparent that the election would turn on which candidate received the electoral votes in the state of Florida. The popular vote in that state had been so close that an automatic machine recount of all ballots cast was conducted. This recount narrowed the race even further, and Gore exercised his statutory right to request manual recounts of votes cast in four counties. Thus began a political drama that lasted weeks and captivated the

nation. The political struggle over the election turned crucially upon a welter of conflicting laws: state statutes, federal laws, and various constitutional provisions, both state and federal.

While all parties to the election dispute concurred on what the relevant laws were, almost none of them agreed upon how those laws were to be interpreted or in what way their overlapping and sometimes conflicting requirements were to be reconciled with one another. In brief, Florida's laws allowed for manual recounts of ballots under certain circumstances, but without set deadlines for the certification of all legal votes; the Florida state constitution granted the people of Florida the right to select electors to the national Electoral College, but U.S. federal laws fixed the conditions under which those electors would be certified; and while Florida courts possessed ultimate authority to interpret state election requirements and procedures, the U.S. Constitution granted the legislature of Florida the power to establish election laws. With such a confusing array of laws to confront, the courts addressing the issues involved were forced to *reason* about the meaning of the law in ways that illustrate many of the complexities of legal interpretation.

Issues in Bush v. Gore

To appreciate how the election case exemplifies problems in legal interpretation, we can examine briefly a sampling of the issues presented by both candidates up to the final disposition of the case by the U.S. Supreme Court on December 12, 2000. To begin with, several provisions of state law were heavily debated. One state law, for instance, allowed for full manual recounts of all votes cast to be conducted by the county canvassing board in the event of an "error in vote tabulation." A sample manual recount in some counties came to totals different from the automatic machine count. But is a discrepancy between a machine count of votes and a sample manual count an "error" in tabulation? The statute which allowed candidates to request and the county boards to authorize a recount of votes failed to specify any time limit for completion of the recount; but another act stipulated that any voting results submitted more than seven days after the election "shall be ignored." But what if the recounting takes more than seven days? To make matters worse, a further provision of state law said that if the returns are not received in time "such returns may be ignored." Do "shall be ignored" and "may be ignored" mean different things? And if so, which controls? If the voting results "may" be ignored, then presumably they "may not" be ignored as well. Are any limits placed upon this implied discretion?

The Florida Supreme Court held that the "may ignore" statute takes priority over the "shall ignore" provision. One reason given by the court for this choice was that, where two statutory provisions conflict, the most recent takes priority. Is this a good principle for interpreting the law? Why? The court further argued that if the "shall ignore" rule were to take priority, manual recounts would be unworkable as a practical matter, since recounts may take considerable time. The legislature, the court reasoned, could not have intended this result. But why is that? Must those who draft laws always be consistent? Finally, according to the Florida court, to prohibit a manual recount would be a restriction upon the electoral process in violation of the state Constitution; hence, the court ruled, the recount should go forward, since otherwise at least some "legal votes" would not be counted at all. The court held that a legal vote is "one in which there is a clear indication of the intent of the voter." But what determines whether the "intent of the voter" is clear? Is a punch-card ballot in which the holes are partially punched through (the infamous "hanging chad") a "clear indication"? Why is this the right way to define a "legal vote"? The U.S. Supreme Court found that, since different counties could use differing criteria to determine what is a "legal vote" under such a vague standard, it would be impossible to ensure that everyone's vote would count "equally" within the electoral process. Thus, manual recounts would violate the federal constitutional guarantee of "equal protection of the laws." (Since it was decided on grounds involving equal protection of the laws, the excerpt from the Supreme Court's ruling in *Bush v. Gore* appears in this text at the end of Chapter 3.)

Statutory Interpretation

As the disputes in the presidential election case make clear, even though the law is expressed in language, that language is nearly always incomplete and must be interpreted before it can be applied to a specific situation. But how should statutes be read? How ought constitutional provisions to be understood?

The intriguing case of *Smith v. U.S.,* which opens the readings for this chapter, nicely explores these problems. John Angus Smith offered to trade a gun for some drugs to a man who, unknown to him, was an undercover police officer. Smith was charged and convicted on various federal firearms offenses, including a term of imprisonment for "use of a firearm" in the commission of a drug trafficking offense. On appeal, Smith's argument was straightforward, if controversial: obviously, Smith reasoned, Congress meant to punish only those drug traffickers who use a gun threateningly or intend to do violence with a gun; thus, Smith insisted, he could not be guilty, since he didn't use the weapon in question *as a weapon,* but only as an item of exchange. Since he didn't employ his gun *as a gun,* he did not really "use a firearm" during the commission of a crime. What conduct is it that constitutes the "use" of a firearm in the commission of an offense? The majority of the U.S. Supreme Court affirmed Smith's conviction. Certainly, says the majority, Smith "used" a gun in some sense—he used it to try to obtain drugs. The fact that he didn't use the weapon *as* a weapon is irrelevant, since the phrase "as a weapon" does not actually appear anywhere in the relevant statute. Moreover, confining the meaning of the statute to use "as a weapon" would be too narrow, for then only the actual firing of it would be a punishable offense. Yet, the majority reasoned, had Smith hit someone over the head with the gun he ought still to have been found guilty. As further support for their reading, the majority also looked to other parts of federal law and to the supposed purposes of Congress in passing such legislation.

Dissenting in *Smith*, Justice Antonin Scalia argues that Smith's conviction should be overturned. The meaning of a statute derives from its context, Scalia observes, and thus "use of a firearm" must mean "use" for the intended purpose of a firearm. Although words can be employed in all manner of ways, in construing laws it is the ordinary use that should be looked to, and this means that using a gun *as* a gun is what the statute in question implies.

The *Smith* case nicely foregrounds problems about what the law means. Does a statute always have a "plain meaning" that is apparent to those to whom it is directed? Is the meaning of a statute something that is set when the statute is enacted? Or can the meaning of a law change and evolve over time? Is a law's meaning decided by the actual intentions of the legislators who voted for it? Or by the pursposes the legislature claims the law was meant to address? Or by what the reader or interpreter of a statute takes it to mean?

We could look at the problem of the meaning of law within the broader context of linguistic meaning generally. One point of departure for resolving questions of linguistic interpretation is to focus upon the intent of the speaker—in a legal context, the intent of the legislative body that enacted the law in question. On this view, what the law says depends upon what I (the author of the law) intended it to say, not upon what you (the reader of the law) think I was saying (or should have said). Of course, in many cases, the author's intent and the reader's understanding will coalesce, given an appropriate shared context of background information and belief. Suppose I shout "fire." Without a clear context, my meaning may be unclear. But if we assume that my remark is made in a context where smoke is present and an alarm is sounding, then it is unlikely that my intent will be misread. But the "speaker's meaning" view invites fresh questions: How important to a conception of

what a statute means are the legislator's ideas or views of what it means? Can a group (for example, a state assembly) be said to have an "intention" with regard to a particular measure or enactment? How did the people who wrote the law think that it should be interpreted? Did they "intend," for example, that their meaning be discerned in one way, rather than another? Is it ever proper to ask what a legislator might have intended about a particular application of a given law, had he or she considered it?

Contrasted with the intent of the speaker, meaning can also be evaluated from the perspective of the reader's understanding. On this view, a statute means what the person to whom it is addressed would reasonably take it to mean. But questions arise here, too: What are the limits to a "reasonable" reading of a statute? Could Smith "reasonably" have assumed that he was not breaking the firearms ban by seeking to barter his gun away, rather than to fire it? Or should he have realized that any "use" of the weapon to facilitate the commission of a drug offense is forbidden? Some texts, for example novels or poems, can be understood in sharply divergent ways by equally "reasonable" readers? Can the same be true of a legal "text"?

In a selection from his scholarly work included here, Supreme Court Justice Antonin Scalia addresses what he takes to be a conflict between certain forms of legal reasoning and interpretation, on the one hand, and a commitment to democracy, on the other. Democracy expresses itself ideally, Scalia thinks, through the legislative process, and in fact much of the body of our law is statutory law. But, Scalia warns, it is simply not compatible with democratic theory that laws are interpreted "to mean whatever they ought to mean," a view that too often prevails, in Scalia's opinion, among judges, lawyers, and legal scholars. Scalia employs an older Supreme Court case, *Church of the Holy Trinity v. U.S.*, as a vehicle for exposing ill-conceived theories of statutory interpretation. In that case, a church had contracted with a minister in England to come to New York and work as a pastor at the church. The church was accused by the government of violating a federal law prohibiting employers to "in any way assist or encourage the importation or migration of any alien or aliens" into the United States. The statute had been passed during an especially xenophobic period in American history, and the Court was faced with the task of determining whether the statute made the church's conduct illegal. The Court held that it did not, since the "obvious" intent of Congress in this case "reaches only to the manual laborer, as distinguished from the professional man."

Scalia is unhappy with theories that appeal to legislative intent or that invoke accounts of legislative history. Always looking past the text to uncover an intent that is alleged to lay beneath the law is too dangerous a method, in Scalia's view. Legislative history is manipulable, and the intent of the legislature may simply not be sufficiently clear. Scalia defends a view he calls "textualism": the idea that "the text is the law, and it is the text that must be observed." The law should be construed "reasonably," based upon its "objective intent." Scalia illustrates this theory in his discussion of both the *Holy Trinity* and *Smith* cases.

Constitutional Interpretation

The fundamental law of the United States is to be found in the federal Constitution, a document that erected a framework of government, set out the terms of state and federal powers, and purported to guarantee to individuals certain rights. Much of the language of the Constitution is, however, abstract and highly general; and it is for this reason that the interpretation of its key provisions is often deeply controversial. Recall, for instance, the Court's resolution of the presidential election case. The Fourteenth Amendment to the Constitution mandates that no citizen be denied "equal protection of the laws." The Supreme Court held that this provision was violated by Florida's manual recount of votes. Critics complained that the Justices had acted irresponsibly by "reading into" the Constitution their own moral, social, and political agendas. Others insisted that they had simply enforced the "true" meaning of the Constitution. But what is the difference between "reading things into" the Constitution and "finding" them there already? What does it mean to interpret a constitution or a statute responsibly? How does one reason from vague and open-ended language such as "due process" or "equal protection" to concrete decisions in particular cases, from general principles to specific results? In what way are judges' decisions guided by the law, rather than by their own opinions?

Perhaps the best way to grasp the issues here is to begin with a brief recitation of a handful of rulings issued by the Supreme Court in the past few years. Among the more controversial holdings are these (many of which we will encounter later in this text): a state that arrests and imprisons homosexuals for practicing sodomy in their bedrooms violates their consti-

tutional rights; a law requiring that "creationism" be taught in the public schools violates the First Amendment because it "establishes a religion"; a statutory rape law providing that only males are punishable for rape does not violate their right to "equal protection of the laws"; there is no constitutionally protected right to use the drug peyote as part of a religious ceremony; no state may execute a person who was under the age of sixteen at the time of a capital offense; no American citizens have a right of privacy in their garbage; neither Congress nor the states may prohibit the burning of the American flag as a form of political protest; irreversibly comatose persons who have not made clearly known their wishes regarding life-sustaining medical interventions have no constitutionally protected "right to die." This is, of course, but a small sampling of an increasingly long list of controversial decisions handed down by the courts each year, decisions touching freedom of speech and of the press, freedom of religion, racial and sexual equality, criminal liability and punishment, personal autonomy and privacy, and so on.

Accustomed as we are to hearing of these controversial rulings, the reaction they provoke in many of us is still the same: Who are the justices of the Supreme Court to lay down the law in a community that purports at least to be a democracy? In making these delicate and often disturbing decisions, many say, the Supreme Court and lower courts are going too far; they are overstepping their legitimate function, which is to "apply" the law, not to "make" it. (This view has since been echoed in calls for judges who would "interpret" the Constitution and not "legislate from the bench.") This common complaint about the courts and their controversial rulings actually disguises two fundamental questions about constitutional interpretation and judicial reasoning. First, in a democracy who should have the right to issue authoritative interpretations of the Constitution? Second, what is the proper method of understanding what the Constitution requires or permits or forbids? The first of these questions has come to be called the "countermajoritarian difficulty": What justifies permitting a body, neither elected nor otherwise politically accountable in any significant way, to overrule the judgments of the people as expressed by their representatives? Why shouldn't interpreting the Constitution itself be a democratic process?

The second question, and the one with which we shall be concerned in this section, is equally daunting. The Constitution, on its face at least, makes absolutely no reference whatever to privacy, garbage, sodomy, creationism, peyote, statutory rape, flag burning, or the irreversibly comatose. It has been made to speak to these issues only through acts of interpretation. But what governs or controls or constrains these acts of interpretation? What tells us whether the interpretation has been done well or badly, correctly or incorrectly? Is there any standard of "correctness" here at all? Or are constitutional decisions simply choices dictated by the private moral and political convictions of the judge?

Griswold, Lawrence, and the Right of Privacy

Few areas of constitutional adjudication have posed these questions about interpretation more acutely than the Supreme Court's "privacy" rulings, dealing primarily with abortion and sexual matters. How should the text of the Constitution and the Court's subsequent decisions be interpreted in regard to privacy and personal sexual autonomy? Is there any principled interpretive methodology that can settle such cases noncontroversially? Are any of the Court's privacy rulings legitimate? These questions were thrust into relief in 2003, when the Supreme Court overruled one of its most controversial opinions and declared, in *Lawrence v. Texas*, that homosexual conduct is constitutionally protected. Two prior privacy cases serve to shed light on the Court's reasoning in *Lawrence* and its contentious aftermath.

In 1961, a Mr. Griswold, the director of the Planned Parenthood League of Connecticut, was arrested for violating a state statute forbidding the dissemination of contraceptive devices and information, even to married persons. Griswold contended that the statute violated the Constitution, and the Supreme Court agreed. Writing for the majority, Justice Douglas argued that the statute violated the general right of privacy granted by the Constitution to all citizens. Douglas was aware that "privacy" occurs nowhere in the text of the Constitution; nonetheless he found a right of privacy in the "penumbras," the faint shadows of several of the amendments to the Constitution. To establish this, Douglas relied partly upon precedent, the authority of prior cases. In the *Pierce* and *Meyer* cases from the 1920s, for example, it had been held that the First Amendment protects the rights of parents to send their children to private schools and to teach them a foreign language. In *NAACP v. Alabama*, the Court had protected the freedom to associate by preventing disclosure of an organization's membership list. The Third and Fourth Amendments protect a person's interest in the privacy and sanctity of the home; and the Fifth Amendment,

Douglas continued, protects people against being forced to disclose things about themselves. Douglas believed that these textual requirements and prior cases add up to a general right of privacy relating to matters of marriage, children, and family; the state of Connecticut must have a good reason for invading this zone of privacy. Douglas insisted that it did not. After all, if the purpose of the statute is to discourage illicit sexual relations (as the state claimed), why make even birth control counseling for married persons punishable?

At least two other arguments were given in *Griswold* to support the finding of a right of privacy in the Constitution. Justice Goldberg asserted one of these arguments by invoking the Ninth Amendment: "The enumeration in the Constitution, of certain rights, shall not be construed to deny or disparage others retained by the people." Goldberg believed privacy to be one of the rights "retained by the people," and he contended that the Connecticut statute violated the "due process" clause of the Fourteenth Amendment, which protects (in Harlan's language) "values implicit in the concept of ordered liberty," rights that are "fundamental." One of these values or rights, Harlan believed, is privacy in the home, and this includes marital privacy. Finally, Justice Black, in dissent, admitted that he found the Connecticut law offensive but that he could find no specific provision of the Constitution protecting a general right of privacy. The majority's arguments, he thought, are little better than a vehicle through which the justices rationalized their invalidation of a law they found personally offensive. This, Black insisted, is not their job. (Excerpts from *Griswold* may be found in the "Cases for Further Reflection" at the end of this chapter.)

A number of significant decisions extending the scope of the right of privacy followed in the wake of *Griswold*, striking down laws prohibiting interracial marriage, extending the right of privacy to include the possession of obscene materials in one's own home, reversing a conviction for public distribution of contraceptives to *unmarried* persons, and invalidating prohibitions on the sale of nonprescription contraceptives to persons under the age of sixteen.[1] By far the most controversial extension of *Griswold*, however, came in 1973 in the case of *Roe v. Wade*, in which the Court struck down criminal abortion statutes that prohibited abortions except to save the life of the mother.

---

[1]See, respectively, *Loving v. Virginia*, 388 U.S. 1 (1967); *Stanley v. Georgia*, 394 U.S. 577 (1969); *Eisenstadt v. Baird*, 405 U.S. 438 (1972); and *Carey v. Population Services*, 431 U.S. 678 (1977).

Justice Blackmun's opinion for the Court applied the privacy right to the decision to abort: "The right of privacy, whether it be founded in the Fourteenth Amendment's concept of personal liberty and restrictions upon state action, as we feel it is, or, as the District Court determined, in the Ninth Amendment's reservation of rights to the people, is broad enough to encompass a woman's decision whether or not to terminate her pregnancy."[2]

Bowers v. Hardwick, decided by the Supreme Court in 1986, raised deep questions about *Griswold* and its sequela: What did *Griswold* really decide? Just what is the scope of the constitutional right of privacy?

Michael Hardwick was observed by a police officer to be engaged in oral sex with another man, an act that is a felony in Georgia. Hardwick was arrested for violating the sodomy statute, and he challenged the law's constitutionality before the Supreme Court. Justice White, writing for the Court, framed the issue in this way: Does the Constitution confer a fundamental right to engage in homosexual sodomy? White answered no. Hardwick's conduct is not protected, White maintained, by the rationale of the line of cases stretching from *Pierce* and *Meyer* through *Griswold* and *Roe*, for those cases dealt only with intimate matters pertaining to family, marriage, and procreation, none of which are at stake in homosexual sodomy. Nor is Hardwick's sexual conduct one of the "fundamental values" or liberties "deeply rooted in our Nation's history and traditions," a point White supported by citing the long history of the criminalization of homosexual conduct. Nor can Hardwick rely on privacy in the home, as not everything that occurs in the home is constitutionally protected.

Dissenting, Justice Blackmun distinguished between two ideas or threads running throughout the privacy cases: privacy in certain decisions involving personal autonomy in intimate matters and privacy in certain locations, such as the home. Blackmun argued that both of these are implicated in *Bowers*. We protect choices regarding marriage, childbearing, and child rearing not because they are the only constitutionally important interests, but because each deals with the most fundamental ways in which individuals define themselves, with the lives that they must make for themselves. Plainly, Blackmun argued, sexual orientation and sexual conduct are crucial parts of one's self-definition. Furthermore, the incident here took place in

Hardwick's bedroom, and there is a textual basis, Blackmun thought, for protecting privacy in the home, as earlier cases made clear.

Blackmun's minority view in 1986 became the majority position in 2003 in *Lawrence v. Texas*. John Lawrence and his gay partner were charged with "deviate sexual intercourse with another individual of the same sex." The Court, construing its prior cases from *Griswold* on, read them broadly to mean that "there are other spheres of our life and existence, outside the home, where the state should not be a dominant presence. . . . Liberty presumes an autonomy of the self that includes freedom of thought, belief, expression, and certain intimate conduct." Arguing that "persons in a homosexual relationship may seek autonomy . . . just as heterosexuals do" and that "the decision in *Bowers* would deny this right," the majority concluded that "*Bowers* was not correct when it was decided and it is not correct today" and it "should be and now is overruled."

The dissenters in *Lawrence* accuse the majority of being overly anxious to jettison an embarrassing ruling at the cost of undermining respect for the authority of precedent, the principle of *stare decisis*. Only "fundamental rights" rooted in American history and traditions merit constitutional protection, and gay sex is not among these. The dissenting justices take the majority to task for resting their ruling on an "emerging awareness" that matters pertaining to sex are within the scope of personal liberty. As a principle of constitutional interpretation, this standard could license any and all constitutional entitlements that a majority of judges believe to be appropriate. (The Court's ruling in *Lawrence* is included in the "Cases for Further Reflection" at the end of this chapter.)

Originalism and the Limits of Privacy

The selection by Robert Bork raises important questions about the source, legitimacy, and scope of the constitutional right of privacy. Bork is concerned with what he (and others) see as the gradual politicizing, or political involvement, of the courts: the pursuit by judges of a political agenda (usually liberal), which should be voted on by legislatures rather than inserted into the law by courts. Such "activism" threatens the legitimacy of the rule of law. Bork would have courts follow "the only thing that can be called law," namely, "the principles of the text, whether Constitution or statute, as generally understood at

---

[2]410 U.S. 153, 164–165.

the time of enactment."[3] This is the premise of Bork's theory of constitutional interpretation, what he calls a jurisprudence of "original understanding."

Bork roundly criticizes Douglas's argument in *Griswold,* arguing that no number of specific constitutional freedoms, even including their "penumbras," add up to a distinct and general "right of privacy," a right that Douglas simply created and that, Bork alleges, hovers uncertainly over the only rights with a genuine constitutional basis. Bork repeatedly presses the question of what the right of privacy includes, given that it has no actual basis in the Constitution. He concludes that no major case in the Court's privacy jurisprudence has the support, by way of precedent, of anything in the constitutional text or in the holdings or of any of the earlier cases in the series. Each is a fresh act of judicial policy making, and this is nowhere more evident, Bork believes, than in Justice Blackmun's dissent in *Bowers.*

Elsewhere, Bork asserts that the privacy decisions, along with other "activist" holdings, violate three core requirements of permissible constitutional interpretation: that constitutional principles and rights be neutrally derived, defined, and applied.[4] Privacy is not neutrally derivable from the text but read into it by judges with a particular moral bias. Nor has constitutional privacy been neutrally defined; indeed, its scope has not been defined at all. And at what level of generality should a right like that of privacy be understood and applied? Should it be viewed narrowly, following White in *Bowers*? Or should it be viewed expansively and at a higher level of generality or abstraction, as per the majority in *Lawrence*? Because the right of privacy has not been neutrally derived from the Constitution to begin with, Bork reasons, it is no wonder that these questions have no answer.

One important theory of constitutional interpretation has a long history. This is the view often referred to as a jurisprudence of "original understanding" or more simply "originalism." The basic idea behind originalism is fairly straightforward: The courts should always strive to interpret statutory and constitutional language by seeking to discover, resurrect, and apply the intent of the authors of the statute or of the Constitution. The search for authorial intent (which has its advocates elsewhere—for example, in literary theory), although requiring the gathering of

historical evidence of various kinds, relies chiefly upon the language of the written text as the most important source of evidence regarding that intent.

Originalists defend their theory as a coherent and nonarbitrary interpretive methodology: The written text has an objective meaning that can be found, not made up. Originalists such as Bork insist that "there is a historical Constitution that was understood by those who enacted it to have a meaning of its own. The intended meaning has an existence independent of anything judges may say."[5] By deriving and applying this meaning, courts can settle problems that otherwise plague current constitutional decision making—for example, the difficulty of determining at what level of generality a constitutional principle or right is to be defined. Original understanding avoids the problem, Bork claims, by "finding the level of generality that interpretation of the words, structure, and history of the Constitution fairly supports."[6] Bork sums up the view this way: "What is the meaning of a rule . . . ? It is the meaning understood at the time of the law's enactment. . . . Law is a public act. Secret reservations and intentions count for nothing. All that counts is how the words used in the Constitution would have been understood at the time. The original understanding is thus manifested in the words used and in the secondary materials, such as debates at the conventions, public discussion, newspaper articles, dictionaries in use at the time, and the like."[7]

Originalism, as an interpretive methodology, raises a number of questions and has been subjected to a variety of criticisms. The theory says that we are to look for the original intent, the intent of the "authors" of the Constitution. But this hides a crucial problem. Who are the authors? The framers of the document, those who actually wrote it in Philadelphia? Or perhaps the adopters, the people in the various colonial conventions who voted to ratify the document? There are reasons for discounting either group. It is not clear why the intent of the framers, an elite group of wealthy property owners, unelected by anyone, should be privileged in this way, especially if one of the driving forces behind originalism is to square constitutional interpretation with democracy. On the other hand, people vote for things, including constitutions, with all manner of purposes and motives. What reason

---

[3] Bork, *The Tempting of America* (New York: Free Press, 1990), Chap. 7.

[4] *Ibid.,* Chap. 7.

[5] Bork, *op. cit.,* 176.

[6] *Ibid.,* p. 150.

[7] *Ibid.,* p. 144.

is there to think that the majority of New Yorkers who voted to ratify the Constitution expressed any uniform "intention" with regard to anything on which the Constitution speaks? These are the *epistemological* difficulties posed by originalism, that is, problems dealing with what we can know of the intentions of the authors of a statute or a constitution. How can we know the intent of people who lived so long ago? And even if we could unearth their thoughts, might we not find that they neither intended nor did not intend for (say) garbage to be private or for "creationism" to be taught—that is, that they simply never thought about the constitutionality of these matters at all?

Despite its problems, the originalist theory of constitutional interpretation is a response to a serious difficulty: If we don't look to the intent of the drafters or framers of a statute or a constitution to give meaning to vague or open-ended language, what anchors a reading or an interpretation to the text at all? Can we permit judges or other constitutional interpreters to rely solely and directly upon their own value judgments in their role as interpreters? Or to appeal to the precepts of "natural law" or the principles of "correct moral reasoning"? To invoke America's "fundamental traditions"? To defer to public consensus or majoritarian sentiment? The basic difficulty with all of these ways of reasoning within and from the Constitution is, according to the originalist, the same in every case: None yields any real constraint on the task of interpreting the Constitution because each can be employed or invoked to support almost any decision. Our "traditions" are many and various, the "correct" moral theory notoriously difficult to find, and the view of the majority often that which the constitutional language (particularly in the Bill of Rights) seeks to protect us against.

The reading from Justice Scalia also addresses constitutional interpretation. Consistent with his view that legal texts have an "objective" meaning, Scalia urges us not to follow "original intent" so much as "original meaning." But both of these are to be preferred to the search for "current meaning," defended by those who believe in a "living Constitution" the content of which evolves over time. Those who defend this misguided view, Scalia protests, have no criteria to guide their interpretations of constitutional language, and their view comes dangerously close to holding that, if the Constitution *should* say something, then it *does*. Legal philosopher Ronald Dworkin argues that Scalia's textualism is indefensible. Scalia fails to distinguish between (1) what the framers of the Constitution intended to say—the meaning of their words—and (2) what they expected the impact or consequences of their words to be. Dworkin's point is that these can be separated. Taking up one of Scalia's examples, the framers of the Eighth Amendment to the Constitution did not forbid only punishment "cruel and unusual as of the date of 1791." Rather, their language was meant to forbid whatever punishments are truly cruel and unusual. In this way, Dworkin argues, later generations could discover that the abstract principle embedded in the Eighth Amendment actually prohibits (say) capital punishment, despite the fact that the framers themselves (wrongly) believed that the death penalty was not cruel and unusual.

Smith v. U.S.

JUSTICE O'CONNOR delivered the opinion of the Court.

We decide today whether the exchange of a gun for narcotics constitutes "use" of a firearm "during and in relation to . . . [a] drug trafficking crime" within the meaning of 18 U.S.C. § 924(c)(1). We hold that it does.

---

508 U.S. 223 (1993), United States Supreme Court.

I

Petitioner John Angus Smith and his companion went from Tennessee to Florida to buy cocaine; they hoped to resell it at a profit. While in Florida, they met petitioner's acquaintance, Deborah Hoag. Hoag agreed to, and in fact did, purchase cocaine for petitioner. She then accompanied petitioner and his friend to her motel room, where they were joined by a drug dealer. While Hoag listened, petitioner and the dealer discussed petitioner's MAC–10 firearm, which had been modified to operate as an automatic. The MAC–10 apparently is a favorite among criminals. It is small and compact, lightweight, and can be equipped with a silencer. Most important of all, it can be devastating: A fully automatic MAC–10 can fire more than 1,000 rounds per minute. The dealer expressed his interest in becoming the owner of a MAC–10, and petitioner promised that he would discuss selling the gun if his arrangement with another potential buyer fell through.

Unfortunately for petitioner, Hoag had contacts not only with narcotics traffickers but also with law enforcement officials. In fact, she was a confidential informant. Consistent with her post, she informed the Broward County Sheriff's Office of petitioner's activities. The Sheriff's Office responded quickly, sending an undercover officer to Hoag's motel room. Several others were assigned to keep the motel under surveillance. Upon arriving at Hoag's motel room, the undercover officer presented himself to petitioner as a pawnshop dealer. Petitioner, in turn, presented the officer with a proposition: He had an automatic MAC–10 and silencer with which he might be willing to part. Petitioner then pulled the MAC–10 out of a black canvas bag and showed it to the officer. The officer examined the gun and asked petitioner what he wanted for it. Rather than asking for money, however, petitioner asked for drugs. He was willing to trade his MAC–10, he said, for two ounces of cocaine. The officer told petitioner that he was just a pawnshop dealer and did not distribute narcotics. Nonetheless, he indicated that he wanted the MAC–10 and would try to get the cocaine. The officer then left, promising to return within an hour.

Rather than seeking out cocaine as he had promised, the officer returned to the Sheriff's Office to arrange for petitioner's arrest. But petitioner was not content to wait. The officers who were conducting surveillance saw him leave the motel room carrying a gun bag; he then climbed into his van and drove away. The officers reported petitioner's departure and began following him. When law enforcement authorities tried to stop petitioner, he led them on a high-speed chase. Petitioner eventually was apprehended.

. . .

A grand jury sitting in the District Court for the Southern District of Florida returned an indictment charging petitioner with, among other offenses, two drug trafficking crimes. . . . Most important here, the indictment alleged that petitioner knowingly used the MAC–10 and its silencer during and in relation to a drug trafficking crime. Under 18 U.S.C. § 924(c)(1), a defendant who so uses a firearm must be sentenced to five years' incarceration. And where, as here, the firearm is a "machinegun" or is fitted with a silencer, the sentence is 30 years. . . . The jury convicted petitioner on all counts.

On appeal, petitioner argued that § 924(c)(1)'s penalty for using a firearm during and in relation to a drug trafficking offense covers only situations in which the firearm is used as a weapon. According to petitioner, the provision does not extend to defendants who use a firearm solely as a medium of exchange or for barter. The Court of Appeals for the Eleventh Circuit disagreed. The plain language of the statute, the court explained, imposes no requirement that the firearm be used as a weapon. Instead, any use of "the weapon to facilitate *in any manner* the commission of the offense" suffices. . . .

Section 924(c)(1) requires the imposition of specified penalties if the defendant, "during and in relation to any crime of violence or drug trafficking crime[,] uses or carries a firearm." By its terms, the statute requires the prosecution to make two showings. First, the prosecution must demonstrate that the defendant "use[d] or carrie[d] a firearm." Second, it must prove that the use or carrying was "during and in relation to" a "crime of violence or drug trafficking crime."

Petitioner argues that exchanging a firearm for drugs does not constitute "use" of the firearm within the meaning of the statute. He points out that nothing in the record indicates that he fired the MAC–10, threatened anyone with it, or employed it for self-protection. In essence, petitioner argues that he cannot be said to have "use[d]" a firearm unless he used it as a weapon, since that is how firearms most often are used. . . . [W]e confine our discussion to what the parties view as the dispositive issue in this case: whether trading a firearm for drugs can constitute "use" of the firearm within the meaning of § 924(c)(1).

When a word is not defined by statute, we normally construe it in accord with its ordinary or natural meaning. . . . Surely petitioner's treatment of his MAC–10 can be described as "use" within the everyday meaning of that term. Petitioner "used" his MAC–10 in an attempt to obtain drugs by offering to trade it for cocaine. Webster's defines "to use" as "[t]o convert to one's service" or "to employ." Black's Law Dictionary contains a similar definition: "[t]o make use of; to convert to one's service; to employ; to avail oneself of; to utilize; to carry out a purpose or action by means of." Indeed, over 100 years ago we gave the word "use" the same gloss, indicating that it means "to employ" or "to derive service from." Petitioner's handling of the MAC–10 in this case falls squarely within those definitions. By attempting to trade his MAC–10 for the drugs, he "used" or "employed" it as an item of barter to obtain cocaine; he "derived service" from it because it was going to bring him the very drugs he sought.

In petitioner's view, § 924(c)(1) should require proof not only that the defendant used the firearm, but also that he used it *as a weapon*. But the words "as a weapon" appear nowhere in the statute. Rather, § 924(c)(1)'s language sweeps broadly, punishing any "us[e]" of a firearm, so long as the use is "during and in relation to" a drug trafficking offense. . . . Had Congress intended the narrow construction petitioner urges, it could have so indicated. It did not, and we decline to introduce that additional requirement on our own.

Language, of course, cannot be interpreted apart from context. The meaning of a word that appears ambiguous if viewed in isolation may become clear when the word is analyzed in light of the terms that surround it. Recognizing this, petitioner and the dissent argue that the word "uses" has a somewhat reduced scope in § 924(c)(1) because it appears alongside the word "firearm." Specifically, they contend that the average person on the street would not think immediately of a guns-for-drugs trade as an example of "us[ing] a firearm." Rather, that phrase normally evokes an image of the most familiar use to which a firearm is put—use as a weapon. Petitioner and the dissent therefore argue that the statute excludes uses where the weapon is not fired or otherwise employed for its destructive capacity. . . . Indeed, relying on that argument—and without citation to authority—the dissent announces its own, restrictive definition of "use." "To use an instrumentality," the dissent argues, "ordinarily means to use it for its intended purpose."

There is a significant flaw to this argument. It is one thing to say that the ordinary meaning of "uses a firearm" *includes* using a firearm as a weapon, since that is the intended purpose of a firearm and the example of "use" that most immediately comes to mind. But it is quite another to conclude that, as a result, the phrase also *excludes* any other use. Certainly that conclusion does not follow from the phrase "uses . . . a firearm" itself. As the dictionary definitions and experience make clear, one can use a firearm in a number of ways. That one example of "use" is the first to come to mind when the phrase "uses . . . a firearm" is uttered does not preclude us from recognizing that there are other "uses" that qualify as well. In this case, it is both reasonable and normal to say that petitioner "used" his

MAC–10 in his drug trafficking offense by trading it for cocaine; the dissent does not contend otherwise.

The dissent's example of how one might "use" a cane, suffers from a similar flaw. To be sure, "use" as an adornment in a hallway is not the first "use" of a cane that comes to mind. But certainly it does not follow that the *only* "use" to which a cane might be put is assisting one's grandfather in walking. . . . [T]he use of a cane as an instrument of punishment was once so common that "to cane" has become a verb meaning "[t]o beat with a cane." In any event, the only question in this case is whether the phrase "uses . . . a firearm" in § 924(c)(1) is most reasonably read as *excluding* the use of a firearm in a gun-for-drugs trade. The fact that the phrase clearly *includes* using a firearm to shoot someone, as the dissent contends, does not answer it.

We are not persuaded that our construction of the phrase "uses . . . a firearm" will produce anomalous applications. . . . § 924(c)(1) requires not only that the defendant "use" the firearm, but also that he use it "during and in relation to" the drug trafficking crime. As a result, the defendant who "uses" a firearm to scratch his head, or for some other innocuous purpose, would avoid punishment for that conduct altogether: Although scratching one's head with a gun might constitute "use," that action cannot support punishment under § 924(c)(1) unless it facilitates or furthers the drug crime; that the firearm served to relieve an itch is not enough. . . .

In any event, the "intended purpose" of a firearm is not that it be used in any offensive manner whatever, but rather that it be used in a particular fashion—by firing it. The dissent's contention therefore cannot be that the defendant must use the firearm "as a weapon," but rather that he must fire it or threaten to fire it, "as a gun." Under the dissent's approach, then, even the criminal who pistol-whips his victim has not used a firearm within the meaning of § 924(c)(1), for firearms are intended to be fired or brandished, not used as bludgeons. The universal view of the courts of appeals, however, is directly to the contrary. No court of appeals ever has held that using a gun to pistol-whip a victim is anything but the "use" of a firearm; nor has any court ever held that trading a firearm for drugs falls short of being the "use" thereof. . . . We therefore hold that a criminal who trades his firearm for drugs "uses" it during and in relation to a drug trafficking offense within the meaning of § 924(c)(1). Because the evidence in this case showed that petitioner "used" his MAC–10 machine gun and silencer in precisely such a manner, proposing to trade them for cocaine, petitioner properly was subjected to § 924(c)(1)'s 30-year mandatory minimum sentence. The judgment of the Court of Appeals, accordingly, is affirmed.

It is so ordered.

JUSTICE SCALIA, with whom JUSTICE STEVENS and JUSTICE SOUTER join, dissenting.

Section 924(c)(1) mandates a sentence enhancement for any defendant who "during and in relation to any crime of violence or drug trafficking crime . . . uses . . . a firearm." 18 U.S.C. § 924(c)(1). The Court begins its analysis by focusing upon the word "use" in this passage, and explaining that the dictionary definitions of that word are very broad. It is, however, a "fundamental principle of statutory construction (and, indeed, of language itself) that the meaning of a word cannot be determined in isolation, but must be drawn from the context in which it is used." That is particularly true of a word as elastic as "use," whose meanings range all the way from "to partake of" (as in "he uses tobacco") to "to be wont or accustomed" (as in "he used to smoke tobacco").

In the search for statutory meaning, we give nontechnical words and phrases their ordinary meaning. To use an instrumentality ordinarily means to use it for its intended purpose. When someone asks "Do you use a cane?," he is not inquiring whether you have your grandfather's silver-handled walking stick on display in the hall; he wants to know whether you *walk* with a cane. Similarly, to speak of "using a firearm" is to speak of using it for its distinctive purpose, *i.e.,* as a weapon. To be sure, "one can use a firearm in a number of ways," including as an article of exchange, just as one can "use" a cane as a hall decoration—but that is not the ordinary meaning of "using" the one or the other. The Court does not appear to grasp the distinction between how a word *can be* used and how it *ordinarily is* used. It would, indeed, be "both reasonable and normal to say that petitioner 'used' his MAC–10 in his drug trafficking offense by trading it for cocaine." It would also be reasonable and normal to say that he "used" it to scratch his head. When one wishes to describe the action of employing the instrument of a firearm for such unusual purposes, "use" is assuredly a verb one could select. But that says nothing about whether the *ordinary* meaning of the phrase "uses a firearm" embraces such extraordinary employments. It is unquestionably *not* reasonable and normal, I think, to say simply "do not use firearms" when one means to prohibit selling or scratching with them.

Given our rule that ordinary meaning governs, and given the ordinary meaning of "uses a firearm," it seems to me inconsequential that "the words 'as a weapon' appear nowhere in the statute," they are reasonably implicit. Petitioner is not, I think, seeking to introduce an "additional requirement" into the text, but is simply construing the text according to its normal import.

The Court seeks to avoid this conclusion by referring to the next subsection of the statute, § 924(d), which does not employ the phrase "uses a firearm," but provides for the confiscation of firearms that are "used in" referenced offenses which include the crimes of transferring, selling, or transporting firearms in interstate commerce. The Court concludes from this that *whenever* the term appears in this statute, "use" of a firearm must include nonweapon use. I do not agree. We are dealing here not with a technical word or an "artfully defined" legal term, but with common words that are, as I have suggested, inordinately sensitive to context. Just as adding the direct object "a firearm" to the verb "use" *narrows* the meaning of that verb (it can no longer mean "partake of"), so also adding the modifier "in the offense of transferring, selling, or transporting firearms" to the phrase "use a firearm" *expands* the meaning of that phrase (it then includes, as it previously would not, nonweapon use). But neither the narrowing nor the expansion should logically be thought to apply to *all* appearance of the affected word or phrase. Just as every appearance of the word "use" in the statute need not be given the narrow meaning that word acquires in the phrase "use a firearm," so also every appearance of the phrase "use a firearm" need not be given the expansive connotation that phrase acquires in the broader context "use a firearm in crimes such as unlawful sale of firearms." When, for example, the statute provides that its prohibition on certain transactions in firearms "shall not apply to the loan or rental of a firearm to any person for temporary use for lawful sporting purposes," I have no doubt that the "use" referred to is *only* use as a sporting *weapon,* and not the use of pawning the firearm to pay for a ski trip. Likewise when, in § 924(c)(1), the phrase "uses . . . a firearm" is not employed in a context that necessarily envisions the unusual "use" of a firearm as a commodity, the normally understood meaning of the phrase should prevail. . . .

Even if the reader does not consider the issue to be as clear as I do, he must at least acknowledge, I think, that it is eminently debatable—and that is enough, under the rule of lenity, to require finding for the petitioner here. . . .

For the foregoing reasons, I respectfully dissent.

Church of the Holy Trinity v. U.S.

Mr. Justice Brewer Delivered the Opinion of the Court

Plaintiff in error is a corporation, duly organized and incorporated as a religious society under the laws of the State of New York. E. Walpole Warren was, prior to September, 1887, an alien residing in England. In that month the plaintiff in error made a contract with him, by which he was to remove to the city of New York and enter into its service as rector and pastor; and in pursuance of such contract, Warren did so remove and enter upon such service. It is claimed by the United States that this contract on the part of the plaintiff in error was forbidden by the act of February 26, 1885, 23 Stat. 332, c. 164, and an action was commenced to recover the penalty prescribed by that act. The Circuit Court held that the contract was within the prohibition of the statute, and rendered judgment accordingly (36 Fed. Rep. 303) and the single question presented for our determination is whether it erred in that conclusion.

The first section describes the act forbidden, and is in these words:

> Be it enacted by the Senate and House of Representatives of the United States of America in Congress assembled, That from and after the passage of this act it shall be unlawful for any person, company, partnership, or corporation, in any manner whatsoever, to prepay the transportation, or in any way assist or encourage the importation or migration of any alien or aliens, any foreigner or foreigners, into the United States, its Territories, or the District of Columbia, under contract or agreement, parol or special, express or implied, made previous to the importation or migration of such alien or aliens, foreigner or foreigners, to perform labor or service of

> any kind in the United States, its Territories, or the District of Columbia.

It must be conceded that the act of the corporation is within the letter of this section, for the relation of rector to his church is one of service, and implies labor on the one side with compensation on the other. Not only are the general words labor and service both used, but also, as it were to guard against any narrow interpretation and emphasize a breadth of meaning, to them is added "of any kind"; and, further, as noticed by the Circuit Judge in his opinion, the fifth section, which makes specific exceptions, among them professional actors, artists, lecturers, singers and domestic servants, strengthens the idea that every other kind of labor and service was intended to be reached by the first section. While there is great force to this reasoning, we cannot think Congress intended to denounce with penalties a transaction like that in the present case. It is a familiar rule, that a thing may be within the letter of the statute and yet not within the statute, because not within its spirit, nor within the intention of its makers. This has been often asserted, and the reports are full of cases illustrating its application. This is not the substitution of the will of the judge for that of the legislator, for frequently words of general meaning are used in a statute, words broad enough to include an act in question, and yet a consideration of the whole legislation, or of the circumstances surrounding its enactment, or of the absurd results which follow from giving such broad meaning to the words, makes it unreasonable to believe that the legislator intended to include the particular act. . . .

Among other things which may be considered in determining the intent of the legislature is the title of the act. We do not mean that it may be used to add to or take from the body of the statute, *Hadden v. The Collector*, 5 Wall. 107, but it may help to interpret its meaning. In the case of *United States v. Fisher*, 2 Cranch, 358, 386, Chief Justice Marshall said: "On the influence which the title ought to have in construing the enacting clauses much has been said; and yet it is not easy to discern the point of difference between the opposing

143 U.S. 457 (1892), United States Supreme Court.

counsel in this respect. Neither party contends that the title of an act can control plain words in the body of the statute; and neither denies that, taken with other parts, it may assist in removing ambiguities. Where the intent is plain, nothing is left to construction. Where the mind labors to discover the design of the legislature, it seizes everything from which aid can be derived; and in such case the title claims of degree of notice, and will have its due share of consideration." . . .

It will be seen that words as general as those used in the first section of this act were by that decision limited, and the intent of Congress with respect to the act was gathered partially, at least, from its title. Now, the title of this act is, "An act to prohibit the importation and migration of foreigners and aliens under contract or agreement to perform labor in the United States, its Territories and the District of Columbia." Obviously the thought expressed in this reaches only to the work of the manual laborer, as distinguished from that of the professional man. No one reading such a title would suppose that Congress had in its mind any purpose of staying the coming into this country of ministers of the gospel, or, indeed, of any class whose toil is that of the brain. The common understanding of the terms labor and laborers does not include preaching and preachers; and it is to be assumed that words and phrases are used in their ordinary meaning. So whatever of light is thrown upon the statute by the language of the title indicates an exclusion from its penal provisions of all contracts for the employment of ministers, rectors and pastors.

Again, another guide to the meaning of a statute is found in the evil which it is designed to remedy; and for this the court properly looks at contemporaneous events, the situation as it existed, and as it was pressed upon the attention of the legislative body. *United States v. Union Pacific Railroad*, 91 U.S. 72, 79. The situation which called for this statute was briefly but fully stated by Mr. Justice Brown when, as District Judge, he decided the case of *United States v. Craig*, 28 Fed. Rep. 795, 798: "The motives and history of the act are matters of common knowledge. It had become the practice for large capitalists in this country to contract with their agents abroad for the shipment of great numbers of an ignorant and servile class of foreign laborers, under contracts, by which the employer agreed, upon the one hand, to prepay their passage, while, upon the other hand, the laborers agreed to work after their arrival for a certain time at a low rate of wages. The effect of this was to break down the labor market, and to reduce other laborers engaged in

like occupations to the level of the assisted immigrant. The evil finally became so flagrant that an appeal was made to Congress for relief by the passage of the act in question, the design of which was to raise the standard of foreign immigrants, and to discountenance the migration of those who had not sufficient means in their own hands, or those of their friends, to pay their passage."

It appears, also, from the petitions, and in the testimony presented before the committees of Congress, that it was this cheap unskilled labor which was making the trouble, and the influx of which Congress sought to prevent. It was never suggested that we had in this country a surplus of brain toilers, and, least of all, that the market for the services of Christian ministers was depressed by foreign competition. Those were matters to which the attention of Congress, or of the people, was not directed. So far, then, as the evil which was sought to be remedied interprets the statute, it also guides to an exclusion of this contract from the penalties of the act.

A singular circumstance, throwing light upon the intent of Congress, is found in this extract from the report of the Senate Committee on Education and Labor, recommending the passage of the bill: "The general facts and considerations which induce the committee to recommend the passage of this bill are set forth in the Report of the Committee of the House. The committee report the bill back without amendment, although there are certain features thereof which might well be changed or modified, in the hope that the bill may not fail of passage during the present session. Especially would the committee have otherwise recommended amendments, substituting for the expression "labor and service," whenever it occurs in the body of the bill, the words "manual labor" or "manual service," as sufficiently broad to accomplish the purposes of the bill, and that such amendments would remove objections which a sharp and perhaps unfriendly criticism may urge to the proposed legislation. The committee, however, believing that the bill in its present form will be construed as including only those whose labor or service is manual in character, and being very desirous that the bill become a law before the adjournment, have reported the bill without change." 6059, *Congressional Record*, 48th Congress. And, referring back to the report of the Committee of the House, there appears this language: "It seeks to restrain and prohibit the immigration or importation of laborers who would have never seen our shores but for the inducements and allurements of men whose only object is to obtain labor at the lowest possible rate, regardless of the social and material well-being of our own citizens and regardless of the evil consequences which result to American laborers from such immigration. This class of immigrants care nothing about our institutions, and in many instances never even heard of them; they are men whose passage is paid by the importers; they come here under contract to labor for a certain number of years; they are ignorant of our social condition, and that they may remain so they are isolated and prevented from coming into contact with Americans. They are generally from the lowest social stratum, and live upon the coarsest food and in hovels of a character before unknown to American workmen. They, as a rule, do not become citizens, and are certainly not a desirable acquisition to the body politic. The inevitable tendency of their presence among us is to degrade American labor, and to reduce it to the level of the imported pauper labor." Page 5359, *Congressional Record*, 48th Congress.

We find, therefore, that the title of the act, the evil which was intended to be remedied, the circumstances surrounding the appeal to Congress, the reports of the committee of each house, all concur in affirming that the intent of Congress was simply to stay the influx of this cheap unskilled labor. . . .

Suppose in the Congress that passed this act some member had offered a bill which in terms declared that,

if any Roman Catholic church in this country should contract with Cardinal Manning to come to this country and enter into its service as pastor and priest; or any Episcopal church should enter into a like contract with Canon Farrar; or any Baptist church should make similar arrangements with Rev. Mr. Spurgeon; or any Jewish synagogue with some eminent Rabbi, such contract should be adjudged unlawful and void, and the church making it be subject to prosecution and punishment, can it be believed that it would have received a minute of approving thought or a single vote? Yet it is contended that such was in effect the meaning of this statute. The construction invoked cannot be accepted as correct. It is a case where there was presented a definite evil, in view of which the legislature used general terms with the purpose of reaching all phases of that evil, and thereafter, unexpectedly, it is developed that the general language thus employed is broad enough to reach cases and acts which the whole history and life of the country affirm could not have been intentionally legislated against. It is the duty of the courts, under those circumstances, to say that, however broad the language of the statute may be, the act, although within the letter, is not within the intention of the legislature, and therefore cannot be within the statute.

The judgment will be reversed, and the case remanded for further proceedings in accordance with this opinion.

The Role of U.S. Federal Courts in Interpreting the Constitution

ANTONIN SCALIA

"Intent of the Legislature"

Statutory interpretation is such a broad subject that the substance of it cannot be discussed comprehensively here. It is worth examining a few aspects, how-

From Antonin Scalia, *A Matter of Interpretation: Federal Courts and the Law* (Princeton: Princeton University Press, 1997), pp. 16–25, 37–38, 41–47. Reprinted by permission of Princeton University Press.

ever, if only to demonstrate the great degree of confusion that prevails. We can begin at the most fundamental possible level. So utterly unformed is the American law of statutory interpretation that not only is its methodology unclear, but even its very *objective* is. Consider the basic question: What are we looking for when we construe a statute?

You will find it frequently said in judicial opinions of my court and others that the judge's objective in interpreting a statute is to give effect to "the intent of the legislature." This principle, in one form or another, goes back at least as far as Blackstone. Unfortunately, it does not square with some of the (few) generally accepted concrete rules of statutory construction. One is the rule that when the text of a statute is clear, that is the end of the matter. Why should that be so, if what the legislature *intended*, rather than what it *said*, is the object of our inquiry? In selecting the words of the statute, the legislature might have misspoken. Why not permit that to be demonstrated from the floor debates? Or indeed, why not accept, as proper material for the court to consider, later explanations by the legislators—a sworn affidavit signed by the majority of each house, for example, as to what they *really* meant?

Another accepted rule of construction is that ambiguities in a newly enacted statute are to be resolved in such fashion as to make the statute, not only internally consistent, but also compatible with previously enacted laws. We simply assume, for purposes of our search for "intent," that the enacting legislature was aware of all those other laws. Well, of course that is a fiction, and if we were really looking for the subjective intent of the enacting legislature we would more likely find it by paying attention to the text (and legislative history) of the new statute in isolation.

The evidence suggests that, despite frequent statements to the contrary, we do not really look for subjective legislative intent. We look for a sort of "objectified" intent—the intent that a reasonable person would gather from the text of the law, placed alongside the remainder of the *corpus juris*. . . . And the reason we adopt this objectified version is, I think, that it is simply incompatible with democratic government, or indeed, even with fair government, to have the meaning of a law determined by what the lawgiver meant, rather than by what the lawgiver promulgated. That seems to me one step worse than the trick the emperor Nero was said to engage in: posting edicts high up on the pillars, so that they could not easily be read. Government by unexpressed intent is similarly tyrannical. It is the *law* that governs, not the intent of the lawgiver. That seems to me the essence of the famous American ideal set forth in the Massachusetts constitution: A government of laws, not of men. Men may intend what they will; but it is only the laws that they enact which bind us.

In reality, however, if one accepts the principle that the object of judicial interpretation is to determine the intent of the legislature, being bound by genuine but unexpressed legislative intent rather than the law is only the *theoretical* threat. The *practical* threat is that, under the guise or even the self-delusion of pursuing unexpressed legislative intents, common-law judges will in fact pursue their own objectives and desires, extending their lawmaking proclivities from the common law to the statutory field. When you are told to decide, not on the basis of what the legislature said, but on the basis of what it *meant*, and are assured that there is no necessary connection between the two, your best shot at figuring out what the legislature meant is to ask yourself what a wise and intelligent person *should* have meant; and that will surely bring you to the conclusion that the law means what you think it *ought* to mean—which is precisely how judges decide things under the common law. . . .

Church of the Holy *Trinity*

To give some concrete form to the danger I warn against, let me describe what I consider to be the prototypical case involving the triumph of supposed "legislative intent" (a handy cover for judicial intent) over the text of the law. It is called *Church of the Holy Trinity v. United States* and was decided by the Supreme Court of the United States in 1892. The Church of the Holy Trinity, located in New York City, contracted with an Englishman to come over to be its rector and pastor. The United States claimed that this agreement violated a federal statute that made it unlawful for any person to "in any way assist or encourage the importation or migration of any alien . . . into the United States, . . . under contract or agreement . . . made previous to the importation or migration of such alien . . . , to perform labor or service of any kind in the United States. . . ." The Circuit Court for the Southern District of New York held the church liable for the fine that the statute provided. The Supreme Court reversed.

· · ·

The Court proceed[ed] to conclude from various extratextual indications, including even a snippet of legislative history (highly unusual in those days), that the statute was intended to apply only to *manual* labor—which renders the exceptions for actors, artists, lecturers, and singers utterly inexplicable. The Court then shifts gears and devotes the last seven pages of its opinion to a lengthy description of how and why we are a religious nation. That being so, it says, "[T]he construction invoked cannot be accepted as correct."

· · ·

Well, of course I think that the act was within the letter of the statute, and was therefore within the statute: end of case. Congress can enact foolish statutes as well as wise ones, and it is not for the courts to decide which is which and rewrite the former.... *Church of the Holy Trinity* is cited to us whenever counsel wants us to ignore the narrow, deadening text of the statute, and pay attention to the life-giving legislative intent. It is nothing but an invitation to judicial lawmaking....

Another modern and forthright approach to according courts the power to revise statutes is set forth in Professor Eskridge's recent book, *Dynamic Statutory Interpretation*. The essence of it is acceptance of the proposition that it is proper for the judge who applies a statute to consider "'not only what the statute means abstractly, or even on the basis of legislative history, but also what it ought to mean in terms of the needs and goals of our present day society.'"[1] The law means what it ought to mean.

I agree ... that many decisions can be cited which, by subterfuge, accomplish precisely what ... Eskridge and other honest nontextualists propose. As I have said, "legislative intent" divorced from text is one of those subterfuges; and as I have described, *Church of the Holy Trinity* is one of those cases. What I think is needed, however, is not rationalization of this process but abandonment of it. It is simply not compatible with democratic theory that laws mean whatever they ought to mean, and that unelected judges decide what that is.

It may well be that the statutory interpretation adopted by the Court in *Church of the Holy Trinity* produced a desirable result; and it may even be (though I doubt it) that it produced the unexpressed result actually intended by Congress, rather than merely the one desired by the Court. Regardless, the decision was wrong because it failed to follow the text. The text is the law, and it is the text that must be observed....

Textualism

The philosophy of interpretation I have described above is known as textualism. In some sophisticated circles, it is considered simpleminded—"wooden," "unimaginative," "pedestrian." It is none of that. To be a textualist in good standing, one need not be too dull to perceive the broader social purposes that a statute is designed, or could be designed, to serve; or too hidebound to realize that new times require new laws. One need only hold the belief that judges have no authority to pursue those broader purposes or write those new laws.

Textualism should not be confused with so-called strict constructionism, a degraded form of textualism that brings the whole philosophy into disrepute. I am not a strict constructionist, and no one ought to be—

though better that, I suppose, than a nontextualist. A text should not be construed strictly, and it should not be construed leniently; it should be construed reasonably, to contain all that it fairly means. The difference between textualism and strict constructionism can be seen in a case my Court decided four terms ago.[2] The statute at issue provided for an increased jail term if, "during and in relation to . . . [a] drug trafficking crime," the defendant "uses . . . a firearm." The defendant in this case had sought to purchase a quantity of cocaine; and what he had offered to give in exchange for the cocaine was an unloaded firearm, which he showed to the drug-seller. The Court held, I regret to say, that the defendant was subject to the increased penalty, because he had "used a firearm during and in relation to a drug trafficking crime." The vote was not even close (6–3). I dissented. Now I cannot say whether my colleagues in the majority voted the way they did because they are strict-construction textualists, or because they are not textualists at all. But a proper textualist, which is to say my kind of textualist, would surely have voted to acquit. The phrase "uses a gun" fairly connoted use of a gun for what guns are normally used for, that is, as a weapon. As I put the point in my dissent, when you ask someone, "Do you use a cane?" you are not inquiring whether he has hung his grandfather's antique cane as a decoration in the hallway.

But while the good textualist is not a literalist, neither is he a nihilist. Words do have a limited range of meaning, and no interpretation that goes beyond that range is permissible. My favorite example of a departure from text—and certainly the departure that has enabled judges to do more freewheeling lawmaking than any other—pertains to the Due Process Clause found in the Fifth and Fourteenth Amendments of the United States Constitution, which says that no person shall "be deprived of life, liberty, or property without due process of law." It has been interpreted to prevent the government from taking away certain liberties *beyond* those, such as freedom of speech and of religion, that are specifically named in the Constitution.... Well, it may or may not be a good thing to guarantee additional liberties, but the Due Process Clause quite obviously does not bear that interpretation. By its inescapable terms, it guarantees only process. Property can be taken by the state; liberty can be taken; even life can be taken; but not without the *process* that our traditions require—notably, a validly enacted law and a fair trial. To say otherwise is to abandon textualism, and to render democratically adopted texts mere springboards for judicial lawmaking.

Of all the criticisms leveled against textualism, the most mindless is that it is "formalistic." The answer to that is, *of course it's formalistic!* The rule of law is *about* form. If, for example, a citizen performs an act—let us say the sale of certain technology to a foreign country—which is prohibited by a widely publicized bill proposed by the administration and passed by both houses of Congress, *but not yet signed by the President*, that sale is lawful. It is of no consequence that everyone knows both houses of Congress and the President wish to prevent that sale. Before the wish becomes a binding law, it must be embodied in a bill that passes both houses and is signed by the President. Is that not formalism? A murderer has been caught with blood on his hands, bending over the body of his victim; a neighbor with a video camera has filmed the crime; and the murderer has confessed in writing and on videotape. We nonetheless insist that before the state can punish this miscreant, it must conduct a full-dress criminal trial that results in a verdict of guilty. Is that not formalism? Long live formalism. It is what makes a government a government of laws and not of men. . . .

Interpreting Constitutional Texts

Without pretending to have exhausted the vast topic of textual interpretation, I wish to address a final subject: the distinctive problem of constitutional interpretation. The problem is distinctive, not because special principles of interpretation apply, but because the usual principles are being applied to an unusual text. Chief Justice Marshall put the point as well as it can be put in *McCulloch v. Maryland:*

> A constitution, to contain an accurate detail of all the subdivisions of which its great powers will admit, and of all the means by which they may be carried into execution, would partake of the prolixity of a legal code, and could scarcely be embraced by the human mind. It would probably never be understood by the public. Its nature, therefore, requires that only its great outlines should be marked, its important objects designated, and the minor ingredients which compose those objects be deduced from the nature of the objects themselves.[3]

In textual interpretation, context is everything, and the context of the Constitution tells us not to expect nitpicking detail, and to give words and phrases an expansive rather than narrow interpretation—though not an interpretation that the language will not bear.

Take, for example, the provision of the First Amendment that forbids abridgment of "the freedom of speech, or of the press." That phrase does not list the full range of communicative expression. Handwritten letters, for example, are neither speech nor press. Yet surely there is no doubt they cannot be censored. In this constitutional context, speech and press, the two most common forms of communication, stand as a sort of synecdoche for the whole. That is not strict construction, but it is reasonable construction.

· · ·

[T]he Great Divide with regard to constitutional interpretation is not that between Framers' intent and objective meaning, but rather that between *original* meaning (whether derived from Framers' intent or not) and *current* meaning. The ascendant school of constitutional interpretation affirms the existence of what is called The Living Constitution, a body of law that (unlike normal statutes) grows and changes from age to age, in order to meet the needs of a changing society. And it is the judges who determine those needs and "find" that changing law. Seems familiar, doesn't it? Yes, it is the common law returned, but infinitely more powerful than what the old common law ever pretended to be, for now it trumps even the statutes of democratic legislatures.

· · ·

Flexibility and Liberality of the Living Constitution

The argument most frequently made in favor of The Living Constitution is a pragmatic one: Such an evolutionary approach is necessary in order to provide the "flexibility" that a changing society requires; the Constitution would have snapped if it had not been permitted to bend and grow. This might be a persuasive argument if most of the "growing" that the proponents of this approach have brought upon us in the past, and are determined to bring upon us in the future, were the *elimination* of restrictions upon democratic government. But just the opposite is true. Historically, and particularly in the past thirty-five years, the "evolving" Constitution has imposed a vast array of new constraints—new inflexibilities—upon administrative, judicial, and legislative action. To mention only a few things that formerly could be done or not done, as the society desired, but now cannot be done:

- admitting in a state criminal trial evidence of guilt that was obtained by an unlawful search,[4]
- permitting invocation of God at public-school graduations,[5]
- electing one of the two houses of a state legislature the way the United States Senate is elected, i.e., on a basis that does not give all voters numerically equal representation, [6]
- terminating welfare payments as soon as evidence of fraud is received, subject to restoration after hearing if the evidence is satisfactorily refuted,[7]
- imposing property requirements as a condition of voting,[8]
- prohibiting anonymous campaign literature,[9]
- prohibiting pornography.[10]

And the future agenda of constitutional evolutionists is mostly more of the same—the creation of *new* restrictions upon democratic government, rather than the elimination of old ones. *Less* flexibility in government, not *more*. As things now stand, the state and federal government may either apply capital punishment or abolish it, permit suicide or forbid it—all as the changing times and the changing sentiments of society may demand. But when capital punishment is held to violate the Eighth Amendment, and suicide is held to be protected by the Fourteenth Amendment, all flexibility with regard to those matters will be gone. No, the reality of the matter is that, generally speaking, devotees of The Living Constitution do not seek to facilitate social change but to prevent it.

. . .

Several terms ago a case came before the Supreme Court involving a prosecution for sexual abuse of a young child. The trial court found that the child would be too frightened to testify in the presence of the (presumed) abuser, and so, pursuant to state law, she was permitted to testify with only the prosecutor and defense counsel present, with the defendant, the judge, and the jury watching over closed-circuit television. A reasonable enough procedure, and it was held to be constitutional by my Court. I dissented, because the Sixth Amendment provides that "[i]n *all* criminal prosecutions the accused shall enjoy the right . . . to be confronted with the witnesses against him" (emphasis added). There is no doubt what confrontation meant—or indeed means today. It means face-to-face, not watching from another room. And there is no doubt what one of the major purposes of that provision was: to induce *precisely* that pressure upon the witness which the little girl found it difficult to endure. It is

difficult to accuse someone to his face, particularly when you are lying. Now no extrinsic factors have changed since that provision was adopted in 1791. Sexual abuse existed then, as it does now; little children were more easily upset than adults, then as now; a means of placing the defendant out of sight of the witness existed then as now (a screen could easily have been erected that would enable the defendant to see the witness, but not the witness the defendant). But the Sixth Amendment nonetheless gave *all* criminal defendants the right to *confront* the witnesses against them, because that was thought to be an important protection. The only significant things that *have* changed, I think, are the society's sensitivity to so-called psychic trauma (which is what we are told the child witness in such a situation suffers) and the society's assessment of where the proper balance ought to be struck between the two extremes of a procedure that assures convicting 100 percent of all child abusers, and a procedure that assures acquitting 100 percent of those falsely accused of child abuse. I have no doubt that the society is, as a whole, happy and pleased with what my Court decided. But we should not pretend that the decision did not *eliminate* a liberty that previously existed.

Lack of a Guiding Principle for Evolution

My pointing out that the American people may be satisfied with a reduction of their liberties should not be taken as a suggestion that the proponents of The Living Constitution *follow* the desires of the American people in determining how the Constitution should evolve. They follow nothing so precise; indeed, as a group they follow nothing at all. Perhaps the most glaring defect of Living Constitutionalism, next to its incompatibility with the whole antievolutionary purpose of a constitution, is that there is no agreement, and no chance of agreement, upon what is to be the guiding principle of the evolution. *Panta rei* is not a sufficiently informative principle of constitutional interpretation. What is it that the judge must consult to determine when, and in what direction, evolution has occurred? Is it the will of the majority, discerned from newspapers, radio talk shows, public opinion polls, and chats at the country club? Is it the philosophy of Hume, or of John Rawls, or of John Stuart Mill, or of Aristotle? As soon as the discussion goes beyond the issue of whether the Constitution is static, the evolutionists divide into as many camps as there are individual views of the good, the true, and the beautiful. I think that is inevitably so, which means that evolutionism is simply not a practicable constitutional philosophy.

I do not suggest, mind you, that originalists always agree upon their answer. There is plenty of room for disagreement as to what original meaning was, and even more as to how that original meaning applies to the situation before the court. But the originalist at least knows what he is looking for: the original meaning of the text. Often—indeed, I dare say usually—that is easy to discern and simple to apply. Sometimes (though not very often) there will be disagreement regarding the original meaning; and sometimes there will be disagreement as to how that original meaning applies to new and unforeseen phenomena. How, for example, does the First Amendment guarantee of "the freedom of speech" apply to new technologies that did not exist when the guarantee was created—to sound trucks, or to government-licensed over-the-air television? In such new fields the Court must follow the trajectory of the First Amendment, so to speak, to determine what it requires—and assuredly that enterprise is not entirely cut-and-dried but requires the exercise of judgment.

But the difficulties and uncertainties of determining original meaning and applying it to modern circumstances are negligible compared with the difficulties and uncertainties of the philosophy which says that the Constitution *changes*; that the very act which it once prohibited it now permits, and which it once permitted it now forbids; and that the key to that change is unknown and unknowable. The originalist, if he does not have all the answers, has many of them. The Confrontation Clause, for example, requires confrontation. For the evolutionist, on the other hand, every question is an open question, every day a new day. No fewer than three of the Justices with whom I have served have maintained that the death penalty is unconstitutional, *even though its use is explicitly contemplated in the Constitution*. The Due Process Clause of the Fifth and Fourteenth Amendments says that no person shall be deprived of life without due process of law; and the Grand Jury Clause of the Fifth Amendment says that no person shall be held to answer for a capital crime without grand jury indictment. No matter. Under The Living Constitution the death penalty may have *become* unconstitutional. And it is up to each Justice to decide for himself (under no standard I can discern) when that occurs.

In the last analysis, however, it probably does not matter what principle, among the innumerable possibilities, the evolutionist proposes to determine in what direction The Living Constitution will grow. Whatever he might propose, at the end of the day an evolving constitution will evolve the way the majority wishes. The people will be willing to leave interpretation of the Constitution to lawyers and law courts so long as the people believe that it is (like the interpretation of a statute) essentially lawyers' work—requiring a close examination of text, history of the text, traditional understanding of the text, judicial precedent, and so forth. But if the people come to believe that the Constitution is *not* a text like other texts; that it means, not what it says or what it was understood to mean, but what it *should* mean, in light of the "evolving standards of decency that mark the progress of a maturing society"—well, then, they will look for qualifications other than impartiality, judgment, and lawyerly acumen in those whom they select to interpret it. More specifically, they will look for judges who agree with *them* as to what the evolving standards have evolved to; who agree with *them* as to what the Constitution *ought* to be.

It seems to me that that is where we are heading, or perhaps even where we have arrived. Seventy-five years ago, we believed firmly enough in a rock-solid, unchanging Constitution that we felt it necessary to adopt the Nineteenth Amendment to give women the vote. The battle was not fought in the courts, and few thought that it could be, despite the constitutional guarantee of Equal Protection of the Laws; that provision did not, when it was adopted, and hence did not in 1920, guarantee equal access to the ballot but permitted distinctions on the basis not only of age but of property and of sex. Who can doubt that if the issue had been deferred until today, the Constitution would be (formally) unamended, and the courts would be the chosen instrumentality of change? The American people have been converted to belief in The Living Constitution, a "morphing" document that means, from age to age, what it ought to mean. And with that conversion has inevitably come the new phenomenon of selecting and confirming federal judges, at all levels, on the basis of their views regarding a whole series of proposals for constitutional evolution. If the courts are free to write the Constitution anew, they will, by God, write it the way the majority wants; the appointment and confirmation process will see to that. This, of course, is the end of the Bill of Rights, whose meaning will be committed to the very body it was meant to protect against: the majority. By trying to make the Constitution do everything that needs doing from age to age, we shall have caused it to do nothing at all.

Endnotes

[1] William N. Eskridge, Jr., *Dynamic Statutory Interpretation* 50 (1994) [quoting Arthur Phelps, *Factors Influencing Judges in Interpreting Statutes,* 3 Vand. L. Rev. 456, 469 (1950)].

[2] *Smith v. United States,* 508 U.S. 223 (1993).

[3] *McCulloch v. Maryland,* 17 U.S. (4 Wheat.) 316, 407 (1819).

[4] See *Mapp v. Ohio,* 367 U.S. 643 (1961).

[5] See *Lee v. Weisman,* 505 U.S. 577 (1992).

[6] See *Reynolds v. Sims,* 377 U.S. 533 (1964).

[7] See *Goldberg v. Kelly,* 397 U.S. 254 (1970).

[8] See *Kramer v. Union Free Sch. Dist.,* 395 U.S. 621 (1969).

[9] See *McIntyre v. Ohio Elections Comm'n,* 115 S. Ct. 1511 (1995).

[10] Under current doctrine, pornography may be banned only if it is "obscene," see *Miller v. California,* 413 U.S. 15 (1973), a judicially crafted term of art that does not embrace material that excites "normal, healthy sexual desires," *Brockett v. Spokane Arcades, Inc.,* 472 U.S. 491, 498 (1985).

Comment on Scalia

Ronald A. Dworkin

Justice Scalia has managed to give two lectures about meaning with no reference to Derrida or Gadamer or even the hermeneutic circle, and he has set out with laudable clarity a sensible account of statutory interpretation. These are considerable achievements. But I believe he has seriously misunderstood the implications of his general account for constitutional law, and that his lectures therefore have a schizophrenic character. He begins with a general theory that entails a style of constitutional adjudication which he ends by denouncing.

His initial argument rests on a crucial distinction between law and intention. "Men may intend what they will," he says, "but it is only the laws that they enact which bind us," and he is scornful of decisions like *Holy Trinity,* in which the Supreme Court, conceding that the "letter" of a statute forbade what the church had done, speculated that Congress did not intend that result. Indeed, he is skeptical about the very idea of a corporate legislative "intention"; most members of Congress, he says, have never thought about the unforeseen issues of interpretation that courts must face. A careless reader might object, however, that any coherent account of

statutory interpretation *must* be based on assumptions about someone's (or some body's) intention, and that Scalia's own account accepts this at several points. Scalia admits that courts should remedy "scrivener's error." He rejects "strict constructionism"—he thinks the Supreme Court's "literalist" decision in the "firearm" case, *Smith v. United States,* was silly. He credits at least some of the "canons" of interpretation as being an "indication" of meaning. And he says that it would be absurd to read the First Amendment's protection of speech and press as not applying to handwritten notes, which are, technically, neither.

Each of these clarifications allows respect for intention to trump literal text, and the careless objection I am imagining therefore claims an inconsistency. Scalia's defenders might say, in reply to the objection, that he is not an *extreme* textualist, and that these adjustments are only concessions to common sense and practicality. But that misunderstands the objection, which is that the concessions undermine Scalia's position altogether, because they recognize not only the intelligibility but the priority of legislative intention, both of which he begins by denying. If judges can appeal to a presumed legislative intent to add to the plain meanings of "speech" and "press," or to subtract from the plain meaning of "uses a firearm," why can they not appeal to the same legislative intent to allow a priest to enter the country? Scalia's answer to this objection must not rely on any self-destructive "practicality" claim.

From Antonin Scalia, *A Matter of Interpretation: Federal Courts and the Law* (Princeton: Princeton University Press, 1997), pp. 115–127. Reprinted by permission of Princeton University Press.

It must rely instead on a distinction between *kinds* of intention, a distinction he does not make explicitly, but that must lie at the heart of his theory if the theory is defensible at all.

This is the crucial distinction between what some officials intended to *say* in enacting the language they used, and what they intended—or expected or hoped—would be the *consequence* of their saying it. Suppose a boss tells his manager (without winking) to hire the most qualified applicant for a new job. The boss might think it obvious that his own son, who is an applicant, is the most qualified; indeed he might not have given the instruction unless he was confident that the manager would think so too. Nevertheless, what the boss *said*, and *intended* to say, was that the most qualified applicant should be hired, and if the manager thought some other applicant better qualified, but hired the boss's son to save his own job, he would not be following the standard the boss had intended to lay down.

So what I called the careless objection is wrong. The supposed lapses from Scalia's textualism it cites are not lapses at all, because textualism insists on deference to one kind of intention—semantic intention—and in all his remarks so far cited Scalia is deferring to that. Any reader of anything must attend to semantic intention, because the same sounds or even words can be used with the intention of saying different things. If I tell you (to use Scalia's own example) that I admire bays, you would have to decide whether I intended to say that I admire certain horses or certain bodies of water. Until you had, you would have no idea what I had actually said even though you would know what sounds I had uttered. The phrase "using a firearm" might naturally be used, in some contexts, with the intention of describing only situations in which a gun is used as a threat; the same phrase might be used, in other contexts, to mean using a gun for any purpose including barter. We do not know what Congress actually said, in using a similar phrase, until we have answered the question of what it is reasonable to suppose, in all the circumstances including the rest of the statute, it intended to say in speaking as it did.

When we are trying to decide what someone meant to say, in circumstances like these, we are deciding which clarifying *translation* of his inscriptions is the best. It is a matter of complex and subtle philosophical argument what such translations consist in, and how they are possible—how, for example, we weave assumptions about what the speaker believes and wants, and about what it would be rational for him to believe and want, into decisions about what he meant to say. The difficulties are greatly increased when we are translating not the utterances of a real person but those of an institution like a legislature. We rely on personification—we suppose that the institution has semantic intentions of its own—and it is difficult to understand what sense that makes, or what special standards we should use to discover or construct such intentions. Scalia would not agree with my own opinions about these matters. But we do agree on the importance of the distinction I am emphasizing: between the question of what a legislature intended to say in the laws it enacted, which judges applying those laws must answer, and the question of what the various legislators as individuals expected or hoped the consequences of those laws would be, which is a very different matter.

Holy Trinity illustrates the difference and its importance. There can be no serious doubt that Congress meant to say what the words it used would naturally be understood to say. It is conceivable—perhaps even likely—that most members would have voted for an exception for English priests had the issue been raised. But that is a matter of (counterfactual) expectations, not of semantic intention. The law, as Scalia emphasizes, is what Congress has said, which is fixed by the best interpretation of the language it used, not by what some proportion of its members wanted or expected or assumed would happen, or would have wanted or expected or assumed if they had thought of the case. Not everyone agrees with that judgment. Some lawyers think that it accords better with democracy if judges defer to reasonable assumptions about what most legislators wanted or would have wanted, even when the language they used does not embody those actual or hypothetical wishes. After all, these lawyers argue, legislation should reflect what those who have been elected by the people actually think best for the country. Scalia disagrees with that judgment: he thinks it more democratic to give semantic intention priority over expectation intention when the two conflict, as they putatively did in *Holy Trinity*.

Now consider the implications of textualism so understood for the most important part of Scalia's judicial duties: interpreting the exceedingly abstract clauses of the Bill of Rights and later rights-bearing amendments. Scalia describes himself as a constitutional "originalist." But the distinction we made allows us a further distinction between two forms of originalism: "semantic" originalism, which insists that the rights-granting clauses be read to say what those who made them intended to say, and "expectation" originalism, which holds that these clauses should be understood to have the consequences that those who made them expected them to have. Consider, to see the difference, the *Brown* question: does the Fourteenth Amendment guarantee of "equal protection of the laws" forbid racial segregation in public schools? We know that the majority of the members of Congress who voted for that amendment did not expect or intend it to have that consequence: they themselves sustained racial segregation in the schools of the District of Columbia. So an expectation-originalist would interpret the Fourteenth Amendment to permit segregation and would declare the Court's decision wrong. But there is no plausible interpretation of what these statesmen meant to *say*, in laying down the language "equal protection of the laws," that entitles us to conclude that they *declared* segregation constitutional. On the contrary, as the Supreme Court held, the best understanding of their semantic intentions supposes that they meant to, and did, lay down a general principle of political morality which (it had become clear by 1954) condemns racial segregation. So, on that ground, a semantic-originalist would concur in the Court's decision.

If Scalia were faithful to his textualism, he would be a semantic-originalist. But is he? Notice his brief discussion of whether capital punishment offends the Eighth Amendment's prohibition against "cruel and unusual" punishments. An expectation-originalist would certainly hold that it does not, for the reasons Scalia cites. The "framers" would hardly have bothered to stipulate that "life" may be taken only after due process if they thought that the Eighth Amendment made capital punishment unconstitutional anyway. But the question is far more complicated for a semantic-originalist. For he must choose between two clarifying translations—two different accounts of what the framers intended to *say* in the Eighth Amendment. The first reading supposes that the framers intended to say, by using the words "cruel and unusual," that punishments generally thought cruel at the time they spoke were to be prohibited—that is, that they would have expressed themselves more clearly if they had used the phrase "punishments widely regarded as cruel and unusual at the date of this enactment" in place of the misleading language they actually used. The second reading supposes that they intended to lay down an abstract principle forbidding whatever punishments are in fact cruel and unusual. Of course, if the correct translation is the first version, then capital punishment does not violate the Eighth Amendment. But if the second, principled, translation is a more accurate account of what they intended to say, the question

remains open. Just as the manager in my story could only follow his boss's principled instruction by using his own judgment, so judges could then only apply the Eighth Amendment by deciding whether capital punishment is in fact cruel and has now become (as in fact it has become, at least among democracies) unusual.

The textual evidence Scalia cites would be irrelevant for a semantic-originalist who translated the Eighth Amendment in a principled rather than a concrete and dated way. There is no contradiction in the following set of claims. The framers of the Eighth Amendment laid down a principle forbidding whatever punishments are cruel and unusual. They did not themselves expect or intend that that principle would abolish the death penalty, so they provided that death could be inflicted only after due process. But it does not follow that the abstract principle they stated does not, contrary to their own expectation, forbid capital punishment. Suppose some legislature enacts a law forbidding the hunting of animals that are members of "endangered species" and then, later in its term, imposes special license requirements for hunting, among other animals, minks. We would assume that the members who voted for both provisions did not think that minks were endangered. But we would not be justified in concluding from that fact that, as a matter of law, minks were excluded from the ban even if they plainly *were* endangered. The latter inference would be an example of *Holy Trinity* thinking.

You will now understand my concern about Scalia's consistency. For he cites the view that capital punishment is unconstitutional as so obviously preposterous that it is cause for wonder that three justices who served with him actually held such an opinion. If he were an expectation-originalist, we would not be surprised at that view, or at the evidence he offers to support it. But for a semantic-originalist the question just *cannot* be foreclosed by references to the death penalty in the rest of the Constitution. A semantic-originalist would also have to think that the best interpretation of the Eighth Amendment was the dated rather than the principled translation, and even someone who might be drawn to that dated interpretation could not think the principled one *preposterous*.

On the contrary, it is the dated translation that seems bizarre. It is near inconceivable that sophisticated eighteenth-century statesmen, who were familiar with the transparency of ordinary moral language, would have used "cruel" as shorthand for "what we now think cruel." They knew how to be concrete when they intended to be: the various provisions for criminal and civil process in the Fourth, Fifth, Sixth, and Seventh Amendments do not speak of "fair" or "due" or "usual" procedures but lay down very concrete provisions. If they had intended a dated provision, they could and would have written an explicit one. Of course, we cannot imagine Madison or any of his contemporaries doing that: they wouldn't think it appropriate to protect what they took to be a fundamental right in such terms. But that surely means that the dated translation would be a plain mistranslation.

So Scalia's impatience with what seems the most natural statement of what the authors of the Eighth Amendment intended to say is puzzling. Part of the explanation may lie in his fear of what he calls a "morphing" theory of the Constitution—that the rights-bearing clauses are chameleons which change their meaning to conform to the needs and spirit of new times. He calls this chameleon theory "dominant," but it is hardly even intelligible, and I know of no prominent contemporary judge or scholar who holds anything like it. True, a metaphorical description of the Constitution as "living" has figured in constitutional rhetoric of the past, but this metaphor is much better understood as endorsing, not the chameleon theory, but the view I just described as the one that Scalia, if he were a semantic-originalist, might be expected to hold himself—that key constitutional provisions, as a matter of their original meaning, set out abstract principles rather than concrete or dated rules. If so, then the application of these abstract principles to particular cases, which takes fresh judgment, must be continually reviewed, not in an attempt to find substitutes for what the Constitution says, but out of respect for what it says. . . .

Scalia argues that the First Amendment should be read not as abstract but as dated—that it should be read, that is, as guaranteeing only the rights it would have been generally understood to protect when it was enacted. He makes three points: first, that since many parts of the Bill of Rights are plainly concrete—the Third Amendment's prohibition against quartering troops during peacetime, for example—the "framers" probably intended to make them all so; second, that the "framers" would presumably be anxious to insure that their own views about free speech were respected even if later generations no longer agreed; and, third, that in any case the "framers" would not have wanted to leave the development of a constitutionalized moral principle to judges.

These are all arguments for ignoring the natural semantic meaning of a text in favor of speculations about the expectations of its authors, and the Scalia of the preconstitutional part of these lectures would have

ridiculed those arguments. First, why shouldn't the "framers" have thought that a combination of concrete and abstract rights would best secure the (evidently abstract) goals they set out in the preamble? No other national constitution is written at only one level of abstraction, and there is no reason to suppose the authors of the Bill of Rights would have been tempted by that kind of stylistic homogeneity. Second, as I said, Enlightenment statesmen were very unlikely to think that their own views represented the last word in moral progress. If they really were worried that future generations would protect rights less vigorously than they themselves did, they would have made plain that they intended to create a dated provision. Third, we must distinguish the question of what the Constitution means from the question of which institution has final authority to decide what it means. If, as many commentators think, the "framers" expected judges to have that authority, and if they feared the consequences for abstract rights, they would have taken *special* care to write concrete, dated clauses. If, on the contrary, they did not expect judicial review, then Scalia's third argument fails for that reason. The First Amendment turns out to be his *Holy Trinity*.

He ignores, moreover, an apparently decisive argument against a translation of the First Amendment as dated. There *was* no generally accepted understanding of the right of free speech on which the framers could have based a dated clause even if they had wanted to write one. On the contrary, the disagreement about what that right comprises was much more profound when the amendment was enacted than it is now. When the dominant Federalist party enacted the Sedition Act in 1798, its members argued, relying on Blackstone, that "the freedom of speech" meant only freedom from "prior restraint"—in effect, freedom from an advance prohibition—and did not include any protection at all from punishment *after* publication. The opposing Republicans argued for a dramatically different view of the amendment: as Albert Gallatin (Jefferson's future secretary of the treasury) pointed out, it is "preposterous to say, that to punish a certain act was not an abridgment of the liberty of doing that act." All parties to the debate *assumed* that the First Amendment set out an abstract principle and that fresh judgment would be needed to interpret it. The Federalists relied, not on contemporary practice, which hardly supported their reading, but on the moral authority of Blackstone. The Republicans relied, not on contemporary practice either, but on the logic of freedom. No one supposed that the First Amendment codified some current and settled understanding, and the deep division among them showed that there was no settled understanding to codify. . . .

What has happened? Why does the resolute text-reader, dictionary-minder, expectation-scorner of the beginning of these lectures change his mind when he comes to the most fundamental American statute of them all? He offers, in his final pages, an intriguing answer. He sees, correctly, that if we read the abstract clauses of the Bill of Rights as they were written—if we read them to say what their authors intended them to say rather than to deliver the consequences they expected them to have—then judges must treat these clauses as enacting abstract moral principles and must therefore exercise moral judgment in deciding what they *really* require. That does not mean ignoring precedent of textual or historical integrity or morphing the Constitution. It means, on the contrary, enforcing it in accordance with its text, in the only way that this can be done. Many conservative judges therefore reject semantic originalism as undemocratic; elected judges, they say, should not have that responsibility. Scalia gives nearly the opposite reason: he says the moral reading gives the people not too little but too much power, because it politicizes the appointment of Supreme Court justices and makes it more likely that justices will be appointed who reflect the changing moods of the majority. He fears that the constitutional rights of individuals will suffer.

History disagrees. Justices whose methods seem closest to the moral reading of the Constitution have been champions, not enemies, of individual rights, and, as the political defeat of Robert Bork's nomination taught us, the people seem content not only with the moral reading but with its individualist implications. Scalia is worried about the decline of what he believes to be property rights embedded in the Constitution but ignored in recent decades. He reminds liberals that rights of criminal defendants may also be at risk. But even if we were persuaded that the Court has gone too far in neglecting property rights, and also that *Maryland v. Craig* compromised a valid constitutional right, these assumed mistakes would hardly outweigh the advantages to individual freedom that have flowed from judges' treatment of the great clauses as abstract.

It is, however, revealing that this is the scale on which Scalia finally wants his arguments to be weighed, and it may provide a final explanation, if not justification, for the inconsistency of his lectures as a whole. His most basic argument for textualism is drawn from majoritarian theory: he says that it is undemocratic when a statute is interpreted other than in accordance with the public text that was before legislators when they voted and is available to everyone in the community afterwards. His most basic argument for rejecting textualism in constitutional interpretation, on the other hand, reflects his *reservations* about majority rule. As with most of us, Scalia's attitudes about democracy are complex and ambivalent. I disagree with his judgment about which individual rights are genuine and important, and about whether the moral reading is a threat or an encouragement to freedom. But I agree with him that in the end the magnet of political morality is the strongest force in jurisprudence. The power of that magnet is nowhere more evident than in the rise and fall of his own love affair with textual fidelity.

The Right of Privacy

Robert Bork

The 1965 decision in *Griswold v. Connecticut*[1] was insignificant in itself but momentous for the future of

constitutional law. Connecticut had an ancient statute making it criminal to use contraceptives. The state also had a general accessory statute allowing the punishment of any person who aided another in committing an offense. On its face, the statute criminalizing the use of contraceptives made no distinction between married couples and others. But the statute also had never been enforced against anyone who used contraceptives, married or not. There was, of course, no prospect that it ever would be enforced. If any Connecticut official had been mad enough to attempt enforcement, the law would at once have been removed from the books and the official from his office. Indeed, some Yale law professors had gotten the statute all the way to the Supreme Court a few years previously, and the Court had refused to decide it precisely because there was no showing that the law was ever enforced. The professors had some difficulty arranging a test case but finally managed to have two doctors who gave birth control information fined $100 apiece as accessories.

Such enforcement in the area as there was consisted of the occasional application of the accessory statute against birth control clinics, usually clinics that advertised. The situation was similar to the enforcement of many antigambling laws. They may cover all forms of gambling on their faces, but they are in fact enforced only against commercial gambling. An official who began arresting the priest at the church bingo party or friends having their monthly poker game at home would have made a most unwise career decision and would be quite unlikely to get a conviction. There are a number of statutes like these in various state codes, such as the statutes flatly prohibiting sodomy and other "unnatural practices," which apply on their faces to all couples, married or unmarried, heterosexual or homosexual. The statutes are never enforced, but legislators, who would be aghast at any enforcement effort, nevertheless often refuse to repeal them.

There is a problem with laws like these. They are kept in the codebooks as precatory statements, affirmations of moral principle. It is quite arguable that this is an improper use of law, most particularly of criminal law, that statutes should not be on the books if no one intends to enforce them. It has been suggested that if anyone tried to enforce a law that had moldered in disuse for many years, the statute should be declared void by reason of desuetude or that the defendant should go free because the law had not provided fair warning.

But these were not the issues in *Griswold.* Indeed, getting off on such grounds was the last thing the defendants and their lawyers wanted. Since the lawyers had a difficult time getting the state even to fine two doctors as accessories, it seems obvious that the case was not arranged out of any fear of prosecution, and certainly not the prosecution of married couples. *Griswold* is more plausibly viewed as an attempt to enlist the Court on one side of one issue in a cultural struggle. Though the statute was originally enacted when the old Yankee culture dominated Connecticut politics, it was now quite popular with the Catholic hierarchy and with many lay Catholics whose religious values it paralleled. The case against the law was worked up by members of the Yale law school faculty and was supported by the Planned Parenthood Federation of America, Inc., the Catholic Council on Civil Liberties, and the American Civil Liberties Union. A ruling of unconstitutionality may have been sought as a statement that opposition to contraception is benighted and, therefore, a statement about whose cultural values are dominant. Be that as it may, the upshot was a new constitutional doctrine perfectly suited, and later used, to enlist the Court on the side of moral relativism in sexual matters.

Justice Douglas's majority opinion dealt with the case as if Connecticut had devoted itself to sexual fascism. "Would we allow the police to search the sacred precincts of marital bedrooms for telltale signs of the use of contraceptives? The very idea is repulsive to the notions of privacy surrounding the marriage relationship."[2] That was both true and entirely irrelevant to the case before the Court. Courts usually judge statutes by the way in which they are actually enforced, not by imagining horrible events that have never happened, never will happen, and could be stopped by courts if they ever seemed about to happen. Just as in *Skinner* he had treated a proposal to sterilize three-time felons as raising the specter of racial genocide, Douglas raised the stakes to the sky here by treating Connecticut as though it was threatening the institution of marriage. "We deal with a right of privacy older than the Bill of Rights—older than our political parties, older than our school system." The thought was incoherent. What the right of privacy's age in comparison with that of our political parties and school system had to do with anything was unclear, and where the "right" came from if not from the Bill of Rights it is impossible to understand. No court had ever invalidated a statute on the basis of the right Douglas described. That makes it all the more perplexing that Douglas in fact purported to derive the right of privacy not from some pre-existing right or law of nature, but from the Bill of Rights. It is important to understand Justice Douglas's argument both because the method, though without merit, continually recurs in constitutional adjudication and because the "right of privacy" has become a loose canon in the law. Douglas began by pointing out that "specific guarantees in the Bill of Rights have

penumbras, formed by emanations from those guarantees that help give them life and substance." There
is nothing exceptional about that thought, other than
the language of penumbras and emanations. Courts
often give protection to a constitutional freedom by
creating a buffer zone, by prohibiting a government
from doing something not in itself forbidden but
likely to lead to an invasion of a right specified in the
Constitution. Douglas cited *NAACP v. Alabama*,[3] in
which the Supreme Court held that the state could not
force the disclosure of the organization's membership
lists since that would have a deterrent effect upon the
members' first amendment rights of political and legal
action. That may well have been part of the purpose of
the statute. But for this anticipated effect upon guaranteed freedoms, there would be no constitutional objection to the required disclosure of membership. The
right not to disclose had no life of its own independent
of the rights specified in the first amendment.

Douglas named the buffer zone or "penumbra" of
the first amendment a protection of "privacy," although,
in *NAACP v. Alabama*, of course, confidentiality of membership was required not for the sake of individual privacy but to protect the public activities of politics and
litigation. Douglas then asserted that other amendments
create "zones of privacy." These were the first, third (soldiers not to be quartered in private homes), fourth (ban
on unreasonable searches and seizures), and fifth (freedom from self-incrimination). There was no particularly
good reason to use the word "privacy" for the freedoms
cited, except for the fact that the opinion was building
toward those "sacred precincts of marital bedrooms."
The phrase "areas of freedom" would have been more
accurate since the provisions cited protect both private
and public behavior.

None of the amendments cited, and none of their
buffer or penumbral zones, covered the case before the
Court. The Connecticut statute was not invalid under
any provision of the Bill of Rights, no matter how
extended. Since the statute in question did not threaten
any guaranteed freedom, it did not fall within any
"emanation." *Griswold v. Connecticut* was, therefore,
not like *NAACP v. Alabama*. Justice Douglas bypassed
that seemingly insuperable difficulty by simply asserting that the various separate "zones of privacy" created by each separate provision of the Bill of Rights
somehow created a general but wholly undefined
"right of privacy" that is independent of and lies outside any right or "zone of privacy" to be found in the
Constitution. Douglas did not explain how it was that
the Framers created five or six specific rights that

could, with considerable stretching, be called "privacy," and, though the Framers chose not to create
more, the Court could nevertheless invent a general
right of privacy that the Framers had, inexplicably, left
out. It really does not matter to the decision what the
Bill of Rights covers or does not cover.

Douglas closed the *Griswold* opinion with a burst of
passionate oratory. "Marriage is a coming together for
better or for worse, hopefully enduring, and intimate to
the degree of being sacred. It is an association that promotes a way of life, not causes; a harmony in living,
not political faiths; a bilateral loyalty, not commercial
or social projects. Yet it is an association for as noble a
purpose as any involved in our prior decisions."[4] It
is almost a matter for regret that Connecticut had
not threatened the institution of marriage, or even
attempted to prevent anyone from using contraceptives,
since that left some admirable sentiments, expressed
with rhetorical fervor, dangling irrelevantly in mid-air.
But the protection of marriage was not the point of
Griswold. The creation of a new device for judicial power
to remake the Constitution was the point.

The *Griswold* opinion, of course, began by denying that any such power was being assumed. "[W]e
are met with a wide range of questions that implicate
the Due Process Clause of the 14th Amendment.
Overtones of some arguments suggest that [*Lochner v.
New York*] should be our guide. But we decline that
invitation. . . . We do not sit as a super-legislature to
determine the wisdom, need, and propriety of laws
that touch economic problems, business affairs, or
social conditions."[5] *Griswold*, as an assumption of judicial power unrelated to the Constitution is, however,
indistinguishable from *Lochner*. And the nature of that
power, its lack of rationale or structure, ensured that it
could not be confined.

The Court majority said there was now a right of
privacy but did not even intimate an answer to the
question, "Privacy to do what?" People often take
addictive drugs in private, some men physically abuse
their wives and children in private, executives conspire
to fix prices in private, Mafiosi confer with their button
men in private. If these sound bizarre, one professor at
a prominent law school has suggested that the right of
privacy may create a right to engage in prostitution.
Moreover, as we shall see, the Court has extended the
right of privacy to activities that can in no sense be said
to be done in private. The truth is that "privacy" will
turn out to protect those activities that enough Justices
to form a majority think ought to be protected and not
activities with which they have little sympathy.

If one called the zones of the separate rights of the Bill of Rights zones of "freedom," which would be more accurate, then, should one care to follow Douglas's logic, the zones would add up to a general right of freedom independent of any provision of the Constitution. A general right of freedom—a constitutional right to be free of regulation by law—is a manifest impossibility. Such a right would posit a state of nature, and its law would be that of the jungle. If the Court had created a general "right of freedom," we would know at once, therefore, that the new right would necessarily be applied selectively, and, if we were given no explanation of the scope of the new right, we would know that the "right" was nothing more than a warrant judges had created for themselves to do whatever they wished. That, as we shall see in the next chapter, is precisely what happened with the new, general, undefined, and unexplained "right of privacy."

Justice Black's dissent stated: "I like my privacy as well as the next one, but I am nevertheless compelled to admit that government has a right to invade it unless prohibited by some specific constitutional provision."[6] He found none. "The Court talks about a constitutional 'right of privacy' as though there is some constitutional provision or provisions forbidding any law ever to be passed which might abridge the 'privacy' of individuals. But there is not." He pointed out that there are "certain specific constitutional provisions which are designed in part to protect privacy at certain times and places with respect to certain activities." But there was no general right of the sort Douglas had created. Justice Stewart's dissent referred to the statute as "an uncommonly silly law" but noted that its asininity was not before the Court.[7] He could "find no such general right of privacy in the Bill of Rights, in any other part of the Constitution, or in any case ever before decided by this Court." He also observed that the "Court does not say how far the new constitutional right of privacy announced today extends." That was twenty-four years ago, and the Court still has not told us.

. . .

Endnotes

[1] 381 U.S. 479 (1965).

[2] *Id.* at 485–86.

[3] 357 U.S. 449 (1958).

[4] 381 U.S. at 486.

[5] *Ibid.* at 481–482.

[6] [*Ibid.*] at 507, 508, 510 (Black, [Justice], dissenting).

[7] [*Ibid.*] at 527, 530 n. 7 (Stewart, [Justice], dissenting).

Study Questions

1. One criticism of the reader's understanding approach to ascertaining legal meaning is that, since differing readers are variously situated with respect to the values and beliefs they bring to a particular text, this theory leads to a thorough-going relativism about legal meaning. Do you agree? Why or why not?

2. What does Justice Scalia see as the central problem with the theory that statutory interpretation should proceed on the basis of discerning the intent of the legislature?

3. What guides does Scalia give as to how the "objective intent" of a law, like the one at stake in *Smith v. U.S.*, is to be ascertained?

4. What differences does Scalia see between his "textualist" view and the "strict constructionism" advocated by earlier, conservative jurists?

5. Would you vote to convict John Smith of "using" a firearm during his crime? What kind of "use" do you think Congress intended when it passed the law under which Smith was prosecuted?

6. Justice Scalia's dissent in *Smith* includes this example: "When someone asks 'Do you use a cane?,'" he is not asking whether you have it mounted on the wall as a decoration: "he wants to know whether you *walk* with a cane. Similarly, to speak of 'using a firearm' is to speak of using it for its distinctive purpose, i.e., as a weapon." Do you agree?

7. What role, if any, would you grant to the (apparent) objectives of Congress in enacting the statute in *Holy Trinity* as regards the interpretation of that statute? Could Congress have passed a law the consequences of which it failed fully to foresee? If so, is it legitimate for a judge to "correct" for that oversight?

8. Should it matter, in your view, whether Reverend Warren deprived anyone else of a job in accepting the position at Holy Trinity Church? What view of congressional intent might make this a relevant question?

9. At various points throughout the privacy cases, appeal is made to the Ninth Amendment: "The enumeration in the Constitution, of certain rights, shall not be construed to deny or disparage others retained by the people." The suggestion has been made that privacy is one of these "retained" rights. But the Ninth is the focus of controversy. Some scholars argue that its appearance in the text of the Constitution is prophylactic only: at the time of adoption there was some concern that the inclusion of a bill of rights would be taken to imply that the federal power (granted in section 8 of Article I) is not limited but extends all the way up to the edge of the rights enumerated; that is, that the federal government has the power to do everything except infringe upon those listed rights. The Ninth Amendment was meant merely to preclude that inference. On its face, however, the Ninth seems to be a clear invitation to look beyond the text and structure of the Constitution to locate fundamental rights still retained by the people. The difficulty, of course, is that we are not told where to look for such rights; the text of the amendment provides no guidelines. How would you determine to what rights the Ninth Amendment refers? Should the Ninth be relied upon at all in interpreting the Constitution?

10. Justice Blackmun, dissenting in *Bowers*, argued that the Court should protect our fundamental interests in "controlling the nature of [our] intimate associations with others." Bork objects to this formulation of the right of privacy as it would make it impossible consistently to criminalize adultery, incest, or other sex crimes so long as they are committed in the home. Is Bork correct?

11. Why, according to Bork, is the right of privacy neither neutrally derived, defined, nor applied?

12. Bork insists that the "original understanding" or original intent behind the language of the Constitution cannot be taken to reflect the specific opinions or views of any particular person or group. Why does Bork make this claim?

13. The concept of judicial review, according to which courts may sit in judgment on the constitutionality of legislative acts, is not (as is often remarked) explicitly mentioned in the Constitution. How could a textualist like Scalia square the viability of judicial review with that theory?

14. State Justice Scalia's reasons for disagreeing with the Court's decision in *Church of the Holy Trinity*. Do you agree? Is Scalia's critique of the Court's argument in *Holy Trinity* consistent with his criticisms of the Court's ruling in *Smith*? How might someone argue that they are inconsistent?

15. Explain Dworkin's distinction between "semantic intention" and "expectation intention." Give an example of each. Which of these concepts plays the crucial role in legal interpretation, according to Dworkin?

16. According to Dworkin, the broad clauses of the Constitution "set out abstract principles" of political morality (for example, that segregation is inherently unequal) rather than "concrete or dated rules." Relate this view to Dworkin's "interpretive" theory of law, discussed in Chapter 1.

17. In December 1998, then-President Bill Clinton was impeached by the House of Representatives on several articles: (1) that he had perjured himself before a grand jury concerning the nature of his relationship with Monica Lewinsky and in a deposition made in the Paula Jones case, and (2) that he had improperly influenced witnesses. Article II of the Constitution provides that the President shall be removed from office upon impeachment by a majority vote in the House and a two-thirds vote of the Senate. Impeachment of the President is specified for treason, bribery, or "other high crimes and misdemeanors." As many legal commentators pointed out, "high crimes and misdemeanors" is not defined in the Constitution, and there does not appear to be a settled usage. "High" crime is ambiguous and may refer to a "serious offense" or an "offense by a high-ranking official." A "misdemeanor," in modern terminology, is generally considered to be a lesser offense (as contrasted, say, with a felony). How should "high crimes and misdemeanors" be interpreted? Must the crime alleged to be impeachable conduct be punishable by a minimum number of years in prison? Suppose, as Richard Posner has hypothesized, "the President moved to Saudi Arabia so that he could have four wives, intending to run the government of the United States by e-mail and telephone." (Richard Posner, *An Affair of State* [Cambridge: Harvard University Press, 1999], p. 99.) Would this be impeachable conduct even though it is not a crime? Must impeachable

conduct be related to an abuse of office? Suppose that Clinton "using none of the resources of his office and so being innocent of any misuse of Presidential power, had killed Monica Lewinsky with his bare hands in order to prevent her from cooperating with the Independent Counsel . . ." (*op. cit.*, p. 105). Would he not be subject to impeachment? What about lying under oath? Is that a "high crime" or only a "middle-level" offense? How would an originalist about constitutional interpretation try to resolve these questions? How would a Scalia-type "textualist" view them? What would Dworkin's theory of constitutional interpretation recommend?

18. Randolph Lee received a traffic citation that he falsely signed in the name of his deceased brother, Edward Watson. A few weeks later, Lee was again stopped for various traffic infractions. Lee told officers that he was Edward Watson, and argued that, since he had received the previous citation in that

name, "he had to be Mr. Watson." When his subterfuge was discovered, Lee was charged with violating a section of the California penal code that made it an offense to "falsely impersonate another either in his private or official capacity." Lee insisted upon his innocence, arguing that a deceased person "has no private of official capacity" and therefore it could not be a crime to impersonate a dead person. Lee claimed that the obvious purpose of the statute was to prohibit forms of impersonation that could result in actual harm to another *existing* individual. The prosecution countered that the legislature must have intended to make impersonation of the dead punishable, as in the case of protecting the interests of the deceased during the period between her death and the settling of her estate. (*Lee v. Superior Court* 22 Cal. 4th 41 [2000]). How would you decide this case? Is it clear what the statute means? Is the legislative intent behind this law clear? Why or why not?

B. *Boundaries of the Law: Freedom of Expression and Enforcing Morality*

Law and Morality

Laws and moral standards differ in some significant ways. Laws, for example, come into existence when enacted by a legislature or expressed by a court; they take effect at a particular time and place and are enforced by specific procedures. Moral standards, on the other hand, don't seem to share these features. Moreover, laws may apply to activities that have no apparent moral significance. Such laws are called *mala prohibita* ("bad because forbidden") and include statutes requiring that one must drive on the right side of the road or pay one's taxes by April 15.

Law and morality do overlap, however, and deliberately so. Both legal statutes and moral rules, for

example, forbid harming others in certain ways; both require that people honor their promises, and both protect rights to property, privacy, and many other things. Laws can also be brought into conformity to moral standards by being changed or repealed when they are believed to be wrong. Some would argue (as we saw in Chapter 1) that areas of vagueness or open texture in the law may have to be filled in by reference to moral concepts.

More controversial than these obvious connections between law and morality is the claim that the law should be used to enforce the moral opinions of the majority concerning certain areas of social life. Often these issues concern behavior that a minority views as morally acceptable and thus not the law's

business. Examples of such areas include sexual behavior, religious practices, suicide, and drug use.
Questions about what this category should or should
not include, how the things included are to be defined,
and whether the category should exist at all are the
subject of much legal and philosophical debate. Often contentious in this regard are (1) activities that
allegedly harm only oneself, such as smoking or
drinking, failing to wear a seat belt or motorcycle
helmet, and (2) activities that offend others, as in the
case of public nudity or obscene speech.

In this section of Chapter 2, we focus upon the use
of the law to "enforce" the moral views and beliefs of a
community, with special emphasis on the constitutionally protected freedoms of expression and religious
exercise.

The Case of Public Nudity

The case of *South Florida Free Beaches* begins the readings with an unusual claim embodying many of the
issues explored in this section: that public nudity is a
form of expressing oneself that deserves constitutional
protection. Should those who wish to sunbathe nude
at public beaches have the liberty to do so? What reasons could be used to justify a legal ban on such conduct? Is it permissible to use the law to enforce the
moral beliefs of a majority who find public nudity
wrong or offensive?

Mill and the Harm Principle

John Stuart Mill's famous essay *On Liberty* aims
to give a broad philosophical justification for wide-
ranging individual freedom of thought and action.
The core of Mill's position, stated in the opening paragraph of our selection, has come to be called the
"harm principle." This states that the only justification
for limiting a person's freedom of thought and action
is to prevent that person from harming others. His or
her own good is never a sufficient reason for restricting a person's freedom, either physically or through
use of the law. (Mill recognizes only two narrow
exceptions to this principle: children and "backward"
peoples.) Only when actions threaten to harm others is
interference legitimate; where conduct is primarily
"self-regarding," it cannot be prohibited. That which
is primarily self-regarding defines the sphere of individual liberty.

Mill isolates three types of liberty: (1) liberty of
"tastes and pursuits," or freedom to frame and pursue
a plan of life, to make a variety of personal, career, and
lifestyle choices; (2) liberty of "association," or freedom to come together with others for purposes ranging from marriage to clubs, from church to business;
and (3) liberty of "thought and feeling," or freedom of
conscience and expression. Mill is especially concerned with the last of these because he believes it
contributes crucially to the well-being of individuals
and society. For all we know, Mill claims, any given
opinion or view may express the truth; if we squelch
that opinion we are robbed of the opportunity to learn
the truth, thus harming ourselves. Furthermore, the
collision of differing and contrasting points of view
and lifestyles is helpful in challenging us to justify our
own convictions to ourselves; views that must be
defended are thereby invigorated. And finally, if an
opinion is false or a choice a poor one, these facts will
be discovered sooner or later in their clash with contending perspectives; the truth will win out in the end.

Mill's theory firmly repudiates the view known as
paternalism, the idea that interference with a person's
liberty is justified in order to protect that person's own
welfare or needs or interests; a restriction of your freedom for your own good. No one, Mill believes, should
be told what to do with his or her life, assuming of
course that he or she is a competent adult. Each of us
has the best knowledge of what is in our own interests. The evil of paternalistic interference far outweighs any evil that a person may visit upon himself.
This does not mean that Mill argues for a callous
egoism: we certainly should encourage and assist
others to take better care of themselves, to give up
dangerous habits, and to enrich their lives, but we
may not coerce them into such things with the instrument of the law. Where the majority seeks to coerce the
minority, Mill observes, the result is frequently intolerance, prejudice, and pain.

Some writers have suggested that the decisions of
courts in many cases dealing with pornography, religious freedom, and so on, illustrate how the First
Amendment "constitutionalizes" Mill's harm principle, so that the Constitution is read as an endorsement
of the conception of liberty articulated by Mill. When
reading the material throughout this chapter, you
should ask yourself whether this is the case and
whether such a reading of the Constitution is desirable.

Is it possible, for example, to frame or draft
statutes or interpret constitutional language in a way
that adequately defines what constitutes "harm" to

another? Certain forms of harm are of course obvious and uncontroversial: deprivation of property and physical injury, for example. But to limit harm to such obvious forms would be unacceptably narrow. Most of us would agree that the law should prohibit assault (placing another in reasonable fear of imminent bodily harm) or libel (publication of facts about another with the aim of injuring his or her reputation). Plainly there are ways of "harming" someone without stealing his stereo or punching him in the nose. Harm, it seems, must include certain forms of psychological injury or distress, but this gives rise to another difficulty: How to shape the law so that further harms fall within the prohibitions of the harm principle without weakening that standard altogether by counting as "harmful" anything that displeases or offends. The freedom to do only that to which no one has any objection is limited indeed.

Responses to Mill

British judge Patrick Devlin, in a work that is now classic, argues that Mill's demand that society afford the maximum scope possible for individual thought and action, consistent with a prohibition on harm to others, is indefensible. The impetus for Devlin's essay stemmed from the publication in Britain of a report recommending the decriminalization of homosexual acts on grounds largely derived from Mill. Devlin used the occasion to develop a forceful critique of Mill.

In his essay, Devlin asks us to think about the idea of society. What is a society? It is not, Devlin answers, merely a geographical locality or a political structure. A society is a community of ideas and ideals—an interconnected network of shared values and beliefs. Not only must a society have a political structure to be viable, it must also have a moral structure. This shared body of values—what Devlin calls the "public morality"—is essential to the preservation of a viable community. Devlin uses the institution of marriage as an example of one element of the public morality. Marriage is both a legal and a political institution. It is also the basis of various moral prohibitions on certain behaviors (for example, adultery and polygamy). Society may legitimately use the law to support these moral proscriptions in order to preserve an important part of the social fabric. Of course, Devlin is aware that not every deviation from these values will pose a threat to the public morality. How, then, do we determine when something is so vital to

the public morality that it must be protected? We must look, says Devlin, to the views of the ordinary person. We must find out, or try to imagine, what the reaction of the average, reasonable person would be to a given action or behavior. If that person has a deep-seated feeling of revulsion or disgust at some activity, this is a signal that the limits of social toleration have been reached. Devlin elaborates on this idea by appealing to the notion of the juror in the jury room. Just as a jury typically must come to a unanimous decision, so it must be that everyone (or nearly everyone) is disgusted by some practice before society has a right to step in with the law. Also, people on a jury are supposed to deliberate calmly and carefully before reaching a verdict, rather than being carried away by their prejudices.

What does Devlin's theory mean in practical terms? Suppose Jane Roe is arrested and charged with committing acts of ritual animal sacrifice. If, upon careful reflection, nearly everyone in Jane's community is repulsed by the idea of such a practice, the community would be justified (according to Devlin) in making Jane's conduct illegal, even over her protest that animal sacrifice is part of her religion.

In a response to Devlin included here, philosopher H. L. A. Hart charges that Devlin wrongly conceives of the public morality as a kind of seamless web, so that deviation from any part of it (for example, a rejection of traditional sexual mores) weakens the entire fabric. Devlin also seems mistakenly to move from the claim that a viable society must have some shared moral values to the claim that a society is identical with its shared morality as defined at a given point, so any disruption in the public morality would amount to the destruction of society. But this conception, Hart reasons, would make change within a society impossible—any change would signal the end of one society and the beginning of another. Nothing is gained by thinking about the situation in this way.

Mill and Hart are often regarded as defenders of *liberalism* in political morality: roughly, the view that the function of a legal system of governance is to secure basic rights and freedoms to citizens and thus establish a zone within which each individual can chose her own conception of the "good," that is, her own set of values and beliefs about how to conduct parts of her life, such as religious convictions and intimate relationships. Contemporary legal philosopher Gerald Dworkin seeks in his selection to challenge the efforts of liberals to defend this position. While not necessarily agreeing with Devlin on the specifics of, say, gay sex or marriage, Dworkin does agree with Devlin that no clear, principled line can be drawn distinguishing between conduct which is legitimately punishable, because harmful, and that which is merely "immoral" but within the liberal's zone of freedom or autonomy. Even liberalism accepts the "enforcement" morality in some sense—for example, by endorsing laws that protect people from harm. But to "harm" another is to act wrongly, that is, immorally. So, Dworkin asks, how do we distinguish, in the way Mill and Hart want, those parts of morality that may properly be enforced from those that may not? Dworkin questions the liberal view that certain "ideals" of virtue and sexual conduct, for instance, may never be enforced with the power of the law.

Offense and Artistic Freedom

In the summer of 1998, police in Sacramento, California, arrested "Gangsta" rapper Shawn Thomas, who performs under the name C-BO, for violating conditions of parole for a previous offense. The arrest sparked controversy and outrage among advocates of free speech, for Thomas had been jailed because of violent, anti-police lyrics released on a new CD. Over his lawyer's objections, Thomas had earlier been required as a condition of parole not to record lyrics that "promote the gang lifestyle [or are] anti-law enforcement." Lyrics on the CD included the following: "You better swing, batter, batter swing/'Cause once you get your third felony,/Yeah, 50 years you gotta bring/It's a deadly game of baseball/So when they try to pull you over, shoot 'em in the face, y'all." Police authorities insisted that the parole conditions were a justifiable effort to stem gang violence; critics argued that authorities should never have the power to jail a person based solely on the content of his or her speech.

Just one year after the Thomas controversy in California, another ignited in New York. Then-mayor Rudy Giuliani threatened to pull taxpayer-subsidized funding from the Brooklyn Museum of Art. At issue was an exhibit entitled "Sensation," which included, among other works, a portrait of the Virgin Mary decorated with elephant dung, mannequins with genitals as facial features, and a glass tank featuring a fake cow's head and 20,000 live maggots. Giuliani and many other New Yorkers found the exhibit vulgar and offensive. Defenders of the museum asserted the First Amendment rights of artists creatively to express themselves, even at the expense of public sensibilities.

Freedom of Expression and the First Amendment

The legal questions raised by cases such as these turn on whether artists and performers have a right to express themselves or to use public money to convey ideas that taxpayers or their authorities may find deeply offensive. But the controversies raise other questions as well: Should my creative freedom as an artist take priority over your demand that such freedom be curtailed? For what reasons, if any, may society properly restrict an artist's—or anyone's—expressive freedom? Probing further, we may ask whether the ideal of freedom of expression protects all forms of expression. What about obscene language or pornographic literature? What about racist insults? Or the symbols and chants of hate groups and bigots? What justifies the law's attempt to draw lines dividing permissible from impermissible speech? May only speech that harms others be restricted?

At the most basic philosophical level, the foregoing questions converge on the demand to know what justifies or legitimates placing coercive restraints or criminal penalties on any of the myriad ways in which people choose to act, think, or express themselves. For what reasons may society restrict my liberty to think or act as I please? Political and legal philosophers have defended a variety of answers to these most basic questions. It is always a good reason for restricting someone's liberty, the answers go, if doing so is necessary to (1) prevent harm to others, (2) prevent serious and profound offense to others, (3) prevent harm to the actor himself or herself, or (4) prevent the occurrence of something inherently wrong or immoral even if neither harm nor profound offense to the actor or others is likely. Which, if any, of these proffered grounds (or some combination) are sufficient to justify curtailing individual liberty? Which of these alternatives (or some combination) should we seek to implement through the vehicle of the law? In our system of jurisprudence, such basic issues concerning individual liberty and collective authority arise most sharply at the constitutional level—for example, in applying the First Amendment to the U.S. Constitution: "Congress shall make no law . . . abridging freedom of speech. . . ."

The interpretation of and rationales for a legal regime strongly protective of free speech raise many more questions. What is "speech"? Is it whatever is spoken? But surely the First Amendment applies as much to the written word as to an oral exchange. Is speech whatever is (in any way) "communicated"? This interpretation seems too broad; after all, physical assault can "communicate" ideas (on some level), but surely a robber cannot rely on the First Amendment as a defense. Yet courts have protected a range of "symbolic speech"—wearing armbands, burning flags—involving conduct commonly recognized as expressing a message. Why should freedom of speech be protected? Is it to promote democratic self-government? But how much speech would actually be covered by this rationale? Is it to generate and sustain a "marketplace of ideas"? Or to further the search for truth? Will truth always win out in the marketplace?

Of course, not all expression should be protected: threats, bribes, and false advertising are all forms of "speech," but no one would seriously doubt that they should properly be made illegal. Over a number of decades, the courts have fashioned a framework to distinguish protected from unprotected speech: If communication is expressive (whether spoken, written, or "symbolic"), the government may not prohibit it unless (1) the government has a compelling or overriding interest or purpose and (2) the restriction or suppression of the expression is unrelated to the content of what is said (i.e., the restriction is not based on the content of the communication). The state can prohibit bribes, for it has a compelling interest in discouraging such things; and the state can prohibit the use of loudspeakers at 2 A.M., because this limitation is imposed regardless of what I use my loudspeaker to say. Throughout this section, we will have occasion to consider how this basic framework applies to a variety of cases.

The Cohen Case

The case of Robert Cohen, included in the readings of this section, squarely raises the question: What is constitutionally protected expression? Cohen had been charged with "disturbing the peace . . . through offensive conduct" for wearing a jacket bearing the words "Fuck the draft" into the Los Angeles County courthouse. Cohen appealed the conviction, and the U.S. Supreme Court eventually overturned it. Justice

Harlan, writing for the court, raised a number of points. The state cannot punish Cohen merely for the underlying content of his message (i.e., "I don't like the draft"), as doing so would plainly violate the First Amendment. Cohen's speech did not fall within the generally recognized areas in which restrictions on speech are appropriate (for example, Cohen did not "incite a riot" or engage in "fighting words" or defamatory remarks against a specific person). Nor was Cohen's message unavoidable to those who might be offended by it. Finally, Harlan attacks the California statute at stake in the case. That law is far too vague: What does "offensive" mean? The term is dangerously flexible, such that almost any offense or distress could become grounds for prohibition. The language of the California law is so vague that it fails to give people adequate notice of what the law requires. Harlan here appeals to a crucially important notion in the law: It is a fundamental principle that criminal offenses be specified as precisely as possible, so that people can know with reasonable certainty what is against the law and what isn't. Statutes are sometimes held "void for vagueness"—so unclear that they are unconstitutional.

Speech and Hate

Among the most recent and divisive disputes concerning the scope of freedom of expression revolves around how institutions of higher learning ought to respond to the much-publicized rise in incidents of racial and sexual "hate-speech" on college and university campuses. Many college campuses in the last few years have experienced an alarming increase in various racial incidents, from racial graffiti in dorms to confrontational racial slurs and epithets in the quad. As a consequence, several campuses have experimented with policies prohibiting "discriminatory harassment" or "personal vilification." Generally, such "speech codes" have tended to fall into two categories. Some seek to suppress the broadest range of hate-speech, from the lowliest gutter epithets and slurs to more disguised, veiled, or sophisticated expressions of racial hatred and contempt. Others aim to isolate and suppress only the crudest forms of racial insults: those directed at specific persons with the intent to vilify and degrade their target.

Critics have argued that such policies run afoul of the First Amendment, and in 1988 a federal court in Michigan struck down a policy of the University of

Michigan that prohibited "stigmatizing or victimizing" individuals or groups on the basis of "race, ethnicity, religion, sex, sexual orientation, creed, national origin, ancestry, age, marital status, handicap, or Vietnam-era veteran status" by creating an "intimidating, hostile, or demeaning" educational environment. The court claimed that the terms of the policy were so vague and broad as to fail to pass constitutional muster.[1]

The courts have held that certain categories of expression do not deserve free-speech protection. These categories include, for example, defamatory speech, "fighting words," and speech that is "directed to inciting or producing imminent lawless action" where such lawlessness is likely. Does abusive, racist speech deserve full free-speech protection? Or is it sufficiently close to one or another of the forms of expression traditionally excluded from such protection? Much of the difficulty here lies in deciding what "hate-speech" is; it is best to look at specific examples. (*Warning:* To discuss concrete cases, it is necessary to employ the language used by bigots. I will need to do so here.) One case involved a group of White students who trailed a Black female across campus saying, "I've never tried a nigger before." Another involved a swastika and the words "die faggot" scrawled on a dormitory door. These kinds of cases are arguably close to conduct already prohibited (for example, sexual harassment or assault). Other cases are not so clear. Suppose two students, one White and the other Black, are involved in a heated classroom discussion of affirmative action (the White student is against it; the Black student supports it). At one point, the White student angrily points a finger at the Black student and says, "You just want a handout because you're a [expletive deleted] nigger, and lazy niggers always want a handout." By itself, this is not conduct rising to the level of an assault. Nor does it suffice to display a pattern of discriminatory behavior. It certainly is direct vilification based on race. If the White student defends his statement on free-speech grounds, should this defense be credited?

Much of the legal dispute concerning hate speech seems to turn on whether such expression can be said to cause harm of the sort that the law should prohibit. But what of the argument that hate speech should be banned on the grounds that it is deeply offensive to the vast majority of citizens? The question of offensiveness as a justification for restricting liberty is directly taken up by Joel Feinberg in his imaginative example of a bus ride shared with people engaging in a panoply of disgusting behaviors. As you read through Feinberg's list of "gross" doings, ask yourself which, if any, you would prohibit and why.

Religious Free Expression

Just as artistic and political expression are protected under the First Amendment to the Constitution, so religious expression is as well, and in two ways: under the so-called "Establishment" Clause of the First Amendment, no level of government is permitted to designate an official church or religion; under the "Free Exercise" clause, every citizen is guaranteed the right freely to exercise his or her religion. However, these general claims hide some tough questions: What constitutes a "religion"? Must a "religion" include a belief in God? Can deeply held moral or ethical convictions constitute a religion? Does government "establish a religion" when it (for example) gives financial aid to activities conducted by a religious organization, or when it displays religious symbols during a holiday season? When, if ever, may government exempt a person or group from, or make special accommodations regarding, the requirement of a generally applicable law—for example, laws requiring attendance at school, payment of taxes, or performance of military service, as well as those prohibiting drug use or animal sacrifice?

This section of readings ends with a case that explores just one of these many issues. In 2002, Michael Newdow successfully sued the California public school district in which his daughter was enrolled as an elementary student, alleging that the district's requirement that students shall recite the Pledge of Allegiance to the Flag each day is a violation of the Establishment Clause of the First Amendment. In a ruling that shocked many, the U.S. Ninth Circuit Court of Appeals agreed. The pledge, which contains the words "under God," the court found, improperly endorses a particular religious viewpoint. Moreover, it sends a message to those who don't share this perspective that they are "not one of us." The court goes on to argue that the pledge exercise places coercive pressure upon students to participate, for fear of being ostrasized by their peers.

---

[1] See *Doe v. University of Michigan*, 721 F. Supp. 852 (1989).

South Florida Free Beaches, Inc., v. City of Miami, Florida

OPINION: Albert J. Henderson, Circuit Judge:

South Florida Free Beaches, Inc. (South Florida) and Gary Bryant sought a declatory judgment and injunctive relief in the United States District Court for the Southern District of Florida, alleging that various state statutes and city of Miami ordinances unconstitutionally infringed on their right to sunbathe in the nude.

After a non-jury trial, the district court held that nude sunbathing was not a form of expression protected by the first amendment. . . .

We *affirm*.

· · ·

The bare facts in the record show that Bryant and other members of South Florida for several years regularly swam and sunbathed in the nude on a public beach within the corporate limits of the city of Miami. Although a number of statutes and local ordinances restricted such conduct, they were not consistently enforced. Recently, however, Miami officials expressed an intent to prosecute any person who violates these statutes and ordinances. Dade County and the state of Florida, while disclaiming any current intent to arrest the plaintiffs, contend the laws are valid and enforceable. The plaintiffs assert that the city's threat of prosecution chills the exercise of their first amendment right of expression. Nude sunbathing, the plaintiffs claim, is the practice by which they advocate and communicate their philosophy that the human body is wholesome and that nudity is not indecent.

· · ·

As noted above, the district court, in a revealing evaluation, held that "nude sunbathing *per se* is not a constitutionally protected activity." Examining the challenged laws for vagueness, the district court noted that although some of the language may be unclear in the abstract, they clearly proscribed nudity. Employing an overbreadth analysis, the district court upheld all the challenged statutes and ordinances, except that part of Fla.Stat. § 877.03 proscribing actions "as of a nature to corrupt the public morals, or outrage the sense of public decency. . . .

South Florida and Bryant initially assign as error the district court's failure to accord constitutional protection to their activities. Because they allegedly are advocating an idea, they maintain that the government cannot absolutely prohibit the form chosen to express it. Although that may be true in other contexts, we agree that nudity is protected as speech only when combined with some mode of expression which itself is entitled to first amendment protection.

All of the reported cases adhere to this view that the constitution does not protect unassociated nudity from exposure to governmental limitations. . . .

The plaintiffs point to a number of cases for the proposition that nudity, as a means of expression, is constitutionally permissible. All of these cases, however, involved nudity in combination with a protected form of expression. Nudity alone does not place otherwise protected material outside the mantle of the First Amendment.

Stripped of constitutional protection, nude sunbathing is subject to legitimate governmental proscriptions. Thus, we hold that the first amendment does not clothe these plaintiffs with a constitutional right to sunbathe in the nude. Neither do they possess a constitutional right of associating in the nude. They remain able to advocate the benefits of nude sunbathing, albeit while fully dressed.

· · ·

734 F.2d 608 (1984), United States Court of Appeals, Eleventh Circuit.

On Liberty

John Stuart Mill

The object of this Essay is to assert one very simple principle, as entitled to govern absolutely the dealings of society with the individual in the way of compulsion and control, whether the means used be physical force in the form of legal penalties, or the moral coercion of public opinion. That principle is, that the sole end for which mankind are warranted, individually or collectively, in interfering with the liberty of action of any of their number, is self-protection. That the only purpose for which power can be rightfully exercised over any member of a civilized community, against his will, is to prevent harm to others. His own good, either physical or moral, is not a sufficient warrant. He cannot rightfully be compelled to do or forbear because it will be better for him to do so, because it will make him happier, because, in the opinions of others, to do so would be wise, or even right. These are good reasons for remonstrating with him, or reasoning with him, or persuading him, or entreating him, but not for compelling him, or visiting him with any evil in case he do otherwise. To justify that, the conduct from which it is desired to deter him must be calculated to produce evil to some one else. The only part of the conduct of any one, for which he is amenable to society, is that which concerns others. In the part which merely concerns himself, his independence is, of right, absolute. Over himself, over his own body and mind, the individual is sovereign.

It is, perhaps, hardly necessary to say that this doctrine is meant to apply only to human beings in the maturity of their faculties. We are not speaking of children, or of young persons below the age which the law may fix as that of manhood or womanhood. Those who are still in a state to require being taken care of by others, must be protected against their own actions as well as against external injury. For the same reason, we may leave out of consideration those backward states of society in which the race itself may be considered as in its nonage. The early difficulties in the way of spontaneous progress are so great, that there is seldom any choice of means for overcoming them; and a ruler full of the spirit of improvement is warranted in the use of any expedients that will attain an end, perhaps otherwise unattainable. Despotism is a legitimate mode of government in dealing with barbarians, provided the end be their improvement, and the means justified by actually effecting that end. Liberty, as a principle, has no application to any state of things anterior to the time when mankind have become capable of being improved by free and equal discussion. Until then, there is nothing for them but implicit obedience to an Akbar or a Charlemagne, if they are so fortunate as to find one. But as soon as mankind have attained the capacity of being guided to their own improvement by conviction or persuasion (a period long since reached in all nations with whom we need here concern ourselves), compulsion, either in the direct form or in that of pains and penalties for non-compliance, is no longer admissible as a means to their own good, and justifiable only for the security of others.

It is proper to state that I forego any advantage which could be derived to my argument from the idea of abstract right, as a thing independent of utility. I regard utility as the ultimate appeal on all ethical questions; but it must be utility in the largest sense, grounded on the permanent interests of man as a progressive being. Those interests, I contend, authorise the subjection of individual spontaneity to external control, only in respect to those actions of each, which concern the interest of other people. If any one does an act hurtful to others, there is a *prima facie* case for punishing him, by law, or, where legal penalties are not safely applicable, by general disapprobation. There are also many positive acts for the benefit of others, which he may rightfully be compelled to perform; such as to give evidence in a court of justice; to bear his fair share in the common defense, or in any other

---

From John Stuart Mill, *On Liberty*, Chapter 1. First published in 1859.

joint work necessary to the interest of the society of which he enjoys the protection; and to perform certain acts of individual beneficence, such as saving a fellow-creature's life, or interposing to protect the defenseless against ill-usage, things which whenever it is obviously a man's duty to do, he may rightfully be made responsible to society for not doing. A person may cause evil to others not only by his actions but by his inaction, and in either case he is justly accountable to them for the injury. The latter case, it is true, requires a much more cautious exercise of compulsion than the former. To make any one answerable for doing evil to others is the rule; to make him answerable for not preventing evil is, comparatively speaking, the exception. Yet there are many cases clear enough and grave enough to justify that exception. In all things which regard the external relations of the individual, he is *de jure* amenable to those whose interests are concerned, and, if need be, to society as their protector. There are often good reasons for not holding him to the responsibility; but these reasons must arise from the special expediencies of the case: either because it is a kind of case in which he is on the whole likely to act better, when left to is own discretion, than when controlled in any way in which society have it in their power to control him; or because the attempt to exercise control would produce other evils, greater than those which it would prevent. When such reasons as these preclude the enforcement of responsibility, the conscience of the agent himself should step into the vacant judgment seat, and protect those interests of others which have no external protection; judging himself all the more rigidly, because the case does not admit of his being made accountable to the judgment of his fellow-creatures.

But there is a sphere of action in which society, as distinguished from the individual, has, if any, only an indirect interest; comprehending all that portion of a person's life and conduct which affects only himself, or if it also affects others, only with their free, voluntary, and undeceived consent and participation. When I say only himself, I mean directly, and in the first instance; for whatever affects himself, may affect others *through* himself; and the objection which may be grounded on this contingency, will receive consideration in the sequel. This, then, is the appropriate region of human liberty. It comprises, first, the inward domain of consciousness; demanding liberty of conscience in the most comprehensive sense; liberty of thought and feeling; absolute freedom of opinion and sentiment on all subjects, practical or speculative, scientific, moral, or theo-

logical. The liberty of expressing and publishing opinions may seem to fall under a different principle, since it belongs to that part of the conduct of an individual which concerns other people; but, being almost of as much importance as the liberty of thought itself, and resting in great part on the same reasons, is practically inseparable from it. Secondly, the principle requires liberty of tastes and pursuits; of framing the plan of our life to suit our own character, of doing as we like, subject to such consequences as may follow; without impediment from our fellow creatures, so long as what we do does not harm them, even though they should think our conduct foolish, perverse or wrong. Thirdly, from this liberty of each individual, follows the liberty, within the same limits, of combination among individuals; freedom to unite, for any purpose not involving harm to others; the persons combining being supposed to be of full age, and not forced or deceived.

No society in which these liberties are not, on the whole, respected, is free, whatever may be its form of government; and none is completely free in which they do not exist absolute and unqualified. The only freedom which deserves the name, is that of pursuing our own good in our own way, so long as we do not attempt to deprive others of theirs, or impede their efforts to obtain it. Each is the proper guardian of his own health, whether bodily, or mental and spiritual. Mankind are greater gainers by suffering each other to live as seems good to themselves, than by compelling each to live as seems good to the rest.

Though this doctrine is anything but new, and, to some persons, may have the air of a truism, there is no doctrine which stands more directly opposed to the general tendency of existing opinion and practice. Society has expended fully as much effort in the attempt (according to its lights) to compel people to conform to its notions of personal as of social excellence. The ancient commonwealths thought themselves entitled to practise, and the ancient philosophers countenanced, the regulation of every part of private conduct by public authority, on the ground that the State had a deep interest in the whole bodily and mental discipline of every one of its citizens; a mode of thinking which may have been admissible in small republics surrounded by powerful enemies, in constant peril of being subverted by foreign attack or internal commotion, and to which even a short interval of relaxed energy and self-command might so easily be fatal that they could not afford to wait for the salutary permanent effects of freedom. In the modern world, the greater size of political communities, and, above all, the separation between spiritual and temporal authority (which placed the direction of men's consciences in other hands than those which controlled their worldly affairs), prevented so great an interference by law in the details of private life; but the engines of moral repression have been wielded more strenuously against divergence from the reigning opinion in self-regarding, than even in social matters; religion, the most powerful of the elements which have entered into the formation of moral feeling, having almost always been governed either by the ambition of a hierarchy, seeking control over every department of human conduct, or by the spirit of Puritanism. And some of those modern reformers who have placed themselves in strongest opposition to the religions of the past, have been in no way behind either churches or sects in their assertion of the right of spiritual domination: M. Comte, in particular, whose social systems, as unfolded in his *Système de Politique Positive*, aims at establishing (though by moral more than by legal appliances) a despotism of society over the individual, surpassing anything contemplated in

the political ideal of the most rigid disciplinarian among the ancient philosophers.

Apart from the peculiar tenets of individual thinkers, there is also in the world at large an increasing inclination to stretch unduly the powers of society over the individual, both by the force of opinion and even by that of legislation; and as the tendency of all the changes taking place in the world is to strengthen society, and diminish the power of the individual, this encroachment is not one of the evils which tend spontaneously to disappear, but, on the contrary, to grow more and more formidable. The disposition of mankind, whether as rulers or as fellow-citizens, to impose their own opinions and inclinations as a rule of conduct on others, is so energetically supported by some of the best and by some of the worst feelings incident to human nature, that it is hardly ever kept under restraint by anything but want of power; and as the power is not declining, but growing, unless a strong barrier of moral conviction can be raised against the mischief, we must expect, in the present circumstances of the world, to see it increase.

The Enforcement of Morals

Patrick Devlin

The report of the Committee on Homosexual Offences and Prostitution, generally known as the Wolfenden Report, is recognized to be an excellent study of two very difficult legal and social problems. But it has also a particular claim to the respect of those interested in jurisprudence; it does what law reformers so rarely do; it sets out clearly and carefully what in relation to its subjects it considers the function of the law to be. Statutory additions to the criminal law are too often made on the simple principle that "there ought to be a law against it." The greater part of the law relating to sexual offences is the creation of statute and it is diffi-

cult to ascertain any logical relationship between it and the moral ideas which most of us uphold. Adultery, fornication, and prostitution are not, as the Report points out, criminal offences: homosexuality between males is a criminal offence but between females it is not. Incest was not an offence until it was declared so by statute only fifty years ago. Does the legislature select these offences haphazardly or are there some principles which can be used to determine what part of the moral law should be embodied in the criminal? There is, for example, being now considered a proposal to make A.I.D., that is, the practice of artificial insemination of a woman with the seed of a man who is not her husband, a criminal offence; if, as is usually the case, the woman is married, this is in substance, if not in form, adultery. Ought it to be made punishable when adultery is not?

From Patrick Devlin, *The Enforcement of Morals* in "Proceedings of the British Academy" (London: The British Academy, 1959), vol. xiv, pp. 129–151. Reprinted by permission.

This sort of question is of practical importance, for a law that appears to be arbitrary and illogical, in the end and after the wave of moral indignation that has put it on the statute book subsides, forfeits respect. As a practical question it arises more frequently in the field of sexual morals than in any other, but there is no special answer to be found in that field. The inquiry must be general and fundamental. What is the connection between crime and sin and to what extent, if at all, should the criminal law of England concern itself with the enforcement of morals and punish sin or immorality as such?

. . .

It is true that for many centuries the criminal law was much concerned with keeping the peace and little, if at all, with sexual morals. But it would be wrong to infer from that that it had no moral content or that it would ever have tolerated the idea of a man being left to judge for himself in matters of morals. The criminal law of England has from the very first concerned itself with moral principles. A simple way of testing this point is to consider the attitude which the criminal law adopts towards consent.

Subject to certain exceptions inherent in the nature of particular crimes, the criminal law has never permitted consent of the victim to be used as a defence. In rape, for example, consent negatives an essential element. But consent of the victim is no defence to a charge of murder. It is not a defence to any form of assault that the victim thought his punishment well deserved and submitted to it; to make a good defence the accused must prove that the law gave him the right to chastise and that he exercised it reasonably. Likewise, the victim may not forgive the aggressor and require the prosecution to desist; the right to enter a *nolle prosequi* belongs to the Attorney-General alone.

Now, if the law existed for the protection of the individual, there would be no reason why he should avail himself of it if he did not want it. The reason why a man may not consent to the commission of an offence against himself beforehand or forgive it afterwards is because it is an offence against society. It is not that society is physically injured; that would be impossible. Nor need any individual be shocked, corrupted, or exploited; everything may be done in private. Nor can it be explained on the practical ground that a violent man is a potential danger to others in the community who have therefore a direct interest in his apprehension and punishment as being necessary to their own protection. That would be true of a man

whom the victim is prepared to forgive but not of one who gets his consent first; a murderer who acts only upon the consent, and maybe the request, of his victim is no menace to others, but he does threaten one of the great moral principles upon which society is based, that is, the sanctity of human life. There is only one explanation of what has hitherto been accepted as the basis of the criminal law and that is that there are certain standards of behaviour or moral principles which society requires to be observed; and the breach of them is an offence not merely against the person who is injured but against society as a whole.

Thus, if the criminal law were to be reformed so as to eliminate from it everything that was not designed to preserve order and decency or to protect citizens (including the protection of youth from corruption), it would overturn a fundamental principle. It would also end a number of specific crimes. Euthanasia or the killing of another at his own request, suicide, attempted suicide, and suicide pacts, duelling, abortion, incest between brother and sister, are all acts which can be done in private and without offence to others and need not involve the corruption or exploitation of others. Many people think that the law on some of these subjects is in need of reform, but no one hitherto has gone so far as to suggest that they should all be left outside the criminal law as matters of private morality. They can be brought within it only as a matter of moral principle. It must be remembered also that although there is much immorality that is not punished by law, there is none that is condoned by the law. The law will not allow its processes to be used by those engaged in immorality of any sort. For example, a house may not be let for immoral purposes; the lease is invalid and would not be enforced. But if what goes on inside there is a matter of private morality and not the law's business, why does the law inquire into it at all?

I think it is clear that the criminal law as we know it is based upon moral principle. In a number of crimes its function is simply to enforce a moral principle and nothing else. The law, both criminal and civil, claims to be able to speak about morality and immorality generally. Where does it get its authority to do this and how does it settle the moral principles which it enforces? Undoubtedly, as a matter of history, it derived both from Christian teaching. But [the] law can no longer rely on doctrines in which citizens are entitled to disbelieve. It is necessary therefore to look for some other source.

In jurisprudence, as I have said, everything is thrown open to discussion and, in the belief that they cover the whole field, I have framed three interrogatories addressed to myself to answer:

1. Has society the right to pass judgment at all on matters of morals? Ought there, in other words, to be a public morality, or are morals always a matter for private judgment?

2. If society has the right to pass judgment, has it also the right to use the weapon of the law to enforce it?

3. If so, ought it to use that weapon in all cases or only in some; and if only in some, on what principles should it distinguish?

I shall begin with the first interrogatory and consider what is meant by the right of society to pass a moral judgment, that is, a judgment about what is good and what is evil. The fact that a majority of people may disapprove of a practise does not of itself make it a matter for society as a whole. Nine men out of ten may disapprove of what the tenth man is doing and still say that it is not their business. There is a case for a collective judgment (as distinct from a large number of individual opinions which sensible people may even refrain from pronouncing at all if it is upon somebody else's private affairs) only if society is affected. Without a collective judgment there can be no case at all for intervention. Let me take as an illustration the Englishman's attitude to religion as it is now and as it has been in the past. His attitude now is that a man's religion is his private affair; he may think of another man's religion that it is right or wrong, true or untrue, but not that it is good or bad. In earlier times that was not so; a man was denied the right to practise what was thought of as heresy, and heresy was thought of as destructive of society.

The language used in the passages I have quoted from the Wolfenden Report suggests the view that there ought not to be a collective judgment about immorality *per se*. Is this what is meant by "private morality" and "individual freedom of choice and action"? Some people sincerely believe that homosexuality is neither immoral nor unnatural. Is the "freedom of choice and action" that is offered to the individual, freedom to decide for himself what is moral or immoral, society remaining neutral; or is it freedom to be immoral if he wants to be? The language of the Report may be open to question, but the conclusions at which the Committee arrive answer this question unambiguously. If society is not prepared to say that homosexuality is morally wrong,

there would be no basis for a law protecting youth from "corruption" or punishing a man for living on the "immoral" earnings of a homosexual prostitute, as the Report recommends. This attitude the Committee makes even clearer when they come to deal with prostitution. In truth, the Report takes it for granted that there is in existence a public morality which condemns homosexuality and prostitution. What the Report seems to mean by private morality might perhaps be better described as private behaviour in matters of morals.

This view—that there is such a thing as public morality—can also be justified by *a priori* argument. What makes a society of any sort is community of ideas, not only political ideas but also ideas about the way its members should behave and govern their lives; these latter ideas are its morals. Every society has a moral structure as well as a political one: or rather, since that might suggest two independent systems, I should say that the structure of every society is made up both of politics and morals. Take, for example, the institution of marriage. Whether a man should be allowed to take more than one wife is something about which every society has to make up its mind one way or the other. In England we believe in the Christian idea of marriage and therefore adopt monogamy as a moral principle. Consequently the Christian institution of marriage has become the basis of family life and so part of the structure of our society. It is there not because it is Christian. It has got there because it is Christian, but it remains there because it is built into the house in which we live and could not be removed without bringing it down. The great majority of those who live in this country accept it because it is the Christian idea of marriage and for them the only true one. But a non-Christian is bound by it, not because it is part of Christianity but because, rightly or wrongly, it has been adopted by the society in which he lives. It would be useless for him to stage a debate designed to prove that polygamy was theologically more correct and socially preferable; if he wants to live in the house, he must accept it as built in the way in which it is.

We see this more clearly if we think of ideas or institutions that are purely political. Society cannot tolerate rebellion; it will not allow argument about the rightness of the cause. Historians a century later may say that the rebels were right and the Government was wrong and a percipient and conscientious subject of the State may think so at the time. But it is not a matter which can be left to individual judgment.

The institution of marriage is a good example for my purpose because it bridges the division, if there is one, between politics and morals. Marriage is part of the structure of our society and it is also the basis of a moral code which condemns fornication and adultery. The institution of marriage would be gravely threatened if individual judgments were permitted about the morality of adultery; on these points there must be a public morality. But public morality is not to be confined to those moral principles which support institutions such as marriage. People do not think of monogamy as something which has to be supported because our society has chosen to organize itself upon it; they think of it as something that is good in itself and offering a good way of life and that it is for that reason that our society has adopted it. I return to the statement that I have already made, that society means a community of ideas; without shared ideas on politics, morals, and ethics no society can exist. Each one of us has ideas about what is good and what is evil; they cannot be kept private from the society in which we live. If men and women try to create a society in which there is no fundamental agreement about good and evil they will fail; if, having based it on common agreement, the agreement goes, the society will disintegrate. For society is not something that is kept together physically; it is held by the invisible bonds of common thought. If the bonds were too far relaxed the members would drift apart. A common morality is part of the bondage. The bondage is part of the price of society; and mankind, which needs society, must pay its price.

. . .

I think, therefore, that it is not possible to set theoretical limits to the power of the State to legislate against immorality. It is not possible to settle in advance exceptions to the general rule or to define inflexibly areas of morality into which the law is in no circumstances to be allowed to enter. Society is entitled by means of its laws to protect itself from dangers, whether from within or without. Here again I think that the political parallel is legitimate. The law of treason is directed against aiding the king's enemies and against sedition from within. The justification for this is that established government is necessary for the existence of society and therefore its safety against violent overthrow must be secured. But an established morality is as necessary as good government to the welfare of society. Societies disintegrate from within more frequently than they are broken up by external pressures. There is disintegration when no common

morality is observed and history shows that the loosening of moral bonds is often the first stage of disintegration, so that society is justified in taking the same steps to preserve its moral code as it does to preserve its government and other essential institutions. The suppression of vice is as much the law's business as the suppression of subversive activities; it is no more possible to define a sphere of private morality than it is to define one of private subversive activity. It is wrong to talk of private morality or of the law not being concerned with immorality as such or to try to set rigid bounds to the part which the law may play in the suppression of vice. There are no theoretical limits to the power of the State to legislate against treason and sedition, and likewise I think there can be no theoretical limits to legislation against immorality. You may argue that if a man's sins affect only himself it cannot be the concern of society. If he chooses to get drunk every night in the privacy of his own home, is any one except himself the worse for it? But suppose a quarter or a half of the population got drunk every night, what sort of society would it be? You cannot set a theoretical limit to the number of people who can get drunk before society is entitled to legislate against drunkenness. The same may be said of gambling. The Royal Commission on Betting, Lotteries, and Gaming took as their test the character of the citizen as a member of society. They said: "Our concern with the ethical significance of gambling is confined to the effect which it may have on the character of the gambler as a member of society. If we were convinced that whatever the degree of gambling this effect must be harmful we should be inclined to think that it was the duty of the State to restrict gambling to the greatest extent practicable."

In what circumstances the State should exercise its power is the third of the interrogatories I have framed. But before I get to it I must raise a point which might have been brought up in any one of the three. How are the moral judgments of society to be ascertained? By leaving it until now, I can ask it in the more limited form that is now sufficient for my purpose. How is the law-maker to ascertain the moral judgments of society? It is surely not enough that they should be reached by the opinion of the majority; it would be too much to require the individual assent of every citizen. English law has evolved and regularly uses a standard which does not depend on the counting of heads. It is that of the reasonable man. He is not to be confused with the rational man. He is not expected to reason about anything and his judgment may be largely a matter of feeling. It is the viewpoint of the man in the street—or to use an archaism familiar to all lawyers—the man in the Clapham omnibus. He might also be called the right-minded man. For my purpose I should like to call him the man in the jury box, for the moral judgment of society must be something about which any twelve men or women drawn at random might after discussion be expected to be unanimous. This was the standard the judges applied in the days before Parliament was as active as it is now and when they laid down rules of public policy. They did not think of themselves as making law but simply as stating principles which every right-minded person would accept as valid. It is what Pollock called "practical morality," which is based not on theological or philosophical foundations but "in the mass of continuous experience half-consciously or unconsciously accumulated and embodied in the morality of common sense." He called it also "a certain way of thinking on questions of morality which we expect to find in a reasonable civilized man or a reasonable Englishman, taken at random."

Immorality then, for the purpose of the law, is what every right-minded person is presumed to consider to be immoral. Any immorality is capable of affecting society injuriously and in effect to a greater or lesser extent it usually does; this is what gives the law its *locus standi*. It cannot be shut out. But—and this brings me to the third question—the individual has a *locus standi* too; he cannot be expected to surrender to the judgment of society the whole conduct of his life. It is the old and familiar question of striking a balance between the rights and interests of society and those of the individual. This is something which the law is constantly doing in matters large and small. To take a very down-to-earth example, let me consider the right of the individual whose house adjoins the highway to have access to it; that means in these days the right to have vehicles stationary in the highway, sometimes for a considerable time if there is a lot of loading or unloading. There are many cases in which the courts have had to balance the private right of access against the public right to use the highway without obstruction. It cannot be done by carving up the highway into public and private areas. It is done by recognizing that each have rights over the whole; that if each were to exercise their rights to the full, they would come into conflict; and therefore that the rights of each must be curtailed so as to ensure as far as possible that the essential needs of each are safeguarded.

I do not think that one can talk sensibly of a public and private morality any more than one can of a public or private highway. Morality is a sphere in which there is a public interest and a private interest, often in conflict, and the problem is to reconcile the two. This does not mean that it is impossible to put forward any general statements about how in our society the balance ought to be struck. Such statements cannot of their nature be rigid or precise; they would not be designed to circumscribe the operation of the law-making power but to guide those who have to apply it. While every decision which a court of law makes when it balances the public against the private interest is an *ad hoc* decision, the cases contain statements of principle to which the court should have regard when it reaches its decision. In the same way it is possible to make general statements of principle which it may be thought the legislature should bear in mind when it is considering the enactment of laws enforcing morals.

· · ·

This indicates a general sentiment that the right to privacy is something to be put in the balance against the enforcement of the law. Ought the same sort of consideration to play any part in the formation of the law? Clearly only in a very limited number of cases. When the help of the law is invoked by an injured citizen, privacy must be irrelevant; the individual cannot ask that his right to privacy should be measured against injury criminally done to another. But when all who are involved in the deed are consenting parties and the injury is done to morals, the public interest in the moral order can be balanced against the claims of privacy. The restriction on police powers of investigation goes further than the affording of a parallel; it means that the detection of crime committed in private and when there is no complaint is bound to be rather haphazard and this is an additional reason for moderation. These considerations do not justify the exclusion of all private immorality from the scope of the law. I think that, as I have already suggested, the test of "private behaviour" should be substituted for "private morality" and the influence of the factor should be reduced from that of a definite limitation to that of a matter to be taken into account. Since the gravity of the crime is also a proper consideration, a distinction might well be made in the case of homosexuality between the lesser acts of indecency and the full offense, which on the principles of the Wolfenden Report it would be illogical to do.

Law, Liberty, and Morality

H. L. A. Hart

When we turn [to] the positive grounds held to justify the legal enforcement of morality it is important to distinguish a moderate and an extreme thesis, though critics of Mill have sometimes moved from one to the other without marking the transition. Lord Devlin seems to me to maintain, for most of his essay, the moderate thesis and Stephen the extreme one.[1]

According to the moderate thesis, a shared morality is the cement of society; without it there would be aggregates of individuals but no society. "A recognized morality" is, in Lord Devlin's words, "as necessary to society's existence as a recognized government," and though a particular act of immorality may not harm or endanger or corrupt others nor, when done in private, either shock or give offence to others, this does not conclude the matter. For we must not view conduct in isolation from its effect on the moral code: if we remember this, we can see that one who is "no menace to others" nonetheless may by his immoral conduct "threaten one of the great moral principles on which society is based." In this sense the breach of moral principle is an offence "against society as a whole," and society may use the law to preserve its morality as it uses it to safeguard anything else essential to its existence. This is why "the suppression of vice is as much the law's business as the suppression of subversive activities."

By contrast, the extreme thesis does not look upon a shared morality as of merely instrumental value analogous to ordered government, and it does not justify the punishment of immorality as a step taken, like the punishment of treason, to preserve society from dissolution or collapse. Instead, the enforcement of morality is regarded as a thing of value, even if immoral acts harm no one directly, or indirectly by weakening the moral cement of society. I do not say

that it is possible to allot to one or other of these two theses every argument used, but they do, I think characterise the main critical positions at the root of most arguments, and they incidentally exhibit an ambiguity in the expression "enforcing morality as such." Perhaps the clearest way of distinguishing the two theses is to see that there are always two levels at which we may ask whether some breach of positive morality is harmful. We may ask first, Does this act harm anyone independently of its repercussion on the shared morality of society? And secondly we may ask, Does this act affect the shared morality and thereby weaken society? The moderate thesis requires, if the punishment of the act is to be justified, an affirmative answer at least at the second level. The extreme thesis does not require an affirmative answer at either level.

Lord Devlin appears to defend the moderate thesis. I say "appears" because, though he says that society has the right to enforce a morality as such on the ground that a shared morality is essential to society's existence, it is not at all clear that for him the statement that immorality jeopardizes or weakens society is a statement of empirical fact. It seems sometimes to be an *a priori* assumption, and sometimes a necessary truth and a very odd one. The most important indication that this is so is that, apart from one vague reference to "history" showing that "the loosening of moral bonds is often the first stage of disintegration," no evidence is produced to show that deviation from accepted sexual morality, even by adults in private, is something which, like treason, threatens the existence of society. No reputable historian has maintained this thesis, and there is indeed much evidence against it. As a proposition of fact it is entitled to no more respect than the Emperor Justinian's statement that homosexuality was the cause of earthquakes. Lord Devlin's belief in it, and his apparent indifference to the question of evidence, are at points traceable to an undiscussed assumption. This is that all morality—sexual morality together with the morality that forbids acts injurious to others such as killing, stealing, and dishonesty—forms a single seamless web, so that those who deviate from any part are likely or perhaps bound to deviate from the whole. It is of course clear (and one of the oldest insights of political theory) that society could not exist without a morality which mirrored and supplemented the law's proscription of conduct injurious to others. But there is again no evidence to support, and much to refute, the theory that those who deviate from conventional sexual morality are in other ways hostile to society.

There seems, however, to be central to Lord Devlin's thought something more interesting, though no more convincing, than the conception of social morality as a seamless web. For he appears to move from the acceptable proposition that *some* shared morality is essential to the existence of any society to the unacceptable proposition that a society is identical with its morality as that is at any given moment of its history, so that a change in its morality is tantamount to the destruction of a society. The former proposition might be even accepted as a necessary rather than an empirical truth depending on a quite plausible definition of society as a body of men who hold certain moral views in common. But the latter proposition is absurd. Taken strictly, it would prevent us saying that the morality of the given society had changed, and would compel us instead to say that one society had disappeared and another one taken its place. But it is only on this absurd criterion of what it is for the same society to continue to exist that it could be asserted without evidence that any deviation from a society's shared morality threatens its existence.

It is clear that only this tacit identification of a society with its shared morality supports Lord Devlin's denial that there could be such a thing as private immorality and his comparison of sexual immorality, even when it takes place "in private," with treason. No doubt it is true if deviations from conventional sexual morality are tolerated by the law and come to be known, the conventional morality might change in a permissive direction, though this does not seem to be the case with homosexuality in those European countries where it is not punishable by law. But even if the conventional morality did so change, the society in question would not have been destroyed or "subverted." We should compare such a development not to the violent overthrow of government but to a peaceful constitutional change in its form, consistent not only with the preservation of a society but with its advance.

· · ·

The extreme thesis has many variants, and it is not always clear which of them its advocates are concerned to urge. According to some variants, the legal enforcement of morality is only of instrumental value: it is merely a means, though an indispensable one, for preserving of morality, whereas the preservation of morality is the end, valuable in itself, which justifies its legal enforcement. According to other variants, there is something intrinsically valuable in the legal enforcement of morality. What is common to all varieties of the extreme thesis is that, unlike the moderate thesis, they do not hold the enforcement of morality or its preservation to be valuable merely because of their beneficial consequences in securing the existence of society.

It is to be observed that Lord Devlin hovers somewhat ambiguously between one form of the extreme thesis and the moderate thesis. For if we interpret his crucial statement that the preservation of a society's morality is necessary for its existence as a statement of fact (as the analogy with the suppression of treason suggests we should), then the continued existence of society is something distinguishable from the preservation of its morality. It is, in fact, a desirable consequence of the preservation of its morality, and, on the assumption that the enforcement of morality is identical with or required for its preservation, this desirable consequence justifies the enforcement of morality. So interpreted, Lord Devlin is an advocate of the moderate thesis and his argument is a utilitarian one. The objection to it is that his crucial statement of fact is unsupported by evidence; it is Utilitarianism without benefit of facts. If, on the other hand, we interpret his statement that any immorality, even in private, threatens the existence of society, not as an empirical statement but as a necessary truth (as the absence of evidence suggests we should), then the continued existence of a society is not something different from the preservation of its morality; it is identical with it. On this view the enforcement of morality is not justified by its valuable consequences in securing society from dissolution or decay. It is justified simply as identical with or required for the preservation of the society's morality. This is a form of the extreme thesis, disguised only by the tacit identification of a society with its morality which I criticised.

Stephen is, I think, a more consistent defender of certain forms of the extreme thesis than Lord Devlin is of the moderate one.

It is important for the understanding of Stephen's views on the legal enforcement of morality to notice that he, like Lord Devlin, assumes that the society to which his doctrine is to apply is marked by a considerable degree of moral solidarity, and is deeply disturbed by infringements of its moral code. Just as for Lord Devlin the morality to be enforced by law must be "public," in the sense that it is generally shared and identifiable by the triple marks of "intolerance, indignation, and disgust," so for Stephen "you cannot punish anything which public opinion as expressed in the common practice of society does not strenuously and unequivocally condemn . . . To be able to punish a moral majority must be overwhelming." It is possible that in mid-Victorian England these conditions were satisfied in relation to "that considerable number of acts" which according to Stephen were treated as crimes merely because they were regarded as grossly immoral. Perhaps an "overwhelming moral majority" then actually did harbour the healthy desire for revenge of which he speaks and which is to be gratified by the punishment of the guilty. But it would be sociologically naïve to assume that these conditions obtain in contemporary England at least as far as sexual morality is concerned. The fact that there is lip service to an official sexual morality should not lead us to neglect the possibility that in sexual, as in other matters, there may be a number of mutually tolerant moralities, and that even where there is some homogeneity of practice and belief, offenders may be viewed not with hatred or resentment but with amused contempt or pity.

In a sense, therefore, Stephen's doctrine, and much of Lord Devlin's, may seem to hover in the air above the *terra firma* of contemporary social reality; it may be a well-articulated construction, interesting because it reveals the outlook characteristic of the English judiciary but lacking application to contemporary society.

Endnote

[1] Ed. James Fitzjames Stephen was a British lawyer and judge who was sharply critical of the democratic and secular society for which Mill had argued. Stephen's criticisms of Mill can be found in his book, *Liberty, Equality, Fraternity*, published in 1873.

Devlin Was Right: Law and the Enforcement of Morality

GERALD DWORKIN

It is now thirty-five years since H. L. A. Hart published *Law, Liberty and Morality*,[1] which marked the beginning of the Hart-Devlin debate concerning the enforcement of morality by the criminal law. It is 125 years since James Fitzjames Stephen published *Liberty, Equality, Fraternity*, which initiated a similar debate with John Stuart Mill.[2] Both of these debates concerned the legitimate role of the use of criminal sanctions to punish immoral conduct. As Hart framed the issue, the question can be formulated as: Ought immorality as such be a crime? It is claimed that Mill and Hart say that the answer is "No"; it is said that Fitzjames Stephen and Devlin say "Yes." Contemporary liberal theorists such

From Gerald Dworkin, "Devlin Was Right: Law and the Enforcement of Morality," *William and Mary Law Review*, Vol. 40 (1999), pp. 927–946. Reprinted by permission of William and Mary Law Review.

as Joel Feinberg, Thomas Nagel, and Ronald Dworkin are united in agreement with Mill and Hart that it is not a legitimate function of the state to punish conduct simply on the grounds that it is immoral.

Contemporary legal opinion also divides as to the constitutionality of various statutes that forbid conduct based on the alleged right of the state to enforce moral views. Whether the issue is consensual homosexual conduct between adults, nude dancing in bars, or the ritual sacrifice of animals, judges disagree about whether the state should regulate conduct based on its moral status.

In this essay, I want to distinguish two issues. The first is the substantive question of whether the state actually should regulate particular conduct, e.g., homosexual sex, on the grounds that it considers the conduct immoral. The second is the question of whether it is illegitimate "in principle" for the state to do so. On most issues concerning specific laws, I side with Hart, against Devlin, in believing that the conduct in question should not be criminalized. I side with Devlin, however, in believing that there is no principled line following the contours of the distinction between immoral and harmful conduct such that only grounds referring to the latter may be invoked to justify criminalization.

I.

My first task is to attempt to clarify what divides Devlin and his opponents. We know that this division concerns whether a principled line can be drawn between the kinds of reasons that the state gives to justify coercive restrictions on behavior. What does it mean, though, for there is to be a principled line? I shall begin by looking at the line that liberals—my term for those who oppose Devlin—claim to be the right one, and I will then look at what they mean by that line being the correct one.

The historical context for the Hart-Devlin debate was the release of the Report of the Committee on Homosexual Offences and Prostitution—popularly referred to as the Wolfenden Report, after its chairman. The Committee defended a particular conception of the function of the criminal law:[3]

> [I]ts function, as we see it, is to preserve
> public order and decency, to protect the citizen from what is offensive or injurious, and
> to provide sufficient safeguards against
> exploitation and corruption of others, particularly those who are specially vulnerable
> because they are young, weak in body or
> mind, inexperienced, or in a state of special
> physical, official or economic dependence.[4]

Having said what the law allows by way of reasons for coercion, the report made clear at least one ground that is not allowed: "It is not the duty of the law to concern itself with immorality as such."[5]

The usual rubric under which one discusses these issues is that of the enforcement of morality by the criminal law. The specific formulation attributed to the above claims is that the law ought not to be in the business of enforcing morality. The obvious rejoinder, however, is: Why then does the law protect citizens against, among others, injury, harm, offense, and indecency? Surely, it is because for someone to inflict these on another without adequate justification and excuse is to act wrongly, i.e., immorally. Indeed, if one begins to examine some of the more specific categories, the most prominent of which is "harm," one reaches the conclusion that the term itself is a normative one. Not every setback to a person's interests counts as harmful for the purposes of justifying coercion. Only those that are "wrongs" count.

One answer that is sometimes given—that although rape is both harmful and immoral, the reason the law prohibits it is only that it is harmful—is not available to liberals who wish to reject some thesis about the enforcement of morality. The thesis has to be formulated in terms of different parts of morality. Some parts may be enforced by the law; some parts may not.

Where the line is drawn may differ from liberal to liberal, but they all agree that various rights may be enforced in order to protect individuals against attacks on interest. Indeed, on some views this is part of the notion of a right itself. Other notions that are invoked include the protection of autonomy and respect for persons. What are the parts of morality that may not be enforced? Here, matters are less clear, but they seem to include various ideals, such as ideals of virtue and character, certain ideals of fairness or fittingness, and ideals of sexual conduct.

With respect to certain issues, liberals may divide. Consider Good Samaritan laws—laws requiring so-called "easy rescue." Some liberals, such as Feinberg, approve of such laws because they think that people are harmed by not being rescued. Others who think of harm as being lowered from some status quo believe that failure to rescue is not a harm. They believe that people do not have a right to be rescued, but that it is "indecent" to fail to come to someone's aid in such circumstances. If they wish to require such rescue, they are willing to enforce some ideals, but not others. To defend their thesis, then, liberals have to be able to specify some division of morality into parts and argue that only some of the parts may be protected legitimately and promoted by coercion.

For our purposes, we shall draw the line more or less as Feinberg does—the protection of autonomy and equal respect for persons. This line is not one that is more vague or fuzzy than others we use, yet it does seem to separate the activities that many liberals believe may be regulated from those that may not be. We now need to see what kinds of arguments are available to justify such a line, and whether they are adequate.

II.

Devlin's views differ from those of liberals in at least two respects. There are substantive differences and differences of theory. Devlin often looks like a consequentialist who has a different view about the consequences. His famous equation of immorality with treason and his advocacy of the right of any state to defend against either make a claim about the harm that would occur if the actual moral code of a society were allowed to be attacked and weakened. Hart has said all that needs to be said about the various forms the thesis "an established morality is as necessary as good government to the welfare of society" may take, and the evidence (or lack of it) for various claims to protect the shared moral views of society. The trouble with many of Devlin's claims is the same as that faced by the strategic theorist who, when asked about his various "calculated risks," admitted that he had never done the calculations.

Even when Devlin comes to the view, based on consequentialist considerations, that some form of conduct may be regulated, he often agrees with the liberals that it should not be. He does so because he believes that

> [t]he arm of the law is an instrument to be used by society, and the decision about what particular cases it should be used in is essentially a practical one. Since it is an instrument, it is wise before deciding to use it to have regard to the tools with which it can be fitted and to the machinery which operates it.[6]

In addition to these practical matters, however, Devlin refers to "general statements of principle which it may be thought the legislature should bear in mind when it is considering the enactment of laws enforcing morals."[7] These include: "toleration of the maximum individual freedom that is consistent with the integrity of society . . . that in any new matter of morals the law should be slow to act . . . [and] more tentatively . . . that as far as possible privacy should be respected."[8]

In spite of the fact that Devlin refers to these as "principles," it is quite clear from the context that these are considerations of value that he thinks ought to be used in deciding when matters that are legitimately within the province of the law actually should be enforced. He distinguishes among three questions:

1. Has society the right to pass judgment at all on matters of morals?

2. If a society has the right to pass judgment, has it also the right to use the weapon of the law to enforce it?

3. If so, ought it to use that weapon in all cases or only in some; and if only in some, on what principles should it distinguish?[9]

Devlin offers an answer to the last question:

> [M]y third interrogatory should be answered—not by the formulation of hard and fast rules, but by a judgment in each case taking into account the sort of factors I have been mentioning. The line that divides the criminal law from the moral is not determinable by the application of any clear-cut principle. . . . There is no logic to be found in this. The boundary between the criminal law and the moral law is fixed by balancing in the case of each particular crime the pros and cons of legal enforcement in accordance with the sort of considerations I have been outlining.[10]

This passage is a bit of a mess. The problem is that Devlin is giving an answer to his third interrogatory, but frames it in terms appropriate for the second. He states that the line dividing the criminal law from the moral should not be determined by clear-cut principle. What he should be saying, though, if he is answering the third question, is that the line between what the state has a right to regulate and what it actually ought to regulate is not a matter of principle. This, however, is a matter on which any sensible liberal would agree. Given that it clearly is immoral for men to lie to women about their affections in order to secure sexual favors, and given that any woman so lied to has a personal grievance, it is something we might debate about criminalizing. Considerations of prudence, of efficient use of scarce resources, or of the value of privacy may lead us not to use the criminal law in this case. Both liberals and "Devlinites" can agree about this.

The issue that divides Devlin and the liberals is the second interrogatory. I take it that Devlin believes the answer to his second interrogatory is "yes" and for liberals it is "no." The debate concerns whether one can draw a principled line designating which matters the state has a "right" to regulate by means of the criminal law. What exactly is a principled line, and are there other conditions that liberals impose on whatever principle(s) they put forward?

III.

What is being contrasted with "a principled line" when these issues are at stake? The contrast is not with no line at all, but with a line justified in some different fashion. Of course, it is not being claimed that the alternatives are unprincipled—merely nonprincipled.

To tighten up the question, it is useful to consider Mill's views about principled line-drawing. Mill calls his harm principle "one very simple principle,"[11] and he is clear that the principle is supposed to settle the issue of the state's jurisdiction, not the question of when the state should exercise its power:

> If anyone does an act hurtful to others, there is a prima facie case for punishing him by law or, where legal penalties are not safely applicable, by general disapprobation. . . . . There are often good reasons for not holding him to the responsibility; but these reasons must arise from the special expediencies of the case: either because it is a kind of case in which he is on the whole likely to act better when left to his own discretion than when controlled in any way in which society have it in their power to control him; or because the attempt to exercise control would produce other evils, greater than those which it would prevent.[12]

The reference to "cases" is not determinative of what to do about specific offenders but about types of acts and deciding whether they are the right types to be the subject of legal coercion. Based on this explanation, one might think that we have a principled line with exceptions based on "special expediencies." The problem here is that Mill says his principled line is also based on expediencies, i.e., what will promote utility: "I forego any advantage which could be derived to my argument from the idea of abstract right as a thing independent of utility. I regard utility as the ultimate appeal on all ethical questions."[13]

So when Devlin writes,

> I think, therefore, that it is not possible to set theoretical limits to the power of the State to legislate against immorality. It is not possible to settle in advance exceptions to the general rule or to define inflexibly areas of morality into which the law is in no circumstance to be allowed to enter.[14]

Devlin certainly disagrees substantively with Mill, yet both appeal to "expediencies" and consequences. Basically, their dispute is between direct and indirect consequentialism. As we have seen, Devlin thinks that for each proposed type of immorality one must balance the pros and cons of enforcement. Mill thinks that there is an argument from the long-range consequences

"grounded on the permanent interests of man as a progressive being" for setting up general categories (e.g., harm to self) and claims that we can draw a line determining the illegitimacy of enforcement against acts falling into that category in advance. Correspondingly, there are general categories (e.g., harm to others) that bring the conduct within the scope of state action, although determining whether a given range of acts in such a category ought actually to be criminalized is left to more particular calculation. One might raise some questions about whether any line drawn in advance on the basis of the balance of benefits over harms is a "principled" one. Unless one is going to beg the question against consequentialists, though, it seems reasonable to adopt a broad definition of "principled."

The last preliminary question that needs to be addressed is whether a liberal, principled view should include some restrictions on the nature of the principles to which we appeal. By this I mean some qualification on the appeal of the principle in question. Liberals address their arguments to people, such as Devlin, who disagree with them about many things. They have factual disagreements, and they have disagreements about the rational status of religion; they have different ideals of sexuality, and they may have different views of moral reasoning. If the arguments are to be persuasive, there must be enough common ground to allow for a shared starting point. This is one meaning of the widely used (and misused) term "neutrality." Of course, a liberal simply may be looking for a line of argument that she finds convincing; she may be satisfied if her argument is sound.

The issue of legitimacy concerns the basic framework for a society; therefore it is reasonable to assume that a liberal wishes to adopt some kind of "justifiable to" restriction on her arguments. It could be a Rawlsian "only principles that all citizens may reasonably be expected to endorse," or a Scanlonian "only principles which are not reasonably rejectable," or a Larmorian "principles . . . must be ones which are justifiable to everyone whom they are to bind." Whichever of these one adopts, the idea is to avoid, if possible, appealing to any controversial conception of what is intrinsically valuable.

IV.

There seem to be only two possible ways to argue against the idea of a principled restriction of enforcing morality. The first is to consider all the various arguments put forward in favor of such a restriction and to show in each case that they are not sound. I obviously cannot do that here. Here, I propose a brief examination of Feinberg's argument, and then suggest that it is implausible to suppose that any such argument can succeed.

To avoid begging the question against the legal moralist, Feinberg must produce definitions of "harm" and "wrongdoing" acceptable to the legal moralist such that there are cases of harmless wrongdoing. Feinberg distinguishes between "A harms1 B," which means that "A adversely affects B's interest" and "A harms2 B" which means that "A adversely affects B's interest and in so doing wrongs B (violates B's right)."[15] An example of the former, but not the latter, would be A breaking B's leg at B's request (e.g., because B is trying to avoid the draft). This distinction now allows Feinberg to state that

> there are two ways in which an act can be an instance of harmless wrongdoing. It can be a wrongful act that adversely affects no one else's interest, or it can be a wrongful act that does adversely affect the interest of another person but does so without wronging that person.[16]

In the first case the act, while wrong, does not harm1 (and *a fortiori* does not harm2) anyone, with the possible exception of the person who commits the wrongful act. In the second case the wrongful act does harm1 someone besides the agent but does not harm2 anyone else.

First, let us note that the claim that harmless wrongdoing is possible is the claim that we have an understanding of morality according to which there can be wrongful acts that do not harm1 or do not harm2 anyone other than the agent who performs the acts. This means that there can be wrongful acts that either do not set back interests, or if they do, they do not violate anyone's rights. Let us consider these in turn.

As possible examples of wrongful acts that do not set back interests, Feinberg suggests a "wrongly broken promise that redounds by a fluke to the promisee's advantage" and "[t]respassing on another's land (a violation of his property right) while actually improving his property (advancing his interests)."[17] The problem with these examples is that anyone who wants to defend some kind of identification of harm and wrongdoing is not likely to do so on this level. As the interminable discussions of rule versus act utilitarianism have shown, only die-hard act utilitarians would want to link the

wrongness of particular acts to the specific harmful consequences of those acts. The more plausible version is to consider an act wrong if it is of a type, the general performance of which is harmful. The level of these examples seems particularly ill-chosen because, for the purposes of legislation, it is always act-types that are in question. What we need are examples of types of acts which, while wrongful, do not (usually, tend to) set back interests. Whether it is possible for such acts to exist depends upon one's views about the nature of morality.

What about examples of the second kind, that is, acts that are wrongful but do not harm2 anyone else although they may harm1 someone else? As examples, Feinberg considers acts that set back interests but to which the adversely affected party consents. Here it is crucial that Feinberg identifies wronging someone with violating that person's rights. He also often thinks in terms of there being no "victim" or nobody who has a complaint. In these cases, there are wrongful acts with nobody being wronged, hence the notion of harmless immorality—harmless because harm2 requires that there be somebody who is wronged, immoral because it is wrong in the abstract. Thus the defender of the enforcement of morality must accept the idea of an immoral, wrongful act that is harmless—not because of a lack of setback to interest but because there is no one who is wronged.

The defender of enforcement might adopt several strategies at this point. He might disagree as to whether rights have been violated. Someone who believes in inalienable, nonwaivable rights in a strong sense would deny that the Volenti maxim—to one who has consented no wrong has been done—is correct. Alternatively, he might concede that no rights have been violated but not accept Feinberg's stipulation that it is only when rights have been violated that somebody is wronged. Feinberg would not claim that rights exhaust the realm of morality. Why then stipulate that someone has been wronged only when her rights have been violated?

An important substantive thesis about criminalization underlies the stipulation. For Feinberg, the law should be limited to the protection of particular values, namely personal autonomy and respect for persons:

> The harm principle mediated by the Volenti maxim protects personal autonomy and the moral value of "respect for persons" that is associated with it . . . . But there are other moral principles, other normative judgments, other ideals, other values—some

well-founded, some not—that the harm principle does not enforce, since its aim is only to respect personal autonomy and protect human rights, not to vindicate correct evaluative judgments of any and all kinds.[18]

V.

We have a clear thesis. What is the argument for it? Why may the law not protect ideals? In truth, I cannot find a clear argument in Feinberg. He makes statements such as the following:

[M]uch of what we call morality consists of rules designed to prevent evils of a kind whose existence would not be the basis of any assignable person's grievance. . . . [T]hey are evils that "float free" and are incapable of grounding personal grievances. . . . To prevent them with the iron fist of legal coercion would be to impose suffering and injury for the sake of no one else's good at all. For that reason the enforcement of most non-grievance morality strikes many of us as morally perverse.[19]

The liberal then should be willing to concede that the desirability of preventing such evils is a consideration of some weight on the scales, while insisting nevertheless that its weight is insufficient to counterbalance the case for liberty, since it is impossible to name anyone who can demand "protection" from the evils in question.[20]

Their free-floating character makes it doubtful indeed that they could ever be sufficiently evil to warrant legal coercion by means of the criminal law. That blunt and undiscriminating instrument, unless aimed at serious harms and wrongs, is quite likely to cause more evil than it can possibly prevent.[21]

The last point is hardly a matter of principle. Devlin can agree that it is prudent not to use the law in such cases but still insist that, as a matter of principle, it cannot be ruled out. As for the previous quotes, they seem to either beg the question or to be conclusory.

It is a rather complicated question to decide whether Feinberg's view is a principled objection to legal moralism. His initial view of legal moralism is that "it is always a relevant reason of at least minimal cogency in support of penal legislation that it will prevent genuine evils other than harm and offense."[22] On this view,

Feinberg concedes that legal moralism is correct. He believes, however, that the liberal can salvage his position by insisting that "as reasons go it is not much of one . . . rarely if ever enough to offset the presumptive case for liberty. . . . In specific cases of proposed legislation then, liberals, despite their grudging concession, can nearly always oppose moralistic statutes."[23]

The most plausible interpretation of Feinberg is that moralistic considerations are almost never good reasons. If reason exists to suppose that attempts to determine the few cases in which moralistic considerations are good reasons result in more errors than drawing a line in advance and ruling them all out, the result is the antimoralism Feinberg wants.

Turning to his argument, it is striking that it is unlike his argument against paternalism. That argument involves a fair bit of theory about the nature of personal sovereignty and contends that drawing the boundaries as the paternalist suggests is in conflict with a conception—an ideal—of the autonomous person. His argument against legal moralism, however, consists largely of making various illuminating distinctions about kinds of evils and then simply asserting that some of them are not serious enough to warrant preventing by coercion.

His general argument is that, given the importance of personal liberty, if we are unable to justify a restriction of liberty by pointing to someone who can complain, we cannot restrict liberty. Various ideals, though, are at least as important to us as some of our minor grievances. If it is inappropriate to view children as commodities, if surrogacy implicates this attitude, and if it is worth paying the costs of preventing some couples from having children in this way, the burden of proof that must be overcome before restricting liberty seems as easily surmounted as it would be in the case of many harms.

Looking at what forms the great part of Feinberg's discussion—the treatment of specific cases of harmless immoralities—strengthens this point. For a number of such cases, he is forced either to disagree with the existing law or to find explanations other than legal moralism. In what he calls the "[s]tubborn counterexample," he considers Irving Kristol's story of consenting gladiatorial contests in Yankee Stadium before consenting adults. Feinberg claims that although there is "evil" involved, it is "a free-floating one, an evil not directly linked to human interests and sensibilities. That evil consists in the objective regrettability of millions deriving pleasure from brutal bloodshed and others getting rich exploiting their moral weakness."[24]

The evil is not directly linked in that there is no causal link to making people worse in terms of their sensibilities, but if it is a bad thing for people to derive pleasure from brutality, the evil is still connected to human interests and sensibilities because people's sensibilities are exhibiting a degraded character. Why don't we all have a complaint and a legitimate claim not to have such events take place in our society? Ultimately, Feinberg argues either that there are sufficient questions of voluntariness and sufficient dangers such that we can invoke the harm principle or that, if we cannot, we have to swallow the poison pill and "boldly insist . . . that the law be kept from interfering, and thereby reject the force of the story as a counterexample.[25]

One counterexample does not make a refutation. There are sufficiently many, however, ultimately to force the liberal into implausible positions. A few of my favorite things that have been criminalized include the following: dwarf-tossing, informational blackmail (the threat to reveal true information about the sordid part of a reformed person), the sale of one's heart (for transplantation), and consensual slavery. All of these share the feature of inflicting harms on consenting persons. Of course, a liberal who opposes legal moralism may try to use a notion of moral paternalism to explain these cases. This suggests that liberals such as Hart who support (limited) paternalism are already on shaky grounds, as Feinberg clearly recognizes. No such interferences are grounded on the basis of a victim who has a complaint. Once one abandons the grounding in individual complaint, however, the extension to legal moralism seems plausible.

VI.

In the final part of this essay, I will outline an argument that, while by no means conclusive, suggests why there may not be a good argument in favor of the liberal's position. It is an argument that depends upon a plausible idea of what making moral judgments involves. Let me start with a well-known quotation: "We do not call anything wrong, unless we mean to imply that a person ought to be punished in some way or other for doing it; if not by law, by the opinion of his fellow creatures; if not by opinion, by the reproaches of his own conscience."

This passage links the idea of right and wrong with the idea of punishment. Indeed, it makes the connection conceptual in character. It comes not from a "Devlinite" but from the patron saint of liberalism, John Stuart Mill. It seems to me not only to enjoy a good liberal pedigree but also to embody a correct insight into the idea of moral wrongness. If an action is wrong, that provides a reason—perhaps conclusive, perhaps not—for not doing it. It also provides a reason—perhaps conclusive, perhaps not—for discouraging the performance of such actions.

Of course, it does not follow from the fact that an action ought not to be done that any third party ought to discourage it, to criticize it, or to forbid it by means of the criminal law. All of these, however, seem appropriate responses. Wrong (immoral) actions are not to be done, but that means that they are the appropriate targets of our criticism and our discouragement.

Of course, there may be good reasons in particular cases for not criticizing someone who acts wrongly even though the action itself remains criticizable. It surely, then, cannot be the case that we could claim some principled reason for never actually criticizing those who act wrongly.

Again, the issues of whether an action is criticizable and whether one ought actually to criticize it are distinct from the issue of whether one ought to try to stop it in some more direct fashion. Questions of interference by means of moral and social pressure require rather different treatment. There seem to be spheres of autonomy within which we believe it wrong for others to interfere, even with actions that are wrong and therefore ought not to be done. What this shows, however, is that the step from "wrong" to "subject to interference" requires additional argument. Of course, the step from "harmful" to "subject to interference" or from "deeply offensive" to "subject to interference" requires additional argument as well. All I am claiming is that, because "wrongful" implies "ought not to be done," the category of immoral acts establishes the same threshold for the legitimacy of state interference as does the category of harmful or offensive acts.

Could there be, in principle, reasons for not discouraging immoral actions by means of the criminal law? Could the nature of the sanctions make a difference? Is it the fact that criminal sanctions involve the loss of liberty, and in extreme cases life, that makes that kind of difference?

The first thing to note is that the criminal law operates with more than the sanctions of deprivation of life or liberty. It also imposes monetary fines. Unless liberals really mean to defend a weaker thesis, e.g., that the threat of loss of freedom or life may not be used to enforce morality, they are arguing that enforcing morality by means of criminal fines is illegitimate. It also cannot be the severity of the sanction that accounts for a principled restriction. Most of us would rather spend a week in prison for assaulting a colleague than face the aversion and ostracism of our professional peers.

Is it perhaps the condemnatory or expressive function of the criminal law? We have already seen that the immoral is what is not to be done. Those who do such wrongs are to be condemned, at least in the sense that they are condemnable. The distinct questions of who is, or ought to be, in a position to condemn and of whether it would do good or harm to condemn remain. Perhaps it is a good idea, in general, for the state to restrict the amount of condemnation in which it engages. These questions, however, seem to be matters of good judgment and prudence, not matters of principle.

The criminal law is an institution whose central rationales include making it less likely that acts that ought not to be done are not done and serving as a vehicle for condemning those who do what ought not to be done. The existence of principled reasons for ruling out (in advance) the criminal process as a means of discouragement therefore seems quite implausible.

Principled reasons do exist for excluding certain subclasses of immoral actions from the criminal law. A good example is free speech. Here we find a class of actions that are immoral (e.g., denials of the holocaust, racial insults) and that we seek to immunize from criminal prosecution. Such acts pass the initial threshold for being considered legitimate objects of state interference. We believe, however, that there are reasons for maintaining a sphere of autonomy for individuals to engage in such actions. Some of these reasons are what I would consider policy rather than principle. Consider, for example, the claim that, though it would be within our right to interfere with such acts, granting interference powers to the state is too dangerous. Some of these arguments are matters of right themselves. Note, however, that this class of acts is not merely immoral but also harmful, so that it constitutes an exception to the harm principle as well. If the existence of such a protected class counts as proof that the state ought not interfere with immoral acts, it also shows that the state ought not interfere with harmful acts.

We may recognize a "right to do wrong in other spheres," but these are consistent with believing that the "mere immorality" of an action brings it within the legitimate sphere of the criminal law. It is not that there is some further set of features (harm, offense, etc.) that must be added to immorality in order to bring the conduct within the legitimate sphere of state regulation. It may be that there are further features that, linked to a suitable principle, exclude it. This is just what is true for other features such as harm and offense.

The nonenforcement thesis has been popular with liberals because they think the prospect of convincing others about the morality or immorality of various controversial acts is dim. If I am right, however, the prospect of convincing them of the nonenforcement thesis is even dimmer. As Bertrand Russell observed with respect to logical matters, postulation has all "the advantages of theft over honest toil." I encourage liberals who wish to argue against, for example, the criminalization of homosexual sex, to engage in the honest toil of arguing that the reason such conduct ought not be criminalized is that there is nothing immoral in it.

Endnotes

[1] H. L. A. Hart, *Law, Liberty and Morality* (1963).

[2] James Fitzjames Stephen, *Liberty, Equality, Fraternity* (R. J. White ed., Cambridge University Press, 1967) (1873).

[3] In fact, the Committee displayed typical English caution by adding the qualifier "so far as it concerns the subjects of this enquiry." Patrick Devlin, *The Enforcement of Morals 2* (1965) (quoting Report of the Committee on Homosexual Offences and Prostitution (1957) [hereinafter Wolfenden Report]). Devlin himself noted, however, that the conclusions of the Committee "are made in general terms and there seems to be no reason why, if they are valid, they should not be applied to the criminal law in general." Id. p. 3.

[4] Id. at 1 (quoting Wolfenden Report, *supra* note 3).

[5] Id. (quoting Wolfenden Report, *supra* note 3). Another claim that I shall ignore for the most part, as it seems to me to have led the discussion into less fruitful paths, is the view that "there must remain a realm of private morality and immorality which is . . . not the law's business." Id. p. 3 (quoting Wolfenden Report, *supra* note 3). The introduction of the private/public distinction addresses where behavior takes place rather than its status as moral or immoral.

[6] See Devlin, *supra* note 3 p. 20.

[7] Id. p. 16.

[8] Id. p. 18.

[9] Id. pp. 7–8.

[10] Id. pp. 21–22.

[11] John Stuart Mill, *On Liberty* 13 (Currin V. Shields ed., Liberty Arts Press, 1956) (1859).

[12] Id. pp. 14–15.

[13] Id. p. 14.

[14] Devlin, *supra* note 3, at 12–13. There is a certain complication here that is connected with the idea of "areas of morality" into which the law is not to enter. My own view is that there are areas of conduct that are immoral and with which the state ought not interfere. The category of free speech,

however, is not an area of morality. In similar fashion, I believe that there are areas of conduct that are harmful to others but that ought not to be regulated. Examples of such areas are some kinds of consented-to harm. I do not believe, though, that one can—to parallel Devlin—settle in advance areas of harm into which the law is in no circumstance to be allowed to enter.

[15] Joel Feinberg, *Harmless Wrongdoing* (New York: Oxford University Press, 1990) p. xxix.

[16] Id.

[17] Id. p. xxviii.

[18] Joel Feinberg, *The Moral Limits of the Criminal Law: Harmless Wrongdoing* (1988), p. 12.

[19] Id. pp. 79–80.

[20] Id. p. 174 (emphasis added).

[21] Id. p. 220.

[22] Id. p. 5.

[23] Id. pp. 5–6.

[24] Id. p. 130.

[25] Id. p. 329.

Cohen v. California

Opinion of the Court

Mr. Justice Harlan delivered the opinion of the Court.

This case may seem at first blush too inconsequential to find its way into our books, but the issue it presents is of no small constitutional significance.

Appellant Paul Robert Cohen was convicted in the Los Angeles Municipal Court of violating that part of California Penal Code § 415 which prohibits "maliciously and willfully disturb[ing] the peace or quiet of any neighborhood or person . . . by . . . offensive conduct. . . ."[1] He was given 30 days' imprisonment. The facts upon which his conviction rests are detailed in the opinion of the Court of Appeal of California, Second Appellate District, as follows:

"On April 26, 1968, the defendant was observed in the Los Angeles County Courthouse in the corridor outside of division 20 of the municipal court wearing a jacket bearing the words 'Fuck the Draft' which were plainly visible. There were women and children present in the corridor. The defendant was arrested. The defendant testified that he wore the jacket knowing that the words were on the jacket as a means of informing the public of the depth of his feelings against the Vietnam War and the draft.

"The defendant did not engage in, nor threaten to engage in, nor did anyone as the result of his conduct in fact commit or threaten to commit any act of vio-

lence. The defendant did not make any loud or unusual noise, nor was there any evidence that he uttered any sound prior to his arrest."

In affirming the conviction the Court of Appeal held that "offensive conduct" means "behavior which has a tendency to provoke *others* to acts of violence or to in turn disturb the peace," and that the State had proved this element because, on the facts of this case, "[i]t was certainly reasonably foreseeable that such conduct might cause others to rise up to commit a violent act against the person of the defendant or attempt to forcibly remove his jacket." The California Supreme Court declined review by a divided vote. We brought the case here, postponing the consideration of the question of our jurisdiction over this appeal to a hearing of the case on the merits. We now reverse.

In order to lay hands on the precise issue which this case involves, it is useful first to canvass various matters which this record does *not* present.

The conviction quite clearly rests upon the asserted offensiveness of the *words* Cohen used to convey his message to the public. The only "conduct" which the State sought to punish is the fact of communication. Thus, we deal here with a conviction resting solely upon "speech," not upon any separately identifiable conduct which allegedly was intended by Cohen to be perceived by others as expressive of particular views but which, on its face, does not necessarily convey any message and hence arguably could be regulated without effectively repressing Cohen's ability to express himself. Further, the State certainly lacks power to

---

408 U.S. 15 (1971), United States Supreme Court.

punish Cohen for the underlying content of the message the inscription conveyed. At least so long as there is no showing of an intent to incite disobedience to or disruption of the draft, Cohen could not, consistently with the First and Fourteenth Amendments, be punished for asserting the evident position on the inutility or immorality of the draft his jacket reflected.

Appellant's conviction, then, rests squarely upon his exercise of the "freedom of speech" protected from arbitrary governmental interference by the Constitution and can be justified, if at all, only as a valid regulation of the manner in which he exercised that freedom, not as a permissible prohibition on the substantive message it conveys. This does not end the inquiry, of course, for the First and Fourteenth Amendments have never been thought to give absolute protection to every individual to speak whenever or wherever he pleases, or to use any form of address in any circumstances that he chooses. In this vein, too, however, we think it important to note that several issues typically associated with such problems are not presented here.

In the first place, Cohen was tried under a statute applicable throughout the entire State. Any attempt to support this conviction on the ground that the statute seeks to preserve an appropriately decorous atmosphere in the courthouse where Cohen was arrested must fail in the absence of any language in the statute that would have put appellant on notice that certain kinds of otherwise permissible speech or conduct would nevertheless, under California law, not be tolerated in certain places. No fair reading of the phrase "offensive conduct" can be said sufficiently to inform the ordinary person that distinctions between certain locations are thereby created.[2]

In the second place, as it comes to us, this case cannot be said to fall within those relatively few categories of instances where prior decisions have established the power of government to deal more comprehensively with certain forms of individual expression simply upon a showing that such a form was employed. This is not, for example, an obscenity case. Whatever else may be necessary to give rise to the States' broader power to prohibit obscene expression, such expression must be, in some significant way, erotic. It cannot plausibly be maintained that this vulgar allusion to the Selective Service System would conjure up such psychic stimulation in anyone likely to be confronted with Cohen's crudely defaced jacket.

This court has also held that the States are free to ban the simple use, without a demonstration of additional justifying circumstances, of so-called "fighting words," those personally abusive epithets which, when addressed to the ordinary citizen, are, as a matter of common knowledge, inherently likely to provoke violent reaction. While the four-letter word displayed by Cohen in relation to the draft is not uncommonly employed in a personally provocative fashion, in this instance it was clearly not "directed to the person of the hearer." No individual actually or likely to be present could reasonably have regarded the words on appellant's jacket as a direct personal insult. Nor do we have here an instance of the exercise of the State's police power to prevent a speaker from intentionally provoking a given group to hostile reaction. There is, as noted above, no showing that anyone who saw Cohen was in fact violently aroused or that appellant intended such a result.

Finally, in arguments before this Court much has been made of the claim that Cohen's distasteful mode of expression was thrust upon unwilling or unsuspecting viewers, and that the State might therefore legitimately act as it did in order to protect the sensitive from otherwise unavoidable exposure to appellant's crude form of protest. Of course, the mere presumed presence of unwitting listeners or viewers does not serve automatically to justify curtailing all speech capable of giving offense. While this Court has recognized that government may properly act in many situations to prohibit intrusion into the privacy of the home of unwelcome views and ideas which cannot be totally banned from the public dialogue, we have at the same time consistently stressed that "we are often 'captives' outside the sanctuary of the home and subject to objectionable speech." The ability of government, consonant with the Constitution, to shut off discourse solely to protect others from hearing it is, in other words, dependent upon a showing that substantial privacy interests are being invaded in an essentially intolerable manner. Any broader view of this authority would effectively empower a majority to silence dissidents simply as a matter of personal predilections.

In this regard, persons confronted with Cohen's jacket were in a quite different posture than, say, those subjected to the raucous emissions of sound trucks blaring outside their residences. Those in the Los Angeles courthouse could effectively avoid further bombardment of their sensibilities simply by averting their eyes. And, while it may be that one has a more substantial claim to a recognizable privacy interest when walking through a courthouse corridor than, for example, strolling through Central Park, surely it is nothing like the interest in being free from unwanted expression in the confines of one's own home. Given the subtlety and complexity of the factors involved, if Cohen's "speech" was otherwise entitled to constitutional protection, we do not think the fact that some unwilling "listeners" in a public building may have been briefly exposed to it can serve to justify this breach of the peace conviction where, as here, there was no evidence that persons powerless to avoid appellant's conduct did in fact object to it, and where that portion of the statute upon which Cohen's conviction rests evinces no concern, either on its face or as construed by the California courts, with the special plight of the captive auditor, but, instead, indiscriminately sweeps within its prohibitions all "offensive conduct" that disturbs "any neighborhood or person."

Against this background, the issue flushed by this case stands out in bold relief. It is whether California can excise, as "offensive conduct," one particular scurrilous epithet from the public discourse, either upon the theory of the court below that its use is inherently likely to cause violent reaction or upon a more general assertion that the States, acting as guardians of public morality, may properly remove this offensive word from the public vocabulary.

The rationale of the California court is plainly untenable. At most it reflects an "undifferentiated fear or apprehension of disturbance [which] is not enough to overcome the right to freedom of expression." We have been shown no evidence that substantial numbers of citizens are standing ready to strike out physically at whomever may assault their sensibilities with execrations like that uttered by Cohen. There may be some persons about with such lawless and violent proclivities, but that is an insufficient base upon which to erect, consistently with constitutional values, a governmental power to force persons who wish to ventilate their dissident views into avoiding particular forms of expression. The argument amounts to little more than the self-defeating proposition that to avoid physical censorship of one who has not sought to provoke such a response by a hypothetical coterie of the violent and lawless, the States may more appropriately effectuate that censorship themselves.

Admittedly, it is not so obvious that the First and Fourteenth Amendments must be taken to disable to States from punishing public utterance of this unseemly expletive in order to maintain what they regard as a suitable level of discourse within the body politic. We think, however, that examination and reflection will reveal the shortcomings of a contrary viewpoint.

At the outset, we cannot overemphasize that, in our judgment, most situations where the State has a justifiable interest in regulating speech will fall within one or more of the various established exceptions, discussed above but not applicable here, to the usual rule that governmental bodies may not prescribe the form or content of individual expression. Equally important to our conclusion is the constitutional backdrop against which our decision must be made. The constitutional right of free expression is powerful medicine in a society as diverse and populous as ours. It is designed and intended to remove governmental restraints from the arena of public discussion, putting the decision as to what views shall be voiced largely into the hands of each of us, in the hope that use of such freedom will ultimately produce a more capable citizenry and more perfect polity and in the belief that no other approach would comport with the premise of individual dignity and choice upon which our political system rests.

To many, the immediate consequence of this freedom may often appear to be only verbal tumult, discord, and even offensive utterance. These are, however, within established limits, in truth necessary side effects of the broader enduring values which the process of open debate permits us to achieve. That the air may at times seem filled with verbal cacophony is, in this sense, not a sign of weakness but of strength. We cannot lose sight of the fact that, in what otherwise might seem a trifling and annoying instance of individual distasteful abuse of a privilege, these fundamental societal values are truly implicated. That is why "[w]holly neutral futilities . . . come under the protection of free speech as fully as do Keats' poems or Donne's sermons," *Winters v. New York* (1948) (Frankfurter, J., dissenting), and why "so long as the means are peaceful, the communication need not meet standards of acceptability," *Organization for a Better Austin v. Keefe* (1971).

Against this perception of the constitutional policies involved, we discern certain more particularized considerations that peculiarly call for reversal of this conviction. First, the principle contended for by the State seems inherently boundless. How is one to distinguish this from any other offensive word? Surely the State has no right to cleanse public debate to the point where it is grammatically palatable to the most squeamish among us. Yet no readily ascertainable general principle exists for stopping short of that result were we to affirm the judgment below. For, while the particular four-letter word being litigated here is perhaps more distasteful than most others of its genre, it is nevertheless often true that one man's vulgarity is another's lyric. Indeed, we think it is largely because governmental officials cannot make principled distinctions in this area that the Constitution leaves matters of taste and style so largely to the individual.

Additionally, we cannot overlook the fact, because it is well illustrated by the episode involved here, that much linguistic expression serves a dual communicative function: it conveys not only ideas capable of relatively precise, detached explication, but otherwise inexpressible emotions as well. In fact, words are often chosen as much for their emotive as their cognitive force. We cannot sanction the view that the Constitution, while solicitous of the cognitive content of individual speech, has little or no regard for that emotive function which, practically speaking, may often be the more important element of the overall message sought to be communicated. Indeed, as Mr. Justice Frankfurter has said, "[o]ne of the prerogatives of American citizenship is the right to criticize public men and measures—and that means not only informed and responsible criticism but the freedom to speak foolishly and without moderation." *Baumgartner v. United States* (1944).

Finally, and in the same vein, we cannot indulge the facile assumption that one can forbid particular words without also running a substantial risk of suppressing ideas in the process. Indeed, governments might soon seize upon the censorship of particular words as a convenient guise for banning the expression of unpopular views. We have been able, as noted above, to discern little social benefit that might result from running the risk of opening the door to such grave results.

It is, in sum, our judgment that, absent a more particularized and compelling reason for its actions, the State may not, consistently with the First and Fourteenth Amendments, make the simple public display here involved of this single four-letter expletive a criminal offense. Because that is the only arguably sustainable rationale for the conviction here at issue, the judgment below must be reversed.

Separate Opinion

Mr. Justice Blackmun, with whom The Chief Justice and Mr. Justice Black join.

I dissent, and I do so for two reasons:

1. Cohen's absurd and immature antic, in my view, was mainly conduct and little speech. The California Court of Appeal appears so to have described it, and I cannot characterize it otherwise. Further, the case appears to me to be well within the sphere of *Chaplinsky v. New Hampshire,* where Mr. Justice Murphy, a known champion of First Amendment freedoms, wrote for a unanimous bench. As a consequence, this Court's agonizing First Amendment values seems misplaced and unnecessary.

2. I am not at all certain that the California Court of Appeal's construction of § 415 is now the authoritative California construction. . . .

Endnotes

[1] The statute provides in full:

"Every person who maliciously and willfully disturbs the peace or quiet of any neighborhood or person, by loud or unusual noise, or by tumultuous or offensive conduct, or threatening, traducing, quarreling, challenging to fight, or fighting, or who, on the public streets of any unincorporated town, or upon the public highways in such unincorporated town, run any horse race, either for a wager or for amusement, or fire any gun or pistol is such unincorporated town, or use any vulgar language within the presence or hearing of women or children, in a loud and boisterous manner, is guilty of a misdemeanor, and upon conviction by any Court of competent jurisdiction shall be punished by fine not exceeding two hundred dollars, or by imprisonment in the County Jail for not more than ninety days, or by both fine and imprisonment, or either, at the discretion of the Court."

[2] It is illuminating to note what transpired when Cohen entered a courtroom in the building. He removed his jacket and stood with it folded over his arm. Meanwhile, a policeman sent the presiding judge a note suggesting that Cohen be held in contempt of court. The judge declined to do so and Cohen was arrested by the officer only after he emerged from the courtroom.

A Ride on the Bus

Joel Feinberg

There is a limit to the power of abstract reasoning to settle questions of moral legitimacy. The question raised by this chapter is whether there are any human experiences that are harmless in themselves yet so unpleasant that we can rightly demand legal protection from them even at the cost of other persons' liberties. The best way to deal with that question at the start is to engage our imaginations in the inquiry, consider hypothetically the most offensive experiences we can imagine, and then sort them into groups in an effort to isolate the kernel of the offense in each category. Accordingly, this section will consist of a number of vividly sketched imaginary tales, and the reader is asked to project himself into each story and determine as best he can what his reaction would be. In each story the reader should think of himself as a passenger on a normally crowded public bus on his way to work or to some important appointment in circumstances such that if he is forced to leave the bus prematurely, he will not only have to pay another fare to get where he is going, but he will probably be late, to his own disadvantage. If he is not exactly a captive on the bus, then, he would nevertheless be greatly inconvenienced if he had to leave the bus before it reached his destination. In each story, another passenger, or group of passengers, gets on the bus, and proceeds to cause, by their characteristics or their conduct, great offense to *you*. The stories form six clusters corresponding to the kind of offense caused.

A. Affronts to the Senses

Story 1. A passenger who obviously hasn't bathed in more than a month sits down next to you. He reeks of a barely tolerable stench. There is hardly room to stand elsewhere on the bus and all other seats are occupied.

Story 2. A passenger wearing a shirt of violently clashing orange and crimson sits down directly in your forward line of vision. You must keep your eyes down to avoid looking at him.

Story 3. A passenger sits down next to you, pulls a slate tablet from his briefcase, and proceeds to scratch his fingernails loudly across the slate, sending a chill up your spine and making your teeth clench. You politely ask him to stop, but he refuses.

Story 4. A passenger elsewhere in the bus turns on a portable radio to maximum volume. The sounds it emits are mostly screeches, whistles, and static, but occasionally some electronically amplified rock and roll music blares through.

B. Disgust and Revulsion

Story 5. This is much like story 1 except that the malodorous passenger in the neighboring seat continually scratches, drools, coughs, farts, and belches.

Story 6. A group of passengers enters the bus and shares a seating compartment with you. They spread a table cloth over their laps and proceed to eat a picnic lunch that consists of live insects, fish heads, and pickled sex organs of lamb, veal, and pork, smothered in garlic and onions. Their table manners leave almost everything to be desired.

Story 7. Things get worse and worse. The itinerant picnickers practice gluttony in the ancient Roman manner, gorging until satiation and then vomiting on to their table cloth. Their practice, however, is a novel departure from the ancient custom in that they eat their own and one another's vomit along with the remaining food.

Story 8. A coprophagic sequel to story 7.

Story 9. At some point during the trip the passenger at one's side quite openly and nonchalantly changes her sanitary napkin and drops the old one into the aisle.

C. *Shock to Moral, Religious, or Patriotic Sensibilities*

Story 10. A group of mourners carrying a coffin enters the bus and shares a seating compartment with you. Although they are all dressed in black their demeanor is by no means funereal. In fact they seem more angry than sorrowful, and refer to the deceased as "the old bastard," and "the bloody corpse." At one point they rip open the coffin with hammers and proceed to smash the corpse's face with a series of hard hammer blows.

Story 11. A strapping youth enters the bus and takes a seat directly in your line of vision. He is wearing a T-shirt with a cartoon across his chest of Christ on the cross. Underneath the picture appear the words "Hang in there, baby!"

Story 12. After taking the seat next to you a passenger produces a bundle wrapped in a large American flag. The bundle contains, among other things, his lunch, which he proceeds to eat. Then he spits into the star-spangled corner of the flag and uses it first to clean his mouth and then to blow his nose. Then he uses the main striped part of the flag to shine his shoes.

D. *Shame, Embarrassment (Including Vicarious Embarrassment), and Anxiety*

Story 13. The passenger who takes the seat directly across from you is entirely naked. On one version of the story, he or she is the same sex as you; on the other version of the story, he or she is the opposite sex.

Story 14. The passenger in the previous story proceeds to masturbate quietly in his or her seat.

Story 15. A man and woman, more or less fully clothed to start, take two seats directly in front of you, and then begin to kiss, hug, pet, and fondle one another to the accompaniment of loud sighs

and groans of pleasure. They continue these activities throughout the trip.

Story 16. The couple of the previous story, shortly before the bus reaches their destination, engage in acts of mutual masturbation, with quite audible instructions to each other and other sound effects.

Story 17. A variant of the previous story which climaxes in an act of coitus, somewhat acrobatically performed as required by the crowded circumstances.

Story 18. The seat directly in front of you is occupied by a youth (of either sex) wearing a T-shirt with a lurid picture of a copulating couple across his or her chest.

Story 19. A variant of the previous story in which the couple depicted is recognizable (in virtue of conventional representations) as Jesus and Mary.

Story 20. The couple in stories 15–17 perform a variety of sadomasochistic sex acts with appropriate verbal communications ("Oh, that hurts so sweet! Hit me again! Scratch me! Publicly humiliate me!").

Story 21. The two seats in front of you are occupied by male homosexuals. They flirt and tease at first, then kiss and hug, and finally perform mutual fellatio to climax.

Story 22. This time the homosexuals are both female and they perform cunnilingus.

Story 23. A passenger with a dog takes an aisle seat at your side. He or she keeps the dog calm at first by petting it in a familiar and normal way, but then petting gives way to hugging, and gradually goes beyond the merely affectionate to the unmistakably erotic, culminating finally with oral contact with the canine genitals.

E. *Annoyance, Boredom, Frustration*

Story 24. A neighboring passenger keeps a portable radio at a reasonably low volume, and the sounds it emits are by no means offensive to the senses. Nor is the content of the program offensive to the sensibilities. It is, however, a low quality "talk show" which you find intensely boring, and there is no possible way for you to disengage your attention.

Story 25. The two seats to your left are occupied by two persons who put on a boring "talk show" of their own. There is no way you can avoid hearing every animated word of their inane conversation, no way your mind can roam to its own thoughts, problems, and reveries.

Story 26. The passenger at your side is a friendly bloke, garrulous and officious. You quickly tire of his conversation and beg leave to read your newspaper, but he persists in his chatter despite repeated requests to desist. The bus is crowded and there are no other empty seats.

F. *Fear, Resentment, Humiliation, Anger (from Empty Threats, Insults, Mockery, Flaunting, or Taunting)*

Story 27. A passenger seated next to you reaches into a military kit and pulls out a "hand grenade" (actually only a realistic toy), and fondles and juggles it throughout the trip to the accompaniment of menacing leers and snorts. Then he pulls out a (rubber) knife and "stabs" himself and others

repeatedly to peals of maniacal laughter. He turns out to be harmless enough. His whole intent was to put others in apprehension of harm.

Story 28. A passenger sits next to you wearing a black arm band with a large white swastika on it.

Story 29. A passenger enters the bus straight from a dispersed street rally. He carries a banner with a large and abusive caricature of the Pope and an anti-Catholic slogan. (You are a loyal and pious Catholic.)

Story 30. Variants of the above. The banner displays a picture of a black according to some standard offensive stereotype (Step 'n' Fetchit, Uncle Tom, etc.) with an insulting caption, or a picture of a sneering, sniveling, hook-nosed Fagin or Shylock, with a scurrilous anti-Jewish caption, or a similar offensive denunciation or lampooning of groups called "Spicks," "Dagos," "Polacks", etc.

Story 31. Still another variant. A counter-demonstrator leaves a feminist rally to enter the bus. He carries a banner with an offensive caricature of a female and the message, in large red letters: "Keep the bitches barefoot and pregnant."

Michael A. Newdow v. United States of America

GOODWIN, Circuit Judge:

Michael Newdow appeals a judgment dismissing his challenge to the constitutionality of the words "under God" in the Pledge of Allegiance to the Flag. Newdow argues that the addition of these words by a 1954 federal statute to the previous version of the Pledge of Allegiance (which made no reference to God) and the daily recitation in the classroom of the Pledge of Allegiance, with the added words included, by his daughter's public school teacher are violations of the Establishment Clause of the First Amendment to the United States Constitution.

U.S. Circuit Court of Appeals for the Ninth Circuit, 328 F.3d 446 (2002).

Factual and Procedural Background

Newdow is an atheist whose daughter attends public elementary school in the Elk Grove Unified School District ("EGUSD") in California. In accordance with state law and a school district rule, EGUSD teachers begin each school day by leading their students in a recitation of the Pledge of Allegiance ("the Pledge"). The California Education Code requires that public schools begin each school day with "appropriate patriotic exercises" and that "[t]he giving of the Pledge of Allegiance to the Flag of the United States of America shall satisfy" this requirement. To implement the California statute, the school district that Newdow's daughter attends has promulgated a policy that states, in pertinent part: "Each elementary school class [shall] recite the pledge of allegiance to the flag once each day."

The classmates of Newdow's daughter in the EGUSD are led by their teacher in reciting the Pledge codified in federal law. On June 22, 1942, Congress first codified the Pledge as "I pledge allegiance to the flag of the United States of America and to the Republic for which it stands, one Nation indivisible, with liberty and justice for all." On June 14, 1954, Congress amended Section 172 to add the words "under God" after the word "Nation." The Pledge is currently codified as "I pledge allegiance to the Flag of the United States of America, and to the Republic for which it stands, one nation under God, indivisible, with liberty and justice for all."

Newdow does not allege that his daughter's teacher or school district requires his daughter to participate in reciting the Pledge. Rather, he claims that his daughter is injured when she is compelled to "watch and listen as her state-employed teacher in her state-run school leads her classmates in a ritual proclaiming that there is a God, and that our's [sic] is 'one nation under God.'"

Newdow's complaint in the district court challenged the constitutionality, under the First Amendment, of the 1954 Act, the California statute, and the school district's policy requiring teachers to lead willing students in recitation of the Pledge. He sought declaratory and injunctive relief, but did not seek damages.

The school districts and their superintendents (collectively, "school district defendants") filed a Federal Rule of Civil Procedure 12(b)(6) motion to dismiss for failure to state a claim. . . . District Judge Milton L. Schwartz approved the recommendation and entered a judgment of dismissal. This appeal followed. . . .

The Establishment Clause of the First Amendment states that "Congress shall make no law respecting an establishment of religion". . . . Over the last three decades, the Supreme Court has used three interrelated tests to analyze alleged violations of the Establishment Clause in the realm of public education: the three-prong test set forth in *Lemon v. Kurtzman* 403 U.S. 602, 612–13 (1971); the "endorsement" test, first articulated by Justice O'Connor in her concurring opinion in *Lynch*, and later adopted by a majority of the Court in *County of Allegheny v. ACLU*, 492 U.S. 573 (1989); and the "coercion" test first used by the Court in *Lee v. Weisman* 505 U.S. 577 (1992).

In 1971, in the context of unconstitutional state aid to nonpublic schools, the Supreme Court in *Lemon*

set forth the following test for evaluating alleged Establishment Clause violations. To survive the "*Lemon* test," the government conduct in question (1) must have a secular purpose, (2) must have a principal or primary effect that neither advances nor inhibits religion, and (3) must not foster an excessive government entanglement with religion.

In the 1984 *Lynch* case, which upheld the inclusion of a nativity scene in a city's Christmas display, Justice O'Connor wrote a concurring opinion in order to suggest a "clarification" of Establishment Clause jurisprudence. Justice O'Connor's "endorsement" test effectively collapsed the first two prongs of the *Lemon* test:

> The Establishment Clause prohibits government from making adherence to a religion relevant in any way to a person's standing in the political community. Government can run afoul of that prohibition in two principal ways. One is excessive entanglement with religious institutions . . . . The second and more direct infringement is government endorsement or disapproval of religion. Endorsement sends a message to nonadherents that they are outsiders, not full members of the political community, and an accompanying message to adherents that they are insiders, favored members of the political community.

The Court formulated the "coercion test" when it held unconstitutional the practice of including invocations and benedictions in the form of "nonsectarian" prayers at public school graduation ceremonies. . . .

[W]e will analyze the school district policy and the 1954 Act under all three tests.

We first consider whether the 1954 Act and the EGUSD's policy of teacher-led Pledge recitation survive the endorsement test. The magistrate judge found that "the ceremonial reference to God in the pledge does not convey endorsement of particular religious beliefs." Supreme Court precedent does not support that conclusion.

In the context of the Pledge, the statement that the United States is a nation "under God" is an endorsement of religion. It is a profession of a religious belief, namely, a belief in monotheism. The recitation that ours is a nation "under God" is not a mere acknowledgement that many Americans believe in a deity. Nor is it merely descriptive of the undeniable historical significance of religion in the founding of the Republic.

Rather, the phrase "one nation under God" in the context of the Pledge is normative. To recite the Pledge is not to describe the United States; instead, it is to swear allegiance to the values for which the flag stands: unity, indivisibility, liberty, justice, and—since 1954—monotheism. The text of the official Pledge, codified in federal law, impermissibly takes a position with respect to the purely religious question of the existence and identity of God. A profession that we are a nation "under God" is identical, for Establishment Clause purposes, to a profession that we are a nation "under Jesus," a nation "under Vishnu," a nation "under Zeus," or a nation "under no god," because none of these professions can be neutral with respect to religion. Furthermore, the school district's practice of teacher-led recitation of the Pledge aims to inculcate in students a respect for the ideals set forth in the Pledge, and thus amounts to state endorsement of these ideals. Although students cannot be forced to participate in recitation of the Pledge, the school district is nonetheless conveying a message of state endorsement of a religious belief when it requires public school teachers to recite, and lead the recitation of, the current form of the Pledge.

The Supreme Court recognized the normative and ideological nature of the Pledge in *Barnette*, 319 U.S. 624. There, the Court held unconstitutional a school district's wartime policy of punishing students who refused to recite the Pledge and salute the flag. The Court noted that the school district was compelling the students "to declare a belief," and "require[ing] the individual to communicate by word and sign his acceptance of the political ideas [the flag] . . . bespeaks." "[T]he compulsory flag salute and pledge requires affirmation of a belief and an attitude of mind." The Court emphasized that the political concepts articulated in the Pledge[1] were idealistic, not descriptive: "'[L]iberty and justice for all,'" if it must be accepted as descriptive of the present order rather than an ideal, might to some seem an overstatement." The Court concluded that: "If there is any fixed star in our constitutional constellation, it is that no official, high or petty, can prescribe what shall be orthodox in politics, nationalism, religion, or other matters of opinion or force citizens to confess by word or act their faith therein."

The Pledge, as currently codified, is an impermissible government endorsement of religion because it sends a message to unbelievers "that they are outsiders, not full members of the political community, and an accompanying message to adherents that they are insiders, favored members of the political community."

Similarly, the policy and the Act fail the coercion test. Just as in *Lee*, the policy and the Act place students in the untenable position of choosing between participating in an exercise with religious content or protesting. . . .

Although the defendants argue that the religious content of "one nation under God" is minimal, to an atheist or a believer in certain non-Judeo-Christian religions or philosophies, it may reasonably appear to be an attempt to enforce a "religious orthodoxy" of monotheism, and is therefore impermissible. The coercive effect of this policy is particularly pronounced in the school setting given the age and impressionability of schoolchildren, and their understanding that they are required to adhere to the norms set by their school, their teacher and their fellow students. Furthermore, under *Lee*, the fact that students are not required to participate is no basis for distinguishing *Barnette* from the case at bar because, even without a recitation requirement for each child, the mere fact that a pupil is required to listen every day to the statement "one nation under God" has a coercive effect. The coercive effect of the Act is apparent from its context and legislative history, which indicate that the Act was designed to result in the daily recitation of the words "under God" in school classrooms. President Eisenhower, during the Act's signing ceremony, stated: "From this day forward, the millions of our school children will daily proclaim in every city and town, every village and rural schoolhouse, the dedication of our Nation and our people to the Almighty." Therefore, the policy and the Act fail the coercion test.

Finally we turn to the *Lemon* test, the first prong of which asks if the challenged policy has a secular purpose. Historically, the primary purpose of the 1954 Act was to advance religion, in conflict with the first prong of the *Lemon* test. The federal defendants "do not dispute that the words 'under God' were intended" "to recognize a Supreme Being," at a time when the government was publicly inveighing against atheistic communism. Nonetheless, the federal defendants argue that the Pledge must be considered as a whole when assessing whether it has a secular purpose. They claim that the Pledge has the secular purpose of "solemnizing public occasions, expressing confidence in the future, and encouraging the recognition of what is worthy of appreciation in society."

[T]he legislative history of the 1954 Act reveals that the Act's *sole* purpose was to advance religion, in order to differentiate the United States from nations under communist rule. . . . Such a purpose runs counter to the Establishment Clause, which prohibits the government's endorsement or advancement not only of one particular religion at the expense of other religions, but also of religion at the expense of atheism.

Similarly, the school district policy also fails the *Lemon* test. Although it survives the first prong of *Lemon* because, as even Newdow concedes, the school district had the secular purpose of fostering patriotism in enacting the policy, the policy fails the second prong. . . . Given the age and impressionability of schoolchildren, as discussed above, particularly within the confined environment of the classroom, the policy is highly likely to convey an impermissible message of endorsement to some and disapproval to others of their beliefs regarding the existence of a monotheistic God. Therefore the policy fails the effects prong of *Lemon*, and fails the *Lemon* test. In sum, both the policy and the Act fail the *Lemon* test as well as the endorsement and coercion tests.

In conclusion, we hold that (1) the 1954 Act adding the words "under God" to the Pledge, and (2) EGUSD's policy and practice of teacher-led recitation of the Pledge, with the added words included, violate the Establishment Clause. The judgment of dismissal is vacated with respect to these two claims, and the cause is remanded for further proceedings consistent with our holding. Plaintiff is to recover costs on this appeal.

REVERSED AND REMANDED.

Endnote

[1] *Barnette* was decided before "under God" was added, and thus the Court's discussion was limited to the political ideals contained in the Pledge.

Study Questions

1. On what grounds does the court in *South Florida Free Beaches* reject the plaintiff's argument that public nudity is a constitutionally protected form of expression?

2. How would you decide *South Florida*? Is nude sunbathing expressive conduct? Does it convey a message? What message were the plaintiffs in the case allegedly conveying? Is that a message that the reasonable viewer is likely to understand when confronted by public nudity? Should public nudity be regarded as a form of "symbolic" speech?

3. What interests can the City of Miami invoke to justify the ban on nude sunbathing in public?

4. Mill insists that even false speech must be tolerated in a free society. What grounds does Mill give for this claim?

5. Mill claims that liberty should not be restricted unless the actor threatens harm to others. What clues does Mill give as to how he thinks "harm" should be interpreted?

6. Mill rests his case for the "harm principle" on a utilitarian moral and social theory: The harm principle is "right" just because it promotes the greatest good for society overall (or at least more good than any other arrangement). Can you see problems in attempting to justify such a stringent principle on utilitarian grounds?

7. How does Devlin determine when something becomes a matter of public morality? Is the reaction of the average person on the street a reliable indicator that some standard is central to the public morality?

8. Is Devlin making a utilitarian argument that government has a right to promote virtue and condemn vice only where this will promote the good of social cohesion? Or is he arguing that society has a right to instill virtues irrespective of utility?

9. Some people would argue that the rise in divorce rates and the breakdown of the traditional nuclear family in America in the decades since Devlin wrote have contributed to a variety of other social ills: growing poverty, child neglect, increasing juvenile delinquency, joblessness, drug use, and so on. Do these trends (if correctly perceived) support Devlin's argument about the centrality of the institution of marriage to the public morality?

10. Consider the following cases: (a) You enjoy listening to rap music, particularly music by rap groups that use what some people would consider violent and lewd lyrics. Your neighbor Joe knows that you listen to such music nightly (he never hears it, though, as you never play it too loudly), and this knowledge drives him to distraction. Joe hates rap music. He believes it is the root of all evil. He can't sleep at night because he is lying awake greatly distressed by the thought that you

are polluting your mind with the hateful chatter. (b) One day you take your portable stereo and your rap music tapes to the beach, set them up, and turn on the music while snoozing in the sun. Joe is a few yards away; he hears the music and is disgusted; his day is ruined. (c) A friend of yours joins you on the beach and is so taken by the music that she removes all of her clothing and prances about the beach naked, moving to the music. Joe witnesses this display and is, predictably, distressed and offended. Question: Have you (or your friend) "harmed" Joe in any of these cases? If not, why not? What difference is there between the psychological distress produced by assaulting or defaming someone (which most of us, and certainly the law, recognize as real forms of harm) and the various forms of distress experienced by Joe? Many communities have ordinances prohibiting public nudity. Can such ordinances be justified on Mill's grounds?

11. Imagine that I am a budding genius at chemistry and that I discover a recipe for making a deadly nerve gas from household ingredients. I then decide to publish my results in a letter to the editor of the local newspaper. Should I be allowed to do so? On what grounds could my "speech" be curtailed?

12. Lawrence Horn and James Perry were convicted for the 1993 murders of Horn's ex-wife and disabled son. Horn arranged for Perry to do the killing so that Horn could collect insurance money. One aspect of the case raised unusual freedom-of-expression claims concerning what terrorism experts call "mayhem manuals" —books and magazines available from small, independent publishers (and increasingly online) with "how to" instructions on making bombs, silencers, sniper weapons, and other devices. Police discovered in Horn's apartment a copy of a 130-page mail-order guidebook for murder: *Hit Man: A Technical Manual for Independent Contractors*. In the book, the pseudonymous author announces that "the professional hit man fills a need in society and is, at times, the only alternative for personal justice." The killer need feel "no twinge of guilt," because "the hit man is merely the executioner, an enforcer who carries out the sentence." Prosecutors found that Horn and Perry had followed twenty-two of the book's steps in committing their crime. The killers used an AR-7 rifle, recommended by *Hit Man* because it "breaks down

easily." The book advises that the killer fire "at least three shots to ensure quick and easy death. Aim for the head," the book suggests, "preferably the eye sockets. Close kills enable you to determine right away whether you have successfully fulfilled your part in the contract." The victims died from three shots to the face by a powerful rifle. The publisher of *Hit Man*, Paladin Press, argued that it could not be held liable for abetting the murders, because it had no knowledge of Horn's intentions. Paladin also claimed that mystery writers and other law-abiding citizens buy *Hit Man*. A number of major publishers sided with Paladin for fear that a decision against *Hit Man* would be a vote for censorship. Should the First Amendment shield the publication of such materials? Did Paladin Press, by virtue of publishing *Hit Man*, incite criminal acts? Do such publications pose a "clear and present danger" of imminent lawlessness? Is there any reason for the publication of *Hit Man* other than as a manifestation of the intent to assist in the commission of murder?

13. Controversial radio talk show personality Howard Stern was the subject of a 1996 lawsuit for intentional infliction of emotional distress based on Stern's alleged handling of and remarks about the cremated remains of the plaintiff's sister. The deceased woman, Debbie Tay, had been a frequent guest on Stern's show before her death from a drug overdose. Stern persuaded a friend of Tay's, Chaunce Hayden, to appear on the show and to bring Ms. Tay's cremated remains, which he did. Hayden had been a close friend of Tay and had been given a portion of the remains by Tay's next-of-kin. Relatives of Ms. Tay alleged that Hayden appeared on the radio show on July 18, 1995, with a decorative box containing some of Ms. Tay's remains, and that Stern shook and rattled the box, played with some of the bone fragments, and joked about Ms. Tay. The deceased's relatives sued Stern, claiming that his intentional and outrageous conduct caused them emotional harm. The court dismissed the suit, finding that "while the program which is the predicate of the complaint was certainly vulgar and disrespectful, the acts complained of cannot be characterized as being beyond all bounds of decency, atrocious and utterly intolerable in a civilized society." The court also found that Stern could not be sued for inflicting emotional harm resulting from the

negligent mishandling of a corpse, since the deceased had been cremated. The court further concluded that "since a gift was made [to Mr. Hayden] of Ms. Tay's remains, whatever property interest [Tay's relatives] had in [the remains] was forfeited. Mr. Hayden . . . was then free to do as he saw fit with his share of the remains." Do you agree with the court's ruling? Do you agree that Mr. Hayden is free to do anything he wishes with the remains? Can he sell them? Feed them to his dog? An unsubstantiated allegation accused Stern of daring Hayden to eat some of the remains. Should that kind of treatment of human remains be prohibited by law? If so, on what grounds? Is there any "harm" in such behavior? Does such conduct threaten the "public morality"?

14. Both Hart and Mill seem to assume that the cost of enforcing the common, public morality is necessarily too great. Are they correct, in your judgment?

15. The dissenters in *Cohen v. California* argued that the case involved "mainly conduct and little speech" and that the conduct could legitimately be prohibited as likely to provoke violence. Is wearing a jacket bearing a four-letter word "conduct," rather than "speech"? Suppose there had been evidence that someone who saw Cohen's jacket became violent. Is that a convincing argument for restricting Cohen's right to express himself (assuming that that was what he was doing)?

16. In 1977, residents of the Chicago suburb of Skokie were shocked to learn that the American Nazi Party was planning to stage a "white power" rally on the steps of Skokie's village hall on May 1. Nearly half of Skokie's population at that time was Jewish, and as many as twelve hundred of those were actual survivors of Hitler's persecution of European Jews. The members of the community forced village officials to obtain a court order preventing the rally and to pass ordinances prohibiting the dissemination of any material "which promotes and incites hatred against persons by reason of their race, national origin, or religion" or strives to "incite violence, hatred, abuse or hostility toward anyone based on race, religion, or ethnicity." Skokie maintained that neo-Nazi chants and signs or armbands bearing the swastika were racial slurs and thus were unprotected by the First Amendment. Frank Collin, then head of the Nazi Party, challenged the ordinances in federal court

and won. The court found that the ordinances impermissibly limited freedom of speech. Collin was quoted as stating: "The key to Skokie is that the right to free speech was denied us here. . . . We fought in the courts from 1975 onward. We were constantly denied. . . . I've got to come up with something within the law, to use the law against our enemy, the Jew. . . . I used it [the First Amendment] at Skokie. I planned the reaction of the Jews. They are hysterical." [Quoted in Donald Alexander Downs, *Nazis in Skokie* (Notre Dame, Ind.: University of Notre Dame Press, 1985), p. 28.] Did the courts correctly invalidate the Skokie ordinances, in your view? Suppose the Nazis had marched through Skokie and some of the citizens had reacted violently. Would this mean that the Nazis had "incited a riot" or that their march posed a "clear and present danger" of immediate violence? Or would the violence be the fault of the onlookers who chose to react in that manner?

17. In the early 1990s, Stanford University approved a modification to university policies regarding racist speech. Titled "Free Expression and Discriminatory Harassment," the policy prevented harassment by "personal vilification," defined as "words or nonverbal symbols . . . commonly understood to convey direct and visceral hatred or contempt for human beings on the basis of their sex, race, color, handicap, religion, sexual orientation, or national and ethnic origin." The harassing conduct must have been "intended to stigmatize an individual or small number of individuals" and addressed directly to those it stigmatized. Similar anti-harassment policies have been implemented at universities and colleges across the country. The Stanford policy remained in effect for five years but was invalidated by a California court after a group of students filed suit alleging that the policy prohibited speech on the basis of its content and thus was constitutionally impermissible. The court agreed, finding that "on its face, the Speech Code prohibits words which will not only cause people to react violently, but also cause them to feel insulted or stigmatized . . . [Stanford] cannot proscribe speech that merely hurts the feelings of those who hear it." [*Corry v. Stanford*, No. 740309 (Cal. Super. Ct. Santa Clara County Feb. 27, 1995.)] Do you agree with the court's judgment? Should the Stanford policy have been judged constitutionally permissible?

18. Many communities now allow local organizations and businesses to contribute to road maintenance in and around their towns and cities through the "Adopt a Highway" program. Sponsors like the program because they are acknowledged by signs posted along the roadway—a form of publicly assisted advertising. Suppose that the Ku Klux Klan contributes to the program and demands that a sign be posted acknowledging its help: "Highway Maintenance Courtesy of the KKK." Officials refuse to honor the request. What should be the result under the First Amendment?

19. Some scholars have suggested that the cases in which the courts have permitted states to limit religious freedom nearly always involve activities important to minority religious groups: the use of peyote by Native Americans, the practice of polygamy among Mormons, the refusal to salute the flag among Jehovah's Witnesses, and so on. These critics contend that the courts would not be likely to permit similar restrictions if they impacted "mainstream" religious groups in America, such as Catholics or Jews. Is this criticism fair?

20. In December 1995, Chia Thai Moua, a Hmong immigrant from Laos now living in Fresno, California, pled no contest to a charge of felony animal cruelty. Moua admitted to clubbing a three-month-old German shepherd puppy to death on the front steps of his home. Moua is a Hmong shaman and, like other Hmong, believed that the soul of a dog, when released from its body, can track down and destroy evil spirits that bring disease. Moua contended at trial that his wife had been seriously ill during the time leading up to the incident, and that none of his other treatments had cured her. Moua had previously sacrificed a pig and a chicken and had burned paper money. "But still my wife gets no better. What was I to do? I am a shaman and this is what I believe." Moua unsuccessfully sought to defend himself by arguing that he was exercising his religious beliefs and did not kill the dog with "malice." A lower court refused to allow the religious freedom defense. [*Los Angeles Times*, Dec. 16, 1995, p. A1.] Should Hmong people continue to be prosecuted for practices dictated by their apparently sincere religious convictions?

21. In the aftermath of the 9–11 terrorist attacks on the United States, heightened security measures increasingly came into conflict with civil liberties. In early 2001, a Florida woman of Muslim descent, Sultaana Freeman, was permitted to wear her niqab, a traditional facial veil that leaves only the eyes exposed, for the photo on her Florida state driver's license. After September 11 of that year, the state Department of Motor Vehicles reviewed its driver's license database. Freeman was ordered to have another photo taken without the veil. She refused and sued the state for violation of her First Amendment right of religious free expression. Should she win her lawsuit, in your view? (*National Law Journal*, Sept. 16, 2002, p. A20.)

22. Barry Black, Richard Elliott, and Jonathan O'Mara were convicted of violating Virginia's cross-burning statute, § 18.2–423. That statute provides:

It shall be unlawful for any person or persons, with the intent of intimidating any person or group of persons, to burn, or cause to be burned, a cross on the property of another, a highway or other public place. Any person who shall violate any provision of this section shall be guilty of a Class 6 felony. Any such burning of a cross shall be prima facie evidence of an intent to intimidate a person or group of persons.

On August 22, 1998, Black led a Ku Klux Klan rally in rural southwestern Virginia. Twenty-five to thirty people attended this gathering, which occurred on private property with the permission of the owner, who was in attendance. The property was located on an open field. Eight to ten houses were located in the vicinity of the rally. One nearby witness testified that she watched the Klan rally from a nearby house. During the rally, the witness heard Klan members speak about "what they were" and "what they believed in." The speakers "talked real bad about the blacks and the Mexicans." One speaker told the assembled gathering that "he would love to take a .30/.30 and just randomly shoot the blacks." The speakers also talked about "President Clinton and Hillary Clinton," and about how their tax money "goes to . . . the black people." The witness testified that this language made her "very . . . scared." Black and his co-defendants challenged the Virginia law as a violation of their First Amendment right to freedom of expression. In June 2003, the U.S.

Supreme Court disagreed, holding that the First Amendment permits Virginia to outlaw cross burnings done with the intent to intimidate because burning a cross is a "particularly virulent form of intimidation" with a "long and pernicious history as a signal of impending violence." [*Virginia v. Black* 123 S. Ct. 1536; 2003 U.S. LEXIS 2715 (2003)].

Suppose the defendants had alleged (as other accused KKK members have done in similar cases) that they had a lawful burning permit and that the gathering in question was a "cross-lighting" ceremony for "religious purposes." Should this be a legitimate defense? Why or why not? Do you agree with the Supreme Court's decision?

C. *Obscenity and Pornography*

Indecency and Obscenity on the Internet

The emergence of the Internet as a mainstream medium of communication, education, and entertainment, together with the concomitant rise in the amount of sexually explicit material available online, has generated much legislative activity in recent years, leading to a confusing array of legal acronyms. To begin with, in 1996, Congress passed the Communications Decency Act (or CDA). The CDA prohibited the knowing transmission over the Internet of obscene or indecent messages to any recipient under 18 years of age. It also forbade any individual from knowingly sending over or displaying on the Internet certain "patently offensive" material in a manner available to persons under 18. The U.S. Supreme Court struck down the CDA in 1997 as an unconstitutional infringement of First Amendment rights. The law did not precisely define the nature of "indecent" or "patently offensive material," the Court found; and, "in order to deny minors access to potentially harmful speech," the Court wrote, "the CDA effectively suppressed a large amount of speech that adults had a constitutional right to receive and to address to one another."[1] Subsequently, Congress enacted the Child Online Protection Act (or COPA). COPA made it a crime to post

on the Web "for commercial purposes" sexually explicit material that is "available to any minor" and that is "harmful to minors." COPA defined "material that is harmful to minors" as "any communication, picture, image, graphic image file, article, recording, writing, or other matter of any kind" that the average person, applying "contemporary community standards," would deem obscene and that "lacks serious literary, artistic, political, or scientific value for minors." In ruling on this statute, the Supreme Court held that COPA's reliance on community standards to identify material that was harmful to minors did not, by itself, violate the First Amendment.[2]

The latest of the Court's important decisions dealing with obscenity and pornography is *Ashcroft v. The Free Speech Coalition*, which was decided in 2002 and is the first reading for this section. The Child Pornography Prevention Act of 1996 (or CPPA) expanded existing federal prohibitions on child pornography to include not only pornographic images made using actual children, but also "any visual depiction, including any photograph, film, video, picture, or computer or computer- generated image or picture" that "is, or appears to be, of a minor engaging in sexually explicit conduct." The CPPA attempted to ban "virtual" child pornography, made with the use of computer-generated

---

[1] See *Reno v. American Civil Liberties Union*, 521 U.S. 844 (1997).

[2] See *Ashcroft v. American Civil Liberties Union*, 122 S. Ct. 1700 (2002).

imagery. Earlier decisions had upheld prohibitions upon the use of actual children in the production of pornographic images or films, but no living children need have been employed in the creation of the material targeted by CPPA. Rejecting arguments that virtual child pornography can lead to child sexual abuse, the Court ruled that the provisions of the CPPA were overly broad and thus unconstitutional. The law goes too far, the justices ruled, in applying to images that are not obscene under legal standards, and by proscribing any depiction of sexually explicit activity, no matter how it is presented. The CPPA would also have prohibited speech that has value. After all, the Court observed, many works of literature, as well as popular films, depict the idea of teenagers engaging in sexual activity.

The argument in *Ashcroft v. The Free Speech Coalition* presupposes familiarity with some basics of obscenity law. We can turn to these briefly.

Legal Definitions

Many people believe that speech that is "pornographic" or "obscene" (whether the two concepts are the same is one of the topics of this section) should not be protected by the law. Such speech might include (but would not necessarily be limited to) (1) depictions, on film or in still pictures, of human genitalia or of contact between genitals, anus, and mouth (in various combinations) or descriptions of such activities; (2) depictions or descriptions of homosexual intercourse; and (3) depictions or descriptions of bestiality. Many would also include in such prohibited categories of "speech" depictions or descriptions of violence in connection with any of the above (for example, mutilation, binding and gagging, sexual penetration with implements, drawing of blood, infliction of pain).

The term *pornography* can be broadly defined to refer to any form of sexually explicit material. In this sense, any of the items falling within the categories listed above would be "pornographic." The focus of this section is what legal implications, if any, should flow from that description. As all parties to the debate about the legality of pornography are willing to admit, existing law construes pornography as a special case of the "obscene"; and many of the pornography cases that have come before the courts in the past several decades have posed the issue of whether, and to what extent, obscenity is constitutionally protected speech. The basic standard governing current obscenity law was handed down by the Supreme Court in 1973 in *Miller v. California.* The Court held that "the basic guidelines for the trier of fact must be: (a) whether 'the average person, applying contemporary community standards,' would find that the work, taken as a whole, appeals to the prurient interest, (b) whether the work depicts or describes in a patently offensive way, sexual conduct specifically defined by the applicable state law, and (c) whether the work, taken as a whole, lacks serious literary, artistic, political, or scientific value."[3]

The Court confined the permissible scope of the state regulation of the obscene to "works which depict or describe sexual conduct," and urged that "patently offensive representations or descriptions of ultimate sexual acts, normal or perverted, actual or simulated," or "patently offensive representations or descriptions of masturbation, excretory functions, and lewd exhibition of the genitals" would likely fall within the ambit of material deemed "obscene" by the *Miller* standard. State regulations of obscene materials have been upheld under the *Miller* test to protect audiences whose members are unwilling, "captive" (for example, prohibitions on showing pornographic films at drive-in movie theaters visible from the street or of broadcasting "dirty words" over the radio), or minors.[4] Zoning ordinances for "adult theaters" and restrictions on "live" sexual performances have also been permitted.[5] Nonetheless, a great many works that many people might find obscene (*Playboy, Hustler,* "triple-X" films available at the local video store) are plainly at present constitutionally protected forms of expression.

The Hudnut Case

In 1984, the city of Indianapolis, Indiana, enacted an unusual anti-pornography ordinance. The ordinance was based on the city council's finding that pornography is "a systematic practice of exploitation and subordination based on sex which differentially harms women," and pornography was accordingly defined as "the graphic sexually explicit subordination of women, whether in pictures or in words." Based on this conception of pornography, the ordinance prohibited a variety of activities, including "trafficking" in pornography

---

[3] 413 U.S. 15 (1973).

[4] See *Erznoznik v. Jacksonville,* 422 U.S. 205 (1975), *F.C.C. v. Pacific Foundation,* 438 U.S. 726 (1978), and *Pinkus v. United States,* 436 U.S. 293 (1978).

[5] See *Young v. American Mini Theaters,* 427 U.S. 50 (1976) and *California v. Larue,* 409 U.S. 109 (1972).

and "forcing" pornography on a person in any place of employment, school, home, or public place. The ordinance further prohibited "coercion into pornographic performance." The law gave to any woman aggrieved by trafficking or coercion a right to file a complaint "as a woman acting against the subordination of women."

In the *Hudnut* case, reprinted here, federal appellate judge Frank Easterbrook, writing for the court, affirms a lower court's decision that the Indianapolis ordinance is unconstitutional under the First Amendment because it discriminates on the grounds of speech content, permitting only speech "treating women in the approved way." Judge Easterbrook concedes that pornographic materials can reinforce beliefs of male domination and female submission; but, he insists, pornography's impact on people's beliefs can be only through the vehicle of ideas—ideas that must receive First Amendment protection.

Pornography and Harm

Should pornography be legally permissible? In his selection, philosopher Joel Feinberg explores various factors bearing on this question. Feinberg argues for a generally liberal position, consistent with the overall view of Mill: Pornographic works may be prohibited only if they can be shown to be directly harmful or at least profoundly offensive to many in a way that cannot be avoided. Feinberg criticizes what he takes to be the courts' confusion of pornography with the obscene. This has led, among other things, to debates about the status of pornographic materials. Are they forms of art or literature or simply "sex aids"? The concept of the "obscene," according to Feinberg, encompasses that which is blatant, flagrant, or shameless. Can sex ever be described in these ways? Perhaps in some cases; but much pornography, Feinberg thinks, is not actually obscene.

Feinberg discusses two general grounds for banning or at least greatly restricting the production and distribution of pornographic materials: that they bring about violence and that they are profoundly offensive. With respect to the latter ground, Feinberg considers the suggestion that the prohibition of pornography could be defended by appeal to what he calls the "offense principle": the idea that conduct that is profoundly or extremely obscene, offensive, or revolting may legitimately be forbidden as a form of public nuisance (similar, for example, to creating a horrible stench), at least where the conduct is unavoidable by

reasonable means. Here, of course, the question of the status of works of pornography as art or literature may be used to offset their offensiveness. However, even pornography lacking any such "redeeming" characteristics, Feinberg maintains, rarely rises to the level of revulsion necessary to be preventable under the offense principle. And even if it does, such material is usually avoidable.

Does pornography cause harm? And if so, can its production and use be restricted on Mill's grounds? It is here that Feinberg takes up the challenge of feminist arguments in favor of banning pornography. The feminist critique of pornography is, as Feinberg sees it, defended on two grounds: Pornography harms women either by "defaming" them (holding them up to ridicule and derision) as a group or by inciting violence against them (for example, rape). Feinberg responds that a connection between neither pornography and defamation nor pornography and instances of actual violence can be closely enough forged to pass muster under the harm principle, properly understood. If pornography depicts women as subordinate in a way that gives rise to a cause of action for defamation, so do many other things, from television shows to novels. On the other hand, to prohibit pornography on the ground that it brings about violence requires both a likelihood of serious harm and a direct link between the pornographic expression (the film or magazine) and the violence. The connection between pornography and violence cannot be merely suggestive; it must be tight. Feinberg is doubtful that such a tight link can be established; the closest that one can come to such proof, he admits, is in the case of "violent" pornography, of which he provides several gruesome examples.

Yet even in the case of especially violent pornography, the question can still be raised: Does it *cause* violence against women? No, says Feinberg, because the direction of causation is not from violent pornography to violent acts against women. Instead, violent pornography and rape are both effects of a deeper causal agency: the "cult of macho." Pornography and rape are both products of a set of underlying beliefs about and attitudes toward women that are associated with "machismo." Pornography is a symptom, and therefore its suppression will likely have little effect. Nor is it possible to argue, by analogy to concepts in the criminal law, that the makers or distributors of pornographic materials are guilty of "incitement" to violence or "solicitation" of rape, for vendors of pornography do not counsel or advise customers to rape—not, at least, in a way the law currently would recognize.

Finally, Feinberg rejects the feminist argument that the profound offense felt by women through their awareness of degrading and humiliating pornographic films and magazines is sufficient to justify the suppression of pornography. Even if not reasonably avoidable, such feelings of offense "at the thought" that members of one's sex are being degraded fails to establish that anyone in particular is really being victimized by such portrayals.

The Feminist Critique of Pornography

In her essay, feminist legal scholar Catherine MacKinnon defends the general position taken by the Indianapolis ordinance (of which she was a principal author) addressed in the *Hudnut* case. Like Feinberg, MacKinnon also challenges the law's identification of pornography with the obscene, but for very different reasons. Equating pornography with obscenity, MacKinnon claims, obscures its true nature by representing it as just one more form of expression, one more way of conveying an idea, belief, or attitude. From a moral point of view, this reduces the debate about pornography to whether such material is in good or bad taste; legally it has the effect of making pornography an issue under the First Amendment. As against this, MacKinnon defends the "civil rights" conception of pornography implicit in the Indianapolis law: Pornography is a discriminatory practice, not simply a certain type of offensive picture or text; pornography is not a political or social or religious "idea," and as such it does not deserve First Amend-

ment protection, any more than does the now-outlawed practice of racial segregation. Displays of violent pornography are not invitations to engage in a dialogue with the "marketplace of ideas"; they are, rather, acts of disempowerment.

Pornography, MacKinnon believes, reflects and reinforces the way men in general tend to regard women; it is not linked only with a cult of machismo, as even men who don't think of themselves as especially macho nonetheless participate in a culture that regards women as essentially commodities for use by men. The problem with obscenity law is that it is made by men and reflects male ideals and standards. This is especially obvious, MacKinnon thinks, in the case of the *Miller* standards: the "average person" is a male; "community standards" are already infected with sexism; "lacking serious . . . merit" effectively permits much that is demeaning to women.

At a deeper level, MacKinnon challenges Feinberg's Millian premises as they apply to the pornography question. Mill and other liberal political philosophers assume that people will not be silenced socially so long as no legal restrictions are placed upon their freedom of expression. But this, MacKinnon claims, is false: Permitting pornographers to "speak" silences women. Finally, MacKinnon argues that pornography does "contribute causally" to harm to women; and she urges that the law's understanding of "harm," derived from the simple transitive model of "A hit B," is unduly narrow and fails to account for a larger sense in which a discriminatory practice, whether it be pornography or racial segregation, can result in a "collective harm."

Ashcroft v. The Free Speech Coalition

JUSTICE KENNEDY delivered the opinion of the Court.

We consider in this case whether the Child Pornography Prevention Act of 1996 (CPPA), abridges the freedom of speech. The CPPA extends the federal prohibition against child pornography to sexually

explicit images that appear to depict minors but were produced without using any real children. The statute prohibits, in specific circumstances, possessing or distributing these images, which may be created by using adults who look like minors or by using computer imaging. The new technology, according to Congress, makes it possible to create realistic images of children who do not exist. . . .

535 U.S. 234 (2002), United States Supreme Court.

By prohibiting child pornography that does not depict an actual child, the statute goes beyond *New York v. Ferber*, 458 U.S. 747 (1982), which distinguished child pornography from other sexually explicit speech because of the State's interest in protecting the children exploited by the production process. . . . As a general rule, pornography can be banned only if obscene, but under *Ferber*, pornography showing minors can be proscribed whether or not the images are obscene under the definition set forth in *Miller v. California*. . . .

While we have not had occasion to consider the question, we may assume that the apparent age of persons engaged in sexual conduct is relevant to whether a depiction offends community standards. Pictures of young children engaged in certain acts might be obscene where similar depictions of adults, or perhaps even older adolescents, would not. The CPPA, however, is not directed at speech that is obscene . . . Like the law in *Ferber*, the CPPA seeks to reach beyond obscenity, and it makes no attempt to conform to the *Miller* standard. For instance, the statute would reach visual depictions, such as movies, even if they have redeeming social value.

The principal question to be resolved, then, is whether the CPPA is constitutional where it proscribes a significant universe of speech that is neither obscene under *Miller* nor child pornography under *Ferber*.

Before 1996, Congress defined child pornography as the type of depictions at issue in *Ferber*, images made using actual minors. . . . The CPPA retains that prohibition at 18 U.S.C. § 2256(8)(A) and adds three other prohibited categories of speech, of which the first, § 2256(8)(B), and the third, § 2256(8)(D), are at issue in this case. Section 2256(8)(B) prohibits "any visual depiction, including any photograph, film, video, picture, or computer or computer-generated image or picture" that "is, or appears to be, of a minor engaging in sexually explicit conduct." The prohibition on "any visual depiction" does not depend at all on how the image is produced. The section captures a range of depictions, sometimes called "virtual child pornography," which include computer-generated images, as well as images produced by more traditional means. For instance, the literal terms of the statute embrace a Renaissance painting depicting a scene from classical mythology, a "picture" that "appears to be, of a minor engaging in sexually explicit conduct." The statute also prohibits Hollywood movies, filmed without any child actors, if a jury believes an actor "appears to be" a minor engaging in "actual or simulated . . . sexual intercourse."

These images do not involve, let alone harm, any children in the production process; but Congress decided the materials threaten children in other, less direct, ways. Pedophiles might use the materials to encourage children to participate in sexual activity. . . . Furthermore, pedophiles might "whet their own sexual appetites" with the pornographic images, "thereby increasing the creation and distribution of child pornography and the sexual abuse and exploitation of actual children." . . . Under these rationales, harm flows from the content of the images, not from the means of their production. In addition, Congress identified another problem created by computer-generated images: Their existence can make it harder to prosecute pornographers who do use real minors. . . . As imaging technology improves, Congress found, it becomes more difficult to prove that a particular picture was produced using actual children. . . .

Section 2256(8)(C) prohibits a more common and lower tech means of creating virtual images, known as computer morphing. Rather than creating original images, pornographers can alter innocent pictures of real children so that the children appear to be engaged in sexual activity. Although morphed images may fall within the definition of virtual child pornography, they implicate the interests of real children and are in that sense closer to the images in *Ferber*. Respondents do not challenge this provision, and we do not consider it.

. . . [A] law imposing criminal penalties on protected speech is a stark example of speech suppression. The CPPA's penalties are indeed severe. A first offender may be imprisoned for 15 years. . . . A repeat offender faces a prison sentence of not less than 5 years and not more than 30 years in prison. . . . While even minor punishments can chill protected speech, . . . this case provides a textbook example of why we permit facial challenges to statutes that burden expression. With these severe penalties in force, few legitimate movie producers or book publishers, or few other speakers in any capacity, would risk distributing images in or near the uncertain reach of this law. The Constitution gives significant protection from overbroad laws that chill speech within the First Amendment's vast and privileged sphere. Under this principle, the CPPA is unconstitutional on its face if it prohibits a substantial amount of protected expression. . . .

. . . [S]peech may not be prohibited because it concerns subjects offending our sensibilities. . . .

As a general principle, the First Amendment bars the government from dictating what we see or read or speak or hear. The freedom of speech has its limits; it does not embrace certain categories of speech, including defamation, incitement, obscenity, and pornography produced with real children. . . . While these categories may be prohibited without violating the First Amendment, none of them includes the speech prohibited by the CPPA. . . .

As we have noted, the CPPA is much more than a supplement to the existing federal prohibition on obscenity . . . . The CPPA . . . , extends to images that appear to depict a minor engaging in sexually explicit activity without regard to the *Miller* requirements. . . . Any depiction of sexually explicit activity, no matter how it is presented, is proscribed. The CPPA applies to a picture in a psychology manual, as well as a movie depicting the horrors of sexual abuse. . . .

. . . The statute proscribes the visual depiction of an idea—that of teenagers engaging in sexual activity—that is a fact of modern society and has been a theme in art and literature throughout the ages. Under the CPPA, images are prohibited so long as the persons appear to be under 18 years of age. This is higher than the legal age for marriage in many States, as well as the age at which persons may consent to sexual relations. . . .

. . . Both themes—teenage sexual activity and the sexual abuse of children—have inspired countless literary works. William Shakespeare created the most famous pair of teenage lovers, one of whom is just 13 years of age. . . . The work has inspired no less than 40 motion pictures, some of which suggest that the teenagers consummated their relationship. . . .

Contemporary movies pursue similar themes. Last year's Academy Awards featured the movie, *Traffic,* which was nominated for Best Picture. . . . The film portrays a teenager, identified as a 16-year-old, who becomes addicted to drugs. The viewer sees the degradation of her addiction, which in the end leads her to a filthy room to trade sex for drugs. The year before, *American Beauty* won the Academy Award for Best Picture. . . . In the course of the movie, a teenage girl engages in sexual relations with her teenage boyfriend, and another yields herself to the gratification of a middle-aged man. . . .

. . . Whether or not the films we mention violate the CPPA, they explore themes within the wide sweep of the statute's prohibitions. If these films, or hundreds of others of lesser note that explore those subjects, contain a single graphic depiction of sexual activity within the statutory definition, the possessor of the film would be subject to severe punishment without inquiry into the work's redeeming value. This

is inconsistent with an essential First Amendment rule: The artistic merit of a work does not depend on the presence of a single explicit scene. . . .

The Government seeks to address this deficiency by arguing that speech prohibited by the CPPA is virtually indistinguishable from child pornography, which may be banned without regard to whether it depicts works of value. . . . *Ferber* recognized that the State had an interest in stamping it out without regard to any judgment about its content. . . . The production of the work, not its content, was the target of the statute. The fact that a work contained serious literary, artistic, or other value did not excuse the harm it caused to its child participants. . . .

. . . First, as a permanent record of a child's abuse, the continued circulation itself would harm the child who had participated. Like a defamatory statement, each new publication of the speech would cause new injury to the child's reputation and emotional well-being. . . . Second, because the traffic in child pornography was an economic motive for its production, the State had an interest in closing the distribution network. . . . Under either rationale, the speech had what the Court in effect held was a proximate link to the crime from which it came.

. . . [T]he CPPA prohibits speech that records no crime and creates no victims by its production. Virtual child pornography is not "intrinsically related" to the sexual abuse of children, as were the materials in *Ferber*. . . . While the Government asserts that the images can lead to actual instances of child abuse, . . . the causal link is contingent and indirect. The harm does not necessarily follow from the speech, but depends upon some unquantified potential for subsequent criminal acts.

The Government says these indirect harms are sufficient because, as *Ferber* acknowledged, child pornography rarely can be valuable speech. . . . This argument, however, suffers from two flaws. First, *Ferber*'s judgment about child pornography was based upon how it was made, not on what it communicated. . . .

The second flaw in the Government's position is that *Ferber* did not hold that child pornography is by definition without value. On the contrary, the Court recognized some works in this category might have significant value, . . . but relied on virtual images—the very images prohibited by the CPPA—as an alternative and permissible means of expression . . . *Ferber*, then, not only referred to the distinction between actual and virtual child pornography, it relied on it as a reason supporting its holding. *Ferber* provides no support for a statute that eliminates the distinction and makes the alternative mode criminal as well.

. . . The Government . . . argues that the CPPA is necessary because pedophiles may use virtual child pornography to seduce children. . . . The Government, of course, may punish adults who provide unsuitable materials to children and it may enforce criminal penalties for unlawful solicitation. The precedents establish, however, that speech within the rights of adults to hear may not be silenced completely in an attempt to shield children from it . . . .

Here, the Government wants to keep speech from children not to protect them from its content but to protect them from those who would commit other crimes. The principle, however, remains the same: The Government cannot ban speech fit for adults simply because it may fall into the hands of children. The evil in question depends upon the actor's unlawful conduct, conduct defined as criminal quite apart from any link to the speech in question. This establishes that the speech ban is not narrowly drawn. The objective is to prohibit illegal conduct, but this restriction goes well beyond that interest by restricting the speech available to law-abiding adults.

The Government submits further that virtual child pornography whets the appetites of pedophiles and encourages them to engage in illegal conduct. This rationale cannot sustain the provision in question. The mere tendency of speech to encourage unlawful acts is not a sufficient reason for banning it. . . . First Amendment freedoms are most in danger when the government seeks to control thought or to justify its laws for that impermissible end. The right to think is the beginning of freedom, and speech must be protected from the government because speech is the beginning of thought.

. . . There is here no attempt, incitement, solicitation, or conspiracy. The Government has shown no more than a remote connection between speech that might encourage thoughts or impulses and any resulting child abuse. Without a significantly stronger, more direct connection, the Government may not prohibit speech on the ground that it may encourage pedophiles to engage in illegal conduct.

The Government next argues that its objective of eliminating the market for pornography produced using real children necessitates a prohibition on virtual images as well. Virtual images, the Government contends, are indistinguishable from real ones; they are part of the same market and are often exchanged. In this way, it is said, virtual images promote the trafficking in works produced through the exploitation of real children. The hypothesis is somewhat implausible. If virtual images were identical to illegal child pornography, the illegal images would be driven from the market by the indistinguishable substitutes. Few pornographers would risk prosecution by abusing real children if fictional, computerized images would suffice.

In the case of the material covered by *Ferber*, the creation of the speech is itself the crime of child abuse; the prohibition deters the crime by removing the profit motive. . . . [H]ere, there is no underlying crime at all. Even if the Government's market deterrence theory were persuasive in some contexts, it would not justify this statute.

Finally, the Government says that the possibility of producing images by using computer imaging makes it very difficult for it to prosecute those who produce pornography by using real children. Experts, we are told, may have difficulty in saying whether the pictures were made by using real children or by using computer imaging. The necessary solution, the argument runs, is to prohibit both kinds of images. The argument, in essence, is that protected speech may be banned as a means to ban unprotected speech. This analysis turns the First Amendment upside down.

The Government may not suppress lawful speech as the means to suppress unlawful speech. Protected speech does not become unprotected merely because it resembles the latter. The Constitution requires the reverse. . . . The overbreadth doctrine prohibits the Government from banning unprotected speech if a substantial amount of protected speech is prohibited or chilled in the process.

To avoid the force of this objection, the Government would have us read the CPPA not as a measure suppressing speech but as a law shifting the burden to the accused to prove the speech is lawful. In this connection, the Government relies on an affirmative defense under the statute, which allows a defendant to avoid conviction for nonpossession offenses by showing that the materials were produced using only adults and were not otherwise distributed in a manner conveying the impression that they depicted real children. . . .

The Government raises serious constitutional difficulties by seeking to impose on the defendant the burden of proving his speech is not unlawful. . . . If the evidentiary issue is a serious problem for the Government, as it asserts, it will be at least as difficult for the innocent possessor. . . .

We need not decide, however, whether the Government could impose this burden on a speaker.

Even if an affirmative defense can save a statute from First Amendment challenge, here the defense is incomplete and insufficient, even on its own terms. . . . A defendant charged with possessing, as opposed to distributing, proscribed works may not defend on the ground that the firm depicts only adult actors. . . . So while the affirmative defense may protect a movie producer from prosecution for the act of distribution, that same producer, and all other persons in the subsequent distribution chain, could be liable for possessing the prohibited work. Furthermore, the affirmative defense provides no protection to persons who produce speech by using computer imaging, or through other means

that do not involve the use of adult actors who appear to be minors. . . . In these cases, the defendant can demonstrate no children were harmed in producing the images, yet the affirmative defense would not bar the prosecution For this reason, the affirmative defense cannot save the statute, for it leaves unprotected a substantial amount of speech not tied to the Government's interest in distinguishing images produced using real children from virtual ones.

. . .

. . . [T]he prohibitions of §§ 2256(8)(B) and 2256(8)(D) are overbroad and unconstitutional. . . .

The judgment of the Court of Appeals is affirmed.

American Booksellers Association v. Hudnut

Easterbrook, Circuit Judge.

Indianapolis enacted an ordinance defining "pornography" as a practice that discriminates against women. "Pornography" is to be redressed through the administrative and judicial methods used for other discrimination. The City's definition of "pornography" is considerably different from "obscenity," which the Supreme Court has held is not protected by the First Amendment.

. . . To be "obscene" under *Miller v. California*, 413 U.S. 15 . . . (1973), "a publication must, taken as a whole, appeal to the prurient interest, must contain patently offensive depictions or descriptions of specified sexual conduct, and on the whole have no serious literary, artistic, political, or scientific value.". . . Offensiveness must be assessed under the standards of the community. Both offensiveness and an appeal to something other than "normal, healthy sexual desires" . . . are essential elements of "obscenity."

"Pornography" under the ordinance is "the graphic sexually explicit subordination of women, whether in pictures or in words, that also includes one or more of the following:

1. Women are presented as sexual objects who enjoy pain or humiliation; or

2. Women are presented as sexual objects who experience sexual pleasure in being raped; or

3. Women are presented as sexual objects tied up or cut up or mutilated or bruised or physically hurt, or as dismembered or truncated or fragmented or severed into body parts; or

4. Women are presented as being penetrated by objects or animals; or

5. Women are presented in scenarios of degradation, injury, abasement, torture, shown as filthy or inferior, bleeding, bruised, or hurt in a context that makes these conditions sexual; or

6. Women are presented as sexual objects for domination, conquest, violation, exploitation, possession, or use, or through postures or positions of servility or submission or display.

The Indianapolis ordinance does not refer to the prurient interest, to offensiveness, or to the standards of the community. It demands attention to particular depictions, not to the work judged as a whole. It is irrelevant under the ordinance whether the work has literary, artistic, political, or scientific value. The City and many amici point to these omissions as virtues.

771 F. 2d 323 (1985), United States Court of Appeals, Seventh Circuit.

They maintain that pornography influences attitudes, and the statute is a way to alter the socialization of men and women rather than to vindicate community standards of offensiveness. And as one of the principal drafters of the ordinance has asserted, "if a woman is subjected, why should it matter that the work has other value?" Catherine A. MacKinnon, *Pornography, Civil Rights, and Speech*, 20 HarvCiv.Rts.—Civ.Lib.L. Rev. 1, 21 (1985).

Civil rights groups and feminists have entered this case as amici on both sides. Those supporting the ordinance say that it will play an important role in reducing the tendency of men to view women as sexual objects, a tendency that leads to both unacceptable attitudes and discrimination in the workplace and violence away from it. Those opposing the ordinance point out that much radical feminist literature is explicit and depicts women in ways forbidden by the ordinance and that the ordinance would reopen old battles. It is unclear how Indianapolis would treat works from James Joyce's *Ulysses* to Homer's *Iliad*; both depict women as submissive objects for conquest and domination.

We do not try to balance the arguments for and against an ordinance such as this. The ordinance discriminates on the ground of the content of the speech. Speech treating women in the approved way—in sexual encounters "premised on equality" (MacKinnon, *supra*, at 22)—is lawful no matter how sexually explicit. Speech treating women in the disapproved way—as submissive in matters sexual or as enjoying humiliation—is unlawful no matter how significant the literary, artistic, or political qualities of the work taken as a whole. The state may not ordain preferred viewpoints in this way. The Constitution forbids the state to declare one perspective right and silence opponents.

The ordinance contains four prohibitions. People may not "traffic" in pornography, "coerce" others into performing in pornographic works, or "force" pornography on anyone. Anyone injured by someone who has seen or read pornography has a right of action against the maker or seller.

Trafficking is defined in § 16–3(g)(4) as the "production, sale, exhibition, or distribution of pornography." The offense excludes exhibition in a public" or educational library, but a "special display" in a library may be sex discrimination. Section 16–3(g)(4)(c) provides that the trafficking paragraph "shall not be construed to make isolated passages or isolated parts actionable."

"Coercion into pornographic performance" is defined in § 16–3(g)(5) as "[c]oercing, intimidating or fraudulently inducing any person . . . into performing for pornography. . . ." The ordinance specifies that proof of any of the following "shall not constitute a defense: I. That the person is a woman; . . . VI. That the person has previously posed for sexually explicit pictures . . . with anyone . . . ; . . . VIII. That the person actually consented to a use of the performance that is changed into pornography; . . . IX. That the person knew that the purpose of the acts or events in question was to make pornography; . . . XI. That the person signed a contract, or made statements affirming a willingness to cooperate in the production of pornography; XII. That no physical force, threats, or weapons were used in the making of the pornography; or XIII. That the person was paid or otherwise compensated."

"Forcing pornography on a person," according to § 16–3(g)(5), is the "forcing of pornography on any woman, man, child, or transsexual in any place of employment, in education, in a home, or in any public place." The statute does not define forcing, but one of its authors states that the definition reaches pornography shown to medical students as part of their education or given to language students for translation. MacKinnon, *supra*, at 4–41.

Section 16–3(g)(7) defines as a prohibited practice the "assault, physical attack, or injury of any woman, man, child, or transsexual in a way that is directly caused by specific pornography."

For purposes of all four offenses, it is generally "not . . . a defense that the respondent did not know or intend that the materials were pornography. . . ." Section 16–3(g)(8). But the ordinance provides that damages are unavailable in trafficking cases unless the complainant proves "that the respondent knew or had reason to know that the materials were pornography." It is a complete defense to a trafficking case that all of the materials in question were pornography only by virtue of category (6) of the definition of pornography. In cases of assault caused by pornography, those who seek damages from "a seller, exhibitor or distributor" must show that the defendant knew or had reason to know of the material's status as pornography. By implication, those who seek damages from an author need not show this.

A woman aggrieved by trafficking in pornography may file a complaint "as a woman acting against the subordination of women" with the office of equal opportunity. Section 16–17(b). A man, child, or transsexual also may protest trafficking "but must prove injury in the same way that a woman is injured. . . ." *Ibid.* Subsection (a) also provides, however, that "any person claiming to be aggrieved" by trafficking, coercion, forcing, or assault may complain against the "perpetrators." We need not decide whether § 16–17(b) qualifies the right of action § 16–17(a).

The office investigates and within 30 days makes a recommendation to a panel of the equal opportunity advisory board. The panel then decides whether there is reasonable cause to proceed (§ 16–24(2) and may refer the dispute to a conciliation conference or to a complaint adjudication committee for a hearing (§§ 16–24(3), 16–26 (a)). The committee uses the same procedures ordinarily associated with civil rights litigation. It may make findings and enter orders, including both orders to cease and desist and orders "to take further affirmative action . . . including but not limited to the power to restore complainant's losses. . . ." Section 16–26(d). Either party may appeal the committee's decision to the board, which reviews the record before the committee and may modify its decision.

Under Indiana law an administrative decision takes effect when rendered, unless a court issues a stay. . . . The board's decisions are subject to review in the ordinary course. . . . Judicial review in pornography cases is to be de novo . . . , which provides a second complete hearing. When the board finds that a person has engaged in trafficking or that a seller, exhibitor, or distributor is responsible for an assault, it must initiate judicial review of its own decision, . . . and the statute prohibits injunctive relief in these cases in advance of the court's final decision. . . .

The district court held the ordinance unconstitutional. . . . The court concluded that the ordinance regulates speech rather than the conduct involved in making pornography. The regulation of speech could be justified, the court thought, only by a compelling interest in reducing sex discrimination, an interest Indianapolis had not established. The ordinance is also vague and overbroad, the court believed, and establishes a prior restraint of speech.

. . . "If there is any fixed star in our constitutional constellation, it is that no official, high or petty, can prescribe what shall be orthodox in politics, nationalism, religion, or other matters of opinion or force citizens to confess by word or act their faith therein." *West Virginia State Board of Education v. Barnette*, 319 U.S. 624, 642 . . . (1943). Under the First Amendment the government must leave to the people the evaluation of ideas. Bald or subtle, an idea is as powerful as the audience allows it to be. A belief may be pernicious—the beliefs of Nazis led to the death of millions, those of the Klan to the repression of millions. A pernicious belief may prevail. Totalitarian governments today rule much of the planet, practicing suppression of billions and spreading dogma that may enslave others. One of the things that separates our society from theirs is our absolute right to propagate opinions that the government finds wrong or even hateful. . . .

Under the ordinance, graphic sexually explicit speech is "pornography" or not depending on the perspective the author adopts. Speech that "subordinates" women and also, for example, presents women as enjoying pain, humiliation, or rape, or even simply presents women in "positions of servility or submission or display" is forbidden, no matter how great the literary or political value of the work taken as a whole. Speech that portrays women in positions of equality is lawful, no matter how graphic the sexual content. This is thought control. It establishes an "approved" view of women, of how they may react to sexual encounters, of how the sexes may relate to each other. Those who espouse the approved view may use sexual images; those who do not, may not.

Indianapolis justifies the ordinance on the ground that pornography affects thoughts. Men who see women depicted as subordinate are more likely to treat them so. Pornography is an aspect of dominance. It does not persuade people so much as change them. It works by socializing, by establishing the expected and the permissible. In this view pornography is not an idea; pornography is the injury.

There is much to this perspective. Beliefs are also facts. People often act in accordance with the images and patterns they find around them. People raised in a religion tend to accept the tenets of that religion, often without independent examination. People taught from birth that black people are fit only for slavery rarely rebelled against that creed; beliefs coupled with the self-interest of the masters established a social structure that inflicted great harm while enduring for centuries. Words and images act at the level of the subconscious before they persuade at the level of the conscious. Even the truth has little chance unless a statement fits within the framework of beliefs that may never have been subjected to rational study. . . .

Yet this simply demonstrates the power of pornography as speech. All of these unhappy effects depend on mental intermediation. Pornography affects how people see the world, their fellows, and social relations. If pornography is what pornography does, so is other speech. Hitler's orations affected how some Germans saw Jews. Communism is a world view, not simply a *Manifesto* by Marx and Engels or a set of speeches. Efforts to suppress communist speech in the United States were based on the belief that the public acceptability of such ideas would increase the likelihood of totalitarian government. Religions affect socialization in the most pervasive way. The opinion in *Wisconsin v. Yoder*, 406 U.S. 205 . . . 1526 . . . (1972), shows how a religion can dominate an entire approach to life, governing much more than the relation between the sexes. Many people believe that the existence of television, apart from the content of specific programs, leads to intellectual laziness, to a penchant for violence, to many other ills. The Alien and Sedition Acts passed during the administration of John Adams rested on a sincerely held belief that disrespect for the government leads to social collapse and revolution—a belief with support in the history of many nations. Most governments of the world act on this empirical regularity, suppressing critical speech. In the United States, however, the strength of the support for this belief is irrelevant. . . .

Racial bigotry, anti-Semitism, violence on television, reporters' biases—these and many more influence the culture and shape our socialization. None is directly answerable by more speech, unless that speech too finds its place in the popular culture. Yet all is protected as speech, however insidious. Any other answer leaves the government in control of all of the institutions of culture, the great censor and director of which thoughts are good for us.

Sexual responses often are unthinking responses, and the association of sexual arousal with the subordination of women therefore may have a substantial effect. But almost all cultural stimuli provoke unconscious responses. Religious ceremonies condition their participants. Teachers convey messages by selecting what not to cover; the implicit message about what is off limits or unthinkable may be more powerful than the messages for which they present rational argument. Television scripts contain unarticulated assumptions. People may be conditioned in subtle ways. If the fact that speech plays a role in a process of conditioning were enough to permit governmental regulation, that would be the end of freedom of speech.

It is possible to interpret the claim that the pornography is the harm in a different way. Indianapolis emphasizes the injury that models in pornographic films and pictures may suffer. The record contains materials depicting sexual torture, penetra-

tion of women by red-hot irons and the like. These concerns have nothing to do with written materials subject to the statute, and physical injury can occur with or without the "subordination" of women . . . [A] state may make injury in the course of producing a film unlawful independent of the viewpoint expressed in the film.

The more immediate point, however, is that the image of pain is not necessarily pain. In *Body Double*, a suspense film, directed by Brian DePalma, a woman who has disrobed and presented a sexually explicit display is murdered by an intruder with a drill. The drill runs through the woman's body. The film is sexually explicit and a murder occurs—yet no one believes that the actress suffered pain or died. In *Barbarella* a character played by Jane Fonda is at times displayed in sexually explicit ways and at times shown "bleeding, bruised, [and] hurt in a context that makes these conditions sexual"—and again no one believes that Fonda was actually tortured to make the film. In *Carnal Knowledge* a woman grovels to please the sexual whims of a character played by Jack Nicholson; no one believes that there was a real sexual submission, and the Supreme Court held the film protected by the First Amendment . . . And this works both ways. The description of women's sexual domination of men in *Lysistrata* was not real dominance. Depictions may affect slavery, war, or sexual roles, but a book about slavery is not itself slavery, or a book about death by poison a murder.

Much of Indianapolis's argument rests on the belief that when speech is "unanswerable," and the metaphor that there is a "marketplace of ideas" does not apply, the First Amendment does not apply either. The metaphor is honored; Milton's *Aeropagitica* and John Stuart Mill's *On Liberty* defend freedom of speech on the ground that the truth will prevail, and many of the most important cases under the First Amendment recite this position. The Framers undoubtedly believed it. As a general matter it is true. But the Constitution does not make the dominance of truth a necessary condition of freedom of speech. To say that it does would be to confuse an outcome of free speech with a necessary condition for the application of the amendment.

A power to limit speech on the ground that truth has not yet prevailed and is not likely to prevail implies the power to declare truth. At some point the government must be able to say (as Indianapolis has said): "We know what the truth is, yet a free exchange of speech has not driven out falsity so that we must now prohibit falsity." If the government may declare the truth, why wait for the failure of speech? Under the First Amendment, however, there is no such thing as a false idea [*Gertz v. Robert Welch, Inc.*, 418 U.S. 323 . . . (1974)], so the government may not restrict speech on the ground that in a free exchange truth is not yet dominant.

. . .

Obscenity as Pornography

JOEL FEINBERG

1. *The Feminist Case Against Pornography*

In recent years a powerful attack on pornography has been made from a different quarter and on different, but often shifting grounds. Until 1970 or so, the demand for legal restraints on pornography came mainly from "sexual conservatives," those who regarded the pursuit of erotic pleasure for its own sake to be immoral or degrading, and its public depiction obscene. The new attack, however, comes not from prudes and bluenoses, but from women who have been in the forefront of the sexual revolution. We do not hear any of the traditional complaints about pornography from this group—that erotic states in themselves are immoral, that sexual titillation corrupts character, and that the spectacle of "appeals to prurience" is repugnant to moral sensibility. The new charge is rather that pornography degrades, abuses, and defames women, and contributes to a general climate of attitudes toward women that makes violent sex crimes more frequent. Pornography, they claim, has come to pose a threat to public safety, and its legal restraint can find justification either under the harm principle, or, by analogy with Nazi parades in Skokie and K.K.K. rallies, on some theory of profound (and personal) offense.

. . .

There is no necessity . . . that pornography *as such* be degrading to women. . . . [W]e can imagine easily

enough an ideal pornography in which men and women are depicted enjoying their joint sexual pleasures in ways that show not a trace of dominance or humiliation of either party by the other. The materials in question might clearly satisfy my previous definition of "pornography" as materials designed entirely and effectively to induce erotic excitement in observers, without containing any of the extraneous sexist elements.

. . .

. . . Some degrading pornography is also violent, glorifying in physical mistreatment of the woman, and featuring "weapons, of torture or bondage, wounds and bruises."[1] "One frightening spread from *Chic Magazine* showed a series of pictures of a woman covered with blood, masturbating with a knife. The title was "'Columbine Cuts Up.'"[2] A movie called "Snuff" in which female characters (and, it is alleged, the actresses who portrayed them) are tortured to death for the sexual entertainment of the audiences, was shown briefly in a commercial New York theatre. The widely circulated monthly magazine *Hustler* once had a cover picture of a nude woman being pushed head first into a meat grinder, her shapely thighs and legs poised above the opening to the grinder in a sexually receptive posture, while the rest comes out of the bottom as ground meat. The exaggeration of numbers in Kathleen Barry's chilling description hardly blunts its horror: "In movie after movie women are raped, ejaculated on, urinated on, anally penetrated, beaten, and, with the advent of snuff films, murdered in an orgy of sexual pleasure."[3] The examples, alas, are abundant and depressing. . . .

. . .

May the law legitimately be used to restrict the liberty of pornographers to produce and distribute, and their customers to purchase and use, erotic materials that are violently abusive of women? (I am assuming that no strong case can be made for the proscription of materials that are merely degrading in one of the relatively subtle and nonviolent ways.) Many feminists answer, often with reluctance, in the affirmative. Their arguments can be divided into two general classes. Some simply invoke the harm principle. Violent pornography wrongs and harms women, according to these arguments, either by defaming them as a group, or (more importantly) by inciting males to violent crimes against them or creating a cultural climate in which such crimes are likely to become more frequent. The two traditional legal categories involved in these harm-principle arguments, then, are *defamation* and *incitement*. The other class of arguments invoke[s] the offense principle, not in order to prevent mere "nuisances," but to prevent profound offense analogous to that of the Jews in Skokie or the blacks in a town where the K.K.K. rallies.

2. *Violent Pornography, the Cult of Macho, and Harm to Women*

I shall not spend much time on the claim that violent and other extremely degrading pornography should be banned on the ground that it *defames* women. In a skeptical spirit, I can begin by pointing out that there are immense difficulties in applying the civil law of libel and slander as it is presently constituted in such a way as not to violate freedom of expression. Problems with *criminal* libel and slander would be even more unmanageable, and *group* defamation, whether civil or criminal, would multiply the problems still further. The argument on the other side is that pornography is essentially propaganda—propaganda against women. It does not slander women in the technical legal sense by asserting damaging falsehoods about them, because it *asserts* nothing at all. But it spreads an image of women as mindless playthings or "objects," inferior beings fit only to be used and abused for the pleasure of men, whether they like it or not, but often to their own secret pleasure. This picture lowers the esteem men have for women, and for that reason (if defamation is the basis of the argument) is sufficient ground for proscription even in the absence of any evidence of tangible harm to women caused by the behavior of misled and deluded men.

If degrading pornography defames (libels or slanders) women, it must be in virtue of some beliefs

about women—false beliefs—that it conveys, so that in virtue of those newly acquired or reinforced false beliefs, consumers lower their esteem for women in general. If a work of pornography, for example, shows a woman (or group of women) in exclusively subservient or domestic roles, that may lead the consumer to *believe* that women, in virtue of some inherent female characteristics, are only fit for such roles. There is no doubt that much pornography does portray women in subservient positions, but if that is defamatory to women in anything like the legal sense, then so are soap commercials on TV. So are many novels, even some good ones. (A good novel may yet be about some degraded characters.) That some groups are portrayed in unflattering roles has not hitherto been a ground for the censorship of fiction or advertising. Besides, it is not clearly the *group* that is portrayed at all in such works, but only one individual (or small set of individuals) and fictitious ones at that. Are fat men defamed by Shakespeare's picture of Falstaff? Are Jews defamed by the characterization of Shylock? Could any writer today even hope to write a novel partly about a fawning corrupted black, under group defamation laws, without risking censorship or worse? The chilling effect on the practice of fiction-writing would amount to a near freeze. . . .

What looks like sexual subservience to some looks like liberation from sexual repression to others. It is hard to imagine how a court could provide a workable, much less fair, test of whether a given work has sufficiently damaged male esteem toward women for it to be judged criminally defamatory, when so much of the viewer's reaction he brings on himself, and viewer reactions are so widely variable.

It is not easy for a single work to defame successfully a group as large as 51% of the whole human race. (Could a misanthrope "defame" the whole human race by a false statement about "the nature of man"? Would every human being then be his "victim"?) Perhaps an unanswered barrage of thousands of tracts, backed by the prestige of powerful and learned persons without dissent might successfully defame any group no matter how large, but those conditions would be difficult to satisfy so long as there is freedom to speak back on the other side. In any case, defamation is not the true gravamen of the wrong that women in general suffer from extremely degrading pornography. When a magazine cover portrays a woman in a meat grinder, *all* women are insulted, degraded, even perhaps endangered, but few would naturally complain that they were *libeled* or *slandered*.

Those terms conceal the point of what has happened. If women are harmed by pornography, the harm is surely more direct and tangible than harm to "the interest in reputation."

The major argument for repression of violent pornography under the harm principle is that it promotes rape and physical violence. In the United States there is a plenitude both of sexual violence against women and of violent pornography. According to the F.B.I. Uniform Crime Statistics (as of 1980), a 12-year-old girl in the United States has one chance in three of being raped in her lifetime; studies only a few years earlier showed that the number of violent scenes in hard-core pornographic books was as high as 20% of the total, the number of violent cartoons and pictorials in leading pornographic magazines was as much as 10% of the total. This has suggested to some writers that there must be a direct causal link between violent pornography and sexual violence against women; but causal relationships between pornography and rape, if they exist, must be more complicated than that.

. . .

On the other hand, there is evidence that novel ways of committing crimes are often suggested (usually inadvertently) by bizarre tales in films or TV . . . , and even factual newspaper reports of crimes can trigger the well-known "copy-cat crime" phenomenon. But if the possibility of copy-cat cases, by itself, justified censorship or punishment, we would have grounds for suppressing films of *The Brothers Karamozov* and the TV series *Roots* (both of which have been cited as influences on imitative crimes). . . . A violent episode in a pornographic work may indeed be a causally necessary condition for the commission of some specific crime by a specific perpetrator on a specific victim at some specific time and place. But for his reading or viewing that episode, the perpetrator may not have done precisely what he did in just the time, place, and manner that he did it. But so large a part of the full causal explanation of his act concerns his own psychological character and predispositions, that it is likely that some similar crime would have suggested itself to him in due time. It is not likely that non-rapists are converted into rapists *simply* by reading and viewing pornography. If pornography has a serious causal bearing on the occurrence of rape (as opposed to the trivial copy-cat effect) it must be in virtue of its role (still to be established) in implanting the appropriate cruel dispositions in the first place.

Rape is such a complex social phenomenon that there is probably no one simple generalization to account for it. Some rapes are no doubt ineliminable, no matter how we design our institutions. Many of these are the product of deep individual psychological problems, transferred rages, and the like. But for others, perhaps the preponderant number, the major part of the explanation is sociological, not psychological. In these cases the rapist is a psychologically normal person well adjusted to his particular subculture, acting calmly and deliberately rather than in a rage, and doing what he thinks is expected of him by his peers, what he must do to acquire or preserve standing in his group. His otherwise inexplicable violence is best explained as a consequence of the peculiar form of his socialization among his peers, his pursuit of a prevailing ideal of manliness, what the Mexicans have long called *machismo,* but which exists to some degree or other among men in most countries, certainly in our own.

The macho male wins the esteem of his associates by being tough, fearless, reckless, wild, unsentimental, hard-boiled, hard drinking, disrespectful, profane, willing to fight whenever his honor is impugned, and fight without fear of consequences no matter how extreme. He is a sexual athlete who must be utterly dominant over "his" females, who are expected to be slavishly devoted to him even though he lacks gentleness with them and shows his regard only by displaying them like trophies; yet he is a hearty and loyal companion to his "teammates" (he is always on a "team" of some sort). Given the manifest harm the cult of macho has done to men, women, and to relations between men and women, it is difficult to account for its survival in otherwise civilized nations. Perhaps it is useful in time of war, and war has been a preoccupation of most generations of young men, in most nations, up to the present. If so, then the persistence of *machismo* is one of the stronger arguments we have (among many others) for the obsolescence of war.

The extreme character of macho values must be understood before any sense can be made of the appeal of violent pornography. The violent porn does not appeal to prurience or lust as such. Indeed, it does not appeal at all to a psychologically normal male who is not in the grip of the macho cult. In fact these pictures, stories, and films have no other function but to express and reinforce the macho ideology. "Get your sexual kicks," they seem to say, "but make sure you get them by humiliating the woman, and showing her who's boss. Make sure at all costs not to develop any tender feelings toward her that might give her a subtle form of control over you and thus destroy your standing with the group. Remember to act in the truly manly manner of a 'wild and crazy guy.'"

In her brilliant article on this subject, Sarah J. McCarthy cites some horrible examples from *Penthouse* magazine of the macho personality structure which is peculiarly receptive to, and a necessary condition for, the appeal of violent porn:

> "There's still something to be said for bashing a woman over the head, dragging her off behind a rock, and having her," said one of the guys in the February 1980 *Penthouse*. . . . "Women Who Flirt With Pain" was the cover hype for a *Penthouse* interview with an assortment of resident Neanderthals (a name that would swell them with pride).
>
> "We're basically rapists because we're created that way," proclaims Dale. "We're irrational, sexually completely crazy. Our sexuality is more promiscuous, more immediate, and more fleeting, possibly less deep. We're like stud bulls that want to mount everything in sight. . . ."

The letters-to-the-editor in the February *Penthouse* contains an ugly letter from someone who claims to be a sophomore at a large midwestern university and is "into throat-fucking." He writes of Kathy and how he was "ramming his huge eleven-inch tool down her throat." [Sexual bragging, pornography style.] Kathy "was nearly unconscious from coming." [Deceit and self-deception, pornography style.] Gloria Steinem writes in the May 1980 *Ms.*: "Since *Deep Throat*, a whole new genre of pornography has developed. Added to the familiar varieties of rape, there is now an ambition to rape the throat. . . ."

Another issue of *Penthouse* contains an article about what they have cleverly called "tossing." A college student from Albuquerque, who drives a 1974 Cadillac and who is "attracted to anything in a skirt," tells how it's done. "How did you get into tossing?" the *Penthouse* interviewer asks. "It just happened," says Daryl. "I was doing it in high school two years ago and didn't know what it was. I'd date a chick once, fuck her in my car, and just dump her out. Literally."[4]

These repugnant specimens are not examples of make-believe violent pornography. Rather, they are examples of the attitudes and practices of persons who are antecedently prone to be appreciative consumers of violent pornography. These grisly sentiments are perhaps found more commonly among working class youths in military barracks and factories but they are only slightly more familiar than similar bravado heard by middle class Americans in fraternity houses and dormitories. These remarks are usually taken as meant to impress their male auditors; they are uttered with a kind of aggressive pride. The quotations from *Penthouse* capture the tone exactly.

. . .

Would it significantly reduce sexual violence if violent pornography were effectively banned? No one can know for sure, but if the cult of macho is the main source of such violence, as I suspect, then repression of violent pornography, whose function is to pander to the macho values already deeply rooted in society, may have little effect. Pornography does not cause normal decent chaps, through a single exposure, to metamorphize into rapists. Pornography-reading machos commit rape, but that is because they already have macho values, not because they read the violent pornography that panders to them. Perhaps then *constant* exposure to violent porn might turn a decent person into a violence-prone macho. But that does not seem likely either, since the repugnant violence of the materials could not have any appeal in the first place to one who did not already have some strong macho predispositions, so "constant exposure" could not begin to become established. Clearly, other causes, and more foundational ones, must be at work, if violent porn is to have any initial purchase. Violent pornography is more a symptom of *machismo* than a cause of it, and treating symptoms merely is not a way to offer protection to potential victims of rapists. At most, I think there may be a small spill-over effect of violent porn on actual violence. Sometimes, a bizarre new sadistic trick (like "throat-fucking"?) is suggested by a work of violent pornography and taken up by those prone to cruel violence to begin with. More often, perhaps, the response to an inventive violent porno scene may be like that of the college *Penthouse* reader to "tossing": "I was doing it in high school two years ago, and I didn't know what it was." He read *Penthouse* and learned "what it was," but his conduct, presumably, was not significantly changed.

If my surmise about causal connections is correct they are roughly as indicated in the . . . diagram.

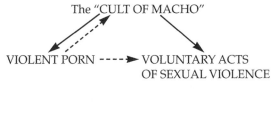

= causal direction

- - - ▶ = possible "spill-over effects"

The primary causal direction is not from violent pornography to violent real-life episodes. Neither is it from violent pornography to the establishment and reinforcement of macho values. Rather, the cult of macho expectations is itself the primary cause *both* of the existence of violent porn (it provides the appreciative audience) and of the real-life sexual violence (it provides the motive). The dotted arrows express my acknowledgement of the point that there might be some small spill-over effect from violent pornography back on the macho values that spawn it, in one direction, and on real-life violence in the other, but the pornography cannot be the primary causal generator. Sexual violence will continue to fester so long as the cult of macho flourishes, whether or not we eliminate legal violent pornography.

How then can we hope to weaken and then extirpate the cultish values at the root of our problem? The criminal law is a singularly ill-adapted tool for that kind of job. We might just as well legislate against entrepreneurship on the grounds that capitalism engenders "acquisitive personalities," or against the military on the grounds that it produces "authoritarian personalities," or against certain religious sects on the ground that they foster puritanism, as criminalize practices and institutions on the grounds that they contribute to *machismo*. But macho values are culturally, not instinctively, transmitted, and the behavior that expresses them is learned, not inherited, behavior. What is learned can be unlearned. Schools should play a role. Surely, learning to see through machismo and avoid its traps should be as important a part of a child's preparation for citizenship as the acquisition of patriotism and piety. To be effective, such teaching should be frank and direct, not totally reliant on general moral platitudes. It should talk about the genesis of children's attitudes toward the other sex, and invite discussion of male insecurity, resentment of women, cruelty, and even specific odious examples. Advertising firms and film companies should be asked (at first), then pressured (if necessary) to cooperate, as they did in the successful campaign to deglamorize cigarette smoking. Fewer exploitation films should be made that provide attractive models of youths flashing knives, playing chicken or Russian roulette, or "tossing" girls. Materials (especially films) should be made available to clergymen as well as teachers, youth counselors, and parole officers. A strong part of the emphasis of these materials should be on the harm that bondage to the cult of macho does to men too, and how treacherous a trap *machismo* can be. The new moral education must be careful, of course, not to preach dull prudence as a preferred style for youthful living. A zest for excitement, adventure, even danger, cannot be artificially removed from adolescent nature. Moreover, teamwork, camaraderie, and toughness of character need not be denigrated. But the cult of macho corrupts and distorts these values in ways that can be made clear to youths. The mistreatment of women, when its motivation is clearly revealed and understood, should be a sure way of eliciting the contempt of the group, not a means to greater prestige within it.

Rape is a harm and a severe one. Harm prevention is definitely a legitimate use of the criminal law. Therefore, if there is a clear enough causal connection to rape, a statute that prohibits violent pornography would be a morally legitimate restriction of liberty. But it is not enough to warrant suppression that pornography as a whole might have some harmful consequences to third parties, even though most specific instances of it do not.

. . .

Those instances of sexual violence which may be harmful side-effects of violent pornography are directly produced by criminals (rapists) acting voluntarily on their own. We already have on the statute books a firm prohibition of rape and sexual assault. If, in addition, the harm principle permits the criminalization of actions only indirectly related to the primary harm, such as producing, displaying or selling violent pornography, then there is a danger that the law will be infected with unfairness; for unless certain further conditions are fulfilled, the law will be committed to punishing some parties for the entirely voluntary criminal conduct of other parties. . . . Suppose that *A* wrongfully harms (e.g., rapes) *B* in circumstances such that (1) *A* acts fully voluntarily on his own initiative, and (2) nonetheless, but for what *C* has communicated to him, he would not have done what he did to *B*. Under what further conditions, we must ask, can *C* be rightfully held criminally responsible along with *A* for the harm to *B*? Clearly *C* can be held responsible if the information he communicated was helpful assistance to *A* and intended to be such. In that case *C* becomes a kind of collaborator. Under traditional law, *C* can also incur liability if what he communicated to *A* was some kind of encouragement to commit a crime against *B*. The clearest cases are those in which *C* solicits *A*'s commission of the criminal act by offering inducements to him. "Encouragement" is also criminal when it takes the form of active urging. Sometimes mere advice to commit the act counts as an appropriate sort of encouragement. When the encouragement takes a general form, and the harmful crime is recommended to "the general reader" or an indefinite audience, then the term "advocacy" is often used. Advocating criminal conduct is arguably a way of producing such conduct, and is thus often itself a crime. An article in a pornographic magazine advocating the practice of rape (as opposed to advocating a legislative change of the rape laws) would presumably be a crime if its intent were serious and its audience presumed to be impressionable to an appropriately dangerous degree.

Violent pornography, however, does not seem to fit any of these models. Its authors and vendors do not solicit rapes; nor do they urge or advise rapes; nor do they advocate rape. If some of their customers, some of the time, might yet "find encouragement" in their works to commit rapes because rape has been portrayed in a way that happens to be alluring to them, that is their own affair, the pornographer might insist, and their own responsibility.

. . .

3. *Violent Pornography and Profound Offense*

The harm principle grounds for legally banning pornography do not appear sufficient. Does the offense principle do any better? Pornographic displays *can* be public nuisances, of course, and when the balancing tests tip in the nuisance direction, the offending activities may fairly be prohibited, or redirected to less offensive channels. The manner in which degrading and violent pornography offends women (and men who support women's rights) is substantially different from that in which erotica as such offend the prudish. The shame, embarrassment, shock, disgust, and irritation of the latter group can be effectively avoided if the erotic displays are concealed from their view. The offense to a woman's sensibilities when her whole sex is treated as grist for the meat grinder, however, is deeply repugnant to her moral sensibilities whether out of view or not. Feminist writers often make this point by means of analogies to racist literature and films.

Suppose some unscrupulous promoters decide that they can make large profits by pandering to the latent hatred against blacks which they suppose to be endemic in a substantial minority of the white community. Since explicitly racist remarks and overt racist behavior are no longer widely acceptable in American society, many secret black-haters might enjoy an occasional night at the movies where they can enjoy to their heart's content specially made films that lampoon minstrel-style "darkies" "with wide eyes as white as moons, hair shot straight in the air like Buckwheat's, afraid of everything—spiders, [their] own shadows, ghosts."[5] So much for comic openers. The main features could be stories of uppity blacks put in their place by righteous whites, taunted and hounded, tarred and feathered, tortured and castrated, and in the climactic scenes, hung up on gallows to the general rejoicing of their betters. The aim of the films would be to provide a delicious catharsis of pent-up hatred. It would be prudent, on business grounds, to keep advertisements discreet, and to use euphemistic descriptions like "folk films" (analogous to "adult films").

I don't imagine that many blacks would be placated by the liberal lawmaker who argues in support of his refusal to enact prohibitive legislation that there is little evidence of actual harm done to blacks by the films, that they do not advocate violence to blacks or incite mobs to fury, and that for all we know they will make the racists less dangerous by providing a harmless outlet for their anti-social impulses. Neither would many blacks be assuaged by the liberal assurance that we should all be wary of possible harmful effects anyway, continue to look for evidence thereof, and use educational campaigns as a more effective means of exposing the evils of racism. "That is all well and good," the blacks might reply, "but first we must lance this painful boil on our sensibilities. The 'folk films,' whether we are in the audience or not, are morally abominable affronts to us. Their very existence in our midst is a perpetual laceration of our feelings. We aren't present to be humiliated, but they degrade the very atmosphere in which we breathe and move."

The analogy to violent pornographic films is close though not perfect. (It is an interesting fact to ponder that although there undoubtedly is a large racist underground in this country, no promoter has yet found a way of exploiting it in the manner of our example.) The pornographic films do serve an erotic interest of their customers, and that gives them, *ceteris paribus*, a personal value greater perhaps than that of the "folk films." The racist films, on the other hand, may be easier to disguise as genuine works of drama, thus making it much more difficult for a line to be drawn between them and genuine attempts at dramas about odious people and their victims. The bare-knowledge offense in the two cases seems almost equally profound, going well beyond anything called "mere nuisance," to touch the chord of moral sensibility.

It does not express an unsympathetic attitude toward the offended parties, however, to deny a basis in either the harm or offense principles for the use of legal force to "lance the boil." Profound offense . . . , is either an impersonal and disinterested moral outrage or else an aggrieved response on one's own behalf because of the unpleasant mental states one has been forced to experience. If it is an impersonal response, then it can warrant legal force against its cause only on the basis of the principle of legal moralism which is unacceptable to liberals. We would have to argue in that case that the very showing of violent films to appreciative audiences is an evil in itself and one of such magnitude that it can be rightly prevented by legal force if necessary, even though it is not the kind of evil that *wrongs* anyone. . . . If, on the other hand, the profound offense is a felt personal wrong voiced on one's own behalf as its "victim," then the complaint is that the offending materials cause one to suffer unpleasant states that are a nuisance to avoid. But that offense will not have much weight on the scales if one is not forced to witness the showings, or lurid announcements of the showings, and is not forced to take irritating and inconveniencing detours to avoid them. The offense principle, in short, will not warrant legal prohibition

of the films unless the offense they cause is not reasonably avoidable. It is only in its character as disinterested moral outrage that it is not reasonably avoidable, but we cannot ban everything that is thought to be outrageous, whether right-violating or not, without recourse to legal moralism.

. . .

Racist and porno films do not directly insult specific individuals, but rather large groups, thus diluting the impact of the insult, or at least its directed personal character, proportionately. The "folk films" might be more serious affronts in this respect than the porno films since their target is a much smaller group than half of the human race, and one which has historically been brutalized by slavery and cruel repression. A black man might be more likely to feel a *personal* grievance at the folk film he does not witness than a woman would to a porno film she does not witness, for these reasons. This personal aspect of his offense would overlay the more general disinterested moral indignation he shares with the women who are offended by their bare knowledge of the existence of violent pornographic displays. Nonetheless, understandable as the black's felt grievance may be, the insulting film shown to a willing audience in a private or commercial theatre is in the same boat as the insulting conversations among willing friends in a private home or club. In both cases the conduct is morally execrable, but in neither case do liberal principles warrant state intervention to punish the mischief.

. . .

Endnotes

[1] Gloria Steinem, "Erotica and Pornography, A Clear and Present Difference," *Ms.*, November, 1978, p. 54.

[2] Lisa Lehrman, *op. cit.* (footnote 2), pp. 181–82.

[3] Kathleen Barry, *Female Sexual Slavery* (New York: Avon Books, 1979), p. 206.

[4] Sarah J. McCarthy, "Pornography, Rape, and the Cult of Macho," *The Humanist*, Sept./Oct., 1980, p. 15.

[5] *Ibid.*, p. 11.

Pornography: On Morality and Politics

Catherine MacKinnon

Possession and use of women through the sexualization of intimate intrusion and access to them is a central feature of women's social definition as inferior and feminine. Visual and verbal intrusion, access, possession, and use is predicated upon and produces physical and psychic intrusion, access, possession, and use. In contemporary industrial society, pornography is an industry that mass produces sexual intrusion on, access to, possession and use of women by and for men for profit. It exploits women's sexual and economic inequality for gain. It sells women to men as and for sex. It is a technologically sophisticated traffic in women.

This understanding of the reality of pornography must contend not only with centuries of celebratory intellectual obfuscation. It must contend with a legal tradition of neutralization through abstraction from the realities of power, a tradition that has authoritatively defined pornography as not about women as such at all, but about sex, hence about morality, and as not about acts or practices, but about ideas. Uncovering gender in this area of law reveals women to be most invisible when most exposed and most silent when used in defense of speech. In both pornography and the law of obscenity, women are seen only as sex and heard only when mouthing a sexual script. When pornography and the law of pornography are investigated together, it becomes clear that pornography is to women's status, hence its critique is to feminism, as its preservation is to male supremacy in its liberal legal guise.

The law of obscenity is the state's approach to addressing the pornography problem, which it construes as an issue of regulation of expression under the First Amendment. Nudity, explicitness, excess of

candor, arousal or excitement, prurience, unnaturalness—these qualities raise concerns under obscenity law when sex is depicted or portrayed. . . . Obscenity as such probably does little harm. Pornography contributes causally to attitudes and behaviors of violence and discrimination which define the treatment and status of half the population.

Obscenity law is concerned with morality, meaning good and evil, virtue and vice. The concerns of feminism with power and powerlessness are first political, not moral. From the feminist perspective, obscenity is a moral idea; pornography is a political practice. Obscenity is abstract; pornography is concrete. Obscenity conveys moral condemnation as a predicate to legal condemnation. Pornography identifies a political practice that is predicated on power and powerlessness—a practice that is, in fact, legally protected. The two concepts represent two entirely different things.

In accounting for gender inequality as part of the socially constructed relationship between power—the political—on the one hand and knowledge of truth and reality—the epistemological—on the other, the classic description Justice Stewart once offered of the obscenity standard, "I know it when I see it,"[1] becomes even more revealing than it is usually taken to be. Taken as a statement that connects epistemology with power, if one asks, from the point of view of women's experience, does he know what women know when we see what we see, one has to doubt it, given what is on the newsstands. How does his point of view keep what is there, there? To liberal critics, his admission exposed the relativity, the partiality, the insufficient abstractness of the obscenity standard. Not to be emptily universal, to leave your concreteness showing, is a sin among men. Their problem with Justice Stewart's formulation is that it implies that anything, capriciously, could be suppressed. In fact, almost nothing is. The meaning of what his view permits, as it turns out, is anything but capricious. It is entirely systematic and determinate. His statement is

From Catherine MacKinnon, *Toward a Feminist Theory of the State* (Cambridge: Harvard University Press, 1989), pp. 195–214. Reprinted by permission of the author.

precisely descriptively accurate; its candor is why it has drawn so much criticism. He admitted what courts do epistemologically all the time. In so doing, he both did it and gave it the stature of doctrine (if only dictum). That is, he revealed that the obscenity standard—and it is not unique—is built on what the male standpoint sees. The problem is, so is pornography. In this way, the law of obscenity reproduces the pornographic point of view of women on the level of constitutional jurisprudence.

Pornography, in the feminist view, is a form of forced sex, a practice of sexual politics, an institution of gender inequality. In this perspective, pornography, with the rape and prostitution in which it participates, institutionalizes the sexuality of male supremacy, which fuses the eroticization of dominance and submission with the social construction of male and female. Gender is sexual. Pornography constitutes the meaning of that sexuality. Men treat women as whom they see women as being. Pornography constructs who that is. Men's power over women means that the way men see women defines who women can be. Pornography is that way. In this light, obscenity law can be seen to treat morals from the male point of view, meaning the standpoint of male dominance. The feminist critique of pornography, by contrast, proceeds from women's point of view, meaning the standpoint of the subordination of women to men.

. . .

Obscenity law proposes to control what and how sex can be publicly shown. In practice, its standard centers upon the same features that feminism and pornography both reveal as key to male sexuality: the erect penis and penetration. Historically, obscenity law was vexed by restricting such portrayals while protecting great literature. (Nobody considered protecting women.) Solving this problem by exempting works of perceived value, obscenity restrictions relaxed—some might say collapsed—revealing a significant shift in the last decade. Under the old law, pornography was publicly repudiated yet privately consumed and actualized: do anything to women with impunity in private behind a veil of public denial and civility. Under the new law, in a victory for Freudian derepression, pornography is publicly celebrated. The old private rules have become the new public rules. Women were sex and are still sex. Greater efforts of brutality have become necessary to eroticize the taboo—each taboo being a hierarchy in disguise— since the frontier of the taboo keeps vanishing as one crosses it. Put another way, more and more violence

has become necessary to keep the progressively desensitized consumer aroused to the illusion that sex (and he) is daring and dangerous. Making sex with the powerless "not allowed" is a way of keeping "getting it" defined as an act of power, an assertion of hierarchy, which keeps it sexy in a sexual system in which hierarchy is sexy. In addition, pornography has become ubiquitous. Sexual terrorism has become democratized. Pornography has become truly available to women for the first time in history. Among other effects, this central mechanism of sexual subordination, this means of systematizing the definition of women as a sexual class, has now become available to its victims for scrutiny and analysis as an open public system, not just as a private secret abuse. Hopefully, this was a mistake.

. . .

In 1973, obscenity under law came to mean that which "the average person applying contemporary standards, would find that, taken as a whole, appeals to the prurient interest; that [which] depicts or describes, in a patently offensive way, sexual conduct as defined by the applicable state law; and that which, taken as a whole, lacks serious literary, artistic, political, or scientific value." Feminism doubts whether "the average person," gender neutral, exists; has more questions about the content and process of definition of community standards than about deviations from them; wonders why prurience counts but powerlessness does not, why sensibilities are better protected from offense than women are from exploitation; defines sexuality, hence its violation and expropriation, more broadly than does any state law; and wonders why a body of law which cannot in practice tell rape from intercourse should be entrusted with telling pornography from anything less. In feminist perspective, one notices that although the law of obscenity says that sex on streetcorners is not supposed to be legitimated "by the fact that the persons are simultaneously engaged in a valid political dialogue,"[2] the requirement that the work be considered "as a whole" legitimates something very like that on the level of publications such as *Playboy*,[3] even though experimental evidence is beginning to support what victims have long known: legitimate settings diminish the injury perceived to be done to the women whose trivialization and objectification it contextualizes. Besides, if a woman is subjected, why should it matter that the work has other value? Perhaps what redeems a work's value among men enhances its injury to women. Existing standards of literature, art, science, and politics are, in feminist light, remarkably consonant with pornography's mode, meaning, and message. Finally and foremost, a feminist approach reveals that although the content and dynamic of pornography concerns women—the sexuality of women, women as sexuality—in the same way that the vast majority of "obscenities" refer specifically to women's bodies, women's invisibility has been such that the law of obscenity has never even considered pornography a women's issue.

To appeal to "prurient interest" means to give a man an erection. Men are scared to make it possible for some men to tell other men what they can and cannot have sexual access to, because men have power. Men believe that if you do not let them have theirs, they might not let you have yours. This is why the indefinability of pornography—all the "one man's this is another man's that"—is so central to pornography's definition. It is not because all men are such great liberals, but because those other men might be able to do to them whatever *they* can do to *them,* which may explain why the liberal principle is what it is.

What this frame on the issue obscures, because the fought-over are invisible, is that the fight over a definition of pornography is a fight among men over the terms of access to women, hence over the best means to guarantee male power as a system. The tacit questions become: Whose sexual practices threaten this system? Are they men whose sexual access can be sacrificed in the interest of maintaining it for the rest? Public sexual access by men to anything other than women is far less likely to be protected speech. This is not to say that male sexual access to anything—children, other men, women with women, objects, animals—is not the real rule. The issue is rather how public, hence how express in law, that system will be.

In this light, the "prurient interest" prong of the obscenity standard has a built-in bind. To find prurience as a fact, someone has to admit sexual arousal by the materials; but male sexual arousal signals the importance of protection. Men put themselves in this position and then wonder why they cannot agree. Sometimes it seems that what is obscene is what does not turn on the Supreme Court, or what revolts them more, which is rare, since revulsion is eroticized. Sometimes it seems that what is obscene is what turns on those men whom the men in power think they can afford to ignore. Sometimes it seems that what is obscene is what makes dominant men see themselves as momentary potential targets of male sexual aggression. Sometimes it seems that anything can be done to

a woman, but obscenity is sex that makes male sexuality look bad.

Courts' difficulties in framing workable standards to separate "prurient" from other sexual interest, commercial exploitation from art or advertising, sexual speech from sexual conduct, and obscenity from great literature make the feminist point. These lines have proved elusive in law because they do not exist in life. Commercial sex resembles art because both exploit women's sexuality. The liberal slippery slope is the feminist totality. Politically speaking, whatever obscenity may do, pornography converges with more conventionally acceptable depictions and descriptions just as rape does with intercourse, because both are acts within the same power relation. Just as it is difficult to distinguish literature or art against a background, a standard, of objectification, it is difficult to discern sexual freedom against a background, a standard, of sexual coercion. This does not mean that it cannot be done. It means that legal standards will be practically unenforceable, will reproduce this problem rather than solve it, until they address its fundamental issue—gender inequality—directly.

To define the pornographic as the "patently offensive" further misconstrues its harm. Pornography is not bad manners or poor choice of audience; obscenity is. Pornography is also not an idea; obscenity is. The legal fiction whereby the obscene is "not speech" has deceived few; it has effectively avoided the need to adjudicate pornography's social etiology. But obscenity law got one thing right: pornography is more actlike than thoughtlike. The fact that pornography, in a feminist view, furthers the idea of the sexual inferiority of women, a political idea, does not make pornography a political idea. That one can express the idea a practice expresses does not make that practice an idea. Pornography is not an idea any more than segregation or lynching are ideas, although both institutionalize the idea of the inferiority of one group to another. The law considers obscenity deviant, antisocial. If it causes harm, it causes antisocial acts, acts against the social order. In a feminist perspective, pornography is the essence of a sexist social order, its quintessential social act. . . .

The success, therefore the harm, of pornography, is invisible to the male state in its liberal guise and so has been defined out of the customary approach taken to, and the dominant values underlying, the First Amendment. The theory of the First Amendment under which most pornography is protected from governmental restriction proceeds from liberal assumptions that do not apply to the situation of women. First Amendment theory, like virtually all liberal legal theory, presumes the validity of the distinction between public and private: the "role of law [is] to make and guard the line between the sphere of social power, organized in the form of the state, and the arena of private right." On this basis, courts distinguish between obscene billboards ("thrust upon the unwilling viewer") and the private possession of obscenity at home. The problem is that not only the public but also the private is a "sphere of social power" of sexism. On paper and in life, pornography is thrust upon unwilling women in their homes. The distinction between public and private does not cut the same for women as for men. As a result, it is men's right to inflict pornography upon women in private that is protected.

The liberal theory underlying First Amendment law proceeds on the belief that free speech, including pornography, helps discover truth. Censorship, in its view, restricts society to partial truths. Laissez-faire might be an adequate theory of the social preconditions for knowledge in a nonhierarchical society. In a society of gender inequality, the speech of the powerful impresses its view upon the world, concealing the truth of powerlessness under a despairing acquiescence that provides the appearance of consent and makes protest inaudible as well as rare. Pornography can invent women because it has the power to make its vision into reality, which then passes, objectively, for truth. So while the First Amendment supports pornography on the belief that consensus and progress are facilitated by allowing all views, however divergent and unorthodox, it fails to notice that pornography (like the racism, including anti-Semitism, of the Nazis and the Klan) is not at all divergent or unorthodox. It is the ruling ideology. Feminism, the dissenting view, is suppressed by pornography. Thus, while defenders of pornography argue that allowing all speech, including pornography, frees the mind to fulfill itself, pornography freely enslaves women's minds and bodies inseparably, normalizing the terror that enforces silence on women's point of view.

In liberalism, speech must never be sacrificed for other social goals. But liberalism has never understood this reality of pornography: the free so-called speech of men silences the free speech of women. It is the same social goal, just other people. This is what a real inequality, a real conflict, a real disparity in social power looks like. First, women do not simply have freedom of speech on a social level. The most basic

assumption underlying First Amendment adjudication is that, socially, speech is free. The First Amendment itself says, "Congress shall make no law . . . abridging the freedom of speech." Free speech exists. The problem for government is to avoid constraining that which, if unconstrained by government, is free. This tends to presuppose that whole segments of the population are not systematically silenced socially, prior to government action. Second, the law of the First Amendment comprehends that freedom of expression, in the abstract, is a system but fails to comprehend that sexism (and racism), in the concrete, are also systems. As a result, it cannot grasp that the speech of some silences the speech of others in a way that is not simply a matter of competition for airtime. That pornography chills women's expression is difficult to demonstrate empirically because silence is not eloquent. Yet on no more of the same kind of evidence, the argument that suppressing pornography might chill legitimate speech has supported its protection.

First Amendment logic has difficulty grasping harm that is not linearly caused in the "John hit Mary" sense. The idea is that words or pictures can be harmful only if they produce harm in a form that is considered an action. Words work in the province of attitudes, actions in the realm of behavior. Words cannot constitute harm in themselves—never mind libel, invasion of privacy, blackmail, bribery, conspiracy, most sexual harassment, and most discrimination. What is saying "yes" in Congress—a word or an act? What is saying "Kill" to a trained guard dog? What is its training? What is saying "You're fired" or "We have enough of your kind around here"? What is a sign that reads "Whites Only"? What is a real estate advertisement that reads "Churches Nearby"? What is a "Help Wanted—Male" ad? What is a letter that states: "Constituent interests dictate that the understudy to my administrative assistant be a man"? What is "Sleep with me and I'll give you an 'A'"? These words, printed or spoken, are so far from legally protecting the cycle of events they actualize that they are regarded as evidence that acts occurred, in some cases as actionable in themselves. Is a woman raped by an attitude or a behavior? Which is sexual arousal? Which is cross burning? The difficulty of the distinction in the abstract has not prevented the law from acting when the consequences were seen to matter. When words are tantamount to acts, they are treated as acts.

· · ·

The dominant view is that pornography must cause harm just as car accidents cause harm, or its effects are not cognizable as harm. The trouble with this individuated, atomistic, linear, exclusive, isolated, narrowly tortlike—in a word, positivistic—conception of injury is that the way pornography targets and defines women for abuse and discrimination does not work like this. It does hurt individuals, just not as individuals in a one-at-a-time sense, but as members of the group *women*. Individual harm is caused one woman and not another essentially as one number rather than another is caused in roulette; but on a group basis, the harm is absolutely selective and systematic. Its causality is essentially collective and totalistic and contextual. To reassert atomistic linear causality as a sine qua non of injury—you cannot be harmed unless you are harmed through this etiology—is to refuse to respond to the true nature of this specific kind of harm. Such refusals call for explanation. Morton Horowitz has written that the issue of causality in tort law is "one of the pivotal ideas in a system of legal thought that sought to separate private law from politics and to insulate the legal system from the threat of redistribution." Perhaps causality in the law of obscenity is an attempt to privatize the injury pornography does to women in order to insulate the same system from the threat of gender equality.

Women are known to be brutally coerced into pornographic performances. But so far it is only with children, usually male children, that courts see that the speech of pornographers was once someone else's life. Courts and commissions and legislatures and researchers have searched largely in vain for the injury of pornography in the mind of the (male) consumer or in "society," or in empirical correlations between variations in levels of "antisocial' acts and liberalization in obscenity laws. Speech can be regulated "in the interest of unwilling viewers, captive audiences, young children, and beleaguered neighborhoods," but the normal level of sexual force—force that is not seen as force because it is inflicted on women and called sex—has never been a policy issue in the pornography area. Until the last few years experimental research never approached the question of whether pornographic stimuli might support sexual aggression against women or whether violence per se might be sexually stimulating or have sexual sequelae. Research is just beginning on the consequences for women of sexual depictions that show consensual dominance and submission. We know the least about the impact of female-only nudity, depictions of specific acts like penetration, or sex that appears mutual in a social context of gender inequality. We know even less about

why sex—that is, women—*must*, seemingly, be experienced through a traffic in pictures and words.

. . .

Because obscenity law so evades the reality of pornography, it is difficult to show that the male state, hegemonically liberal whether in the hands of conservatives or of liberals, actually protects pornography. The deception that the state is hostile to sexual derepression and eager to repress pornography, the fantasy that an authoritarian state restricts pornography rather than protects it, lay clearly exposed when the courts were confronted with the real damage pornography does to women's status and treatment as the basis for making it civilly actionable to its victims. The courts accepted the harm but held the pornography more important than those it harms—hence protected it as speech. In *American Booksellers Assn. Inc. v. Hudnut* the Seventh Circuit Court of Appeals held that an ordinance that makes the injuries of pornography actionable as sex inequality is unconstitutional under the First Amendment because it prohibits expression of a point of view.[4]

Acts became ideas and politics became morals as the court transformed coercion, force, assault, and trafficking in subordination into "thought control" and second-class citizenship on the basis of gender into "ideas that can be expressed about sexuality."[5] Obscenity law, which is based upon nothing but value judgments about morality, was presented as the standard for constitutional point-of-viewlessness. The court saw legal intervention against acts (most of which are already crimes) as "point of view" discrimination without doubting the constitutionality of state intervention against obscenity, which has no connection with acts and is expressly defined on the basis of point of view about sex. The court saw civil action by individual women as censorship threatening freedom, yet saw no threat to freedom and no censorship in criminal prosecutions of obscenity. When is a point of view not a point of view? When it is yours—especially when your words, like those of the pornographers, are words in power. In the epistemologically hermetic doublethink of the male point of view, prohibiting advances toward sex equality under law is state neutrality. From the male standpoint, it looks neutral because the state mirrors the inequality of the social world. Under the aegis of this neutrality, state protection of pornography becomes official policy.

The law of pornography thus has the same surface theme and the same underlying theme as pornography itself. Superficially both involve morality: rules made and transgressed for purposes of sexual arousal.

Actually, both are about power: the equation between the erotic and the control of women by men, *women* made and transgressed for purposes of sexual arousal. It seems essential to the kick of pornography that it be to some degree against the rules, but never truly unavailable or truly illegitimate. Thus obscenity law, like the law of rape, preserves both the value and the ability to get what it purports to devalue and restrict access to by prohibition. Obscenity law helps keep pornography sexy by putting state power—force, hierarchy—behind its purported prohibition on what men can have sexual access to. The law of obscenity is to pornography as pornography is to sex: a map that purports to be a mirror, a practice that pretends to represent a practice, a legitimation and authorization and set of directions and guiding controls that project themselves onto social reality, while purporting merely to reflect an image of what is already there. Pornography presents itself as fantasy or illusion or idea, which can be good or bad as it is accurate or inaccurate while it actually, hence accurately, distributes power. Liberal morality cannot deal with illusions that constitute reality because its theory of reality, lacking a substantive critique of the distribution of social power, cannot get behind the empirical word, truth by correspondence. On the surface, both pornography and the law of obscenity are about sex. But it is the status of women that is at stake.

Endnotes

[1] *Jacobellis v. Ohio*, 378 U.S. 184, 197 (1964) (Stewart, J., concurring).

[2] *Paris Adult Theatre I v. Slayton*, 413 U.S. 49, 67 (1973). See also "a quotation from Voltaire in the fly-leaf of a book will not constitutionally redeem an other-wise obscene publication." *Kois v. Wisconsin*, 408 U.S. 229, 231 (1972), quoted in *Miller v. California*, 413 U.S. at 25 n. 7.

[3] *Penthouse International v. McAuliffe*, 610 F. 2d 1353 (5th Cir. 1980). For a study in enforcement, see *Coble v. City of Birmingham*, 389 Sol. 2d 527 (Ala. Ct. App. 1980).

[4] *American Booksellers Assn., Inc. v. Hudnut*, 771 F. 2d 323 (7th Cir. 1985).

[5] 771 F. 2d at 328.

Study Questions

1. The court majority in *Ashcroft v. The Free Speech Coalition* asserts that the CPPA is overbroad because it "prohibits speech that records no crime and creates no victims by its production." Do you agree? Do you think MacKinnon would agree?

2. Does the majority in *The Free Speech Coalition* give sufficient credit, in your view, to the contentions of the CPPA's backers that the production and consumption of virtual child pornography is likely to "whet the sexual appetites" of pedophiles, "thereby increasing the creation and distribution of child pornography and the sexual abuse and exploitation of actual children"?

3. The court in *Hudnut* declares that the Indianapolis anti-pornography ordinance is a form of "thought-control." How does the court arrive at this conclusion?

4. How does the *Hudnut* court respond to the feminist argument that pornography is a practice whose result is the continuation and deepening of the subordination and domination of women by men? Do you find the court's response convincing?

5. On what grounds does Feinberg criticize the courts' confusion of pornography with obscenity?

6. What, according to Feinberg, are the causal relationships between pornography (especially violent pornography) and the "cult of macho"? Is Feinberg's defense of his view of the causal relationship sound?

7. Imagine a video store run by the Ku Klux Klan. The store sells racist videos, magazines, and films with titles such as *Beat Them Niggers,* in which whites are shown (among other things) verbally abusing, beating, and urinating upon blacks. Should the distribution and sale of such materials be allowed? Is there a difference, relevant for First Amendment purposes, between these kinds of films and the examples of violent pornography described by Feinberg and MacKinnon?

8. Some courts have argued for a shift in the law away from an exclusive focus upon the viewers of pornography and toward its participants, who are often victims of the industry. People like MacKinnon want to protect those who are exploited by pornographers. In a 1982 case, the Supreme Court ruled unanimously that "child pornography"—sexually explicit films depicting children involved in sex acts—deserves no constitutional protection. The Court's argument summed up a number of factors concerning child pornography that place it

outside the protection of the First Amendment: the need to safeguard the physical and psychological well-being of minors; the claim that pornographic material is "intrinsically" related to the sexual abuse of children; and the fact that child pornography has no literary, scientific, or educational value. Could it be argued that the same factors apply in the case of women who participate in the making of pornography? If not, why not? Could it be argued that the women who participate in the pornography industry are being harmed, even though many of them may not fully realize that fact, just as the children involved in "kiddie porn" are being harmed without their awareness?

Cases for Further Reflection
Griswold v. Connecticut

Griswold is often cited as the foundation of modern "substantive due process" jurisprudence, sometimes referred to as "privacy" cases. Questions to consider as you read this case: Does Justice Douglas's appeal to the "penumbras and emanations" of the Bill of Rights in *Griswold* constitute good constitutional interpretation, in your view? Is such an appeal a license to ignore the text of the Constitution? Why or why not? Take note of the Third Amendment, which prohibits the quartering of soldiers in someone's home without the owner's consent, and of the Fourth Amendment, which guarantees the right "of the people to be secure in their person, houses, papers, and effects, against unreasonable searches and seizures." Note that the kind of intrusion prohibited by both amendments is a physical intrusion, not a regulation of behavior. Is it stretching the meaning of these amendments to make them prohibit statutes regulating behavior, as the Connecticut statute did?

Douglas, [Justice].

Appellant Griswold is Executive Director of the Planned Parenthood League of Connecticut. Appellant Buxton is a licensed physician and a professor at the Yale Medical School who served as Medical Director for the League at its Center in New Haven—a center open and operating from November 1 to November 10, 1961, when appellants were arrested.

They gave information, instruction, and medical advice to *married persons* as to the means of preventing conception. They examined the wife and prescribed the best contraceptive device or material for her use. Fees were usually charged, although some couples were serviced free.

The statutes whose constitutionality is involved in this appeal are §§53-32 and 54-196 of the General Statutes of Connecticut (1958 rev.). The former provides: "Any person who uses any drug, medicinal article or instrument for the purpose of preventing conception shall be fined not less than fifty dollars or imprisoned not less than sixty days nor more than one year or be both fined and imprisoned."

Section 54-196 provides: "Any person who assists, abets, counsels, causes, hires or commands another to commit any offense may be prosecuted and punished as if he were the principal offender."

The appellants were found guilty as accessories and fined $100 each, against the claim that the accessory statute as so applied violated the Fourteenth Amendment. The Appellate Division of the Circuit Court affirmed. The Supreme Court of Errors affirmed that judgment. We noted probable jurisdiction. . . .

381 U.S. 479 (1965), United States Supreme Court.

Coming to the merits, we are met with a wide range of questions that implicate the Due Process Clause of the Fourteenth Amendment. Overtones of some arguments suggest that *Lochner v. New York* should be our guide. But we decline that invitation. . . . We do not sit as a superlegislature to determine the wisdom, need, and propriety of laws that touch economic problems, business affairs, or social conditions. This law, however, operates directly on an intimate relation of husband and wife and their physician's role in one aspect of that relation.

The association of people is not mentioned in the Constitution nor in the Bill of Rights. The right to educate a child in a school of the parents' choice—whether public or private or parochial—is also not mentioned. Nor is the right to study any particular subject or any foreign language. Yet the First Amendment has been construed to include certain of those rights.

By *Pierce v. Society of Sisters* the right to educate one's children as one chooses is made applicable to the States by the force of the First and Fourteenth Amendments. By *Meyer v. Nebraska* the same dignity is given the right to study the German language in a private school. In other words, the State may not consistently with the spirit of the First Amendment, contract the spectrum of available knowledge. The right of freedom of speech and press includes not only the right to utter or to print, but the right to distribute, the right to receive, the right to read and freedom of inquiry, freedom of thought, and freedom to teach—indeed the freedom of the entire university community. Without those peripheral rights the specific rights would be less secure. And so we reaffirm the principle of the *Pierce* and the *Meyer* cases.

In *NAACP v. Alabama*, 357 U.S. 449 (1958), we protected the "freedom to associate and privacy in one's associations," noting that freedom of association was a peripheral First Amendment right. Disclosure of membership lists of a constitutionally valid association, we held, was invalid, "as entailing the likelihood of a substantial restraint upon the exercise by petitioner's members of their right to freedom of association." In other words, the First Amendment has a penumbra where privacy is protected from governmental intrusion. In like context, we have protected forms of "association" that are not political in the customary sense but pertain to the social, legal, and economic benefit of the members [*NAACP v. Button*, 371 U.S. 415 (1963)]. In *Schware v. Board of Bar Examiners*, 353 U.S. 232 (1957), we held it not permissible to bar a lawyer from practice, because he had once been a member of the Communist Party. . . .

Those cases involved more than the "right of assembly"—a right that extends to all irrespective of their race or ideology. The right of "association," like the right of belief, is more than the right to attend a meeting; it includes the right to express one's attitudes or philosophies by membership in a group or by affiliation with it or by other lawful means. Association in that context is a form of expression of opinion; and while it is not expressly included in the First Amendment its existence is necessary in making the express guarantees fully meaningful.

The foregoing cases suggest that specific guarantees in the Bill of Rights have penumbras, formed by emanations from those guarantees that help give them life and substance. . . . Various guarantees create zones of privacy. The right of association contained in the penumbra of the First Amendment is one, as we have seen. The Third Amendment in its prohibition against the quartering of soldiers "in any house" in time of peace without the consent of the owner is another facet of that privacy. The Fourth Amendment explicitly affirms the "right of the people to be secure in their persons, houses, papers, and effects, against unreasonable searches and seizures." The Fifth Amendment in its Self-Incrimination Clause enables the citizen to create a zone of privacy under which government may not force him to surrender to his detriment. The Ninth Amendment provides: "The enumeration in the Constitution, of certain rights, shall not be construed to deny or disparage others retained by the people."

The Fourth and Fifth Amendments were described in *Boyd v. United States*, 116 U.S. 616 (1886), as protection against all governmental invasions "of the sanctity of a man's home and the privacies of life." We recently referred . . . to the Fourth Amendment as creating a "right to privacy, no less important than any other right carefully and particularly reserved to the people." . . .

The present case, then, concerns a relationship lying within the zone of privacy created by several fundamental constitutional guarantees. And it concerns a law which, in forbidding the use of contraceptives rather than regulating their manufacture or sale, seeks to achieve its goals by means having a maximum destructive impact upon that relationship. Such a law cannot stand in light of the familiar principle, so often applied by this Court, that a "governmental purpose to control or prevent activities constitutionally subject to state regulation may not be achieved by means which sweep unnecessarily broadly and thereby invade the area of protected freedoms." . . . Would we allow the police to search the sacred precincts of marital bedrooms for telltale signs of the use of contraceptives? The very idea is repulsive to the notions of privacy surrounding the marriage relationship.

We deal with a right of privacy older than the Bill of Rights—older than our political parties, older than our school system. Marriage is a coming together for better or for worse, hopefully enduring, and intimate to the degree of being sacred. It is an association that promotes a way of life, not causes; a harmony in living, not political faiths; a bilateral loyalty, not commercial or social projects. Yet it is an association for as noble a purpose as any involved in our prior decisions.

Reversed.

Goldberg, [Justice], joined by Warren, [Chief Justice], and Brennan, [Justice], concurring.

I agree with the Court that Connecticut's birth-control law unconstitutionally intrudes upon the right of marital privacy, and I join in its opinion and judgment. Although I have not accepted the view that "due process" as used in the Fourteenth Amendment incorporates all of the first eight amendments, I do agree that the concept of liberty protects those personal rights that are fundamental, and is not confined to the specific terms of the Bill of Rights. My conclusion that the concept of liberty is not so restricted and that it embraces the right of marital privacy though that right is not mentioned explicitly in the Constitution is supported . . . by the language and history of the Ninth Amendment. . . .

The Ninth Amendment . . . was proffered to quiet expressed fears that a bill of specifically enumerated rights could not be sufficiently broad to cover all essential rights and that the specific mention of certain rights would be interpreted as a denial that others were protected. . . . [T]he Framers did not intend that the first eight amendments be construed to exhaust the basic and fundamental rights which the Constitution guaranteed to the people.

. . . To hold that a right so basic and fundamental and so deep-rooted in our society as the right of privacy in marriage may be infringed because that right is not guaranteed in so many words by the first eight amendments to the Constitution is to ignore the Ninth Amendment and to give it no effect whatsoever. . . .

I do not mean to imply that the Ninth Amendment is applied against the States by the Fourteenth. Nor do I mean to state that the Ninth Amendment constitutes an independent source of rights protected from infringement by either the States or the Federal Government. Rather the Ninth Amendment simply lends strong support to the view that the "liberty" protected by the Fifth and Fourteenth Amendments from infringement by the Federal Government or the States is not restricted to rights specifically mentioned in the first eight amendments. . . .

In determining which rights are fundamental, judges are not left at large to decide cases in light of their personal and private notions. Rather, they must look to the "traditions and [collective] conscience of our people" to determine whether a principle is "so rooted [there] . . . as to be ranked as fundamental." The inquiry is whether a right involved "is of such a character that it cannot be denied without violating those 'fundamental principles of liberty and justice which lie at the base of all our civil and political institutions.'"

The entire fabric of the Constitution and the purposes that clearly underlie its specific guarantees demonstrate that the rights to marital privacy and to marry and raise a family are of similar order and magnitude as the fundamental rights specifically protected.

Although the Constitution does not speak in so many words of the right of privacy in marriage, I cannot believe that it offers these fundamental rights no protection. The fact that no particular provision of the Constitution explicitly forbids the State from disrupting the traditional relation of the family—a relation as old and as fundamental as our entire civilization—surely does not show that the Government was meant to have the power to do so. . . .

The logic of the dissents would sanction federal or state legislation that seems to me even more plainly unconstitutional than the statute before us. Surely the Government, absent a showing of a compelling subordinating state interest, could not decree that all husbands and wives must be sterilized after two children have been born to them. Yet by their reasoning such an invasion of marital privacy would not be subject to constitutional challenge because, while it might be "silly," no provision of the Constitution specifically prevents the Government from curtailing the marital right to bear children and raise a family. . . .

In a long series of cases this Court has held that where fundamental personal liberties are involved, they may not be abridged by the States simply on a showing that a regulatory statute has some rational relationship to the effectuation of a proper state purpose. "Where there is a significant encroachment upon personal liberty, the State may prevail only upon showing a subordinating interest which is compelling." . . . The law must be shown "necessary, and not merely rationally related, to the accomplishment of a permissible state policy." . . .

Although the Connecticut birth-control law obviously encroaches upon a fundamental personal liberty, the State does not show that the law serves any "subordinating [state] interest which is compelling" or that it is "necessary . . . to the accomplishment of a permissible state policy." The State, at most, argues that there is some rational relation between this statute and what is admittedly a legitimate subject of state concern—the discouraging of extra-marital relations. It says that preventing the use of birth-control devices by married persons helps prevent the indulgence by some in such extra-marital relations. The rationality of this justification is dubious, particularly in light of the admitted widespread availability to all persons in the State of Connecticut, unmarried as well as married, of birth-control devices for the prevention of disease, as distinguished from the prevention of conception. But, in any event, it is clear that the state interest in safeguarding marital fidelity can be served by a more discriminately tailored statute, which does not, like the present one, sweep unnecessarily broadly, reaching far beyond the evil sought to be dealt with and intruding upon the privacy of all married couples. . . . The State of Connecticut does have statutes, the constitutionality of which is beyond doubt, which prohibit adultery and fornication. These statutes demonstrate that means for achieving the same basic purpose of protecting marital fidelity are available to Connecticut without the need to "invade the area of protected freedoms." . . .

In sum, I believe that the right to privacy in the marital relation is fundamental and basic—a personal right "retained by the people" within the meaning of the Ninth Amendment. Connecticut cannot constitutionally abridge this fundamental right, which is protected by the Fourteenth Amendment from infringement by the States. I agree with the Court that petitioners' convictions must therefore be reversed.

. . .

Harlan, [Justice], concurring. . . .

In my view, the proper constitutional inquiry in this case is whether this Connecticut statute infringes the Due Process Clause of the Fourteenth Amendment because the enactment violates basic values "implicit in the concept of ordered liberty. . . ." For reasons state[d] at length in my dissenting opinion in *Poe v. Ullman* ([367 U.S. 487 (1961)], I believe that it does. While the relevant inquiry may be aided by resort to one or more of the provisions of the Bill of Rights, it is not dependent on them or any of their radiations. The

Due Process Clause of the Fourteenth Amendment stands, in my opinion, on its own bottom.

. . .

White, [Justice], concurring. . . .

In my view, this Connecticut law as applied to married couples deprives them of "liberty" without due process of law, as that concept is used in the Fourteenth Amendment. I therefore concur in the judgment of the Court reversing these convictions under Connecticut's aiding and abetting statute. . . .

[T]his is not the first time this Court has had occasion to articulate that the liberty entitled to protection under the Fourteenth Amendment includes the right "to marry, establish a home and bring up children." . . . and "the liberty . . . to direct the upbringing and education of children," . . . and that these are among "the basic civil rights of man." . . . These decisions affirm that there is a "realm of family life which the state cannot enter" without substantial justification. . . . Surely the right invoked in this case, to be free of regulation of the intimacies of the marriage relationship, "come[s] to this Court with a momentum for respect lacking when appeal is made to liberties which derive merely from shifting economic arrangements." . . .

An examination of the justification offered, however, cannot be avoided by saying that the Connecticut anti-use statute invades a protected area of privacy and association or that it demeans the marriage relationship. The nature of the right invaded is pertinent, to be sure, for statutes regulating sensitive areas of liberty do, under the cases of this Court, require "strict scrutiny," *Skinner v. Oklahoma*, and "must be viewed in the light of less drastic means for achieving the same basic purpose." "Where there is a significant encroachment upon personal liberty, the State may prevail only upon showing a subordinating interest which is compelling." But such statutes, if reasonably necessary for the effectuation of a legitimate and substantial state interest, and not arbitrary or capricious in application, are not invalid under the Due Process Clause.

As I read the opinions of the Connecticut courts and the argument of Connecticut in this Court, the State claims but one justification for its anti-use statute. . . . [T]he statute is said to serve the State's policy against all forms of promiscuous or illicit sexual relationships, be they premarital or extramarital, concededly a permissible and legitimate legislative goal.

Without taking issue with the premise that the fear of conception operates as a deterrent to such relationships in addition to the criminal proscriptions Connecticut has against such conduct, I wholly fail to see how the ban on the use of contraceptives by married couples in any way reinforces the State's ban on illicit sexual relationships. Connecticut does not bar the importation or possession of contraceptive devices; they are not considered contraband material under state law, and their availability in that State is not seriously disputed. The only way Connecticut seeks to limit or control the availability of such devices is through its general aiding and abetting statute whose operation in this context has been quite obviously ineffective and whose most serious use has been against birth-control clinics rendering advice to married, rather than unmarried, persons. . . . Moreover, it would appear that the sale of contraceptives to prevent disease is plainly legal under Connecticut law.

In these circumstances one is rather hard pressed to explain how the ban on use by married persons in any way prevents use of such devices by persons engaging in illicit sexual relations and thereby contributes to the State's policy against such relationships. . . . At most the broad ban is of marginal utility to the declared objective. A statute limiting its prohibition on use to persons engaging in the prohibited relationship would serve the end posited by Connecticut in the same way, and with the same effectiveness, or ineffectiveness, as the broad antiuse statute under attack in this case. I find nothing in this record justifying the sweeping scope of this statute, with its telling effect on the freedoms of married persons, and therefore conclude that it deprives such persons of liberty without due process of law.

. . .

Black, [Justice], joined by Stewart, [Justice], dissenting. . . .

In order that there may be no room at all to doubt why I vote as I do, I feel constrained to add that the law is every bit as offensive to me as it is to my Brethren of the majority. . . . There is no single one of the graphic and eloquent strictures and criticisms fired at the policy of this Connecticut law either by the Court's opinion or by those of my concurring Brethren to which I cannot subscribe—except their conclusion that the evil qualities they see in the law make it unconstitutional. . . .

The Court talks about a constitutional "right of privacy" as though there is some constitutional provision or provisions forbidding any law ever to be passed which might abridge the "privacy" of individuals. But there is not. There are, of course, guarantees in certain specific constitutional provisions which are designed in part to protect privacy at certain times and places with respect to certain activities. Such, for example, is the Fourth Amendment's guarantee against "unreasonable searches and seizures." But I think it belittles that Amendment to talk about it as though it protects nothing but "privacy." . . .

One of the most effective ways of diluting or expanding a constitutionally guaranteed right is to substitute for the crucial word or words of a constitutional guarantee another word or words, more or less flexible and more or less restricted in meaning. . . . "Privacy" is a broad, abstract and ambiguous concept which can easily be shrunken in meaning but which can also, on the other hand, easily be interpreted as a constitutional ban against many things other than searches and seizures. . . . For these reasons I get nowhere in this case by talk about a constitutional "right of privacy" as an emanation from one or more constitutional provisions. I like my privacy as well as the next one, but I am nevertheless compelled to admit that government has a right to invade it unless prohibited by some specific constitutional provision. . . .

I discuss the due process and Ninth Amendment arguments together because on analysis they turn out to be the same thing—merely using different words to claim for this Court and the federal judiciary power to invalidate any legislative act which the judges find irrational, unreasonable or offensive. . . .

Of the cases on which my Brothers White and Goldberg rely so heavily, undoubtedly the reasoning of two of them supports their result here—as would that of a number of others which they do not bother to name. . . . The two they do cite and quote from, *Meyer v. Nebraska*, and *Pierce v. Society of Sisters*, were both decided in opinions by Mr. Justice McReynolds which elaborated the same natural law due process philosophy found in *Lochner v. New York*, one of the cases on which he relied in *Meyer*, along with such other long discredited decisions as, e.g., *Adkins v. Children's Hospital*. . . . Without expressing an opinion as to whether either of those cases reached a correct result in light of our later decisions applying the First Amendment to the States through the Fourteenth, I merely point out that the reasoning stated in *Meyer* and *Pierce* was the same natural law due process philosophy which many later opinions repudiated, and which I cannot accept. . . .

My Brother Goldberg has adopted the recent discovery that the Ninth Amendment as well as the Due Process Clause can be used by this Court as authority to strike down all state legislation which this court thinks violates "fundamental principles of liberty and justice," or is contrary to the "traditions and [collective] conscience of our people." He also states, without proof satisfactory to me, that in making decisions on this basis judges will not consider "their personal and private notions." One may ask how they can avoid considering them. Our Court certainly has no machinery with which to take a Gallup Poll. And the scientific miracles of this age have not yet produced a gadget which the Court can use to determine what traditions are rooted in the "[collective] conscience of our people." Moreover, one would certainly have to look far beyond the language of the Ninth Amendment to find that the Framers vested in this Court any such awesome veto powers over lawmaking, either by the States or by the Congress. . . . That Amendment was passed not to broaden the powers of this Court or any other department of "the General Government," but, as every student of history knows, to assure the people that the Constitution in all its provisions was intended to limit the Federal Government to the powers granted expressly or by necessary implication. . . .

The Due Process Clause with an "arbitrary and capricious" or "shocking to the conscience" formula was liberally used by this Court to strike down economic legislation in the early decades of this century, threatening, many people thought, the tranquility and stability of the Nation. That formula, based on subjective considerations of "natural justice," is no less dangerous when used to enforce this Court's view about personal rights than those about economic rights. . . .

Lawrence et al. v. Texas

In this case, decided in 2003, the U.S. Supreme Court held that a Texas statute making it a crime for two persons of the same sex to engage in certain intimate sexual conduct violated the Due Process Clause of the Constitution. In reading this case, consider the following questions: How much weight should be given to majority's contention that early sodomy laws were not especially directed at homosexuals? Why should that fact, if it is correct, take precedence over what laws the state of Texas seeks to impose upon homosexuals today? If the Court is right, and "non-procreative" sex was in fact the target of early anti-sodomy laws, could a state legitimately pass a law banning all forms of consensual sexual activity that are not for the purpose of procreation? The Court reads the line of cases descending from *Griswold* to stand for the "autonomy of the self" regarding "intimate conduct." Is this too broad an interpretation of the precedents, in your view? Try to determine how the interpretive theories of Dworkin, Scalia, and Bork would approach this question.

JUSTICE KENNEDY delivered the opinion of the Court.

Liberty protects the person from unwarranted government intrusions into a dwelling or other private places. In our tradition the State is not omnipresent in the home. And there are other spheres of our lives and existence, outside the home, where the State should not be a dominant presence. Freedom extends beyond spatial bounds. Liberty presumes an autonomy of self that includes freedom of thought, belief, expression, and certain intimate conduct. The instant case involves liberty of the person both in its spatial and more transcendent dimensions.

The question before the Court is the validity of a Texas statute making it a crime for two persons of the same sex to engage in certain intimate sexual conduct.

In Houston, Texas, officers of the Harris County Police Department were dispatched to a private residence in response to a reported weapons disturbance.

---

539 U.S.—; 123 S. Ct. 2472 (2003).

They entered an apartment where one of the petitioners, John Geddes Lawrence, resided. The right of the police to enter does not seem to have been questioned. The officers observed Lawrence and another man, Tyron Garner, engaging in a sexual act. The two petitioners were arrested, held in custody overnight, and charged and convicted before a Justice of the Peace.

The complaints described their crime as "deviate sexual intercourse, namely anal sex, with a member of the same sex (man)." The applicable state law is Tex. Penal Code Ann. § 21.06(a) (2003). It provides: "A person commits an offense if he engages in deviate sexual intercourse with another individual of the same sex." The statute defines "[d]eviate sexual intercourse" as follows:

(A) any contact between any part of the genitals of one person and the mouth or anus of another person; or
(B) the penetration of the genitals or the anus of another person with an object.

The petitioners exercised their right to a trial *de novo* in Harris County Criminal Court. They challenged the statute as a violation of the Equal Protection Clause of the Fourteenth Amendment and of a like provision of the Texas Constitution (Tex. Const., Art. 1, § 3a). Those contentions were rejected. . . .

We conclude the case should be resolved by determining whether the petitioners were free as adults to engage in the private conduct in the exercise of their liberty under the Due Process Clause of the Fourteenth Amendment to the Constitution. For this inquiry we deem it necessary to reconsider the Court's holding in *Bowers*.

There are broad statements of the substantive reach of liberty under the Due Process Clause in earlier cases, including *Pierce v. Society of Sisters*, 268 U.S. 510 (1925), and *Meyer v. Nebraska*, 262 U.S. 390 (1923); but the most pertinent beginning point is our decision in *Griswold v. Connecticut*, 381 U.S. 479 (1965).

In *Griswold* the Court invalidated a state law prohibiting the use of drugs or devices of contraception and counseling or aiding and abetting the use of contraceptives. The Court described the protected interest as a right to privacy and placed emphasis on the marriage relation and the protected space of the marital bedroom.

After *Griswold* it was established that the right to make certain decisions regarding sexual conduct extends beyond the marital relationship. In *Eisenstadt v. Baird*, 405 U.S. 438 (1972), the Court invalidated a law prohibiting the distribution of contraceptives to unmarried persons. The case was decided under the Equal Protection Clause, *id.*, at 454; but with respect to unmarried persons, the Court went on to state the fundamental proposition that the law impaired the exercise of their personal rights. . . .

The opinions in *Griswold* and *Eisenstadt* were part of the background for the decision in *Roe v. Wade*, 410 U.S. 113 (1973). As is well known, the case involved a challenge to the Texas law prohibiting abortions, but the laws of other States were affected as well. Although the Court held the woman's rights were not absolute, her right to elect an abortion did have real and substantial protection as an exercise of her liberty under the Due Process Clause. The Court cited cases that protect spatial freedom and cases that go well beyond it. *Roe* recognized the right of a woman to make certain fundamental decisions affecting her destiny and confirmed once more that the protection of liberty under the Due Process Clause has a substantive dimension of fundamental significance in defining the rights of the person.

In *Carey v. Population Services Int'l*, 431 U.S. 678 (1977), the Court confronted a New York law forbidding sale or distribution of contraceptive devices to persons under 16 years of age. Although there was no single opinion for the Court, the law was invalidated. Both *Eisenstadt* and *Carey*, as well as the holding and rationale in *Roe*, confirmed that the reasoning of *Griswold* could not be confined to the protection of rights of married adults. This was the state of the law with respect to some of the most relevant cases when the Court considered *Bowers v. Hardwick*.

The facts in *Bowers* had some similarities to the instant case. A police officer, whose right to enter seems not to have been in question, observed Hardwick, in his own bedroom, engaging in intimate sexual conduct with another adult male. The conduct was in violation of a Georgia statute making it a criminal offense to engage in sodomy. One difference between the two cases is that the Georgia statute prohibited the conduct whether or not the participants were of the same sex, while the Texas statute, as we have seen, applies only to participants of the same sex. Hardwick was not prosecuted, but he brought an action in federal court to declare the state statute invalid. He alleged he was a practicing homosexual and that the criminal prohibition violated rights guaranteed to him by the Constitution. The Court, in an opinion by Justice White, sustained the Georgia law. . . .

The Court began its substantive discussion in *Bowers* as follows: "The issue presented is whether the Federal Constitution confers a fundamental right upon homosexuals to engage in sodomy and hence invalidates the laws of the many States that still make such conduct illegal and have done so for a very long time." That statement, we now conclude, discloses the Court's own failure to appreciate the extent of the liberty at stake. To say that the issue in *Bowers* was simply the right to engage in certain sexual conduct demeans the claim the individual put forward, just as it would demean a married couple were it to be said marriage is simply about the right to have sexual intercourse. The laws involved in *Bowers* and here are, to be sure, statutes that purport to do no more than prohibit a particular sexual act. Their penalties and purposes, though, have more far-reaching consequences, touching upon the most private human conduct, sexual behavior, and in the most private of places, the home. The statutes do seek to control a personal relationship that, whether or not entitled to formal recognition in the law, is within the liberty of persons to choose without being punished as criminals.

This, as a general rule, should counsel against attempts by the State, or a court, to define the meaning of the relationship or to set its boundaries absent injury to a person or abuse of an institution the law protects. It suffices for us to acknowledge that adults may choose to enter upon this relationship in the confines of their homes and their own private lives and still retain their dignity as free persons. When sexuality finds overt expression in intimate conduct with another person, the conduct can be but one element in a personal bond that is more enduring. The liberty protected by the Constitution allows homosexual persons the right to make this choice.

At the outset it should be noted that there is no long-standing history in this country of laws directed at homosexual conduct as a distinct matter. Beginning in colonial times there were prohibitions of sodomy derived from the English criminal laws passed in the first instance by the Reformation Parliament of 1533. The English prohibition was understood to include relations between men and women as well as relations between men and men. . . . Thus early American sodomy laws were not directed at homosexuals as such but instead sought to prohibit non-procreative sexual activity more generally. This does not suggest approval of homosexual conduct. It does tend to show that this particular form of conduct was not thought of as a separate category from like conduct between heterosexual persons. . . .

[Far] from possessing "ancient roots," American laws targeting same-sex couples did not develop until the last third of the 20th century.

It was not until the 1970s that any State singled out same-sex relations for criminal prosecution, and only nine States have done so. . . . Over the course of the last decades, States with same-sex prohibitions have moved toward abolishing them. . . . In all events we think that our laws and traditions in the past half century are of most relevance here. These references show an emerging awareness that liberty gives substantial protection to adult persons in deciding how to conduct their private lives in matters pertaining to sex. . . .

The sweeping references by Chief Justice Burger to the history of Western civilization and to Judeo-Christian moral and ethical standards did not take account of other authorities pointing in an opposite direction. A committee advising the British Parliament recommended in 1957 repeal of laws punishing homosexual conduct [The Wolfenden Report: Report of the Committee on Homosexual Offenses and Prostitution (1963)]. Parliament enacted the substance of those recommendations 10 years later. . . . The 25 States with laws prohibiting the relevant conduct referenced in the *Bowers* decision are reduced now to 13, of which 4 enforce their laws only against homosexual conduct. In those States where sodomy is still proscribed, whether for same-sex or heterosexual conduct, there is a pattern of nonenforcement with respect to consenting adults acting in private. The State of Texas admitted in 1994 that as of that date it had not prosecuted anyone under those circumstances. . . .

In *Planned Parenthood of Southeastern Pa. v. Casey,* 505 U.S. 833 (1992), the Court reaffirmed the substantive force of the liberty protected by the Due Process Clause. The *Casey* decision again confirmed that our laws and tradition afford constitutional protection to personal decisions relating to marriage, procreation, contraception, family relationships, child rearing, and education. In explaining the respect the Constitution demands for the autonomy of the person in making these choices, we stated as follows:

> These matters, involving the most intimate and personal choices a person may make in a lifetime, choices central to personal dignity and autonomy, are central to the liberty protected by the Fourteenth Amendment. At the heart of liberty is the right to define one's own concept of existence, of meaning, of the

universe, and of the mystery of human life. Beliefs about these matters could not define the attributes of personhood were they formed under compulsion of the State.

Persons in a homosexual relationship may seek autonomy for these purposes, just as heterosexual persons do. The decision in *Bowers* would deny them this right.

To the extent *Bowers* relied on values we share with a wider civilization, it should be noted that the reasoning and holding in *Bowers* have been rejected elsewhere. The European Court of Human Rights has followed not *Bowers* but its own decision in *Dudgeon v. United Kingdom*. . . . Other nations, too, have taken action consistent with an affirmation of the protected right of homosexual adults to engage in intimate, consensual conduct. . . . The right the petitioners seek in this case has been accepted as an integral part of human freedom in many other countries. There has been no showing that in this country the governmental interest in circumscribing personal choice is somehow more legitimate or urgent.

Bowers was not correct when it was decided, and it is not correct today. It ought not to remain binding precedent. *Bowers v. Hardwick* should be and now is overruled.

The present case does not involve minors. It does not involve persons who might be injured or coerced or who are situated in relationships where consent might not easily be refused. It does not involve public conduct or prostitution. It does not involve whether the government must give formal recognition to any relationship that homosexual persons seek to enter. The case does involve two adults who, with full and mutual consent from each other, engaged in sexual practices common to a homosexual lifestyle. The petitioners are entitled to respect for their private lives. The State cannot demean their existence or control their destiny by making their private sexual conduct a crime. Their right to liberty under the Due Process Clause gives them the full right to engage in their conduct without intervention of the government. "It is a promise of the Constitution that there is a realm of personal liberty which the government may not enter." . . . The Texas statute furthers no legitimate state interest which can justify its intrusion into the personal and private life of the individual.

Had those who drew and ratified the Due Process Clauses of the Fifth Amendment or the Fourteenth Amendment known the components of liberty in its

manifold possibilities, they might have been more specific. They did not presume to have this insight. They knew times can blind us to certain truths and later generations can see that laws once thought necessary and proper in fact serve only to oppress. As the Constitution endures, persons in every generation can invoke its principles in their own search for greater freedom.

The judgment of the Court of Appeals for the Texas Fourteenth District is reversed, and the case is remanded for further proceedings not inconsistent with this opinion.

It is so ordered.

JUSTICE SCALIA, with whom THE CHIEF JUSTICE and JUSTICE THOMAS join, dissenting.

"Liberty finds no refuge in a jurisprudence of doubt." *Planned Parenthood of Southeastern Pa. v. Casey,* 505 U.S. 833, 844 (1992). That was the Court's sententious response, barely more than a decade ago, to those seeking to overrule *Roe v. Wade.* The Court's response today, to those who have engaged in a 17-year crusade to overrule *Bowers v. Hardwick,* is very different. The need for stability and certainty presents no barrier.

Most of the rest of today's opinion has no relevance to its actual holding—that the Texas statute "furthers no legitimate state interest which can justify" its application to petitioners under rational-basis review. . . . Though there is discussion of "fundamental proposition[s]," and "fundamental decisions," nowhere does the Court's opinion declare that homosexual sodomy is a "fundamental right" under the Due Process Clause; nor does it subject the Texas law to the standard of review that would be appropriate (strict scrutiny) if homosexual sodomy *were* a "fundamental right." . . . Instead the Court simply describes petitioners' conduct as "an exercise of their liberty"—which it undoubtedly is—and proceeds to apply an unheard-of form of rational-basis review that will have far-reaching implications beyond this case.

I begin with the Court's surprising readiness to reconsider a decision rendered a mere 17 years ago in *Bowers v. Hardwick.*

Today's approach to *stare decisis* invites us to overrule an erroneously decided precedent (including an "intensely divisive" decision) *if:* (1) its foundations have been "eroded" by subsequent decisions, (2) it has been subject to "substantial and continuing" criticism, and (3) it has not induced "individual or societal reliance" that counsels against overturning. The problem is that *Roe* itself—which today's majority surely has no disposition to overrule—satisfies these conditions to at least the same degree as *Bowers*. . . . "[T]here has been," the Court says, "no individual or societal reliance on *Bowers* of the sort that could counsel against overturning its holding . . . ." It seems to me that the "societal reliance" on the principles confirmed in *Bowers* and discarded today has been overwhelming. Countless judicial decisions and legislative enactments have relied on the ancient proposition that a governing majority's belief that certain sexual behavior is "immoral and unacceptable" constitutes a rational basis for regulation. We ourselves relied extensively on *Bowers* when we concluded, in *Barnes v. Glen Theatre, Inc.*, 501 U.S. 560, 569 (1991), that Indiana's public indecency statute furthered "a substantial government interest in protecting order and morality." State laws against bigamy, same-sex marriage, adult incest, prostitution, masturbation, adultery, fornication, bestiality, and obscenity are likewise sustainable only in light of *Bowers*' validation of laws based on moral choices. Every single one of these laws is called into question by today's decision; the Court makes no effort to cabin the scope of its decision to exclude them from its holding. (Noting "an emerging awareness that liberty gives substantial protection to adult persons in deciding how to conduct their private lives *in matters pertaining to sex*" (emphasis added)). The impossibility of distinguishing homosexuality from other traditional "morals" offenses is precisely why *Bowers* rejected the rational-basis challenge. "The law," it said, "is constantly based on notions of morality, and if all laws representing essentially moral choices are to be invalidated under the Due Process Clause, the courts will be very busy indeed."

Texas Penal Code Ann. § 21.06(a) (2003) undoubtedly imposes constraints on liberty. So do laws prohibiting prostitution, recreational use of heroin, and, for that matter, working more than 60 hours per week in a bakery. But there is no right to "liberty" under the Due Process Clause, though today's opinion repeatedly makes that claim. The Fourteenth Amendment *expressly allows* States to deprive their citizens of "liberty," *so long as "due process of law" is provided*:

> "No state shall . . . deprive any person of life, liberty, or property, *without due process of law.*" Amdt. 14 (emphasis added).

Our opinions applying the doctrine known as "substantive due process" hold that the Due Process Clause prohibits States from infringing *fundamental* liberty interests, unless the infringement is narrowly tailored to serve a compelling state interest. We have held repeatedly, in cases the Court today does not overrule, that *only* fundamental rights qualify for this so-called "heightened scrutiny" protection—that is, rights which are "'deeply rooted in this Nation's history and tradition.'" . . . All other liberty interests may be abridged or abrogated pursuant to a validly enacted state law if that law is rationally related to a legitimate state interest. . . . *Bowers* concluded that a right to engage in homosexual sodomy was not "'deeply rooted in this Nation's history and tradition.'"

The Court today does not overrule this holding. Not once does it describe homosexual sodomy as a "fundamental right" or a "fundamental liberty interest," nor does it subject the Texas statute to strict scrutiny. Instead, having failed to establish that the right to homosexual sodomy is "'deeply rooted in this Nation's history and tradition,'" the Court concludes that the application of Texas's statute to petitioners' conduct fails the rational-basis test, and overrules *Bowers'* holding to the contrary. "The Texas statute furthers no legitimate state interest which can justify its intrusion into the personal and private life of the individual."

. . .

After discussing the history of antisodomy laws, the Court proclaims that, "it should be noted that there is no longstanding history in this country of laws directed at homosexual conduct as a distinct matter." This observation in no way casts into doubt the "definitive [historical] conclusion," on which *Bowers* relied: that our Nation has a longstanding history of laws prohibiting *sodomy in general*—regardless of whether it was performed by same-sex or opposite-sex couples. . . . It is (as *Bowers* recognized) entirely irrelevant whether the laws in our long national tradition criminalizing homosexual sodomy were "directed at homosexual conduct as a distinct matter." Whether homosexual sodomy was prohibited by a law targeted at same-sex sexual relations or by a more general law prohibiting both homosexual and heterosexual sodomy, the only relevant point is that it *was* criminalized—which suffices to establish that homosexual sodomy is not a right "deeply rooted in our Nation's history and tradition". . . .

Realizing that fact, the Court instead says: "[W]e think that our laws and traditions in the past half century are of most relevance here. These references show *an emerging awareness* that liberty gives substantial protection to adult persons in deciding how to conduct their private lives *in matters pertaining to sex*." Apart from the fact that such an "emerging awareness" does not establish a "fundamental right," the statement is factually false. States continue to prosecute all sorts of crimes by adults "in matters pertaining to sex": prostitution, adult incest, adultery, obscenity, and child pornography. . . .

In any event, an "emerging awareness" is by definition not "deeply rooted in this Nation's history and tradition[s]," as we have said "fundamental right" status requires. Constitutional entitlements do not spring into existence because some States choose to lesson or eliminate criminal sanctions on certain behavior. Much less do they spring into existence, as the Court seems to believe, because *foreign nations* decriminalize conduct. The *Bowers* majority opinion *never* relied on "values we share with a wider civilization," but rather rejected the claimed right to sodomy on the ground that such a right was not "'deeply rooted in *this Nation's* history and tradition.'" *Bowers'* rational-basis holding is likewise devoid of any reliance on the views of a "wider civilization." The Court's discussion of these foreign views (ignoring, of course, the many countries that have retained criminal prohibitions on sodomy) is therefore meaningless dicta. Dangerous dicta, however, since "this Court . . . should not impose foreign moods, fads, or fashions on Americans." . . .

I turn now to the ground on which the Court squarely rests its holding: the contention that there is no rational basis for the law here under attack. This proposition is so out of accord with our jurisprudence—indeed, with the jurisprudence of *any* society we know—that it requires little discussion.

The Texas statute undeniably seeks to further the belief of its citizens that certain forms of sexual behavior are "immoral and unacceptable," the same interest furthered by criminal laws against fornication, bigamy, adultery, adult incest, bestiality, and obscenity. *Bowers* held that this *was* a legitimate state interest. The Court today reaches the opposite conclusion. The Texas statute, it says, "furthers *no legitimate state interest* which can justify its intrusion into the personal and private life of the individual." The Court embraces instead Justice Stevens' declaration in his *Bowers* dissent, that "the fact that the governing majority in a State has traditionally viewed a particular practice as immoral is not a sufficient reason for upholding a law prohibiting the practice." This effectively decrees the end of all morals legislation. If, as the Court asserts, the promotion of majoritarian sexual morality is not even a *legitimate* state interest, none of the above-mentioned laws can survive rational-basis review.

Let me be clear that I have nothing against homosexuals, or any other group, promoting their agenda through normal democratic means. Social perceptions of sexual and other morality change over time, and every group has the right to persuade its fellow citizens that its view of such matters is the best. That homosexuals have achieved some success in that enterprise is attested to by the fact that Texas is one of the few remaining States that criminalize private, consensual homosexual acts. But persuading one's fellow citizens is one thing, and imposing one's views in absence of democratic majority will is something else. I would no more *require* a State to criminalize homosexual acts—or, for that matter, display *any* moral disapproval of them—than I would *forbid* it to do so. What Texas has chosen to do is well within the range of traditional democratic action, and its hand should not be stayed through the invention of a brand-new "constitutional right" by a Court that is impatient of democratic change. It is indeed true that "later generations can see that laws once thought necessary and proper in fact serve only to oppress," and when that happens, later generations can repeal those laws. But it is the premise of our system that those judgments are to be made by the people, and not imposed by a governing caste that knows best.

One of the benefits of leaving regulation of this matter to the people rather than to the courts is that the people, unlike judges, need not carry things to their logical conclusion. The people may feel that their disapprobation of homosexual conduct is strong enough to disallow homosexual marriage, but not strong enough to criminalize private homosexual acts—and may legislate accordingly. The Court today pretends that it possesses a similar freedom of action, so that we need not fear judicial imposition of homosexual marriage, as has recently occurred in Canada (in a decision that the Canadian Government has chosen not to appeal). At the end of its opinion—after having laid waste the foundations of our rational-basis jurisprudence—the Court says that the present case "does not involve whether the government must give formal recognition to any relationship that homosexual persons seek to enter." Do not believe it. More illuminating than this bald, unreasoned disclaimer is the progression of thought displayed by an earlier passage in the Court's opinion, which notes the constitutional protections afforded to "personal decisions relating to *marriage*, procreation, contraception, family relationships, child rearing, and education," and then declares that "[p]ersons in a homosexual relationship may seek autonomy for these purposes, just as heterosexual persons do." Today's opinion dismantles the structure of constitutional law that has permitted a distinction to be made between heterosexual and homosexual unions, insofar as formal recognition in marriage is concerned. If moral disapproval of homosexual conduct is "no legitimate state interest" for purposes of proscribing that conduct, and if, as the Court coos (casting aside all pretense of neutrality), "[w]hen sexuality finds overt expression in intimate conduct with another person, the conduct can be but one element in a personal bond that is more enduring," what justification could there possibly be for denying the benefits of marriage to homosexual couples exercising "[t]he liberty protected by the Constitution"? Surely not the encouragement of procreation, since the sterile and the elderly are allowed to marry. This case "does not involve" the issue of homosexual marriage only if one entertains the belief that principle and logic have nothing to do with the decisions of this Court. Many will hope that, as the Court comfortingly assures us, this is so.

The matters appropriate for this Court's resolution are only three: Texas's prohibition of sodomy neither infringes a "fundamental right" (which the Court does not dispute), nor is unsupported by a rational relation to what the Constitution considers a legiti-mate state interest, nor denies the equal protection of the laws. I dissent.

. . .

JUSTICE THOMAS, dissenting.

I join JUSTICE SCALIA's dissenting opinion. I write separately to note that the law before the Court today "is . . . uncommonly silly." *Griswold v. Connecticut*, 381 U.S. 479, 527 (1965) (Stewart, J., dissenting). If I were a member of the Texas Legislature, I would vote to repeal it. Punishing someone for expressing his sexual prefer-ence through noncommercial consensual conduct with another adult does not appear to be a worthy way to expend valuable law enforcement resources.

Notwithstanding this, I recognize that as a member of this Court I am not empowered to help petitioners and others similarly situated. My duty, rather, is to "decide cases 'agreeably to the Constitu-tion and laws of the United States.'" *Id.*, at 530. And, just like Justice Stewart, I "can find [neither in the Bill of Rights nor any other part of the Constitution a] gen-eral right of privacy," *ibid.*, or as the Court terms it today, the "liberty of the person both in its spatial and more transcendent dimensions," *ante*, at 1.

Minersville School District v. Gobitis

The *Gobitis* case involved two students, ages ten and twelve, who refused to par-ticipate in a daily classroom flag salute. The Gobitis children were Jehovah's Wit-nesses, and believed, in the words of Billy Gobitis, "that I must not worship anything out of harmony with God's commandments . . . I do not salute the flag because I do not like my country. I love my country but I love God more." The children were expelled from school, and the father brought suit. In a famous opin-ion (subsequently overturned), Supreme Court Justice Felix Frankfurter upheld the flag salute requirement on the ground that it promotes national unity and this takes priority over accommodating religious scruple. Frankfurter's justification for limiting the religious freedom of the Jehovah's Witness children should be compared with Patrick Devlin's appeal to "public morality" in the context of free-dom of expression.

Mr. Justice Frankfurter delivered the opinion of the Court.

---

310 U.S. 586 (1940), United States Supreme Court.

A grave responsibility confronts this Court when-ever in course of litigation it must reconcile the con-flicting claims of liberty and authority. But when the liberty invoked is liberty of conscience, and the author-ity is authority to safeguard the nation's fellowship, judicial conscience is put to its severest test. Of such a nature is the present controversy.

Lillian Gobitis, aged twelve, and her brother William, aged ten, were expelled from the public schools of Minersville, Pennsylvania, for refusing to salute the national flag as part of a daily school exercise. The local Board of Education required both teachers and pupils to participate in this ceremony. The ceremony is a familiar one. The right hand is placed on the breast and the following pledge recited in unison: "I pledge allegiance to my flag, and to the Republic for which it stands; one nation indivisible, with liberty and justice for all." While the words are spoken, teachers and pupils extend their right hands in salute to the flag. The Gobitis family are affiliated with "Jehovah's Witnesses," for whom the Bible as the Word of God is the supreme authority. The children had been brought up conscientiously to believe that such a gesture of respect for the flag was forbidden by command of Scripture.[1]

The Gobitis children were of an age for which Pennsylvania makes school attendance compulsory. Thus they were denied a free education, and their parents had to put them into private schools. To be relieved of the financial burden thereby entailed, their father, on behalf of the children and in his own behalf, brought this suit. He sought to enjoin the authorities from continuing to exact participation in the flag-salute ceremony as a condition of his children's attendance at the Minersville school.

We must decide whether the requirement of participation in such a ceremony, exacted from a child who refuses upon sincere religious grounds, infringes without due process of law the liberty guaranteed by the Fourteenth Amendment.

Centuries of strife over the erection of particular dogmas as exclusive or all-comprehending faiths led to the inclusion of a guarantee for religious freedom in the Bill of Rights. The First Amendment, and the Fourteenth through its absorption of the First, sought to guard against repetition of those bitter religious struggles by prohibiting the establishment of a state religion and by securing to every sect the free exercise of its faith. So pervasive is the acceptance of this precious right that its scope is brought into question, as here, only when the conscience of individuals collides with the felt necessities of society.

Certainly the affirmative pursuit of one's convictions about the ultimate mystery of the universe and man's relation to it is placed beyond the reach of law. Government may not interfere with organized or individual expression of belief or disbelief. Propagation of belief—or even of disbelief—in the supernatural is protected, whether in church or chapel, mosque or synagogue, tabernacle or meeting-house. Likewise the Constitution assures generous immunity to the individual from imposition of penalties for offending, in the course of his own religious activities, the religious views of others, be they a minority or those who are dominant in government.

But the manifold character of man's relations may bring his conception of religious duty into conflict with the secular interests of his fellow-men. When does the constitutional guarantee compel exemption from doing what society thinks necessary for the promotion of some great common end, or from a penalty for conduct which appears dangerous to the general good? To state the problem is to recall the truth that no single principle can answer all of life's complexities. The right to freedom of religious belief, however dissident and however obnoxious to the cherished beliefs of others—even of a majority—is itself the denial of an absolute. But to affirm that the freedom to follow conscience has itself no limits in the life of a society would deny that very plurality of principles which, as a matter of history, underlies protection of religious toleration. Our present task, then, as so often the case with courts, is to reconcile two rights in order to prevent either from destroying the other. But, because in safeguarding conscience we are dealing with interests so subtle and so dear, every possible leeway should be given to the claims of religious faith.

In the judicial enforcement of religious freedom we are concerned with a historic concept. The religious liberty which the Constitution protects has never excluded legislation of general scope not directed against doctrinal loyalties of particular sects. Judicial nullification of legislation cannot be justified by attributing to the framers of the Bill of Rights views for which there is no historic warrant. Conscientious scruples have not, in the course of the long struggle for religious toleration, relieved the individual from obedience to a general law not aimed at the promotion or restriction of religious beliefs. The mere possession of religious convictions which contradict the relevant concerns of a political society does not relieve the citizen from the discharge of political responsibilities. The necessity for this adjustment has again and again been recognized. In a number of situations the exertion of political authority has been sustained, while basic considerations of religious freedom have been left inviolate. *Reynolds v. United States*, 98 U.S. 145. . . . In all these cases the general laws in question, upheld in their application to those who refused obedience from religious conviction, were manifestations of specific powers of government deemed by the legislature essential to secure and maintain the orderly, tranquil, and free society without which religious toleration itself is unattainable. Nor does the freedom of speech assured by Due Process move in a more absolute circle of immunity than that enjoyed by religious freedom. Even if it were assumed that freedom of speech goes beyond the historic concept of full opportunity to utter and to disseminate views, however heretical or offensive to dominant opinion, and includes freedom from conveying what may be deemed an implied but rejected affirmation, the question remains whether school children, like the Gobitis children, must be excused from conduct required of all the other children in the promotion of national cohesion. We are dealing with an interest inferior to none in the hierarchy of legal values. National unity is the basis of national security. To deny the legislature the right to select appropriate means for its attainment presents a totally different order of problem from that of the propriety of subordinating the possible ugliness of littered streets to the free expression of opinion through distribution of handbills.

· · ·

Unlike the instances we have cited, the case before us is not concerned with an exertion of legislative power for the promotion of some specific need or interest of secular society—the protection of the family, the promotion of health, the common defense, the raising of public revenues to defray the cost of government. But all these specific activities of government presuppose the existence of an organized political society. The ultimate foundation of free society is the binding tie of cohesive sentiment. Such a sentiment is fostered by all those agencies of the mind and spirit which may serve to gather up the traditions of a people, transmit them from generation to generation, and thereby create that continuity of a treasured common life which constitutes a civilization. "We live by symbols." The flag is the symbol of our national unity, transcending all internal differences, however large, within the framework of the Constitution. This Court has had occasion to say that . . . the flag is the symbol of the Nation's power, the emblem of freedom in its truest, best sense. . . . It signifies government resting on the consent of the governed; liberty regulated by law; the protection of the weak against the strong; security against the exercise of arbitrary power; and absolute safety for free institutions against foreign aggression.

· · ·

The wisdom of training children in patriotic impulses by those compulsions which necessarily pervade so much of the educational process is not for our independent judgment. Even were we convinced of the folly of such a measure, such belief would be no proof of its unconstitutionality. For ourselves, we might be tempted to say that the deepest patriotism is best engendered by giving unfettered scope to the most crotchety beliefs. Perhaps it is best, even from the standpoint of those interests which ordinances like the one under review seek to promote, to give to the least popular sect leave from conformities like those here in issue. But the courtroom is not the arena for debating issues of educational policy. It is not our province to choose among competing considerations in the subtle process of securing effective loyalty to the traditional ideals of democracy, while respecting at the same time individual idiosyncrasies among a people so diversified in racial origins and religious allegiances. So to hold would in effect make us the school board for the country. That authority has not been given to this Court, nor should we assume it.

· · ·

The preciousness of the family relation, the authority and independence which give dignity to parenthood, indeed the enjoyment of all freedom, presuppose the kind of ordered society which is summarized by our flag. A society which is dedicated to the preservation of these ultimate values of civilization may in self-protection utilize the educational process for inculcating those almost unconscious feelings which bind men together in a comprehending loyalty, whatever may be their lesser differences and difficulties. That is to say, the process may be utilized so long as men's right to believe as they please, to win others to their way of belief, and their right to assemble in their chosen places of worship for the devotional ceremonies of their faith, are all fully respected.

Reversed.

Endnote

[1] Reliance is especially placed on the following verses from Chapter 20 of Exodus:

"3. Thou shalt have no other gods before me.

"4. Thou shalt not make unto thee any graven image, or any likeness of any thing that is in heaven above, or that is in the earth beneath, or that is in the water under the earth:

"5. Thou shalt not bow down thyself to them, nor serve them: . . ."

Texas v. Johnson

The following case dealt with flag-burning and political protest. Arguing that the government may not "prohibit the expression of an idea simply because society finds the idea itself offensive or disagreeable," the Court majority held that Johnson's act of flag-burning was a constitutionally protected form of "speech." Do you agree that Johnson's conduct was "expressive" of a message? What message? Why does the majority reject the assertion that flag-burning may be prohibited because of the unique nature of the flag as a symbol of our nation? Do you agree with Justice Rehnquist that burning the flag is akin to a "fighting word" an insult undeserving of constitutional protection?

Justice Brennan delivered the opinion of the Court.

After publicly burning an American flag as a means of political protest, Gregory Lee Johnson was convicted of desecrating a flag in violation of Texas law. This case presents the question whether his conviction is consistent with the First Amendment. We hold that it is not.

While the Republican National Convention was taking place in Dallas in 1984, respondent Johnson participated in a political demonstration dubbed the "Republican War Chest Tour." As explained in literature distributed by the demonstrators and in speeches made by them, the purpose of this event was to protest the policies of the Reagan administration and of certain Dallas-based corporations. The demonstrators marched through the Dallas streets, chanting political slogans and stopping at several corporate locations to stage "die-ins" intended to dramatize the consequences of nuclear war. On several occasions they spray-painted the walls of buildings and overturned potted plants, but Johnson himself took no part in such activities. He did, however, accept an American flag handed to him by a fellow protestor who had taken it from a flag pole outside one of the targeted buildings.

The demonstration ended in front of Dallas City Hall, where Johnson unfurled the American flag, doused it with kerosene, and set it on fire. While the flag burned, the protestors chanted, "America, the red, white, and blue, we spit on you." After the demonstrators dispersed, a witness to the flag-burning collected

109 S. Ct. 2533 (1989), United States Supreme Court.

the flag's remains and buried them in his backyard. No one was physically injured or threatened with injury, though several witnesses testified that they had been seriously offended by the flag-burning.

Of the approximately 100 demonstrators, Johnson alone was charged with a crime. The only criminal offense with which he was charged was the desecration of a venerated object in violation of Tex. Penal Code Ann. § 42.09(a)(3)(1989).[1] After a trial, he was convicted, sentenced to one year in prison, and fined $2,000. The Court of Appeals for the Fifth District of Texas at Dallas affirmed Johnson's conviction, . . . but the Texas Court of Criminal Appeals reversed, . . . holding that the State could not, consistent with the First Amendment, punish Johnson for burning the flag in these circumstances.

. . .

Johnson was convicted of flag desecration for burning the flag rather than for uttering insulting words. This fact somewhat complicates our consideration of his conviction under the First Amendment. We must first determine whether Johnson's burning of the flag constituted expressive conduct, permitting him to invoke the First Amendment in challenging his conviction. . . .

The First Amendment literally forbids the abridgement only of "speech," but we have long recognized that its protection does not end at the spoken or written word. While we have rejected "the view that an apparently limitless variety of conduct can be labeled 'speech' whenever the person engaging in the conduct intends thereby to express an idea," . . . we have acknowledged that conduct may be "sufficiently imbued with elements of communication to fall within the scope of the First and Fourteenth Amendments." . . .

Especially pertinent to this case are our decisions recognizing the communicative nature of conduct relating to flags. Attaching a peace sign to the flag . . . saluting the flag . . . and displaying a red flag . . . we have held, all may find shelter under the First Amendment. . . . Pregnant with expressive content, the flag as readily signifies this Nation as does the combination of letters found in "America."

The State of Texas conceded for purposes of its oral argument in this case that Johnson's conduct was expressive conduct, . . . and this concession seems to us prudent. . . . Johnson burned an American flag as part—indeed, as the culmination—of a political demonstration that coincided with the convening of the Republican Party and its renomination of Ronald Reagan for President. The expressive, overtly political nature of this conduct was both intentional and overwhelmingly apparent. At his trial, Johnson explained his reasons for burning the flag as follows: "The American Flag was burned as Ronald Reagan was being renominated as President. And a more powerful statement of symbolic speech, whether you agree with it or not, couldn't have been made at that time. It's quite a just position [juxtaposition]. We had new patriotism and no patriotism." . . . In these circumstances, Johnson's burning of the flag was conduct "sufficiently imbued with elements of communication" . . . to implicate the First Amendment.

. . . [W]e must decide whether Texas has asserted an interest in support of Johnson's conviction that is unrelated to the suppression of expression. . . . The State offers two separate interests to justify this conviction: preventing breaches of the peace, and preserving the flag as a symbol of nationhood and national unity. We hold that the first interest is not implicated on this record and that the second is related to the suppression of expression.

Texas claims that its interest in preventing breaches of peace justifies Johnson's conviction for flag desecration. However, no disturbance of the peace actually occurred or threatened to occur because of Johnson's burning of the flag. . . .

The State's position, therefore, amounts to a claim that an audience that takes serious offense at particular expression is necessarily likely to disturb the peace and that the expression may be prohibited on this basis. Our precedents do not countenance such a presumption. On the contrary, they recognize that a principal "function of free speech under our system of government is to invite dispute. It may indeed best serve its high purpose when it induces a condition of unrest, creates dissatisfaction with conditions as they are, or even stirs people to anger." . . .

Nor does Johnson's expressive conduct fall within that small class of "fighting words" that are "likely to provoke the average person to retaliation, and thereby cause a breach of the peace." No reasonable onlooker would have regarded Johnson's generalized expression of dissatisfaction with the policies of the Federal Government as a direct personal insult or an invitation to exchange fisticuffs. . . .

We thus conclude that the State's interest in maintaining order is not implicated on these facts. . . .

It remains to consider whether the State's interest in preserving the flag as a symbol of nationhood and national unity justifies Johnson's conviction.

. . . Johnson was not, we add, prosecuted for the expression of just any idea; he was prosecuted for his expression of dissatisfaction with the policies of this country, expression situated at the core of our First Amendment values. . . .

Moreover, Johnson was prosecuted because he knew that his politically charged expression would cause "serious offense." If he had burned the flag as a means of disposing of it because it was dirty or torn, he would not have been convicted of flag desecration under this Texas law: federal law designates burning as the preferred means of disposing of a flag "when it is in such condition that it is no longer a fitting emblem for display," and Texas has no quarrel with this means of disposal. . . . The Texas law is thus not aimed at protecting the physical integrity of the flag in all circumstances, but is designed instead to protect it only against impairments that would cause serious offense to others. . . .

Texas argues that its interest in preserving the flag as a symbol of nationhood and national unity survives this close analysis. Quoting extensively from the writings of this Court chronicling the flag's historic and symbolic role in our society, the State emphasizes the "special place" reserved for the flag in our Nation. . . . The State's argument is not that it has an interest simply in maintaining the flag as a symbol of *something*, no matter what it symbolizes; indeed, if that were the State's position, it would be difficult to see how that interest is endangered by highly symbolic conduct such as Johnson's. Rather, the State's claim is that it has an interest in preserving the flag as a symbol of *nationhood* and *national unity*, a symbol with a determinate range of meanings. . . . According to Texas, if one physically treats the flag in a way that would tend to cast doubt on either the idea that nationhood and national unity are the flag's referents or that national unity actually exists, the message conveyed thereby is a harmful one and therefore may be prohibited.

If there is a bedrock principle underlying the First Amendment, it is that Government may not prohibit the expression of an idea simply because society finds the idea itself offensive or disagreeable.

In short, nothing in our precedents suggests that a State may foster its own view of the flag by prohibiting expressive conduct relating to it.

Texas'[s] focus on the precise nature of Johnson's expression, moreover, misses the point of our prior decisions: Their enduring lesson, that the Government may not prohibit expression simply because it disagrees with its message, is not dependent on the particular mode in which one chooses to express an idea. If we were to hold that a State may forbid flag-burning wherever it is likely to endanger the flag's symbolic role, but allow it wherever burning a flag promotes that role—as where, for example, a person ceremoniously burns a dirty flag—we would be saying that when it comes to impairing the flag's physical integrity, the flag itself may be used as a symbol—as a substitute for the written or spoken word or a "short cut from mind to mind"—only in one direction. We would be permitting a State to "prescribe what shall be orthodox" by saying that one may burn the flag to convey one's attitude toward it and its referents only if one does not endanger the flag's representation of nationhood and national unity. . . .

. . . To conclude that the Government may permit designated symbols to be used to communicate only a limited set of messages would be to enter territory having no discernible or defensible boundaries. Could the Government, on this theory, prohibit the burning of state flags? Of copies of the Presidential seal? Of the Constitution? In evaluating these choices under the First Amendment, how would we decide which symbols were sufficiently special to warrant this unique status? To do so, we would be forced to consult our own political preferences, and impose them on the citizenry, in the very way that the First Amendment forbids us to do. . . .

There is, moreover, no indication—either in the text of the Constitution or in our cases interpreting it—that a separate juridical category exists for the American flag alone. Indeed, we would not be surprised to learn that the persons who framed our Constitution and wrote the Amendment that we now construe were not known for their reverence for the Union Jack. The First Amendment does not guarantee that other concepts virtually sacred to our Nation as a whole—such as the

principle that discrimination on the basis of race is odious and destructive—will go unquestioned in the marketplace of ideas. . . . We decline, therefore, to create for the flag an exception to the joust of principles protected by the First Amendment. . . .

We are tempted to say, in fact, that the flag's deservedly cherished place in our community will be strengthened, not weakened, by our holding today. Our decision is a reaffirmation of the principles of freedom and inclusiveness that the flag best reflects, and of the conviction that our toleration of criticism such as Johnson's is a sign and source of our strength. Indeed, one of the proudest images of our flag, the one immortalized in out own national anthem, is of the bombardment it survived at Fort McHenry. It is the Nation's resilience, not its rigidity, that Texas sees reflected in the flag—and it is that resilience that we reassert today.

The way to preserve the flag's special role is not to punish those who feel differently about these matters. It is to persuade them that they are wrong. . . .

. . . We can imagine no more appropriate response to burning a flag than waving one's own, no better way to counter a flag-burner's message than by saluting the flag that burns, no surer means of preserving the dignity even of the flag that burned than by—as one witness here did—according its remains a respectful burial. We do not consecrate the flag by punishing its desecration, for in doing so we dilute the freedom that this cherished emblem represents.

Chief Justice Rehnquist, with whom Justice White and Justice O'Connor join, dissenting.

· · ·

The American flag, throughout more than 200 years of history, has come to be the visible symbol embodying our Nation. It does not represent the views of any particular political party, and it does not represent any particular political philosophy. The flag is not simply another "idea" or "point of view" competing for recognition in the marketplace of ideas. Millions and millions of Americans regard it with an almost mystical reverence regardless of what sort of social, political, or philosophical beliefs they may have. I cannot agree that the First Amendment invalidates the Act of Congress, and the laws of 48 of the 50 States, which make criminal the public burning of the flag.

· · ·

Johnson's public burning of the flag in this case . . . obviously did convey Johnson's bitter dislike of his country. But his act . . . conveyed nothing that could not have been conveyed and was not conveyed just as forcefully in a dozen different ways. As with "fighting words," so with flag burning, for purposes of the First

Amendment: it is "no essential part of any exposition of ideas, and [is] of such slight social value as a step to truth that any benefit that may be derived from [it] is clearly outweighed" by the public interest in avoiding probable breach of the peace. The highest courts of several States have upheld state statutes prohibiting the public burning of the flag on the grounds that it is so inherently inflammatory that it may cause a breach of public order. . . .

The result of the Texas statute is obviously to deny one in Johnson's frame of mind one of many means of "symbolic speech." Far from being a case of "one picture being worth a thousand words," flag burning is the equivalent of an inarticulate grunt or roar that, it seems fair to say, is most likely to be indulged in not to express any particular idea, but to antagonize others. Only five years ago we said . . . that "the First Amendment does not guarantee the right to employ every conceivable method of communication at all times and in all places." The Texas statute deprived Johnson of only one rather inarticulate symbolic form of protest—a form of protest that was profoundly offensive to many—and left him with a full panoply of other symbols and every conceivable form of verbal expression to express his deep disapproval of national policy. Thus, in no way

can it be said that Texas is punishing him because his hearers—or any other group of people—were profoundly opposed to the message that he sought to convey. Such opposition is no proper basis for restricting speech or expression under the First Amendment. It was Johnson's use of this particular symbol, and not the idea that he sought to convey by it or by his many other expressions, for which he was punished.

Endnotes

[1] Tex. Penal Code Ann. §42.09 (1989) provides in full: "§42.09. Desecration of Venerated Object

"(a) A person commits an offense if he intentionally or knowingly desecrates:

"(1) a public monument;

"(2) a place of worship or burial; or

"(3) a state or national flag.

"(b) For purposes of this section, 'desecrate' means deface, damage, or otherwise physically mistreat in a way that the actor know will seriously offend one or more persons likely to observe or discover his action.

"(c) An offense under this section is a Class A misdemeanor."

People of the State of Michigan v. Timothy Joseph Boomer

> Timothy Boomer, a rafting enthusiast, became too enthusiastic for his own good! Canoeing down a river in Michigan, Boomer fell overboard and proceeded to utter "a stream of profanities" while extricating himself from the water. Boomer's colorful exasperation was overheard by other recreationists, some of whom included children. Boomer was arrested for violating a Michigan law that made it a misdemeanor to use "indecent" or "vulgar" language "in the presence or hearing of any woman or child." Boomer challenged the law on First Amendment grounds. How might Devlin's view be used to develop a justification for this kind of law? Would you find that justification convincing?

MURPHY, J.

Defendant appeals by leave granted his misdemeanor conviction, following a district court jury trial,

---

467 Mich. 889; 653 N.W.2d 406 (2002).

of using indecent and vulgar language. MCL 750.337. The district court imposed a sentence of four days' community service, plus fines and costs of $75 or three days in jail. Defendant's conviction was affirmed on appeal to the circuit court. Defendant argues, as he did below, that MCL 750.337 is unconstitutional. We reverse defendant's conviction because MCL 750.337 is unconstitutionally vague.

1. Basic Facts and Procedural History

Defendant's conviction arose out of events that occurred on the Rifle River in Arenac County on August 15, 1998. Witness Michael Smith was canoeing down the Rifle River with his wife and two children approximately forty yards behind defendant's party, which consisted of five canoes. Smith testified that he saw defendant fall out of his canoe and into the river, at which point defendant loudly uttered a stream of profanities, while slapping the water and throwing his hands in the air.

Kenneth Socia, a road patrol deputy for the Arenac County Sheriff's Department who was on duty at the Rifle River that day, testified that he heard a "loud commotion" and "vulgar language" coming from approximately one-quarter mile up the river. Socia looked up and saw defendant chasing a group of canoes, splashing water at them with his paddle, and repeatedly swearing at them. Socia and Smith both testified that the river was crowded with families and children, and that defendant would have been able to see Smith's two children, who were under five years old. Socia issued defendant a citation for violating MCL 750.337.

MCL 750.337 provides:

> Any person who shall use any indecent, immoral, obscene, vulgar or insulting language in the presence or hearing of any woman or child shall be guilty of a misdemeanor.

Before trial in the district court, defendant moved to dismiss the charge on the grounds that the statute was unconstitutionally vague and overbroad, and was also unconstitutional as applied to this case. The district court denied the motion, and the case went to the jury. Defendant was convicted. . . .

II. Defendants Arguments on Appeal

Defendant argues that his conviction must be reversed because MCL 750.337 is facially unconstitutional on both overbreadth and vagueness grounds. Defendant further argues that his conviction must be reversed because MCL 750.337 is unconstitutional as applied to the circumstances of this case. Finally, defendant argues that his conviction must be reversed because the district court severed the portion of MCL 750.337 concerning "the presence or hearing of any woman," thereby violating the Legislature's intent in enacting the statute.

III. Analysis

We find it unnecessary to address defendant's overbreadth arguments, or to undertake an extensive First Amendment analysis, because we hold that MCL 750.337 is unconstitutionally vague.

MCL 750.337 was enacted, in its present form, in 1931, with its legislative origins dating back to an earlier version enacted in 1897. . . . The earlier version of the statute contained the same language as the present version, except that it provided that it applied to language used within the limits of any township, village, or city in the state of Michigan. 1897 PA 219. Throughout the one hundred plus years of its existence, there have been no published Michigan cases addressing the statute.

In considering defendant's challenge to the constitutionality of MCL 750.337, this Court adheres to the well-established rule that a statute is presumed to be constitutional and is so construed unless its unconstitutionality is clearly apparent. The fact that a statute may appear undesirable, unfair, unjust, or inhumane does not of itself render a statute unconstitutional and empower a court to override the Legislature.

In *People v. Lino*, 447 Mich 567, 575, n 2: 527 NW2d 434 (1994), our Supreme Court noted that a constitutional challenge based on vagueness "is brought under the Due Process Clause of the Fourteenth Amendment of the United States Constitution." The *Lino* Court, explaining the vagueness doctrine, stated that "[i]n order to pass constitutional muster, a penal statute must define the criminal offense 'with sufficient definiteness that ordinary people can understand what conduct is prohibited and in a manner that does not encourage arbitrary and discriminatory enforcement.'"

"[T]here are at least three ways a penal statute may be found unconstitutionally vague: (1) failure to provide fair notice of what conduct is prohibited, (2) encouragement of arbitrary and discriminatory enforcement, or (3) being overbroad and impinging on First Amendment freedoms."

The explanation of the void-for-vagueness doctrine enunciated by the United States Supreme Court . . . clearly points out the reasons for the doctrine:

> It is a basic principle of due process that an enactment is void for vagueness if its prohibitions are not clearly defined. Vague laws

offend several important values. First, because we assume that man is free to steer between lawful and unlawful conduct, we insist that laws give the person of ordinary intelligence a reasonable opportunity to know what is prohibited, so that he may act accordingly. Vague laws may trap the innocent by not providing fair warning. Second, if arbitrary and discriminatory enforcement is to be prevented, laws must provide explicit standards for those who apply them. A vague law impermissibly delegates basic policy matters to policemen, judges, and juries for resolution on an ad hoc and subjective basis, with the attendant dangers of arbitrary and discriminatory application. Third, but related, where a vague statute "abut[s] upon sensitive areas of basic First Amendment freedoms," it "operates to inhibit the exercise of [those] freedoms." Uncertain meanings inevitably lead citizens to "'steer far wider of the unlawful zone' . . . than if the boundaries of the forbidden areas were clearly marked."

Here, it would be difficult to conceive of a statute that would be more vague than MCL 750.337. There is no restrictive language whatsoever contained in the statute that would limit or guide a prosecution for indecent, immoral, obscene, vulgar, or insulting language. Allowing a prosecution where one utters "insulting" language could possibly subject a vast percentage of the populace to a misdemeanor conviction.

MCL 750.337 contains no . . . legislative guidance. Even if the statute were judicially construed to apply only to speech that a reasonable person should know is indecent, immoral, or vulgar when used in the presence of a child, as plaintiff urges, in our opinion, it would remain vague. This construction would require every person who speaks audibly where children are present to guess what a law enforcement officer might consider too indecent, immoral, or vulgar for a child's ears. Children aside, it is far from obvious what the reasonable adult considers to be indecent, immoral, vulgar, or insulting. As a result, a judicially imposed "reasonable person" limitation would not, in our opinion, cure the vagueness of the statute. . . . Here, we find it unquestionable that MCL 750.337, as drafted, reaches constitutionally protected speech, and it operates to inhibit the exercise of First Amendment rights.

MCL 750.337 is an unconstitutional enactment in violation of the Due Process Clause of the Fourteenth Amendment of the United States Constitution because the statute is facially vague. Therefore, because defendant's conviction was based on the unconstitutional statute, we reverse the conviction.

Reversed.

Reynolds v. United States

Living in what is now the state of Utah in 1878, George Reynolds was charged and convicted of the offense of bigamy (entering into a state of marriage with a person when one already has a living spouse). On appeal, Reynolds argued that he was a member of the Mormon Church and that polygamy was not only permissible by the tenets of that faith (at the time), but actually mandatory "where circumstances permit." He claimed that he had a right freely to exercise his religion. The Supreme Court disagreed, cautioning that, while "mere religious belief and opinion" cannot be interfered with, religious practices are not always shielded by the Constitution. Is there a principled way to decide which religious practices must be allowed and which must not be tolerated? What guidance does the Court give in addressing this question? What do you think Mill would say of this case? What about a church whose members believe that Scripture commands them to handle poisonous snakes? What of a church whose rituals involve the consumption of illegal substances? Or one that denies traditional forms of medical care to children?

This is an indictment found in the District Court for the third judicial district of the Territory of Utah, charging George Reynolds with bigamy, in violation of sect. 5352 of the Revised Statutes, which, omitting its exceptions, is as follows:

> Every person having a husband or wife living, who marries another, whether married or single, in a Territory, or other place over which the United States have exclusive jurisdiction, is guilty of bigamy, and shall be punished by a fine of not more that $500, and by imprisonment for a term of not more than five years.

. . .

On the trial, the plaintiff in error, the accused, proved that at the time of his alleged second marriage he was, and for many years before had been, a member of the Church of Jesus Christ of Latter-Day Saints, commonly called the Mormon Church, and a believer in its doctrines; that it was an accepted doctrine of that church "that it was the duty of male members of said church, circumstances permitting, to practise polygamy; . . . that this duty was enjoined by different books which the members of said church believed to be to divine origin, and among others the Holy Bible, and also that the members of the church believed that the practice of polygamy was directly enjoined upon the male members thereof by the Almighty God, in a revelation to Joseph Smith, the founder and prophet of said church; that the failing or refusing to practise polygamy by such male members of said church, when circumstances would admit, would be punished, and the penalty for such failure and refusal would be damnation in the life to come." He also proved "that he had received permission from the recognized authorities in said church to enter into polygamous marriage; . . . that Daniel H. Wells, one having authority in said church to perform the marriage ceremony, married the said defendant on or about the time the crime is alleged to have been committed, to some woman by the name of Schofield, and that such marriage ceremony was performed under and pursuant to the doctrines of said church."

Upon this proof he asked the court to instruct the jury that if they found from the evidence that he "was married as charged—if he was married—in pursuance of and in conformity with what he believed at the time

to be a religious duty, that the verdict must be 'not guilty.'" This request was refused, and the court did charge "that there must have been a criminal intent, but that if the defendant, under the influence of a religious belief that it was right—under an inspiration, if you please, that it was right—deliberately married a second time, having a first wife living, the want of consciousness of evil intent—the want of understanding on his part that he was committing a crime—did not excuse him; but the law inexorably in such case implies the criminal intent."

Upon this charge and refusal to charge the question is raised, whether religious belief can be accepted as a justification of an overt act made criminal by the law of the land. The inquiry is not as to the power of Congress to prescribe criminal laws for the Territories, but as to the guilt of one who knowingly violates a law which has been properly enacted, if he entertains a religious belief that the law is wrong.

Congress cannot pass a law for the government of the Territories which shall prohibit the free exercise of religion. The first amendment to the Constitution expressly forbids such legislation. Religious freedom is guaranteed everywhere throughout the United States, so far as congressional interference is concerned. The question to be determined is, whether the law now under consideration comes within this prohibition.

Polygamy has always been odious among the northern and western nations of Europe, and, until the establishment of the Mormon Church was almost exclusively a feature of the life of Asiatic and of African people. At common law, the second marriage was always void (2 Kent, Com. 79), and from the earliest history of England polygamy has been treated as an offence against society. After the establishment of the ecclesiastical courts, and until the time of James I, it was punished through the instrumentality of those tribunals, not merely because ecclesiastical rights had been violated, but because upon the separation of the ecclesiastical courts from the civil the ecclesiastical were supposed to be the most appropriate for the trial of matrimonial causes and offences against the rights of marriage, just as they were for testamentary causes and the settlement of the estate of Deceased persons.

By the statute of 1 James I (c. 11), the offence, if committed in England or Wales, was made publishable in the civil courts, and the penalty was death. As this statute was limited in its operation to England and Wales, it was at a very early period re-enacted, generally with some modifications, in all

---

98 U.S. 145 (1878), United States Supreme Court.

the colonies. In connection with the case we are now considering, it is a significant fact that on the 8th of December, 1788, after the passage of the act establishing religious freedom, and after the convention of Virginia had recommended as an amendment to the Constitution of the United States the declaration in a bill of rights that "all men have an equal, natural, and unalienable right to the free exercise of religion, according to the dictates of conscience," the legislature of that State substantially enacted the statute of James I, death penalty included, because, as recited in the preamble, "it hath been doubted whether bigamy or polygamy be punishable by the laws of this Commonwealth." 12 Hening's Stat. 691. From that day to this we think it may safely be said there never has been a time in any State of the Union when polygamy has not been an offence against society, cognizable by the civil courts and punishable with more or less severity. In the face of all this evidence, it is impossible to believe that the constitutional guaranty of religious freedom was intended to prohibit legislation in respect to this most important feature of social life. Marriage, while from its very nature a sacred obligation, is nevertheless, in most civilized nations, a civil contract, and usually regulated by law. Upon it society may be said to be built, and out of its fruits spring social relations and social obligations and duties, with which government is necessarily required to deal. In fact, according as monogamous or polygamous marriages are allowed,

do we find the principles on which the government of the people to a greater or less extent, rests.

· · ·

[T]he only question which remains is, whether those who make polygamy a part of their religion are excepted from the operation of the statute. If they are, then those who do not make polygamy a part of their religious belief may be found guilty and punished, while those who do, must be acquitted and go free. This would be introducing a new element into criminal law. Laws are made for the government of actions, and while they cannot interfere with mere religious belief and opinions, they may with practices. Suppose one believed that human sacrifices were a necessary part of religious worship, would it be seriously contended that the civil government under which he lived could not interfere to prevent a sacrifice? Or if a wife religiously believed it was her duty to burn herself upon the funeral pyre of her dead husband, would it be beyond the power of the civil government to prevent her carrying her belief into practice?

So here, as a law of the organization of society under the exclusive dominion of the United States, it is profited that plural marriages shall not be allowed. Can a man excuse his practices to the contrary because of his religious belief? To permit this would be to make the professed doctrines of religious belief superior to the law of the land, and in effect to permit every citizen to become a law unto himself. Government could exist only in name under such circumstances.

Chapter 3

Constitutional Law: Equal Protection of the Laws

The ideals of equality and justice are among the most powerful of those by which we purport to live. Many believe that the highest purpose of our law is to bring about justice and to treat persons equally; the central place given to these principles in the Constitution and the Declaration of Independence testifies to their importance. Yet, as with the guarantees of freedom of speech and religion, the aspiration to equality brings with it a host of deep and perplexing philosophical problems. Chapter 3 introduces us to these dilemmas.

Just what is the condition of "equality"? And can the law bring it about? The material in Section A investigates these questions, focusing on the constitutional requirement of "equal protection of the laws" and its implementation through antidiscrimination law and programs of preferential treatment or "affirmative action." What kind of equality does the Constitution guarantee? Should it tolerate any differences in treatment based on race? Should it be "color-blind"? Or must the law recognize and respond to racial differences in order to bring about a more equitable distribution of social wealth in the future? The Supreme Court's most recent ruling on affirmative action, in *Grutter v. Bollinger*, is followed by readings which explore not only the pros and cons of preferential treatment programs, but also basic questions about the meaning and reality of race as a way of categorizing individuals, and the recently disputed issue of reparations for the enslavement of African Americans.

Section B looks at discrimination based on sexual orientation and gender. What concept of sexual equality does the Constitution endorse? What forms of gender bias exist in the law? And should all distinctions based upon sex be impermissible? The section begins with a state court ruling that generated much disagreement and which addressed this question: Are existing bans on same-sex marriage a violation of equal protection? This controversy is framed and further examined by law professor Cass Sunstein. Subsequent essays argue against various forms of gender-bias in the law. The section ends with one contributor's concept of a society in which ideal gender equality has been achieved.

The final section of this chapter surveys some issues in the field of family law. The rights of an unwed father are the subject of *Michael H. v. Gerald D.*; other selections review how legislatures and courts have tried to sort out the legal implications of emerging reproductive technologies.

The "Cases for Further Reflection" at the end of the chapter include a variety of court cases dealing with difficult issues of equality, discrimination, and fairness: Did the Supreme Court's decision in *Bush v. Gore* isolate a genuine violation of equality? Does it discriminate against either partner in an interracial relationship to forbid them to marry? May a state offer education at a state-sponsored university yet forbid women to enroll as students?

A. *Equal Protection Law, Racial Discrimination, and Affirmative Action*

The idea of equality is deceptively simple. As an illustration, consider the following case. Florida Power, a regional utility, laid off more than 1,200 employees during the mid-1990s. The layoffs were necessary, the utility argued, in order to maintain the company's competitiveness in a deregulated market. Of the 1,200, more than 70 percent were over 40 years old. A number of the former employees then sued Florida Power, alleging that the company had engaged in age discrimination. Under both state and federal law, it is discriminatory to treat persons in differing ways merely because of their age, gender, or race. To do so is to fail to accord "equal protection" to all.

Did Florida Power treat its employees unequally on the basis of age? Certainly, it laid off a proportionately higher number of older workers. Is this fact sufficient to show that Florida Power intended to discriminate against people on the basis of age? Suppose the utility contends that its layoffs were justified on grounds other than age. As you can see, the questions of just what "equal protection" means, and of how to establish violations of it, are difficult indeed.

It is surprising to many to learn that the original Constitution of 1789 makes no mention of "equality." Nor does the term appear in any of the first ten Amendments—the so-called "Bill of Rights." The original document arguably does address religious discrimination, at least indirectly, in the form of the "Establishment" and "Free Exercise" clauses of the First Amendment. (See Chapter 2 for more on these notions.) And the Constitution prohibits "titles of nobility." These aspects of the original Constitution very much reflect the aspirations and concerns of its Enlightenment authors, who believed in the equal opportunity to pursue happiness without the impediment of legal restrictions based on heredity or religious affiliation. It was not until the aftermath of the Civil War, however, that equality became part of the amended Constitution.

Today, the ultimate source and focus for the philosophically difficult legal issues regarding equality is the Fourteenth Amendment to the Constitution, and in particular, the so-called *Equal Protection* clause, guaranteeing that no state shall "deny to any person within its jurisdiction the equal protection of the laws." A brief discussion of the background to and subsequent development of this clause will set the stage for exploring the difficulties it poses.

The Fourteenth Amendment

Following the Civil War, the Congress passed a number of constitutional amendments with the aim of "reconstructing" the South and healing the nation. The Thirteenth Amendment prohibited slavery and gave Congress the power to take steps to eradicate it. In response, many of the Southern states passed harsh and restrictive laws applying to Blacks, curtailing their civil rights in various ways, though short of an outright return to slavery. To eliminate these "Black Codes," Congress enacted the Civil Rights Act of 1866. This act granted to newly freed Blacks a small number of specifically enumerated but limited rights: to enter into contracts, to sue, to hold and convey property, to move about without threat of arrest. While the original draft language of the act apparently included a reference to general "civil rights and immunities," this was later dropped.

According to some scholars, the majority of the supporters of the 1866 act were against the idea of full political and social equality for Blacks, and this may have been a factor in the passage of the Fourteenth Amendment. According to legal historian Raoul

Berger, one group of legislators, concerned that the act have a proper foundation in the Constitution, proposed the Fourteenth Amendment to serve that purpose; and it was their view that the Equal Protection Clause guaranteed to Blacks no more than the few specific rights listed in the act. Other factions, however, seemingly had larger ambitions and may have intended that "equal protection of the law" be broadly read to ensure full political and social equality for Blacks.

Throughout the rest of the nineteenth century and well into this one, the narrow conception of equality predominated in the courts. In 1896, in *Plessy v. Ferguson*,[1] the Supreme Court held that the segregation of Blacks and Whites on public transit facilities (and by implication in various other public facilities) did not violate the guarantee of equal protection, provided that such separate facilities were roughly similar; and the Court noted that many of the states that supported the Fourteenth Amendment had, for example, segregated their schools and prohibited racial intermarriage. This "separate-but-equal" doctrine prevailed until 1954 and the landmark case *Brown v. Board of Education*.[2] Finding that the practice of segregation stamped Blacks with "a badge of inferiority," the Court concluded that separate but equal "is inherently unequal." Later cases prohibited racial segregation in a whole variety of public facilities and settings.

The significance for us of the history just sketched is twofold. First, it seems clearly to show that the understanding of equality now endorsed by the courts, and presumably by the great majority of Americans, moves well beyond any views reasonably attributable to the framers of the Fourteenth Amendment; they, it appears, may well have regarded *Plessy* as correctly decided and *Brown* as a misinterpretation of the amendment's language. Second, the fact of two such divergent interpretations as *Plessy* and *Brown* reveals just how flexible and open-ended is the language of the Equal Protection Clause. If we acknowledge that the guarantee of equality may mean more than its authors took it to mean, and if we recognize the breadth and sweep of the text itself, we are brought to the edge of a basic issue in social and political philosophy: What is equality? What concept of equality should we understand our law to endorse? Why is equality desirable?

---

[1] 163 U.S. 537 (1896).
[2] 347 U.S. 483 (1954).

The Concept of Equality

Thinking about the idea of equality quickly leads to puzzlement. This fact is demonstrated in the selection reprinted here by Peter Westen. Westen employs a series of illustrations to show that treating people equally is not as easy as it seems. What, for example, can it mean to treat people equally when making them equal in one way has the effect of making them unequal in another respect? Westen's aim is to highlight this and similar questions.

Even assuming that we understand what equality means, why is it important to treat people equally? Suppose that you and I are both hungry. We have both gone without food for the same length of time and for the same reasons. We are physically quite alike and both extremely weak. What gives each of us an equal claim to a piece of food? The answer given by many philosophers going back to Aristotle invokes a basic moral principle that has been thought by some to be self-evidently true: *Those who are the same in relevant respects ought to be treated the same with regard to those respects;* or *Those similarly situated should be similarly treated.* This *formal principle of equality* reveals an important feature of the concept of equality: When we ask whether two things or two people are "equal," we must always be assumed to be asking this question relative to an aspect of the things or people that we judge to be relevant. It is not enough simply to ask "Are A and B equal?" The question makes no sense until we further specify the traits in which A and B are to be judged equal or unequal. Are A and B equal with respect to height, weight, shoe size, intelligence, bravery, moral worth? We must have in mind, in other words, the parameters within which they are to be judged similar or dissimilar, the relevant respects in which they are the same or different.

One way to understand the Equal Protection Clause of the Constitution is as a confirmation or implementation of the formal principle of equality: The clause says that legislatures must treat similarly those who are similarly situated with respect to the purposes of the laws they pass. After a legislature decides which people are to be affected by a new law, for example, it must further ensure that those people are treated equally with respect to that law.

The problem in all of this, of course, is that the formal principle of equality and the Equal Protection Clause understood simply as a guarantee of formal equality say nothing by themselves about which are the traits that matter. They merely lay down a requirement of fair administration, prohibiting differences in treatment among those who have already been determined to be the same in the relevant way. In one crucial respect, however, the Equal Protection Clause of the Fourteenth Amendment is not merely a guarantee of formal equality, for that clause actually rules out altogether, as ever relevant to how people should be treated, one trait or characteristic: the fact of being Black.

It is obvious that people differ from each other in a variety of ways, for example, in their physical characteristics and abilities, and in their talents, aptitudes, and interests. And it is also apparent that when people notice or recognize ways in which others are different from themselves, they often use that recognition as a reason for treating the others less well. The recognition of difference both supports and further reinforces prejudicial attitudes and biases. The concept of equality, however, demands that differences in how people are treated must be justified by sufficiently compelling reasons. Under existing law, this demand precludes the acknowledgment of at least some differences from becoming prejudicial practices, and the law does this by disallowing that certain differences matter. In this way, the concept of equality is connected to the idea of *justice*. In one sense, treating people justly means that all are given a fair share of the goods, services, and opportunities that society has to offer. If I am denied an opportunity based on an irrelevant difference, I am the victim of injustice. In another sense, justice may demand that I be compensated for something of which I have been unfairly deprived. If I have been wrongly treated on the basis of an irrelevant characteristic, I may demand compensation from those who wronged me. As we will see, both of these forms of justice are relevant to contemporary debates, for example, over programs of affirmative action.

But the problem remains: How do we specify the differences among people that matter or are relevant to how people should be treated? Generally speaking, the law has sought to solve this problem through a negative process of elimination: Instead of trying to settle on all of the ways in which, ideally, people should be regarded as similarly situated, the law has contented itself with seeking to identify and root out the respects that should *not* matter, the traits or characteristics that do not justify differences in treatment. This approach derives support from the basic aim of the post–Civil War amendments to the

Constitution: to prohibit at least some forms of discrimination against Blacks, "race, color, or previous condition of servitude" are traits on which the Constitution says it is unfair or unjust to base differences in treatment. Other parts of the Constitution, and of our law generally, would add national origin, religious affiliation, and status as an illegitimate child to the list of proscribed traits. Any law that classifies people on the basis of these traits automatically becomes "suspect" and must be subjected to "strict scrutiny" to determine whether it is justified by a "compelling" interest of the state. To treat people differently or unequally on the basis of these characteristics without such a compelling reason is to practice discrimination.

Many of us think of discrimination on the basis of race or religion as the most fundamental violation of equality, yet the concept of discrimination is not without its own difficulties. How is discrimination to be identified and remedied? When does a practice that disadvantages a particular population or group become "discriminatory"? School districts in many parts of the country were at one time racially segregated by law, yet even when such deliberately discriminatory efforts were ended, their effects lingered through segregated housing patterns and school attendance zones. Is this "de facto" segregation a violation of the equal protection of the laws that should be remedied by, for example, forced busing of students? Or is it the consequence of private "choice" for which government is not responsible? Consider the example of a state that enacts a law requiring a passing score on a literacy test as a prerequisite to registration as a voter. The test has the effect of disqualifying almost all of the Latinos in the state, but nearly all Whites pass the exam. How should a law that has a disproportionate racial impact but is nonetheless nondiscriminatory "on its face" be viewed? Should it automatically be presumed invalid? Should it be taken as evidence of racial prejudice operating behind the scenes? Should the fact that it is color-blind on its face be sufficient to let it stand? Finally, there is the issue of remedies for discrimination. Should the victims of past discrimination be given some kind of favored treatment? Should a firm or other employer shown to have discriminated in the past be required to hire a fixed percentage of its workforce from among members of the minority group against which it discriminated? Should it matter if the actual minority persons hired were not the individuals originally turned down for a job?

Anti-Discrimination Law and Race

The format of the 2000 Census generated much disagreement. Attempting to reflect the growing multiracial character of the U.S. population, Census officials decided to add new, mixed-race categories to the survey, bringing the total number of racial categories to fifty-seven. Historians point out that the census has frequently played a significant role in defining ethnicities. In the early 1800s, for example, Irish immigrants were classified as "Negroes," whereas Armenian immigrants were "raced" as "white"; the term "Hispanic" was incorporated in the 1970s to cover people from a number of specific backgrounds. No one was sure how the new census data would affect racial demographics or the legal distinctions and doctrines incorporating them. For example, it was argued that, with many Americans claiming some degree of Native American heritage, the total number of Native Americans could double or triple in one year. Also unclear were the implications for anti-discrimination law. If a mixed-race individual makes a discrimination complaint, does it matter which race, or combination of races, is alleged to be the target of the discriminatory conduct? How would affirmative-action programs be implemented in the face of a burgeoning number of "races"? If an employer is ordered to hire additional Black workers, for example, will it have complied with the order if the person is of mixed-race background? Would it matter if the person was hired "as Black" or as a member of some other category?

For some scholars, the foregoing disputes only highlight what they now maintain should be obvious: the entire notion of "race" as a name for a discrete, biological category is a sham. Race, these scholars argue, is a thoroughly social construct. Summarizing the views of these scholars in her essay, Naomi Zack explains that no physical property has ever been identified that picks out all and only people otherwise believed to be members of a single race. Zack looks at various cultural meanings of race and how those meanings have affected important legal classifications and distinctions.

The Grutter Case and Affirmative Action

Among the most hotly contested issues concerning equality is the use of race as a basis for differential treatment. Is it *always* impermissible to use traits such as ethnic or national origin as factors on the basis of which to treat people differently or unequally? This query has been given sharp focus with respect to programs of "preferential treatment" or "affirmative action" policies in education and employment. Supporters argue that such programs are required by ideas of fairness and the greater social good; opponents contend that such practices disserve the ideal of equality.

In June 2003, the U.S. Supreme Court handed down a much-anticipated ruling that is the latest word on the legal dimensions of the preferential treatment controversy. The Law School at the University of Michigan followed a formal admissions policy that sought to achieve student body diversity along a number of dimensions, but with particular reference to ethnic diversity, and the inclusion of African American, Hispanic, and Native American students. By enrolling a "critical mass" of underrepresented students, the policy sought to enhance the character of the student body and, ultimately, the legal profession. Grutter, a white resident of Michigan, filed suit alleging the Law School had discriminated against her on the basis of race, since the admissions policy used race as a "predominant" factor in the selection process.

Grutter's claim had been made before, and rulings in these prior cases became important precedents explored by the Court in its ruling in *Grutter*. In one of these cases, the plaintiff, Cheryl Hopwood, applied for admission to the University of Texas law school. She had a 3.8 grade point average (GPA) and scored in the 83rd percentile on the LSAT. In the early 1990s, the Texas law school admitted about 500 students a year, accepting students who scored better than 85 percent of all college graduates who took the LSAT and had a 3.5 GPA. Texas, like other law schools, sought to recruit a "diverse" class of incoming students. In 1992, however, only eighty-eight African American and fifty-two Mexican American students in the entire nation satisfied these standards. To achieve diversity, Texas therefore segregated its admissions process, reviewing separately applications from African American and Mexican American students. Hopwood, who was white, was denied admission and filed suit, alleging racial discrimination by the law school.

Hopwood argued that only one of the forty-one African American students and three of the Mexican American students admitted to Texas in 1992 had scores that matched hers. Hopwood insisted that the university operated a virtual "quota system" for certain students. University officials countered that the

African American and Mexican American students it admitted were qualified, with average GPAs of around 3.3. It also pointed out that the population of the state of Texas is nearly 50 percent African and Mexican American, and that the university would not be doing its job if it enrolled students on the numbers alone. In March 1996, the Fifth U.S. Circuit Court of Appeals accepted Hopwood's arguments and struck down the University of Texas plan on the grounds that it failed to pass the test of "strict scrutiny." In June 1996, the U.S. Supreme Court, in a move widely viewed as further repudiation of affirmative action, refused to hear an appeal.

The most significant precedent debated in *Grutter*, however, was decided in 1978. The medical school at the University of California at Davis ran two admissions programs, one for "regular" applicants and one for "special," disadvantaged students. Sixteen of the 100 seats in the entering class were set aside for students from the special program, which had a lower minimum grade point average requirement than the regular program. Alan Bakke was twice rejected under the regular program, although students with lower overall scores were admitted through the special program. Bakke sued the university, alleging that he was unjustifiably excluded from the medical school in violation of both the equal protection clause of the Constitution and the Civil Rights Act of 1964. The trial court agreed with Bakke but refused to order the school to admit him; this was done by the Supreme Court of California.

The United States Supreme Court split badly on the issues involved in *Bakke*, with Justice Powell emerging as the key figure. (Powell voted against "quotas" but in favor of using race as a factor in medical school admissions. Four other justices held that the Civil Rights Act, and by implication the Equal Protection Clause, prohibits any consideration of race as a relevant factor, joining with Powell to make a majority against quotas; another four justices held that Davis-type preferential treatment programs are permissible under both the act and the Constitution, joining with Powell in asserting that consideration of race and ethnicity is allowable.) Because Powell was the key vote, much of the subsequent legal discussion of preferential treatment programs has concentrated on his view.

As we saw earlier, the courts have long held that any ordinance, policy, or practice that treats a person's race as a factor relevant to how he or she is to be treated by the government must be subjected to "strict scrutiny," meaning that the law must be shown necessary to the realization of a "compelling" objective if it

is to have any hope of being upheld. Justice Powell argued that such scrutiny must be applied to the Davis program, and he carefully reviewed the various arguments given by Davis to support preferential treatment: to increase the representation of minority students in medical school; to "cure" societal discrimination; to better serve the health needs of the minority community. Powell rejected these as constitutionally impermissible grounds for preferential treatment but argued that another purpose—to promote diversity—is legitimate and may permit the use of race as one factor among many in admissions decisions. The Constitution will not tolerate, however, policies that unduly burden the rights of particular, innocent individuals such as Bakke simply to further the social standing of certain groups.

Equality and Preferential Treatment

Two of the arguments most commonly offered in support of preferential treatment programs are based on the idea of justice. The first argument appeals to the obvious inequalities of material condition and opportunity currently existing between Whites and members of other ethnic and racial groups and claims that such differences are the result of *distributive injustice,* an unequal distribution of benefits stemming from the use of race as a relevant factor in the distribution of social wealth: jobs, educational opportunities, and so forth. Preferences are therefore needed now to place Blacks and other minorities in positions they would have had but for the discrimination, positions they would presumably have attained under conditions of fair competition.

Those favoring affirmative action point to significant evidence of continuing disparities, ethnic and gendered, among the nation's educational institutions and within the workforce. In 2001, the National Center for Education Statistics reported that the "earnings gap" between Blacks and Whites remained significant, with Blacks on average making 32 percent less than Whites.[3] Blacks had a 10 percent lower rate of college attendance in the early 1990s than Whites; and college completion rates were consistently lower for Blacks than for Whites.[4] In primary and secondary education, compared with White children, Blacks scored lower

---

[3] See http://nces.ed.gov/pubs2001/inequality/4.asp
[4] See http://nces.ed.gov/pubs2001/inequality/5.asp

both on math and readings tests than Whites at every level, from grade 1 through grade 12.[5] *Business Week*'s directory of 1,000 publicly held companies lists only one Black and two female executive officers.[6] Of two million engineers in America, only 2 percent are Hispanic. Of 225,000 physical scientists, 3 percent are Black and less than 2 percent are Hispanic. Blacks and Hispanics comprise less than 21.2 percent of the lawyers in the nation's largest law firms. According to another recent survey, seven out of ten Blacks and Latinos remain in low-level jobs. Nearly 80 percent of all skilled jobs are still held by White males.[7]

Nor have women fared much better. Many women continue to be relegated to poor-paying "pink-collar" jobs or are stranded in entry-level positions at the bottom of the corporate ladder. According to one university study, one quarter of the 1,300 women polled earn a poverty-level income. In 2001, it was reported that pay discrepancy between White men and woman is larger than that between men and woman who are Black or Hispanic.[8] Women, on average, still earn only 79 cents for every dollar earned by men.[9]

The foregoing figures are taken to reveal significant and continuing disparities in material resources and prestige between Whites and non-Whites, and between men and women. The reasons for these disparities are rarely overt or blatant discrimination; proponents of affirmative action suggest that the disparities are much more likely the result of institutional barriers: the use of qualification requirements, employment networks and tradition, and the effects of previous legal segregation. Employers who use race- or gender-neutral qualifications as the basis of their hiring practices might create a disadvantage for minorities. Nearly all employers insist that they want to hire the most qualified candidates; yet qualifications justifiable on grounds of ensuring productivity may also put at a comparative disadvantage individuals whose education was second-rate. This problem is particularly acute for Blacks in the labor force who attended legally segregated schools in which there was likely a presumption of Black inferiority, or for

women who were taught that analytical and scientific reasoning are unfeminine and that their proper role in society is to get married and become housewives.

Another argument maintains that the case for preferential treatment rests on the notion of *reparation:* we must institute programs to aid minorities not because we want to achieve some ideal of equal opportunity but because the present condition of Blacks in America is a direct result of a history of injustices committed against them by Whites and because reparation, so understood, is owed by Whites as a group to Blacks as a group.

Those opposed to affirmative action programs also make arguments of justice. Recall the formal principle of equality, which affirms that individuals who are equal under the law should be treated in the same manner. This principle means that people who are governed by the same laws must have the same rights and obligations; the fact that some may possess greater economic power than others should have no bearing on whether and how the law applies to each. Critics of affirmative action argue that the demands of formal justice require that one's race and gender (and perhaps other characteristics as well) be deemed irrelevant to possession of the opportunity to participate equally in the benefits and burdens of society. Yet affirmative action programs seem to entail a violation of this very requirement. For if it was a violation of equality to discriminate *against* people in the past, it is also wrong to discriminate *in favor* of them now by means of programs that give preferential treatment. Affirmative action destroys equality under the law, say the opponents, and in so doing might even open the door to further discrimination. Members of groups not preferred by special admissions or hiring programs are themselves treated unjustly by being denied access to schools or jobs based on *their* race. The guarantee of equality is a promise of neutrality and color blindness, and this applies no matter what policy or whose race is at stake.

Arguments based upon the notion of social utility, or overall social good, frequently complement arguments for or against preferential treatment based on considerations of justice. Utilitarian supporters of preferential treatment have asserted, for example, that such programs are necessary to bring larger numbers of minorities into the professions, thereby enriching and benefiting the lives of those who participate in them. The presence of women and people of color in universities and professional schools, for example, enhances the likelihood that important perspectives on life will

[5] See http://nces.ed.gov/pubs2001/inequality/6.asp

[6] See *Business Week*, October 19, 1990.

[7] See *Los Angeles Times*, Sept. 10, 1995.

[8] See "Diversity in the Workforce," Wellesley Center for Women, Wellesley College, 2001.

[9] See Victor D. Infante, "Why Women Still Earn Less Than Men," *Workforce*, April, 2001.

not go unrepresented in the classroom. It is further claimed, as by U.C. Davis in *Bakke,* that greater numbers of minorities in medical, law, and business schools will result in improved service to minority communities currently underserved by these professions. And it is asserted that "successful" minority persons who have been aided by preferential treatment can serve as valuable role models for young people from disadvantaged backgrounds. Opponents of affirmative action respond that such programs will not bring about the greatest good for society as a whole. They point to the potential for resentment among those members of non-preferred groups who, like Bakke, are passed over in favor of minority individuals, and they raise the concern that minority graduates of professional schools who are admitted with lower grade point averages and test scores may not be as qualified to dispense beneficial, and sometimes vital, services as the rejected applicants would have been.

Philosopher Thomas Nagel gives a guarded defense of affirmative action policies. Nagel begins by distinguishing efforts to enhance the diversity of applicant pools and training programs to make minority candidates competitive, which he calls "weak affirmative action," from definite preferences in employment and education given to members of minority groups over other equally or even better-qualified candidates, which he calls "strong affirmative action." Nagel evaluates three objections to programs of strong affirmative action, concluding that only significant moral arguments in favor of affirmative action can overcome these objections. He concludes by presenting his own arguments seeking to justify strong affirmative action. Nagel argues that such programs are justified in the short term but only for Blacks, whose unique history of oppression justifies extraordinary measures. Women and members of other minority groups have not suffered in the same way as Blacks, Nagel believes, and therefore strong affirmative action in their case is unjustified.

As a counterpoint to Nagel, writer Shelby Steele makes a case against affirmative action. Steele believes that programs of affirmative action have done more to harm Blacks than to help them, and in the selection included here he tries to establish this. Affirmative action, Steele asserts, has shifted from simply ensuring equality of opportunity to proportionate representation of races in schools and professions without regard for whether those who benefit were victims of past discrimination. Nor has achieving proportionate representation ameliorated the social and economic disparities between Blacks and Whites. Steele rejects the argument that preferential treatment is justified on the basis of reparations owed by Whites to Blacks. On another level, Steele insists, affirmative action preferences actually harm Blacks by sustaining the assumption that Blacks are inferior and wouldn't be able to make it without reliance upon preferences. Preferential treatment encourages them to play the role of victim and to rely on others instead of doing for themselves.

Reparations For Slavery

The legacy of slavery returned to the courts in several novel lawsuits filed in state and federal courts since the year 2000. Acting as representatives of slave descendants, small groups of plaintiffs have filed suits against corporations that allegedly profited from slavery. Insurance companies have been one target. In 2002, Aetna Inc. was sued on the basis that it was "unjustly enriched" by selling insurance policies to slave-owners to guard against the loss of the slave. Aetna expressed "deep regret" that, in the years after its founding in 1853, the company insured the lives of slaves. Supporters of these lawsuits argue that reparations for the wrongs of slavery are overdue, and they urge that both the federal and state governments, as well as private corporations, be targeted. Reparations for slavery have also been supported by members of Congress. Representative John Conyers, a principal advocate of reparations, has sponsored resolutions in the House to

> study the institution of slavery in this country from 1619 to 1865, and subsequent de jure and de facto racial and economic discrimination against African Americans, as well as the impact of these forces on living African Americans, and to make recommendations to the Congress on appropriate remedies.[10]

Following the text of Conyers' Resolution in our readings is the record of a federal court case in which reparations supporters attempted to sue the United States for damages due to the enslavement of African Americans and for subsequent discrimination against them. The plaintiffs maintained that the Thirteenth

---

[10] From 143 *Congressional Record* E1548-E1549, 105th Congress, 1st Session (July 29, 1997).

Amendment to the Constitution, which banned slavery, was intended also to eliminate its "vestiges"—an obligation that the government has failed to fulfill.

The Ninth Circuit Court of Appeals dismissed the suit, finding that it raised a "non-justiciable" and essentially "political" issue.

Barbara Grutter v. Lee Bollinger, et al.

JUSTICE O'CONNOR delivered the opinion of the Court.

This case requires us to decide whether the use of race as a factor in student admissions by the University of Michigan Law School (Law School) is unlawful.

The Law School ranks among the Nation's top law schools. It receives more than 3,500 applications each year for a class of around 350 students. Seeking to admit a group of students who individually and collectively are among the most capable, the Law School looks for individuals with substantial promise for success in law school and a strong likelihood of succeeding in the practice of law and contributing in diverse ways to the well-being of others. More broadly, the Law School seeks a mix of students with varying backgrounds and experiences who will respect and learn from each other. In 1992, the dean of the Law School charged a faculty committee with crafting a written admissions policy to implement these goals. In particular, the Law School sought to ensure that its efforts to achieve student body diversity complied with this Court's most recent ruling on the use of race in university admissions. See *Regents of Univ. of Cal. v. Bakke*, 438 U.S. 265 (1978). Upon the unanimous adoption of the committee's report by the Law School faculty, it became the Law School's official admissions policy.

The hallmark of that policy is its focus on academic ability coupled with a flexible assessment of applicants' talents, experiences, and potential to contribute to the learning of those around them. The policy requires admissions officials to evaluate each applicant based on all the information available in the file, including a personal statement, letters of recommendation, and an essay describing the ways in which the applicant will contribute to the life and diversity of the Law School. In reviewing an applicant's file,

admissions officials must consider the applicant's undergraduate grade point average (GPA) and Law School Admissions Test (LSAT) score because they are important (if imperfect) predictors of academic success in law school. The policy stresses that no applicant should be admitted unless we expect that applicant to do well enough to graduate with no serious academic problems.

The policy makes clear, however, that even the highest possible score does not guarantee admission to the Law School. Nor does a low score automatically disqualify an applicant. Rather, the policy requires admissions officials to look beyond grades and test scores to other criteria that are important to the Law School's educational objectives. So-called "soft" variables such as the enthusiasm of recommenders, the quality of the undergraduate institution, the quality of the applicant's essay, and the areas and difficulty of undergraduate course selection are all brought to bear in assessing an applicant's likely contributions to the intellectual and social life of the institution.

The policy aspires to achieve that diversity which has the potential to enrich everyone's education and thus make a law school class stronger than the sum of its parts. The policy does not restrict the types of diversity contributions eligible for "substantial weight" in the admissions process, but instead recognizes many possible bases for diversity admissions. The policy does, however, reaffirm the Law School's long-standing commitment to one particular type of diversity, that is, racial and ethnic diversity with special reference to the inclusion of students from groups which have been historically discriminated against, like African Americans, Hispanics and Native Americans, who without this commitment might not be represented in our student body in meaningful numbers. By enrolling a "critical mass" of [underrepresented] minority students, the Law School seeks to ensur[e] their ability to make unique contributions to the character of the Law School.

539 U.S.__(2003), 2003 U.S. LEXIS 4800, United States Supreme Court.

The policy does not define diversity solely in terms of racial and ethnic status. Nor is the policy insensitive to the competition among all students for admission to the [L]aw [S]chool. Rather, the policy seeks to guide admissions officers in producing classes both diverse and academically outstanding, classes made up of students who promise to continue the tradition of outstanding contribution by Michigan Graduates to the legal profession.

Petitioner Barbara Grutter is a white Michigan resident who applied to the Law School in 1996 with a 3.8 grade point average and 161 LSAT score. The Law School initially placed petitioner on a waiting list, but subsequently rejected her application. In December 1997, petitioner filed suit in the United States District Court for the Eastern District of Michigan against the Law School. . . . Petitioner alleged that respondents discriminated against her on the basis of race in violation of the Fourteenth Amendment. . . .

Petitioner further alleged that her application was rejected because the Law School uses race as a predominant factor, giving applicants who belong to certain minority groups a significantly greater chance of admission than students with similar credentials from disfavored racial groups. Petitioner also alleged that respondents had no compelling interest to justify their use of race in the admissions process. Petitioner requested compensatory and punitive damages, an order requiring the Law School to offer her admission, and an injunction prohibiting the Law School from continuing to discriminate on the basis of race.

· · ·

During the 15-day bench trial, the parties introduced extensive evidence concerning the Law School's use of race in the admissions process. Dennis Shields, Director of Admissions when petitioner applied to the Law School, testified that he did not direct his staff to admit a particular percentage or number of minority students, but rather to consider an applicant's race along with all other factors. Shields testified that at the height of the admissions season, he would frequently consult the so-called "daily reports" that kept track of the racial and ethnic composition of the class (along with other information such as residency status and gender). This was done, Shields testified, to ensure that a critical mass of underrepresented minority students would be reached so as to realize the educational benefits of a diverse student body. Shields stressed, however, that he did not seek to admit any particular number or percentage of underrepresented minority students.

Erica Munzel, who succeeded Shields as Director of Admissions, testified that "critical mass" means "meaningful numbers" or "meaningful representation," which she understood to mean a number that encourages underrepresented minority students to participate in the classroom and not feel isolated. Munzel stated there is no number, percentage, or range of numbers or percentages that constitute critical mass. Munzel also asserted that she must consider the race of applicants because a critical mass of underrepresented minority students could not be enrolled if admissions decisions were based primarily on undergraduate GPAs and LSAT scores.

The current Dean of the Law School, Jeffrey Lehman, also testified. Like the other Law School witnesses, Lehman did not quantify critical mass in terms of numbers or percentages. He indicated that critical mass means numbers such that underrepresented minority students do not feel isolated or like spokespersons for their race. When asked about the extent to which race is considered in admissions, Lehman testified that it varies from one applicant to another. In some cases, according to Lehman's testimony, an applicant's race may play no role, while in others it may be a "'determinative'" factor.

· · ·

In the end, the District Court concluded that the Law School's use of race as a factor in admissions decisions was unlawful. Applying strict scrutiny, the District Court determined that the Law School's asserted interest in assembling a diverse student body was not compelling because the attainment of a racially diverse class . . . was not recognized as such by *Bakke* and is not a remedy for past discrimination.

Sitting en banc, the Court of Appeals reversed the District Court's judgment and vacated the injunction.

· · ·

We granted certiorari, 537 U.S. 1043 (2002), to resolve the disagreement among the Courts of Appeals on a question of national importance: Whether diversity is a compelling interest that can justify the narrowly tailored use of race in selecting applicants for admission to public universities.

We last addressed the use of race in public higher education over 25 years ago. In the landmark *Bakke* case, we reviewed a racial set-aside program that reserved 16 out of 100 seats in a medical school class for members of certain minority groups. The decision produced six separate opinions, none of which commanded a majority of the Court. . . .

Since this Court's splintered decision in *Bakke,* Justice Powell's opinion announcing the judgment of the Court has served as the touchstone for constitutional analysis of race-conscious admissions policies.

. . .

[T]oday we endorse Justice Powell's view that student body diversity is a compelling state interest that can justify the use of race in university admissions. . . .

We have held that all racial classifications imposed by government must be analyzed by a reviewing court under strict scrutiny. This means that such classifications are constitutional only if they are narrowly tailored to further compelling governmental interests. . . . Although all governmental uses of race are subject to strict scrutiny, not all are invalidated by it. As we have explained, "whenever the government treats any person unequally because of his or her race, that person has suffered an injury that falls squarely within the language and spirit of the Constitution's guarantee of equal protection." But that observation says nothing about the ultimate validity of any particular law; that determination is the job of the court applying strict scrutiny. When race-based action is necessary to further a compelling governmental interest, such action does not violate the constitutional guarantee of equal protection so long as the narrow-tailoring requirement is also satisfied. . . .

With these principles in mind, we turn to the question whether the Law School's use of race is justified by a compelling state interest. Before this Court, as they have throughout this litigation, respondents assert only one justification for their use of race in the admissions process: obtaining "the educational benefits that flow from a diverse student body." In other words, the Law School asks us to recognize, in the context of higher education, a compelling state interest in student body diversity.

We first wish to dispel the notion that the Law School's argument has been foreclosed, either expressly or implicitly, by our affirmative-action cases decided since *Bakke.* It is true that some language in those opinions might be read to suggest that remedying past discrimination is the only permissible justification for race-based governmental action. . . . But we have never held that the only governmental use of race that can survive strict scrutiny is remedying past discrimination. Nor, since *Bakke,* have we directly addressed the use of race in the context of public higher education. Today, we hold that the Law School has a compelling interest in attaining a diverse student body.

The Law School's educational judgment that such diversity is essential to its educational mission is one to which we defer. The Law School's assessment that diversity will, in fact, yield educational benefits is substantiated by respondents and their *amici.* Our scrutiny of the interest asserted by the Law School is no less strict for taking into account complex educational judgments in an area that lies primarily within the expertise of the university. Our holding today is in keeping with our tradition of giving a degree of deference to a university's academic decisions, within constitutionally prescribed limits. . . .

We have long recognized that, given the important purpose of public education and the expansive freedoms of speech and thought associated with the university environment, universities occupy a special niche in our constitutional tradition. . . . Our conclusion that the Law School has a compelling interest in a diverse student body is informed by our view that attaining a diverse student body is at the heart of the Law School's proper institutional mission, and that "good faith" on the part of a university is presumed, absent a showing to the contrary.

As part of its goal of "assembling a class that is both exceptionally academically qualified and broadly diverse," the Law School seeks to "enroll a 'critical mass' of minority students." The Law School's interest is not simply to assure within its student body some specified percentage of a particular group merely because of its race or ethnic origin. That would amount to outright racial balancing, which is patently unconstitutional. Rather, the Law School's concept of critical mass is defined by reference to the educational benefits that diversity is designed to produce.

These benefits are substantial. As the District Court emphasized, the Law School's admissions policy promotes "cross-racial understanding," helps to break down racial stereotypes, and enables [students] to better understand persons of different races. These benefits are important and laudable, because classroom discussion is livelier, more spirited, and simply more enlightening and interesting when the students have the greatest possible variety of backgrounds.

The Law School's claim of a compelling interest is further bolstered by its *amici,* who point to the educational benefits that flow from student body diversity. In addition to the expert studies and reports entered into evidence at trial, numerous studies show that student body diversity promotes learning outcomes, and better prepares students for an increasingly diverse workforce and society, and better prepares them as professionals. . . .

These benefits are not theoretical but real, as major American businesses have made clear that the skills needed in today's increasingly global marketplace can only be developed through exposure to widely diverse people, cultures, ideas, and viewpoints. . . .

We have repeatedly acknowledged the overriding importance of preparing students for work and citizenship, describing education as pivotal to sustaining our political and cultural heritage with a fundamental role in maintaining the fabric of society.

· · ·

In order to cultivate a set of leaders with legitimacy in the eyes of the citizenry, it is necessary that the path to leadership be visibly open to talented and qualified individuals of every race and ethnicity. All members of our heterogeneous society must have confidence in the openness and integrity of the educational institutions that provide this training. . . .

The Law School does not premise its need for critical mass on "any belief that minority students always (or even consistently) express some characteristic minority viewpoint on any issue." To the contrary, diminishing the force of such stereotypes is both a crucial part of the Law School's mission, and one that it cannot accomplish with only token numbers of minority students. Just as growing up in a particular region or having particular professional experiences is likely to affect an individual's views, so too is one's own, unique experience of being a racial minority in a society, like our own, in which race unfortunately still matters. The Law School has determined, based on its experience and expertise, that a "critical mass" of underrepresented minorities is necessary to further its compelling interest in securing the educational benefits of a diverse student body.

Even in the limited circumstance when drawing racial distinctions is permissible to further a compelling state interest, government is still constrained in how it may pursue that end: [T]he means chosen to accomplish the [government's] asserted purpose must be specifically and narrowly framed to accomplish that purpose.

To be narrowly tailored, a race-conscious admissions program cannot use a quota system—it cannot insulat[e] each category of applicants with certain desired qualifications from competition with all other applicants. Instead, a university may consider race or ethnicity only as a "plus" in a particular applicant's file, without insulat[ing] the individual from comparison with all other candidates for the available seats. In other words, an admissions program must be flexible enough to consider all pertinent elements of diversity in light of the particular qualifications of each applicant, and to place them on the same footing for consideration, although not necessarily according them the same weight.

We find that the Law School's admissions program bears the hallmarks of a narrowly tailored plan. As Justice Powell made clear in *Bakke*, truly individualized consideration demands that race be used in a flexible, nonmechanical way. It follows from this mandate that universities cannot establish quotas for members of certain racial groups or put members of those groups on separate admissions tracks. Nor can universities insulate applicants who belong to certain racial or ethnic groups from the competition for admission. Universities can, however, consider race or ethnicity more flexibly as a "plus" factor in the context of individualized consideration of each and every applicant.

We are satisfied that the Law School's admissions program, like the Harvard plan described by Justice Powell, does not operate as a quota.

· · ·

The Law School's goal of attaining a critical mass of underrepresented minority students does not transform its program into a quota. As the Harvard plan described by Justice Powell recognized, there is of course "some relationship between numbers and achieving the benefits to be derived from a diverse student body, and between numbers and providing a reasonable environment for those students admitted." [S]ome attention to numbers, without more, does not transform a flexible admissions system into a rigid quota. Nor, as JUSTICE KENNEDY posits, does the Law School's consultation of the "daily reports," which keep track of the racial and ethnic composition of the class (as well as of residency and gender), suggest there was no further attempt at individual review save for race itself during the final stages of the admissions process. To the contrary, the Law School's admissions officers testified without contradiction that they never gave race any more or less weight based on the information contained in these reports. Moreover, as JUSTICE KENNEDY concedes, between 1993 and 2000, the number of African American, Latino, and Native American students in each class at the Law School varied from 13.5 to 20.1 percent, a range inconsistent with a quota. . . .

That a race-conscious admissions program does not operate as a quota does not, by itself, satisfy the requirement of individualized consideration. When using race as a "plus" factor in university admissions, a university's admissions program must remain flexible enough to ensure that each applicant is evaluated as an individual and not in a way that makes an applicant's race or ethnicity the defining feature of his or her application. The importance of this individualized consideration in the context of a race-conscious admissions program is paramount. . . .

Here, the Law School engages in a highly individualized, holistic review of each applicant's file, giving serious consideration to all the ways an applicant might contribute to a diverse educational environment. The Law School affords this individualized consideration to applicants of all races. There is no policy, either *de jure* or *de facto,* of automatic acceptance or rejection based on any single "soft" variable.

We also find that, like the Harvard plan Justice Powell referenced in *Bakke,* the Law School's race-conscious admissions program adequately ensures that all factors that may contribute to student body diversity are meaningfully considered alongside race in admissions decisions. With respect to the use of race itself, all underrepresented minority students admitted by the Law School have been deemed qualified. By virtue of our Nation's struggle with racial inequality, such students are both likely to have experiences of particular importance to the Law School's mission, and less likely to be admitted in meaningful numbers on criteria that ignore those experiences.

. . .

We acknowledge that there are serious problems of justice connected with the idea of preference itself. Narrow tailoring, therefore, requires that a race-conscious admissions program not unduly harm members of any racial group. Even remedial race-based governmental action generally remains subject to continuing oversight to assure that it will work the least harm possible to other innocent persons competing for the benefit. To be narrowly tailored, a race-conscious admissions program must not unduly burden individuals who are not members of the favored racial and ethnic groups.

We are satisfied that the Law School's admissions program does not. Because the Law School considers all pertinent elements of diversity, it can (and does) select nonminority applicants who have greater potential to enhance student body diversity over underrepresented minority applicants. . . . We agree that, in the context of its individualized inquiry into the possible diversity contributions of all applicants, the Law School's race-conscious admissions program does not unduly harm nonminority applicants.

We are mindful, however, that a core purpose of the Fourteenth Amendment was to do away with all governmentally imposed discrimination based on race. Accordingly, race-conscious admissions policies must be limited in time. This requirement reflects that racial classifications, however compelling their goals, are potentially so dangerous that they may be employed no more broadly than the interest demands. Enshrining a permanent justification for racial preferences would offend this fundamental equal protection principle. We see no reason to exempt race-conscious admissions programs from the requirement that all governmental use of race must have a logical end point. The Law School, too, concedes that all race-conscious programs must have reasonable durational limits.

. . .

The requirement that all race-conscious admissions programs have a termination point assures all citizens that the deviation from the norm of equal treatment of all racial and ethnic groups is a temporary matter, a measure taken in the service of the goal of equality itself. . . .

We take the Law School at its word that it would like nothing better than to find a race-neutral admissions formula and will terminate its race-conscious admissions program as soon as practicable. . . . It has been 25 years since Justice Powell first approved the use of race to further an interest in student body diversity in the context of public higher education. Since that time, the number of minority applicants with high grades and test scores has indeed increased. We expect that 25 years from now, the use of racial preferences will no longer be necessary to further the interest approved today.

In summary, the Equal Protection Clause does not prohibit the Law School's narrowly tailored use of race in admissions decisions to further a compelling interest in obtaining the educational benefits that flow from a diverse student body. . . . The judgment of the Court of Appeals for the Sixth Circuit, accordingly, is affirmed.

It is so ordered.

JUSTICE THOMAS, concurring in part and dissenting in part.

Frederick Douglass, speaking to a group of abolitionists almost 140 years ago, delivered a message lost on today's majority:

"[I]n regard to the colored people, there is always more that is benevolent, I perceive, than just, manifested towards us. What I ask for the negro is not benevolence, not pity, not sympathy, but simply *justice.* The American people have always been anxious to know what they shall do with us. . . . I have had but one answer from the beginning. Do nothing with us! Your doing with us has already played the mischief with us. Do nothing with us! If the apples will not remain on the tree of their own strength, if they are worm-eaten at the core, if they are early ripe and disposed to fall, let them fall! . . . And if the negro cannot stand on his own legs, let him fall also. All I ask is, give him a chance to stand on his own legs! Let him alone! . . . [Y]our interference is doing him positive injury." What the Black Man Wants: An Address Delivered in Boston, Massachusetts, on 26 January 1865, reprinted in 4 The Frederick Douglass Papers 59, 68 (J. Blassingame & J. McKivigan eds. 1991) (emphasis in original).

Like Douglass, I believe blacks can achieve in every avenue of American life without the meddling of university administrators. Because I wish to see all students succeed whatever their color, I share, in some respect, the sympathies of those who sponsor the type of discrimination advanced by the University of Michigan Law School (Law School). The Constitution does not, however, tolerate institutional devotion to the status quo in admissions policies when such devotion ripens into racial discrimination. Nor does the Constitution countenance the unprecedented deference the Court gives to the Law School, an approach inconsistent with the very concept of "strict scrutiny."

No one would argue that a university could set up a lower general admission standard and then impose heightened requirements only on black applicants. Similarly, a university may not maintain a high admission standard and grant exemptions to favored races. The Law School, of its own choosing, and for its own purposes, maintains an exclusionary admissions system that it knows produces racially disproportionate results. Racial discrimination is not a permissible solution to the self-inflicted wounds of this elitist admissions policy.

The majority upholds the Law School's racial discrimination not by interpreting the people's Constitution, but by responding to a faddish slogan of the cognoscenti. Nevertheless, I concur in part in the Court's opinion. First, I agree with the Court insofar as its decision, which approves of only one racial classification, confirms that further use of race in admissions remains unlawful. Second, I agree with the Court's holding that racial discrimination in higher education admissions will be illegal in 25 years. I respectfully dissent from the remainder of the Court's opinion and the judgment, however, because I believe that the Law School's current use of race violates the Equal Protection Clause and that the Constitution means the same thing today as it will in 300 months.

. . .

Unlike the majority, I seek to define with precision the interest being asserted by the Law School before determining whether that interest is so compelling as to justify racial discrimination. The Law School maintains that it wishes to obtain educational benefits that flow from student body diversity. This statement must be evaluated carefully, because it implies that both "diversity" and "educational benefits" are components of the Law School's compelling state interest. Additionally, the Law School's refusal to entertain certain changes in its admissions process and status indicates that the compelling state interest it seeks to validate is actually broader than might appear at first glance.

Undoubtedly there are other ways to "better" the education of law students aside from ensuring that the student body contains a "critical mass" of underrepresented minority students. Attaining "diversity," whatever it means,[1] is the mechanism by which the Law School obtains educational benefits, not an end of itself. The Law School, however, apparently believes that only a racially mixed student body can lead to the educational benefits it seeks. How, then, is the Law School's interest in these allegedly unique educational "benefits" *not* simply the forbidden interest in "racial balancing," that the majority expressly rejects?

A distinction between these two ideas (unique educational benefits based on racial aesthetics and race for its own sake) is purely sophistic—so much so that the majority uses them interchangeably. . . . The Law School's argument, as facile as it is, can only be understood in one way: Classroom aesthetics yields educational benefits, racially discriminatory admissions policies are required to achieve the right racial mix, and therefore the policies are required to achieve the educational benefits. It is the *educational benefits* that are the end, or allegedly compelling state interest, not "diversity." . . .

One must also consider the Law School's refusal to entertain changes to its current admissions system that might produce the same educational benefits. The Law School adamantly disclaims any race-neutral alternative that would reduce "academic selectivity," which would in turn "require the Law School to become a very different institution, and to sacrifice a core part of its educational mission." In other words, the Law School seeks to improve marginally the education it offers without sacrificing too much of its exclusivity and elite status.

The proffered interest that the majority vindicates today, then, is not simply "diversity." Instead the Court upholds the use of racial discrimination as a tool to advance the Law School's interest in offering a marginally superior education while maintaining an elite institution. Unless each constituent part of this state interest is of pressing public necessity, the Law School's use of race is unconstitutional. I find each of them to fall far short of this standard.

. . .

. . . Today, the Court insists on radically expanding the range of permissible uses of race to something as trivial (by comparison) as the assembling of a law school class. I can only presume that the majority's failure to justify its decision by reference to any principle arises from the absence of any such principle.

Under the proper standard, there is no pressing public necessity in maintaining a public law school at all and, it follows, certainly not an elite law school. Likewise, marginal improvements in legal education do not qualify as a compelling state interest. . . .

Finally, even if the Law School's racial tinkering produces tangible educational benefits, a marginal improvement in legal education cannot justify racial discrimination where the Law School has no compelling interest in either its existence or in its current educational and admissions policies.

The interest in remaining elite and exclusive that the majority thinks so obviously critical requires the use of admissions "standards" that, in turn, create the Law School's "need" to discriminate on the basis of race.

. . .

The Court's deference to the Law School's conclusion that its racial experimentation leads to educational benefits will, if adhered to, have serious collateral consequences. The Court relies heavily on social science evidence to justify its deference. . . . The Court never acknowledges, however, the growing evidence that racial (and other sorts) of heterogeneity actually impairs learning among black students. See,

e.g., Flowers & Pascarella, Cognitive Effects of College Racial Composition on African American Students After 3 Years of College, 40 *J. of College Student Development* 669, 674 (1999) (concluding that black students experience superior cognitive development at Historically Black Colleges (HBCs) and that, even among blacks, "a substantial diversity moderates the cognitive effects of attending an HBC"); Allen, The Color of Success: African-American College Student Outcomes at Predominantly White and Historically Black Public Colleges and Universities, 62 *Harv. Educ. Rev.* 26, 35 (1992) (finding that black students attending HBCs report higher academic achievement than those attending predominantly white colleges).

. . .

. . . Today . . . the majority ignores the "experience" of those institutions that have been forced to abandon explicit racial discrimination in admissions.

The sky has not fallen at Boalt Hall at the University of California, Berkeley, for example. Prior to Proposition 209's adoption of Cal. Const., Art. 1, § 31(a), which bars the State from "grant[ing] preferential treatment . . . on the basis of race . . . in the operation of . . . public education," Boalt Hall enrolled 20 blacks and 28 Hispanics in its first-year class for 1996. In 2002, without deploying express racial discrimination in admissions, Boalt's entering class enrolled 14 blacks and 36 Hispanics. Total underrepresented minority student enrollment at Boalt Hall now exceeds 1996 levels. Apparently the Law School cannot be counted on to be as resourceful. The Court is willfully blind to the very real experience in California and elsewhere, which raises the inference that institutions with reputation[s] for excellence, rivaling the Law School's have satisfied their sense of mission without resorting to prohibited racial discrimination.

Putting aside the absence of any legal support for the majority's reflexive deference, there is much to be said for the view that the use of tests and other measures to "predict" academic performance is a poor substitute for a system that gives every applicant a chance to prove he can succeed in the study of law. The rallying cry that in the absence of racial discrimination in admissions there would be a true meritocracy ignores the fact that the entire process is poisoned by numerous exceptions to "merit." For example, in the national debate on racial discrimination in higher education admissions, much has been made of the fact that elite institutions utilize a so-called "legacy" preference to give the children of alumni an advantage in admissions. This, and other, exceptions to a "true" meritocracy give the lie to protestations that merit admissions are in fact the order of the day at the Nation's universities. The Equal Protection Clause does not, however, prohibit the use of unseemly legacy preferences or many other kinds of arbitrary admissions procedures. What the Equal Protection Clause does prohibit are classifications made on the basis of race. So while legacy preferences can stand under the Constitution, racial discrimination cannot. I will not twist the Constitution to invalidate legacy preferences or otherwise impose my vision of higher education admissions on the Nation. The majority should similarly stay its impulse to validate faddish racial discrimination the Constitution clearly forbids.

. . .

. . . [N]o modern law school can claim ignorance of the poor performance of blacks, relatively speaking, on the Law School Admissions Test (LSAT). Nevertheless, law schools continue to use the test and then attempt to "correct" for black underperformance by using racial discrimination in admissions so as to obtain their aesthetic student body. The Law School's continued adherence to measures it knows produce racially skewed results is not entitled to deference by this Court. The Law School itself admits that the test is imperfect, as it must, given that it regularly admits students who score at or below 150 (the national median) on the test. . . . And the Law School's *amici* cannot seem to agree on the fundamental question whether the test itself is useful. . . .

Having decided to use the LSAT, the Law School must accept the constitutional burdens that come with this decision. The Law School may freely continue to employ the LSAT and other allegedly merit-based standards in whatever fashion it likes. What the Equal Protection Clause forbids, but the Court today allows, is the use of these standards hand-in-hand with racial discrimination. An infinite variety of admissions methods are available to the Law School. Considering all of the radical thinking that has historically occurred at this country's universities, the Law School's intractable approach toward admissions is striking.

The Court will not even deign to make the Law School try other methods, however, preferring instead to grant a 25-year license to violate the Constitution. And the same Court that had the courage to order the desegregation of all public schools in the South now fears, on the basis of platitudes rather than principle, to force the Law School to abandon a decidedly imperfect admissions regime that provides the basis for racial discrimination.

The absence of any articulated legal principle supporting the majority's principal holding suggests another rationale. I believe what lies beneath the Court's decision today are the benighted notions that one can tell when racial discrimination benefits (rather than hurts) minority groups and that racial discrimination is necessary to remedy general societal ills. This Court's precedents supposedly settled both issues, but clearly the majority still cannot commit to the principle that racial classifications are *per se* harmful and that almost no amount of benefit in the eye of the beholder can justify such classifications.

Putting aside what I take to be the Court's implicit rejection of *Adarand*'s holding that beneficial and burdensome racial classifications are equally invalid, I must contest the notion that the Law School's discrimination benefits those admitted as a result of it. The Court spends considerable time discussing the impressive display of *amicus* support for the Law School in this case from all corners of society. But nowhere in any of the filings in this Court is any evidence that the purported "beneficiaries" of this racial discrimination prove themselves by performing at (or even near) the same level as those students who receive no preferences. . . .

The silence in this case is deafening to those of us who view higher education's purpose as imparting knowledge and skills to students, rather than a communal, rubber-stamp, credentialing process. The Law School is not looking for those students who, despite a lower LSAT score or undergraduate grade point average, will succeed in the study of law. The Law School seeks only a facade—it is sufficient that the class looks right, even if it does not perform right.

The Law School tantalizes unprepared students with the promise of a University of Michigan degree and all of the opportunities that it offers. These overmatched students take the bait, only to find that they cannot succeed in the cauldron of competition. And this mismatch crisis is not restricted to elite institutions. . . . Indeed, to cover the tracks of the aestheticists, this cruel farce of racial discrimination must continue—in selection for the Michigan Law Review, and in hiring at law firms and for judicial clerkships—until the "beneficiaries" are no longer tolerated. While these students may graduate with law degrees, there is no evidence that they have received a qualitatively better legal education (or become better lawyers) than if they had gone to a less "elite" law school for which they were better prepared. And the aestheticists will never address the real problems facing "underrepresented minorities," instead continuing their social experiments on other people's children.

Beyond the harm the Law School's racial discrimination visits upon its test subjects, no social science has disproved the notion that this discrimination engender[s] attitudes of superiority or, alternatively, provoke[s] resentment among those who believe that they have been wronged by the government's use of race. These programs stamp minorities with a badge of inferiority and may cause them to develop dependencies or to adopt an attitude that they are "entitled" to preferences.

It is uncontested that each year, the Law School admits a handful of blacks who would be admitted in the absence of racial discrimination. Who can differentiate between those who belong and those who do not? The majority of blacks are admitted to the Law School because of discrimination, and because of this policy all are tarred as undeserving. This problem of stigma does not depend on determinacy as to whether those stigmatized are actually the "beneficiaries" of racial discrimination. When blacks take positions in the highest places of government, industry, or academia, it is an open question today whether their skin color played a part in their advancement. The question itself is the stigma—because either racial discrimination did play a role, in which case the person may be deemed "otherwise unqualified," or it did not, in which case asking the question itself unfairly marks those blacks who would succeed without discrimination. Is this what the Court means by "visibly open"?

Finally, the Court's disturbing reference to the importance of the country's law schools as training grounds meant to cultivate "a set of leaders with legitimacy in the eyes of the citizenry" through the use of racial discrimination deserves discussion. As noted earlier, the Court has soundly rejected the remedying of societal discrimination as a justification for governmental use of race. For those who believe that every racial disproportionality in our society is caused by some kind of racial discrimination, there can be no distinction between remedying societal discrimination and erasing racial disproportionalities in the country's leadership caste. And if the lack of proportional racial representation among our leaders is not caused by societal discrimination, then "fixing" it is even less of a pressing public necessity.

The Court's civics lesson presents yet another example of judicial selection of a theory of political representation based on skin color—an endeavor I have previously rejected. The majority appears to believe that broader utopian goals justify the Law School's use of race, but the Equal Protection Clause commands the elimination of racial barriers, not their creation in order to satisfy our theory as to how society ought to be organized.

Endnote

[1]"[D]iversity," for all of its devotees, is more a fashionable catch-phrase than it is a useful term, especially when something as serious as racial discrimination is at issue. Because the Equal Protection Clause renders the color of one's skin constitutionally irrelevant to the Law School's mission, I refer to the Law School's interest as an "aesthetic." That is, the Law School wants to have a certain appearance, from the shape of the desks and tables in its classrooms to the color of the students sitting at them.

I also use the term "aesthetic" because I believe it underlines the ineffectiveness of racially discriminatory admissions in actually helping those who are truly underprivileged. . . . It must be remembered that the Law School's racial discrimination does nothing for those too poor or uneducated to participate in elite higher education and therefore presents only an illusory solution to the challenges facing our nation.

Puzzles About Equality

Peter Westen

One day, while on vacation in Guatemala, I go to a *campesino* market to buy food for dinner. I ask a vendor for one pound of black beans. He puts a brass weight marked "one pound" in one pan of a hand-held balance and pours beans into the other pan until the two come into balance. "Bueno," he says, "ya son iquales" ("Good, now they're equal").

What does the vendor mean when he says that the two pans of the scale are "equal"? Does he mean that they are absolutely identical in weight? Does he mean that they are highly similar in weight? Or does "equal" mean something different from—something in between—"identical," on the one hand, and "similar," on the other?

I try to buy a newspaper, but the vendor cannot make change for a $10 bill. I ask the pharmacist for change. She takes the $10 bill and gives me two $5 bills, while counting aloud, "5 + 5 = 10."

What does the pharmacist mean by saying "5 + 5 = 10"? Does "equal" have the same meaning in arithmetic as it does for the *campesino*? If the pharmacist means something different, where does the difference lie—in the meaning of the word "equal" or in something to which the "equal" refers? Is there any core meaning of "equality" that remains constant in both usages?

After buying snacks for my three children, I sit in a cafe and read the newspaper. I read that the people of Guatemala have recently adopted a new constitution, which states that "in Guatemala, all people are free and equal." What does it mean to say in law that all people are equal? Does the legal equality of one Guatemalan to another differ from the mathematical equality of "5 + 5 = 10" and the descriptive equality of the two pans of the balance scale? Is there any sense in which the meaning of equality remains the same in all

three instances? Why does the concept of equality in the Guatemalan constitution seem more elusive, more complex, and more controversial than the equality of "5 + 5 = 10"? And if the former equality is more enigmatic than the latter, where does the enigma lie—in the concept of equality itself, or somewhere else?

I return home with the snacks for the children—chocolate for my son, gum for my daughters. "Because I want to treat you all equally," I say, "I have brought each of you your favorite treat." My son likes the chocolate but not my explanation. "I agree that you're treating us fairly," he says, "but you're not treating us equally because you're bringing us different things." Who is right? Am I right that I treated my children equally, or is my son right that I did not? Or is it possible that both of us are right?

My older daughter has a different problem with the gum. Like her younger sister she would rather have gum than chocolate, but unlike her sister, she does not care much for any kind of sweet. She would rather have the money than the gum. "I know you're trying to be fair," she says, "but it's not really equal to give the same thing to both of us if it's something she likes more than I do."

Am I right in thinking that I am treating my daughters equally by giving the same quantity of gum to each without further distinguishing between them? Or is the older child right when she says that no distribution is really equal which has a disparate impact on them by giving one more pleasure than the other? Are we both right? Or does the answer lie in the distinction some commentators draw between treating people "equally," on the one hand, and treating them "as equals," on the other? Have I succeeded in treating the girls equally and yet failed to treat them as equals? Or is it sophistic to distinguish between equal treatment and treatment as equals?

The older daughter's complaint also raises a question about the relationship between fair treatment and equal treatment. What is the connection between treating a person fairly and treating her equally? Why does

From Peter Westen, *Speaking of Equality* (Princeton: Princeton University Press, 1990), pp. 3–7. Reprinted by permission of Princeton University Press.

she regard it as a form of moral criticism to call the treatment "unequal"? Is unequal treatment a moral concept, or is it a purely descriptive concept? Is it both?

I am still thinking about the relationship between equal treatment and fair treatment when my wife calls us to dinner. My wife serves the meal to the children by giving the largest portion to our son, who is a teenager and has the largest appetite, the next largest portion to the older daughter, who is going through a growth spurt, and the smallest portion to the youngest, who never eats much at dinner. She also gives everyone a glass of water. Everything goes smoothly until I suggest that we have treated the children equally by treating them in accordance with their needs. My son does not like my use of "equal."

"I don't get it," he says. "The more you talk about equality, the less I understand it. 'Equal' means giving us each the same amount: It means taking food and dividing it by the number of people at the table. What Mom did with the glasses of water was equal. What she did with the meal was proportional—dividing the meal in proportion to our needs. 'Equal' is equal; it's not proportional."

I resist the temptation to say that while some commentators agree with him, others (including Aristotle) disagree. Some agree that per-capita distributions are the only truly equal distributions. Others believe that, while per-capita distributions differ in substance from distributions in accord with needs (or in accord with merit, or effort, or wants), per-capita distributions are no more inherently equal than other principled distributions.

Nor do I tell my son that some commentators would question the proposition he regards as self-evident, namely, that his mother treated him and his sisters equally by giving them each a glass of water. Whether it is truly equal, they would say, depends upon her *reason* for giving him a glass of water. If she gave him the glass of water because (and *only* because) she had already given water to his sisters, then she treated him equally. If, however, she gave him the glass of water because she believes every child is entitled to at least one glass of water per meal (and not because she had already given glasses of water to his sisters), then she did not treat him equally with his sisters. This is so, they say, because treatment is equal if and only if it is treatment to which a person is entitled only by virtue of its having already been given to others.

After dinner several children from the neighborhood come to the door soliciting contributions for their parish church's Lenten celebration. Each holds out a tin can asking that we favor him with our donation. Our girls both want to give a portion of their allowance, but they don't know how they should distribute it. My wife, not seeing any basis for distinguishing among the children, feels we should divide the donation among them equally. "Unless someone gives me a good reason for preferring one child over the others," she says, "I really think we have to treat them the same."

My son, who is embarrassed by the throng of children, doesn't feel presumptively obliged to treat them equally. "I don't see why it's up to us to find reasons for treating them differently; it's up to them to show us reasons for treating them the same. Why do we have to resolve doubts in their favor?"

The difference of opinion between my wife and son is the difference between competing normative propositions—competing maxims—regarding equality. My wife is proceeding in accord with what some call "the presumption of equality," that is, the normative proposition that "people ought to be treated equally unless there are good reasons for treating them differently." My son, feeling no presumption one way or the other, may be unconsciously proceeding in accord with what is sometimes called the "principle of equality," namely, the principle that "equals should be treated equally, and unequals should be treated unequally."

Which of the two propositions of equality is the more persuasive? Are they consistent with one another? What do they both mean in the context at hand? Who are the "people" who are to be treated equally within the meaning of the "presumption of equality"—only those children who are soliciting contributions at our door, or all the door-to-door solicitors in town? What would constitute a "good reason" for treating the children unequally within the meaning of the presumption? Is a personal preference for redheads a good reason? Who are the "equals" who are to be treated equally within the meaning of the "principle of equality"—the first child to approach us, or the one we wish most to please? And what is the meaning of "equal treatment" within both propositions of equality—to donate to the most courteous child, or to all the children per capita?

I turn on the evening news to hear about a controversial campaign by Guatemalan women in favor of affirmative action. Advocates on both sides of the controversy adopt the language of equality. I am reminded of other controversies in which both sides invoke "equality" in support of their contrary positions—controversies over the use of sex tables in computing life insurance, the use of height and strength requirements for fire departments, and the maintenance of separate athletic events for men and women. How does the concept of equality accommodate such mutually exclusive positions, and what is the source of its compelling rhetorical force? Why is it easier to argue in favor of equality than against it? Why is inequality always on the defensive? Is it because equality is inherently desirable, or presumptively desirable? If either, how can equality also lend itself to the most controverted of social causes? How can equality be simultaneously both desirable and controversial?

In one sense, these questions regarding equality differ significantly. Some involve descriptive statements of equality, others involve prescriptive statements of equality. Some look to whether rules are equal on their face, others to whether rules are equal as applied. Some concern the meaning of "equals," others the meaning of "equal treatment." Some probe the relationship between equality and rights of nondiscrimination. Some involve propositions of equality.

Yet in another sense the questions are also the same. They all call for an analysis of language—an inquiry into ordinary usages of the word "equality." Their answers turn not on contested moral propositions but on linguistic analysis of the concept of equality in moral and legal discourse.

It is fitting that these questions of equality should differ from one another and yet be the same, for equality is itself a relationship that uniquely straddles the gap between "different" and "same": things that are equal, being distinct things, are necessarily different; and yet, being equal, they are also the same. Moreover, the general concept of equality that underlies particular relationships of equality has both a fixed element, which remains the same in all its usages (at least regarding persons and things we perceive through the sense), and a variable term, which can differ greatly from one statement of equality to another. The key to understanding the meaning and rhetorical force of "equality" in law and morals, I believe, lies in identifying the kinds of variable terms that enter into moral and legal statements of equality.

What Is Race?

Naomi Zack

We take *race* for granted in the United States, and someone's race may be the first thing you notice about a person you do not know. We acknowledge that there are serious "racial tensions" and "racial problems" in our society. If pressed, what most of us understand by those expressions is that people of different races react to one another with hostility because they are of different races, and that members of each race have problems that are the result of being members of their race. We do not usually think that there is anything wrong with the ways in which people are sorted into races— that is, with the *criteria* for membership in different races—because we think that what race a person

From Naomi Zack, *Thinking About Race* (Belmont: Wadsworth Publishing Co., 1998), pp. 1–7.

belongs to is obvious from looking at him or her. We do not question the *naturalness* of racial differences or the very existence of races. We go on about our business as though there always have been human races and there always will be human races. We assume that the physical differences that make up the different races have always been the same and always been thought about in the same ways.

In fact, the word *race* and the idea the word stands for have meant very different things throughout Western European and American history. Section A is an analysis of some of those different historical meanings. The core meaning of race at present would seem to be distinctive biological types of human beings that can be studied by scientists. This suggests that scientists must have an idea of race that could give our ordinary thinking about racial difference some stability. But the biological sciences do not have useful or verified concepts of race at this time and there is no reason to believe that they ever will. In Section B, the problems with race in the biological sciences are analyzed. Despite the lack of a physical, scientific foundation, categories of race remain deeply embedded in common sense and social reality. Section C analyzes the definitions of black, white, Indian, and Asian race that have been in use in American society since about 1900, and then offers some observations about broad cultural ideas of race.

A. The History of the Concept of Race

A *word* is a sign or sound that stands for something else, usually a thing that exists outside of the mind, an image in the mind, or a *concept*. A concept is an idea or the meaning of a word. Concepts change over time and these changes depend on the historical situations in which they are used. Words may be spelled and pronounced the same from one century to the next, or they may look and sound different. In both cases, the same concepts can sometimes be traced. In translations between different languages, a word may look and sound the same and stand for a different concept, or look and sound different but stand for the same concept. Throughout European history, until the eighteenth and nineteenth centuries, the word *race* (and its synonyms and the words for it in different languages) meant family or national group. In ancient Greece and Rome, a person's race was the group to which he or she belonged, associated with an ancestral place and culture. During the Middle Ages, a person's race was literally his or her family and ancestors, in the sense of a *line*, which was an English synonym for race. By the seventeenth century, the start of the modern period in which nation-states began to emerge, the word race was associated with cultures and civilizations in particular geographic areas. Through the eighteenth century, while physical differences such as the darker skin hues of Africans were associated with race, racial divisions were based on differences in religion and cultural tradition rather than on human biology. Indeed, the modern science of biology, with systematic methods for dividing living things into genus, species, and subspecies, was not developed until the late eighteenth and early nineteenth centuries. Ancestry, culture, biology: each of these was a different historical concept of race.

By the second half of the nineteenth century all the earlier concepts were combined, and *race* came to mean a distinct biological group of human beings who were not all members of the same family but who shared inherited physical and cultural traits that were different from those shared within other races. This meaning of race was constructed by American scientists during slavery and segregation. The claims of these scientists of race were used as justifications for black chattel slavery and white social and economic dominance over Negroes. Based on reports of *empirical* findings that were often incomplete or even falsified, hierarchies of human races were postulated. Always, the black race was on the bottom and the white race on the top, with Asians and Indians in the middle. Nineteenth-century racial theory posited inherited *racial essences* as the cause of superior or inferior intellectual, aesthetic, spiritual, and moral qualities. This concept of race was more *abstract* than the older family line concept, because it posited race as the cause of characteristics that were inherited through family descent. It was also more *general* because each of the main racial groups included many family lines within them. The notion of essence did not allow for mixed essences; in cases of racial mixture it was assumed that offspring inherited the essence of the hierarchically "inferior" race. During the early twentieth century, social scientists began to realize that differences in human culture, behavior, intellect, morality, and spirituality were the result of environment, education, and history rather than biology. As a result, the concept of race shrank to mean biological differences only. That is, at present, as a factual basis for individual and group identification, "race" still means inheritable physical characteristics only.

B. The Problems with Race in Science

If you ask adult Americans what race is, you might be told that races are different *breeds* of human beings and that the elementary school books used to say that there were three of them: Negro, Caucasian, and Mongoloid, or in current language, black, white, and Asian. The U.S. census and most public institutions gather information and keep records based on the racial categories of black, white, Asian or Pacific Islander, and American Indian or Alaska Native. In recent decades, everyone who has been a student or an employee, or filled out an application to participate in a large public institution has been required to indicate what their race is at some stage in complying with requests for information. As well as information on race, *Hispanic* or non-Hispanic *ethnicity* has to be indicated.

The Hispanic category was artificially created by the U.S. government and it contains wide racial variation. Some members of the group whom the government considers Hispanic claim that they should be identified as *Latino[/a]* or *Chicano[/a]*. People who are *biracial* or *multiracial* are often frustrated by the bureaucratic system of racial classification that these forms represent because they are usually asked to designate themselves by one race only. Their only alternative to this is to *identify* as *"other."*

Still, most Americans believe that the information requested on such forms has a factual basis apart from its interest to officials. The 1990 U.S. census recorded the following data for a population of 249 million: 200 million whites; 30 million blacks; 7 million Asians and Pacific Islanders; 2 million Native Americans, Eskimos, and Aleut; 10 million who were "other." Additionally, there were 22 million Hispanics. The presumption that these figures mean something is very strong. They are taken seriously as a basis for *entitlement* programs for nonwhite minority groups, and used for information about the population by business and educational institutions. They are also a source for national, group, and individual self-images. Individuals believe that their types of skin color, hair texture, facial features, and bone structure are the results of belonging to the race to which they belong. And the race to which you belong, even if it is that cryptic category of "other," has a place on the national map of races.

If it were true that being black, white, Asian, or Indian caused human beings to have the types of physical traits they do, then there ought to be some physical marker for race, apart from those traits, that scientists can identify. Otherwise, there would be nothing general about a race that could cause distinctive types of physical traits in individuals. However, neither biologists, nor anthropologists, nor physiologists, nor geneticists, nor any of the other scientists who have studied physical race have ever identified any general racial characteristics shared by all members of any particular race. There are no genes or other hereditary factors shared by every member of any of the main racial groups. In this sense, race provides an interesting contrast to biological sex. There are chromosomal markers of XY and XX, respectively, for male and female biological sex. Given the presence of XY or XX, the presence of more specific sexual traits, such as testicles or ovaries, can be predicted. But there is nothing analogous for race. When scientists study physical traits or diseases that are more prevalent in people of some races, they depend on the social definitions of race in order to pick out the members of the race they are studying.

The colloquial association of "blood" with race, as in the expressions, "She has black blood" or "He has some Indian blood" is no more than a metaphor, left over from the nineteenth-century pseudosciences of race. The four major human blood groups were identified in the early 1900s and it has been known since then that these blood types do not correspond to membership in races. There is some correspondence over the surface of the globe between geographical areas and blood types, but this is no more than a loose statistical association. We do think about the main racial groups as having originated in specific continental areas, such as Caucasians from northern Europe, Negroes from Africa, Asians from Asia, and Indians from the Americas. However, human populations have been in constant movement all over the globe for millions of years. And, the ordinary idea of race purports to tell us something about people as they are now, not about where their ancestors may have lived at some time in the past. Also, geographical origins of ancestors could not be reliable indicators of race because all races have been present on all continents over recorded history. Furthermore, most anthropologists now believe that human beings originated in Africa.

Racial membership has been culturally associated with some inherited physical characteristics, such as skin color and types of facial features, but these traits are no different in principle from other physical traits that have no racial significance, such as height. Moreover, the traits that are considered racial traits do not all get inherited together for any race, but are subject to dispersal and recombination each time a child is conceived.

Not only is there no general characteristic that determines racial membership, but the specific traits of skin color, hair texture, and bone structure vary more within any of the main racial groups than they do between any two racial groups. Indeed, scientists now speak of *populations* when referring to groups that the layperson would call races. Such populations may share more of some inherited physical traits than other populations. But the distribution of these traits within the membership of a population changes over generations and the human physical trait boundaries between populations cannot be sharply drawn. Even when the physical traits that are considered racial traits are compared within the general human population, they represent very small variations in genetic material, on the order of one ten-thousandth of all human genetic material.

What the foregoing amounts to is that there is no scientific basis for our idea of race as a human biological difference. Race, as something general about a person or a group, is a social overlay on actual physical traits. This is not to deny that people perceive what they think are racial traits or that race has a powerful social reality. But it means that what we think of as race is solely a matter of convention and imagination. We follow a convention of imagining the existence of races and sorting people into these imaginary categories. Once this realization of the imaginary nature of race sinks in, the human differences that are attributed to race have to be explained and understood in other terms. The physical differences of skin, hair, and bone that have been associated with race are not important enough, in relation to biological function, to require a deep explanation. However, many of the intellectual and moral differences that have been attributed to race are very important in terms of social status and individual well-being and it is those alleged differences that require careful study.

C. *The Cultural Meanings of Race*

Even though race does not have the biological foundation it is assumed to have in common sense, not only is race very important in the United States but most adult Americans know what race they are and how to sort other people into their appropriate races. The question is, how do they—we—do that if there is greater physical variation within races than between races? Generally, people rely on the race of their close family members as a source of their own racial identity. And they generally rely on physical appearance for classifying others. That is, we have fairly clear images, in our minds and presented to us through the mass media, of how blacks, whites, Asians, and Indians are "supposed" to look. We expect people of our own and different races to conform to these images, and most of the time they seem to do so. Nonetheless, the images or stereotypes of racial appearance have varied historically and geographically in the United States and they do not work for classifying people who do not look "typical."

When physical appearance is ambiguous or atypical, the race of kin, of parents and other forebears, is

the determining factor for racial classification. This family-inheritance aspect of race is also at work in determining the race of people whose appearance is racially "clear." It's just that if someone looks black and has black kin, or looks white and has white kin, there need be no explicit reference to the race of his or her ancestors. The ambiguous cases draw out the formal basis that underlines all racial classification. The formal basis for black and white racial identity amounts to this:

> *Black:* A person is black if he or she has a black ancestor anywhere in family history. This is known as the "one-drop rule" of black classification because it is based on a myth that one drop of "black blood" is sufficient to determine racial blackness. The one-drop rule is a legacy of nineteenth-century ideas of racial essences that results in hypodescent for racial mixture. A social system of hypodescent in cases of racial mixture means that offspring have the race of the parent with the lower racial status. Thus, Americans with both white and black ancestry are always officially classified as black and often encouraged to identify as black in personal and social contexts.

> *White:* A person is white if he or she has no black ancestry anywhere in family history. This means that in order to be white, a person has to be purely white. This is a condition impossible to prove because it would be proving a negative, in this case the absence of black ancestors. Before about 1900, definitions of whiteness were less restricted in some states because definitions of blackness rested on having one black grandparent, great-grandparent, or great-great-grandparent. This meant that someone could be white if he or she had a black ancestor one generation back from the generation in which a black ancestor would result in being black. (For example, in a state such as Virginia, where one black grandparent determined blackness, someone with one black great-grandparent and no known black ancestry more recent than that would have been classified as white.)

The formal one-drop rule definitions of black and white race that have been in effect during the twentieth century posit those two races as *logical contradictories* of one another. This entails that everyone is either black or white and that no one is both. However, it has been acknowledged since at least the beginning of the nineteenth century that other races besides black and white exist, so black and white cannot be logical contradictories. Therefore, the formal definitions are misleading, if not actually false.

Like the definitions of black and white, American cultural definitions of Asian and Indian rely on physical appearance and the race of ancestors. Indigenous American Indian cultures did not have biological concepts of race, and rules for tribal membership allowed generously for adoption into tribes other than those to which one or both biological parents belonged. However, because American Indians have entitlements based on treaty law, the U.S. federal government has sometimes imposed requirements for blood quanta of at least 50 percent ancestry from one tribe in order to be classified as an Indian. As a result of this policy, and due to loyalty to traditional cultural identities, many American Indian tribes have developed their own criteria for full bloods.

Asian Americans have been present in the United States since the mid-nineteenth century. Since that time, new immigrants have been sources of cheap labor and those born here have met with varied barriers to success. However, Asian Americans have not been as visible as American blacks or American Indians in liberatory literary and activist traditions that resist dominance by the white majority. At this time, Asian American groups include Cambodian, Chinese, Japanese, Filipino, Hmong and Laotian, Indian, Korean, Pacific Islander, Thai, and Vietnamese. Whether, and to what extent, these groups are perceived as one race depends on where they live and other specific cultural contexts.

Despite the formal one-drop rule definitions of American blackness and whiteness, in reality there is considerable racial mixture in this country. Only a minority of American Indians can prove they are full bloods; half of all Asian Americans marry non-Asians; approximately 6 percent of all whites have some black ancestry; approximately 90 percent of American blacks have nonblack ancestry; and the so-called Hispanic population has included wide racial variations of black, white, and Indian for hundreds of years. Still, few Americans choose to identify as mixed race and the idea of mixed race as a positive identity is relatively new. That Americans still use a system of three or four main races despite these commonly known facts about mixed race suggests either that the false

nineteenth-century biological theory of racial essences is deeply embedded in "folk wisdom," or else that Americans suspend their rational disbeliefs about this theory for pragmatic reasons, or both.

Where the false nineteenth-century biological theory of racial essences is still believed, it is appropriate to refer to the scientific evidence against it, or rather, the lack of scientific evidence for it. This lack of evidence for biological race is not proof that such evidence will never be found. Nonetheless, and this is the conceptual point worth taking, most folk ideas about race are based on the false assumption that the evidence already exists.

Pragmatic reasons for believing in racial categories have always been fairly obvious from the standpoint of the group supporting the belief. Black slavery was accepted by the founders of the U.S. Constitution at a time when it was believed that all human beings had natural rights to freedom. It was written into the Constitution that for purposes of electing representatives based on population size, each black slave would be counted as two-thirds of a person. One way to justify slavery was to insist that blacks were inferior or incomplete human beings. Slavery, segregation, and other forms of injustice against blacks benefited whites economically, politically, and socially at the expense of blacks. Beliefs in human differences based on natural divisions of race were thus a convenient basis on which to rationalize unjust treatment that had motives of self-interest which could not otherwise be admitted or defended. The systematic theft of American Indian land and the destruction of native cultures, as well as the exploitation of the cheap labor of Asian immigrants, were similarly rationalized by myths of white racial superiority.

However, there is another side to this pragmatic coin of racial categorization. Nonwhite Americans who have been categorized in biological racial terms have found it useful to use their categories as identities from which to protest and resist injustice based on race. Nineteenth-century pseudoscience falsely connected unsubstantiated ideas of biological race with ideas of less advanced or degenerate inherited cultural traits and practices. Speculation was substituted for empirical methodology and connections were made between biology and culture that had no empirical or logical justification. There was no biological foundation even for ideas of biological race. But, the groups thus racialized have included positive and valued aspects of their cultures as part of their racial identities. Indeed, what black Americans often mean by the word *race* is a shared history of survival and struggle. American Indians, when they identify as *full-bloods*, often use the racial classification to indicate loyalty to traditional Indian religious beliefs and ways of living, although identities based on indigenism are independent of EuroAmerican classifications. Asian Americans also have group and individual interests in preserving traditional lifestyles and religions, although they have less often presented themselves as racially distinct on that basis.

The pragmatic importance of racial identification, for all groups, also derives from an association of racial identity with family relations. Almost all human beings claim to value their family members and their family relationships. The false biological concept of race was attached to real, physical, inherited traits. These physical inherited traits are anchored in family descent, which is also real.

The real and fulfilling, political, cultural, and familial associations with racial classification and belonging suggest that not all the connotations and associations of race are ungrounded or humanly dimin- ishing. Therefore, care and skill must be used in dissolving the ignorant and unjust aspects of racial classification. The important question to consider and reconsider is this: Do differences among human groups require a taxonomy or classification scheme that creates the kind of strong divisions associated with the idea of race in the false biological sense?

A Defense of Affirmative Action

Thomas Nagel

The term "affirmative action" has changed in meaning since it was first introduced. Originally it referred only to special efforts to ensure equal opportunity for members of groups that had been subject to discrimination. These efforts included public advertisement of positions to be filled, active recruitment of qualified applicants from the formerly excluded groups, and special training programs to help them meet the standards for admission or appointment. There was also close attention to procedures of appointment, and sometimes to the results, with a view to detecting continued discrimination, conscious or unconscious.

More recently the term has come to refer also to some degree of definite preference for members of these groups in determining access to positions from which they were formerly excluded. Such preference might be allowed to influence decisions only between candidates who are otherwise equally qualified, but usually it involves the selection of women or minority members over other candidates who are better qualified for the position.

Let me call the first sort of policy "weak affirmative action" and the second "strong affirmative action." It is important to distinguish them, because the distinction is sometimes blurred in practice. It is strong affirmative action—the policy of preference—that arouses controversy. Most people would agree that weak or precautionary affirmative action is a good thing, and worth its cost in time and energy. But this does not imply that strong affirmative action is also justified.

I shall claim that in the present state of things it is justified, most clearly with respect to blacks. But I also believe that a defender of the practice must acknowledge that there are serious arguments against it, and that it is defensible only because the arguments for it have great weight. Moral opinion in this country is sharply divided over the issue because significant values are involved on both sides. My own view is that while strong affirmative action is intrinsically undesirable, it is a legitimate and perhaps indispensable method of pursuing a goal so important to the national welfare that it can be justified as a temporary, though not short-term, policy for both public and private

From testimony before the Subcommittee on the Constitution of the Senate Judiciary Committee, June 18, 1981. Reprinted by permission of the author.

institutions. In this respect it is like other policies that impose burdens on some for the public good.

Three Objections

I shall begin with the argument against. There are three objections to strong affirmative action: that it is inefficient; that it is unfair; and that it damages self-esteem.

The degree of inefficiency depends on how strong a role racial or sexual preference plays in the process of selection. Among candidates meeting the basic qualifications for a position, those better qualified will on the average perform better, whether they are doctors, policemen, teachers, or electricians. There may be some cases, as in preferential college admissions, where the immediate usefulness of making educational resources available to an individual is thought to be greater because of the use to which the education will be put or because of the internal effects on the institution itself. But by and large, policies of strong affirmative action must reckon with the costs of some lowering in performance level: the stronger the preference, the larger the cost to be justified. Since both the costs and the value of the results will vary from case to case, this suggests that no one policy of affirmative action is likely to be correct in all cases, and that the cost in performance level should be taken into account in the design of a legitimate policy.

The charge of unfairness arouses the deepest disagreements. To be passed over because of membership in a group one was born into, where this has nothing to do with one's individual qualifications for a position, can arouse strong feelings of resentment. It is a departure from the ideal—one of the values finally recognized in our society—that people should be judged so far as possible on the basis of individual characteristics rather than involuntary group membership.

This does not mean that strong affirmative action is morally repugnant in the manner of racial or sexual discrimination. It is nothing like those practices, for though like them it employs race and sex as criteria of selection, it does so for entirely different reasons. Racial and sexual discrimination are based on contempt or even loathing for the excluded group, a feeling that certain contacts with them are degrading to members of the dominant group, that they are fit only for subordinate positions or menial work. Strong affirmative action involves none of this: it is simply a means of increasing the social and economic strength of formerly victimized groups, and does not stigmatize others.

There is an element of individual unfairness here, but it is more like the unfairness of conscription in wartime, or of property condemnation under the right of eminent domain. Those who benefit or lose out because of their race or sex cannot be said to deserve their good or bad fortune.

It might be said on the other side that the beneficiaries of affirmative action deserve it as compensation for past discrimination, and that compensation is rightly exacted from the group that has benefited from discrimination in the past. But this is a bad argument, because as the practice usually works, no effort is made to give preference to those who have suffered most from discrimination, or to prefer them especially to those who have benefited most from it, or been guilty of it. Only candidates who in other qualifications fall on one or the other side of the margin of decision will directly benefit or lose from the policy, and these are not necessarily, or even probably, the ones who especially deserve it. Women or blacks who don't have the qualifications even to be considered are likely to have been handicapped more by the effects of discrimination than those who receive preference. And the marginal white male candidate who is turned down can evoke our sympathy if he asks, "Why me?" (A policy of explicitly *compensatory* preference, which took into account each individual's background of poverty and discrimination, would escape some of these objections, and it has its defenders, but it is not the policy I want to defend. Whatever its merits, it will not serve the same purpose as direct affirmative action.)

The third objection concerns self-esteem, and is particularly serious. While strong affirmative action is in effect, and generally known to be so, no one in an affirmative action category who gets a desirable job or is admitted to a selective university can be sure that he or she has not benefited from the policy. Even those who would have made it anyway fall under suspicion, from themselves and from others: it comes to be widely felt that success does not mean the same thing for women and minorities. This painful damage to esteem cannot be avoided. It should make any defender of strong affirmative action want the practice to end as soon as it has achieved its basic purpose.

Justifying Affirmative Action

I have examined these three objections and tried to assess their weight, in order to decide how strong a countervailing reason is needed to justify such a policy.

In my view, taken together they imply that strong affirmative action involving significant preference should be undertaken only if it will substantially further a social goal of the first importance. While this condition is not met by all programs of affirmative action now in effect, it is met by those which address the most deep-seated, stubborn, and radically unhealthy divisions in the society, divisions whose removal is a condition of basic justice and social cohesion.

The situation of black people in our country is unique in this respect. For almost a century after the abolition of slavery we had a rigid racial caste system of the ugliest kind, and it only began to break up twenty-five years ago. In the South it was enforced by law, and in the North, in a somewhat less severe form, by social convention. Whites were thought to be defiled by social or residential proximity to blacks, intermarriage was taboo, blacks were denied the same level of public goods—education and legal protection—as whites, were restricted to the most menial occupations, and were barred from any positions of authority over whites. The visceral feelings of black inferiority and untouchability that this system expressed were deeply ingrained in the members of both races, and they continue, not surprisingly, to have their effect. Blacks still form, to a considerable extent, a hereditary social and economic community characterized by widespread poverty, unemployment, and social alienation.

When this society finally got around to moving against the caste system, it might have done no more than to enforce straight equality of opportunity, perhaps with the help of weak affirmative action, and then wait a few hundred years while things gradually got better. Fortunately it decided instead to accelerate the process by both public and private institutional action, because there was wide recognition of the intractable character of the problem posed by this insular minority and its place in the nation's history and collective consciousness. This has not been going on very long, but the results are already impressive, especially in speeding the advancement of blacks in the middle class. Affirmative action has not done much to improve the position of poor and unskilled blacks. That is the most serious part of the problem, and it requires a more direct economic attack. But increased access to higher education and upper-level jobs is an essential part of what must be achieved to break the structure of drastic separation that was left largely undisturbed by the legal abolition of the caste system.

Changes of this kind require a generation or two. My guess is that strong affirmative action for blacks will continue to be justified into the early decades of the next century, but that by then it will have accomplished what it can and will no longer be worth the costs. One point deserves special emphasis. The goal to be pursued is the reduction of a great social injustice, not proportional representation of the races in all institutions and professions. Proportional racial representation is of no value in itself. It is not a legitimate social goal, and it should certainly not be the aim of strong affirmation action, whose drawbacks make it worth adopting only against a serious and intractable social evil.

This implies that the justification for strong affirmative action is much weaker in the case of other racial and ethnic groups, and in the case of women. At least, the practice will be justified in a narrower range of circumstances and for a shorter span of time than it is for blacks. No other group has been treated quite like this, and no other group is in a comparable status. Hispanic Americans occupy an intermediate position, but it seems to me frankly absurd to include persons of oriental descent as beneficiaries of affirmative action, strong or weak. They are not a severely deprived and excluded minority, and their eligibility serves only to swell the numbers that can be included on affirmative action reports. It also suggests that there is a drift in the policy toward adopting the goal of radical proportional representation for its own sake. This is a foolish mistake, and should be resisted. The only legitimate goal of the policy is to reduce egregious racial stratification.

With respect to women, I believe that except over the short term, and in professions or institutions from which their absence is particularly marked, strong affirmative action is not warranted and weak affirmative action is enough. This is based simply on the expectation that the social and economic situation of women will improve quite rapidly under conditions of full equality of opportunity. Recent progress provides some evidence for this. Women do not form a separate hereditary community, characteristically poor and uneducated, and their position is not likely to be self-perpetuating in the same way as that of an outcast race. The process requires less artificial acceleration, and any need for strong affirmative action for women can be expected to end sooner than it ends for blacks.

I said at the outset that there was a tendency to blur the distinction between weak and strong affirmative action. This occurs especially in the use of numerical quotas, a topic on which I want to comment briefly.

A quota may be a method of either weak or strong affirmative action, depending on the circumstances. It amounts to weak affirmative action—a safeguard against discrimination—if, and only if, there is independent evidence that average qualifications for the positions being filled are no lower in the group to which minimum quota is being assigned than in the applicant group as a whole. This can be presumed true of unskilled jobs that most people can do, but it becomes less likely, and harder to establish, the greater the skill and education required for the position. At these levels, a quota proportional to population, or even to representation of the group in the applicant pool, is almost certain to amount to strong affirmative action. Moreover it is strong affirmative action of a particularly crude and indiscriminate kind, because it permits no variation in the degree of preference on the basis of costs in efficiency, depending on the qualification gap. For this reason I should defend quotas only where they serve the purpose of weak affirmative action. On the whole, strong affirmative action is better implemented by including group preference as one factor in appointment or admission decisions, and letting the results depend on its interaction with other factors.

I have tried to show that the arguments against strong affirmative action are clearly outweighed at present by the need for exceptional measures to remove the stubborn residues of racial caste. But advocates of the policy should acknowledge the reasons against it, which will ensure its termination when it is no longer necessary. Affirmative action is not an end in itself, but a means of dealing with a social situation that should be intolerable to us all.

Affirmative Action

SHELBY STEELE

In a few short years, when my two children will be applying to college, the affirmative action policies by which most universities offer black students some form of preferential treatment will present me with a dilemma. I am a middle-class black, a college professor, far from wealthy but also well-removed from the kind of deprivation that would qualify my children for the label "disadvantaged." Both of them have endured racial insensitivity from whites. They have been called names, have suffered slights, and have experienced firsthand the peculiar malevolence that racism brings out in people. Yet, they have never experienced racial discrimination, have never been stopped by their race on any path they have chosen to follow. Still their society now tells that if they will only designate themselves as black on their college applications they will likely do better in the college lottery than if they conceal this fact. I think there is something of a Faustian bargain in this.

Of course, many blacks and a considerable number of whites would say that I was sanctimoniously making affirmative action into a test of character. They would say that this small preference is the meagerest recompense for centuries of unrelieved oppression. And to these arguments other very obvious facts must be added. In America, many marginally competent or flatly incompetent whites are hired every day—some because their white skin suits the conscious or unconscious racial preference of their employer. The white children of alumni are often grandfathered into elite universities in what can only be seen as a residual benefit of historic white privilege. Worse, white incompetence is always an individual matter, while for blacks it is often confirmation of ugly stereotypes. The Peter Principle was not concerned with only blacks in mind. Given that unfairness cuts both ways, doesn't it only balance the scales of history that my children now receive a slight preference over whites? Doesn't this repay, in a small way,

From Shelby Steele, *The Content of Our Character* (New York: St. Martin's Press, 1990), pp. 111–125. Reprinted by permission of St. Martin's Press.

the systematic denial under which their grandfather lived out his days?

So, in theory, affirmative action certainly has all the moral symmetry that fairness requires—the injustice of historical and even contemporary white advantage is offset with black advantage; preference replaces prejudice, inclusion answers exclusion. It is reformist and corrective, even repentant and redemptive. And I would never sneer at these good intentions. Born in the late forties in Chicago, I started my education (a charitable term in this case) in a segregated school and suffered all the indignities that come to blacks in a segregated society. My father, born in the South, only made it to the third grade before the white man's fields took permanent priority over his formal education. And though he educated himself into an advanced reader with an almost professorial authority, he could only drive a truck for a living and never earned more than ninety dollars a week in his entire life. So yes, it is crucial to my sense of citizenship, to my ability to identify with the spirit and the interests of America, to know that this country, however imperfectly, recognizes its past sins and wishes to correct them.

Yet good intentions, because of the opportunity for innocence they offer us, are very seductive and can blind us to the effects they generate when implemented. In our society, affirmative action is, among other things a testament to white goodwill and to black power, and in the midst of these heavy investments, its effects can be hard to see. But after twenty years of implementation, I think affirmative action has shown itself to be more bad than good and that blacks—whom I will focus on in this essay—now stand to lose more from it than they gain.

In talking with affirmative action administrators and with blacks and whites in general, it is clear that supporters of affirmative action focus on its good intentions while detractors emphasize its negative effects. Proponents talk about "diversity" and "pluralism"; opponents speak of "reverse discrimination," the unfairness of quotas and set-asides. It was virtually impossible to find people outside either camp. The closest I came was a white male manager at a large computer company who said, "I think it amounts to reverse discrimination, but I'll put up with a little of that for a little more diversity." I'll live with a little of the effect to gain a little of the intention, he seemed to be saying. But this only makes him a halfhearted supporter of affirmative action. I think many people who don't really like affirmative action support it to one degree or another anyway.

I believe they do this because of what happened to white and black Americans in the crucible of the sixties when whites were confronted with their racial guilt and blacks tasted their first real power. In this stormy time white absolution and black power coalesced into virtual mandates for society. Affirmative action became a meeting ground for these mandates in the law, and in the late sixties and early seventies it underwent a remarkable escalation of its mission from simple anti-discrimination enforcement to social engineering by means of quotas, goals, timetables, set-asides and other forms of preferential treatment.

Legally, this was achieved through a series of executive orders and EEOC guidelines that allowed racial imbalances in the workplace to stand as proof of racial discrimination. Once it could be assumed that discrimination explained racial imbalances, it became easy to justify group remedies to presumed discrimination, rather than the normal case-by-case redress for proven discrimination. Preferential treatment through quotas, goals, and so on is designed to correct imbalances based on the assumption that they always indicate discrimination. This expansion of what constitutes discrimination allowed affirmative action to escalate into the business of social engineering in the name of anti-discrimination, to push society toward statistically proportionate racial representation, without any obligation of proving actual discrimination.

What accounted for this shift, I believe, was the white mandate to achieve a new racial innocence and the black mandate to gain power. Even though blacks had made great advances during the sixties without quotas, these mandates, which came to a head in the very late sixties, could no longer be satisfied by anything less than racial preferences. I don't think these mandates in themselves were wrong, since whites clearly needed to do better by blacks and blacks needed more real power in society. But, as they came together in affirmative action, their effect was to distort our understanding of racial discrimination in a way that allowed us to offer the remediation of preference on the basis of mere color rather than actual injury. By making black the color of preference, these mandates have reburdened society with the very marriage of color and preference (in reverse) that we set out to eradicate. The old sin is reaffirmed in a new guise.

But the essential problem with this form of affirmative action is the way it leaps over the hard business of developing a formerly oppressed people to the point where they can achieve proportionate representation on their own (given equal opportunity) and goes straight for the proportionate representation. This may satisfy some whites of their innocence and some blacks of their power, but it does very little to truly uplift blacks.

A white female affirmative action officer at an Ivy League university told me what many supporters of affirmative action now say: "We're after diversity. We ideally want a student body where racial and ethnic groups are represented according to their proportion in society." When affirmative action escalated into social engineering, diversity became a golden word. It grants whites an egalitarian fairness (innocence) and blacks an entitlement to proportionate representation (power). *Diversity* is a term that applies democratic principles to races and cultures rather than to citizens, despite the fact that there is nothing to indicate that real diversity is the same thing as proportionate representation. Too often the result of this on campuses (for example) has been a democracy of colors rather than of people, an artificial diversity that gives the appearance of an educational parity between black and white students that has not yet been achieved in reality. Here again, racial preferences allow society to leapfrog over the difficult problem of developing blacks to parity with whites and into a cosmetic diversity that covers the blemish of disparity—a full six years after admission, only about 26 percent of black students graduate from college.

Racial representation is not the same thing as racial development, yet affirmative action fosters a confusion of these very different needs. Representation can be manufactured; development is always hard-earned. However, it is the music of innocence and power that we hear in affirmative action that causes us to cling to it and to its distracting emphasis on representation. The fact is that after twenty years of racial preferences, the gap between white and black median income is greater than it was in the seventies. None of this is to say that blacks don't need policies that ensure our right to equal opportunity, but what we need more is the development that will let us take advantage of society's efforts to include us.

I think that one of the most troubling effects of racial preferences for blacks is a kind of demoralization, or put another way, an enlargement of self-doubt. Under affirmative action the quality that earns us preferential treatment is an implied inferiority. However this inferiority is explained—and it is easily enough explained by the myriad deprivations that grew out of our oppression—it is still inferiority. There are explanations, and then there is the fact. And the fact must

be borne by the individual as a condition apart from the explanation, apart even from the fact that others like himself also bear this condition. In integrated situations where blacks must compete with whites who may be better prepared, these explanations may quickly wear thin and expose the individual to racial as well as personal self-doubt.

All of this is compounded by the cultural myth of black inferiority that blacks have always lived with. What this means in practical terms is that when blacks deliver themselves into integrated situations, they encounter a nasty little reflex in whites, a mindless, atavistic reflex that responds to the color black with alarm. Attributions may follow this alarm if the white cares to indulge them, and if they do, they will most likely be negative—one such attribution is intellectual ineptness. I think this reflex and the attributions that may follow it embarrass most whites today, therefore, it is usually quickly repressed. Nevertheless, on an equally atavistic level, the black will be aware of the reflex his color triggers and will feel a stab of horror at seeing himself reflected in this way. He, too, will do a quick repression, but a lifetime of such stabbings is what constitutes his inner realm of racial doubt.

The effects of this may be a subject for another essay. The point here is that the implication of inferiority that racial preferences engender in both the white and black mind expands rather than contracts this doubt. Even when the black sees no implication of inferiority in racial preferences, he knows that whites do, so that—consciously or unconsciously—the result is virtually the same. The effect of preferential treatment—the lowering of normal standards to increase black representation—puts blacks at war with an expanded realm of debilitating doubt, so that the doubt itself becomes an unrecognized preoccupation that undermines their ability to perform, especially in integrated situations. On largely white campuses, blacks are five times more likely to drop out than whites. Preferential treatment, no matter how it is justified in the light of day, subjects blacks to a midnight of self-doubt, and so often transforms their advantage into a revolving door.

Another liability of affirmative action comes from the fact that it indirectly encourages blacks to exploit their own past victimization as a source of power and privilege. Victimization, like implied inferiority, is what justifies preference, so that to receive the benefits of preferential treatment one must, to some extent, become invested in the view of one's self as a victim. In this way, affirmative action nurtures a victim-focused identity in blacks. The obvious irony here is that we become inadvertently invested in the very condition we are trying to overcome. Racial preferences send us the message that there is more power in our past suffering than our present achievements—none of which could bring us a *preference* over others.

When power itself grows out of suffering, then blacks are encouraged to expand the boundaries of what qualifies as racial oppression, a situation that can lead us to paint our victimization in vivid colors, even as we receive the benefits or preference. The same corporations and institutions that give us preference are also seen as our oppressors. At Stanford University minority students—some of whom enjoy as much as $15,000 a year in financial aid—recently took over the president's office demanding, among other things, more financial aid. The power to be found in victimization, like any power, is intoxicating and can lend itself to the creation of a new class of supervictims who can feel the pea of victimization under twenty mattresses. Preferential treatment rewards us for being underdogs rather than for moving beyond that status—a misplacement of incentives that, along with its deepening of our doubt, is more a yoke than a spur.

But, I think, one of the worst prices that blacks pay for preference has to do with an illusion. I saw this illusion at work recently in the mother of a middle-class black student who was going off to his first semester of college. "They owe us this, so don't think for a minute that you don't belong there." This is the logic by which many blacks, and some whites, justify affirmative action—it is something "owed," a form of reparation. But this logic overlooks a much harder and less digestible reality, that it is impossible to repay blacks living today for the historic suffering of the race. If all blacks were given a million dollars tomorrow morning it would not amount to a dime on the dollar of three centuries of oppression, nor would it obviate the residues of that oppression that we still carry today. The concept of historic reparation grows out of man's need to impose a degree of justice on the world that simply does not exist. Suffering can be endured and overcome, it cannot be repaid. Blacks cannot be repaid for the injustice done to the race, but we can be corrupted by society's guilty gestures of repayment.

Affirmative action is such a gesture. It tells us that racial preferences can do for us what we cannot do for ourselves. The corruption here is in the hidden incentive *not* to do what we believe preferences will do. This is an incentive to be reliant on others just as we are struggling for self-reliance. And it keeps alive the illusion that we can find some deliverance in repayment. The hardest thing for any sufferer to accept is that his suffering excuses him from very little and never has enough currency to restore him. To think otherwise is to prolong the suffering.

Several blacks I spoke with said they were still in favor of affirmative action because of the "subtle" discrimination blacks were subject to once on the job. One photojournalist said, "They have ways of ignoring you." A black female television producer said, "You can't file a lawsuit when your boss doesn't invite you to the insider meetings without ruining your career. So we still need affirmative action." Others mentioned the infamous "glass ceiling" through which blacks can see the top positions of authority but never reach them. But I don't think racial preferences are a protection against this subtle discrimination; I think they contribute to it.

In any workplace, racial preferences will always create two-tiered populations composed of preferreds and unpreferreds. This division makes automatic a perception of enhanced competence for the unpreferreds and of questionable competence for the preferreds—the former earned his way, even though others were given preference, while the latter made it by color as much as by competence. Racial preferences implicitly mark whites with an exaggerated superiority just as they mark blacks with an exaggerated inferiority. They not only reinforce America's oldest racial myth but, for blacks, they have the effect of stigmatizing the already stigmatized.

I think that much of the "subtle" discrimination that blacks talk about is often (not always) discrimination against the stigma of questionable competence that affirmative action delivers to blacks. In this sense, preferences scapegoat the very people they seek to help. And it may be that at a certain level employers impose a glass ceiling, but this may not be against the race so much as against the race's reputation for having advanced by color as much as by competence. Affirmative action makes a glass ceiling virtually necessary as a protection against the corruptions of preferential treatment. This ceiling is the point at which corporations shift the emphasis from color to competency and stop playing the affirmative action game. Here preference backfires for blacks and becomes a taint that holds them back. Of course, one could argue that this taint, which is, after all, in the minds of whites, becomes nothing more than an excuse to discriminate against blacks. And certainly the result is the same in either case—blacks don't get past the glass ceiling. But this argument does not get around the fact that racial preferences now taint this color with a new theme of suspicion that makes it even more vulnerable to the impulse in others to discriminate. In this crucial yet gray area of perceived competence, preferences make whites look better than they are and blacks worse, while doing nothing whatever to stop the very real discrimination that blacks may encounter. I don't wish to justify the glass ceiling here, but only to suggest the very subtle ways that affirmative action revives rather than extinguishes the old rationalizations for racial discrimination.

In education, a revolving door; in employment, a glass ceiling.

I believe affirmative action is problematic in our society because it tries to function like a social program. Rather than ask it to ensure equal opportunity we have demanded that it create parity between the races. But preferential treatment does not teach skills, or educate or instill motivation. It only passes out entitlement by color, a situation that in my profession has created an unrealistically high demand for black professors. The social engineer's assumption is that this high demand will inspire more blacks to earn Ph.D.'s and join the profession. In fact, the number of blacks earning Ph.D.'s has declined in recent years. A Ph.D. must be developed from preschool on. He requires family and community support. He must acquire an entire system of values that enables him to work hard while delaying gratification. There are social programs, I believe, that can (and should) help blacks *develop* in all these areas, but entitlement by color is not a social program; it is a dubious reward for being black.

It now seems clear that the Supreme Court, in a series of recent decisions, is moving away from racial preferences. It has disallowed preferences except in instances of "identified discrimination," eroded the precedent that statistical racial imbalances are *prima facie* evidence of discrimination, and in effect granted white males the right to challenge consent degrees that use preference to achieve racial balances in the workplace. One civil rights leader said, "Night has fallen on civil rights." But I am not so sure. The effect of these decisions is to protect the constitutional rights of everyone rather than take rights away from blacks. What they do take away from blacks is the special entitlement to more rights than others that preferences always grant. Night has fallen on racial preferences, not on the fundamental rights of black Americans. The reason for this shift, I believe, is that the white mandate for absolution from past racial sins has weakened considerably during the eighties. Whites are now less

willing to endure unfairness to themselves in order to grant special entitlements to blacks, even when these entitlements are justified in the name of past suffering. Yet the black mandate for more power in society has remained unchanged. And I think part of the anxiety that many blacks feel over these decisions has to do with the loss of black power they may signal. We had won a certain specialness and now we are losing it.

But the power we've lost by these decisions is really only the power that grows out of our victimization—the power to claim special entitlements under the law because of past oppression. This is not a very substantial or reliable power, and it is important that we know this so we can focus more exclusively on the kind of development that will bring enduring power. There is talk now that Congress will pass new legislation to compensate for these new limits on affirmative action. If this happens, I hope that their focus will be on development and anti-discrimination rather than entitlement, on achieving racial parity rather than jerry-building racial diversity.

I would also like to see affirmative action go back to its original purpose of enforcing equal opportunity—a purpose that in itself disallows racial preferences. We cannot be sure that the discriminatory impulse in America has yet been shamed into extinction, and I believe affirmative action can make its greatest contribution by providing a rigorous vigilance in this area. It can guard constitutional rather than racial rights, and help institutions evolve standards of merit and selection that are appropriate to the institution's needs yet as free of racial bias as possible (again, with the understanding that racial imbalances are not always an indication of racial bias). One of the most important things affirmative action can do is to define exactly what racial discrimination is and how it might manifest itself within a specific institution. The impulse to discriminate *is* subtle and cannot be ferreted out unless its many guises are made clear to people. Along with this there should be monitoring of institutions and heavy sanctions brought to bear when actual discrimination is found. This is the sort of affirmative action that America owes to blacks and to itself. It goes after the evil of discrimination itself, while preferences only sidestep the evil and grant entitlement to its *presumed* victims.

But if not preferences, then what? I think we need social policies that are committed to two goals: the educational and economic development of disadvantaged people, regardless of race, and the eradication from our society—through close monitoring and severe sanctions—of racial, ethnic, or gender discrimination. Preferences will not deliver us to either of these goals, since they tend to benefit those who are not disadvantaged—middle-class white women and middle-class blacks—and attack one form of discrimination with another. Preferences are inexpensive and carry the glamour of good intentions—change the numbers and the good deed is done. To be against them is to be unkind. But I think the unkindest cut is to bestow on children like my own an advantage while neglecting the development of those disadvantaged children on the East Side of my city who will likely never be in a position to benefit from a preference. Give my children fairness; give disadvantaged children a better shot at development—better elementary and secondary schools, job training, safer neighborhoods, better

financial assistance for college, and so on. Fewer blacks go to college today than ten years ago; more black males of college age are in prison or under the control of the criminal justice system than in college. This despite racial preferences.

The mandates of black power and white absolution out of which preferences emerged were not wrong in themselves. What was wrong was that both races focused more on the goals of these mandates than on the means to the goals. Blacks can have no real power without taking responsibility for their own educational and economic development. Whites can have no racial innocence without earning it by eradicating discrimination and helping the disadvantaged to develop. Because we ignored the means, the goals have not been reached, and the real work remains to be done.

House Resolution 40: Reparations to African Americans

Be it enacted by the Senate and House of Representatives of the United States of America in Congress assembled,

Section 1. Short Title

This Act may be cited as the "Commission to Study Reparation Proposals for African Americans Act."

Section 2. Findings and Purpose

(a) Findings: The Congress finds that—

    (1) approximately 4,000,000 Africans and their descendants were enslaved in the United States and the colonies that became the United States from 1619 to 1865;

    (2) the institution of slavery was constitutionally and statutorily sanctioned by the Government of the United States from 1769 through 1865;

From 143 *Congressional Record* E1548-E1549, 105th Congress, 1st Session (July 29, 1997).

    (3) the slavery that flourished in the United States constituted an immoral and inhumane deprivation of Africans' life, liberty, African citizenship rights, and cultural heritage, and denied them the fruits of their own labor; and

    (4) sufficient inquiry has not been made into the effects of the institution of slavery on living African Americans and society in the United States.

(b) Purpose: The purpose of this Act is to establish a commission to—

    (1) examine the institution of slavery which existed from 1619 through 1865 within the United States and the colonies that became the United States, including the extent to which the Federal and State Governments constitutionally and statutorily supported the institution of slavery;

    (2) examine de jure and de facto discrimination against freed slaves and their descendants from the end of the Civil War to the present, including economic, political, and social discrimination;

(3) examine the lingering negative effects of the institution of slavery and the discrimination described in paragraph (2) on living African Americans and on society in the United States;

(4) recommend appropriate ways to educate the American public of the Commission's findings;

(5) recommend appropriate remedies in consideration of the Commission's findings on the matters described in paragraphs (1) and (2); and

(6) submit to the Congress the results of such examination, together with such recommendations.

Section 3. Establishment and Duties

(a) Establishment: There is established the Commission to Study Reparation Proposals for African Americans (hereinafter in this Act referred to as the "Commission").

(b) Duties: The Commission shall perform the following duties:

. . .

(7) Recommended appropriate remedies. . . . In making such recommendations, the Commission shall address, among other issues, the following questions:

(A) Whether the Government of the United States should offer a formal apology on behalf of the people of the United States for the perpetration of gross human rights violations on African slaves and their descendants.

(B) Whether African Americans still suffer from the lingering effects of . . . [slavery and Jim Crow].

(C) Whether, in consideration of the Commission's findings, any form of compensation to the descendants of African slaves is warranted.

(D) If the Commission finds that such compensation is warranted, what should be the amount of compensation, what form of compensation should be awarded, and who should be eligible for such compensation.

Cato v. U.S.

RYMER, Circuit Judge:

Two groups of plaintiffs, Jewel Cato, Joyce Cato, Howard Cato and Edward Cato; and Leerma Patterson, Charles Patterson, and Bobbie Trice Johnson (collectively "Cato"), filed nearly identical complaints *in forma pauperis* against the United States for damages due to the enslavement of African Americans and subsequent discrimination against them, for an acknowledgment of discrimination, and for an apology. The district court in both cases dismissed the complaints prior to service pursuant to 28 U.S.C. § 1915(d).

We have carefully considered Cato's pleading and the arguments of appellate counsel. On our own, we

70 F.3d 1103 (1995). United States Court of Appeals for the Ninth Circuit.

have tried to conceive of possibilities for stating a cognizable claim. As Judge Armstrong stated so well:

> Discrimination and bigotry of any type is intolerable, and the enslavement of Africans by this Country is inexcusable. This Court, however, is unable to identify any legally cognizable basis upon which plaintiff's claims may proceed against the United States. While plaintiff may be justified in seeking redress for past and present injustices, it is not within the jurisdiction of this Court to grant the requested relief. The legislature, rather than the judiciary, is the appropriate forum for plaintiff's grievances.

To us, as to the district court, it is clear that this complaint cannot be cured by amendment. Cato's theories of liability either fall outside the limited waiver of sovereign immunity by the United States, or otherwise are not within the jurisdiction of the federal courts. Because the district court did not abuse its discretion, we affirm.

I

Cato's complaint seeks compensation of $100,000,000 for forced, ancestral indoctrination into a foreign society; kidnapping of ancestors from Africa; forced labor; breakup of families; removal of traditional values; deprivations of freedom; and imposition of oppression, intimidation, miseducation and lack of information about various aspects of their indigenous character. She also requests that the court order an acknowledgment of the injustice of slavery in the United States and in the 13 American colonies between 1619 and 1865, as well as of the existence of discrimination against freed slaves and their descendants from the end of the Civil War to the present. In addition, she seeks an apology from the United States.

The complaint itself does not refer to any basis upon which the United States might have consented to suit. However, because Cato was proceeding *pro se,* the district court construed her papers liberally and surveyed the most likely authorities for waiver, but found them unavailing. Specifically, the court noted that the waiver of sovereign immunity in tort actions against the government in the Federal Tort Claims Act (FTCA), is limited to claims accruing on and after January 1, 1945, and that the Civil Rights Act applies to individual federal officials but not to the United States. The court also observed that while Cato's action appears to be patterned after the reparations authorized by Congress for individuals of Japanese ancestry who were forced into internment camps during World War II, those reparations were not awarded as damages in court but rather were enacted into law in the Civil Liberties Act of 1988. The court concluded that Cato's claims are barred by sovereign immunity, and that the appropriate forum for policy questions of the sort raised by her complaint is Congress, rather than the courts. Cato timely appealed.

II

First, Cato contends that dismissal of her action was premature in that she was given no opportunity to be heard on the adequacy of her complaint, or to amend.

She also argues that the complaint should not have been dismissed merely because the court has doubts that the plaintiff will prevail.

We do not read the district court's order as dismissing Cato's complaint on account of doubts about her ability to succeed. Rather, the court determined that Cato had not met her burden of showing a waiver of sovereign immunity, and that her claims were not legally cognizable because they raise a "policy question" which the judiciary "has neither the authority nor wisdom to address." For these reasons, the court concluded that while Cato may be justified in seeking redress for past and present injustices from the Congress, the court lacked jurisdiction to grant the requested relief.

As Cato's complaint neither identifies any constitutional or statutory right that was violated, nor asserts any basis for federal subject matter jurisdiction or waiver of sovereign immunity, it was properly dismissed. . . .

The critical question, however, for the district court as for us, is whether leave to amend should have been given. . . . Accordingly, we turn to Cato's disagreements with the court's ruling and to the possibilities for amendment that she suggests on appeal.

III

Cato first contends that we should not affirm the district court's dismissal on statute of limitations grounds. Strictly speaking, we don't. The dispositive question is whether her theories of liability are barred by sovereign immunity, or otherwise fall outside the district court's jurisdiction.

B

We take Cato's argument that her action is not barred by the statute of limitations in this context to mean that no time constraint (whether as a condition of the government's waiver of sovereign immunity or otherwise, should apply to her claims. She offers two reasons: First, that courts should not sustain dismissal of actions on statute of limitations grounds where the wrong sued upon is based on a constitutional or statutory prohibition. For this proposition she analogizes the wrongs about which she complains to recent cases arising under the Indian Trade and Intercourse Act, which prohibited the sale of land by Indians unless it was by treaty made under the authority of the United States, where the federal courts have addressed Indian land claims that are hundreds of years old. Cato locates the relevant prohibition in her case in the Thirteenth Amendment.

To the extent her argument is that we should for the same reason ignore time limitations on the government's waiver of sovereign immunity, we can't agree. Analogy to Indian land claim cases is not persuasive, for the courts' willingness to hear the kind of claim exemplified by *Oneida* does not turn on whether the claims were based on a prohibition. Rather, *Oneida*, for example, turned on the well-established rule that a suit by the United States as trustee on behalf of an Indian Tribe is not subject to state delay-based defenses, and the anomalous result that would otherwise obtain if the trustee were allowed to sue under more favorable conditions than those afforded the tribes themselves. Further, the circumstances under which an action *by* the United States can be brought sheds no light on the circumstances under which an action *against* the United States can be brought. In any event, as the government points out, regardless of whether there are factual similarities between the treatment accorded Indian Tribes and African American slaves and their descendants (as Cato contends), there is nothing in the relationship between the United States and any other persons, including African American slaves and their descendants, that is legally comparable to the unique relationship between the United States and Indian Tribes. Courts have recognized fiduciary responsibilities running from the United States to Indian Tribes because of specific treaty obligations and a network of statutes that by their own terms impose specific duties on the government. Similar strictures do not appear in the Thirteenth Amendment alone, or in combination with the other Civil War amendments and the various Civil Rights Acts which have been enacted in the meantime. We therefore see no basis in the Indian land cases, or the relationship between the federal government and Indian Tribes, for relieving a private plaintiff such as Cato of the need to show that her action against the United States meets all the conditions, including time constraints, of the consent by the United States to be sued.

C

As a second ground for avoiding affirmance on the basis of the statute of limitations, Cato argues that she need not allege discrimination within any particular time period because discrimination is a continuing act.

She submits that African Americans continue to face virtually unfettered police activity and intolerance by others; none has been elected President and only three to the Senate; and Congress has failed to pass legislation that would eliminate disparity in executions of African Americans for capital crimes. From this, she contends, the continuing violations doctrine applies because African Americans are still subjected to the badges and indicia of slavery.

IV

Cato argues that the action is justiciable because the Thirteenth Amendment created a national right for African Americans to be free of the badges and indicia of slavery, they continue to suffer from the lingering incidents of slavery, and there are theories of relief available under the FTCA for intentionally inflicted harm and violation of duty by the federal government. She first draws on the legislative history of the Thirteenth Amendment and the Civil Rights Act of 1866 to contend that the federal government had an obligation to end the vestiges of slavery, but has failed to keep the promise. As she puts it, "this action is the means to seek the remedy which has been prescribed by Congress and the Court and which is long overdue."

Then, in addition to disparities in employment, income, and education, Cato identifies two contemporary actions, or inactions, by Congress which she contends evince its failure to fulfill its duty under the Thirteenth Amendment: Congress's failure to pass the Racial Justice Act (introduced as HR 4017 in the House on March 11, 1994, to amend Title 28 of the United States Code to prevent racially discriminatory capital sentencing) and legislation introduced in the United States Senate that would repeal federal affirmative action programs (introduced February 22, 1995, as S. 497, called an "Act to End Unfair Preferential Treatment."

These theories afford no basis for curing the complaint, for two main reasons. First, Cato proceeds on a generalized, class-based grievance; she neither alleges, nor suggests that she might claim, any conduct on the part of any specific official or as a result of any specific program that has run afoul of a constitutional or statutory right and caused her a discrete injury. Without a concrete, personal injury that is not abstract and that is fairly traceable to the government conduct that she challenges as unconstitutional, Cato lacks standing. . . .

Neither does Cato have standing to litigate claims based on the stigmatizing injury to all African

Americans caused by racial discrimination. In any case, she does not trace the presence of discrimination and its harm to the United States rather than to other persons or institutions. Accordingly, Cato lacks standing to bring a suit setting forth the claims she suggests.

V

Cato submits that sovereign immunity does not bar her action because the United States can be sued directly under the Thirteenth Amendment, because it can be sued through its agents even where there is no express statutory provision, and because the United States waives its sovereign immunity whenever Congress has explicitly provided a private right of action in a statute or through legislative history.

Cato argues that the first clause of the Thirteenth Amendment ends slavery and its vestiges, while the second allows Congress to enact appropriate legislation to fulfill the obligation set out in the first. In her view, this gives rise to a right to sue the United States directly because otherwise, the Thirteenth Amendment's obligation is meaningless. . . . Cato argues that when an important constitutional right has been violated and there is no explicit Congressional declaration barring suit, an action for damages against the United States may lie. Finally, she infers in the adoption of the Thirteenth Amendment a promise by Congress to enforce these articles (which she claims that Congress has failed to fulfill), thereby waiving sovereign immunity. We cannot agree.

VI

. . . [Cato] seeks an acknowledgment of discrimination and an apology from the United States. For reasons we have already explained, however, Cato lacks standing to seek relief premised on the stigmatizing injury of discrimination in general. As the district court indicated, the legislature, rather than the judiciary, is the appropriate forum for this relief. Accordingly, her requests for non-monetary relief were properly dismissed.

VII

As the United States has not waived its sovereign immunity with respect to any of Cato's theories of relief that might fall within the Federal Tort Claims Act or any other source that we can identify, and

under well-established principles Cato lacks standing to pursue claims in court arising out of the government's failure to do right as she sees it, we conclude that the district court did not abuse its discretion in dismissing both complaints with prejudice. . . .

AFFIRMED.

Study Questions

1. Do the reasons leading us to believe that racial discrimination against Blacks and others is wrong and unconstitutional also apply in the case of the discrimination involved in affirmative action practices? Should the classifications utilized in such programs (being a Black, being a woman, etc.) be subjected to "strict scrutiny"? What would be the result?

2. Justice Powell, in his opinion in the *Bakke* case, seemed to think it makes a difference whether an applicant is turned down for medical or law school because of a quota system or because race is used as a factor in an admissions policy. Is this right? Why should that matter to someone like Bakke or Grutter who, after all, lose out either way and apparently as a consequence of their race?

3. Do you agree with the argument that the interest in obtaining a diverse student body cannot pass the test of "strict scrutiny"? Should such a purpose be subjected to that test?

4. The majority in *Grutter* argues that race-based classifications, when "necessary to further a compelling governmental interest," are permissible under the Constitution. Does the Court make a convincing case that the Michigan Law School has met this burden?

5. Imagine a law school with an entirely racially homogeneous student body (say, all White). Under the Court's rationale in *Grutter*, could such a school entirely ban all White applicants for a certain term of years in order to obtain the educational benefits of a diverse student body? If so, would you agree that this should be tolerated under the Equal Protection Clause?

6. The law school in *Grutter* argued, and the majority of the Court agreed, that the interest in exposing law school students to a "critical mass" of

diversity "requires more than a token number of minority students." Are these statements tantamount to fixing a quota? Is it just picking a minimum number of students for diversity purposes to which the Court majority objects? What is a "quota" in this context?

7. Why is Justice Thomas skeptical of the Michigan Law School's claim that racial diversity brings educational benefits to students at the school? Does Thomas think that the purported benefits are illusory? Or that they are an insufficiently compelling state interest in the face of an otherwise discriminatory practice?

8. Is Justice Thomas fair in characterizing the Law School's interest in this case as maintaining an "elite institution"? Why is elite stature, if that is what is at stake, not a "compelling" interest?

9. Thomas argues that university admissions policies giving weight to an applicant's race actually burden, rather than benefit, the minority students at whom they are aimed. Are you convinced by Thomas's arguments?

10. If Zack is correct and "race" does not signify a genuine, biological category, should all references to "race" in the law be jettisoned? What implications would such a purge have upon the law?

11. Zack maintains that, even though it is not a genuine biological feature of reality race nonetheless has performed a "pragmatic" role in our law and culture. Can you think of a pragmatic justification for retaining racial classifications that you would find convincing? What is it?

12. Supposing that racial groupings are arbitrary in the way Zack suggests, what result would this have for programs like the one at issue in *Grutter v. Bollinger* which seek "diversity" based upon race?

13. Many adoption agencies attempt to "match" prospective adoptive parents to their children on the basis of several factors, including religion, race, and ethnic background. Should use of such factors be viewed as racial discrimination? Why must a White child be raised "as White"? Why must a Black child be raised "as Black"? Is this what the matching system seeks to achieve? If desegregation of schools is thought to be justified in order to overcome the effects upon children of a "separate-but-equal" education, why shouldn't

families be "desegregated" through policies of transracial adoption? If the state may seek to block a White family from adopting a Black child, why then shouldn't the state be allowed to block a White person from marrying a Black? (See *Loving v. Virginia*, in the "Cases for Further Reflection" at the end of this chapter.)

14. James O'Connor worked for Consolidated Coin Caterers from 1978 until August 19, 1990 when he was fired at age 56. Believing that he had been fired because of his age, O'Connor filed a suit in federal court, alleging that Coin Caterers had violated the Age Discrimination in Employment Act (ADEA). The court dismissed his suit. The ADEA limits its protection to individuals forty years of age and older and this, the court reasoned, meant that, to prove discrimination, plaintiffs such as O'Connor must show that they were replaced by someone with comparable qualifications who was *under* forty years old. Because the person who replaced O'Connor was exactly forty, a *prima facie* case of discrimination could not be made. O'Connor appealed to the U.S. Supreme Court. In April 1996, the Court ruled in O'Connor's favor. According to Justice Scalia, writing for the majority, "the fact that one person in the protected class [40 or older] has lost out to another person in the protected class is . . . irrelevant, so long as he has lost out *because of his age*. . . . There can be no greater inference of *age* discrimination (as opposed to "40 or over" discrimination) when a 40-year-old is replaced by a 39-year-old than when a 56-year-old is replaced by a 40-year-old." Do you agree with Justice Scalia's argument? How much of a disparity in ages must be present before you would be persuaded that discrimination on the basis of age has occurred? Is ten years' difference sufficient? Five? Three? Suppose O'Connor had been thirty-five years old and that he was fired and replaced by someone who was twenty. Would this suggest age discrimination?

15. A Michigan police academy used physical performance tests on its male and female recruits. The tests were "gender-normed" to take into account physiological differences between men and women. Two male candidates at the academy were "washed out" because they failed the physical tests. They filed suit alleging that they were victims of gender discrimination since, although they failed the tests by *male* standards, they would

have qualified under the *female* standards. [*Alspaugh v. Michigan Law Enforcement Officers Training Council*, 246 Mich. App. 547 (2002).] Do you agree with the candidates? Why or why not?

16. What, for Nagel, distinguishes "weak" from "strong" affirmative action policies?

17. What three objections to strong affirmative action does Nagel consider?

18. Why does Nagel think that strong affirmative action is not justified in the case of women? Are you convinced?

19. What does Steele mean when he says of affirmative action programs that "the old sin is reaffirmed in a new guise"?

20. What does Steele think is wrong with the appeal to one's status as a victim of past injustice as a way of justifying preferential treatment?

21. Imagine that you are a congressional Representative and are asked to vote on the House Resolution to look into reparations for African Americans. Would you support the Resolution? Why or why not?

22. Why are reparations to descendents of slaves a "policy question" rather than a claim justiciable in court? Courts have, in the past, ordered various remedies for racial discrimination, including desegregation of schools and other public facilities, and busing of students. Why should these be within a court's jurisdiction but not reparations for the wrongs of slavery?

23. The plaintiffs in *Cato v. U.S.* sought to vindicate their view that the claims of African Americans for reparations are within the jurisdiction of the courts by pointing out that the courts have adjudicated disputes concerning Native American claims for many decades. Why does the court reject this argument?

24. Do you agree with the complaint in *Cato* that the government has failed to eliminate, under the Thirteenth Amendment to the Constitution, the "lingering incidents of slavery"? If the court were to agree with the plaintiffs, what remedy would be appropriate? How could a proper remedy be implemented? To whom, for instance, should the reparations sought be paid? To all African Americans? Only to those African Americans who can demonstrate that their ancestors lived in former slave states? Only to those whose relatives were actually slaves?

B. *Sexual Orientation, Gender, and Equality*

Equality and Same-Sex Marriage

In 1996, Congress passed and President Clinton signed into law the Defense of Marriage Act (DOMA). DOMA was only one among many similar initiatives sponsored in a number of state legislatures. The key section of DOMA forbade any federal recognition of same-sex marriages for matters such as income tax filing status and Social Security benefits. DOMA and its offspring were the result of mounting fears that some states might actually allow same-sex unions. The controversy was ignited first in Hawaii. There, several gay and lesbian couples sued that state, asserting that to prohibit them from entering into a state of marriage was a denial of equal protection of the laws, a guarantee made by the Hawaii Constitution, just as in the federal Constitution. A ban on same-sex marriages is discriminatory, the plaintiffs alleged, since it denies to them a range of benefits open to heterosexual couples and pertaining, *inter alia*, to taxes, inheritance, and health insurance. In its ruling, which begins the readings for this section, the state Supreme Court agreed in principle with the plaintiffs. Sex is a "suspect classification" under the law, the Court argued, and thus any law banning same-sex unions must be narrowly tailored to satisfy a compelling state interest. The case was remanded, or sent back, to lower courts to determine if such a compelling interest really could be demonstrated. The voters of Hawaii intervened, however, and passed an amendment to the state Constitution which reserved marriage to opposite-sex couples. While other states, such as Massachusetts, Indiana, and New Jersey, continued to debate the legality of same-sex marriage, the Hawaii Supreme Court then ruled that the status of same-sex marriage had been settled by the passage of the amendment prohibiting them.

Is telling a gay or lesbian couple that they may not marry an act of discrimination? Law professor Cass Sunstein believes it is. Sunstein's analysis of *Loving v. Virginia* (included in the "Cases For Further Reflection" at the conclusion of this chapter) sets the stage for his argument. *Loving* involved a Virginia law banning interracial marriage. In response to the complaint that such a ban amounted to racial discrimination, the state reasoned that neither Blacks nor Whites were victims of discrimination, since members of both races were equally disabled from marrying members of the other. This argument was rejected on the grounds that anti-miscegenation laws were an attempt to keep the races separate, thus perpetuating the underlying system of racial inequality between Blacks and Whites. Sunstein argues that same-sex marriages are forbidden in a parallel way: prohibitions on them are designed to further the illicit purpose of suppressing sexual autonomy and supporting a system of gender-caste which discriminates against same-sex relations. Just as interracial unions were once condemned as "unnatural," same-sex relations are viewed as unsettling a "natural" separation of sexual beings into "active" (or male) and "passive" (or female) roles.

Gender and Equality

What does it mean to treat men and women "equally"? Consider the following cases. In 1993 The Citadel, South Carolina's formerly all-male military academy, accepted—and then tried to reject—Shannon Faulkner, a female high school student. (The school apparently mistook Faulkner's name for that of a male.) Faulkner filed suit, alleging that The Citadel's policy of excluding women was an equal-protection

violation. Faulkner won the suit but left The Citadel only two days after the beginning of the school year, alleging that she was the victim of brutal hazing and sexual harassment. Faulkner's story paralleled that of several women who sought admission to Virginia Military Institute (VMI), another state-supported, single-sex academy. In that case, the federal government filed suit against VMI. After a lower court had ruled in the school's favor, a federal appellate court reversed. It found that VMI had a unique program that would be significantly affected by coeducation. It ruled, however, that Virginia had failed convincingly to justify having such a unique military academy for men only. The appellate court ordered that plans be drawn either to admit women to VMI or to establish a separate but equal academy for women. In response to the ruling, Virginia created Virginia Women's Institute for Leadership (VWIL), intended to be an all-female version of VMI. Alleging that VWIL was not an equal facility, the government again brought a challenge, which made its way to the Supreme Court. The opinion by Justice Ruth Ginsburg (in the "Cases For Further Reflection" at the end of the chapter) ruled that VMI had no justification for refusing to admit women and that creating VWIL did not substitute for admitting women to VMI.

In 1978 a jury in Sonoma County, California, convicted a young man named Michael M. (his last name being withheld to shield his identity) for violating the section of the California Penal Code then defining statutory rape: unlawful sexual intercourse "accomplished with a female not the wife of the perpetrator, where the female is under the age of eighteen years." California, like most states, criminalizes "statutory rape," so called because the act is unlawful even if both parties consent to it. Appealing to reverse his conviction, Michael M. made an unusual and intriguing argument: The California law is unconstitutional and violates the guarantee of equal protection since only men can be held criminally liable for its violation. California's statutory rape law is an example of sex discrimination. Although California has since changed its law on statutory rape to incorporate a gender-neutral definition of the crime, the issues posed by *Michael M.* are, as we shall see, still very much a part of the law.

In his opinion for the United States Supreme Court (included in "Cases For Further Reflection"), Chief Justice Rehnquist began by stating what the Court (and California) took to be the purpose of the statute: to prevent illegitimate teenage pregnancy. The Court found that this is an important objective (citing statistics regarding teenage pregnancy and its attendant social effects). Can the state seek to meet this objective by punishing only the male? The court answered yes, since most of the burden of the pregnancy falls on the female. A gender-neutral statute, permitting the punishment of the female as well as the male, would frustrate the law's enforcement since the female is unlikely to notify the authorities if she, too, faces a penalty. The statute therefore does not violate the equal protection guarantee. Males and females are not similarly situated with respect to the risks of sex and pregnancy, and therefore it is not a violation of equal protection to treat them differently.

Justice Brennan, in a dissenting opinion, countered that even if the goal here is an important one, the statute is not "substantially related"—does not come close enough—to the achievement of that goal. Other states have switched to gender-neutral statutes without much difficulty, and a gender-neutral law might well have a greater deterrent effect, because both participants would be liable. It is irrational, the dissenters seem to believe, to take illicit sexual activity so seriously and yet exempt from punishment 50 percent of the violators.

Critics of the Court's decision in *Michael M.* are suspicious of the declared purpose in retaining the statutory rape law. Is it to prevent teenage pregnancy? If so, why not punish both people involved? They suggest a more sinister purpose. On a deeper level, they claim, the statute reinforces a range of damaging and morally unacceptable sexual stereotypes: that men are always the aggressors in sexual encounters, that women are submissive and naive, that women need to have their chastity protected. In short, the Court assumes that the problem of teenage pregnancy is important and thereby acquiesces in a sexist law. The Court invokes the physiological difference of pregnancy, together with socially imposed sex-role expectations, with the consequence that deeper and potentially more damaging prejudices against women are retained.

Sexism in the Law

The *Michael M.* and *VMI* cases serve as useful points of departure for an exploration of the whole question of "equality between the sexes" and what that means (or should mean) under our Constitution and laws. Any discussion of sexual equality must begin, however, with the history of legalized sexual discrimination,

justified by what were thought to be "legitimate" or "real" differences between the sexes. Throughout the nineteenth century and the early part of this century, the law treated women as separate and distinct from men. Women were thought to possess a separate, distinct, and immutable "nature" that made them unfit for many of the positions and occupations traditionally held by men; women properly belonged to a separate social and legal sphere, consisting primarily if not exclusively of domestic life and child rearing. The law excluded women from many aspects of public life and left them unprotected within the private, domestic world. This ideology was succinctly expressed by the Supreme Court in 1873 when it ruled that Myra Bradwell could not be admitted to the practice of law in Illinois. Concurring in the Court's decision, Justice Bradley wrote:

> [T]he civil law as well as nature itself, has always recognized a wide difference in the respective spheres and destinies of man and woman. Man is, or should be woman's protector and defender. The natural and proper timidity and delicacy which belongs to the female sex evidently unfits it for many of the occupations of civil life. . . . The paramount destiny and mission of woman are to fulfill the noble and benign offices of wife and mother. This is the law of the Creator.[1]

With increasing industrialization, many states passed legislation regulating a variety of working conditions for women. Typical was a law challenged in *Muller v. Oregon*,[2] which upheld restrictions on the number of hours women could work.

> [T]hat woman's physical structure and the performance of maternal functions place her at a disadvantage in the struggle for subsistence is obvious. . . . Differentiated by these matters from the other sex, she is properly placed in a class by herself, and legislation designed for her protection may be sustained, even when the legislation is not necessary for men.[3]

As late as 1948, the Supreme Court upheld a Michigan law forbidding a woman to work as a bartender unless she was the "wife or daughter of the

---

[1] *Bradwell v. Illinois*, 83 U.S. 130 (1873).
[2] 208 U.S. 412 (1908).
[3] 208 U.S. 412 (1908) at 421–22.

male owner."[4] The blatant stereotyping of and discrimination against women exemplified by the foregoing cases is now no longer legal. However, despite legal protections and gains in such areas as employment, many women still encounter barriers reflecting sexist assumptions and prejudices. For example, some women perceive that their work is still undervalued relative to that of men. Traditional women's professions, such as nursing, teaching, and social work, have become targets of recent efforts to cut budgets and trim spending; and more women than men are relegated to part-time work with little job security and few benefits. Stereotyped views about women also still prevail. In the late 1980s, for example, a group of female workers at Johnson Controls, a Milwaukee-based manufacturer of automotive batteries, accused the company of sex discrimination.[5] Car batteries are made with lead, and studies had shown that exposure to certain levels of lead can seriously impair female reproductive abilities and injure developing fetuses. Johnson Controls, along with many other large manufacturing corporations, instituted a fetal protection policy. Under the policy, all female employees, unless they provided proof of sterility, were barred from any job with a level of lead exposure alleged to pose reproductive hazards; no such restrictions were placed on male employees, regardless of their fertility and level of lead exposure. The policy had the effect of excluding women workers from virtually all of the typically higher-paying assembly-line positions in the company. The women who challenged the company in court claimed that the policy reflected some of the same paternalistic and condescending attitudes toward women prevalent a century ago, evident, for example, in the assumption that women, unlike men, are incapable of deciding for themselves whether to accept a job that poses certain risks.

Only recently have the courts begun consistently to strike down gender-based classifications as violative of women's equal-protection rights. Even here, however, the courts have generally refused to require that laws that distinguish between people on the basis of their sex must be "strictly scrutinized." Instead, they have settled on a weaker, intermediate standard of review: It is enough if such laws are "substantially related to an important governmental objective."

To many, these rulings are morally indefensible; nonetheless, they do raise important questions: Does rejecting these rulings mean that *any* laws that differentiate between the sexes are impermissible? Is it a violation of equal protection to prohibit women from serving as guards at male, maximum-security prisons?[6] To ban women from military combat? To refuse to admit women to all-male military academies or the Boy Scouts? These questions are explored in this section.

Difference and Sameness

In what ways are men and women the same? What are the "real" differences between men and women? Given that judgments about the relevance of differences can vary, how are so-called "real" differences to be distinguished from the effects of stereotypes and sexist assumptions that have been or should be rejected? Recent literature on this topic, much of it by feminist legal scholars, struggles with two contrasting views of "sameness" and "difference." The "equal treatment" view reasons that treating men and women equally means treating them the same. There are no "real" differences between the sexes that matter, only ways in which society and culture have made differences matter when they shouldn't. Legal equality, therefore, means behaving the same toward each sex. The contrasting view says that ensuring true sexual and gender equality requires giving women (and conceivably men as well) "special treatment." The law should recognize and accommodate the real, biological differences between men and women so that women are not disadvantaged relative to men with regard to employment and education. The distinction between these two views can best be seen through an illustrative case.

Company C offers all employees, regardless of sex, a benefits package that includes insurance benefits covering a variety of disabilities. Mr. M. is an employee who requires prostate surgery and will be off work for ten weeks. Another employee, Ms. W., is pregnant; with delivery and postnatal care she will also be out for ten weeks. The company's disability insurance package covers prostate surgery but excludes disabilities incident to normal pregnancy. Has the company treated Ms. W. and Mr. M. equally? The company can argue that it has given equal treatment here because it offers the same benefits package to all employees—women

---

[4] See *Goesaert v. Cleary*, 335 U.S. 464 (1948).

[5] *International Union, UAW v. Johnson Controls*, 111 S. Ct. 1196 (1991).

[6] See *Dothard v. Rawlinson*, 433 U.S. 321 (1977).

are not discriminated against in terms of being covered as much by the policy as are men. This argument by the company was supported by the Supreme Court in *Geduldig v. Aiello*,[7] in which the Court upheld the exclusion of pregnancy from a disability insurance scheme. "There is no risk from which men are protected and women are not," the Court wrote, and "there is no risk from which women are protected and men are not." The Court's reasoning in this case followed the "equal treatment" model, arguing that "equality" just means giving the same benefits to men and women. Ms. W., on the other hand, can argue that Company C is in reality imposing a double standard: it limits the disabilities for which women employees may receive coverage, and from which they alone suffer, while extending full coverage to male employees, even for specifically male conditions, such as prostate surgery. This has happened, Ms. W. can claim, because the entire benefits package was arrived at in a gender-biased manner in that it was created with men in mind, with the model of the male employee as its standard or norm. Women were then covered to the degree that they conformed to or were "like" men. But women are not the same as men; women have special capacities and burdens, and "equal protection" means adjusting for these through law. Ms. W. thus relies on the "special treatment" model.

The argument between Company C and Ms. W. can be examined on another level. Suppose the state forbids employers to refuse granting pregnancy leaves of up to four months (as some states now do). Company C does refuse to grant Ms. W. a pregnancy leave, relying on the principle that "equal protection" means that all forms of workplace discrimination based on pregnancy are impermissible. In court, Company C argues that its decision is even-handed and deals with all workers equally—it doesn't give men any comparable extended disability leave either. All it has to do, says the company, is give leaves to everyone or no one. But, responds Ms. W., the company's choice is not equitable, for it is still assuming that where women really do have different needs from men, those differences don't count, and this is a form of bias against women.

Underlying both of these theories of difference and sameness is the problem of fixing the standard or norm used to determine in what ways men and women are similar or different. Suppose the military requires that all fighter pilots be at least 5′ 11″ in

height, arguing that fighter-plane cockpits necessitate that the pilot be this tall to reach and work the controls for the aircraft properly. If the military permits both men and women to apply for fighter-pilot positions, has it treated them equally even if the height requirement disqualifies many more women than men? The military can insist that it denies no one a spot as a pilot merely on the grounds of sex. But suppose it can be shown that the height requirement is not just "the way things are," but that the cockpit requires a pilot at least 5′ 11″ in height because for years cockpit dimensions have been normed after men, most of whom average 5′ 11″? A solution here would be to use *androgynous* norms as the appropriate standards against which to judge men and women, that is, norms not arrived at by reference to traits specific to either gender. This might be accomplished in the jet-fighter case by reconfiguring cockpits around a height dimension close to average for men *and* women. Knowing how to identify the appropriate androgynous standard, however, might not be as apparent in other cases.

The Dilemma of Difference

In her selection included here, legal scholar Martha Minow explains and illustrates what she considers the central problem in the legal and conceptual understanding of equality—what she terms the "dilemma of difference." The dilemma arises because both recognizing and failing to recognize a way in which people are different can perpetuate prejudice and stigma attached to that difference, thus frustrating the goal of achieving equality. As we have already seen, some contend that the *Michael M.* case exemplifies this difficulty: California's statutory rape law, in recognizing the difference of pregnancy and seeking to deal with both sexes fairly by treating women and men dissimilarly with regard to the risk of pregnancy, may at the same time serve to reinforce stereotypes that undercut the very fairness and equality at which the law aims in the first place. Minow thinks dilemmas of difference occur throughout the law as a result of hidden or unconscious assumptions about the nature and significance of difference that have worked their way into the fabric of the law. Minow carefully explains and illustrates each of these assumptions with the aim of clarifying the challenges confronting the law's effort to ensure equality, especially equality between the sexes.

---

[7] 417 U.S. 484 (1974).

The Assimilationist Ideal

Philosopher and lawyer Richard Wasserstrom explores a broader question: In what way would differences in race and sex be viewed in an "ideal" society? Wasserstrom investigates and compares three possibilities.

The first, or "assimilationist," ideal seeks a society in which differences among the races or between the sexes are treated the same as differences in eye color. Because no one thinks that eye color should be relevant in any way to the distribution of social benefits or burdens, the assimilationist society would be one in which nothing turns on one's race or sex. The second ideal, that of "diversity," analogizes sex and race to the current legal status of religion. One's religious identity, we believe, should make no difference to political rights and benefits; yet we still permit (and encourage) people to recognize and celebrate their differing religious identities. Similarly, in this view people could still define themselves in terms of gender differences, although no political or social stigma would be attached to doing so. The last of the three ideals would take sexual equality much as we have it now, with considerable sex-role differentiation.

Which ideal is the most attractive? Would assimilationism be too radical a break with our current set of beliefs and traditions? These questions cannot be answered, Wasserstrom thinks, without facing the further question of whether the "differences" between the sexes are "natural" or "social." Wasserstrom argues that they are largely, if not entirely, social in origin because almost none of the obvious physical differences between men and women really make a difference in our technologically advanced society. He then constructs a positive case for the assimilationist ideal: The assimilationist society allows all of its members a degree of individual autonomy that cannot be present in a society that, like ours, defines people's prospects and limits their possibilities ahead of time, simply by confining them to "preprogrammed" sex roles.

Intersectionality and the Experience of Black Women

In the final reading for this section, Kimberle Crenshaw examines the issues of gender equality and discrimination from the standpoint of Critical Race Theory (CRT) (see Chapter 1 for background on CRT). Crenshaw argues that the dominant perspective of the law of equal protection toward gender issues systematically excludes the situation of those who are both black and female. The dominant framework must be modified, Crenshaw maintains, to ensure genuinely equal protection to people at the "intersection" of two dimensions of discrimination: racial and sexual.

Baehr v. Lewin

LEVINSON, J. [announcing the judgment of the Court]:

[In 1991, three plaintiff couples, Ninia Baehr and Genora Dancel, Tammy Rodrigues and Antoinette Pregil, and Pat Lagon and Joseph Melilio, filed a lawsuit for a declaratory judgment that Hawaii's Marriage Law, Hawaii Revised Statutes §572-1, unconstitutionally denied same-sex couples the same marriage rights as different-sex couples. The plaintiffs challenged the statute under Hawaii's equal protection and privacy guarantees: Article I, section 5 of the Hawaii Constitution provides: "No person shall be deprived of life, liberty or property without due process of law, nor be denied the equal protection of the laws, nor be denied the enjoyment of the person's civil rights or be discriminated against in the exercise thereof because of race, religion, sex or ancestry." Article I, section 6 provides: "The right of the people to privacy is recognized and shall not be infringed without the showing of a compelling state interest. The legislature shall take affirmative steps to implement this right."]

[T]here is no doubt that, at a minimum, article I, section 6 of the Hawaii Constitution encompasses all of the fundamental rights expressly recognized as being subsumed within the privacy protections of the United States Constitution. . . . The issue in the present case is,

---

852 P.2d 44 (1993), Supreme Court of Hawaii.

therefore, whether the "right to marry" protected by article I, section 6 of the Hawaii Constitution extends to same-sex couples. . . . The United States Supreme Court has set forth its most detailed discussion of the fundamental right to marry in [prior rulings]:

> It is not surprising that the decision to marry has been placed on the same level of importance as decisions relating to procreation, childbirth, child rearing, and family relationships. . . . [I]t would make little sense to recognize a right of privacy with respect to other matters of family life and not with respect to the decision to enter the relationship that is the foundation of the family in our society. The woman whom appellee desired to marry had a fundamental right to seek an abortion of their expected child, see *Roe v. Wade*, or to bring the child into life to suffer the myriad social, if not economic, disabilities that the status of illegitimacy brings. . . . Surely, a decision to marry and raise the child in a traditional family setting must receive equivalent protection. And, if appellee's right to procreate means anything at all, it must imply some right to enter the only relationship in which the State of Wisconsin allows sexual relations legally to take place.

Implicit in [these prior rulings is the] court's link between the right to marry, on the one hand, and the fundamental rights of procreation, childbirth, abortion, and child rearing, on the other, is the assumption that the one is simply the logical predicate of the others. [T]he federal construct of the fundamental right to marry . . . presently contemplates unions between men and women. . . . In effect, as the applicant couples frankly admit, we are being asked to recognize a new fundamental right.

[W]e do not believe that a right to same-sex marriage is so rooted in the traditions and collective conscience of our people that failure to recognize it would violate the fundamental principles of liberty and justice that lie at the base of all our civil and political institutions. Neither do we believe that a right to same-sex marriage is implicit in the concept of ordered liberty, such that neither liberty nor justice would exist if it were sacrificed. Accordingly, we hold that the applicant couples do not have a fundamental constitutional right to same-sex marriage arising out of the right to privacy or otherwise.

[T]he applicant couples contend that they have been denied the equal protection of the laws as guaranteed by article I, section 5 of the Hawaii Constitution. [T]he circuit court erred when it concluded, as a matter of law, that: (1) homosexuals do not constitute a "suspect class" for purposes of equal protection analysis [so that] (2) the classification created by HRS §572-1 is not subject to "strict scrutiny," but must satisfy only the "rational relationship" test; and [that] (3) HRS §572-1 satisfies the rational relationship test because the legislature "obviously designed [it] to promote the general welfare interests of the community by sanctioning traditional man-woman family units and procreation."

[M]arriage is a state-conferred legal status, the existence of which gives rise to rights and benefits reserved exclusively to that particular relationship. . . . So zealously has this court guarded the state's role as the exclusive progenitor of the marital partnership that it declared, over seventy years ago, that "common law" marriages—i.e., "marital" unions existing in the absence of a state-issued license and not performed by a person or society possessing governmental authority to solemnize marriages—would no longer be recognized in the Territory of Hawaii. . . .

The applicant couples correctly contend that . . . refusal to allow them to marry on the basis that they are members of the same sex deprives them of access to a multiplicity of rights and benefits that are contingent upon that status [, including] (1) a variety of state income tax advantages, including deductions, credits, rates, exemptions, and estimates; (2) public assistance from and exemptions relating to the Department of Human Services; (3) control, division, acquisition, and disposition of community property; (4) rights relating to dower, curtesy, and inheritance; (5) rights to notice, protection, benefits, and inheritance under the Uniform Probate Code; (6) award of child custody and support payments in divorce proceedings; (7) the right to spousal support; (8) the right to enter into premarital agreements; (9) the right to change of name; (10) the right to file a nonsupport action; (11) post-divorce rights relating to support and property division; (12) the benefit of the spousal privilege and confidential marital communications; (13) the benefit of the exemption of real property from attachment or execution; and (14) the right to bring a wrongful death action. For present purposes, it is not disputed that the applicant couples would be entitled to all of these marital rights and benefits, but for the fact that they are denied access to the state-conferred legal status of marriage.

HRS §572-1, on its face, discriminates based on sex against the applicant couples in the exercise of the civil right of marriage. . . . Article I, section 5 of the

Hawaii Constitution provides in relevant part that "[n]o person shall . . . be denied the equal protection of the laws, *nor be denied the enjoyment of the person's civil rights or be discriminated against in the exercise thereof* because of race, religion, sex, or ancestry." (Emphasis added). Thus, by its plain language, the Hawaii Constitution prohibits state-sanctioned discrimination against any person in the exercise of his or her civil rights on the basis of sex.

. . .

. . . Lewin contends that "the fact that homosexual partners cannot form a state-licensed marriage is not the product of impermissible discrimination" implicating equal protection considerations, but rather "a function of their biologic inability as a couple to satisfy the definition of the status to which they aspire." . . . Lewin proposes that "the right of persons of the same sex to marry one another does not exist because marriage, by definition and usage, means a special relationship between a man and a woman." We believe Lewin's argument to be circular and unpersuasive. . . .

[In *Loving v. Virginia*] the Virginia courts declared that interracial marriage simply could not exist because the Deity had deemed such a union intrinsically unnatural, and, in effect, because it had theretofore never been the "custom" of the state to recognize mixed marriages, marriage "always" having been construed to presuppose a different configuration. With all due respect to the Virginia courts of a bygone era, we do not believe that trial judges are the ultimate authorities on the subject of Divine Will, and, as *Loving* amply demonstrates, constitutional law may mandate, like it or not, that customs change with an evolving social order. . . .

[W]e hold that sex is a "suspect category" for purposes of equal protection analysis under article I, section 5 of the Hawaii Constitution and that HRS §572-1 is subject to the "strict scrutiny" test. It therefore, follows, and we so hold, that (1) HRS §572-1 is presumed to be unconstitutional (2) unless Lewin, as an agent of the State of Hawaii, can show that (a) the statute's sex-based classification is justified by compelling state interests and (b) the statute is narrowly drawn to avoid unnecessary abridgments of the applicant couples' constitutional rights.

Judge Heen [dissents] based on his belief that "HRS §572-1 treats everyone alike and applies equally to both sexes[,]" with the result that "[n]either sex is being granted a right or benefit the other does not have, and neither sex is being denied a right or benefit that the other has." The rationale underlying Judge

Heen's belief, however, was expressly considered and rejected in *Loving v. Virginia*:

> Thus, the State contends that, because its miscegenation statutes punish equally both the white and the Negro participants in an interracial marriage, these statutes, despite their reliance on racial classifications do not constitute an invidious discrimination based upon race. . . . [W]e reject the notion that the mere "equal application" of a statute containing racial classifications is enough to remove the classifications from the Fourteenth Amendment's proscriptions of all invidious discriminations. . . . In the case at bar, . . . we deal with statutes containing racial classifications, and the fact of equal application does not immunize the statute from the very heavy burden of justification which the Fourteenth Amendment has traditionally required of state statutes drawn according to race.

Substitution of "sex" for "race" and article I, section 5 for the fourteenth amendment yields the precise case before us together with the conclusion that we have reached. . . .

[W]e vacate the circuit court's order and judgment and remand this matter for further proceedings consistent with this opinion. On remand, in accordance with the "strict scrutiny" standard, the burden will rest on Lewin to overcome the presumption that HRS §572-1 is unconstitutional by demonstrating that it furthers compelling state interests and is narrowly drawn to avoid unnecessary abridgments of constitutional rights.

Vacated and remanded.

HEEN, J., dissenting:

[T]he plaintiff in *Loving* was not claiming a right to a same sex marriage. Loving involved a marriage between a white male and a black female whose marriage, which took place in Washington, D.C., was refused recognition in Virginia under that state's miscegenation laws. . . . In *Zablocki* an application for a marriage license by a male and a female was denied because the male was not able to show, pursuant to a Wisconsin statute's requirement, that he was in compliance with all existing obligations for child support.

Although appellants suggest an analogy between the racial classification involved in *Loving* . . . the alleged sexual classification involved in the case at bar, we do not find such an analogy. The operative distinction lies in the relationship which is described by the term "marriage" itself, and that relationship is the legal union of one man and one woman. [As one Washington decision put it,] "[A]ppellants are not being denied entry into the marriage relationship because of their sex; rather, they are being denied entry into the marriage relationship because of the recognized definition of that relationship as one which may be entered into only by two persons who are members of the opposite sex." . . .

HRS §572-1 treats everyone alike and applies equally to both sexes. The effect of the statute is to prohibit same sex marriages on the part of professed or non-professed heterosexuals, homosexuals, bisexuals, or asexuals, and does not effect an invidious discrimination.[1] . . .

HRS §572-1 does not establish a "suspect" classification based on gender because all males and females are treated alike. A male cannot obtain a license to marry another male, and a female cannot obtain a license to marry another female. Neither sex is being *granted* a right or benefit the other does not have, and neither sex is being *denied* a right or benefit that the other has.

My thesis is well illustrated by the case of *Phillips v. Wisconsin Personnel Comm'n*, 482 N.W.2d 121 (Ct. App. 1992). In that case, the plaintiff, an unmarried female, was denied medical benefits for her unmarried female "dependent" lesbian companion because Phillips' state health plan defined "dependent" as spouse or children. Phillips appealed the commission's dismissal of her

gender discrimination complaint and the Wisconsin Court of Appeals, in striking down her claim, stated that dependent insurance coverage is unavailable to unmarried companions of both male and female employees. A statute is only subject to a challenge for gender discrimination under the equal protection clause when it discriminates on its face, or in effect, between males and females.

Similarly, HRS §572-1 does not discriminate on the basis of gender. The statute applies equally to all unmarried persons, both male and female, who desire to enter into a legally recognized marriage . . . .

In my view, the statute's classification is clearly designed to promote the legislative purpose of fostering and protecting the propagation of the human race through heterosexual marriages and bears a reasonable relationship to that purpose. I find nothing unconstitutional in that.

Endnote

[1] Appellants' sexual preferences or lifestyles are completely irrelevant. Although the plurality appears to recognize the irrelevance, the real thrust of the plurality opinion disregards the true import of the statute. The statute treats everyone alike and applies equally to both sexes.

Homosexuality and the Constitution

CASS R. SUNSTEIN

A *True Story*

In 1958, Richard Loving, a white man, and Mildred Jeter, a black woman, were married in the District of Columbia. Soon thereafter they returned to their home

From Cass R. Sunstein, "Homosexuality and the Constitution," in David M. Estlund and Martha C. Nussbaum (eds.), *Sex, Preference, and Family,* copyright 1997 by Oxford University Press, Inc. Used by permission of Oxford University Press, Inc.

in Virginia. They were promptly indicted. Their crime was to have married in violation of Virginia's prohibition on interracial marriage. They pleaded guilty to the charge and were sentenced to a year in jail. The trial judge suspended the sentence on condition that the Lovings leave Virginia and not return for twenty-five years. The judge said: "Almighty God creates the races white, black, yellow, malay and red, and he placed them on separate continents. And but for the interference with his arrangement there would be no cause for such marriages. The fact that he separated the races shows that he did not intend for the races to mix."

The Lovings challenged the miscegenation law on constitutional grounds. They claimed that the law deprived them of the "equal protection of the laws." Thus was born the most aptly titled case in the entire history of American law, *Loving v. Virginia.*[1]

In the United States Supreme Court, the legal issues were relatively straightforward. In 1954, the Court had decided *Brown v. Board of Education.*[2] There the Court had made clear that racial discrimination is constitutionally unacceptable and that "separate but equal" is not equal. The Brown Court held that under the Constitution, the government could not discriminate against blacks. This was the issue in *Loving:* Was the ban on racial intermarriage a form of discrimination in the relevant sense?

On this question, there was sharp dispute. Virginia thought that the answer was, "Clearly not." Virginia's lawyers argued that miscegenation laws punished whites and blacks equally. They claimed that there was no discrimination against blacks. The only relevant discrimination was against people who sought to participate in mixed marriages, and such people were racially diverse, including members of all races. Unlike in *Brown,* where racial separation marked racial inequality, here separation was truly equal. Discrimination against people who seek to participate in mixed marriages is not "racial discrimination" at all. It does not draw a line between blacks and whites. It is a form of discrimination, to be sure—but not at all of the form that justifies special judicial skepticism under the Constitution. Because blacks and whites were treated exactly alike, that kind of skepticism was unwarranted.

From the standpoint of the 1990s, the argument may seem odd, even otherworldly. But if we linger over it, we will see that its logic is straightforward and even plausible. How did the Supreme Court respond? The key sentence in *Loving v. Virginia* says that "the racial classifications [at issue] must stand on their own justification, as measures designed to maintain White Supremacy." This striking reference to White Supremacy—by a unanimous Court, capitalizing both words and speaking in these terms for the only time in the nation's history was designed to get at the core of Virginia's argument that discrimination on the basis of participation in mixed marriages was not discrimination on the basis of race.

The Court appeared to be making the following argument. Even though the ban on racial marriage treats blacks and whites alike—even though there is formal equality—the ban is transparently an effort to keep the races separate and, by so doing, to maintain the form and the conception of racial difference that are indispensable to white supremacy. Viewed in its context—in light of its actual motivations and its actual effects—the ban was thus part of a system of racial caste. Virginia really objected to racial intermixing because it would confound racial boundaries, thus defeating what the district judge saw as "natural" differences produced by God's plan.

In a world with miscegenation, natural differences between blacks and whites would become unintelligible; the very word "miscegenation" would lose its meaning. Indeed, in a world with racial mixing, it would be unclear who was really black and who was really white. The categories themselves would be unsettled—revealed to be a matter of convention rather than nature. In such a world, white supremacy could not maintain itself. And because this was the assumption behind Virginia's law, the law stood revealed as an unacceptable violation of the equal protection principle.

A Hypothetical Story

Now let us imagine a hypothetical case. Two women seek to marry. They are prevented from doing so by a law forbidding same-sex marriage. They argue first that the relevant law violates the right to be free from sex discrimination. This seems to be a good strategic choice on their part. It is of course well-established that laws discriminating on the basis of sex will be subject to careful judicial scrutiny, and will generally be invalidated. By contrast, it also seems clear that laws discriminating on the basis of sexual orientation will be subject to deferential judicial scrutiny, and will generally be validated. Our hypothetical couple would therefore do very well to argue that they are subject to discrimination on the basis of sex, not sexual orientation. They might try to establish this argument by saying what seems clearly true, that if one of them were a man, there would be no barrier to the marriage. The law therefore seems to contain explicit discrimination on the basis of sex. It treats one person differently from another simply because of gender. It is therefore a form of sex discrimination.

This argument appears straightforward; but under current constitutional law, the argument gets nowhere. The prohibition on same-sex marriage, it is said, discriminates on the basis of sexual orientation rather than on the basis of sex. There is no sex discrimination, because women and men are treated exactly the same. If a man wants to marry a man, he is barred; a woman seeking to marry a woman is barred in precisely the same way. For this reason, women and men are not treated differently. From this we see that the complaint in our hypothetical case is "really" about discrimination on the basis of sexual orientation, not at all about discrimination on the basis of sex. Since discrimination on the basis of sexual orientation is subject to highly deferential "rational basis" review, under which almost all statutes are upheld, the barrier to same-sex marriages and relations is constitutionally acceptable.

. . .

It will readily appear that this is the same answer offered by the state of Virginia in the *Loving* case. To the extent that *Loving v. Virginia* is now believed inapposite, it is for the following reason. We can now see that a law forbidding racial intermarriage is an effort to promote white supremacy. The separation of the races, especially in matters of sexuality and marriage, was part and parcel of the subordination of blacks to whites. That separation was part of the creation of a fixed category of racial differences. No one really denies this. It seems clear that if racial mixing were common, no one would know who is black and white, indeed the categories would lose much of their meaning. (It even seems reasonably clear that issues of sex discrimination are at work in this context, since the availability of black women to white men was common, and since the miscegenation laws seem especially inspired by the effort to prevent black men from having relations with white women.) The effort to promote "white purity" was conspicuously intended to prevent the various results that would come about from racial mixing. The Supreme Court's reference to "White Supremacy" was thus both necessary and sufficient to defeat Virginia's argument. It was readily shown that the miscegenation laws were connected to that constitutionally unacceptable social institution.

At least for participants in the current legal system, it is much harder to say this for same-sex relations. Exactly how is the prohibition on same-sex marriage an effort to promote male supremacy? How can the one have anything to do with the other? We can see that racial intermarriage was objectionable because of its effects on the racial difference, deemed natural and desirable, but thought (by the 1960s) to have social consequences only because of social institutions productive of something like a caste system based on race. Surely, it might be suggested, the question of same-sex relations raises no analogous issues.

I believe that it is puzzlement about such matters that accounts for the failure to see that *Loving v. Virginia* is a relevant or even decisive precedent for the view that the prohibition on same-sex relations is impermissible sex discrimination. In the end, however, I think that *Loving v. Virginia* is in fact a decisive precedent. Very briefly: A ban on racial intermarriage is part of an effort to insist that with respect to race there are just "two kinds." The separation of humanity into two rigidly defined kinds, white and black, is part of what white supremacy means. Even though some people have darker skin color than others, and even though genes do diverge, this separation is in important respects a social artifact.

To say that there are just "two kinds" of people, black and white, is hardly a simple report on the facts; the division of the world into two kinds is emphatically social. Whatever we may say about genes and colors, that particular division is the construction of a distinctive social state of affairs. It is tempting to think that the same cannot be said for the separation of humanity into two kinds, women and men. Perhaps that separation is genuinely ordained by nature; perhaps it is not a social artifact at all, or at least not at all in the same way. Who would deny that the distinction between men and women is fundamental in this sense?

But perhaps this argument goes by too quickly. It is indeed true that some people are black and others are white; this is no less true, or less "factual," than the division of humanity into men and women. The question is what society does with these facts. I believe that the prohibition on same-sex marriages, as part of the social and legal insistence on "two kinds," is as deeply connected with male supremacy as the prohibition on racial intermarriage is connected with white supremacy. Same-sex marriages are banned because of what they do to—because of how they unsettle—gender categories.

This is not merely a philosophical or sociological observation; it is highly relevant to the legal argument. It suggests that, like the ban on racial intermarriage, the ban on same-sex marriages is doomed by a constitutionally illegitimate purpose. The ban has everything to do with constitutionally unacceptable stereotypes about the appropriate role of men and women.

Moreover, the ban has constitutionally unacceptable effects. It is part of a system of sex-role stereotyping that is damaging for men and women, heterosexual and homosexual alike, though in quite different ways. Indeed, one of the most interesting issues has to do with the distinctive ways in which the ban differentially harms heterosexual men, gay men, heterosexual women, and lesbians.

On Sex Difference and Sexual Orientation

. . . [T]he ban on same-sex marriages is not now thought to raise a problem of sex inequality under the American Constitution. But might the legal ban (and the social taboo) not be a product of a desire to maintain a system of gender hierarchy, a system that same-sex marriages tend to undermine by complicating traditional and still-influential ideas about "natural difference" between men and women? Here is my thesis: In terms of their purposes and effects, bans on same-sex marriage have very much the same connection to gender caste as bans on racial intermarriage have to racial caste. I am speaking here of the real-world motivations for these bans, and I am assuming, as does current law, that impermissible motivations are fatal to legislation. The claim from neutrality is implausible in this context for exactly the same reason that it was implausible in *Loving*. To say this is not to say that the ban on same-sex marriages is necessarily unacceptable in all theoretically possible worlds. In our world, the ban is like a literacy test motivated by a discriminatory purpose, or a veterans' preference law designed to exclude women from employment.

In this space, I will not be able fully to defend this thesis, on which much work remains to be done. Certainly the thesis is not belied by the fact that some "macho" cultures do not stigmatize male homosexuality as much as (say) the United States. Even in such cultures, a sharp distinction is drawn between passivity and activity in sexual relations, and cultural understandings of passive and active operate in highly gendered terms. Thus the passive role is both stigmatized and identified with femininity, whereas the active role is socially respectable and identified with masculinity. In such cultures, sex-role distinctions have somewhat different manifestations, but sex discrimination is fully operative in thinking both about men and women and about sexuality.

My claim about the reasons behind the ban on same-sex marriages is in part an empirical one; and it has suggestive empirical support in psychological studies. For example, one social psychologist, capturing much of the general view, finds that "a major determinant of negative attitudes toward homosexuality is the need to keep males masculine and females feminine, that is, to avoid sex-role confusion. . ."[3] The evidence taken as a whole suggests that the prohibition on homosexual relations is best seen as an effort to insist on and to rigidify "natural difference," in part by crisply separating gender roles.[4] This occurs largely by ensuring that there are firm and clear lines, defined in terms of gender, about sexual (and social) activity as opposed to sexual (and social) receptivity or passivity.

Thus it is that the definition of men as essentially active, in social and sexual arenas, and of women as essentially passive in both places, helps undergird the caste system based on sex. It simultaneously helps account for the prohibition of same-sex relations. The social opprobrium directed against homosexuals is an outgrowth of the ways in which, for heterosexuals, the existence of homosexuality draws into question familiar ideas about the sex difference.

There appear to be important distinctions here between the reasons that underlie the stigmatization or prohibition on male homosexual relations on the one hand and those that account for bans on female homosexual relations on the other. The evidence suggests that the social stigmatization of male homosexuality comes in large part from the perceived unnaturalness of male passivity in sex. It is this feature of male homosexuality that accounts for the social opprobrium directed against it. Thus it is well-established that the male heterosexual opposition to male homosexuality stems largely from the desire to stigmatize male sexual passivity (especially male receptivity in anal intercourse). We might speculate that subjection to sexual aggression of this kind is especially troublesome because, socially speaking, it turns men into women, and in this way complicates ordinary views about the sex difference. Thus it is a familiar part of violent male encounters that the victim will be feminized, as in the boxer Mike Tyson's remark to a challenger, "I'm going to make you my girlfriend." I suggest that far from being an oddity, this comment says something deeply revealing about the relationship between same-sex relations and the system of caste based on gender. The comment is tightly connected with Chief Justice Burger's approval of Blackstone's statement about the greater malignity of sodomy than rape.

The ban on lesbian relations stems from quite different concerns. Part of the purpose of such bans is to ensure that women are sexually available to men; the institution of lesbianism has been problematic (or invisible) largely for this reason. Another part of the concern stems from the fact that lesbianism also complicates gender difference by creating a sexually active role for women, one that also undermines existing conceptions of natural difference. It is for this reason familiar to see that socially active women—women prominent in politics or public life—are often stigmatized as lesbian. Indeed, a charge of lesbianism is a standard delegitimating device operating against women who have assumed stereotypically male social roles. There is thus a close connection between the caste system based on gender and the prohibition on lesbianism.

I claim that considerations of this sort help to maintain the legal and social taboo on homosexuality, in a way that might well be damaging to both men and women, and to both heterosexual and homosexual alike, though of course in very different ways and to quite different degrees. The distinction between the rigid categories "male" and "female," with the accompanying social and sexual traits "active" and "passive," has especially conspicuous harmful effects for gay men and lesbians. But for all of us, the categories and the traits are much too crude to account for social and sexual life when both of these are going well. For heterosexual women as well, the distinction can be highly damaging, because it is rigidly confining and untrue to the complexity of their experience, even when their sexual attraction is directed to men. The damage is closely connected to the caste-like features of the current system of gender relations. For heterosexual men, very much the same is true, since a degree of passivity in society and in sexual relations is both an inevitable and a desirable part of life, and since it is such an unnecessary burden to be embarrassed by or ashamed of this.

Speculative and brisk as they are, these various points suggest that the division of gender into "two kinds" may be as artificial and unfortunate for gender as it is for race. There are men and women, to be sure. But the division of humanity into only "two kinds," with accompanying features, is far too rough a basis for understanding the diversity of human character, in both the private and the public spheres. The insistence on two kinds in turn undergirds the system of caste based on gender; it is also part and parcel of practices of discrimination against same-sex relations. For this reason, the prohibition on such relations is a form of discrimination on the basis of sex, just as the prohibition on miscegenation was a form of discrimination on the basis of race. Both prohibitions are invalid under the equal protection clause.

Conclusion

In almost all countries, including the United States, there is a system with caste-like features based on gender. This is the target of the equal protection clause, rightly understood. If we shift our attention from the unhelpful and misleading question of difference to the relevant question of caste, we will see a tight connection between discrimination on the basis of sexual orientation and discrimination on the basis of sex. In the long run, I believe, the ban on same-sex relations will be seen as having the same relationship to male supremacy as did the ban on mixed marriages have to white supremacy. *Loving v. Virginia* is therefore a key case for those seeking to use the Constitution to counteract both sex discrimination and discrimination on the basis of sexual orientation.

This does not mean that current courts should require states to allow same-sex marriages. Under contemporary conditions, a judicial holding of this sort would probably be a large mistake, even though the basic principle is sound. Elected officials, including the President, have somewhat more flexibility. As part of their constitutional duty, elected officials and citizens themselves should clearly state the basic governing principle, which is that discrimination on the basis of sexual orientation is morally and legally unacceptable. But in producing social reform in this area, public officials should be selective, strategic, and occasionally cautious. This course may well disappoint people who are firmly committed to the basic principle and who conflate caution with ambivalence. The conflation is unnecessary and misleading. If we are to dismantle the system of caste based on gender—a system that goes so deep into both law and life—we should sometimes be cautious about implementation even as we stand firm on principle.

Endnotes

[1] 388 U.S. 12 (1967).

[2] 347 U.S. 483 (1954).

[3] See MacDonald and Games, "Some Characteristics of Those Who Hold Positive and Negative Attitudes Toward Homosexuals," 1 *Journal of Homosexuality* 9, 19 (1974). See also Whitley, "The Relationship of Sex-Role Orientation to Heterosexuals' Attitudes Toward Homosexuals," 17 *Sex Roles* 103 (1987).

[4] Ibid.

The Dilemma of Difference

Martha Minow

. . . [W]hen does treating people differently emphasize their differences and stigmatize or hinder them on that basis? And when does treating people the same become insensitive to their difference and likely to stigmatize or hinder them on *that* basis?

I call this question "the dilemma of difference." The stigma of difference may be recreated both by ignoring and by focusing on it. Decisions about education, employment, benefits, and other opportunities in society should not turn on an individual's ethnicity, disability, race, gender, religion, or membership in any other group about which some have deprecating or hostile attitudes. Yet refusing to acknowledge these differences may make them continue to matter in a world constructed with some groups, but not others, in mind. The problems of inequality can be exacerbated both by treating members of minority groups the same as members of the majority and by treating the two groups differently.

The dilemma of difference may be posed as a choice between integration and separation, as a choice between similar treatment and special treatment, or as a choice between neutrality and accommodation. Governmental neutrality may be the best way to assure equality, yet governmental neutrality may also freeze in place the past consequences of differences. Do the public schools fulfill their obligation to provide equal opportunities by including all students in the same integrated classroom, or by offering some students special programs tailored to their needs? Special needs arise from "differences" beyond language proficiency and physical or mental disability. Religious differences also raise questions of same versus different treatment. Students who belong to religious minorities may seek exemption from courses in sex education or other subjects that conflict with

their religious teachings. Religiously observant students may ask to use school time and facilities to engage in religious activities, just as other students engage in other extra-curricular activities. But the legal obligation of neutrality is explicit here, in policy committed to separating church and state. Do the schools remain neutral toward religion by balancing the teaching of evolution with the teaching of scientific arguments about creation? Or does this accommodation of a religious viewpoint depart from the requisite neutrality?

The difference dilemma also arises beyond the schoolhouse. If women's biological differences from men justify special benefits in the workplace—such as maternity leave—are women thereby helped or hurt? Are negative stereotypes reinforced, in violation of commitments to equality? Or are differences accommodated, in fulfillment of the vision of equality? Members of religious groups that designate Saturday as the Sabbath may desire accommodation in the workplace. Is the commitment to a norm of equality advanced through such an accommodation, or through neutral application of a Saturday work requirement that happens to burden these individuals differently from others?

. . .

Dilemmas of difference appear unresolvable. The risk of nonneutrality—the risk of discrimination—accompanies efforts both to ignore and to recognize difference in equal treatment and special treatment. Difference can be recreated in color or gender blindness and in affirmative action; in governmental neutrality and in governmental preferences; and in discretionary decisions and in formal constraints on discretion. Why does difference seem to pose choices each of which undesirably revives difference or the stigma or disadvantage associated with it?

In this last question lies a clue to the problem. The possibility of reiterating difference, whether by acknowledgment or nonacknowledgment, arises as long as difference itself carries stigma and precludes equality. Buried in the questions about difference are

From Martha Minow, *Making All the Difference* (Ithaca: Cornell University Press, 1990), pp. 19–20, 49–62, 64–66, 69–70, 73–78. Reprinted with permission of Cornell University Press.

assumptions that difference is linked to stigma or deviance and that sameness is a prerequisite for equality. Perhaps these assumptions themselves must be identified and assessed if we are to escape or transcend the dilemmas of difference.

If to be equal one must be the same, then to be different is to be unequal or even deviant. But any assignment of deviance must be made from the vantage point of some claimed normality: a position of equality implies a contrasting position used to draw the relationship—and it is a relationship not of equality and inequality but of superiority and inferiority. To be different is to be different in relationship to someone or something else—and this point of comparison must be so taken for granted, so much the "norm," that it need not even be stated.

At least five closely related but unstated assumptions underlie difference dilemmas. Once articulated and examined, these assumptions can take their proper place among other choices about how to treat difference, and we can consider what we might do to challenge or renovate them.

Five Unstated Assumptions

Assumption 1: Difference Is Intrinsic, Not a Comparison

Can and should questions about who is different be resolved by a process of discovering intrinsic differences? Is difference something intrinsic to the different person or something constructed by social attitudes? By posing legal claims through the difference dilemma, litigants and judges treat the problem of difference as what society or a given decision-maker should do about the "different person"—a formulation that implicitly assigns the label of difference to that person.

The difference inquiry functions by pigeonholing people in sharply distinguished categories based on selected facts and features. Categorization helps people to cope with complexity and to understand one another. Devising categories to simplify a complicated world may well be an inevitable feature of human cognition.

When lawyers and judges analyze difference and use categories to do so, they import a basic method of legal analysis. Legal analysis, cast in a judicial mode, typically asks whether a given situation "fits" in a category defined by a legal rule or, instead, belongs outside it. Questions presented for review by the Supreme Court, for example, often take the form "Is this a

that?" For example, are Jews a race? Is a contagious disease a handicap? Other questions take the form "Is doing x really doing y?" For example, is offering a statutory guarantee of job reinstatement after maternity leave really engaging in gender discrimination? Is denying unemployment benefits to someone who left work because of pregnancy also really discriminating on the basis of gender? . . .

. . .

Some have argued that the assignment of differences in Western thought entails not just relationships and comparisons but also the imposition of hierarchies. To explore this idea, we need the next unstated assumption: the implicit norm or reference point for the comparison through which difference is assigned.

Assumption 2: The Norm Need Not Be Stated

To treat someone as different means to accord him treatment that is different from the treatment of someone else, to describe someone as "the same" implies "the same as" someone else. When differences are discussed without explicit reference to the person or trait on the other side of the comparison, an unstated norm remains. Usually, this default reference point is so powerful and well established that specifying it is not thought necessary.

When women argue for rights, the implicit reference point used in discussions of sameness and difference is the privilege accorded some men—typically, white men who are well established in the society. . . . Unfortunately for the reformers, embracing the theory of "sameness" meant that any sign of difference between women and the men used for comparison could be used to justify treating women differently from those men.

A prominent "difference" assigned to women by implicit comparison with men, is pregnancy—especially pregnancy experienced by women working for pay outside their homes. The Supreme Court's treatment of issues concerning pregnancy a and the workplace highlights the power of the unstated norm in analyses of problems of difference. In 1975 the Court accepted an appeal to a male norm in striking down a Utah statute that disqualified a woman from receiving unemployment compensation for a specified period surrounding childbirth, even if her reasons for leaving work were unrelated to the pregnancy. Although the capacity to become pregnant is a difference between women and men, this fact alone did not justify treating women and men differently on matters unrelated to pregnancy. Using men as the norm, the Court reasoned that any woman who can perform like a man can be treated like a man. A woman could not be denied unemployment compensation for different reasons than a man would.

What, however, is equal treatment for the woman who is correctly identified within the group of pregnant persons, not simply stereotyped as such, and temporarily unable to work outside the home for that reason? The Court first grappled with these issues in two cases that posed the question of whether discrimination on the basis of pregnancy—that is, employers' denial of health benefits—amounted to discrimination on the basis of sex. In both instances the Court answered negatively, reasoning that the employers drew a distinction not on the forbidden basis of sex but only on the basis of pregnancy; and since women could be both pregnant and nonpregnant, these were not instances of sex discrimination. Only from a point of view that regards pregnancy as a strange occurrence, rather than an ongoing bodily potential, would its relationship to female experience be made so tenuous; and only from a vantage point that regards men as the norm would the exclusion of pregnancy from health insurance coverage seem unproblematic and free from gender discrimination.

Congress responded by enacting the Pregnancy Discrimination Act, which amended Title VII (the federal law forbidding gender discrimination in employment) to include discrimination on the basis of pregnancy within the range of impermissible sex discrimination. Yet even under these new statutory terms, the power of the unstated male norm persists in debates over the definition of discrimination. Indeed, a new question arose under the Pregnancy Discrimination Act: if differential treatment on the basis of pregnancy is forbidden, does the statute also forbid any state requirement for pregnancy or maternity leaves—which are, after all, distinctions drawn on the basis of pregnancy, even though drawn to help women?

A collection of employers launched a lawsuit in the 1980s arguing that even favorable treatment on the basis of pregnancy violated the Pregnancy Discrimination Act. The employers challenged a California statute that mandated a limited right to resume a prior job following an unpaid pregnancy disability leave. The case—*California Federal Savings & Loan Association v. Guerra*, which became known as "Cal/Fed"[1]—in a real and painful sense divided the community of advocates for women's rights. Writing briefs on opposing sides,

women's rights groups went public with the division. Some maintained that any distinction on the basis of pregnancy—any distinction on the basis of sex—would perpetuate the negative stereotypes long used to demean and exclude women. Others argued that denying the facts of pregnancy and the needs of new mothers could only hurt women; treating women like men in the workplace violated the demands of equality. What does equality demand—treating women like men, or treating women specially?

What became clear in these arguments was that a deeper problem had produced this conundrum: a work world that treats as the model worker the traditional male employee who has a full-time wife and mother to care for his home and children. The very phrase "special treatment," when used to describe pregnancy or maternity leave, posits men as the norm and women as different or deviant from that norm. The problem was not women, or pregnancy, but the effort to fit women's experiences and needs into categories forged with men in mind.

The case reached the Supreme Court. Over a strenuous dissent, a majority of the justices reconceived the problem and rejected the presumption of the male norm which had made the case seem like a choice between "equal treatment" and "special treatment." Instead, Justice Marshall's opinion for the majority shifted from a narrow workplace comparison to a broader comparison of men and women in their dual roles as workers and as family members. The Court found no conflict between the Pregnancy Discrimination Act and the challenged state law that required qualified reinstatement of women following maternity leaves, because "California's pregnancy disability leave statute allows women, as well as men, to have families without losing their jobs." The Court therefore construed the federal law to permit states to require that employers remove barriers in the workplace that would disadvantage pregnant people compared with others. Moreover, reasoned the majority, if there remains a conflict between a federal ban against sex-based discrimination and a state law requiring accommodation for women who take maternity leaves, that conflict should be resolved by the extension to men of benefits comparable to those available to women following maternity or pregnancy leaves. Here, the Court used women's experiences as the benchmark and called for treating men equally in reference to women, thus reversing the usual practice. The dissenters, however remained convinced that the federal law prohibited preferential treatment on the basis of pregnancy; they persisted in using the male norm as the measure for equal treatment in the workplace. . . .

Assumption 3: The Observer Can See Without a Perspective

This assumption builds on the others. Differences are intrinsic, and anyone can see them; there is one true reality, and impartial observers can make judgments unaffected and untainted by their own perspective or experience. The facts of the world, including facts about people's traits, are knowable truly only by someone uninfluenced by social or cultural situations. Once legal rules are selected, regardless of prior disputes over the rules themselves, society may direct legal officials to apply them evenhandedly and to use them to discover and categorize events, motives, and culpability as they exist in the world. This aspiration to impartiality in legal judgments, however, is just that—an aspiration, not a description. The aspiration even risks obscuring the inevitable perspective of any given legal official, or of anyone else, and thereby makes it harder to challenge the impact of perspective on the selection of traits used to judge legal consequences.

The ideal of objectivity itself suppresses the coincidence between the viewpoints of the majority and what is commonly understood to be objective or unbiased. For example, in an employment discrimination case the defendant, a law firm, sought to disqualify Judge Constance Baker Motley from sitting on the case because she, as a black woman who had once represented plaintiffs in discrimination cases, would identify with those who suffer race or sex discrimination. The defendant assumed that Judge Motley's personal identity and her past political work had made her different, lacking the ability to perceive without a perspective. Judge Motley declined, however, to recuse herself and explained; "If background or sex or race of each judge were, by definition, sufficient grounds for removal, no judge on this court could hear this case, or many others, by virtue of the fact that all of them were attorneys, of a sex, often with distinguished law firm or public service backgrounds."[2]

Because of the aspiration to impartiality and the prevalence of universalist language in law, most observers of law have been reluctant to confront the arguments of philosophers and psychologists who challenge the idea that observers can see without a perspective. Philosophers such as A. J. Ayer and W. V. Quine note that although we can alter the theory we use to frame our perceptions of the world, we cannot see the world unclouded by preconceptions. What interests us, given who we are and where we stand, affects our ability to perceive.

The impact of the observer's unacknowledged perspective may be crudely oppressive. When a municipality includes a nativity creche in its annual Christmas display, the majority of the community may perceive no offense to non-Christians in the community. If the practice is challenged in court as a violation of the Constitution's ban against establishment of religion, a judge who is Christian may also fail to see the offense to anyone and merely conclude, as the Supreme Court did in 1984, that Christmas is a national holiday. Judges may be peculiarly disabled from perceiving the state's message about a dominant religious practice because judges are themselves often members of the dominant group and therefore have the luxury of seeing their perspectives mirrored and reinforced in major social and political institutions. Similarly, members of a racial majority may miss the impact of their own race on their perspective about the race of others.

. . .

Assumption 4: Other Perspectives Are Irrelevant

. . . Many people who judge differences in the world reject as irrelevant or relatively unimportant the experience of "different people." William James put it this way: "We have seen the blindness and deadness to each other which are our natural inheritance."[3] People often use stereotypes as though they were real and complete, thereby failing to see the complex humanity of others. Stereotyped thinking is one form of the failure to imagine the perspective of another. Glimpsing contrasting perspectives may alter assumptions about the world, as well as about the meaning of difference.

. . .

A perspective may go unstated because it is so unknown to those in charge that they do not recognize it as a perspective. Judges in particular often presume that the perspective they adopt is either universal or superior to others. Indeed, a perspective may go unstated because it is so powerful and pervasive that it may be presumed without defense. It has been said that Aristotle could have checked out—and corrected—his faulty assertion that women have fewer teeth than men. He did not do so, however, because he thought he knew. Presumptions about whose perspective ultimately matters arise from the fifth typically unarticulated assumption, that the status quo is the preferred situation.

Assumption 5: The Status Quo Is Natural, Uncoerced, and Good

Connected with many of the other assumptions is the idea that critical features of the status quo—general social and economic arrangements—are natural and desirable. From this assumption follow three propositions. First, the goal of governmental neutrality demands the status quo because existing societal arrangements are assumed to be neutral. Second, governmental actions that change the status quo have a different status from omissions, or failures to act, that maintain the status quo. Third, prevailing societal arrangements are not forced on anyone. Individuals are free to make choices and to assume responsibility for those choices. These propositions are rarely stated, both because they are deeply entrenched and because they treat the status quo as good, natural, and freely chosen—and thus not in need of discussion.

Difference may seem salient, then, not because of a trait intrinsic to the person but because the dominant institutional arrangements were designed without that trait in mind—designed according to an unstated norm reconfirmed by the view that alternative perspectives are irrelevant or have already been taken into account. The difference between buildings built without considering the needs of people in wheelchairs and buildings that are accessible to people in wheelchairs reveals that institutional arrangements define whose reality is to be the norm and what is to seem natural. Sidewalk curbs are not neutral or natural but humanly constructed obstacles. Interestingly, modifying what has been the status quo often brings unexpected benefits as well. Inserting curb cuts for the disabled turns out to help many others, such as bike riders and parents pushing baby strollers. (They can also be positioned to avoid endangering a visually impaired person who uses a cane to determine where the sidewalk ends.)

Yet the weight of the status quo remains great. Existing institutions and language already shape the world and already express and recreate attitudes about what counts as a difference, and who or what is the relevant point of comparison. Assumptions that the status quo is natural, good, and uncoerced make proposed changes seem to violate the commitment to neutrality, predictability, and freedom.

. . .

. . . An extensive dispute about the role of women's choices in the gender segregation of the workplace arose in a sex discrimination charge pursued by the federal Equal Employment Opportunity Commission against Sears, Roebuck & Co.[4] Did the absence of women from jobs as commission salespersons result from women's own choices and preferences, or from societal discrimination and employers' refusals to make those jobs available? The legal framework in the case seemed to force the issue into either/or questions: women's workforce participation was due either to their own choices or to forces beyond their control; women's absence from certain jobs was either due to employers' discrimination or not; either women lacked the interest and qualifications for these jobs, or women had the interest and qualifications for the jobs.

Would it be possible to articulate a third view? Consider this one: choices by working women and decisions by their employers were both influenced by larger patterns of economic prosperity and depression and by shifting social attitudes about appropriate roles for women. These larger patterns became real in people's lives when internalized and experienced as individual choice. Assuming that the way things have been resulted either from people's choices or from nature helps to force legal arguments into these alternatives and to make legal redress of historic differences a treacherous journey through incompatible alternatives.

Sometimes, judges have challenged the assumption that the status quo is natural and good; they have occasionally approved public and private decisions to take difference into account in efforts to alter existing conditions and to remedy their harmful effects. But for the most part, unstated assumptions work in subtle and complex ways. They fill a basic human need to simplify and make our world familiar and unsurprising, yet by their very simplification, assumptions exclude contrasting views. Moreover, they contribute to the dilemma of difference by frustrating legislative and constitutional commitments to change the treatment of differences in race, gender, ethnicity, religion, and handicap.

. . .

Endnotes

[1] 107 S. Ct. 683 (1987).

[2] *Blank v. Sullivan & Cromwell*, 418 F. Supp. 1 (S.D.N.Y. 1975); accord *Commonwealth v. Local Union 542*, Int'l Union of Operating Eng'rs, 388 F. Supp. 115 (F.D.Pa. 1974)(Higginbotham, J.)(denying defendant's motion to disqualify the

judge from a race discrimination case because of the judge's racial identity as a black person). Judge Higginbotham noted that "black lawyers have litigated in federal courts almost exclusively before white judges, yet they have not urged the white judges should be disqualified on matters of race relations" (id. at 177).

[3] James, "What Makes a Life Significant," in *On Some of Life's Ideals*, pp. 49, 81. I want to acknowledge here that "blindness" as a metaphoric concept risks stigmatizing people who are visually impaired.

[4] 628 F. Supp. 1264 (N.D. Ill. 1986).

The Assimilationist Ideal

Richard Wasserstrom

Just as we can and must ask what is involved in our or any other culture in being of one race or one sex rather than the other, and how individuals are in fact viewed and treated, we can also ask a different question, namely, what would the good or just society make of an individual's race or sex, and to what degree, if at all, would racial and sexual distinctions ever properly be taken into account there? Indeed, it could plausibly be argued that we could not have a wholly adequate idea of whether a society was racist or sexist unless we had some conception of what a thoroughly nonracist or nonsexist society would look like. This question is an extremely instructive as well as an often neglected one. Comparatively little theoretical literature that deals with either racism or sexism has concerned itself in a systematic way with this issue, but as will be seen it is in some respects both a more important and a more complicated one where sex is concerned than where race is involved. Moreover, as I shall argue, many discussions of sexual differences which touch upon this question do so inappropriately by concentrating upon the relatively irrelevant question of whether the differences between males and females are biological rather than social in origin.

The inquiry that follows addresses and seeks to answer two major questions. First, what are the major, plausible conceptions of what the good society would look like in respect to the race and sex of individuals, and how are these conceptions to be correctly characterized and described? And second, given a delineation of the alternatives, what is to be said in favor or against one or another of them? . . .

. . .

[O]ne conception of a nonracist society is that which is captured by what I shall call the assimilationist ideal: a nonracist society would be one in which the race of an individual would be the functional equivalent of the eye color of individuals in our society today. In our society no basic political rights and obligations are determined on the basis of eye color. No important institutional benefits and burdens are connected with eye color. Indeed, except for the mildest sort of aesthetic preferences, a person would be thought odd who even made private, social decisions by taking eye color into account. It would, of course, be unintelligible, and not just odd, were a person to say today that while he or she looked blue-eyed, he or she regarded himself of herself as really a brown-eyed person. Because eye color functions differently in our culture than does race, there is no analogue to passing for eye color. Were the assimilationist ideal to become a reality, the same would be true of one's race. In short, according to the assimilationist ideal, a nonracist society would be one in which an individual's race was of no more significance in any of these three areas than is eye color today.

What is a good deal less familiar is an analogous conception of the good society in respect to sexual differentiation—one in which an individual's sex were to become a comparably unimportant characteristic. An assimilationist society in respect to sex would be one in which an individual's sex was of no more significance in any of the three areas than is eye color today. There would be no analogue to transsexuality, and, while physiological or anatomical sex differences would remain, they would possess only the kind and degree of significance that today attaches to the physiologically distinct eye colors persons possess.

It is apparent that the assimilationist ideal in respect to sex does not seem to be as readily plausible and obviously attractive here as it is in the case of race. In fact, many persons invoke the possible realization of the assimilationist ideal as a reason for rejecting the Equal Rights Amendment and indeed the idea of women's liberation itself. . . .

To begin with, it must be acknowledged that to make the assimilationist ideal a reality in respect to sex would involve more profound and fundamental revisions of our institutions and our attitudes than would be the case in respect to race. On the institutional level we would, for instance, have to alter significantly our practices concerning marriage. If a nonsexist society is a society in which one's sex is no more significant than eye color in our society today, then laws which require the persons who are getting married to be of different sexes would clearly be sexist laws.

More importantly, given the significance of role differentiation and ideas about the psychological differences in temperament that are tied to sexual identity, the assimilationist ideal would be incompatible with all psychological and sex-role differentiation. That is to say, in such a society the ideology of the society would contain no proposition asserting the inevitable or essential attributes of masculinity or femininity; it would never encourage or discourage the ideas of sisterhood or brotherhood; and it would be unintelligible to talk about the virtues or the disabilities of being a woman or a man. In addition, such a society would not have any norms concerning the appropriateness of different social behavior depending upon whether one were male or female. There would be no conception of the existence of a set of social tasks that were more appropriately undertaken or performed by males or by females. And there would be no expectation that the family was composed of one adult male and one adult female, rather than, say, just two adults—if two adults seemed the appropriate number. To put it simply, in the assimilationist society in respect to sex, persons would not be socialized so as to see or understand themselves or others as essentially or significantly who they were or what their lives would be like because they were

either male or female. And no political rights or social institutions, practices, and norms would mark the physiological differences between males and females as important.

Were sex like eye color, these kinds of distinctions would make no sense. Just as the normal, typical adult is virtually oblivious to the eye color of other persons for all significant interpersonal relationships, so, too, the normal, typical adult in this kind of nonsexist society would be equally as indifferent to the sexual, physiological differences of other persons for all significant interpersonal relationships. Bisexuality, not heterosexuality or homosexuality, would be the typical intimate, sexual relationship in the ideal society that was assimilationist in respect to sex.

To acknowledge that things would be very different is, of course, hardly to concede that they would thereby be undesirable—or desirable for that matter. But still, the problem is, perhaps, with the assimilationist ideal. And the assimilationist ideal is certainly not the only possible, plausible ideal.

There is, for instance, another one that is closely related to, but distinguishable from that of the assimilationist ideal. It can be understood by considering how religion rather than eye color tends to be thought about in our culture today and incorporated within social life today. If the good society were to match the present state of affairs in respect to one's religious identity, rather than the present state of affairs in respect to one's eye color, the two societies would be different, but not very greatly so. In neither would we find that the allocation of basic political rights and duties ever took an individual's religion into account. And there would be a comparable indifference to religion even in respect to most important institutional benefits and burdens—for example, access to employment in the desirable vocations, the opportunity to live where one wished to live, and the like. Nonetheless, in the good society in which religious differences were to some degree socially relevant, it would be deemed appropriate to have some institutions (typically those which are connected in an intimate way with these religions) which did in a variety of ways properly take the religion of members of the society into account. . . .

. . .

[I]t may be that in respect to sex, and conceivably, in respect to race, too, something more like this ideal of diversity in respect to religion is the right one. But one problem then—and it is a more substantial one than is sometimes realized—is to specify with a good deal of precision and care what the ideal really comes to in the matter of sexual or racial identity and degree of acceptable sexual or racial differentiation. Which institutional and personal differentiations would properly be permissible and which would not be? Which attitudes, beliefs, and role expectations concerning the meaning and significance of being male or female would be properly introduced and maintained in the good society and which would not be?

. . .

. . . Some persons might think the right ideal was one in which substantially greater sexual differentiation and sex-role identification were retained than would be the case within a good society of that general type. Thus, someone might believe, for instance, that the good society was, perhaps, essentially like the one they think we now have in respect to sex: equality of basic political rights, such as the right to vote, but all of the sexual differentiation in both legal and nonlegal, formal and informal institutions, all of the sex-role socialization and all of the differences in matters of temperament that are characteristic of the way in which our society has been and still is ordered. And someone might also believe that the prevailing ideological concomitants of these arrangements are the correct and appropriate ones to perpetuate. . . .

[T]he next question is that of how a choice is rationally to be made among these different, possible ideals. One general set of issues concerns the empirical sphere, because the question of whether something is a plausible and attractive ideal does turn in part on the nature of the empirical world. If it is true, for example, that any particular characteristic, such as an individual's race or sex, is not only a socially significant category in our culture but that it is largely a socially created one as well, then for many people a number of objections to the assimilationist ideal appear immediately to disappear. The other general set of issues concerns the relevant normative considerations. Here the key questions concern the principles and considerations by which to assess and evaluate different conceptions of how persons ought to be able to live and how their social institutions ought to be constructed and arranged. I begin with the empirical considerations and constraints, although one heuristic disadvantage in doing so is that this decision may appear to give them greater weight than, as I shall argue, they in fact deserve.

What opponents of assimilationism and proponents of schemes of strong sexual differentiation seize upon is that sexual difference appears to be a naturally occurring category of obvious and inevitable relevance for the construction of any plausible conception of the nature of the good society. The problems with this way of thinking are twofold. To begin with, a careful and thorough analysis of the social realities would reveal, I believe, that it is the socially created sexual differences which constitute most of our conception of sex differences and which tend in fact to matter the most in the way we live our lives as persons of one sex or the other. For, it is, I think, sex-role differentiation and socialization, not the physiological and related biological differences—if there are any—that make men and women as different as they are from each other, and it is these same sex-role-created differences which are invoked to justify the necessity or the desirability of most sexual differentiation proposed to be maintained at any of the levels of social arrangements and practices described earlier.

It is important, however, not to attach any greater weight than is absolutely necessary to the truth or falsity of this causal claim about the source of the degree of sexual distinctions that exist[s] in our or other cultures. For what is significant, although seldom recognized, is the fact that the answer to that question almost never goes very far in settling the question of what the good society should look like in respect to any particular characteristic of individuals. And the answer certainly does not go as far as many persons appear to believe it does to settle that question of the nature of the good society.

Let us suppose that there are what can be called "naturally occurring" sexual differences and even that they are of such a nature that they are in some sense of direct prima facie social relevance. It is essential to see that this would by no means settle the question of whether in the good society sex should or should not be as minimally significant as eye color. Even if there are major or substantial biological differences between men and women that are in this sense "natural" rather than socially created, this does not determine the question of what the good society can and should make of these differences—without, that is, begging the question by including within the meaning of "major" or "substantial" or "natural" the idea that these are things that ought to be retained, emphasized, or otherwise normatively taken into account. It is not easy to see why, without begging the question, it should be thought that this fact, if it is a fact, settles the question adversely to anything like the assimilationist ideal. Persons might think that truths of this sort about nature or biology do affect, if not settle, the question of what the good society should look like for at least two different reasons.

In the first place, they might think the differences are of such a character that they substantially affect what would be *possible* within a good society of human persons. Just as the fact that humans are mortal necessarily limits the features of any possible good society, so, they might argue, the fact that males and females are physiologically or biologically different limits in the same way the features of any possible good society.

In the second place, they might think the differences are of such a character that they are relevant to the question of what would be *desirable* in the good society. That is to say, they might not think that the differences determine or affect to a substantial degree what is possible, but only that the differences are appropriately taken into account in any rational construction of an ideal social existence.

The second reason seems to be a good deal more plausible than the first. For there appear to be very few, if any, respects in which the ineradicable, naturally occurring differences between males and females *must* be taken into account. The industrial revolution has certainly made any of the general differences in strength between the sexes capable of being ignored by the good society for virtually all significant human activities. And even if it were true that women are naturally better suited than men to care for and nurture children, it is also surely the case that men can be taught to care for and nurture children well. Indeed, the one natural or biological fact that seems *required* to be taken into account is the fact that reproduction of the human species requires that the fetus develop *in utero* for a period of months. Sexual intercourse is not necessary, for artificial insemination is available. Neither marriage nor the nuclear family is necessary either for conception or child rearing. Given the present state of medical knowledge and what might be termed the natural realities of female pregnancy, it is difficult to see why any important institutional or interpersonal arrangements are constrained to take the existing biological differences as to the phenomenon of *in utero* pregnancy into account.

But to say all this is still to leave it a wholly open question to what degree the good society *ought* to build upon any ineradicable biological differences, or to create ones in order to construct institutions and sex-roles which would thereby maintain a substantial degree of sexual differentiation. The way to answer that question is to consider and assess the arguments

for and against doing so. What is significant is the fact that many of the arguments for doing so are less persuasive than they appear to be upon the initial statement of this possibility.

It might be argued, for instance, that the fact of menstruation could be used as a premise upon which to base the case for importantly different social roles for females than for males. But this could only plausibly be proposed if two things were true: first, that menstruation would be debilitating to women and hence relevant to social role even in a culture which did not teach women to view menstruation as a sign of uncleanliness or as a curse; and, second, that the way in which menstruation necessarily affected some or all women was in fact necessarily related in an important way to the role in question. But even if both of these were true, it would still be an open question whether any sexual differentiation ought to be built upon these facts. The society could still elect to develop institutions that would nullify the effect of these natural differences and it would still be an open question whether it ought to do so. Suppose, for example, what seems implausible—that some or all women will not be able to perform a particular task while menstruating, e.g., guard the border of a country. It would be possible, even easy, if the society wanted to, to arrange for substitute guards for the women who were incapacitated. We know that persons are not good guards when they are sleepy, and we make arrangements so that persons alternate guard duty to avoid fatigue. The same could be done for menstruating women, even given the implausibly strong assumptions about menstruation.

The point that is involved here is a very general one that has application in contexts having nothing to do with the desirability or undesirability of maintaining substantial sexual differentiation. It has to do with the fact that humans possess the ability to alter their natural and social environment in distinctive, dramatic, and unique ways. An example from the nonsexual area can help bring out this too seldom recognized central feature. It is a fact that some persons born in human society are born with congenital features such that they cannot walk or walk well on their legs. They are born naturally crippled or lame. However, humans in our society certainly possess the capability to devise and construct mechanical devices and institutional arrangements which render this natural fact about some persons relatively unimportant in respect to the way they and others will live together. We can bring it about, and in fact are in the process of bringing it about, that persons who are confined to wheelchairs can move down sidewalks and across streets because the curb stones at corners of intersections have been shaped so as to accommodate the passage of wheelchairs. And we can construct and arrange buildings and events so that persons in wheelchairs can ride elevators, park cars, and be seated at movies, lectures, meetings, and the like. Much of the environment in which humans live is the result of their intentional choices and actions concerning what that environment shall be like. They can elect to construct an environment in which the natural incapacity of some persons to walk or walk well is a major difference or a difference that will be effectively nullified vis-à-vis the lives that they, too, will live. . . .

There are, though, several other arguments based upon nature, or the idea of the "natural" that also must be considered and assessed. First, it might be argued that if a way of doing something is natural, then it ought to be done that way. Here, what may be meant by "natural" is that this way of doing the thing is the way it would be done if culture did not direct or teach us to do it differently. It is not clear, however, that this sense of "natural" is wholly intelligible; it supposes that we can meaningfully talk about how humans would behave in the absence of culture. And few if any humans have ever lived in such a state. Moreover, even if this is an intelligible notion, the proposal that the natural way to behave is somehow the appropriate or desirable way to behave is strikingly implausible. It is, for example, almost surely natural, in this sense of "natural," that humans would eat their food with their hands, except for the fact that they are, almost always, socialized to eat food differently. Yet, the fact that humans would naturally eat this way, does not seem in any respect to be a reason for believing that that is thereby the desirable or appropriate way to eat food. And the same is equally true of any number of other distinctively human ways of behaving.

Second, someone might argue that substantial sexual differentiation is natural not in the sense that it is biologically determined nor in the sense that it would occur but for the effects of culture, but rather in the sense that substantial sexual differentiation is a virtually universal phenomenon in human culture. By itself, this claim of virtual universality, even if accurate, does not directly establish anything about the desirability or undesirability of any particular ideal. But it can be made into an argument by the addition of the proposition that where there is a widespread, virtually universal social practice or institution, there is

probably some good or important purpose served by the practice or institution. Hence, given the fact of substantial sex-role differentiation in all, or almost all, cultures, there is on this view some reason to think that substantial sex-role differentiation serves some important purpose for and in human society.

This is an argument, but it is hard to see what is attractive about it. The premise which turns the fact of sex-role differentiation into any kind of a strong reason for sex-role differentiation is the premise of conservatism. And it is no more or less convincing here than elsewhere. There are any number of practices or institutions that are typical and yet upon reflection seem without significant social purpose. Slavery was once such an institution; war perhaps still is.

· · ·

If the chief thing to be said in favor of something like the assimilationist society in respect to sex is that some arguments against it are not very relevant, that does not by itself make a very convincing case. Such is not, however, the way in which matters need be left. There is an affirmative case of sorts for something like the assimilationist society.

One strong, affirmative moral argument on behalf of the assimilationist ideal is that it does provide for a kind of individual autonomy that a substantially nonassimilationist society cannot provide. The reason is because any substantially nonassimilationist society will have sex roles, and sex roles interfere in basic ways with autonomy. The argument for these two propositions proceeds as follows.

Any nonassimilationist society must have some institutions and some ideology that distinguishes between individuals in virtue of their sexual physiology, and any such society will necessarily be committed to teaching the desirability of doing so. That is what is implied by saying it is nonassimilationist rather than assimilationist. And any substantially nonassimilationist society will make one's sexual identity an important characteristic so that there will be substantial psychological, role, and status differences between persons who are male and those who are female. That is what is implied by saying that it is substantially nonassimilationist. Any such society will necessarily have sex roles, a conception of the places, characteristics, behaviors, etc., that are appropriate to one sex or the other but not both. That is what makes it a *sex* role.

Now, sex roles are, I think, morally objectionable on two or three quite distinct grounds. One such ground is absolutely generic and applies to all sex roles. The other grounds are less generic and apply only to the kinds of sex roles with which we are familiar and which are a feature of patriarchal societies, such as our own. I begin with the more contingent, less generic objections.

We can certainly imagine, if we are not already familiar with, societies in which the sex roles will be such that the general place of women in that society can be described as that of the servers of men. In such a society individuals will be socialized in such a way that women will learn how properly to minister to the needs, desires, and interests of men; women and men will both be taught that it is right and proper that the concerns and affairs of men are more important than and take precedence over those of women; and the norms and supporting set of beliefs and attitudes will be such that this role will be deemed the basic and appropriate role for women to play and men to expect. Here, I submit, what is objectionable about the connected set of institutions, practices, and ideology—the structure of the prevailing sex role—is the role itself. It is analogous to a kind of human slavery. The fundamental moral defect—just as is the case with slavery—is not that women are being arbitrarily or capriciously assigned to the social role of server, but that such a role itself has no legitimate place in the decent or just society. As a result, just as is the case with slavery, the assignment on *any* basis of individuals to such a role is morally objectionable. A society arranged so that such a role is a prominent part of the structure of the social institutions can be properly characterized as an *oppressive* one. It consigns some individuals to lives which have no place in the good society, which restrict unduly the opportunities of these individuals, and which do so in order improperly to enhance the lives and opportunities of others.

But it may be thought possible to have sex roles and all that goes with them without having persons of either sex placed within a position of general, systemic dominance or subordination. Here, it would be claimed, the society would not be an oppressive one in this sense. Consider, for example, the kinds of sex roles with which we are familiar and which assign to women the primary responsibilities for child rearing and household maintenance. It might be argued first that the roles of child rearer and household maintainer are not in themselves roles that could readily or satisfactorily be eliminated from human society without the society itself being deficient in serious, unacceptable ways. It might be asserted, that is, that these are roles or tasks that simply must be filled if children are

to be raised in a satisfactory way. Suppose this is correct, suppose it is granted that society would necessarily have it that these tasks would have to be done. Still, if it is also correct that, relatively speaking, these are unsatisfying and unfulfilling ways for humans to concentrate the bulk of their energies and talents, then, to the degree to which this is so, what is morally objectionable is that if this is to be a *sex* role, then women are unduly and unfairly allocated a disproportionate share of what is unpleasant, unsatisfying, unrewarding work. Here the objection is the degree to which the burden women are required to assume is excessive and unjustified vis-à-vis the rest of society, i.e., the men. Unsatisfactory roles and tasks, when they are substantial and pervasive, should surely be allocated and filled in the good society in a way which seeks to distribute the burdens involved in a roughly equal fashion.

Suppose, though, that even this feature were eliminated from sex roles, so that, for instance, men and women shared more equally in the dreary, unrewarding aspects of housework and child care, and that a society which maintained sex roles did not in any way have as a feature of that society the systemic dominance or superiority of one sex over the other, there would still be a generic moral defect that would remain. The defect would be that any set of sex roles would necessarily impair and retard an individual's ability to develop his or her own characteristics, talents, capacities, and potential life-plans to the extent to which he or she might desire and from which he or she might derive genuine satisfaction. Sex roles, by definition, constitute empirical and normative limits of varying degrees of strength—restrictions on what it is that one can expect to do, be, or become. As such, they are, I think, at least prima facie objectionable.

To some degree, all role-differentiated living is restrictive in this sense. Perhaps, therefore, all role differentiation in society is to some degree troublesome, and perhaps all strongly role-differentiated societies are objectionable. But the case against sex roles and the concomitant sexual differentiation they create and require need not rest upon this more controversial point. For one thing that distinguishes sex roles from many other roles is that they are wholly involuntarily assumed. One has no choice about whether one shall be born a male or female. And if it is a consequence of one's being born a male or a female that one's subsequent emotional, intellectual, and material development will be substantially controlled by this fact, then it is necessarily the case that substantial, permanent, and involuntarily assumed restraints have been imposed on some of the most central factors concerning the way one will shape and live one's life. The point to be emphasized is that this would necessarily be the case, even in the unlikely event that substantial sexual differentiation could be maintained without one sex or the other becoming dominant and developing oppressive institutions and an ideology to support that dominance and oppression. Absent some far stronger showing than seems either reasonable or possible that potential talents, abilities, interests, and the like are inevitably and irretrievably distributed between the sexes in such a way that the sex roles of the society are genuinely congruent with and facilitative of the development of those talents, abilities, interests, and the like that individuals can and do possess, sex roles are to this degree incompatible with the kind of respect which the good or the just society would accord to each of the individual persons living within it. It seems to me, therefore, that there are persuasive reasons to believe that no society which maintained what I have been describing as *substantial* sexual differentiation could plausibly be viewed as a good or just society.

What remains more of an open question is whether a society in which sex functioned in the way in which eye color does (a strictly assimilationist society in respect to sex) would be better or worse than one in which sex functioned in the way in which religious identity does in our society (a nonoppressive, more diversified or pluralistic one). For it might be argued that especially in the case of sex and even in the case of race much would be gained and nothing would be lost if the ideal society in respect to these characteristics succeeded in preserving in a nonoppressive fashion the attractive differences between males and females and the comparably attractive differences among ethnic groups. Such a society, it might be claimed, would be less bland, less homogeneous and richer in virtue of its variety.

I do not think there is any easy way to settle this question, but I do think the attractiveness of the appeal to diversity, when sex or race are concerned, is less alluring than is often supposed. The difficulty is in part one of specifying what will be preserved and what will not, and in part one of preventing the reappearance of the type of systemic dominance and subservience that produces the injustice of oppression. Suppose, for example, that it were suggested that there are aspects of being male and aspects of being female that are equally attractive and hence desirable to maintain and perpetuate: the kind of empathy that is associated with women and the kind of self-control associated with men. It does not matter what the characteristic is, the problem is one of seeing why the characteristic should be tied by the social institutions to the sex of the individuals of the society. If the characteristics are genuinely ones that all individuals ought to be encouraged to display in the appropriate circumstances, then the social institutions and ideology ought to endeavor to foster them in all individuals. If it is good for everyone to be somewhat empathetic all of the time or especially empathetic in some circumstances, or good for everyone to have a certain degree of self-control all of the time or a great deal in some circumstances, then there is no reason to preserve institutions which distribute these psychological attributes along sexual lines. And the same is true for many, if not all, vocations, activities, and ways of living. If some, but not all persons would find a life devoted to child rearing genuinely satisfying, it is good, surely, that that option be open to them. Once again, though, it is difficult to see the argument for implicitly or explicitly encouraging, teaching, or assigning to women, as opposed to men, that life simply in virtue of their sex. Thus, while substantial diversity in individual characteristics, attitudes, and ways of life is no doubt an admirable, even important feature of the good society, what remains uncertain is the necessity or the desirability of continuing to link attributes or behaviors such as these to the race or sex of individuals. And for the reasons I have tried to articulate there are significant moral arguments against any conception of the good society in which such connections are pursued and nourished in the systemic fashion required by the existence and maintenance of *sex* roles.

A Black Feminist Critique of Antidiscrimination Law

Kimberle Crenshaw

One way to approach the problem at the intersection of race and sex is to examine how courts frame and interpret the stories of Black women plaintiffs. Indeed, the way courts interpret claims made by Black women is itself part of Black women's experience; consequently, a cursory review of cases involving Black female plaintiffs is quite revealing. To illustrate the difficulties inherent in judicial treatment of intersectionality, I will consider three employment discrimination cases: *DeGraffenreid v. General Motors, Moore v. Hughes Helicopter* and *Payne v. Travenol.*[1]

In *DeGraffenreid*, five Black women brought suit against General Motors, alleging that the employer's seniority system perpetuated the effects of past discrimination against Black women. Although General Motors did not hire Black women prior to 1964, the court noted that "General Motors has hired . . . female employees for a number of years prior to the enactment of the Civil Rights Act of 1964." Because General Motors did hire women—albeit *white women*—during the period that no Black women were hired, there was, in the court's view, no sex discrimination that the seniority system could conceivably have perpetuated. Moreover, reasoning that Black women could choose to bring either a sex or a race discrimination claim, but not both, the court stated:

> The legislative history surrounding Title VII does not indicate that the goal of the statute was to create a new classification of "black women" who would have greater standing than, for example, a black male. The prospect of the creation of new classes of protected minorities, governed only by the mathematical principles of permutation and combination, clearly raises the prospect of opening the hackneyed Pandora's box.

The court's conclusion that Congress did not intend to allow Black women to make a compound claim arises from its inability to imagine that discrimination against Black women can exist independently from the experiences of white women or of Black men. Because the court was blind to this possibility, it did not question whether Congress could have meant to leave this form of discrimination unredressed. Assuming therefore that there was no distinct discrimination suffered by Black women, the court concluded that to allow plaintiffs to make a compound claim would unduly advantage Black women over Black men or white women.

This negative conclusion regarding Black women's ability to bring compound claims has not been replicated in another kind of compound discrimination case—"reverse discrimination" claims brought by white males. Interestingly, no case has been discovered in which a court denied a white male's reverse discrimination claims on similar grounds—that is, that sex and race claims cannot be combined because Congress did not intend to protect compound classes. Yet, white males challenging affirmative action program that benefit minorities and women are actually in no better position to make a race and gender claim than the Black women in *DeGraffenreid*: If white men are required to make their claims separately, they cannot prove race discrimination because white women are not discriminated against, and they cannot prove sex discrimination because Black males are not discriminated against. One would think, therefore, that the logic of *DeGraffenreid* would complicate reverse discrimination cases. That Black women's claims raise the question of compound discrimination while white males' reverse discrimination claims do not suggests that the notion of "compound class" is somehow relative or contingent on some presumed norm rather than definitive and absolute. If that norm is understood to be white male, one can understand how Black women, being "two steps removed" from being white men, are deemed to be a compound class while white men are not. Indeed, if assumptions about objectivity of law are replaced with the subjective perspective of white males, one can understand better not only why Black women are viewed as compound classes and white men are not, but also why the boundaries of sex and race discrimination doctrine are defined respectively by the experiences of white women and Black men. Consider first that when a white male imagines being a female, he probably imagines being a white female. Similarly, a white male who must project himself as Black will no doubt imagine himself to be a Black male, thereby holding constant all other characteristics except race.

Antidiscrimination law is similarly constructed from the perspective of white males. Gender discrimination, imagined from the perspective of white men, is what happens to white women; race discrimination is what happens to Black men. The dominance of the single-axis framework, most starkly represented by *DeGraffenreid*, not only marginalizes Black women but simultaneously privileges the subjectivity of white men. Under this view, Black women are protected only to the extent that their experiences coincide with those of either of the two groups. Where their experiences are distinct, Black women will encounter difficulty articulating their claims as long as approaches prevail which completely obscure problems of intersectionality.

Moore v. Hughes Helicopters, Inc. presents a different way in which courts fail to understand or recognize Black women's claims. *Moore* is typical of cases in which courts refused to certify Black females as class representative in race *and* sex discrimination actions. In *Moore*, the plaintiff alleged that the employer, Hughes Helicopter, practiced race and sex discrimination in promotions to upper-level craft positions and to supervisory jobs. Moore introduced statistical evidence establishing a significant disparity between men and women, and somewhat less of a disparity between Black and white men in supervisory jobs.

Affirming the district court's refusal to certify Moore as the class representative in the sex discrimination complaint on behalf of all women at Hughes, the Ninth Circuit noted approvingly:

> . . . Moore had never claimed before the EEOC that she was discriminated against as a female, *but only* as a Black female. . . . [T]his raised serious doubts as to Moore's ability to adequately represent white female employees.

The curious logic in *Moore* reveals not only the narrow scope of antidiscrimination doctrine and its failure to embrace intersectionality, but also the centrality of white female experiences in the conceptualization of gender discrimination. The court rejected Moore's bid to represent all females apparently because her attempt to specify her race was seen as being at odds with the standard allegation that the employer simply discriminated "against females." However, the court failed to see that the absence of a racial referent does not necessarily mean that the claim being made is a more inclusive one. A white woman claiming discrimination against females may be in no better position to represent all women than a Black woman who claims discrimination as a Black female and wants to represent all females. The court's preferred articulation of "against females" is not necessarily more inclusive—it just appears to be so because the racial contours of the claim are not specified.

The court's preference for "against females" rather than "against Black females" reveals the implicit grounding of white female experiences in the doctrinal conceptualization of sex discrimination. For white women, claiming sex discrimination is simply a statement that but for gender, they would not have been disadvantaged. For them there is no need to specify discrimination as *white* females because their race does not contribute to the disadvantage for which they seek redress. The view of discrimination that is derived from this grounding takes race privilege as a given.

Discrimination against a white female is thus the standard sex discrimination claim; claims that diverge from this standard appear to present some sort of hybrid claim. More significantly, because Black females' claims are seen as hybrid, they sometimes cannot represent those who may have "pure" claims of sex discrimination. The effect of this approach is that even though a challenged policy or practice may clearly discriminate against all females, the fact that it has particularly harsh consequences for Black females places Black plaintiffs at odds with white females.

The *Moore* court also denied the plaintiffs' bid to represent Black males, leaving Moore with the task of supporting her race and sex discrimination claims with statistical evidence of discrimination against Black females alone. Because she was unable to represent white women or Black men, she could not use overall statistics on sex disparity at Hughes, nor could she use statistics on race. Proving her claim using statistics on Black women alone was no small task, due to the fact that she was bringing the suit under a disparate impact theory of discrimination.

The court's rulings on Moore's sex and race claim left her with such a small statistical sample that even if she had proved that there were qualified Black women, she could not have shown discrimination under a disparate impact theory. *Moore* illustrates yet another way that antidiscrimination doctrine essentially erases Black women's distinct experiences and, as a result, deems their discrimination complaints groundless.

Finally, Black female plaintiffs have sometimes encountered difficulty in their efforts to win certification as class representatives in some race discrimination actions. This problem typically arises in cases where statistics suggest significant disparities between Black and white workers and further disparities between Black men and Black women. Courts in some cases have denied certification based on logic that mirrors the rationale in *Moore:* The sex disparities between Black men and Black women created such conflicting interests that Black women could not possibly represent Black men adequately. In one such case, *Payne v. Travenol,* two Black female plaintiffs alleging race discrimination brought a class action suit on behalf of all Black employees at a pharmaceutical plant. The court refused, however, to allow the plaintiffs to represent Black males and granted the defendant's request to narrow the class to Black women only. Ultimately, the district court found that there had been extensive racial discrimination at the plant and awarded back pay and constructive seniority to the class of Black female employees. But, despite its finding of general race discrimination, the court refused to extend the remedy to Black men for fear that their conflicting interests would not be adequately addressed; the Fifth Circuit affirmed.[2]

Even though *Travenol* was a partial victory for Black women, the case specifically illustrates how antidiscrimination doctrine generally creates a dilemma for Black women. It forces them to choose between specifically articulating the intersectional aspects of their subordination, thereby risking their ability to represent Black men, or ignoring intersectionality in order to state a claim that would not lead to the exclusion of Black men. When one considers the political consequences of this dilemma, there is little wonder that many people within the Black community view the specific articulation of Black women's interests as dangerously divisive.

In sum, several courts have proved unable to deal with intersectionality, although for contrasting reasons. In *DeGraffenreid,* the court refused to recognize the possibility of compound discrimination against Black women and analyzed their claim using the employment of white women as the historical base. As a consequence, the employment experiences of white women obscured the distinct discrimination that Black women experienced.

Conversely, in *Moore,* the court held that a Black woman could not use statistics reflecting the overall sex disparity in supervisory and upper-level labor jobs because she had not claimed discrimination as a woman, but "only" as a Black woman. The court would not entertain the notion that discrimination experienced by Black women is indeed sex discrimination—provable through disparate impact statistics on women.

Finally, courts such as the one in *Travenol* have held that Black women cannot represent an entire class of Blacks due to presumed class conflicts in cases where sex additionally disadvantaged Black women. As a result, in the few cases where Black women are allowed to use overall statistics indicating racially disparate treatment, Black men may not be able to share in the remedy.

Perhaps it appears to some that I have offered inconsistent criticisms of how Black women are treated in antidiscrimination law: I seem to be saying that in one case, Black women's claims were rejected and their experiences obscured because the court refused to acknowledge that the employment experience of Black women can be distinct from that of white women, while in other cases, the interests of Black women were harmed because Black women's claims were viewed as so distinct from the claims of either white women or Black men that the court denied to Black females representation of the larger class. It seems that I have to say that Black women are the same and harmed by being treated differently, or that they are different and harmed by being treated the same. But I cannot say both.

This apparent contradiction is but another manifestation of the conceptual limitations of the single-issue analyses that intersectionality challenges. The point is that Black women can experience discrimination in any number of ways and that the contradiction arises from our assumptions that their claims of exclusion must be unidirectional. Consider an analogy to traffic in an intersection, coming and going in all four directions. Discrimination, like traffic through an intersection, may flow in one direction, and it may flow in another. If an accident happens in an intersection, it can be caused by cars traveling from any number of directions and, sometimes, from all of them. Similarly, if a Black woman is harmed because she is in the intersection, her injury could result from sex discrimination or race discrimination or both.

Providing legal relief only when Black women prove that their claims are based on race or on sex is analogous to calling an ambulance for the victim only after the driver responsible for the injuries is identified. But it is not always easy to identify the driver: sometimes the skid marks and the injuries simply indicate that they occurred simultaneously, frustrating efforts to determine which driver caused the harm. In these cases the tendency seems to be that no driver is held responsible, no treatment is administered, and the involved parties simply get back in their cars and zoom away.

I am suggesting that Black women can experience discrimination in ways that are both similar to and different from those experienced by white women and Black men. Black women sometimes experience discrimination in ways similar to white women's experiences; sometimes they share very similar experiences with Black men. Yet often they experience double discrimination—the combined effects of practices which discriminate on the basis of race, and on the basis of sex. And sometimes, they experience discrimination as Black women—not the sum of race and sex discrimination, but as Black women.

DeGraffenreid, Moore, and *Travenol* are doctrinal manifestations of a common political and theoretical approach to discrimination which operates to marginalize Black women. Unable to grasp the importance of Black women's intersectional experiences, not only courts, but feminist and civil rights thinkers as well have treated Black women in ways that deny both the unique compoundedness of their situation and the centrality of their experiences to the larger classes of women and Blacks. Consequently, their needs and perspectives have been relegated to the margin of the feminist and Black liberationist agendas. While it could be argued that this marginalization represents an absence of political will to include Black women, I believe that it reflects an uncritical and disturbing acceptance of dominant ways of thinking about discrimination.

Underlying dominant conceptions of discrimination, which have been challenged by a developing approach called critical race theory, is a view that the wrong which antidiscrimination law addresses is the use of race or gender factors to interfere with decisions that would otherwise be fair or neutral. This process-based definition is not grounded in a bottom-up commitment to improve the substantive conditions for those who are victimized by the interplay of numerous factors. Instead, the dominant message of antidiscrimination law is that it will regulate only the limited extent to which race or sex interferes with the process of determining outcomes. This narrow objective is facilitated by the top-down strategy of using a singular "but for" analysis to ascertain the effects of race or sex. Because the scope of antidiscrimination law is so limited, sex and race discrimination have come to be defined in terms of the experiences of those who are privileged *but for* their racial or sexual characteristics. Put differently, the paradigm of sex discrimination tends to be based on the experiences of white women; the model of race discrimination tends to be based on the experiences of the most privileged Blacks. Notions of what constitutes race and sex discrimination are, as a result, narrowly tailored to embrace only a small set of circumstances which do not explicitly include the experiences of Black women.

To the extent that this general description is accurate, the following analogy can be useful in describing how Black women are marginalized in the interface between antidiscrimination law and race and gender hierarchies: imagine a basement which contains all people who are disadvantaged on the basis of race, sex, class, sexual preference, age and/or physical ability. These people are stacked—feet standing on shoulders—with those on the bottom being disadvantaged by the full array of factors, up to the very top, where the heads of all those disadvantaged by a singular factor brush up against the ceiling. Their ceiling is actually the floor above on which only those who are *not* disadvantaged in any way reside. In efforts to correct some aspects of domination, those above the ceiling admit from the basement only those who can say that "but for" the ceiling, they too would be in the upper room. A hatch is developed through which those placed immediately below can crawl. Yet this hatch is generally available only to those who—due to the singularity of their burden and their otherwise privileged position relative to those below—are in the position to crawl through. Those who are multiply burdened are generally left below unless they can somehow pull themselves into the groups that are permitted to squeeze through the hatch.

As this analogy translates for Black women, the problem is that they can receive protection only to the extent that their experiences are recognizably similar to those whose experiences tend to be reflected in antidiscrimination doctrine. If Black women cannot conclusively say that "but for" their race or "but for" their gender they would be treated differently, they are not invited to climb through the hatch but told to wait in the unprotected margin until they can be absorbed into the broader, protected categories of race and sex.

Despite the narrow scope of this dominant conception of discrimination and its tendency to marginalize those whose experiences cannot be described within its tightly drawn parameters, this approach has been regarded as the appropriate framework for addressing a range of problems. In much of feminist theory and, to some extent, in antiracist politics, this framework is reflected in the belief that sexism or racism can be meaningfully discussed without paying attention to the lives of those other than the race-, gender-, or class-privileged. As a result, both feminist theory and antiracist politics have been organized, in part, around the equation of sexism with what happens to white women and the equation of racism with what happens to the Black middle class or to Black men.

Looking at historical and contemporary issues in both the feminist and the civil rights communities, one can find ample evidence of how both communities' acceptance of the dominant framework of discrimination has hindered the development of an adequate theory and praxis to address problems of intersectionality. Not only does this adoption of a single-issue framework for discrimination marginalize Black women within the very movements that claim them as part of their constituency but it also makes the elusive goal of ending racism and patriarchy even more difficult to attain.

. . .

Endnotes

[1] 673 F.2d 798 (5th Cir. 1983). These are all statutory cases pursuant to Title VII of the Civil Rights Act of 1964, 42 U.S.C. §2000e, *et seq.* as amended (1982).

[2] 416 F. Supp. 248 (N.D. Miss. 1976), aff'd., 673 F.2d 798 (5th Cir. 1982).

Study Questions

1. Do you agree that the prohibition on same-sex marriage, at stake in *Grutter*, is an instance of discrimination based on sex? Consider the following two arguments: (1) "There is no sex discrimination in this case, for neither sex is being favored: members of both sexes are treated equally in the sense that men cannot marry men and women

cannot marry women." (2) "There is sex discrimination in this case, for the law prohibits a man from doing what a woman may do—that is, marry a man. Thus, the law discriminates against men because they are men." (A parallel argument shows that the law discriminates against women because they are women.) Which of these arguments is correct, in your view?

2. Does Sunstein convincingly make his case that bans on same-sex marriage are a way of reinforcing a gender "caste" system or hierarchy, analogous to the racial hierarchy implicit (so he argues) in anti-miscegenation laws?

3. Opponents of same-sex marriage in Hawaii argued that the state's compelling interest in maintaining the institution of marriage is procreation; hence, they reasoned, the restriction to heterosexual unions is entirely justified. Is this a good argument? If procreation is the reason for preserving marriage, then could marriage licenses still be granted to infertile, heterosexual couples? Or to elderly couples?

4. If same-sex unions are permitted on the grounds that to forbid them would be discriminatory, what about those who wish to enter into a polygamous relationship? Could they maintain that bans on polygamy must be lifted for similar reasons? What about consensual, incestuous relationships?

5. Read *U.S. v. Virginia* in the "Cases For Further Reflection." VMI won its case initially at appellate level, though this verdict was overturned by the Supreme Court. The appellate court had found that coeducation at VMI would change the nature of the educational experience furnished there, and had therefore concluded that it is not "maleness" that justifies the program but "the homogeneity of gender . . . regardless of which sex is considered." Does the state have an interest in restricting such "adversative" training to men only?

6. In *U.S. v. Virginia*, why does the Supreme Court reject Virginia's argument that the "adversative" method of military training at VMI requires an all-male environment? Why, according to the Court, is an education at VWIL not comparable to one at VMI?

7. What does Minow mean by the "dilemma of difference"? Can you think of an example of such a dilemma other than those given by Minow?

8. According to Minow, dilemmas of difference rest on five unacknowledged assumptions. What are these assumptions? Are these assumptions made only by courts, or do we all make them?

9. Why does Wasserstrom think the assimilationist ideal is less attractive in the case of sex than in the case of race?

10. How does Wasserstrom respond to the objection against assimilationism that sex-role differentiation is necessary because it is almost universally present throughout the range of human culture?

11. Is sex discrimination bad or wrong for the same reasons as racial discrimination? Is sex discrimination rooted in assumptions of inferiority and prejudice? Do the various familiar stereotypes of women (that they are weak, overly emotional, dependent, less intellectual than men) add up to the suspicion that laws that maintain (or even encourage) these stereotypes are motivated by a hatred of women, similar to race hatred in the case of Blacks?

12. In 1972 the Congress proposed an amendment to the Constitution stating that "equality of rights under the law shall not be denied or abridged by the United States or by any State on account of sex." Because it was not ratified by a sufficient number of states (some even withdrew their initial support), the Equal Rights Amendment (ERA) failed to become part of the Constitution. What changes might it have made to the law of sex discrimination? If you had been a judge faced with interpreting the amendment, what would you have taken to be its meaning? It is worth noting that some opponents of the ERA sought to defeat it by arguing that it would lead ultimately to some of the same consequences that Wasserstrom says would follow in an "assimilationist" society. Would the ERA have required an assimilationist society? Does the equal protection clause of the Fourteenth Amendment require assimilationism?

13. Hooters of America, Inc. operates a chain of restaurants. For years, the company has had a strict policy of hiring only women to work as servers in its restaurants. The women hired by the company are called "Hooters Girls," and are chosen (among other things) for their large bust size and how good they look in a skimpy uniform. The Equal Employment Opportunity Com-

mission filed a gender bias complaint against Hooters. The company reportedly was willing to invest as much as $10 million in resisting the complaint. "A little good clean wholesome female sexuality," according to a company spokesperson, "is what our customers come for." Company supporters argue that the EEOC's bias suit was misplaced and that its reasoning would dictate that "men would have to be allowed to try out for the Dallas Cheerleaders." Critics of Hooters respond that similar arguments were once used by airlines to justify hiring only women as flight attendants (for example, women's unique "nurturing" abilities were essential to comfort passengers); they also argue that female waitresses make up a disproportionately large segment of servers in the poorly paying fast-food sector. Should customer preferences be used to justify sex-based hiring? And does such hiring necessarily reflect a negative stereotype?

14. Many states are currently experiencing a sharp rise in prison populations; many new prisons are under construction, and states are hiring to fill a variety of jobs associated with these facilities. Imagine that a number of women have recently applied with the state department of corrections for positions as correctional officers, whose basic role is to serve as prison guards. Correctional officer jobs are highly sought after; since they are much better compensated than other positions with the department. The state, however, refuses to hire the female applicants, pointing to a state policy that assigns guards to maximum-security facilities based upon their gender; since the overwhelming majority of the state's prisoners are men, women are virtually excluded from correctional officer positions. The state defends its policy by arguing that the essence of a correctional officer's job is to maintain prison security and that this job simply could not be adequately performed by a woman, regardless of her size, strength, and ability. Sex offenders, for example, who have assaulted women before might well do so again if access to female guards were possible; and other inmates, "deprived of the normal heterosexual environment," might assault women guards "just because they were women." The female applicants insist that the state's reasoning is simply a rationalization for its perpetuation of sexist thinking: namely, that women are unwitting

sex objects who need to be protected from male inmates. Does the state policy at issue here discriminate against women? How would you decide that question? Suppose the job of a correctional officer were to include observing prisoners as they took showers. Is it justifiable to limit this duty to members of the same sex as the prisoners?

15. In the 1980s, the Equal Employment Opportunity Commission (EEOC) brought charges against the Sears, Roebuck corporation, alleging that the giant retailer had, over a period of a decade or more, engaged in a nationwide pattern of discrimination against women by failing to promote its female employees into commission sales positions on the same basis as males and by paying female management employees less than similarly situated male employees. Commission selling at Sears typically involved high-cost merchandise such as major appliances, furnaces, and roofing, whereas merchandise sold on a non-commission basis was generally low-cost and included such items as clothing, jewelry, and cosmetics. Non-commission salespeople were paid a straight hourly wage. Commission sales offered greater financial reward. The EEOC relied heavily upon statistical evidence revealing a significant gender disparity among Sears' sales positions, with the great majority of the commission sales positions being held by men. Such a disparity went beyond what would be expected under fair employment conditions. Sears admitted these facts but contested the EEOC explanation, arguing instead that women had little interest in commission sales but preferred to sell soft-line products, such as clothing and housewares, rather than fencing, refrigeration equipment, or tires. Women also like jobs that are less stressful, risky, and competitive than commission selling tends to be, Sears claimed, because women prefer social contact and the cooperative aspects of the workplace. Does evidence of the disparity between men and women in commission sales jobs reflect a sexist bias on the part of Sears, resulting in far fewer opportunities presented to women than to men? Or does the evidence merely reflect the general preferences of most women in society? Sears had developed a statement of qualifications for commission sales: the salesperson should be aggressive and competitive, have lots of drive, and have technical knowledge and fluency. Does this profile accurately state the qualifications necessary for the job? Or does it describe the type of people who had been doing the job up to that point, almost all of whom were men?

16. A federal court ruled in 1997 that the Alabama prison system did not violate the Equal Protection clause by placing only male inmates in chain gangs. The court held that excluding women from working while shackled was not unconstitutional, due to the low ratio of female to male prisoners in Alabama: of 20,000 state prisoners, only 776 were female. Is this a convincing argument? Can male prisoners make an equal protection argument that *they* are being treated unequally?

17. Ms. Feeney, a woman who was not a veteran, worked for twelve years as a Massachusetts state employee. She had taken and passed a number of civil service exams for better jobs, but because of a veterans' preference law in Massachusetts, each time she was ranked below male veterans who had earned lower test scores than she had. Under the Massachusetts law, all veterans who qualified for state civil service jobs had to be considered for appointment ahead of any qualified non-veteran. The law defined a veteran as "any person, male or female, including a nurse," who was honorably discharged from the armed forces after at least ninety days of active service, at least one day of which was during "wartime." The law operated to the overwhelming advantage of males. Feeney brought suit in federal court, alleging that the state's absolute preference for veterans constituted discrimination and thus violated the Equal Protection Clause of the Fourteenth Amendment. Should she win, in your view? [See *Personnel Administrator of Massachusetts v. Feeney*, 442 U.S. 256 (1979).]

C. Equality, Parenthood, and Family Law

Previous sections of this chapter have dealt with problems of racial equality, discrimination with regard to gender-roles, and the law's treatment of same-sex partnerships. Related to and often intertwined with these issues are problems in the area known as family law.

It is obvious that many dimensions of family life find expression in and are shaped by the law. The formation and dissolution of marriages, the distribution of property and wealth, and the rights of and responsibilities to children are all centrally configured and clarified by the law. Consider, for example, the very definition of the family. What is a family for purposes of the law? And what is the justification for thinking of families as having a degree of legal salience? In *Village of Belle Terre v. Boraas*, a small group of unrelated college students had been living in a house in a quiet bedroom community.[1] The students challenged a local land ordinance restricting land use to one-family dwellings, where "family" was defined to exclude more that two unrelated people living together. Could the students have argued that they were just "one big, happy family"? In another case, the city of East Cleveland, in an apparent effort to minimize traffic and parking congestion and prevent overcrowding, passed an ordinance limiting occupancy of a dwelling unit to members of a single family—but "family" here meant a nuclear family of parents and children. The plaintiff lived with her son and two grandsons, and was convicted for failing to evict her grandsons as "illegal occupants."[2] What justification could the city give for its ordinance? Is the city guilty of discrimination against those living in extended family situations? Should the constitution of the family—and who is or is not a member of it—be a purely private matter?

_____

[1] 416 U.S. 1 (1974).
[2] See *Moore v. City of East Cleveland*, 431 U.S. 494 (1977).

Issues in Family Law

The scope of family law is wide. Some of the issues dealt with in family law include: (1) What is the justification of the institution of marriage? Who should be allowed to enter into a marriage? What benefits should marital status confer upon the parties? Typically, the law takes notice of marriage in various ways: by conferring rights pertaining to child-rearing and adoption, by securing survivors' benefits and providing insurance coverage, and by granting leaves from work for the birth or death of a family member, among many other provisions. But should any of these benefits be available to domestic partners who are unmarried cohabitants? What conditions, if any, should the community place upon the dissolution of marriages? (2) What barriers may the law erect regarding procreation? May the law permissibly restrict certain forms of technologically assisted reproduction, for instance? Ought society to permit surrogate parenting contracts? (3) What limitations or restrictions may legitimately be placed upon the power of parents vis-à-vis their children? How much freedom may parents have, for example, in directing their children's education or in making decisions about their health and medical needs? (4) What regulations should govern the adoption of children or the terms of child custody?

Conceptions of Family Law

In the book from which her selection is taken here, law professor Janet Dolgin explores the development of two competing conceptions of the family, traceable through a series of cases and doctrines. The models have differing understandings of, and implications for, how families are constituted, changed, or dissolved. One view, which Dolgin calls the "traditional" model, sees the family as a unit determined primarily by biological connections and a marital status conferred by the law for the good of the larger community. Since the institution of marriage is, in this view, justified by a utilitarian appeal to the common good, family members have fewer options and choices. Historically, for example, marriages were treated as nearly indissoluble, with few grounds considered as a basis for divorce. The terms of marriage were largely set independently of the marital partners; they were not negotiated by them. In the "modern" view, by contrast, a family is less like an institution of fixed status and more like a private arrangement between contracting parties. A marriage involves limited commitments undertaken for the sake of mutual advantage. Here the autonomy of the parties is the most salient feature of family life. The parties themselves may set the terms of their relationships and can mutually abrogate their agreement should they chose to do so.

Existing family law is an unsteady blend of both of these models, and this instability is reflected in many areas. Antenuptial agreements, for example, in which the partners set out their respective claims to the property each brings to the impending marriage, were less common in times when marriage was more traditionally viewed as a status and contracts "in contemplation of divorce" were seen as improper. Divorce itself is widely tolerated to the degree that marriage is seen as a contractual arrangement; and so-called "no-fault" divorces, where the marriage is ended by a simple decision to conclude it, are now regarded as socially acceptable. The distribution of marital property upon dissolution is also handled differently by the two models. Traditionally, the law often required that property go to the spouse in whose name title was held. Since this was nearly always the husband, these traditional arrangements often left former wives (and their dependent children) with little or no property. Many who support the "contract" model of the family argue that the law of marriage should follow community property rules, whereby property belongs to both spouses and thus must be divided between them no matter who formerly owned the property or whose funds had been used to acquire it. Where children are concerned, the traditional view, conceiving of marriage as a union of male and female and the consecration of a sexual relationship, has been less amenable to surrogate parenting relationships and to adoption by gay and lesbian couples. And, since marriage traditionally reflected widespread social understandings and expectations rooted in fixed gender roles, same-sex unions were rejected as unacceptable. Under the

contract view, however, choice of partner and lifestyle are given greater weight. Thus, for example, cohabiting individuals may have enforceable rights against one another, even though they are not married.[3]

The remainder of the readings in this chapter focus on two specific issues in family law: the rights of unwed biological fathers and non-marital children to maintain a relationship; and the definition of parental status in light of emerging reproductive technologies.

Michael H. v. Gerald D.

In *Michael H. v. Gerald D.*, the case which opens our readings, the U.S. Supreme Court upheld a California statute providing that "the issue of a wife cohabiting with her husband is conclusively presumed to be a child of the marriage." Michael had fathered a daughter, Victoria, out of wedlock during an affair with Carole. When Carole returned to her husband, Gerald, Michael was cut off from his daughter, since California law operated to make Gerald the legal father of the child. Michael challenged the law.

What rights should unwed mothers and fathers have in adoption proceedings? Does "equal protection of the laws" require that both should have equal rights? Should the law give priority to the rights of one? What are the elements that should matter legally for the purposes of establishing a parental relationship? The Court's ruling in *Michael H.* is scrutinized by legal scholar J. M. Balkin. Balkin specifically attacks Justice Scalia's opinion, which placed much reliance upon the "history and tradition" of legal marriage. Balkin questions why the "traditions" of protecting the marital unit must take priority over the bond between parent and child.

Parenthood, Reproductive Technology, and the Law

Advances in reproductive medicine have made possible ways of creating a human being that would scarcely have been imaginable to people of earlier generations. The process of artificial insemination, in which ova are combined with sperm outside the uterus, can now be coupled with other techniques in

---

[3] See *Marvin v. Marvin*, 557 P.2d 106 (Cal. 1976).

such a way that many people could be involved in the process that results in the birth of one child. It is this fragmentation of the reproductive process that has created many issues concerning the "parenthood" of the several parties involved. Commercial "surrogate mothering" arrangements, for example, involve a woman who agrees to be inseminated and birth a child, and then to surrender the child to a couple who agree to act as the child's custodial parents. In these cases, the child is often the product of the husband's sperm; however, as the *Johnson v. Calvert* case demonstrates, it is possible for the husband and the wife each to donate gametes, or reproductive material, which is then combined in a laboratory and implanted in the uterus of another woman who agrees to carry to term and birth the baby, who is entirely unrelated to her genetically. (Even more complex arrangements are possible: For example, ova and sperm could be collected from two anonymous donors and the resulting embryo implanted into the uterus of another woman, who then births the child and turns him or her over to two other persons, who then act as the custodial parents. Five individuals thus collaborate to produce and raise one human being.)

The law has predictably struggled to keep up with these permutations of the reproductive process. Consider artificial insemination. Once AID ("artificial insemination by donor") became widely available, the law was changed to reflect that reality. The Uniform Parentage Act (adopted in most states) stipulates that when a woman is inseminated with donor sperm, the woman's husband (and not the donor) is treated in law as if he were the natural father. But the Act did not settle other problems: Suppose *in vitro* fertilization is performed using a sperm source and the ova of one woman; the resulting embryo is then placed in the uterus of another woman. Who are the parents? Under existing law, the sperm donor would not be a father (unless he is married to the woman into whom the embryo is implanted); his parental claims are nullified. Should the law also nullify the parental status of the "ovum" donor? Should providing an ovum be regarded as an activity on a par with providing sperm? (Unlike sperm donation, ovum donation involves drugs and an invasive surgical procedure.) If the ovum donor is not treated as the mother, should the "uterine donor" be so regarded? While it is true that there is no male activity comparable to carrying a baby to term and birthing it, should the law regard someone who has no genetic tie to the baby as the mother? Even when parentage is not at issue, other legal and moral

problems can still arise. Traditionally, a man who had no living offspring upon his demise had no natural children who could inherit his estate. Suppose a husband's sperm is collected and stored ("frozen") until it is later used by his wife to conceive a child. But before the conception can take place, the husband dies. Does the child become the heir to his or her father's estate? Or consider a procedure common at fertility clinics. It is now possible to harvest ova from women, combine them with sperm in a laboratory setting, and then cryopreserve (or "freeze") the resulting embryos, thus arresting embryonic development at an early stage. For couples with difficulty in conceiving, this procedure can be used to create a number of embryos, some of which are then implanted into the uterus with the hope of achieving viable pregnancy. But suppose the couple separate and divorce before the "frozen" embryos can be implanted. What, then, is the legal status of the embryos? Are they property? If so, to whom do they belong?[4]

Johnson v. Calvert and Beyond

Mark Calvert and his wife, Chris, were unable to conceive a child because Chris had undergone a hysterectomy. Ova harvested from her ovaries, however, were combined at a fertility clinic with sperm from Mark. The Calverts had contracted with Anna Johnson to assist them. Johnson agreed to have the Calverts' embryo implanted in her uterus, in exchange for $10,000, paid in installments. Johnson would give birth and relinquish all claims regarding the child, whom Mark and Chris would then raise. But mounting misunderstandings during pregnancy led Johnson to threaten to refuse to give up the child. Mark and Chris filed suit asking for a declaration that they were the legal parents; Johnson filed a countersuit asking to be declared the mother. Thus the California court was faced with the dilemma: Who is the mother? The woman who gestates and births the child? Or the woman whose egg is implanted in the woman who gestates and gives birth?

Mark argues that maternity ought to be established on the same basis as paternity—that is, by a blood test. Since Mark's wife, Chris, is genetically consanguineous with the child, she is the mother. Anna responds that Mark is, in effect, a semen donor, and a

---

[4] See *Davis v. Davis*, 842 S.W.2d 588 (Supreme Court of Tennessee, 1992).

semen donor's paternity rights are nullified and vested in the spouse of the recipient of the semen (which would be Anna's husband). Hence, Mark is not the father. Anna relies on a provision of California law which stipulates that the "natural mother" is the person who gives birth to the child. Hence, Anna concludes, she is the mother. Drawing distinctions between gestational motherhood and "intending" or social motherhood, the court decides that Chris must be the mother under California law.

The final reading is from medical ethicist and law professor Alex Capron, who critiques both the result in *Calvert* and an even more complicated subsequent case, *In re Buzzanca*.

Michael H. *v. Gerald* D.

SCALLA, J., announced the judgment of the Court and delivered an opinion in which the Chief Justice joined, and in all but note [f] of which Justice O'Connor and Justice Kennedy joined.

[Carole D., while married to Gerald D., had an affair with Michael H. In September 1980, she gave birth to Victoria. Gerald was listed as father on the birth certificate and always treated Victoria as his daughter. However, a blood test indicated with near certainty (98%) that Michael was Victoria's father. Carole and Michael intermittently lived together, and he presented Victoria as his daughter. In turn, Victoria apparently referred to him as "Daddy."

After Carole and Victoria permanently returned to Gerald, Michael's attempts to visit Victoria were rebuffed. He therefore filed a filiation action in a California court to establish his paternity and right to visitation. Victoria, represented by a guardian ad litem, cross-complained that she had a right to maintain a relationship with both "fathers."

A court-ordered psychological exam recommended that Michael be allowed continued contact as long as Carole retained sole custody of Victoria. At this point, Gerald intervened and moved for summary judgment on the ground that there were no triable issues of fact as to Victoria's paternity. He invoked Cal. Evid. Code §621, which provides that "the issue of a wife cohabiting with her husband, . . . is conclusively presumed to be a child of the marriage," unless within two years of the birth, paternity has been established in another man.

The Superior Court rejected Michael and Victoria's constitutional challenges to §621, and denied their motions for continued visitation. On appeal, Michael and Victoria raised a due process challenge to the statute, but the California Court of Appeals affirmed the lower court judgment and upheld the statute.]

The California statute that is the subject of this litigation is, in substance, more than a century old. . . .

Michael was seeking to be declared the father of Victoria. The immediate benefit he evidently sought to obtain from that status was visitation rights. . . . But if Michael were successful in being declared the father, other rights would follow—most importantly, the right to be considered as the parent who should have custody, a status which "embrace(s) the sum of parental rights with respect to the rearing of a child." All parental rights, including visitation, were automatically denied by denying Michael status as the father. . . . The [California courts] held that California law denies visitation, against the wishes of the mother, to a putative father who has been prevented by §621 from establishing his paternity.

Michael contends as a matter of substantive due process that because he has established a parental relationship with Victoria, protection of Gerald's and Carole's marital union is an insufficient state interest to support termination of that relationship. This argument is, of course, predicated on the assertion that Michael has a constitutionally protected liberty interest in his relationship with Victoria.

It is an established part of our constitutional jurisprudence that the term "liberty" in the Due Process Clause extends beyond freedom from physical restraint.

---

491 U.S. 110 (1989), United States Supreme Court.

In an attempt to limit and guide interpretation of the Clause, we have insisted not merely that the interest denominated as a "liberty" be "fundamental" (a concept that, in isolation, is hard to objectify), but also that it be an interest traditionally protected by our society. As we have put it, the Due Process Clause affords only those protections "so rooted in the traditions and conscience of our people as to be ranked as fundamental." Our cases reflect "continual insistence upon respect for the teachings of history [and] solid recognition of the basic values that underlie our society. . . ." *Griswold.*

This insistence that the asserted liberty interest be rooted in history and tradition is evident, as elsewhere, in our cases according constitutional protection to certain parental rights. Michael reads [our prior cases] as establishing that a liberty interest is created by biological fatherhood plus an established parental relationship—factors that exist in the present case as well. We think that distorts the rationale of those cases. As we view them, they rest not upon such isolated factors but upon the historic respect—indeed, sanctity would not be too strong a term—traditionally accorded to the relationships that develop within the unitary family.

Thus, the legal issue in the present case reduces to whether the relationship between persons in the situation of Michael and Victoria has been treated as a protected family unit under the historic practices of our society, or whether on any other basis it has been accorded special protection. We think it impossible to find that it has. In fact, quite to the contrary, our traditions have protected the marital family (Gerald, Carole, and the child they acknowledge to be theirs) against the sort of claim Michael asserts.

The presumption of legitimacy was a fundamental principle of the common law. Traditionally, that presumption could be rebutted only by proof that a husband was incapable of procreation or had had no access to his wife during the relevant period. . . . And, under the common law both in England and here, "neither husband nor wife [could] be a witness to prove access or nonaccess." The primary policy rationale underlying the common law's severe restrictions on rebuttal of the presumption appears to have been an aversion to declaring children illegitimate, thereby depriving them of rights of inheritance and succession, and likely making them wards of the state. A secondary policy concern was the interest in promoting the "peace and tranquility of States and families," a goal that is obviously impaired by facilitating suits against husband and wife asserting that their children are illegitimate. . . .

We have found nothing in the older sources, nor in the older cases, addressing specifically the power of the natural father to assert parental rights over a child born into a woman's existing marriage with another man. Since it is Michael's burden to establish that such a power (at least where the natural father has established a relationship with the child) is so deeply embedded within our traditions as to be a fundamental right, the lack of evidence alone might defeat his case. But the evidence shows that even in modern times— when . . . the rigid protection of the marital family has in other respects been relaxed—the ability of a person in Michael's position to claim paternity has not been generally acknowledged. . . .

Moreover, even if it were clear that one in Michael's position generally possesses, and has generally always possessed, standing to challenge the marital child's legitimacy, that would still not establish Michael's case. As noted earlier, what is at issue here is not entitlement to a state pronouncement that Victoria was begotten by Michael. It is no conceivable denial of constitutional right for a State to decline to declare facts unless some legal consequence hinges upon the requested declaration. What Michael asserts here is a right to have himself declared the natural father and thereby to obtain parental prerogatives. What he must establish, therefore, is not that our society has traditionally allowed a natural father in his circumstances to establish paternity, but that it has traditionally accorded such a father parental rights, or at least has not traditionally denied them. Even if the law in all States had always been that the entire world could challenge the marital presumption and obtain a declaration as to who was the natural father, that would not advance Michael's claim. Thus, it is ultimately irrelevant, even for purposes of determining current social attitudes towards the alleged substantive right Michael asserts, that the present law in a number of States appears to allow the natural father—including the natural father who has not established a relationship with the child—the theoretical power to rebut the marital presumption. What counts is whether the States in fact award substantive parental rights to the natural father of a child conceived within and born into an extant marital union that wishes to embrace the child. We are not aware of a single case, old or new, that has done so. This is not the stuff of which fundamental rights qualifying as liberty interests are made. . . .

We do not accept Justice Brennan's criticism that this result "squashes" the liberty that consists of "the freedom not to conform." It seems to us that reflects the erroneous view that there is only one side to this controversy—that one disposition can expand a "liberty" of sorts without contracting an equivalent "liberty" on the other side. Such a happy choice is rarely available. Here, to provide protection to an adulterous natural father is to deny protection to a marital father, and vice versa. If Michael has a "freedom not to conform" (whatever that means), Gerald must equivalently have a "freedom to conform." One of them will pay a price for asserting that "freedom"—Michael by being unable to act as father of the child he has adulterously begotten, or Gerald by being unable to preserve the integrity of the traditional family unit he and Victoria have established. Our disposition does not choose between these two "freedoms," but leaves that to the people of California. . . .

We have never had occasion to decide whether a child has a liberty interest, symmetrical with that of her parent, in maintaining her filial relationship. We need not do so here because, even assuming that such a right exists, Victoria's claim must fail. Victoria's due process challenge is, if anything, weaker than Michael's. Her basic claim is not that California has erred in preventing her from establishing that Michael, not Gerald, should stand as her legal father. Rather, she claims a due process right to maintain filial relationships with both Michael and Gerald. This assertion merits little discussion, for, whatever the merits of the guardian ad litem's belief that such an arrangement can be of great psychological benefit to a child, the claim that a State must recognize multiple fatherhood has no support in the history or traditions of this country. Moreover, even if we were to construe Victoria's argument as forwarding the lesser proposition that, whatever her status vis-à-vis Gerald, she has a liberty interest in maintaining a filial relationship with her natural father, Michael, we find that, at best, her claim is the obverse of Michael's and fails for the same reasons.

BRENNAN, J., with whom Marshall and Blackmun, JJ., join, dissenting.

Once we recognized that the "liberty" protected by the Due Process Clause of the Fourteenth Amendment encompasses more than freedom from bodily restraint, today's plurality opinion emphasizes, the concept was cut loose from one natural limitation on its meaning. This innovation paved the way, so the plurality hints, for judges to substitute their own preferences for those of elected officials. Dissatisfied with this supposedly unbridled and uncertain state of affairs, the plurality casts about for another limitation on the concept of liberty.

It finds this limitation in "tradition." Apparently oblivious to the fact that this concept can be as malleable and as elusive as "liberty" itself, the plurality pretends that tradition places a discernible border around the Constitution. The pretense is seductive; it would be comforting to believe that a search for "tradition" involves nothing more idiosyncratic or complicated than poring through dusty volumes on American history. Yet, as Justice White observed in his dissent in *Moore v. East Cleveland*, 431 U.S. 494, 549 (1977): "What the deeply rooted traditions of the country are is arguable." Indeed, wherever I would begin to look for an interest "deeply rooted in the country's traditions," one thing is certain: I would not stop (as does the plurality) at Bracton, or Blackstone, or Kent, or even the American Law Reports in conducting my search.

. . .

It is ironic that an approach so utterly dependent on tradition is so indifferent to our precedents. Citing barely a handful of this Court's numerous decisions defining the scope of the liberty protected by the Due Process Clause to support its reliance on tradition, the plurality acts as though English legal treatises and the American Law Reports always have provided the sole source for our constitutional principles. They have not.

It is not that tradition has been irrelevant to our prior decisions. Throughout our decisionmaking in this important area runs the theme that certain interests and practices—freedom from physical restraint, marriage, childbearing, childrearing, and others—form the core of our definition of "liberty." Our solicitude for these interests is partly the result of the fact that the Due Process Clause would seem an empty promise if it did not protect them, and partly the result of the historical and traditional importance of these interests in our society. In deciding cases arising under the Due Process Clause, therefore, we have considered whether the concrete limitation under consideration impermissibly impinges upon one of these more generalized interests.

Today's plurality, however, does not ask whether parenthood is an interest that historically has received our attention and protection; the answer to that question is too clear for dispute. Instead, the plurality asks whether the specific variety of parenthood under consideration—a natural father's relationship with a child whose mother is married to another man—has enjoyed such protection.

If we had looked to tradition with such specificity in past cases, many a decision would have reached a different result. . . .

The plurality's interpretive method is more than novel; it is misguided. It ignores the good reasons for limiting the role of "tradition" in interpreting the Constitution's deliberately capacious language. In the plurality's constitutional universe, we may not take notice of the fact that the original reasons for the conclusive presumption of paternity are out of place in a world in which blood tests can prove virtually beyond a shadow of a doubt who sired a particular child and in which the fact of illegitimacy no longer plays the burdensome and stigmatizing role it once did. Nor, in the plurality's world, may we deny "tradition" its full scope by pointing out that the rationale for the conventional rule has changed over the years; . . . instead, our task is simply to identify a rule denying the asserted interest and not to ask whether the basis for that rule—which is the true reflection of the values undergirding it—has changed too often or too recently to call the rule embodying that rationale a "tradition." Moreover, by describing the decisive question as whether Michael and Victoria's interest is one that has been "traditionally *protected by* our society," rather than one that society traditionally has thought important (with or without protecting it), and by suggesting that our sole function is to "*discern the society's views*," the plurality acts as if the only purpose of the Due Process Clause is to confirm the importance of interests already protected by a majority of the States. Transforming the protection afforded by the Due Process Clause into a redundancy mocks those who, with care and purpose, wrote the Fourteenth Amendment.

. . .

[T]o describe the issue in this case as whether the relationship existing between Michael and Victoria "has been treated as a protected family unit under the historic practices of our society, or whether on any other basis it has been accorded special protection," is to reinvent the wheel. The better approach—indeed, the one commanded by our prior cases and by common sense—is to ask whether the specific parent-child relationship under consideration is close enough to the interests that we already have protected to be deemed an aspect of "liberty" as well. . . .

On four prior occasions, we have considered whether unwed fathers have a constitutionally protected interest in their relationships with their children. Though different in factual and legal circumstances, these cases have produced a unifying theme: although an unwed father's biological link to his child does not, in and of itself, guarantee him a constitutional stake in his relationship with that child, such a link combined with a substantial parent-child relationship will do so. . . .

The evidence is undisputed that Michael, Victoria, and Carole did live together as a family; that is, they shared the same household, Victoria called Michael "Daddy," Michael contributed to Victoria's support, and he is eager to continue his relationship with her. Yet they are not, in the plurality's view, a "unitary family," whereas Gerald, Carole, and Victoria do compose such a family. The only difference between these two sets of relationships, however, is the fact of marriage. . . . However, the very premise of [our prior cases is] that marriage is not decisive in answering the question whether the Constitution protects the parental relationship under consideration. . . .

[The plurality's] pinched conception of "the family," crucial as it is in rejecting Michael and Victoria's claim of a liberty interest, is jarring in light of our many cases preventing the States from denying important interests or statuses to those whose situations do not fit the government's narrow view of the family. From *Loving v. Virginia* to . . . *Moore v. East Cleveland*, we have declined to respect a State's notion, as manifested in its allocation of privileges and burdens, of what the family should be. . . .

The plurality's focus on the "unitary family" is misdirected for another reason. It conflates the question whether a liberty interest exists with the question what procedures may be used to terminate or curtail it. It is no coincidence that we never before have looked at the relationship that the unwed father seeks to disrupt, rather than the one he seeks to preserve, in determining whether he has a liberty interest in his relationship with his child. To do otherwise is to allow the State's interest in terminating the relationship to play a role in defining the "liberty" that is protected by the Constitution. According to our established framework under the Due Process Clause, however, we first ask whether the person claiming constitutional protection has an interest that the Constitution recognizes; if we find that she does, we next consider the State's interest in limiting the extent of the procedures that will attend the deprivation of that interest. By stressing the need to preserve the "unitary family" and by focusing not just on the relationship between Michael and Victoria but on their "situation" as well, today's plurality opinion takes both of these steps at once.

The plurality's premature consideration of California's interests is evident from its careful limitation of its holding to those cases in which "the mother is, at the time of the child's conception and birth, married to and cohabitating with another man, *both of whom wish to raise the child as the offspring of their union*" (emphasis added). . . . The highlighted language suggests that if Carole or Gerald alone wished to raise Victoria, or if both were dead and the State wished to raise her, Michael and Victoria might be found to have a liberty interest in their relationship with each other.

But that would be to say that whether Michael and Victoria have a liberty interest varies with the State's interest in recognizing that interest, for it is the State's interest in protecting the marital family—and not Michael and Victoria's interest in their relationship with each other—that varies with the status of Carole and Gerald's relationship. It is a bad day for due process when the State's interest in terminating a parent-child relationship is reason to conclude that that relationship is not part of the "liberty" protected by the Fourteenth Amendment.

The plurality has wedged itself between a rock and a hard place. If it limits its holding to those situations in which a wife and husband wish to raise the child together, then it necessarily takes the State's interest into account in defining "liberty"; yet if it extends that approach to circumstances in which the marital union already has been dissolved, then it may no longer rely on the State's asserted interest in protecting the "unitary family" in denying that Michael and Victoria have been deprived of liberty. . . .

The atmosphere surrounding today's decision is one of make-believe. Beginning with the suggestion that the situation confronting us here does not repeat itself every day in every corner of the country, moving on to the claim that it is tradition alone that supplies the details of the liberty that the Constitution protects, and passing finally to the notion that the Court always has recognized a cramped vision of "the family," today's decision lets stand California's pronouncement that Michael—whom blood tests show to a 98 percent probability to be Victoria's father—is not Victoria's father. When and if the Court awakes to reality, it will find a world very different from the one it expects.

A *Critique of Michael H. v. Gerald D.*

J. M. BALKIN

I begin with a recent decision of the United States Supreme Court, *Michael H. v. Gerald D.* This case is especially interesting to constitutional scholars because its various opinions offer a number of contrasting theories about the meaning of the "liberty" protected by the due process clause of the Constitution. For those not familiar with the case, it involves an attempt by one Michael H. to establish parental rights to a little girl, Victoria, who Michael claimed was his biological daughter, and who had lived with him as his daughter

on and off for three years. Michael sued to establish his paternity and obtain visitation rights. Victoria, however, was conceived and born while her mother Carole was married to another man, Gerald D. Michael H. offered genetic tests establishing to a 98.07 percent certainty that he, and not Gerald D., was the biological father. Nevertheless, the United States Supreme Court upheld a California statute which established a presumptive conclusion that a child is the offspring of the man who is married to the mother at the time of the child's birth, unless the mother or her husband wish to deny the husband's paternity. Neither Gerald nor Carole wished to contest paternity in this case because they did not want Michael to visit Victoria.

Michael H. argued that California's statutory presumption denied him a liberty guaranteed by the due

From J. M. Balkin, "Tradition, Betrayal, and the Politics of Deconstruction: Michael H. v. Gerald D.," *Cardozo Law Review,* 11 (1990), pp. 1613, 1614–1629. Reprinted by permission of the Cardozo Law Review.

process clause of the fourteenth amendment. The Supreme Court held, in a plurality opinion written by Justice Scalia, that Michael had no liberty interest in a continuing relationship with Victoria. Justice Scalia argued that the concept of liberty is amorphous, and that to give it content one must refer to existing traditions of liberty in the United States. He argued that one must look to "the most specific level at which a relevant tradition protecting, or denying protection to, the asserted right can be identified." Thus, it was not enough for Justice Scalia that American society traditionally protected the interests of biological fathers in relationships with their children. Justice Scalia argued that there was no liberty interest in this case because society has not traditionally protected the parental rights of adulterous fathers of children born during marriage of the mother to another man. Moreover, there was a traditional interest in the protection of what Justice Scalia called the "unitary family"—one husband, one wife, one or many children. Therefore, despite the virtual certainty that Victoria was Michael's biological daughter, despite the fact that she lived with him over many months and he held her out as his own child, despite the fact that she even called him "Daddy," California was constitutionally justified in cutting off all of Michael's parental rights in the interest of preserving the unitary family.

I suspect that many people will think that this opinion is wrong-headed in the extreme. For some it will appear to be nothing more than the product of a rather intolerant jurist who apparently believes that familial relations have always been conducted according to the rules first laid down by June and Ward Cleaver. Indeed, one hardly needs all of the philosophical artillery of deconstruction to see why Justice Scalia's arguments are problematic. Nevertheless, I do think that one can learn something from deconstructing this opinion. But what one will learn is as much about deconstruction—and its possible political uses— as it is about constitutional law.

We could deconstruct this opinion in many ways. We might note that Justice Scalia's opinion relies upon a distinction between more or less specific traditions, a distinction which is, as Justice Brennan points out, manipulable and difficult to maintain. I shall return to this criticism in a moment. Nevertheless, we should first take seriously the reasons why Justice Scalia wants to read the concept of tradition narrowly. He makes clear that the search for the most specific tradition is tied to his fears about the open-ended character of the concept of liberty and the great power given to

judges who must interpret this concept. Justice Scalia is greatly concerned that courts will use such open-ended terms to make value-laden choices inappropriate to their institutional role. The more specific the inquiry into tradition, the more likely it is that a court is protecting something that already is in place, rather than simply creating a tradition, or stretching an existing tradition further than is historically permissible. For persons with the same general philosophy as Justice Scalia, an example of such an unwarranted extension of tradition might be extending the traditional respect for the privacy of marriage to protect extramarital sexual relations. Thus, specific traditions are more reliable guides to the contours of liberty than are general traditions because they are more easily identifiable, and because they involve less danger of countermajoritarian value choices by the judiciary.

Ultimately, however, these very justifications undermine Justice Scalia's test of the most specific tradition. His test assumes that constitutionally protected liberties match or do not match existing traditions in an unproblematic way. For each asserted right there either is or is not a specific tradition associated with its protection. Yet there are many different ways of describing a liberty, and many different ways of characterizing a tradition. For example, we might point out that under this test, there has been no established tradition in California for protecting Justice Scalia's own rights to visit his children, since there is no tradition of affording protection to fathers who are children of Italian immigrants and who graduated from Ivy League law schools before 1965, were appointed to the United States Supreme Court by former governors of the state of California and have more than two children but less than thirteen. Indeed, the question has hardly ever come up. Justice Scalia would no doubt respond that these are the wrong factors to consider in matching liberty to tradition. And we might reply: How do you, oh purveyor of neutral principles, know this?

To be sure, Justice Scalia has a plausible response. When Justice Scalia claims parental rights to his children, the liberty he claims is the parental right of fathers with respect to biological children born while the father was married to the child's mother. This has been traditionally protected. The rights of adulterous fathers, however, have not been traditionally protected.

But this answer reveals that Justice Scalia's theory is not simply a preference for narrower traditions over broader traditions. It rests upon an important metaphysical set of assumptions—that traditions or (more importantly) the absences of traditions, come in discrete units with discrete boundaries. To describe a tradition accurately is to respect the preexisting boundaries of the tradition. Similarly, to describe a liberty tradition- ally protected is to describe its actual contours. Thus, one cannot simply divide up traditions and liberties any way one wants.

. . .

Moreover, Justice Scalia's vision of tradition as- sumes that traditions are not only discrete, but pre- sumptively normatively correct. What is traditional is worthy of constitutional protection, and what is not traditional is not, whether it be marital privacy, the rights of married fathers to visit their children, sexual harassment in the workplace or racial segregation. This, too, is a potential source of embarrassment.

Justice Scalia's metaphysics of tradition produces sufficiently troublesome counter-examples that we must pause and consider whether we have stumbled upon a serious difficulty concerning the concept of tra- dition itself. What is tradition? How do we determine its boundaries or entailments, and what is its norma- tive status? If there is a tradition of protecting marital privacy, but not a more specific tradition of protecting marital purchase of contraceptives, how do we know whether the latter situation is nevertheless subsumed under the former for purposes of constitutionally pro- tected liberty? Might one not conclude instead that the real historical tradition was protection of marital pri- vacy in the home, so that the purchase of contracep- tives in the open marketplace could be regulated or even proscribed consistent with the tradition? Would this not be more consistent with the experiences of Margaret Sanger and her followers, who publicly advocated birth control in the early twentieth century, and were met with incredible resistance? Again, if sexual harassment directed toward women in the workplace and respect for marital privacy are both tra- ditions, but only one is worth protecting, how do we tell the difference? If back alley abortions are a tradi- tion in response to the "traditional" prohibition on abortion in America, does this make abortion (in or out of a back alley) a tradition worth protecting and sustaining? In short, what normative status should be assigned to a set of values given the fact that many people have held these values at one point or another in our nation's history?

. . .

In fact, what is most troubling about Justice Scalia's call for respecting the most specific tradition available is that our most specific historical traditions may often by opposed to our more general commit-

ments to liberty or equality. Curiously, then, different parts of the American tradition may conflict with each other. And, indeed, this is one of the untidy facts of historical experience. The Fourteenth Amendment's abstract commitment to racial equality was accom- panied by simultaneous acceptance of segregated public schools in the District of Columbia and acqui- escence in antimiscegenation laws. The establish- ment clause and the principle of separation of church and state have coexisted with presidential proclama- tions of national days of prayer, official congressional chaplains, and national Christmas trees. Traditions do not exist as integrated wholes. They are a mot- ley collection of principles and counterprinciples, standing for one thing when viewed narrowly and standing for another when viewed more generally. Tradition never speaks with one voice, although, to be sure, persons of particular predilections may hear only one.

Michael H. v. Gerald D. . . . is all about tradition and betrayal. It is about the sexual betrayal that led to the conception of Victoria. It is about the emotional betrayal of Michael H. by the mother, Carole, who, after living with him and allowing him to foster a rela- tionship with his own daughter, denied him the right to continue that relationship. It is about the legal tradi- tion and betrayal—that is, the handing over—of a child from her biological father to another man, a tra- dition and betrayal enforced in the name of protecting the tradition of the family—the raising of children by their parents.

Finally, *Michael H.* is about the tradition and the betrayal of the concept of liberty protected by the due process clause. For here, Justice Scalia, preaching about the great traditions that the clause protects, and the obligations of previous precedents, believes he is following those traditions and those precedents at the same time that his colleagues on the Court argue that he is betraying them. As Justice Brennan succinctly states, "[i]t is ironic that an approach so utterly depen- dent on tradition is so indifferent to our precedents." When one thinks of tradition in law, one thinks natu- rally of the principle of stare decisis—the develop- ment of law through precedent and reasoning by analogy. Yet is this particular tradition—this handing down of precedential rules from one case to the next— not also a form of betrayal? And is not every betrayal also the beginning of a new tradition? When a judge produces a reading of preceding cases, her reading is always similar to and different from what came before. Sometimes this is deliberate—sometimes it is simply a result of the alterations produced by reading authoritative materials in new contexts. As the tradition grows and develops, it alters itself. And as it alters itself, it is both true and false to itself. It is both a handing down and a modification, however slight or subtle, of what came before. It is the simultaneous production of similarity and difference. It is both tradition and betrayal.

. . .

From these remarks, it should be clear that I, too, am unsatisfied with Justice Scalia's opinion in *Michael H.*, and in particular with his reliance on tradition, which smacks of sexual and cultural intolerance and an almost willful blindness to the many different layers of tradition and countertradition in American

society. And it should also be fairly clear that one could use deconstruction to critique Justice Scalia's opinion on many different levels—showing how, in his attempt to protect traditional family values, he destroys the possibility of a bond between a child and her biological father. One might also note that while the Court appears to be the protector of family values, it does so by allowing parent-child relations to be severed by legal technicalities. Here the supreme law of the land (the Constitution) is claimed to reflect general traditional values, but in fact destroys particular parental bonds. The acknowledgement of one story about family relations is at the expense and exclusion of other, less "respectable" but no less extant versions.

Family Law in Transition

Janet L. Dolgin

During the nineteenth century, an interest in stemming social changes in traditional patterns of domestic life provided one encouragement to the growth of family law as a discrete area of American civil law. Even so, the response of the law in the United States to changing family patterns has not been without deviations and regional differences. However, during the nineteenth century the appearance within the family of similarities to forms of interaction in the marketplace threatened a society that more and more defined the family through contrasts with the world of work, and the explicit separation of family law from all forms of commercial law provided one defense against the possibility that the form of relationships in the marketplace could be imported into the home and could begin to affect relationships there.

Thus, one important response of the law to changes in family patterns during the nineteenth century involved the imposition of harsh new definitions

and prohibitions. For instance, acknowledging and responding to a rise in the rate of divorce by the late nineteenth century, state legislatures widely reduced the grounds and toughened the procedures by which people could divorce. At the same time and for similar reasons, states widely restricted the availability of contraception and forbade abortion at any point during a pregnancy. Abortion had been made a statutory crime in the United States about fifty years earlier, but the early anti-abortion statutes generally preserved the common-law rule that had no quarrel with termination of a pregnancy before "quickening" (the mother's first recognition of fetal movement).

In 1873, the U.S. Congress passed the Comstock Law (named after New York's "purity campaigner," Anthony Comstock). This law severely punished the transmission or importation of material providing information about contraception or abortion. Thus, for many decades lawmakers refused to endorse the new realities emerging in social and domestic life in the United States. However, the harsh statutes promulgated during the nineteenth century were somewhat less rigidly applied in practice because courts, though generally following legislative direction, were reluctant

From Janet L. Dolgin, *Defining the Family* (New York: New York University Press, 1997), pp. 33–39. Reprinted by permission of New York University Press and the author.

in particular cases to enforce the stringent new laws. Ultimately, such legislative restrictions and prohibitions failed to contain the processes of change. Despite the promulgation of laws that prohibited contraception and abortion, family size continued to decline; actual husbands and wives noted the new, stiff laws that expressly prohibited contraception and abortion, but spoke in opposition through "silent practice."

Faced with a growing gap between legal rules and life, the law eventually relented, and especially by the second half of the twentieth century began to tolerate, and often actively to endorse, changes in the family that reflected individualism and that valued choice over tradition. By this time, more than half of American marriages ended in divorce, and only about one-third of families consisted of two parents and their minor children.

With astonishing rapidity, beginning in the late 1960s the legislative bulwark, erected in the previous century to thwart changes in the family and represented especially by prohibitions against divorce, contraception, and abortion, collapsed. Within a decade family law reversed course almost completely. By the late 1970s family law, at least as regards adults and the relation between adults within families, provided for broadened understandings of familial relationships. Moreover, family law began, if hesitantly and only partially, to amalgamate with contract, tort, and property law. The process occurred rapidly, though not without lingering ambivalence.

With regard to children and the parent-child relationship in particular, the law has been slower to sanction shifts away from tradition. That process is occurring as well but is more obviously riddled with deep ambivalence, and consequently with contradiction. This process can be seen perhaps most clearly in the responses of the law to disputes involving reproductive technology because there the parent-child bond is being created in transparently new ways, socially and biologically. If this relationship can be *created* in contractual terms and on commercial grounds, perhaps it can, and will, become indistinguishable from commercial relationships in its actualization as well as in its creation. The consequent fear that babies, and the women who produce them, will be commodified is only the most frequently voiced lament about the development of assisted reproduction to surrogacy and the new reproductive technologies.

At present, the law remains reluctant to allow the parent-child bond to be created in terms of the marketplace. But with regard to adults, family law, beginning in the late 1960s, expressly approved the creation—and to some, though a lesser, extent, the operation—of families governed by the predicates of contract (individualism and choice).

The shift in family law toward the acceptance of nontraditional forms of interaction appeared dramatically in the so-called "divorce revolution." In the late 1960s state legislators began to permit divorce upon agreement of the parties: no-fault divorce. California was the first state to recognize no-fault divorce. In less than a decade, almost every state provided for some sort of divorce that at least lessened the need for accusations of fault between the parties. Previously, divorce was never available simply because the parties chose to separate, but only in cases in which the state deemed the actions of one party to the marriage so aberrant as to render the relationship nonexistent. Under laws that permitted divorce only upon accusations of fault, grounds included acts such as adultery, willful desertion, and absence long enough to lead to a presumption of death. Along with the shift from fault to no-fault divorce came a set of procedural changes making it far easier for couples to divorce. A few states even began to provide for summary dissolution proceedings that can be used in cases involving no minor children and that require no divorce hearing at all.

So, within a decade the law transferred a great part of the responsibility for regulating marriage and divorce from the state to the parties involved. In consequence, no-fault divorce, . . . is also "no-responsibility" divorce—at least no responsibilities enforced by legal sanction. As with business partners, spouses can design the terms of their relationships' beginnings and endings, and the law will enforce the agreements they reach.

Legal acknowledgment that the spousal relationship is no longer uniquely defined by an encompassing and fixed set of rights and obligations is further indicated by the increasing willingness of courts and legislatures to recognize cohabitation agreements between parties never formally married. These agreements suggest that couples who choose not to marry may enjoy the benefits of cohabitation and may determine, and ask the law to ensure, the financial and other consequences of a potential separation, much as business partners may determine the consequences of their firm's dissolution. *Marvin v. Marvin,* decided in California in 1976, was the first case to recognize and agree to enforce cohabitation contracts in contemplation of the cohabitation's termination. Other states followed the *Marvin* example and thereby gave unmarried cohabitants some of the protection that the law had already provided to couples upon the termination of marital relationships.

A further example of the process of defining and treating the family as a collection of separate individuals rather than as a unit of social value beyond the individuals involved, appears in antenuptial agreements in contemplation of divorce. Dismissed by courts everywhere only a few decades ago as violative of state public policy, such agreements are now widely recognized and enforced. Moreover, several of the courts that first recognized antenuptial agreements in contemplation of divorce justified their decisions with reference to shifts in the character of the family and increases in the frequency of divorce. In *Posner v. Posner,* for example, a Florida court in 1970 took judicial notice of the increase in the ratio of divorce to marriage within the society. In these cases, courts enforcing premarital agreements largely relied on principles of standard contract law. As one review of changes in family law published in 1988 explained, states generally enforce antenuptial agreements if they are (1) free from fraud and overreaching, (2) reflect a full and fair disclosure by and between the parties of their respective assets, and in some states, (3) not unconscionable as to property division or spousal support. This account could refer to almost any unexceptional contract case.

The law has further begun to consider contracts between couples that define the character and terms of ongoing relationships as well as the terms of the creation or termination of relationships. The Uniform Premarital Agreement Act allows couples to establish certain aspects of an ongoing marriage in an antenuptial agreement. This possibility provides expressly for the contractualization of the terms of marriage as a continuing relationship and represents a change at least as unsettling to traditional understandings of family as that permitting premarital negotiations providing for the terms of a marriage's dissolution. Legal recognition of bargained negotiations between parties to a marriage over the terms of their relationship completely contradicts a long-standing assumption, deeply embedded in nineteenth-century liberalism, that family relationships, unlike almost all other relationships, were not to be regulated by consent but by the natural subordination of one kind of person (wives) to another (husbands).

A further upheaval in assumptions about the nature of families is indicated by a decision of the Hawaii Supreme Court in 1993 which provided that under the state's constitution even the definition of marriage, traditionally understood as a bond between one man and one woman, must be open to revisions based on choice. In *Baehr v. Lewin,* Hawaii's highest court agreed with a group of six litigants protesting the state's prohibition against same-sex marriage, that the definition of marriage can no longer be limited by traditional understandings of the marital relationship. The court held the state's marriage statute presumptively unconstitutional in restricting marriage to opposite-sex parties because the statute violated the equal protection clause of the state's constitution. In earlier cases, decided in other states, courts had always concluded that marriage *by definition* includes a man and a woman.

Thus, more and more the American legal system has come to view adult family members as it views business associates—as autonomous individuals free to negotiate the terms of their relationships and the terms of their relationships' demise. With regard to children and to the parent-child tie, the legal system has been less ready to sanction the amalgamation of family law with the laws of the market. But even here change is occurring.

The pressure to redefine the essence of the parent-child connection is nowhere stronger than in cases involving reproductive technology. But other examples exist as well. Cases of relatively young children attempting to initiate the termination of their relationships with their parents illustrate dramatically the scope of potential shifts in the meaning of the parent-child tie and in the status of children. In *In re Kingsley,* a ten-year-old boy in Florida hired a lawyer (actually his foster father) to help him terminate his biological mother's parental rights and to effect his adoption by the family that had been housing him as a foster child. The trial court decision, although overturned on appeal, is significant because in the decision the legal system recognized the child and his relation to his parents in terms of contract, rather than biological status. Despite the way that the media framed the case, it did not actually involve the creation of a "divorce" action between parents and their children. Rather, the importance of the case lay in the standing given the young boy, Gregory Kingsley, to argue that his biological mother's parental rights should be terminated because she was unfit to be a parent. In one sense, the case can be described as nothing more than a minor transformation of a far more familiar abuse or neglect action. However, the trial court's decision for the boy, which provided for the termination of the biological mother's rights and for the child's adoption by his foster parents, was significant because it suggested that in the future children could initiate termination and adoption actions. The trial court's decision rested on its recognition of the child as an autonomous actor able to engage an attorney and to initiate the legal process that would determine his own parentage.

An older example of choice, rather than biology, determining the parent-child bond is that of adoption. Legal approaches to adoption during most of this century were designed to reflect the model of the nuclear family composed of married parents and their biological children. Present changes in adoption law, and even more, proposals to reform adoption law in ways that would differentiate adoptive families from biological families, suggest widespread confusion about the essence of the bond between parents and their children in general.

For the common law, the significance of biology in the definition of family precluded the recognition of adoptive families. By the late nineteenth century, statutory law provided for adoptive families in the United States and Great Britain, and only in the twentieth century were such families afforded real protection by the law. To some extent, the legal recognition of adoptive families represented an early acknowledgment that the love and intimacy that are supposed to characterize the parent-child relationship need not be anchored in biology. For decades, however, the law continued to insist that adoption be structured "in imitation of biology."

Now, open adoptions in which biological and adoptive parents join together in parenting a child have become increasingly acceptable. The move toward unsealing adoption records represents a similar trend. However, both open adoptions and the so-called "search movement," which advocates unsealing adoption records, can be, and are being, read to support contradictory conclusions about the essence of the family and therefore suggest that society and the law are not consistently embracing negotiations and choice in family matters. These recent changes in approaches to adoption are variously interpreted to suggest that no one model need dictate how family members are related to one another and to suggest that relations founded in biological connections *are* more real than other relations. Generally, controversies about how the law should define and regulate adoption dramatically illustrate the society's ambivalence and confusion about changing understandings of children in families and of the parent-child bond.

Thus, it appears that for the law even the once inviolate core of the family unit, the parent-child connection, has become subject to the pressures of individualism in ways that would have been unimaginable three or four decades ago. The process of change in the parent-child tie is occurring more slowly and amidst much stronger emotion, confusion, and opposition than the parallel process regarding relations among adults. But even here, at the core of the family unit, at least as that unit has been understood for the past century and a half, a new vision, or rather a variety of new visions, of family are being recognized and actualized. This process is occurring, but amidst considerable confusion and uncertainty.

. . .

Johnson v. Calvert

Mark and Crispina Calvert are a married couple who desired to have a child. Crispina was forced to undergo a hysterectomy in 1984. Her ovaries remained capable of producing eggs, however, and the couple eventually considered surrogacy. In 1989 Anna Johnson heard

851 P.2d 776 (1993), Supreme Court of California.

about Crispina's plight from a coworker and offered to serve as a surrogate for the Calverts.

On January 15, 1990, Mark, Crispina, and Anna signed a contract providing that an embryo created by the sperm of Mark and the egg of Crispina would be implanted in Anna and the child born would be taken into Mark and Crispina's home "as their child." Anna agreed she would relinquish "all parental rights" to the child in favor of Mark and Crispina. In return, Mark and Crispina would pay Anna $10,000 in a series of installments, the last to be paid six weeks after the child's birth. Mark and Crispina were also to pay for a $200,000 life insurance policy on Anna's life.

The zygote was implanted on January 19, 1990. Less than a month later, an ultrasound test confirmed Anna was pregnant.

Unfortunately, relations deteriorated between the two sides. Mark learned that Anna had not disclosed she had suffered several stillbirths and miscarriages. Anna felt Mark and Crispina did not do enough to obtain the required insurance policy. She also felt abandoned during an onset of premature labor in June.

In July 1990, Anna sent Mark and Crispina a letter demanding the balance of the payments due her or else she would refuse to give up the child. The following month, Mark and Crispina responded with a lawsuit, seeking a declaration they were the legal parents of the unborn child. Anna filed her own action to be declared the mother of the child, and the two cases were eventually consolidated. The parties agreed to an independent guardian ad litem for the purposes of the suit.

The child was born on September 19, 1990, and blood samples were obtained from both Anna and the child for analysis. The blood test results excluded Anna as the genetic mother. The parties agreed to a court order providing that the child would remain with Mark and Crispina on a temporary basis with visits by Anna.

. . . [W]e are left with the undisputed evidence that Anna, not Crispina, gave birth to the child and that Crispina, not Anna, is genetically related to him. Both women thus have adduced evidence of a mother and child relationship as contemplated by the [Uniform Parentage] Act. Yet for any child California law recognizes only one natural mother, despite advances in reproductive technology rendering a different outcome biologically possible.

We decline to accept the contention of amicus curiae . . . that we should find the child has two mothers. Even though rising divorce rates have made multiple parent arrangements common in our society, we see no compelling reason to recognize such a situation here. The Calverts are the genetic and intending parents of their son and have provided him, by all accounts, with a stable, intact, and nurturing home. To recognize parental rights in a third party with whom the Calvert family has had little contact since shortly after the child's birth would diminish Crispina's role as mother.

We see no clear legislative preference in [the statutory law] as between blood testing evidence and proof of having given birth.

. . .

Because two women each have presented acceptable proof of maternity, we do not believe this case can be decided without enquiring into the parties' intentions as manifested in the surrogacy agreement. Mark and Crispina are a couple who desired to have a child of their own genes but are physically unable to do so without the help of reproductive technology. They affirmatively intended the birth of the child, and took the steps necessary to effect in vitro fertilization. But for their acted-on intention, the child would not exist. Anna agreed to facilitate the procreation of Mark's and Crispina's child. The parties' aim was to bring Mark's and Crispina's child into the world, not for Mark and Crispina to donate a zygote to Anna. Crispina from the outset intended to be the child's mother. Although the gestative function Anna performed was necessary to bring about the child's birth, it is safe to say that Anna would not have been given the opportunity to gestate or deliver the child had she, prior to implantation of the zygote, manifested her own intent to be the child's mother. No reason appears why Anna's later change of heart should vitiate the determination that Crispina is the child's natural mother.

We conclude that although the Act recognizes both genetic consanguinity and giving birth as means of establishing a mother and child relationship, when the two means do not coincide in one woman, she who intended to procreate the child—that is, she who intended to bring about the birth of a child that she intended to raise as her own—is the natural mother under California law.[1]

. . .

Anna urges that surrogacy contracts violate several social policies. Relying on her contention that she is the child's legal, natural mother, she cites the public policy embodied in [the] Penal Code prohibiting the payment for consent to adoption of a child. She argues further that the policies underlying the adoption laws of this state are violated by the surrogacy contract because it in effect constitutes a prebirth waiver of her parental rights.

We disagree. Gestational surrogacy differs in crucial respects from adoption and so is not subject to the adoption statutes. The parties voluntarily agreed to participate in in vitro fertilization and related medical procedures before the child was conceived; at the time when Anna entered into the contract, therefore, she was not vulnerable to financial inducements to part with her own expected offspring. As discussed above, Anna was not the genetic mother of the child. The payments to Anna under the contract were meant to compensate her for her services in gestating the fetus and undergoing labor, rather than for giving up "parental" rights to the child. Payments were due both during the pregnancy and after the child's birth.

. . .

Finally, Anna and some commentators have expressed concern that surrogacy contracts tend to exploit or dehumanize women, especially women of lower economic status. Anna's objections center around the psychological harm she asserts may result from the gestator's relinquishing the child to whom she has given birth. Some have also cautioned that the practice of surrogacy may encourage society to view children as commodities, subject to trade at their parents' will.

We are unpersuaded that gestational surrogacy arrangements are so likely to cause the untoward results Anna cites as to demand their invalidation on public policy grounds. Although common sense suggests that women of lesser means serve as surrogate mothers more often than do wealthy women, there has been no proof that surrogacy contracts exploit poor women to any greater degree than economic necessity in general exploits them by inducing them to accept lower-paid or otherwise undesirable employment. We are likewise unpersuaded by the claim that surrogacy will foster the attitude that children are mere commodities; no evidence is offered to support it.

The argument that a woman cannot knowingly and intelligently agree to gestate and deliver a baby for intending parents carries overtones of the reasoning that for centuries prevented women from attaining equal economic rights and professional status under the law. To resurrect this view is both to foreclose a personal and economic choice on the part of the surrogate mother, and to deny intending parents what may be their only means of procreating a child of their own genes.

. . .

Anna argues at length that her right to the continued companionship of the child is protected under the federal Constitution.

. . .

Anna relies mainly on theories of substantive due process, privacy, and procreative freedom, citing a number of decisions recognizing the fundamental liberty interest of natural parents in the custody and care of their children. These cases do not support recognition of parental rights for a gestational surrogate.

Anna's argument depends on a prior determination that she is indeed the child's mother. Since Crispina is the child's mother under California law because she, not Anna, provided the ovum for the in vitro fertilization procedure, intending to raise the child as her own, it follows that any constitutional interests Anna possesses in this situation are something less than those of a mother. . . .

. . .

The judgment of the Court of Appeal is affirmed.

KENNARD, J., dissenting.

When a woman who wants to have a child provides her fertilized ovum to another woman who carries it through pregnancy and gives birth to a child, who is the child's legal mother? Unlike the majority, I do not agree that the determinative consideration should be the intent to have the child that originated with the woman who contributed the ovum. In my view, the woman who provided the fertilized ovum and the woman who gave birth to the child both have substantial claims to legal motherhood. Pregnancy entails a unique commitment, both psychological and emotional, to an unborn child. No less substantial, however, is the contribution of the woman from whose egg the child developed and without whose desire the child would not exist.

For each child, California law accords the legal rights and responsibilities of parenthood to only one "natural mother." When, as here, the female reproductive role is divided between two women, California law requires courts to make a decision as to which woman is the child's natural mother, but provides no standards by which to make that decision. The majority's resort to "intent" to break the "tie" between the genetic and gestational mothers is unsupported by statute, and, in the absence of appropriate protections in the law to guard against abuse of surrogacy arrangements, it is ill-advised. To determine who is the legal mother of a child born of a gestational surrogacy arrangement, I would apply the standard most protective of child welfare—the best interests of the child.

The majority offers four arguments in support of its conclusion to rely on the intent of the genetic mother as the exclusive determinant for deciding who is the natural mother of a child born of gestational surrogacy. Careful examination, however, demonstrates that none of the arguments mandates the majority's conclusion.

The first argument that the majority uses in support of its conclusion that the intent of the genetic mother to bear a child should be dispositive of the question of motherhood is "but-for" causation. Specifically, the majority relies on a commentator who writes that in a gestational surrogacy arrangement, "the child would not have been born but for the efforts of the intended parents." [But the resort to the "but-for" test derived from tort law is unprecedented and unjustified here.]

. . .

Behind the majority's reliance on "but-for" causation as justification for its intent test is a second, closely related argument: The mental concept of the child is a controlling factor of its creation, and the originators of that concept merit full credit as conceivers.

. . .

[This concept is taken from the law of intellectual property.] The problem with this argument, of course, is that children are not property. Unlike songs or inventions, rights in children cannot be sold for consideration, or made freely available to the general public.

Next, the majority offers as its third rationale the notion that bargained-for expectations support its conclusion regarding the dispositive significance of the genetic mother's intent. Specifically, the majority states that "intentions that are voluntarily chosen, deliberate, express and bargained-for ought presumptively to determine legal parenthood."

. . . But the courts will not compel performance of all contract obligations. The unsuitability of applying the notion that, because contract intentions are "voluntarily chosen, deliberate, express and bargained-for," their performance ought to be compelled by the courts is even more clear when the concept of specific performance is used to determine the course of the life of a child. Just as children are not the intellectual property of their parents, neither are they the personal property of anyone, and their delivery cannot be ordered as a contract remedy on the same terms that a court would, for example, order a breaching party to deliver a truckload of nuts and bolts.

. . .

The majority's final argument in support of using the intent of the genetic mother as the exclusive determinant of the outcome in gestational surrogacy cases is that preferring the intending mother serves the child's interests, which are "[u]nlikely to run contrary to those of adults who choose to bring [the child] into being."

I agree with the majority that the best interests of the child is an important goal. . . . The problem with the majority's rule of intent is that application of this inflexible rule will not serve the child's best interests in every case.

. . .

In the absence of legislation that is designed to address the unique problems of gestational surrogacy, this court should look not to tort, property or contract law, but to family law, as the governing paradigm and source of a rule of decision. The allocation of parental rights and responsibilities necessarily impacts the welfare of a minor child. And in issues of child welfare, the standard that courts frequently apply is the best interests of the child. This "best interests" standard serves to assure that in the judicial resolution of disputes affecting a child's well-being, protection of the minor child is the foremost consideration. Consequently, I would apply "the best interests of the child" standard to determine who can best assume the social and legal responsibilities of motherhood for a child born of a gestational surrogacy arrangement.

. . .

Factors that are pertinent to good parenting, and thus that are in a child's best interests, include the ability to nurture the child physically and psychologically and to provide ethical and intellectual guidance. Also crucial to a child's best interests is the "well recognized right" of every child "to stability and continuity." The intent of the genetic mother to procreate a child is certainly relevant to the question of the child's best interests; alone, however, it should not be dispositive.

Endnote

[1] Thus, under our analysis, in a true "egg donation" situation, where a woman gestates and gives birth to a child formed from the egg of another woman with the intent to raise the child as her own, the birth mother is the natural mother under California law.

The dissent would decide parentage based on the best interests of the child. Such an approach raises the repugnant specter of governmental interference in matters implicating our most fundamental notions of privacy, and confuses concepts of parentage and custody. Logically, the determination of parentage must precede, and should not be dictated by, eventual custody decisions. The implicit assumption of the dissent is that a recognition of the genetic intending mother as the natural mother may sometimes harm the child. This assumption overlooks California's dependency laws, which are designed to protect all children irrespective of the manner of birth or conception. Moreover, the best interests standard poorly serves the child in the present situation: it fosters instability during litigation and, if applied to recognize the gestator as the natural mother, results in a split of custody between the natural father and the gestator, an outcome not likely to benefit the child. Further, it may be argued that, by voluntarily contracting away any rights to the child, the gestator has, in effect, conceded the best interests of the child are not with her.

Too Many Parents

ALEXANDER MORGAN CAPRON

Biomedical developments have generated countless challenges for the law. While the legal system's response is not always awe-inspiring, its confused and faltering reaction to medically assisted reproduction is in a class by itself. Perhaps this is not surprising, since of late virtually every bizarre possibility hypothesized in the early days of artificial baby-making has materialized, first in the fertility clinics and then in the courthouses.

Yet even courts that have responded with some semblance of ad hoc justice have failed to respect the central interests at stake, which are not those of the warring adults but of the children who are and will be produced using the new reproductive methods. Two recent cases from opposite coasts demonstrate the limitations of the contract law model on which the courts have relied with increasing frequency and make clear the need to read present legislation wisely and to craft new legislation that is astute as well as comprehensive.

In re Marriage of Buzzanca

Orange County, California, which has given rise to the most widely discussed surrogate motherhood cases—occasionally involving facts so weird the cases have gone straight to the talk-show circuit without first being litigated—recently outdid itself. On 10 June 1998, the state's highest court declined to review a Court of Appeal decision reversing a trial court holding that a little girl with eight people who could arguably be called her parents was actually parentless.

Behind the birth of that little girl, Jaycee Buzzanca, lies a convoluted tale. About five years ago, Erin Davidson agreed to become an egg donor, on the condition that she and her husband, who have four children, would approve who got her eggs. Once Mr. and Mrs. X (who remain anonymous) passed muster, seventeen eggs harvested from Mrs. Davidson were fertilized with Mr. X's sperm. Four were implanted in Mrs. X, who then gave birth to twins; the remaining embryos were kept in frozen storage. After the twins' birth, the fertility center offered the Xs three choices: destroy the embryos, donate them for research, or donate them for other couples. Mr. and Mrs. X checked off the third option. The Davidsons seem to have been unaware any further donation might occur.

Meanwhile, John and Luanne Buzzanca had failed to produce a child with five different surrogate mothers. On 13 August 1994, one of the Xs' frozen embryos was implanted in the uterus of "professional surrogate" Pamela Snell, who had served that role in the birth of three previous babies. Twelve days later, John and Luanne Buzzanca and Pamela and her husband Randy Snell signed a written surrogacy agreement, which—in what proved an understatement—warned that the peculiar circumstances of the case made parenthood legally unpredictable. The delay in formalizing the agreement was eventually found by the appellate court to be without legal significance, but its psychological meaning shortly emerged when John separated from Luanne. Eight months later, just weeks before Jaycee's birth on 26 April 1995, he filed for divorce.

From *Hastings Center Report* (September-October 1998), pp. 22–24. Reprinted by permission of the Hastings Center Report and the author.

In that filing, John alleged the marriage had produced no children, which Luanne denied in her response. Her attempt to get temporary child support was initially rebuffed by the family court because John was not Jaycee's biological father nor was she born to Luanne during the course of the marriage (the two ways the law typically establishes fatherhood). In February 1996, however, an appellate panel ruled that Luanne had made sufficient showing that she would prevail at trial to entitle her to child support pending the litigation.

In March 1997 the lower court heard John's petition for divorce as well as a petition Luanne had filed in September 1996 to establish herself as Jaycee's legal mother. Based only on oral arguments, the court ruled that John was not the legal father because he had not contributed the sperm, that Luanne was not the legal mother because she had neither contributed the egg nor borne Jaycee, and that the surrogate was not the legal mother because the parties had so stipulated. The gamete donors and their spouses were unknown to the court and not parties to the case.

In reversing these conclusions, the appellate panel looked to the Uniform Parentage Act as enacted in California. The act does not directly address the tangled circumstances of the case, but the court extrapolated a basic principle from the act: people should be held responsible for the reproductive outcomes of their actions. In addition to the two bases for establishing fatherhood that John Buzzanca failed to meet, the act provides that if a man consents to his wife's artificial insemination by donor (AID), he is deemed the father, and the donor of the semen "is treated in law as if he were not the natural father of a child thereby conceived."[1] While John's wife was not the one who bore Jaycee, Presiding Justice David Sills concluded that John fit within the act's assignment of fatherhood to one "who intends to raise [a] child but who otherwise does not have any biological tie" to the child whose procreation he "contemplate[d] by [his] consent to a medical procedure."[2]

The appellate court faced a bigger hurdle when it turned to Luanne's relationship with Jaycee because the act does not address the female equivalent of AID. Furthermore, in the leading California case on surrogate motherhood, *Johnson v. Calvert*,[3] the state supreme court had set forth only two ways to establish maternity: giving birth to a child or following the procedures (blood tests) used to determine paternity, neither of which applied to Luanne. Yet as the *Buzzanca* panel

noted, the *Johnson* court had reached its conclusions about maternity through reasoning by parity from "statutes which, on their face, referred only to paternity." Having decided that an unrelated man could be deemed the father of a child because he intended the child to be born, the panel by a parity of reasoning ruled the same was true of a woman. Hence Luanne is Jaycee's mother.

Making Policy, Not Reading Statutes

This would be a sensible result, were the sole question whether John and Luanne could be held to have financial obligations to support Jaycee, but much more is actually at stake, especially as regards the assignment of maternity. Although presented as statutory interpretation, the opinion not merely makes up law out of whole cloth but actually goes against the policies embodied in the parentage and adoption laws.

First, the California Supreme Court itself stretched the parentage act beyond recognition in *Johnson* when it treated the law's two ways of identifying the natural mother as though they were separate "definitions" of motherhood that could yield two separate mothers, when in fact they are simply two ways of establishing that a woman is the "natural mother" because she gave birth to the child. The identity of a birth mother is not usually in doubt, but when it is, it may be resolved through genetic tests.

Although the act's drafters did not contemplate that biological motherhood could have two facets, genetic and gestational, that has come to be the reality in many assisted reproduction cases. A policy decision must now be made about when if ever to rely on genetics over gestation. While the act does not address this issue directly, the only hint of the weight the legislature would give to these competing considerations favors the birth mother, since under the act genetic testing was in service of establishing birth, not the other way around. To reach the opposite conclusion, as the *Johnson* court did, and to premise the result on treating men and women "in parity," fails to recognize that women make a different contribution to reproduction than men and profoundly devalues the gestational aspect of that contribution.

Second, the *Buzzanca* court carried this illogic one step further by generalizing a narrow statutory provision. It interpreted the AID provision to embody the principle that obligation follows intention, whereas in fact the act simply bars a husband who has consented to AID performed by a physician from using a paternity test to defeat the presumption that a child born to his wife during the marriage is his legal issue. The act does not, however, govern the relationship of a man to a child not borne by his wife, much less the relationship of the wife to a child who is not the product of her womb and to whom neither she nor her husband are genetically related.

During gestation and at the moment of birth, the only mother-child relationship that is beyond question is that of child and birth mother, and the interests of the child will be best served if all concerned, including "professional surrogates," keep that mother-child relationship in mind. Recognizing this recognizes the need for responsible *maternal* behavior during pregnancy and for having someone clearly authorized to make *maternal* decisions about the newborn, without having first to sort through contracts or genetic relationships with the child that others claim to hold, on the basis of which they claim entitlement to make decisions about the pregnancy or the newborn child.

This is the issue that *Buzzanca* elides by going beyond assigning financial responsibility to imply parental status. Not surprisingly, the panel read the AID provision of the parentage act as expressing the age-old doctrine of estoppel, that a person who consents to an act should not be able to disclaim responsibility when others act accordingly. But it is one thing to say that a husband who consents to his wife's AID shoulders the responsibility of fatherhood, and quite another to say that the woman who commissions a surrogate contract is more entitled to be the mother of the resulting child than either the surrogate who bears the child or the woman whose egg is used.

The appellate panel in *Buzzanca* did not have to tackle this issue directly because the gamete donors remained out of the picture, and because Pamela Snell, who had filed for custody of Jaycee around the same time that Luanne petitioned to be named Jaycee's mother, apparently withdrew, and because by February 1997 the trial court had accepted the parties' stipulation that the Snells were not Jaycee's "biological parents." But had Pamela not relented—indeed, had she refused to turn over Jaycee at birth to a divorcing couple (as Luanne apparently feared, since she forged a "forwarding" order on Pamela's mail to keep her from receiving notice of the divorce action)—it goes well beyond any existing statute to conclude that Luanne's intent to be a mother should necessarily outweigh Pamela's undeniable biological relationship with Jaycee.

Broadening Responsibility

A further difficulty with the "intent" model of parenthood is that its reliance on contract law not only turns children into commodities (in a marketplace where fertility centers charge ever higher prices for "elite" gametes and surrogates) but treats public decisions as private, especially by evading adoption laws. People wishing to become parents of unrelated children can now sidestep the child-protective regimen established by the adoption laws simply by contracting for adoption prenatally.

Of course, draconian prohibitions on all forms of surrogacy may simply lead to ingenious evasions, as illustrated by *Doe v. Doe,* a divorce case decided in April by the Connecticut Supreme Court.[4] Though that case involved fewer participants, it was also very peculiar and actually began before the Does got married. Plaintiff "Jane Doe," who had several children from a first marriage, had become infertile, so defendant "John Doe" advertised in the local paper for a surrogate, who was then inseminated with the defendant's semen, using a syringe but not under medical supervision. When the surrogate was four months' pregnant, Jane and John Doe married, and the surrogate assumed Jane's identity for purposes of receiving prenatal care and delivery.

The child was twelve years old by the time the superior and probate courts came to rule on John Doe's divorce complaint and his petitions to be declared the child's lawful father and to terminate the parental rights of the surrogate mother and her by-then ex-husband. Therefore, both in the interests of the child and in recognition of the maternal role long played by Mrs. Doe, the Connecticut court was right to accept a probate court ruling that John was the child's father and to utilize a state statute under which Jane could enjoy the status of an interested third party with "a powerful, albeit nonparental, claim to custody." In determining child custody issues, a "court's paramount consideration," as Justice David M. Borden noted, "is the child's welfare."[5]

Like many cases in which the new reproductive technologies have been examined legally, *Doe* is a divorce case; in such cases, children's status and needs are often pawns in the divorcing couple's battles over money, power, and revenge for hurt feelings. Given these circumstances, the steps needed to protect the interests of children in the context of a divorce action may not be the steps that best protect the children of the new reproductive technology at or before birth or even before conception. Furthermore, the claims of the other germinal and gestational participants in assisted reproduction are not best worked out in the context of a divorce case, which directly involves only the "social" parents. Indeed, the surrogate mother in *Doe* had apparently not sought to establish her legal parentage earlier, despite her dissatisfaction. Shortly after the child's birth, the surrogate wrote to the Does expressing deep "hurt" over their failure to live up to assurances that the relationship was more than a "business deal" and would involve their providing pictures of, and visits with, the baby. Seven years later, after the surrogate's own daughter had died, she asked John Doe's help in traveling to conceive a child with a Florida man; she also stated that she still considered the child to be hers and his (and not Jane Doe's) and that she desired to see "our daughter" but did not want a visit with Jane, who "is not a part of this as far as I am concerned. . . . My feelings towards our daughter concern you and I, and no one else."[6]

If society really wants to hold all the parties involved responsible for the consequences of their intentional acts, at least three steps are needed. First, it should make it clear to all those involved that they are at risk of financial and other responsibilities, while the benefits they gain will always be tempered by the goal of achieving what is best for the innocent third parties involved, namely, the children.

Second, the incentives to carry out artificial reproduction under medical supervision could then be increased by minimizing the financial and other risks of certain parties (particularly gamete donors) who participate in assisted reproduction run by legitimate fertility centers operated under supervision both by physicians and by adoption authorities or other agencies concerned with child welfare.

Third, the law should make the fertility centers that arrange for gamete donation, in vitro fertilization, and surrogate gestation responsible for the consequences. Of course, a center could insist that "intended" parents agree to indemnify the center for the child-support payments and other expenses that arise when death, divorce, or disagreement complicates the outcomes sought. But the effect of an indemnity agreement would still be to leave the first obligation on the centers' shoulders, giving them an incentive to screen all participants well and to structure arrangements in the way that would be most protective of the children produced. Any inability or unwillingness of the adults involved to make good on their responsibilities would be at the expense of the fertility center, not the innocent victims. Fertility centers, as the "repeat players" in assisted reproduction, are easier to supervise than the individuals involved; moreover, it would be much easier and more cost-effective for centers to obtain the necessary liability coverage. More even than the "intended" parents, the fertility centers are responsible for bringing these children into existence since they assemble the necessary participants and carry out the key laboratory and clinical procedures. Thus, it is not only fair to hold the centers ultimately responsible should the children's interests be placed at risk, but it would be most protective of the children, since it would induce greater caution and care on the part of the leading actors. Success has many parents, disaster only one: in the case of assisted reproduction, protecting the well-being of those most at risk from disasters means that the role of "the one parent" should be placed on the fertility centers, which will be most able—and available—to pay the piper.

Endnotes

[1] Uniform Parentage Act § 5.

[2] In re Marriage of Buzzanca, 61 Cal. App. 4th 1410, 1418 (1998).

[3] 5 Cal. 4th 84, 851 P.2d 776 (1993).

[4] 244 Conn. 403, 710 A.2d 1297 (1998).

[5] 244 Conn. at 441, citing Manter v. Manter, 185 Conn. 502, 441 A.2d 146 (1981).

[6] 244 Conn. at 445, n. 47.

Study Questions

1. The Court's ruling in *Michael H. v. Gerald D.* holds that the state may give preference for parenting purposes to a man who is currently married to the child's mother over the child's biological father. Suppose you are asked to defend this preference. What would you say?

2. Are you convinced that Balkin persuasively uncovers the "contradictions" inherent in the Court's ruling in *Michael H. v. Gerald D.*? Does the Court permit "legal technicalities" to sever the parent-child relation in this case?

3. Balkin accuses Justice Scalia of "sexual and cultural intolerance." What evidence does he have for this accusation? Do you agree with him? Why?

4. Is Justice Scalia, in *Michael H.*, concerned that Michael poses a threat to the marriage of Carole and Gerald? If so, is that a legitimate worry? Why? What about the interests of Victoria, the child? Is it a fair criticism to say that the Court potentially sacrifices her interests in order to promote desirable public policy goals?

5. The Court rejects the child's claim in *Michael H.* that she has a right to "maintain a filial relationship" with Michael, insisting that state recognition of "multiple fatherhood" has no support in the history or traditions of this country. Is the Court correct? What about stepparent relationships? The ruling in *Michael M.* has been interpreted to mean that a stepfather's rights can prevail over the rights of the biological father. Are you convinced that this result is what our legal "tradition" endorses?

6. It has been held that DNA or other forms of scientific testing may be used to establish paternity (in other words, to prove that a given man is the father of a child) for various legal purposes (for example, in awarding child support). If biological tests are sufficient to establish paternity for these purposes, why isn't Michael's biological connection with Victoria adequate in his case against Gerald D.?

7. Studies have shown that, in the great majority of divorce cases, the mother becomes the custodial parent subsequent to the dissolution of the marriage. Hence, many of these women become single parents, with the associated burdens, whereas the fathers become simply single. Moreover, some such fathers are "deadbeat" dads who do not pay the full amount they owe in child support. How, if at all, should the law be changed to help eliminate these inequities? Do you see them as inequities?

8. How important is it, in your opinion, to challenge traditional views of marriage in order to achieve gender equality?

9. The Uniform Parentage Act specifies the following: "If, under the supervision of a licensed physician and with the consent of her husband, a wife is inseminated artificially with semen donated by a man not her husband, the husband is treated in law as if he were the natural father of the child thereby conceived." Under this Act, would a child born of donor semen to an unmarried woman (or to a woman who did not consent to the procedure) have no father?

10. What is the significance of the genetic connection between Crispina Calvert and the child at issue in *Calvert v. Johnson*? Why is that connection of greater significance than the bond developed between the surrogate (Anna) and the child whom she carried for nine months of pregnancy and then gave birth?

11. The California court in *Calvert* holds that the significance of and basis for being a mother can only be established in the same way as the basis for being a father—that is, by genetic consanguinity. Should motherhood be established in the same way as fatherhood? Is this an equal application of the law? Can the contributions of the "uterine donor" be compared to those of a semen donor?

12. The justices in *Calvert* agreed on one point: that the child should not have two mothers. But why not? Is a convincing argument for this claim given? Many children today are being raised in large, "blended" families. How is this environment substantially different from having multiple parents?

Cases for Further Reflection
Bush v. Gore

Issued on December 12, 2000, the Supreme Court's opinion in the presidential election case brought the legal proceedings—and the election—to a close. The Court argued that the manual recounts of votes in some Florida counties were proceeding under uneven standards, since similar ballots might be counted differently in different counties. Does this lack of uniformity, in your opinion, violate the Equal Protection Clause of the Fourteenth Amendment? Why wouldn't other elections be equally flawed under the Court's reasoning? For example, differing counties and differing states employ varying voting methods, from machines that scan paper ballots, to punch-card machines, and even machines that use no paper or card at all. Does this lack of uniformity give rise to other forms of inequality in the electoral process? Why or why not?

PER CURIAM

On December 8, 2000, the Supreme Court of Florida ordered that the Circuit Court of Leon County tabulate by hand 9,000 ballots in Miami-Dade County. It also ordered the inclusion in the certified vote totals of 215 votes identified in Palm Beach County and 168 votes identified in Miami-Dade County for Vice President Albert Gore, Jr., and Senator Joseph Lieberman, Democratic Candidates for President and Vice President. The Supreme Court noted that petitioner, Governor George W. Bush asserted that the net gain for Vice President Gore in Palm Beach County was 176 votes, and directed the Circuit Court to resolve that dispute on remand. The court further held that relief would require manual recounts in all Florida counties where so-called "undervotes" had not been subject to manual tabulation. The court ordered all manual recounts to begin at once. Governor Bush and Richard Cheney, Republican Candidates for the Presidency and Vice Presidency, filed an emergency application for a stay of this mandate. On December 9, we granted the application, treated the application as a petition for a writ of certiorari, and granted certiorari.

The petition presents the following questions: whether the Florida Supreme Court established new standards for resolving Presidential election contests,

thereby violating Art. II, § 1, cl. 2, of the United States Constitution . . . and whether the use of standardless manual recounts violates the Equal Protection and Due Process Clauses. With respect to the equal protection question, we find a violation of the Equal Protection Clause.

. . . On November 8, 2000, the day following the Presidential election, the Florida Division of Elections reported that petitioner, Governor Bush, had received 2,909,135 votes, and respondent, Vice President Gore, had received 2,907,351 votes, a margin of 1,784 for Governor Bush. Because Governor Bush's margin of victory was less than "one-half of a percent . . . of the votes cast," an automatic machine recount was conducted under § 102.141(4) of the election code, the results of which showed Governor Bush still winning the race but by a diminished margin. Vice President Gore then sought manual recounts in Volusia, Palm Beach, Broward, and Miami-Dade Counties. . . . A dispute arose concerning the deadline for local county canvassing boards to submit their returns to the Secretary of State. The Secretary declined to waive the November 14 deadline imposed by statute. The Florida Supreme Court, however, set the deadline at November 26. . . .

On November 26, the Florida Elections Canvassing Commission certified the results of the election and declared Governor Bush the winner of Florida's 25 electoral votes. On November 27, Vice President Gore, pursuant to Florida's contest provisions, filed a

531 U.S. 98 (2000), United States Supreme Court.

complaint in Leon County Circuit Court contesting the certification. . . .

The Supreme Court held that Vice President Gore had satisfied his burden of proof . . . with respect to his challenge to Miami-Dade County's failure to tabulate, by manual count, 9,000 ballots on which the machines had failed to detect a vote for President ("undervotes").

. . .

The court therefore ordered a hand recount of the 9,000 ballots in Miami-Dade County. . . . The individual citizen has no federal constitutional right to vote for electors for the President of the United States unless and until the state legislature chooses a statewide election as the means to implement its power to appoint members of the Electoral College. U.S. Const., Art. II, § 1. . . . History has now favored the voter, and in each of the several States the citizens themselves vote for Presidential electors. When the state legislature vests the right to vote for President in its people, the right to vote as the legislature has prescribed is fundamental; and one source of its fundamental nature lies in the equal weight accorded to each vote and the equal dignity owned to each voter. . . .

The right to vote is protected in more than the initial allocation of the franchise. Equal protection applies as well to the manner of its exercise. Having once granted the right to vote on equal terms, the State may not, by later arbitrary and disparate treatment, value one person's vote over that [of another] . . . The question before us . . . is whether the recount procedures the Florida Supreme Court has adopted are consistent with its obligation to avoid arbitrary and disparate treatment of the members of its electorate.

Much of the controversy seems to revolve around ballot cards designed to be perforated by a stylus but which, either through error or deliberate omission, have not been perforated with sufficient precision for a machine to count them. In some cases a piece of the card—a chad—is hanging, say by two corners. In other cases there is no separation at all, just an indentation.

The Florida Supreme Court has ordered that the intent of the voter be discerned from such ballots. For purposes of resolving the equal protection challenge, it is not necessary to decide whether the Florida Supreme Court had the authority under the legislative scheme for resolving election disputes to define what a legal vote is and to mandate a manual recount implementing that definition. The recount mechanisms implemented in response to the decisions of the Florida Supreme Court do not satisfy the minimum requirement for non-arbitrary treatment of voters necessary to secure the fundamental right. Florida's basic command for the count of legally cast votes is to consider the "intent of the voter." This is unobjectionable as an abstract proposition and a starting principle. The problem inheres in the absence of specific standards to ensure its equal application. The formulation of uniform rules to determine intent based on these recurring circumstances is practicable and, we conclude, necessary.

The law does not refrain from searching for the intent of the actor in a multitude of circumstances; and in some cases the general command to ascertain intent is not susceptible to much further refinement. In this instance, however, the question is not whether to believe a witness but how to interpret the marks or holes or scratches on an inanimate object, a piece of cardboard or paper which, it is said, might not have registered as a vote during the machine count. The factfinder confronts a thing, not a person. The search for intent can be confined by specific rules designed to ensure uniform treatment.

The want of those rules here has led to unequal evaluation of ballots in various respects. . . . As seems to have been acknowledged at oral argument, the standards for accepting or rejecting contested ballots might vary not only from county to county but indeed within a single county from one recount team to another.

The State Supreme Court ratified this uneven treatment. It mandated that the recount totals from two counties, Miami-Dade and Palm Beach, be included in the certified total. The court also appeared to hold *sub silentio* that the recount totals from Broward County, which were not completed until after the original November 14 certification by the Secretary of State, were to be considered part of the new certified vote totals even though the county certification was not contested by Vice President Gore. Yet each of the counties used varying standards to determine what was a legal vote. Broward County used a more forgiving standard than Palm Beach County, and uncovered almost three times as many new votes, a result markedly disproportionate to the difference in population between the counties.

. . . [T]he actual process by which the votes were to be counted under the Florida Supreme Court's decision raises further concerns. That order did not specify who would recount the ballots. The county canvassing boards were forced to pull together ad hoc teams comprised of judges from various Circuits who had no previous training in handling and interpreting ballots. Furthermore, while others were permitted to observe, they were prohibited from objecting during the recount.

The recount process, in its features here described, is inconsistent with the minimum procedures necessary to protect the fundamental right of each voter in the special instance of a statewide recount under the authority of a single state judicial officer. Our consideration is limited to the present circumstances, for the problem of equal protection in election processes generally presents many complexities.

Upon due consideration of the difficulties identified to this point, it is obvious that the recount cannot be conducted in compliance with the requirements of equal protection and due process without substantial additional work. It would require not only the adoption (after opportunity for argument) of adequate statewide standards for determining what is a legal vote, and practicable procedures to implement them, but also orderly judicial review of any disputed matters that might arise. . . .

. . . None are more conscious of the vital limits on judicial authority than are the members of this Court, and none stand more in admiration of the Constitution's design to leave the selection of the President to the people, through their legislatures, and to the political sphere. When contending parties invoke the process of the courts, however, it becomes our unsought responsibility to resolve the federal and constitutional issues the judicial system has been forced to confront.

The judgment of the Supreme Court of Florida is reversed, and the case is remanded for further proceedings not inconsistent with this opinion. . . .

It is so ordered.

Loving v. Virginia

The following case, *Loving v. Virginia*, involved an antimiscegenation law, that is, a law forbidding racial intermarriage. The Supreme Court unanimously struck down the law as a violation of the Equal Protection clause of the Fourteenth Amendment. When reading the brief excerpt from the Court's ruling, consider the following: The Virginia law did not prohibit all racial intermarriage—it prohibited those who were White from marrying anyone who was not White. Passed in 1924, during the peak of the eugenics movement in the United States, the law was entitled "An Act to Preserve Racial Integrity." Its stated intention was to prevent the "corruption of blood" and a "mongrel breed of citizens." The Court found that the law drew a "racial classification" and lacked a rational basis.

Although blatantly racist, such a law raises interesting questions: Did the law classify on the basis of race in a way that disadvantaged racial minorities? Whites could not marry non-Whites; Blacks, Asians, Latinos, and other non-White persons could intermarry without restriction. Given that fact, how can it be argued that the law reflects racial prejudice? *Loving* involved a Black woman and a White man. The Virginia law, "on its face, " applied equally to Blacks and to Whites: neither could marry the other. If Blacks can't marry Whites and Whites can't marry Blacks, isn't everyone being treated equally? Could these facts be used to argue that the law actually treated Whites *unequally* with respect to members of other racial groups?

Mr. Chief Justice Warren delivered the opinion of the Court.

388 U.S. 1 (1967), United States Supreme Court.

This case presents a constitutional question never addressed by this Court: whether a statutory scheme adopted by the State of Virginia to prevent marriages between persons solely on the basis of racial classifications violates the Equal Protection and Due Process

Clauses of the Fourteenth Amendment. For reasons which seem to us to reflect the central meaning of those constitutional commands, we conclude that these statutes cannot stand consistently with the Fourteenth Amendment.

In June 1958, two residents of Virginia, Mildred Jeter, a Negro woman, and Richard Loving, a white man, were married in the District of Columbia pursuant to its laws. Shortly after their marriage, the Lovings returned to Virginia and established their marital abode in Caroline County. At the October Term, 1958, of the Circuit Court of Caroline County, a grand jury issued an indictment charging the Lovings with violating Virginia's ban on interracial marriages. On January 6, 1959, the Lovings pleaded guilty to the charge and were sentenced to one year in jail; however, the trial judge suspended the sentence for a period of 25 years on the condition that the Lovings leave the State and not return to Virginia together for 25 years. He stated in an opinion that:

"Almighty God created the races white, black, yellow, malay and red, and he placed them on separate continents. And but for the interference with his arrangement there would be no cause for such marriages. The fact that he separated the races shows that he did not intend for the races to mix."

The Supreme Court of Appeals upheld the constitutionality of the antimiscegenation statutes, and, after modifying the sentence, affirmed the convictions. The Lovings appealed this decision, and we noted probable jurisdiction. . . .

The two statutes under which appellants were convicted and sentenced are part of a comprehensive statutory scheme aimed at prohibiting and punishing interracial marriages. The Lovings were convicted of violating § 20–58 of the Virginia Code:

"*Leaving State to evade law.*—If any white person and colored person shall go out of this State, for the purpose of being married, and with the intention of returning, and be married out of it, and afterwards return to and reside in it, cohabiting as man and wife, they shall be punished as provided in § 20–59, and the marriage shall be governed by the same law as if it had been solemnized in this State. The fact of their cohabitation here as man and wife shall be evidence of their marriage."

Section 20–59, which defines the penalty for miscegenation, provides:

"*Punishment for marriage.*—If any white person intermarry with a colored person, or any colored person intermarry with a white person, he shall be guilty of a felony and shall be punished by confinement in the penitentiary for not less than one nor more than five years."

Other central provisions in the Virginia statutory scheme are § 20–57, which automatically voids all marriages between "a white person and a colored person" without any judicial proceeding, and §§ 20–54 and 1–14 which, respectively, define "white persons" and "colored persons and Indians" for purposes of the statutory prohibitions. The Lovings have never disputed in the course of this litigation that Mrs. Loving is a "colored person" or that Mr. Loving is a "white person" within the meanings given those terms by the Virginia statutes.

Virginia is now one of 16 States which prohibit and punish marriages on the basis of racial classifications. Penalties for miscegenation arose as an incident to slavery and have been common in Virginia since the colonial period. The present statutory scheme dates from the adoption of the Racial Integrity Act of 1924, passed during the period of extreme nativism which followed the end of the First World War. The central features of this Act, and current Virginia law, are the absolute prohibition of a "white person" marrying other than another "white person," a prohibition against issuing marriage licenses until the issuing official is satisfied that the applicants' statements as to their race are correct, certificates of "racial composition" to be kept by both local and state registrars, and the carrying forward of earlier prohibitions against racial intermarriage. . . .

[T]he State does not contend in its argument before this Court that its powers to regulate marriage are unlimited notwithstanding the commands of the Fourteenth Amendment. . . . Instead, the State argues that the meaning of the Equal Protection Clause, as illuminated by the statements of the Framers, is only that state penal laws containing an interracial element as part of the definition of the offense must apply equally to whites and Negroes in the sense that members of each race are punished to the same degree. Thus, the State contends that, because its miscegenation statutes punish equally both the white and the Negro participants in an interracial marriage, these statutes, despite their reliance on racial classifications, do not constitute an invidious discrimination based upon race. The second argument advanced by the State assumes the validity of its equal application theory. The argument is that, if the Equal Protection Clause does not outlaw miscegenation statutes because of their reliance on racial classifications, the question of constitutionality would thus become whether there was any rational basis for a State to treat interracial marriages differently from other marriages. On this question, the State argues, the scientific evidence is substantially in doubt and, consequently, this Court should defer to the wisdom of the state legislature in adopting its policy of discouraging interracial marriages.

Because we reject the notion that the mere "equal application" of a statute containing racial classifications is enough to remove the classifications from the Fourteenth Amendment's proscription of all invidious racial discriminations, we do not accept the State's contention that these statutes should be upheld if there is any possible basis for concluding that they serve a rational purpose. The mere fact of equal application does not mean that our analysis of these statutes should follow the approach we have taken in cases involving no racial discrimination. . . .

The State argues that statements in the Thirty-ninth Congress about the time of the passage of the Fourteenth Amendment indicate that the Framers did not intend the Amendment to make unconstitutional state miscegenation laws. . . . While these statements have some relevance to the intention of Congress in submitting the Fourteenth Amendment, it must be understood that they pertained to the passage of specific statutes and not to the broader, organic purpose of a constitutional amendment. As for the various statements directly concerning the Fourteenth Amendment, we have said in connection with a related problem, that although these historical sources "cast some light" they are not sufficient to resolve the problem;" [at] best, they are inconclusive. . . .

There can be no question but that Virginia's miscegenation statutes rest solely upon distinctions drawn according to race. The statutes proscribe generally accepted conduct if engaged in by members of different races. Over the years, this Court has consistently repudiated distinctions between citizens solely because of their ancestry as being odious to a free people whose institutions are founded upon the doctrine of equality. At the very least, the Equal Protection Clause demands that racial classifications, especially suspect in criminal statutes, be subjected to the most rigid scrutiny, and, if they are ever to be upheld, they must be shown to be necessary to the accomplishment of some permissible state objective, independent of the racial discrimination which it was the object of the Fourteenth Amendment to eliminate. . . .

There is patently no legitimate overriding purpose independent of invidious racial discrimination which justifies this classification. The fact that Virginia prohibits only interracial marriages involving white persons demonstrates that the racial classifications must stand on their own justification, as measures designed to maintain White Supremacy. We have consistently denied the constitutionality of measures which restrict the rights of citizens on account of race. There can be no doubt that restricting the freedom to marry solely because of racial classifications violates the central meaning of the Equal Protection Clause.

These statutes also deprive the Lovings of liberty without due process of law in violation of the Due Process Clause of the Fourteenth Amendment. The freedom to marry has long been recognized as one of the vital personal rights essential to the orderly pursuit of happiness by free men.

Marriage is one of the "basic civil rights of man," fundamental to our very existence and survival. To deny this fundamental freedom on so unsupportable a basis as the racial classifications embodied in these statutes, classifications so directly subversive of the principle of equality at the heart of the Fourteenth Amendment, is surely to deprive all the State's citizens of liberty without due process of law. The Fourteenth Amendment requires that the freedom of choice to marry not be restricted by invidious racial discriminations. Under our Constitution, the freedom to marry, or not marry, a person of another race resides with the individual and cannot be infringed by the State.

These convictions must be reversed.
It is so ordered.

U.S. *v. Virginia*

Virginia Military Institute (VMI), a state-supported, single-sex military academy, was sued by the federal government for discrimination. A federal appellate court found that VMI had a unique program of "adversative" training that would be significantly affected by coeducation. It ruled, however, that Virginia had failed convincingly to justify having such a unique military academy for men only. The appellate court ordered that plans be drawn either to admit women to VMI or to establish a separate but equal academy for women. In response to the ruling, Virginia created Virginia Women's Institute for Leadership (VWIL), intended to be an all-female version of VMI. Alleging that VWIL was not an equal facility, the government again brought a challenge, which made its way to the Supreme Court. The opinion by Justice Ruth Ginsburg ruled that VMI had no justification for refusing to admit women and that VWIL did not compensate for that exclusion. Do you agree with the Court's decision? Does the state have an interest in restricting such "adversative" training to men only?

Justice Ginsburg delivered the opinion of the Court.

Virginia's public institutions of higher learning include an incomparable military college, Virginia Military Institute (VMI). The United States maintains that the Constitution's equal protection guarantee precludes Virginia from reserving exclusively to men the unique educational opportunities VMI affords. We agree.

Founded in 1839, VMI is today the sole single-sex school among Virginia's 15 public institutions of higher learning. VMI's distinctive mission is to produce "citizen-soldiers," men prepared for leadership in civilian life and in military service. VMI pursues this mission through pervasive training of a kind not available anywhere else in Virginia, an "adversative method" [that] constantly endeavors to instill physical and mental discipline in its cadets and impart to them a strong moral code. [Neither] the goal of producing citizen-soldiers nor VMI's implementing methodology is inherently unsuitable to women. And the school's impressive record in producing leaders has made admission desirable to some women. Nevertheless, Virginia has elected to preserve exclusively for men the advantages and opportunities a VMI education affords.

From its establishment in 1839, [VMI] has remained financially supported by Virginia. [Today, it] enrolls about 1300 men as cadets. [Its] "adversative, or doubting, model of education" [features] "physical rigor, mental stress, absolute equality of treatment, absence of privacy, minute regulation of behavior, and indoctrination in desirable values." [VMI] cadets live in spartan barracks where surveillance is constant and privacy nonexistent; they wear uniforms, eat together in the mess hall, and regularly participate in drills. Entering students are incessantly exposed to the rat line, "an extreme form of the adversative model," comparable in intensity to Marine Corps boot camp. Tormenting and punishing, the rat line bonds new cadets to their fellow sufferers and, when they have completed the 7-month experience, to their former [tormentors]. In 1990, prompted by a complaint filed [by] a female high-school student seeking admission to VMI, the United States sued, [alleging] that VMI's exclusively male admission policy violated [equal protection]. The District Court ruled in favor of VMI, [but the Court of Appeals reversed and remanded, suggesting] these options for the State: Admit women to VMI; establish parallel institutions or programs; or abandon state support, leaving VMI free to pursue its policies as a private institution. [In response,] Virginia proposed a parallel program for women: Virginia Women's Institute for Leadership (VWIL). The 4-year, state-sponsored

518 U.S. 515 (1996), United States Supreme Court.

undergraduate program would be located at Mary Baldwin College, a private liberal arts school for women, and would be open, initially, to about 25 to 30 students. Although VWIL would share VMI's mission—to produce "citizen-soldiers"—the VWIL program would differ, as does Mary Baldwin College, from VMI in academic offerings, methods of education, and financial resources. [The] District Court [decided] the plan met the requirements of [equal protection]. [A] divided Court of Appeals [affirmed].

The cross-petitions in this case present two ultimate issues. First, does Virginia's exclusion of women from the educational opportunities provided by VMI—extraordinary opportunities for military training and civilian leadership development—deny to women "capable of all of the individual activities required of VMI cadets" the equal protection of the [laws]? Second, if VMI's "unique" situation—as Virginia's sole single-sex public institution of higher education—offends the Constitution's equal protection principle, what is the remedial requirement?

Parties who seek to defend gender-based government action must demonstrate an "exceedingly persuasive justification" for that action. Today's skeptical scrutiny of official action denying rights or opportunities based on sex responds to volumes of history. [Since] Reed, the Court has repeatedly recognized that neither federal nor state government acts compatibly with the equal protection principle when a law or official policy denies to women, simply because they are women, full citizenship stature—equal opportunity to aspire, achieve, participate in and contribute to society based on their individual talents and capacities. Without equating gender classifications, for all purposes, to classifications based on race or national origin, the court, in post-Reed decisions, has carefully inspected official action that closes a door or denies opportunity to women (or to men). . . .

. . . Measuring the record in this case against the review standard just described, we conclude that Virginia has shown no "exceedingly persuasive justification" for excluding all women from the citizen-soldier training afforded by VMI. We therefore affirm the Fourth Circuit's initial judgment. [Because] the remedy proffered by Virginia—the Mary Baldwin VWIL program—does not cure the constitutional violation, [we] reverse the fourth Circuit's final judgment in this case.

[Virginia] asserts two justifications in defense of VMI's exclusion of women. First, "[single-sex] education provides important educational benefits," and the option of single-sex education contributes to "diversity in educational approaches." Second, "[the] unique VMI method of character development and leadership training," the school's adversative approach, would have to be modified were VMI to admit women. We consider these [in] turn.

Single-sex education affords pedagogical benefits to at least some students, Virginia emphasizes, and that reality is uncontested in this litigation. Similarly, it is not disputed that diversity among public educational institutions can serve the public good. But Virginia has not shown that VMI was established, or has been maintained, with a view to diversifying, by its categorical exclusion of women, educational opportunities within the State. In cases of this genre, our precedent instructs that "benign" justifications proffered in defense of categorical exclusions will not be accepted automatically; a tenable justification must describe actual state purposes, not rationalizations for actions in fact differently grounded. [Neither] recent nor distant history bears out Virginia's alleged pursuit of diversity through single-sex educational options. . . .

[In] sum, we find no persuasive evidence in this record that VMI's male-only admission policy "is in furtherance of a state policy of 'diversity.'" [A] purpose genuinely to advance an array of educational options [is] not served by VMI's historic and constant plan—a plan to "afford a unique educational benefit only to males." However "liberally" this plan serves the State's sons, it makes no provision whatever for her daughters. That is not equal protection.

Virginia next argues that VMI's adversative method of training provides educational benefits that cannot be made available, unmodified, to women. Alterations to accommodate women would necessarily be [so] "drastic," Virginia asserts, as to transform, indeed "destroy," VMI's program. Neither sex would be favored by the transformation, Virginia maintains: Men would be deprived of the unique opportunity currently available to them; women would not gain that opportunity because their participation would "eliminate the very aspects of [the] program that distinguish [VMI from] other institutions of higher education in Virginia." The District Court forecast from expert witness testimony, and the Court of Appeals accepted, that coeducation would materially affect "at least these three aspects of VMI's program—physical training, the absence of privacy, and the adversative approach." And it is uncontested that women's admission would require accommodations, primarily in arranging housing assignments and physical training programs for female cadets. It is also undisputed, however, that "the VMI methodology could be used to educate women." The District Court even allowed that some women may prefer it to the methodology a women's college might pursue. The parties, furthermore, agree that "some women can meet the physical standards [VMI] now imposes on men." [In] support of its initial judgment for Virginia, [the] District Court made "findings" on "gender-based developmental differences" [that] restate the opinions of Virginia's expert witnesses, opinions about typically male or typically female "tendencies." For example, "males tend to need an atmosphere of adversativeness," while "females tend to thrive in a cooperative atmosphere." [The] United States emphasizes that [we] have cautioned reviewing courts to take a "hard look" at generalizations or "tendencies" of the kind pressed by [Virginia]. State actors controlling gates to opportunity [may] not exclude qualified individuals based on "fixed notions concerning the roles and abilities of males and females."

It may be assumed [that] most women would not choose VMI's adversative method. [However,] it is also probable that "many men would not want to be educated in such an environment." (On that point, even our dissenting colleague might agree.) [The] issue, however, is not whether "women—or men— should be forced to attend VMI" [but] whether the State can constitutionally deny to women who have the will and capacity, the training and attendant opportunities that VMI uniquely affords. The notion that admission of women would downgrade VMI's stature, destroy the adversative system and, with it, even the school, is a judgment hardly proved, a prediction hardly different from other "self-fulfilling prophecies" once routinely used to deny rights or opportunities. When women first sought admission to the bar and access to legal education, concerns of the same order were [expressed]. Medical faculties similarly resisted men and women as partners in the study of medicine. [Surely,] the State's great goal [of producing citizen-soldiers] is not substantially advanced by women's categorical exclusion, in total disregard of their individual merit, from the State's premier "citizen-soldier" corps. Virginia, in sum, "has fallen far short of establishing the 'exceedingly persuasive justification'" that must be the solid base for any gender-defined classification.

In the second phase of the litigation, Virginia presented its remedial plan—maintain VMI as a male-only college and create VWIL as a separate program for women. . . . The constitutional violation in this case is the categorical exclusion of women from an extraordinary educational opportunity afforded men. A proper remedy for an unconstitutional exclusion, we have explained, aims to "eliminate [so far as possible] the discriminatory effects of the past" and to "bar like discrimination in the future." [VWIL] affords women no opportunity to experience the rigorous military training for which VMI is famed. Instead, the VWIL program "deemphasizes" military education, and uses a "cooperative method" of education "which reinforces self-esteem." VWIL students participate in ROTC and a "largely ceremonial" Virginia Corps of Cadets, but Virginia deliberately did not make VWIL a military institute. The VWIL House is not a military-style residence and VWIL students need not live together throughout the 4-year program, eat meals together, or wear uniforms during the school day. VWIL students thus do not experience the "barracks" life "crucial to the VMI experience," the spartan living arrangements designed to foster an "egalitarian ethic." [VWIL] students receive their "leadership training" in seminars [etc.] lacking the "physical rigor, mental stress, [minute] regulation of behavior, and indoctrination in desirable values" made hallmarks of VMI's citizen-soldier training. Kept away from the pressures, hazards, and psychological bonding characteristic of VMI's adversative training, VWIL students will not know the "feeling of tremendous accomplishment" commonly experienced by VMI's successful cadets. Virginia maintains that these methodological differences are "justified pedagogically," based on "important differences between men and women in learning and developmental needs," "psychological and sociological differences" [that] Virginia describes as "real" and "not stereotypes." [Generalizations] about "the way women are," estimates of what is appropriate for most women, no longer justify denying opportunity to women whose talent and capacity place them outside the average description. [In] contrast to the generalizations about women on which Virginia rests, we note against these dispositive realities: VMI's "implementing methodology" is not "inherently unsuitable to women," "some women [do] well under [the] adversative model," "some women, at least, would want to attend [VMI] if they had the opportunity," "some women are capable of all of the individual activities required of VMI cadets," and "can meet the physical standards [VMI] now imposes on men." It is on behalf of these women that the United States has instituted this suit, and it is for them that a remedy must be crafted, a remedy that will end their exclusion from a state-supplied educational opportunity for which they are [fit].

In myriad respects other than military training, VWIL does not qualify as VMI's equal. VWIL's student body, faculty, course offerings, and facilities hardly match VMI's. Nor can the VWIL graduate anticipate the benefits associated with VMI's 157-year history, the school's prestige, and its influential alumni network. Virginia, in sum, while maintaining VMI for men only, has failed to provide any "comparable single-gender women's institution." Instead the Commonwealth has created a VWIL program fairly appraised as a "pale shadow" of VMI in terms of the range of curricular choices and faculty stature, funding, prestige, alumni support and influence.... We rule here that Virginia has not shown substantial equality in the separate educational opportunities the State supports at VWIL and VMI. [The] Fourth Circuit plainly erred in exposing Virginia's VWIL plan to a deferential analysis, for "all gender-based classification today" warrant "heightened scrutiny." Valuable as VWIL may prove for students who seek the program offered, Virginia's remedy affords no cure at all for the opportunities and advantages withheld from women who want a VMI education and can make the grade. In sum, Virginia's remedy does not match the constitutional violation; the State has shown no "exceedingly persuasive justification" for withholding from women qualified for the experience premier training of the kind VMI affords.

. . .

Justice Scalia, dissenting.

Today the Court shuts down an institution that has served the people of [Virginia] with pride and distinction for over a century and a half. To achieve that desired result, it [rejects] the factual findings of two courts below, sweeps aside the precedents of this Court, and ignores the history of our people. As to facts: it explicitly rejects the finding that there exist "gender-based developmental differences" supporting Virginia's restriction of the "adversative" method to only a men's institution, and the finding that the all-male composition of [VMI] is essential to that institution's character. As to precedent: it drastically revises our established standards for reviewing sex-based classifications. And as to history: it counts for nothing the long tradition [of] men's military [colleges]. Much of the Court's opinion is devoted to deprecating the closed-mindedness of our forebears with regard to women's [education]. Closed-minded they were—as

every age is, including our [own]. The virtue of a democratic system [is] that it readily enables the people, over time, to be persuaded that what they took for granted is not so, and to change their laws accordingly. That system is destroyed if the smug assurances of each age are removed from the democratic process and written into the Constitution. Since [the Constitution]—the old one—takes no sides in this educational debate, I dissent.

I shall devote most of my analysis to evaluating the Court's opinion on the basis of our current equal-protection [jurisprudentce]. [I] have no problem with a system of abstract tests such as rational-basis, intermediate, and strict scrutiny (though I think we can do better than applying strict scrutiny and intermediate scrutiny whenever we feel like it). [But] the function of this Court is to preserve our society's values, [not] to revise them; to prevent backsliding from the degree of restriction the Constitution imposed upon democratic government, not to prescribe, on our own authority, progressively higher degrees. [Whatever] abstract tests we may choose to devise, they cannot supersede—and indeed ought to be crafted so as to reflect—those constant and unbroken national traditions that embody the people's understanding of ambiguous constitutional texts. [The] tradition of having government-funded military schools for men is as well rooted in the traditions of this country as the tradition of sending only men into military combat. The people may decide to change the one tradition, like the other, through democratic processes; but the assertion that either tradition has been unconstitutional through the centuries is not law, but politics-smuggled-into-law. And the same applies, more broadly, to single-sex education in general which [is] threatened by today's decision with the cut-off of all state and federal support. Today, however, change is forced upon Virginia, and reversion to single-sex education is prohibited nationwide, not by democratic processes but by order of this Court. Even while bemoaning the sorry, bygone days of "fixed notions" concerning women's education, the Court favors current notions so fixedly that it is willing to write them into the [Constitution] by application of custom-built "tests." This is not the interpretation of a Constitution, but the creation of one.

. . .

[I] now proceed to describe how the analysis should have been conducted. The question to be answered [is] whether the exclusion of women from VMI is "substantially related to an important governmental objective." It is beyond question that Virginia has an important state interest in providing effective college education for its citizens. That single-sex instruction is an approach substantially related to that interest should be evident enough from the long and continuing history in this country of men's and women's colleges. [But] beside its single-sex constitution, VMI is different from other colleges [in employing] a "distinctive educational method." [A] State's decision to maintain within its system one school that provides the adversative method is "substantially related" to its goal of good education. Moreover, it was uncontested that "if the state were to establish a women's VMI-type [i.e., adversative] program, the program would attract an insufficient number of participants to make the program work"; and it was found by the District Court that if Virginia were to include women in VMI, the school "would eventually find it necessary to drop the adversative system altogether." Thus, Virginia's options were an adversative method that excludes women or no adversative method at all. [Virginia's] election to fund one public all-male institution and one on the adversative model—and to concentrate its resources in a single entity that serves both these interests in diversity—is substantially related to the State's important educational interests.

. . .

As is frequently true, the Court's decision today will have consequences that extend far beyond the parties to the case. What I take to be the Court's unease with these consequences, and its resulting unwillingness to acknowledge them, cannot alter the reality. [Under] the constitutional principles announced and applied today, single-sex public education is unconstitutional. By going through the motions of applying a balancing test—asking whether the State has adduced an "exceedingly persuasive justification" for its sex-based classification—the Court creates the illusion that government officials in some future case will have a clear shot at justifying some sort of single-sex public education. Indeed, the Court seeks to create even a greater illusion than that: It purports to have said nothing of relevance to other public schools at all. "We address specifically and only an educational opportunity recognized [as 'unique']." [But] the rationale of today's decision is sweeping: for sex-based classifications, a redefinition of intermediate scrutiny that makes it indistinguishable from strict scrutiny. Indeed, the Court indicates that if any program restricted to one sex is "unique," it must be opened to members of the opposite sex "who have the will and

capacity" to participate in it. [T]he single-sex program that will not be capable of being characterized as "unique" [is] nonexistent. [R]egardless of whether the Court's rationale leaves some small amount of room for lawyers to argue, it ensures that single-sex public education is functionally dead. [The] enemies of single-sex education have won; by persuading only seven Justices [that] their view of the world is enshrined in the Constitution, they have effectively imposed that view on all 50 States.

There are few extant single-sex public educational programs. The potential of today's decision for widespread disruption of existing institutions lies in its application to *private* single-sex education. Government support is immensely important to private educational institutions. Charitable status under the tax law is also highly significant for private [colleges,] and it is certainly not beyond the Court that rendered today's decision to hold that a donation to a single-sex college should be deemed contrary to [public policy]. The Court adverts to private single-sex education only briefly, and only to make the assertion that "we address specifically and only an educational opportunity recognized by the District Court and the Court of Appeals as 'unique.'" As I have already remarked, [the Court's] assurance [that this case concerns only a "unique" educational opportunity] assures nothing, unless it is to be taken as a promise that in the future the Court will disclaim the reasoning it has used today to destroy VMI. The Government, in its briefs to this Court, at least purports to address the consequences of its attack on VMI for public support of private single-sex education. It contends that private colleges which are the direct or indirect beneficiaries of government funding are not thereby necessarily converted into state actors to which [equal protection] is then applicable. That is true. It is also virtually meaningless. The issue will be not whether government assistance turns private colleges into state actors, but whether the government itself would be violating the Constitution by providing state support to single-sex colleges. [The] only hope for state-assisted single-sex private schools is that the Court will not apply in the future the principles of law it has applied today. That is a substantial hope, I am happy and ashamed to say. [It] will certainly be possible for this Court to write a future opinion that ignores the broad principles of law set forth today, and that characterizes as utterly dispositive the opinion's perceptions that VMI was a uniquely prestigious all-male institution, conceived in chauvinism, etc., etc. I will not join that [opinion].

Michael M. *v.* Superior Court of Sonoma County

Michael M. raises many fascinating questions about the legal recognition of gender discrimination. When reading this case, consider these questions: In what ways is California's statutory rape law "sexist"? Under the statute, intercourse with a female under the age of eighteen is criminal but intercourse with a male under eighteen is not. Therefore, any female under eighteen who has sex with an older male participates in an unlawful activity (even though she cannot be punished for it); whereas any male under eighteen, as long as he has sex with a woman above that age, participates in a perfectly lawful activity. Teenage boys, in other words, seem to have more sexual freedom than teenage girls. Was this an intended consequence of the statute? How can we tell? Is this further evidence of prejudice against women?

Justice Rehnquist announced the judgment of the Court and delivered an opinion, in which The Chief Justice, Justice Stewart, and Justice Powell joined.

The question presented in this case is whether California's "statutory rape" law, § 261.5 of the Cal. Penal Code Ann ... violates the Equal Protection Clause of the Fourteenth Amendment. Section 261.5 defines unlawful sexual intercourse as "an act of sexual intercourse accomplished with a female not the wife of the perpetrator, where the female is under the age of 18 years." The statute thus makes men alone criminally liable for the act of sexual intercourse.

In July 1978, a complaint was filed in the Municipal Court of Sonoma County, California, alleging that petitioner, then a $17^1/_2$-year-old male, had had unl0awful sexual intercourse with a female under the age of 18, in violation of § 261.5. The evidence adduced at a preliminary hearing showed that at approximately midnight on June 3, 1978, petitioner and two friends approached Sharon, a $16^1/_2$-year-old female, and her sister as they waited at a bus stop. Petitioner and Sharon, who had already been drinking, moved away from the others and began to kiss. After being struck in the face for rebuffing petitioner's initial advances, Sharon submitted to sexual intercourse with petitioner. Prior to trial, petitioner sought to set aside the information on both state and federal constitutional grounds, asserting that § 261.5 unlaw-

fully discriminated on the basis of gender. The trial court and the California Court of Appeal denied petitioner's request for relief and petitioner sought review in the Supreme Court of California.

The Supreme Court held that "section 261.5 discriminates on the basis of sex because only females may be victims, and only males may violate the section." ... The court then subjected the classification to "strict scrutiny," stating that it must be justified by a compelling state interest. It found that the classification was "supported not by mere social convention but by the immutable physiological fact that it is the female exclusively who can become pregnant." ... Canvassing "the tragic human costs of illegitimate teenage pregnancies," including the large number of teenage abortions, the increased medical risk associated with teenage pregnancies, and the social consequences of teenage childbearing, the court concluded that the State has a compelling interest in preventing such pregnancies. Because males alone can "physiologically cause the result which the law properly seeks to avoid," the court further held that the gender classification was readily justified as a means of identifying offender and victim. For the reasons stated below, we affirm the judgment of the California Supreme Court.

As is evident from our opinions, the Court has had some difficulty in agreeing upon the proper approach and analysis in cases involving challenges to gender-based classifications. ...

... Unlike the California Supreme Court, we have not held that gender-based classifications are "inherently

450 U.S. 464 (1981), United States Supreme Court.

suspect" and thus we do not apply so-called "strict scrutiny" to those classifications. . . . Our cases have held, however, that the traditional minimum rationality test takes on a somewhat "sharper focus" when gender-based classifications are challenged. See *Craig v. Boren*, 429 U.S. 190, 210 (1976). . . . In *Reed v. Reed*, 404 U.S. 71 (1971), for example, the Court stated that a gender-based classification will be upheld if it bears a "fair and substantial relationship" to legitimate state ends, while in *Craig v. Boren*. . . . the Court restated the test to require the classification to bear a "substantial relationship" to "important governmental objectives."

Underlying these decisions is the principle that a legislature may not "make overbroad generalizations based on sex which are entirely unrelated to any differences between men and women or which demean the ability or social status of the affected class." . . . But because the Equal Protection Clause does not "demand that a statute necessarily apply equally to all persons" or require "'things which are different in fact . . . to be treated in law as though they were the same,'" . . . this Court has consistently upheld statutes where the gender classification is not invidious, but rather realistically reflects the fact that the sexes are not similarly situated in certain circumstances. . . . As the Court has stated, a legislature may "provide for the special problems of women." . . .

Applying those principles to this case, the fact that the California Legislature criminalized the act of illicit sexual intercourse with a minor female is a sure indication of its intent or purpose to discourage that conduct. Precisely why the legislature desired that result is of course somewhat less clear. This Court has long recognized that "[i]nquiries into congressional motives or purposes are a hazardous matter." . . .

. . . Here, for example, the individual legislators may have voted for the statute for a variety of reasons. Some legislators may have been concerned about preventing teenage pregnancies, others about protecting young females from physical injury or from the loss of "chastity," and still others about promoting various religious and moral attitudes towards premarital sex.

The justification for the statute offered by the State and accepted by the Supreme Court of California, is that the legislature sought to prevent illegitimate teenage pregnancies.

. . .

We are satisfied not only that the prevention of illegitimate pregnancy is at least one of the "purposes" of the statute, but also that the State has a strong interest in preventing such pregnancy. At the risk of stating the obvious, teenage pregnancies, which have increased dramatically over the last two decades, have significant social, medical, and economic consequences for both the mother and her child, and the State.

. . .

. . . Of particular concern to the state is that approximately half of all teenage pregnancies end in abortion. And of those children who are born, their illegitimacy makes them likely candidates to become wards of the State.

We need not be medical doctors to discern that young men and young women are not similarly situated with respect to the problems and the risks of sexual intercourse. Only women may become pregnant, and they suffer disproportionately the profound physical, emotional, and psychological consequences of sexual activity. The statute at issue here protects women from sexual intercourse at an age when those consequences are particularly severe.

The question thus boils down to whether a State may attack the problem of sexual intercourse and teenage pregnancy directly by prohibiting a male from having sexual intercourse with a minor female. We hold that such a statute is sufficiently related to the State's objectives to pass constitutional muster.

Because virtually all of the significant harmful and inescapably identifiable consequences of teenage pregnancy fall on the young female, a legislature acts well within its authority when it elects to punish only the participant who, by nature, suffers few of the consequences of his conduct. It is hardly unreasonable for a legislature acting to protect minor females to exclude them from punishment. Moreover, the risk of pregnancy itself constitutes a substantial deterrence to young females. No similar natural sanctions deter males. A criminal sanction imposed solely on males thus serves to roughly "equalize" the deterrents on the sexes.

We are unable to accept petitioner's contention that the statute is impermissibly underinclusive and must, in order to pass judicial scrutiny, be *broadened* so as to hold the female as criminally liable as the male. It is argued that this statute is not *necessary* to deter teenage pregnancy because a gender-neutral statute, where both male and female would be subject to prosecution, would serve that goal equally well. The relevant inquiry, however, is not whether the statute is drawn as precisely as it might have been, but whether the line chosen by the California Legislature is within constitutional limitations. . . .

In any event, we cannot say that a gender-neutral statute would be as effective as the statute California has chosen to enact. The State persuasively contends that a gender-neutral statute would frustrate its interest in effective enforcement. Its view is that a female is surely less likely to report violations of the statute if she herself would be subject to criminal prosecution. In an area already fraught with prosecutorial difficulties, we decline to hold that the Equal Protection Clause requires a legislature to enact a statute so broad that it may well be incapable of enforcement.

We similarly reject petitioner's argument that § 261.5 is impermissibly overbroad because it makes unlawful sexual intercourse with prepubescent females, who are, by definition, incapable of becoming pregnant. Quite apart from the fact that the statute could well be justified on the grounds that very young females are particularly susceptible to physical injury from sexual intercourse . . . , it is ludicrous to suggest that the Constitution requires the California Legislature to limit the scope of its rape statute to older teenagers and exclude young girls.

There remains only petitioner's contention that the statute is unconstitutional as it is applied to him because he, like Sharon, was under 18 at the time of sexual intercourse. Petitioner argues that the statute is flawed because it presumes that as between two persons under 18, the male is the culpable aggressor. We find petitioner's contentions unpersuasive. Contrary to his assertions, the statute does not rest on the assumption that males are generally the aggressors. It is instead an attempt by a legislature to prevent illegitimate teenage pregnancy by providing an additional deterrent for men. The age of the man is irrelevant since young men are as capable as older men of inflicting the harm sought to be prevented.

In upholding the California statute we also recognize that this is not a case where a statute is being challenged on the grounds that it "invidiously discriminates" against females. To the contrary, the statute places a burden on males which is not shared by females. But we find nothing to suggest that men, because of past discrimination or peculiar disadvantages, are in need of the special solicitude of the courts. Nor is this a case where the gender classification is made "solely for . . . administrative convenience" . . . , or rests on "the baggage of sexual stereotypes." . . . As we have held, the statute instead reasonably reflects the fact that the consequences of sexual intercourse and pregnancy fall more heavily on the female than on the male. . . .

Accordingly the judgment of the California Supreme Court is
Affirmed.

. . .

Justice Brennan, with whom Justices White and Marshall join, dissenting. . . . It is disturbing to find the Court so splintered on a case that presents such a straightforward issue: Whether the admittedly gender-based classification in Cal. Penal Code Ann. § 261.5 . . . bears a sufficient relationship to the State's asserted goal of preventing teenage pregnancies to survive the "mid-level" constitutional scrutiny mandated by *Craig v. Boren.* . . . Applying the analytical framework provided by our precedents, I am convinced that there is only one proper resolution for this issue: the classification must be declared unconstitutional. I fear that the plurality opinion . . . reach[es] the opposite result by placing too much emphasis on the desirability of achieving the State's asserted statutory goal—prevention of teenage pregnancy—and not enough emphasis on the fundamental question of whether the sex-based discrimination in the California statute is *substantially* related to the achievement of that goal.

. . .

The State of California vigorously asserts that the "important governmental objective" to be served by § 261.5 is the prevention of teenage pregnancy. It claims that its statute furthers this goal by deterring sexual activity by males—the class of persons it considers more responsible for causing those pregnancies. But even assuming that prevention of teenage pregnancy is an important governmental objective and that it is in fact an objective of § 261.5 . . . , California still has the burden of proving that there are fewer teenage pregnancies under its gender-based statutory rape law than there would be if the law were gender-neutral. To meet this burden, the State must show that because its statutory rape law punishes only males, and not females, it more effectively deters minor females from having sexual intercourse.

The plurality assumes that a gender-neutral statute would be less effective than § 261.5 in deterring sexual activity because a gender-neutral statute would create significant enforcement problems. . . .

. . . However, a State's bare assertion that its gender-based statutory classification substantially furthers an important government interest is not enough to meet its burden of proof under *Craig v. Boren.* Rather, the State must produce evidence that will persuade the court that its assertion is true. . . .

The State has not produced such evidence in this case. Moreover, there are at least two serious flaws in the State's assertion that law enforcement problems created by a gender-neutral statutory rape law would make such a statute less effective than a gender-based statute in deterring sexual activity. . . .

. . . There are now at least 37 States that have enacted gender-neutral statutory rape laws. . . .

. . . California has introduced no evidence that those States have been handicapped by the enforcement problems the plurality finds so persuasive. . . .

The second flaw in the State's assertion is that even assuming that a gender-neutral statute would be more difficult to enforce, the State has still not shown that those enforcement problems would make such a statute less effective than a gender-based statute in deterring minor females from engaging in sexual intercourse. Common sense, however, suggests that a gender-neutral statutory rape law is potentially a *greater* deterrent of sexual activity than a gender-based law, for the simple reason that a gender-neutral law subjects both men and women to criminal sanctions and thus arguably has a deterrent effect on twice as many potential violators. Even if fewer persons were prosecuted under the gender-neutral law, as the State suggests, it would still be true that twice as many persons would be *subject* to arrest. The state's failure to prove that a gender-neutral law would be a less effective deterrent than a gender-based law, like the State's failure to prove that a gender-neutral law would be difficult to enforce, should have led this court to invalidate § 261.5. . . .

. . . Until very recently, no California court or commentator had suggested that the purpose of California's statutory rape law was to protect young women from the risk of pregnancy. Indeed, the historical development of § 261.5 demonstrates that the law was initially enacted on the premise that young women, in contrast to young men, were to be deemed legally incapable of consenting to an act of sexual intercourse. Because their chastity was considered particularly precious, those young women were felt to be uniquely in need of the State's protection. In contrast, young men were assumed to be capable of making such decisions for themselves; the law therefore did not offer them any special protection.

It is perhaps because the gender classification in California's statutory rape law was initially designed to further these outmoded sexual stereotypes, rather than to reduce the incidence of teenage pregnancies, that the State has been unable to demonstrate a substantial relationship between the classification and its newly asserted goal. . . . But whatever the reason, the State has not shown that Cal. Penal Code § 261.5 is any more effective than a gender-neutral law would be in deterring minor females from engaging in sexual intercourse. It has therefore not met its burden of proving that the statutory classification is substantially related to the achievement of its asserted goal.

I would hold that § 261.5 violates the Equal Protection Clause of the Fourteenth Amendment, and I would reverse the judgment of the California Supreme Court.

U.S. *v. Clary*

James Clary pled guilty to a charge of possession with intent to distribute cocaine. Federal law set the level of punishment of possession of crack cocaine at 100 times the level of severity for possession of powder cocaine, per gram of the drug. Possession of over 50 grams of crack carried a mandatory term of 10 years imprisonment. After Clary's guilty plea but before sentencing, he filed a motion arguing that the ten-year mandatory minimum sentence contained in the crack cocaine statute violated his Equal Protection rights guaranteed by the Constitution. Clary presented eleven witnesses who testified about the profound impact of the crack statute and its ten-year mandatory minimum sentence on African Americans. The district court agreed with Clary, finding that, nationwide,

92.6 percent of those convicted of possession of crack were African American, whereas only 4.7 percent were white. The percentages were nearly reversed for possession of powder cocaine. Do you agree with the district court that the disparate racial impact reveals that Congress acted with a discriminatory purpose in setting the penalties for crack? Do you agree with the Eighth Circuit Court that "a belief that racial animus was a motivating factor, based on disproportionate impact, is simply not enough" for an Equal Protection violation?

John R. Gibson, Senior Circuit Judge: The [district] court outlined the events leading up to passage of the crack statute. The court cited several news articles submitted by members of Congress for publication in the Congressional Record which portrayed crack dealers as unemployed, gang-affiliated, gun-toting, young black males. Legislators, the court reasoned, used these media accounts as informational support for the statute. The district court also pointed to perceived procedural irregularities surrounding Congress' approval of the crack sentencing provisions. For instance, few hearings were held in the House on the enhanced penalties for crack. While many Senators called for a more measured response, the Senate committee conducted a single morning hearing. Finally, although the penalties were originally set at 50 to 1, they were arbitrarily doubled.

The district court also observed that 98.2 percent of defendants convicted of crack cocaine charges in the Eastern District of Missouri between the years 1988 and 1992 were African American. Nationally, 92.6 percent of those convicted of crack cocaine charges were African American, as opposed to 4.7 percent who were white. With respect to powder cocaine, the percentages were largely reversed. The court found that this statistical evidence demonstrated both the disparate impact of the 100 to 1 ratio and the probability that "the subliminal influence of unconscious racism had permeated federal prosecution throughout the nation."

While the government directed the court to evidence that Congress considered crack to be more dangerous because of its potency, addictiveness, affordability and prevalence, the court found evidence in the record contradicting many of the legislators' beliefs. In particular, the court questioned Congress' conclusion that crack was 100 times more potent or dangerous than powder cocaine, referring to testimony that there is no reliable medical evidence that crack cocaine is more addictive than powder cocaine. In light of these

factors, the court found the punishment of crack at 100 times greater than powder cocaine to be a "frenzied, irrational response." The court repeatedly stressed that "cocaine is cocaine.". . .

[In] past decisions by this court [we found] that Congress clearly had rational motives for creating the distinction between crack and powder cocaine. Among the reasons were "the potency of the drug, the ease with which drug dealers can carry and conceal it, the highly addictive nature of the drug, and the violence which often accompanies trade in it." [We also] squarely reject[ed] the argument that crack cocaine sentences disparately impact on African Americans. [Under] Personnel Administrator of Massachusetts v. Feeney, 442 U.S. 256 (1979), . . . even if a neutral law has a disproportionate adverse impact on a racial minority, it is unconstitutional only if that effect can be traced to a discriminatory purpose. discriminatory purpose "implies that the decisionmaker, in this case [Congress], selected or reaffirmed a particular course of action at least in part 'because of' not merely 'in spite of,' its adverse effects upon an identifiable group." [T]here was no evidence that Congress or the Sentencing Commission had a racially discriminatory motive when it crafted the Guidelines with extended sentences for crack cocaine felonies.

[At congressional hearings on crack cocaine] Dr. Robert Byck, Professor of Psychiatry and Pharmacology at Yale University, . . . contrasted inhaling crack vapor to packing a nose with cocaine powder (the most common form of using cocaine powder). Byck stated that crack is more dangerous than cocaine powder because as a person breathes crack vapor, an almost unlimited amount of the drug can enter the body. "Moreover, the speed of the material going to the brain is very rapid." He also commented on the marketability of crack cocaine, stating that "here suddenly, we have cocaine available in a little package, in unit dosage, available at a price that kids can pay initially." . . .

This case undoubtedly presents the most complete record on this issue to come before this court. Nevertheless, we are satisfied that both the record before the

---

34 F.3d 709 (1994). United States Court of Appeals for the Eighth Circuit.

district court and the district court's findings fall short of establishing that Congress acted with a discriminatory purpose in enacting the statute, and that Congress selected or reaffirmed a particular course of action "at least in part 'because of,' not merely 'in spite of' its adverse effects upon an identifiable group." . . .

We . . . question the district court's reliance on "unconscious racism." The court reasoned that a focus on purposeful discrimination will not show more subtle and deeply-buried forms of racism. The court's reasoning, however, simply does not address the question whether Congress acted with a discriminatory purpose. Similar failings affect the court's statement that although intent per se may not have entered into Congress' enactment of the crack statutes, Congress' failure to account for a substantial and foreseeable disparate impact on African Americans nonetheless violates the spirit and letter of equal protection.

We also question the court's reliance on media-created stereotypes of crack dealers and its conclusion that this information "undoubtedly served as the touchstone that influenced racial perceptions held by legislators and the public as related to the 'crack epidemic.'" Although the placement of newspaper and magazine articles in the Congressional Record indicates that this information may have affected at least some legislators, these articles hardly demonstrate that the stereotypical images "undoubtedly" influenced the legislators' racial perceptions. It is too long a leap from newspaper and magazine articles to an inference that Congress enacted the crack statute because of its adverse effect on African American males, instead of the stated purpose of responding to the serious impact of a rapidly-developing and particularly-dangerous form of drug use. Similarly, the evidence of the haste with which Congress acted and the action it took is as easily explained by the seriousness of the perceived problem as by racial animus. . . .

Other testimony before the district court demonstrates the particular lack of support for the court's conclusion about Congress' motivation in passing the statute. . . . Eric E. Sterling, [who was] Counsel to the Subcommittee of Criminal Justice of the House of Representatives at the time the statutes in question were passed . . . stated that the members of Congress did not have racial animus, but rather "racial consciousness," an awareness that the "problem in the inner cities . . . was about to explode into the white part of the country." Sterling believed that Congress wanted the penalties to be applied wherever crack was being trafficked, although Congress was aware that crack was used primarily by minorities. He further described the seriousness of the problem as reported by the popular press, and stated his view that the creation and promulgation of the law was based on "crass political interest." His opinion was that the motivating factor for the legislation was a perception that crack cocaine posed a unique and unprecedented problem for American narcotics enforcement. . . .

For the most part, the other witnesses that testified before the district court were medical witnesses, several of whom contested the medical information before the Senate that showed differences between crack and powder cocaine. Scientific disagreement with testimony in congressional hearings, offered at a later time and after additional research, simply does not establish discriminatory purpose, or for that matter, a lack of scientific support for Congress' action.

We reverse and remand to the district court for resentencing consistent with this opinion.

Chapter 4

Criminal Law

Many of us are better acquainted with the basic language and aims of the criminal law than with any other part of our jurisprudence. Unfortunately, most of that familiarity fails to extend much beyond the latest TV show or movie mystery. Sensational criminal trials, such as those of O. J. Simpson and Theodore Kaczynski, the confessed Unabomber, also distort the public's perception of the criminal process. All of this is regrettable, for the criminal law raises some of the most troubling and yet fascinating philosophical difficulties anywhere in the law—problems sharpened in their urgency by the obvious extent to which the criminal law can affect the course of a human life, or, in the extreme case, end it.

In 1995, a New York jury awarded Darrell Cabey $43 million in his suit against Bernhard Goetz. Goetz had shot and paralyzed Cabey in a notorious clash in a New York subway. A few days before Christmas 1984, the slightly built Goetz entered a subway car in New York City. Four youths, apparently looking for trouble, asked him for money. Goetz responded with a .38-caliber revolver, wounding each of the four and paralyzing one of them. The media quickly branded Goetz the "subway vigilante," and his eventual trial on multiple counts of assault and attempted murder highlighted difficult issues: Did Goetz intend to kill the youths? Could he be convicted of "attempted" murder? Did he act in self-defense? Did he endanger others unjustifi-

ably? Should he be punished? These questions prompt larger ones: Under what conditions should a person be held responsible for his or her acts? Under what conditions may one be excused? Suppose I simply made a mistake? Or was merely careless? Or was mentally unstable? Is it fair to punish me for a harm I caused but did not intend? If I try but fail to commit a crime, should I be punished as severely as if I had succeeded? What is the aim of punishment in the first place? Must the punishment always "fit" the crime? Is that always possible? If, for example, my crime consists in subjecting you to a chance of injury, would it be fair to subject me in similar fashion to a risk of harm? Are there punishments that ought never to be inflicted?

Section A begins our exploration of these issues. *People v. Dlugash* is a study in liability for criminal "attempts," exploring how attempts to commit a crime should be punished. Douglas Husak reviews the perplexities of the "criminal intent" requirement in the law. Sanford Kadish questions why criminal defendants who, through "luck," fail to cause harm, should be rewarded with a lesser penalty than those who succeed.

Section B examines the role of the "mental element" in crime and its relationship to the concepts of excuse and justification. The burgeoning variety of excuses advanced by criminal defendants is reviewed, and two specific excuses are discussed in detail. The court's opinion in the case of Janice

Leidholm and the essay by Cathryn Jo Rosen each weigh the arguments for and against the battered woman's defense; the remaining selections examine the role of mental illness and the insanity defense, with Norval Morris arguing for its abolition and Stephen J. Morse for its retention.

Section C turns to larger issues about punishment and sentencing. The Supreme Court's recent opinion in *Lockyer v. Andrade* raises questions about the ultimate purpose of punishment and what it means for a penalty to be excessive. The selection from the writings of Jeremy Bentham outlines the case for a utilitarian approach to the justification of punishment; Michael Moore seeks to defend the retributive theory, and H. L. A. Hart seeks an account which "mixes" aspects of both utilitarian and retributive concerns.

Section D examines the complex issues surrounding the death penalty. The Supreme Court's controversial decision in *Atkins v. Virginia*, banning capital punishment in the case of individuals who are mentally retarded, is followed by readings addressing the constitutional issues posed by capital punishment: whether it is "cruel and unusual," and whether it is imposed in a discriminatory way. The moral and policy dimensions of these issues are debated by Ernest van den Haag, Hugo Bedau, and Randall Kennedy.

The "Cases for Further Reflection" deal with issues ranging from the meaning of "cruel and unusual punishment" to the death penalty, habitual offender statutes, the role of victim-impact statements in criminal sentencing, and even a case involving the criminal punishment of a dog.

A. *What Is a Crime?*

The Elements of Criminality

Bernhard Goetz was accused of having committed at least four separate and distinct crimes, all arising out of his use of a gun on the subway that morning: possessing a loaded gun in public, recklessly endangering the lives of others, criminal assault, and attempted murder. How can one action produce such a wealth of "crimes"? The answer is that each offense was based upon one or another aspect of Goetz's conduct together with his state of mind at the time of the incident, as these were defined by the relevant laws. Notorious as Goetz's case was, it nonetheless illustrates both procedural and substantive aspects of the criminal law. Because these concepts figure prominently in the material for this section, it will be useful to pause a moment over them.

You will recall from Chapter 1 that *procedural* law is concerned with the rules governing how civil and criminal cases are begun, conducted, and resolved. In a criminal case, the procedural aspects begin with the apprehension of a person (or persons) suspected of wrongdoing. Although criminal procedure is complex and the precise steps followed may differ greatly from one case to the next, all criminal cases resulting in a conviction must pass through some basic steps, illustrated in the following chart:[1]

Procedural Elements of Conviction and Punishment

1. Defendant's (D's) allegedly wrongful conduct is detected or is confessed.

---

[1] I would like to thank Prof. Jim Nickel for the charts used here.

2. D is apprehended by, or otherwise comes into the custody of authorities.

3. D is indicted and arraigned, with charges formally presented and a plea entered.

4. D pleads guilty and is sentenced, *or* D's plea results in a trial.

5. D is tried and convicted.

6. D is sentenced by the judge.

7. D's sentence is carried out.

Goetz initially fled, later to turn himself in to authorities and offer a confession. He was indicted (as we have seen) for committing multiple crimes and entered a plea of "not guilty." The subsequent trial resulted in a conviction on one count (illegal possession of a firearm). He was then sentenced and served 250 days in jail. Years later, Darrell Cabey, the young man whom Goetz paralyzed with his final shot, sued Goetz in civil court for damages. This is not an unknown state of affairs, because a criminal conviction (or acquittal) does not bar a private lawsuit concerning injuries sustained by victims of crime.

Although procedural law raises important issues, this section focuses largely on problems raised by the *substantive* law. What are the elements of *substantive* law in a case such as Goetz's? What is involved in showing that a defendant is guilty of having committed a crime? Some of the basic elements are listed below.

Substantive Elements of a Crime

1. A valid, publicly known, and non-retroactive law prohibits a given act (A).

2. Defendant (D) committed A.

3. D committed A with the state of mind defined by the law prohibiting A.

4. D has neither a justification nor an excuse for committing A (i.e., D is responsible for committing A).

Several aspects of this list of conditions are important. The first element or condition seems to state the obvious, but some significant principles are in play here. One is the *Principle of Legality,* which requires that people subject to the law be given clear and adequate notice of what the law expects of them so that they can have a fair opportunity to conform their conduct to its requirements. As interpreted by the courts, the demand of legality is a component of *due process* and

requires that statutes and other enactments be sufficiently definite to provide both a standard of conduct for the average citizen to follow, and a clear standard for police enforcement. Statutes have been found to violate this principle. In *Lanzetta v. New Jersey* (306 U.S. 451 [1939]), for example, the defendants were arrested pursuant to a statute that read: "any person not engaged in any lawful occupation, known to be a member of a gang consisting of two or more persons, who has been convicted of any crime in . . . any state" has violated the law. The Supreme Court held that this statute was "repugnant" to the *Due Process* clause of the Constitution because of its vagueness: It simply isn't clear what one is not supposed to do here. Not be unemployed? Not "associate" with two other people? *Lanzetta* also illustrates another important aspect of conditions (1) and (2), above: namely, that the law prohibits what people *do* (e.g., shooting a police officer; reckless driving), not *who they are* (e.g., an unemployed "gangster"). The reference in (1), above, to retroactivity also has a constitutional dimension: the Constitution explicitly forbids laws that are *"ex post facto,"* that is, laws prohibiting actions that took place before the laws were enacted. Clearly such laws cannot pass the test of legality, because no one can conform his or her conduct to a law that has yet to exist.

Together, conditions (2) and (3) above express the core of the substantive notion of a crime: the central feature of the criminal law is its attempt to rest liability upon the conjunction of two elements: outward behavior and inner state of mind.

Act and Intent

These two basic elements of criminality are marked by their Latin names: *actus reus* and *mens rea. Actus reus* refers to an act of wrongdoing: running a red light, shooting someone, taking a television set without the owner's permission (and not returning it). The criminal law is concerned with conduct, with things people *do.* You might wonder why this is so. Must something be *done* before the criminal law can respond? Why not (for example) focus on thoughts or emotions? Why not subject to punishment those who possess, though they have not yet manifested, "poor character"? Why can't a person be punished for having "evil thoughts"? (Consider in this connection that several centuries ago, it was a criminal offense in England to "imagine the King's death.") It is of course difficult to prove what thoughts or feelings people have (unless they are willing to tell you), and perhaps thoughts, by themselves, are less dangerous than actual conduct. Certainly they are difficult to control, whereas acts are, at least usually, something over which we have some power.

Even if we agree that the criminal law should confine its attention to acts, this still leaves the problem of understanding what an "act" is. Acts can be difficult to define. How many "acts" did Bernhard Goetz commit? Is imagining the King's death an "act"? The Model Penal Code (MPC), a proposed uniform criminal statute written by a number of lawyers and legal scholars, defines an "act" as a "muscular movement under conscious control." Is "possessing a loaded gun" an "act" under this definition?

The expression *mens rea* literally means "guilty mind" or "evil mind," and is generally taken to refer to the *mental* element of a crime. The basic idea is that one must have had a culpable or blameworthy state of mind before one can be said to have committed a crime. This requirement is frequently explained in terms of the idea that a criminal acts with the *intent to commit the offense*. It doesn't take much reflection to see that this requirement raises a whole range of fresh difficulties and problems: How can it be determined what X intended or thought or believed or wanted? Aren't there different states of mind that a person can have when he or she performs an action that constitutes an *actus reus*? Should all states of mind be regarded as equally culpable? If not, how can we distinguish between the relevant states of mind and grade them appropriately? What states of mind excuse people from liability altogether?

Douglas Husak, in his selection for this section, illustrates the philosophical dimensions of intention in the law by raising a number of questions. What does it mean to perform an action intentionally? Is everything that I do voluntarily an intentional action? Suppose that I am subject to epileptic seizures. A seizure hits while I am driving down the highway, and I swerve from the road and injure a pedestrian. Did I act voluntarily? Intentionally? In what sense? When? Or, to pick a fanciful example, suppose I wish to harass a former lover who lives in an apartment building. I am knowledgeable about electricity, and, out of spite, I manage to shut off the power to the entire building for hours. Unknown to me, however, an elderly man on a respirator lives in the building. With the power cut off, the respirator quits and the man dies. Is it fair to say that I intended the man's death? Could I have foreseen his death? Could a reasonable person have done so? Would it have made a

difference if I had known of the man's condition? Does it matter that my motive was simply to annoy my ex-lover, not to injure or kill anyone? As Husak goes on to explore, some courts and commentators have even questioned why intent should be an element of criminality at all.

Plainly there are some conditions under which a person cannot be held accountable for an act of wrongdoing. This ties *mens rea* to the last of the conditions, (4), noted above. An *excuse* is a factor that, if proven, establishes that the actor did not have the required state of mind and is therefore not properly subject to the sanctions of the criminal law. Typical excuses include infancy (being a minor), duress (being forced or pressured by another), mistake (being unaware of crucial facts or circumstances), and insanity (suffering from some kind of mental disability or defect). To say that a defendant has a *justification* for his conduct makes even a stronger claim: namely, that the defendant made the correct choice, all things considered.

Strict Criminal Liability

For all rules there are exceptions, and this holds true for the conditions defining a substantive criminal offense. One important exception worth noting applies to condition (3), the requirement that the defendant acted with a certain state of mind with regard to the offense charged. Common as this principle is, there are important and controversial exceptions to it, such as the doctrine of *felony-murder*.

Generally speaking, to be convictable of murder, one must either have acted with the intent to kill or have exhibited extreme recklessness with regard to human life (for example, by emptying a revolver into a crowded room). To be convicted of first-degree murder it is usually necessary to have acted in a premeditated fashion or to have committed the crime under circumstances presumed to be premeditated, such as by administering poison. The felony-murder doctrine is an exception to these requirements. This doctrine says that if, in the course of the commission of a felony a killing occurs, all accomplices in the felony can be charged with murder. X, Y, and Z decide to rob a bank. Z waits in the getaway car while X and Y commit the holdup. A security guard makes a menacing gesture, and Y shoots him. Z is guilty of felony-murder even if he was nowhere near the scene and did not pull the trigger.

The felony-murder concept has numerous permutations and complexities. Suppose that, after X and Y leave the bank, one of the tellers dies of a fright-induced heart attack. California has held that Z is guilty of felony-murder.[2] What if X turns on Y in the bank and shoots him? Some states, again including California, have held that Z can be convicted for this murder as well.[3] Finally, what if neither the person killed nor the person doing the killing is one of the felons? Should felony-murder still apply?

Other crimes are similar to felony-murder in a critical respect: Statutory rape (unlawful intercourse with a female minor), bigamy (being married to more than one person at a time), and various "public welfare" offenses (for example, mishandling or mislabeling drug products), along with the felony-murder rule, have traditionally been among the offenses imposing *strict criminal liability,* the defining feature of which is the refusal to require proof of the actor's state of mind as a prerequisite to liability.

The principal justifications offered for the creation of strict liability offenses have been utilitarian in nature, appealing to the supposed good consequences of imposing such liability. Those who favor strict criminal liability on these grounds argue that it will deter crime by inducing those contemplating felonious conduct to think again, and that it will protect the public by provoking those who engage in dangerous but socially beneficial activities (such as drug manufacture) to be especially cautious. Others argue that strict liability is more efficient than the traditional emphasis upon the requirement of *mens rea* since it is burdensome to inquire into a defendant's state of mind. It has also been argued that a person who begins a series of events that terminates in the death of another incurs a kind of moral stain or taint that must then be expiated through punishment appropriate to the crime of murder. Alternatively, it might be urged that those who commit felonies run the risk that things might turn out worse than they expected.

Opponents of strict liability offenses object that it is wrong and unfair to thus use the defendant as an expedient to promote the greater good. People should be punished, the critics insist, only when they manifest a culpable state of mind for the offense with which they have been charged.

---

[2] *People v. Stampe,* 2 Cal. App. 3d 203 (1969).
[3] *People v. Cabaltero,* 31 Cal. App. 2d 52 (1939).

The Model Penal Code

To have before us a useful framework for the analysis of problems having to do with states of mind, consider the manner in which the drafters of the Model Penal Code sought to handle the mental element. The Code proposes that every criminal offense be specified in terms of a breakdown of its constituent elements. Take burglary as an example. Most jurisdictions define burglary in this way: Knowingly breaking and entering the dwelling house of another with the intent to commit a felony therein. This crime has several elements: (1) breaking and entering; (2) dwelling house; (3) of another; (4) intent to commit a felony. The Code proposes that, to be convictable of this offense, I must have the requisite state of mind with respect to each element of the offense. In this case, that means that I must, with intent or conscious purpose, have broken in and entered property; have done so in the awareness that it was a dwelling house, and the dwelling house of another; and have intended to commit a felony when I got inside. Failure to possess the relevant state of mind in conjunction with any of the elements would mean that I could not be convicted of the offense. Suppose I leave my house late at night, intending to burglarize some homes down the street. It is unusually dark and foggy; I break into my own house. Have I committed burglary? No. Although I acted with the purpose or conscious intent to enter, I did not do so with respect to the dwelling house of *another.* (I may be convictable of *attempting* burglary, of course, but that is a separate matter.) Frustrated, I try again the next night. Hours of effort and no success wear me out and I decide to return home. It is dark and even foggier than the night before. I walk through the unlocked door of what I think is my house. But it is not my house. Have I committed burglary? No. I entered the dwelling of another, but I did not act with the "purpose to enter the house of another"; I acted with the purpose to go home, even though that's not where I wound up.

Conflicting Conceptions of Criminal Wrongdoing

Why should consequences matter in defining a criminal offense? Recall the substantive elements of a crime listed above. Conditions (1) and (2) refer to an act prohibited by law. As we saw in the discussion of the enforcement of morality in Chapter 2, there is a lively debate about what specific kinds of acts should be so proscribed. Should they, for example, always be acts that cause harm? And if so, what about acts that pose a *risk* of harm, even if they do not actually bring it about? Two contrasting approaches to theorizing about substantive criminal law reflect conflicting answers to these questions. The more traditional approach focuses upon the *suffering* of the crime victim, the actual harm done. This concern was reflected in the charges brought against Bernhard Goetz for assault. The traditional view is less inclined to consider, for example, the imposition of a risk of harm—reflected in the reckless endangerment charge—as deserving of criminal punishment. But if an injury occurs, even if it was not specifically intended by the perpetrator, the suffering of the victim demands a response. In this way, the traditional view construes the mental element or "intent" requirement broadly: If the "natural and probable" consequence of shooting at a man at close range is that you might sever his spinal cord, and if that happens, you "intended" it, even if there was no conscious aim to bring about that consequence. The traditional approach holds that the suffering of the victim demands that the perpetrator "pay" for his wicked deed.

A contrasting view of criminality is reflected in the charges brought against Goetz for attempted murder and reckless endangerment. Here the concern is not with the harm done to the victim but with the assailant's act itself, with the act that caused the harm, and with the degree of control the assailant had over that act. If I shoot at you, intending to kill you, but I miss, why should the absence of a victim mitigate the seriousness of what I have done? Am I not just as guilty of endangering your life, putting you at risk? This more modern view thus settles on a rationale for punishing the *attempt* to commit a crime and for punishing such attempts with severity equal to that for successfully completed crimes. Which approach to defining and responding to criminality is best? Which is morally right?

Liability and Punishment for Attempts

How should people who *attempt* to break the law, but who don't succeed, be dealt with by the law? Focusing on the law of attempts usefully brings many of the questions we have been examining into focus.

The common law position for some time has been that those who (unsuccessfully) attempt to commit a crime should be punished less severely than those who succeed in the commission of the crime. That this has been the general practice of our law is indisputable, but the reasons for it are less clear. Imagine that two people shoot at me. One hits me; the other misses by inches. Both tried equally hard and acted with equal malice (evil intent). Insofar as we want to punish the wicked or deter the dangerous, both of my attackers would seem to merit equal punishment. Does it make sense to punish less harshly the person who missed the target than the one who got the "bull's eye"? Doesn't this seem to make guilt or innocence a function of luck? Is the one who missed more likely to try again? Does the fact that both tried and only one succeeded show that the successful attempter tried harder—was "wholehearted" in his efforts—so he deserves more punishment or manifests greater danger?

Dlugash and the "Impossible" Attempt

The facts of *People v. Dlugash* raise a further question: Should attempts to commit crimes be punished at all if what the actor sought to do was impossible under the circumstances? During an argument in the early morning hours, Joe Bush shoots Mike Geller three times in the chest. Roughly five minutes later, Bush's companion, Dlugash, walks over the prone Geller and empties five shots into and about his head and vital organs. Dlugash later testifies that he acted because he was "afraid of Joe Bush." Dlugash is convicted of murder; but an appellate court reverses the conviction on the grounds that the state did not prove beyond a reasonable doubt that Geller was alive at the time Dlugash pulled the trigger. However Dlugash is also convicted of the "lesser included offense" of attempted murder. Dlugash now presents the appellate court with an unusual question: Can you attempt to murder a man who is already dead?

The common law of England—many of the central principles and distinctions of which were adopted early in the history of this country—made it a criminal offense to attempt to commit a crime: the unsuccessful effort to bring about the intended harm. Like most crimes, attempt has both *actus reus* and *mens rea* components. The *mens rea* requirement for attempts is fairly straightforward: One must have acted with the purpose of committing the object crime. (There are some difficult cases here, however. If I throw a bomb at a car, hoping and desiring to kill the driver but killing the passenger instead, did I intend the passenger's death?) The *actus reus* requirement for attempts is more complex, the principal difficulty being how to draw a line successfully between merely *preparing* to commit a crime (for example, buying burglar's tools) and *beginning the attempt* (heading off to the bank with the tools in my backpack). How much do I have to do, how far do I have to go, in order to have "made the attempt"?

Certainly the thorniest problem in the law of attempts, however, has been that posed by the following question: If what you are trying to do would constitute a crime if completed, should you be convicted of attempt if the crime was impossible to commit? Should it matter why the crime could not be committed? One obvious sort of reason for the "impossibility" involved here is that the facts might not be as you take them to be. X shoots at a shape lying under the blankets on a bed, intending to kill the person he believes to be asleep on it, but the lump under the sheets is merely a pile of pillows. Y is a pickpocket looking for easy prey; he reaches into your pocket, intending to steal your wallet, but the pocket is empty. Has X attempted murder or simply engaged in target practice with the bedclothes? Should Y be convicted of attempted robbery or merely admonished to keep his hands to himself?

What if the facts that make it impossible to complete your attempt relate to the legal definition or classification of a thing? Z tries to buy what he thinks are stolen goods from a "fence"; yet the goods are not stolen but really Z's own. Must Z be acquitted on the grounds that no amount of effort exerted in "buying" one's own things will make that conduct into the crime of receiving stolen property? Or should Z be judged guilty, since only an unforeseeable contingency (no thanks to him) kept his act from being a crime? If we let every such contingency exonerate the attempter, does that mean that the only attempts punishable will be (paradoxically) the successful ones? Traditionally, the law called the impossibility faced by X and Y "factual" and that facing Z "legal." The grounds for this distinction are not clear; they are explored by the court in *Dlugash.*

In *Dlugash,* the court notes that the law of attempt in New York has been modified to reflect the position adopted by the Model Penal Code. MPC section 5.01 effectively does away with the legal-factual impossibility distinction. It focuses on what the defendant intended or believed, not what actually happened. How does this approach apply to Dlugash? If he believed the victim to be alive at the moment of the shooting, he is guilty of attempted murder, even if Geller was in fact dead at the time. And, the Court holds, there is evidence here to support the claim that Dlugash *did* believe Geller to be alive. (It is also worth noting that the MPC, unlike the code in many states, would punish Dlugash's attempt with the same degree of severity as the crime that was his object.)

Luck and the Criminal Law

In the final reading of this section, law professor Sanford Kadish argues against a view pervasive in the criminal law. What Kadish calls the "harm doctrine" says that a defendant who intends a harm that never actually occurs deserves less punishment than a defendant who intends the same harm but where that harm does obtain. Unsuccessful attempts to commit crimes, for example, seem, under this doctrine, to give defendants a "reward" for failure. Kadish thinks that the doctrine of imposing a lesser punishment where no harm is done neither serves the purposes of the law nor is justified by moral principle. Kadish illustrates the operation of the resulting harm doctrine with the law of attempts and of endangerment, and evaluates them in light of such penal goals as prevention of criminal activity and deterrence. Lastly, Kadish contends, rewarding failure may actually disserve the goals of the practice of punishment.

People v. Dlugash

Jasen, Judge.

The criminal law is of ancient origin, but criminal liability for attempt to commit a crime is comparatively recent. At the root of the concept of attempt liability are the very aims and purposes of penal law. The ultimate issue is whether an individual's intentions and actions, though failing to achieve a manifest and malevolent criminal purpose, constitute a danger to organized society of sufficient magnitude to warrant the imposition of criminal sanctions. Difficulties in theoretical analysis and concomitant debate over very pragmatic questions of blameworthiness appear dramatically in reference to situations where the criminal attempt failed to achieve its purpose solely because the factual or legal context in which the individual acted was not as the actor supposed them to be. Phrased somewhat differently, the concern centers on whether an individual should be liable for an attempt to commit a crime when, unknown to him, it was impossible to successfully complete the crime attempted. For years, serious studies have been made on the subject in an effort to resolve the continuing controversy when, if at all, the impossibility of successfully completing the criminal act should preclude liability for even making the futile attempt. The 1967 revision of the Penal law approached the impossibility defense to the inchoate crime of attempt in a novel fashion. The statute provides that, if a person engages in conduct which would otherwise constitute an attempt to commit a crime, "it is no defense to a prosecution for such attempt that the crime charged to have been attempted was, under the attendant circumstances, factually or legally impossible of commission, if such crime could have been committed had the attendant circumstances been as such person believed them to be." (Penal Law, §110.10.) This appeal presents to us, for the first time, a case involving the application of the modern statute. We hold that, under the proof presented by the People at trial, defendant Melvin Dlugash may be held for attempted murder, though the

target of the attempt may have already been slain, by the hand of another, when Dlugash made his felonious attempt.

On December 22, 1973, Michael Geller, 25 years old, was found shot to death in the bedroom of his Brooklyn apartment. The body, which had literally been riddled by bullets, was found lying face up on the floor. An autopsy revealed that the victim had been shot in the face and head no less than seven times. Powder burns on the face indicated that the shots had been fired from within one foot of the victim. Four small caliber bullets were recovered from the victim's skull. The victim had also been critically wounded in the chest. One heavy caliber bullet passed through the left lung, penetrated the heart chamber, pierced the left ventricle of the heart upon entrance and again upon exit, and lodged in the victim's torso. Although a second bullet was damaged beyond identification, the bullet tracks indicated that these wounds were also inflicted by a bullet of heavy caliber. A tenth bullet, of unknown caliber, passed through the thumb of the victim's left hand. The autopsy report listed the cause of death as "[m]ultiple bullet wounds of head and chest with brain injury and massive bilateral hemothorax with penetration of [the] heart." Subsequent ballistics examination established that the four bullets recovered from the victim's head were .25 caliber bullets and that the heart-piercing bullet was of .38 caliber.

Detective Joseph Carrasquillo of the New York City Policy Department was assigned to investigate the homicide. On December 27, 1973, five days after the discovery of the body, Detective Carrasquillo and a fellow officer went to the defendant's residence in an effort to locate him. The officers arrived at approximately 6:00 P.M. The defendant answered the door and, when informed that the officers were investigating the death of Michael Geller, a friend of his, defendant invited the officers into the house. Detective Carrasquillo informed defendant that the officers desired any information defendant might have regarding the death of Geller and, since defendant was regarded as a suspect, administered the standard

363 N. E. 2d 1155 (1977), Court of Appeals of New York.

preinterrogation warnings. The defendant told the officers that he and another friend, Joe Bush, had just returned from a four- or five-day trip "upstate someplace" and learned of Geller's death only upon his return. Since Bush was also a suspect in the case and defendant admitted knowing Bush, defendant agreed to accompany the officers to the station house for the purposes of identifying photographs of Bush and of lending assistance to the investigation. Upon arrival at the police station, Detective Carrasquillo and the defendant went directly into an interview room. Carrasquillo advised the defendant that he had witnesses and information to the effect that as late as 7:00 P.M. on the day before the body was found, defendant had been observed carrying a .25 caliber pistol. Once again, Carrasquillo administered the standard preinterrogation statement of rights. The defendant then proceeded to relate his version of the events which culminated in the death of Geller. Defendant stated that on the night of December 21, 1973, he, Bush and Geller had been out drinking. Bush had been staying at Geller's apartment and, during the course of the evening, Geller several times demanded that Bush pay $100 towards the rent on the apartment. According to defendant, Bush rejected these demands, telling Geller that "you better shut up or you're going to get a bullet." All three returned to Geller's apartment at approximately midnight, took seats in the bedroom, and continued to drink until sometime between 3:00 and 3:30 in the morning. When Geller again pressed his demand for rent money, Bush drew his .38 caliber pistol, aimed it at Geller and fired three times. Geller fell to the floor. After the passage of a few minutes, perhaps two, perhaps as much as five, defendant walked over to the fallen Geller, drew his .25 caliber pistol, and fired approximately five shots in the victim's head and face. Defendant contended that, by the time he fired the shots, "it looked like Mike Geller was already dead." After the shots were fired, defendant and Bush walked to the apartment of a female acquaintance. Bush removed his shirt, wrapped the two guns and a knife in it, and left the apartment, telling Dlugash that he intended to dispose of the weapons. Bush returned 10 or 15 minutes later and stated that he had thrown the weapons down a sewer two or three blocks away.

After Carrasquillo had taken the bulk of the statement, he asked the defendant why he would do such a thing. According to Carrasquillo, the defendant said, "Gee, I really don't know." Carrasquillo repeated the question 10 minutes later, but received the same response. After a while, Carrasquillo asked the question for a third time and defendant replied, "Well, gee, I guess it must have been because I was afraid of Joe Bush."

At approximately 9:00 P.M., the defendant repeated the substance of his statement to an Assistant District Attorney. Defendant added that at the time he shot at Geller, Geller was not moving and his eyes were closed. While he did not check for a pulse, defendant stated that Geller had not been doing anything to him at the time he shot because "Mike was dead."

Defendant was indicted by the Grand Jury of Kings County on a single count of murder in that, acting in concert with another person actually present, he intentionally caused the death of Michael Geller. At the trial, there were four principal prosecution witnesses: Detective Carrasquillo, the Assistant District Attorney who took the second admission, and two physicians from the office of the New York City Chief Medical Examiner. For proof of defendant's culpability, the prosecution relied upon defendant's own admissions as related by the detective and the prosecutor. From the physicians, the prosecution sought to establish that Geller was still alive at the time defendant shot at him. Both physicians testified that each of the two chest wounds, for which defendant alleged Bush to be responsible, would have caused death without prompt medical attention. Moreover, the victim would have remained alive until such time as his chest cavity became fully filled with blood. Depending on the circumstances, it might take 5 to 10 minutes for the chest cavity to fill. Neither prosecution witness could state, with medical certainty, that the victim was still alive when, perhaps five minutes after the initial chest wounds were inflicted, the defendant fired at the victim's head. The defense produced but a single witness, the former Chief Medical Examiner of New York City. This expert stated that, in his view, Geller might have died of the chest wounds "very rapidly" since, in addition to the bleeding, a large bullet going through a lung and the heart would have other adverse medical effects. "Those wounds can be almost immediately or rapidly fatal or they may be delayed in there, in the time it would take for death to occur. But I would say that wounds like that which are described here as having gone through the lungs and the heart would be fatal wounds and in most cases they're rapidly fatal."

The jury found the defendant guilty of murder. The defendant then moved to set the verdict aside. He submitted an affidavit in which he contended that he "was absolutely, unequivocally and positively certain that Michael Geller was dead before [he] shot him." This motion was denied.[1]

On appeal, the Appellate Division reversed the judgment of conviction on the law and dismissed the indictment. The court ruled that "the People failed to prove beyond a reasonable doubt that Geller had been alive at the time he was shot by defendant; defendant's conviction of murder thus cannot stand." Further, the court held that the judgment could not be modified to reflect a conviction for attempted murder because "the uncontradicted evidence is that the defendant, at the time that he fired the five shots into the body of the decedent, believed him to be dead, and . . . there is not a scintilla of evidence to contradict his assertion in that regard."

While the defendant admitted firing five shots at the victim approximately two to five minutes after Bush had fired three times, all three medical expert witnesses testified that they could not, with any degree of medical certainty, state whether the victim had been alive at the time the latter shots were fired by the defendant. Thus, the People failed to prove beyond a reasonable doubt that the victim had been alive at the time he was shot by the defendant. Whatever else it may be, it is not murder to shoot a dead body.

The distinction between "factual" and "legal" impossibility is a nice one indeed and the courts tend to place a greater value on legal form than on any substantive danger the defendant's actions pose for society. The approach of the draftsmen of the Model Penal Code was to eliminate the defense of impossibility in virtually all situations. Under the code provision, to constitute an attempt, it is still necessary that the result intended or desired by the actor constitute a crime. However, the code suggested a fundamental change to shift the locus of analysis to the actor's mental frame of reference and away from undue dependence upon external considerations. The basic premise of the code provision is that what was in the actor's own mind should be the standard for determining his dangerousness to society and, hence, his liability for attempted criminal conduct.

In the belief that neither of the two branches of the traditional impossibility arguments detracts from the offender's moral culpability, the Legislature substantially carried the code's treatment of impossibility into the 1967 revision of the Penal Law. Thus, a person is guilty of an attempt when, with intent to commit a crime, he engages in conduct which tends to effect the commission of such crime. (Penal Law, §110.10.) Thus,

if defendant believed the victim to be alive at the time of the shooting, it is no defense to the charge of attempted murder that the victim may have been dead.

Turning to the facts of the case before us, we believe that there is sufficient evidence in the record from which the jury could conclude that the defendant believed Geller to be alive at the time defendant fired shots into Geller's head. Defendant admitted firing five shots at a most vital part of the victim's anatomy from virtually point blank range. Although defendant contended that the victim had already been grievously wounded by another, from the defendant's admitted actions, the jury could conclude that the defendant's purpose and intention was to administer the coup de grace.

Defendant argues that the jury was bound to accept, at face value, the indications in his admissions that he believed Geller dead. Certainly, it is true that the defendant was entitled to have the entirety of the admissions, both the inculpatory and the exculpatory portions, placed in evidence before the trier of facts.

However, the jury was not required to automatically credit the exculpatory portions of the admissions. The general rule is, of course, that the credibility of witnesses is a question of fact and the jury may choose to believe some, but not all, of a witness' testimony.

In this case, there is ample other evidence to contradict the defendant's assertion that he believed Geller dead. There were five bullet wounds inflicted with stunning accuracy in a vital part of the victim's anatomy. The medical testimony indicated that Geller may have been alive at the time defendant fired at him. The defendant voluntarily left the jurisdiction immediately after the crime with his coperpetrator. Defendant did not report the crime to the police when left on his own by Bush. Instead, he attempted to conceal his and Bush's involvement with the homicide. In addition, the other portions of defendant's admissions make his contended belief that Geller was dead extremely improbable. Defendant, without a word of instruction from Bush, voluntarily got up from his seat after the passage of just a few minutes and fired five times point blank into the victim's face, snuffing out any remaining chance of life that Geller possessed. Certainly, this alone indicates a callous indifference to the taking of a human life. His admissions are barren of any claim of duress[2] and reflect, instead, an unstinting co-operation in efforts to dispose of vital incriminating evidence. Indeed, defendant maintained a false version of the occurrence until such time as the police informed him that they had evidence that he lately possessed a gun of the same caliber as one of the weapons involved in the shooting. From all of this, the jury was certainly warranted in concluding that the defendant acted in the belief that Geller was yet alive when shot by defendant.

The jury convicted the defendant of murder. Necessarily, they found that defendant intended to kill a live human being. Subsumed within this finding is the conclusion that defendant acted in the belief that Geller was alive. Thus, there is no need for additional fact findings by a jury. Although it was not established beyond a reasonable doubt that Geller was, in fact, alive, such is no defense to attempted murder since a murder would have been committed "had the attendant circumstances been as [defendant] believed them to be." (Penal Law, §110.10.) The jury necessarily found that defendant believed Geller to be alive when defendant shot at him.

The Appellate Division erred in not modifying the judgment to reflect a conviction for the lesser included offense of attempted murder. An attempt to commit a murder is a lesser included offense of murder and the Appellate Division has the authority, where the trial evidence is not legally sufficient to establish the offense of which the defendant was convicted, to modify the judgment to one of conviction for a lesser included offense which is legally established by the evidence.

Endnotes

[1] It should be noted that Joe Bush pleaded guilty to a charge of manslaughter in the first degree. At the time he entered his plea, Bush detailed his version of the homicide. According to Bush, defendant Dlugash was a dealer in narcotic drugs and Dlugash claimed that Geller owed him a large sum of money from drug purchases. Bush was in the kitchen alone when Geller entered and threatened him with a shotgun. Bush pulled out his .38 caliber pistol and fired five times at Geller. Geller slumped to the floor. Dlugash then entered, withdrew his .25 caliber pistol and fired five shots into the deceased's face. Bush, however, never testified at Dlugash's trial.

[2] Notwithstanding the Appellate Division's implication to the contrary, the record indicates that defendant told the Assistant District Attorney that Bush, after shooting Geller, kept his gun aimed at Geller, and not at Dlugash. As defendant stated, "this was after Joe had his .38 on him, I started shooting on him."

Intent

Douglas N. Husak

The philosophical and the legal literature about intention rarely intersect. Philosophers have been largely interested in the ontological status of intentions and their place within a theory of mind. Legal theorists have been more concerned to identify the conditions under which an act is intentional or unintentional. To accomplish this objective, they have not tended to believe that they must resolve the deeper philosophical questions about the nature of intentions.

From Douglas N. Husak, "Intent," in Christopher Berry (ed.), *The Philosophy of Law: An Encyclopedia* (New York: Garland Publishing, 1999), pp. 425–428. Reproduced by permission of Routledge/Taylor & Francis Books, Inc.

Intention is important to the criminal law primarily because action that intentionally brings about a harm is thought to be the paradigm of culpable action. A person who intentionally kills or intentionally injures is widely believed to be more blameworthy and deserving of a more severe punishment than a person who performs these acts unintentionally. The most serious offenses for which persons deserve the most severe punishments—murder, for example—frequently require intention. This clear connection between intention and culpability has led to a disagreement about whether the concept of intention is partly ascriptive or wholly descriptive. Does a judgment of whether a person is responsible for something affect an assessment of what that person did intentionally? On the other hand, does an assessment of what a person did intentionally simply describe an inner state or process that is independent of a judgment of responsibility?

Despite the centrality of the concept of intention, criminal theorists lack a clear account of its meaning, and disagree about whether its meaning in the criminal law differs from its meaning in ordinary usage. The problem surfaces in at least three contexts. First, what does it mean to perform an act intentionally? The locution "Person D performed action A intentionally" cannot be analyzed without imposing some constraints on how to interpret the action variable "A." According to accounts of action inspired by Donald Davidson, all actions are intentional under some description: if D performed A, then there must be some description under which D did A intentionally. The account of action endorsed by most criminal theorists, however, simply construes an action as a bodily movement and supposes that these bodily movements are voluntary actions when they are caused by volitions. A theory of action must be invoked to settle these issues.

Second, what does it mean to intend to perform an action in the future? An analysis of "D does A with the intention to do B" is required to interpret statutes that prohibit doing some act with a further intention. Burglary, for example, is defined in the common law as a breaking and entering of the dwelling house of another at night with the intent to commit a felony therein. In terminology that has given rise to much confusion, the further intention to do B has sometimes been called a "specific intention," to contrast with the alleged "general intention" to do A. How does this further intention differ from a hope or expectation?

Third, what does it mean to bring about the consequence of an action intentionally; how should "brings about the consequence of A intentionally" be analyzed? This question has stimulated the greatest interest from courts and philosophical commentators. Presumably, D's action A intentionally brings about whatever consequences he wants or desires to occur, and these consequences constitute his aim or objective in performing A. However, does D intentionally bring about those consequences, which he foresees will occur, even when he does not want or desire them? This dispute is about whether what Jeremy Bentham called "oblique intentions," in contrast to "direct intentions," are really a kind of intention at all. Suppose that a defendant is aware that a victim will

be killed if he burns down a house. If he sets the fire in order to collect the insurance he has taken on the structure, and not because he wants or desires to cause death, does he intend to kill, and thus commit murder, simply because he foresees that his action will cause someone to die? If so, must the defendant have foreseen a consequence with practical certainty, or does foresight of a high degree of probability suffice for that consequence to have been brought about intentionally? Courts and commentators divide over this issue.

In order to avoid such difficulties, the *Model Penal Code* and most of the state criminal codes that have followed it have all but abandoned the use of the concept of intention. If intention is so ambiguous and troublesome, why not replace it with comparatively clear concepts such as purpose and knowledge? A person brings about a consequence *purposely* when his conscious object is to cause that consequence. A person brings about a consequence *knowingly* when he is practically certain that his action will cause that consequence. If this reform is adopted, one need not take a stance on whether those results that are brought about knowingly are brought about intentionally. Murder, for example, need not be defined to require an intentional killing. Instead, murder might be defined as a purposeful killing, or (as in the *Model Penal Code*) to include killings performed either purposely or knowingly. One of the most significant questions in drafting a statute or a whole criminal code is to determine whether to follow the *Model Penal Code* in this respect and to delete reference to intention.

If the concept of intention is retained in criminal statutes and theorists decide that the agent has not killed intentionally simply because he foresaw that his act would cause death, there is room for doubt about whether the most serious offenses, such as murder, should continue to require intention. Why should intention be the paradigm of culpability? Legal philosophers have brought many different kinds of challenges to the centrality of intention. If intention is agreed to be so important, should not all crimes—or at least, all serious crimes—require it? Why are there kinds of culpability or mens rea other than intention? Many offenses can be committed even though a defendant does not intentionally cause harm but is merely reckless about whether that harm will occur. Offenses that may be committed recklessly at least require that a defendant is conscious of the risk that his action will cause harm. Even more controversial are offenses that may be committed with mere negligence. These offenses impose criminal liability when the defendant should have been aware of the risk that his conduct would result in harm—that is, when a reasonable person in the defendant's situation would have been aware of the risk—even though the defendant himself may have been unaware of that risk. The most controversial offenses are those of "strict liability" that require no culpability at all. To the extent that they are persuaded that intention is the paradigm culpable state and that culpability is essential to criminal liability, theorists are likely to oppose the punishment of persons whose mental state diverges further and further from intention.

A different question about the importance of intention can be raised by theorists who inquire why motives are so widely believed to be immaterial to criminal liability. Do not motives as well as intentions affect the blameworthiness of defendants? Given that intentions are so hard to distinguish from motives, why should the criminal law be so preoccupied with the former and so totally uninterested in the latter?

In addition, the centrality of intention can be challenged by noting that the criminal law occasionally accepts a number of substitutes for intention. A few of these have been widely discredited. Most jurisdictions have replaced "objective" standards of intention with a "subjective" standard. That is, a defendant is no longer taken to have intended what a reasonable person in his circumstances would have intended. Instead, the trend has been to seek to ascertain the actual mental state of the particular defendant. However, other substitutes for intention have persisted; sometimes a crime that generally requires an intention can be committed despite the absence of the appropriate intention. Two such devices are noteworthy. The first is the "felony-murder rule." According to the least qualified version of this rule, a person is deemed to have intended to kill, and thus is guilty of murder, whenever death results from his commission of a felony.

The second device is the "doctrine of transferred intent." According to this doctrine, a defendant who intends to harm V1, but accidentally harms V2, is treated as intentionally harming V2. The justifiability of both these devices is subject to dispute.

A number of theorists have concluded that intention should not be so central to the criminal law. Some of these reservations about intention have arisen from the practical difficulties of proving that a defendant acted intentionally. Other reservations derive from a view about the function or purpose of the criminal law. If the criminal law is designed to deter harmful conduct, why should it be so important whether a harm is brought about intentionally or unintentionally? Following Barbara Wootton, some theorists have proposed that all offenses should become instances of "strict liability." Although this sweeping proposal has gained few adherents, there is little consensus as to exactly why it is objectionable. H. L. A. Hart has emphasized that the implementation of this proposal would result in the loss of control over whether persons would incur criminal liability and thus would undermine planning and predictability in human affairs. Although this response is clearly correct, it does not seem to capture why theorists are so convinced that mental states in general and intention in particular should be used in the definitions of serious offenses. What is required is a theory of culpability, a justification for regarding intention as the paradigm culpable state, and a reason to conclude that persons should be punished only for those acts for which they are culpable.

Although philosophers have contested the general significance of intention to the criminal law, a number of important questions about intention arise in the context of particular offenses. Which offenses should require intention, and which can be committed despite the absence of intention? The acts prohibited by some statutes necessarily require intention; it seems impossible to "bribe" or to "kidnap," for example, without intending to do so. In many other cases, however, there is controversy about the degree of culpability that should be required to give rise to liability. Rape is one such example. Should a defendant be liable for rape when he consciously disregards the risk that consent has not been given, or must he actually know that his victim has not consented? Possessory offenses are another example. Should they require an intention to possess the proscribed item, or should recklessness be sufficient to give rise to liability?

Disagreement has long been expressed about whether liability for the various inchoate offenses should require intention (construed as purpose). Consider liability for a criminal attempt. Is the degree of culpability required for an attempt to commit a given crime identical to the degree of culpability that is required to commit that crime? If so, D attempts to murder V when he tries to perform an action that he foresees will kill V, even though his purpose is not to cause V to die. But perhaps a criminal attempt requires an intention (that is, a purpose) to commit the completed offense, even though the completed offense requires no such intention. If to attempt to commit a crime is to try to commit that crime, then it would seem that attempts necessarily require purpose. Much the same question arises in the context of conspiracy or solicitations. If D performs an act that he knows will encourage E to commit a crime, is D liable for solicitation, even though his purpose in performing the act was to make money and not to encourage E? These are only a few of the examples involving disputes about whether the definitions of particular offenses should include or dispense with intention.

The Criminal Law and the Luck of the Draw

Sanford H. Kadish

I propose to consider what to make of a doctrine of the criminal law that seems to me not rationally supportable notwithstanding its near universal acceptance in Western law, the support of many jurists and philosophers, and its resonance with the intuitions of lawyers and lay people alike. This is the doctrine—the harm doctrine, I'll call it—that reduces punishment for intentional wrongdoers (and often precludes punishment for negligent and reckless wrongdoers) if by chance the harm they intended or risked does not occur. I will also consider a corollary of the harm doctrine which offers a full defense if it so happens that, unbeknownst to the defendants, the harm they intended could not possibly have been done.

Whether the harm doctrine can be justified is, as George Fletcher has said, a "deep, unresolved issue in the theory of criminal liability."[1] . . . The debate over the issue remains unresolved notwithstanding the earnest attention of generations of scholars. But though the ground is well trod, the subject continues to have a fascination for those of us who worry about the criminal law (perhaps just because it has defied successful resolution), and I am not immune to its attraction.

I should explain at the start what I mean by saying that the harm doctrine is not rationally supportable. I mean that it is a doctrine that does not serve the crime preventive purposes of the criminal law, and is not redeemed by any defensible normative principle. Suppose, for example, the law provided that any crime committed during the night of a half-moon may not be punished with more than one-half the punishment appropriate on all other occasions. This distinction is patently irrelevant to any crime preventive purpose of the criminal law. Yet it might still be rationally supportable if it could be justified by moral principle. But no such principle can relate guilt or desert to the phases of the moon. Here, then, we would have an extreme instance of a rationally indefensible doctrine. One qualification: sometimes the law must defer to people's irrationalities to maintain the acceptance needed to govern. This might possibly be the case even with my half-moon doctrine of punishment. The doctrine, however, would still be rationally indefensible, even though its adoption by the law would not be.

Of course our criminal law has for centuries included many irrational doctrines—whole Augean stables full. Some of them were that way from the start. Others got that way when changed conditions made them anomalous, like the murder rule requiring the victim to have died within a year and a day of the injury. But these differ from the harm doctrine in that they are widely recognized as insupportable, and their long persistence in the law is simply evidence that the law is slow to change. The harm doctrine is special (although, as we will see, not singular) in that large segments of the legal and lay community regard it as sound.

I will begin by setting out the law that most clearly exhibits the harm doctrine at work. This is the law governing the punishment of failed efforts to

From Sanford H. Kadish, "The Criminal Law and the Luck of the Draw" *Journal of Criminal Law and Criminology*, Winter 1994, pp. 679–702. Reprinted by permission of the author.

do some prohibited harm (the law of attempts) and of actions that create the risk of the harm without producing it (the law of culpable risk creation). These rules are well known and I will only sketch them briefly.

First, the law of attempts. Consider the case of a man who stabbed his son in anger, pleaded guilty and was convicted of a crime equivalent for our purposes to attempted murder. After serving several months of a two year sentence he was paroled. However, three months later his son, who had been hospitalized since the attack, took a turn for the worse and died, whereupon the prosecutor, quite within the law, charged the father with murder, a crime punishable with life imprisonment or death.

What did the father do in jail or on parole that merited the greater punishment? Not a thing. If a good constitution or a good surgeon had saved the son, the father could not have been further punished. The occurrence of the resulting death alone raises the crime and the punishment. In most jurisdictions this same principle operates for all crimes, not just homicidal crimes. In California, for example, an attempt to commit a crime is punishable with half the punishment for the completed crime. Thus, the reward for failing, no matter how hard you try to succeed or how close you come, is a lesser punishment.

Now consider crimes of culpable risk creation—crimes in which a person is punished, not for attempting a harm, but for culpably risking it. The punishment of these crimes is also made to depend on chance. Take the case of Mr. Malone. He and his friend decided to play a game of Russian Roulette in which each took turns spinning the chamber of a revolver, with one round in it, and firing at the other. When Malone's turn came to pull the trigger the gun fired and killed his friend. Malone was convicted of second degree murder, based on the egregious risk to life he needlessly created.

That sounds fair enough. But suppose instead, that the bullet only inflicted a flesh wound, or that the bullet was not in the firing chamber when Malone pulled the trigger. Could Malone then have been convicted of any crime? Perhaps he could have been convicted of some ad hoc statutory offense concerning firearms, but such an offense would carry nothing like the penalty for murder. And if there had been no special statute of this kind, he could not be convicted of any crime at all, since traditionally just recklessly endangering another was itself not criminal—except in specific contexts, like driving a

car. Some jurisdictions have in recent years made it criminal to recklessly endanger another person in all situations, but even these statutes treat the offense as a minor one.

Finally, I need to mention one more doctrine that exhibits the law's preoccupation with a resulting harm. It is the doctrine of impossibility, which takes the harm doctrine one step further. The harm doctrine calls for a lesser punishment when no harm was done; the impossibility doctrine calls for no punishment at all when the harm could not possibly have been done. Though now a minority view, it still has its defenders, both on and off the bench.

The gist of this doctrine is that a serious effort to commit a crime, even one which includes what the actor thought was the last thing he needed to do to commit it, is not punishable if the crime could not have succeeded. For example, assume a person uses lies and deceit to dupe another into giving up his property, but all to no avail because the owner sees the lies for what they are. Can the would-be deceiver be convicted of attempting to obtain the property of another by false pretenses? Not under the impossibility doctrine—since the owner saw through the lies, the defendant could not possibly have succeeded. In another example a hunter, meaning to shoot a deer before the hunting season, shoots at a straw dummy the game warden erected, with reflectors for eyes to give it verisimilitude. Is this an attempt to take a deer out of season? No, said the court: "If the state's evidence showed an attempt to take the dummy, it fell far short of proving an attempt to take a deer."[2] A final example: Professor Moriarty shoots at what he takes to be Sherlock Holmes, but which in reality is the shadow of Holmes' paper cutout profile that Holmes has set revolving on a phonograph in front of a lamp. Too clever by half, Mr. Holmes. Moriarty escapes again, this time thanks to the impossibility doctrine, since his action—shooting at a shadow—couldn't possibly kill Holmes.

Today, these impossibility cases would go the other way in most jurisdictions—though the attachment of courts to the doctrine is sometimes remarkable. But with the exception of the impossibility doctrine, all of the doctrines I have described are essentially still the law in most places.

Having illustrated the workings of the harm doctrine, the two major tasks I have set for myself lie ahead. First I must make good, if I can, my claim that the doctrine, in all its applications, is not rationally defensible. Second, I need to consider what to make of the durability of this doctrine.

The Rational Indefensibility of the Harm Doctrine

To make my case that the harm doctrine cannot be rationally defended, I must establish two things: (a) that the doctrine cannot be justified in terms of the crime preventive purposes of criminal punishment; and (b) that neither can it be justified in terms of any convincing principle of justice.

Does the harm doctrine further the law's interest in crime prevention? There are two main ways in which criminal punishment is thought to reduce crime. One is by preventing further criminal acts by the offender. The other is by discouraging criminal acts by others. How far the law succeeds in particular times and places in attaining this goal is an empirical question I need not pursue here, for the question is whether, on the law's premise that punishment does work in this way, the distinction in punishment required by the harm doctrine is defensible. Let's first consider the goal of preventing further crime by the offender being punished.

Convicting offenders serves to identify those who have shown themselves to threaten further breaches of the law, and punishing them constitutes a response to the threat they constitute. The response may take the form of efforts to alter their criminal proclivities (reformation), or to teach them a lesson (special deterrence), or to physically keep them from doing harm for a while (incapacitation). The question is whether the actual occurrence of harm is relevant in assessing the dangerousness of the offenders and their suitability as subjects for reformation, special deterrence or incapacitation in the interest of public protection.

Consider in this light the attempt cases I presented a moment ago. Take the father who stabbed his son. He is now out on parole from his attempted murder conviction. Has he suddenly become more dangerous because the son finally succumbed? Or consider the Russian Roulette player, Mr. Malone. Would he have been less dangerous if the bullet had not fired because it was in another chamber? Of course not. And the same is surely true of the impossibility cases I just described. Whether the property owner did or did not have the wit to see through the defendant's lies, whether the object the hunters shot at turns out to be a dummy or a live deer, whether the revolving shadow was really that of Holmes or only a cutout—in none of these cases does it make a whit of difference so far as identifying the actor as prima facie requiring protective measures or as

indicating the length of time the actor should be held. It may be conceded that a different response may be called for if the impossibility would be obvious to any sane person—trying to open a safe with incantations, for example—or where the evidence of criminal intent is doubtful. But neither is true in any of my cases.

One might argue that we need the harm to happen in order to be sure of the dangerousness of the actors. Without it, the argument might go, we would have to speculate on whether they would actually go forward and do the harm, and thereby deprive actors of the freedom to make a final choice. This argument has no force, however, in cases where the defendants have done the last act they thought necessary to cause the harm—consider, for example, one who shoots to kill another but misses, or cases like those of Professor Moriarty and the hunters. Furthermore, even if the defendant has more to do, the law of attempts requires substantial acts—traditionally defined as acts that come proximately close to success—precisely to meet this concern. Finally, the argument is misdirected, for its logic leads not to punishing attempts less, but to not punishing them at all: freedom to make a final choice whether to take the last step or to desist is at stake whether the punishment is two years or four.

Is culpable risk creation any different? Do we need the harm to assure us of the culpability and dangerousness of the actor when the act is unintentional? Surely not in all cases. We do not need the gun to fire and kill someone to be certain of the danger of Russian Roulette. We don't need someone to be killed to know that wild, drunken driving through congested city streets is dangerous.

Therefore, reducing punishment in all cases, just because luckily no harm occurs, makes no sense in terms of the purpose of punishment to identify dangerous behavior and to prevent its perpetrators from repeating it. My point is not that a rational criminal law would increase the punishment for attempts; it may as well be that the law should reduce the punishment for completed offenses. Rather, my point is simply that punishing attempts and completed crimes differently makes no sense insofar as the goal of the criminal law is to identify and deal with dangerous offenders who threaten the public.

Now let's look at the second way criminal punishment may reduce crime, through general deterrence. This works not by protecting the public from the offender, but by providing others who might be tempted to commit a like crime with a warning of what may happen to them if they do. The question here is the same as before: whether it makes any sense to punish attempted and completed crimes differently, insofar as the goal of the law is to deter others from committing the crime.

It seems evident that in crimes of culpable risk creation, like that of my Russian Roulette player or my reckless driver, the lesser punishment for attempts reduces the deterrent efficacy of the law. Since the actors are not planning on doing the harm, the threat of punishment if they do is discounted for them by its improbability. The only way to maintain its full deterrent force is to threaten punishment whether or not the harm occurs. But in crimes of intention like attempts—for example, Professor Moriarty trying to kill Holmes, or the father trying to kill his son—some argue that we do not lose deterrence, because people who try to commit a crime expect to succeed, and if the punishment for success does not deter them, an equal punishment for failure certainly will not. By punishing them less for attempt when they fail, therefore, we economize on the use of punishment without loss of deterrence.

There is something to this, but not enough, I think, to justify the law's prevailing punishment patterns. Isn't it plausible to suppose that at least in some cases the threat of equally severe punishment for an attempt may increase the law's deterrent effect? I have in mind cases where potential offenders know there is a greater chance of being caught and punished if they fail than if they succeed. Sting operations, for example, are of this kind, because they are generally directed at consensual behavior such as narcotic sales or bribery that usually goes undetected and unpunished when it succeeds. Treason is another example. As the well-known couplet puts it, "Treason doth never prosper: what's the reason? For if it prosper, none dare call it treason." Moreover, even to the extent the harm doctrine may economize on punishment without loss of deterrence, there are the other objectives of punishment—reformation, special deterrence and incapacitation—that are indeed disserved by rewarding chance failure with less punishment, as I've indicated.

There is indeed an appeal in the argument that reducing punishment for attempt is justified insofar as it economizes on the use of punishment. It is an appeal, however, primarily because our punishments tend to be indefensibly high—any way to reduce them seems a move in the right direction. If statutory punishments were more nearly optimal, however, a reduction based simply on failure would have much less to be said for it, for the reasons I've tried to suggest.

Finally, some argue that the harm doctrine would serve crime preventive purposes by offering the prospect of lesser punishment as an inducement for the defendant to desist. This is an argument more appealing on first sight than on second thought. It doesn't apply to those who culpably create risks since, having already created the risk, it's too late for desisting. Neither does it carry weight with those who believe they have already taken the last step needed to do the harm. And even with those who know they still have more to do, the argument is really weaker than it seems. First, by the time the defendant has done the substantial acts toward carrying out the crime that the law of attempt requires, there is very little chance of a change of heart. Second, even if the defendant might have a moment of doubt at the last instant, reducing the punishment from say, six to three years imprisonment, hardly does much to reinforce it. Third, if providing a motive to desist were really the objective, one would expect the law to offer a defense of total exculpation where the defendant voluntarily desists. But only a minority of jurisdictions allow voluntary abandonment as a complete defense. And even in those that do, the practice of reducing punishment for failed attempts persists.

My argument to this point has been that attributing legal significance to the chance happening of harm either undercuts or is irrelevant to the crime prevention purposes of criminal punishment. Even so, as I said at the outset, a practice may be justified by some relevant principle of justice. Now I take the principle that limits punishment to what the offender deserves to be such a principle, and one which those subscribing to the harm doctrine would want to rely on. The question, then, is whether wrongdoers deserve less punishment (or none at all) because the harm they intended or culpably risked happens not to occur, or could not have occurred, for reasons unknown to them.

Isn't desert the same whether or not the harm occurs? It is commonly accepted that punishment is deserved if persons are at fault, and that fault depends on their choice to do the wrongful action, not on what is beyond their control. Reconsider my attempt cases. Would the father who stabbed his son deserve less punishment if a skillful doctor had been available to save the son's life? Would the Russian Roulette player deserve less punishment if the bullet happened to be in another chamber when he fired? Or consider my impossibility cases. Do the hunters who shot the dummy believing it was a deer, or Professor Moriarty, who shot the shadow thinking it was Sherlock Holmes, deserve no punishment because they were mistaken?

While in principle it's difficult to find good reasons for making desert turn on chance, here's the rub: most of us do in fact make judgments precisely of this kind. Doesn't it seem natural for a parent to want to punish her child more for spilling his milk than for almost spilling it, more for running the family car into a wall than for almost doing so? That's the way our unexamined intuitions run. The sight of the harm arouses a degree of anger and resentment that far exceeds that aroused by apprehension of the harm.

What should we make of this paradox? Is there something to be said after all for the popular sentiment that fortuitous results do have a bearing on blameworthiness, something that is missed by treating it simply as an irregularity? Can attributing punishment significance to the occurrence of harm be justified in terms of the desert principle?

Obviously, the foundation of my argument against making punishment turn on the chance happening of harm rests on the incompatibility of luck and desert. But perhaps this assumption is mistaken. A distinguished philosopher, Thomas Nagel, has advanced the paradoxical notion of "moral luck."[3] His point is that we do commonly make and defend judgments of moral desert despite the presence of substantial elements of chance. So if the harm principle is irrational because it makes moral desert turn on chance, then so are many of our considered moral judgments.

Nagel instances four situations in which moral desert turns on chance. Two of the four are based on a determinist premise; namely, that you may be lucky or unlucky in the antecedent factors that determine the kind of person you turn out to be and in how you choose to exercise your will. True enough if one accepts determinism. But, first, that explanation of human action is highly contestable, and second, the criminal law, with its concepts of personal responsibility and desert, plainly rejects it.

A third instance Nagel gives of moral luck is that you may be lucky or not in whether circumstances present you with an occasion to make a moral choice that will reveal your moral shortcomings; for example, luck in whether you are ever presented with the need to choose to betray a friend or break a promise. But I don't believe that this threatens our sense of justice in blaming in the same way that luck in the fortuitous outcome of an action (the harm doctrine) threatens it. The settled moral understanding is that what you deserve is a function of what you choose. It may be that you would not have had occasion to make a choice that revealed your badness if you had better

luck. Nonetheless, you did make a choice—nobody made you—and it is that choice for which you are blamed. It is a different matter, however, to say that chance occurrences that follow after you have made your choice determine what you deserve, for that is to rest desert upon factors other than what you chose to do. Fortuity prior to choice, therefore, may be accommodated to our notions of just desert; fortuity thereafter cannot. As I see it, that leaves the harm doctrine, Nagel's fourth instance of moral luck, as the one deep challenge to the desert principle. . . .

I turn now to arguments designed to justify the harm doctrine in terms of the principle of desert. . . . One argument proceeds as follows: our prevailing punishment practice with respect to results is no different than a penal lottery in which the amount of punishment for a crime depends on some such chance event as the drawing of long and short straws. To appreciate this, the argument goes, we need to cease thinking of the lesser punishment for failing to complete the crime as attributable to lesser guilt, and think of it merely as the chance event that determines the losers and winners of the lottery. Thought of as a penal lottery, then, there is no unfairness, for in leaving punishment to chance all attempters are treated alike. They all, in effect, draw straws. If they draw the short straw (that is, they succeed) they get the greater punishment. If they draw the long straw (that is, they fail) they get lesser punishment. There is no unfairness in treating the winners better than the losers so long as the lottery is unrigged.

But even unrigged, the basic injustice of a lottery in allocating punishment remains: to allow one of two offenders equally deserving of punishment to receive less punishment if she wins a lottery detaches punishment from desert. It would be the same if we allowed every equally guilty offender a throw of the dice—a throw of six or less and we halve the punishment. The two offenders end up being punished differently even though they are identical in every non-arbitrary sense. That is what is crucial, not the fact that they both had an equal chance of getting a lesser punishment when they threw the dice.

One might object that while punishing a person more than he deserves is unjust, punishing him less because he lucked out is not. Of course, the offender who lucked out can't complain. But the one who got what would otherwise be his just punishment may well complain, as any child knows who sees his sibling spanked once while he is spanked twice for the same offense. You wouldn't convince the child he wasn't unfairly treated by explaining to him that you left it to chance and he lost. He'd feel wronged, and rightly so. The parent's punishment action was arbitrary, in the sense that punishment of the children was left to chance, and thus forfeited any claim that the child should respect it as fair punishment.

A different defense of the harm doctrine rests on the judgment that given two people who try to do a harm or to risk it, the one who succeeds becomes a worse person than the one who fails, and thus deserves more punishment. So it has been argued that "in doing something evil one becomes something evil," and the one who fails to kill does not become what success in killing would have made him—an attempted murderer is not a murderer.

I do understand how most people would have heavier hearts if their blow had killed another than if it luckily only wounded. But I rather think they'd be kidding themselves to think themselves better persons because their victim happened to have a good constitution or a good doctor. Even if I'm wrong, though, I don't see how the difference warrants a difference in punishment. The principle of proportional punishment requires that the amount of punishment should bear some relation to the degree of blameworthiness of the defendants' actions, not to what they think of themselves or to what they have become in some existential sense.

Finally, I will mention two recent efforts to bring our intuitions about the harm doctrine into harmony with our reason. The first draws upon the recently popular retributive justification of punishment that views punishing the offender as restoring the imbalance of benefits and burdens created by the crime. There is, of course, one readily understandable imbalance produced by most crimes: the criminal profits from a loss he imposes on the victim—he steals or damages the victim's property, he causes the victim to suffer an economic loss, or he injures him physically. If punishment can justifiably be seen as somehow restoring the victim's loss, then less punishment for an attempt, where the victim has suffered no (or, arguably less) loss, could make sense. It is hard to see, however, how inflicting pain on the criminal restores anything—certainly it doesn't restore the victim to his property or compensate him for his economic loss or for his medical expenses and pain and suffering. And even if it somehow did, in the unpalatable sense that the victim received a restorative amount of pleasure from the offender's suffering, it is not the morality of retributive punishment that would have been demonstrated,

but the desirability of satisfying the vengeful feelings of the victim, which is not the same thing.

However, the image of righting the imbalance is more often construed by those who use it in a different way—not as compensating the victim for physical injury or economic loss, but rather as depriving the offender of an unfair advantage; namely, the advantage of releasing himself from restraints the rest of us accept to allow the social enterprise to go forward. Punishment of the wrongdoer, then, deprives him of the parasitic advantage he has taken, somewhat analogously to the way a penalty in a competitive game is designed to negate any advantage gained by unsporting conduct. Using this as a justification for retributive punishment, Michael Davis has fashioned an ingenious argument to justify a lesser punishment for attempt.[4] He draws an analogy to an imagined auction of licenses that permit the holder to act free of social restraints. Such an auction would reveal that a license to fail is worth less than a license to succeed, because people would naturally bid less for it. One who succeeds in committing a crime has unfairly imposed on the rest of us to the extent of the value of the license to succeed, while one who fails has imposed on us to the lesser extent of the value of a license to try and fail. Less is needed in the latter case, therefore, to rectify the unfairness.

There are many intriguing questions that may be pursued in connection with the working of this hypothetical auction, but my basic disquiet with Davis' argument arises from the premise on which it rests. For the psychoanalyst, it is plausible to conceive of people as spurred on by their deepest urges to ravage and plunder their neighbors, but held in check by social and legal constraints. On this view, presumably, the law-abiding have this grievance against the law-defying: "We played by the rules and held ourselves back from larceny, assault, rape and so forth. But you disregarded the implicitly agreed-on rules and did what the rest might have wanted to do. For taking this unfair advantage of the rest of us it is only right that you should be penalized."

As I said, this is the explanation some psychoanalysts give for the prevalence of the retributive urge. However, the contention that in punishing the criminal we are only cancelling the advantage the offender took of the rest of us in not restraining his anti-social impulses, as the rest of us do most of the time, seems an unlikely moral justification. No doubt there are some crimes for which this analysis is apt—for example, those in which the offender and others are indeed competing to win some goal, such as business people bidding for a contract. The one who cheats by finding out what the others have bid in order to be sure he submits the winning bid does derive precisely the kind of unfair advantage that Davis has in mind. The same can be said of income tax evasion. But, it seems unrealistic and demeaning to the rest of us to treat all crimes in this manner. What the law-abiding feel when they read of a child abduction, a rape, a murder, a vicious assault, is not that the offender has gotten an unfair advantage over them for which he should be penalized (and penalized proportionately to the price a license to commit these crimes would fetch at an auction). It is the evil of the offender and the harm he has imposed on the victim which moves them, not their own loss. So the theory of punishment as restoration of the unfair advantage the offender has taken of the rest of us ultimately fails, as does the notion of auctioned licenses which rests on it.

The second recent effort to justify the harm doctrine comes from R. A. Duff.[5] He suggests that in punishing an attempt less than a completed crime the law serves to communicate to the offender that, although subjectively he is as culpable as one who does the harm, in fact all should be grateful that the harm he intended did not come to pass. The lesser punishment communicates the law's judgment that a worse state of affairs would have existed if the offender had achieved his objective—in other words, things are not as bad as they might have been. Perhaps the force of this argument turns on Duff's theory of justified punishment as communication directed towards the offender's repentance, but I find it hard to accept that we need the lesser punishment to keep us (and the offender) aware, for example, that things would be worse if the attempted rapist had succeeded in raping his victim.

What to Make of Rationally Indefensible Doctrines

This, then, is my case against the harm doctrine. If I'm right, what should we make of it? What might it signify that an irrational doctrine like this perdures in the law and continues to have such a strong intuitive appeal outside the law, and what, if anything, should be done about it? I have no big answers, only some speculations.

The first important thing to notice is that the harm doctrine is not a singular anomaly in the criminal law. There are other rationally indefensible standard

criminal law doctrines that have widespread intuitive appeal. In speculating on the whys and wherefores of the harm doctrine it may be instructive to take them into account as well. Let me instance two doctrines that seem to me to be of this character.

This first goes under different names and has a variety of applications. I will refer to it as the lesser-wrong doctrine, for it rests on the premise that if I do something I should not—something wrong or unlawful—I become guilty of any harm my action produced, even though I wouldn't have been responsible for it had I been doing something legal. One finds the principle widely manifested in the law. For example, in the law of homicide, it is known as the misdemeanor-manslaughter or felony-murder rule. A hunter, first looking around to be sure no one will be endangered, shoots at game. The bullet unpredictably ricochets off a rock, killing a person who was hiding behind a bush. So far no crime has been committed, only an accident. But suppose the hunting season had not yet started or the animal was of a protected species. Now the hunter would be guilty not only of hunting out of season and killing an endangered species but of culpable homicide as well. Under the traditional common law rules, if the hunting offenses were misdemeanors the hunter would be guilty of manslaughter; if they were felonies the hunter would be guilty of murder. While the severity of these doctrines has been moderated in modern times, they are still part of the law. The lesser-wrong principle affects thinking in non-homicide cases as well. For example: A man deserts his pregnant wife. Under this doctrine he is guilty of the crime of deserting a pregnant wife even if he had no reason to know she was pregnant. Why? Because deserting one's wife is itself a wrong thing to do. A man absconds with a girl under sixteen without parental approval. Under this doctrine he is guilty of the crime of doing so even if he reasonably thought she was over sixteen. Why? Because running off with a young woman is itself a wrongful action.

I needn't labor what's wrong with these doctrines. The pursuit of crime-preventive purposes scarcely justifies them. To speak of the homicide doctrines, for example, if we want to deter life-threatening actions, then those are the types of acts that we should punish—not non-threatening acts just because they're done in the course of some lesser crime and happen to kill by some fluke. The doctrines only serve to raise the punishment for the lesser crimes during which death chances to result. . . . Nor does the desert principle support these doctrines. What the offender deserves is punishment for the lesser crimes, not for the deaths, which are, by stipulation, wholly accidental. Of course, the same reasoning also applies to the non-homicidal instances of the lesser wrong principle, as in the cases of the husband deserting his wife and the man taking out a young woman without permission. If anything, these are even more objectionable since they result not just in arbitrarily raising the punishment, but in making a legally innocent action a crime.

Here then we have another instance of an irregularity in our sentiments producing a rationally indefensible doctrine—not, like the harm doctrine, the diminution of resentment when no harm is done, but its augmentation when it is, so great that one who is not culpable of the harm is made accountable nonetheless, because that person has done something else that is wrong. To be sure, the lesser-wrong doctrine does not have so widespread an intuitive appeal as the harm doctrine, and is not so deeply rooted in the law. But it is to be found more than occasionally, particularly in Anglo-American law, and it does respond to a not uncommon intuition that someone who has done wrong can't complain if he gets blamed for harms that happen as a consequence, even if he didn't intend them or couldn't reasonably expect them.

It is obvious enough that these irrational doctrines are not indigenous to the law. The doctrines of criminal liability and punishment represent a system of assessing legal blame which the law models upon the principles that govern assessing moral blame in our everyday social life. If I am right that some of the law's doctrines are not rationally defensible, that is because, as Adam Smith observed, it is our moral judgments that are irregular. For it is clear that these intuitions—that chance results do matter in assessing blame, that in doing wrong you take on all the consequences, foreseeable or not, and that it is right that wrongdoers should be made to suffer—are ingrained in our moral sensibilities, and that the law I have been describing only reflects them. The track of the irrational in the criminal law leads back to our moral culture itself.

. . . Not only are our laws instruments for achieving our purposes; they are also a medium for expressing our cultural and moral sensibilities just like our art, religion, language, literature, myths, and ceremonies. Justice Holmes no doubt had something like this in mind when he observed that "the law is the witness and external deposit of our moral life." There are limits, therefore, particularly in a democratic community like ours, to how far the law can or should be bent by reformers to express a moral outlook different from that of the deeply held intuitive perceptions of the great mass of humanity, irrational though they may seem to some. . . .

Endnotes

[1] George P. Fletcher, *Rethinking Criminal Law*, 473–474 (1978).

[2] *State v. Guffey*, 262 S.W.2d 152 (Mo. Ct. App. 1955).

[3] Thomas Nagel, *Mortal Questions*, 24–38 (1979). See also Bernard Williams, *Moral Luck*, 20–39 (1981).

[4] Michael Davis, *To Make the Punishment Fit the Crime*, 101 (1992).

[5] R. A. Duff, "Auctions, Lotteries, and the Punishment of Attempts," 9 *Law & Phil.* 1 (1990), pp. 30–37.

Study Questions

1. Why, according to the court in *Dlugash,* can't Dlugash be convicted of murder?

2. What evidence convinced the court that Dlugash did believe Geller was alive at the time Dlugash fired his shots?

3. *Hyam v. Director of Public Prosecutions* involved a British woman who was charged with murder. Hyam went to the apartment of her former lover, stuffed gasoline-soaked newspapers through a mail slot in the door, and ignited them. A fire resulted, in which two children inside the apartment died. Hyam testified that she had intended only to scare off a woman who had taken up with Hyam's ex-boyfriend, and that she had no idea that a fire would result or that any children were inside the apartment. To be guilty of murder, Hyam had to have acted with the "intent to kill." Was that her intention? How would you decide that question? More generally, do people intend only the things that they have immediately in mind (e.g., scaring off the new girlfriend)? What about the means one uses and the ultimate consequences of one's acts? If I act through means that lead to consequences I did not foresee (even though others might have), did I "intend" those consequences?

4. Mildred Pruner, a sixty-seven-year-old woman, was robbed at gunpoint. When Pruner appeared to testify at the trial of her alleged assailant, she became so distraught at describing the assault that she suffered a heart attack on the witness

stand and died on the floor of the courtroom. The state's chief medical examiner determined that Pruner was literally "scared to death." The court subsequently ruled Pruner's death a homicide. Should the defendant be held responsible for the witness's death? Did he perform an "act" of killing her? Is some kind of strict criminal liability being imposed here?

5. Philosopher David Lewis has argued that punishing (unsuccessful) attempters less harshly than those who complete the crime is justified as a form of *penal lottery*, subjecting a person to a risk of harm. Attempts to commit a crime, whether or not they succeed, do impose risks (perhaps of death) on their intended victims. So, Lewis proposes, our law appropriately deals with attempters in the same way, exposing *them* to a risk of greater punishment (perhaps even death): the risk that they may hit the target, rather than miss, and wind up in the electric chair rather than a jail cell. Lewis proposes that we make the element of chance operating in the law of attempt more explicit and overt by instituting a penal lottery in which those convicted of attempt draw lots, the loser perhaps being executed. The worse the crime you attempt, the worse the odds for you. [See Lewis, "The Punishment that Leaves Something to Chance," *Philosophy and Public Affairs*, Vol. 18 (1989): 53–67.] Is a penal lottery unfair or unjust? If so, how? Is it fair to subject all attempters, successful or not, to a risk of death? Does it matter that we subject them *equally* to such a risk of death? If people's lives are affected by chance in a whole variety of other ways (which they indisputably are), why not in this way?

6. Victor is unhappily married to Esmeralda. In fact, Victor so despises his wife that he has on more than one occasion seriously thought of killing her. Victor was raised on a small island in the Caribbean and, as a young boy, was initiated into the black-magic cults of the native peoples. Victor still retains deep beliefs in the power of voodoo magic. One day, when he feels he can stand his wife no longer, Victor retires to his secret workshop, where he has over the years meticulously collected the accoutrements of the black arts. Carefully he prepares a tiny, doll-like replica of the despised Esmeralda. When at last the doll is finished, Victor takes a deep breath and, with nervous fingers and a look of hatred, viciously and

repeatedly stabs the doll with "sacred" needles. Exhausted by his deed, Victor collapses. When he awakens, he is overcome with remorse and disgust at what he has done. He promptly leaves his workshop, marches to the local police station, and turns himself in, believing with all sincerity that he has murdered his wife. Question: Is Victor guilty of attempted murder? Why not? Consider the language of the Model Penal Code, section 5.01: "(1) *Definition of Attempt.* A person is guilty of an attempt to commit a crime if, acting with the kind of culpability otherwise required for commission of the crime, he: (a) purposely engages in conduct which would constitute the crime if the attendant circumstances were as he believes them to be; or (b) when causing a particular result is an element of the crime, does or omits to do anything with the purpose of causing or with the belief that it will cause such result without further conduct on his part; or (c) purposely does or omits to do anything which, under the circumstances as he believes them to be, is an act or omission constituting a substantial step in a course of conduct planned to culminate in his commission of the crime." Is Victor convictable of attempt under this language? If so, does this make sense?

7. Do you agree with Kadish that a defendant need not actually harm an intended victim in order to assure us of his culpability or dangerousness?

8. Are you persuaded by Kadish's argument against the resulting harm doctrine. If not, how would you defend that doctrine?

9. Scott Falter, a former head of a church in Arizona, was charged with murder in the death of his wife. The victim had been stabbed multiple times and dragged in the family swimming pool. Falter defended himself with the aid of witness who claimed that Falter was a sleepwalker. Sleep-disorder specialists also testified that Falter met the profile of a sleepwalker, capable of unconscious behavior. If you were the judge hearing this case, would you rule that Falter did not commit an "act" for which he could be held accountable because of his sleepwalking? Consider the language of Model Penal Code 2.01: "the following are not voluntary acts . . . (a) a reflex or convulsion; (b) a bodily movement during unconsciousness or sleep . . ."

10. The headline read "Man Convicted of Attempted Rape of Fictitious Child." Steven Peterman, age

45, was convicted and sentenced in November 2002 to twelve years in prison for attempting to have sex with a ten-year-old girl who did not exist. Evidence had suggested that Peterman was involved in a child pornography ring. Prosecutors worked with a female acquaintance of Peterman to arrest him. They invented a ten-year-old girl, whom the acquaintance then pretended to know. The woman indicated she would give Peterman access to the girl if he would come to her residence. Peterman arrived at the woman's home with several photographs, characterized by police as child pornography, along with a variety of sex toys. Prosecutors claimed that taking sex toys to the woman's home was proof of criminal intent to have sex with a child. "This is about whether Mr. Peterman had the intent to commit

an overt act in furtherance of such a crime," officials claimed. "When he went to the residence where he believed the child was waiting, he had purchased several items that he intended to use in committing a crime." According to officials, since Peterman believed that the girl was real, and intended to have sex with her, he could be charged with attempted rape. Though admitting having to engage in a "bit of legal gymnastics" to file the charge, authorities insisted that Peterman wasn't prosecuted for simply thinking about raping a child. (See CNN.com Law Center, Friday, November 29, 2002. See also *The Wichita Eagle Online*, "Rape Conviction, Minus Victim," posted Friday, November 29, 2002.) Do you agree that Peterman was properly convictable of attempted rape?

B. *Justification and Excuse*

"It Wasn't Really My Fault"

Andrea Yates, Theodore Kaczynski, Robert Alton Harris, and Jeffrey Dahmer. Each of these defendants, central figures in some of the most highly publicized and notorious criminal trials of the last decade, enraged many by seeking, to one degree or another, to *excuse* their violent conduct.

In everyday life, most of us are willing to excuse a friend who arrives late for an important meeting or a student who turns in a late paper, but only if the excuse is reasonable under the circumstances (the teacher gets to decide what's reasonable!). The law is willing to listen to excuses, too. But under what circumstances and for what reasons should it do so? This is the central question examined in this section.

Three Cases

In March 2002, a Texas jury, rejecting her insanity plea, convicted Andrea Yates of capital murder in the

drowning deaths of her five children. Yates had waited until her husband left for work. She then filled the bathtub and drowned each of her children, one at a time. Yates was described as deeply psychotic by some experts: she had scratched "666"—the so-called "sign of Satan"—into her scalp and suffered hallucinations of cartoon characters talking to her from the television screen. Yates believed that Satan had urged her to drown the children: "I felt that I had done all of the other sins and now this would be the last one . . . It was something I was told to do [by] Satan."[1] Yates had reportedly experienced hearing voices and having delusions previous to the killings, but had told no one for fear that Satan would hear her and harm her children. Did the jury rightly reject her insanity plea? Should she have been held responsible for her conduct simply because she was aware, in some sense, that what she did was wrong?

---

[1] *Newsday*, March 8, 2002, p. A18.

Theodore Kaczynski, the confessed "Unabomber," pled guilty in January 1998 to thirteen charges, including murder. Kaczynski was overwhelmingly implicated in a string of attacks dating back to the 1970s, which resulted in three deaths and twenty-nine injuries. Excerpts from his own journals revealed that Kaczynski intended "to start killing people" and referred to his mail bombs as "experiments." Of one of the attacks, Kaczynski's journal entry reported that his experiment was a "success at last" and that he was "producing good results."

Aided by his brother, authorities found Kaczynski living in a rustic, one-room cabin in a remote part of Montana. Fearful that they would seek to portray him as "sick," Kaczynski fought with his court-appointed lawyers and even threatened to act in his own defense. A key issue confronting the judge and the lawyers in the case turned on Kaczynski's mental state. Defense experts argued that Kaczynski was a paranoid schizophrenic who had lived for years as a hermit; had no electricity, phone, or running water; and ate squirrel and porcupine roasted over a fire. The lawyers cited Kaczynksi's erratic behavior concerning his own case and how it should be handled, as well as an apparent suicide attempt while in police custody. The judge in the case, however, initially found the former math professor to be lucid, calm, and intelligent, with a clear understanding of the legal issues at stake in his own case.

Kaczynski's case presented the court with several questions: Does he suffer from mental illness? Did he suffer from mental illness at the time of the crimes? Were his intentions, although clearly apparent from his diaries, nonetheless the product of mental disease?

Robert Alton Harris was convicted of brutally murdering two teenage boys (after which he casually ate the remainder of their lunches). Harris had a ghastly childhood. His father was an abusive alcoholic who beat his wife and children and sexually molested his daughters. Harris was born prematurely after the father kicked Harris's mother in the stomach. Harris was repeatedly kicked, hit, and emotionally abused. He was slated for execution in California's gas chamber when the horror of his upbringing was used in making a plea for clemency to then-governor Pete Wilson. Wilson denied the clemency request with these words:

> It is argued on his behalf that Robert Harris must be judged to be in effect a child who cannot be held accountable under California law. . . . Experts contend that Harris has suffered organic brain damage both as a result

of his mother's abuse of alcohol during pregnancy and as a result of trauma inflicted by his parents, mostly by an especially vicious father. . . . The application for clemency adequately demonstrates that Mr. Harris' childhood was a living nightmare. He suffered monstrous child abuse that would have a brutalizing effect on him. . . . But victimized though he may have been, Harris was not deprived of the capacity to premeditate, to plan or to understand the consequences of his actions. . . . For the protection of its most vulnerable members, society must hold accountable and hold to a minimum level of personal responsibility Robert Harris and all members of society—excepting only those who have been clearly shown to lack the capacity to meet that minimum level of responsibility. . . . Harris' own conduct [includes] clear and chilling evidence of his capacity to think, to conceive a plan, to understand the consequences of his actions, to dissemble and deceive and destroy evidence to avoid apprehension and punishment. . . . He was capable of planning to do wrong, and taking precautions to conceal his wrongdoing. . . . Robert Harris, the child, had no choice. He was a victim of serious and inexcusable abuse. Robert Harris, the man, did have a choice. He chose to take a life, two lives. . . .The decision of the jury was correct . . . Clemency is denied.

Excuse and Justification

The Kaczynski and Harris cases illustrate ways in which the law of excuse and justification involves serious questions concerning a defendant's responsibility for his or her actions. Suppose that I am charged with the robbery of an elderly man in a city park. Recognized defenses or legitimate excuses under the law to such a charge would be that I was *entrapped* into committing the crime, a police officer having planted the idea of it in my mind, an idea to which I was not otherwise predisposed; I was *coerced* into the robbery through a threat of death or serious bodily harm; I was a *minor* under the age of seven. In *Richardson v. U.S.*,[2] the defendant was charged with robbery for having

---

[2] 403 F.2d 574 (1968).

stopped a man named Snowden and removing $98 from his (Snowden's) wallet. On appeal of his conviction, Richardson claimed that Snowden owed him (Richardson) a long-standing gambling debt, amounting to $270, which Richardson had been seeking to collect for some time. Richardson's conviction was reversed on the grounds that he had made an honest mistake: he thought that, as a result of the outstanding debt, the money in Snowden's wallet was his (Richardson's) property. To engage in robbery, one must act with the intent (purpose) to take the property of another; since Richardson thought the property belonged to him, his mistake negated the *mens rea* required for the offense. Mistakes can excuse.

A distinction long made in the criminal law is the distinction between conditions or circumstances *excusing* a defendant's conduct and those serving as a *justification* for that conduct. In both cases, the defendant admits to causing a result forbidden by law but argues nonetheless that she should not be punished. The defendant can claim justification in situations in which she did something the law forbids under circumstances that did no harm to society but actually advanced a social interest in a way society wishes to encourage. For example, it was typically held by courts that acting under authority of law may provide a justification for what would otherwise be a criminal wrong. So, for instance, a police office may use force in the performance of her official duties that might not be justified were she an ordinary citizen. The actor can claim excuse when she did cause harm to society but did so under conditions that mark her as less deserving of punishment. As noted above, coercion or duress are traditionally regarded as excuses; acting in self-defense is often classified as a justification, although, as the readings in this section explore, this is not a classification without critics.

The Unknowingly Justified Actor and the Theory of Justification

In his selection, Paul Robinson helps us to understand the competing accounts of just what a justification is with a fascinating case. Defendant steals a backpack left in a crowded, public area, believing he has successfully committed a theft. Taking the item to a quiet location, Defendant opens it and discovers a bomb. He summons the police, who successfully defuse the device. Had it exploded in its original location, many lives would have been lost. What should become of

Defendant? Of course, had he known all along that the backpack contained a bomb he would have been justified in facilitating its removal, and he would have had a defense to any charge that he had stolen someone's property. But he was in fact unaware of the facts that serve to afford a justification. Should he have one anyway? Or should he go to jail for theft?

Robinson distinguishes two accounts of why and when circumstances should afford a justification. The "deeds" theory says that a justification attaches if the actor's conduct avoids a harm, regardless of his culpability or state of mind. The "reasons" theory insists that a justification attaches only if the actor's conduct was referable to reasons which show that he acted with a justificatory purpose. On the deeds theory, Defendant goes free; on the reasons theory, he goes to jail. Robinson argues in favor of the deeds account, maintaining that Defendant, much like the actor who attempts a crime but fails, should get the benefit of the fact that a lesser harm was done, even though the actor himself did not see it that way when he acted.

The Proliferation of Excuses

The last twenty years have seen a dramatic expansion in both the kinds of excuses and justifications offered by criminal defendants and their successful deployment in high-profile cases. Among the recent entrants is the so-called "abuse excuse." Lyle and Erik Menendez, accused in the shotgun slayings of their wealthy parents, won a deadlocked jury and a mistrial with their claim of excuse that the killings were fear-induced, brought on by years of sexual abuse and molestation on the part of their father. Lorena Bobbit, charged with mutilating her husband's genitals while he slept, insisted that her marriage was an abusive "reign of terror" that provoked her to act in self-defense. Recent cases invoking other excuses include the following: (1) In May 1979, while working at a pub in England, the defendant, a woman, got into a fight with a barmaid and stabbed her to death. Charged with murder, her record indicated a history of uncontrolled behavior resulting in nearly thirty convictions in the preceding ten years. It was noticed that her uncontrollable disruptive behavior followed a definite monthly pattern. Doctors later diagnosed her condition as "premenstrual syndrome" [PMS].[3]

---

[3] See D. Brahams, "Premenstrual Syndrome: A Disease of the Mind." *The Lancet*, Vol. 11 (Nov. 28, 1981): 1238–1240.

(2) In 1984 a defendant was charged with attempted bank robbery and larceny. In defense, he pled insanity in the form of "pathological gambling disorder."[4] (3) Ann Green was charged with murder in the suffocation deaths of her two infants. She testified that she had seen hands she did not recognize holding pillows over the infants' faces. In 1989 a jury found Ms. Green "not responsible" for the deaths on the grounds that she suffered from "postpartum psychosis." (4) In 1989 Terrence Frank successfully avoided a conviction for first-degree murder in the shooting deaths of two people on the Navajo reservation in Arizona. Mr. Frank's attorney convinced the jury that his client was temporarily insane at the time of the killing as a result of brain damage he had sustained from childhood exposure to uranium radiation leaking from mines surrounding his home. Frank's father and grandfather had both died from radiation-induced cancer, and an abnormally high rate of birth defects was recorded in the area. (Frank was convicted of second-degree, unpremeditated murder.)[5] (5) In April 1994, a Texas jury returned no verdict against a defendant accused of shooting two unarmed men who had purportedly threatened him. The defense argued that "urban survival syndrome," created by life on the inner-city streets, led to the shooting. As yet, few of these excuses have received widespread acceptance. Which, if any, should be acknowledged?

Battered Woman's Defense

One excuse that has increasingly been recognized by many jurisdictions involves the tragic spread of domestic violence and spousal abuse. "Battered woman's syndrome" has been invoked by female defendants, victims of repeated physical and emotional abuse, who injure or kill their abusers. Women exhibiting the syndrome frequently lack self-esteem. They want to leave abusive relationships but feel they cannot, often because they are unable to support themselves and fear that their abusers will track them down and beat them worse than before should they attempt to leave. Battered woman's syndrome is often treated as a justification, analogous to self-defense. But

as Cathryn Jo Rosen points out in her essay, this choice raises some problems.

The exercise of force to repel an attacker in self-defense has traditionally been regarded as a full-fledged justification, rather than an excuse. To defend yourself against an immediate threat to your life where no other option exists, the law has said, is the "right" thing to do. (Whether a convincing moral argument can be given to support this position is explored in our readings.) Historically, the use of defensive force has been evaluated in terms of the following criteria:

Traditional Criteria for the Use of Defensive Force

1. There must be an imminence of violent attack threatening death or great bodily injury.

2. Only the immediate context of the situation may be used to justify self-defense.

3. The force used to repel the attack can be no greater than the attacking force itself.

4. The previous three criteria are to be judged from the standpoint of the objective, "reasonable" person.

Taken together, these criteria show that the law of self-defense typically has been conceived by the law on the model of the momentary, face-to-face encounter between armed strangers, where the defendant has a reasonable belief that he is in imminent danger to which he must respond in kind. However, this model often fails to describe the realities of spousal abuse or women's responses to it. Lorena Bobbit claimed she acted in self-defense in mutilating her husband because he had threatened to track her down and rape her if she left him. Yet Mr. Bobbit was asleep when attacked, not brandishing a gun. If an abused woman chooses a moment when she is most likely to prevail over her victimizer, can she still argue that her action was justified? Those who think so maintain that the law must take account of the woman's perspective, and they point to the law of rape as an example of how and why this is to be done.

Feminist theorists such as Susan Estrich[6] have argued that for too long the law's understanding of

---

[4] *U.S. v. Gould,* 741 F. 2d 45 (4th Cir. 1984).

[5] See "'Toxin Defense' Successful," *The National Law Journal,* May 1, 1989, p. 5.

[6] See Susan Estrich, *Real Rape* (Cambridge: Harvard University Press, 1987).

whether a woman consented to sex was to be assessed in terms of how hard she resisted, how seriously her life was threatened, or how reasonable her belief was that she was in mortal danger. But, say critics of rape law, what counts as resistance or force, what is understood to be a threat, and what is taken to be unreasonable about a belief—all are substantially, if not entirely, *gendered:* they are conceived (in the case of existing law) from a male point of view and reflect distorted images of women and of sexuality.

The widely discussed *Rusk*[7] case from the early 1980s drives home the point. The defendant met his victim at a bar and asked her for a ride home. She agreed. When they arrived, it was late at night in a neighborhood unfamiliar to the woman. The defendant asked her up to his apartment; she refused. He asked again. After her second refusal, he reached over and took her car keys. She accompanied him upstairs, where he pulled her by the arms onto the bed and began to undress her. Crying, she testified, "I was really scared, because I can't describe, you know, what was said. It was more the look in his eyes . . . and I said 'If I do what you want, will you let me go without killing me?' . . . He said yes and I proceeded to do what he wanted me to."[8] Although ultimately his conviction was sustained, many of the judges hearing this case found, in the words of one judge, "no conduct by the defendant reasonably calculated to make the victim so fearful that she should fail to resist."[9] No force was employed; the victim's alleged fear sprang from nothing of substance. In this view, the defendant committed not rape but a seduction; his belief that she "went along with it" was not unreasonable from *his* point of view. Requiring that juries examine a similar series of events from the standpoint of the *reasonable woman,* however, might well lead to very different results.

---

[7] 289 Md. 230, 424 A. 2d 720 (1981).

[8] *Ibid.,* p. 722.

[9] *Ibid.,* p. 733 (Cole, J., dissenting). The dissent further observes: She also testified that she was afraid of "the way he looked," and afraid of his statement, "come on up, come on up." But what can the majority conclude from this statement coupled with a "look" that remained undescribed? There is no evidence whatsoever to suggest that this was anything other than a pattern of conduct consistent with the ordinary seduction of a female acquaintance who at first suggests her disinclination. (*Ibid.,* p. 733.) The majority cites the lower court, finding that "'the way he looked' fails utterly to support the fear required by [law]." (*Ibid,* p. 724.)

Asking juries to consider what a reasonable woman would do when faced with an assailant like Rusk or an abusive husband will, in the view of some, introduce a much-needed corrective into the criminal law. With regard to the battered woman's defense, however, Cathryn Jo Rosen is not fully convinced. Rosen focuses on this question: Will looking only at the subjective perspective of the female victim result in justifying any killing she believes necessary to defend herself? Rosen insists that, to say of Defendant's killing that it is justified assumes the truth of the following claim: the life of the aggressor (the person against whom defensive force is used) is necessarily less valuable to society than the life of the defender. This, Rosen believes, is a very difficult claim to support. Neither the battered woman's defense nor self-defense more generally, Rosen argues, should be regarded as justification for what would otherwise be criminal conduct. Rosen shows how her concerns regarding the battered woman's defense connect with deeper questions about how to justify any form of self-defense in the law. She concludes that evidence of spousal abuse should be cautiously considered, and then only as an excuse, not a justification.

Cultural Defenses

Recent changes in the law of rape and sexual harassment and the introduction of the battered woman's defense stem from the awareness that women experience the world, and especially sexuality, in ways different from men. In the same fashion but on a much broader scale, peoples of differing cultures may regard as excusable, or even fully justified, conduct proscribed by the criminal law.

In 1997 a California court sentenced a Korean missionary, Sung Soo Choi, to involuntary manslaughter in the death of a woman upon whom Sung had performed an exorcism ritual. Sung believed the woman to be possessed by demons that made her disobedient to her husband. Sung and the husband agreed that the woman should be treated with a ritual combining prayer and a laying on of hands. The victim was discovered to have suffered sixteen broken ribs, deep bruises, and internal injuries resulting from the five-hour ritual. In 1985 a woman of Japanese ancestry walked into the ocean near Santa Monica, California, with her two children after learning that her husband was having an affair. She survived, but the children drowned. Experts testified at trial that the woman's actions were consistent with the traditional practice of *oyakoshinju,* or parent-child suicide, for which she would be charged with involuntary manslaughter in Japan today. The first-degree murder charge initially filed against her was dropped, and she was allowed to plead guilty to voluntary manslaughter. She received five years' probation with psychiatric treatment.[10] A Yoruban woman who immigrated to England from Nigeria was arrested after she scarred her child's face with a razor to initiate the child into their tribe. She argued in her defense that it would be abuse *not* to practice this ritual.[11] A Hmong man, tried by California for kidnapping and rape after abducting a woman at a college campus, defended himself by arguing that in Hmong culture, *zij poj niam,* or "marriage by bride-capture," was considered an acceptable way of obtaining a bride.[12]

Should a person's cultural background be invocable to show that he or she did not have the *mens rea* for a crime with which he or she is charged? Should the introduction of evidence bearing on a defendant's culture be permitted as an excusing condition in mitigation of punishment?

The Insanity Plea

As the case of Theodore Kaczynski, the admitted Unabomber, reveals, no claim of excuse has provoked such contentious debate as the claim that a defendant must be acquitted, even for a wrongdoing he plainly committed, because at the time of the offense he was *insane.*

Lorena Bobbit's jury acquitted her on grounds of temporary insanity, finding that an "irresistible impulse" provoked her to attack her husband; yet in Wisconsin, a jury refused to accept an insanity plea by Jeffrey Dahmer, accused (and eventually convicted) of killing, dismembering, and even eating the body parts of fifteen young men and boys. To understand these results, we conclude this section with a discussion of two prominent issues: How is "insanity" to be understood, and why should it be an excuse at all? The

Cameron case serves as a point of departure for these questions.

The facts of Marie Cameron's gruesome murder need no elaboration. Marie's stepson, Gary, was arrested and charged with the crime. At trial he raised the defense that he was insane at the time of the murder, and evidence was introduced to show he was a "paranoid schizophrenic." As is always the case in a criminal proceeding before a jury, the closing arguments of the prosecution and the defense are followed by the phase of the trial in which the judge "instructs" the jury, that is, informs the jury of the rules of the law that they must apply to their determination of the facts of the case. In *Cameron,* the trial judge instructed the jury regarding the rules governing the defense of insanity, as these rules were then structured by the law of Washington state. Applying the judge's instructions, the jury convicted Cameron. The appellate court affirmed the conviction. Cameron appealed to the Supreme Court of Washington, alleging that the instructions given to the jury incorrectly stated the "law" governing the insanity plea. Before we delve more deeply into the issues raised by Cameron's appeal, we must understand something of the broader history of the insanity defense and the various attempts to fashion and define an appropriate test for insanity.

"Insanity" is a legal rather than a medical term, and the efforts to clarify its meaning have been many and varied. The modern law of insanity begins with the famed *M'Naghten Case,* decided by the British House of Lords in 1843. Daniel M'Naghten had been charged with shooting and killing Edward Drummond, whom M'Naghten mistakenly believed to be the prime minister of England, Sir Robert Peel. M'Naghten pled not guilty, his lawyer insisting that M'Naghten suffered from delusions that undermined his perception of right and wrong. Upon considering the matter, the House of Lords articulated what came to be called the *M'Naghten Rule,* as intended to govern pleas of insanity. They held that:

> in all cases a man is presumed to be sane and to possess sufficient degree of reason to be responsible for his crimes, until the contrary be proved to the juror's satisfaction; and to establish a defense on the grounds of insanity it must be clearly proved that, at the time of committing the act, the party accused was laboring from such a defect of reason, from a disease of the mind, as not to know the

[10] See "'Cultural' Defenses Draw Fire," *The National Law Journal,* April 17, 1989, pp. 3, 28.

[11] See "Judges Debate Cultural Defense," *American Bar Association Journal,* December 1992, p. 28.

[12] See "Cultural Defense—A Legal Tactic," *L. A. Times,* July 15, 1988, pt. I, p. 1.

nature and quality of the act he was doing; or, if he did know it, that he did not know he was doing what was wrong.[13]

The substance of the M'Naghten Rule can be reduced to four elements: (1) defect of reason; (2) disease of the mind; (3) failure to know the nature and quality of one's act; and (4) failure to know that the act was wrong. As the rule is generally interpreted, elements 1 and 2 are necessary for a determination of insanity; either 3 or 4, together with 1 and 2, is sufficient. Typically, the "mental disease" spoken of in 2 must be a comparatively permanent condition, including such things as congenital defects and traumatic injury. There are at least two divergent interpretations of "know" as it is employed in 3 and 4. One view holds that "know" refers only to formal cognition or intellectual awareness (as in "I know that two plus two equals four"); the other holds that "know" is to be understood in a wider sense to mean that one appreciates the total setting (including the feelings and emotions of oneself and others) in which one's actions take place, and that one can evaluate the impact of one's actions upon others (as in "He knew that the match would cause a fire and the people would be burned").

The M'Naghten Rule was widely adopted throughout the jurisdictions of the common law world as the appropriate test for legal insanity, and many states, including Washington state at the time of *Cameron*, rely on some variant of it. Yet the M'Naghten Rule has been subjected to severe criticism over the years. Contemporary criminologists and jurists argue that it relies heavily on an outmoded psychology according to which the mental life of a person can be neatly divided into "cognitive," "affective," and "volitional" components. Such a model ignores the complexity of our psychic lives—how the ways in which we seek to understand the world and what we believe about it both influence and are influenced by our deepest desires, goals, and feelings. Other critics point out that *M'Naghten* stresses only cognitive impairment as relevant to insanity, with the result that the insanity defense often is unavailable to those who are seriously disturbed even though cognitively they may function on a near-normal level. A person suffering from kleptomania, for instance, would be such a case. It was for these reasons that, early on, some jurisdictions sought

to supplement *M'Naghten* with an "irresistible impulse" test: One is exempt from criminal liability if one either fits the *M'Naghten* definition or at the time of the offense could not control the urge to act as one did. This ancillary test was not without critics of its own. Is it really possible for a jury to ascertain whether a given "impulse" was irresistible? How can we tell when someone could have resisted if only he or she had tried a little harder? How do we know that he or she *could* have tried harder?

An alternative test for insanity was proposed by federal judge David Bazelon in 1954 in *Durham v. U.S.*[14] Durham was a habitual offender who underwent numerous psychiatric treatments, none of which seemed to be effective. When Durham was arrested and convicted for yet another offense, Judge Bazelon took advantage of Durham's appeal to state a new test: The accused is not criminally responsible if his or her unlawful act was the "product of mental disease or mental defect." The court believed this rule to be superior to those it supplanted because it treated the mind as a functional unit, thus bringing the legal standards up to date with developments in modern psychiatry and psychology and allowing experts to present the relevant scientific and medical data to the jury. *Durham* represented a sharp departure from the old tests of criminal insanity; nevertheless, several jurisdictions adopted it. The rule created problems, however, and was ultimately rejected by the U.S. Supreme Court. The most frequent criticism of the rule was that it gave no standards or guidelines to the jury. As a result of its breadth, inordinate weight was given to the testimony of "experts," whose conflicting testimony often left juries in a state of bewilderment. Is the defendant crazy or not?

Some states, frustrated with the lengthy trials and inconsistent testimony of professional witnesses, have moved to limit the circumstances under which a successful insanity defense may be mounted. For example, the Texas statute under which Andrea Yates was prosecuted incorporated only one portion of the M'Naghten rules: A defense is available only if "at the time of the conduct charged, the actor, as a result of severe mental disease or defect, did not know that his conduct was wrong."[15] Yates had admitted what she did was a "sin," and, hence, seemed not to satisfy the Texas definition.

---

[13] 8 Eng. Rep. 718 (1843).

[14] 214 F. 2d 862 (D.C. Cir. 1954).
[15] Tex. Penal Code, Sec. 8.01 (2002).

The test for insanity proposed by the Model Penal Code is rapidly gaining acceptance as a remedy for the defects of the *M'Naghten, Durham,* and irresistible impulse tests. Section 4.01 of the code provides that "a person is not responsible for criminal conduct if at the time of such conduct as a result of mental disease or defect he lacks substantial capacity either to appreciate the criminality [wrongfulness] of his conduct or to conform his conduct to the requirements of the law." The central issue in *Cameron* has to do with the applicability of the M'Naghten Rule to the defendant's conduct and, in particular, to the third and fourth elements of the test: Did Cameron understand the nature and quality of his actions? Plainly, he understood in some sense what he was doing and comprehended its implications (why else would one stab a victim more than seventy times?). On the other hand, he may have thought he was killing Satan. Did Cameron know that what he was doing was wrong? The narrow issue in the case centers on the trial court's definition of "wrong," which it took to be knowledge that the act was "contrary to law." Did Cameron realize that what he was doing violated the law? Perhaps. The Supreme Court of Washington reversed Cameron's conviction, holding that one who believes he is acting under a divine command is no less insane because he knows or realizes (in some sense) that murder is against the law.

Should the Insanity Defense Be Abolished?

Some people are outraged that a person such as Cameron should be found "not guilty by reason of insanity." The deliberate and vicious nature of the crime seems to them to demand a guilty verdict. Dissatisfaction with the realities of the insanity defense, together with the obvious difficulty in framing an acceptable and workable test for it, have moved some to condemn the defense as misconceived from the outset and to push for its abolition. The debate over abolition is joined here in the selections by Norval Morris and Stephen J. Morse.

Morris defends the abolitionist position. What does this actually amount to, and what are the arguments for it? Under existing law, a plea of insanity is a special defense. This means that it excuses an individual from responsibility for conduct that otherwise satisfies the (*actus reus* and *mens rea*) requirements for a crime. Morris proposes that the special defense of insanity be eliminated. In his view, mental illness

would be relevant to a person's guilt or innocence only insofar as it might show that the defendant lacked the specific *mens rea* for the offense with which he or she is charged. An example serves to illustrate Morris's scheme and how it would differ from the current regime: In *People v. Wetmore,*[16] the victim of a burglary returned home after a three-day absence to find the defendant living in his (the victim's) apartment. The defendant, Wetmore, was wearing the victim's clothes and cooking his food. The lock on the door had been broken, and the place was a shambles. Psychiatric examiners found that the homeless Wetmore suffered from the delusion that he "owned" the property and that he was "directed" to the victim's apartment, where he promptly moved in. Wetmore's conviction on burglary charges was reversed, the court finding that Wetmore could not be held accountable for breaking and entering the house of another if he thought it was his own.

Wetmore's mental illness precluded his having the state of mind necessary for the offense with which he was charged. However, mental illness does not always have this effect, and Cameron's case shows us why: In spite of his illness, it is beyond dispute that Cameron acted with the intent and purpose to kill. Under the abolitionist proposal, then, Wetmore is acquitted but Cameron is not. This is the difference between eliminating and retaining the insanity plea as a special defense.

Should the law distinguish in this way between Wetmore and Cameron? Why should the special defense be abolished? As Morris indicates, the principal argument made for eliminating the defense asserts that it is simply unworkable. "Insanity" defies any attempt at a meaningful definition; it confuses judges and juries; and it is very costly. Moreover, Morris alleges, the special defense is rarely raised and then only in connection with particularly heinous crimes. Morris concludes on a larger theme: The very idea of attempting to draw a bright line between the sick and the bad is misguided because it obscures the reality that social factors and determinants of behavior impair the capacity of people to conform to the law much more severely than insanity ever does.

The abolition of the special defense of insanity will have the consequence that people like Cameron are convicted. But, one might ask, what is the real difference here? After all, whether or not he is found

---

[16] 149 Cal. Rptr. 265 (1978).

"guilty," Cameron is not likely simply to "go free." Mentally ill individuals who are acquitted, like Wetmore, frequently are taken into custody again under the procedure of "civil commitment" and subjected to treatment. If they wind up in custody in either case, what is the difference between the law's handling of Wetmore and Cameron? One reply says that criminal conviction and a verdict of guilt, unlike civil commitment, carry with them a *moral stigma;* they represent a judgment that the individual's conduct is evil or wicked, properly deserving of blame and condemnation. This way of understanding a guilty verdict is reflected elsewhere in our law—for instance, in the refusal to permit convicted felons to vote. Yet if people such as Cameron truly are "sick," one might reason, they should not be blamed or condemned in this way. Cameron is not a proper object of that kind of moral response. And all of this is quite independent of whether Cameron should be detained for his and others' safety.

Stephen J. Morse argues in favor of retaining the insanity defense on explicitly moral grounds. Actors who possess "minimal cognitive and volitional competence," Morse contends, ought not to be subject to criminal punishment. Morse tries to explicate the troublesome notions of rational action and of acting under compulsion, and to determine how much irrationality and compulsion, evident in an actor's conduct, should be sufficient to afford him or her a legal excuse of insanity.

To better appreciate the moral intuition animating Morse's position, consider the following: It seems that for many centuries in Europe, from the early Middle Ages through the close of the eighteenth century, animals were routinely tried, convicted, and punished for a variety of "crimes," including eating crops, destroying livestock, and attacking humans.[17] Typical of these animal cases is that of the dog Provetie. (See "Cases for Further Reflection" at the conclusion of this chapter.)

On May 5, 1595, Provetie bit the hand of a young child who was carrying a piece of meat. The child died, and Provetie was apprehended, tried, and convicted of murder. In passing sentence, the judge proclaimed that Provetie must be severely punished "as an example to others and more especially to evilly disposed dogs," and in consequence he ordered Provetie to be hanged "at the plain of Gravesteijn . . . where evildoers are customarily punished." (In this case the dog got off easily; other punishments routinely involved torture.)

Various hypotheses have been offered to explain this bizarre chapter of legal history, but its relevance for us lies in this observation: Although many of us might want this dog off the streets, few if any of us would regard the procedure of charging and convicting the dog, condemning it as an evildoer, and hanging it in order to deter other dogs as anything but silly. Most of us would find something peculiarly inappropriate about such treatment of a dog. Such conduct is inappropriate because it reflects a way of regarding dogs that seems simply to be mistaken: Dogs are not capable of understanding the requirements of law or good morals, nor are they able to conform their behavior to such standards. Those opposing the abolition of the insanity defense ask us to imagine a case involving a person who, with respect to the law, is in substantially the same position as the dog—that is, someone who is unable either to understand fully its requirements or to conform his or her behavior to them.

Morris concedes that there is something to the claim that conviction in a case such as *Cameron* is inappropriate, but he regards this claim as vague and ill-founded. Every day we punish people whose capacity to conform their behavior to the law is impaired by a variety of factors: parental neglect, social and economic deprivation, and the like. Yet no one thinks, he points out, that we should have a special defense of "growing up in a ghetto."

---

[17] For a thorough and entertaining discussion, see E. P. Evans, *The Criminal Prosecution and Capital Punishment of Animals* (London: Faber and Faber, 1987).

The Bomb Thief and the Theory of Justification Defenses

Paul H. Robinson

Is a justification defense, such as self-defense, law enforcement authority, or lesser evil, given because of an actor's good motive—his justificatory purpose—for doing what otherwise would be an offense? Or, is a justification defense given because, given the special justifying circumstances, the law tolerates and even encourages the actor's conduct? The answer to these questions has implications for how justification defenses are formulated. The bomb thief case nicely illustrates the tension between these two ways of characterizing the justification defense, and helps illustrates why one theory is better then the other.

The Bomb Thief

Motti Ashkenazi, a thin, almost gaunt-looking man from a poor, crime-ridden South Tel Aviv neighborhood, is strolling along a crowded Jerusalem beach between Tel Aviv and Jaffa on a hot Friday afternoon in June 1997. A drug addict and petty thief who only a week ago had been arrested after bungling a car burglary, Ashkenazi has been thinking for a while about getting off drugs and putting his life together. But the going has been tough even with the support of his family.

As he walks, he sees that someone has left a black backpack unattened in an open area by the sidewalk. The 30-year-old Ashkenazi looks around but sees no one watching. He picks up the backpack and quickly sneaks off, pleased by his good fortune. Without opening the backpack to inspect his loot, he walks down nearby Geula Street to a rundown apartment building and slips inside. There in the stairwell, he unzips the backpack. Inside he sees a clock with wires connected to a cookie tin, with loose nails surrounding

the contraption. Ashkenazi quickly realizes he just stole a bomb.

Panicked but in control, he runs into the nearby Savoy Hotel and rushes up to the reception desk. He tells the clerk what he found and the clerk calls the Tel Aviv police. The bomb squad arrives in minutes and starts trying to deactivate the bomb in the apartment building stairwell. Meanwhile, Ashkenazi stands outside the building, keeping the street clear of passersby and warning a group of children to stay away. The bomb squad finds that the bomb is packed with nearly 3 kilograms of explosives. They successfully neutralize it. Police officers search the beach for more bombs but find none.

At first, Ashkenazi lies to the police and tells them he found the backpack in the apartment building stairwell, where he had gone to urinate, but later confesses to having stolen the backpack. Considering the amount of explosives and the number of people in the area where the bomb was left, police estimate that the bomb would have killed many people in a major terrorist attack.[1]

What criminal liability should Ashkenazi have for the theft of the backpack, if any? Ashkenazi's conduct constitutes theft; he has taken another's property without the owner's permission. All jurisdictions and scholars agree that, if he had known at the time of the offense what he discovered later—that the bag contained a terrorist bomb—he clearly would have been justified in taking the bag. Indeed, his knowing of the actual circumstances would have made his conduct not just justified but heroic. Of what effect is the fact that he did not know that his taking the bag was justified, that he in fact thought he was committing theft? Should he be liable for theft, which he thought he was committing? Or, should he be exempt from liability because his act, while it normally would have caused a net harm, in this instance caused a net benefit, probably saving many lives?

These questions frame an ongoing dispute in criminal law theory over the nature of justification

From Paul H. Robinson, "The Bomb Thief and the Theory of Justification Defenses," *Criminal Law Forum*, vol. 8 (1997), pp. 387–409. Reprinted with kind permission from Kluwer Academic Publishers.

defenses. Is a justification defense given because the actor's deed in fact avoids a greater harm, the *deeds theory* of justification, or because of the actor's reason for acting, his justificatory purpose, the *reasons theory*?

In most cases of justification, both theories are satisfied: the justifying circumstances exist; the actor knows of them and performs the offense conduct because of them. She performs the right deed for the right reason. But in two kinds of cases, the two theories conflict: mistake as to a justification and an unknowingly justified actor.

Where an actor mistakenly believes she is justified, the reasons theory would give a justification defense—for it is only the actor's subjective intent that matters—while the deeds theory would deny a justification defense. But this conflict between the theories ends primarily in a labeling dispute. The actor denied a justification defense under the deeds theory nonetheless will be exculpated under an excuse defense for her mistake as to a justification, assuming the mistake is reasonable.

The reverse case, where an actor mistakenly believes that she is not justified, actually gives different liability results under the two theories. An unknowingly justified actor has no defense under the reasons theory, with its subjective focus, for she believed her conduct was unjustified. Under the deeds theory, in contrast, her conduct will be justified, because the deeds theory looks to the objective nature of the conduct. The unknowingly justified actor would be liable at most for trying to act unjustifiably—what I will argue later is a standard form of impossible attempt. Thus, while the reasons theory imposes liability for the full substantive offense, the deeds theory imposes only the reduced liability of attempt.

It is for this reason that the case of Motti Ashkenazi, the bomb thief—perhaps the cleanest case available of the unknowingly justified actor—is so interesting and so important. . . .

Current Law Governing the Unknowingly Justified Actor

Most, but not all, American state criminal codes appear to follow the reasons theory, although the apparent clarity of first appearances does not always survive close inspection. The American Law Institute's Model Penal Code uses a reasons formulation in its justification defenses: an actor is *justified* if she *believes* that her conduct is necessary for defense. Current English law also appears to adopt the reasons theory. . . .

Most academic writers have signed on in support of the reasons theory and in opposition to the deeds theory, some suggesting that the latter is "absurd," unfair, or unduly burdensome.

Disagreements over the Proper Liability for the Unknowingly Justified Actor

Recall the differing results from the two theories. The reasons theory gives no justification defense because the actor does not believe that the justifying circumstances exist. Whether the circumstances actually exist or not is irrelevant. Thus, Ashkenazi's theft is not justified even though it was necessary for the protection of other persons' lives. Ashkenazi's reason for acting was wrong; that his deed was in fact objectively justified is irrelevant. Under the deeds theory, in contrast, the actual nature of the deed is central: Ashkenazi would receive a justification defense even though he did not realize at the time that his conduct was objectively justified. As discussed more fully below . . . , however, he nonetheless may be liable for an attempt, and thereby receive some, albeit reduced, liability.

Disagreement over the Significance of Resulting Harm

It may be that this disagreement over the proper liability level for the unknowingly justified actor is simply a manifestation of a larger dispute going beyond the nature of justification defenses. The grading disagreement may be simply another battleground in the dispute over the significance of resulting harm. Those who believe that the criminal law ought to focus on conduct and culpable state of mind alone, and that the fortuity of resulting harm ought not affect liability, will naturally prefer the result of the reasons theory. Their view is that only the actor's subjective state of mind should matter to liability. That the unknowingly justified actor believes that his conduct is unjustified is enough in itself to impose full liability, they would argue, just as the person who thinks he has bought illegal drugs or believes he has lit a fuse on dynamite sticks ought to be fully liable even if it turns out that the powder is talcum and the dynamite sticks are wooden. The Model Penal Code, for one, seems to take this view when it adopts a rule that generally punishes attempts to the same extent as the substantive offense.

If this is the reason for one's support of a reasons theory of justification, then there is little more to be said on the liability issue. Even if one were to adopt a deeds theory, which gives only attempt liability, under such a pure subjectivist approach attempts would be graded the same as the substantive offense, thereby erasing any difference in the liability results between the theories. . . .

Further . . . there are other important reasons beyond liability results for preferring the conceptual scheme and terminology of the deeds theory. Only the deeds conceptualization of justification allows the law clearly to identify, with the label "justified," conduct that it condones and will tolerate by others in similar situations in the future. The reasons conceptualization, by including under the same label both justified conduct and mistake as to a justification, frustrates this important ex ante function of law. Conduct performed under a mistaken belief it is justified is not conduct the law wishes to signal as approved in similar circumstances in the future. In fact, it wishes to signal the opposite, that such conduct is to be avoided in the future. By combining both objectively justified conduct and mistaken justification under the same label, "justified," the law hides this important distinction. Under the reasons approach, then, case adjudications in which the defendant is acquitted as "justified" obscure and confuse the public as to the rules of conduct rather than clarify and educate. On these grounds, even the pure subjectivist may conclude that a deeds theory of justification is preferable.

Whatever the logical appeal of the pure subjectivist view, it is a view that exists (and will probably always exist) only in academia. . . . I know of no jurisdiction that actually takes a pure subjectivist view, whatever code drafters may say they prefer. All American jurisdictions, even many of those adopting the Model Penal Code, reject that code's notion that attempts should be punished the same as the substantive offense. Even the Model Penal Code itself a ambivalent in its apparent commitment to a pure subjectivist view. It creates an exception for attempts to commit a first-degree felony, such as murder. Thus, attempted murder is graded less than murder. More important, if the code really believed in the pure subjectivist view, it would drop all result elements from its offenses, as irrelevant to liability. In fact, it commonly defines offenses as containing a result element. Further, the Model Panel Code drafters selected the most demanding, traditional definition of causation, the necessary cause ("but for") test. If the drafters truly were unabashed subjectivists, they would at the very least have adopted a weaker causation test, perhaps a sufficient cause test (as was proposed during the American Law Institute floor debate on the causa-

tion section). If results ought to be irrelevant but for some unpleasant reason must be maintained, would not the drafters at least want to make it as easy as possible to satisfy those irrelevant result requirements?

It may be that the Model Penal Code drafters grudgingly added result elements to offense definitions and adopted the strong, necessary cause test of causation, because they thought the public would demand it of their criminal law. But this only concedes that the pure subjectivist view of criminal law is one that cannot be sold to those who are to be governed by that law. To insist on a pure subjectivist view would be to undercut the criminal law's moral authority with the public, which in turn would endanger the law's effectiveness.

Israeli Penal Law section 27 grades attempts in a way that is similar in some respects to that of the Model Penal Code. It allows judges to impose the same penalty for an attempt as for the substantive offense, which might be taken to suggest a pure subjectivist view. But the section exempts attempts from any mandatory or minimum penalty that would apply to the substantive offense. The true subjectivist would provide no such exemption, of course, for the exemption concedes that attempts are different from the substantive offense in an important way, a way that suggests a liability discount is appropriate where the harm does not come about. In practice, under section 27, a judge may provide a substantial reduction in all attempt cases. The empirical evidence presented below suggests the community would prefer such a reduction. Thus, if judges concur in the community view, they will follow such a practice. The only effect of section 27, then, is to take away the traditional provision that set the maximum penalty for attempt at less than that for the substantive offense. Given how rarely offenders are sentenced to the statutory maximum, section 27 may be of little effect.

Nor can one take the provision as a symbolic commitment to the pure subjectivist view. For, if that were the drafters' intention, there would be no reason for them to retain the result elements of offense definitions. If every substantive offense and attempt deserve the same punishment upon the same conduct and culpable state of mind, on what ground does the law retain a result element in substantive offenses? At best, one can conclude that the Israeli Penal Law leaves the issue of the significance of resulting harm to sentencing judges.

Given this, as well as the Model Penal Code's ambivalence on the same issue, it is worth considering the implications for the unknowingly justified actor of a world where it is conceded that resulting harm does matter to liability.

The Unknowingly Justified Actor in a World Where Resulting Harm Matters

If we assume, as the world we know does, that resulting harm ought to increase liability, what theory of justification is preferable? If people generally think that resulting harm should matter to liability, why do so many writers and code drafters seem to prefer the reasons theory of justification? If state code drafters routinely reject the manifestations of the pure subjectivist view, as in rejecting the Model Penal Code call for grading attempts the same as the complete offense, why would they not also reject the code's subjective formulation of justification defenses? Is this simply the product of an untidy world, where the minority subjectivist view is adopted in the formulation of justification defenses simply because the state code drafters do not see the connection between the issues of subjectivist attempt grading and subjectivist justification formulations? In short, probably yes.

If a jurisdiction admits the significance of resulting harm in assessing liability, if resulting harm may give rise to greater liability than no resulting harm, it seems difficult to see how a jurisdiction can reject the deeds theory of justification, which gives attempt liability to the unknowingly justified actor, in favor of the reasons theory, which ignores the fact that the conduct in reality causes no net harm. The actor may have thought he or she was causing a net societal harm but be surprised to find that no such net harm occurs. If the unknowingly justified actor is to be held liable, the liability is analogous to that of the attempter who thinks he is committing an offense, only to be surprised to find out that he is not.

Unknowing Justification as a Legally Impossible Attempt

The propriety of viewing the unknowingly justified actor as an instance of impossible attempt is confirmed by the fact that such an actor clearly comes within the language of modern attempt provisions. He clearly would be liable for attempt under sections 25 and 26 of the Israeli Penal Law. Similarly, Model Penal Code section 5.01(1)(a) provides: "A person is guilty of an attempt to commit a crime if, acting with the kind of culpability otherwise required for commission of the crime, he purposely engages in conduct which would constitute the crime if the attendant circumstances were as he believes them to be . . . ." Under the circumstances as Ashkenazi believed them to be, he is liable for theft. The harm that normally flows from a theft is outweighed in this instance by the benefit derived because of the justifying circumstances. To hold Ashkenazi liable for theft, as the reasons theory would do, is to ignore this central fact. The existence or resulting net harm does matter. Nonetheless, Ashkenazi has the culpable state of mind required for theft and has shown his willingness to act upon it. These are the central characteristics of and rationale for punishing an impossible attempter, and Ashkenazi accordingly deserves to be held liable for attempt.

To deny the status of the unknowingly justified actor as an impossible attempter, and the strength of the conceptual analogy between the two, creates a challenge for reasons theorists. They must argue that the fortuitous lack of harm that undercuts an offense element—the shooter misses because the intended shooting victim bends down just as the trigger is squeezed—ought to reduce the offense grade to that of an attempt, but that the fortuitous lack of a net harm in a justification case—Ashkenazi's theft saves lives—ought not reduce the grade to that of an attempt. On what grounds could such a distinction—between the absence of a harm and the absence of a net harm—be defended?

George Fletcher argues that there is an important difference between violating an offense norm and violating a justification norm; . . . I concede that the two certainly are different. Fletcher's arguments in this respect are persuasive, but then few would disagree with the claim that offenses are conceptually distinct from justification defenses. What Fletcher must show is why offense rules and justification rules are different in a way that drives us to deviate from our general rule that the presence of resulting harm ought to increase liability over that of an unsuccessful attempt to cause it. I find nothing in his analysis that addresses this central point.

To put the offense-justification distinction in a factual context, consider the following two cases. The actor believes a wind storm is coming but ignores the risk and burns a field's harvest stubble (a common practice by farmers as a low-cost way to increase the fertility of the ground) despite the likelihood that the wind storm will cause the fire he sets to spread to a nearby town. It turns out that the actor is wrong about the wind storm. There never existed any danger to the nearby town, at least no more than the usual, no wind storm, stubble burning creates. Is the actor guilty of reckless endangerment because he mistakenly believed that he was creating an unlawful danger? I think most would say no—reckless endangerment requires proof of a real, not just an imagined unreasonable, risk of harm. At most, the actor could be liable for *attempted* reckless endangerment, provided such an offense were recognized.

Now assume the same actor maliciously burns his neighbor's cornfield, but the burning serves as a fire-break to an oncoming forest fire about which he did not know. The burning ends up saving the nearby town and is, therefore, justified on the objective facts; in other words, a standard unknowingly justified actor case. I would argue, by analogy to the case above, that the actor ought not be held liable for the full offense— that is, he ought to get a justification defense—because no net harm occurred. He could be held liable for an attempt, unjustifiably to burn the field (there is no justifying good that comes from his externalized *intention* unjustifiably to burn the field). If the absence of real danger means the stubble-burner can be punished only for his externalized culpable intention (as an attempt), how, in the absence of any net harm, can the cornfield-burner who saved the town be punished for more than *his* externalized culpable intention (as an attempt)?

Note that Professor Fletcher's claim that the issue should be resolved differently in the justification context than in the offense definition context runs into some practical difficulty in modern codes. The Model Penal Code defines recklessness (and negligence) in a way that incorporates the concept of justification: it is criminal to disregard a risk (or, in the case of negligence, to be unaware of a risk of which a reasonable person would be aware) that is "substantial and *unjustified*." Thus, the application of statutes requiring recklessness or negligence requires an assessment of the justification of the risk, making it impossible to isolate justifications for special treatment apart from offense definitions.

. . .

Liability for Resisting an Unknowingly Justified Actor

Beyond the issue of liability for the unknowingly justified actor, the competing theories of justification have implications for the lawfulness of resisting the unknowingly justified actor. Assume the terrorist in the Ashkenazi case is watching his planted backpack from a distance, waiting to see the bomb go off and the resulting mayhem. He sees Ashkenazi steal the bag and confronts him, demanding its return. Can the terrorist or an accomplice lawfully use force against Ashkenazi to regain control of the bag? In other words, should one be able lawfully to resist a person who one knows is an unknowingly justified actor?

Under the deeds theory, Ashkenazi's conduct is justified, and therefore the terrorist cannot lawfully resist it. But the reasons theory makes the actual justified nature of the deed irrelevant. Because he acts for the wrong reason, the unknowingly justified actor is not justified. He is acting "unlawfully," which traditionally creates a right lawfully to resist the conduct. Yet logic tells us here again that reasons theory gives improper results. Whether the deed is or is not actually justified ought to be central to whether the law authorizes resistance to it.

An analysis of the statutory provisions confirms these results: the reasons-based Model Penal Code would give the terrorist a right forcibly to resist Ashkenazi's taking; the deeds-based Draft Criminal Code of England and Wales would not.

Because Ashkenazi does not have the "belief" required for a justification, his theft, even though it is necessary to save the people on the beach, is not "justified" under the Model Penal Code. Under the code, an actor can interfere with conduct that is "unlawful." (Israeli Penal Law section 34 has a similar requirement that defensive conduct is permitted only against "unlawful" attack.) Is Ashkenazi's unjustified conduct "unlawful"? Model Penal Code section 3.11(1) defines "unlawful force" as: "force . . . which . . . would constitute [an] offense . . . except for a defense . . . not amounting to a privilege to use the force." Ashkenazi has no defense to his theft; he will in fact be held fully liable for it under the Model Penal Code. Thus, his theft is "unlawful" and, therefore, the terrorist lawfully *can* resist his taking under the code, even though he (the terrorist) knows of the justifying facts! In other words, even the contorted definition of "unlawful force" in section 3.11(1) does not save the Model Penal Code from improper results. In the context of the unknowingly justified actor, the code's reasons formulation of justification has a real and a detrimental effect. While its effect is likely inadvertent—it is hard to believe that the drafters actually intended such a result—it demonstrates the dangers of constructing a code using the reasons approach.

Note that the Draft Criminal Code for England and Wales avoids this error by providing an objective form of justification. Whether the terrorist lawfully may interfere with Ashkenazi's theft under the proposed code depends upon whether Ashkenazi's theft is "unlawful," as defined by section 44(3). Ashkenazi would have a defense to his theft under section 44(1)(c); the circumstances exist that make his theft necessary to protect others even though he does not know of those circumstances. But his defense will not be one of those enumerated in section 44(3), situations in which, despite resulting in an acquittal, the conduct nonetheless is held to be "unlawful." Ashkenazi's defense is not that he thought his theft was necessary, as would be relevant under section 44(1)(c), for example, but rather that his theft was in fact necessary. Therefore, his conduct is not "unlawful" under section 44(3) and, therefore, the terrorist cannot lawfully resist it—the proper result.

Summary and Conclusion

The deeds and reasons theories give different results for both an unknowingly justified actor and a person resisting such an actor. The reasons theory gives no defense to an unknowingly justified actor; thus full liability. The deeds theory gives a justification defense, but the unknowingly justified actor nonetheless is liable for an impossible attempt in most modern code jurisdictions. The deeds approach, then, generates the proper result, a conclusion confirmed by the empirical study showing that lay persons see the unknowingly justified actor as liable at the reduced attempt level, not at the level of full substantive liability that the reasons theory would provide.

The two theories also give different liability results for a person who resists an unknowingly justified actor. The reasons theory, having concluded that the unknowingly justified actor's conduct is unjustified, allows a person lawfully to resist the justified conduct. This is the result under the Model Penal Code, but surely it is the wrong result (and may not have been intended by the drafters) for it allows a person lawfully to engage in conduct that the person knows to be against society's interest. The deeds theory, in contrast, properly denies a defense to one who resists one he knows to be an unknowingly justified actor.

These liability results, together with the labeling advantages of the deeds theory in distinguishing objective justification from subjective, mistaken justification, suggest that justification theory and law ought to follow a deeds theory rather than the reasons theory currently more popular.

What is the implication of the reasons-deeds dispute for Motti Ashkenazi? Because of the lives saved by his actions, the police decide not to charge Ashkenazi in the theft, and allow him an easy plea bargain in another case pending against him. Ashkenazi becomes a bit of a hero in Tel Aviv.

On the other hand, there is criticism of the police and prosecutors for letting him off easy. He becomes a bit of a comic hero. He is lampooned on a late-night talk show for his "good deed." The talk show host envisions a drugged-out Ashkenazi invited to meet the president and reimbursed for the income he lost when the backpack did not contain valuables. The conflicting feelings about the Ashkenazi case are understandable.

Under a deeds theory, Ashkenazi's conduct is recognized as beneficial, and it is given a legal status reflecting that benefit: it is justified, and therefore beyond lawful interference by others. Much of the expressed public admiration for what Ashkenazi did bespeaks this feeling.

But the deeds theory also draws an important distinction between Ashkenazi's conduct, which is admirable, and his motivation, which is reprehensible. The deeds theory would privilege the conduct against interference but would impose liability and punishment on Ashkenazi for his demonstrated willingness to commit what he thought was an unjustified theft. While the terrorist could not lawfully interfere with him, Ashkenazi himself would be liable for attempted theft.

While public admiration for Ashkenazi's deed can easily spill over to admiration for the man, it ought to be resisted. There is societal value in publicly admiring the conduct, for it signals to all that such conduct would be encouraged in the future, even would be thought of as heroic. But there is also societal value in making clear that Ashkenazi himself is to be condemned, for it is only in this way that the norm against theft can be unambiguously reinforced.

By defining justifications subjectively, the reasons theory obscures this key distinction: it allows the law to announce only whether an *actor* is "justified"; it allows the law no mechanism by which it can announce the character of the *act*. The deeds theory, in contrast, highlights the distinction between the act and the actor. Ashkenazi's act may be praised, while Ashkenazi is condemned.

The reasons theory also misses the mark when it sees Ashkenazi as no different from other thieves, and thus liable for full substantive liability. Ashkenazi and other thieves *are* different, as different as are an attempted murderer and a murderer. The latter has caused a net harm; the former has only tried to. One may hope that, if exposed to the deeds theory of justification—and its implication that Ashkenazi is properly treated as an attempter—reason theory supporters may find the deeds view more appealing.

Endnote

[1] This factual account is based on Raine Marcus, *"Petty Thief's 'Good Deed' Saves Lives on Crowded Tel Aviv Beach,"*

Jerusalem Post, June 22, 1997; Arutz Sheva, *"Stealing a Blast,"* June 22, 1997 (*Judean Voice News and Commentary* computer bulletin board posting); Dod Lebia, "First Time in My Life That I Went to the Police without Handcuffs" *Ma'ariv,* June 23, 1997; Buki Na'eh & Erin Navon, "Sometimes Crime Can Pay Off," *"Ma'ariv,"* June 23, 1997; Erin Navon, "Reveals Bomb, Starts Rehab, *Ma'ariv,"* June 23, 1997; Chana Kaylm, "The Luck of Motti Ashkenazi," *Ha'Arets,* June 23, 1997; Reuvan Shapira, "Addict Took a Bag on the Tel Aviv Beach, Found a Bomb Inside, and Alerted the Police," *Ha'Arets,* June 22, 1997; Interview by Jon Van Samek with Raine Marcus, *Jerusalem Post* reporter (July 22, 1997).

State v. Leidholm

Vande Walle, Justice.

Janice Leidholm was charged with murder for the stabbing death of her husband, Chester Leidholm, in the early morning hours of August 7, 1981, at their farm home near Washburn. She was found guilty by a McLean County jury of manslaughter and was sentenced to five years' imprisonment in the State Penitentiary with three years of the sentence suspended. Leidholm appealed from the judgment of conviction. We reverse and remand the case for a new trial.

I

According to the testimony, the Leidholm marriage relationship in the end was an unhappy one, filled with a mixture of alcohol abuse, moments of kindness toward one another, and moments of violence. The alcohol abuse and violence was exhibited by both parties on the night of Chester's death.

Early in the evening of August 6, 1981, Chester and Janice attended a gun club party in the city of Washburn where they both consumed a large amount of alcohol. On the return trip to the farm, an argument developed between Janice and Chester which continued after their arrival home just after midnight. Once

inside the home, the arguing did not stop; Chester was shouting, and Janice was crying.

At one point in the fighting, Janice tried to telephone Dave Vollan, a deputy sheriff of McLean County, but Chester prevented her from using the phone by shoving her away and pushing her down. At another point, the argument moved outside the house, and Chester once again was pushing Janice to the ground. Each time Janice attempted to get up, Chester would push her back again.

A short time later, Janice and Chester re-entered their home and went to bed. When Chester fell asleep, Janice got out of bed, went to the kitchen, and got a butcher knife. She then went back into the bedroom and stabbed Chester. In a matter of minutes Chester died from shock and loss of blood.

II

. . . The first, and controlling, issue we consider is whether or not the trial court correctly instructed the jury on self-defense.

. . .

A defense of justification is the product of society's determination that the *actual existence* of certain circumstances will operate to make proper and legal what otherwise would be criminal conduct. A defense of excuse, contrarily, does not make legal and proper conduct which ordinarily would result in criminal

334 N.W. 2d 811 (1983), Supreme Court of North Dakota.

liability; instead, it openly recognizes the criminality of the conduct but excuses it because the actor believed that circumstances actually existed which would justify his conduct when in fact they did not. In short, had the facts been as he supposed them to be, the actor's conduct would have been justified rather than excused. . . .

In the context of self-defense, this means that a person who believes that the force he uses is necessary to prevent imminent unlawful harm is *justified* in using such force if his belief is a *correct* belief; that is to say, if his belief corresponds with what actually is the case. If, on the other hand, a person *reasonably* but incorrectly believes that the force he uses is necessary to protect himself against imminent harm, his use of force is *excused.*

. . .

Courts have traditionally distinguished between standards of reasonableness by characterizing them as either "objective" or "subjective." An objective standard of reasonableness requires the factfinder to view the circumstances surrounding the accused at the time he used force from the standpoint of a hypothetical reasonable and prudent person. Ordinarily, under such a view, the unique physical and psychological characteristics of the accused are not taken into consideration in judging the reasonableness of the accused's belief.

This is not the case, however, where a subjective standard of reasonableness is employed. See *State v. Wanrow*, 88 Wash. 2d 221, 559 P.2d 548 (1977). Under the subjective standard the issue is not whether the circumstances attending the accused's use of force would be sufficient to create in the mind of a reasonable and prudent person the belief that the use of force is necessary to protect himself against immediate unlawful harm, but rather whether the circumstances are sufficient to induce in the accused an honest and reasonable belief that he must use force to defend himself against imminent harm.

. . .

Because (1) the law of self-defense as developed in past decisions of this court has been interpreted to require the use of a subjective standard of reasonableness, and (2) we agree with the court in *Hazlett* that a subjective standard is the more just, and (3) our current law of self-defense . . . does not require a contrary conclusion, that is to say, our current law of self-defense is consistent with either a subjective or objective standard, we now decide that the finder of fact must view the circumstances attending an accused's use of force

from the standpoint of the accused to determine if they are sufficient to create in the accused's mind an honest and reasonable belief that the use of force is necessary to protect himself from imminent harm. . . .

The practical and logical consequence of this interpretation is that an accused's actions are to be viewed from the standpoint of a person whose mental and physical characteristics are like the accused's and who sees what the accused sees and knows what the accused knows. For example, if the accused is a timid, diminutive male, the factfinder must consider these characteristics in assessing the reasonableness of his belief. If, on the other hand, the accused is a strong, courageous, and capable female, the factfinder must consider these characteristics in judging the reasonableness of her belief.

In its statement of the law of self-defense, the trial court instructed the jury:

> The circumstances under which she acted must have been such as to produce in the mind of reasonably prudent persons, regardless of their sex, similarly situated, the reasonable belief that the other person was then about to kill her or do serious bodily harm to her.

In view of our decision today, the court's instruction was a misstatement of the law of self-defense. A correct statement of the law to be applied in a case of self-defense is:

> [A] defendant's conduct is not to be judged by what a reasonably cautious person might or might not do or consider necessary to do under the like circumstances, but what he himself in good faith honestly believed and had reasonable ground to believe was necessary for him to do to protect himself from apprehended death or great bodily injury.

The significance of the difference in viewing circumstances from the standpoint of the "defendant alone" rather than from the standpoint of a "reasonably cautious person" is that the jury's consideration of the unique physical and psychological characteristics of an accused allows the jury to judge the reasonableness of the accused's actions against the accused's subjective impressions of the need to use force rather than against those impressions which a jury determines that a hypothetical reasonably cautious person would have under similar circumstances. . . .

Hence, a correct statement of the law of self-defense is one in which the court directs the jury to assume the physical and psychological properties peculiar to the accused, viz., to place itself as best it can in the shoes of the accused, and then decide whether or not the particular circumstances surrounding the accused at the time he used force were sufficient to create in his mind a sincere and reasonable belief that the use of force was necessary to protect himself from imminent and unlawful harm. . . .

Leidholm argued strongly at trial that her stabbing of Chester was done in self-defense and in reaction to the severe mistreatment she received from him over the years. Because the court's instruction in question is an improper statement of the law concerning a vital issue in Leidholm's defense, we conclude it amounts to reversible error requiring a new trial.

. . .

The expert witness in this case testified that Janice Leidholm was the victim in a battering relationship which caused her to suffer battered woman syndrome manifested by (1) a psychological condition of low self-esteem and (2) a psychological state of "learned helplessness." . . .

The instruction on battered woman syndrome was designed to support Leidholm's claim of self-defense by focusing the jury's attention on the psychological characteristics common to women who are victims in abusive relationships, and by directing the jury that it may consider evidence that the accused suffered from battered woman syndrome in determining whether or not she acted in self-defense. The instruction correctly points out that battered woman syndrome is not of itself defense. In other words, "The existence of the syndrome in a marriage does not of itself establish the legal right of the wife to kill the husband, the evidence must still be considered in the context of self-defense." . . .

There is nothing in the proposed instruction at issue which would add to or significantly alter a correct instruction on the law of self-defense. The jury's use of a subjective standard of reasonableness in applying the principles of self-defense to the facts of a particular case requires it to consider expert testimony, once received in evidence, describing battered woman syndrome and the psychological effects it produces in the battered spouse when deciding the issue of the existence and reasonableness of the accused's belief that force was necessary to protect herself from imminent harm. If an instruction given is modeled after the law of self-defense which we adopt today, the court need not include a specific instruction on battered woman syndrome in its charge to the jury. . . .

The judgment of conviction is reversed and the case is remanded . . . for a new trial.

The Battered Woman's Defense

Cathryn Jo Rosen

Defining the battered woman's defense is not an easy task. The literature is full of claims that the defense is misconceived. Yet, even those authors who bemoan the misconceptions have difficulty arriving at a cogent

From Cathryn Jo Rosen, "The Excuse of Self-Defense: Correcting a Historical Accident on Behalf of Battered Women Who Kill," *American University Law Review*, Vol. 36 (1986): 11–33. Reprinted by permission of the American University Law Review.

definition of the term. Indeed, use of the term at all is widely disparaged. A number of writers repeatedly emphasize that the theory should be denominated "women's self-defense," perhaps to dispel the notion that there is a special exception to the normal rules of self-defense for battered women. Nonetheless, courts and the media relentlessly choose to adhere to the battered woman's defense phraseology.

One explanation for some of the confusion between "self-defense," "women's self-defense," and "battered woman's defense" may lie in the defense's historical development. The best descriptions of the battered woman's defense are by feminist lawyers who based their strategy on lessons learned while representing women who defended themselves against male aggression under circumstances that fell outside the setting of traditional self-defense. Self-defense rules were developed to acquit a man who kills to protect himself or his family against a threatened attack from a man of similar size and strength with whom the defender usually has had only a single encounter. Rules requiring like force, imminency of the threatened harm, consideration of only the circumstances surrounding the single encounter, and use of an objective reasonable man standard are more than adequate in such circumstances. Women, however, usually use deadly force to protect themselves under very different circumstances. Usually their male victims are larger and stronger and are not strangers. The woman's fear of the man will be influenced by her knowledge of his character and reputation for violence. Rules requiring like force, imminency, consideration of only the circumstances immediately surrounding the killing, and use of an objective reasonable man standard necessarily defeat the woman's claim.

The first successes for the notion of women's self-defense were not battered women's cases. In the early 1970s, feminists rallied to support the defense of Joan Little, a prisoner in a North Carolina jail who stabbed and killed a male guard. Little claimed that she stabbed the unarmed guard because he threatened to rape her. Ms. Little was acquitted on the theory of self-defense despite the arguable absence of equal force.

Two years later, Inez Garcia was acquitted by a jury after her second trial on homicide charges. She claimed a self-defense. Garcia was physically and sexually assaulted by two male acquaintances. Before leaving the scene, the men threatened to return and rape Garcia again. She took her shotgun and went to search for her assailants. Several hours later she found one of the men on a street and shot and killed him. Judged by an objective standard of reasonableness, Garcia's motive appeared to be vengeance rather than self-defense. The jury, however, was permitted to consider the defendant's ethnic background, her rape, and the men's threat to repeat their attack when determining whether she reasonably believed that the use of deadly force was necessary to avoid an imminent threat of serious bodily harm.

Soon acquittals of women, including battered women, who pleaded self-defense became common in many jurisdictions. The most important appellate victory for the feminist advocates of women's self-defense was in a case that did not involve a battered woman. In 1977, the Washington Supreme Court reversed Yvonne Wanrow's second-degree murder conviction in a decision holding that use of the reasonable man objective standard of self-defense violated Wanrow's right to equal protection of the law. Wanrow shot an intoxicated, unarmed man whom she knew had a reputation for violence when he approached her in a threatening manner. At the time, Wanrow, who was five-foot-four, had a broken leg and was using a crutch. Recognizing that Wanrow's fear and perception of danger was affected by her status as a woman, the court held that use of the reasonable man standard in the jury instruction was improper because it deprived Wanrow of the right to have the jury consider her conduct in light of her own perceptions. The court directed that the jury on retrial should be instructed to apply a subjective, sex-specific standard of reasonableness.

Little, *Garcia*, and *Wanrow* involved situations in which an objectively reasonable observer of the confrontation would not have perceived that the aggressor threatened imminent death or serious bodily harm to the defendant nor have believed that defensive use of deadly force was the only alternative available. Application of traditional rules of self-defense inevitably would lead to a murder conviction. Defense counsel were able to persuade the courts that their mistaken beliefs that the circumstances justified self-help were subjectively reasonable given the particular experiences and perceptions of the defendants.

The same problems occur in battered women's cases, often in more extreme forms. In the late 1970s, feminist lawyers began to outline a defense strategy for battered women who kill their abusers. They combined the women's self-defense theory developed in cases like *Little*, *Garcia*, and *Wanrow* with the use of expert testimony on the psychological impact of an abusive relationship on battered women. The feminists assumed from the start that homicides committed by women are equally reasonable as homicides committed by men. The defense strategy is to persuade the judge and jury that a variety of social factors cause women to perceive imminent, lethal danger in situations where men would not. Although stemming from unique factors, women's perceptions of danger demand equal recourse to deadly force. This argument is necessary because traditional self-defense, permeated as it is by male experience, does not acknowledge that a woman's response to a set of circumstances could be reasonable even though it was different than a man's response to the same set of circumstances. Rather than requesting that battered women receive special treatment from the law, the creators of the defense hoped to encourage application of the law of self-defense in a sex-neutral, individualized manner to all women, including those who kill their abusers.

The feminists proposed to obtain equality under the law by removing stereotypical myths and misconceptions about battered women from the trial process. Yet their self-defense theory for battered women who kill depends upon persuading the judge and the jury to accept an alternate set of factual generalizations about women in general, battered women in particular, the efficacy of the criminal justice system, and society. These assumptions, which serve to remedy the failure of battered women who kill to prove the traditional elements of self-defense, include the following:

1. Women find it necessary to resort to self-help because the courts and police do not provide them with adequate protection from their abusers. Therefore, even in the absence of an imminent or immediate threat of harm, their belief that self-defense is necessary may be reasonable.

2. A woman's perception of danger will be affected by her smaller size, socialization regarding passive attributes of femininity, and poor physical training. Therefore, it is perfectly reasonable for a woman to believe an unarmed man may be able to kill her.

3. A woman may reasonably feel the need to use a weapon to protect herself from an unarmed assailant.

4. Consideration of surrounding circumstances should not be limited to the time immediately preceding the killing. Prior conduct of the victim toward defendant will influence her perception of the dangerous nature of his behavior at the time of the homicide. Prior specific acts of violence should be admissible as well as the victim's general reputation for violence.

5. Defendant's rage and desire for revenge is not inconsistent with self-defense.

These assumptions widen the scope of relevant testimony and constitute the framework for the argument that the defendant's belief that self-defense was necessary was subjectively reasonable. Borrowing from Fletcher's writings, the feminists argued that the reasonableness of the woman's act of self-help should be adjudged in a sex-neutral, individualized manner in which the individual defendant's characteristics and culpability are relevant. The jurors should be instructed to place themselves in defendant's shoes and determine under all the circumstances, including defendant's history as a battered woman, the reasonableness of defendant's belief that use of deadly force was necessary.

Among the trial tactics the creators of the battered woman's defense recommend is the careful and strategic use of lay and expert testimony to neutralize stereotypical prejudices and ideas that may interfere with the jury's ability to perceive the defendant's conduct as a reasonable act of self-defense. Although the expert testimony may take numerous forms, many defense attorneys have used expert psychiatrist or psychological testimony. Often it consists primarily of a description of Dr. Lenore E. Walker's cycle of violence and learned helplessness theories which together constitute the battered woman syndrome. The expert will describe the battered woman syndrome in general terms after which she may be permitted to testify that the defendant suffers from battered woman syndrome.

Expert testimony is used to show why, under the particular circumstances of the case, the defendant's conduct was reasonable and, therefore, justified. Theoretically, the woman's defensive action will be proved necessary and proportionate by showing how the defendant could perceive a threat of imminent danger in verbal threats alone, in a nondeadly attack from an unarmed spouse, or from a sleeping man. The testimony explains why the woman stayed with her spouse despite the abusive relationship and why, on the occasion in question, she may not have run away or sought assistance from friends, relatives, or the police despite an apparent opportunity to do so. Finally, the testimony explains why the woman cannot be faulted for becoming involved in an abusive relationship. Rather, she is a victim of her social reality, responding to circumstances in accordance with the values of femininity and life-long marriage to which she was acculturated.

The problem is that such an inquiry is inconsistent with the theory of justification which assumes that anyone who does the same act under the same external circumstances has done the right thing. By including a certain psychological trait of the individual in the circumstances, we have moved closer to the theory of excuse than to justification. Nonetheless, the feminist theory is based on the premise that explanation of the reasonableness of defendant's belief that use of deadly force was proportionate and necessary will establish that the woman's act was justified rather than excused. Feminists argue that recognition of the woman's act as justified rather than excused is crucial.

> [E]xcusable self-defense would imply that her response was typically and idiosyncratically emotional. The doctrine would perpetuate the views that the woman could not have been rational in assessing the danger and that the legal system must compensate for her mental and physical weaknesses. . . .
>
> Justification, on the other hand, would assume that society values a woman's and a man's lives equally, and thus considers women's lives worthy of self-defense. It would recognize that a woman has the capacity to correctly and reasonably perceive that the act is warranted, legitimate, and justified. Justification would encourage, indeed would compel, a legal recognition that a woman's capacity for reasonable judgment—comparable to that of a man's—can be the basis for engaging in the "correct behavior" of self-defense.[1]

This doctrinaire insistence on treatment of the battered woman's defense as a justification is unnecessary and may be fatal to widespread and successful use of the battered woman's defense. Most battered woman's defense cases involve situations in which the defendant was not, in fact, in imminent danger of death or serious bodily harm at her victim's hands. The defense relies on persuading the jury that the defendant suffered from an identifiable psychological syndrome that caused her to assess the dangerousness of the situation in a different manner than an average, ordinary person—including a woman who does not suffer from battered woman syndrome. In other words, acquittal is dependent upon proving that defendant had . . . a disability that caused a mistaken, but reasonable, belief in the existence of circumstances that would justify self-defense. It is a theory of excuse rather than of justification. Because defendant responded to internal and external coercive pressures, for which she was not responsible but which were created by her social reality as a battered woman, she is not to blame for her conduct. A person who did not suffer from battered woman syndrome, however, would be culpable under identical external circumstances. Indeed, successful use of the battered woman's

defense theory depends in part on defense counsel's ability to persuade the court and jury that a person who did not suffer from battered woman syndrome would not be justified under identical objectively identifiable circumstances. This, however, is inherently inconsistent with the concept of justification.

Efforts to characterize artificially the battered woman's defense as a justification must ultimately lead to some of the current misapprehensions as to its nature and the fears that its adoption will ultimately lead to justification of all killings that the defendant subjectively believed were necessary and proportionate. Conversely, it may explain, in part, the tendency to incorrectly view battered women as bearing a special right to self-defense based on their victimized status alone. Recognition that the defense is categorized properly as an excuse rather than a justification may enhance the ability of battered women who kill to win acquittals. To present a complete defense, a defendant would still have to show that her belief that justificatory circumstances existed was subjectively reasonable. Because the defendant is excused rather than justified, however, there would be no chance that the conduct will be encouraged.

The fact that the battered woman's defense is more consistent with excuse theory does not answer the feminist concern that excusing battered women who kill, in circumstances they believe create a right of self-defense, may perpetuate undesirable views that women are by nature irrational and that their lives are unworthy of self-defense against a man. First, however, these concerns are overblown. Treatment of the battered woman's defense as an excuse does not preclude justifying women who kill men under objectively identifiable circumstances more akin to traditional self-defense. Second, for the same reasons that battered women should be excused for killing their spouses, men who kill under mistaken beliefs as to justifying circumstances should also be excused. Third, even if treatment of the battered woman's defense as an excuse does lead to perpetuation of sex discrimination under the current law, it may be that the problem should be cured in a different manner than the feminists recommend. All self-defense should be treated as excused rather than justified conduct. Indeed, the difficulties that the courts and commentators have encountered with the battered woman's defense vividly illustrate the need for such a reconceptualization of the defense. Excused self-defense would better meet the needs of battered women, of the criminal justice system, and of society in general.

. . .

Today, most American jurisdictions classify self-defense as a justification even though it traditionally developed as an excuse. As a result, principles of excuse have become merged with principles of justification in the law of self-defense. Consequently, results in some cases are illogical and inconsistent with basic principles of criminal law. The problem is particularly apt to arise when demands are made to justify self-help behavior that is harmful to society in instances where the actor cannot fairly be held blameworthy because of circumstances particular to that individual. Battered women who kill their abusers present the paradigm example of such cases. Although the defendant's conduct is understandable, and absolving her from moral blame is not difficult, we are hesitant to proclaim that the act was justified and therefore to be encouraged. Even in traditional cases, self-defense is, at most, permissible and tolerated. Treatment of all self-defense as an excuse would further the criminal justice system's interest in discouraging self-help, promote society's interest in preserving the sanctity of human life, and fulfill the feminist goal of absolving battered women who kill of guilt without proclaiming that such women are inferior to men.

Justification requires that the actor chose to violate the criminal law only because it was the lesser of a necessary choice of evils. Classification of self-defense as a justification, therefore, requires that the defender's interest in life be regarded as superior to that of the unlawful aggressor's. The act is accordingly one that is encouraged because it was beneficial to society or at least created no harm. The qualitative balancing act required to justify killings in self-defense, however, is not easy to perform.

The law's prohibition against intentional killing coincides with contemporary society's emphasis on the importance of human life as the most valuable interest protected by the criminal law. Clearly, however, there are also circumstances when intentional killing is justified because of the benefit it confers upon society as a whole. The intentional killings originally justified by the criminal law illustrate such situations. For example, one who kills a military enemy in battle is justified, as is the officer who kills to prevent an act of terrorism or to apprehend a person who has taken others hostage. Similarly, if we assume for the moment that capital punishment is acceptable, the executioner's act of killing the condemned is certainly justified. In all of these circumstances (the list is not exclusive), one life is taken to save many lives and to enhance the power of the rule of law. And, except in the instance of war, arguably the person whose life has been taken already has been shown to be dangerous and a threat to society as a whole.

A classic self-defense case involves a situation in which the actor takes the life of another to save the actor's life. One life has been chosen over one other life and the choice has been made in contravention of the legal rule generally prohibiting intentional killings. In the best of cases, it is difficult to identify any benefit that might accrue to society in general as a result of the killing. Moreover, the common law has always had great difficulty making judgments that one human life is more valuable than another. The result is the rule that a person can only defend against unlawful force. Yet, even this rule, the basis of which is uncertain, does not entirely solve the problem. First, modern criminal codes, for the most part, classify at least those cases in which the mistake was reasonable as justified self-defense. The closer the law moves toward a subjective standard of reasonableness, the greater the threat to the attacker's basic human rights. The extent of the attacker's rights would be defined solely by the victim's judgment of what was the right response under the circumstances. Indeed, cases involving mistake regarding the perception that the victim was threatening unlawful deadly force could result in the taking of an entirely innocent life. The killing of an innocent victim cannot be justified rationally. Society has been harmed by the taking of an innocent life and the actor can only be acquitted under an excuse theory. Second, even an unlawful aggressor is not necessarily a threat to all society. The attacker may only be a threat to one other person, the defender. Therefore, self-defense can only be the lesser evil if the interests of the defender that the aggressor threatens are greater than the aggressor's interest in life.

A variety of theories have been suggested to support the relative devaluation of the unlawful aggressor's life. Robinson[2] postulates that, although the relative physical harms to be suffered by the defender and the aggressor are equal, the defender also has an interest in bodily integrity. When the right to bodily integrity is added to the defender's right to be free from physical injury, the aggressor's interest in freedom from physical injury is outweighed. This view, however, is problematic because it blithely ignores the fact that the aggressor must also have a right to bodily integrity.

Essentially, Robinson's theory is a forfeiture theory. The idea behind the moral forfeiture theory that self-defense is correctly classified as a justification is that by virtue of his act of aggression, the aggressor forfeits some interest or right he would otherwise have had—such as the right to bodily integrity, his interest in life, or his right to freedom from aggression. The forfeiture theories cannot withstand a number of difficulties. If the defender is mistaken as to the unlawfulness of the aggression, his act will still be justified. Yet, it is difficult to say that one whose aggression was not unlawful has waived any rights. Even when the aggressor's conduct is actually unlawful there are difficulties. The criminal law generally does not permit express consent to one's own death. Yet, any forfeiture theory presumes that the victim's act of aggression constitutes implied consent to the use of defensive force.

Ultimately, there probably is no acceptable calculus to support treatment of self-defense as a justification. Its modern classification as such is likely the product of historical accident. If the law were to recognize that even traditional self-defense is properly considered an excuse, the nonculpable defensive acts of many more people could be excepted from punishment without the threat of escalating societal violence.

The difficulty in devaluing the life of the aggressor is particularly acute in some battered women's cases. Many men who abuse their spouses never display aggressive or violent behavior outside the confines of their homes. Certainly, perpetrators of domestic violence are not nice people. Yet, it is doubtful that anyone seriously could argue that ridding society of people merely because they are not nice benefits all. Feminists assert that the abuser's intent to kill or seriously injure his wife makes his death nonharmful rather than his character as a wife-beater. A victim of battered woman syndrome, however, may be mistaken as to the true nature of her spouse's threats on a particular occasion. Even if the mistake is reasonable or if there is no mistake, the difficulty with the calculus remains. Proponents of the battered woman's defense sympathize so much with the defendant that they have a tendency to focus exclusively on the psychological and physical harm suffered by the woman while forgetting the abuser. His right to life, though, is equally important as the woman's.

One of the most difficult problems confronted by legal theorists is the question of whether killing a legally insane aggressor in self-defense can be justified. Forfeiture theories of self-defense that rely on devaluing the aggressor's interest in life, freedom from aggression, or bodily integrity because of his wrongful conduct disintegrate in cases where the aggressor is not culpable. This problem is particularly acute in battered woman's defense cases. If we sympathize with the women as being victims of their social reality, we must sympathize with the batterers as well. Abusers are not entirely morally reprehensible. According to psychological and sociological literature, they also are victims of "disease" or of their social reality. This makes it even more difficult for the legal system to determine that the abuser's life is less valuable than his victim's.

The most that can be said in battered woman's defense cases, as in all self-defense cases, is that society is neutral with respect to the killing. By treating such cases as instances of excuse rather than justification, the difficulties created by weighing qualitative values of human lives and according a lesser interest to a potentially "innocent" person can be avoided. An excuse analysis would lead to identical results—acquittal—but do so by focusing on the pressure confronted by the defendant and the lack of available options.

It is difficult to identify a positive benefit that accrues to anyone other than the killer from the taking of an aggressor's life in self-defense. Thus, there is no reason for the law affirmatively to encourage such conduct. To the contrary, classification of self-defense as a justification may be detrimental to society. The early common law failed to recognize self-defense as either a justification or an excuse because self-help was inimical to the goal of creating respect for the rule of law and, in turn, for governmental authority. Although lack of respect for properly constituted legal authority is not generally a problem today, the law still serves a vital function of discouraging self-help.

There are a number of reasons why self-help is contrary to the interests of modern society. Reliance on self-help tends to diminish respect for the rule of law. Self-help in the form of self-defense carries the additional problem of increasing the quantum of violence in an already violent society. More troublesome is the possibility that the more widespread resort to self-help becomes, the more often innocent people may be killed erroneously.

It is troublesome even when a person who is guilty of a crime becomes the victim of proper self-help. The constant decline in the number of capital crimes throughout American history attests to the general view that only the most vicious of intentional killers deserve to die for their deeds. We cling to the hope that criminals can be reformed, or at least deterred, if only they are subjected to incarceration, institutionalization, or community corrections. Most persons killed in self-defense would not have been eligible for capital punishment if duly convicted of their threatened crimes. This is particularly true of many of the abusive husbands in battered woman's defense cases.

The proportionate force, necessity, and imminence prerequisites for self-defense are designed to quiet the law's uneasiness about encouraging self-help. The requirement that deadly force only be used to counter deadly force is geared to ensure that the aggressor, in fact, will commit an intentional homicide if not met with defensive force. One must suffer non-deadly harm if use of deadly force would be the only way to avoid it. The necessity rule seeks to limit the use of self-help to circumstances in which there is absolutely no other alternative to striking back against the aggressor. It is intended to encourage the defendant to seek, in the first instance, nonviolent or nondeadly defensive means. By requiring strict necessity, it is hoped that use of deadly force in self-defense will be considered only as a last resort. Finally, the imminence requirement is meant to restrict self-defense to those situations where there is no time to turn to actors in the criminal justice system to do their designated job and save the defendant from the need to resort to self-defense. Relaxation of any of these strict, narrow requirements raises the specter of justifying, and thus encouraging, self-help—conduct that the law and society prefer to discourage.

The battered woman's defense requires relaxation of all of these requirements. Rather than limiting the determination of whether these elements of the defense have been met to very limited, objectively ascertainable circumstances, defenders of battered women ask the courts to consider circumstances that would be unknown to the casual observer. Factors such as relative strength, the defendant's physical training, and the defendant's prior experiences with and knowledge about her victim are neither external nor objectively identifiable. Consideration of such circumstances is not compatible with the notion of self-defense as behavior that is justified and should be encouraged.

Even more worrisome, however, is the assumption underlying the battered woman's defense that self-defense is necessary in some situations—even when the threatened attack is not imminent—because the criminal justice system has not adequately protected women. This assertion supports the feminist demand that the concepts of imminence and necessity be broadened. Yet, it is exactly this notion that the law must suppress. For the logical corollary is that any person who believes, reasonably or unreasonably, that the criminal justice system does not offer adequate protection can resort to self-help even though there may have been sufficient time to summon the aid of lawful authority. Even when we understand the actor's unusual need to resort to self-help, the actor's behavior may still be dangerous to society. If self-defense is a justification and if justified conduct is conduct we consistently encourage because it benefits society whenever similar circumstances arise, the defense cannot rationally be expanded to encompass the battered woman's defense. Indeed, it may be that if those who suffer from battered woman syndrome or other psychological trauma induced by their social reality are more likely to kill in self-help, the criminal law should be doing even more than it currently does to prevent them from doing so. Domestic abuse is a serious societal problem but promotion of vigilantism is certainly not the solution. Treatment of self-defense as an excuse allows the judge to make a determination that it would be unjust to convict the defendant while at the same time avoiding a determination that the defendant did the right and just thing and the consequent risk of increasing the quantum of violence in an all too violent society.

Just as the early common law's difficulty with condoning self-help has survived into late twentieth century America, the conflicting recognition that an individual whose life is threatened cannot be expected to die meekly also has survived. When self-defense is categorized as an excuse, it reflects the community's understanding that, under all circumstances, the defendant understandably believed that she had no option but to kill or be killed. Although self-help should not be affirmatively encouraged, the pressure to resort to self-help can be understood. A person who submits to these pressures is not culpable and should not be convicted of any crime.

. . .

Battered women who kill their abusers in perceived self-defense present a special challenge to the criminal justice system, especially to the evolution of the law of self-defense. Although self-defense first appeared in the common law as an excuse, in the twentieth century it has been classified as a justification. Justified conduct is otherwise criminal conduct that under particular external, objectively identifiable circumstances did not harm society. Under these circumstances it was the exact opposite of a discouraged criminal act; it was an encouraged desirable course of conduct. Few cases in which self-defense is claimed, however, fit the model of a justification. The problem is that self-defense constitutes self-help, and self-help is inimical to the rule of law.

Battered woman's defense cases are illustrative of this policy conflict. Often battered women use deadly force in self-defense under external circumstances where their act is not objectively reasonable. The woman's status as a battered woman makes her resort to deadly force understandable; it is subjectively reasonable. It is, therefore, easy to conclude that the woman is not to be blamed for her actions and should not be convicted of homicide. To hold that she acted in self-defense, however, is a determination that her act was justified. To justify such conduct may result in the encouragement of self-help as the preferred solution to domestic abuse. On the other hand, to convict or to excuse women who act in self-defense is to treat women as inferior to men whose defensive acts are justified.

The solution to this dilemma is to return self-defense to its original theoretical basis as an excuse in all cases. Excuse recognizes that, even though self-help may not be desirable and may harm society, such conduct often results from a person's understandable inability to choose an alternative course of action due to overwhelming external or internal pressures. Treatment of self-defense as an excuse accommodates the defensive needs of battered women and other individuals who act in subjectively reasonable fear given their social reality. It allows the fact-finder to consider the defender's subjective beliefs without risking the possibility that all bona fide defensive acts, no matter how objectively unreasonable, will be condoned by the criminal law. Concomitantly, it furthers the criminal law's goals of preserving life and discouraging self-help.

Endnotes

[1] Crocker, "The Meaning of Equality for Battered Women Who Kill Men in Self-Defense," 8 *Harvard Women's Law Journal* 121 (1985), no. 20 at 131 (footnotes omitted).

[2] Paul Robinson, "Criminal Law Defenses: A Systematic Analysis," 82 *Columbia Law Review* (1982): 199–291.

State v. Cameron

Petitioner, Gary Cameron, was charged with the premeditated first degree murder of his stepmother, Marie Cameron. His principal defense was that he was insane at the time he committed the offense. The Court of Appeals affirmed a guilty verdict and this court granted Cameron's petition for review. We reverse the trial court and the Court of Appeals. In doing so, we shall discuss only those issues on which reversal is granted.

At the outset it should be noted that petitioner does not challenge the charge that he stabbed Marie Cameron numerous times or that she died as a result of those wounds. Further, there does not seem to be any serious question that, except for the defense of insanity, the stabbing was done with an intent to kill. Rather, the challenge focuses on three errors alleged to have denied him a fair trial: (1) the definition of insanity in such a way as to prevent the jury's consideration of his insanity defense; (2) the admission of foreign pubic hairs found on the victim's body; and (3) the admission of hearsay evidence of an alleged statement made by the victim 2 months prior to her murder. . . .

Turning first to the insanity defense, it is clear there is evidence running counter to petitioner's contention. This however, does not detract from petitioner's challenge to the trial court's insanity instruction. The question is whether there is evidence of insanity which the jury could have considered but for the court's instruction. We hold there is.

The basic facts reveal that on the morning of June 9, 1980, petitioner stabbed Marie Cameron in excess of 70 times, leaving the knife sticking in her heart. The body was left in the bathtub with no apparent attempt to conceal it. Later that day a

---

100 Wash. 2d 520 (1983), Supreme Court of Washington.

police officer saw petitioner in downtown Shelton wearing only a pair of women's stretch pants, a woman's housecoat, a shirt and no shoes. He was stopped and questioned. After first giving a false name, he corrected it and explained he was dressed that way because "I just grabbed what I could . . . My mother-in-law turned vicious." He also stated he was headed for California. Having no known reason to detain petitioner, the officer released him to continue hitchhiking.

The next day petitioner was detained by the Oregon State Police as he wandered along the shoulder of Interstate 5 near Salem. Since he was wearing only the stretch pants and one shoe he was thought to be an escapee from a nearby mental hospital. A check revealed petitioner was wanted in Shelton for the death of Marie Cameron.

Petitioner was arrested and informed of his constitutional rights. He then gave two confessions, the first being a tape-recorded oral confession and the second a signed written confession. Neither is challenged by petitioner.

In the oral confession petitioner stated generally that he was living in or about the home of his father and stepmother. He left home dressed as he was because his stepmother had become violent. "[S]he's into different types of sorcery. She's just strictly a very evil person . . . and she became very violent with me, with a knife in her hand, and so, uh, I don't deny that I'm the one that did what went on out there." He indicated that when he walked into the bathroom he had not expected her. When he saw her, she had the knife which he was able to take from her easily by bending her wrist back. Then, as he stated, "I took the knife and really stabbed her."

In describing the stabbing, petitioner related: "I just kept stabbing her and stabbing her, because she wasn't feeling . . . it was as if she was laughing . . . as if she was up to something that morning, and I don't know . . . she plays around with witchcraft and that stuff . . ." The last place he saw her was in the bathtub about which he said "she kept moving and moving and moving, and kind of grabbed me like this, but laughing, as if she was enjoying . . . and it was kind of sickening, but it was really maddening to me, because of her offense towards me, it was like . . . you know, it was almost like she was mechanical . . . I mean, the thing was set up that, that's what she wanted to happen. . . . I feel that deep inside she was asking somebody to put her out of her misery . . . she was very symbolic with the 'Scarlet Whore Beast' she was very much into sorcery

very, uh, anti-God, not really anti-God but takes the God's truth and twists it into sorcery."

Concerning his feelings about the incident petitioner said: "I felt confused . . . I felt no different from the beginning than the end there was no difference . . . legally I know, that it is against the law, but as far as right and wrong in the eye of God, I would say I felt no particular wrong."

When asked further about the incident petitioner responded: "I washed the blood off me, and I changed clothes, and then I looked back at her and she was, uh, she was still moving around, after being stabbed, what I thought was in the heart, and the throat . . . about seven or eight times, and she just . . . she kept moving. It was like . . . there was a smile on her face, she kept lunging for me, while she was dead . . . I wasn't trying to be vicious . . . it would look that way, but that wasn't the intent, but she kept lunging at me, over and over again, and the nature of her attack, I was, ah, mad enough I wanted to kill her. I felt that I was justified in self-defense at that point . . ." The last petitioner saw of the knife, "I tried to stick it in her heart . . . she's some kind of an animal."

Petitioner explained further "she's into a very strong sorcery trip, and that's why so many stab wounds . . . I'm not a goring [sic] person . . . I've never been violent in my life, but for some reason . . . there was some evil spirit behind her that was . . . it was like, it was like there was some thing within her that, that wasn't really part of her body . . . she was smiling . . . she was almost like enjoying playing and it was disgusting."

When petitioner subsequently gave the written confession he added: "My attack wasn't a vicious attack the first time. I was trying to stop the spirit that was moving in her. She kept saying, 'Gary, Gary, Gary,' as if she was enjoying it." When she stopped moving he washed himself, changed his clothes and then "My stepmother started moving again as if a spirit was in her. I took the knife and started stabbing her again. When I realized there was something in her that wouldn't stop moving, I started stabbing her in the head and heart. I wanted to kill the spirit that seemed to be attacking my spirit." Once again he changed his clothes but again found her moving and again stabbed her numerous times until all movement stopped. He then changed clothes once more and left.

As with the petitioner's testimony we note the testimony of the psychiatrists and psychologists is not without some disparity. Nevertheless, there is ample evidence which, under a proper insanity instruction, could have been considered by the jury as a matter of defense.

Prior to trial, petitioner made a motion to acquit on the ground of insanity pursuant to RCW 10.77.080. Three psychiatrists, Doctors Jarvis, Allison and Bremner and a psychologist, Dr. Trowbridge, were called to testify. They agreed petitioner suffered from paranoid schizophrenia both at the time of the killing and at the time of trail. Although stating it differently, all four appeared to agree that petitioner believed he was an agent of God, required to carry out God's directions. They also agreed that petitioner believed God commanded him to kill his stepmother and that he was therefore obligated to kill the "evil spirit." Consequently, all doctors concurred he was legally insane at the time of the murder.

The trial court denied the motion for acquittal and submitted the issue of insanity to the jury. At trial, the four doctors repeated their earlier testimony. All agreed that at the time of the killing, and at the time of trial, petitioner suffered from the mental disease of paranoid schizophrenia. While expressing their views in slightly different ways, they agreed petitioner understood that, as a mechanical thing, he was killing his stepmother and knew it was against the laws of man. They stressed, however, that at the time, he was preoccupied with the delusional belief that his stepmother was an agent of satan who was persecuting him, as were others like Yasser Arafat and the Ayatollah Khomeini. He believed he was being directed by God to kill satan's angel and that by so doing, he was obeying God's higher directive or law. At this time he believed himself to be a messiah and in fact compared himself with Jesus Christ.

The doctors pointed out, in different ways, that because of his delusional beliefs, petitioner felt God had directed him to send her from this life to another. He had no remorse over the killing. He felt it was justified by God and that he was merely doing a service. "He felt he would generally be protected from any difficulties . . . because 'God would not allow it to happen.'"

Concerning the legal tests for insanity the mental health experts opined that while he understood it was against the law to kill, he believed he was responding to God's directive and thus had an obligation to rid the world of this "demon," "sorceress" or "evil spirit." Thus, while technically he understood the mechanical nature of the act he did not have the capacity to discern between right and wrong with reference to the act. Some of the doctors expressed the clear view that at the time of the killing, he was unable to appreciate the nature and quality of his acts. No doctor contended otherwise.

Concerning petitioner's insanity defense the trial court gave standard . . . pattern jury instruction . . . but, over petitioner's exception, added a last paragraph which defines "right and wrong."

> In addition to the plea of not guilty, the defendant has entered a plea of insanity existing at the time of the act charged.
>
> Insanity existing at the time of the commission of the act charged is a defense.
>
> For a defendant to be found not guilty by reason of insanity you must find that, as a result of mental disease or defect the defendants mind was affected to such an extent that the defendant was unable to perceive the nature and quality of the acts with which the defendant is charged or was unable to tell right from wrong with reference to the particular acts with which defendant is charged.
>
> *What is meant by the terms "right and wrong" refers to knowledge of a person at the time of committing an act that he was acting contrary to the law.* (Italics ours.)

Petitioner, on the other hand, proposed the use of [an alternative] jury instruction . . . which does not contain the last paragraph.

Petitioner argues that the trial court should have left the term "right and wrong" undefined as provided by the Legislature in RCW 9A.12.010. At the very least, it is urged, "right and wrong" should not have been defined in such a way as to exclude from the jury's deliberation the consideration of "right and wrong" in terms of one's ability to understand the moral qualities of the act.

[The court held that the instruction was wrong.]

At the time this case was tried, the Court of Appeals had just issued *State v. Crenshaw* . . . 617 P.2d 1041 (1980) which approved the instruction challenged herein. Subsequent thereto this court affirmed the Court of Appeals opinion. . . .

Insofar as the instant case is concerned, however, our discussion of *Crenshaw* also recognized an exception to the alternative grounds set forth therein. That exception is controlling here:

> A narrow exception to the societal standard of moral wrong has been drawn for instances wherein a party performs a criminal act,

knowing it is morally and legally wrong, but believing, because of a mental defect, that the act is ordained by God: such would be the situation with a mother who kills her infant child to whom she is devotedly attached, believing that God has spoken to her and decreed the act. Although the woman knows that the law and society condemn the act, it would be unrealistic to hold her responsible for the crime, since her free will has been subsumed by her belief in the deific decree.

. . . Consequently, as we held in *Crenshaw*, one who believes that he is acting under the direct command of God is no less insane because he nevertheless knows murder is prohibited by the laws of man. Indeed, it may actually emphasize his insanity. . . .

In the instant case there is considerable evidence (although not unanimous) from which the jury could have concluded that petitioner suffered from a mental disease; that he believed his stepmother was satan's angel or a sorceress; that he believed God directed him to kill his stepmother; that because of the mental disease it was impossible for him to understand that what he was doing was wrong; and . . . that his free will had "been subsumed by [his] belief in the deific decree." The last paragraph of the trial court's challenged instruction precluded the jury's consideration of these factors and thus runs afoul of the *Crenshaw* exception. In short, the instruction prevented the jury from considering those essential relevant facts that formed the petitioner's theory of the case. To this extent the trial court erred by adding the definitional paragraph to the instruction.

The Abolition of the Insanity Defense

Norval Morris

Abolition of the defense of insanity has received exhaustive attention in the literature; the informed reader is entitled, therefore, to be notified of where the argument leads so that he may avoid the sharper irritations of redundancy. In accordance with the thesis of separation of the mental health law and the criminal-law powers to incarcerate, I propose the abolition of the special defense of insanity. A fall-back alternative position, in no way conflicting with the separation thesis, is for the abolition of the special defense and for legislative substitution of a qualified defense of diminished responsibility to a charge of murder having the effect, if successful, of a conviction of manslaughter with the usual sentencing discretion attached to that crime.

The argument will be presented in broad perspective, the nuances of difference between the competing defenses of insanity being glossed over. The sequence will be (a) the general argument for abolition, (b) an analysis of how the law would operate under the proposed abolition and the alternative substitution of diminished responsibility, and (c) a consideration and repudiation of the main criticisms of the abolition proposal.

The problem is to cut through the accumulated cases, commentaries, and confusions to the issues of principle underlying the responsibility of the mentally ill for conduct otherwise criminal. The issues are basically legal, moral, and political, not medical or psychological, though, of course, the developing insights of psychiatry and psychology are of close relevance to those legal, moral, and political issues.

. . .

I must stress that in advocating the abolition of the special defense of insanity, the nuances of difference among the *McNaughtan* Rules, the *Durham* Rule, the rules offered by the American Law Institute and accepted in *Brawner* and in many state criminal codes, the irresistible impulse test, the recommendations of

From Norval Morris, *Madness and the Criminal Law* (Chicago: University of Chicago Press, 1982), pp. 53–70. Reprinted by permission of the University of Chicago Press.

the Group for the Advancement of Psychiatry, and other suggested special defenses, though important in practice and meriting close analysis, are not essential to the present discussion. All vary around the following structure: a definition of mental illness, as a threshold to the invocation of the defense, and a statement of a required causal relationship between that "mental illness" and the otherwise criminal behavior of the accused. My thesis stands, whatever definition of illness and whatever language to capture a causal relationship are offered. And, of course, variations on where the burdens of proof are placed on those two issues, and on how heavy are those burdens, are also irrelevant.

. . .

Why, then, go beyond the simple rule, to give mental illness the same exculpatory effect as, say, blindness or deafness? Evidence of the latter afflictions may be admitted as indicative of lack of both the *actus reus* (prohibited act) and the *mens rea* of a crime. Why go further? The answer lies in the pervasive moral sense that when choice to do ill is lacking, it is improper to impute guilt. And hence there is pressure for a special defense of insanity, just as there is pressure for a special defense of infancy or duress.

. . .

One is left . . . with the feeling that the special defense is a genuflection to a deep-seated moral sense that the mentally ill lack freedom of choice to guide and govern their conduct and that therefore blame should not be imputed to them for their otherwise criminal acts nor should punishment be imposed. To the validity of this argument we will several times return, but it is important not to assume that those who advocate the abolition of the special defense of insanity are recommending the wholesale punishment of the sick. They are urging rather that mental illness be given the same exculpatory effect as other adversities that bear upon criminal guilt. And they add the not unfair criticism of the conventional position that they observe the widespread conviction and punishment of the mentally ill, the special defense being an ornate rarity, a tribute to our capacity to pretend to a moral position when pursuing profoundly different practices.

The number held as not guilty by reason of insanity in the United States as a whole and in some states will illustrate the relative rarity of the special defense. Nationally, in the 1978 census of state and federal facilities, 3,140 persons were being held as not guilty by reason of insanity.[1] In Illinois, at the time of writing

127 are so held. In New York, between 1965 and 1976 inclusive, 278 persons were found not guilty by reason of insanity (53 in the first five years, 225 in the second six years—the increase being explicable presumably by constitutionally imposed relaxation of the *Brawner* rules for, and processes of, releasing those found not guilty by reason of insanity). No one acquainted with the work of the criminal courts can think that these numbers remotely approximate the relationship between serious mental illness and criminal conduct. The defense is pleaded only where it may be advantageous to the accused and that balance of advantage fluctuates with sentencing practice and rules and practices relating to the release of those found not guilty by reason of insanity. Hence statistics will not lead us to principle in this matter; a more fundamental inquiry is necessary.

A useful entering wedge to principle is to inquire, What is the irreducible minimum relationship between mental illness and criminal guilt? What is the least the criminal law could do in this matter?

It is unthinkable that mental illness should be given a lesser reach than drunkenness. If a given mental condition (intent, recklessness) is required for the conviction of a criminal offense, then, as a proposition requiring no discussion, in the absence of that mental condition there can be no conviction. This holds true whether the absence of that condition is attributable to blindness, deafness, drunkenness, mental illness or retardation, linguistic difficulties, or, if it could be established, hypnotic control. But this states basic principles of criminal law, not a special defense. The main reasons for defining a "special defense" beyond the traditional common-law relationship between mental illness and the *actus reus* and *mens rea* of crime are, I think, twofold: expediency in crime control and fairness.

The expediency rationale can be quickly advanced and disposed of; the fairness rationale is more difficult.

In an important article in 1963, "Abolish 'The Insanity Defense'—Why Not?"[2] J. Goldstein and J. Katz accurately perceived that "the insanity defense is not a defense, it is a device for triggering indeterminate restraint"[3] of those who were mentally ill at the time of the crime but are not civilly committable now. In considerable part, that has been its role since 1800 when the emergence of the special defense in England led to the Criminal Lunatics Act of 1800, which provided indeterminate custody for those found not guilty by reason of insanity, with similar legislation spreading in the states and federal systems in this country.

Few are prepared any longer to justify the special defense on this crime control basis, as a means of confining the dangerous though not civilly committable. It would be a strange "defense," an unusual benevolence, whose purpose is confinement of those who could not otherwise be confined.

Hence we are brought to the central issue—the question of fairness, the sense that it is unjust and unfair to stigmatize the mentally ill as criminals and to punish them for their crimes. The criminal law exists to deter and to punish those who would or who do choose to do wrong. If they cannot exercise choice, they cannot be deterred and it is a moral outrage to punish them.[4] The argument sounds powerful but its premise is weak.

Choice is neither present nor absent in the typical case where the insanity defense is currently pleaded; what is at issue is the degree of freedom of choice on a continuum from the hypothetically entirely rational to the hypothetically pathologically determined—in states of consciousness neither polar condition exists.

The moral issue sinks into the sands of reality. Certainly it is true that in a situation of total absence of choice it is outrageous to inflict punishment; but the frequency of such situations to the problems of criminal responsibility becomes an issue of fact in which tradition and clinical knowledge and practice are in conflict. The traditions of being possessed of evil spirits, of being bewitched, confront the practices of a mental health system which increasingly fashions therapeutic practices to hold patients responsible for their conduct. And suppose we took the moral argument seriously and eliminated responsibility in those situations where we thought there had been a substantial impairment of the capacity to choose between crime and no crime (I set aside problems of strict liability and of negligence for the time being). Would we not have to, as a matter of moral fairness, fashion a special defense of gross social adversity? The matter might be tested by asking which is the more criminogenic, psychosis or serious social deprivation? In an article in 1968 on this topic I raised the question of whether there should be a special defense of dwelling in a black ghetto.[5] Some literal-minded commentators castigated me severely for such a recommendation, mistaking a form of argument, the *reductio ad absurdum*, for a recommendation. But let me again press the point. If one were asked how to test the criminogenic effect of any factor in man or in the environment, the answer would surely follow empirical lines. . . .

Hence, at first blush, it seems a perfectly legitimate correlational and, I submit, causal inquiry, whether psychosis, or any particular type of psychosis, is more closely related to criminal behavior than, say, being born to a one-parent family living on welfare in a black inner-city area. And there is no doubt of the empirical answer. Social adversity is grossly more potent in its pressure toward criminality, certainly toward all forms of violence and street crime as distinct from white-collar crime, than is any psychotic condition. As a factual matter, the exogenous pressures are very much stronger than the endogenous.

But the argument feels wrong. Surely there is more to it than the simple calculation of criminogenic impact. Is this unease rationally based? I think not, though the question certainly merits further consideration. As a rational matter it is hard to see why one should be more responsible for what is done to one than for what one is. Yet major contributors to jurisprudence and criminal-law theory insist that it is necessary to maintain the denial of responsibility on grounds of mental illness to preserve the moral infrastructure of the criminal law.[6] For many years I have struggled with this opinion by those whose work I deeply respect, yet I remain unpersuaded. Indeed, they really don't try to persuade, but rather affirm and reaffirm with vehemence and almost mystical sincerity the necessity of retaining the special defense of insanity as a moral prop to the entire criminal law.

And indeed I think that much of the discussion of the defense of insanity is the discussion of a myth rather than of a reality. It is no minor debating point that in fact we lack a defense of insanity as an operating tool of the criminal law other than in relation to a very few particularly heinous and heavily punished offenses. There is not an operating defense of insanity in relation to burglary or theft, or the broad sweep of index crimes generally; the plea of not guilty on the ground of insanity is rarely to be heard in city courts of first instance which handle the grist of the mill of the criminal law—though a great deal of pathology is to be seen in the parade of accused and convicted persons before these courts. As a practical matter we reserve this defense for a few sensational cases where it may be in the interest of the accused either to escape the possibility of capital punishment (though in cases where serious mental illness is present, the risk of execution is slight) or where the likely punishment is of a sufficient severity to make the indeterminate commitment of the accused a preferable alternative to a criminal conviction. Operationally the defense of insanity is a tribute, it seems to me, to our hypocrisy rather than to our morality.

To be less aggressive about the matter and to put aside anthropomorphic allegations of hypocrisy, the special defense of insanity may properly be indicted as producing a morally unsatisfactory classification on the continuum between guilt and innocence. It applies in practice to only a few mentally ill criminals, thus omitting many others with guilt-reducing relationships between their mental illness and their crime; it excludes other powerful pressures on human behavior, thus giving excessive weight to the psychological over the social. It is a false classification in the sense that if a team of the world's most sensitive and trained psychiatrists and moralists were to select from all those found guilty of felonies and those found not guilty by reason of insanity any given number who should not be stigmatized as criminals, very few of those found not guilty by reason of insanity would be selected. How to offer proof of this? The only proof, I regret, is to be found by personal contact with a flow of felony cases through the courts and into the prisons. No one of serious perception will fail to recognize both the extent of mental illness and retardation among the prison population and the overwhelming weight of adverse social circumstances on criminal behavior. This is, of course, not an argument that social adversities should lead to acquittals; they should be taken into account in sentencing. And the same is true of the guilt and sentencing of those pressed by psychological adversities. The special defense is thus a morally false classification. And it is a false classification also in the sense that it does not select from the prison population those most in need of psychiatric treatment.

. . .

There are three points to be made in favor of a legislatively introduced rule of "diminished responsibility" in this country of the type now well tested by English juries.

First, for some exceptional murder charges *mens rea* principles and even rules like the Illinois 9-2-(b) may not suffice to reduce murder to manslaughter in cases where such a reduction is desirable. I hypothesize an accused who is clearly psychotic and paranoiac believing he is commanded by God to kill, as Hadfield and some others have believed. He has heard voices to that effect and is in no doubt of his moral duty. He probably does not fall within any *mens rea* provisions which would reduce his crime from murder to manslaughter (unless one sets out on the unacceptable path of California case law) and does not fall within analogues of Illinois section 9-2-(b) since he does not believe he has a defense to a criminal charge. Yet such cases are, it is submitted, better treated and sentenced as manslaughter than as murder. A legislative provision modeled on the English Homicide Act of 1957 would achieve that result.

Secondly, where states impose mandatory sentences on those convicted of murder, some escape mechanisms from those sentences for the mentally ill (other than frustration by charge bargaining) are desirable. The evil to be remedied here lies in the mandatory sentence, not in the criminal law relating to mentally ill criminals; but the only politically acceptable remedy may be legislative enunciation of a doctrine of diminished responsibility.

Thirdly, diminished responsibility is, on close analysis, apart from the two special problems in the two previous paragraphs, a shift of sentencing discretion to a degree from judge to jury, the jury under diminished responsibility lowering the maximum (and sometimes the minimum) sentencing range within which the judge will impose sentence. In some states there may be advantages in such a limitation of judicial discretion.

I now try to draw the analysis to a close. For the reasons offered above I urge the legislative abolition of the special defense of insanity. For those who find persuasive the three reasons last offered for a special legislatively introduced doctrine of diminished responsibility to flush out ordinary *mens rea* doctrines I recommend a formula akin to that in the English Homicide Act of 1957 with the accused who falls within it being convicted of and sentenced for manslaughter, his sentence taking into account his mental illness at the time of the crime.

. . .

Endnotes

[1] Steadman, Monahan, Hartstone, Davis & Clark, "Mentally Disordered Offenders: A National Survey of Patients and Facilities," *Law and Human Behavior.*

[2] 72 *Yale L. J.* 853 (1963).

[3] *Id.* at 868.

[4] Arguments for the retention of the special defense of insanity as a moral foundation of the criminal law are offered by Herbert Wechsler (see, for example, 37 F.R.D. 365 (2d Cir. 1964))

and by Sanford Kadish ("The Decline of Innocence," 26 *Camb. L. J.* 273 (1968)). A more cautious support of retention is advanced by Francis A. Allen (*Law, Intellect and Education*, at 114–18 (1979)). Contrary views, generally supporting the abolitionist position taken in this chapter, are advanced by H. L. A. Hart, Chief Justice Weintraub, Lady Barbara Wooton, Joel Feinberg, Dr. Seymour Halleck, and Dr. Thomas Szasz. (Their views are summarized in the appendix to N. Morris, "Psychiatry and the Dangerous Criminal," 41 *S. Cal. L. Rev.*

514 (1968), prepared by Gary Lowenthal; see n. 13 of that article). The list of those favoring abolition lengthens with the Butler Committee Report . . . and the Carnahan Report . . . as well as the apparently unending debates of the various proposals for a Federal Criminal Code. [Report of the Committee on Mentally Abnormal Offenders, Cmd. 6244 (1975).]

[5] Morris, note 4 *supra*.

[6] See note 4 *supra*.

Excusing the Crazy: The Insanity Defense Reconsidered

Stephen J. Morse

The Moral Basis of the Insanity Defense

The basic moral issue regarding the insanity defense is whether it is just to hold responsible and punish a person who was extremely crazy at the time of the offense.[1] Those who believe that the insanity defense should be abolished must claim either that no defendant is extremely crazy at the time of the offense or that it is morally proper to convict and punish such people. Neither claim is easy to justify.

In all societies some people at some times behave crazily—that is, the behavior at those times is recognizably, aberrantly irrational. A small number of these people behave extremely crazily on occasion, including those times when an offense is committed. A hypothetical defendant with a delusional belief that he is the object of a murderous plot, who kills one of the alleged plotters after hallucinating that he hears the plotter's foul threats, is crazy. Such cases are rare, but clearly exist; the influence of extreme craziness on some criminal behavior cannot be denied. . . .

The insanity defense is rooted in moral principles of excuse that are accepted in both ordinary human interaction and criminal law. Our intuition is that minimal rationality (a cognitive capacity) . . . or lack of com-

pulsion (no hard choice) are the essential preconditions for responsibility. Young children are not considered responsible for the harms they cause precisely because they lack these capacities. Similarly, adults who cause harm while terrifically distraught because of a personal tragedy, for instance, will typically be thought less responsible and culpable for the harm than if they had been normally rational and in control. Aristotle recognized these fundamental requirements for responsibility by noting that persons may be less blameworthy for actions committed under the influence of mistake (a cognitive problem) or compulsion. . . .

Criminal law defenses that focus on the moral attributes of the defendant are based on these same intuitions and principles. Even if the defendant's conduct fulfills the usual requirements for prima facie guilt—that is, act, mental state, causation, result—the defendant will be found not guilty, not culpable, if the acts committed were the products of cognitive (e.g., infancy) or [hard choice] circumstances (e.g., duress) that were not under the defendant's control. . . . To convict a person with a meritorious defense would offend our conception of the relationship between legal guilt and blameworthiness. . . .

In sum, the moral basis of the insanity defense is that there is no just punishment without desert and no desert without responsibility. Responsibility is, in turn, based on minimal cognitive and volitional competence. Thus, an actor who lacks such competence is not responsible, does not deserve punishment, and cannot justly be punished.

From Stephen J. Morse, "Excusing the Crazy: The Insanity Defense Reconsidered," *Southern California Law Review,* Vol. 58 (1985): 777–791. Reprinted by permission of the Southern California Law Review.

The discussion so far has been premeditatedly vague about two issues that must now be clarified: the meanings of rationality and compulsion and the extent to which these factors affect moral accountability. Rationality is notoriously hard to define, but a reasonable working definition would include reference to both the sensibleness of the actor's goals and the logic of the means chosen to achieve them. It is, of course, difficult to say that the preferences or goals of another are irrational or not sensible, but there is no alternative to making these judgments within the social context in which those preferences are held. In a rough-and-ready fashion, we may ask whether, given the social context, any sense can be made of the actor's goals, whether any reasonable person could hold them, whether they are logically or empirically intelligible. Thus, in our society, it is generally considered rational to be a member of a so-called "fringe" religion because our society approves of diverse religious beliefs. In contrast, it does not make sense to want (truly) to be a Martian. These judgments about the intelligibility or rationality of goals can be made so long as we recognize that few goals are rational or irrational in an ultimate sense and we make a general presumption in favor of rationality.

It is easier to assess the rationality of the means an actor chooses to achieve goals because this assessment involves factual beliefs about the world or logical relationships. The inquiry becomes whether instrumental behavior is rationally connected to achieving identified goals. In Aristotelian terms, is the actor a good "practical reasoner"? . . .

. . . If one tests this framework with cognitive craziness, say a delusional belief system, it works very well indeed. For instance, the person who gouges his eye out because he believes he is the Lord's prophet and that mutilating himself will produce peace on earth, surely has an intelligible, rational goal, but the means chosen violates instrumental rationality in a number of ways. If the actor has beliefs that are simply not justifiable on any reasonable view of the world and seems incapable of correcting the errors by logic or evidence, then it is fair to conclude that the actor is irrational with respect to the behavior in question.

Now let us turn to a discussion of the criteria for compulsion. Although it is a vague concept at best, we may define compulsion generally as hard choices that society cannot ask defendants to make at their peril. But what are the criteria of choices so hard that a defendant's "wrong" choice should be excused? First, it must be the case that the defendant will experience substantially greater physical or psychological pain if he or she behaves lawfully/rightly than if he or she behaves unlawfully/wrongly. In other words, the pain produced by performing the lawful/right act must outweigh the pain produced by performing the unlawful/wrong act, the latter of which is usually a strong counterweight to wrongdoing. Let us consider a range of examples. First, the typical case of duress fits this criterion: the defendant will suffer greater pain if he or she does not perform the commanded, wrongful deed than if he or she does. Now consider the drug-dependant person (DDP) who is physically addicted to the drug. A DDP who does not take the drug will undergo the psychological and physical pain of withdrawal. This pain may very well be greater than the pain produced by fear of violating the law or by other psychological factors such as the loss of self-respect. Finally, take the hypothetical of a driver who rounds a turn on a mountain road and sees two children lying in the road. If the driver runs over the children, surely killing both of them, the driver lives; if the driver swerves to avoid them, the driver will go over the edge of the cliff, plunging to a certain death. Although theoretically all lives are equal, the immediate pain of losing one's own life is greater than the pain produced by the possibility that the law may punish the driver in the future. In all these cases, the actor is reasonably rational: the practical syllogism leading to action is logically intact, but the actor faces a very hard choice. . . .

The criteria I have offered for compulsion comport with our moral intuitions and practices. If a choice is too hard, it is *unfair* to blame and punish the actor who has no reasonable alternative. This is not to say that the actor has no choice. Saintly persons might be willing to undergo any pain rather than harm another, but the criminal law cannot expect such saintly behavior from ordinary persons. In addition, possible future criminal punishment will have little deterrent effect on a person faced with the immediate and severe pain of making the "right" choice in a hard-choice situation.

How much irrationality and compulsion are necessary for moral and legal excuse? The degree of rationality or self-control that may be involved in a specific act is rarely an all-or-none matter, and these factors may vary in degree over time during one's life. Similarly, the degree of rationality or self-control that society and the law require for responsibility may vary over time within a society and among societies. One need not be totally irrational or compelled to be excused, but at various times and in various places more or less may generally be expected from people.

The most important point to recognize, however, is that mental health science cannot set the legal standard for irrationality or compulsion in the context of legal accountability because setting the standard is not a scientific issue. The standard is a moral and social standard, to be set by those legal institutions empowered by a society to make individual moral and social decisions. In our society, for example, the substantive standards for legal insanity should be set largely by the legislature and interpreted by the courts, and individual cases should be decided by juries and judges.

The criteria for lack of responsibility also include the requirement that the irrationality or compulsion must be nonculpable. In other words, the actor should not be excused if the irrationality or compulsion was the result of the person's rational, voluntary act. If the irrationality is produced by the voluntary and knowing ingestion of a hallucinogen, for example, the actor is entirely responsible for the subsequent irrationality and will therefore not be excused. Similarly, a mentally disordered person who is able to control the disorder or its effects will be held responsible if such a person could have taken medicine, exercised willpower, or whatever.

The insanity defense issue, then, is whether in some cases extreme craziness (involved in the defendant's offensive conduct) so compromises the defendant's rationality or creates such compulsion that it would be unjust to hold the defendant responsible. Whatever skepticism exists about the scientific status of psychiatry and psychology, it is clear that a small number of persons commit offenses under the influence of extremely crazy states of mind. Even resolute opponents of the insanity defense, such as Norval Morris, admit that there "is indeed some quite florid psychopathology [i.e., crazy behavior] . . . among those for whom these pleas are made." The law should mitigate the punishment of such people because, presumably, they are less responsible. These admissions concede that craziness can affect the foundational capacities for responsibility. In light of such a concession, opponents of the insanity defense should have the burden to demonstrate that no mentally disordered defendant should be excused entirely.

Norval Morris has presented the most recent, important, nonconsequentialist argument for abolishing the insanity defense in his book *Madness and the Criminal Law*. Professor Morris suggests numerous consequentialist arguments for rejecting the insanity defense, but, believing in desert as a limiting principle in criminal law, he confronts directly "the question of fairness, the sense that it is unjust and unfair to stigmatize the mentally ill as criminals and to punish them for their crimes." Professor Morris denies that the mentally disordered lack the capacity to choose their behavior. In brief, he argues that other causes, such as social disadvantage, are far more criminogenic than mental disorder (including severe disorder), yet we do not excuse those who are poor or the products of broken homes. Professor Morris concludes, "[a]s a rational matter it is hard to see why one should be more responsible for what is done to one than for what one is." This conclusion is surely correct. It does not follow from the argument presented for it, however, which makes a morally irrelevant comparison between the poor and the mentally disordered.

Professor Morris confuses causation with excuse, a confusion that has consistently bedeviled criminal law theorists. Causation is not an excuse, however, for all behavior is caused. If causation were an excuse no one would be held responsible for *any* behavior, criminal or not. Moreover, causation is not the equivalent of the subspecies of excuse that we term compulsion. Compulsion exists when the person faces a regrettable hard choice that leaves one with no reasonable alternative to wrongdoing. Again, if causation were the equivalent of compulsion, no one would be responsible because all would be compelled. Causation is not the issue; nonculpable lack of rationality and compulsion is. Understood in these terms, Professor Morris's conclusion that a person should not be more responsible for what is done to one than for what one is does indeed follow. These are not the terms in which he makes his argument, however.

Consider the case of a person whose extreme irrationality stems from the involuntary ingestion of a powerful hallucinogen. Such a defendant, who is not responsible for the ingestion of the drug, is not held responsible for a consequent crime. How can we distinguish this case from that of a person who commits a crime in response to motivations produced by severe mental disorder, say, a sudden command hallucination buttressed by a consistent delusional belief that the action is necessary? Crazy defendants who are not responsible for what they are should also be excused. In both cases the defendant is excused not because the behavior was caused—all behavior is caused—but because the defendant was sufficiently irrational and was not responsible for the irrationality.

The reason we do not excuse most disadvantaged criminals (or those whose criminal behavior can be explained by powerful causes) is not because we lack sympathy for their unfortunate background or because we fail to recognize that social disadvantage is a powerful cause of crime, as it surely is. Rather, most disadvantaged defendants are held responsible because they possess minimal rationality and are not compelled to offend. A disadvantaged defendant driven sufficiently crazy by circumstances will be excused because that defendant is crazy, not because the crazy behavior is caused and the defendant is disadvantaged. Similarly, most mentally disordered persons are held responsible for acts influenced by their disorders because they are sufficiently rational to meet the low threshold standards for responsibility. In sum, the criteria for moral autonomy and responsibility are rationality and lack of compulsion, whereas the criterion for excuse is that the actor is nonculpably lacking either reasonable rationality or is compelled.

The other major recent attack on the insanity defense, the American Medical Association's (AMA) report recommending abolition of the "special" defense of insanity, provides another instructive but confused counterargument to the defense's moral basis. The AMA's most important argument is that the insanity defense undermines the moral integrity of the criminal law because it impermissibly confuses psychiatric and legal concepts. The AMA writes:

> A defense premised on psychiatric models represents a singularly unsatisfactory, and inherently contradictory approach to the issue of accountability. . . .
>
> The essential goal of an exculpatory test for insanity is to identify the point at which a defendant's mental condition has become so impaired that society may confidently conclude that he has lost his free will. . . . Because free will is an article of faith, rather than a concept that can be explained in medical terms, it is impossible for psychiatrists to determine whether a mental impairment has affected the defendant's capacity for voluntary choice, or caused him to commit the particular act in question. Accordingly, since models of mental illness are indeterminant in this respect, they can provide no reliable measure of responsibility.

Rather than being a persuasive argument against the moral basis of the defense, this quote exhibits a confusion about moral responsibility akin to Professor Morris's equation of causation with excuse. The AMA believes that the insanity defense confuses moral and legal concepts with medical concepts, but it is the AMA analysis that is guilty of this confusion.

The legal defense of insanity is not based on the psychiatric premise of determinism, and the essential goal of the defense is not to identify those actors who lack free will. The legal defense of insanity is based on the premise that rationality and lack of compulsion are the touchstones of moral responsibility, and the various tests seek to identify those actors who lack these attributes. The AMA correctly notes that free will cannot be explained in medical terms or identified medically, but this is entirely beside the point. Medical models cannot provide a "reliable measure of responsibility" because they are not meant to do so. The AMA errs by claiming that free will is the basis for responsibility and that mental disorder is somehow necessarily the antithesis of free will. Free will is not the basis for responsibility, and mental disorder per se does not negate responsibility: irrationality or compulsion negate responsibility.

Endnote

[1] I use the word "crazy" advisedly and with no lack of respect for either disordered persons or the professionals who try to help them. It refers to behavior that is weird, loony, or nuts; less colloquially, it is behavior that seems inexplicably irrational. I chose the word "crazy" because I believe that it is the best generic term to describe the type of behavior that leads to a diagnosis or label of mental disorder. At the same time, it avoids begging questions about whether the crazy person was capable of behaving less crazily. When one engages in the discourse of illness, disease, or disorder, it is often assumed that the phenomena being discussed are uncontrollable manifestations of abnormal biological processes. But the truth is that our understanding of behavior, including very crazy behavior, is limited, and neither mental health scientists nor laypersons really know to what degree behavior of any sort can actually be controlled. Thus, I prefer to use a nonjargon word to describe the type of behavior—crazy behavior—with which the law is concerned in insanity defense cases.

Study Questions

1. Do you agree with Robinson that the "reasons" theory of justification—that an actor is justified only if he knows the circumstances that afford a justification—is a view "that exists only in academia"? Can you imagine someone arguing that Ashkenazi (the defendant in the bomb case) should be punished for stealing the backpack containing the bomb?

2. According to Rosen, what rationales are typically given in support of treating self-defense as a justification?

3. How does Rosen respond to the objection that simply excusing women who kill their abusers, rather than justifying their conduct as appropriate self-defense, will reinforce stereotypes of women as irrational?

4. In 1990, nine children of Hmong parents in the U.S. died from cardiac arrest after contracting measles. The parents had initially sought the aid of shamans and had waited until the children were near death before taking them to a hospital. In other incidents, Hmong immigrants have refused corrective surgery or chemotherapy for their children. In one case, a shaman told the family that the child's condition was to atone for sins committed by ancestors, and that medical intervention would pass these sins on to the next generation. Assuming that the parents in such cases were to face criminal charges related to medical neglect of their children, should they be able to invoke their sincerely held religious beliefs and cultural practices as an excuse?

5. What is the argument for a cultural defense to criminal liability? Is it based on an assumption that members of a minority subculture are ignorant of the applicable law? Although ignorance of governing law is generally not an excuse, should it be used to excuse those raised in a foreign culture? If cultural factors are presented to the jury in an effort to show that the defendant should be excused for breaking the law, what limits should be placed upon such an excuse? Should people always be judged by the standards of their native culture?

6. In *Regina v. Machekequonabe* (28 O.R. 309 [1897]), a Native American was charged with manslaughter for killing what he took to be an evil spirit clothed in human form, called a "Wendigo," which the defendant believed would eat a human being. The defendant saw what appeared to be a tall human form running in the distance, gave chase, challenged the victim, and then fired. The defense argued that the defendant lacked the "intention even to harm a human being, much less to kill." Was the court correct in refusing to consider the defendant's argument?

7. What does it mean to say that a plea of insanity should be retained by the law as a "special defense"?

8. What two arguments does Morris think support retention of the special defense of insanity? How does he seek to counter each of these arguments?

9. What does Morse see as the moral basis of the insanity defense?

10. As part of his argument in support of the insanity defense, Morse contends that "if the actor has beliefs that are simply not justifiable on any reasonable view of the world and seems incapable of correcting the errors by logic or evidence, then it is fair to conclude that the actor is irrational with respect to the behavior in question." Do you agree with this criterion? Why or why not?

11. Morse says it is clear, at least, that a "small number of persons" commit offenses in which they are sufficiently irrational or compulsive to merit mitigation of their sentences. Do you agree that the number is likely to be "small"? And if so, should the number of people able to raise the insanity defense somehow be limited?

12. Morse criticizes Morris for improperly comparing "the poor and the mentally disordered." What comparison was Morris making? Is the comparison unfair, in your view?

13. In response to growing frustration with the existing tests for insanity, some jurisdictions, rather than abolish the defense altogether, have created a new verdict—"guilty but mentally ill"—as an alternative to the traditional options, "guilty" and "not guilty by reason of insanity." This verdict allows the jury to find that a person was sufficiently culpable to be said to have committed the crime, but at the same time to have suffered from a mental illness. Under this verdict, the accused is convicted and sentenced as a normal offender. He or she may then be moved to a treatment facility for all or part of the sentence, and any time remaining after the completion of treatment must be spent back in prison. Does this compromise verdict make sense? Is it morally defensible?

14. In March 1991, a jury convicted Norma Valentin on drug possession charges despite a defense based on the claim that she suffered from multiple personality disorder. According to Ms. Valentin, her other personalities include "Vicki," a drug dealer; "Ayessa," an Indian fortune-teller; and "Virginia," the personality involved in relationships with men. Ms. Valentin's counsel contended that her "core"

personality should not be criminally liable for crimes committed by one of her "secondary" personalities (see "Don't Try This Defense," *The National Law Journal*, March 25, 1991, p. 6). Assuming that Ms. Valentin's multiple personality disorder is genuine, as attested by psychiatrists, should the law attempt to apportion responsibility among the various personalities "housed" within a single body? Why or why not?

15. A man calling himself Mr. "V" is a sixty-two-year-old who, until recently, lived in a quiet suburb of Denver, Colorado. Mr. V had been living on a small retirement income. His children are grown and his wife is ill and requires care at home, which Mr. V had been providing. You are an assistant district attorney in Los Angeles County, and your boss has assigned you to follow-up on unsolved crimes and cases that have never officially been "closed." One such case involved a crime committed in L.A. thirty-five years ago. A man, then in his late twenties, had been seen burglarizing a number of grocery and department stores in the valley. This man, known then as Mr. S, was indicted but never caught or brought to trial. Recently, unmistakable evidence has come to light that Mr. V is, in reality, Mr. S. Mr. V was arrested in Denver and sent to L.A. The news media is full of stories about Mr. V. Many people believe he should be punished. Mr. V's supporters point out that, after he moved to Colorado and changed his name, he lived for thirty-five years as

a devoted father and husband, a volunteer firefighter, and Boy Scout leader. Mr. V has raised money for homeless shelters in Denver and was active on the local school board. As a young man, Mr. V was the only support for his single mother and her other children (Mr. V's younger siblings). Mr. V says he was driven to desperate measures to obtain food, clothing, and other necessities for his family. As the prosecutor, would you argue that Mr. V should be tried and punished for the crimes he committed as Mr. S? Why or why not?

16. In *U.S. v. Haynes* (143 F.3d 1089 [1998]) the defendant, an inmate at a federal prison, suddenly attacked another prisoner by pouring scalding oil on the other inmate's head as he played dominoes. In defense, Haynes claims that the victim had threatened more than once to sexually assault Haynes. The day before the attack, the victim had thrown Haynes to the ground within sight of a guard, who did nothing. On the day of the attack, the victim had threatened to "finish what he started." The court held that Haynes could not argue self-defense in the form of a "pre-emptive strike." "Under the law of the jungle, a good offense may be the best defense," the court wrote, "but although prisons are nasty places, they are not jungles." Because Haynes "was not faced with an imminent use of force" by the victim, he should have used other, lawful alternatives. Do you agree with the court's decision in this case?

C. *Punishment and Responsibility*

Criminal defendants who are indicted and convicted of an offense are then subject to punishment. Most of the time we simply assume that those who are convicted are properly subject to punishment, although we often disagree on what that punishment should be. What does it take to justify the legal infliction of

punishment? What, for example, would you say of the following items?

1. Under California's "three-strikes" law, a stiff, habitual offender statute approved by voters in 1994 and upheld by the U.S. Supreme Court in

2003, an offender who commits a felony and who has two prior convictions for "serious" felonies must be sentenced to a minimum of twenty-five years to life imprisonment. In 1995 a Los Angeles man faced a twenty-five-year sentence on petty theft for stealing a slice of pepperoni pizza; a parolee who broke into a restaurant and stole four chocolate chip cookies received twenty-six years.

2. California recently became the only state in the nation to require that convicted child molesters be punished through chemical castration. Under the law, molesters with two convictions will be forced to receive weekly injections of a synthetic hormone called Depo-Provera, which is intended to suppress their sex drive.

Are the punishments inflicted or proposed in these cases justifiable? If so, on what grounds?

Recent issues and emerging trends in the practice of criminal punishment are reviewed in our readings in the brief selection from David Dolinko. Among the more salient shifts and changes, Dolinko includes a rapidly growing prison population and increasing reliance upon recidivist and "three-strikes" measures. "Mandatory minimums" in criminal sentencing, trying adolescent offenders as adults, and use of civil property forfeiture are also on the rise.

The Nature and Purposes of Punishment

The question of how to justify the infliction of punishment presupposes that we know what punishment is. How, then, can we characterize punishment? Most legal philosophers are in agreement that most, if not all, of the following features are properties of punishment: (1) punishment involves the imposition of unpleasant consequences upon the person punished, among them, the loss of rights, freedoms, or even life; (2) punishment also expresses the community's disapproval of the offender's conduct, a public expression of condemnation; (3) punishment is imposed for a violation of existing law where the offender has caused the violation to occur; and (4) punishment is inflicted by agents authorized by law to impose it. This last condition differentiates criminal punishment from the misfortune brought on (say) by a "punishing storm."

Clearly, punishment seems by its very nature to involve hard treatment—the coercive infliction of pain and suffering. Normally, such a way of treating another

person would be wrong. Hence, the practice of punishing persons seems to need some justifying account. What makes it right when punishment is involved?

Courts and lawmakers have traditionally considered a variety of social goals and moral claims in addressing the question of how to justify the institution of criminal punishment. Some argue that the only legitimate concern of the criminal justice system is the *rehabilitation* of the offender. The purpose of fixing responsibility, in this view, is simply to locate individuals who need preventive detention and therapy. Others contend that the aim of the law is to *deter* crime, by either incapacitating or specifically deterring an individual, thus preventing him or her from engaging in further criminality, or by generally deterring others, seeking to induce them to avoid acting as the offender did. Finally, some insist that the practice of punishment is grounded in the *retributive* idea that punishment is what the offender deserves and may be inflicted only on that ground, not on the theory that punishment will benefit society in some way. Retributivists maintain that their view is not to be equated with a primitive and thinly disguised lust for vengeance; rather, the motivation is the desire to do justice, to see that the moral balance is restored and the criminal's debt repaid.

As Michael Moore explains in his selection, the goals and principles appealed to in the effort to justify criminal punishment tend to align themselves with one or the other of the two general moral and social theories reviewed at the beginning of Chapter 1: *utilitarianism* and *deontology*. As we saw in Chapter 1, utilitarianism on the most abstract level is one of a family of views that takes the *consequences* or results produced or likely to be produced by an act or a policy to be the measure of its moral correctness. Deontological ethics, in contrast, measures the rightness or correctness of conduct by the degree to which it conforms to the duties or obligations we have to treat others in appropriate ways. The deontologist Kant held a deontological theory of punishment called *retributivism,* which can be formulated more precisely as the view that punishing a person is justifiable only if it gives to him or her what he or she deserves. Let's examine these theories more fully.

Theories of Punishment

Recall that a consequentialist says that an action is right or wrong depending upon its overall consequences. To justify a system of criminal punishment, in this view, would require showing that punishment does some good or prevents some evil, and that it does so better than any alternative for handling criminal behavior. As we saw in Chapter 1, proponents of consequentialism differ among themselves as to the precise nature of the "good" to be promoted, and this difference spills over into consequentialist reasoning about punishment. Consequentialists have argued that legal punishment is necessary to achieve the greatest happiness or to secure the maximum degree of liberty for all citizens; more specifically, they have contended that punishment is aimed at incapacitating identified wrongdoers, rehabilitating those with criminal propensities, and deterring potential offenders. Deterrence, incapacitation, and so on are, according to consequentialists, *goals,* to which a system of punishment is (supposedly) the most effective *means.* The goals of utilitarian consequentialists have in the past had an important impact on actual penological practice: sentencing reform and experiments with various rehabilitative programs are but two of the ways in which utilitarians since Jeremy Bentham have sought to align the penal system more closely with legitimate consequentialist goals.

In the selection from his *Introduction to the Principles of Morals and Legislation* included here, Bentham explores cases where the infliction of punishment would be "unmeet" or inappropriate. These include cases where the infliction of punishment would be ineffectual or would be outweighed by other considerations. Bentham sets down basic guidelines for the enlightened legislator to follow in restructuring the criminal law. The guidelines focus particularly upon setting the proportionality between the offense and the penalty, including the requirement that "the punishment ought in no case to be more than what is necessary to bring it into conformity with the rules here given." In Bentham's utilitarian view, the infliction of punishment is justifiable if and only if it brings about a net gain in good (pleasure) for society; the proper amount of punishment is that which produces the most good. Bentham's theory imagines that the legislator will devise a proposed procedure and schedule for inflicting fines or imprisonment based upon a kind of quantitative analysis: he or she will add up the pleasures that such a procedure and schedule would inflict, discounted by the pain or discomfort produced, and adopt the proposal only if there is a net gain in utility.

Advocates of the retributive conception of punishment make at least two basic claims: (1) Only those who are guilty should be subject to punishment, and (2) Punishment may be inflicted only if it gives to the guilty person what he or she deserves. These basic principles are, again, fleshed out in various ways by various retributivists. Some argue that giving an offender his or her "just deserts" is a way of removing an unfair advantage that the wrongdoer has taken over those who obey the law; other retributivists assert that the moral censure or opprobrium represented by the infliction of punishment is the essential factor. It is important to note that retributivists who refer to registering moral censure or erasing an unfair advantage are insisting that the imposition of censure or annulment of an advantage are *intrinsic features* of punishment itself, not simply goals achievable through the means of punishment, as the consequentialists would have it. Retributivism has also had a significant effect on criminal justice, particularly in the form of calls to lessen the discretion of courts by requiring determinate sentencing, and in the enactment of stiff sentencing guidelines at both the state and federal levels.

Utilitarianism vs. Retributivism

As an initial matter, both the utilitarian and the retributive conceptions of punishment possess some degree of attractiveness. A utilitarian holds that for an instance of punishment to be justified it is necessary that it do some good. Suppose an old man steals some bread from a supermarket to feed his hungry children. A utilitarian asks us to temper the reaction to punish the man for his choice and to consider the larger circumstances within which he acted: What good will it do to penalize him? The problem with Kant's retributivism, the utilitarian might say, is that it requires that we punish such persons even when it clearly won't do any good, and this is inconsistent with a humane and enlightened approach to criminality. Moreover, the retributivist must show, in detail, how to draw up a procedure and schedule for the infliction of punishment based upon the concept of desert. Determining exactly what a defendant deserves is no easy task. The Kantian, on the other hand, claims that it is necessary that punishment be deserved, and, he points out, this is an imperative that the utilitarian will not always observe. Suppose we inform you that we have decided to punish you with life imprisonment for the crime of running a stop sign. We are doing this not because you deserve or merit such a punishment, but rather to use you as an example to others. (Tired of the widespread failure to obey stop signs, we reason that the frequency of such lawlessness will decrease dramatically at the sight of your awful plight.) Even assuming that subjecting you to such punishment would serve the goal of deterrence, surely you would demand to know what gives us the right to use you in this way—and it is this demand that lies at the heart of the retributivist insistence that punishment must be deserved. The difficulty with the utilitarian preoccupation with deterrence, it seems, is that it may allow people to be punished out of all proportion to their guilt, or even in the absence of any guilt whatever, when it serves the interests of society. More generally, the retributivist complains that the question of whether the accused deserves punishment is not something that can be captured by the kind of quantitative analysis Bentham suggests. Culpability and innocence are basic moral features of persons and their actions and choices.

In his selection for this section, Michael Moore defends the retributive theory of punishment. Moore defines retributivism as the view that "punishment is justified only if the person receiving it deserves it." He contrasts the "pure retributivist" theory with both utilitarianism and a "mixed" theory of punishment that seeks to combine the retributive and utilitarian views. Through an argument by elimination, Moore seeks to show that retributivism is the only viable candidate among the competing theories.

The selection from H. L. A. Hart attempts to combine aspects of both utilitarian and retributive theories of punishment. For Hart, the general institution of punishment is justified on broadly utilitarian grounds, whereas the application of that general practice to particular individuals is the province of retributivism.

Proportionality and "Three Strikes"

Many of the complexities in the theory of punishment can usefully be explored in a recent and controversial ruling from the U.S. Supreme Court. On November 4, 1995, Leandro Andrade was apprehended stealing five videotapes worth $84.70 from a Kmart store in Ontario, California. Later that month, Andrade entered a different Kmart store in Montclair and placed four videotapes worth $68.84 in the rear waistband of his pants. Police subsequently arrested Andrade for these crimes. In 1990, Andrade had been convicted in state court for a misdemeanor petty theft offense. Together with his prior felonies, Andrade's thefts exposed him to punishment under California's "three strikes law," which stipulated that any felony could constitute the third strike, and thus could subject a defendant to a term of 25 years to life in prison. The trial judge sentenced Andrade to two consecutive terms of 25 to life. A California Court of Appeal rejected Andrade's assertion that the sentence violated the Constitution's Eighth Amendment prohibition against cruel and unusual

punishment. In 2003, the U.S. Supreme Court, in an opinion by Justice O'Connor, upheld California's three-strikes law and Andrade's sentence. The issue for the Court was whether Andrade's penalty—two consecutive terms of 25 years to life—is "grossly disproportionate" to the wrong Andrade committed: stealing $150 worth of videos. The majority, reviewing several of its precedents, held that the "gross disproportionality" principle lacked "precise contours" and is applicable in "exceedingly rare" and "extreme" cases. Given the lack of precision in defining a "cruel and unusual punishment," the sentence handed to Andrade was not a violation of "clearly established" federal law.

"Scarlet-Letter" Punishments

Many crimes are punished through the imposition of jail sentences, payment of fines, or a combination of both. An interesting test case for utilitarian and retributivist theories of punishment concerns more novel forms of punishment with which courts in various parts of the United States have begun to experiment. Windell McDowell was convicted in a California court of purse snatching and was placed on probation on the condition that he not go out of his house without wearing shoes with metal taps on the soles.[1] In Oregon Thomas Kirby pled guilty to a charge of first-degree burglary and was placed on probation on the condition that he publish, at his own expense, an advertisement, accompanied by a picture, in the local newspaper. The ad was to read "Criminal's Apology."[2] Richard Bateman was convicted on two counts of first-degree sexual abuse in 1985. He faced a maximum sentence of five years' imprisonment and a large fine, but an Oregon court instead suspended his sentence and placed him on probation. As one of the conditions of his sentence, Bateman was required to place on the door of his residence and on both doors of any vehicle he might drive, in three-inch lettering, the words "DANGEROUS SEX OFFENDER—NO CHILDREN ALLOWED."[3] In other cases, offenders have been asked to wear sandwich boards proclaiming their guilt or place "DUI" on their license plates; one

---

[1] *People v. McDowell*, 59 Cal. App. 3d 807 (1976).

[2] *State v. Kirby*, No. 85–1649 (Or. Cir. Ct. for Lincoln County, Oregon [1986]).

[3] *State v. Bateman*, Nos. C85-08-33209 and C85-10-34220 (Or. Cir. Ct. for Multnomah County, Oregon [1986]).

man convicted of murder was required to place family photos of his victim on the walls of his cell.

In one of his most famous stories, nineteenth-century American author Nathaniel Hawthorne described the punishment inflicted upon an adulteress in early America: She was forced for the rest of her days to wear on her chest a scarlet letter A, plainly visible to all, as a sign of her crime. Judicial "scarlet letters" are becoming increasingly common, and they raise troublesome questions: Is humiliation a useful form of punishment? Is subjecting a person to disgrace and public ridicule justifiable in a utilitarian theory of punishment? In a retributive view? Do such sentences constitute "cruel and unusual" punishment"? Even more broadly, are there some forms of punishment that our law should never inflict?

Lockyer v. Andrade

JUSTICE O'CONNOR . . .

This case raises the issue whether the United States Court of Appeals for the Ninth Circuit erred in ruling that the California Court of Appeal's decision affirming Leandro Andrade's two consecutive terms of 25 years to life in prison for a "third strike" conviction is contrary to, or an unreasonable application of, clearly established federal law as determined by this Court. . . .

On November 4, 1995, Leandro Andrade stole five videotapes worth $84.70 from a Kmart store in Ontario, California. Security personnel detained Andrade as he was leaving the store. On November 18, 1995, Andrade entered a different Kmart store in Montclair, California, and placed four videotapes worth $68.84 in the rear waistband of his pants. Again, security guards apprehended Andrade as he was existing the premises. Police subsequently arrested Andrade for these crimes.

These two incidents were not Andrade's first or only encounters with law enforcement. According to the state probation officer's presentence report, Andrade has been in and out of state and federal prison since 1982. In January 1982, he was convicted of a misdemeanor theft offense and was sentenced to 6 days in jail with 12 months' probation. Andrade was arrested again in November 1982 for multiple counts of first-degree residential burglary. He pleaded guilty to at least three of those counts, and in April of the following year he was sentenced to 120 months in prison. In 1988, Andrade was convicted in federal court of "[t]ransportation of [m]arijuana," and was sentenced to eight years in federal prison. In 1990, he was convicted in state court for a misdemeanor petty theft offense and was ordered to serve 180 days in jail. In September 1990, Andrade was convicted again in federal court for the same felony of "[t]ransportation of [m]arijuana" and was sentenced to 2,191 days in federal prison. And in 1991, Andrade was arrested for a state parole violation—escape from federal prison. He was paroled from the state penitentiary system in 1993. . . .

Because of his 1990 misdemeanor conviction, the State charged Andrade in this case with two counts of petty theft with a prior conviction. . . . Under California law, petty theft with a prior conviction is a so-called "wobbler" offense because it is punishable either as a misdemeanor or as a felony. . . . The decision to prosecute petty theft with a prior conviction as a misdemeanor or as a felony is in the discretion of the prosecutor. . . .

Under California's three strikes law, any felony can constitute the third strike, and thus can subject a defendant to a term of 25 years to life in prison. . . . In this case, the prosecutor decided to charge the two counts of theft as felonies rather than misdemeanors. The trial court denied Andrade's motion to reduce the offenses to misdemeanors, both before the jury verdict and again in state habeas proceedings.

A jury found Andrade guilty of two counts of petty theft with a prior conviction. According to California law, a jury must also find that a defendant has

538 U.S. 63 (2003), United States Supreme Court.

been convicted of at least two serious or violent felonies that serve as qualifying offenses under the three strikes regime. In this case, the jury made a special finding that Andrade was convicted of three counts of first-degree residential burglary. A conviction for first-degree residential burglary qualifies as a serious or violent felony for the purposes of the three strikes law. . . . As a consequence, each of Andrade's convictions for theft. . . . triggered a separate application of the three strikes law. Pursuant to California law, the judge sentenced Andrade to two consecutive terms of 25 years to life in prison.

On direct appeal in 1997, the California Court of Appeal affirmed Andrade's sentence. . . . Andrade filed a petition for a writ of habeas corpus in Federal District Court. The District Court denied his petition. The Ninth Circuit granted Andrade a certificate of appealability as to his claim that his sentence violated the Eighth Amendment, and subsequently reversed the judgment of the District Court. . . .

Andrade's argument in this Court is that two consecutive terms of 25 years to life for stealing approximately $150 in videotapes is grossly disproportionate in violation of the Eighth Amendment. Andrade similarly maintains that the state court decision affirming his sentence is "contrary to, or involved an unreasonable application of, clearly established Federal law, as determined by the Supreme Court of the United States."

As a threshold matter here, we first decide what constitutes "clearly established Federal law, as determined by the Supreme Court of the United States." Andrade relies upon a series of precedents from this Court—*Rummel v. Estelle*, 445 U.S. 263 (1980), *Solem v. Helm*, 463 U.S. 277 (1983), and *Harmelin v. Michigan*, 501 U.S. 957 (1991)—that he claims clearly establish a principle that his sentence is so grossly disproportionate that it violates the Eighth Amendment. . . .

Through this thicket of Eighth Amendment jurisprudence, one governing legal principle emerges as "clearly established": A gross disproportionality principle is applicable to sentences for terms of years.

Our cases exhibit a lack of clarity regarding what factors may indicate gross disproportionality. In *Solem* (the case upon which Andrade relies most heavily), we stated: "It is clear that a 25-year sentence generally is more severe than a 15-year sentence, but in most cases it would be difficult to decide that the former violates the Eighth Amendment while the latter does not." . . .

The final question is whether the California Court of Appeal's decision affirming Andrade's sentence is "contrary to, or involved an unreasonable application of," this clearly established gross disproportionality principle. . . . In terms of length of sentence and availability of parole, severity of the underlying offense, and the impact of recidivism, Andrade's sentence implicates factors relevant in both *Rummel* and *Solem*. Because *Harmelin* and *Solem* specifically stated that they did not overrule *Rummel*, it was not contrary to our clearly established law for the California Court of Appeal to turn to *Rummel* in deciding whether a sentence is grossly disproportionate. . . .

Andrade's sentence also was not materially indistinguishable from the facts in *Solem*. The facts here fall in between the facts in *Rummel* and the facts in *Solem*. *Solem* involved a sentence of life in prison without the possibility of parole. The defendant in *Rummel* was sentenced to life in prison with the possibility of parole. Here, Andrade retains the possibility of parole. *Solem* acknowledged that *Rummel* would apply in a "similar factual situation." 463 U.S., at 304, n. 32. And while this case resembles to some degree both *Rummel* and *Solem*, it is not materially indistinguishable from either. . . . Consequently, the state court did not "confron[t] a set of facts that are materially indistinguishable from a decision of this Court and nevertheless arriv[e] at a result different from our precedent." . . .

The gross disproportionality principle reserves a constitutional violation for only the extraordinary case. [I]t was not an unreasonable application of our clearly established law for the California Court of Appeal to affirm Andrade's sentence of two consecutive terms of 25 years to life in prison.

The judgment of the United States Court of Appeals for the Ninth Circuit, accordingly, is reversed.

It is so ordered.

JUSTICE SOUTER, with whom JUSTICE STEVENS, JUSTICE GINSBURG, and JUSTICE BREYER join, dissenting.

The application of the Eighth Amendment prohibition against cruel and unusual punishment to terms of years is articulated in the "clearly established" principle acknowledged by the Court: a sentence grossly disproportionate to the offense for which it is imposed is unconstitutional. . . . Andrade's sentence cannot survive Eighth Amendment review. Although *Solem* is important for its instructions about applying objective proportionality analysis, the case is controlling here because it established a benchmark in applying the general principle. We specifically held that a sentence of life imprisonment without parole for uttering a $100 "no account" check was disproportionate to the crime, even though the defendant had committed six prior nonviolent felonies. In explaining our proportionality review, we contrasted the result with *Rummel's* on the ground that the life sentence there had included parole eligibility after 12 years.

The facts here are on all fours with those of *Solem* and point to the same result. Andrade, like the defendant in *Solem,* was a repeat offender who committed theft of fairly trifling value, some $150, and their criminal records are comparable, including burglary (though Andrade's were residential), with no violent crimes or crimes against the person. The respective sentences, too, are strikingly alike. Although Andrade's petty thefts occurred on two separate occasions, his sentence can only be understood as punishment for the total amount he stole. The two thefts were separated by only two weeks; they involved the same victim; they apparently constituted parts of a single, continuing effort to finance drug sales; their seriousness is measured by the dollar value of the things taken; and the government charged both thefts in a single indictment. . . . The state court accordingly spoke of his punishment collectively as well, carrying a 50-year minimum before parole eligibility. . . . and because Andrade was 37 years old when sentenced, the substantial 50-year period amounts to life without parole. . . . The results under the Eighth Amendment should therefore be the same in each case. The only ways to reach a different conclusion are to reject the practical equivalence of a life sentence without parole and one with parole eligibility at 87. . . . The former is unrealistic; an 87-year-old man released after 50 years behind bars will have no real life left, if he survives to be released at all. And the latter, disparaging *Solem* as a point of reference on Eighth Amendment analysis, is wrong as a matter of law.

The second reason that relief is required even under the unreasonable application standard rests on the alternative way of looking at Andrade's 50-year sentence as two separate 25-year applications of the three-strikes law, and construing the challenge here as going to the second, consecutive 25-year minimum term triggered by a petty theft. To understand why it is revealing to look at the sentence this way, it helps to recall the basic difficulty inherent in proportionality review. We require the comparison of offense and penalty to disclose a truly gross disproportionality before the constitutional limit is passed, in large part because we believe that legislatures are institutionally equipped with better judgment than courts in deciding what penalty is merited by particular behavior. In this case, however, a court is substantially aided in its

reviewing function by two determinations made by the State itself.

The first is the State's adoption of a particular penological theory as its principal reason for shutting a three-strikes defendant away for at least 25 years. Although the State alludes in passing to retribution or deterrence . . . its only serious justification for the 25-year minimum treats the sentence as a way to incapacitate a given defendant from further crime; the underlying theory is the need to protect the public from a danger demonstrated by the prior record of violent and serious crime. The State, in other words, has not chosen 25 to life because of the inherent moral or social reprehensibility of the triggering offense in isolation; the triggering offense is treated so seriously, rather, because of its confirmation of the defendant's danger to society and the need to counter his threat with incapacitation. As to the length of incapacitation, the State has made a second helpful determination, that the public risk or danger posed by someone with the specified predicate record is generally addressed by incapacitation for 25 years before parole eligibility. . . . The three-strikes law, in sum, responds to a condition of the defendant shown by his prior felony record, his danger to society, and it reflects a judgment that 25 years of incapacitation prior to parole eligibility is appropriate when a defendant exhibiting such a condition commits another felony.

Whether or not one accepts the State's choice of penological policy as constitutionally sound, that policy cannot reasonably justify the imposition of a consecutive 25-year minimum for a second minor felony committed soon after the first triggering offense. Andrade did not somehow become twice as dangerous to society when he stole the second handful of videotapes; his dangerousness may justify treating one minor felony as serious and warranting long incapacitation, but a second such felony does not disclose greater danger warranting substantially longer incapacitation. . . . no one could seriously argue that the second theft of videotapes provided any basis to think that Andrade would be so dangerous after 25 years, the date on which the consecutive sentence would begin to run, as to require at least 25 years more. I know of no jurisdiction that would add 25 years of imprisonment simply to reflect the fact that the two temporally related thefts took place on two separate occasions, and I am not surprised that California has found no such case, not even under its three-strikes law. . . . In sum, the argument that repeating a trivial crime justifies doubling a 25-year minimum incapacitation sentence based on a threat to the public does not raise a seriously debatable point on which judgments might reasonably differ. The argument is irrational, and the state court's acceptance of it in response to a facially gross disproportion between triggering offense and penalty was unreasonable within the meaning of §2254(d).

This is the rare sentence of demonstrable gross disproportionality, as the California Legislature may well have recognized when it specifically provided that a prosecutor may move to dismiss or strike a prior felony conviction "in the furtherance of justice." In this case, the statutory safeguard failed, and the state court was left to ensure that the Eighth Amendment prohibition on grossly disproportionate sentences was met. If Andrade's sentence is not grossly disproportionate, the principle has no meaning. The California court's holding was an unreasonable application of clearly established precedent.

The Future of Punishment

DAVID DOLINKO

I want to say a few words . . . about . . . the future of punishment. For reasons that I hope will become clear, . . . this is a crucially important and very timely topic, and yet one that might well give pause to the bravest among us.

For a special brand of courage—or perhaps of dollop of madness—is required to prophesy the future of a social institution as volatile, as controversial, and as prone to unforeseen change as the institution of criminal punishment. . . . [In the early 1970s] "the future of punishment" would have looked dim indeed. For most of the twentieth century, the concepts of punishing criminals and giving them their just deserts had been yielding ground to the notions of reforming or rehabilitating offenders through individualized, therapeutic methods. Almost all of the innovations in American criminal justice since 1900 had borne the stamp of this "rehabilitative ideal": the "juvenile court, the indeterminate sentence, systems of probation and parole, the youth authority, and the promise (if not the reality) of therapeutic programs in prisons, juvenile institutions, and mental hospitals."[1] The Supreme Court had placed its imprimatur on these developments with its 1949 declaration that "retribution is no longer the dominant objective of the criminal law" and that "a strong motivating force for the

changes" was "the belief that by careful study of the lives and personalities convicted offenders many could be less severely punished and restored sooner to complete freedom and useful citizenship"—a belief, the Court added, which "to a large extent has been justified."[2] An influential report on penal justice, issued by the American Friends Service Committee in 1971, noted that "the treatment approach receives nearly unanimous support from those working in the field of criminal justice."[3] As recently as 1973, the criminal law scholar Jeffrie Murphy structured an anthology of readings about punishment theory around the issue of whether the criminal process should be completely replaced, as society's response to crime, by therapeutic rehabilitation[4]—as had been advocated, for example, by the noted psychiatrist Karl Menninger in his widely read 1968 book *The Crime of Punishment*.[5] In the same year as Menninger's book there appeared *Punishment and Responsibility*, a collection of essays by the preeminent English legal philosopher H. L. A. Hart. In one of those essays we find Hart describing how the novels of Dostoyevsky "make real to us . . . a conception of punishment which, since he wrote, has come to occupy a much diminished place in . . . penal policy and practice"—a conception that "makes primary the meting out to a responsible wrongdoer of his just deserts."[6] Hart noted that "many of us here today—perhaps most of us—may hate these ideas as useless obstructions to rational thought," but he added sagely that "we still need to understand the moral and

From David Dolinko, "The Future of Punishment," *UCLA Law Review*, Vol. 46 (1999): 1719–1726. Reprinted by permission of the UCLA Law Review.

psychological appeal which these ideas have, for they have not disappeared yet."[7]

From our perspective today, we can see that those seemingly antiquated retributive notions of which Hart spoke have not only failed to disappear, but have come roaring back with—one might say—a vengeance. Therapy, reform, and rehabilitation have fallen into discredit and disrepute. "The new retributivists . . . gained the ascendency in the punishment debate during the 1970s,"[8] and retributivism "can fairly be regarded today as the leading philosophical justification of the institution of criminal punishment."[9] And that institution itself, far from withering away, flourishes in America today as perhaps never before. Indeed, punishment has become one of our most impressive growth industries.

In 1970, when the future of punishment seemed so tenuous, there were less than 200,000 inmates in state and federal prisons. As of June 30, 1998, that figure had swollen to 1,277,866. This increase is all the more remarkable given that the violent crime rate has declined every year since 1991, the property crime rate has dropped steadily since 1975, and the levels of both of these types of crime fell last year to their lowest point since 1973.

Of course, a good part of the explanation for this seeming anomaly lies in the unrelenting "War on Drugs." Sixty percent of federal prison inmates, and 23% of state prisoners, are serving time for drug violations. More people are behind bars for drug offenses in the United States than are in prison for all crimes in England, France, Germany, and Japan combined. The FBI reported for 1995 a total of 1,476,100 arrests for drug-law violations, a 65% increase since 1986. More than a third of those arrests—some 503,000—were for marijuana possession: more than the combined total of arrests for murder, manslaughter, robbery, rape, arson, and all sex offenses including prostitution.

This zealous drug war helps explain why nearly one of every 150 persons in this country is in jail or prison, why state prisons are operating at between 15% and 24% above capacity and the federal prison system at 19% above capacity, and why an American born this year stands a one in twenty chance of spending some part of life in a correctional facility—a one in four chance if that American is black. But the drug war is only part of the explanation. One must also take into account the general increase in harshness, punitiveness, and "tough on crime" policies that has been rampant since the decline of therapeutic rehabilitation.

Consider, for example, the spread of "three-strikes" laws designed to impose greatly increased

prison terms on recidivists. Since Washington state pioneered the concept in 1993, twenty-two other states have passed some form of three-strikes law. California's is the most draconian, requiring a twenty-five-year-to-life sentence for any third felony as long as the two priors were "violent" or "serious." As of July 1998 nearly a quarter of California's prisoners were serving terms for second or third strikes. Despite a $5 billion investment in a massive prison-building program over the last fifteen years, the California system is more overcrowded now than it was before.

Consider, too, the spread of mandatory minimum sentencing laws. Every state has now enacted some law of this type. Federal law includes about sixty such statutes, several of which have real bite. Most notorious, perhaps, is the law that imposes a mandatory ten-year minimum prison sentence for trafficking in 5000 grams of powder cocaine or 50 grams of crack, and a mandatory five-year term for 500 grams of powder or 5 grams of crack. There is little evidence in the legislative history that this 100-to-1 disparity was adopted on rational grounds. Furthermore, there is little scientific support for the disparity, and the U.S. Sentencing Commission has called for its abolition. Yet the disparity survives, and because over 90% of federal crack defendants are black while almost half the powder cocaine defendants are white, this anomaly helps explain why there were, at the end of 1996, 1571 sentenced black inmates per 100,000 blacks in the United States compared to 193 white inmates per 100,000 whites.

There are other ways in which American punishment practices have grown harsher over the last three decades. Twenty states have eliminated parole release, and many states, responding to federal incentives, now require prisoners to serve at least 85% of their sentences. Thirty-five states have made it easier to transfer juveniles to adult courts, either by adding specific offenses that can result in such a transfer or by lowering the upper age limit of juvenile court jurisdiction. The federal government's decade-old sentencing guidelines authorize increasing a defendant's sentence on the basis of crimes with which he was never charged, and even crimes of which he was acquitted, as long as the sentencing judge—not a jury—finds by a preponderance of the evidence—not beyond a reasonable doubt—that the defendant committed these crimes.

The most dramatic sign of America's turn toward harsher punishment, however, has to be the contemporary revival of the death penalty. From 1968 through 1976, not a single execution took place in this country, as capital punishment underwent a series of legal challenges that it ultimately withstood. Executions had been declining during the fifties and sixties, and a public-opinion poll in July 1966 had found only 42% of respondents favoring death for convicted murderers, with 47% opposed. Similar polls nowadays routinely report 70% to 80% of Americans favoring capital punishment, and since George Pataki defeated Mario Cuomo for the New York governorship in 1994 on a pro-death-penalty platform, it is rare to find an American politician opposing capital punishment. From the time executions resumed in January 1977 through the end of last year, an even 500 persons had been put to death in the United States. Most astoundingly, as of April 1, 1999, there were 3565 inmates under sentence of death in American prisons—a number more than twice as great as the total number of persons executed in this country in the fifty years of my life to date!

When I remarked earlier that punishment has become an impressive growth industry, I had in mind more than the stirring output statistics with which I have been bombarding you, however. There is, for example, the growth of privately owned prisons. Some 120 prisons and jails, including some under construction, are now privately run, and the number of inmates in these facilities rose from 3000 in 1987 to more than 85,000 in 1996. The stock price of the nation's largest private jailer, the Corrections Corporation of America, has increased tenfold since 1994. On the other hand, there is the increasing clout of unions representing prison guards—the fastest-growing public employee associations in many states, which generally oppose private prisons because they employ nonunion labor. In California, the California Correctional Peace Officers Association sustained some unpleasant publicity from its efforts to derail a state investigation into alleged abuses at Pelican Bay, the state's highest-security prison. But the association doubled its membership in the past decade and, according to one recent report, "made deft use of a staggering $4.5 million in bipartisan political contributions" to win support in last year's state elections.

I imagine I have said more than enough to drive home the point that criminal punishment in this country today is a thriving activity with a powerful impact on the shape and spirit of our national life. What adds to the timeliness of the present [discussion], even as it complicates any effort at prognostication, is the changing nature of our punishment practices. Let me just mention two aspects of these changes: the blurring of the borderline between criminal punishment and noncriminal methods of responding to offenders, and the rise in popularity of nontraditional, unusual modes of punishment, often with a strong component of public shaming.

In theory, punishment is imposed through the distinctive mechanism of the criminal law, with its array of special procedural protections for those who find themselves exposed to this most coercive exercise of official power. But in practice the strength of the criminal-civil distinction appears to be eroding. One striking illustration of this trend is the phenomenal expansion, over the last three decades, of the use of civil property forfeiture as a tool against drug criminals. From a 1970 federal statute authorizing the seizure and forfeiture of drugs, drug-manufacturing and storage equipment, and conveyances used to transport drugs, anti-drug forfeiture provisions have grown to include proceeds traceable to drug transactions as well as real property "used, or intended to be used" in drug felonies. Because forfeiture proceedings are classified as "civil," they offer a way to impose what for all intents and purposes is a punishment, often a severe one, on suspected drug offenders even where the evidence is insufficient to allow a criminal conviction—indeed, even in cases where the property owner has been tried and acquitted. There is no presumption of innocence, no right to appointed counsel, no proof beyond a reasonable doubt: Once the government establishes probable cause that the property is subject to forfeiture, the burden is on the property owner to prove by a preponderance of the evidence that the property has not been used for criminal purposes.

Another example of the erosion of the criminal-civil distinction can be found in the spread of "sexually violent predator" laws, enacted in sixteen states in recent years. These statutes allow states to confine "sexually violent predators" after they have served their sentences. In *Kansas v. Hendricks*,[10] the Supreme Court upheld the application of such a statute to a repeat child molester who was nearing the end of his criminal sentence when the state secured his indefinite confinement in the psychiatric wing of the prison hospital. The Court held this commitment not to be "punishment"— and hence neither an ex post facto measure nor a double jeopardy violation—even though the preamble to the Kansas statute itself explained that it applied to persons who did not have the kind of mental disorder that would qualify them for traditional civil commitment, and whose personality disorders "are unamenable to existing treatment modalities." The Court stated that confining such a person would be nonpunitive even on the assumption that there was in fact no treatment at all for his condition.

As for nontraditional, "creative" punishments, a recent Op-Ed piece in the New York Times offered a number of provocative examples of "shaming" penalties imposed as conditions of probation. A California judge required a burglar to wear a T-shirt proclaiming "I am a felon on probation for theft"; an Illinois farmer convicted of assault had to erect a sign warning "A Violent Felon Lives Here"; Arkansas and Wisconsin judges have had shoplifters stand in front of stores with signs admitting their crimes; a Florida woman was ordered to take out an advertisement in her local paper confessing that she had bought drugs in front of her children; and a Long Island drunk driver was made to display a license plate branding him a convicted felon. And let us not forget the revival of the chain gang in recent years in Florida, Alabama, and Lewis County, Washington—nor the California statute conditioning parole for repeat child molesters on "chemical castration."

To sum it up: Criminal punishment is an institution that is large, growing, and quite possibly mutating into new and surprising forms. . . .

From Jeremy Bentham, *An Introduction to the Principles of Morals and Legislation* (London: W. Pickering, 1823), Chapter 1.

Endnotes

[1] Francis A. Allen, *The Decline of the Rehabilitative Ideal: Penal Policy and Social Purpose* 6 (1981).

[2] *Williams v. New York*, 337 U.S. 241, 248, 249 (1949).

[3] American Friends Service Committee, *Struggle for Justice* 83 (1971).

[4] See Jeffrie G. Murphy, *Introduction to Punishment and Rehabilitation* 10 n.6 (Jeffrie G. Murphy ed., 1973).

[5] Karl Menninger, *The Crime of Punishment* (1968).

[6] H. L. A. Hart, *Punishment and Responsibility: Essays in the Philosophy of Law* 158 (1968).

[7] *Id.* at 159.

[8] John Braithwaite and Philip Pettit, *Not Just Deserts: A Republican Theory of Criminal Justice* 4 (1990).

[9] David Dolinko, "Three Mistakes of Retributivism," 39 *UCLA L. Rev.* 1623 (1992).

[10] 521 U.S. 346 (1997).

A Utilitarian Theory of Punishment

Jeremy Bentham

I. *Cases Unmeet for Punishment*

General View of Cases Unmeet for Punishment

The general object which all laws have, or ought to have, in common, is to augment the total happiness of the community; and therefore, in the first place, to exclude, as far as may be, every thing that tends to subtract from that happiness: in other words, to exclude mischief.

But all punishment is mischief: all punishment in itself is evil. Upon the principle of utility, if it ought at all to be admitted, it ought only to be admitted in as far as it promises to exclude some greater evil.

It is plain, therefore, that in the following cases punishment ought not to be inflicted.

1. Where it is *groundless;* where there is no mischief for it to prevent; the act not being mischievous upon the whole.

2. Where it must be *inefficacious;* where it cannot act so as to prevent the mischief.

3. Where it is *unprofitable,* or too *expensive;* where the mischief it would produce would be greater than what it prevented.

4. Where it is *needless;* where the mischief may be prevented, or cease of itself, without it; that is, at a cheaper rate.

Cases in Which Punishment Is Groundless

These are,

(1) Where there has never been any mischief: where no mischief has been produced to any body by the act in question. Of this number are those in which the act was such as might, on some occasions, be mischievous or disagreeable, but the person whose interest it concerns gave his *consent* to the performance of it. This consent, provided it be free, and fairly obtained, is the best proof that can be produced, that, to the person who gives it, no mischief, at least no immediate mischief, upon the whole, is done. For no man can be so good a judge as the man himself, what it is gives him pleasure or displeasure.

(2) Where the mischief was *outweighed:* although a mischief was produced by that act, yet the same act was necessary to the production of a benefit which was of greater value than the mischief. This may be the case with any thing that is done in the way of precaution against instant calamity, as also with any thing that is done in the exercise of the several sorts of powers necessary to be established in every community, to wit, domestic, judicial, military, and supreme.

(3) Where there is a certainty of an adequate compensation; and that in all cases where the offense can be committed. This supposes two things: 1. That the offense is such as admits of an adequate compensation; 2. That such a compensation is sure to be forthcoming. Of these suppositions, the latter will be found to be a merely ideal one: a supposition that cannot, in the universality here given to it, be verified by fact. It cannot, therefore, in practice, be numbered amongst the grounds of absolute impunity. It may, however, be admitted as a ground for an abatement of that punishment, which other considerations, standing by themselves, would seem to dictate.

Cases in Which Punishment Must be Inefficacious

These are,

(1) Where the penal provision is *not established* until after the act is done. Such are the cases, 1. Of an *ex-post-facto* law; where the legislator himself appoints not a punishment till after the act is done; 2. Of a sentence beyond the law; where the judge, of his own authority, appoints a punishment which the legislator had not appointed.

(2) Where the penal provision, though established, in *not conveyed* to the notice of the person on whom it seems intended that it should operate. Such is the case where the law has omitted to employ any of the expedients which are necessary, to make sure that every person whatsoever, who is within the reach of the law, be apprized of all the cases whatsoever, in which (being in the station of life he is in) he can be subjected to the penalties of the law.

(3) Where the penal provision, though it were conveyed to a man's notice, *could produce no effect* on him, with respect to the preventing him from engaging in any act of the *sort* in question. Such is the case, 1. In extreme *infancy;* where a man has not yet attained that state or disposition of mind in which the prospect of evils so distant as those which are held forth by the law, has the effect of influencing his conduct; 2. In *insanity;* where the person, if he has attained to that disposition, has since been deprived of it through the influence of some permanent though unseen cause; 3. In *intoxication;* where he has been deprived of it by the transient influence of a visible cause; such as the use of wine, or opium, or other drugs, that act in this manner on the nervous system; which condition is indeed neither more nor less than a temporary insanity produced by an assignable cause.

(4) Where the penal provision (although, being conveyed to the party's notice, it might very well prevent his engaging in acts of the sort in question, provided he knew that it related to those acts) could not have this effect, with regard to the *individual* act he is about to engage in: to wit, because he knows not that it is of the number of those to which the penal provision relates. This may happen 1. In the case of *unintentionality;* where he intends not to engage, and thereby knows not that he is about to engage, in the *act* in which eventually he is about to engage; 2. In the case of *unconsciousness;* where, although he may know that he is about to engage in the *act* itself, yet, from not knowing all the material *circumstances* attending it, he knows not of the *tendency* it has to produce that mischief, in contemplation of which it has been made penal in most instances; 3. In the case of *missupposal;* where, although he may know of the tendency the act has to produce that degree of mischief, he supposes it, though mistakenly, to be attended with some circumstances, or set of circumstances, which, if it had been attended with, it would either not have been productive of that mischief, or have been productive of such a greater degree of good, as he determined the legislator in such a case not to make it penal.

(5) Where, though the penal clause might exercise a full and prevailing influence, were it to act alone, yet by the *predominant* influence of some opposite cause upon the will, it must necessarily be ineffectual; because the

evil which he sees himself about to undergo, in the case of his *not* engaging in the act, is so great, that the evil denounced by the penal clause, in case of his engaging in it, cannot appear greater. This may happen, 1. In the case of *physical danger;* where the evil is such as appears likely to be brought about by the unassisted powers of *nature;* 2. In the case of a *threatened mischief;* where it is such as appears likely to be brought about through the intentional and conscious agency of *man.*

(6) Where (though the penal clause may exert a full and prevailing influence over the *will* of the party) yet his *physical faculties* (owing to the predominant influence of some physical clause) are not in a condition to follow the determination of the will insomuch that the act is absolutely *involuntary.* Such is the case of physical *compulsion* or *restraint,* by whatever means brought about; where the man's hand, for instance, is pushed against some object which his will disposes him *not* to touch; or tied down from touching some object which his will disposes him to touch.

Cases Where Punishment is Unprofitable

These are,

(1) Where, on the one hand, the nature of the offense, on the other hand, that of the punishment, are, *in the ordinary state of things,* such, that when compared together, the evil of the latter will turn out to be greater than that of the former.

Now the evil of the punishment divides itself into four branches, by which so many different sets of persons are affected. 1. The evil of *coercion* or *restraint;* or the pain which it gives a man not to be able to do the act, whatever it be, which by the apprehension of the punishment he is deterred from doing. This is felt by those by whom the law is *observed;* 2. The evil of *apprehension;* or the pain which a man, who has exposed himself to punishment, feels at the thoughts of undergoing it. This is felt by those by whom the law has been *broken,* and who feel themselves in *danger* of its being executed upon them; 3. The evil of *sufferance;* or the pain which a man feels, in virtue of the punishment itself, from the time when he begins to undergo it. This is felt by those by whom the law is broken, and upon whom it comes actually to be executed; 4. The pain of sympathy, and the other *derivative* evils resulting to the persons who are in *connection* with the several classes of original sufferers just mentioned. Now of these four lots of evil, the first will be

greater or less, according to the nature of the punishment which stands annexed to that offense.

On the other hand, as to the evil of the offense, this will also, of course, be greater or less, according to the nature of each offense. The proportion between the one evil and the other will therefore be different in the case of each particular offense. The cases, therefore, where punishment in unprofitable on this ground, can by no other means be discovered, than by an examination of each particular offense; which is what will be the business of the body of the work.

(2) Where, although in the *ordinary state* of things, the evil resulting from the punishment is not greater than the benefit which is likely to result from the force with which it operates, during the same space of time, towards the excluding the evil of the offense, yet it may have been rendered so by the influence of some *occasional circumstances.* In the number of these circumstances may be, 1. The multitude of delinquents at a particular juncture; being such as would increase, beyond the ordinary measure, the *quantum* of the second and third lots, and thereby also of a part of the fourth lot, in the evil of the punishment; 2. The extraordinary value of the services of some one delinquent; in the case where the effect of the punishment would be to deprive the community of the benefit of those services; 3. The displeasure of the *people;* that is, of an indefinite number of the members of the *same* community, in cases where (owing to the influence of some occasional incident) they happen to conceive, that the offense or the offender ought not to be punished at all, or at least ought not to be punished in the way in question; 4. The displeasure of *foreign powers;* that is, of the governing body, or a considerable number of the members of some *foreign* community or communities, with which the community in question, is connected.

Cases Where Punishment is Needless

These are,

(1) Where the purpose of putting an end to the practice may be attained as effectually at a cheaper rate; by instruction, for instance, as well as by terror; by informing the understanding, as well as by exercising an immediate influence on the will. This seems to be the case with respect to all those offenses which consist in the disseminating pernicious principles in matters of *duty;* of whatever kind the duty be; whether political, or

moral, or religious. And this, whether such principles be disseminated *under,* or even *without,* a sincere persuasion of their being beneficial. I say, even *without;* for though in such a case it is not instruction that can prevent the writer from endeavoring to inculcate his principles, yet it may [prevent] the readers from adopting them; without which, his endeavoring to inculcate them will do no harm. In such a case, the sovereign will commonly have little need to take an active part; if it be the interest of *one* individual to inculcate principles that are pernicious, it will as surely be the interest of *other* individuals to expose them. But if the sovereign must needs take a part in the controversy, the pen is the proper weapon to combat error with, not the sword.

II. *Of the Proportion Between Punishments and Offenses*

We have seen that the general object of all laws is to prevent mischief; that is to say, when it is worth while; but that, where there are no other means of doing this than punishment, there are four cases in which it is *not* worth while.

When it *is* worth while, there are four subordinate designs or objects, which, in the course of his endeavors to compass, as far as may be, that one general object, a legislator, whose views are governed by the principle of utility, comes naturally to propose to himself.

1. His first, most extensive, and most eligible object, is to prevent, in as far as it is possible, and worth while, all sorts of offenses whatsoever; in other words, so to manage, that no offense whatsoever may be committed.

2. But if a man must needs commit an offense of some kind or other, the next object is to induce him to commit an offense *less* mischievous, *rather* than one *more* mischievous; in other words, to choose always the *least* mischievous, of two offenses that will either of them suit his purpose.

3. When a man has resolved upon a particular offense, the next object is to dispose him to do *no more* mischief than is *necessary* to his purpose; in other words, to do as little mischief as is consistent with the benefit he has in view.

4. The last object is, whatever the mischief be, which it is proposed to prevent, to prevent it at as *cheap* a rate as possible.

Subservient to these four objects, or purposes, must be the rules or canons by which the proportion of punishments to offenses is to be governed.

The first object, it has been seen, is to prevent, in as far as it is worth while, all sorts of offenses; therefore,

> *The value of the punishment must not be less in any case than what is sufficient to outweigh that of the profit of the offense.*

If it be, the offense (unless some other considerations, independent of the punishment, should intervene and operate efficaciously in the character of tutelary motives) will be sure to be committed not withstanding; the whole lot of punishment will be thrown away; it will be altogether *inefficacious.*

The above rule has been often objected to, on account of its seeming harshness; but this can only have happened for want of its being properly understood. The strength of the temptation, *caeteris paribus,* is as the profit of the offense; the quantum of the punishment must rise with the profit of the offense; *caeteris paribus,* it must therefore rise with the strength of the temptation. This there is no disputing. True it is, that the stronger the temptation, the less conclusive is the indication which the act of delinquency affords of the depravity of the offender's disposition. So far then as the absence of any aggravation, arising from extraordinary depravity of disposition, may operate, or at the utmost, so far as the presence of a ground of extenuation, resulting from the innocence or beneficence of the offender's disposition, can operate, the strength of the temptation may operate in abatement of the demand for punishment. But it can never operate so far as to indicate the propriety of making the punishment ineffectual, which it is sure to be when brought below the level of the apparent profit of the offense.

The partial benevolence which should prevail for the reduction of it below this level, would counteract as well those purposes which such a motive would actually have in view, as those more extensive purposes which benevolence ought to have in view; it would be cruelty not only to the public, but to the very persons in whose behalf it pleads; in its effects, I mean, however opposite in its intention. Cruelty to the public, that is cruelty to the innocent, by suffering them, for want of an adequate protection, to lie exposed to the mischief of the offense; cruelty even to the offender himself, by punishing him to no purpose, and without the chance of compassing that beneficial end, by which alone the introduction of the evil of punishment is to be justified.

But whether a given offense shall be prevented in a given degree by a given quantity of punishment, is never any thing better than a chance; for the purchasing of which, whatever punishment is employed, is so much expended in advance. However, for the sake of giving it the better chance of outweighing the profit of the offense,

The greater the mischief of the offense, the greater is the expense, which it may be worth while to be at, in the way of punishment.

The next object is, to induce a man to choose always the least mischievous of two offenses; therefore

Where two offenses come in competition, the punishment for the greater offense must be sufficient to induce a man to prefer the less.

When a man has resolved upon a particular offense, the next object is, to induce him to do no more mischief than what is necessary for his purpose; therefore

The punishment should be adjusted in such manner to each particular offense, that for every part of the mischief there may be a motive to restrain the offender from giving birth to it.

The last object is, whatever mischief is guarded against, to guard against it at as cheap a rate as possible; therefore

The punishment ought in no case to be more than what is necessary to bring it into conformity with the rules here given.

It is further to be observed, that owing to the different manners and degrees in which persons under different circumstances are affected by the same exciting cause, a punishment which is the same in name will not always either really produce, or even so much as appear to others to produce, in two different persons the same degree of pain; therefore,

That the quantity actually inflicted on each individual offender may correspond to the quantity intended for similar offenders in general, the several circumstances influencing sensibility ought always to be taken into account.

Of the above rules of proportion, the four first, we may perceive, serve to mark out the limits on the side of diminution; the limits *below* which a punishment ought not to be *diminished*; the fifth, the limits on the side of increase; the limits *above* which it ought not to be *increased*. The five first are calculated to serve as guides to the legislator; the sixth is calculated, in some measure, indeed, for the same purpose; but principally for guiding the judge in his endeavors to conform, on both sides, to the intentions of the legislator.

. . .

The Argument for Retributivism

Michael Moore

A Taxonomy of Purposes of Punishment

The Prima Facie Justifications of Punishment

. . .

Retributivism, the final theory used to justify punishment, is the view that punishment is justified by the

From *Law and Psychiatry: Rethinking the Relationship* (Cambridge: Cambridge University Press, 1984): 233–243. Reprinted with permission of the author.

desert of the offender. The good that is achieved by punishing, in this view, has nothing to do with future states of affairs, such as the prevention of crime or the maintenance of social cohesion. Rather, the good that punishment achieves is that someone who deserves it gets it.

Retributivism is quite distinct from a view that urges that punishment is justified because a majority of citizens feel that offenders should be punished. Rather, retributivism is a species of objectivism in ethics that asserts that there is such a thing as desert and that the presence of such a (real) moral quality in a person justifies punishment of that person. What a populace may think or feel about vengeance on an offender is one thing; what treatment an offender deserves is another. And it is only this last notion that is relevant to retributivism.

Retributivism is also distinct from what it sometimes called "revenge utilitarianism." This is the view that the state must punish because private citizens otherwise will take the law into their own hands and that such private vengeance leads to chaos and disorder. Punishment in such a view is justified by its ability to prevent these bad things. Retributivism has nothing to do with this essentially forward-looking justification. Moreover, this "prevention of private vengeance" theory is to my mind not even a prima facie justifying reason for punishment. The obvious thing to do if citizens are going to violate the law by taking it into their own hands, is to deter those citizens by punishing them, not by punishing someone else. It places retributivism in an unnecessarily bad light to think that it justifies punishment only because of the shadow cast by a threat of illegal violence by vengeful citizens.

The Two Pure Theories of Punishment

It is common to reduce the survivors on this list of prima facie justifications of punishment to two general theories, the utilitarian theory and the retributive theory. To see how this is done, one need only consider the good state of affairs that is to be achieved by incarceration, special deterrence, general deterrence, and rehabilitation (to the extent that it is of the first sort of rehabilitative theory, and not the second). For all four of these rationales for punishment share the prevention of crime as the beneficial end that justifies punishment. In each case, the ultimate justification for inflicting the harm of punishment is that it is outweighed by the good to be achieved, namely, the prevention of future crimes by that offender or by others. This justification of an institution by the social welfare it will enhance make all such theories instances of the utilitarian theory of punishment.

Thus, the denunciation theory of punishment is a second kind of utilitarian theory of punishment, insofar as the good it seeks to achieve is not simply the prevention of crime. To the extent one grants intrinsic value to social cohesion, and does not regard that as a value only because it contributes to the maintenance of public order, the denunciation theory can be distinguished from the other utilitarian theories just considered by the differing social good it seeks to achieve.

Nonetheless, it is still a utilitarian theory, since it outweighs the harm that is punishment by some form of net social gain that punishment achieves.

Both crime prevention and the maintenance of social cohesion are types of collective good. The general utilitarian theory of punishment is one that combines these and other forms of collective good that punishment might achieve, and calls them all a "social gain." Whenever the social gain outweighs the harm punishment causes to offenders or their families, such a theory would say that there is a net social gain. Such a vocabulary allows us a succinct definition of any form of utilitarian theory: Punishment is justified if and only if some net social gain is achieved by it.

A retributivist theory is necessarily nonutilitarian in character, for it eschews justifying punishment by its tendency to achieve any form of net social gain. Rather, retributivism asserts that punishment is properly inflicted because, and only because, the person deserves it. That some people deserve punishment in such a theory is both a necessary and a sufficient condition justifying criminal sanctions. A succinct definition of the retributivist theory of punishment, paralleling that given of the utilitarian theory, is that punishment is justified if and only if the persons receiving it deserve it.

The Mixed Theory of Punishment

Once one grants that there are two sorts of prima facie justifications of punishment—effecting a net social gain (utilitarian) and giving just deserts (retributivist)—one can also see that in addition to the two pure theories of punishment there can also be mixed theories. There are two logically possible mixed theories, although only one of these merits any serious attention. There is first of all the popular form of mixed theory that asserts that punishment is justified if and only if it achieves a net social gain *and* is given to offenders who deserve it. Giving just deserts and achieving a net social gain, in such a case, are each individually necessary but only jointly sufficient conditions justifying punishment. The second logically possible mixed theory would be one asserting that punishment is justified if and only if it achieves a net social gain, *or* if it is given to offenders who deserve it. Such a theory has no name, because there is no one, to my knowledge, who has ever adopted it. Such a theory is unnamed and unclaimed because it shares the defects of each of the pure theories, utilitarianism and retributivism. I shall accordingly put this "mixed theory" aside from further consideration.

The first kind of mixed theory itself has two branches. By far the most usual and popular form of the theory asserts that we do not punish people *because* they deserve it. Desert enters in, this theory further asserts, only as a limit on punishment: We punish offenders *because* some net social gain is achieved, such as the prevention of crime, but only if such offenders deserve it. It is, in other words, the achieving of a net social gain that justifies punishment, whereas the desert of offenders serves as a limiting condition on punishment but as not part of its justification. The alternative branch of the mixed theory is just the converse: One would urge that we punish *because* offenders deserve it, but *only if* some net social gain is achieved by doing so. In such a case, the roles of net social gain and desert are simply reversed: Giving offenders their just deserts serves as the justification of punishment, and the achieving of a net social gain as the limiting condition.

A cynic might view these two branches of the mixed theory as nothing more than an uncomfortable shuffle by mixed theorists. When accused of barbarism for punishing persons for retributivist reasons, they assert the first branch of the theory (they punish not because some persons deserve it, but because of a collective good that is achieved). When accused of immorality for imposing harsh treatment on someone as a means of making everyone else better off, such theorists shift to the other foot, and claim they do not punish someone to achieve a net social gain, but only to give offenders their just deserts. The cynic has a point here, because there is a sense in which the two branches of the theory are the same, namely, the sense that they justify exactly the same kinds of treatment for all cases. The only difference in theories is in the motivations of those who hold them. And while that may make a difference in our moral judgments of those who hold the different branches of the mixed theory of punishment, it does not make a difference in terms of the actual social institutions and judgments such theories will justify. I shall accordingly lump both of these branches together and call them the mixed theory of punishment.

The Argument for Retributivism

The Argument Against the Pure Utilitarian Theory

In exploring one's thoughts about punishment, it is perhaps easiest to start with some standard kinds of thought experiments directed against a pure utilitarian theory of punishment. A thought experiment is essentially a device allowing one to sort out one's true reasons for believing that certain propositions are true. To be successful, such a thought experiment need not involve any actual case or state of affairs, nor need the cases envisioned even be very likely; they only need be conceivable in order to test our own thoughts.

It is standard fare in the philosophy of punishment to assert, by way of several thought experiments, counterexamples to the utilitarian thesis that punishment is justified if and only if some net social gain is achieved. I mention only two such counterexamples: scapegoating and preventive detention. With regard to the first, it might be recalled that D. B. Cooper successfully skyjacked an aircraft some years ago, and that this successful, unsolved crime apparently encouraged the mass of skyjackings that have cost so much in terms of dollars, lives, and convenience. Cooper wore large sunglasses in his escapade, and there was accordingly only a very limited description available of him. Imagine that shortly after his skyjacking we had the benefit of the knowledge we now have by hindsight, and we decided that it would be better to punish someone who looked like Cooper (and who had no good alibi) in order to convince others that skyjacking did not pay. For a consistent utilitarian, there is a net social gain that would be achieved by punishing such an innocent person, and there is no a priori reason that the net social gain in such a case might not outweigh the harm that is achieved by punishing an innocent person.

The preventive detention kind of counterexample is very similar: Imagine that a psychiatrist discovers that a patient has extremely dangerous propensities. The patient is also the accused in a criminal trial. It turns out, however, that the accused is not guilty of the crime for which he is charged and in fact has committed no crime whatsoever. Should a judge who, we may suppose, is the only one who knows that the man is both dangerous and innocent find the accused guilty? Doing so will prevent the defendant's predicted criminal behavior because he will be incarcerated. In a utilitarian theory, it is difficult to see why such a judgment would not be perfectly appropriate, as long as the prediction is reliable enough, and as long as the crimes predicted are sufficiently serious that the good of their prevention outweighs the harm of punishing that person, even though he has committed no crime as yet.

The general form of the argument arising from these kinds of thought experiments is that of a reductio ad absurdum argument. The argument has three premises:

1. Punishment should be inflicted if and only if doing so achieves a net social gain.

2. A net social gain would be achieved in this case by the infliction of punishment.

3. Punishment should not be inflicted in this case.

Each of these premises corresponds to steps in both of the foregoing thought experiments. The first premise is simply a restatement of the utilitarian theory of punishment. The second premise presupposes that there are some cases where a net social gain can be achieved by punishing an innocent person and asserts that this is such a case. The third premise asserts our intuition that such persons ought not to be punished.

All three premises together yield a contradiction:

4. Punishment should not be inflicted and punishment should be inflicted.

The first two premises have as their joint conclusion that the person should be punished; this conclusion, when conjoined with the third premise, produces the contradictory conclusion.

The strongest possible form of a reductio ad absurdum argument is one that ends in a formal contradiction. To avoid the contradiction, there are only three possibilities, corresponding to each of the three premises. One could give up the third premise and simply admit that in such cases the persons should be punished, despite their innocence. This move is a rather implausible one, inasmuch as it commits one to admitting that one will punish an entirely innocent person. The second possibility is to deny that there will be cases where there will be a net social gain from punishing an innocent person. This move is usually associated with the name of rule utilitarianism and involves the idea that one cannot make a general practice of punishing the innocent, because then the harm of so doing (in terms of demoralization costs in society and the like) will outweigh any possible good to be achieved, even the prevention of skyjacking. The problem with this response, popular as it is, is that it fails to deal fairly with the nature of the thought experiment. That is, suppose there are some risks of detection of punishment of innocent persons, and, thus, some risks of demoralization costs; such risk will only allow utilitarians to say that the number of cases in which punishment of the innocent will maximize utility is somewhat diminished. It does not foreclose as somehow impossible that there are such cases. Such cases are conceivable, and if in them one is still not willing to punish, one thereby shows oneself not to be a utilitarian about punishment.

This brings us to the third possibility: One can simply give up the first premise, that is, one can repudiate the utilitarian theory of punishment. Such thought experiments, I think, when clearly conceived and executed, show almost all of us that we are not pure utilitarians about punishment.

Arguments Against the Mixed Theory of Punishment

The arguments against the pure utilitarian theory of punishment do not by themselves drive one into retributivism. For one can alleviate the injustice of the pure utilitarian theory of punishment by adopting the mixed theory. Since under the mixed theory the desert of the offender is a necessary condition of punishment, it will follow from the mixed theory that in each of the kinds of counterexamples considered (where punishment is not deserved), punishment should not be given. No contradictions will be generated, because the premises are consistent:

1. Punishment should be inflicted if and only if doing so achieves both a net social gain and gives an offender his just deserts.

2. A net social gain would be achieved in this case by the infliction of punishment.

3. It is not the case that punishment would give an offender his just deserts in this case.

4. Punishment should not be inflicted.

From the first three of these premises, the conclusion is deducible that there should be no punishment. This is also what the fourth premise asserts, so that there is no contradiction when one substitutes the mixed theory for the utilitarian theory of punishment.

There is, nonetheless, another sort of thought experiment that tests whether one truly believes the mixed theory, or is in fact a pure retributivist. Such thought experiments are the kind that fill the editorial pages where outrage is expressed at the lightness of sentence in a particular case, or the lightness of sentencing generally in the courts of some communities. An example is provided by *State v. Chaney* wherein the defendant was tried and convicted of two counts of forcible rape and one count of robbery. The defendant and a companion had picked up the prostitute at a downtown location in Anchorage. After driving the victim around in their car, the defendant and his companion beat her and forcibly raped her four times, also forcing her to perform an act of fellatio with the defendant's companion.

During this same period of time, the victim's money was removed from her purse, and she only then was allowed to leave the vehicle after dire threats of reprisals if she attempted to report the incident to the police.

Despite this horrendous series of events, the trial judge imposed the minimum sentence on the defendant for each of the three counts and went out of his way to remark that he (the trial judge) was "sorry that the (military) regulations would not permit keeping (defendant) in the service if he wanted to stay because it seems to me that is a better setup for everybody concerned than putting him in the penitentiary." The trial judge also mentioned that as far as he was concerned, there would be no problem for the defendant to be paroled on the very first day of his sentence, if the parole board should so decide. The sentence was appealed by the state under a special Alaska procedure, and the attorney general urged the Alaska Supreme Court to disapprove the sentence.

The thought experiment such a case begins to pose for us is as follows: Imagine in such a case that after the rape but before sentencing the defendant has gotten into an accident so that his sexual desires are dampened to such an extent that he presents no further danger of rape; if money is also one of his problems, suppose further that he has inherited a great deal of money, so that he no longer needs to rob. Suppose, because of both of these facts, we are reasonably certain that he does not present a danger of either forcible assault, rape, robbery, or related crimes in the future. Since Chaney is (by hypothesis) not dangerous, he does not need to be incapacitated, specially deterred, or reformed. Suppose further that we could successfully pretend to punish Chaney, instead of actually punishing him, and that no one is at all likely to find out. Our pretending to punish him will thus serve the needs of general deterrence and maintain social cohesion, and the cost to the state will be less than if it actually did punish him. Is there anything in the mixed theory of punishment that would urge that Chaney nonetheless should really be punished? I think not, so that if one's conclusion is that Chaney and people like him nonetheless should be punished, one will have to give up the mixed theory of punishment.

The argument structure is again that of a reductio and is as follows:

1. Punishment should be inflicted if and only if doing so both achieves a net social gain and gives an offender his just deserts.

2. A net social gain would not be achieved in this case by the infliction of punishment.

3. Punishment should be inflicted.

Again, these three premises generate a contradiction:

4. Punishment should not be inflicted and punishment should be inflicted.

From the first two premises, it follows that there should be no punishment; this contradicts the third premise that there nonetheless should be punishment.

One again has the choice of giving up one of the three premises of the argument. To give up the third premise is very unappealing to most people; doing so requires that people like Chaney should not be punished at all. Again, the tempting move is to assert that there will be no cases in which one will be sure enough that the danger is removed, or the ends of general deterrence served, that one can ever successfully assert the second premise. But as in the earlier case, this is simply to misunderstand the nature of the thought experiment. One only need think it conceivable that such dangers could be removed, or such ends of deterrence served, in order to test one's theory of punishment. And nothing in utilitarianism can guarantee that utility is always maximized by the punishment of the guilty. The only other way to avoid the contradiction is to give up the first premise. Yet this means that one would have to give up the mixed theory of punishment.

The Argument for Retributivism

If one follows the predicted paths through these thought experiments, the end result is that one finds oneself, perhaps surprisingly, to be a retributivist. We might call this an argument through the back door for retributivism, because the argument does not assert in any positive way the correctness of retributivism. It only asserts that the two theories of punishment truly competitive with retributivism, namely, the pure utilitarian theory and the mixed theory, are each unacceptable to us. That leaves retributivism as the only remaining theory of punishment we can accept.

It has seemed to some theorists that there is a limited amount of positive argument that can be given in favor of a retributivist theory and still have the theory remain truly retributivist. Hugo Bedau has recently reminded us, for example, that the retributivist faces a familiar dilemma:

Either he appeals to something else—some good end—that is accomplished by the practice of punishment, in which case he is open to the criticism that he has nonretributivist, consequentialist justification for the practice of punishment. Or his justification does not appeal to something else, in which case it is open to the criticism that is circular and futile.[1]

In this respect, however, retributivism is no worse off than any other nonutilitarian theories in ethics, each of which seeks to justify an institution or practice not by the good consequences it may engender, but rather by the inherent rightness of the practice. The justification for any such theories is one that appeals to both our particular judgments and our more general principles, in order to show that the theory fits judgments that on reflection we are sure of, and principles that on reflection we are proud of.

. . .

Endnote

[1] Hugo Bedau, "Retribution and the Theory of Punishment," *Journal of Philosophy*, Vol. 75 (1978): 601–620.

Punishment and Responsibility

H. L. A. HART

Many are now troubled by the suspicion that the view that there is just one supreme value or objective (e.g., Deterrence, Retribution or Reform) in terms of which *all* questions about the justification of punishment are to be answered, is somehow wrong; yet, from what is said on such occasions no clear account of what the different values or objectives are, or how they fit together in the justification of punishment, can be extracted. . . .

. . . It is likely that in our inherited ways of talking or thinking about punishment there is some persistent drive towards an over-simplification of multiple issues which require separate consideration. To counter this drive what is most needed is *not* the simple admission that instead of a single value or aim (Deterrence, Retribution, Reform or any other) a plurality of different values and aims should be given as a conjunctive answer to some *single* question concerning the justification of punishment. What is needed is the realization that different principles (each of which may in a sense be called a "justification") are relevant at different points in any morally acceptable account of punishment. What we should look for are answers to a number of different questions such as: What justifies the general practice of punishment? To whom may punishment be applied? How severely may we punish? In dealing with these and other questions concerning punishment we should bear in mind that in this, as in most other social institutions, the pursuit of one aim may be qualified by or provide an opportunity, not to be missed, for the pursuit of others. Till we have developed this sense of the complexity of punishment (and this prolegomenon aims only to do this) we shall be in no fit state to assess the extent to which the whole institution has been eroded by, or needs to be adapted to, new beliefs about the human mind.

Justifying Aims and Principles of Distribution

There is, I think, an analogy worth considering between the concept of punishment and that of property. In both cases we have to do with a social institution of which the centrally important form is a structure of *legal* rules, even if it would be dogmatic to deny the names of punishment or property to the similar though more rudimentary rule-regulated practices within groups such as a family, or a school, or in customary societies whose

From H. L. A. Hart, *Punishment and Responsibility* (Oxford: Oxford University Press, 1962), pp. 2–4, 6–13. Reprinted by courtesy of the Editor of the Aristotelian Society.

customs may lack some of the standard or salient features of law (e.g., legislation, organized sanctions, courts). In both cases we are confronted by a complex institution presenting different interrelated features calling for separate explanation; or, if the morality of the institution is challenged, for separate justification. In both cases failure to distinguish separate questions or attempting to answer them all by reference to a single principle ends in confusion. Thus in the case of property we should distinguish between the question of the *definition* of property, the question why and in what circumstance it is a *good* institution to maintain, and the questions in what ways individuals may become *entitled* to acquire property and *how much* they should be allowed to acquire. These we may call questions of *Definition, General Justifying Aim,* and *Distribution,* with the last subdivided into questions of *Title* and *Amount.*

The Nature of an Offence

Before we reach any question of justification we must identify a preliminary question to which the answer is so simple that the question may not appear worth asking; yet it is clear that some curious "theories" of punishment gain their only plausibility from ignoring it, and others from confusing it with other questions. This question is: Why are certain kinds of action forbidden by law and so made crimes or offences? The answer is: To announce to society that these actions are not to be done and to secure that fewer of them are done. These are the common immediate aims of making any conduct a criminal offence and until we have laws made with these primary aims we shall lack the notion of a "crime" and so of a "criminal." Without recourse to the simple idea that the criminal law sets up, in its rules, standards of behaviour to encourage certain types of conduct and discourage others we cannot distinguish a punishment in the form of a fine from a tax on a course of conduct. This indeed is one grave objection to those theories of law which in the interests of simplicity or uniformity obscure the distinction between primary laws setting standards for behaviour and secondary laws specifying what officials must or may do when they are broken. Such theories insist that all legal rules are "really" directions to officials to exact "sanctions" under certain conditions, e.g., if people kill. Yet only if we keep alive the distinction (which such theories thus obscure) between the primary objective of the law in encouraging or discouraging certain kinds of behaviour, and its merely ancillary sanction or remedial steps, can we give sense to the notion of a crime or offence.

It is important however to stress the fact that in thus identifying the immediate aims of the criminal law we have not reached the stage of justification. There are indeed many forms of undesirable behaviour which it would be foolish (because ineffective or too costly) to attempt to inhibit by use of the law and some of these may be better left to educators, trades unions, churches, marriage guidance councils, or other nonlegal agencies. Conversely there are some forms of conduct which we believe cannot be effectively inhibited without use of the law. But it is only too plain that in fact the law may make activities criminal which it is morally important to promote and the suppression of these may be quite unjustifiable. Yet confusion between the simple immediate aim of any criminal legislation and the justification of punishment seems to be the most charitable explanation of the claim that punishment is *justified* as an "emphatic denunciation by the community of a crime." Lord Denning's dictum that this is the ultimate justification of punishment can be saved . . . only if it is treated as a blurred statement of the truth that the aim not of punishment, but of criminal legislation is indeed to denounce certain types of conduct as something not to be practised. Conversely the immediate aim of criminal legislation cannot be any of the things which are usually mentioned as justifying punishment: for until it is settled what conduct is to be legally denounced and discouraged we have not settled from what we are to *deter* people, or who are to be considered *criminals* from whom we are to exact *retribution,* or on whom we are to wreak *vengeance,* or whom we are to *reform.*

Even those who look upon human law as a mere instrument for enforcing "morality as such" (itself conceived as the law of God or Nature) and who at the stage of justifying punishment wish to appeal not to socially beneficial consequences but simply to the intrinsic value of inflicting suffering on wrong-doers who have disturbed by their offence the moral order, would not deny that the aim of criminal legislation is to set up types of behaviour (in this case conformity with a preexisting moral law) as legal standards of behaviour and to secure conformity with them. No doubt in all communities certain moral offences—e.g., killing—will always be selected for suppression as crimes and it is conceivable that this may be done not to protect human beings from being killed but to save the potential murderer from sin; but it would be paradoxical to look upon the law as designed not to discourage murder at all (even conceived as sin rather than harm) but simply to extract the penalty from the murderer.

General Justifying Aim

I shall not here criticize the intelligibility or consistency or adequacy of those theories that are united in denying that the practice of a system of punishment is justified by its beneficial consequences and claim instead that the main justification of the practice lies in the fact that when breach of the law involves moral guilt the application to the offender of the pain of punishment is itself a thing of value. A great variety of claims of this character, designating "Retribution" or "Expiation" or "Reprobation" as the justifying aim, fall in spite of differences under this rough general description. Though in fact I . . . [think] that these all either avoid the question of justification altogether or are in spite of their protestations disguised forms of Utilitarianism, I shall assume that Retribution, defined simply as the application of the pains of punishment to an offender who is morally guilty, may figure among the conceivable justifying aims of a system of punishment. Here I shall merely insist that it is one thing to use the word Retribution *at this point* in an account of the principle of punishment in order to designate the General Justifying Aim of the system, and quite another to use it to secure that to the question "To whom may punishment be applied?" (the question of Distribution), the answer given is "Only to an offender for an offence." Failure to distinguish Retribution as a General Justifying Aim from retribution as the simple insistence that only those who have broken the law—and voluntarily broken it—may be punished, may be traced in many writers. . . . We shall distinguish the latter from Retribution in General Aim as "retribution in Distribution." Much confusing shadow-fighting between utilitarians and their opponents may be avoided if it is recognized that it is perfectly consistent to assert *both* that the General Justifying Aim of the practice of punishment is its beneficial consequences *and* that the pursuit of this General Aim should be qualified or restricted out of deference to principles of Distribution which require that punishment should be only of an offender for an offence. Conversely it does not in the least follow from the admission of the latter principle of retribution in Distribution that the General Justifying Aim of punishment is Retribution though of course Retribution in General Aim entails retribution in Distribution.

We shall consider later the principles of justice lying at the root of retribution in Distribution. Meanwhile it is worth observing that both the old-fashioned Retributionist (in General Aim) and the most modern sceptic often make the same (and, I think, wholly mistaken) assumption that sense can only be made of the restrictive principle that punishment be applied only to an offender for an offence if the General Justifying Aim of the practice of punishment is Retribution. The sceptic consequently imputes to all systems of punishment (when they are restricted by the principle of retribution in Distribution) all the irrationality he finds in the idea of Retribution as a General Justifying Aim; conversely the advocates of the latter think the admission of retribution in Distribution is a refutation of the utilitarian claim that the social consequences of punishment are its Justifying Aim.

The most general lesson to be learnt from this extends beyond the topic of punishment. It is, that in relation to any social institution, after stating what general aim or value its maintenance fosters we should enquire whether there are any and if so what principles limiting the unqualified pursuit of that aim or value. Just because the pursuit of any single social aim always has its restrictive qualifier, our main social institutions always possess a plurality of features which can only be understood as a compromise between partly discrepant principles. This is true even of relatively minor legal institutions like that of a contract. In general this is designed to enable individuals to give effect to their wishes to create structures of legal rights and duties, and so to change, in certain ways, their legal position. Yet at the same time there is need to protect those who, in good faith, understand a verbal offer made to them to mean what it would ordinarily mean, accept it, and then act on the footing that a valid contract has been concluded. As against them, it would be unfair to allow the other party to say that the words he used in his verbal offer or the interpretation put on them did not express his real wishes or intention. Hence principles of "estoppel" or doctrines of the "objective sense" of a contract are introduced to prevent this and to qualify the principle that the law enforces contracts in order to give effect to the joint wishes of the contracting parties.

Distribution

This as in the case of property has two aspects: (i) Liability (Who may be punished?) and (ii) Amount. In this section I shall chiefly be concerned with the first of these.

From the foregoing discussions two things emerge. First, though we may be clear as to what value the practice of punishment is to promote, we have still to answer as a question of Distribution. "Who may be punished?"

Secondly, if in answer to this question we say "only an offender for an offence," this admission of retribution in Distribution is not a principle from which anything follows as to the severity or amount of punishment; in particular it neither licenses nor requires, as Retribution in General Aim does, more severe punishments than deterrence or other utilitarian criteria would require.

The root question to be considered is, however, why we attach the moral importance which we do to retribution in Distribution. Here I shall consider the efforts made to show that restriction of punishment to offenders is a simple consequence of whatever principles (Retributive or Utilitarian) constitute the Justifying Aim of punishment.

The standard example used by philosophers to bring out the importance of retribution in Distribution is that of a wholly innocent person who has not even unintentionally done anything which the law punishes if done intentionally. It is supposed that in order to avert some social catastrophe officials of the system fabricate evidence on which he is charged, tried, convicted and sent to prison or death. Or it is supposed that without resort to any fraud more persons may be deterred from crime if wives and children of offenders were punished vicariously for their crimes. In some forms this kind of thing may be ruled out by a consistent sufficiently comprehensive utilitarianism.[1] Certainly expedients involving fraud or faked charges might be very difficult to justify on utilitarian grounds. We can of course imagine that a negro might be sent to prison or executed on a false charge of rape in order to avoid widespread lynching of many others; but a *system* which openly empowered authorities to do this kind of thing, even if it succeeded in averting specific evils like lynching, would awaken such apprehension and insecurity that any gain from the exercise of these powers would by any utilitarian calculation be offset by the misery caused by their existence. But official resort to this kind of fraud on a particular occasion in breach of the rules and the subsequent indemnification of the officials responsible might save many lives and so be thought to yield a clear surplus of value. Certainly vicarious punishment of an offender's family might do so and legal systems have occasionally though exceptionally resorted to this. An example of it is the Roman *Lex Quisquis* providing for the punishment of the children of those guilty of *majestas*. In extreme cases many might still think it right to resort to these expedients but we should do so with the sense of sacrificing an important principle. We should be conscious of choosing the lesser of two evils, and this would be inexplicable if the principle sacrificed to utility were itself only a requirement of utility.

Similarly the moral importance of the restriction of punishment to the offender cannot be explained as merely a consequence of the principle that the General Justifying Aim is Retribution for immorality involved in breaking the law. Retribution in the Distribution of punishment has a value quite independent of Retribution as Justifying Aim. This is shown by the fact that we attach importance to the restrictive principle that only offenders may be punished, even where breach of this law might not be thought immoral. Indeed even where the laws themselves are hideously immoral as in Nazi Germany—e.g., forbidding activities (helping the sick or destitute of some racial group) which might be thought morally obligatory—the absence of the principle restricting punishment to the offender would be a further *special* iniquity; whereas admission of this principle would represent some residual respect for justice shown in the administration of morally bad laws.

Endnote

[1] See J. Rawls, "Two Concepts of Rules," *Philosophical Review* (1955), pp. 4–13.

Study Questions

1. Does Justice Souter, dissenting in *Lockyer v. Andrade*, make a convincing case that the Court majority has misunderstood its own precedents?

2. Why isn't the punishment inflicted in *Lockyer v. Andrade* an "exceedingly rare" and "extreme" case of a disproportionality between the crime and the penalty? Do you agree with the dissenters that, "if Andrade's sentence is not grossly disproportionate, the principle has no meaning"?

3. Suppose that I am a masochist and claim to enjoy "unpleasant consequences": I like pain, and I relish the feeling of being condemned by and disapproved of in the minds of others. Is it possible to "punish" me, given the characteristics that punishment seems to have?

4. Explain whether you believe that any of the following ought to count as legitimate cases of inflicting punishment. If they are not instances of punishment, say why: commitment of the mentally ill

against their will; military conscription in time of war; quarantine of those with highly communicable diseases.

5. Give at least one specific example of each of the four general situations in which Bentham thinks that punishment ought not to be inflicted.

6. Bentham says that punishment would be "inefficacious" in cases where the defendant is either insane or intoxicated. Why does Bentham say this? Do you agree?

7. Should armed robbery be punished more than unarmed robbery? Would Bentham's theory give any guidance here? What answer would it give?

8. Bentham claims that the "general object which all laws . . . ought to have . . . is to augment the total happiness of the community." Do you agree? What might a retributivist say to this?

9. What two kinds of counterexamples does Moore develop as arguments against the utilitarian theory of punishment?

10. What argument does Moore use to reject the mixed theory of punishment?

11. The popular science-fiction film, *Minority Report*, imagines a world in which crime-fighters are able, with the assistance of "precognitive" beings who can foresee the future, to apprehend and prosecute individuals *before* they commit criminal offenses. Assuming it were possible, could a utilitarian justification be articulated for "prospective" infliction of punishment? What would be the objections to such a practice? Are there objections that do not turn, in one way or another, on the suspicion that the evidence used to apprehend the suspects would not be infallibly reliable? Is this the reason why the law limits infliction of punishment to cases where the person has already acted and "the deed been done"?

12. State in your own words the distinction that Hart tries to draw between the "general justifying aim" of a practice and the "principle of distribution" operating within that practice. Are you convinced by Hart's reasons for allocating the general aim to utilitarian considerations and the distributive aspect to retributivism?

13. In 1996, the California State Assembly narrowly defeated a bill that would have reinstituted corporal punishment for youthful offenders. The bill provided that juveniles found to have vandalized property with graffiti would be whacked on the bottom up to ten times with a wooden paddle wielded by a parent. If the parent refused to mete out the punishment or to deliver a sufficient blow, the judge could empower the bailiff to administer the punishment. Proponents argued that the measure would give the judge an additional tool in the effort to combat vandalism; opponents claimed that corporal punishment would backfire by breeding anger and resentment. Can corporal punishment be justified on utilitarian grounds? What assumptions would be necessary in the utilitarian view to show the justifiability of such punishment? Could corporal punishment be justified on retributive grounds? Would you have endorsed the bill? Why or why not?

14. In *U.S. v. Bello* [2d U.S. Cir. Ct. of Appeals No. 01-1682 (2002)] the defendant was convicted of conspiracy to commit credit-card fraud. Since he was the sole breadwinner for his family, the judge declined to send him to prison. Instead, the judge imposed a ten-month home detention. As one condition of the detention, however, the defendant was forbidden to watch any television during the entire ten months, so that, according to the judge, he would not be distracted from the self-reflection necessary to prevent the further commission of crimes. Is this an unjustified restriction? Is it "cruel and unusual"?

15. The Women's Coalition of Pasadena, California, proposed in 1997 to seek legislation requiring that permanent, lifetime cuffs be affixed to sexual offenders after they leave prison. The cuffs would contain an anti-tampering microchip to avoid removal. Children could then be taught to recognize the bracelet and avoid those who wear it. Do you think such restraints would be justified, assuming that the cuffs could be shown to reduce the rate of child molestation?

16. In 1995, two Native American teenagers of the Tlingit tribe were convicted in the beating and robbery of a pizza deliveryman. Rather than sentence them for the crime, however, the Washington state judge turned the youths over to tribal authorities who proposed to deal with the offenders in a way more consistent with their tribal traditions. The two eighteen-year-olds were given the punishment of banishment: provided with the basics, a Bible, and a book on Tlingit culture, the

boys were sent to live for a year on uninhabited islands in Alaska. Tribal authorities argued that banishment is integral to a process of rehabilitation. Restitution was also to be a part of the punishment: the families of the teenagers gave money to the victim, and the boys were forced to carve objects for sale toward restitution. Is such a form of punishment justifiable? If so, on what grounds?

D. *The Death Penalty*

Few legal issues polarize views quite as readily as the debate over the constitutionality of capital punishment. In December 2002, a federal appeals court reversed the findings of a district court judge in New York. The lower court had declared unconstitutional the federal death penalty law on grounds that too many condemned inmates have turned out to be innocent: "Our system of criminal justice, for all its protections, is sufficiently fallible that innocent people are convicted of capital crimes with some frequency."[1] The ruling came on the heels of a widely publicized moratorium on executions, imposed by then Illinois Governor George Ryan. A state commission appointed by Ryan to investigate how capital cases had been administered in that state, concluded with assertions of unfairness occurring at nearly every stage of the process. In 1997, the American Bar Association passed a resolution against the execution of the mentally retarded in order to "ensure that death penalty cases are administered fairly and impartially . . . and minimize the risk that innocent persons may be executed." Opponents of the death penalty seized on these developments, arguing that, under existing capital punishment law, it is possible that an individual could be executed before she had a full opportunity to demonstrate her innocence, thus being deprived of "due process" of law. Opponents cited evidence that 12 men sentenced to death had been exonerated by DNA testing since the early 1980s.

The Case of Karla Faye Tucker

One out of every three executions in the United States occurs in the state of Texas. In early February 1998, one scheduled execution drew intense scrutiny from both opponents and proponents of the death penalty. Karla Faye Tucker was scheduled to die as punishment for her participation in a double murder. In 1983 Tucker, then twenty-three years old, along with her boyfriend, broke into the apartment of an acquaintance to steal motorcycle parts. Tucker killed the acquaintance with a pickax, claiming that she experienced an orgasm with each blow; a woman found in the apartment was killed by Tucker's boyfriend. Subsequent to her capture, Tucker confessed her crimes and testified against her boyfriend. She expressed remorse—even to the point of admitting that she should die for her wrongdoing. Central to Tucker's cooperation was a religious conversion, which Tucker claimed she underwent while awaiting trial. Fourteen years later, on the eve of her execution, supporters described Tucker as a caring, repentant, and deeply religious person; she had married the prison minister in 1993. Tucker, along with those opposed to her execution, argued that she could help save troubled youth through spiritual counseling. Some objected to leniency for Tucker, alleging that the public outcry on her behalf was due to her gender and race (Tucker was White). Texas had not executed a woman since the Civil War, the critics contended, and had Tucker been a Black male (as are the majority of death row inmates across the country), no one would have cared. Tucker died in the Texas death chamber on February 3, 1998, after Governor George W. Bush refused to commute her sentence.

---

[1] See *United States v. Quinones*, 196 F. Supp. 2d 416, 420 [S.D.N.Y. 2002].

The Complexity of Capital Punishment

The Tucker case acted as a lens to focus public attention on the death penalty and the legal and moral questions it raises. Among these questions are: What purpose is capital punishment supposed to serve? Does it deter crime? Is it a form of just retribution? Should a genuinely repentant person be executed? Is capital punishment administered in a racially or sexually discriminatory fashion?

The debate concerning capital punishment is complex in that it blends issues at once constitutional, moral, and empirical. Of constitutional importance is the question of whether death is a "cruel and unusual" punishment. Morally, the death penalty involves questions about the sanctity of life, the power of the state, and the justice of fitting crime to punishment. Empirically, the controversies over the death penalty turn on whether and to what extent credible evidence shows capital punishment to be a greater deterrent than life imprisonment and on how statistical evidence of disproportionality between White and non-White defendants sentenced to death is to be explained. These issues are explored in the readings for this section.

Cruelty, Proportionality, and the Eighth Amendment

Hours before his scheduled execution in 1992, Robert Alton Harris made a last-minute plea to the Supreme Court of the United States. His argument was simple: death in California's gas chamber, which exposes the condemned to cyanide gas, is an unconstitutional form of cruel and unusual punishment. The Court refused to stay the execution, but two justices dissented, arguing in part that when California began use of the gas chamber,

> it was considered a humane method of execution. Fifty-five years of history and moral development have superseded that judgment. The barbaric use of cyanide gas in the Holocaust, the development of cyanide agents as chemical weapons, our contemporary understanding of execution by lethal gas, and the development of less cruel methods of execution all demonstrate that execution by cyanide gas is unnecessarily cruel.[2]

---

[2] *Gomez v. U.S. District Court,* 112 S. Ct. 1652 (1992).

After his execution, Harris's argument won over state legislators, who modified the law to permit the alternative of lethal injection. The Harris case nonetheless raises questions about the humaneness of certain forms of punishment, and about the meaning of the Eighth Amendment. Because these notions also relate importantly to the debate concerning capital punishment, it is worth exploring them a bit further.

What kinds of punishment does the Eighth Amendment ban? How can we flesh out the meaning of "cruel and unusual" punishment? A number of possibilities exist. It might be suggested, for example, that the language simply be taken at face value: only punishments that are painful and infrequently administered are forbidden. But this won't work; a punishment does not become licit if done only painlessly and often. Another suggestion turns to the constitutional theory of original intent (see the discussion in Chapter 1) and urges that "cruel and unusual" means whatever the framers of the Constitution thought it meant, that is, whatever *they* would have deemed cruel and unusual. This interpretation, however, is subject to all of the problems confronting originalism as a general interpretive method (see Chapter 2). Nor, some would argue, is it reasonable to let the meaning of "cruel and unusual" reflect the consensus of public opinion at any one time. The Eighth and similar amendments were supposed to serve as a check or constraint on the sentiments of the majority, not an implementation of them. A utilitarian might argue that a punishment is "cruel and unusual" if it levies a penalty in excess of what is warranted by the goal of bringing about the greatest happiness, say, by deterring others. But here the problem is that the language and subsequent interpretation of the clause make it clear that it was meant to rule out certain punishments altogether, even if they would have an extra deterrent effect if carried out. Finally, others propose that the meaning of "cruel and unusual" punishment be interpreted in light of the Kantian, retributive conception of punishment. Cruel and unusual punishments are those that may not be inflicted, no matter how advantageous to society, because they are inconsistent with a proper regard for human dignity and a respect for people as autonomous and responsible beings. The clause thus acts as a "side constraint," setting the permissible outer boundaries of social policy.

Central both to the retributive theory and to the approach of many courts to the Eighth Amendment is the *principle of proportionality.* This states that the severity of the punishment inflicted must be proportional to the gravity of the offense; the punishment, in other words, must "fit the crime." Familiar as this saying is, the principle it represents is not entirely clear.

In early 1993, the state of Washington executed convicted triple-murderer Westley Allan Dodd by hanging. Because he had hanged one of the three boys he confessed to killing, Dodd insisted that his own execution be by hanging rather than the available alternative of lethal injection. Dodd evidently felt that this mode of punishment "fit" his crime. In his writings on the state of Virginia, Thomas Jefferson recorded, among other things, some proposed revisions to the state's criminal code.[3] The revised code assigned specific punishments to types of offenses: treason and murder were to be punished with death, rape and sodomy with "dismemberment," and maiming and disfiguring with "retaliation." The proposed penal code constituted an attempt to carry out the retributive requirement that the punishment fit the crime on at least two levels. First, the schedule of proposed punishments attempted to ensure that the mode or kind of punishment be appropriate to the crime committed: reparation for larceny, physical beatings for battery, and so on. Second, this principle was applied concretely to the specific manner in which crimes and their matching punishments were to be carried out: murder by poison, for example, was to be punished with death by poison.

How closely must punishment match crime? Would it be possible to carry out the logic of the Virginia Code across the board? In some cases, this would be impossible; for example, a blind man who attacks and blinds another can't be blinded in return. But are there certain punishments that must remain unacceptable even if they are literally workable as a return of like for like? May we torture the torturer? Rape the rapist? (Neither Kant nor the Virginia Code is willing to insist upon literal sameness here; both recommend castration as a punishment for rape.) Some retributivists answer that their theory should be understood to recommend only that crimes and punishments be ranked in severity, with the most serious crimes getting the most serious punishment, the second most serious crime getting the second most serious punishment, and so on, with no further requirement that the crime be precisely mirrored, detail for detail, in the punishment.

The Death Penalty and the Eighth Amendment

Is the death penalty a constitutionally permissible punishment? A brief review of several prior Supreme Court rulings will help clarify the terrain of the debate.

It is widely agreed that the Constitution itself certainly contemplates the death penalty, which was commonly used in the eighteenth century, even for crimes other than murder. The document says, for example, that no one shall be held "to answer for a capital . . . crime" except upon indictment, and it insists that no one shall be deprived of "life" without due process of law. In 1972, however, the Supreme Court, in *Furman v. Georgia*,[4] struck down all state capital punishment laws as they then operated. Differing explanations were given for the ruling. Some justices took the position that death, for whatever crime, is always cruel and unusual because it fails to comport with "evolving standards of decency." The plurality took the view that death is not unconstitutional *per se*, but that the unbridled discretion then given to juries to impose death as a punishment had resulted in a racially prejudicial administration of the penalty, making its imposition "arbitrary and capricious" and violating the Eighth Amendment on that ground.

Subsequent to *Furman*, most states enacted statutes to control jury deliberations in death penalty cases, providing for "guided discretion." These new procedural laws created a separate "penalty phase" in any trial resulting in conviction for a capital offense, permitting juries to recommend execution only if they found "aggravating circumstances" (for example, that the murder was committed for monetary gain or by a prisoner under a sentence of life imprisonment). In most states, the same jury that found the defendant guilty hears the evidence about aggravation and mitigation and then returns a verdict of life or death.[5] It is these laws that were upheld by the Court in *Gregg v. Georgia*.[6] The plurality opinion in *Gregg* echoed the views of pro-death-penalty advocates like Ernest van den Haag: the constitutional judgment that a punish-

---

[3] Thomas Jefferson, "Notes on the State of Virginia: Proposed Revised Code of Virginia," reprinted in S. Presser and J. Zainalden (eds.), *Law in American History: Cases and Materials* (St. Paul, Minn.: West, 1980).

[4] 408 U.S. 238 (1972).

[5] Under the Court's recent ruling in *Ring v. Arizona* [122 S. Ct. 2428 (2002)] this judgment must be rendered by the jury, not the judge.

[6] 428 U.S. 153 (1976).

ment is or is not excessive or inhumane must be based on the public consensus. Because most people favor the death penalty, execution cannot be *per se* unconstitutional. Subsequent to the ruling in *Gregg*, the Court has refused to allow states to limit the kinds of mitigating circumstances that juries can consider in deliberating on whether to impose death; and it has been held that no crime can carry a mandatory death penalty—execution can result only when a jury has been permitted to weigh the considerations for and against death.[7]

Proportionality and the Mentally Disabled

The Court's latest opinion on the death penalty is included in this section. In *Atkins v. Virginia*, the Court reversed an earlier precedent and held that a national consensus has emerged that executing the mentally retarded amounts to cruel and unusual punishment in violation of the Eighth Amendment to the Constitution. As early as 1958, the Court had maintained that the prohibition of cruel and unusual punishment "must draw its meaning from the evolving standards of decency that mark the progress of a maturing society."[8] In *Atkins*, the Court pointed to several developments demonstrating, in the majority's view, that contemporary standards of decency had evolved to the point where execution of the retarded was no longer acceptable. In the late 1980s, for instance, Congress had outlawed the use of the federal death penalty against the mentally disabled; as many as 17 states had followed suit. When these states are added to those that ban execution altogether, the Court reasoned, a clear majority exists against executing retarded defendants.

According to the Court, the growing consensus among the states "reflects a widespread judgment about the relative culpability of mentally retarded offenders." Moreover, it was doubtful, in the Court's view, whether justifications for capital punishment in the form of appeals to deterrence or retribution could properly be applied to mentally retarded defendants.

The Argument for the Death Penalty

Both retributive and utilitarian arguments are made to support the death penalty. Famous among retributive arguments is that made by Kant, who insisted that one who murders must be punished with death. There is no "sameness of kind" between death (of the victim) and continued life (of the murderer). No amount of imprisonment for the living, Kant maintained, would "equal" being dead. Van den Haag suggests a similar argument in our readings: wanton murder is the worst of offenses and thus deserves the worst punishment. And, although it is true that a mistaken execution would be irredeemable, this does not distinguish death from life imprisonment, for lost years cannot be restored to one unjustly imprisoned any more than life can to those who are gone.

The retributive claim is not that death is imposed as an act of revenge; it is, rather, that justice demands it. Nor is execution inconsistent with respect for the "sanctity of life," say retributive supporters of capital punishment. Kant, for example, reasoned that part of what it means to treat a condemned murderer as an autonomous person is that society must give to that person what he or she deserves (death)—to do less would be to use that person's fate (which she has chosen) as a vehicle for our own needs (for example, to lessen our own discomfort at the thought of execution).

The utilitarian argument in support of capital punishment turns on the various "goods" that execution is supposed to confer. Chief among these alleged goods are the ideas that the death penalty is an efficient *preventive* and a better *deterrent* than alternative forms of punishment, such as life imprisonment. The notions of prevention and deterrence are fraught with confusion, however, and it is important to consider carefully what these concepts mean in their application to capital punishment. To say that any form of punishment is *preventive* of crime means that the infliction of punishment makes it impossible for the individual punished to commit the crimes that he or she would have committed had the punishment not been inflicted. To say that a form of punishment is a *deterrent* is to assert that the example of inflicting punishment in a given case will induce others inclined toward criminal acts to refrain from criminality.

It is a frequently made but often unsubstantiated claim that capital punishment is a perfect preventative measure. After all, dead people don't commit crimes. This is true, of course, but it doesn't follow simply

---

[7] See *Lockett v. Ohio*, 438 U.S. 586 (1978); *Woodson v. North Carolina*, 428 U.S. 280 (1976).

[8] *Trop v. Dulles*, 356 U.S. 86 (1958).

from this fact that in executing someone you have thereby prevented any crimes. To license this claim you would have to know whether the person executed would have committed further crimes had he or she been allowed to live. Because this kind of "counterfactual" statement can never be known with certainty, it is false to insist that capital punishment is in every case necessarily a crime preventive measure. Capital punishment may be definitively *incapacitative* (since the dead person is powerless), but that is a different claim from the assertion that it prevents future crimes.

Is the death penalty a more effective deterrent than any alternative—for example, life imprisonment? Here, again, it is tempting to try to answer this question *a priori* by insisting that death *must* be a deterrent, given that everyone is afraid to die. However, the question that must be answered is whether the fear of death will affect the incentives that criminals might have to commit capital crimes. This issue must be assessed on the basis of the empirical evidence. As the readings by van den Haag and Hugo Bedau make clear, the evidence relating to the deterrence value of the death penalty is highly contested. Van den Haag and Bedau debate the results of numerous studies that have been done—studies comparing crime rates in jurisdictions with capital punishment with those that do not impose it, and studies comparing crime rates in a single jurisdiction both before and after capital punishment was imposed (or abandoned).

The Argument Against the Death Penalty

Both the utilitarian and the retributive grounds for the institution of the death penalty have been challenged by opponents. To begin with, the opponents say, the existing research has not convincingly shown capital punishment to be a significantly more effective deterrent than life imprisonment without parole. But even aside from that problem, the critics caution, capital punishment brings with it negative costs that utilitarians must face. First, capital punishment is extremely expensive. Currently more than 3,000 people are on death row nationwide, and the number is growing by roughly 200 per year. Because of the lengthy appeals frequently pursued by death-row inmates, the average time spent on death row is six years. Long-term incarceration, attorneys' fees, and the laborious procedures required by law to put someone to death have pushed the cost of some executions well into the millions. A different type

of cost, according to death-penalty foes, is in human terms. Innocent people have been and will continue to be executed, and life cannot be restored once taken. Finally, opponents of capital punishment such as Bedau contend that the deterrence arguments, if correct, prove too much: even supposing that torture were found to be an extremely effective deterrent, that would not legitimate its use. Bedau observes in this connection that neither Kant nor van den Haag approves death-by-torture.

The primary objection to the retributive case for capital punishment turns on the requirement of proportionality. Ensuring that the punishment "fits the crime" is not something that retributivists are willing to do in all cases (as noted above), but if it is not permissible to dismember one who killed others by dismemberment, why is it permissible to kill at all? Retributivists are unwilling to follow the dictates of proportionality in every case, so why must death be punished with death? Wouldn't proportionality be satisfied as long as the most severe crime was linked to the most severe sanction short of capital punishment, namely, life imprisonment without parole? Critics also worry that retributivists wrongly assume that murderers autonomously choose to kill and thus "will" their own deaths. The reality, they contend, is that a high proportion of murders are correlated with drug use and mental disorders, thereby undermining the moral imperative that those who commit murder must die.

Race and the Death Penalty

The claim that the death penalty is administered arbitrarily and capriciously—the claim at the center of the Court's ruling in *Furman v. Georgia*—has not gone away. Years after capital punishment was reinstated, many of those opposed to it maintain that death is meted out in a deeply discriminatory fashion. Various researchers have claimed to discover disturbing patterns in the ways juries and judges impose capital punishment.[9] The facts cited by the researchers include these: more than 48 percent of death row inmates are non-White, even though minorities make up less than 20 percent of the total United States population; the number of Blacks put to death since 1930 is

---

[9] See, for example, Gross and Mauro, "Patterns of Death," *Stanford Law Review,* Vol. 37 (1984): 27–101; Bowers and Pierce, "Arbitrariness and Discrimination under Post-*Furman* Capital Statutes," *Crime and Delinquency,* Vol. 26 (1980): 563–635.

greater than that of Whites executed, although Blacks account for less than 12 percent of the total population; and in some states a murderer of a White person is more than ten times more likely to be sentenced to death than a murderer of a Black person. Critics of capital punishment allege that these and similar statistical results cannot be explained on any ground other than race. Judges and juries, they contend, clearly value White lives more than Black lives, and this bias leads them to execute a disproportionate number of Blacks and spare a disproportionate number of murderers of Blacks. Are these allegations warranted? These questions are taken up in the *McCleskey* case and in the essay by Randall Kennedy.

McCleskey v. Kemp involved a Black defendant convicted and sentenced to death for a murder committed during an armed robbery. McCleskey argued that Georgia's capital punishment statute violated the Equal Protection clause of the Fourteenth Amendment to the Constitution. McCleskey relied upon an extensive study of death-penalty convictions in Georgia. That study had purported to find many racial disparities in the imposition of the death penalty in Georgia. McCleskey argued that those who murder Whites are

more likely to be sentenced to death, and that Black defendants are more likely to be sentenced to death than White defendants convicted of the same offense. The Supreme Court rejected McCleskey's argument, insisting that proof of discrimination in capital sentencing cannot be merely general and statistical, but must demonstrate that those involved in McCleskey's own case acted with racial bias. No such proof, according to the Court, was forthcoming.

In his essay, Randall Kennedy subjects the Court's reasoning in *McCleskey* to careful scrutiny. Kennedy is critical of the Court's refusal to concede that racial bias has been shown to be a likely factor in McCleskey's fate, given that the disparities confirmed by researchers can be explained in no other way. Kennedy then looks at a deeper issue: Assuming that it had ruled in favor of McCleskey, what should the Court have done? What follows from the discrimination argument upon which the critics of the death penalty rely? That all forms of capital punishment should be abolished? Or that states be required to increase the number of people executed for murdering Blacks? Kennedy examines these and several other responses to the inequality of capital punishment.

Atkins v. Virginia

JUSTICE STEVENS delivered the opinion of the Court.

Those mentally retarded persons who meet the law's requirements for criminal responsibility should be tried and punished when they commit crimes. Because of their disabilities in areas of reasoning, judgment, and control of their impulses, however, they do not act with the level of moral culpability that characterizes the most serious adult criminal conduct. Moreover, their impairments can jeopardize the reliability and fairness of capital proceedings against mentally retarded defendants. Presumably for these reasons, in the 13 years since we decided *Penry v. Lynaugh*, 492 U.S. 302 (1989), the American public, legislators, scholars, and judges have deliberated over

the question whether the death penalty should ever be imposed on a mentally retarded criminal. The consensus reflected in those deliberations informs our answer to the question presented by this case: whether such executions are "cruel and unusual punishments" prohibited by the Eighth Amendment to the Federal Constitution.

Petitioner, Daryl Renard Atkins, was convicted of abduction, armed robbery, and capital murder, and sentenced to death. At approximately midnight on August 16, 1996, Atkins and William Jones, armed with a semi-automatic handgun, abducted Eric Nesbitt, robbed him of the money on his person, drove him to an automated teller machine in his pickup truck where cameras recorded their withdrawal of additional cash, then took him to an isolated location where he was shot eight times and killed. . . . At the

536 U.S., 304 (2002), United States Supreme Court.

penalty phase of the trial, the State introduced victim impact evidence and proved two aggravating circumstances: future dangerousness and "vileness of the offense." To prove future dangerousness, the State relied on Atkins' prior felony convictions as well as the testimony of four victims of earlier robberies and assaults. To prove the second aggravator, the prosecution relied upon the trial record, including pictures of the deceased's body and the autopsy report.

In the penalty phase, the defense relied on one witness, Dr. Evan Nelson, a forensic psychologist who had evaluated Atkins before trial and concluded that he was "mildly mentally retarded." His conclusion was based on interviews with people who knew Atkins, a review of school and court records, and the administration of a standard intelligence test which indicated that Atkins had a full scale 1Q of 59. The jury sentenced Atkins to death. . . .

Because of the gravity of the concerns expressed by the dissenters, and in light of the dramatic shift in the state legislative landscape that has occurred in the past 13 years, we granted certiorari to revisit the issue that we first addressed in the *Penry* case.

The Eighth Amendment succinctly prohibits "excessive" sanctions. It provides: "Excessive bail shall not be required, nor excessive fines imposed, nor cruel and unusual punishments inflicted." In *Weems v. United States*, 217 U.S. 349 (1910), we held that a punishment of 12 years jailed in irons at hard and painful labor for the crime of falsifying records was excessive. We explained "that it is a precept of justice that punishment for crime should be graduated and proportioned to the offense." . . .

A claim that punishment is excessive is judged not by the standards that prevailed in 1685 when Lord Jeffreys presided over the "Bloody Assizes" or when the Bill of Rights was adopted, but rather by those that currently prevail. . . .

Proportionality review under those evolving standards should be informed by '"objective factors to the maximum possible extent'". . . .

[W]e shall first review the judgment of legislatures that have addressed the suitability of imposing the death penalty on the mentally retarded and then consider reasons for agreeing or disagreeing with their judgment.

The parties have not called our attention to any state legislative consideration of the suitability of imposing the death penalty on mentally retarded offenders prior to 1986. In that year, the public reaction to the execution of a mentally retarded murderer in

Georgia apparently led to the enactment of the first state statute prohibiting such executions. In 1988, when Congress enacted legislation reinstating the federal death penalty, it expressly provided that a "sentence of death shall not be carried out upon a person who is mentally retarded." In 1989, Maryland enacted a similar prohibition. . . .

Much has changed since then. Responding to the national attention received by the Bowden execution and our decision in *Penry*, state legislatures across the country began to address the issue. In 1990 Kentucky and Tennessee enacted statutes similar to those in Georgia and Maryland, as did New Mexico in 1991, and Arkansas, Colorado, Washington, Indiana, and Kansas in 1993 and 1994. In 1995, when New York reinstated its death penalty, it emulated the Federal Government by expressly exempting the mentally retarded. Nebraska followed suit in 1998. There appear to have been no similar enactments during the next two years, but in 2000 and 2001 six more States—South Dakota, Arizona, Connecticut, Florida, Missouri, and North Carolina—joined the procession. The Texas Legislature unanimously adopted a similar bill, and bills have passed at least one house in other States, including Virginia and Nevada.

It is not so much the number of these States that is significant, but the consistency of the direction of change. Given the well-known fact that anticrime legislation is far more popular than legislation providing protections for persons guilty of violent crime, the large number of States prohibiting the execution of mentally retarded persons (and the complete absence of States passing legislation reinstating the power to conduct such executions) provides powerful evidence that today our society views mentally retarded offenders as categorically less culpable than the average criminal. The evidence carries even greater force when it is noted that the legislatures that have addressed the issue have voted overwhelmingly in favor of the prohibition. Moreover, even in those States that allow the execution of mentally retarded offenders, the practice is uncommon. Some States, for example New Hampshire and New Jersey, continue to authorize executions, but none have been carried out in decades. Thus there is little need to pursue legislation barring the execution of the mentally retarded in those States. And it appears that even among those States that regularly execute offenders and that have no prohibition with regard to the mentally retarded, only five have executed offenders possessing a known IQ less than 70 since we decided *Penry*. The practice, therefore, has become truly unusual, and it is fair to say that a national consensus has developed against it.

To the extent there is serious disagreement about the execution of mentally retarded offenders, it is in determining which offenders are in fact retarded. In this case, for instance, the Commonwealth of Virginia disputes that Atkins suffers from mental retardation. Not all people who claim to be mentally retarded will be so impaired as to fall within the range of mentally retarded offenders about whom there is a national consensus. . . .

This consensus unquestionably reflects widespread judgment about the relative culpability of mentally retarded offenders, and the relationship between mental retardation and the penological purposes served by the death penalty. Additionally, it suggests that some characteristics of mental retardation undermine the strength of the procedural protections that our capital jurisprudence steadfastly guards.

As discussed above, clinical definitions of mental retardation require not only subaverage intellectual functioning, but also significant limitations in adaptive skills such as communication, self-care, and self-direction that became manifest before age 18. Mentally retarded persons frequently know the difference between right and wrong and are competent to stand trial. Because of their impairments, however, by definition they have diminished capacities to understand and process information, to communicate, to abstract from mistakes and learn from experience, to engage in logical reasoning, to control impulses, and to understand the reactions of others. There is no evidence that they are more likely to engage in criminal conduct than others, but there is abundant evidence that they often act on impulse rather than pursuant to a premeditated plan, and that in group settings they are followers rather than leaders. Their deficiencies do not warrant an exemption from criminal sanctions, but they do diminish their personal culpability.

In light of these deficiencies, our death penalty jurisprudence provides two reasons consistent with the legislative consensus that the mentally retarded should be categorically excluded from execution. First, there is a serious question as to whether either justification that we have recognized as a basis for the death penalty applies to mentally retarded offenders. *Gregg v. Georgia*, 428 U.S. 153, 183 (1976), identified "retribution and deterrence of capital crimes by prospective offenders" as the social purposes served by the death penalty. . . .

With respect to retribution—the interest in seeing that the offender gets his "just deserts"—the severity of the appropriate punishment necessarily depends on the culpability of the offender. Since *Gregg*, our jurisprudence has consistently confined the imposition of the death penalty to a narrow category of the most serious crimes. . . . If the culpability of the average murderer is insufficient to justify the most extreme sanction available to the State, the lesser culpability of the mentally retarded offender surely does not merit that form of retribution. Thus, pursuant to our narrowing jurisprudence, which seeks to ensure that only the most deserving of execution are put to death, an exclusion for the mentally retarded is appropriate.

With respect to deterrence—the interest in preventing capital crimes by prospective offenders—"it seems likely that 'capital punishment can serve as a deterrent only when murder is the result of premeditation and deliberation.'" Exempting the mentally retarded from that punishment will not affect the "cold calculus that precedes the decision" of other potential murderers. Indeed, that sort of calculus is at the opposite end of the spectrum from behavior of mentally retarded offenders. The theory of deterrence in capital sentencing is predicated upon the notion that the increased severity of the punishment will inhibit criminal actors from carrying out murderous conduct. Yet it is the same cognitive and behavioral impairments that make these defendants less morally culpable—for example, the diminished ability to understand and process information, to learn from experience, to engage in logical reasoning, or to control impulses—that also make it less likely that they can process the information of the possibility of execution as a penalty and, as a result, control their conduct based upon that information. Nor will exempting the mentally retarded from execution lessen the deterrent effect of the death penalty with respect to offenders who are not mentally retarded. Such individuals are unprotected by the exemption and will continue to face the threat of execution. Thus, executing the mentally retarded will not measurably further the goal of deterrence.

The reduced capacity of mentally retarded offenders provides a second justification for a categorical rule making such offenders ineligible for the death penalty. The risk that the death penalty will be imposed in spite of factors which may call for a less severe penalty, is enhanced, not only by the possibility of false confessions, but also by the lesser ability of mentally retarded defendants to make a persuasive showing of mitigation in the face of prosecutorial evidence of one or more aggravating factors. Mentally retarded defendants may be less able to give meaningful assistance to their counsel and are typically poor witnesses, and their demeanor may create an unwarranted impression of lack of remorse for their crimes. As *Penry* demonstrated, moreover, reliance on mental retardation as a mitigating factor can be a two-edged sword that may enhance the likelihood that the aggravating factor of future dangerousness will be found by the jury. Mentally retarded defendants in the aggregate face a special risk of wrongful execution.

Our independent evaluation of the issue reveals no reason to disagree with the judgment of "the legislatures that have recently addressed the matter" and concluded that death is not a suitable punishment for a mentally retarded criminal. We are not persuaded that the execution of mentally retarded criminals will measurably advance the deterrent or the retributive purpose of the death penalty. Construing and applying the Eighth Amendment in the light of our "evolving standards of decency," we therefore conclude that such punishment is excessive and that the Constitution "places a substantive restriction on the State's power to take the life" of a mentally retarded offender.

The judgment of the Virginia Supreme Court is reversed and the case is remanded for further proceedings not inconsistent with this opinion.

It is so ordered.

JUSTICE SCALIA, with whom the CHIEF JUSTICE and JUSTICE THOMAS join, dissenting.

Today's decision is the pinnacle of our Eighth Amendment death-is-different jurisprudence. Not only does it, like all of that jurisprudence, find no support in the text or history of the Eighth Amendment; it does not even have support in current social attitudes regarding the conditions that render an otherwise just death penalty inappropriate. Seldom has an opinion of this Court rested so obviously upon nothing but the personal views of its members.

As the foregoing history demonstrates, petitioner's mental retardation was a *central issue* at sentencing. The jury concluded, however, that his alleged retardation was not a compelling reason to exempt him from the death penalty in light of the brutality of his crime and his long demonstrated propensity for violence. "In upsetting this particularized judgment on the basis of a constitutional absolute," the Court concludes that no one who is even slightly mentally retarded can have sufficient "moral responsibility to be subjected to capital punishment for any crime. As a sociological and moral conclusion that is implausible;

and it is doubly implausible as an interpretation of the United States Constitution."

Under our Eighth Amendment jurisprudence, a punishment is "cruel and unusual" if it falls within one of two categories: "those modes or acts of punishment that had been considered cruel and unusual at the time that the Bill of Rights was adopted," and modes of punishment that are inconsistent with modern "standards of decency," as evinced by objective indicia, the most important of which is "legislation enacted by the country's legislatures."

The Court makes no pretense that execution of the mildly mentally retarded would have been considered "cruel and unusual" in 1791. Only the *severely* or *profoundly* mentally retarded, commonly known as "idiots," enjoyed any special status under the law at that time. They, like lunatics, suffered a "deficiency in will" rendering them unable to tell right from wrong. . . .

The Court is left to argue, therefore, that execution of the mildly retarded is inconsistent with the "evolving standards of decency that mark the progress of a maturing society." *Trop v. Dulles*, 356 U.S. 86, 101 (1958) (plurality opinion) (Warren, C. J.). Before today, our opinions consistently emphasized that Eighth Amendment judgments regarding the existence of social standards should be informed by objective factors to the maximum possible extent and should not be, or appear to be, merely the subjective views of individual Justices. . . .

The Court pays lipservice to these precedents as it miraculously extracts a "national consensus" forbidding execution of the mentally retarded, *ante*, at 12, from the fact that 18 States—less than *half* (47%) of the 38 States that permit capital punishment (for whom the issue exists)—have very recently enacted legislation barring execution of the mentally retarded. . . .

But let us accept, for the sake of argument, the Court's faulty count. That bare number of States alone—*18*—should be enough to convince any reasonable person that no "national consensus" exists. How is it possible that agreement among 47% of the death penalty jurisdictions amounts to "consensus"? Our prior cases have generally required a much higher degree of agreement before finding a punishment cruel and unusual on "evolving standards" grounds. . . .

The Court attempts to bolster its embarrassingly feeble evidence of "consensus" with the following: "It is not so much the number of these States that is significant, but the *consistency* of the direction of change." But in what *other* direction *could we possibly* see change? Given that 14 years ago *all* the death penalty statutes included the mentally retarded, *any* change (except precipitate undoing of what had just been done) was *bound to be* in the one direction the Court finds significant enough to overcome the lack of real consensus. . . .

The genuinely operative portion of the opinion, then, is the Court's statement of the reasons why it agrees with the contrived consensus it has found, that the "diminished capacities" of the mentally retarded render the death penalty excessive. The Court's analysis rests on two fundamental assumptions: (1) that the Eighth Amendment prohibits excessive punishments, and (2) that sentencing juries or judges are unable to account properly for the "diminished capacities" of the retarded. The first assumption is wrong. . . . The Eighth Amendment is addressed to always-and-everywhere "cruel" punishments, such as the rack and the thumbscrew. But where the punishment is in itself permissible, the Eighth Amendment is not a ratchet, whereby a temporary consensus on leniency for a particular crime fixes a permanent constitutional maximum, disabling the States from giving effect to altered beliefs and responding to changed social conditions. The second assumption—inability of judges or juries to take proper account of mental retardation—is not only unsubstantiated, but contradicts the immemorial belief, here and in England, that they play an *indispensable* role in such matters. . . .

Proceeding from these faulty assumptions, the Court gives two reasons why the death penalty is an excessive punishment for all mentally retarded offenders. First, the "diminished capacities" of the mentally retarded raise a "serious question" whether their execution contributes to the "social purposes" of the death penalty, viz., retribution and deterrence. . . . Retribution is not advanced, the argument goes, because the mentally retarded are *no more culpable* than the average murderer, whom we have already held lacks sufficient culpability to warrant the death penalty. Who says so? Is there an established correlation between mental acuity and the ability to conform one's conduct to the law in such a rudimentary matter as murder? Are the mentally retarded really more disposed (and hence more likely) to commit willfully cruel and serious crime than others? In my experience, the opposite is true: being childlike generally suggests innocence rather than brutality.

Assuming, however, that there is a direct connection between diminished intelligence and the inability to refrain from murder, what scientific analysis can possibly show that a mildly retarded individual who commits an exquisite torture-killing is "no more cul-

pable" than the "average" murderer in a holdup-gone-wrong or a domestic dispute? Or a moderately retarded individual who commits a series of 20 exquisite torture-killings? Surely culpability, and deservedness of the most severe retribution, depends not merely (if at all) upon the mental capacity of the criminal (above the level where he is able to distinguish right from wrong) but also upon the depravity of the crime—which is precisely why this sort of question has traditionally been thought answerable not by a categorical rule of the sort the Court today imposes upon all trials, but rather by the sentencer's weighing of the circumstances (both degree of retardation and depravity of crime) in the particular case. The fact that juries continue to sentence mentally retarded offenders to death for extreme crimes shows that society's moral outrage sometimes demands execution of retarded offenders. By what principle of law, science, or logic can the Court pronounce that this is wrong? There is none. Once the Court admits (as it does) that mental retardation does not render the offender morally *blameless*, there is no basis for saying that the death penalty is *never* appropriate retribution, no matter *how* heinous the crime. As long as a mentally retarded offender knows "the difference between right and wrong," only the sentencer can assess whether his retardation reduces his culpability enough to exempt him from the death penalty for the particular murder in question.

As for the other social purpose of the death penalty that the Court discusses, deterrence: That is not advanced, the Court tells us, because the mentally retarded are "less likely" than their non-retarded counterparts to "process the information of the possibility of execution as a penalty and . . . control their conduct based upon that information." Of course this leads to the same conclusion discussed earlier—that the mentally retarded (because they are less deterred) are more likely to kill—which neither I nor the society at large believes. In any event, even the Court does not say that *all* mentally retarded individuals cannot "process the information of the possibility of execution as a penalty and . . . control their conduct based upon that information"; it merely asserts that they are "less likely" to be able to do so. But surely the deterrent effect of a penalty is adequately vindicated if it successfully deters many, but not all, of the target class. Virginia's death penalty, for example, does not fail of its deterrent effect simply because *some* criminals are unaware that Virginia *has* the death penalty. In other words, the supposed fact that *some* retarded criminals cannot fully appreciate the death penalty has nothing to do with the deterrence rationale, but is simply an echo of the arguments denying a retribution rationale, discussed and rejected above. I am not sure that a murderer is somehow less blameworthy if (though he knew his act was wrong) he did not fully appreciate that he could die for it; but if so, we should treat a mentally retarded murderer the way we treat an offender who may be "less likely" to respond to the death penalty because he was abused as a child. We do not hold him immune from capital punishment, but require his background to be considered by the sentencer as a mitigating factor.

Today's opinion adds one more to the long list of substantive and procedural requirements impeding imposition of the death penalty imposed under this Court's assumed power to invent a death-is-different jurisprudence. None of those requirements existed when the Eighth Amendment was adopted, and some of them were not even supported by current moral consensus. . . .

There is something to be said for popular abolition of the death penalty; there is nothing to be said for its incremental abolition by this Court.

I respectfully dissent.

The Death Penalty Once More

Ernest van den Haag

People concerned with capital punishment disagree on essentially three questions: (1) Is it constitutional? (2) Does the death penalty deter crime more than life imprisonment? (3) Is the death penalty morally justifiable?

I. Is *the Death Penalty Constitutional?*

The fifth amendment, passed in 1791, states that "no person shall be deprived of life, liberty, or property, without due process of law." Thus, with "due process of law," the Constitution authorizes depriving persons "of life, liberty or property." The fourteenth amendment, passed in 1868, applies an identical provision to the states. The Constitution, then, authorizes the death penalty. It is left to elected bodies to decide whether or not to retain it.

The eighth amendment, reproducing almost verbatim a passage from the English Bill of Rights of 1689, prohibits "cruel and unusual punishments." This prohibition was not meant to repeal the fifth amendment since the amendments were passed simultaneously. "Cruel" punishment is not prohibited unless "unusual"

as well, that is, new, rare, not legislated, or disproportionate to the crime punished. Neither the English Bill of Rights, nor the eighth amendment, hitherto has been found inconsistent with capital punishment.

A. Evolving Standards

Some commentators argue that, in *Trop v. Dulles*, the Supreme Court indicated that "evolving standards of decency that mark the progress of a maturing society" allow courts to declare "cruel and unusual," punishments authorized by the Constitution. However, *Trop* was concerned with expatriation, a punishment that is not specifically authorized by the Constitution. The death penalty is. *Trop* did not suggest that "evolving standards" could de-authorize what the Constitution repeatedly authorizes. Indeed, Chief Justice Warren, writing for the majority in *Trop*, declared that "the death penalty . . . cannot be said to violate the constitutional concept of cruelty."[1] Furthermore, the argument based on "evolving standards" is paradoxical: the Constitution would be redundant if current views, enacted by judicial fiat, could supersede what it plainly says. If "standards of decency" currently invented or evolved could, without formal amendment, replace or repeal the standards authorized by the Constitution, the Constitution would be superfluous.

This work was originally published in 29 U.C. Davis L. Rev. 957 (1985). © 1985 by The Regents of the University of California. Reprinted by permission.

It must be remembered that the Constitution does not force capital punishment on the population but merely authorizes it. Elected bodies are left to decide whether to use the authorization. As for "evolving standards," how could courts detect them without popular consensus as a guide? Moral revelations accepted by judges, religious leaders, sociologists, or academic elites, but not by the majority of voters, cannot suffice. The opinions of the most organized, most articulate, or most vocal might receive unjustified deference. Surely the eighth amendment was meant to limit, but was not meant to replace, decisions by the legislative branch, or to enable the judiciary to do what the voters won't do. The general consensus on which the courts would have to rely could be registered only by elected bodies. They favor capital punishment. Indeed, at present, more than seventy percent of the voters approve of the death penalty. The state legislatures reflect as much. Wherefore, the Supreme Court, albeit reluctantly, rejected abolition of the death penalty by judicial fiat. This decision was subsequently qualified by a finding that the death penalty for rape is disproportionate to the crime, and by rejecting all mandatory capital punishment.

B. Caprice

Laws that allowed courts too much latitude to decide, perhaps capriciously, whether to actually impose the death penalty in capital cases also were found unconstitutional. In response, more than two-thirds of the states have modified their death penalty statutes, listing aggravating and mitigating factors, and imposing capital punishment only when the former outweigh the latter. The Supreme Court is satisfied that this procedure meets the constitutional requirements of noncapriciousness. However, abolitionists are not.

. . . Professor Charles Black contends that the death penalty is necessarily imposed capriciously, for irremediable reasons. If he is right, he has proved too much, unless capital punishment is imposed more capriciously now than it was in 1791 or 1868, when the fifth and fourteenth amendments were enacted. He does not contend that it is. Professor Black also stresses that the elements of chance, unavoidable in all penalization, are least tolerable when capital punishment is involved. But the irreducible chanciness inherent in human efforts does not constitutionally require the abolition of capital punishment, unless the framers were less aware of chance and human frailty than Professor Black is. . . .

C. Discrimination

Sociologists have demonstrated that the death penalty has been distributed in a discriminatory pattern in the past: black or poor defendants were more likely to be executed than equally guilty others. This argues for correction of the distributive process, but not for abolition of the penalty it distributes, unless constitutionally excessive maldistribution ineluctably inheres in the penalty. There is no evidence to that effect. Actually, although we cannot be sure that it has disappeared altogether, discrimination has greatly decreased compared to the past.

However, recently the debate on discrimination has taken a new turn. Statistical studies have found that, *ceteris paribus*, a black man who murders a white has a much greater chance to be executed than he would have had, had his victim been black. This discriminates against black *victims* of murder: they are not as fully, or as often, vindicated as are white victims. However, although unjustified per se, discrimination against a class of victims need not, and here does not, amount to discrimination against their victimizers. The pattern discriminates *against* black murderers of whites and *for* black murderers of blacks. One may describe it as discrimination for, or discrimination against, just as one may describe a glass of water as half full or half empty. Discrimination against one group (here, blacks who kill whites) is necessarily discrimination in favor of another (here, blacks who kill blacks).

Most black victims are killed by black murderers, and a disproportionate number of murder victims is black. Wherefore the discrimination in favor of murderers of black victims more than offsets, numerically, any remaining discrimination against other black murderers.

D. Comparative Excessiveness

Recently lawyers have argued that the death penalty is unconstitutionally disproportionate if defendants, elsewhere in the state, received lesser sentences for comparable crimes. But the Constitution only requires that penalties be appropriate to the gravity of the crime, not that they cannot exceed penalties imposed elsewhere. Although some states have adopted "comparative excessiveness" reviews, there is no constitutional requirement to do so.

Unavoidably, different courts, prosecutors, defense lawyers, judges and juries produce different penalties even when crimes seem comparable. Chance plays a great role in human affairs. Some offenders are never caught or convicted, while others are executed; some are punished more than others guilty of worse crimes. Thus, a guilty person, or group of persons, may get away with no punishment, or with a light punishment, while others receive the punishment they deserve. Should we let these others go too, or punish them less severely? Should we abolish the penalty applied unequally or discriminatorily?

The late Justice Douglas suggested an answer to these questions:

> A law that . . . said that blacks, those who never went beyond the fifth grade in school, those who made less than $3,000 a year, or those who were unpopular or unstable should be the only people executed [would be wrong]. A law which in the overall view reaches that result in practice has no more sanctity than a law which in terms provides the same.[2]

Justice Douglas' answer here conflates an imagined discriminatory law with the discriminatory application of a non-discriminatory law. His imagined law would be inconsistent with the "equal protection of the laws" demanded by the fourteenth amendment, and the Court would have to invalidate it ipso facto. But discrimination caused by uneven application of non-discriminatory death penalty laws may be remedied by means other than abolition, as long as the discrimination is not intrinsic to the laws.

Consider now, albeit fleetingly, the moral as distinguished from the constitutional bearing of discrimination. Suppose guilty defendants are justly executed, but only if poor, or black and not otherwise. This unequal justice would be morally offensive for what may be called tautological reasons: if any punishment for a given crime is just, then a greater or lesser punishment is not. Only one punishment can be just for all persons equally guilty of the same crime. Therefore, different punishments for equally guilty persons or group members are unjust: some offenders are punished more than they deserve, or others less.

Still, equality and justice are not the same. "Equal justice" is not a redundant phrase. Rather, we strive for two distinct ideals, justice and equality. Neither can replace the other. We want to have justice and, having it, we want to extend it equally to all. We would not want equal injustice. Yet, sometimes, we must choose between equal injustice and unequal justice. What should we prefer? Unequal justice is justice still, even if

only for some, whereas equal injustice is injustice for all. If not every equally guilty person is punished equally, we have unequal justice. It seems preferable to equal injustice—having no guilty person punished as deserved. Since it is never possible to punish equally all equally guilty murderers, we should punish, as they deserve, as many of those we apprehend and convict as possible. Thus, even if the death penalty were inherently discriminatory—which is not the case—but deserved by those who receive it, it would be morally just to impose it on them. If, as I contend, capital punishment is just and not inherently discriminatory, it remains desirable to eliminate inequality in distribution, to apply the penalty to all who deserve it, sparing no racial or economic class. But if a guilty person or group escaped the penalty through our porous system, wherein is this an argument for sparing others?

If one does not believe capital punishment can be just, discrimination becomes a subordinate argument, since one would object to capital punishment even if it were distributed equally to all the guilty. If one does believe that capital punishment for murderers is deserved, discrimination against guilty black murderers and in favor of equally guilty white murderers is wrong, not because blacks receive the deserved punishment, but because whites escape it.

Consider a less emotionally charged analogy. Suppose traffic police ticketed all drivers who violated the rules, except drivers of luxury cars. Should we abolish tickets? Should we decide that the ticketed drivers of nonluxury cars were unjustly punished and ought not to pay their fines? Would they become innocent of the violation they are guilty of because others have not been ticketed? Surely the drivers of luxury cars should not be exempted. But the fact that they were is no reason to exempt drivers of nonluxury cars as well. Laws could never be applied if the escape of one person, or group, were accepted as ground for not punishing another. To do justice is primarily to punish as deserved, and only secondarily to punish equally.

Guilt is personal. No one becomes less guilty or less deserving of punishment because another was punished leniently or not at all. That justice does not catch up with all guilty persons understandably is resented by those caught. But it does not affect their guilt. If some, or all, white and rich murderers escape the death penalty, how does that reduce the guilt of black or poor murderers, or make them less deserving of punishment, or deserving of a lesser punishment?

Some lawyers have insisted that the death penalty is distributed among those guilty of murder as though by a lottery and that the worst may escape it. They exaggerate, but suppose one grants the point. How do those among the guilty selected for execution by lottery become less deserving of punishment because others escaped it? What is wrong is that these others escaped, not that those among the guilty who were selected by the lottery did not.

Those among the guilty actually punished by a criminal justice system unavoidably are selected by chance, not because we want to so select them, but because the outcome of our efforts largely depends on chance. No murderer is punished unless he is unlucky enough both to be caught and to have convinced a court of his guilt. And courts consider evidence not truth. They find truth only when the evidence establishes it. Thus they may have reasonable doubts about the guilt of an actually guilty person. Although we may strive to make justice as equal as possible, unequal justice will remain our lot in this world. We should not give up justice, or the death penalty, because we cannot extend it as equally to all the guilty as we wish. If we were not to punish one offender because another got away because of caprice or discrimination, we would give up justice for the sake of equality. We would reverse the proper order of priorities.

II. Is *the Death Penalty More Deterrent Than Other Punishments?*

Whether or not the death penalty deters the crimes it punishes more than alternative penalties—in this case life imprisonment with or without parole—has been widely debated since Isaac Ehrlich broke the abolitionist ranks by finding that from 1933–65 "an additional execution per year . . . may have resulted on the average in seven or eight fewer murders."[3] Since his article appeared, a whole cottage industry devoted to refuting his findings has arisen. Ehrlich, no slouch, has been refuting those who refuted him. The result seems inconclusive. Statistics have not proved conclusively that the death penalty does or does not deter murder more than other penalties. Still, Ehrlich has the merit of being the first to use a sophisticated statistical analysis to tackle the problem, and of defending his analysis, although it showed deterrence. . . . His predecessors cannot be accused of mathematical sophistication. Yet the academic community uncritically accepted their abolitionist results. I myself have no contribution to make to the mathematical analyses of deterrent effects. Perhaps this is why I have come to believe that

they may becloud the issue, leading us to rely on demonstrable deterrence as though decisive.

Most abolitionists believe that the death penalty does not deter more than other penalties. But most abolitionists would abolish it, even if it did. I have discussed this matter with prominent abolitionists. . . . Each told me that, even if every execution were to deter a hundred murders, he would oppose it. I infer that, to these abolitionist leaders, the life of every murderer is more valuable than the lives of a hundred prospective victims, for these abolitionists would spare the murderer, even if doing so would cost a hundred future victims their lives.

Obviously, deterrence cannot be the decisive issue for these abolitionists. It is not necessarily for me either, since I would be for capital punishment on grounds of justice alone. On the other hand, I should favor the death penalty for murderers, if probably deterrent, or even just possibly deterrent. To me, the life of any innocent victim who might be spared has great value; the life of a convicted murderer does not. This is why I would not take the risk of sacrificing innocents by not executing murderers.

Even though statistical demonstrations are not conclusive, and perhaps cannot be, I believe that capital punishment is likely to deter more than other punishments because people fear death more than anything else. They fear most death deliberately inflicted by law and scheduled by the courts. Whatever people fear most is likely to deter most. Hence, I believe that the threat of the death penalty may deter some murderers who otherwise might not have been deterred. And surely the death penalty is the only penalty that could deter prisoners already serving a life sentence and tempted to kill a guard, or offenders about to be arrested and facing a life sentence. Perhaps they will not be deterred. But they would certainly not be deterred by anything else. We owe all the protection we can give to law enforcers exposed to special risks.

Many murders are "crimes of passion" that, perhaps, cannot be deterred by any threat. Whether or not they can be would depend on the degree of passion; it is unlikely to be always so extreme as to make the person seized by it totally undeterrable. At any rate, offenders sentenced to death ordinarily are guilty of premeditated murder, felony murder, or multiple murders. Some are rape murderers, or hit men, but, to my knowledge, no one convicted of a "crime of passion" is on death row. Whatever the motive, some prospective offenders are not deterrable at all, others are easily deterred, and most are in between. Even if only some murders were, or could be, deterred by capital punishment, it would be worthwhile.

Sometimes an anecdote, invented in the 19th Century, is told to suggest that the threat of the death penalty does not deter. Some pickpockets are said to have gone eagerly about their business in a crowd assembled to see one of them hang. We are not told what the level of their activity was, compared to the level in crowds of similar size assembled for different purposes. Thus, the anecdote merely shows that the death penalty does not deter some criminals. This never was contested.

Almost all convicted murderers try to avoid the death penalty by appeals for commutation to life imprisonment. However, a minuscule proportion of convicted murderers prefer execution. It is sometimes argued that they murdered for the sake of being executed, of committing suicide via execution. More likely, they prefer execution to life imprisonment. Although shared by few, this preference is not irrational per se. It is also possible that these convicts accept the verdict of the court, and feel that they deserve the death penalty for the crimes they committed, although the modern mind finds it hard to imagine such feelings. But not all murderers are ACLU humanists.

Because those sentenced to death tend to sedulously appeal the verdict of the trial courts, executions are correctly said to be costly. It is doubtful, however, that they are most costly than life imprisonment. Contrary to widely shared assumptions, life prisoners spend much of their time preparing habeas corpus appeals (not to speak of other lawsuits) just as prisoners condemned to death do. But even if execution were more costly than life imprisonment, it should not be abandoned if it is just. If unjust, execution should not occur, even if it were cheap and imprisonment costly. But execution probably is less costly than life imprisonment.

III. Is *the* Death *Penalty Moral?*

A. *Miscarriages*

Miscarriages of justice are rare, but do occur. Over a long enough time they lead to the execution of some innocents. Does this make irrevocable punishments morally wrong? Hardly. Our government employs trucks. They run over innocent bystanders more frequently than courts sentence innocents to death. We do not give up trucks because the benefits they produce outweigh the harm, including the death of innocents. Many human activities, even quite trivial ones, foreseeably cause wrongful deaths. Courts may cause fewer wrongful deaths than golf. Whether one sees the benefit of doing justice by imposing capital punishment as moral, or as material, or both, it outweighs the loss of innocent lives through miscarriages, which are as unintended as traffic accidents.

B. *Vengeance*

Some abolitionists feel that the motive for the death penalty is an un-Christian and unacceptable desire for vengeance. But though vengeance be the motive, it is not the purpose of the death penalty. Doing justice and deterring crime are the purposes, whatever the motive. Purpose (let alone effect) and motive are not the same.

The Lord is often quoted as saying "Vengeance is mine." He did not condemn vengeance. He merely reserved it to Himself—and to the government. For, in the same epistle He is also quoted as saying that the ruler is "the minister of God, a revenger, to execute wrath upon him that doeth evil." The religious notion of hell indicates that the biblical God favored harsh and everlasting punishment for some. However, particularly in a secular society, we cannot wait for the day of judgment to see murderers consigned to hell. Our courts must "execute wrath upon him that doeth evil" here and now.

C. *Charity and Justice*

Today many religious leaders oppose capital punishment. This is surprising, because there is no biblical warrant for their opposition. The Roman Catholic Church and most Protestant denominations traditionally have supported capital punishment. Why have their moral views changed? When sharing secular power, the churches clearly distinguished between justice, including penalization as deserved, a function of the secular power, and charity, which, according to religious doctrine, we should feel for all those who suffer for whatever reasons. Currently, religious leaders seem to conflate justice and charity, to conclude that the death penalty and, perhaps, all punishment, is wrong because uncharitable. Churches no longer share secular power. Perhaps bystanders are more ready to replace justice with charity than are those responsible for governing.

D. *Human Dignity*

Let me return to the morality of execution. Many abolitionists believe that capital punishment is "degrading to human dignity" and inconsistent with the "sanctity of life." Justice Brennan, concurring in *Furman*, stressed these phrases repeatedly. He did not explain what he meant.

Why would execution degrade human dignity more than life imprisonment? One may prefer the latter; but it seems at least as degrading as execution. Philosophers, such as Immanuel Kant and G. F. W. Hegel, thought capital punishment indispensable to redeem, or restore, the human dignity of the executed. Perhaps they were wrong. But they argued their case, whereas no one has explained why capital punishment degrades. Apparently those who argue that it does degrade dignity simply define the death penalty as degrading. If so, degradation (or dehumanization) merely is a disguised synonym for their disapproval. Assertion, reassertion, or definition do not constitute evidence or argument, nor do they otherwise justify, or even explain, disapproval of capital punishment.

Writers, such as Albert Camus, have suggested that murderers have a miserable time waiting for execution and anticipating it. I do not doubt that. But punishments are not meant to be pleasant. Other people suffer greatly waiting for the end, in hospitals, under circumstances that, I am afraid, are at least as degrading to their dignity as execution. These sufferers have not deserved their suffering by committing crimes, whereas murderers have. Yet, murderers suffer less on death row, unless their consciences bother them.

E. Lex Talionis

Some writers insist that the suffering the death penalty imposes on murderers exceeds the suffering of their victims. This is hard to determine, but probably true in some cases and not in other cases. However, the comparison is irrelevant. Murderers are punished, as are all offenders, not just for the suffering they caused their victims, but for the harm they do to society by making life insecure, by threatening everyone, and by requiring protective measures. Punishment, ultimately, is a vindication of the moral and legal order of society and not limited by the *Lex Talionis*, meant to limit private retaliation for harms originally regarded as private.

F. Sanctity of Life

We are enjoined by the Declaration of Independence to secure life. How can this best be achieved? The Constitution authorizes us to secure innocent life by taking the life of murderers, so that any one who deliberately wants to take an innocent life will know that he risks forfeiting his own. The framers did not think that taking the life of a murderer is inconsistent with the "sanctity of life" which Justice Brennan champions. He has not indicated why they were wrong.

G. Legalized Murder?

Ever since Cesare Bonesana, Marchese di Beccaria, wrote *Die Delitti e Delle Pene*, abolitionists have contended that executing murderers legitimizes murder by doing to the murderer what he did to his victim. Indeed, capital punishment retributes, or pays back the offender. Occasionally we do punish offenders by doing to them what they did to their victims. We may lock away a kidnapper who wrongfully locked away his victim, and we may kill the murderer who wrongfully killed his victim. To lawfully do to the offender what he unlawfully did to his victim in no way legitimizes his crime. It legitimizes (some) killing, and not murder. An act does not become a crime because of its physical character, which, indeed, it may share with the legal punishment, but because of its social, or, better, antisocial, character—because it is an unlawful act.

H. Severity

Is the death penalty too severe? It stands in a class by itself. But so does murder. Execution is irreparable. So is murder. In contrast, all other crimes and punishments are, at least partly or potentially, reparable. The death penalty thus is congruous with the moral and material gravity of the crime it punishes.

Still, is it repulsive? Torture, however well deserved, now is repulsive to us. But torture is an artifact. Death is not, since nature has placed us all under sentence of death. Capital punishment, in John Stuart Mill's phrase, only "hastens death"—which is what the murderer did to his victim. I find nothing repulsive in hastening the murderer's death, provided it be done in a nontorturous manner. Had he wished to be secure in his life, he could have avoided murder.

To believe that capital punishment is too severe for any act, one must believe that there can be no act horrible enough to deserve death. I find this belief difficult to understand. I should readily impose the death penalty on a Hitler or a Stalin, or on anyone who does what they did, albeit on a smaller scale.

Conclusion

The death penalty has become a major issue in public debate. This is somewhat puzzling, because quantitatively it is insignificant. Still, capital punishment has separated the voters as a whole from a small, but influential, abolitionist elite. There are, I believe, two reasons that explain the prominence of the issue.

First, I think, there is a genuine ethical issue. Some philosophers believe that the right to life is equally imprescriptible for all, that the murderer has as much right to live as his victim. Others do not push egalitarianism that far. They believe that there is a vital difference, that one's right to live is lost when one intentionally takes an innocent life, that everyone has just the right to one life, his own. If he unlawfully takes that of another, he, *eo ipso*, loses his own right to life.

Second, and perhaps as important, the death penalty has symbolic significance. Those who favor it believe that the major remedy for crime is punishment. Those who do not, in the main, believe that the remedy is anything but punishment. They look at the causes of crime and conflate them with compulsions, or with excuses, and refuse to blame. The majority of the people are less sophisticated, but perhaps they have better judgment. They believe that everyone who can understand the nature and effects of his acts is responsible for them, and should be blamed and punished, if he could know that what he did was wrong. Human beings are human because they can be held responsible, as animals cannot be. In that Kantian sense the death penalty is a symbolic affirmation of the humanity of both victim and murderer.

Endnotes

[1] 356 U.S. 86 (1958) at 99.

[2] *Furman v. Georgia*, 408 U.S. 238, 256 (1972) (Douglas, J., concurring).

[3] Ehrlich, *The Deterrent Effect of Capital Punishment: A Question of Life or Death*, 65 Am. Econ. Rev. 397, 414 (1975).

A *Reply to van den* Haag

H. A. BEDAU

Ernest van den Haag divides his defense of the death penalty into three sections: its constitutionality, its preventive effects, and its moral status. It will be convenient to address his criticisms in the order in which he presents them, even though that may make for somewhat tedious reading. . . .

I

Van den Haag argues five different issues on the constitutionality of the death penalty, the first of which rests on the text of the Fifth Amendment in the Bill of Rights (1791). Since "due process of law" is mentioned there in connection with lawful deprivation of

From *Death Penalty in America: Current Controversies* by Hugo Adam Bedau. © 1997 by Hugo Adam Bedau. Used by permission of Oxford University Press, Inc.

"life, limb, or liberty," he concludes that "the Constitution . . . authorizes the death penalty." But this is triply wrong.

First, the text in question does not *authorize* the death penalty; instead, it presents us with a conditional proposition: *If* life is to be taken as a punishment, then it *must* be done with due process of law. In effect, this text presents the government with a choice: Either repeal the death penalty or carry it out according to the requirements of due process. As for any "authorization" of the death penalty, or any other punishment, that depends on the exercise of legislative power within the constraints of the Constitution. As for this mention of the death penalty in the Fifth Amendment, I agree that it shows that the Framers did not consider the possibility that there might be an inconsistency between permitting this mode of punishment under the constraint of due process and any of the other provisions of the Bill of Rights. In any case, it is essential to realize that this conditional proposition is consistent with the rejection of the death penalty (in standard logic, the truth of a conditional neither depends upon nor implies accepting the antecedent).

Second, van den Haag passes over the crucial question whether our current procedures for imposing the death penalty really do satisfy the requirements of due process. I take his silence on the point to imply that he has no qualms here. Well, I do. . . . To be sure, due process of law is a complex and contested concept, and reasonable people can disagree over its requirements. Former Supreme Court Justice Harry Blackmun is not the only erstwhile supporter of the death penalty in America who has abandoned hope that "the machinery of death" can be operated according to the requirements of due process of law.

Finally, by parity of reasoning to van den Haag's own argument, if a state legislature were to enact corporal punishments of extreme cruelty, say cutting off the hand of a thief after his third felony conviction, the legislature could count on the reference to deprivation of "limb" in this clause of the Fifth Amendment to enable such a punishment to pass the Supreme Court's scrutiny—so long as the maiming were done with "due process of law." Are we seriously to believe that the Court would endorse such reasoning? I cannot; nothing in the Fifth Amendment precludes the Court from relying on the Eighth Amendment, prohibiting "cruel and unusual punishments," to rule out as unconstitutional any punishments that maim. The same is true of punishments that kill.

Van den Haag next attacks the argument that the Eighth Amendment prohibition against "cruel and unusual punishments" undermines the legitimacy of the death penalty in our day, even if it did not do so when the amendment was passed, because the clause must be interpreted (in the language of the Court's ruling in *Trop v. Dulles* [1958]) according to "evolving standards of decency." He dismisses this judicial language as "paradoxical" if used to interpret the Constitution in order to repeal punishments having statutory authority, since it would make the Constitution as written "superfluous." Van den Haag seems to think *Trop* was nonetheless correctly decided because the punishment ruled out by the Court in that case was "expatriation, a punishment not specifically authorized by the Constitution." But the Eighth Amendment nowhere mentions (and certainly doesn't "authorize") capital punishment, either.

The issue here is twofold: how to interpret the "cruel and unusual punishment" clause of that amend-

ment, and how to apply that interpretation to the death penalty in light of the relevant facts. As the ratification discussions in 1789 show, it was even then anticipated that at some future date this language might plausibly be used to strike down the death penalty. Nothing in either the Fifth or the Eighth Amendments prohibits the Supreme Court from concluding that two hundred years of experience with capital punishment reveals that it is, after all, cruel and unusual, that its administration makes a mockery of due process of law, and that it also violates "the equal protection of the law" (Fourteenth Amendment).

In this regard it is important to notice that van den Haag mentions in passing (though without implying his approval) that the Supreme Court has declared the death penalty for rape (in *Coker v. Georgia* [1977]) and the mandatory death penalty for murder (in *Woodson v. North Carolina* [1976]) to be in violation of the Eighth Amendment. Consistent with his prior argument here, he must reject the legitimacy of these rulings. On his view, any legislature that wants to have the death penalty for rape is constitutionally "authorized" to do so, whether or not it is "disproportionate" to the crime. And the same is true of any other crime—armed robbery, kidnapping, treason, espionage, arson, train robbery, desecration of a grave— each of them punishable by death earlier in this century in one or another American jurisdiction. But by van den Haag's reasoning, since disproportionality is nowhere mentioned in the Eighth Amendment (having been invented by the Supreme Court in *Weems v. United States* [1910] as an appropriate interpretive principle to explain what a "cruel and unusual punishment" is), he must infer that courts have no authority to invoke disproportionality as a ground for declaring *any* penalties unconstitutional. Thus, he implicitly rejects the Supreme Court's authority to nullify the death penalty for murder by means of an argument that prevents the Court from applying the Eighth Amendment to invalidate *any* penalty, so long as that penalty is carried out by "due process of law" and was tolerated by the Framers.

Van den Haag next addresses the objection that the death penalty as administered is too capricious to be tolerated on constitutional grounds. (As his essay preceded the Court's decision in *McCleskey v. Kemp* by two years, he had no opportunity to mention that this decision supports his own views.) He replies in two steps: First, he endorses the Supreme Court's decision in *Gregg* that the post-*Furman* statutory reforms have eliminated whatever caprice infected the administration of pre-*Furman* death penalties. This judgment simply will not withstand scrutiny. The good-faith hopes of the *Gregg* majority in 1976 (especially evident in the concurring opinion by Justice White) have simply not been borne out in practice in the two decades since then. No serious and informed student of the administration of the death penalty believes these statutes have so far accomplished more than cosmetic reforms, however well-intentioned they may have been when enacted.

The next objection van den Haag raises is that unless we are to believe the administration of the death penalty today is *more* capricious than it was in the previous century, its capriciousness today fails to show any constitutionally relevant defect. This is a bad argument because it ignores the holding in *Furman*, which was based above all on the capricious, arbitrary, and discriminatory administration of the death penalty of that day. Unless there is *less*—indeed, little or no—caprice in the death penalty as administered today, in contrast to what there was when *Furman* was decided, the post-*Furman* statutes ought to be invalidated by the reasoning that prevailed in *Furman*. One way around this, of course, is to argue that *Furman* was wrongly decided in the first place and ought to be overruled—an argument I am sure van den Haag would want to make. The fact that the Supreme Court has so far failed to reverse its ruling in *Gregg*, or to hold the states on a short tether where the death penalty is concerned, tells us more about the ideology and politics of the majority of the Court since 1975 than it does about the constitutionality of the death penalty.

Van den Haag devotes two paragraphs to attacking the claim that racial discrimination in administering the death penalty establishes that penalty's unconstitutionality. (Subsequent to his essay, David Baldus and his two coauthors published *Equal Justice and the Death Penalty: A Legal and Empirical Analysis* [1990], amply establishing just such discrimination.) Van den Haag concedes that there is some racial discrimination in the way this penalty is administered. The importance of this concession is not to be underestimated; few defenders of the death penalty today are willing to concede as much. Van den Haag probably attaches little weight to it because he probably would also concede that the whole criminal justice system is tilted slightly against nonwhites, thus reducing to relative insignificance whatever racial discrimination the death penalty involves. He insists that the remedy is not to abolish the death penalty but to abolish the discrimination (which, he adds, favor murderers of blacks and therefore favors blacks over whites, since most black murder victims are killed by blacks). When this is taken as an abstract proposition, one must agree with van den Haag: Since capital statutes as they are written do not discriminate on racial grounds, they ought not to be repealed just because they are administered with discriminatory results.

But this remedy of nondiscrimination, which van den Haag so easily proposes, simply flies in the face of everything we know about the history of the death penalty in this nation, and especially in the South. Are we seriously to think that in Texas or Alabama or South Carolina (or even outside the South, in California, Illinois, or New York) prosecutors and trial juries will remedy their history of racial discrimination by meting out death penalties regardless of the race of the victim or the offender? No, we are not. Van den Haag's argument is simply beside the point; it is a frivolous appeal to an abstract possibility that two centuries of experience tell us will not be put into practice, not in our lifetimes and not in those of our children or their children. If we really want to improve on the rough justice of our current practices involving the death penalty, the only way to do so is to abolish it and sentence *all* convicted murderers to prison, whatever their race and the race of their victim(s). No doubt inequities will remain, but their magnitude will have been dramatically reduced.

Van den Haag's final and lengthiest constitutional consideration takes up proportionality review. A year after his essay was published, the Supreme Court ruled in *Pulley v. Harris* (1984) as he would have wished, rejecting the argument to make proportionality review a constitutional requirement in capital cases. However, nowhere in his discussion does he address the equal protection clause of the Fourteenth Amendment and what relevance it may have, although that ought to be his chief, if not his sole, concern here. Instead, he invites us to consider which is worse—giving some murderers their just deserts (a death penalty) even when we do not give it to all murderers, or giving it to none because we cannot give it to all. Van den Haag favors, he says, justice over equality if we cannot have both. Again, taken abstractly, his position here is plausible.

But, also once again, why take the matter so abstractly? We have ample empirical evidence, based on actual research on prosecutorial decision making, the deliberations of capital juries, and the conduct of clemency hearings in capital cases, to believe that the disproportionality in sentencing is *not* the result of a random "lottery" or of mere "chance" (van den Haag's favorite explanatory factors). Rather, it is due to illegitimate factors of race, class, and social policy. This is why the decision to execute a given capital offender is vulnerable to criticism on equal protection grounds.

. . .

II

With constitutional issues disposed of, van den Haag addresses deterrence and the empirical research on which judgments of deterrence are and ought to be made. Oddly, he says nothing explicit about incapacitation, although the special incapacitative effects of the death penalty are usually touted by those of its defenders who attach importance to deterrence. He concludes that the results of all the empirical research are "inconclusive," and so he is inclined to advise partisans on each side of the death penalty debate to distrust reliance on research of this sort. This is a minimalist interpretation of the evidence if ever there was one, since it wrongly encourages the inexperienced student of this subject to think that the empirical pros and cons about the special deterrent effects of the death penalty are at a standoff. Van den Haag and others who support the death penalty on deterrent grounds need to ponder [other research] to see just how completely without foundation is any belief in the deterrent efficacy of the death penalty in the United States during the past half century.

Van den Haag then insists that despite the lack of empirical evidence he still believes the death penalty is a better deterrent. Why? "[B]ecause people fear death more than anything else." Perhaps they would say they do, if they were asked to answer the question, Which do you fear more, a death penalty or life in prison? But armed robbers, gangland hit men, kids in cars hell-bent on drive-by shootings, and other persons really interested in murdering someone are not thinking about that question. They are thinking instead about this question: "What's the best way for me to commit the crime and not get caught?" Van den Haag also argues that the death penalty must be a better deterrent because death row convicts would rather have their sentences commuted to life in prison. This preference tends to show that life imprisonment is believed to be a less *severe* punishment than death. It does not show that death is a better *deterrent*—unless

you accept as an axiom that the more severe a punishment is thought to be, the better a deterrent it is. The truth of that belief matters not at all if rational people will be deterred from murder as well by a long prison sentence as by a death sentence.

Van den Haag concedes that many murderers are undeterrable but adds: "Even if only some murders were, or could be, deterred by capital punishment, it would be worthwhile." Many agree with him. But one must ask, What cost are you prepared to pay to gain this elusive extra deterrence? The dollar costs, as Richard Dieter has shown, are mounting rapidly, with no end in sight. Quite apart from these costs are the moral costs, chief of which is the great risk of executing the innocent (I will return to this later).

Before turning to his third category of issues, van den Haag addresses the relative costs of execution versus imprisonment. He argues that imprisonment is the more costly of the two and that, even if it weren't we should pay the extra cost of justice—which involves putting to death all who are sentenced to death, preferably with more dispatch than we currently do. We all should agree with him about paying what justice costs, but it remains to be shown that executing prisoners *is* what justice requires (an issue to which I will return in the following). And on the empirical question of the relative costs, the best current information and research, summarized by Dieter, suggest van den Haag is simply wrong—just as he is wrong in claiming that it is primarily the postconviction appeals that run up the economic costs of capital punishment.

Throughout his discussion of deterrence, van den Haag fails to address a crucial question: If the death penalty is to be defended on grounds of its superior deterrence (or incapacitation), what stops us from defending even more savage penalties if they prove (or seem likely to prove) to be an even better deterrent than the death penalty as currently used? Later in his essay, he dismisses torture on the subjective ground that it is "repulsive to us." Well, it is not repulsive to torturers, and to them van den Haag evidently has nothing to say except to express his personal disapproval. It's of no use to his argument that everyone agrees the Constitution prohibits such "cruel and unusual punishments" as boiling in oil or crucifixion or burning at the stake. He has to explain, consistent with his endorsement of the importance of extra deterrence, how and why he respects the moral basis of the constitutional prohibition. He fails to do that; his ethical subjectivism prevents him from doing so. Like every other defender of the death penalty on deterrent grounds, van den Haag has nursed an asp to his bosom that will destroy whatever limits he thinks might be morally appropriate on cruel punishments—limits that in any case he can treat as nothing more than collective subjective preferences.

I complete my criticism of van den Haag's view on deterrence by responding to his claim that I and other abolitionists who oppose the death penalty on principle would evidently tolerate the murder of hundreds rather than execute any convicted murderers even if we knew that by doing so we could have prevented those murders by the extra deterrence the death penalty provides. I cannot speak for the others whom van den Haag mentions in this connection. . . . But speaking only for myself, I would point out two things.

First, my unwillingness to execute (or to have the state hire someone to execute) a convicted murderer is not the same as someone else's decision to commit murder. Neither is it in any sense the cause of such a decision. My refusal to authorize killing the guilty is not equivalent to my authorizing the death of the innocent. So my refusal to authorize executions does not make me responsible for murder, even if those executions would have deterred murderers that imprisonment would not.

Second, as is evident from contemporary philosophical discussion, it is extremely difficult to resist the lure of torture, murder, and other dark deeds when it can be argued that without such acts thousands, or millions, of innocents will surely die. Where the death penalty today is concerned, however, any version of this dilemma is so conjectural that worrying about it is as implausible as worrying about sharks on dry land. Van den Haag is right that I oppose the death penalty in principle and without exceptions; he is wrong in implying that I would tolerate with equanimity the deaths of innocents simply to avoid lawful execution of one who is guilty. I favor abolition, not least because I am confident that zero deterrence would be lost.

III

In the final and most important (but briefest and least coherent) part of his argument, van den Haag raises eight scattered issues collected under the heading of the morality of the death penalty. On the first of these, miscarriages of justice, he concedes that in the long run the death penalty "lead[s] to the execution of some innocents." This is another important concession. . . . But these losses are rare and worth it, he argues, because of the offsetting advantages that *only* the death penalty provides—at which point he recycles his belief in the deterrent superiority of the death penalty. As for his analogy (we tolerate high-speed highways despite our knowledge that they increase traffic deaths), all one can say is that there is *no* analogy between a morally defensible practice in which lethal accidents do occur that take statistical lives and a morally dubious practice in which lethal events are designed for particular individuals in the mistaken belief that they deserve it.

Van den Haag turns next to the role of "vengeance." [H]is interest in this concept arises from its role in Judeo-Christian religious morality. . . . I am troubled by van den Haag's endorsement of vengeance as a legitimate "motive" for the death penalty, even if not its real "purpose." Insofar as vengeance is the motive, does he want us to believe that only supporters of the death penalty *can* act from this motive? Or that only they are *entitled* to act from it? Neither is plausible. That to one side, vengeance is too eruptive and violent an emotion to encourage in ourselves and others. It cannot be confined and channeled to tolerate, much less support, due process of law in punishment, and is likely to spill over into private violence. However, as van den Haag rightly notes, subjective "motives" such as vengeance are not what is at issue in evaluating punitive policy; it is the objective "purposes" that govern the discussion. So, asking us to tolerate vengeance as a legitimate motive for the death penalty is really a red herring, and a dangerous one.

Van den Haag rebukes Christian religious leaders who oppose the death penalty, reminding them that "there is no biblical warrant for their opposition." However, even if van den Haag is right about how to read and interpret the Bible, all he has done is put in question the legitimacy of professing Christians opposing the death penalty on narrowly biblical (constructing "biblical" to mean "literally textual") grounds. This does nothing to undermine any nonreligious moral arguments against the death penalty, which Jews and Christians are as entitled to advance as well as anyone else.

Van den Haag next tackles the concept and role of "human dignity" and denies that there is any mileage for abolitionists to be gained by invoking this value. He adds that "no one has explained why capital punishment degrades" human dignity, and he implies that no one can. In an essay published some years after his and designed to explain the idea of the death penalty as a violation of human dignity, I began by using the four principles Justice Brennan introduced in his concurring opinion in *Furman* in order to explain why the death penalty was an affront to human dignity and thus in violation of the Eighth Amendment's prohibition of "cruel and unusual punishments." The essential part of my argument, taken out of the context of a rather long discussion, was this:

> Let us reformulate Brennan's four principles in a more uniform manner that emphasizes their connection to human dignity. Taking them in the order in which he mentions them, this is what we get: First, it is an affront to the dignity of a person to be forced to undergo catastrophic harm at the hands of another when, before the harm is imposed, the former is entirely at the mercy of the latter, as is always the case with legal punishment. Second, it offends the dignity of a person who is punished according to the will of a punisher free to pick and choose arbitrarily among offenders so that only a few are punished very severely when all deserve the same severe punishment if any do. Third, it offends the dignity of a person to be subjected to a severe punishment when society shows by its actual conduct in sentencing that it no longer regards this severe punishment as appropriate. Finally, it is an affront to human dignity to impose a very severe punishment on an offender when it is known that a less severe punishment will achieve all the purposes it is appropriate to try to achieve by punishing anyone in any manner whatsoever.

These reformulations link the concept of human dignity explicitly with the concept of "cruel and unusual punishments" via the notion of appropriate limits to the permissible severity of punishments. This is easily seen if we recall several of the constitutive elements of human dignity discussed earlier: Respect for the autonomy of rational creatures forbids its needless curtailment in the course of deserved punishment. Respect for the equal worth of persons forbids inequitable punishments of convicted offenders equally guilty. The fundamental

equal rights of persons, including convicted offenders, precludes treating some offenders as if they had ceased to be persons.

Van den Haag turns to the law of retaliation, *lex talionis*, only to reject its authority. This is another important concession because it deprives him of arguing from this general principle of retaliatory punishments to the special case of the death penalty for murder, in which we take "a life for a life." (Of course, his disavowal of *lex talionis* also spares him the embarrassment of trying to cope with the inapplicability and absurdity of this law for a wide range of crimes, just as it frees him to defend the death penalty, should he wish to, for crimes that include no murder.) Instead, he argues that "[p]unishment, ultimately, is a vindication of the moral and legal order of society." No doubt it ought to be, although it behooves those who would defend punishment in these terms to convince us that the current moral and legal order is sufficiently just to warrant our punitive practices. But of course one can grant van den Haag's claim about the nature or ultimate purpose of state punishment without for one moment suggesting that law and moral order can be vindicated *only* or *best* by the use of death penalties or any other unnecessary punishment. This is precisely what I would deny and what van den Haag apparently believes and ought to defend. But he doesn't.

Before turning to the next of van den Haag's moral considerations, we should notice how the fundamental principle of much of his overall argument is badly neglected. He makes it clear in passing that murderers *deserve* to die, and that the principal justification of the death penalty is *justice*. He seems to believe that *desert* tells us *whom* to punish (guilty criminals), *what* they deserve as their punishment (murderers deserve death), and *why* this is what they deserve (justice). Yet his position on these issues is incomplete and unsatisfactory, for at least two reasons. First, he does not defend a mandatory death penalty; in principle that ought to prevent the arbitrariness, which he concedes, of our current discretionary death penalty, just as it ought to increase deterrence and retribution. So why doesn't he support it? Because a mandatory death penalty "risks jury cancellations." Historically, there is evidence to support this worry, but it is a silly reason for him to endorse, unless he believes that the future death penalties likely to be canceled by this route are so many that they vastly exceed in number the future death penalties not meted out under the current discretionary system, with the result that a return to mandatory death penalties would achieve less deterrence and retribution than the current system. Why van den Haag would believe this, when he believes the public overwhelmingly favors the death penalty and when he knows that opponents of the death penalty are routinely excluded from capital trial juries, beats me. And how our current arbitrary and discretionary death penalty system "vindicates the moral and legal order" in a manner of which we can be proud remains a mystery.

Second, what are we to make of his fundamental proposition that *murderers deserve the death penalty*? Is it supposed to be a necessary moral truth that anyone can see to be true simply by understanding the concepts used to express it, an analytic a priori proposition? I hope van den Haag would not take this route to defend this proposition because it will be difficult to prevent turning it into a mere prejudice. To avoid that, this proposition must be somehow established by derivation from more fundamental norms. What are they? Since he has rejected *lex talionis*—the obvious if unsatisfactory answer—and supplied no alternative, we are left to guess. It is interesting to note that in the face of a resurgent approval among philosophers during the past two decades for a retributive justification of punishment, only a few have gone on to endorse a purely or primarily retributive defense of capital punishment.

The next target of his critique is the ideal of "the sanctity of life," which some abolitionists (notably, Justice Brennan) insist the death penalty violates. He does not try to explain this ideal or why one might think it is inconsistent with the death penalty. Instead, he recycles constitutional considerations, purporting to show that the Framers, who accepted this ideal, did so in a manner that did not rule out capital punishment. But none of this really speaks to the moral issues involved. For my part, I would put this ideal to one side in the present discussion because the *sanctity* of life (all life? only human life? only innocent human life?) is not a secular concept but a religious one—unlike the *right* to life, which is a secular concept. For some reason, van den Haag has virtually nothing to say about this idea (but see my penultimate paragraph below). Whatever role the sanctity of life properly plays in a religiously based morality, it really cannot be used as a building block for a secular morality. Nor can it be properly used to evaluate from a secular perspective such controversial issues as suicide, euthanasia, abortion, war—or the death penalty. Since van den Haag does not discuss the

bearing of our right to life on the morality of the death penalty, I will excuse myself from doing so here.

Van den Haag's penultimate barb is directed at those abolitionists who think that executing murderers "legitimizes murder by doing to the murderer what he did to his victim." He rejects this objection because it confuses the legitimate killing of convicted murderers with the illegitimate killing by murderers. This strikes me as completely begging the question. The point of the objection he wishes to refute is that where the legitimacy of killing lies in the eye of the killer, we must be very careful what killings we are prepared to permit.

Consider by contrast for a moment the idea of killing in self-defense. Opponents of the death penalty do not condemn such killings, arguing that killing in self-defense legitimates murder. (Notice, by the way, that van den Haag nowhere claims that when society uses the death penalty, it does so in self-defense. Perhaps he would grant that this is an implausible claim for defenders of the death penalty to advance, because nowhere in Europe today, or in Michigan for a century and a half, to cite but one local example, has social defense required reliance on the death penalty.) The reason abolitionists believe the death penalty legitimates murder in the eyes of some is that the grounds on which the government acts in deciding whom to prosecute for a death sentence, whom to convict of capital murder, whom to sentence to death, whom to refuse clemency, looks suspiciously vindictive, arbitrary, and illegitimate. This invites some to reason as follows: "If the government is permitted to kill for its reasons, then I should be permitted to kill for mine." Van den Haag's argument is not with abolitionists, who do not endorse this reasoning, but with whoever does reason in the manner. Simply declaring that murder is wrong and the death penalty legitimate is hardly sufficient.

Finally, van den Haag turns to the question whether the death penalty is "too severe" and concludes that it is not. Yes, it is "irreparable"—but so is murder. No, it is not "repulsive"—since we all must die someday. And he ends by informing us how readily he would put to death a Hitler, a Stalin, or "anyone who does what they did, albeit on a smaller scale." But whether the death penalty is too severe depends on what one thinks the purpose and rationale of its severity is. Whatever that purpose or rationale, I think it is unnecessary for deterrence or incapacitation, arbitrary and discriminatory in the retribution it inflicts, and therefore an affront to our civilized sensibilities.

As to whether the death penalty is repulsive, I suggest that van den Haag inform himself more vividly about what happens during a typical electrocution—a pretty ugly affair at best . . . and as demonstrated by the repulsive 1990 electrocution of Jesse Tafero in Florida. I would grant . . . that the physical act of execution by lethal injection is not repulsive typically or necessarily—no doubt, a widely shared belief and a significant factor in explaining the popularity of lethal injection with American legislatures during the past twenty years. But this emphasis on the details of particular executions or on techniques for carrying out the death penalty obscures what is arguably repulsive about executions as such: It is not only that the prisoner dies, or dies in agony, or dies with ugly disfigurement, but that the lethal act itself is the result of calculated planning by the impersonal state in which the state's overwhelming power is on display against the helplessness of the prisoner.

When van den Haag reminds us that death is inevitable in the nature of things, he does not make a very persuasive point. Human disappointment, pain, loneliness, bereavement, and other forms of misery and suffering are part of the human condition and virtually inevitable for each of us. Yet is that a good reason for complacency in their face if it is within our power to remedy or mitigate, even if only briefly or slightly, these inevitabilities? Van den Haag does not address this question.

As for Hitler and Stalin, they are often the trump card used by modern defenders of the death penalty who cannot believe that anyone really would oppose *all* executions. The trouble is that appealing to Hitler and Stalin sheds no light on whether to execute all or some or none of the more than three thousand prisoners on American death rows today. For myself, I would be glad to make an exception to my absolute rejection of the death penalty by permitting van den Haag to destroy tyrants such as these if he would give me the lives of those actually under sentence of death today, whose crimes are pathetically insignificant if measured against genocide, aggressive warfare, and the other crimes against humanity of which these dictators and their henchmen were guilty.

Van den Haag ends his essay by making two points with which abolitionists ought to agree—in part. First, he insists that the national debate over the death penalty is important because it involves "a genuine ethical issue." He is right, but what is this issue as he sees it? It is whether "the right to life" extends to all humans and cannot ever be forfeited. He thinks it can be; I think it cannot. Even if I am right, I suggest that this is not the important ethical issue in the debate. The paramount ethical issue posed by the death penalty is this: Whether or not everyone has an unforfeitable right to life, do *we* do the right thing in authorizing killing some criminals when we know there is an adequate alternative punishment (imprisonment), or do we do the right thing when we refuse to kill any, no matter how guilty they are? The issue, in short, is not the right to life; it is the right to *kill*.

Second, van den Haag insists that we are rightly concerned about the death penalty because it has important "symbolic significance," a significance far beyond its practical import. Again, this is correct. For him, however, this symbolic significance lies in its "affirmation of the humanity of both victim and murderer." Van den Haag here has the support of no less a philosopher than Immanuel Kant, though he does not mention this. I, on the other hand, think the whole idea is bizarre. The very thought that I affirm the humanity of a murderer by treating him more or less as he treated his innocent and undeserving victim would be funny were it not so momentous. For me, the death penalty symbolizes *unlimited impersonal power* over the individual, with dramatically final and irreversible results whenever it is expressed. As long as we choose to hang this moral albatross around our necks, I see no way for us to enjoy, much less help the rest of the world to enjoy, the benefits of a truly human community.

McCleskey v. Kemp

Justice Powell delivered the opinion of the Court, in which Rehnquist, C. J., and White, O'Connor, and Scalia, J. J., joined.

This case presents the question whether a complex statistical study that indicates a risk that racial considerations enter into capital sentencing determinations proves that petitioner McCleskey's capital sentence is unconstitutional under the Eighth or Fourteenth Amendment.

McCleskey, a black man, was convicted of two counts of armed robbery and one count of murder in the Superior Court of Fulton County, Georgia, on October 12, 1978. McCleskey's convictions arose out of the robbery of a furniture store and the killing of a white police officer during the course of the robbery. The evidence at trial indicated that McCleskey and three accomplices planned and carried out the robbery. All four were armed. McCleskey entered the front of the store while the other three entered the rear. McCleskey secured the front of the store by rounding up the customers and forcing them to lie face down on the floor. The other three rounded up the employees in the rear and tied them up with tape. The manager was forced at gunpoint to turn over the store receipts, his watch, and $6. During the course of the robbery, a police officer, answering a silent alarm, entered the store through the front door. As he was walking down the center aisle of the store, two shots were fired. Both struck the officer. One hit him in the face and killed him.

Several weeks later, McCleskey was arrested in connection with an unrelated offense. He confessed that he had participated in the furniture store robbery, but denied that he had shot the police officer. At trial, the State introduced evidence that at least one of the bullets that struck the officer was fired from a .38 caliber Rossi revolver. This description matched the description of the gun that McCleskey had carried during the robbery. The State also introduced the testimony of two witnesses who had heard McCleskey admit to the shooting.

The jury convicted McCleskey of murder. At the penalty hearing, the jury heard arguments as to the appropriate sentence. Under Georgia law, the jury could not consider imposing the death penalty unless it found beyond a reasonable doubt that the murder was accompanied by one of the statutory aggravating circumstances. . . . The jury in this case found two aggravating circumstances to exist beyond a reasonable doubt: the murder was committed during the course of an armed robbery . . . ; and the murder was committed upon a peace officer engaged in the performance of his duties. . . . McCleskey offered no mitigating evidence. The jury recommended that he be sentenced to death on the murder charge and to consecutive life sentences on the armed robbery charges. The court followed the jury's recommendation and sentenced McCleskey to death.

On appeal, the Supreme Court of Georgia affirmed the convictions and the sentences. . . .

McCleskey next filed a petition for a writ of habeas corpus in the Federal District Court for the Northern District of Georgia. His petition raised 18 claims, one of which was that the Georgia capital sentencing process is administered in a racially discriminatory manner in violation of the Eighth and Fourteenth Amendments to the United States Constitution. In support of his claim, McCleskey proffered a statistical study performed by Professors David C. Baldus, Charles Pulaski, and George Woodworth (the Baldus study) that purports to show a disparity in the imposition of the death sentence in Georgia based on the race of the murder victim and, to a lesser extent, the race of the defendant. The Baldus study is actually two sophisticated statistical studies that examine over 2,000 murder cases that occurred in Georgia during the 1970's. The raw numbers collected by Professor Baldus indicate that defendants charged with killing white persons received the death penalty in 11% of the

481 U.S. 279 (1986), United States Supreme Court.

cases, but defendants charged with killing blacks received the death penalty in only 1% of the cases. The raw numbers also indicate a reverse racial disparity according to the race of the defendant: 4% of the black defendants received the death penalty, as opposed to 7% of the white defendants.

Baldus also divided the cases according to the combination of the race of the defendant and the race of the victim. He found that the death penalty was assessed in 22% of the cases involving black defendants and white victims; 8% of the cases involving white defendants and white victims; 1% of the cases involving black defendants and black victims; and 3% of the cases involving white defendants and black victims. Similarly, Baldus found that prosecutors sought the death penalty in 70% of the cases involving black defendants and white victims; 32% of the cases involving white defendants and white victims; 15% of the cases involving black defendants and black victims; and 19% of the cases involving white defendants and black victims.

Baldus subjected his data to an extensive analysis, taking account of 230 variables that could have explained the disparities on nonracial grounds. One of his models concludes that, even after taking account of 39 nonracial variables, defendants charged with killing white victims were 4.3 times as likely to receive a death sentence as defendants charged with killing blacks. According to this model, black defendants were 1.1 times as likely to receive a death sentence as other defendants. Thus, the Baldus study indicates that black defendants, such as McCleskey, who kill white victims have the greatest likelihood of receiving the death penalty.

The District Court . . . denied the petition insofar as it was based upon the Baldus study. . . . The Court of Appeals affirmed the denial. . . .

We . . . now affirm.

McCleskey's first claim is that the Georgia capital punishment statute violates the Equal Protection Clause of the Fourteenth Amendment. He argues that race has infected the administration of Georgia' statute in two ways: persons who murder whites are more likely to be sentenced to death than persons who murder blacks, and black murderers are more likely to be sentenced to death than white murderers. As a black defendant who killed a white victim, McCleskey claims that the Baldus study demonstrates that he was discriminated against because of his race and because of the race of his victim. In its broadest form, McCleskey's claim of discrimination extends to every actor in the Georgia capital sentencing process, from the prosecutor who sought the death penalty and the jury that imposed the sentence, to the State itself that enacted the capital punishment statute and allows it to remain in effect despite its allegedly discriminatory application. We agree with the Court of Appeals, and every other court that has considered such a challenge, that this claim must fail.

Our analysis begins with the basic principle that a defendant who alleges an equal protection violation has the burden of proving "the existence of purposeful discrimination." . . . Thus, to prevail under the Equal Protection Clause, McCleskey must prove that the decisionmakers in his case acted with discriminatory purpose. He offers no evidence specific to his own case that would support an inference that racial considerations played a part in his sentence. Instead, he relies solely on the Baldus study. McCleskey argues that the Baldus study compels an inference that his sentence rests on purposeful discrimination. McCleskey's claim that these statistics are sufficient proof of discrimination, without regard to the facts of a particular case, would extend to all capital cases in Georgia, at least where the victim was white and the defendant is black.

The Court has accepted statistics as proof of intent to discriminate in certain limited contexts. First, this Court has accepted statistical disparities as proof of an equal protection violation in the selection of the jury venire in a particular district. . . . Second, this Court has accepted statistics in the form of multiple-regression analysis to prove statutory violations under Title VII of the Civil Rights Act of 1964. . . .

But the nature of the capital sentencing decision, and the relationship of the statistics to that decision, are fundamentally different from the corresponding elements in the venire-selection or Title VII cases. Most importantly, each particular decision to impose the death penalty is made by a petit jury selected from a properly constituted venire. Each jury is unique in its composition, and the Constitution requires that its decision rest on consideration of innumerable factors that vary according to the characteristics of the individual defendant and the facts of the particular capital offense. . . . Thus, the application of an inference drawn from the general statistics to a specific decision in a trial and sentencing simply is not comparable to the application of an inference drawn from general statistics to a specific venire-selection or Title VII case. In those cases, the statistics relate to fewer entities, and fewer variables are relevant to the challenged decisions. . . .

Because discretion is essential to the criminal justice process, we would demand exceptionally clear proof before we would infer that the discretion has been abused. The unique nature of the decisions at issue in this case also counsels against adopting such an inference from the disparities indicated by the Baldus study. Accordingly, we hold that the Baldus study is clearly insufficient to support an inference that any of the decisionmakers in McCleskey's case acted with discriminatory purpose.

McCleskey also suggests that the Baldus study proves that the State as a whole has acted with a discriminatory purpose. He appears to argue that the State has violated the Equal Protection Clause by adopting the capital punishment statute and allowing it to remain in force despite its allegedly discriminatory application. But "'discriminatory purpose' . . . implies more than intent as volition or intent as awareness of consequences. It implies that the decisionmaker, in this case a state legislature, selected or reaffirmed a particular course of action at least in part 'because of,' not merely 'in spite of,' its adverse effects upon an identifiable group." . . . For this claim to prevail, McCleskey would have to prove that the Georgia Legislature enacted or maintained the death penalty statute because of an anticipated racially discriminatory effect. In *Gregg v. Georgia*, . . . this Court found that the Georgia capital sentencing system could operate in a fair and neutral manner. There was no evidence then, and there is none now, that the Georgia Legislature enacted the capital punishment statute to further a racially discriminatory purpose. . . . Nor has McCleskey demonstrated that the legislature maintains the capital punishment statute because of the racially disproportionate impact suggested by the Baldus study. . . .

Accordingly, we reject McCleskey's equal protection claims. . . .

Justice Brennan, with whom Justice Marshall joins, and with whom Justice Blackmun and Justice Stevens join in all but Part I, dissenting.

It is important to emphasize at the outset that the Court's observation that McCleskey cannot prove the influence of race on any particular sentencing decision is irrelevant in evaluating his Eighth Amendment claim. Since *Furman v. Georgia*, . . . The Court has been concerned with the risk of the imposition of an arbitrary sentence, rather than the proven fact of one. . . . This emphasis on risk acknowledges the difficulty of divining the jury's motivation in an individual case. In addition, it reflects the fact that concern for arbitrariness focuses on the rationality of the system as a whole, and that a system that features a significant probability that sentencing decisions are influenced by impermissible considerations cannot be regarded as rational. . . . As we said in *Gregg v. Georgia* . . . , "the petitioner looks to the sentencing system as a whole (as the Court did in *Furman* and we do today)": a constitutional violation is established if a plaintiff demonstrates a "pattern of arbitrary and capricious sentencing." . . .

Defendants challenging their death sentences thus never have had to prove that impermissible considerations have actually infected sentencing decisions. We have required instead that they establish that the system under which they were sentenced posed a significant risk of such an occurrence. McCleskey's claim does differ, however, in one respect from these earlier cases: it is the first to base a challenge not on speculation about how a system might operate, but on empirical documentation of how it does operate.

The Court assumes the statistical validity of the Baldus study, and acknowledges that McCleskey has demonstrated a risk that racial prejudice plays a role in capital sentencing in Georgia. . . . Nonetheless, it finds the probability of prejudice insufficient to create constitutional concern. . . . Close analysis of the Baldus study, however, in light of both statistical principles and human experience, reveals that the risk that race influenced McCleskey's sentence is intolerable by any imaginable standard.

The Baldus study indicates that, after taking into account some 230 nonracial factors that might legitimately influence a sentencer, the jury more likely than not would have spared McCleskey's life had his victim been black. The study distinguishes between those cases in which (1) the jury exercises virtually no discretion because the strength or weakness of aggravating factors usually suggests that only one outcome is appropriate; and (2) cases reflecting an "intermediate" level of aggravation, in which the jury has considerable discretion in choosing a sentence. McCleskey's case falls into the intermediate range. In such cases, death is imposed in 34% of white-victim crimes and 14% of black-victim crimes, a difference of 139% in the rate of imposition of the death penalty. . . . In other words, just under 59%—almost 6 in 10—defendants comparable to McCleskey would not have received the death penalty if their victims had been black. . . .

Of the more than 200 variables potentially relevant to a sentencing decision, race of the victim is a powerful explanation for variation in death sentence rates—as powerful as nonracial aggravating factors such as a prior murder conviction or acting as the principal planner of the homicide. . . .

Evaluation of McCleskey's evidence cannot rest solely on the numbers themselves. We must also ask whether the conclusion suggested by those numbers is consonant with our understanding of history and human experience. Georgia's legacy of a race-conscious criminal justice system, as well as this Court's own recognition of the persistent danger that racial attitudes may affect criminal proceedings, indicates that McCleskey's claim is not a fanciful product of mere statistical artifice. . . .

The Court cites four reasons for shrinking from the implications of McCleskey's evidence: the desirability of discretion for actors in the criminal justice system, the existence of statutory safeguards against abuse of that discretion, the potential consequences for broader challenges to criminal sentencing, and an understanding of the contours of the judicial role. While these concerns underscore the need for sober deliberation, they do not justify rejecting evidence as convincing as McCleskey has presented.

The Court maintains that petitioner's claim "is antithetical to the fundamental role of discretion in our criminal justice system." . . . It states that "where the discretion that is fundamental to our criminal process is involved, we decline to assume that what is unexplained is invidious." . . . Reliance on race in imposing capital punishment, however, is antithetical to the very rationale for granting sentencing discretion. Discretion is a means, not an end. It is bestowed in order to permit the sentencer to "trea[t] each defendant in a capital case with that degree of respect due the uniqueness of the individual." . . . Considering the race of a defendant or victim in deciding if the death penalty should be imposed is completely at odds with this concern that an individual be evaluated as a unique human being. . . .

The Court also declines to find McCleskey's evidence sufficient in view of "the safeguards designed to minimize racial bias in the [capital sentencing] process." . . . [T]he Court cannot rely on the statutory safeguards in discounting McCleskey's evidence, for it is the very effectiveness of those safeguards that such evidence calls into question. While we may hope that a model of procedural fairness will curb the influence of race on sentencing, "we cannot simply assume that the model works as intended; we must critique its performance in terms of its results." . . .

The Court next states that its unwillingness to regard petitioner's evidence as sufficient is based in part on the fear that recognition of McCleskey's claim would open the door to widespread challenges to all aspects of criminal sentencing. . . . Taken on its face, such a statement seems to suggest a fear of too much justice. . . . In fairness, the Court's fear that McCleskey's claim is an invitation to descend a slippery slope also rests on the realization that any humanly imposed system of penalties will exhibit some imperfection. Yet to reject McCleskey's powerful evidence on this basis is to ignore both the qualitatively different character of the death penalty and the particular repugnance of racial discrimination, considerations which may properly be taken into account in determining whether various punishments are "cruel and unusual." Furthermore, it fails to take account of the unprecedented refinement and strength of the Baldus study. . . .

Finally, the Court justifies its rejection of McCleskey's claim by cautioning against usurpation of the legislatures' role in devising and monitoring criminal punishment. The Court is, of course, correct to emphasize the gravity of constitutional in-tervention and the importance that it be sparingly employed. The fact that "capital punishment is now the law in more than two thirds of our States,". . . however, does not diminish the fact that capital punishment is the most awesome act that a State can perform. The judiciary's role in this society counts for little if the use of governmental power to extinguish life does not elicit close scrutiny. . . . Those whom we would banish from society or from the human community itself often speak in too faint a voice to be heard above society's demand for punishment. It is the particular role of courts to hear these voices, for the Constitution declares that the majoritarian chorus may not alone dictate the conditions of social life. The Court thus fulfills, rather than disrupts, the scheme of separation of powers by closely scrutinizing the imposition of the death penalty, for no decision of a society is more deserving of "sober second thought." . . .

Homicide, Race, and Capital Punishment

Randall Kennedy

No issues concerning race and criminal law are more sobering than those raised by allegations that racial selectivity affects the administration of capital punishment. First, sentencing a person to death as punishment for crime is a unique flexing of state power that inevitably reflects the society's deepest values, emotions, and neuroses. Second, the legal system has shown itself to be largely incapable of acknowledging the influence of racial sentiment in the meting out of punishment even in circumstances in which the presence of such bias is obvious. In no other area of criminal law have judges engaged in more obfuscation, delusion, evasion, and deception. Third, addressing racial discrimination in capital sentencing poses a daunting task for those seeking to craft appropriate remedies.

If a jurisdiction tends to punish more harshly murderers of whites than murderers of blacks, is the appropriate response to abolish capital punishment, to more narrowly limit the circumstances in which capital punishment is imposed, or to execute more people who murder blacks? Even if such a tendency exists, should it be the basis for granting relief to a convicted murderer who fails to show that racial discrimination affected the punishment meted out in his particular case? Is such a tendency a remediable wrong or, instead, an inevitable social trait whereby people unavoidably identify more with the victimization of "their own" as opposed to the victimization of "others"? If this tendency is a wrong, is remedying it within the capacity of courts or is remedying this wrong best left to the legislative and executive branches of government?

. . .

The Supreme Court decided *Coker* at a critical moment in the history of capital punishment. In 1972,

in *Furman v. Georgia*, a closely divided (5 to 4) Court invalidated most existing state laws authorizing the death sentence on the grounds that they violated the Eighth Amendment's prohibition against cruel and unusual punishments. All nine justices wrote opinions in *Furman*. . . . Amid the cacophony, however, a main chord is discernible—that the principal failing of then-existing capital sentencing regimes was the absence of a meaningful basis for distinguishing the few cases in which [capital punishment] is imposed from the many cases in which it is not. "These death sentences," Justice Potter Steward complained, were "cruel and unusual in the same way that being struck by lightning is cruel and unusual."

Furman suggested to some observers that the United States might join the trend of other advanced, Western, industrial democracies toward disavowal of capital punishment. Many state legislatures responded to *Furman*, however, by enacting new death penalty statutes which they believed might overcome the Court's objections. In 1976, in yet another case from Georgia, *Gregg v. Georgia*, the Supreme Court affirmed the constitutionality of at least some of these new "improved" capital punishment laws. The Court validated capital punishment as long as it was implemented by procedures that, in its view, "suitably directed and limited" the discretion of sentencers to preclude arbitrary or capricious punishment. The most salient and significant feature of the approved death penalty statutes is the bifurcaton of trials into a phase directed solely to determining whether the defendant is guilty and then a phase directed solely to determining whether he should be sentenced to death. At the sentencing phase, the defendant is given wide latitude to argue to a judge or jury that his life should be spared. The state, on the other hand, must persuade the judge or jury that the crime meets certain statutorily defined criteria that distinguish it from other crimes, and therefore justifies a death sentence.

In the aftermath of *Gregg*, and particularly as states began aggressively to seek the execution of condemned prisoners, civil rights activists redoubled their efforts. A central feature of their attack, in courts of public opinion as well as courts of law, was and remains their allegation that death sentences tend to be applied in a racially discriminatory fashion. The Court declined to adjudicate the issue on several occasions but finally agreed to consider it in 1987 in yet a third landmark case from Georgia, *McCleskey v. Kemp*.

On May 13, 1978, Warren McCleskey, a black man, helped to rob the Dixie Furniture Store in Atlanta, Georgia. A white police officer, Frank Schlatt, attempted to foil the robbery but was killed by a shot to the head. Sometime later, McCleskey was arrested in connection with another armed robbery. Under questioning, he admitted to participating in the furniture store heist but denied shooting Officer Schlatt. After further investigation, it emerged that McCleskey had stolen a revolver capable of shooting the type of bullet that killed Officer Schlatt. McCleskey also reportedly admitted shooting Schlatt to both a codefendant and a neighboring inmate in jail, both of whom later testified against him.

A jury of eleven whites and one black sentenced McCleskey to life imprisonment for the robbery and death for the murder. His subsequent appeals followed the normal, dreary route of post-conviction proceedings in capital cases. An aspect of his appeal, however, contained a challenge to the entire system of capital punishment in Georgia and beyond. Supported by the most comprehensive statistical analysis ever done on the racial demographics of sentencing in a single state, McCleskey's attorneys argued that their client's sentence should be invalidated because there was a constitutionally impermissible risk that both his race and that of his victim had played a significant role in the decision to sentence him to death.

McCleskey's claim was largely predicated on a study organized and overseen by David C. Baldus, an expert in the application of statistics to legal problems. The Baldus study was derived from records involving the disposition of more than two thousand murder cases between 1973 and 1979. The Georgia Department of Pardons and Paroles and other state agencies provided Baldus with police reports, parole board records, prison files, and other items that evidenced the process by which state authorities handled criminal homicides.

Three findings of the Baldus study are especially pertinent. First, viewing the evidence on a statewide basis, Baldus found "neither strong nor consistent" evidence of discrimination directed against black defendants because of their race. That did not prevent McCleskey's attorneys from asserting that the race of the defendant—especially when the defendant is black and victim white—influences Georgia's capital sentencing process. In their argument to the Supreme Court, however, McCleskey's attorneys clearly subordinated the claim of race-of-the-defendant discrimination to the claim of race-of-the-victim discrimination.

Second, Baldus found that among the variables that might plausibly influence capital sentencing—age, level of education, criminal record, military record, method of killing, motive for killing, relationship of defendant to victim, strength of evidence, and so forth—the race of the victim emerged as the most consistent and powerful factor. Initially, simple correlations suggested the importance of this variable. Without attempting to control for the possible effects of competing variables, Baldus found that perpetrators in white-victim cases were eleven times more likely to be condemned to death than perpetrators in black-victim cases.

Professor Baldus and his associates subjected this striking correlation to extensive statistical analysis to test whether the seemingly racial nature of this disparity was explainable in terms of hidden factors confounded with race. He eventually took into account some 230 nonracial variables that might have influenced the pattern of sentencing. He concluded that even after accounting for every nonracial variable that might have mattered substantially, the race of the victim continued to have a statistically significant correlation with the imposition of capital sentences. Applying a statistical model that included the thirty-nine nonracial variables believed most likely to play a role in capital punishment in Georgia, the Baldus study concluded that the odds of being condemned to death were 4.3 times greater for defendants who killed whites than for defendants who killed blacks, a variable nearly as influential as a prior conviction for armed robbery, rape, or even murder.

Third, Baldus concluded that racial disparities in capital sentencing are most dramatic in that category containing neither the most aggravated nor the least aggravated homicides. Racial disparities are greatest, he argued, in the middle range of aggravated homicides. In the most aggravated cases, decisionmakers typically impose the death sentence regardless of racial variables, and in the least aggravated cases decisionmakers typically spare the defendant regardless of racial variables. In the middle range of aggravation, however, where a decision could go either way, the influence of racial variables emerges more powerfully. This hypothesis is particularly relevant to *McCleskey* because, in Baldus's view, McCleskey's crime was situated in the middle range of aggravated homicide.

After an evidentiary hearing, U.S. District Judge J. Owen Forrester rejected McCleskey's race discrimination claim primarily on the ground that the Baldus study did not represent "good statistical methodology." He objected to what he viewed as significant omissions, errors, and inconsistencies in Baldus's data base and inadequacies in the design of Baldus's statistical models. Judge Forrester's findings were subsequently eclipsed because the court of appeals and the Supreme Court resolved the case without reviewing them; the appellate courts assumed arguendo that the Baldus study was valid. Judge Forrester's findings, however, continue to be relevant insofar as much of the criticism of *McCleskey* and support for legislative responses to it is premised on a belief in the validity of the Baldus study.

· · ·

The factual core of the Baldus study withstands even a skeptical analysis, however. To some extent I am moved to this conclusion by the study's evident carefulness and its authors' insistence on making their data, premises, and calculations available and transparent to the public. I am also influenced by the sworn testimony of respected experts in Baldus's field, notwithstanding the risk of ideological taint identified above. The Baldus study, moreover, is consistent with findings published by a large body of prior research. Even commentators who generally deride allegations of racial discrimination in the administration of criminal law concede that in the context of capital punishment the race of the victim consistently influences sentencing decisions.

· · ·

The Court of Appeals for the Eleventh Circuit assumed the validity of the Baldus study but nevertheless affirmed the district court's race discrimination holding on the grounds that the statistical disparities and supplemental evidence failed to prove a constitutional violation.

Justice Lewis Powell's opinion for a bare majority (5 to 4) of the Supreme Court largely followed the Eleventh Circuit's analysis. The Supreme Court, too, assumed, arguendo, the validity of the Baldus study. Similarly, the Court insisted that the constitutionality of McCleskey's sentence must be determined by asking whether officials in *his* case purposefully discriminated on the basis of race. The Court concluded that no such inference could be drawn from the Baldus statistics. Justice Powell noted that in some contexts a "stark" pattern of statistical disparities may create a prima facie case which shifts onto the state the burden of rebutting an allegation of racial discrimination. He observed, however, that in the context of capital sentencing, "decisions at the heart of the State's criminal justice system," the Court would demand "exceptionally clear proof" before inferring that a sentencing authority had abused its discretion. In the Court's view, the racial correlations revealed by the Baldus study did not meet that standard. Powell declared that "because of the risk that the factor of race may enter the criminal justice process, [the Court has] engaged in 'unceasing efforts' to eradicate racial prejudice from our criminal justice system." In this instance, though, no clear showing had been made that racial prejudice animated the death sentence imposed upon McCleskey. Nor, according to Powell, did the Baldus statistics even show that racial prejudices played a significant role in other cases in Georgia. "At most," Powell averred, "the Baldus study indicates a discrepancy that appears to correlate with race."

Justice Powell noted several reasons of policy that pushed the Court to rule as it did. One was the need to give ample latitude for sentencers to use their discretion in making the unique decision as to whether to end the life of a human being as punishment for a crime. Another concern was that accepting McCleskey's challenge would open a Pandora's box of litigation. "McCleskey's claim, taken to its logical conclusion," Powell remarked with alarm, "throws into serious question the principles that underlie our entire criminal justice system," because, if accepted, the Court "could soon be faced with similar claims as to other types of penalty" from members of other groups alleging bias. Finally, Powell invoked considerations of judicial competence and judicial restraint as reasons for avoiding intervention. "McCleskey's arguments," he declared, "are best presented to legislative bodies. . . . It is the legislatures, the elected representatives of the people, that are constituted to respond to the will and consequently the moral values of the people."

With the exception of Thurgood Marshall, each of the dissenting justices (William J. Brennan, Harry A. Blackmun, and John Paul Stevens) wrote opinions explaining their disagreement with the Court. Maintaining that "we cannot pretend that in three decades we have completely escaped the trap of a historical legacy spanning centuries," Justice Brennan declared that "Warren McCleskey's evidence confronts us with the subtle and persistent influence of the past." Crediting the Baldus study "in light of both statistical principles and human experience," Brennan concluded that "the risk that race influenced McCleskey's sentence is intolerable by any imaginable standard." Responding to the Court's concern that accepting McCleskey's claim would open the door to challenges attacking all aspects of criminal sentencing, Brennan remarked that it displayed "a fear of too much justice. . . . The prospect that there may be more widespread abuse than McCleskey documents may be dismaying, but it does not justify complete abdication of [the] judicial role."

In his dissent, Justice Blackmun wrote that he was "disappointed with the Court's action not only because of its denial of constitutional guarantees to petitioner McCleskey individually, but also because of its departure from . . . well-developed constitutional jurisprudence." Blackmun concluded that "the Court . . . sanctions the execution of a man despite his presentation of evidence that establishes a constitutionally intolerable level of racially based discrimination leading to the imposition of his death sentence." . . .

. . .

A sign of the difficulties posed by *McCleskey* is that none of the justices' opinions is altogether satisfactory. The worst of the lot is also the one backed by the most power: Justice Powell's opinion for the Court. Powell strives to convey the impression that the conclusion he and his four associates reached is the only sensible alternative. He therefore gives the false impression that the case is easy. He responds to the parties' briefs, which one expects to be one-sided, with yet another tendentious brief, although his is styled an "opinion" and thus part of the constitutional law of the United States.

Two features of Powell's opinion are especially troubling. One is his minimization of the facts behind McCleskey's claim. Confronted by statistics indicating that people who kill whites in Georgia are four times more likely to be sentenced to death than people who kill blacks, Powell blandly remarked that "at most [this] indicates a discrepancy that appears to correlate with race"—a statement as vacuous as one declaring, say, that "at most" studies on lung cancer indicate a discrepancy that appears to correlate with smoking. Another example of the resolute evasiveness that emerges time and again in Powell's opinion is his statement that the Court should "decline to assume that what is unexplained is invidious." The petitioner, of course, was not asking the Court to make any such

assumption. Rather, McCleskey's attorneys offered into evidence a comprehensive study showing that certain patterns in capital sentencing cannot plausibly be explained by any variable other than race. . . .

The second outstanding feature of Powell's opinion is his resolute unwillingness to recognize the uniqueness of two distinctions that the Court had previously periodically acknowledged. One was that *McCleskey* involved a peculiarly irrevocable punishment; as various justices have noted, "death is different." The other is that the case involved an allegation that capital punishment in Georgia was systematically meted out according to an especially toxic social demarcation, the race line. Powell refused to recognize these two distinctions as limiting boundaries, probably because doing so would undercut his demagogic assertion that accepting McCleskey's claim would necessarily open a Pandora's box from which limitless disruption would ensue. Fretting that an acceptance of McCleskey's racial claim would invite members of other groups—"even" women—to launch equal protection challenges, Powell and the Court majority resolutely shut the door to any statistics-driven, class-based challenge to the administration of punishment. To justify this action in the context of a case involving blacks, the paradigmatic "out-group" in American political culture, Powell argued that no "logical" reason exists for distinguishing racial or gender bias from any other sort of bias—a bias, for instance, against facial unattractiveness. The life of the law, however, includes not only logic but also experience, and experience teaches that in the United States, racial sentiment displays an intensity and persistence that is distinguishable from all other biases. There exists, moreover, a textual warrant in the Constitution for distinguishing racial and, to a lesser extent, gender bias from other sorts of preference and prejudice.

A similar slamming of the door greeted the oft-voiced claim that allegations of unfairness with respect to death penalties are entitled to special judicial solicitude. As Blackmun complained in dissent, Powell's opinion for the Court gave "new meaning" to the notion that death is different by applying *lesser* scrutiny to the decisionmaking process that leads to death sentences than to decisions affecting employment or the selection of juries.

Powell's *McCleskey* opinion was haunted by anxiety over the consequences of acknowledging candidly the large influence of racial sentiment in the administration of capital punishment in Georgia. Powell did not want to concede facts that might prompt the Court to question the racial fairness of capital sentencing, trigger additional *McCleskey*-like challenges, and perhaps even lead to judicially directed reforms of sentencing in general. Nor did he want to concede facts that indicate that the Court was knowingly willing to countenance a regime of capital punishment in which race significantly influenced decisions as to who would be spared and who would be killed. So Powell and his associates acted as if the Baldus study uncovered a minor discrepancy as opposed to an alarming anomaly. It would have been better if the Court openly declared that, for reasons of policy, it declined to grant relief to McCleskey notwithstanding the disturbing facts revealed by the Baldus study. Doing so would have performed the tremendous benefit of educating the public about the real world of capital sentencing and the real world of Supreme Court decisionmaking.

The dissenters rebuked the *McCleskey* Court for what they saw as its betrayal of established traditions. Justice Blackmun maintained, for instance, that he was "disappointed with the Court's action . . . because of its departure from . . . well-developed constitutional jurisprudence." There is much in the claim of disappointment, however, that smells of rank sentimentality. True, the Court could have decided differently; had there been the will, available precedent could have lit the way. In the context of equal protection challenges to jury commissioners authorized to select jury pools on the basis of vague standards, for example, the Supreme Court has shown a marked skepticism toward unexplained racial disparities. It has shifted the burden of explanation to the state when presented with evidence indicating significant discrepancies between the percentage of the population of eligible racial minorities in a given jurisdiction and the percentage of racial minorities selected for possible jury service. The Court could have deployed this same methodology in *McCleskey*—if it had possessed the will to do so. On the other hand, Powell's opinion for the Court was well within the ambit of expectations reasonably derived from prior rulings. *McCleskey* did not begin the Supreme Court's deregulation of the death penalty; it reflected and accelerated a process that had already begun and developed momentum. Although some justices had intimated that the Court should subject to special rigor death sentences challenged on grounds of racial fairness, a stronger tradition, exemplified by the Martinsville Seven case, favored the ethos that prevailed.

If *McCleskey* disappoints, it should do so on some basis other than tradition, for the majority cannot rightly be accused of promulgating a startling ruling.

To the contrary, *McCleskey* was all too predictable. Its critics must face the fact that, as far as reported cases disclose, defendants rarely, verging on never, succeed in challenging punishments using arguments of the sort voiced by Warren McCleskey's attorneys.

The central concern that dictated the Court's resolution of *McCleskey* was anxiety about what judges might have to face if it acknowledged that the influence of racial sentiment in sentencing represents a distortion and unfairness of constitutional dimension. Pretend for a moment, however, that the Supreme Court reversed the district court's rejection of the Baldus study and, based on the study's conclusions, declared a violation of the Equal Protection Clause. Assuming that the Court could have reached this point, what should it have done next?

One alternative would have been to abolish capital punishment entirely on the grounds that racial selectivity is an inextricable part of the administration of capital punishment in the United States and that it would be better to have no death penalty than one unavoidably influenced consistently by racial sentiment.

A more reserved variant would have involved vacating all death sentences in Georgia. Such a response would have fallen short of the ultimate aim of abolitionists since it would apply only to a single state. However, this response would surely have given a tremendous boost to the abolitionist movement by placing a large question mark over the legitimacy of any death penalty system generating unexplained racial disparities of the sort at issue in *McCleskey*. Since studies suggest that *McCleskey*-like statistics exist in several death penalty states, especially those with the largest death rows, the implementation of even a limited abolitionist remedy would have been significant indeed.

For those opposed to capital punishment anyway, abolishing it to vindicate the norms of equal protection is a costless enterprise. Abolition, however, is a costly prospect to the extent that one views the death penalty—as most Americans do—as a useful and highly valued public good. Polls indicate that, at least since the 1980s, upwards of 70 percent of Americans indicate that they favor capital punishment. Moreover, since 1988, the number of crimes punishable by death has increased dramatically, mainly as a result of federal legislation. From the perspective of a proponent of capital punishment, abolition as a remedy for race-of-the-victim discrimination is equivalent to reducing to darkness a town in which streetlights have been provided on a racially unequal basis. From this perspective, it would make more sense to remedy the inequality by installing lights in the parts of town which have been wrongly deprived of illumination. Carrying on the analogy, it would be better to remedy the problem outlined by the Baldus statistics by leveling up—increasing the number of people executed for murdering blacks—rather than leveling down—abolishing capital punishment altogether.

Before turning to the level-up solution, however, notice should be paid to still other possibilities. One is the idea, embraced by Justices Stevens and Blackmun, of limiting the class of persons eligible for execution to those who commit only the most aggravated homicides. The problem with this proposal is that it seems merely to replicate what the Court sought to accomplish by permitting the revival of capital punishment pursuant to procedures that, theoretically, limited and informed sentencers so that similarly situated criminals would be punished according to some tolerably coherent pattern. One point upon which both death penalty deregulators and death penalty abolitionists agree is that the task of selecting in some objective way those persons who should be condemned to die . . . remains beyond the capacities of the criminal justice system. The facts of *McCleskey* itself highlight this problem with the Stevens and Blackmun proposal. According to Professor Baldus, McCleskey's murder was located in the middle range of aggravated murders. In his view, the crime was not among the most heinous murders for which people have been condemned to death in Georgia. It is difficult, however, to see why this is so. McCleskey's crime involved, after all, the murder of a policeman during a robbery by a recidivist who is said to have boasted of the killing. Surely there are many, including potential judges and jurors, who would rank this crime in the same category of heinousness as some of the murders which Professor Baldus does place in the "worst case" category.

Another alternative would be for the Court to retract its rejection of mandatory death sentences. As we have seen, in 1972 the Court struck down all existing state death penalty statutes on the grounds that, by delegating unguided discretionary power to sentencing authorities, they provided insufficient protection against arbitrariness or discrimination. Ten states responded by enacting statutes prescribing capital punishment as the mandatory sentence for the commission of certain crimes. In 1976, the Court invalidated these laws on the grounds that they were inconsistent with fundamental trends in social mores, encouraged juries to shape their verdicts to avoid the harshness of mandatory sentences, and that the procedures established by mandatory sentencing failed to consider each defendant in a sufficiently individualized manner. The justices imposed a constitutional requirement that sentences in capital trial be provided with discretion to extend mercy. Yet it is precisely this power to grant leniency that opens the door to the *McCleskey* problem. . . .

It is by no means clear, moreover, that mandatory capital sentencing would affect racial disparities. First, even if mandatory capital sentencing were allowed, there would remain the possibility that juries would continue to extend relatively more leniency to the killers of blacks, declining more frequently to convict such killers of crimes that trigger automatic death sentences. Second, and probably more important, the institutional actors who have the most to do with the prevalence and incidence of capital sentences are prosecutors, not jurors. Prosecutors decide whether and for what to charge a defendant. Prosecutors further decide whether to charge a person with a capital crime or to accept a plea bargain for a noncapital offense. That prosecutors can be strongly influenced by racial bias is clear. Yet mandatory sentencing schemes do little to address the problem of race-dependent leniency on the part of prosecutors. Although mandatory sentencing provisions would limit, to some extent, the discretion of jurors or judges in responding to choices framed by prosecutors, such laws would do nothing to constrain the prior exercise of prosecutorial discretion. . . .

The level-up solution to the *McCleskey* problem would entail purposefully securing more death sentences against murderers of blacks. One way to pursue this aim would be to impose a choice upon jurisdictions with *McCleskey*-like sentencing patterns: Either respond as vigorously to the murders of blacks by condemning perpetrators of such crimes to death (as is done to murderers of whites), or relinquish the power to put anyone to death.

One problem with using race-conscious measures to reform the administration of capital punishment is that to many observers doing so will seem bizarre at first blush. That reaction, however, is likely to be based, at least in part, upon an exaggerated perception of the extent to which notions of individual desert currently infuse sentencing practices. Sentencing is typically keyed not only to the perceived moral desert of individual defendants but also to utilitarian calculations regarding society's needs. Punishment is used by those pronouncing sentence upon convicted defendants to instruct an onlooking society.

Another problem with the level-up alternative is that even those who favor, or at least tolerate, race-conscious remedies in some contexts reach a point where they find that such remedies are simply too severe to impose upon individuals who themselves played no direct part in inflicting the initial injury. The Supreme Court, for instance, has drawn a bright line of prohibition against affirmative action in the context of employment layoffs. Affirmative action for racial minorities that decreases the chances that white applicants will be *hired* is sometimes allowable, because the burden to be borne "is diffused to a considerable extent among society generally." Affirmative action that results in the *layoff* of white workers, however, is deemed a burden that is "too intrusive" to accept. Transposed to the death penalty, acting pursuant to a race-conscious plan to equalize the provision of death penalty services is simply too harsh a social tax to impose even upon convicted murderers who are, because of their own conduct, "eligible" for execution.

This argument, however, rests heavily upon the "death is different" distinction. It loses considerable force to the extent that one sees the death penalty as part of a continuum of punishments rather than a unique phenomenon occupying a wholly different moral plane. For those who eschew the "death is different" idea, it is not self-evident why, if race can and should be taken into account in redressing racial injustice in employment, housing, voting, and education, race cannot also be taken into account in reforming capital sentencing. They might well recognize the real danger of creating incentives to sentence certain defendants to death primarily to create "good" statistics. They might conclude, however, that this is a danger worth risking in order to encourage officials to take more seriously the security and suffering of black communities and in order to symbolize the affirmative constitutional obligation to insure some rough measure of substantive racial equality in every sphere of American life—including the provision of law enforcement resources.

Study Questions

1. The Court in *Atkins* claims that

> mentally retarded persons frequently know the difference between right and wrong and are competent to stand trial. Because of their impairments, however, by definition they have diminished capacities to understand and process information, to communicate, to abstract from mistakes and

learn from experience, to engage in logical reasoning, to control impulses, and to understand the reactions of others.

Assume that the Court's characterization of the retarded is correct. Why should these facts militate against execution of such persons? On what theory of punishment would these facts be of greatest importance? Of least importance?

2. Do you agree that "evolving standards of decency" condemn execution of the mentally retarded? Suppose public outrage at violent crimes were to grow to the point that states began to reverse their bans on executing the retarded. Would this show that "standards had evolved" in the other direction? Or that the majority was simply becoming "indecent"?

3. Justice Scalia, dissenting in *Atkins*, states that

> the Eighth Amendment is addressed to always-and-everywhere "cruel" punishments, such as the rack and the thumbscrew . . . [it] is not a ratchet, whereby a temporary consensus on leniency for a particular crime fixes a permanent constitutional maximum, disabling the States from giving effect to altered beliefs and responding to changed social conditions.

Suppose that public views regarding punishment "alter" along the following lines: Growing frustration with drug-related crimes has prompted several state legislators to introduce bills with harsh punishments. One such bill, introduced in the Texas legislature, would have punished convicted drug dealers by cutting off their fingers, one finger for each conviction. A bill introduced in Delaware would have required felony drug offenders to receive "no fewer than five nor more than 40 lashes well laid on" a bare back. Would mutilation and flogging then be constitutionally permissible, in Scalia's view? Why or why not? Do you think that such punishments should be tolerated? Why?

4. In a famous passage in his *Metaphysics of Morals*, Kant presented the following argument to demonstrate the necessity of death as a punishment for murder:

> If . . . he has committed a murder, he must die. In this case, there is no substitute that will satisfy the requirements of legal justice. There is no sameness of kind between death and remaining alive even under the most miserable conditions, and consequently there is also no equality between the crime and the retribution unless the criminal is put to

death. . . . Even if a civil society were to dissolve itself by common agreement of all its members (for example, if the people inhabiting an island decided to separate and disperse themselves around the world), the last murderer remaining in prison must first be executed, so that everyone will duly receive what his actions are worth. (John Ladd, trans., *The Metaphysical Elements of Justice* [Indianapolis, Ind.: Bobbs-Merrill, 1965], p. 102)

In what respects is this argument convincing? In what respects is it not?

5. Which crimes should be punished with death, according to van den Haag? Why those and not others?

6. How does van den Haag respond to the argument that the death penalty is administered in a way that is arbitrary? In a way that is discriminatory? Are his responses adequate in your view?

7. Does van den Haag's case for the death penalty place greater weight on utilitarian or on retributive reasons?

8. What criticisms does Bedau raise of van den Haag's claim that murderers deserve the death penalty? Does Bedau dismiss this claim too quickly? Why or why not?

9. Bedau claims that he favors abolition of capital punishment, "not the least because I am confident that zero deterrence would be lost." Does Bedau adequately defend this claim, in your judgment?

10. According to Bedau, "nothing [in the Constitution] prohibits the Supreme Court from concluding that two hundred years of experience with capital punishment reveals that it is, after all, cruel and unusual punishment. . . ." Assume that the majority of Americans consistently vote for and support the death penalty. Would a moral consensus on the permissibility of capital punishment undermine Bedau's claim about its constitutionality?

11. Can the Court's language concerning "evolving standards of decency" be interpreted in a way that does not invoke a societal consensus? In *Thompson v. Oklahoma* (487 U.S. 815 [1988]) the Court held that there was a clear social consensus that executing a person under the age of sixteen violates evolving standards of decency. (Thompson had been sentenced to death for a murder he committed when he was fifteen.) Do you agree? What if there is no clear consensus on an age limit? Does that mean that executing a nine-year-old would not violate the Constitution?

12. Should the death penalty, if it is to be used at all, ever be imposed for crimes other than murder? If so, to which crimes should it apply, and why?

13. Do you agree that statistical evidence of racial disparities in the imposition of capital punishment in a given jurisdiction is sufficient to prove racial discrimination in a death sentence handed down in a particular case?

14. What problems does Kennedy see with what he calls the "level-up" solution to the recognition of discriminatory imposition of the death penalty?

15. What specific criticisms does Kennedy lodge against the majority opinion in the *McCleskey* case? Do you agree?

16. Horace Kelly was sentenced to death in a California court for the 1984 murder of two women and an eleven-year-old boy. Kelly's scheduled execution in April 1998 was stayed by a federal judge, pending a review of arguments by Kelly's lawyers that he had become insane while on death row. Under current doctrine, a criminal cannot be subjected to capital punishment if he or she is insane *at the time of execution*, regardless of his or her mental state when convicted. When asked whether he felt guilty or bad, Kelly is reported to have replied: "the word guilty goes to litification examination. You also can defend a person. Guilt runs three different words and magnetize self." Court-appointed psychiatrists described Kelly's thinking as "illogical and bizarre," and his speech as an incomprehensible "word salad." Kelly's lawyers asserted that he was unable to understand the punishment he was slated to suffer or why he was to suffer it. (See *Los Angeles Times*, April 10, 1998, p. A1.) In your view, should someone in Kelly's mental condition be executed? Why should it matter whether a death-row inmate is able to understand why he is being executed? Is the only explanation for this requirement a retributive one? If this requirement is appropriate, why shouldn't it be required that the condemned individual not only understand why he is being executed, but agree that he should be?

Cases for Further Reflection
Goldschmitt v. Florida

Arthur Goldschmitt was convicted of driving under the influence of alcohol. The trial court placed Goldschmitt on probation (releasing him into the community under the supervision of a court officer) but on the grounds that he comply with a condition: that he place on his car a bumper sticker reading "CONVICTED D.U.I.—RESTRICTED LICENSE." Goldschmitt objected to this condition on several grounds, relying primarily on the claim that the humiliation and disgrace of being forced to display such a message on his car amounted to a form of "cruel and unusual" punishment, in violation of the Eighth Amendment to the Constitution. For what reasons does the court in *Goldschmitt* reject the defendant's argument that the condition of his probation amounted to cruel and unusual punishment? What aims does the court find are furthered by such shaming sanctions?

Per Curiam.

Appellant, Arthur Goldschmitt, was convicted of driving under the influence of alcohol to the extent his normal faculties were impaired (D.U.I.). Goldschmitt appeals the trial court's order placing him on probation and requiring as a special condition of probation that he affix to his personal vehicle a bumper sticker reading "Convicted D.U.I.—Restricted License."

. . . We first consider whether section 316.193(4)(a), Florida Statutes (1985), permits the imposition of this or any other special conditions of probation. Goldschmitt urges that the statute authorizes probation for first-time D.U.I. offenders solely to ensure compliance with the concomitant statutory provision that the offender perform fifty hours of community service. Appellee responds that while the community service condition is a special, additional penalty created by the legislature, D.U.I. probation otherwise is no different than any other form of probation. We agree. Section 948.03(4), Florida Statutes (1985), which permits the sentencing court to fashion special conditions of probation, does not distinguish between felony, misdemeanor, and criminal traffic offenses, or between county and circuit courts.

. . . Goldschmitt's argument that the bumper sticker constitutes a judicially developed, new penalty finds additional basis in the fact that this particular condi-

tion has become standard for all first-time D.U.I. offenders sentenced by two of the county's four judges. We would be quicker to accept his argument if we could be persuaded that any of the judges felt duty bound by local custom or rule to require the sticker despite their personal desire to the contrary. However, this obviously is not the case since half the local judiciary disdain the use of the sticker. While we are skeptical of special probation conditions imposed across-the-board, as opposed to being tailored to the needs and circumstances of the individual probationer, we cannot say that a judge may not impose a special condition of probation any time he or she chooses if that special condition otherwise is lawful. Those who do require the bumper sticker apparently are of the opinion the sticker serves some useful purpose and that every first-time offender should have one.

. . . Next, we turn to the various constitutional objections raised by Goldschmitt. First, he advances the theory that the trial court has infringed upon his first amendment rights by forcing him to broadcast an ideological message via the bumper sticker. His principal authority for this proposition is *Wooley v. Maynard*, 430 U.S. 705, 97 . . . (1977), wherein a New Hampshire Jehovah's Witness found objectionable and taped over the "Live Free or Die" motto on his automobile license plate. Suffice it to say we agree with appellee that the message involved in the present case is "no more ideological than a permit to park in a handicapped parking space" as required by section 320.0848, Florida Statutes (1985). Further, in *Wooley v. Maynard*, the issue was

490 So. 2d 123 (Fla. App. 2 Dist. 1986), District Court of Appeal of Florida, Second District.

whether New Hampshire's interest in broadcasting its state motto sufficiently overrode the defendant's objections to the motto that criminal penalties could be imposed for defacing the tag. Here, the criminal behavior has already been committed prior to the requirement that the message be displayed as a form of penance and a warning to other potential wrongdoers.

. . . Goldschmitt's second constitutional argument is that the bumper sticker constitutes cruel and unusual punishment and is therefore violative of the eighth amendment. He likens the sticker to the pillory of colonial times, a form of publicly suffered punishment that most would agree is cruel and unusual by modern standards. . . . However, the differences between the degrading physical rigors of the pillory and a small strip of colorful adhesive far outweigh the similarities. The mere requirement that a defendant display a "scarlet letter" as part of his punishment is not necessarily offensive to the Constitution.

The deterrent, and thus the rehabilitative, effect of punishment may be heightened if it "inflicts disgrace and contumely in a dramatic and spectacular manner." *United States v. William Anderson Co., Inc.*, 698 F.2d 911, 913 (8th Cir. 1983). The court in William Anderson expressed approval of behavioral sanctions imposed as conditions of probation for certain white-collar criminals, including speeches before civic groups on the evils of price fixing. "Measures are effective which have the impact of the 'scarlet letter' described by Nathaniel Hawthorne or the English equivalent of 'wearing papers' in the vicinity of Westminster Hall like a sandwich-man's sign describing the culprit's transgressions." . . . And, in *United States v. Carlston*, 562 F.Supp. 181 (N. D. Cal.1983), a defendant convicted

of tax evasion was ordered to purchase computers and teach their use to probationers and parolees, the court noting that by association with street criminals he would be "constantly reminded that his conduct was legally and socially wrong." . . . Appellee refers to this philosophy, in the context of the present case, as "Pavlovian conditioning."

Of course, such innovative dispositions can be carried to extremes which might offend constitutional standards. In *Bienz v. State*, 343 So.2d 913 (Fla. 4th DCA 1977), a probationer was ordered into a halfway house with directions to obey all instructions. A supervisor accused him of behaving like a baby and directed him to wear diapers over his regular clothing. While the case was resolved on other grounds, the court commented: "[S]uffice it to say that a command . . . that an adult male wear diapers in public would certainly be demeaning in the minds of so-called reasonable men . . . not surprisingly, prior decisions involving such bizarre incidents are sparse." . . . On the other hand, the requirement that a purse snatcher wear taps on his shoes whenever he left his residence was approved in *People v. McDowell*, 59 Cal. App.3d 807 . . . (1976), despite the defendant's plea that this was tantamount to a sign saying "I am a thief."

In the final analysis, we are unable to state as a matter of law that Goldschmitt's bumper sticker is sufficiently humiliating to trigger constitutional objections or, perhaps more to the point, that the lower court's belief that such a sticker is "rehabilitative" is so utterly without foundation that we are empowered to substitute our judgment for its.

Accordingly, we affirm the judgment and order of probation of the trial court.

The Case of the Dog "Provetie"

As explained in Section B, the following case is one among many "animal trials" recorded throughout Europe from the late middle ages up to the eighteenth century. What does our reaction to such cases say about the objectives of criminal punishment? (Also, how did they make the dog "confess"?)

Claim and Conclusion made and taken in the matter of Lot Huygens Gael, Schout of the Town of Leiden, against

Reported in *The South African Law Journal*, Vol. 24 (1907): 232–234.

and in respect of the dog of Jan Jansse van der Poel, named Provetie, with moreover the sentence of the court.

Lot Huygens Gael, Schout of the Town of Leiden, prosecutor on behalf of his lordship [the Count of Holland] in criminal matters, accuses in the open

Court of the Schepenes of the Town of Leiden the dog of Jan Jansse van der Poel, named Provetie, or by whatsoever other name he may be called, now a prisoner, and says that he, the said Provetie, did not scruple on Sunday last, being the 5th of May, 1595, to bite the child of Jan Jacobsz van der Poel, which child was then playing at his uncle's house and had a piece of meat in his hand, and the said Provetie snapping at it did bite the said child and thus inflicted a wound in the second finger of the right hand, going through the skin to the flesh in such manner that the blood flowed therefrom, and the child a few days after died in consequence of fright, for which cause the prosecutor apprehended the said Provetie, all of which appears from the prisoner's own confession, made by him without torture or being put in irons. . . .

Sentence: The Schepenen of Leiden, having seen the claim and conclusion made and taken by Lot Huygens Gael, Schout of this town, against and to the charge of the dog of Jan Jansse van der Poel, named Provetie, or by whatsoever other name or surname he may be known, the prisoner being present, having seen, moreover, the information obtained by the prosecutor for the purpose, besides the prisoner's own confession made without torture or being placed in irons, doing justice in the name of, etc., have condemned and hereby do condemn him to be led and taken to the plain of Gravesteijn in this town, where evildoers are customarily punished, and that he be there hanged by the executioner to the gallows with a rope until death ensues, that further his dead body be dragged on a hurdle to the gallows-field, and that he there remain hanging to the gallows, to the deterring of other dogs and to all as an example; moreover, they declare all his goods, should he have any, to be confiscated and forfeited for the benefit of the countship.

This done in the open court, all schepenen being present, the 15th May, 1595.

Payne v. Tennessee

Under existing procedure, a defendant convicted of a capital crime is brought to a second proceeding where it is determined whether to impose the death penalty based on the presence or absence of both mitigating and aggravating circumstances. In making this determination, should a death-penalty jury also be permitted to weigh evidence pertaining to the personal characteristics of the victim and the emotional impact of the crime on the victim's family? This is the question raised in *Payne*. In *Payne*, the Supreme Court overruled two pervious cases, *Booth v. Maryland* and *South Carolina v. Gathers*, both of which had forbidden the use of victim-impact evidence. Such evidence, the Court had earlier reasoned, violates the defendant's Eighth Amendment right that sentencing decisions be based on an "individualized determination" reflecting the defendant's characteristics, personal responsibility, and moral guilt. What are the things about a crime that properly relate to the perpetrator's blameworthiness? Tennessee permitted the jury to hear testimony about Payne's victims and the devastating effect of the crime upon the victims' family, especially on the small boy, Nicholas. The opinion in *Payne* prompts many questions: Should the age, sex, and other traits of one's victim be considered at sentencing? Would doing so encourage comparative judgments between differing victims? Would those who victimize celebrities, for example, potentially be subject to greater punishment than those who attack the homeless? Is victim-impact evidence legitimately considered by a jury, or is it an improper attempt to sway jurors with irrelevant, emotional testimony? If the defendant is permitted to furnish testimony speaking to his "good character," why can't evidence pertaining to the victim's character also be admissible? How does the majority in *Payne* respond to the argument that the use of victim-impact evidence will encourage juries to assign degrees of punishment to criminal defendants based on the status (wealth, social stainding, etc.) of their victims?

Chief Justice Rehnquist delivered the opinion of the court.

In this case we reconsider our holdings in *Booth v. Maryland*, 482 U.S. 496, . . . (1987), and *South Carolina v. Gathers*, 490 U.S. 805 (1989), that the Eighth Amendment bars the admission of victim impact evidence during the penalty phase of a capital trial.

The petitioner, Pervis Tyrone Payne, was convicted by a jury on two counts of first-degree murder and one count of assault with intent to commit murder in the first degree. He was sentenced to death for each of the murders, and to 30 years in prison for the assault.

The victims of Payne's offenses were 28-year-old Charisse Christopher, her 2-year-old daughter Lacie, and her 3-year-old son Nicholas. The three lived together in an apartment in Millington, Tennessee, across the hall from Payne's girlfriend, Bobbie Thomas. On Saturday, June 27, 1987, Payne visited Thomas' apartment several times in expectation of her return from her mother's house in Arkansas, but found no one at home. . . .

. . . Sometime around 3 p.m., Payne returned to the apartment complex, entered the Christophers' apartment, and began making sexual advances towards Charisse. Charisse resisted and Payne became violent. A neighbor who resided in the apartment directly beneath the Christophers, heard Charisse screaming, "'Get out, get out,' as if she were telling the children to leave." The noise briefly subsided and then began, "'horribly loud.'" The neighbor called the police after she heard a "blood curdling scream" from the Christopher apartment. . . .

Inside the apartment, the police encountered a horrifying scene. Blood covered the walls and floor throughout the unit. Charisse and her children were lying on the floor in the kitchen. Nicholas, despite several wounds inflicted by a butcher knife that completely penetrated through his body from front to back, was still breathing. Miraculously, he survived, but not until after undergoing seven hours of surgery and a transfusion of 1700 cc's of blood—400 to 500 cc's more than his estimated normal blood volume. Charisse and Lacie were dead.

. . .

During the sentencing phase of the trial, Payne presented the testimony of four witnesses: his mother and father, Bobbie Thomas, and Dr. John T. Huston, a clinical psychologist specializing in criminal court evaluation work. Bobbie Thomas testified that she met Payne at church, during a time when she was being abused by her husband. She stated that Payne was a very caring person, and that he devoted much time and attention to her three children, who were being affected by her marital difficulties. She said that the children had come to love him very much and would miss him, and that he "behaved just like a father that loved his kids." She asserted that he did not drink, nor did he use drugs, and that it was generally inconsistent with Payne's character to have committed these crimes.

Dr. Huston testified that based on Payne's low score on an IQ test, Payne was "mentally handicapped." Huston also said that Payne was neither psychotic nor schizophrenic, and that Payne was the most polite prisoner he had ever met. Payne's parents testified that their son had no prior criminal record and had never been arrested. They also stated that Payne had no history of alcohol or drug abuse, he worked with his father as a painter, he was good with children, and that he was a good son.

The State presented the testimony of Charisse's mother, Mary Zvolanek. When asked how Nicholas had been affected by the murders of his mother and sister, she responded:

"He cries for his mom. He doesn't seem to understand why she doesn't come home. And he cries for his sister Lacie. He comes to me many times during the week and asks me, Grandmama, do you miss my Lacie. And I tell him yes. He says, I'm worried about my Lacie."

In arguing for the death penalty during closing argument, the prosecutor commented on the continuing effects of Nicholas' experience, stating:

"But we do know that Nicholas was alive. And Nicholas was in the same room. Nicholas was still conscious. His eyes were open. He responded to the paramedics. He was able to follow their directions. He was able to hold his intestines in as he was carried to the ambulance. So he knew what happened to his mother and baby sister.

"There is nothing you can do to ease the pain of any of the families involved in this case. There is

501 U.S. 808 (1991), United States Supreme Court.

nothing you can do to ease the pain of Bernice or Carl Payne, and that's a tragedy. There is nothing you can do basically to ease the pain of Mr. and Mrs. Zvolanek, and that's a tragedy. They will have to live with it the rest of their lives. There is obviously nothing you can do for Charisse and Lacie Jo. But there is something you can do for Nicholas.

"Somewhere down the road Nicholas is going to grow up, hopefully. He's going to want to know what happened. And he is going to know what happened to his baby sister and his mother. He is going to want to know what type of justice was done. He is going to want to know what happened. With your verdict, you will provide the answer."

. . .

The jury sentenced Payne to death on each of the murder counts.

. . .

We granted certiorari . . . to reconsider our holdings in *Booth* and *Gathers* that the Eighth Amendment prohibits a capital sentencing jury from considering "victim impact" evidence relating to the personal characteristics of the victim and the emotional impact of the crimes on the victim's family.

In *Booth*, the defendant robbed and murdered an elderly couple. As required by a state statute, a victim impact statement was prepared based on interviews with the victims' son, daughter, son-in-law, and granddaughter. The statement, which described the personal characteristics of the victims, the emotional impact of the crimes on the family, and set forth the family members' opinions and characterizations of the crimes and the defendant, was submitted to the jury at sentencing. The jury imposed the death penalty. The conviction and sentence were affirmed on appeal by the State's highest court.

. . .

This Court held by a 5-to-4 vote that the Eighth Amendment prohibits a jury from considering a victim impact statement at the sentencing phase of a capital trial. The Court made clear that the admissibility of victim impact evidence was not to be determined on a case-by-case basis, but that such evidence was *per se* inadmissible in the sentencing phase of a capital case except to the extent that it "related directly to the circumstances of the crime." In *Gathers*, decided two years later, the Court extended the rule announced in *Booth* to statements made by a prosecutor to the sentencing jury regarding the personal qualities of the victim.

The *Booth* Court began its analysis with the observation that the capital defendant must be treated as a "'uniquely individual human bein[g],'" and therefore

the Constitution requires the jury to make an individualized determination as to whether the defendant should be executed based on the "'character of the individual and the circumstances of the crime.'" The Court concluded that while no prior decision of this Court had mandated that only the defendant's character and immediate characteristics of the crime may constitutionally be considered, other factors are irrelevant to the capital sentencing decision unless they have "some bearing on the defendant's 'personal responsibility and moral guilt.'" To the extent that victim impact evidence presents "factors about which the defendant was unaware, and that were irrelevant to the decision to kill," the Court concluded, it has nothing to do with the "blameworthiness of a particular defendant." Evidence of the victim's character, the Court observed, "could well distract the sentencing jury from its constitutionally required task [of] determining whether the death penalty is appropriate in light of the background and record of the accused and the particular circumstances of the crime." The Court concluded that, except to the extent that victim impact evidence relates "directly to the circumstances of the crime," the prosecution may not introduce such evidence at a capital sentencing hearing because "it creates an impermissible risk that the capital sentencing decision will be made in an arbitrary manner."

Booth and *Gathers* were based on two premises: that evidence relating to a particular victim or to the harm that a capital defendant causes a victim's family do not in general reflect on the defendant's "blameworthiness," and that only evidence relating to "blameworthiness" is relevant to the capital sentencing decision. However, the assessment of harm caused by the defendant as a result of the crime charged has understandably been an important concern of the criminal law, both in determining the elements of the offense and in determining the appropriate punishment. Thus, two equally blameworthy criminal defendants may be guilty of different offenses solely because their acts cause differing amounts of harm. "If a bank robber aims his gun at a guard, pulls the trigger, and kills his target, he may be put to death. If the gun unexpectedly misfires, he may not. His moral guilt in both cases is identical; but his responsibility in the former is greater." *Booth*, 482 U.S., at 519 (Scalia, J., dissenting). The same is true with respect to two defendants, each of whom participates in a robbery, each of whom acts with reckless disregard for human life; if the robbery in which the first defendant participated results in the death of a victim, he may be subjected to the death penalty, but if the robbery in which the second defendant participates does not result in the death of a victim, the death penalty may not be imposed.

The principles which have guided criminal sentencing—as opposed to criminal liability—have varied with the times. The book of Exodus prescribes the *Lex talionis*, "An eye for an eye, a tooth for a tooth." Exodus 21:22–23. In England and on the continent of Europe as recently as the 18th century, crimes which would be regarded as quite minor today were capital offenses. Writing in the 18th century, the Italian criminologist Cesare Beccaria advocated the idea that "the punishment should fit the crime." He said that "[w]e have seen that the true measure of crimes is the injury done to society." J. Farrer, *Crimes and Punishments*, 199 (London, 1880).

Gradually the list of crimes punishable by death diminished, and legislatures began grading the severity of crimes in accordance with the harm done by the criminal. The sentence for a given offense, rather than being precisely fixed by the legislature, was prescribed in terms of a minimum and a maximum, with the actual sentence to be decided by the judge. With the increasing importance of probation, as opposed to imprisonment, as a part of the penological process, some States such as California developed the "indeterminate sentence," where the time of incarceration was left almost entirely to the penological authorities rather than to the courts. But more recently the pendulum has swung back. The Federal Sentencing Guidelines, which went into effect in 1987, provided for very precise calibration of sentences, depending upon a number of factors. These factors relate both to the subjective guilt of the defendant and to the harm caused by his acts.

Wherever judges in recent years have had discretion to impose sentence, the consideration of the harm caused by the crime has been an important factor in the exercise of that discretion:

> The first significance of harm in Anglo-American jurisprudence is, then, as a prerequisite to the criminal sanction. The second significance of harm—one no less important to judges—is as a measure of the seriousness of the offense and therefore as a standard for determining the severity of the sentence that will be meted out." S. Wheeler, K. Mann, and A. Sarat, Sitting in Judgment: The Sentencing of White-Collar Criminals 56 (1988).

Whatever the prevailing sentencing philosophy, the sentencing authority has always been free to consider a wide range of relevant material. In the federal system, we observed that "a judge may appropriately conduct an inquiry broad in scope, largely unlimited as to the kind of information he may consider, or the source from which it may come." . . .

The Maryland statute involved in *Booth* required that the presentence report in all felony cases include a "victim impact statement" which would describe the effect of the crime on the victim and his family. Congress and most of the States have, in recent years, enacted similar legislation to enable the sentencing authority to consider information about the harm caused by the crime committed by the defendant. The evidence involved in the present case was not admitted pursuant to any such enactment, but its purpose and effect was much the same as if it had been. While the admission of this particular kind of evidence— designed to portray for the sentencing authority the actual harm caused by a particular crime—is of recent origin, this fact hardly renders it unconstitutional. . . .

"We have held that a State cannot preclude the sentencer from considering 'any relevant mitigating evidence' that the defendant proffers in support of a sentence less than death." *Eddings v. Oklahoma*, 455 U.S. 104, 114 (1982). Thus we have, as the Court observed in *Booth*, required that the capital defendant be treated as a "'uniquely individual human bein[g].'" But it was never held or even suggested in any of our cases preceding Booth that the defendant, entitled as he was to individualized consideration, was to receive that consideration wholly apart from the crime which he had committed. The language quoted from *Woodson* in the *Booth* opinion was not intended to describe a class of evidence that *could not* be received, but a class of evidence which *must* be received. Any doubt on the matter is dispelled by comparing the language in *Woodson* with the language from *Gregg v. Georgia*, quoted above, which was handed down the same day as *Woodson*. This misreading of precedent in *Booth* has, we think, unfairly weighted the scales in a capital trial; while virtually no limits are placed on the relevant mitigating evidence a capital defendant may introduce concerning his own circumstances, the State is barred from either offering "a glimpse of the life" which a defendant "chose to extinguish," *Mills*, 486 U.S. at 397, (REHNQUIST, C. J., dissenting), or demonstrating the loss to the victim's family and to society which have resulted from the defendant's homicide.

Booth reasoned that victim impact evidence must be excluded because it would be difficult, if not impossible, for the defendant to rebut such evidence without shifting the focus of the sentencing hearing away from the defendant, thus creating a "'mini-trial' on the victim's character." *Booth, supra*, at 506–507. In many cases the evidence relating to the victim is already before the jury at least in part because of its relevance at the guilt phase of the trail. But even as to additional evidence admitted at the sentencing phase, the mere fact that for tactical reasons it might not be prudent for the defense to rebut victim impact evidence makes the case no different than others in which a party is faced with this sort of a dilemma. As we explained in rejecting the contention that expert testimony on future dangerousness should be excluded from capital trials, "the rules of evidence generally extant at the federal and state levels anticipate that relevant, unprivileged evidence should be admitted and its weight left to the fact-finder, who would have the benefit of cross examination and contrary evidence by the opposing party." *Barefoot v. Estelle*, 463 U.S. 880, 898 (1983).

Payne echoes the concern voiced in *Booth*'s case that the admission of victim impact evidence permits a jury to find that defendants whose victims were assets to their community are more deserving of punishment than those whose victims are perceived to be less worthy. As a general matter, however, victim impact evidence is not offered to encourage comparative judgments of this kind—for instance, that the killer of a hardworking, devoted parent deserves the death penalty, but that the murderer of a reprobate does not. It is designed to show instead *each* victim's "uniqueness as an individual human being," whatever the jury might think the loss to the community resulting from his death might be. The facts of *Gathers* are an excellent illustration of this: the evidence showed that the victim was an out of work, mentally handicapped individual, perhaps not, in the eyes of most, a significant contributor to society, but nonetheless a murdered human being.

Under our constitutional system, the primary responsibility for defining crimes against state law, fixing punishments for the commission of these crimes, and establishing procedures for criminal trials rests with the States. The state laws respecting crimes, punishments, and criminal procedure are of course subject to the overriding provisions of the United States Constitution. Where the State imposes the death penalty for a particular crime, we have held that the Eighth Amendment imposes special limitations upon that process. . . . But, as we noted in *California v. Ramos*, 463 U.S. 992, 1001 (1983), "[b]eyond these limitations . . . the Court has deferred to the State's choice of substantive factors relevant to the penalty determination."

. . . The States remain free, in capital cases, as well as others, to devise new procedures and new remedies to meet felt needs. Victim impact evidence is simply another form or method of informing the sentencing authority about the specific harm caused by the crime in question, evidence of a general type long considered by sentencing authorities. We think the *Booth* Court was wrong in stating that this kind of evidence leads to the arbitrary imposition of the death penalty. In the majority of cases, and in this case, victim impact evidence serves entirely legitimate purposes. In the event that evidence is introduced that is so unduly prejudicial that it renders the trial fundamentally unfair, the Due Process Clause of the Fourteenth Amendment provides a mechanism for relief. Courts have always taken into consideration the harm done by the defendant in imposing sentence, and the evidence adduced in this case was illustrative of the harm caused by Payne's double murder.

We are now of the view that a State may properly conclude that for the jury to assess meaningfully the defendant's moral culpability and blameworthiness, it should have before it at the sentencing phase evidence of the specific harm caused by the defendant. "[T]he State has a legitimate interest in counteracting the mitigating evidence which the defendant is entitled to put in, by reminding the sentencer that just as the murderer should be considered as an individual, so too the victim is an individual whose death represents a unique loss to society and in particular to his family." By turning the victim into a "faceless stranger at the penalty phase of a capital trial," *Booth* deprives the State of the full moral force of its evidence and may prevent the jury from having before it all the information necessary to determine the proper punishment for a first-degree murder.

The present case is an example of the potential for such unfairness. The capital sentencing jury heard testimony from Payne's girlfriend that they met at church, that he was affectionate, caring, kind to her children, that he was not an abuser of drugs or alcohol, and that it was inconsistent with his character to have committed the murders. Payne's parents testified that he was a good son, and a clinical psychologist testified that Payne was an extremely polite prisoner and suffered from a low IQ. None of this testimony was related to the circumstances of Payne's brutal crimes. In contrast, the only evidence of the impact of Payne's offenses during the sentencing phase was Nicholas' grandmother's description—in response to a single question—that the child misses his mother and baby sister. Payne argues that the Eighth Amendment commands that the jury's death sentence must be set aside because the jury heard this testimony. But the testimony illustrated quite poignantly some of the harm that Payne's killing had caused; there is nothing unfair about allowing the jury to bear in mind that harm at the same time as it considers the mitigating evidence introduced by the defendant.

. . .

We thus hold that if the State chooses to permit the admission of victim impact evidence and prosecutorial argument on that subject, the Eighth Amendment erects no *per se* bar. A State may legitimately conclude that evidence about the victim and about the impact of the murder on the victim's family is relevant to the jury's decision as to whether or not the death penalty should be imposed. There is no reason to treat such evidence differently than other relevant evidence is treated.

. . .

We accordingly affirm the judgment of the Supreme Court of Tennessee.

Affirmed.

Coker v. Georgia

While serving time in prison for murder and other violent crimes, Ehrlich Coker escaped from a Georgia facility and raped a woman. He was tried, convicted, and sentenced to death on the rape charge, the jury finding death to be an appropriate punishment given the presence of certain "aggravating factors." The Supreme Court overturned Coker's conviction, arguing that death as a punishment for rape is grossly disproportionate and thus violative of the Eighth Amendment. The case should be read with an eye to how to understand and apply the retributive requirement of proportionality. This problem surfaces in the Court's opinion in at least two forms. First, should the aggravating factors here, including the previous crimes Coker had committed, bear on the appropriate punishment for his act of rape? And second, does death itself "fit the crime"? Should it matter for these purposes that, although rape is a brutal and violent crime, it does not involve taking a life?

Syllabus [of Majority Opinion][1]

While serving various sentences for murder, rape, kidnaping, and aggravated assault, petitioner escaped from a Georgia prison and, in the course of committing an armed robbery and other offenses, raped an adult woman. He was convicted of rape, armed robbery, and the other offenses and sentenced to death on the rape charge, when the jury found two of the aggravating circumstances present for imposing such a sentence, *viz*, that the rape was committed (1) by a person with prior capital-felony convictions and (2) in the course of committing another capital felony, armed robbery. The Georgia Supreme Court affirmed both the conviction and sentence. *Held: The judgment upholding the death sentence is reversed and the case is remanded.*

Mr. Justice White, joined by Mr. Justice Stewart, Mr. Justice Blackmun, and Mr. Justice Stevens, con-

---

433 U.S. 584 (1977), United States Supreme Court.

cluded that the sentence of death for the crime of rape is grossly disproportionate and excessive punishment and is therefore forbidden by the Eighth Amendment as cruel and unusual punishment.

(a) The Eighth Amendment bars not only those punishments that are "barbaric" but also those that are "excessive" in relation to the crime committed, and a punishment is "excessive" and unconstitutional if it (1) makes no measurable contribution to acceptable goals of punishment and hence is nothing more than the purposeless and needless imposition of pain and suffering; or (2) is grossly out of proportion to the severity of the crime.

(b) That death is a disproportionate penalty for rape is strongly indicated by the objective evidence of present, public judgment, as represented by the attitude of state legislatures and sentencing juries, concerning the acceptability of such a penalty, it appearing that Georgia is currently the only State authorizing the death sentence for rape of an adult woman, that it is authorized for rape in only two other States but only when the victim is a child, and that in the vast majority (9 out of 10) of rape convictions in Georgia since 1973, juries have not imposed the death sentence.

(c) Although rape deserves serious punishment, the death penalty, which is unique in its severity and irrevocability, is an excessive penalty for the rapist who, as such and as opposed to the murderer, does not unjustifiably take human life.

(d) The conclusion that the death sentence imposed on petitioner is disproportionate punishment for rape is not affected by the fact that the jury found the aggravating circumstances of prior capital felony convictions and occurrence of the rape while committing armed robbery, a felony for which the death sentence is also authorized, since the prior convictions do not change the fact that the rape did not involve the taking of life, and since the jury did not deem the robbery itself deserving of the death penalty, even though accompanied by the aggravating circumstances of prior capital felony convictions.

(e) That under Georgia law a deliberate killer cannot be sentenced to death, absent aggravating circumstances, argues strongly against the notion that, with or without such circumstances, a rapist who does not take the life of his victim should be punished more severely than the deliberate killer.

Mr. Justice Brennan concluded that the death penalty is in all circumstances cruel and unusual punishment prohibited by the Eighth and Fourteenth Amendments.

Mr. Justice Marshall concluded that the death penalty is a cruel and unusual punishment prohibited by the Eighth and Fourteenth Amendments.

Mr. Justice Powell concluded that death is disproportionate punishment for the crime of raping an adult woman where, as here, the crime was not committed with excessive brutality and the victim did not sustain serious or lasting injury.

Dissenting Opinion

Mr. Chief Justice Burger, with whom Mr. Justice Rehnquist joins, dissenting.

In a case such as this, confusion often arises as to the Court's proper role in reaching a decision. Our task is not to give effect to our individual views on capital punishment; rather, we must determine what the Constitution permits a State to do under its reserved powers. In striking down the death penalty imposed upon the petitioner in this case, the Court has overstepped the bounds of proper constitutional adjudication by substituting its policy judgment for that of the state legislature. I accept that the Eighth Amendment's concept of disproportionality bars the death penalty for minor crimes. But rape is not a minor crime; hence the Cruel and Unusual Punishment Clause does not give the Members of this Court license to engraft their conceptions of proper public policy onto the considered legislative judgments of the States. Since I cannot agree that Georgia lacked the constitutional power to impose the penalty of death for rape, I dissent from the Court's judgment.

On December 5, 1971, the petitioner, Ehrlich Anthony Coker, raped and then stabbed to death a young woman. Less than eight months later Coker kidnapped and raped a second young woman. After twice raping this 16-year-old victim, he stripped her, severely beat her with a club, and dragged her into a wooded area where he left her for dead. He was apprehended and pleaded guilty to offenses stemming from these incidents. He was sentenced by three separate courts to three life terms, two 20-year terms, and one eight-year term of imprisonment. Each judgment specified that the sentences it imposed were to run consecutively rather than concurrently. Approximately one and one-half years later, on September 2, 1974, petitioner escaped from the state prison where he was serving these sentences. He promptly raped another 16-year-old woman in the presence of her husband, abducted her from her home, and threatened her with death and serious bodily harm. It is this crime for which the sentence now under review was imposed.

The Court today holds that the State of Georgia may not impose the death penalty on Coker. In so doing, it prevents the State from imposing any effective punishment upon Coker for his latest rape. The Court's holding, moreover, bars Georgia from guaranteeing its citizens that they will suffer no further attacks by this habitual rapist. In fact, given the lengthy sentences Coker must serve for the crimes he has already committed, the Court's holding assures that petitioner—and others in his position—will henceforth feel no compunction whatsoever about committing further rapes as frequently as he may be able to escape from confinement and indeed even within the walls of the prison itself. To what extent we have left States "elbow room" to protect innocent persons from depraved human beings like Coker remains in doubt.

My first disagreement with the Court's holding is its unnecessary breadth. The narrow issue here presented is whether the State of Georgia may constitutionally execute this petitioner for the particular rape which he has committed, in light of all the facts and circumstances shown by this record. The plurality opinion goes to great lengths to consider societal mores and attitudes toward the generic crime of rape and the punishment for it; however, the opinion gives little attention [to] the special circumstances which bear directly on whether imposition of the death penalty is an appropriate societal response to Coker's criminal acts: (a) On account of his prior offenses, Coker is already serving such lengthy prison sentences that imposition of additional periods of imprisonment would have no incremental punitive effect; (b) by his life pattern Coker has shown that he presents a particular danger to the safety, welfare and chastity of women, and on his record the likelihood is therefore great that he will repeat his crime at first opportunity; (c) petitioner escaped from prison, only a year and a half after he commenced serving his latest sentences; he has nothing to lose by further escape attempts; and (d) should he again succeed in escaping from prison, it is reasonably predictable that he will repeat his pattern of attacks on women—and with impunity since the threat of added prison sentences will be no deterrent.

Unlike the Court, I would narrow the inquiry in this case to the question actually presented: Does the Eighth Amendment's ban against cruel and unusual punishment prohibit the State of Georgia from executing a person who has, within the space of three years, raped three separate women, killing one and attempting to kill another, who is serving prison terms exceeding his probable lifetime and has not hesitated to escape confinement at the first available opportunity? Whatever one's view may be as to the State's constitutional power to impose the death penalty upon a rapist who stands before a court convicted for the first time, this case reveals a chronic rapist whose continuing danger to the community is abundantly clear.

Mr. Justice Powell would hold the death sentence inappropriate in this case because "there is no indication that petitioner's offense was committed with excessive brutality or that the victim sustained serious or lasting injury." Apart from the reality that rape is inherently one of the more egregiously brutal acts one human being can inflict upon another, there is nothing in the Eighth Amendment that so narrowly limits the factors which may be considered by a state legislature in determining whether a particular punishment is grossly excessive. Surely recidivism, especially the repeated commission of heinous crimes, is a factor which may properly be weighed as an aggravating circumstance, permitting the imposition of a punishment more severe than for one isolated offense. . . . As a factual matter, the plurality

opinion is correct in stating that Coker's "prior convictions do not change the fact that the instant crime being punished is rape not involving the taking of life," . . . however, it cannot be disputed that the existence of these prior convictions make Coker a substantially more serious menace to society than a first-time offender.

. . .

In sum, once the Court has held that "the punishment of death does not invariably violate the Constitution," *Gregg v. Georgia*, 428 U.S., at 169 . . . it seriously impinges upon the State's legislative judgment to hold that it may not impose such sentence upon an individual who has shown total and repeated disregard for the welfare, safety, personal integrity and human worth of others, and who seemingly cannot be deterred from continuing such conduct. I therefore would hold that the death sentence here imposed is within the power reserved to the State and leave for another day the question of whether such sanction would be proper under other circumstances. . . .

. . .

The question of whether the death penalty is an appropriate punishment for rape is surely an open one. It is arguable that many prospective rapists would be deterred by the possibility that they could suffer death for their offense; it is also arguable that the death penalty would have only minimal deterrent effect. It may well be that rape victims would become more willing to report the crime and aid in the apprehension of the criminals if they knew that community disapproval of rapists was sufficiently strong to inflict the extreme penalty; or perhaps they would be reluctant to cooperate in the prosecution of rapists if they knew that a conviction might result in the imposition of the death penalty. Quite possibly, the occasional, well-publicized execution of egregious rapists may cause citizens to feel greater security in their daily lives, or, on the contrary, it may be that members of a civilized community will suffer the pangs of a heavy conscience because such punishment will be perceived as excessive. We cannot know which among this range of possibilities is correct, but today's holding forecloses the very exploration we have said federalism was intended to foster. It is difficult to believe that Georgia would long remain alone in punishing rape by death if the next decade demonstrated a drastic reduction in its incidence of rape, and increased cooperation by rape victims in the apprehension and prosecution of rapists, and a greater confidence in the rule of law on the part of the populace.

. . .

The subjective judgment that the death penalty is simply disproportionate for the crime of rape is even more disturbing than the "objective" analysis discussed *supra*. The plurality's conclusion on this point is based upon the bare fact that murder necessarily results in the physical death of the victim, while rape does not. . . . However, no Member of the Court explains why this distinction has relevance, much less constitutional significance. It is, after all, not irrational—nor constitutionally impermissible—for a legislature to make the penalty more severe than the criminal act it punishes in the hope it would deter wrongdoing. . . .

It begs the question to state, as does the plurality opinion:

> "Life is over for the victim of the murderers; for the rape victim, life may not be nearly so happy as it was, but is not over and normally is not beyond repair." . . .

Until now, the issue under the Eighth Amendment has not been the state of any particular victim after the crime, but rather whether the punishment imposed is grossly disproportionate to the evil committed by the perpetrator. See, *Gregg v. Georgia*, 428 U.S., at 173 . . . ; *Furman v. Georgia*, 408 U.S. . . . (Powell, J., dissenting). As a matter of constitutional principle, that test cannot have the primitive simplicity of "life for life, eye for eye, tooth for tooth." Rather States must be permitted to engage in a more sophisticated weighing of values in dealing with criminal activity which consistently poses serious danger of death or grave bodily harm. If innocent life and limb is to be preserved I see no constitutional barrier in punishing by death all who engage in such activity, regardless of whether the risk comes to fruition in any particular instance. . . .

. . . Rape thus is not a crime "light-years" removed from murder in the degree of its heinousness; it certainly poses a serious potential danger to the life and safety of innocent victims—apart from the devastating psychic consequences. It would seem to follow therefore that, affording the States proper leeway under the broad standard of the Eighth Amendment, murder is properly punishable by death, rape should be also, if that is the considered judgment of the legislators.

. . .

Endnote

[1] The syllabus constitutes no part of the opinion of the Court but has been prepared by the Reporter of Decisions for the convenience of the reader.

Gregg v. Georgia

In this case, the Supreme Court reinstated capital punishment as constitutionally permissible. The plurality opinion argued that whether a punishment is consistent with "evolving standards of decency" is a judgment to be made on the basis of "objective indicia" reflecting the "public attitude toward a given sanction." The Court observed that the reenactment of capital punishment statutes by most states after the *Furman* decision revealed that the majority of Americans believe death to be an appropriate punishment for some crimes. Execution does not violate the proportionality constraint of the retributive theory of punishment, the Court argued, at least where the defendant has been convicted of taking a life himself (as was the case with *Gregg*); and whether the death penalty is an effective deterrent is a judgment to be left to legislators. According to Justice Brennan, why is the death penalty uniquely degrading to human dignity?

Mr. Justice Stewart, with Justices Powell and Stevens concurring:

---

428 U.S. 153 (1976), United States Supreme Court.

We address initially the basic contention that the punishment of death for the crime of murder is, under all circumstances, "cruel and unusual" in violation of the Eighth and Fourteenth Amendments of the Constitution. [Later in] this opinion, we will consider the sentence of death imposed under the Georgia statutes at issue in this case.

The Court on a number of occasions has both assumed and asserted the constitutionality of capital punishment. . . . But until *Furman v. Georgia*, 408 U.S. 238 (1972), the Court never confronted squarely the fundamental claim that the punishment of death always, regardless of the enormity of the offense or the procedure followed in imposing the sentence, is cruel and unusual punishment in violation of the Constitution. Although this issue was presented and addressed in *Furman*, it was not resolved by the Court. Four Justices would have held that capital punishment is not unconstitutional *per se*; two Justices would have reached the opposite conclusion; and three Justices, while agreeing that the statutes then before the Court were invalid as applied, left open the question whether such punishment may ever be imposed. We now hold that the punishment of death does not invariably violate the Constitution. . . .

. . .

It is clear from the foregoing precedents that the Eighth Amendment has not been regarded as a static concept. As Mr. Chief Justice Warren said, in an oft-quoted phrase, "[t]he Amendment must draw its meaning from the evolving standards of decency that mark the progress of a maturing society." . . . Thus, an assessment of contemporary values concerning the infliction of a challenged sanction is relevant to the application of the Eighth Amendment. As we develop below more fully, . . . this assessment does not call for a subjective judgment. It requires, rather, that we look to objective indicia that reflect the public attitude toward a given sanction.

But our cases also make clear that public perceptions of standards of decency with respect to criminal sanctions are not conclusive. A penalty also must accord with "the dignity of man," which is the "basic concept underlying the Eighth Amendment." *Trop v. Dulles*. . . . This means, at least, that the punishment not be "excessive." When a form of punishment in the abstract (in this case, whether capital punishment may ever be imposed as a sanction for murder) rather than in the particular (the propriety of death as a penalty to be applied to a specific defendant for a specific crime) is under consideration, the inquiry into "excessiveness" has two aspects. First, the punishment must not involve the unnecessary and wanton infliction of pain. . . . Second, the punishment must not be grossly out of proportion to the severity of the crime. . . .

The imposition of the death penalty for the crime of murder has a long history of acceptance both in the United States and in England. The common-law rule imposed a mandatory death sentence on all convicted murderers. . . . And the penalty continued to be used into the 20th century by most American States, although the breadth of the common-law rule was diminished, initially by narrowing the class of murders to be punished by death and subsequently by widespread adoption of laws expressly granting juries the discretion to recommend mercy. . . .

It is apparent from the text of the Constitution itself that the existence of capital punishment was accepted by the Framers. At the time the Eighth Amendment was ratified, capital punishment was a common sanction in every State. Indeed, the First Congress of the United States enacted legislation providing death as the penalty for specified crimes. . . .

Four years ago, the petitioners in *Furman* and its companion cases [predicated] their argument primarily upon the asserted proposition that standards of decency had evolved to the point where capital punishment no longer could be tolerated. The petitioners in those cases said, in effect, that the evolutionary process had come to an end, and that standards of decency required that the Eighth Amendment be construed finally as prohibiting capital punishment for any crime regardless of its depravity and impact on society. This view was accepted by two Justices. Three other Justices were unwilling to go so far; focusing on the procedures by which convicted defendants were selected for the death penalty rather than on the actual punishment inflicted, they joined in the conclusion that the statutes before the Court were constitutionally invalid.

The petitioners in the capital cases before the Court today renew the "standards of decency" argument, but developments during the four years since *Furman* have undercut substantially the assumptions upon which their argument rested. Despite the continuing debate, dating back to the 19th century, over the morality and utility of capital punishment, it is now evident that a large proportion of American society continues to regard it as an appropriate and necessary criminal sanction.

The most marked indication of society's endorsement of the death penalty for murder is the legislative response to *Furman*. The legislatures of at least 35 States have enacted new statutes that provide for the death penalty for at least some crimes that result in the death of another person. . . .

. . . [H]owever, the Eighth Amendment demands more than that a challenged punishment be acceptable to contemporary society. The Court also must ask whether it comports with the basic concept of human dignity at the core of the Amendment. . . .

The death penalty is said to serve two principal social purposes: retribution and deterrence of capital crimes by prospective offenders.

In part, capital punishment is an expression of society's moral outrage at particularly offensive conduct. This function may be unappealing to many, but it is essential in an ordered society that asks its citizens to rely on legal processes rather than self-help to vindicate their wrongs. . . . "Retribution is no longer the dominant objective of the criminal law," *Williams v. New York*, 337 U.S. 241, 248 (1949), but neither is it a forbidden objective nor one inconsistent with our respect for the dignity of men. . . . Indeed, the decision that capital punishment may be the appropriate sanction in extreme cases is an expression of the community's belief that certain crimes are themselves so grievous an affront to humanity that the only adequate response may be the penalty of death.

Statistical attempts to evaluate the worth of the death penalty as a deterrent to crimes by potential offenders have occasioned a great deal of debate. The results simply have been inconclusive. . . .

Although some of the studies suggest that the death penalty may not function as a significantly greater deterrent than lesser penalties, there is no convincing empirical evidence either supporting or refuting this view. We may nevertheless assume safely that there are murderers, such as those who act in passion, for whom the threat of death has little or no deterrent effect. But for many others, the death penalty undoubtedly is a significant deterrent. There are carefully contemplated murders, such as murders for hire, where the possible penalty of death may well enter into the cold calculus that precedes the decision to act. And there are some categories of murder, such as murder by a life prisoner, where other sanctions may not be adequate.

The value of capital punishment as a deterrent of crime is a complex factual issue the resolution of which properly rests with the legislatures, which can evaluate the results of statistical studies in terms of their own local conditions and with a flexibility of approach that is not available to the courts. . . . Indeed, many of the post-*Furman* statutes reflect just such a responsible effort to define those crimes and those criminals for which capital punishment is most probably an effective deterrent.

In sum, we cannot say that the judgment of the Georgia Legislature that capital punishment may be necessary in some cases is clearly wrong. Considera-tions of federalism, as well as respect for the ability of a legislature to evaluate, in terms of its particular State, the moral consensus concerning the death penalty and its social utility as a sanction, require us to conclude, in the absence of more convincing evidence, that the infliction of death as a punishment for murder is not without justification and thus is not unconstitutionally severe.

Finally, we must consider whether the punishment of death is disproportionate in relation to the crime for which it is imposed. There is no question that death as a punishment is unique in its severity and irrevocability. . . . When a defendant's life is at stake, the Court has been particularly sensitive to insure that every safeguard is observed. . . . But we are concerned here only with the imposition of capital punishment for the crime of murder, and when a life has been taken deliberately by the offender, we cannot say that the punishment is invariably disproportionate to the crime. It is an extreme sanction, suitable to the most extreme of crimes.

We hold that the death penalty is not a form of punishment that may never be imposed, regardless of the circumstances of the offense, regardless of the character of the offender, and regardless of the procedure followed in reaching the decision to impose it.

. . .

For the reasons expressed in this opinion, we hold that the statutory system under which Gregg was sentenced to death does not violate the Constitution. Accordingly, the judgment of the Georgia Supreme Court is affirmed.

It is so ordered.

Mr. Justice Brennan, dissenting:

. . .

This Court inescapably has the duty, as the ultimate arbiter of the meaning of our Constitution, to say whether, when individuals condemned to death stand before our Bar, "moral concepts" require us to hold that the law has progressed to the point where we should declare that the punishment of death, like punishments on the rack, the screw, and the wheel, is no longer morally tolerable in our civilized society. . . . I emphasize only that foremost among the "moral concepts" recognized in our cases and inherent in the Clause is the primary moral principle that the State, even as it punishes, must treat its citizens in a manner consistent with their intrinsic worth as human beings—a punishment must not be so severe as to be degrading to human dignity. A judicial determination whether the punishment of death comports with human dignity is therefore not only permitted but compelled by the Clause. . . .

The fatal constitutional infirmity in the punishment of death is that it treats members of the human race as nonhumans, as objects to be toyed with and discarded. [It is] thus inconsistent with the fundamental premise of the Clause that even the vilest criminal remains a human being possessed of common human dignity. As such it is a penalty that subjects the individual to a fate forbidden by the principle of civilized treatment guaranteed by the [clause]. I therefore would hold, on that ground alone, that death is today a cruel and unusual punishment prohibited by the Clause. Justice of this kind is obviously no less shocking than the crime itself, and the new "official" murder, far from offering redress for the offense committed against society, adds instead a second defilement to the first.

Mr. Justice Marshall, dissenting:

In *Furman* I concluded that the death penalty is constitutionally invalid for two reasons. First, the death penalty is excessive. And second, the American people, fully informed as to the purposes of the death penalty and its liabilities, would in my view reject it as morally unacceptable.

Since the decision in *Furman*, the legislatures of 35 States have enacted new statutes authorizing the imposition of the death sentence for certain crimes, and Congress has enacted a law providing the death penalty for air piracy resulting in death. . . . I would be less than candid if I did not acknowledge that these developments have a significant bearing on a realistic assessment of the moral acceptability of the death penalty to the American people. But if the constitutionality of the death penalty turns, as I have urged, on the opinion of an *informed* citizenry, then even the enactment of new death statutes cannot be viewed as conclusive. In *Furman*, I observed that the American people are largely unaware of the information critical to a judgment on the morality of the death penalty, and concluded that if they were better informed they would consider it shocking, unjust, and unacceptable. A recent study, conducted after the enactment of the post-*Furman* statutes, has confirmed that the American people know little about the death penalty, and that the opinions of an informed public would differ significantly from those of a public unaware of the consequences and effects of the death penalty.

Even assuming, however, that the post-*Furman* enactment of statutes authorizing the death penalty renders the prediction of the views of an informed citizenry an uncertain basis for a constitutional decision, the enactment of those statutes has no bearing whatever on the conclusion that the death penalty is unconstitutional because it is excessive. An excessive penalty is invalid under the Cruel and Unusual Punishments Clause "even though popular sentiment may favor" it. . . . The inquiry here, then, is simply whether the death penalty is necessary to accomplish the legitimate legislative purposes in punishment, or whether a less severe penalty—life imprisonment—would do as well. . . .

The two purposes that sustain the death penalty as nonexcessive in the Court's view are general deterrence and retribution. In *Furman*, I canvassed the relevant data on the deterrent effect of capital punishment. . . . The state of knowledge at that point, after literally centuries of debate, was summarized as follows by a United Nations Committee:

> It is generally agreed between the retentionists and abolitionists, whatever their opinions about the validity of comparative studies of deterrence, that the data which now exist show no correlation between the existence of capital punishment and lower rates of capital crime.[1]

The available evidence, I concluded in *Furman*, was convincing that "capital punishment is not necessary as a deterrent to crime in our society." . . .

The other principal purpose said to be served by the death penalty is retribution. . . . It is this notion that I find to be the most disturbing aspect of today's unfortunate decisions.

The concept of retribution is a multifaceted one, and any discussion of its role in the criminal law must be undertaken with caution. On one level, it can be said that the notion of retribution or reprobation is the basis of our insistence that only those who have broken the law be punished, and in this sense the notion is quite obviously central to a just system of criminal sanctions. But our recognition that retribution plays a crucial role in determining who may be punished by no means requires approval of retribution as a general justification for punishment. It is the question whether retribution can provide a moral justification for punishment—in particular, capital punishment—that we must consider.

My Brothers Stewart, Powell, and Stevens offer the following explanation of the retributive justification for capital punishment:

> "The instinct for retribution is part of the nature of man, and channeling that instinct in the administration of criminal justice serves an important purpose in promoting the stability of a society governed by law. When people begin to believe that organized

society is unwilling or unable to impose upon criminal offenders the punishment they 'deserve,' then there are sown the seeds of anarchy—of self help, vigilante justice, and lynch law."

This statement is wholly inadequate to justify the death penalty. As my Brother Brennan stated in *Furman*, "[t]here is no evidence whatever that utilization of imprisonment rather than death encourages private blood feuds and other disorders." It simply defies belief to suggest that the death penalty is necessary to prevent the American people from taking the law into their own hands.

In a related vein, it may be suggested that the expression of moral outrage through the imposition of the death penalty serves to reinforce basic moral values—that it marks some crimes as particularly offensive and therefore to be avoided. The argument is akin to a deterrence argument, but differs in that it contemplates the individual's shrinking from antisocial conduct, not because he fears punishment, but because he has been told in the strongest possible way that the conduct is wrong. This contention, like the previous one, provides no support for the death penalty. It is inconceivable that any individual concerned about conforming his conduct to what society says is "right" would fail to realize that murder is "wrong" if the penalty were simply life imprisonment.

The foregoing contentions—that society's expression of moral outrage through the imposition of the death penalty pre-empts the citizenry from taking the law into its own hands and reinforces moral values—are not retributive in the purest sense. They are essentially utilitarian in that they portray the death penalty as valuable because of its beneficial results. These justifications for the death penalty are inadequate because the penalty is, quite clearly I think, not necessary to the accomplishment of those results.

There remains for consideration, however, what might be termed the purely retributive justification for the death penalty—that the death penalty is appropriate, not because of its beneficial effect on society, but because the taking of the murderer's life is itself morally good. Some of the language of the opinion of my Brothers Stewart, Powell, and Stevens in No. 74–6257 appears positively to embrace this notion of retribution for its own sake as a justification for capital punishment. They state:

> [T]he decision that capital punishment may be the appropriate sanction in extreme cases

is an expression of the community's belief that certain crimes are themselves so grievous an affront to humanity that the only adequate response may be the penalty of death.

They then quote with approval from Lord Justice Denning's remarks before the British Royal Commission on Capital Punishment:

> "The truth is that some crimes are so outrageous that society insists on adequate punishment, because the wrong-doer deserves it, irrespective of whether it is a deterrent or not."

Of course, it may be that these statements are intended as no more than observations as to the popular demands that it is thought must be responded to in order to prevent anarchy. But the implication of the statements appears to me to be quite different— namely, that society's judgment that the murderer "deserves" death must be respected not simply because the preservation of order requires it, but because it is appropriate that society make the judgment and carry it out. It is this latter notion, in particular, that I consider to be fundamentally at odds with the Eighth Amendment. . . . The mere fact that the community demands the murderer's life in return for the evil he has done cannot sustain the death penalty, for as Justices Stewart, Powell, and Stevens remind us, "the Eighth Amendment demands more than that a challenged punishment be acceptable to contemporary society." . . . To be sustained under the Eighth Amendment, the death penalty must "compor[t] with the basic concept of human dignity at the core of the Amendment," ibid.; the objective in imposing it must be "[consistent] with our respect for the dignity of [other] men." . . . Under these standards, the taking of life "because the wrongdoer deserves it" surely must fall, for such a punishment has as its very basis the total denial of the wrongdoer's dignity and worth.

The death penalty, unnecessary to promote the goal of deterrence or to further any legitimate notion of retribution, is an excessive penalty forbidden by the Eighth and Fourteenth Amendments. I respectfully dissent from the Court's judgment upholding the sentences of death imposed upon the petitioners in these cases.

Endnote

[1] United Nations, Department of Economic and Social Affairs, Capital Punishment, pt. II, I 159, p. 123 (1968).

Chapter 5

The Law of Tort

This chapter deals with a part of what is commonly referred to as *civil* law, as contrasted with criminal law. Traditionally, civil law was that branch of law concerned with the rights of private parties, as opposed to the claims of the state. The law of *tort* addresses the interests each of us has in obtaining redress for the wrongs that befall us through the carelessness of others.

To understand these interests more clearly, consider a brief example. Suppose that you own a farm on which you grow crops. One day, I take possession of the land immediately adjacent to yours, claiming that I am the owner. I build a factory that makes widgets. (Don't worry about what a "widget" is; nobody has ever seen one, but they have been used as examples in law schools for centuries!) There are several by-products to my manufacture of widgets, particularly air and water pollution. Some of the bad air and polluted water inevitably cross over the boundaries separating our respective parcels of land, and the result is damage to your crops. By a strange twist of fate, your farm operation also turns out to be dangerous to my employees. The insecticides you spray to keep your crops healthy inevitably drift onto my land with the result that workers in my factory experience respiratory difficulties.

Clearly, there is a conflict here involving types of land use. Your right to use your property as you choose is being frustrated by my choice to use my property in a different manner. Several dimensions of tort law are implicated in this case. You, for example, might choose to sue me in tort for creating a nuisance which caused injury to your crops. In evaluating your claim, the law of tort would ask whether I had breached a duty I owed to you, whether the damage to your crops was in fact caused by my actions, and whether the damage was sufficiently serious as to be recognized by the law. Exploring further, tort law produces other questions: suppose, for example, that lightning starts a fire on my property but I do nothing to stop it. Wind spreads the flames, and the fire consumes your crops. Am I responsible for the damage to your farm? Does it matter that I didn't actually "do" anything? Can I be held accountable for "omissions" as well as for "acts"? Suppose the fire began in my factory and I did everything I could to contain it. Nonetheless, an unusually strong wind carried the embers to your farm and your crops were burned. Can I be held liable if I did everything a reasonable person would do to stop the fire from spreading?

A central concern of those theorists who think about the foundations of tort law is how to balance the competing claims of efficiency and justice in resolving questions such as those raised above. Suppose it turns out that your crops and my factory are simply incompatible adjacent land uses. How should society determine which of us will prevail in court? Should that question be settled on utilitarian grounds, by deciding which of the uses most efficiently enhances the overall utility for the community? Or should it be decided by appeal to the antecedently established rights to which each of us lays claim?

The *Holden* case, and the readings by Oliver Wendell Holmes, Richard Posner, and Jules Coleman begin the chapter by exploring the basic aims of tort law and weighing the competing claims of efficiency and justice in tort. The discussion centers on what the law of tort is designed to accomplish. Is it to minimize the cost of injuries and accidents, or to rectify the wrongdoing of "fault" defendants? The selections in Section B pursue questions about causation in the law of tort. The *Lynch* and *Palsgraf* cases present contrasting perspectives on the question of when one thing can be said to have caused

another. The essays by H. L. A. Hart and A. M Honoré, and by Judith Thomson examine a range of further questions: What determines whether my conduct has caused your injury? Am I responsible for all of the harm that I cause? How relevant to my responsibility for your harm is the fact that I caused it? How relevant is the fact that I was at fault or blameworthy in acting as I did? The readings in Section C by Thomas Macaulay and Ernest Weinrib take up a more specific related issue: liability for omissions, or failures to act, and the legal status of a duty to rescue.

"Cases for Further Reflection" close the chapter with some well-known cases in which courts have grappled with the puzzles of causation, duty, negligence, and other elements of tort law.

A. *Justice, Compensation, and Tort*

The Nature of Torts

In 1983 a young woman named Connie Daniell tried to commit suicide by locking herself in the trunk of a 1973 Ford LTD, where she remained for nine days. After being rescued, Daniell took Ford to court, alleging that the company was responsible for the psychological and physical injuries she suffered in the ordeal because the company had not built the trunk with an internal latch.[1] Daniell sought to enlist the law in naming Ford the responsible party. What is the legal basis for such a claim?

To answer this question, imagine the following scenario: You have just landed a new job downtown. As the first day at the new office approaches, you become excited and a bit nervous. The night before your first meeting with the boss, you check that the

alarm clock is set to go off early because you must be at the office on time to make a good first impression. As fate would have it, the clock malfunctions during the night, the alarm doesn't go off, and you leap out of bed in the morning with only a few minutes to get downtown. You catch an "express" bus to the business district. The bus driver seems to be in a hurry, too; in fact, the bus is traveling at an illegal speed. This is all for the good, you think, until the bus approaches a major intersection, rounding the corner at the precise moment when a construction crew lifting a steel beam with a crane loses control of the rig and sends the beam crashing through the side of the bus at exactly where you are seated.

Fanciful as this scenario may seem, accidents equally bizarre and equally costly occur daily. Now you are recovering in Mercy Hospital with broken bones, intravenous tubes, and a mounting medical bill, and you have lost your job. Is anyone but you responsible for your plight? The construction crew?

---

[1] See *Daniell v. Ford Motor Co., Inc.*, 581 F. Supp. 728 (1984).

The bus company? The bus driver? The alarm clock manufacturer? If any of them is responsible in some way, what can you do about it? Have you been wronged by any or all of these parties in a way that the law might recognize? The answer is yes. Any one of these parties (with the probable exception of the alarm clock maker) may have committed a *tort*: a personal harm or wrong to an individual for which the law provides redress.

Connie Daniell alleged that Ford was liable in tort for her injuries because it was careless in the design of the trunk on one of its cars. When consumer goods fail to perform as expected or cause injuries, tort suits often result. Goods ranging from oral contraceptives and silicone breast implants to car batteries and drain cleaners have been the subject of alleged torts, but the field of tort is by no means restricted to actions brought for defective consumer products. A great many types of injuries, to person or to property, can be the basis for a tort claim: infliction of emotional distress, medical malpractice, environmental damage, and invasions of privacy are all "actionable" (the basis for a suit) in tort. Not everyone agrees that such tort actions always have merit. For example, many in the business world were outraged when, in a widely publicized case, a woman was awarded nearly $3 million from McDonald's for burns she suffered after spilling a cup of McDonald's coffee in her lap. The coffee, she claimed, was too hot.[2] Holding the company responsible for consumers' clumsiness, critics argued, is unjustifiable.

Many tort cases raise important questions about responsibility and fairness. Given the inevitability of injuries and accidents in a crowded, highly technological society, who should bear the burden of the costs those injuries and accidents incur? Who should be responsible for the costs of defective merchandise or products, disease caused by ground water pollution, or the negligence of an unsafe driver? Is it fair to leave these costs to those unlucky enough to incur them, or is there a morally defensible basis for shifting the costs to someone other than the injured party?

These larger questions of social policy and public morality lead to critical legal issues. Was Connie Daniell correct in asserting that Ford was careless in the design of its cars? How careful is Ford required to be? Should Ford have foreseen that someone might be injured by doing what Connie Daniell did? Was the risk of injury from being trapped in the trunk so obvious that no warning was necessary? Did Ford cause the injuries Daniell sustained, or did she cause them herself?

Grounds for Liability in Tort

What sort of "wrong" is a tort? Why doesn't the accident in our bus case amount to a *criminal* wrong—crimes that the bus driver and the construction crew have committed and for which they deserve to be punished? The answer is that although these individuals also may have committed certain crimes, being convictable of a crime is not the same thing as being liable under the law of tort. In the criminal law, the state (the "people") collectively seeks to enforce basic standards of behavior by acting to pay back a wrongdoer for his wrongful deed and by working to discourage similar future conduct. In the law of *tort*, it is the individual victim of another's wrongdoing who brings a suit against the perpetrator. This difference between crime and tort marks a deeper difference in the fundamental purposes of the two branches of law.

The aim of the criminal law is, broadly, to ensure compliance with the rules and standards deemed essential to the preservation of society as a whole. When these rules are broken, people are often hurt. However, the criminal law concerns itself with that hurt only insofar as it is reflected in the disrespect shown for society's rules. It is not a necessary condition of criminality that there be an identifiable "victim" in the sense that you in your hospital bed believe you have been made a victim.

Some crimes (conspiracy, illegal possession, unsuccessful attempts) do not have victims who suffer loss in this way, and even crimes that do have victims (robbery, rape, sexual abuse) do not concern themselves with addressing that loss. Thus arises the need for a body of law specifically concerned with determining where the burden of losses created intentionally or even unintentionally should fall. This role is fulfilled by tort law. You, the plaintiff, seek to have the losses or burdens that have befallen you (medical bills, lost wages, "pain and suffering") shifted to and compensated by someone else. A central question is when and under what circumstances this should be done.

Initially, losses "lie where they fall," and the law does not shift them to others without a good reason. These reasons are framed in terms of *liability rules*, which state what an injured plaintiff must show in order to force someone else to pay for his or her

---

[2] See *Lieback v. McDonald's Restaurants, Jury Verdict Research,* #CV 932419.

injuries. The ultimate theoretical justification of these rules is contested, as we shall see. But first, let us look briefly at each of the two main types of liability rules in tort: *strict liability* and *negligence*.

Strict Liability in Tort

In a case covered by strict liability, the plaintiff must show that (1) the defendant did something, (2) the plaintiff was injured, and (3) the injury was caused by what the defendant did. The defining feature of strict liability is the absence of any requirement that the defendant has been somehow *at fault* in his conduct. Traditionally, the common law imposed liability in this strict sense on property owners whose livestock trespassed on the property of adjacent landowners, causing damage. Strict liability was also imposed for abnormally dangerous conditions or activities such as storing explosives or flammable liquids or engaging in blasting or pumping that resulted in a flood. Today the strict liability rule is widely used in product liability cases, in which a consumer is injured by a defectively designed or manufactured product. Strict product liability claims dominate the current landscape of consumer protection litigation. A seller may be strictly liable for defective products introduced into the stream of commerce even though the seller was in no way negligent.

Section 402(A) of the *Restatement of Torts, Second*, is a source of much modern strict liability law. It states that a seller may be held liable when it makes and sells a product in a "defective" condition, "unreasonably dangerous" to the consumer. What do these terms mean? It is generally accepted that a product is defective if it was manufactured incorrectly—for example, with screws missing or parts not in the right place. Manufacturers can also be liable for defects in the design or concept of a product. For example, a company that made buses for commercial transit was held liable when a woman riding in one of its buses fell to the floor and was injured as the bus made a sharp right turn. The bus was said to be defectively designed as there was no "grab bar" or vertical pole for passengers to hold on to next to the plaintiff's seat.[3] Courts have employed at least two criteria to determine whether a design is defective:

1. The product is more dangerous than would be contemplated by an ordinary consumer using common knowledge—in other words, it falls below reasonable consumer expectations.

2. The product sold creates such a risk of serious injury that the cost to make it safe would outweigh the benefits to society.

It is important to see that these tests may yield different results. Recall the case of Connie Daniell, who locked herself in the trunk of an old car. There was no latch or other device with which the trunk could be opened from the inside. Had the car's trunk been defectively designed? To prove her claim under the first test, Daniell would have had to show that most consumers could not have foreseen the type of injury she suffered. Because most people would readily see the danger, however, this would be difficult. Still, this test has limitations: How should we handle cases in which consumers simply don't have any clear expectations about how a product should behave or how safe it is? For this and other reasons, some courts have preferred to ask a different question: Do trunks without inside latches create such a danger that the risk outweighs the utility or value of having such items available at all? The answer here is somewhat less clear and would probably depend on how much inside trunk latches would add to the cost of cars. Assessments of risk and utility are not easy. After all, such common household items as knives and scissors cause many accidents each year, yet few people would argue that we would be better off without them. Some products, of course, cannot be made completely safe. "Unavoidably unsafe" goods such as vaccines nonetheless have great utility.

Sellers of goods have also been held strictly liable in tort for failing to inform or to warn consumers adequately about the possible dangers of their products. Here the question facing producers is how best to transmit such information. How much of the risk must be disclosed? How vivid must a warning be? A woman taking birth-control pills was told by the maker, Ortho Pharmaceutical, that there could be side effects from use, "the most severe of which is abnormal blood-clotting." After several years of taking the pills, the woman suffered a stroke and sued Ortho, arguing that the risk of a "stroke" had not been fully and adequately conveyed to her.[4] Those in favor of holding manufacturers strictly liable in these cases argue that

---

[3] See *Campbell v. General Motors*, 32 Cal.3d 112 (1982).

[4] See *Macdonald v. Ortho Pharmaceutical Corp.*, 475 N.E.2d 65 (1985).

the firm is in the best position to understand the hazards posed by its products and warn of them; others contend that holding companies liable in all cases in which a product user has not understood the warnings will sharply increase the cost of the products in question, such that consumers who use products safely will wind up subsidizing the careless users.

More generally, advocates of strict tort liability argue that mass production of standardized products and the rapidly growing technological complexity of goods available to the public have left consumers increasingly ill-equipped to evaluate the safety and quality of the goods they purchase. The magnitude of harm presented by products increases as our capacity to assess the risks they impose diminishes. For these and other reasons, courts and legislators have felt it fair to impose strict liability on manufacturers, insisting that they pay for injuries sustained by those who use their products even though the seller has exercised all possible care in the design, manufacture, and sale of its products.

Plaintiff's Fault and Product Misuse

Although the producer of a good may be responsible if the item is dangerous or defective, it seems unfair to insist that the producer be held liable even when its commodity is misused by a consumer. A ladder that has been poorly constructed is the builder's problem, but most would say that a ladder placed on obviously uneven ground or clearly overbalanced by the user is the user's problem. Suppose that a plaintiff in a tort suit is injured by a fall from a ladder or from scaffolding after she was warned not to stand on it because it was unstable. If the plaintiff's own carelessness was the immediate cause of her injury, the defendant who supplied the ladder or scaffolding might be able to assert that fact in its defense. Such a claim was traditionally known as the doctrine of *contributory negligence* because, the allegation went, the plaintiff contributed to her own accident. Consumer misconduct is a frequently invoked defense to product liability lawsuits although this defense has been questioned in some cases. Suppose that Seller markets a car capable of traveling at tremendous speeds. Seller can foresee that at least some buyers of its cars will drive them at the dangerous speeds of which they are capable. Should such "foreseeable misuses" of a product be Seller's problem?

The old common law rule held that contributory negligence was a "complete bar" to the award of damages: even if the plaintiff's carelessness was less significant or obvious than that of the defendant, the plaintiff received nothing. Most jurisdictions have now supplanted the common law rule with a regime of *comparative fault*, according to which the plaintiff's overall compensation is diminished, but not entirely eliminated, by an amount proportional to her part in the accident.

The readings for this section open with a fairly typical torts case, *Holden v. Wal-Mart*, which illustrates the doctrine of comparative fault. Debra Holden underwent a total knee replacement procedure, a medical treatment which some testimony indicated she would not have needed to undergo for many years, had she not fallen in the parking lot at Wal-Mart when her foot twisted in a hole in the pavement. Holden sued Wal-Mart to recover medical costs and other related expenses, and as compensation for her pain and suffering. The jury found Holden 40 percent at fault, and Wal-Mart, 60 percent.

Negligence

The *Holden* case also involves the central tort concept of *negligence*. Liability in negligence is established when the plaintiff shows each of the following: (1) the defendant did something, (2) the plaintiff was injured, (3) the injury was caused by what the defendant did, and (4) the defendant was at fault. The last requirement is sometimes referred to as a *breach of duty* to exercise due care or regard for the safety of others, thereby exposing them to an unreasonable risk of harm. To say that a person is negligent is not necessarily to say that he or she is forgetful or inattentive (even though this may be the case). Rather, to be negligent means to fall below the acceptable level of care for the welfare of others that society expects of us all. As such, "fault" in the law of tort is not always equivalent to moral blame or censure. As one commentator has said, negligence may be the result of "ignorance, lack of intelligence, or an honest mistake"; thus the kind of "fault" required "means nothing more than a departure from a standard of conduct required of a person by society for the protection of his neighbors."[5]

---

[5] W. Page Keeton, *Prosser and Keeton on Torts*, 5th ed. (St. Paul: West Publishing Co., 1984), p. 535.

According to the standard doctrine of tort, a defendant is liable for negligent conduct if he or she failed to act as a *reasonable* person would have acted. Courts have typically resolved tort disputes with the device of a hypothetical "reasonable person" whose conduct serves as a measure of what is reasonable behavior under the circumstances. The obvious vagueness of the term "reasonable" is regarded by the law as a benefit, not a drawback, for it allows the jury to consider all of the factors present in a given case in light of what a person of average intelligence and prudence would do. Driving at 70 miles an hour down a slick road may be "unreasonable" conduct for teenagers out for a thrill, but it may be reasonable for paramedics trying to get a dying patient to the hospital.

It is important to see that, with few exceptions, the law evaluates a defendant's conduct based on what was in fact reasonable under the circumstances, not on what the defendant himself may have believed to be reasonable. Wal-Mart, for example, may not have realized that its parking lot contained holes; but if a reasonable retailer would have been aware of this hazard, Wal-Mart's failure to appreciate the condition of its premises may be deemed negligent. The distinction here is sometimes marked by saying that the law employs an *objective,* rather than a *subjective,* test of negligence or fault. Suppose you leave a banana peel on the stairway. I slip on the peel and am injured. When the law asks whether you acted negligently, it does not assess the faultiness of your conduct exclusively from your own (subjective) point of view, taking into account your particular weaknesses or inabilities or beliefs. It doesn't inquire into whether you personally realized the danger presented by the banana peel—perhaps you are mentally slow and just never thought about it. Instead it asks whether a reasonable person would have appreciated the danger. Even though you may have thought that depositing the banana peel on the steps was "reasonable," what matters is whether your actions were reasonable from an objective standpoint. Tort law does make allowances for some individual physical limitations: for example, a blind person cannot be expected to conform to the standards of the sighted, and a child cannot always be expected to act as an adult would.

Why should negligence be measured by an objective test? After all, it may seem unfair to judge people by standards that do not necessarily reflect their individual level of blameworthiness or culpability. Many jurists answer, in utilitarian fashion, that cooperative social life requires a certain minimum standard of average care upon which everyone can rely. People who, because of their constitution, cannot live up to this standard may be forgiven by an enlightened conscience, but because their conduct still poses a threat or danger, they must be held to that average, objective standard.

We can now return to the construction crew in the hypothetical case sketched at the opening of this chapter. Suppose the crew was required by industry standards (in addition to common sense) to hoist the steel beams with a cable of sufficient tensile strength to handle the load, but they were using a cheaper, substandard cable. This is an example of a failure to exercise proper care for the safety of others by exposing workers and pedestrians (and transit passengers) to a risk of serious harm. Does this mean that you can sue the company for its negligence? Not of itself. To establish a *prima facie* case of negligent harm, the law requires a plaintiff to prove, by a preponderance (majority) of the evidence, that: (1) the defendant (here, the construction company) had a duty to exercise reasonable care in the context within which it acted (lifting heavy steel girders), (2) the defendant violated or breached that duty (using cheap, unsafe cable and thereby creating a genuine hazard), and (3) the breach of that duty caused harm to you (permitting the girder to escape and strike you, resulting in injuries), and (4) the defendant was at fault, having exposed you to danger through its carelessness.

Strict Liability vs. Negligence

The central questions in the law of tort concern what kinds of unintended harms or accidents should be dealt with under strict liability and what kinds under negligence, and whether one or the other rule should become the uniform rule for all tort cases or neither rule should govern and the tort system should be modified or abandoned.

One of the principal justifications often advanced in support of a regime of strict tort liability is that such an approach has the effect of taking a cost that initially falls on an individual and *spreading that cost out* by asking manufacturers of defective products or those involved in dangerous activities to absorb the cost. More generally, those who support strict liability appeal to the good consequences that the adoption of such a liability rule will have. To see what this means, imagine a company that manufactures and sells explosives used in mining and construction. What are the costs of placing such items on the market? Clearly one such cost is the expense incurred by the company in the process of manufacture: what it costs to buy the raw materials, to process and assemble the explosives, and so on. It also costs the company money to advertise and market its goods. Just as plainly, however, another cost of having explosives on the market is that they may injure those who use them. Because such costs would not otherwise appear on the ledger books of the company, economists call them *externalities*. The basic idea behind a policy of strict liability, say its defenders, is to make the explosives industry (in this case) cover its own costs or absorb its own externalities—pay its own way in the world. By holding the explosives business liable for injuries caused by its products, society gives the industry an incentive to make its goods as safe as possible. Strict liability makes sense economically as well, since the industry can use its expertise to eliminate or avoid accident costs more cheaply (efficiently) than can consumers. Finally, strict liability affords an effective way of insuring against the costs of accidents; the industry can simply add the costs of covering injuries to the price of its goods, thus spreading the costs out among the large base of consumers rather than leaving the burden concentrated on the few who are injured.

Those who support a negligence theory of tort law challenge each of the foregoing arguments. Strict liability is poor economic policy since it will generate more costs than its proponents acknowledge. Plaintiffs do not have to shoulder the responsibility and the costs of injuries under a system of strict tort liability, so they will tend to be less careful, with the result that the number of accidents and court cases will rise steadily. Insurance premiums will increase. Consumers will be less mindful of product instructions and warnings and will have less incentive to use the products safely. Supporters of a negligence-based theory of tort often rest their case on the moral claim that liability should never be imposed except where there is a finding of fault, even if fault is measured objectively. Even if it could be shown that strict liability will lower the number of accidents or will spread costs more efficiently, why is it fair to use a

defendant in that way? If a company that makes explosives or chain saws is as careful as possible in the design and construction of its wares, why is it nonetheless fair to force it to pay for harm to consumers? Sometimes, say the critics of strict liability, bad things just happen to consumers and are not the manufacturers' fault.

The Basis of Negligence Liability

In a selection taken from his famous work, *The Common Law*, Oliver Wendell Holmes declares that he is searching for "the general principle of civil liability in tort." Tort law deals with non-consensual harms: Wal-Mart did not agree ahead of time to give money to Holden (as it would if the two had entered into a contract). Rather, Wal-Mart was ordered by the court to transfer wealth to Holden. Holmes wants to know what legitimates this re-distribution of wealth. Holmes discusses the familiar idea that tort law addresses itself to *moral wrongdoing*, that is, to the fault of the defendant. Holmes points out that many doctrines in tort resemble strict liability—for example, the notion that we "act at our peril." But strict liability, Holmes responds, "offends" our "sense of justice." Holmes uses a famous, early torts case as an example: In attempting to separate two fighting dogs, the defendant raised a stick to hit the animals and struck the plaintiff—who had suddenly come up behind him—in the eye, causing severe injury. Holmes reasons that, to hold the defendant liable in this situation would be to endorse the principle that actors are liable for all of the consequences of their actions, even those they could not have foreseen. Actions are choices, for Holmes, and holding people responsible for the results of their choices only makes sense if they could foresee them.

But the fault principle, Holmes cautions, is not an assignment of liability based purely on subjective culpability. Fault in the law is measured, as we have seen, by what the average person would judge to be an unreasonable risk. (Holmes uses some terms that are survivals of the old system of "writs," used in England before the advent of modern tort doctrine. Under that system, an intentional, immediate wrong—say, throwing a log at you and hitting you on the head—would be a "trespass"; had I merely left the log in the road and you had then tripped over it later, my liability for your injury would involve "trespass on the case.")

Theories of Tort

The debate over the liability rules of negligence and strict liability is only a portion of a larger philosophical debate over the basic aims and purposes of tort law. That broader discussion is joined here in the readings by Richard Posner and Jules Coleman.

Posner's account of tort law is premised, at least in part, on a picture of the aims of tort that Posner shares with others. According to this view, the function of tort doctrine is to achieve worthy social goals, and is in turn part of a larger requirement that the institutions and practices of society be just. The purpose of tort is to guard against the risks that are created through complex forms of social interaction. The force of this goal is independent of any moral concern with "righting" the wrongs that one person might bring upon another.

In his selection, Posner argues for his long-held contention that the economic policy of maximizing wealth (and minimizing costs) is the theory which best explains the structure and substance of tort law. (To refresh your memory on the animating ideas behind law and economics, see the introduction to Section E of Chapter 1). Posner explores how wealth-maximization intersects with our moral convictions. Posner tries to show how the existing state of tort law—where much liability is assessed on the basis of negligence, together with pockets of strict liability—can be wealth-maximizing, by appeal to the concept of a "Pareto-optimal" distribution: "A change (including a change brought about by an accident or an intentional act) is good if it makes at least one person better off and no one worse off." How could an accident make someone better off? We all take risks, Posner would argue, because we judge them to be worth it. I want to be able to buy products from Wal-Mart, for instance, even though I realize there is a (small) danger in simply walking through their parking lot; and Wal-Mart, of course, wants to sell to me, even though it knows that, by inviting people onto its premises, someone might get hurt. Now notice, Posner would instruct, that it may not be to everyone's long-term advantage to hold Wal-Mart liable in every case where people are hurt on its premises—if we were to do so, most retailers would soon be out of business. So the costs of my medical bills after I fall need to be paid in accordance with whatever rules will keep the overall costs to everyone (including the "*ex ante*" costs of buying

insurance) as low as possible. A system that holds individuals responsible for their negligent behavior may, Posner thinks, be the more optimal policy overall. Posner explains the connections between his wealth-maximization principle and the theory of rule-utilitarianism.

Opposed to the utilitarian account of tort is the view defended here by Jules Coleman. According to Coleman, tort law is be explained in terms of the principle of *corrective justice*, which states that "individuals who are responsible for the wrongful losses of others have a duty to repair the losses." A fair or just allocation of the costs of accidents and injuries, in this view, is one that reflects the bilateral and restitutionary structure of tort. The purpose is not simply to see to it that the injured are somehow compensated or that their losses are nullified, but to guarantee that it is *the defendant* who makes good the loss, who repairs the wrong. The reasons which provide me with a basis for recovery also identify you (the defendant) as the person from whom the recovery must come. Coleman criticizes the economic theory of torts for ignoring these structural features. Since economics is forward-looking, what matters is simply that the loss is shifted—the parties themselves are little more than vehicles for optimizing costs-savings. Posner cannot convincingly explain, for example, why you—the injurer—must be the one to pay damages and "make me whole." Coleman devotes much of his argument to clarifying the demand of corrective justice that one is responsible for the outcomes of one's wrongful actions. This, Coleman contends, is a principle rooted in political, rather than personal, morality.

The final reading for this section turns away from auto accidents to examine problems raised by a new area of tort law. Law professor Roger Cramton outlines the challenges to existing law posed by the emergence of so-called "mass exposure torts." Some of the most difficult legal and moral issues to arise from the expansion of strict liability are raised by society's efforts to handle tens of thousands of similar product-related injuries. Many courts now permit manufacturers of tobacco, asbestos, IUDs, and breast implants to be sued by both actual and prospective victims in a single proceeding. Cramton examines the tension between the societal goals of such "class action" lawsuits and the need for each individual victim to seek compensatory justice. Cramton believes that the current system for dealing with large-scale consumer injuries leaves many questions unanswered.

Holden v. Wal-Mart Stores, Inc.

The appellant, Debra J. Holden, fell after stepping in a hole in the parking lot of a store owned by the appellee, Wal-Mart Stores, Inc. Holden subsequently underwent knee replacement surgery and sustained medical bills of at least $25,000. During trial, Holden offered evidence of instances at other Wal-Mart stores involving falls due to the condition of the pavement in those stores' parking lots. The district court excluded the evidence on the basis that its probative value was outweighed by the potential for prejudice under Neb. Rev. Stat. § 27-403.

Evidence at trial indicated that Holden had a preexisting knee condition but that the fall might have aggravated it. A jury found Wal-Mart to be 60 percent negligent and Holden to be 40 percent negligent, awarding damages in the amount of $6,000. When reduced by Holden's negligence, the damages amounted to $3,600. Holden appeals, contending that the district court erred in refusing to allow her to present evidence of similar falls occurring at other Wal-Mart stores and that the amount of damages was inadequate.

We conclude that Holden failed to show how falls at other locations were substantially similar to her fall and that the damages awarded by the jury were supported by the record.

Background

In July 1992, Holden was injured after she fell in the parking lot of a Wal-Mart in Scottsbluff, Nebraska. Prior to the fall, Holden had been issued a handicapped parking permit dated June 2, 1992, because prior problems with her knees and feet made it difficult for her to walk distances. On the day of the fall, Holden parked in a handicapped parking space at Wal-Mart. When she pulled into the stall, she did not notice any holes in the surface of the parking lot. After she got out of her van and was walking toward the rear of it, she fell and experienced immediate pain, the worst of which was in her right knee. After she composed her-

self, she saw that the cause of the fall was that her foot had twisted in a hole. Following the fall, Holden went to the emergency room. Holden subsequently underwent knee replacement surgery and brought the instant action against Wal-Mart seeking damages.

In her operative petition, Holden alleged that Wal-Mart was negligent because it failed to properly maintain the parking lot, failed to adequately inspect the premises, failed to repair the hole, and failed to warn her of the condition. Wal-Mart denied the allegations and alleged that any dangerous condition in the parking lot was open and obvious, that Holden was contributorily negligent, and that she assumed the risk of injuries.

Prior to trial, Wal-Mart filed a motion seeking an order prohibiting Holden from presenting evidence concerning other parking lot slip-and-fall incidents at other Wal-Mart stores. In the motion, Wal-Mart alleged that such evidence was not relevant and that any probative value was substantially outweighed by the danger of unfair prejudice or was otherwise in violation of § 27–403. The district court concluded that the relevance of such evidence was substantially outweighed by the danger of unfair prejudice and confusion of issues and sustained the motion.

Trial

During trial, the jury saw photographs of the hole that Holden had stepped in. The photographs showed a crack in the surface of the parking lot, along with a hole. A witness to the accident stated that the hole was large enough for Holden's foot to fit in. Holden's mother, also a witness to the accident, described the hole as being difficult to see. Holden presented several witnesses who testified that the hole was a pothole, that such a hole would take some time to develop, that it posed a risk, and that a retailer such as Wal-Mart had a responsibility either to repair it or to warn customers about it.

Following this evidence, Holden sought to introduce into evidence exhibit 67, which consisted of 84 reports of instances involving falls in the parking lots of other Wal-Mart stores. Holden sought to introduce the exhibit to show notice that holes in pavement need to be taken care of and argued that the exhibit was relevant to show notice and danger. Wal-Mart objected on the basis that there was nothing to show that the instances were similar due to differences in items such as the parking lot surfaces and the times of day when the falls occurred. The district court sustained Wal-Mart's objection.

Witnesses for Wal-Mart testified that the hole was not a hazard or danger. A street superintendent with experience in asphalt paving testified that the hole was not a pothole. An engineer also testified as an expert regarding asphalt repairs and maintenance. The engineer testified that in his opinion, the crack did not constitute a pothole and was not a hazard, and that upon inspection, he would not have recommended that the area required immediate attention.

Following this testimony, Holden again sought to introduce exhibit 67. As an offer of proof, Holden provided the engineer's deposition in which he stated that same or similar incidents would be relevant to him to determine whether or not the parking lot at issue was safe, whether the rules and protocols of the store were working, and whether something else needed to be done. The district court refused to admit the exhibit.

The manager of the Wal-Mart where Holden fell testified regarding the safety procedures followed at the store. He also testified that he did not believe the crack in the parking lot was a hazard and did not constitute a pothole. Following his testimony, Holden again offered exhibit 67. Holden argued that the exhibit was necessary to impeach the manager's definition of a pothole because that definition was inconsistent with what Wal-Mart referred to as a "pothole" at other stores. The district court excluded the evidence.

Holden testified that she had noticed cracks, dips, and depressions in the Wal-Mart parking lot prior to July 1992. She further testified that on the day she fell, she did not expect the surface of the lot to be smooth, that nothing was present to prevent her from seeing the hole, and that she had had plenty of opportunity to observe the condition of the lot.

Prior Medical History

Because Holden has asserted that the damages awarded by the jury were inadequate, we set out the evidence presented at trial concerning her past medical history. At the time of trial, Holden was 35 years of age. She had previously injured her right knee in 1976 as a result of an accident at her school. As a result, she underwent surgery to repair the knee. Following the surgery, Holden was able to resume sporting activities and worked for a period of years.

The record reflects that in April 1992, Holden saw Dr. Diane E. Gilles, an orthopedic surgeon. At that time, Holden told Gilles that she had experienced problems with her right knee since she was in seventh grade and that it had gotten worse since then. She also indicated to Gilles that she was recently involved in an accident involving an exercise bike. Gilles noted in her report that Holden was markedly overweight and concluded that Holden had marked posttraumatic changes with bone-on-bone contact in the medial compartment, possible loose-body superlateral aspect of the knee, patellofemoral changes and spurring, and end-stage arthritis. On April 24, 1992, Holden had a follow-up visit during which Gilles suggested that she might need knee replacement surgery some day.

Wal-Mart adduced evidence that on May 13, 1992, Holden applied for disability insurance benefits from the Social Security Administration. In her application, she stated that she was unable to work due to a disabling condition that existed on December 1, 1991. On May 20, 1992, Holden completed a disability report for Social Security in which she stated that as of that date, she experienced severe pain and swelling in her right knee and was unable to be on her feet for long periods of time. Holden was issued her handicapped parking permit on June 2, and on June 26, she received disability benefits due to obesity and traumatic arthritis of the knee.

Following the fall, on July 7, 1992, a Dr. Ropp, a physician in Gilles' office, saw Holden because of the fall. Ropp did a range of motion evaluation and concluded that Holden's range of motion was better than it had been in April. Holden visited Gilles on July 14 as a followup for foot pain, and Holden did not mention any knee pain at that time. A followup visit for both foot and knee pain occurred in August. On September 28, Holden saw Ropp for left-foot pain. She told Ropp she had been standing processing tomatoes over the past 2 weeks but did not mention her knee.

In November 1992, Holden was seen by Gilles for knee pain. At that time, x rays were taken, and a comparison with the x rays from April 1992 showed the same findings. In March 1993, Holden underwent a gastric stapling operation. Gilles testified that one of the reasons for the operation was to enable Holden to lose enough weight to allow for a right-knee replacement.

Gilles testified that if Holden had not fallen, she probably could have waited between 5 to 10 years before requiring a total knee replacement. Gilles also testified that prior to the fall, Holden had an 87-percent lower extremily impairment and a 35-percent whole person impairment and that after the fall, this increased to a 97-percent lower extremity impairment and 39-percent whole person impairment. Gilles' charges for treatment related to the fall were $646.75.

The record reflects that Holden first saw Dr. Mark Alan McFerran, another orthopedic surgeon, on January 10, 1994. McFerran subsequently performed a total knee replacement and placed Holden on maximum medical improvement in May 1995. McFerran testified that following the fall, Holden complained of pain in her right knee, along with a catching and popping in the knee. Holden indicated to McFerran that she was cautious and apprehensive because at times the knee would give out on her. McFerran stated that Holden had a preexisting condition in her knee. He testified that she had severe end-stage arthritis which had completely worn out the cartilage in her knee and that this was true prior to the fall. McFerran testified that he did not think the impairment rating Holden had prior to the fall would have been significantly different afterward. However, McFerran also testified that he thought the fall at Wal-Mart hastened the need for Holden to have her knee replaced.

The total of McFerran's charges was $24,707.91. McFerran testified that the hardware involved in the knee replacement has a lifespan of 15 to 20 years, after which Holden would require another replacement costing between $40,000 and $50,000, barring complications. Holden presented evidence regarding the pain she experienced after the fall and her need for assistance due to the fall.

The jury returned a verdict finding 40 percent negligence on the part of Holden and 60 percent negligence on the part of Wal-Mart. The jury determined total damages to be $6,000. As a result, Holden recovered $3,600. Holden filed a motion for new trial alleging that the verdict was contrary to law and was not supported by sufficient evidence, that an error of law occurred at trial, and that there was an error in the assessment of recovery. The district court overruled the motion. Holden appeals.

Analysis

Holden contends that exhibit 67 was relevant to show that Wal-Mart had notice of the hole or to show notice that the hole was a pothole and a dangerous condition. Wal-Mart objected to the evidence on the basis that it was not relevant, that it did not portray instances that were the same or similar to Holden's fall, and that any probative value of the evidence was outweighed by its potential for prejudice. The trial court excluded the evidence under § 27-403 on the basis that any probative value was outweighed by its

potentially prejudicial effects. We conclude that the evidence was not relevant because Holden failed to show how the prior falls, depicted in exhibit 67, were substantially similar to her own fall.

In this case, the reports of falls portrayed in exhibit 67 occurred at different locations across the country, under a wide variety of circumstances. Although they all involve a fall in a parking lot, conditions vary widely among them. For example, the falls portrayed in exhibit 67 occurred at differing times of the day, under differing lighting conditions, and under differing weather conditions. Further, a review of the photographs attached to the reports shows a variety of different surface conditions. Holden did not attempt, in an offer of proof, to lay foundations showing that each of the incidents portrayed in exhibit 67 were substantially similar to the circumstances surrounding her own fall. Rather, Holden simply offered all the reports as one exhibit. In the alternative, Holden asked the court to enter into evidence the incidents portrayed as involving potholes but did not identify which incidents those were or how they were otherwise similar to the fall in her case. Under these circumstances, Holden did not establish that the incidents documented in exhibit 67 were substantially similar to her fall. Thus, the district court was correct in excluding the evidence.

Holden next contends that the jury erred in its computation of damages, arguing that the jury made a mistake.

> "An award of damages may be set aside as excessive or inadequate when, and not unless, it is so excessive or inadequate as to be the result of passion, prejudice, mistake, or some other means not apparent in the record. . . . If an award of damages shocks the conscience, it necessarily follows that the award was the result of passion, prejudice, mistake, or some other means not apparent in the record."
>
> *Woollen v. State*, 256 Neb. 865, 890, 593, N.W.2d 729, 745 (1999).

We conclude that the award in the instant case was not the result of a mistake. Rather, it was the result of conflicting evidence at trial. Evidence was presented at trial regarding Holden's previous problems with her right knee, and there was conflicting evidence regarding the effect of the fall on this preexisting condition. Holden testified regarding the additional pain and difficulties the fall caused, and her physicians indicated that the fall sped up the need for her to have knee replacement surgery. However, there was also evidence that Holden had been having similar knee pain causing difficulty in her life prior to the fall. However, she did not report the additional pain in several following appointments with her physicians. The evidence was strong that Holden would, at some point, have undergone knee replacement surgery regardless of the fall. However, when she might have done so was unclear.

Based on the conflicts in testimony, the jury could have reached any number of factual conclusions. A jury is entitled to determine what portion of a claimed injury was proximately caused by the incident and what portion of the medical bills was reasonably required. The jury in this case could have determined that the fall was the proximate cause of only a small

portion of Holden's damages. The evidence for such a determination is apparent from the record, and we will not disturb that determination on appeal.

Conclusion

We conclude that Holden failed to show a substantial similarity between the circumstance of her fall and the evidence she sought to introduce of falls at other locations. We further conclude that the amount of damages awarded by the jury is supported by the record. Accordingly, we find no error and affirm.

Affirmed.

The Fault Requirement in Tort

OLIVER WENDELL HOLMES JR.

The object of [this essay] is to discover whether there is any common ground at the bottom of all liability in tort, and if so, what that ground is. Supposing the attempt to succeed, it will reveal the general principle of civil liability at common law. The liabilities incurred by way of contract are more or less expressly fixed by the agreement of the parties concerned, but those arising from a tort are independent of any previous consent of the wrong-doer to bear the loss occasioned by his act. If *A* fails to pay a certain sum on a certain day, or to deliver a lecture on a certain night, after having made a binding promise to do so, the damages which he has to pay are recovered in accordance with his consent that some or all of the harms which may be caused by his failure shall fall upon him. But when *A* assaults or slanders his neighbor, or converts his neighbor's property, he does a harm which he has never consented to bear, and if the law makes him pay for it, the reason for doing so must be found in some general view of the conduct which every one may fairly expect and demand from every other, whether that other has agreed to it or not.

Such a general view is very hard to find. The law did not begin with a theory. It has never worked one out. The point from which it started and that at which I shall try to show that it has arrived, are on different planes. In the progress from one to the other, it is to be expected that its course should not be straight and its direction not always visible. All that can be done is to point out a tendency, and to justify it. The tendency, which is our main concern, is a matter of fact to be gathered from the cases.

The business of the law of torts is to fix the dividing lines between those cases in which a man is liable for harm which he has done, and those in which he is not.

But it cannot enable him to predict with certainty whether a given act under given circumstances will make him liable, because an act will rarely have that effect unless followed by damage, and for the most part, if not always, the consequences of an act are not known, but only guessed at as more or less probable. All the rules that the law can lay down beforehand are

From Oliver Wendell Holmes Jr., *The Common Law,* pp. 77–84, 88–99, 107–110. (Boston: Brown & Company, 1881).

rules for determining the conduct which will be followed by liability if it is followed by harm—that is, the conduct which a man pursues at his peril. The only guide for the future to be drawn from a decision against a defendant in an action of tort is that similar acts, under circumstances which cannot be distinguished except by the result from those of the defendant, are done at the peril of the actor; that if he escapes liability, it is simply because by good fortune no harm comes of his conduct in the particular event.

If, therefore, there is any common ground for all liability in tort, we shall best find it by eliminating the event as it actually turns out, and by considering only the principles on which the peril of his conduct is thrown upon the actor. We are to ask what are the elements, on the defendant's side, which must all be present before liability is possible, and the presence of which will commonly make him liable if damage follows.

The law of torts abounds in moral phraseology. It has much to say of wrongs, of malice, fraud, intent, and negligence. Hence it may naturally be supposed that the risk of a man's conduct is thrown upon him as the result of some moral short-coming. But while this notion has been entertained, the extreme opposite will be found to have been a far more popular opinion—I mean the notion that a man is answerable for all the consequences of his acts, or, in other words, that he acts at his peril always, and wholly irrespective of the state of his consciousness upon the matter. . . .

As has just been hinted, there are two theories of the common-law liability for unintentional harm. Both of them seem to receive the implied assent of popular text-books, and neither of them is wanting in plausibility and the semblance of authority.

The first is that of Austin, which is essentially the theory of a criminalist. According to him, the characteristic feature of law, properly so called, is a sanction or detriment threatened and imposed by the sovereign for disobedience to the sovereign's commands. As the greater part of the law only makes a man civilly answerable for breaking it, Austin is compelled to regard the liability to an action as a sanction, or, in other words, as a penalty for disobedience. It follows from this, according to the prevailing views of penal law, that such liability ought only to be based upon personal fault; and Austin accepts that conclusion, with its corollaries, one of which is that negligence means a state of the party's mind. These doctrines will be referred to later, so far as necessary.

The other theory is directly opposed to the foregoing. It seems to be adopted by some of the greatest common-law authorities, and requires serious discussion before it can be set aside in favor of any third opinion which may be maintained. According to this view, broadly stated, under the common law a man *acts* at his peril. It may be held as a sort of set-off, that he is never liable for omissions except in consequence of some duty voluntarily undertaken. But the whole and sufficient ground for such liabilities as he does incur outside the last class is supposed to be that he has voluntarily acted, and that damage has ensued. If the act was voluntary, it is totally immaterial that the detriment which followed from it was neither intended nor due to the negligence of the actor.

In order to do justice to this way of looking at the subject, we must remember that the abolition of the common-law forms of pleading has not changed the rules of substantive law. Hence, although pleaders now generally allege intent or negligence, anything which would formerly have been sufficient to charge a defendant in trespass is still sufficient, notwithstanding the fact that the ancient form of action and declaration has disappeared.

In the first place, it is said, consider generally the protection given by the law to property, both within and outside the limits of the last-named action. If a man crosses his neighbor's boundary by however innocent a mistake, or if his cattle escape into his neighbor's field, he is said to be liable in trespass *quare clausum fregit*. If an auctioneer in the most perfect good faith, and in the regular course of his business, sells goods sent to his rooms for the purpose of being sold, he may be compelled to pay their full value if a third person turns out to be the owner, although he has paid over the proceeds, and has no means of obtaining indemnity.

Now suppose that, instead of a dealing with the plaintiff's property, the case is that force has proceeded directly from the defendant's body to the plaintiff's body, it is urged that, as the law cannot be less careful of the persons than of the property of its subjects, the only defenses possible are similar to those which would have been open to an alleged trespass on land. You may show that there was no trespass by showing that the defendant did no act; as where he was thrown from his horse upon the plaintiff, or where a third person took his hand and struck the plaintiff with it. In such cases the defendant's body is the passive instrument of an external force, and the bodily motion relied on by the plaintiff is not his act at all. So you may show a justification or excuse in the conduct of the plaintiff himself. But if no such excuse is shown, and the defendant has voluntarily acted, he must answer for the consequences, however little intended and however unforeseen. If, for instance, being assaulted by a third person, the defendant lifted his stick and accidentally hit the plaintiff, who was standing behind him, according to this view he is liable, irrespective of any negligence toward the party injured.

The arguments for the doctrine under consideration are, for the most part, drawn from precedent, but it is sometimes supposed to be defensible as theoretically sound. Every man, it is said, has an absolute right to his person, and so forth, free from detriment at the hands of his neighbors. In the cases put, the plaintiff has done nothing; the defendant, on the other hand, has chosen to act. As between the two, the party whose voluntary conduct has caused the damage should suffer, rather than one who has had no share in producing it. . . .

In spite, however, of all the arguments which may be urged for the rule that a man acts at his peril, it has been rejected by very eminent courts, even under the old forms of action. In view of this fact, and of the further circumstance that, since the old forms have been abolished, the allegation of negligence has spread from the action on the case to all ordinary declarations in tort which do not allege intent, probably many lawyers would be surprised that any one should think it worth while to go into the present discussion. Such is the natural impression to be derived from daily practice. But even if the doctrine under consideration had no longer any followers, which is not the case, it would be well to have something more than daily practice to sustain our views upon so fundamental a question; as it seems to me at least, the true principle is far from being articulately grasped by all who are interested in it, and can only be arrived at after a careful analysis of what has been thought hitherto. It might be thought enough to cite the decisions opposed to the rule of absolute responsibility, and to show that such a rule is inconsistent with admitted doctrines and sound policy. But we may go further with profit, and inquire whether there are not strong grounds for thinking that the common law has never known such a rule, unless in that period of dry precedent which is so often to be found midway between a creative epoch and a period of solvent philosophical reaction. Conciliating the attention of those who, contrary to most modern practitioners, still adhere to the strict doctrine, by reminding them once more that there are weighty decisions to be cited adverse to it, and that, if they have involved an innovation, the fact that it has been made by such magistrats as Chief Justice Shaw goes far to prove that the change was politic, I think I may assert that a little reflection will show

that it was required not only by policy, but by consistency. I will begin with the latter. . . .

. . . So long, at least, as only physical or irresponsible agencies, however unforeseen, co-operated with the act complained of to produce the result, the argument which would resolve the case of accidentally striking the plaintiff, when lifting a stick in necessary self-defense, adversely to the defendant, would require a decision against him in every case where his act was a factor in the result complained of. The distinction between a direct application of force, and causing damage indirectly, or as a more remote consequence of one's act, although it may determine whether the form of action should be trespass or case, does not touch the theory of responsibility, if that theory be that a man acts at his peril. As was said at the outset, if the strict liability is to be maintained at all, it must be maintained throughout. A principle cannot be stated which would retain the strict liability in trespass while abandoning it in case. It cannot be said that trespass is for acts alone, and case for consequences of those acts. All actions of trespass are for consequences of acts, not for the acts themselves. And some actions of trespass are for consequences more remote from the defendant's act than in other instances where the remedy would be case.

An act is always a voluntary muscular contraction, and nothing else. The chain of physical sequences which it sets in motion or directs to the plaintiff's harm is no part of it, and very generally a long train of such sequences intervenes. An example or two will make this extremely clear.

When a man commits an assault and battery with a pistol, his only act is to contract the muscles of his arm and forefinger in a certain way, but it is the delight of elementary writers to point out what a vast series of physical changes must take place before the harm is done. Suppose that, instead of firing a pistol, he takes up a hose which is discharging water on the sidewalk, and directs it at the plaintiff, he does not even set in motion the physical causes which must co-operate with his act to make a battery. Not only natural causes, but a living being, may intervene between the act and its effect. *Gibbons v. Pepper*, which decided that there was no battery when a man's horse was frightened by accident or a third person and ran away with him, and ran over the plaintiff, takes the distinction that, if the rider by spurring is the cause of the accident, then he is guilty. In *Scott v. Shepherd*, . . . trespass was maintained against one who had thrown a squib into a crowd, where it was tossed from hand to hand in self-defence until it burst and injured the plaintiff. Here even human agencies were a part of a chain between the defendant's act and the result, although they were treated as more or less nearly automatic, in order to arrive at the decision.

Now I repeat, that, if principle requires us to charge a man in trespass when his act has brought force to bear on another through a comparatively short train of intervening causes, in spite of his having used all possible care, it requires the same liability, however numerous and unexpected the events between the act and the result. If running a man down is a trespass when the accident can be referred to the rider's act of spurring, why is it not a tort in every case, as was argued in *Vincent v. Stinehour,* seeing that it can always be referred more remotely to his act of mounting and taking the horse out?

Why is a man not responsible for the consequences of an act innocent in its direct and obvious effects, when those consequences would not have followed but for the intervention of a series of extraordinary, although natural, events? The reason is, that, if the intervening events are of such a kind that no foresight could have been expected to look out for them, the defendant is not to blame for having failed to do so. It seems to be admitted by the English judges that, even on the question whether the acts of leaving dry trimmings in hot whether by the side of a railroad, and then sending an engine over the track, are negligent—that is, are a ground of liability—the consequences which might reasonably be anticipated are material. Yet these are acts which, under the circumstances, can hardly be called innocent in their natural and obvious effects. The same doctrine has been applied to acts in violation of statute which could not reasonably have been expected to lead to the result complained of.

But there is no difference in principle between the case where a natural cause or physical factor intervenes after the act in some way not to be foreseen, and turns what seemed innocent to harm, and the case where such a cause of factor intervenes, unknown, at the time; as, for the matter of that, it did in the English cases cited. If a man is excused in the one case because he is not to blame, he must be in the other. The difference taken in *Gibbons v. Pepper,* cited above, is not between results which are and those which are not the consequences of the defendant's acts: it is between consequences which he was bound as a reasonable man to contemplate, and those which he was not. Hard spurring is just so much more likely to lead to harm than merely riding a horse in the

street, that the court thought that the defendant would be bound to look out for the consequences of the one, while it would not hold him liable for those resulting merely from the other; because the possibility of being run away with when riding quietly, though familiar, is comparatively slight. If, however, the horse had been unruly, and had been taken into a frequented place for the purpose of being broken, the owner might have been liable, because "it was his fault to bring a wild horse into a place where mischief might probably be done."

To return to the example of the accidental blow with a stick lifted in self-defence, there is no difference between hitting a person standing in one's rear and hitting one who was pushed by a horse within range of the stick just as it was lifted, provided that it was not possible, under the circumstances, in the one case to have known, in the other to have anticipated, the proximity. In either case there is wanting the only element which distinguishes voluntary acts from spasmodic muscular contractions as a ground of liability. In neither of them, that is to say, has there been an opportunity of choice with reference to the consequence complained of—a chance to guard against the result which has came to pass. A choice which entails a concealed consequence is as to that consequence no choice.

The general principle of our law is that loss from accident must lie where it falls, and this principle is not affected by the fact that a human being is the instrument of misfortune. But relatively to a given human being anything is accident which he could not fairly have been expected to contemplate as possible, and therefore to avoid. In the language of the late Chief Justice Nelson of New York: "No case or principle can be found, or if found can be maintained, subjecting an individual to liability for an act done without fault on his part. . . . All the cases concede that an injury arising from inevitable accident, or, which in law or reason is the same thing, from an act that ordinary human care and foresight are unable to guard against, is but the misfortune of the sufferer, and lays no foundation for legal responsibility." If this were not so, any act would be sufficient, however remote, which set in motion or opened the door for a series of physical sequences ending in damage; such as riding the horse, in the case of the runaway, or even coming to a place where one is seized with a fit and strikes the plaintiff in an unconscious spasm. Nay, why need the defendant have acted at all, and why is it not enough that his existence has been at the expense of the plaintiff? The requirement of an act is the requirement that the defendant should have made a choice. But the only possible purpose of introducing this moral element is to make the power of avoiding the evil complained of a condition of liability. There is no such power where the evil cannot be foreseen. Here we reach the argument from policy. . . .

A man need not, it is true, do this or that act—the term *act* implies a choice—but he must act somehow. Furthermore, the public generally profits by individual activity. As action cannot be avoided, and tends to the public good, there is obviously no policy in throwing the hazard of what is at once desirable and inevitable upon the actor.

The state might conceivably make itself a mutual insurance company against accidents, and distribute the burden of its citizens' mishaps among all its members. There might be a pension for paralytics, and state aid for those who suffered in person or estate from tempest or wild beasts. As between individuals it might adopt the mutual insurance principle pro tanto, and divide damages when both were in fault, as in the *rusticum judicium* of the admiralty, or it might throw all loss upon the actor irrespective of fault. The state does none of these things, however, and the prevailing view is that its cumbrous and expensive machinery ought not to be set in motion unless some clear benefit is to be derived from disturbing the status quo. State interference is an evil, where it cannot be shown to be a good. Universal insurance, if desired, can be better and more cheaply accomplished by private enterprise. The undertaking to redistribute losses simply on the ground that they resulted from the defendant's act would not only be open to these objections, but, as it is hoped the preceding discussion has shown, to the still graver one of offending the sense of justice. Unless my act is of a nature to threaten others, unless under the circumstances a prudent man would have foreseen the possibility of harm, it is no more justifiable to make me indemnify my neighbor against the consequences, than to make me do the same thing if I had fallen upon him in a fit, or to compel me to insure him against lightning.

. . .

Supposing it now to be conceded that the general notion upon which liability to an action is founded is fault or blameworthiness in some sense, the question arises, whether it is so in the sense of personal moral short-coming, as would practically result from Austin's teaching. The language of Rede, J., . . . gives a sufficient answer. "In trespass the intent" (we may say more broadly, the defendant's state of mind) "cannot be construed." Suppose that a defendant were allowed

to testify that, before acting, he considered carefully what would be the conduct of a prudent man under the circumstances, and, having formed the best judgment he could, acted accordingly. If the story was believed, it would be conclusive against the defendant's negligence judged by a moral standard which would take his personal characteristics into account. But supposing any such evidence to have got before the jury, it is very clear that the court would say, Gentlemen, the question is not whether the defendant thought his conduct was that of a prudent man, but whether you think it was.

Some middle point must be found between the horns of this dilemma.

The standards of the law are standards of general application. The law takes no account of the infinite varieties of temperament, intellect, and education which make the internal character of a given act so different in different men. It does not attempt to see men as God sees them, for more than one sufficient reason. In the first place, the impossibility of nicely measuring a man's powers and limitations is far clearer than that of ascertaining his knowledge of law, which has been thought to account for what is called the presumption that every man knows the law. But a more satisfactory explanation is, that, when men live in society, a certain average of conduct, a sacrifice of individual peculiarities going beyond a certain point, is necessary to the general welfare. If, for instance, a man is born hasty and awkward, is always having accidents and hurting himself or his neighbors, no doubt his congenital defects will be allowed for in the courts of Heaven, but his slips are no less troublesome to his neighbors than if they sprang from guilty neglect. His neighbors accordingly require him, at his proper peril, to come up to their standard, and the courts which they establish decline to take his personal equation into account.

The rule that the law does, in general, determine liability by blameworthiness, is subject to the limitation that minute differences of character are not allowed for. The law considers, in other words, what would be blameworthy in the average man, the man of ordinary intelligence and prudence, and determines liability by that. If we fall below the level in those gifts, it is our misfortune; so much as that we must have at our peril, for the reasons just given. But he who is intelligent and prudent does not act at his peril, in theory of law. On the contrary, it is only when he fails to exercise the foresight of which he is capable, or exercises it with evil intent, that he is answerable for the consequences.

There are exceptions to the principle that every man is presumed to possess ordinary capacity to avoid harm to his neighbors, which illustrate the rule, and also the moral basis of liability in general. When a man has a distinct defect of such a nature that all can recognize it as making certain precautions impossible, he will not be held answerable for not taking them. A blind man is not required to see at his peril; and although he is, no doubt, bound to consider his infirmity in regulating his actions, yet if he properly finds himself in a certain situation, the neglect of precautions requiring eyesight would not prevent his recovering for an injury to himself, and, it may be presumed, would not make him liable for injuring another. So it is held that, in cases where he is the plaintiff, an infant of very tender years is only bound to take the precautions of which an infant is capable; the same principle may be cautiously applied where he is defendant. Insanity is a more difficult matter to deal with, and no general rule can be laid down about it. There is no doubt that in many cases a man may be insane, and yet perfectly capable of taking the precautions, and of being influenced by the motives, which the circumstances demand. But if insanity of a pronounced type exists, manifestly incapacitating the sufferer from complying with the rule which he has broken, good sense would require it to be admitted as an excuse.

Taking the qualification last established in connection with the general proposition previously laid down, it will now be assumed that, on the one hand, the law presumes or requires a man to possess ordinary capacity to avoid harming his neighbors, unless a clear and manifest incapacity be shown; but that, on the other, it does not in general hold him liable for unintentional injury, unless, possessing such capacity, he might and ought to have foreseen the danger, or, in other words, unless a man of ordinary intelligence and forethought would have been to blame for acting as he did. . . .

Notwithstanding the fact that the grounds of legal liability are moral to the extent above explained, it must be borne in mind that law only works within the sphere of the senses. If the external phenomena, the manifest acts and omissions, are such as it requires, it is wholly indifferent to the internal phenomena of conscience. A man may have as bad a heart as he chooses, if his conduct is within the rules. In other words, the standards of the law are external standards, and, however much it may take moral considerations into account, it does so only for the purpose of drawing a line between such bodily motions and rests as it permits, and such as it does not. What the law really forbids, and the only thing it forbids, is the act on the wrong side of the line, be that act blameworthy or otherwise. . . .

Wealth Maximization and Tort Law: A Philosophical Inquiry

Richard A. Posner

For more than two decades I have been arguing that what I call "wealth maximization" is the best positive and normative guide to the law of torts. My purpose in this essay is to restate, refine, and amplify the philosophical version of this argument.

From Richard A. Posner, "Wealth Maximization and Tort Law: A Philosophical Inquiry," in David G. Owen (ed.), *Philosophical Foundations of Tort Law* (Oxford: Clarendon Press, 1995), pp. 99–111. Reprinted by permission of Oxford University Press.

I. Introduction

By "wealth maximization" I mean the policy of trying to maximize the aggregate value or all goods and services, whether they are traded in formal markets (the usual "economic" goods and services) or (in the case of "non-economic" goods or services, such as life, leisure, family, and freedom from pain and suffering) not traded in such markets. "Value" is determined by what the owner of the good or service would demand to part with it or what a non-owner would be willing to pay to obtain it—whichever is greater. "Wealth" is the total value of all "economic" and "non-economic" goods and services and is maximized when all goods and services are, so far as is feasible, allocated to their most valuable uses.

The non-pecuniary dimension of wealth is important to emphasize, especially to noneconomists, who are prone to assume that economists care only about goods and services that are priced in the market. Yet I concede the incompleteness of "wealth," even when so broadly defined, as a measure of social welfare. The reason is that the concept of wealth is dependent on the assignment of property rights and—what is closely related, because property rights are a source of wealth—on the distribution of wealth across persons. To illustrate from tort law, the demand for clean air and water, and hence the contours of nuisance doctrine, may vary depending on whether the question is posed as whether the victim of pollution would be willing to "sell" his "right" to be free from pollution for a price that the polluter would be willing to pay or as whether the victim would offer to "buy" the right to clean air or water from the polluter at a price the latter would be willing to accept. Demand is a function of income and wealth as well as of price. An indigent may not be able to pay anything for freedom from pollution, while a wealthy person may demand an astronomical price to surrender his right (if it is his right) to clean air and water.

I want to prescind from these "baseline" problems and examine wealth maximization in the more common tort situations in which such problems are not acute. A small (or for that matter a large) change in tort doctrine is unlikely to so alter the wealth distribution that (as in my pollution example) the efficiency of the two states of doctrine cannot be compared. It is not confining, therefore, to limit consideration to cases in which a "Hand formula" approach—an injurer in an accident situation should be liable to his victim if, but only if, the expected cost of the accident (that is, the loss, both pecuniary and non-pecuniary, caused by the accident if it occurs, multiplied by the probability of its occurring) exceeds the cost (which again might have a non-pecuniary component, such as time) of avoiding the accident—will generate the identical result whichever party to the accident has a *prima facie* right to the legal protection of his activity.

II. *The Positive Theory*

The idea that value should be determined in this way and used to guide social policy toward accidents and other dangerous conduct comes naturally to most economists and economically minded lawyers. The

idea that it *is* the guide that the courts have used in constructing the doctrines of tort law is much more controversial, even among economic analysts. . . . Controversial as it is, the positive side of the wealth maximization theory of tort law does not present very interesting *philosophical* problems. No doubt a philosopher of science could be engaged to evaluate the entitlement of the positive theory to call itself "scientific" and its claims to be better supported than rival theories. And . . . efforts to elide the age-old philosophical disputes over the meaning of intention and of causation by recasting these concepts in economic terms that do not refer to them might raise some philosophers' eyebrows. But the philosophical adequacy of the positive theory is not apt to trouble many people.

It is different with the normative branch of the theory. The idea that to the extent tort law departs from the dictates of wealth maximization it ought to be changed to conform to them has drawn the ire of philosophers and philosophically minded lawyers. . . . The issues of moral and political philosophy raised by the wealth maximization theory are the focus of this essay.

III. *The Normative Theory*

A. *Pragmatic Normativity*

I begin my discussion of the normative theory with three disclaimers. First, partly for the reason given earlier (the dependence of wealth maximization on the prior assignment of property rights and on the distribution of wealth across persons), I neither assert nor believe that the theory is adequate to resolve all issues of social policy, or even all issues of tort law. Secondly, I do not believe that it can be deduced from any overarching moral theory, such as utilitarianism. And thirdly, I do not believe that wealth in the sense in which I use it, broad as that sense is (remember that it is not a pecuniary *concept* although it uses a pecuniary *metric*), has any intrinsic, non-instrumental, plausibly "ultimate" value, as pleasure or happiness or human flourishing or a good will is thought to have in various philosophies.

All this I concede to my critics. But I no longer think that these concessions weaken my position. For I have become profoundly skeptical of efforts to construct coherent moral systems. I have come to believe that in our society moral beliefs to a great extent precede, and are largely unaffected by, the reasons that can be marshaled pro and con them. It would for example be extraordinarily odd for someone to say, "I know and believe that torturing children is bad, but I would like to know *why* it is bad." One might or might not be able to give him a reason; but it is quite unlikely that one could affect his belief. . . . It is unrealistic, as Swift said, to suppose that you can argue a person out of a position that he had not been argued into; and it is weak-minded to abandon a deep-seated moral belief just because you cannot think up a good retort to a clever argument.

I do not mean that people's moral beliefs never change; certainly many of mine have. But they change because of experience rather than argument. I dare say that some professional philosophers have reasoned their way into one moral position or another (vegetarianism, for example), but I think that arriving at moral beliefs through argument is rare even among philosophers and much rarer among the rest of the population.

All systematic moral theories stub their toes on the immovability of bedrock moral beliefs by argument. The consistent utilitarian has trouble showing why it might not be a good idea occasionally to hang someone known to be innocent. A Kantian who . . . believes that only beings endowed with "reason" have moral rights will have trouble explaining why it is wrong to kill profoundly retarded or comatose people. The greatest natural lawyer (Aquinas) reasoned himself into such conclusions as that masturbation is a worse sin than raping one's mother and that lending money at interest is condemned by the same principle that condemns sodomy. A Rawlsian has trouble explaining why our brains are not a collective good. A Nozick-style libertarian has trouble explaining why gladiatorial contests are wrong. And a wealth maximizer will encounter embarrassments very similar to those that both the utilitarian *and* the Nozickian encounter as he explores such topics as slavery, discrimination, and welfare. These topics are not likely to be directly encountered in tort law, but a philosophy that is contradicted by our deep moral intuitions in various testing cases may be thought inadequate to govern any area of moral inquiry.

It seems unlikely that the only reason for the inadequacy of moral theories as persuaders to action in our society is that no one has appeared on the scene yet who is bright enough to think up a compelling theory. A more plausible explanation . . . is that the moral beliefs of modern Americans reflect different and to a significant degree inconsistent traditions of moral thinking: Greek (Platonic, Aristotelian, Stoic, Pyrrhonian, Epicurean), Jewish Catholic, Protestant (includ-

ing Puritan), pragmatic, liberal, utilitarian, scientific (including Darwinian), Freudian, populist, frontier-individualist, humanitarian, egalitarian. These traditions are not, of course, mixed in the same proportions in every American. So varied are the mixtures, indeed, that some Americans seem actually to inhabit different moral universes from others. Very few live entirely in one tradition, moreover, and those who live in more than one are apt to have a set of moral beliefs that is internally inconsistent—for example, for abortion, sexual freedom, euthanasia, and the protection of animal predators, but against infanticide, capital punishment, economic freedom, and humans eating meat; against abortion, but for hunting and capital punishment; for close families, yet also for easy divorce; for democracy, yet also for academic privilege. So there is inconsistency both within and across individuals, and there is nothing that moral theorizing can do about it.

If this is correct, the most constructive philosophical approach to the question whether wealth maximization should guide tort law may be, rather than considering its adequacy or pedigree as a moral theory, to *relate* it to the various moral traditions that might have or imply a position on tort liability. If, as I believe, wealth maximization resonates well with several moral theories and offends none, a tort system founded on wealth maximization may deserve to command the widespread support that it does in fact seem to command in our society. To put this another way, the unreflective public opinion underlying a system of tort law that can be best understood and explained in terms of wealth maximization intersects the principal moral traditions found in our society.

B. Illustrations

Limitations of space and time compel me to confine myself to a brief explanation of the compatibility of wealth maximization with five ethical theories: (1) the Pareto principle, (2) rule utilitarianism, (3) Aristotelian corrective justice, (4) Kantian deontology, and (5) Kantian egalitarianism.

1. The Pareto Principle   I begin with the Pareto principle, which is that a change (including a change brought about by an accident or an intentional act) is good if it makes at least one person better off and no one worse off. This is a "liberal" principle akin to Kant's and Mill's principle that everyone is entitled to as much liberty as is consistent with the liberty of all other people. The Pareto principle protects a person from harmful activities carried on by others by insisting that all persons potentially harmed by those activities consent to the effects upon them. Persons ordinarily will consent to be harmed only if they have received some form of compensation as a result of which, on balance, they are not made worse off by the harmful activity. By requiring unanimity, the Pareto principle in its pure form avoids the objections to majoritarianism.

The Pareto principle may seem inconsistent with a system of tort law that does not require strict liability for all injuries, although it makes a good fit with the provision of damages for negligent and intentional torts. Even a comprehensive regime of strict liability would be suspect to a Paretian because in the case of serious physical injuries, including death, tort compensation is rarely full compensation. And yet a tort system dominated by the negligence principle—resigned to awarding zero recovery in many cases of accidental injury and less than full compensation even in many cases in which liability is imposed, and very costly to operate (our tort system)—may nevertheless approximate Pareto optimality.

To see this requires understanding that compensation can be *ex ante*, in the form of a cost savings, as well as *ex post*, in the form of a judgment or settlement. *Ex ante* the cost (an "expected" cost in economic jargon) of an accident has two components: the expected cost to the potential injurer of being held liable and made to pay damages for causing an injury to someone else, and the expected cost to the potential victim of being injured in an accident. The same person can, of course, be both potential injurer and potential victim; this is common in collision cases; and let me for the sake of simplicity confine attention to this class of case. Let me also eliminate any dubieties associated with the concept of an "expected" cost by noting that expected costs can be transformed into smaller and more certain current costs through insurance: liability insurance in the case of the expected cost of being an injurer, accident insurance in the case of the expected cost of being a victim. No one buys unlimited insurance, so the transformation of expected into current costs is not complete. Subject to this qualification, of which more shortly, an insured will want to minimize the sum of the premiums for the two types of insurance. The balance between the two costs will differ under negligence and under strict liability. The cost of liability insurance will be lower under the former because a smaller proportion of accidents create liability under a regime of negligence than under one of strict liability. But by the same token the cost of accident insurance will be higher under the negligence regime because more accidents are left

uncompensated by the tort system under that regime. If however, the *sum* of liability and accident insurance costs is lower under the negligence regime, it may be the preferred regime. And if it is preferred by *everybody* it will be Pareto optimal even though, *ex post*, some accident victims will be worse off under the negligence regime. They will be worse off because accident insurance does not always provide full compensation, if only because an accident may so reduce the utility of money to the victim that he would not pay for the right to receive insurance proceeds in the event of such an accident.

I say that negligence "may be" rather than "is" the preferable regime in the case I have just put precisely because there are uncompensated accident costs. Even if the insured's total cost of (both accident and liability) insurance is lower under negligence, the sum of his current and expected accident costs may be higher under a negligence regime than under strict liability—or, depending on such factors as differential incentives for safety and different costs of administration, lower.

It is unlikely in any event that *everybody* will be made better off *ex ante* by any particular choice of tort doctrines. But that is true in every situation in which the Pareto concept is invoked: all "voluntary" transactions have some third-party effects—or, if not all *individual* voluntary transactions, all *classes* of such transactions. A series of voluntary contracts between fully informed and consenting adults may alter the prices of the goods or services involved in the contracts (or prices of inputs into those goods or services) and by doing so harm other people. Still, the Pareto concept retains at least some normative force when approximated, which it might be possible to show is the case with regard to one or more doctrinal or institutional features of (or reforms in) the tort system when evaluated by the criterion of wealth maximization. If unanimity is a morally attractive criterion for social action, near unanimity should be attractive too, even if less so.

2. Rule Utilitarianism The next moral system with which I want to compare the wealth maximization theory of tort law is utilitarianism—appropriately next, because as we progressively relax the unanimity criterion of the Pareto principle we slide closer and closer to utilitarianism. I offer wealth maximization as the rule utilitarian's rule for determining tort liability. The offer will be rejected out of hand by anyone who thinks rule utilitarianism inconsistent with utilitarian premises. Not imposing tort liability on an individual or a firm that had caused no injury might be a good utility-maximizing rule, but if in a particular case total utility would be maximized by departing from it in order to enhance the deterrence of harmful acts, on what *utilitarian* basis could one refuse to do so? Utilitarians give various answers. Many are variants of the proposition that whatever hypothetical departure is thrown up by the critic of utilitarianism would not in fact be utility-maximizing in the real world—to which the critic may answer that basic moral principles must, to be such, hold in all conceivable worlds—to which the utilitarian can reply that all moral theories, even one as austere as Rawls' justice as fairness, are contingent upon certain facts about the world and human nature.

I do not want to get sucked into this vortex. It is enough for my purpose that many, probably most, utilitarians believe that it is infeasible to maximize utility at retail, as it were. They believe that a utility-maximizing polity would rely heavily on rules, admitting some exceptions of course but refusing to allow a general exception that would permit any rule to be waived whenever utility would be maximized by doing so. The general exception would make most people feel insecure and therefore unhappy, and, a related point, it would be difficult to find someone or some institution that could be trusted to enforce so far-reaching a discretionary power fairly and intelligently. So the general exception would not be utility-maximizing, and this in turn implies that the hypothetical cases in which applying it would increase utility are not merely hypothetical, but illusory.

It is infeasible to make *ad hoc* judgments concerning the net contribution to aggregate utility of some particular dangerous act or practice that results in injury—to measure the unhappiness caused by the injury and the unhappiness that would have been caused by the precaution that would have averted it. If utility is to be maximized with respect to accident-causing activities, it will have to be done indirectly. To the extent that the costs of a dangerous activity can be monetized through insurance and compared with the costs of minimizing the expense of insurance through changes in liability or regulation, public policies (including liability rules) designed to minimize the sum of all these costs are more likely to be utility-maximizing than policies guided by some other norm. The uninsured costs of accidents—the costs that insurance does not cover—pose greater difficulty. Yet we observe that most people contentedly assume slight risks of serious injury in exchange for modest benefits. It is unlikely that preventing them from assuming

those risks, as by fixing a speed limit of 10 m.p.h. on all roadways, would be a utility-maximizing policy. The risks can be valued, and risky behavior optimized, by the tort system as follows: estimate what a person would charge to assume the risk in question (it might be the risk of being killed by a speeding driver), divide that number by the risk, and award the quotient in damages if the risk materializes. So, if a person would demand $1 to be subjected to a one in a million chance of being killed, the proper award if he were killed and the defendant found liable would be $1 million; if he would demand $25,000 for a one in a hundred risk, the proper damage award would be $2.5 million. Awards calculated in this manner should give potential defendants the "correct" incentive to take safety precautions by confronting them with the expected costs to potential victims of precautions, while a larger award would induce an excessive investment in such precautions and a smaller award an inadequate incentive.

Such a system of tort liability could not be *proved* to maximize utility, since utility is unobservable and unmeasureable. But the common-sense rule utilitarianism that I am defending is based on the idea that it is possible to make rough but adequate guesses as to what rules are likelier than the alternatives (including *ad hoc* utility-maximizing, in lieu of any rule) to be utility-maximizing, and wealth maximization is a good candidate to be that rule, at least in the area of tort law. This should not be a surprising claim, in view of the historically close connection between the economist's idea of "wealth" and the utilitarian philosopher's idea of "utility." Prosperity is not everything, but to most people it is a lot; and because wealth maximization is not a narrowly pecuniary concept, the wealth maximizer's notion of "prosperity" incorporates noneconomic goods, such as safety and clean air and satisfying family relations, along with economic ones. It is possible that some change in tort law would increase total utility even though it resulted in higher insurance costs and, perhaps, no decrease in accidents. This might happen if, for example, the change resulted in a transfer of income to people who gained more utility from the increment to their income than the transferors lost. So a utilitarian who thought that poor people are more likely than rich ones to be accident victims and that they have a higher marginal utility of money might favor the abolition of the defense of contributory negligence. But as there is no way to verify such conjectures, the wealth maximization approach should appeal to the rule utilitarian as a practical solution to the problem of how *feasibly* to maximize utility.

3. Aristotelian Corrective Justice I want to turn my attention now to the moral tradition—for my purposes adequately illustrated by aspects of the moral teachings of Aristotle and of Kant—in which preference satisfaction, either on an aggregate or an individual basis, is rejected as a basis for moral or legal duties. In Aristotle's theory of corrective justice (to which two and a half millennia of further philosophizing have added rather little), the duty to rectify a wrong is simply that—a duty—rather than an instrument for the achievement of a social or even personal end, such as deterrence or happiness. Aristotle's theory is entwined with the concept of *pleonexia*, or trying to get more than one's fair share. The principles of distributive justice establish some pattern of entitlements, and if someone wrongfully disturbs that pattern, corrective justice requires that the just equilibrium be restored.

This intuitively appealing principle provides a more direct route to remedying intentional torts than the wealth maximizer's approach. But when one turns to the detailed articulation of intentional-tort doctrine, the theory of corrective justice quickly runs out of steam, whereas the economic analyst can explain the defenses to these tort's and why they differ in some respects from the defenses to unintentional torts, the details of the remedies (including why they differ from the remedies for other torts), the overlap with unintentional torts (such as, frequently, defamation), the relation to crime at one end and breach of contract at the other, and in short the over-all pattern of liability for these wrongs. Corrective justice may be in the driver's seat, but economics is required to tell the driver when to turn, stop, accelerate, and so forth.

And with regard to unintentional torts, which is to say to liability for (most) accidents, corrective justice has no thrust at all. One can if one wants speak of the speeding driver as "pleonexic"—as wanting more than his fair share as it were of the opportunities for self-fulfillment provided by the road—but it is difficult to see what is gained by this redescription. There are numerous objections to eliminating tort liability for this or that class of dangerous accidents, as is sometimes done, for example, in workmen's compensation laws and in no-fault automobile compensation schemes. But the loss of corrective justice is not one of the objections. The reason is that, as an aspect of the general lack of detail in the theory, it is wholly unclear what institutional arrangements are entailed by correc-

tive justice. If, as opponents of tort liability believe, some alternative regulatory scheme would control accidents more effectively—or at least as effectively, and at lower cost (or more fairly)—than the tort system, there is no purchase in Aristotle's theory for criticism. The theory does not foreclose oblique, wholesale, or otherwise non-traditional modes of rectifying injustices. It is not even clear what basis for objection an Aristotelian would have to the substitution of criminal for tort liability as the legal regime for intentional torts, if the substitution could be persuasively defended as a fairer, more effective, and cheaper method of "correcting" this class of injustices. Even if the victim is not compensated, provided the criminal is punished severely enough, victim and criminal are once again placed on a plane of equality (and here we can sense the connection between corrective and redistributive—"eye for an eye"—justice). So maybe even in its core application, corrective justice provides only weak support for tort law. But that is not the issue. All that is most important here is the consilience between a wealth maximizer's approach to tort law and that of an Aristotelian.

4. Kantian Deontology The most emphatic insistence that moral duties shall not be based on preferences comes from the Kantians, whose basic thesis, so far as bears on my subject, is that it is wrong for one person to use another person as a means to the first person's ends—wrong therefore to use a worker's body as an input into the manufacture of goods, or a pedestrian's body as an input into one's commuting, without their consent. (If they do consent, then they are being "used" for their own ends as well as for those of the user.)

A Kantian, whether or not of egalitarian bent, is unlikely to be pleased with the implication of a wealth maximization theory of tort law that a person should feel free to drive faster in a poor than in a wealthy neighborhood because expected accident costs are on average lower in the former (the magnitude of the loss if an accident occurs being a function in part of the income of the victim), making the optimal expenditure of time and other resources on avoiding accidents in the poor neighborhood also lower. From a Kantian perspective, this analysis appears to treat potential accident victims merely as obstacles to the ends of potential injuries.

But would an alternative system of tort law provide a *better* fit with Kantian moral principles? The Kantian, like the utilitarian, will find it infeasible to apply his principles directly to morally questionable activities, such as fast driving in poor neighborhoods. He needs a rule too. Maybe a system of tort law oriented by the principle of wealth maximization is the best approach for the Kantian. It seeks to accommodate conflicting activities in such a way that the scope for productive activity is maximized. To the extent that it succeeds in this aim, tort law enjoins upon potential injurers and potential victims alike (and often these are the same person) due consideration for the plans, goals, choices, etc. of the other. It requires *mutual* adjustments, and if the tort system satisfies (approximates) the Pareto condition they will be (or will approximate) the mutual adjustments desired by all. An individual who consents to a system of tort law because, although it may leave him uncompensated for some accidents, on the whole it promotes his ends better than any other system would do cannot complain that he is a mere means to the ends of potential injurers.

5. Kantian Egalitarianism   Some Kantians might, however, want to focus on the inegalitarian implications of wealth maximization that the example of driving faster in the poor neighborhood brings to the fore. As the example shows, tort law interpreted in terms of wealth maximization tends to ratify rather than to change the pre-existing distribution of income or wealth. The victim of the negligent driver is to be put back, so far as possible, in the same position in the income distribution that he occupied before the accident; but a corol-lary is that some potential accident victims receive less consideration than others, merely because they are poorer. But an egalitarian has standing to object to this feature of tort law only if he can show that tort law is, potentially at least, an efficient method of making the distribution of wealth more equal—which seems unlikely. If average rather than individual damages were awarded in tort cases, poor victims would be over-compensated and their incentives to safe conduct correspondingly reduced; this consequence aside, homogenization of damages across income classes would result in a capricious redistribution of wealth from wealthy accident victims (who would receive less compensation) to poor ones. The vast majority of poor people would be unaffected. Perhaps the tort system, while wealth maximizing, is as egalitarian as it can be.

IV. Conclusion

I have tried to show, too briefly I fear to carry full conviction, that a system of tort law guided by the norm of wealth maximization is likely to be consistent with the most influential moral traditions in our society. That does not prove that it is the right system to have, but it ought to blunt the philosophical attacks upon it.

Tort Law and Tort Theory

JULES COLEMAN

There is a familiar and clear, if not always clearly understood, distinction between explanation and justification. Explanations seek to illuminate, or to deepen our understanding, whereas justifications seek to defend or legiti-mate actions, rules, institutions, practices, and the like. This could invite the mistaken view that explanation is a descriptive activity, whereas justification is a normative one. In fact, both are norm-governed activities, regulated, however, by different kinds of norms. The norms that govern explanation are theoretical ones like simplicity, coherence, elegance, and consilience, whereas the norms that govern justification are moral—norms of justice, virtue, goodness, and so on.

Some legal theorists, like Ronald Dworkin and Stephen Perry and especially the natural lawyers, believe

From Jules Coleman, "Tort Law and Tort Theory: Preliminary Reflections on Method," in Gerald J. Postema (ed.), *Philosophy and the Law of Torts* (Cambridge: Cambridge University Press, 2001), pp. 183–189, 197–209. Reprinted by permission of Cambridge University Press.

that in the case of law, the projects of explanation and justification are deeply interdependent: that we cannot explain the concept of law without invoking at least some moral norms. While I disagree, this does not mean I believe that a philosophical explanation of the concept of law need not answer to norms of any sort. The debate may be framed in terms of the distinction between the following two kinds of claims: (1) Our concept of X depends in part on what our concept of X should be; (2) our concept of X depends in part on what X should be. My view is that our concept of law depends on what that concept should be; it must, in other words, answer to theoretical norms. This does not mean that our concept of law depends on what *the law* should be. I deny, in other words, that the concept of law must answer to norms of justice, rightness, goodness, and so on.

Though the conflict between these two views lies at the heart of the current debate between the (somewhat misleadingly termed) normative and descriptive methodologies of jurisprudence, the conflict is nonetheless easily misunderstood. It is important that it be made clear at the outset of my project, because my central claim in this essay—that our concept of tort law is best explained by appeal to a principle of corrective justice—could otherwise invite a natural confusion. The claim that tort law expresses and is best understood in terms of a conception of corrective justice does not rest on an endorsement of that conception as morally justified. The normative considerations that support the account are (in the first instance) epistemic or theoretical, not moral.

The principle of corrective justice that forms the core of the account presented here states that *individuals who are responsible for the wrongful losses of others have a duty to repair the losses.* The substantive requirements of that principle, I maintain, are embodied in our institutions of tort law. While I do not mount a thorough defense of the corrective justice account, I do aim to articulate its main elements in a way that I hope is also persuasive.

In addition to presenting the account, a second purpose of this essay is to illustrate a method of legal analysis. In traditional philosophy of law, we would approach the topic of torts by first seeking to determine what justice requires when one person injures or harms another, and then we would examine our institutions of tort law to determine whether, and if so in what ways, they produce outcomes that justice, independently of them, requires. I have called this "top-down" legal theory. It represents the prevalent mode of legal analysis, though not mine.

The method of analysis I adopt is exemplified in the following three claims about the relationship between corrective justice and tort law: (1) The content of corrective justice is given in part by the institutions of tort law: What corrective justice requires depends on the practices of corrective justice, including tort law. (2) In the absence of practices of corrective justice, there can be no moral duties of corrective justice. (3) The justification of corrective justice depends in part on seeing its attractiveness in the institutions that express or articulate it.

The first claim rejects the top-down approach by denying that the requirements of corrective justice can be adequately articulated independent of the social practices that realize corrective justice. The second claim asserts that even if corrective justice could be independently articulated as a "true," "justified," or "valid" principle of morality, that principle would still require practiced instantiations of it in order to impose moral duties of repair. The third claim emphasizes that the attractiveness of corrective justice as a principle of morality depends (in ways that need further clarification and development) on the moral attractiveness of its practiced realizations.

This essay explicates and further develops these claims. Corrective justice articulates the concept of fairness in a certain domain of human activity, namely, keeping track of the costs of those of life's misfortunes owing to human agency. It articulates fairness in terms of other concepts, for example, "wrong," "loss," "responsibility" and "repair." Tort law makes corrective justice more explicit by filling out the content of these concepts. In developing this line of argument, my goal is not only to articulate a coherent view of the relationship between tort law and corrective justice, but also to suggest a general conception of the relationship between legal theory and practice.

Understanding tort law as animated by corrective justice allows us to see it in a particular way: if we explain tort law in terms of the values that it expresses or captures, the question of its justification becomes a question of the place those values ought to occupy in our public life. Even if corrective justice is an independent and independently defensible principle of justice, other concerns of fairness, decency, and beneficence may dictate that many of life's misfortunes—both those owing to human agency and those that are no one's responsibility—should be held in common, their costs distributed among us all, for example, through the tax system. Thus, one of the broader purposes of the corrective justice account is to enable clearer debate about these matters.

Anyone who claims that tort law embodies certain ideals or principles must provide a conception of tort law and of the relevant principles or ideals, as well as an argument to the effect that tort law, so conceived, is best understood in the light of those principles or ideals. The core of tort law is composed of structural and substantive elements. The substantive core is represented by its basic liability rules: fault and strict liability. Any plausible theory of tort law should explain both and the difference between them, provide a defense, if possible, of each, and an explanation of why fault liability provides the appropriate standard of liability and recovery in some cases, while liability in other cases is appropriately strict.

Tort law's structural core is represented by case-by-case adjudication in which particular victims sue those they identify as responsible for the losses for which they seek redress. In the event a victim's claim to recovery is vindicated, her right to recover takes the form of a claim against the defendant (a claim which the defendant can discharge either directly or by some contractual relation, e.g., insurance). The victim is not, in contrast, awarded a claim against society as a whole or against a pool; and, in the event a defendant is judged liable, she is not required to pay into a general pool, or to compensate some randomly chosen victim, but must instead make good her own victim's compensable losses. Any plausible account of tort law must explain why claims are taken up in this case-by-case fashion, and especially the bi-lateral nature of litigation.

Economic analysis provides a forward-looking account of tort law. The costs of any particular tort are sunk. There is nothing to be done about them, no way of annulling or annihilating them. All that is left is to determine their incidence. Should the loss be left the burden of the victim or shifted to someone else, such as the injurer? Because the past cannot be undone, the decision to shift the loss or to leave it where it lies must be informed by a view to the consequences of the choice. Thus, we should ask what social good can be secured by imposing the costs on one person rather than another. With a body of law devoted to accidents and their costs, the natural consequences to which one ought to attend are the effects of loss-shifting rules on the costs of accidents. The relevant social good is thus the reduction of accident costs, and the economic analyst concludes that the correct liability rules are those likely to lead to the optimal reduction in the costs of accidents.

Of course, any theory of tort law that ignores the costs of accidents and the need to reduce those costs

would miss something both obvious and important. Showing that this important feature of our accident law is also an explanation of its existence, endurance and shape is the burden of the economic explanation. The problem that confronts economic analysis, or any entirely forward-looking theory of tort law, is that it seems to ignore the point that litigants are brought together in a case because one alleges that the other has wrongfully harmed her. Litigants do not come to court in order to provide the judge with an opportunity to pursue or refine his vision of optimal risk-reduction policy. Rather, they seek to have their claims vindicated: to secure an official pronouncement concerning who had the right to do what to whom. The judge is there, in some sense to serve them—to do justice between them; they are not there to serve the judge in his policy-making capacity. Or so one might think prior to theorizing about tort law.

Under economic analysis, the litigants to a tort suit bear no normatively significant relationship to one another. What is important is the relationship of each to the goals of tort law, in particular, optimal risk reduction. From that point of view, the important questions include: How good is the injurer (or injurer class) at reducing accidents of this type, and at what cost? How good is the victim (or victim class) at reducing risk, and at what cost? Need incentives be placed on both of them to achieve optimal deterrence? If so, how should that be done? In contrast, tort law is structured so that the important questions it asks are ones about the relationship between the injurer and victim, not ones about the relationship of either or both to the goals of tort law.

There is simply no principled reason, on the economic analysis, to limit the defendant or plaintiff classes to injurers and their respective victims. The classes of victims and injurers are identified entirely by backward-looking features (the harmful event); yet those best able to reduce the costs of accidents are identified by their relationship to the forward-looking goal of cost reduction. The class of optimal cost reducers is not selectable by any event in which *either* participated, much less by an event in which *both* participated—and certainly not by an event in which they both participated *in a particular* way (namely, as victim and injurer). There may be some overlap between the class of injurers and that of optimal cost reducers, but any such overlap can only be accidental. To put it quite simply, in any case in which A hits B, it is an open question whether A, B, C, D, or E . . . is in the best position to reduce the future risks at the lowest cost.

How then does the economist account for the fact that in the typical tort suit the victim sues the alleged injurer and not the alleged cheapest cost-avoider? How does one square the forward-looking goal of tort law (on the economic model) with the backward-looking structure of tort law? The economist cannot appeal to the obvious answer that the victim believes the injurer harmed him wrongfully and, in doing so, incurred a duty to make good the victim's losses. In the economist's account, the victim sues the injurer because the costs of searching for those in the best position to reduce the costs of future accidents is too high.

Next, how does the economist explain the fact that if the victim makes out his case against the injurer, he is entitled to compensation for damages *from the injurer?* Again, the economist cannot call upon the fact that the injurer incurs a duty to repair the victim's loss because he has wrongfully harmed him. It is one thing to ask whether there are good economic reasons for holding the injurer liable to certain costs. It is another question whether similar economic considerations require that *the victim* be compensated for his loss. It is yet another question—assuming that the injurer should be liable and the victim compensated—whether the victim should be compensated *by the injurer.*

The economic explanation cannot avail itself of the natural answer; instead, matters of liability and compensation are to be resolved in the light of their expected impact on the precautions each party—considered separately—will be induced to take. In order to deter the injurer, it is enough that he be made to bear costs sufficient to induce his taking cost-effective precautions. These costs may turn out to be more or less than the damages the victim actually suffers. Moreover, producing this incentive for the injurer does not require that the injurer pay the victim—only that he pay someone an amount sufficient to induce his compliance with the optimal risk-reducing strategy.

It is an open question in every case whether the victim should be encouraged to take precautions and if so, which ones. That will determine whether, on the economic account, he should be compensated; and if so, how much. Therefore, whether the victim is entitled to recover, and how much he should recover, does not depend on whether he was injured wrongfully or the extent of his injury, but on whether compensating him is necessary to avoid over-deterrence (that is, to avoid giving the victim and those in the victim's circumstances incentive to take overly costly precautions), or whether fully compensating him leads to too little deterrence (that is, fails to incite the most effec-

tive level of precaution-taking by the victim and those in the victim's circumstances).

There are other, more general, economic reasons for compensating victims—or at least for holding out the prospect of compensation. In any torts case, the victim acts as a private prosecutor bringing an action not only on his own behalf but also as an "agent" of the state. The state has an interest in discouraging economically inefficient behavior, but has only limited resources for doing so. By providing an avenue through which victims can secure recourse for harm done to them, the state creates an institution of "private enforcement." The expectation (or hope) of compensation induces private prosecutions, necessary to secure the optimal mix of private and public enforcement. However, on the economic analysis, it is no part of the victim's case for compensation that he has absorbed a loss as a result of another's wrongdoing. Rather, compensating him is to be explained as the result of the mix of the goals of inducing victims to litigate, and inducing both victims and injurers to take optimal precautions.

Consider, further, the economic explanation of the fact that in the typical case the victim sues the person she alleges wronged her. Because the point of tort law is (forward-looking) cost avoidance, we need to explain why the victim sues the injurer rather than seeking out the person who is in fact in the best position to reduce accidents at the lowest cost. It is always an open question whether that person is the injurer or someone else. The standard economic explanation is that the costs of searching on a case-by-case basis for the person who might be the better cost avoider is too high; and so, to follow a familiar strategy, a general rule in which the victim sues the alleged injurer is the second best alternative.

This is not a particularly good argument. Because valid causal explanations support counterfactuals, the claim that victims sue injurers only because search costs require them to do so as a second-best alternative implies that in the absence of search costs, victims who wish to sue would have the responsibility of seeking out the cheapest cost avoiders. In other words, were it costless or very cheap to locate the person in the best position to reduce costs, then it would be the duty of the victim who wishes to sue to find that person.

Indeed, it would appear that if search costs are trivial and if the goal is to provide incentives to those in the best position to reduce costs, then not only should the victims who want to sue have a duty to seek out the cheapest cost avoiders, but victims in general should have those duties—whether or not they are personally disposed to litigate. This is in startling contrast to the fact that tort law provides victims with a right of recourse, an opportunity and a power to seek redress if they are so inclined—not a duty to do so. The point of conferring a power rather than imposing a duty is, of course, that powers are left to the control of those who have them.

To generalize about these features of the economic account: Every core feature of the structure of tort law is explained by first disconnecting the injurer from the victim. The injurer and the victim are brought together for no reason having to do with an event that allegedly occurred between them. That is merely accidental (pardon the pun) to the structure of litigation. The victim is involved for reasons having to do with the various goals of tort law (understood from an economic perspective); and the same is true of the injurer. The importance of the fact (if it is one) that the injurer wrongly harmed the victim is epistemic, not normative. It may provide grounds for thinking that the injurer may be a good cost avoider, but is irrelevant beyond that. The economic account has the overall effect of making tort law appear mysterious.

Tort law, I maintain, is not a mysterious social practice. It has a bilateral structure that is pretty well understood and it has a body of liability and procedural rules that are well known and largely unproblematic. In offering an explanation of tort law, we are not seeking to get a handle on a social practice that we find mysterious or difficult to grasp. Quite the contrary, we are trying to deepen our understanding of something we already comprehend.

Prior to theorizing about tort law, most of us believe all of the following: (1) the victim sues the injurer, and not somebody else; (2) the victim presents arguments and evidence to the effect that the injurer acted wrongfully towards him and that, as a result, he (the victim) suffered harm; (3) the wrongfulness of the act, the fact of the harm, and the causal relation between the two are all pertinent to the outcome of the lawsuit; (4) the jury decides—in accordance with instruction by the judge as to what duties, if any, the injurer owed the victim and the relevant standard of compliance with those duties—whether the victim has made out the relevant case in the light of the evidence introduced; and (5) if the victim is found to have made out his case successfully, he is awarded a claim against the injurer, who is in turn required to make good the victim's losses.

These features of tort law are plain to anyone without the benefit of theory, and the purpose of these features seems transparently evident in the light of our ordinary intuitions about corrective justice. The problem with economic analysis is that it renders these obvious and intuitively transparent features of tort law mysterious and opaque. In the absence of any explanatory theory, our intuition is that a victim is entitled to sue *because* he asserts that the injurer has wrongfully harmed him; that the victim must present arguments to that effect *because* the harm and the wrong are recognized by the law as pertinent to the outcome of the lawsuit; and that if the victim's claims are vindicated, he recovers against his injurer *because* the law recognizes wrongful harm as grounds for such recovery. The economic theory tells us, however, that each of these intuitions is wrong; that the apparently transparent purpose of the tort law in each case is not the real purpose; and that the real purpose, efficiency, has nothing at all to do with the fact that injurer may have wrongfully harmed the victim. If the fact of the harm has any significance at all, it is epistemic. Thus, while the corrective justice account of tort law seeks to show how the structural components of tort law are independently intelligible and mutually coherent in the light of a familiar and widely accepted principle of justice, the economic analysis asserts that in the absence of search, administrative and other transaction costs, these structural features of tort law would be incomprehensible.

. . .

My view is that the best explanation of tort law will display its connections to our broader institutions of distributive and corrective justice in a way that illuminates and deepens our understanding of them all. Specifically, the institutions of tort law and distributive justice together articulate the requirements of fairness with respect to keeping track of the costs of life's misfortunes. There is a basic pretheoretical distinction between misfortunes owing to human agency and those that are attributable to no one's agency. The distinction between corrective and distributive justice reflects, among other things, this pretheoretical distinction between kinds of misfortunes.

Corrective justice articulates the requirements of fairness with respect to the misfortunes we attribute to individual human agency; distributive justice articulates the demands of fairness with respect to other forms of misfortune. Many of the "problems" of tort law, corrective justice, and distributive justice are at bottom the same.

Because the domain of distributive justice includes the class of misfortunes for which no one is responsible, whereas the domain of corrective justice is the class of misfortunes for which some human agency is responsible, it is natural to suggest that the difference in the requirements of fairness with respect to both is captured by the role the concept of personal responsibility plays in each.

Corrective justice says, in effect, that fairness in keeping track of the costs of life's misfortunes owing to individual human agency requires the imposition of a duty of repair for the compensable harms for which one is responsible: those owed, in an appropriate way, to one's responsible agency. That is, I have a duty to repair your loss as a matter of corrective justice just because your loss is an outcome for which I am responsible.

In contrast, the scope of one's duties to come to the aid of others is not limited to alleviating the misfortunes for which one is responsible. Many duties of distributive justice require coming to the aid of others to alleviate misfortunes for which one is not causally or otherwise responsible. Corrective justice is a distinct kind of justice in precisely the sense that the duties imposed by it are grounded in the "responsibility for outcome" relationship.

Not every theorist of distributive justice holds that the claims of justice extend beyond the scope of the responsibility for outcomes relationship. The libertarian, for example, does not. According to the libertarian, the concept of responsibility for outcomes governs both distributive and corrective justice. Of course, there are at least as many formulations of libertarianism as there are libertarians. In its most familiar form, the animating concept is self-ownership. Responsibility for outcomes is explicated in terms of self-ownership in conjunction with causation and volition: roughly, X owns his body; X owns all those products (desirable or undesirable) that are the causal upshots of his voluntary doings—and nothing else. Volition and causation distinguish doings from mere happenings: actions from other events.

The concept of responsibility explicated in terms of ownership, volition and causation is general. It specifies the conditions that must be satisfied in order for it to be true that so-and-so is responsible for such-and-such (where "so-and-so" ranges over persons or other responsible agents and "such-and-such" ranges over states of affairs). Not only is the content of the principle of responsibility for outcomes specified independently of political or legal institutions and practices—this principle, for the libertarian, imposes constraints on political and legal institutions. In order to be just, institutions must conform to the demands of the principle of outcome responsibility. Legal institutions of responsibility, like tort law, must embody the principle of outcome responsibility.

For the libertarian, the institutions of property, tort liability and distributive justice—and perhaps more—are constrained by these conceptions of ownership and responsibility. The net effect is that the libertarian supports strict liability (as opposed to fault) in tort law and rejects redistribution of wealth as unjust. Under strict liability the injurer takes back what he rightfully owns, that is, the misfortunes that are the products of his agency. At the same time, redistribution violates the principle of agency by claiming that individuals own the misfortunes that have befallen others though they are not responsible for them in the relevant sense.

Though the libertarian is mistaken about both tort law and distributive justice, his position is not without interest. Three claims in particular warrant consideration: first, that there is a general concept of responsibility for outcomes that applies across contexts; second, that this concept of responsibility for outcomes imposes constraints on political or legal institutions; third, that the underlying problems and principles of distributive and corrective justice are the same.

It might be useful to compare the libertarian view with Stephen Perry's, in part because Perry is a leading critic of the libertarian theory of strict liability in tort law. Perry rejects the libertarian theory of distributive justice. For him the duties of distributive justice are not restricted to alleviating the misfortunes for which one is outcome-responsible. Perry is best known, however, for his criticisms of the libertarian theory of strict liability in torts. As Perry notes, the libertarian reliance on ownership spelled out in terms of causation leads to indeterminacy. If X is liable strictly for the causal upshots of his voluntary actions, then in most cases, both the injurer and the victim own the victim's loss. This is because, in general, some voluntary actions of both parties are "but for" causes of the harm. A principle of strict causal liability leads not to strict injurer liability—as some, like Richard Epstein have thought—but to indeterminate liability. Perry is right about that.

Perry does not object to the view that outcome-responsibility should play a role in the proper account of tort law. His criticism is directed, rather, at the libertarian's conception of outcome-responsibility. Instead of analyzing it in terms of volition and causation, Perry analyzes it in terms of foreseeability and avoidability. Outcomes an agent can foresee and avoid are ones for which he is outcome-responsible. Perry maintains that, in order to be just, liability in torts must be grounded on this notion of outcome-responsibility.

Like the libertarian's conception, liability based on Perry's notion of outcome-responsibility is indeterminate. In most cases both the victim and the injurer will be outcome responsible in this sense. That is why Perry does not believe that strict liability follows from the concept of outcome-responsibility. Outcome-responsibility is, he believes, necessary but not sufficient for liability in torts. The criterion of outcome-responsibility determines the class of persons who can justly be held responsible for an outcome. For most injuries, both the victim and injurer will be members of the class: Both, after all, can typically foresee and avoid the danger. The loss must be imposed on one or the other on other grounds, and that, according to Perry, is where fault comes in. The party who is at fault bears the cost. The fault principle represents or expresses a criterion of "local distributive justice" applicable to the class selected by the criterion of outcome-responsibility.

Setting to one side the merits of Perry's overall position, I want to emphasize its similarities to the libertarian position. First, like the libertarian, Perry believes that there is a general set of conditions which, if satisfied, warrant the assertion that so-and-so is outcome-responsible for such-and-such state of affairs; that the content of these conditions is specifiable independent of the practices in which the concept of outcome-responsibility might figure; that, in other words, the conditions of outcome-responsibility apply across action contexts and are in that sense invariant; and, finally, that in order to be just, institutions in which liability is based on responsibility for outcomes must reflect this particular conception of it.

I reject these claims. Although I share with Perry and the libertarian the sense that the problems and principles of distributive justice and tort law are, in an abstract but important sense, the same, I reject the libertarian view that the bond that ties them together is some causal conception of responsibility for outcomes. More importantly, in contrast with both Perry and the libertarians, I deny that the justice of our tort institutions depends on a "moral" conception of responsibility for outcomes. There is a conception of responsibility for outcomes at the core of the concept of corrective justice and tort law—but this conception is not independent of tort institutions and practices, and its moral standing is of a piece with the moral standing of the institutions that embody it.

Whereas both Perry and the libertarian believe that in order to be just the imposition of liability in legal contexts must reflect the moral conception of outcome-responsibility, the view suggested here is that the concept of outcome-responsibility suitable to legal contexts must reflect the conditions under which the state's exercise of its authority is legitimate. These include constraints imposed by the fair terms of interaction which in turn reflect a fundamental conception of fairness as a kind of reciprocity. It is not obvious that our judgments of moral responsibility for outcomes, or of responsibility more generally, reflect or answer to a similar set of restrictions.

Put roughly, moral and political philosophy are independent in an important sense. The problem of political philosophy is not whether X is morally responsible for a loss, but whether the state would be justified in imposing liability on X for the adverse consequences of his conduct: for those untoward states of affairs for which he is outcome-responsible. Thus, the conditions under which the state is justified in imposing its coercive authority on someone are implicated in the political question (or legal one) in a way in which they are not in the moral one.

It is a further question whether, in order to be just, the politically relevant conception of responsibility should reflect or coincide with the moral conception. The answer to that question must depend on whether the conditions of legitimate political authority require such a relationship between the moral and legal conceptions of responsibility; and that is a question in political philosophy: Do the fair terms of interaction among persons require that responsibility for outcomes in legal contexts reflect the moral conception of outcome-responsibility? This, of course, is very different from the approach Perry and libertarians take, in which the moral conception of outcome-responsibility imposes constraints on the way we can think about political and legal institutions.

To clarify the differences between Perry and the libertarians on the one hand, and me on the other, I shall draw on a useful distinction of Thomas Scanlon's between *attribution* and *allocation*. The attributive question is, who is responsible? The allocation question is, who should bear the costs? Suppose we begin with the latter question. One answer might be: the person who is responsible for the loss should bear it. This would be to say that the allocation question is to be answered in the light of the principle of attribution. More precisely, we might say that the costs of the accident should lie where they fall unless someone is responsible for having brought it about. If someone is responsible for having brought it about, that person must bear the loss. Any other way of allocating the loss would be unfair or unjust.

That the allocation question is to be resolved in terms of the attribution principle is what Perry shares with the libertarian. They differ, however, with respect to the conditions under which persons are outcome-responsible. And they also differ with respect to whether being outcome-responsible is sufficient to determine fully the answer to the allocation question. The libertarian believes being outcome-responsible is sufficient (at least for the *prima facie* case), whereas Perry does not. For him, liability requires both outcome-responsibility and fault.

In my view, the principle of allocation determines the appropriate principle of attribution—not the other way around. Once we determine what the allocative question is that a particular body of law seeks to answer, then we can determine which, if any, criteria of attribution (or responsibility) must be satisfied. The criteria of responsibility (attribution) suitable to create and enforce duties of repair in order to allocate costs that must fall on someone (injurer or victim) might well be different from those appropriate to the imposition of other duties (to apologize, or in other ways come to aid of others).

Corrective justice and tort law articulate the requirements of fairness in the following way. The principle of corrective justice—that each of us has a duty to repair the wrongful losses for which we are responsible—specifies the content of fairness by articulating relationships among concepts central to the idea of fairness, concepts of loss, responsibility, and repair. Tort law in turn informs our concepts of responsibility, wrongful loss and repair.

Here's how I think it works. Some misfortunes owing to human action are the result of mischief whereas others are innocent. This difference matters to fairness. Again, some harms that are caused by mischievous conduct result from that aspect of the conduct that is mischievous, but some harm results from aspects of mischievous conduct that are without fault. It matters in other words whether the fault is responsible for the misfortune. Corrective justice informs fairness by telling us that when mischievous conduct is responsible for misfortune, the way to allocate misfortune's costs is by imposing a duty of repair.

Tort law further articulates the relevant conceptions of wrong, responsibility and the duty of repair. Tort law tells us that the concept of wrong relevant to

fairness is objective: A person can act wrongly without having a wrong intention, and thus, plausibly, without being morally culpable for what he has done. It also tells us that the duty of repair is to make good pecuniary but not necessarily nonpecuniary costs, that the default conception of repair is full compensation, and so on. Most importantly, it specifies the conditions of responsibility implicated by corrective justice.

There is no reason, then, to suppose that the criteria of responsibility in tort or corrective justice should match up with the general requirements of responsibility in criminal law or retributive justice, and so on. More generally, there is no reason why the criteria of responsibility in various areas of the law should coincide with any general moral notion of responsibility: whether responsibility for actions or responsibility for outcomes. There is no reason to think that a body of the law could not be just or fair otherwise. Rather than the institution's justice depending on its embodying an independently specified and independently defended criterion of responsibility for outcomes, the principle of responsibility in tort law helps make explicit the requirements of fairness within a very specific domain: the domain in which state power is brought to bear on individuals in order to allocate the costs of misfortunes resulting from individual agency. Thus I reject the position taken by Perry and the libertarians. There is no principle of outcome-responsibility that constrains tort law. Rather the conception of responsibility appropriate to tort law is partially given by its own institutions and practices, which in turn make explicit the requirements or content of fairness in this domain.

If the conceptual distance between tort law and corrective justice depends on the kind of embodiment relation I have been describing, can this relation really explain the tort law? It may seem as though corrective justice is too "close" to tort law to explain it. Indeed, corrective justice may seem too indeterminate or, in any event, too inadequately specified to explain anything.

There are two distinct but related challenges here: The first asks what kind of an explanation is being offered; the second asks whether it succeeds as the kind of explanation it is. Turning to the first challenge: The embodiment relation purports to explain tort law by showing how its central concepts get their content. Their content is given, in part, by the practical inferences they warrant within the institution of tort law. Corrective justice describes the structure of those inferences in general terms; tort law as a set of practices embodies that general structure and gives it determinate shape. Corrective justice explains the concepts and the shape of the law not by determining them fully, but by showing how they hang together in the practical inferences that do give them determinate content.

This brings us to the second challenge: If the content of corrective justice is indeterminate prior to its practical realization or embodiment, then how can it really show the way the central concepts of the law hang together in warranting certain kinds of inferences and not others? What, to put the point more sharply, would count as a *wrong* inference, one that *didn't* connect the concepts of the law in the way corrective justice says they are connected? Unless corrective justice can exert some kind of "normative pressure" on the practices it explains, then anything goes; nothing that happens in our tort institutions could count as failing to embody corrective justice. That would make corrective justice worthless as an explanation.

The key to meeting this challenge is to see that while *part* of the content of corrective justice gets worked out in the embodiment relation I have described, tort law is not the *only* practice that helps to give content to corrective justice. Recall that corrective justice articulates part of the requirements of fairness with respect to the activity of keeping track of life's misfortunes owing to human agency. The concept of fairness is partly determined by tort law, but it is also determined in part by all of our other moral practices— legal, political, and private—in which fairness figures. The normative pressure fairness exerts in tort law is the pressure of every other practice in which fairness figures. This insures that not every practice of repair qualifies as an instance of or instantiation of corrective justice or fairness.

Fairness requires that no person be permitted to set the terms of cooperative interaction between individuals unilaterally. This assertion alone has a certain content independent of the law—content sufficient for us to say (with an argument) that a system of tort law cannot be fair if it employs a negligence standard understood along the lines of the famous Learned Hand Formula. According to the Learned Hand Formula, a person has a duty of care to another whenever the costs of the harm risked, discounted by the probability of its occurrence, is greater than the costs taking adequate precautions would impose on the risktaker. If precaution costs exceed the expected value of the harm, there is no duty to take precautions and the failure to do so would not be negligent or unreasonable.

The problem is that in the Learned Hand Formula, the degree of security to which the victim is entitled is entirely a function of the degree to which the potential injurer values his liberty. If precaution costs are foregone opportunities to engage in an activity the injurer values, then the measure of those costs is given by the value of the activity to him. The degree of security the victim is entitled to is fixed by the evaluations of the injurer in violation of the criterion of fairness, and, thus, corrective justice. So even though tort law helps make the demands of fairness as expressed in the principle of corrective justice explicit, fairness and corrective justice provide criteria by which the practice of tort law can be assessed.

It should be noted, however, that while the norms of fairness and corrective justice are moral norms, the kind of normative pressure I have been describing is, in the first instance, tied to their theoretical justification rather than their moral justification. The Learned Hand Test is inappropriate to the practice of tort law because it runs afoul of the principle that best explains tort law—namely, the principle of corrective justice. If, in addition to being the best explanation of tort law, corrective justice turns out also to be a justified principle of morality, then the Learned Hand Test may be inappropriate in another way—it may be immoral.

The idea of fairness that has been implicit in the discussion to this point is central to a range of political doctrines whose roots lie in the liberal tradition. In particular, I have relied on a notion of fairness as reciprocity among free and equal individuals. This notion of fairness is bound up with other ideals, such as freedom and equality; and all of these ideals are contested, as regards both their content and their relative priorities. It may lie somewhat beyond the scope of this essay to settle, once and for all, the most fundamental debates of modern political philosophy. I would like to conclude, however, by sketching what seems to me a particularly attractive view of what animates the best parts of the liberal tradition—including the ideal of fairness that is embodied, though imperfectly, in our institutions of corrective and distributive justice.

Libertarianism—to revisit our earlier discussion—could be characterized as that form of liberalism organized around the idea of outcome-responsibility, in which outcome-responsibility is itself to be analyzed in terms of morally prior notions such as self-ownership, agency, and a certain naturalist conception of causation. While I have rejected this conception of liberalism, I have now meant to dismiss the importance to liberalism of the concept of individual responsibility. I not want to suggest that a certain conception of individual responsibility is fundamental to the liberal ideal. This conception expresses the special relationship each of us bears to her own life, and does not bear to the lives of others. We might express the liberal view of the individual's relationship to his own life in the proposition that each of us is responsible for how her life goes.

This could be understood as a kind of moral claim about the accountability of persons—about the fact that we can and sometimes do judge and evaluate individuals or their lives as good or bad, virtuous or vicious, successful or failed, and so on. However, the sense of responsibility I mean is not just accountability. Rather, it strikes me as a kind of conceptual claim at the core of the liberal ideal: that if we are to have a certain concept of the individual as an agent, as a being who acts and is not merely acted upon, then it must be true that the individual can have a certain kind of ultimate responsibility for how his life goes. That is to say, whatever the circumstances of his birth, his social status, nationality, religion, and so on, his authority over the course of his life is superior to these things; they have no ultimate claim on the way he chooses to lead his life.

The idea of responsibility that I am describing is what makes possible a very strong sense in which I can say that my life is *mine*: I lead it, I have made it, it is my doing rather than something that has happened (and keeps happening) to me. This is an ideal of the person, and not a description of how all people necessarily are. Nonetheless, the ideal represents the realization of capacities that all normal persons have. Liberalism, I want to suggest, is the tradition that derives principles of political life from this ideal, and seeks to realize those principles in practice. Liberal political institutions are best understood as attempts to make is possible for individuals to be responsible for their lives, and to make that equally possible for all.

Any life, we might say, reflects a combination of two kinds of factors: What one does, and what merely happens to one. Ronald Dworkin usefully expresses the distinction between these factors as the difference between *choice* and *circumstance*. In order to realize the idea of responsibility implicated in the concept of a life lived rather than a life had, political institutions must be arranged so that individuals' lives reflect to a greater degree, or to the greatest possible degree, their choices rather than their circumstances of birth and the subsequent influences of fortune. The goal of making it equally possible for each to be responsible for the way her life goes is what grounds the centrality of freedom and equality in liberal doctrine: freedom inasmuch as it is necessary to enable a life to reflect individual choice; and equality inasmuch as no individual is entitled to a greater benefit of circumstance than any other.

This is, as I have said, my own view of what is most central as well as what is best in the liberal tradition. I cannot undertake here to defend it against rival views. But if one were to grant the attractiveness of the picture I am describing, the errors both of libertarianism and of a certain extreme egalitarianism would be apparent. By focusing on the idea of self-ownership as primary, the libertarian singles out one of the preconditions of responsibility, namely choice—but fails to equalize those circumstances that do not reflect choice; on the other hand, a crudely egalitarian liberalism that demands absolute equality of material standards tends to eliminate the element of choice in pursuit of equal circumstances.

If the aim is to give choice the preeminent role in human life, and to do so equally for all, then institutions should be arranged so that circumstances are equalized only insofar as they are not the effects of choice. This, I would maintain, is the concept of fairness that explains the distinction between redistributive and corrective institutions, and that is imperfectly embodied in them. It is the distinction between, on the one hand, those of life's misfortunes that are the result of someone's choices—and which are owed therefore to human agency—and on the other hand, those misfortunes that reflect the material conditions of choice. The principles of distributive justice govern the material conditions of choice, whereas the principle of corrective justice articulates the requirements of fairness with respect to the costs of misfortunes owing to human agency. It does so by expressing the fact that fairness in keeping track of those misfortunes requires that the losses be imposed on the person (if any) whose wrongful conduct is responsible for them. Tort law further articulates the relevant conceptions of wrong, responsibility and the duty of repair. Tort law tells us that the concept of wrong relevant to fairness is objective: a person can act wrongly without having a wrong intention—and thus, plausibly, without being morally culpable for what he has done. It also tells us that the duty of repair is to make good pecuniary but not necessarily non-pecuniary costs, that the default conception of repair is full compensation, and so on. Most importantly, tort law specifies the conditions of responsibility implicated by corrective justice. These requirements of fairness become clear to us in the circumstances that are delineated by our actual tort institutions; they could never be deduced from an abstract notion of fairness.

It would be in some ways neater, and might give the appearance of greater analytical power, to have a single principle of justice or efficiency from which one could derive a series of institutional forms and practices that would be defensible, perhaps even required by, the principle in question. But that would be to falsify the relationship between principles and the practices that articulate or realize them. The pragmatic method I have developed in this essay recognizes (for good reasons, but ones I have only been able to touch on here) that practices make the content of the principles determi-

nate, while at the same time the principles themselves hang together as an articulation of a particular liberal ideal of the person and of the relationships among persons. The content of the most abstract and fundamental principles that form a coherent conception of liberalism is only fully determined by the relationship the principles bear to one another and to their practical embodiments. The pragmatic method implies that we can hope for no more than a revisable structure of independently intelligible and mutually coherent principles and practices. Justice requires that we accept no less.

Individualized Justice and Mass Torts

Roger Cramton

The tension between individual justice (party autonomy in an adversary system) and collective justice (aggregated handling of legal claims) is the basic theme of [this essay]. Nowhere is this tension more evident than in recent efforts to use "settlement class actions" as a means for large-scale resolution of personal injury or property damage claims arising out of exposure to defective products or toxic substances. Important and novel issues of tort law, civil procedure, constitutional due process, and lawyer behavior are presented by settlements resolving the tort claims of future as well as current claimants. Pending cases provide a number of examples: (1) a class containing millions of persons occupationally exposed to asbestos, (2) a class of more than one million women who received breast implants, (3) a class containing all of the owners of Ford Bronco all-terrain vehicles, (4) a class of owners of GM pickups with saddlebag gas tanks, and (5) a class of current and future owners of homes that have a polybutylene plumbing system, an allegedly defective plumbing material that has been

installed in three million mobile homes and an estimated four to five million site-built homes.

This use of the class action device, like most other new developments, has both long- and short-term antecedents. Yet, the recent class actions mentioned above, which contain a novel combination of features, illustrate something quite new in degree and kind. For example, the cases were either brought or certified for settlement purposes rather than to be tried; the plaintiff class includes future victims, many of whom have yet to suffer a legally cognizable injury; approved settlements will bind absent class members, many of whom may not have had an effective opportunity to opt out of the class; the settlements affect claims nationwide and may have the effect of a federal decree eliminating claims governed by state law or a state decree eliminating claims governed by federal law; and in some of the cases, the plaintiffs' lawyers representing the class entered into side settlements with the defendants, giving their current clients different and more favorable relief than the class settlement provides to future claimants. A class action settlement with these features would have been unthinkable to lawyers of a decade or so ago. . . .

Recent class action settlements such as those previously mentioned raise several questions. Some of the most central are:

From Roger Cramton, "Individualized Justice, Mass Torts, and Settlement Class Actions." *Cornell Law Review*, Vol. 80 (1995), pp. 811–835. Reprinted by permission of the Cornell Law Review.

(1) Is the individual justice provided by tort law in the courts so delayed, erratic, and inefficient that it should be replaced by schemes of collective justice molded by self-interested parties and approved by a single federal district judge? If administrative schemes are to be substituted for the tort system, should this be accomplished by legislation rather than by private settlements approved by a single judge?

(2) Does a federal district court have authority to enter a decree that eliminates or displaces the personal injury rights, otherwise governed by state law, of individuals who have been exposed to a product or substance but have not yet suffered a legal injury (future claimants whose claims have not yet matured when notice is given of the opportunity to opt out)?

(3) How can adequate notice of opportunity to opt out of a class action, required by due process, be provided to "exposure only" persons who do not and cannot know that they will suffer an injury in the future? Is "adequate representation" provided when a lawyer negotiates cash settlements for the lawyer's current clients simultaneously with a class action settlement providing different terms for future claimants? Do the virtues of private settlement and alternative dispute resolution justify departures from general principles of legal ethics?

The American common-law system emphasizes party control of litigation rather than judicial prosecution and investigation. The adversary system presupposes opposing parties who exercise a wide range of choice on whether, where, and when a lawsuit is filed; what claims and defenses are asserted; what resources should be devoted to the litigation; and whether the case is settled or tried. The common-law judge is envisioned as a neutral, relatively passive arbiter of conflicting private interests who rules on questions of law and supervises the conduct of the litigation. Party initiative and the underlying principle of individual autonomy are supported by the constitutional right of trial by jury, which presupposes a detailed evaluation of particularistic facts bearing on the plaintiff's claim and the defendant's defenses.

The American tort system reflects the same values by requiring proof of fault, causation, and harm before one person's loss is shifted to someone else. The injured plaintiff must establish by a preponderance of the evidence that the defendant's wrongful acts caused the plaintiff's harm. Although tort law serves mixed goals—compensating accident victims, deterring conduct that is wrongful or involves unreasonable risks to the health or safety of others, and punishing wrongdoers—the central notion until quite recently has been one of corrective justice—repairing, to the extent possible with a money award, the harm that one individual's wrongful act has caused another. Proof that the defendant's wrongful act has caused the plaintiff's injury inevitably requires a particularistic assessment of the plaintiff's and defendant's conduct, a causal relationship between their actions and the claimed harm, and a valuation of the plaintiff's resulting injury.

Two developments in the twentieth century threaten to displace the traditional model of individual rights and party autonomy. First, many judges participate more actively in the management, conduct, and settlement of litigation. Second, pressures flow from the volume, complexity, cost, and interrelatedness of what are referred to here as "mass exposure torts."

Since the development of negligence doctrine in the nineteenth century, the paradigm case of the traditional tort is an accident in which an actor's vehicle—whether stage coach, railroad, or automobile—has injured a stranger. The individualized approach to adjudicating such disputes seemed natural, if not inevitable, given the premises of American law and the constitutional right to a jury trial. In today's world, however, America's market economy encourages mass distribution of products of new, and perhaps untested, technology. Thousands of strangers may be injured by the dissemination and use of a single product. Mass exposure to these products or substances creates situations in which a large number of people believe, or are led to believe, that the defendant's product caused their injuries. The resulting volume of litigation poses problems that threaten both the tort system's reliance on individual responsibility and the procedural system's reliance on party initiative and control.

Mass exposure torts threaten these aspects of the tort system for several reasons. First, proving or determining whether exposure to the product or substance caused the claimed injury is difficult. Frequently, the exposure that leads to claims of injury occurs over a substantial period of time, and the injury itself may have a long latency period. Often there is scientific uncertainty as to whether the exposure caused the alleged harm or whether the condition was the result of the individual's conduct (smoking, for example) or the presence of background substances in the natural environment. Frequently, expert witnesses will be able to testify about causation only in terms of statistical probabilities based on scattered or inconclusive epidemiological studies.

Second, in many cases it is difficult or impossible to determine which of multiple actors caused the claimed injury. If the harm has a long latency period, evidence of whose product or substance caused the harm may be unavailable fifteen or thirty years after the product's distribution and consumption. A related problem arises in cases involving long-term occupational exposure, such as in the asbestos field. The worker may have been exposed to several products, each with somewhat different injury characteristics, manufactured by a number of companies over a lengthy period of time. In such a case, it may be difficult for the plaintiff to establish that the named defendant or defendants were responsible for the plaintiff's harm.

Third, it is doubtful whether individualized justice can be provided when thousands or even millions of claims flow from mass exposure to a product or substance. For example, millions of Americans were exposed occupationally to asbestos products from the 1930s through the 1970s, before regulatory and safety controls reduced the future danger. Many of those exposed have died or suffered injuries, and the exposure will claim further victims well into the twenty-first century. As another example, over one million women had silicone gel breast implants between 1979 and 1994. As of yet, only a small portion of this group has suffered injury, and the causal relationship between implants and some injuries remains uncertain.

The sheer number of claims in cases like these creates troublesome problems of judicial delay, repetitive trials, high transaction costs and an inevitable interrelationship among claimants. As indicated earlier, claimants may suffer from a "disease" rather than the type of immediate physical injury associated with a traumatic accident. Causation may be established only by reliance on probabilistic methods. Publicity given to the dangers of use or exposure to the product gives rise to new claims, such as the emotional harm flowing from fear of contracting the disease in the future, and increases the percentage of victims who assert claims. Evidence that defendants knew of the products' risks but failed to warn those exposed to them supports punitive damage claims that threaten producers with large, unpredictable, and recurring judgments based on the same conduct.

Individual trials that replicate evidence of exposure, causation, and injury in case after case burden the courts, create judicial delay, and carry high transaction costs. In conventional tort litigation, approxi-

mately sixty percent of amounts paid go to accident victims. A study of asbestos litigation estimates that plaintiffs only receive about forty percent of each litigation dollar. Critics assert that lawyers, insurance companies, and litigation expenses consume too much of the amounts available to compensate victims. If fault and causation requirements were eliminated entirely from complex, difficult cases of mass tort exposure, as was done in social security disability or workers' compensation cases, transaction costs could be greatly reduced.

The model of individualized justice posits that each claimant should make all relevant decisions with respect to her claim. The existence of a host of other similar claims inevitably affects these decisions because a claimant will "now have to take into account the existence of the other claimants, the extent to which the other claims may deplete the assets of the tortfeasor, and the possible savings which may be achieved by sharing the costs of litigation." If payment of compensatory and punitive damages to early claimants results in a producer's insolvency, future claimants will receive little or nothing. Some courts assume that maintaining the solvency of corporate actors is a desirable objective wholly apart from its effect on future claimants.

The high costs of proving causation in the individual case may be reduced by a collective action that spreads the costs of discovery, expert testimony, and litigation among many claimants. Thus, collective justice appeals to all parties to some degree and to courts and judges almost without exception. Plaintiffs avoid the "free rider" problem by sharing the costs of discovering evidence and proving causation and fault. Defendants benefit from reduced transaction costs and fixed liability, displacing the uncertainty of unpredictable future liability. Courts similarly benefit from reduced caseloads because thousands of individual cases are combined into one large class action, and claims are processed outside the courts.

These characteristics of mass exposure torts produce pressures that result in efforts at aggregative or collective justice. The class action is a procedural technique in which representatives of a group (class representatives) may assert against the defendants both their own claims and similar claims of other persons who share a common interest. [The law] requires that class actions meet four prerequisites, generally referred to as numerosity, commonality, typicality, and adequacy. First, the class must be so numerous that joinder of all members is impracticable. Second, questions of law or fact must be common to the class. Third, the claims or defenses of the representative parties must be typical of the class as a whole. Finally, the representative plaintiffs and their lawyers must "fairly and adequately protect the interests of the class." . . .

Although the legislative history of the [rules creating class actions] states that the class action device is "ordinarily not appropriate" for "[a] 'mass accident' resulting in injuries to numerous persons, federal courts in recent years have authorized class actions in a number of single-incident mass accident cases and a smaller number of mass exposure tort cases. The Agent Orange class action, involving the claimed injuries of Vietnam veterans from battlefield exposure to dioxin manufactured by the defendants, was the first such case. Bankruptcy situations involving a major asbestos defendant and the manufacturer of the Dalkon Shield intrauterine device had class action aspects.

Collective justice . . . has its distinctive vices as well as its virtues. To the extent that compensating victims becomes a major goal, considerations of fault, responsibility, and deterrence are muted or eliminated. Collective action may solve the "free rider" problem of individualized justice—some litigants benefitting from, but not contributing to, the expensive efforts of another litigant in discovering causation and fault. But collective action creates the new and serious problem of the "kidnapped rider," an individual deprived of any freedom of action by being drawn involuntarily into collective litigation. Collective action may also deprive individuals of meaningful control over their own legal claims, pushing them involuntarily into compensation grids and administrative claims-handling processes to whose ministrations they have not consented.

Collective justice also departs from the normal lawyer-client relationship in which the client makes decisions concerning objectives and the client's lawyer makes tactical and procedural decisions. The plaintiff's lawyer in traditional tort litigation is probably more in charge of the case than traditional theory would suggest. But an individual plaintiff represented by a lawyer retained on a contingent-fee basis may discharge the lawyer at will and may decide whether or not to accept a settlement offer. In most class actions, especially those involving large classes of absent persons whose claims are of limited worth or future creation, the lawyers representing the class ("class counsel") are clearly in charge. Class counsel typically pick the class representatives, frame the issues, push or abandon particular claims, and make

settlement decisions. Class action law even permits class counsel to submit a settlement to the court that some or all of the class representatives oppose. Class action lawyers, even more than government lawyers who represent an amorphous "public," are their own clients in the sense that their fiduciary responsibilities to class members are what they determine them to be in the absence of court supervision and scrutiny.

During the last year or two, a spate of mass exposure class actions have raised novel and interesting questions. The major current cases [include] two class action settlements in the asbestos field; the settlement of the silicone gel breast implants litigation; the *Ford Bronco II* property damage case; the similar litigation involving General Motors pickup trucks; and the polybutylene plumbing case in a Texas state court. In each of these cases, defendants facing mass tort claims have combined with class action plaintiffs' lawyers in efforts to settle the claims of current and future claimants. Some of these proposed settlements have been approved by district courts as fair and reasonable, but have not been reviewed by appellate courts. The proposed settlements have been rejected in the two motor vehicle cases. The breast implants case and other class action filings are pending before trial courts. Appellate review has occurred in only one case. These legal innovations will be tested over the next few years until authoritative decisions, new procedural rules, or legislative solutions replace conflicting arguments with stable law—innovations which may be a long time coming.

Study Questions

1. Testimony in *Holden v. Wal-Mart* indicated that the plaintiff's "lower extremity impairment" increased from 87 percent to 97 percent subsequent to her fall at Wal-Mart. Should Wal-Mart be liable for only 10 percent of her impairment? Why or why not?

2. The jury found that Holden herself was partly to blame for her fall. Why should she recover any damages from Wal-Mart at all?

3. Holden presented evidence at trial regarding the pain she experienced subsequent to the fall and the knee replacement surgery. How can a jury know what amount of money damages is appropriate compensation for her pain?

4. Why should a defendant in a tort case only have to pay an amount of money equal to per degree of

negligence rather than an amount of damages equal to the plaintiff's losses?

5. Does Holmes agree with the claim that tort liability is always based upon the personal fault of the defendant? Why or why not?

6. Is Holmes's defense of an objective standard of reasonableness in tort law consistent with his claim that liability should be imposed only where the actor had a choice? Are you convinced by Holmes's efforts to combine the notion of fault with the objective standard?

7. Do you agree with Posner that corrective justice, while it may explain how the law of intentional wrongs operates, nonetheless cannot explain the law of negligence as well as the principle of wealth-maximization?

8. Do you think Coleman's criticisms of the economic theory of torts are warranted? How do you think Posner would respond to them?

9. Does the imposition of strict liability go beyond the principle of corrective justice, as Coleman articulates it? Consider this example: "[S]uppose a long-standing custom in our neighborhood permits any neighbor to borrow garden equipment from any other neighbor, but the custom is equally strong that if the equipment is damaged or lost while in the borrower's possession, the borrower must make the loss good. Suppose I borrow your lawn mower and without my fault it is damaged when a truck backs over it in my driveway. A rule that imposes liability on me would be a strict liability rule because I was not at fault."[1] Is the imposition of strict liability in this case a demand of corrective justice?

10. Does strict liability wrongly use the defendant as a "risk distributor" to spread the social cost of risks imposed by activities from which nearly everyone benefits?

11. Gwendolyn Robbins suffered a severe hip injury when the car in which she was riding veered off the road after the driver fell asleep at the wheel. The driver died. Robbins sued to recover from the insurance company of the deceased driver. The

defendant insurer argued that Robbins should be denied a large part of her recovery due to her failure to "mitigate damages," that is, to use reasonable efforts to minimize the injuries sustained. Evidence revealed that at the time of the accident, Robbins had refused surgical intervention that in all likelihood would have returned her to a near-normal life. Robbins, a devout Jehovah's Witness, insisted that she was obliged by religious teaching to refuse the surgery and the blood transfusions it would have entailed. On appeal, Robbins lost. The trial and appellate courts disagreed as to how the "reasonableness" of Robbins's conduct was to be measured. The trial court instructed the jury to consider whether "it was reasonable for her [Robbins] given her beliefs" to act as she did. The appellate court disagreed, arguing that the proper standard for the jury in such a case is "whether the plaintiff acted as a reasonably prudent person, under all the circumstances confronting her." (See *Williams v. Bright*, 658 N.Y.S2d 910 [1997].) How would you decide this issue?

12. According to Cramton, what are the aspects of mass exposure torts that threaten to undermine what he calls the "traditional" model of product-related tort lawsuits?

13. Consumer advocates have long argued that cigarettes and other tobacco products are dangerous and that the costs associated with tobacco use should be borne by the tobacco industry. Through the late 1980s, tobacco manufacturers argued in court that smoking injuries were the result of "contributory negligence," in effect, the consumer's own fault: if consumers take up smoking despite the obvious and mandated warning, they "assume the risk" of any resulting injury. Users' own personal freedom of choice, not the product, was the cause of injuries sustained. Recent legal actions against cigarette makers have directly attacked the industry's "freedom of choice" defense. These lawsuits do not focus on the alleged addictive qualities of tobacco's central ingredient: nicotine. Plaintiffs in the massive class action case *Castano v. American Tobacco* (84F.3d734), for example, accused the industry of fraud in connection with a number of allegedly related activities: suppressing the industry's own research revealing that nicotine is an addictive substance, refusing to fund the development of a "safer" cigarette, attempting to conceal knowledge of the

---

[1] Dan B. Dobbs and Paul T. Hayden, *Torts and Compensation* (St. Paul: West Group, 2001), p. 5.

addictiveness of cigarettes, and adjusting or manipulating the level of nicotine in cigarettes to keep smokers "hooked." Although the *Castano* case was not permitted to go forward as a class action suit, arguments quite similar to those advanced in *Castano* were used by a number of individual states, each suing the major tobacco manufacturers. Should smoking-related injuries be treated by the law as the plaintiff's own fault? Can a convincing argument be made for holding cigarette manufacturers strictly liable for the harmful results of smoking?

14. Jurors in *Tovias v. Mercy Health Center* [No. 2000CVQ001176D2 (Webb Co., Texas Dist. Ct.)] found for the plaintiff, who had suffered complications after a sponge was left in her abdomen during surgery. The plaintiff had complained of continuing abdominal pain for nine months subsequent to the surgical intervention. A second procedure discovered the sponge. No one on the medical team could explain how the sponge came to be there. Is this an "automatic" case of negligence?

15. By mid-1998 several attempts had been made to achieve a "global settlement" between the tobacco industry and numerous individuals, states, and local governments alleging injuries and financial costs associated with tobacco use. The proposed settlements were criticized as deeply immoral,

given that they excluded any current or future overseas victims of smoking-related illnesses, by most estimates the fastest-growing segment of smokers worldwide. Should such settlements be approved? Would such agreements be more fair to consumers injured by tobacco use than permitting them to pursue an individual remedy through a tort suit?

16. Anthony Northcutt, a resident of Oklahoma City, went to a county-operated health clinic for blood tests to determine if he was infected with HIV. Northcutt was mistakenly told that he had tested positive for the virus. Northcutt claimed that, while undergoing treatment at the clinic, he was not counseled about the risks of reinfection and the preventative measures necessary to protect himself. Northcutt's life spiraled downwards into alcoholism, suicide attempts, and unprotected sex with men known to be infected. When he contracted HIV for certain, Northcutt sued the clinic and county, arguing that their negligence caused him to behave as he did, thinking he had nothing left to lose. The County responded that its negligence was superseded by Northcutt's own carelessness. (*Northcutt v. City-County Board of Health of Oklahoma County*, No. CJ-98-4016-66 Oklahoma Co. Dist. Ct.) How would you decide this case if you were on the jury?

B. *Causation and Liability*

Did the Defendant Cause the Harm?

Two cases involving bizarre events open the readings for this section. In *Lynch v. Fisher*, the defendant ran out of gas while driving his truck down the highway. He negligently parked the truck on the road, failing either to move it completely to the side or to set out flares. He then left the scene in search of a service sta-

tion. A couple, Mr. and Mrs. Gunter, rounded the corner at excessive speed, were unable to avoid collision with the truck, and were injured, Mrs. Gunter severely. Plaintiff Lynch, traveling in the opposite direction, encountered the accident scene soon after the incident occurred and went to aid the Gunters. Helping Mrs. Gunter out of the car, he then went to the driver's side. When Mr. Gunter got out, Lynch leaned inside to remove the floor pad to use as a cushion. There he found a loaded pistol, which he handed to Mr. Gunter. As Lynch prepared to tend to the wife, Mr. Gunter, temporarily deranged from shock, mistook Lynch for an assailant and shot him in the foot. Finally, truck driver Fisher returned to find a confusion of wrecked vehicles, an unconscious woman, a trigger-happy madman, and a footsore Good Samaritan, who promptly slapped Fisher with a hefty bill for his injuries.

In the second case, *Palsgraf v. Long Island Railroad*, Helen Palsgraf purchased a ticket to ride the train from Brooklyn to Rockaway Beach. While she waited on the railway platform, various trains to other destinations arrived and departed. As one of these was pulling away, a man carrying a plain wrapped package emerged from the crowd and sprinted down the platform to catch the train. He appeared to be losing ground when two of the railroad's employees came to his assistance, pulling and pushing him onto the moving train. As they did this, the package—which contained large fireworks—fell to the ground, slid under the tracks, and, ignited by a spark from the train, exploded. Either the explosion of the fireworks or a stampede caused by the explosion (the facts are still unclear, despite what Judge Cardozo says), caused some scales located at the other end of the platform to topple over onto poor Mrs. Palsgraf. She sued the railroad, alleging that it caused her injuries. (Why didn't she sue the man with the package?)

Should the defendants in either of these cases be held liable for the injuries involved? As we have seen, the law of negligence makes the answer to this question turn on another one: Did either of these defendants *cause* the injuries? This question is not easy to answer.

Cause in Fact

When is an act or event the cause of some further act or event? Indeed, when is an act or event even relevant to a question of causation? Suppose that you sneeze and that immediately following this, an elderly man in Peoria has a heart attack. Absent any further knowledge of the matter, a reasonable person would surely deny that these two events were in any way causally linked or related. One way both to explain and to support this obvious reaction would be to point out that the injury (heart attack) would certainly have occurred even if you hadn't sneezed. (After all, what

possible connection could there be?) This observation strongly suggests that for one act or event, A, to be causally relevant to the occurrence of some other act or event, B, it must at least be the case that A is a *necessary condition* for the occurrence of B; that is, B would not have happened "but for" the occurrence of A. Traditionally, the law refers to a factor that is a necessary condition in this sense as a *cause in fact* or *factual cause*.

Courts have long required that a plaintiff in a tort action establish factual causation as part of his or her *prima facie* tort case. In *Rinaldo v. McGovern*[1], for example, the defendant hit a golf ball but failed to announce his shot by shouting the word "fore." The errant ball traveled some distance to a nearby road and struck the plaintiff in his car. The court held that the accident could not be traced to the defendant's failure to warn, because no warning could have been heard from a car traveling on the highway. The failure to shout "fore" was thus not a cause in fact of the plaintiff's injuries.

Proving factual causation does raise important concerns. For instance, which party should shoulder the burden of proof with regard to issues of factual causation? Should the law require the plaintiff to prove it more likely than not that, had the defendant not acted, the plaintiff would not have been injured? (How are such "contrary to fact" conditional statements to be proven?) Or should it be enough if the plaintiff can show that the defendant's act substantially increased the likelihood that the plaintiff would be injured? And on a more theoretical level, the idea that one event would not have occurred "but for" another appears to have some serious limitations. Consider this case: Two fires simultaneously converge on your house and burn it to the ground. Either fire would have destroyed the house in the absence of the other. The fires were negligently started by separate defendants. Which defendant caused the destruction of your house? Puzzling as it may seem, the "but for" test exonerates each defendant: each can insist that his actions were *not* necessary for the damage inflicted, because the other guy's fire would have done the job. (This problem is explored further below.)

Such hypothetical scenarios are far-fetched, and the requirement of cause in fact makes sense in a good many cases. However, although proving factual causation is a start, reflection shows that by itself, the notion won't get us very far. Consider the tragic circumstances surrounding the death of former president

---

[1] 78 N.Y.2d 729 (1991).

John Kennedy. Many people still believe (whether correctly or incorrectly, we may never know) that the pulling of a trigger on a rifle by a man named Lee Harvey Oswald led to Kennedy's death. If they are right, then Oswald's pulling of that trigger at that moment on that day in Dallas was a necessary condition, or *sine qua non* ("that without which there is not") of Kennedy's death. But consider: If the sun hadn't been shining, Oswald would not have been able to see the presidential motorcade; if the motorcade hadn't kept to its prescribed route, it would not have arrived at the point opposite Oswald's location; if the trigger on Oswald's rifle hadn't been working properly . . . if Oswald had not gained entry to the building from which he shot . . . if Kennedy hadn't made it to Dallas or hadn't been elected president . . . if Oswald hadn't been born. . . . The point is obvious enough. If we look into the past of any given event, we will find numerous (perhaps infinitely many?) conditions that, had they not occurred as they did, would have negated the event in question. And for each of these conditions, a seemingly endless number of further events serve as necessary conditions, and on and on. Insofar as each is a necessary condition or *sine qua non* of its successor in the chain, all would seem to have an equal claim to being called a "cause," and we are left with an abundance of causes and of potential defendants.

A related difficulty in understanding legal causation can be seen in a similar way. Presumably, for any given act I perform, that act will continue having consequences indefinitely; that is, it will stand as a necessary condition for the occurrence of an entire series of other acts or events. Take, for example, my act of preparing this book. That act is a necessary condition for your reading it. Suppose, because you are reading this book with such enthusiasm, you stay up too late one night and sleep in too late the next morning, you miss class and the final exam, you flunk the course, your grade point average is ruined, and you can't get into law school as you had planned. Because of this, you don't meet the young attorney who would have been your spouse, and so on. Does it make sense to say that I am responsible for your not having a spouse or a legal career? When do I cease being responsible for what I do, for chains of cause and effect that I initiate? I start a fire in my fireplace, negligently leaving it unattended. A spark ignites my draperies and spreads from there to the wall; soon the entire house is ablaze. From my home, the fire grows and spreads to neighboring houses and eventually to the entire town. Would it make sense to hold me liable for all of the resulting injury and damage?

Plainly, some limitations must be placed on liability for harm that is, loosely speaking, a "consequence" of one's conduct, if for no other reason than that failing to do so would seem to undermine at least one animating purpose of the tort system. If my conduct results in the destruction of an entire town, it would be pointless to hold me liable in tort (although there might be reason for charging me with a crime), because the purpose of fixing liability in tort is to see to it that the victim's losses are compensated. Obviously I can't compensate the entire town. How, then, can these limits be drawn in a philosophically defensible fashion?

Judge Benjamin Cardozo (later to sit on the U.S. Supreme Court), writing for the New York Court of Appeals in *Palsgraf*, puts the central question in the case this way: Was the railroad's act a wrong to *Mrs. Palsgraf* (even if it was a wrong to the man with the package)? Cardozo insists that negligence requires a *relationship* between the parties involved: The negligent act must have been directed to a specific person before that individual may recover from the defendant. To have a "cause of action" (basis for a suit), Mrs. Palsgraf must show that the railroad breached a duty it had to her. Cardozo claims that this did not occur: "The risk reasonably to be perceived defines the duty to be obeyed." Nothing in this case would have suggested to a reasonable person that the parcel wrapped in plain paper posed a risk to the health or safety of the plaintiff. The railroad does, of course, have certain duties to Mrs. Palsgraf, but these all amount to duties not to harm her in *foreseeable* ways. Because she was not harmed in a foreseeable way, none of those duties were violated.

Judge Andrews, dissenting from Cardozo's majority opinion, asserts that negligence is not a relationship between a person and those whom he "might reasonably be expected" to injure but rather to all those whom he "in fact" injures. Andrews rejects the restriction of negligence to the domain of the foreseeable. Such restrictions are vague and ill-defined questions of policy. What we know is that the negligence of the railroad workers was a necessary condition of the resulting harm and that the accident was a direct consequence of the defendant's actions, remote in neither time nor space. The majority in *Lynch* make much the same argument: Although the injury arose in a bizarre and unforeseeable manner, it remains true that Lynch would not have been injured but for the negligence of Fisher. It is true that Gunter did the shooting, but he cannot be accounted the "cause" of the wounded foot, because he was not acting deliberately or voluntarily at the time. The court, concluding that the "chain [linking Fisher's negligence to Lynch's injuries] is complete and whole—link by link," finds Fisher liable.

Proximate Cause

The question of placing limits upon the consequences of my conduct that, for the purposes of tort law, I can correctly be said to have caused, has been transformed by the law into the requirement that the plaintiff actually prove *two* kinds of cause: *cause in fact* and *proximate cause*. In general, the requirement that the plaintiff show proximate cause marks the concern of the courts to contain the limits of causal liability within reasonable, fair, or just boundaries. *D*'s conduct is the proximate cause of *P*'s injury only if the act and the injury are related "closely enough" to make it fair or just to hold *D* liable. Over the years, the courts have devised various limiting principles under the heading of proximate cause, appealing, for example, to whether the injury was a foreseeable result of the defendant's conduct or whether another cause "intervened" to bring about the harm. To appreciate fully the philosophical complexities of proximate causation, we have to look briefly at these limiting principles.

As a useful reference point, consider the facts of *Derdiarian v. Felix Contracting Co.*[2] (included in "Cases for Further Reflection" at the end of the chapter). Plaintiff Derdiarian worked as a subcontractor for Felix Contracting. Felix was installing an underground gas main along a highway, and Derdiarian testified that he requested to set up his work area on the side of the pipeline excavation away from oncoming traffic. Felix's foreman instructed Derdiarian to work on the opposite side, only a few feet from the oncoming lane. A passing motorist suffered an epileptic seizure and lost consciousness as he approached the excavation, hitting the plaintiff and throwing him into the air. When he landed, Derdiarian was splattered over his face, head, and body with 400-degree liquid enamel from a kettle struck by the careening auto. Although he reportedly "ignited into a fireball," Derdiarian miraculously survived. Felix disclaimed all responsibility, arguing that the plaintiff was injured in a freakish accident brought about by the motorist's negligence. (It was determined that the driver was under treatment for seizures but had neglected to take his medication.) Hence, Felix maintained, it had not proximately caused the plaintiff's injuries.

The issue of proximate cause in cases like *Derdiarian* can usefully be analyzed along four dimensions: (1) the type of accident involved, (2) the precise chain of events or causal mechanism, (3) the extent of the damage, and (4) the nature of the victim. A few general principles, corresponding to these dimensions, from the core of the law of proximate cause. However, as we will see, there are unresolved controversies within each area.

Type

A great many courts have held that a plaintiff's injuries are proximately caused by a defendant only if the harm that occurred was of a foreseeable type, meaning that the kind of harm suffered was just the kind of thing the defendant should have been guarding against. According to this rule, the defendant's liability extends only to the foreseeable risks of his or her negligence. In *Derdiarian*, for example, the court concluded that the "foreseeable, normal, and natural result of the risk created by Felix was the injury of a worker by a car," even though the exact sequence of events was unusual. Some courts have read the law differently. In one famous case, the defendant was off-loading planks from a ship's hold. His negligence caused one of the planks to slip and fall into the hold. The plank struck the bottom of the ship, caused a spark, and ignited gas vapors in the hold, resulting in a costly fire. The court acknowledged that a fire is not one of the things one would normally expect a falling plank to cause, but it held the defendant liable anyway, on the grounds that the fire was directly traceable to the defendant's actions.[3]

Causal Mechanism

Related to the foregoing, most courts have said that as long as the harm involved is of a foreseeable type, the precise chain of events leading up to it need not be foreseeable by the defendant in order for the defendant to be held liable. In one case, a barge owner had neglected to clean residue from the inside of an oil barge, leaving it full of explosive gas. A storm developed and a lightning bolt struck the ship, exploded the gas, and injured nearby workers. The lightning strike was unforeseeable, but the danger of an explosion should have been apparent to a reasonable person.[4] Similarly, in *Derdiarian*, the sequence of

---

[2] 414 N.E.2d 666 (1980).

[3] *In Re Polemis* 3 K.B. 560 (1921).
[4] *Johnson v. Kosmos Portland Cement Co.* 64 F.2d 193 (1933).

events was bizarre, but the resulting injury was a clearly foreseeable consequence of a vehicle's crashing into the work area. Yet, here again, there is controversy. How, for example, should the court rule if it is discovered that the explosion of gas in the barge was ignited by an arsonist, instead of by lightning? Wouldn't the explosion then really have been caused by the arsonist? In some cases, an intervening act has been held to "break the causal chain" linking the defendant's original negligence with the final injuries.

Extent of Damage

Suppose that the plaintiff is struck by the defendant in a fight. The defendant's blow would normally cause a bruise, but the wound would not be serious. However, unknown to the defendant, the plaintiff has a very thin skull, and the glancing blow actually kills him. When the extent of the injury goes beyond what the defendant might have expected, courts frequently impose liability anyway, on the theory that "you take your victim as you find him (her)."

Nature of the Victim

Suppose the defendant sets in motion a chain of events that winds up injuring someone the defendant could not have anticipated to be in danger. In most such cases, the rule adhered to is the one articulated by Judge Cardozo in *Palsgraf*: the defendant's actions can proximately injure only individuals foreseeably within the zone of risk created by the defendant's carelessness. Mrs. Palsgraf was not a foreseeable victim in this way, although the unfortunate plaintiff in *Derdiarian* certainly was.

What Should be Foreseen?

Clearly the idea that a harm or event is "foreseeable" plays a big role in the analysis of cause and effect in the law of tort. The *Lynch* and *Palsgraf* cases in your reading afford an opportunity to confront further puzzles concerning that notion. Is it always clear, for example, which harms would and which would not be foreseeable by a reasonable person? How are the foreseeable risks to be defined or described? Did Fisher's conduct in *Lynch* impose the clearly recognizable risk of *injury to motorists*, making Lynch's injury directly traceable to Fisher's conduct? If so, Fisher is liable. But why couldn't the facts be described this way: Fisher's

actions created an unforeseeable (and very small) risk of *bullet wounds to rescuers of deranged and gun-packing injured motorists*. In that way of describing what Fisher did, it seems clear that he could not be held liable. How should questions like this be resolved?

The Theory of Hart and Honoré

In the excerpt from their book *Causation in the Law*, included in the readings, philosophers H. L. A. Hart and A. M. Honoré take us deeper into the philosophical analysis and justification of causal language in the law. Hart and Honoré begin with the obvious fact that we all use causal language to describe the world: "He broke the window," "Oswald killed Kennedy," and so on. We make these kinds of judgments continually—in assigning responsibility, in reconstructing the past. Hart and Honoré defend the thesis that this ordinary causal language, our everyday, working understanding of "cause," includes distinctions and nuances that place limits on what we can truly be said to have caused. Hence, they reject the conclusion of Judge Andrews in *Palsgraf* that drawing such lines or defining such limits is purely a matter of arbitrary policy. The law both can and ought to reflect these common-sense ways of thinking.

Hart and Honoré begin their search for the implicit limiting principles of causal attribution with a paradigmatic case of causation: *A* throws a lighted match on some dry brush and soon a fire is blazing. Can the fire properly be attributed to *A*'s conduct despite the presence of other factors (oxygen in the air, wind, dryness), each of which were equally necessary to the final result? If so, why? We would all agree that *A*'s conduct caused the fire, but why are we justified in this conviction? Because, Hart and Honoré answer, the wind and other factors are merely part of the background circumstances, part of the total context in which *A* acted. The wind and oxygen are mere conditions, rather than causes. And what is the difference? Conditions such as oxygen in the air are not unusual or out of the ordinary. Hart and Honoré argue that the same tacit appeal to "normal" background conditions explains the following kind of case: *A* hits *B*, who falls to the ground, stunned. At precisely that moment, a tree topples on *B* and kills him. The collapse of the tree at that precise moment was not a normal condition, but rather a part of an abnormal conjunction of events, a coincidence for which *A* cannot be blamed. The same idea can be applied in a third kind of case: *A* throws a lighted match on some dry brush; just before the flames die out, *B* arrives and creates a blaze by pouring gasoline on the smoldering embers. Here we would not be inclined to classify *B*'s act as a mere condition or circumstance through which *A* acted. Why? Because *B* is an independent agent acting in the world. His voluntary and deliberate intervention "breaks" the causal chain linking *A* to the fire.

In Hart and Honoré's view, then, an act is the cause of harm if it is both necessary to the occurrence of the harm and sufficient to produce it without the cooperation of the voluntary or deliberate acts of others or abnormal conjunctions of events. In other words, if your conduct was a *sine qua non* of some harm, you caused it, unless another person voluntarily and deliberately intervened to produce the harm or an unusual combination of events conspired to give rise to the harm.

The Decline of Cause

As we have seen, the law of tort has traditionally required that a plaintiff who wishes to recover against a defendant establish three things: (1) that the plaintiff was injured; (2) that the defendant failed to exercise his or her duty of reasonable care; and (3) that, as a result, the defendant caused the plaintiff's injuries.

Exceptions to the second requirement continue to be recognized by the law; these are pockets of strict liability, in which defendants can find themselves liable for injuries brought on by their actions even if they were not "at fault" in failing to act reasonably and to exercise care for the well-being of others. Prominent among cases in which strict tort liability is imposed are those involving "ultrahazardous" activities (such as blasting) and those dealing with the manufacture and distribution of consumer goods (product liability). Strict tort liability endorses a view that Hart and Honoré call "causal maximalism": the view that the question "Who is responsible for this injury" is to be settled exclusively by reference to causal criteria.[5]

What about exceptions to the last of the requirements stated above, the requirement the *D* caused *P*'s injury? To abandon this requirement would be to embrace "causal minimalism": the idea that judgments about who caused an injury should play little or no

role in determining who is to be held responsible or liable for it. You might think that this is a demand the law could not sensibly endorse, but as Judith Thomson chronicles, a small but growing number of recent cases have taken just this position. The *Summers* and *Sindell* cases, explored in detail by Thomson, illustrate this trend. Moreover, as Thomson notes, a growing number of contemporary legal theorists have dismissed the causation requirement as unimportant when the true goals and aims of tort law are placed in proper perspective. The theorists to whom Thomson refers argue that the fundamental purpose of tort law is *economic*: to bring about an efficient allocation of social resources, a cost-justified level of accidents and safety.

Assuming that cause is thus "declining" in the law, is this good or bad from a moral point of view? Thomson's essay sets out to answer this question by taking note of a parallel trend: the decline of cause in moral theory. Thomson is suspicious of both trends and tries to identify the source of her unease.

The ruling in *Summers v. Tice,* Thomson believes, illustrates the declining importance of cause in tort doctrine. The case involved two defendants, Tice and Simonson, who were both hunting quail. A quail was flushed and both defendants fired negligently in the direction of Summers; one shot struck him in the eye. The defendants were roughly equidistant from Summers and were using the same type of gun and shot; it was not possible to determine from which gun the pellet in Summers's eye had come. The Supreme Court of California argued that the standard practice of placing the burden of proof upon the plaintiff to establish that a specific person caused his injury had to be abandoned in this case because to stick with it would leave Summers without a remedy. The burden must be shifted to the defendants to prove that they did not cause the injury. If they cannot, each is liable.

Thomson tries to articulate the moral position of those who agree with *Summers* and similar decisions: It doesn't matter that Tice didn't cause Summers's injury (if in fact it wasn't he) or that Simonson didn't cause Summers's injury (if in fact it wasn't he). What matters is that they both acted (equally) badly; and for that they should each have to pay. Thomson seeks to relate this view to the Kantian position that one's intention, one's "will," and not the results or effects of one's conduct should matter to its moral worth.

Responding to those who support the waning of cause, both in law and in our moral outlook, Thomson attempts to isolate the basis of the conviction that

---

[5]See *Causation in the Law,* 2nd ed. (Oxford: Clarendon Press, 1985), pp. lxxiii–lxxvii.

cause does matter. We simply *do* judge more harshly a person who, while acting badly, causes injury or death than a person who, acting equally badly, does not cause injury or death. Why? Because the first, but not the second, is to blame for what he or she has caused. Thomson tries to blunt the criticism that enhancing or enlarging the liability of the bad actor who just happens to hit the target rather than miss makes liability turn on sheer luck. It is more than sheer bad luck that makes one bad actor the cause of the injury and another not: The actor's own negligence helped to produce that result.

Lynch v. Fisher

Hardy, Judge.

This matter comes before us on appeal from judgment of the Eleventh Judicial District Court of Louisiana sustaining exceptions of no cause or right of action filed on behalf of all defendants and dismissing plaintiff's action as of nonsuit.

The allegations of the petition which are placed at issue as to their sufficiency in setting forth the cause of action in the exceptions referred to, and which set forth the facts upon which plaintiff's action is based, may be summarized as follows:

That about 9:00 P.M. on July 3, 1945, an employee of the defendants, Wheless and Fisher, (whose insurer is the defendant, Lumbermen's Mutual Casualty Company of Chicago, Ill.) at the time engaged within the general scope and course of his employment, parked a pulpwood truck which he was driving on the right-hand side of highway No. 171, some twelve miles north of Mansfield, De Soto Parish, Louisiana;

That, while said truck was thus parked, a passenger car owned and driven by the defendant, Robert Joe Gunter, collided violently with the rear end thereof;

That the driver of the parked truck was guilty of negligence, imputable to his employers, on numerous grounds, specifically in parking the truck entirely on the highway without leaving a clearance of fifteen feet on the pavement; in failing to have warning lights on the parked truck; in leaving the truck parked on the highway, thereby constituting a menace to traffic, and in failing to set out flares, or to have same available and ready for service.

That the negligence of the defendant, Robert Joe Gunter, consisted of driving and operating his automobile at an excessive, unreasonable and unlawful rate of speed; in failing to keep and maintain a proper lookout; operating his vehicle without adequate brakes; and failing to take any action to avoid the collision;

That the concurrent acts of negligence of the driver of the truck and the driver of the passenger car were the proximate causes of the accident;

That plaintiff seeing the collision ran to the scene thereof, succeeded in opening the doors of the badly damaged Gunter car, and, with the aid of another party, extricated both Mrs. Gunter and the defendant, Robert Joe Gunter, from the automobile, which had meanwhile caught fire;

That, in the effort to further assist the fatally injured Mrs. Gunter, plaintiff attempted to pull a floor mat out of the car to be used as a cushion for her head as she lay upon the roadside; that in the performance of this act plaintiff found a pistol on the floor of the car and handed the same to the defendant Gunter, who, being delirious and temporarily mentally deranged by reason of the shock of the accident, fired the pistol at plaintiff, the bullet passing through plaintiff's left ankle and inflicting serious injuries, for which damages are claimed in this action.

. . .

Determination of the issue of proximate cause must of necessity be considered with relation to the allied doctrine of intervening cause which is clearly material under the alleged facts of this case.

It is quite true, as contended by learned counsel for defendants, as a general proposition of law that only that negligence which directly causes the injury is

---

34 So. 2d 513 (1949), Louisiana Court of Appeal.

deemed to be proximate. But a resolution of this point must perforce depend upon the particular facts of each case.

In the matter before us there are three elements that must be determined:

(a) Did the original negligence of the driver of the parked truck set in motion a chain of circumstances following consecutively one upon the other which led to plaintiff's injury?

(b) Was the act of original negligence superseded by an intervening act breaking the chain of causation leading to plaintiff's injury?

(c) Is the fact that plaintiff's injuries resulted from an improbable and unforeseeable incident sufficient to eliminate the original act of negligence from consideration as a proximate cause?

The answer to these queries will dispose of all the claims based upon the doctrines of proximate and intervening causes and foreseeability.

Upon the basis of the allegations there is no room for any reasonable contravention of the proposition that the circumstances following the negligent parking of the truck down to the removal of the pistol from the car by plaintiff were natural, probable and reasonably to be expected. But at this point an imponderable enters into consideration. The rescuer hands a pistol to the rescued and is shot by the latter. Certainly under the general rule, this action could not be within the reasonable contemplation of any normal individual and the specific incident therefore could not be imputed to the negligent truck driver as a probable result flowing from his negligence. But, unfortunately, the proposition does not admit of being disposed of so easily, for it is well established in the jurisprudence of the State of Louisiana and a majority of other jurisdictions that the general rule must yield to specific instances.

Of course, no Court could reasonably hold that the driver of a vehicle, no matter how gross his negligence, could have contemplated the shooting of a third party as a normal and natural result of such negligence. Nor, indeed, could the rescuer himself be held to have assumed the risk of such a strange, unnatural and unusual result flowing from his gallant efforts.

But, if the results of accidents were normal, usual and predictable, the burden of both Bar and Bench would be immeasurably lighter.

To determine whether or not the shooting incident is susceptible of being distinguished and set apart from the general law of proximate cause, we must base our conclusions not upon those elements which would be applicable as between parties to the collision itself but as affecting the injury inflicted upon an innocent third party, himself without fault.

Let us assume that plaintiff in this case, rushing to the aid of helpless parties occupying the automobile involved in the collision, in the darkness of night, and wrenching open the door of the vehicle, had been severely bitten by a dog which was accompanying the occupants of the car and which had been so frightened or injured by the shock of the collision as to have lost its accustomed gentleness. Could it be said that such a result was proximately caused by the negligence of the truck driver because such a possibility was normally an expectable or foreseeable result of such negligence? The answer is obvious. Scores of cars might have collided with the rear end of this particular truck on this particularly well-traveled main highway without producing such a result.

Similarly, the laws of probability were overwhelmingly against the occurrence of the character and nature of the incident and resulting injury to plaintiff under the actual facts of this case. But, certainly, plaintiff is without fault, and, certainly, the negligence of some party or the concurrent negligence of several parties combined to set up the unfortunate situation which resulted in his injury.

In our opinion the general doctrine of proximate cause cannot be applied under the alleged facts and chain of circumstances herein presented. Under the tenor of the allegation it is quite clear that plaintiff would not have been shot if originally the truck driver had not negligently parked his truck in such manner as to constitute a menace and hazard to vehicles rightfully traveling the highway.

. . . The proximate cause of the injury to one who voluntarily interposes to save the lives of persons imperiled by the negligence of others is the negligence which causes the peril. . . .

. . . In determining the question as to the efficiency of the intervening act, that is, in this case, the shooting of plaintiff by one of the defendants, we must consider the well-established principle that an intervening cause is not necessarily a superseding cause. The intervening cause, in order to supersede original negligence, must have alone produced injury.

Under paragraph (B) of the Common on Section 440 of the Restatement of the Law of Torts this proposition is set forth: "Therefore, if in looking back from the harm and tracing the sequence of events by which it was produced, it is found that a superseding cause has operated, there is no need of determining whether the actor's antecedent conduct was or was not a substantial factor in bringing about the harm."

In the instant case there is no question but that in tracing back from the point of the actual injury to plaintiff we would ordinarily be compelled to conclude that the shooting by one of the defendants was unquestionably a superseding cause were it not for the allegation that the defendant inflicting the injury at the time was temporarily insane by reason of shock resulting from the collision caused by the initial negligence of the truck driver.

Section 455 of the Restatement of the Law of Torts submits the principle:

"If the actor's negligent conduct so brings about the delirium or insanity of another as to make the actor liable for it, the actor is also liable for harm done by the other to himself while delirious or insane, if his delirium or insanity.

(a) Prevents him from realizing the nature of his act. . . .

. . . We think it must logically and inevitably follow that under such circumstances the actor is not only liable for harm done in a fit of delirium or insanity by such deranged person to himself, but also for any harm caused by him to another."

In discussing proximate cause the opinion in *Cruze v. Harvey & Jones* . . . : "The nearest independent cause which is adequate to, and does, produce the result, is the proximate cause of the accident, and supersedes all remote causes."

From this principle, with respect to the facts applicable to the case under consideration, the opinion stated: "The nearest independent cause which produced the death of this mule was the open, unprotected well, and this supersedes all other remote causes, among which may have been the open gap through which the mule escaped."

In *Lee v. Powell Bros. & Sanders Co.,* . . . the Court said: "For severing the legal connection between the negligence by which such an imminent danger was created and the injury that has resulted from it the intervening voluntary act of some person responsible for his acts would have to be shown."

In every consideration of the point which has come to our attention in the study of this case, the qualities of the relieving or superseding act are repeatedly and unfailingly designated as being intervening and voluntary, by a person responsible for his acts.

. . . Since we must accept the well pleaded allegations of the petition as being true for the purpose of determining the exception, we are constrained to hold

that plaintiff has met the requirements established by these several factors and has negatived the possibility that the act which immediately resulted in the harm was the voluntary action of a person responsible for his acts.

Under the allegations of the petition it is inescapable that plaintiff has properly alleged that the defendant Gunter was mentally deranged and rendered temporarily insane as the result of the collision of his car with the parked truck. Plaintiff by his allegations has further definitely asserted that such a condition was brought about by the concurrent negligence of the several defendants. In order to affirm the holding of the lower court it would be necessary for us to find that the temporary insanity of the defendant Gunter, which led to the shooting, was not caused by the collision. Clearly, this is a question of fact to be determined by trial on the merits, and, meanwhile, any conclusion must be governed by the plain allegations of the petition.

Any attempt to determine at what point, with relation to the actual injury to plaintiff, the negligence of the original actor, namely, the driver of the truck, ceased and a new and independent tortious act intervened and superseded the original negligence, conclusively impresses us with the impossibility of such a severance of causes. The chain is complete and whole, link by link, and though tested with the utmost care no break is revealed in the succession of circumstances.

The consecutive order of the related circumstances and events may be briefly outlined:

(1) Negligence of the truck driver in parking his truck on the highway, resulting in

(2) Collision, superinduced by the concurrent negligence of the defendant Gunter, resulting in

(3) (a) Attempted rescue by the plaintiff.

(b) Temporary mental derangement of the defendant Gunter as a result of the shock of the collision, resulting in

(4) The shooting of plaintiff and the injury sustained thereby.

If there is any break in the continuity of the incidents flowing from the original act of negligence, we are unable to point out such a circumstance.

. . .

We make no attempt to minimize the unusual and improbable character of the incident which is alleged to have occurred in the case before us.

The facts set forth are additional evidence of the truth of the adage that "truth is stranger than fiction."

We do not believe that the theory of foreseeability is applicable to the facts of this case. Referring again to the Restatement of the Law of Torts, we find in Section 435 a plain and unambiguous statement of the principle which refutes the requirement of foreseeability: "If the actor's conduct is a substantial factor in bringing about harm to another, the fact that the actor neither foresaw nor should have foreseen the extent of the harm or the manner in which it occurred does not prevent him from being liable."

. . .

Palsgraf v. Long Island Railroad

Cardozo, [Chief Judge].

Plaintiff was standing on a platform of defendant's railroad after buying a ticket to go to Rockaway Beach. A train stopped at the station, bound for another place. Two men ran forward to catch it. One of the men reached the platform of the car without mishap, though the train was already moving. The other man, carrying a package, jumped aboard the car, but seemed unsteady as if about to fall. A guard on the car, who had held the door open, reached forward to help him in, and another guard on the platform pushed him from behind. In this act, the package was dislodged, and fell upon the rails. It was a package of small size, about fifteen inches long, and was covered by a newspaper. In fact it contained fireworks, but there was nothing in its appearance to give notice of its contents. The fireworks when they fell exploded. The shock of the explosion threw down some scales at the other end of the platform, many feet away. The scales struck the plaintiff, causing injuries for which she sues.

The conduct of the defendant's guard, if a wrong in its relation to the holder of the package, was not a wrong in its relation to the plaintiff, standing far away. Relatively to her it was not negligence at all. Nothing in the situation gave notice that the falling package had in it the potency of peril to persons thus removed. Negligence is not actionable unless it involves the invasion of a legally protected interest, the violation of a right. "Proof of negligence in the air, so to speak, will not do." "Negligence is the absence of care, according to the circumstances." The plaintiff as she stood upon the platform of the station might claim to be protected against intentional invasion of her bodily security. Such invasion is not charged. She might claim to be protected against unintentional invasion by conduct involving in the thought of reasonable men an unreasonable hazard that such invasion would ensue. These, from the point of view of the law, were the bounds of her immunity, with perhaps some rare exceptions, survivals for the most part of ancient forms of liability, where conduct is held to be at the peril of the actor (*Sullivan v. Dunham* . . .). If no hazard was apparent to the eye of ordinary vigilance, an act innocent and harmless, at least to outward seeming, with reference to her, did not take to itself the quality of a tort because it happened to be a wrong, though apparently not one involving the risk of bodily insecurity, with reference to some one else. "In every instance, before negligence can be predicated of a given act, back of the act must be sought and found a duty to the individual complaining, the observance of which would have averted or avoided the injury." "The ideas of negligence and duty are strictly correlative." (Bowen, L. J., in *Thomas v. Quartermaine* . . .). The plaintiff sues in her own right for a wrong personal to her, and not as the vicarious beneficiary of a breach of duty to another.

A different conclusion will involve us, and swiftly too, in a maze of contradictions. A guard stumbles over a package which has been left upon a platform. It seems to be a bundle of newspapers. It turns out to be a can of dynamite. To the eye of ordinary vigilance, the bundle is abandoned waste, which may be kicked or trod on with impunity. Is a passenger at the other end of the platform protected by the law against the unsuspected hazard concealed beneath the waste? If not, is

248 N.Y. 339 (1928), New York Court of Appeals.

the result to be any different, so far as the distant passenger is concerned, when the guard stumbles over a valise which a truckman or a porter has left upon the walk? The passenger far away, if the victim of a wrong at all, has a cause of action, not derivative, but original and primary. His claim to be protected against invasion of his bodily security is neither greater nor less because the act resulting in the invasion is a wrong to another far removed. In this case, the rights that are said to have been violated, the interests said to have been invaded, are not even of the same order. The man was not injured in his person nor even put in danger. The purpose of the act, as well as its effect, was to make his person safe. If there was a wrong to him at all, which may very well be doubted, it was a wrong to a property interest only, the safety of his package. Out of this wrong to property, which threatened injury to nothing else, there has passed, we are told, to the plaintiff by derivation or succession a right of action for the invasion of an interest of another order, the right to bodily security. The diversity of interests emphasizes the futility of the effort to build the plaintiff's right upon the basis of a wrong to some one else. The gain is one of emphasis, for a like result would follow if the interests were the same. Even then, the orbit of the danger as disclosed to the eye of reasonable vigilance would be the orbit of the duty. One who jostles one's neighbor in a crowd does not invade the rights of others standing at the outer fringe when the unintended contact casts a bomb upon the ground. The wrongdoer, as to them is the man who carries the bomb, not the one who explodes it without suspicion of the danger. Life will have to be made over, and human nature transformed, before prevision so extravagant can be accepted as the norm of conduct, the customary standard to which behavior must conform.

The argument for the plaintiff is built upon the shifting meanings of such words as "wrong" and "wrongful," and shares their instability. What the plaintiff must show is "a wrong" to herself, *i.e.*, a violation of her own right, and not merely a wrong to some one else, nor conduct "wrongful" because unsocial, but not "a wrong" to any one. We are told that one who drives at reckless speed through a crowded city street is guilty of a negligent act and, therefore, of a wrongful one irrespective of the consequences. Negligent the act is, and wrongful in the sense that it is unsocial, but wrongful and unsocial in relation to other travelers, only because the eye of vigilance perceives the risk of damage. If the same act were to be committed on a speedway or a race course, it would lose its wrongful quality. The risk reasonably to be perceived defines the duty to be obeyed, and risk imports relation; it is risk to another or to others within the range of apprehension. . . . This does not mean, of course, that one who launches a destructive force is always relieved of liability if the force, though known to be destructive, pursues an unexpected path. It was not necessary that the defendant should have had notice of the particular method in which an accident would occur, if the possibility of an accident was clear to the ordinarily prudent eye. . . . Some acts such as shooting, are so imminently dangerous to any one who may come within reach of the missile, however unexpectedly, as to impose a duty of prevision not far from that of an insurer. Even today, and much oftener in earlier stages of the law, one acts sometimes at one's peril. Under this head, it may be, fall certain cases of what is known as transferred intent, an act willfully dangerous to A resulting by misadventure in injury to B. These cases aside, wrong is defined in terms of the natural or probable, at least when unintentional. The range of reasonable apprehension is at times a question for the court, and at times, if varying inferences are possible, a question for the jury. Here, by concession, there was nothing in the situation to suggest to the most cautious mind that the parcel wrapped in newspaper would spread wreckage through the station. If the guard had thrown it down knowingly and willfully, he would not have threatened the plaintiff's safety, so far as appearances could warn him. His conduct would not have involved, even then, an unreasonable probability of invasion of her bodily security. Liability can be no greater where the act is inadvertent.

Negligence, like risk, is thus a term of relation. Negligence in the abstract, apart from things related, is surely not a tort, if indeed it is understandable at all. Negligence is not a tort unless it results in the commission of a wrong, and the commission of a wrong imports the violation of a right, in this case, we are told, the right to be protected against interference with one's bodily security. But bodily security is protected, not against all forms of interference or aggression, but only against some. One who seeks redress at law does not make out a cause of action by showing without more that there has been damage to his person. If the harm was not willful, he must show that the act as to him had possibilities of danger so many and apparent as to entitle him to be protected against the doing of it though the harm was unintended. Affront to personality is still the keynote of the wrong. Confirmation of this view will be found in the history and development of the action on the case. Negligence as a basis of civil liability was unknown to medieval law. For damage to the person, the sole remedy was trespass, and trespass did not lie in the absence of aggression, and that direct and personal. Liability for other damage, as where a servant without orders from the master does or omits something to the damage of another, is a plant of later growth. When it emerged out of the legal soil, it was thought of as a variant of trespass, an offshoot of the parent stock. This appears in the form of action, which was known as trespass on the case. The victim does not sue derivatively, or by right of subrogation, to vindicate an interest invaded in the person of another. Thus to view his cause of action is to ignore the fundamental difference between tort and crime. He sues for breach of a duty owing to himself.

The law of causation, remote or proximate, is thus foreign to the case before us. The question of liability is always anterior to the question of the measure of the consequences that go with liability. If there is no tort to be redressed, there is no occasion to consider what damage might be recovered if there were a finding of a tort. We may assume, without deciding, that negligence, not at large or in the abstract, but in relation to the plaintiff, would entail liability for any and all consequences, however novel or extraordinary. There is room for argument that a distinction is to be drawn according to the diversity of interests invaded by the act, as where conduct negligent in that it threatens an insignificant invasion of an interest in property results in an unforeseeable invasion of an interest of another order, as *e.g.*, one of bodily security. Perhaps other distinctions may be necessary. We do not go into the question now. The consequences to be followed must first be rooted in a wrong.

The judgment of the Appellate Division and that of the Trial Term should be reversed, and the complaint dismissed, with costs in all courts.

. . .

Andrews, [Judge] (dissenting).

Assisting a passenger to board a train, the defendant's servant negligently knocked a package from his arms. It fell between the platform and the cars. Of its contents the servant knew and could know nothing. A violent explosion followed. The concussion broke some scales standing a considerable distance away. In falling they injured the plaintiff, an intending passenger.

Upon these facts may she recover the damages she has suffered in an action brought against the master? The result we shall reach depends upon our theory as to the nature of negligence. Is it a relative concept—the breach of some duty owing to a particular person or to particular persons? Or where there is an act which unreasonably threatens the safety of others, is the doer liable for all its proximate consequences, even where they result in injury to one who would generally be thought to be outside the radius of danger? This not a mere dispute as to words. We might not believe that to the average mind the dropping of the bundle would seem to involve the probability of harm to the plaintiff standing many feet away whatever might be the case as to the owner or to one so near as to be likely to be struck by its fall. If, however, we adopt the second hypothesis we have to inquire only as to the relation between cause and effect. We deal in terms of proximate cause, not of negligence.

Negligence may be defined roughly as an act or omission which unreasonably does or may affect the rights of others, or which unreasonably fails to protect oneself from the dangers resulting from such acts. Here I confine myself to the first branch of the definition. Nor do I comment on the word "unreasonable." For present purposes it sufficiently describes that average conduct that society requires of its members.

There must be both the act or the omission, and the right. It is the act itself, not the intent of the actor, that is important. In criminal law both the intent and the result are to be considered. Intent again is material in tort actions, where punitive damages are sought, dependent on actual malice—not on merely reckless conduct. But here neither insanity nor infancy lessens responsibility.

As has been said, except in cases of contributory negligence, there must be rights which are or may be affected. Often though injury has occurred, no rights of him who suffers have been touched. A licensee or trespasser upon my land has no claim to affirmative care on my part that the land be made safe. Where a railroad is required to fence its tracks against cattle, no man's rights are injured should he wander upon the road because such fence is absent. An unborn child may not demand immunity from personal harm.

But we are told that "there is no negligence unless there is in the particular case a legal duty to take care, and this duty must be one which is owed to the plaintiff himself and not merely to others." This, I think too narrow a conception. Where there is the unreasonable act, and some right that may be affected there is negligence whether damage does or does not result. That is immaterial. Should we drive down Broadway at a reckless speed, we are negligent whether we strike an approaching car or miss it by an inch. The act itself is wrongful. It is a wrong not only to those who happen to be within the radius of danger but to all who might have been there—a wrong to the public at large. Such is the language of the street. Such the language of the courts when speaking of contributory negligence. Such again and again their language in speaking of the duty of some defendant and discussing proximate cause in cases where such a discussion is wholly irrelevant on any other theory. As was said by Mr. Justice Holmes many years ago, "the measure of the defendant's duty in determining whether a wrong has been committed is one thing, the measure of liability when a wrong has been committed is another." Due care is a duty imposed on each one of us to protect society from unnecessary danger, not to protect A, B or C alone.

It may well be that there is no such thing as negligence in the abstract. "Proof of negligence in the air, so to speak, will not do." In an empty world negligence would not exist. It does involve a relationship between man and his fellows. But not merely a relationship between man and those whom he might reasonably expect his act would injure. Rather, a relationship between him and those whom he does in fact injure. If his act has a tendency to harm some one, it harms him a mile away as surely as it does those on the scene. We now permit children to recover for the negligent killing of the father. It was never prevented on the theory that no duty was owing to them. A husband may be compensated for the loss of his wife's services. To say the wrongdoer was negligent as to the husband as well as to the wife is merely an attempt to fit facts to theory. An insurance company paying a fire loss recovers its payment of the negligent incendiary. We speak of subrogation—of suing in the right of the insured. Behind the cloud of words is the fact they hide, that the act, wrongful as to the insured, has also injured the company. Even if it be true that the fault of father, wife or insured will prevent recovery, it is because we consider the original negligence not the proximate cause of the injury.

In the well-known *Polemis* case (1921, 3 K. B. 560), Scrutton, L. J., said that the dropping of a plank was negligent for it might injure "workman or cargo or ship." Because of either possibility the owner of the vessel was to be made good for his loss. The act being wrongful the doer was liable for its proximate results. Criticized and explained as this statement may have been, I think it states the law as it should be and as it is.

The proposition is this. Every one owes to the world at large the duty of refraining from those acts that may unreasonably threaten the safety of others. Such an act occurs. Not only is he wronged to whom harm might reasonably be expected to result, but he also who is in fact injured, even if he be outside what would generally be thought the danger zone. There needs to be duty due the one complaining but this is not a duty to a particular individual because as to him harm might be expected. Harm to some one being the natural result of the act, not only that one alone, but all those in fact injured may complain. We have never, I think, held otherwise. Indeed in the *DiCaprio* case we said that a breach of a general ordinance defining the degree of care to be exercised in one's calling is evidence of negligence as to every one. We did not limit this statement to those who might be expected to be exposed to danger. Unreasonable risk being taken, its consequences are not confined to those who might probably be hurt.

If this be so, we do not have a plaintiff suing by "derivation or succession." Her action is original and primary. Her claim is for a breach of duty to herself—not that she is subrogated to any right of action of the owner of the parcel or of a passenger standing at the scene of the explosion.

The right to recover damages rests on additional considerations. The plaintiff's rights must be injured, and this injury must be caused by the negligence. We build a dam, but are negligent as to its foundations. Breaking, it injures property down stream. We are not liable if all this happened because of some reason other than the insecure foundation. But when injuries do result from our unlawful act we are liable for the consequences. It does not matter that they are unusual, unexpected, unforeseen and unforeseeable. But there is one limitation. The damages must be so connected with the negligence that the latter may be said to be the proximate cause of the former.

These two words have never been given an inclusive definition. What is a cause in a legal sense, still more what is a proximate cause, depend in each case upon many considerations, as does the existence of negligence itself. Any philosophical doctrine of causation does not help us. A boy throws a stone into a pond. The ripples spread. The water level rises. The history of that pond is altered to all eternity. It will be altered by other causes also. Yet it will be forever the resultant of all causes combined. Each one will have an influence. How great only omniscience can say. You may speak of a chain, or if you please, a net. An analogy is of little aid. Each cause brings about future events. Without each the future would not be the same. Each is proximate in the sense it is essential. But that is not what we mean by the word. Nor on the other hand do we mean sole cause. There is no such thing.

Should analogy be thought helpful, however, I prefer that of a stream. The spring, starting on its journey, is joined by tributary after tributary. The river, reaching the ocean, comes from a hundred sources. No man may say whence any drop of water is derived. Yet for a time distinction may be possible. Into the clear creek, brown swamp water flows from the left. Later, from the right comes water stained by its clay bed. The three may remain for a space, sharply divided. But at last, inevitably no trace of separation remains. They are so comingled that all distinction is lost.

As we have said, we cannot trace the effect of an act to the end, if end there is. Again, however, we may trace it part of the way. A murder at Sarajevo may be the necessary antecedent to an assassination in London twenty years hence. An overturned lantern may burn all Chicago. We may follow the fire from the shed to the last building. We rightly say the fire started by the lantern caused its destruction.

A cause, but not the proximate cause. What we do mean by the word "proximate" is, that because of convenience, of public policy, of a rough sense of justice, the law arbitrarily declines to trace a series of events beyond a certain point. This is not logic, it is practical politics. Take our rule as to fires. Sparks from my burning haystack set on fire my house and my neighbor's. I may recover from a negligent railroad. He may not. Yet the wrongful act as directly harmed the one as the other. We may regret that the line was drawn just where it was, but drawn somewhere it had to be. We said the act of the railroad was not the proximate cause of our neighbor's fire. Cause it surely was. The words we used were simply indicative of our notions of public policy. Other courts think differently. But somewhere they reach the point where they cannot say the stream comes from any one source.

Take the illustration given in an unpublished manuscript by a distinguished and helpful writer on the law of torts. A chauffeur negligently collides with another car which is filled with dynamite, although he could not know it. An explosion follows. *A*, walking on the sidewalk nearby, is killed. *B*, sitting in a window of a building opposite, is cut by flying glass. *C*, likewise sitting in a window a block away, is similarly injured. And a further illustration. A nursemaid, ten blocks away, startled by the noise, involuntarily drops a baby from her arms to the walk. We are told that *C* may not recover while *A* may. As to *B* it is a question for court or jury. We will all agree that the baby might not. Because, we are again told, the chauffeur had no reason to believe his conduct involved any risk of injuring either *C* or the baby. As to them he was not negligent.

But the chauffeur, being negligent in risking the collision, his belief that the scope of the harm he might do would be limited is immaterial. His act unreasonably jeopardized the safety of any one who might be affected by it. *C*'s injury and that of the baby were directly traceable to the collision. Without that, the injury would not have happened. *C* had the right to sit in his office, secure from such dangers. The baby was entitled to use the sidewalk with reasonable safety.

The true theory is, it seems to me, that the injury to *C*, if in truth he is to be denied recovery, and the injury to the baby is that their several injuries were not the proximate result of the negligence. And here not what the chauffeur had reason to believe would be the result of his conduct, but what the prudent would foresee, may have a bearing. May have some bearing, for the problem of proximate cause is not to be solved by any one consideration.

It is all a question of expediency. There are no fixed rules to govern our judgment. There are simply matters of which we may take account. We have in a somewhat different connection spoken of "the stream of events." We have asked whether that stream was deflected—whether it was forced into new and unexpected channels. This is rather rhetoric than law. There is in truth little to guide us other than common sense.

There are some hints that may help us. The proximate cause, involved as it may be with many other causes, must be, at the least, something without which the event would not happen. The court must ask itself whether there was a natural and continuous sequence between cause and effect. Was the one a substantial factor in producing the other? Was there a direct connection between them, without too many intervening causes? Is the effect of cause on result not too attenuated? Is the cause likely, in the usual judgment of mankind, to produce the result? Or by the exercise of prudent foresight could the result be foreseen? Is the result too remote from the cause, and here we consider remoteness in time and space, where we passed upon the construction of a contract—but something was also said on this subject. Clearly we must so consider, for the greater the distance either in time or space, the more surely do other causes intervene to affect the result. When a lantern is overturned the firing of a shed is a fairly direct consequence. Many things contribute to the spread of the conflagration—the force of the wind, the direction and width of streets, the character of intervening structures, other factors. We draw an uncertain and wavering line, but draw it we must as best we can.

Once again, it is all a question of fair judgment, always keeping in mind the fact that we endeavor to make a rule in each case that will be practical and in keeping with the general understanding of mankind.

Here another question must be answered. In the case supposed it is said, and said correctly, that the chauffeur is liable for the direct effect of the explosion although he had no reason to suppose it would follow a collision. "The fact that the injury occurred in a different manner than that which might have been expected does not prevent the chauffeur's negligence from being in law the cause of the injury." But the natural results of a negligent act—the results which a prudent man would or should foresee—do have a bearing upon the decision as to proximate cause. We have said so repeatedly. What should be foreseen? No human foresight would suggest that a collision itself might injure one a block away. On the contrary, given an explosion, such a possibility might be reasonably expected. I think the direct connection, the foresight of which the courts speak, assumes prevision of the explosion, for the immediate results of which, at least, the chauffeur is responsible.

It may be said this is unjust. Why? In fairness he should make good every injury flowing from his negligence. Not because of tenderness toward him we say he need not answer for all that follows his wrong. We look back to the catastrophe, the fire kindled by the spark, or the explosion. We trace the consequences—not indefinitely, but to a certain point. And to aid us in fixing that point we ask what might ordinarily be expected to follow the fire or the explosion.

This last suggestion is the factor which must determine the case before us. The act upon which defendant's liability rests is knocking an apparently harmless package onto the platform. The act was negligent. For its proximate consequences the defendant is liable. If its contents were broken, to the owner; if it fell upon and crushed a passenger's foot, then to him. If it exploded and injured one in the immediate vicinity, to him also as to A in the illustration. Mrs. Palsgraf was standing some distance away. How far cannot be told from the record—apparently twenty-five or thirty feet. Perhaps less. Except for the explosion, she would not have been injured. We are told by the appellant in his brief, "it cannot be denied that the explosion was the direct cause of the plaintiff's injuries." So it was a substantial factor in producing the result—there was here a natural and continuous sequence—direct connection. The only intervening cause was that instead of blowing her to the ground the concussion smashed the weighing machine which in turn fell upon her. There was no remoteness in time, little in space. And surely, given such an explosion as here it needed no great foresight to predict that the natural result would be to injure one on the platform at no greater distance from its scene than was the plaintiff. Just how no one might be able to predict. Whether by flying fragments, by broken glass, by wreckage of machines or structure no one could say. But injury in some form was most probable.

Under these circumstances I cannot say as a matter of law that the plaintiff's injuries were not the proximate result of the negligence. That is all we have before us. The court refused to so charge. No request was made to submit the matter to the jury as a question of fact, even would that have been proper upon the record before us.

The judgment appealed from should be affirmed, with costs.

Pound, Lehman and Kellogg, [Judges], concur with Cardozo, [Chief Judge], Andrews, [Judge], dissents in opinion in which Crane and O'Brien, [Judges], concur.

Judgment reversed, etc.

Tracing Consequences

H. L. A. Hart and A. M. Honore

Tracing Consequences

"To consequences no limit can be set": "Every event which would not have happened if an earlier event had not happened is the consequence of that earlier event." These two propositions are not equivalent in meaning and are not equally or in the same way at variance with ordinary thought. They have, however, both been urged sometimes in the same breath by the legal theorist and the philosopher: they are indeed sometimes said by lawyers to be "the philosophical doctrine" of causation. It is perhaps not difficult even for the layman to accept the first proposition as a truth about certain physical events; an explosion may cause a flash of light which will be propagated as far as the outer nebulae; its effects or consequences continue indefinitely. It is, however, a different matter to accept the view that whenever a man is murdered with a gun his death was the consequence of (still less an "effect" of or "caused by") the manufacture of the bullet. The first tells a perhaps unfamiliar tale about unfamiliar events; the second introduces an unfamiliar, though, of course, a possible way of speaking about familiar events. It is not that this unrestricted use of "consequence" is unintelligible or never found; it is indeed used to refer to bizarre or fortuitous connections or coincidences: but the point is that the various causal notions employed for the purposes of explanation, attribution of responsibility, or the assessment of contributions to the course of history carry with them implicit limits which are similar in these different employments.

It is, then, the second proposition, defining consequence in terms of "necessary condition," with which theorists are really concerned. This proposition is the corollary of the view that, if we look into the past of any given event, there is an infinite number of events, each of which is a necessary condition of the given event and so, as much as any other, is its cause. This is the "cone"[1] of causation, so called because, since any event has a number of simultaneous conditions, the series fans out as we go back in time. The justification, indeed only partial, for calling this "the philosophical doctrine" of causation is that is resembles Mill's doctrine that "we have no right to give the name of cause to one of the conditions exclusive of the others of them." It differs from Mill's view in taking the essence of causation to be "necessary condition" and not "the sum total"[2] of the sufficient conditions of an event.

Legal theorists have developed this account of cause and consequence to show what is "factual," "objective," or "scientific" in these notions: this they call "cause in fact" and it is usually stressed as a preliminary to the doctrine that any more restricted application of these terms in the law represents nothing in the facts or in the meaning of causation, but expresses fluctuating legal policy or sentiments of what is just or convenient. Moral philosophers have insisted in somewhat similar terms that the consequences of human action are "infinite": this they have urged as an objection against the Utilitarian doctrine that the rightness of a morally right action depends on whether its consequences are better than those of any alternative action in the circumstances. "We should have to trace as far as possible the consequences not only for the persons affected directly but also for those indirectly affected and to these no limit can be set."[3] Hence, so the argument runs, we cannot either inductively establish the Utilitarian doctrine that right acts are "optimific" or use it in particular cases to discover what is right. Yet, however vulnerable at other points Utilitarianism may be as an account of moral judgment, this objection seems to rest on a mistake as to the sense of "consequence." The Utilitarian assertion that the rightness of an action depends on its consequences is not the same as the assertion that it depends on all those later occurrences which would

From H. L. A. Hart and A. M. Honore, *Causation in the Law,* 2nd ed. (Oxford: Clarendon Press, 1985), pp. 68–83. Reprinted by permission of Oxford University Press.

not have happened had the action not been done, to which indeed "no limit can be set." It is important to see that the issue here is not the linguistic one whether the word "consequence" would be understood if used in this way. The point is that, though we could, we do not think in this way in tracing connections between human actions and events. Instead, whenever we are concerned with such connections, whether for the purpose of explaining a puzzling occurrence, assessing responsibility, or giving an intelligible historical narrative, we employ a set of concepts restricting in various ways what counts as a consequence. These restrictions colour *all* our thinking in causal terms; when we find them in the law we are not finding something invented by or peculiar to the law, though of course it is for the law to say when and how far it will use them and, where they are vague, to supplement them.

No short account can be given of the limits thus placed on "consequences" because these limits vary, intelligibly, with the variety of causal connection asserted. Thus we may be tempted by the generalization that consequences must always be something intended or foreseen or at least foreseeable with ordinary care: but counter-examples spring up from many types of context where causal statements are made. If smoking is shown to cause lung cancer, this discovery will permit us to describe past as well as future cases of cancer as the effect or consequence of smoking even though no one foresaw or had reasonable grounds to suspect this in the past. What is common and commonly appreciated and hence foreseeable certainly controls the scope of consequences in certain varieties of causal statement but not in all. Again the voluntary intervention of a second person very often constitutes the limit. If a guest sits down at a table laid with knife and fork and plunges the knife into his hostess's breast, her death is not in any context other than a contrived one[4] thought of as caused by, or the effect or result of the waiter's action in laying the table; nor would it be linked with this action as its consequence for any of the purposes, explanatory or attributive, for which we employ causal notions. Yet as we have seen there are many other types of case where a voluntary action or the harm it does are naturally treated to the consequence of to some prior neglect or precaution. Finally, we may think that a simple answer is already supplied by Hume and Mill's doctrine that causal connection rests on general laws asserting regular connection; yet, even in the type of case to which this important doctrine applies, reference to it alone will

not solve our problem. For we often trace a causal connection between an antecedent and a consequent which themselves very rarely go together: we do this when the case can be broken down into intermediate stages, which themselves exemplify different generalizations, as when we find that the fall of a tile was the cause of someone's death, rare though this be. Here our problem reappears in the form of the question: When can generalizations be combined in this way?

We shall examine first the central type of case where the problem is of this last-mentioned form. Here the gist of the causal connection lies in the general connection with each other of the successive stages; and is not dependent on the special notions of one person providing another with reasons or exceptional opportunities for actions. This form of causal connection may exist between actions and events, and between purely physical events, and it is in such cases that the words "cause" and "causing" used of the antecedent action or event have their most obvious application. It is convenient to refer to cases of the first type where the consequence is harm as cases of "causing harm," and to refer to cases where harm is the consequence of one person providing another with reasons or opportunities for doing harm as cases of "inducing" or "occasioning" harmful acts. In cases of the first type a voluntary act, or a conjunction of events amounting to a coincidence, operates as a limit in the sense that events subsequent to these are not attributed to the antecedent action or event as its consequence even though they would not have happened without it. Often such a limiting action or coincidence is thought of and described as "intervening": and lawyers speak of them as "superseding" or "extraneous" causes "breaking the chain of causation." To see what these metaphors rest on (and in part obscure) and how such factors operate as a limit we shall consider the detail of three simple cases.

(i) A forest fire breaks out, and later investigation shows that shortly before the outbreak A had flung away a lighted cigarette into the bracken at the edge of the forest, the bracken caught fire, a light breeze got up, and fanned the flames in the direction of the forest. If, on discovering these facts, we hesitate before saying that A's action caused the forest fire this would be to consider the alternative hypothesis that in spite of appearances the fire only succeeded A's action in point of time, that the bracken flickered out harmlessly and the forest fire was caused by something else. To dispose of this it may be necessary to examine in further detail the process of events between the ignition of the bracken and the outbreak of fire in the forest and to show that these exemplified certain types of continuous change. If this is shown, there is no longer any room for doubt: A's action *was* the cause of the fire, whether he intended it or not. This seems and is the simplest of cases. Yet it is important to notice that even in applying our general knowledge to a case as simple as this, indeed in regarding it as simple, we make an implicit use of a distinction between types of factor which constitute a limit in tracing consequences and those which we regard as mere circumstances "through" which we trace them. For the breeze which sprang up after A dropped the cigarette, and without which the fire would not have spread to the forest, was not only subsequent to his action but entirely independent of it: it was, however, a common recurrent feature of the environment, and, as such, it is thought of not as an "intervening" force but as merely part of the circumstances in which the cause "operates." The decision so to regard it is implicitly taken when we combine our knowledge of the successive stages of the process and assert the connection.

It is easy to be misled by the natural metaphor of a causal "chain," which may lead us to think that the causal process consists of a series of single events each of which is dependent upon (would not have occurred without) its predecessor in the "chain" and so is dependent upon the initiating action or event. In truth in any causal process we have at each phase not single events but complex sets of conditions, and among these conditions are some which are not only subsequent to, but independent of the initiating action or event. Some of these independent conditions, such as the evening breeze in the example chosen, we classify as mere conditions in or on which the cause operates; others we speak of as "interventions" or "causes." To decide how such independent elements shall be classified is also to decide how we shall combine our knowledge of the different general connections which the successive stages exemplify, and it is important to see that nothing *in* this knowledge itself can resolve this point. We may have to go to science for the relevant general knowledge before we can assert with proper confidence that A's action did cause the fire, but science, though it tells us that an air current was required, is silent on the difference between a current in the form of an evening breeze and one produced by someone who deliberately fanned the flames as they were flick-

ering out in the bracken. Yet an air current in this deliberately induced form is not a "condition" or "mere circumstance" through which we can trace the consequence; its presence would force us to revise the assertion that A caused the fire. Conversely if science helped us to identify as a necessary factor in producing the fire some condition or element of which we had previously been totally ignorant, e.g., the persistence of oxygen, this would leave our original judgment undisturbed if this factor were a common or pervasive feature of the environment or of the thing in question. There is thus indeed an important sense in which it is true that the distinction between cause and conditions is not a "scientific" one. It is not determined by laws or generalizations concerning connections between events.

When we have assembled all our knowledge of the factors involved in the fire, the residual question which we then confront (the attributive question) may be typified as follows: Here is A's action, here is the fire: can the fire be attributed to A's action as its consequence given that there is also this third factor (the breeze or B's intervention) without which the fire would not have happened? It is plain that, both in raising questions of this kind and in answering them, ordinary thought is powerfully influenced by the analogy between the straightforward cases of causal attribution (where the elements required for the production of harm in addition to the initiating action are all "normal" conditions) and even simpler cases of responsibility which we do not ordinarily describe in causal language at all but by the simple transitive verbs of action. These are the cases of the direct manipulation of objects involving changes in them or their position: cases where we say "He pushed it," "He broke it," "He bent it." The cases which we do confidently describe in causal language ("The fire was caused by his carelessness," "He caused a fire") are cases where no other human action or abnormal occurrence is required for the production of the effect, but only normal conditions. Such cases appear as mere long-range or less direct versions or extensions of the most obvious and fundamental case of all for the attribution of responsibility: the case where we can simply say "He did it." Conversely in attaching importance to thus causing harm as a distinct ground of responsibility and in taking certain kinds of factor (whether human interventions or abnormal occurrences), without which the initiating action would not have led to harm, to preclude the description of the case in simple causal terms, common sense is affected by the fact that here, because of the manner in which the harm eventuates, the outcome cannot be represented as a mere extension of the initiating action; the analogy with the fundamental case for responsibility ("He did it") has broken down.

When we understand the power exerted over our ordinary thought by the conception that causing harm is a mere extension of the primary case of doing harm, the interrelated metaphors which seem natural to lawyers and laymen, in describing various aspects of causal connection, fall into place and we can discuss their factual basis. The persistent notion that some kinds of event required in addition to the initiating action for the production of harm "break the chain of causation" is intelligible, if we remember that though such events actually *complete* the *explanation* of the harm (and so *make* rather than *break* the causal explanation) they do, unlike mere normal conditions, break the *analogy* with cases of simple actions. The same analogy accounts for the description of these factors as "new actions" (*novus actus*) or "new causes," "superseding," "extraneous," "intervening forces": and for the description of the initiating action when "the chain of causation" is broken as "no longer operative," "having worn out," *functus officio*.[5] So too when the "chain" is held not to be "broken" the initiating action is said to be still "potent,"[6] "continuing," "contributing," "operative," and the mere conditions held insufficient to break the chain are "part of the background,"[7] "circumstances in which the cause operates,"[8] "the stage set," "part of history."

(ii) *A* throws a lighted cigarette into the bracken which catches fire. Just as the flames are about to flicker out, *B*, who is not acting in concert with *A*, deliberately pours petrol on them. The fire spreads and burns down the forest. *A*'s action, whether or not he intended the forest fire, was not the cause of the fire: *B*'s was.

The voluntary intervention of a second human agent, as in this case, is a paradigm among those factors which preclude the assimilation in causal judgments of the first agent's connection with the eventual harm to the case of simple direct manipulation. Such an intervention displaces the prior action's title to be called the cause and, in the persistent metaphors found in the law, it "reduces" the earlier action and its immediate effects to the level of "mere circumstances" or "part of the history." *B* in this case was not an "instrument" through which *A* worked or a victim of

the circumstances *A* has created. He has, on the contrary, freely exploited the circumstances and brought about the fire without the co-operation of any further agent or any chance coincidence. Compared with this the claim of *A*'s action to be ranked the cause of the fire fails. That this and not the moral appraisal of the two actions is the point of comparison seems clear. If *A* and *B* both intended to set the forest on fire, and this destruction is accepted as something wrong or wicked, their moral wickedness, judged by the criterion of intention, is the same. Yet the causal judgment differentiates between them. If their moral guilt is judged by the outcome, this judgment though it would differentiate between them cannot be the source of the causal judgment; for it presupposes it. The difference just is that *B* has caused the harm and *A* has not. Again, if we appraise these actions as good or bad from different points of view, this leaves the causal judgments unchanged. *A* may be a soldier of one side anxious to burn down the enemy's hide-out: *B* may be an enemy soldier who has decided that his side is too iniquitous to defend. Whatever is the moral judgment passed on these actions by different speakers it would remain true that *A* had not caused the fire and *B* had.

There are, as we have said, situations in which a voluntary action would not be thought of as an intervention precluding causal connection in this way. These are the cases discussed further below where an opportunity commonly exploited for harmful actions is negligently provided, or one person intentionally provides another with the means, the opportunity, or a certain type of reason for wrongdoing. Except in such cases a voluntary intervention is a limit past which consequences are not traced. By contrast, actions which in any of a variety of different ways are less than fully voluntary are assimilated to the means by which or the circumstances in which the earlier action brings about the consequences. Such actions are not the outcome of an informed choice made without pressure from others, and the different ways in which human action may fall short in this respect range from defective muscular control, through lack of consciousness or knowledge, to the vaguer notions of duress and of predicaments, created by the first agent for the second, in which there is no "fair" choice.

In considering examples of such actions and their bearing on causal judgments there are three dangers to avoid. It would be folly to think that in tracing connections through such actions instead of regarding them, like voluntary interventions, as a limit, ordinary thought has clearly separated out their non-voluntary aspect from others by which they are often accompanied. Thus even in the crude case where *A* lets off a gun (intentionally or not) and startles *B*, so that he makes an involuntary movement of his arm which breaks a glass, the commonness of such a reaction as much as its compulsive character may influence the judgment that *A*'s action was the cause of the damage.

Secondly we must not impute to ordinary thought all the fine discriminations that could be made and in fact are to be found in a legal system, or an equal willingness to supply answers to complex questions in causal terms. Where there is no precise system of punishment, compensation or reward to administer, ordinary men will not often have faced such questions as whether the injuries suffered by a motorist who collides with another in swerving to avoid a child are consequences attributable to the neglect of the child's parents in allowing it to wander onto the road. Such questions courts have to answer and in such cases common judgments provide only a general, though still an important indication of what are the relevant factors.

Thirdly, though very frequently non-voluntary actions are assimilated to mere conditions or means by which the first agent brings about the consequences, the assimilation is never quite complete. This is manifested by the general avoidance of many causal locutions which are appropriate when the consequences are traced (as in the first case) through purely physical events. Thus even in the case in which the second agent's role is hardly an "action" at all, e.g., where *A* hits *B,* who staggers against a glass window and breaks it, we should say that *A*'s blow made *B* stagger and break the glass, rather than that *A*'s blow caused the glass to break, though in an explanatory or attributive context the case would be *summarized* by saying that *A*'s action was the cause of the *damage.*

In the last two cases where *B*'s movements are involuntary in the sense that they are not part of any action which he chose or intended to do, their connection with *A*'s action would be described by saying that *A*'s blow *made B* stagger or *caused* him to stagger or that the noise of *A*'s shot *made* him jump or *caused* him to jump. This would be true, whether *A* intended or expected *B* to react in this way or not, and the naturalness of treating *A*'s action as the cause of the ultimate damage is due to the causal character of this part of the process involving *B*'s action. The same is, however, true where *B*'s actions are not involuntary movement but *A* is considered to have made or caused *B* to do

them by less crude means. This is the case if, for example, *A* uses threats or exploits his authority over *B* to make *B* do something, e.g., knock down a door. At least where *A*'s threats are of serious harm, or *B*'s act was unquestionably within *A*'s authority to order, he too has made or forced or (in formal quasi-legal parlance) "caused" *B* to act.

Outside the area of such cases, where *B*'s will would be said either not to be involved at all, or to be overborne by *A*, are cases where *A*'s act creates a predicament for *B narrowing* the area of choice so that he has either to inflict some harm on himself or others, or sacrifice some important interest or duty. Such cases resemble coercion in that *A* narrows the area of *B*'s choice but differ from it in that this predicament need not be intentionally created. *A* sets a house on fire (intentionally or unintentionally): *B* to save himself has to jump from a height involving certain injury, or to save a child rushes in and is seriously burned. Here, of course, *B*'s movements are not involuntary; the "necessity" of his action is here of a different order. His action is the outcome of a choice between two evils forced on him by *A*'s action. In such cases, when *B*'s injuries are thought of as the consequence of the fire, the implicit judgment is made that his action was the lesser of two evils and in this sense a "reasonable" one which he was obliged to make to avoid the greater evil. This is often paradoxically, though understandably, described by saying that here the agent "had no choice" but to do what he did. Such judgments involve a comparison of the importance of the respective interests sacrificed and preserved, and the final assertion that *A*'s action was the cause of the injuries rests on evaluations about which men may differ.

Finally, the ground for treating some harm which would not have occurred without *B*'s action as the consequence of *A*'s action may be that *B* acted in ignorance of or under a mistake as to some feature of the situation created by *A*. Poisoning offers perhaps the simplest example of the bearing on causal judgments of actions which are less than voluntary in this Aristotelian sense. If *A* intending *B*'s death deliberately poisons *B*'s food and *B*, knowing this, deliberately takes the poison and dies, *A* has not, unless he coerced *B* into eating the poisoned food, caused *B*'s death: if, however, *B* does not know the food to be poisoned, eats it, and dies, *A* has caused his death, even if he put the poison in unwittingly. Of course only the roughest judgments are passed in causal terms in such cases outside law courts, where fine degrees of "appreciation" or "reckless shutting of the eyes" may have to be discriminated from "full knowl-edge." Yet, rough as these are, they indicate clearly enough the controlling principles.

Though in the foregoing cases A's initiating action might often be described as "the cause" of the ultimate harm, this linguistic fact is of subordinate importance to the fact that, for whatever purpose, explanatory, descriptive, or evaluative, consequences of an action are traced, discriminations are made (except in the cases discussed later) between free voluntary inter-ventions and less than voluntary reactions to the first action or the circumstances created by it.

(iii) The analogy with single simple actions which guides the tracing of consequences may be broken by certain kinds of conjunctions of physical events. A hits B who falls to the ground stunned and bruised by the blow; at that moment a tree crashes to the ground and kills B. A has certainly caused B's bruises but not his death: for though the fall of the tree was, like the evening breeze in our earlier example, independent of and subsequent to the initiating action, it would be differentiated from the breeze in any description in causal terms of the connection of B's death with A's action. It is to be noticed that this is not a matter which turns on the intention with which A struck B. Even if A hit B inadvertently or accidentally his blow would still be the cause of B's bruises: he would have caused them, though unintentionally. Conversely even if A had intended his blow to kill, this would have been an attempt to kill but still not the cause of B's death, unless A knew that the tree was about to fall just at that moment. On this legal and ordinary judgments would be found to agree; and most legal systems would distinguish for the purposes of punishment an attempt with a fatal upshot, issuing by such chance or anomalous events, from "causing death"—the terms in which the offenses of murder and manslaughter are usually defined.

Similarly the causal description of the case does not turn on the moral appraisal of A's action or the wish to punish it. A may be a robber and a murderer and B a saint guarding the place A hoped to plunder. Or B may be a murderer and A a hero who has forced his way into B's retreat. In both cases the causal judg-ment is the same. A had caused the minor injuries but not B's death, though he tried to kill him. A may indeed be praised or blamed but not for causing B's death. However intimate the connection between responsibility and causation, it does not determine causal judgments in this simple way. Nor does the causal judgment turn on a refusal to attribute grave consequences to actions which normally have less serious results. Had A's blow killed B outright and the tree, falling on his body, merely smashed his watch we should still treat the coincidental character of the fall of the tree as determining the form of causal state-ment. We should then recognize A's blow as the cause of B's death but not the breaking of the watch.

The connection between A's action and B's death in the first case would naturally be described in the language of coincidence. "It was a coincidence: it just happened that, at the very moment when A knocked B down, a tree crashed at the very place where he fell and killed him." The common legal metaphor would describe the fall of the tree as an "extraneous" cause. This, however, is dangerously misleading, as an analy-sis of the notion of coincidence will show. It suggests merely an event which is subsequent to and indepen-dent of some other contingency, and of course the fall of the tree has both these features in relation to A's blow. Yet in these respects the fall of the tree does not differ from the evening breeze in the earlier case where we found no difficulty in tracing causal connec-tion. The full elucidation of the notion of a coincidence is a complex matter for, though it is very important as a limit in tracing consequences, causal questions are not the only ones to which the notion is relevant. The following are its most general characteristics. We speak of a coincidence whenever the conjunction of two or more events in certain spatial or temporal rela-tions (1) is very unlikely by ordinary standards and (2) is for some reason significant or important, pro-vided (3) that they occur without human contrivance and (4) are independent of each other. It is therefore a coincidence if two persons known to each other in London meet without design in Paris on their way to separate independently chosen destinations; or if two persons living in different places independently decide to write a book on the same subject. The first is a coincidence of time and place ("It just happened that we were at the same place at the same time"), and the second a coincidence of time only ("It just happened that they both decided to write on the subject at the same time").

Use of this general notion is made in the special case when the conjunction of two or more events occurs in temporal and/or spatial relationships which are significant, because, as our general knowledge of causal processes shows, this conjunction is required for the production of some given further event. In the language of Mill's idealized model, they form a necessary part of a complex set of jointly sufficient conditions. In the present case the fall of the tree just as *B* was struck down within its range satisfies the four criteria for a coincidence which we have enumerated. First, though neither event was of a very rare or exceptional kind, their conjunction would be rated very unlikely judged by the standards of ordinary experience. Secondly, this conjunction was causally significant for it was a necessary part of the process terminating in *B*'s death. Thirdly, this conjunction was not consciously designed by *A*; had he known of the impending fall of the tree and hit *B* with the intention that he should fall within its range *B*'s death would not have been the result of any coincidence. *A* would certainly have caused it. The common-sense principle that a contrived conjunction cannot be a coincidence is the element of truth in the legal maxim (too broadly stated even for legal purposes) that an intended consequence cannot be too "remote." Fourthly, each member of the conjunction in this case was independent of the other; whereas if *B* had fallen against the tree with an impact sufficient to bring it down on him, this sequence of physical events, though freakish in its way, would not be a coincidence and in most contexts of ordinary life, as in the law, the course of events would be summarized by saying that in this case, unlike that of the coincidence, *A*'s act was the cause of *B*'s death, since each stage is the effect of the preceding stage. Thus, the blow forced the victim against the tree, the effect of this was to make the tree fall and the fall of the tree killed the victim.

One further criterion in addition to these four must be satisfied if a conjunction of events is to rank as a coincidence and as a limit when the consequences of the action are traced. This further criterion again shows the strength of the influence which the analogy with the case of the simple manipulation of things exerts over thought in causal terms. An abnormal *condition* existing at the time of a human intervention is distinguished both by ordinary thought and, with a striking consistency, by most legal systems from an abnormal event or conjunction of events subsequent to that intervention; the former, unlike the latter, are not ranked as coincidences or "extraneous" causes when the consequences of the intervention come to be traced. Thus *A* innocently gives *B* a tap over the head of a normally quite harmless character, but because *B* is then suffering from some rare disease the tap has, as we say, "fatal results." In this case *A* has caused *B*'s death though unintentionally. The scope of the principle which thus distinguishes contemporaneous abnormal conditions from subsequent events is unclear; but at least where a human being initiates some physical change in a thing, animal, or person, abnormal physical states of the object affected, existing at the time, are ranked as part of the circumstances in which the cause "operates." In the familiar controlling imagery these are part of "the stage already set" before the "intervention."

Judgments about coincidences, though we often agree in making them, depend in two related ways on issues incapable of precise formulation. One of these is patent, the other latent but equally important. Just how unlikely must a conjunction be to rank as a coincidence, and in the light of what knowledge is likelihood to be assessed? The only answer is: "very unlikely in the light of the knowledge available to ordinary men." It is, of course, the indeterminacies of such standards, implicit in causal judgments, that make them inveterately disputable, and call for the exercise of discretion or choice by courts. The second and latent indeterminacy of these judgments depends on the fact that the things or events to which they relate do not have pinned to them some uniquely correct description always to be used in assessing likelihood. It is an important pervasive feature of all our empirical judgments that there is a constant possibility of more or less specific description of any event or thing with which they are concerned. The tree might be described not simply as a "tree" but as a "rotten tree" or as a "fir tree" or a "tree sixty feet tall." So too its fall might be described not as a "fall" but as a fall of a specified distance at a specified velocity. The likelihood of conjunctions framed in these different terms would be differently assessed. The criteria of appropriate description like the standard of likelihood are supplied by consideration of common knowledge. Even if the scientist knew the tree to be rotten and could have predicted its fall with accuracy, this would not change the judgment that its fall at the time when *B* was struck down within its range was a coincidence; nor would it make the description "rotten tree" appropriate for the assessment of the chances involved in this judgment. There are other controls over the choice of description derived from the degree of specificity of our interests in the final outcome of the causal process. We are concerned with the fall of an object sufficient to cause "death" by impact and the precise force or direction which may account for the detail of the wounds is irrelevant here.

Opportunities and Reasons

Opportunities. The discrimination of voluntary interventions as a limit is no longer made when the case, owing to the commonness or appreciable risk of such harmful intervention, can be brought within the scope of the notion of providing an opportunity, known to be commonly exploited for doing harm. Here the limiting principles are different. When A leaves the house unlocked the range of consequences to be attributed to this neglect, as in any other case where precautions are omitted, depends primarily on the way in which such opportunities are commonly exploited. An alternative formulation of this idea is that a subsequent intervention would fall within the scope of consequences if the likelihood of its occurring is one of the reasons for holding A's omission to be negligent.

It is on these lines that we would distinguish between the entry of a thief and of a murderer; the opportunity provided is believed to be sufficiently commonly exploited by thieves to make it usual and often morally or legally obligatory not to provide it. Here, in attributing consequences to prior actions, causal judgments are directly controlled by the notion of the risk created by them. Neglect of such precautions is both unusual and reprehensible. For these reasons it would be hard to separate the two ways in which such neglect deviates from the "norm." Despite this, no simple identification can be made of the notion of responsibility with the causal connection which is a ground for it. This is so because the provision of an opportunity commonly taken by others is ranked as the cause of the outcome independently of the wish to praise or blame. The causal judgment may be made simply to assess a contribution to some outcome. Thus, whether we think well or ill of the use made of railways, we would still claim that the greater mobility of the population in the nineteenth century was a consequence of their introduction.

It is obvious that the question whether any given intervention is a sufficiently common exploitation of the opportunity provided to come within the risk is again a matter on which judgments may differ, though they often agree. The courts, and perhaps ordinary thought also, often describe those that are sufficiently common as "natural" consequences of the neglect. They have in these terms discriminated the entry of a

thief from the entry of a man who burnt the house down, and refused to treat the destruction of the house as a "natural" consequence of the neglect.[9]

We discuss later . . . the argument that this easily intelligible concept of "harm within the risk," overriding as it does the distinctions between voluntary interventions and others, should be used as the general test for determining what subsequent harm should be attributed for legal purposes to prior action. The merits of this proposal to refashion the law along these simple lines are perhaps considerable, yet consequences of actions are in fact often traced both in the law and apart from it in other ways which depend on the discrimination of voluntary interventions from others. We distinguish, after all, as differing though related grounds of responsibility, causing harm by one's own action and providing opportunities for others to do harm, where the guiding analogy with the simple manipulation of things, which underlies causal thought, is less close. When, as in the examples discussed above, we trace consequences through the nonvoluntary interventions of others our concern is to show that certain stages of the process have a certain type of connection with the preceding stages, and not, as when the notion of risk is applied, to show that the ultimate outcome is connected in some general way with the initiating action. Thus, when A's shot makes B start and break a glass it is the causal relationship described by the expression "made B start" that we have in mind and not the likelihood that on hearing a shot someone may break a glass. Causal connection may be traced in such cases though the initiating action and the final outcome are not contingencies that commonly go together.

Apart from these conceptual reasons for distinguishing these related grounds for responsibility, it is clear that both in the law . . . and apart from it we constantly treat harm as caused by a person's action though it does not fall "within the risk." If, when B broke the glass in the example given above, a splinter flew into C's eye, blinding him, A's action is indeed the cause of C's injury though we may not always blame him for so unusual a consequence.

Reasons. In certain varieties of interpersonal transactions, unlike the case of coercion, the second action is quite voluntary. A may not threaten B but may bribe or advise or persuade him to do something. Here, A does not "cause" or "make" B do anything: the strongest words we should use are perhaps that he "induced" or "procured" B's act. Yet the law and moral principles alike may treat one person as responsible for the harm which another free agent has done "in consequence" of the advice or the inducements which the first has offered. In such cases the limits concern the range of those actions done by *B* which are to rank as the consequence of *A*'s words or deeds. In general this question depends on *A*'s intentions or on the "plan of action" he puts before *B*. If *A* advises or bribes *B* to break in and steal from an empty house and *B* does so, he acts in consequence of *A*'s advice or bribe. If he deliberately burns down the house this would not be treated as the consequence of *A*'s bribe or advice, legally or otherwise, though it may in some sense be true that the burning would not have taken place without the advice or bribe. Nice questions may arise, which the courts have to settle, where *B* diverges from the detail of the plan of action put before him by *A*.

. . .

Endnotes

[1] Glanville Williams, *Joint Torts and Contributory Negligence*, p. 239.

[2] Mill, Book III, chap. V, s. 2.

[3] Ross, *The Right and the Good*, p. 36.

[4] E.g., if the guest was suspected of being a compulsive stabber and the waiter had therefore been told to lay only a plastic knife in his place.

[5] *Davies v. Swan Motor Co.* [1947], 2 KB 291, 318.

[6] *Minister of Pensions v. Chennell* [1947], KB 250, 256. Lord Wright (1950), 13 MLR 3.

[7] *Norris v. William Moss & Son Ltd.* [1954], 1 WLR 46, 351.

[8] *Minister of Pensions v. Chennell* [1947], KB 250, 256.

[9] *Bellows v. Worcester Storage Co.* (1937), 297 Mass. 188, 7 NE 2d 588.

The Decline of Cause

Judith Jarvis Thomson

I

Once upon a time there was a simple way of characterizing tort law. It could in those days be said that the defendant will be declared liable for the plaintiff's loss if and only if the plaintiff proves the following three things: (1) that he suffered a loss, (2) that an act or failure to act on the part of the defendant was proximate cause of the plaintiff's suffering that loss, and (3) that the defendant was at fault in so acting or failing to act. Proximate cause was a messy business, of course, but one thing that was clear was that a person's act or omission was not proximate cause of another person's loss unless it caused the loss.

So much for once upon a time. Fault went first: it began to be possible in certain kinds of cases for a plaintiff to win his suit if he proved (1) that he suffered a loss, and (2) that an act or failure to act on the part of the defendant proximately caused his loss, even though he did not prove (3) that the defendant was at fault in so acting or failing to act. Now cause is going. In a number of cases in recent years the plaintiff has won his suit on proof (1) that he suffered a loss, and (3) that there was a faulty act or omission on the part of the defendant, but without proving (2) that the defendant's faulty act or omission caused the loss. No doubt the plaintiff has to prove *some* connection between his loss and the defendant's faulty act. If I prove I lost my legs this morning, and that you hit your little brother with a brick yesterday, *that* certainly will not suffice for me to win a suit against you for damages for the loss of my legs. The plaintiff has to connect the faulty act with the loss. But in the kind of case I have in mind, the connection he makes need not be causation.

Which kind of case? A good example is *Sindell v. Abbott Laboratories*,[1] which was decided by the California Supreme Court in 1980. The plaintiff alleged she could prove that she developed cancer as a result of

From Judith Jarvis Thomson, "The Decline of Cause," *The Georgetown Law Journal*, Vol. 76 (1987), pp. 137–150. Reprinted by permission of the Georgetown Law Journal Association.

the DES taken by her mother while pregnant; she alleged she could prove also that the defendants—eleven drug companies—knew or should have known that DES would cause cancer in the daughters of mothers who took it. In other words, she alleged she could prove (1) that she was harmed, and (3) that the defendant drug companies were at fault. But she was unable to prove, after the passage of so many years, which drug company had marketed the very DES her mother took, so she was unable to prove about any of the drug companies (2) that *its* acts had caused the harm she suffered. All the same, she won the right to get a jury on the fact she alleged she could prove, and the right to win if she could prove them.

An earlier California case—*Summers v. Tice*,[2] decided in 1948—presented the problem that confronted the plaintiff in *Sindell* much more starkly and cleanly. The plaintiff Summers had gone hunting with the two defendants, Tice and Simonson. A quail was flushed, and, as Summers alleged, the defendants fired negligently in Summers' direction; as he also alleged, one of the two wounded him. But he was unable to prove which, since the defendants had fired similar pellets from similar guns. Loss yes, fault yes, but causality could not be proved. However he too won his suit.

My own impression is that cases like *Summers* and *Sindell*—in which loss and fault are clear, but causality cannot be proved—were very rarely won until recently. Why are they being won now? It is an excellent question, with, I am sure, a great many answers. Chief among them is probably a mix of four things: first, the very fact that causality *is* hard to prove in them; together with, second, the felt need to regulate the increasing number of activities which impose risk as a byproduct of technological advance; third, an increasing public acceptance of egalitarianism; and fourth, the absence as yet of a mechanism other than the tort suit to regulate those activities and secure a measure of compensation for those who may be being victimized by them.[3]

II

A related phenomenon—at least I think it really must be related—is the increasing dismissiveness about causality that can be seen in legal theorizing. Here are Landes and Posner in an article published in 1983: "causation in the law is an inarticulate groping for economically sound solutions. . . ."[4] In an article published in 1975, Calabresi defends the idea that certain concepts related to causality have a role to play in law, but his defense of that idea would have puzzled many lawyers fifty years ago. He says:

> [I]n law the term "cause" is used in different guises but always to identify those pressure points that are most amenable to the social goals we wish to accomplish. . . . [U]se of such [causal] concepts has great advantages over explicit identification and separation of the goals. Terms with an historical, common law gloss [like "cause"] permit us to consider goals (like spreading) that we do not want to spell out or too obviously assign to judicial institutions.[5]

This dismissiveness about causality is not visible only in those whose legal theorizing is influenced by economics.[6]

III

I am not competent to speak to the question why the law and legal theory have been developing in these ways, or even to the question exactly what forms these developments have taken. What I want to do instead is to mull over one of the sources of the welcome with which these developments have been received by many of the moral philosophers who have taken note of them.

What I have in mind is that there has been a phenomenon equally entitled to be called "The Decline of Cause" in moral theorizing.

The moral sophisticate nowadays is nowhere near as enamored of causality as the ignorant rest of us. Here is an example. Yesterday, Alfred backed his car out of his driveway without looking. Bad of him!—one ought not do that. Today, Bert backed his car out of his driveway without looking, but lo and behold there was a child at the end of the driveway, and Bert ran over the child and crushed its legs. Horrendous—much worse. Or so many people think.

The moral sophisticate regards that as a vulgar error. "Look," he says, "both Alfred and Bert behaved negligently, indeed equally negligently. Bert crushed a child's legs and Alfred did not, but that was just bad luck for Bert, and good luck for Alfred. After all, it wasn't Bert's fault that there was a child at the foot of his driveway; all Bert was at fault for is exactly what Alfred was at fault for, namely backing his car out of his driveway without looking. So Bert acted no worse than Alfred did and—other things being equal—Bert is no worse a person than Alfred is."

The moral sophisticate may concede that the law does well to mark a difference between Alfred and Bert in the following two ways: (1) imposing a more severe punishment on Bert than on Alfred, and (2) making Bert, and not Alfred, compensate the child's parents. But if so, he says it is for reasons extraneous to the *moral* valuation proper to them and their acts.

It is clear that the moral sophisticate is going to hold this same view in other pairs of cases too. Murder and attempted murder, of course. Yesterday Charles fired a gun at a man, to kill him; Charles'[s] intended victim was wearing a bullet proof vest, so Charles did not kill him. Today David fired a gun at a man, to kill him; David's intended victim was not wearing a bullet proof anything, so David did kill him. David murdered a man, and Charles only attempted murder, but the moral sophisticate says that David acted no worse than Charles did—for after all, it was just bad luck for Charles that his intended victim was wearing that vest, and thus nothing that Charles can take any credit for.

It seems to me three principles lie behind this moral attitude. The first concerns itself with *acts*. What we do in the world depends on the world as well as on us. If you fire a gun at a man to kill him, then the question whether you do not merely fire a gun at him, but also kill him turns on whether the world cooperates—thus on whether the bullet actually reaches him, as it might not if some third party intervenes, and on whether it enters him when it reaches him, as it might not if he is wearing bullet proof clothes. The first principle I have in mind says that the moral value of what you do in the world turns on and only on that part of it which is *entirely* under your control. When you fire a gun at a man, what is under your control is at most such things as the kind of gun you fire, the time and place at which you fire it, the direction in which you fire it, and the intention with which you fire it—merely to scare your victim, or merely to wound him, or positively to kill him. The rest that happens is up to the world, and is not something that has any bearing on the moral value of your act.

I said "at most." Let us look again at the kind of gun you fire. Is it new? Is it clean? Is it sufficiently powerful to do the work you want it to do? Strictly speaking, that the gun you fire does or does not have these features is not entirely under your control. What is under your control is only that you have made an effort to be sure that you are firing a suitable gun and now think you are: After all, somebody might have secretly replaced your carefully chosen gun with a different one—whether a person did or did not do this is not under your control. Similarly for the time and place at

which you fire the gun, and the direction in which fire it: Somebody might have secretly altered your clocks and roadmaps, and substituted distorting glasses for the glasses you normally wear—whether a person did or did not do this is also not under your control.

Strictly speaking, all that is entirely under your control are your intentions in acting—what you are at any given time setting yourself to be doing. That is not to say that setting yourself to do this or that is all you actually *do*; it is to say that the normal value of what you do *by* setting yourself to act in this or that way turns entirely on the moral value of those settings of yourself to act.

The second of the three principles concerns itself with *failures to act,* or omissions, for short. Consider two switchmen on different railways, Edward and Frank. Both were under a duty to throw a switch at ten this morning, and both failed to do so because they did not want to be bothered. Edward's omission caused a terrible train crash; Frank's omission caused nothing untoward at all, since the train Frank's switch-throwing was to turn had luckily stalled before the fork in the track. If you think murder no worse than attempted murder, you will surely think Edward's omission no worse than Frank's. It was, after all, no credit to Frank, it was merely good luck for him, that his train had stalled. The second principle says that the moral value of an omission—as of an act—turns on and only on what is entirely under the agent's control. If you could have set yourself to do a thing, and ought to have done so, then your failure to do so is equally bad no matter what your omission does or does not cause.

The cases of Alfred and Bert with which I began are cases to which both principles apply. Alfred and Bert both acted, for they backed their cars down their driveways; and both failed to act, for they failed to look while doing so. Given the two principles, the fact that Bert's acting while failing to act caused a child's legs to be crushed has no bearing at all on the moral value of what he did.

The third of the three principles has to do with the moral value of *persons*. We do think of some people as morally better than others; on what does this judgment turn? Presumably in part on the moral value of what a person does or fails to do. Given the first two principles, however, that is a function only of the moral value of a person's settings of himself to do this or that, and his failures to set himself to do this or that.

But only in part, for there is something else that a friend of these ideas should think bears on a person's moral value. What I have in mind is that if you think that good and bad luck has no bearing on the moral value of an act or omission *or* person, then you should grant that the truth or falsehood of certain counterfactuals is relevant. For example, I do not drive, and a fortiori have never backed my car out of my driveway with *or* without looking. If I had driven, would I on occasion have backed my car out of my driveway without looking? Isn't that relevant to the question how good or bad a person I am?

I am sure that all of us have faced temptations to act badly, and that many of those temptations we have resisted, though some we have not. Most people, however, are lucky enough never to be tempted to do something truly dreadful. For example, I am sure that none of us has ever been in a position of power over prisoners in a concentration camp. I am sure that none of us has been lost at sea in a lifeboat with no provisions other than a plump cabin boy. We have been lucky. How would we behave if we were in such situations? Surely that we would or would not behave in this or that way has a bearing on our moral value as people. One reason why Stanley Milgram's experiments[7] were found so shocking was that they uncovered the fact that a lot of perfectly ordinary people were quite ready to set themselves to cause others a great deal of pain simply on being told by an authority figure in a white coat to do so. Milgram's readers did not think for a moment that the actual absence of pain excused the subjects of the experiments; and they took it that what Milgram had shown was a deep moral failing which may be present in perfectly ordinary people, though without ever in fact showing itself.

How good a person are you? The third principle tells us that to the extent to which you do not know what you would set yourself to do in situations you have been so far lucky as not to have faced, you just do not know how good a person you are.

I described the person who holds these views as the "moral sophisticate," because I think we do think these views more sophisticated than those which tell us to look merely at what happens, more sophisticated even than those which tell us to look *both* at what happens *and* at what is internal to a person—what he sets himself to do, and what he would set himself to do if he were in situations he has never faced. But I might just as well have described the person who holds these views as a Kantian, because it is directly from Kant that they come down to us today. Kant said: "The good will is not good because of what it effects or accomplishes or because of its adequacy to achieve some proposed end; it is good only because of its willing, i.e., it is good of itself. . . . Usefulness or fruitlessness can neither

diminish or augment [its] worth."[8] And so similarly for the bad will: it is not bad because of what it causes, but only of itself. We might redescribe the decline of cause in moral philosophy as the triumph of Kant.

That Kant has triumphed seems clear enough. For example, I rather fancy that all of you have at least some inclination to agree with the three principles I drew attention to. I certainly do.

It is of interest to notice that these Kantian ideas are visible even in contemporary defenders of the most un-Kantian moral theory of all. I have Utilitarianism in mind, of course. Classical Utilitarians—such as John Stuart Mill and G. E. Moore—took the view that you have acted wrongly if and only if your act causes there to be less good in the world than you could have caused by choosing some other alternative act which was open to you at the time. Whether you knew it or not. Mill did explicitly grant that a man's intentions in acting do have a bearing on the moral evaluation *proper* to him; but Mill insisted that the morality of a man's *act* turns on, and only on, a comparison between what it does in fact cause, and what his other available alternatives would have caused. But hardly anyone is a Classical Utilitarian nowadays. Those in favor of its spirit say that the morality of a man's act turns, not on what it in fact causes, but on what he expects it to cause. In short, the morality of action turns, not on actual, but on expected utilities.

Now I think that these Kantian ideas are one source of the welcome with which many moral philosophers have received those developments in law and legal theory that I mentioned at the outset. For example, they think that all of the defendants were at fault in *Sindell* and *Summers*—equally at fault, regardless of whoever in fact caused the harm. So they think that no one can object, on *moral* grounds, to the plaintiffs' winning, and to the defendants' therefore having to share in the plaintiffs' costs.[9]

IV

What should *we* think of all this? It is swimming upstream to try to fight it, but my own feeling is that it smells too much of the study and too little of the open air. Adam Smith said, very plausibly, I think,

> But how well soever we may seem to be persuaded of the truth of [these ideas], when we consider [them] after this manner, in abstract, yet when we come to particular cases, the actual consequences which happen

to proceed from any action, have a very great effect upon our sentiments concerning its merit or demerit, and almost always either enhance or diminish our sense of both.[10]

Alfred backed his car out of his driveway without looking, and luckily for him, nothing untoward happened in consequence. Bad of him, we think. But not horrendous. People do that kind of thing often enough. They ought not, but they do, and it seems no great sin. Bert also backed his car out of his driveway without looking, but *he* ran a child down and crushed its legs. As Adam Smith said, we just *do* think that what Bert did was worse than what Alfred did. How can any philosophy be right which tells us we are mistaken in thinking this?

On the other hand, I think that Adam Smith's remark would not have been at all plausible if he had not said "almost always." He said: "the actual consequences which happen to proceed from any action, have a very great effect upon our sentiments concerning its merit or demerit, and *almost always* either enhance or diminish our sense of both."[11] There seem to me to be two kinds of case in which they do not.

To get at the first kind, let me draw your attention to the fact that in every example I have given, right from the outset, the agent whose act did cause a harm was at fault. In the two court cases I began with, all of the defendants were at fault, the drug companies in *Sindell,* the negligent hunters in *Summers.* Alfred and Bert were both careless. Charles and David, each of whom shot at a man to kill him, were both at least attempting murder. And so on. But what of an agent who causes someone to suffer a harm, but not by negligence or intention or by any wrong at all? A child runs out into the street and is run down by a truck driver who is entirely without fault—he has taken all due care to ensure that his truck, and in particular, his brakes, were in good order, and he was driving with all due care. The child simply ran too suddenly, too close, into the path of his truck. Does the very fact that he caused harm to the child diminish our sense of the merit of his actions? I think not. This example comes from Thomas Nagel, and he says about it: "The driver, if he is entirely without fault, will feel terrible about his role in the event, but will not have to reproach himself."[12] Nor will we reproach him. There is nothing to reproach him for. So here is a case of the first kind I had in mind: it is a case in which an agent was not at fault at all in acting, and that a bad consequence happens to flow from his action does not affect our sense of its merit or demerit.

In particular, the bad consequence does not make us think worse of his driving than we would have thought had that bad consequence not flowed from it.

Symmetrically, we might imagine someone who does something of no particular merit, and something good just happens to flow from his doing it. For example, suppose a man is standing at a street corner, waiting for a bus. As he waits, he is idly tapping his foot. Through some freak of nature, his tapping his foot causes three lives to be saved. This good consequence does not affect our sense of the merit or demerit of his tapping his foot. In particular, it does not make us think better of his tapping his foot than we would have thought had that good consequence not flowed from it.

Let us go back to that truck driver, whom I will call Unlucky No Fault Driver. His not having been at fault must be the crucial fact about him which makes him an exception to Adam Smith's remarks. For let us now contrast him with two other truck drivers. Both of them were at fault. They were supposed to check their brakes before leaving the garage, but did not want to be bothered. So both went out with bad brakes. In the case of the first, nothing untoward happened, and I will call him Lucky Fault Driver. I will call the second Unlucky Fault Driver. A child ran in front of Unlucky Fault Driver's truck and he ran it down. I want to have it be clear about Unlucky Fault Driver that he ran the child down not because the child ran too suddenly, too close, into the path of his truck, but because his brakes were not in good working order. Had his brakes been in good working order, he would have been able to stop his truck in time; but they were not, so he was not. Lucky Fault Driver acted badly, of course; but I think we do feel that Unlucky Fault Driver acted worse. The fact that a bad consequence flowed from his action does seem to affect our sense of its demerit.

Why? I think the answer is quite simply that Unlucky Fault Driver is to blame for the death he caused. Unlucky No Fault Driver also caused a death; but he is not to blame for it, since he was in no way at fault for causing it. It seems right to say that that is why the bad consequence which flowed from Unlucky No Fault Driver's action does not make us think it worse than we would have thought it had that bad consequence not flowed from it. More generally, it seems right to say that a bad consequence of an action makes that action worse *only* where the agent is to blame for that bad consequence which his action causes.

I am sure that the Kantian moral sophisticate would say at this point, "But surely it was mere bad luck for Unlucky Fault Driver that he caused a child's death. And surely one can't plausibly think a man to blame for something that he caused merely out of bad luck." There is a mistake here, and I think it the main source of the trouble. For it was not *mere* bad luck for Unlucky Fault Driver that he caused a child's death. We need a clearer grip on how bad luck figures in these cases. Unlucky No Fault Driver was in two ways unlucky. It was a piece of bad luck for him that a child ran into his path; and second, it was a piece of bad luck for him that he was unable to stop his truck in time. Unlucky Fault Driver was unlucky in only the first of those two ways. It was not a piece of bad luck for him that he was unable to stop his truck in time. His being unable to stop his truck in time was due to his bad brakes, and thus to his own negligence. Lucky Fault Driver did not have that first piece of bad luck, so it remains a counterfactual truth about him that *if* he had had it, then he too would have been unable to stop his truck in time. His being unable to stop would not have been a mere piece of bad luck for him, but would, instead, have been due to his negligence.

And it is the very same thing—namely Unlucky Fault Driver's negligence—that makes it not *mere* bad luck for him that he caused the child's death. Unlucky No Fault Driver, by contrast, was not at fault; and that is why it was mere bad luck for him that he caused a child's death, and therefore also why he is not to blame for the death of the child he killed.

The Kantian moral sophisticate could of course insist that a man cannot be thought to blame for something if bad luck entered *in any way at all* into the history of his bringing it about. But that seems to me even on its face implausible. Consider, for example, a man who is brought to trial for murder. "Look," his lawyer says to the court, "I grant that the victim's death is not *mere* bad luck for my client, since my client fired a gun at him with the intention of killing him. But the victim's death is in part due to my client's bad luck. For unbeknownst to my client, the victim almost always wore a bullet proof vest, and it was just bad luck for my client that the victim's bullet proof vest happened to be at the cleaners' on the day my client shot at him. So my client cannot be thought to blame for his victim's death." Whatever else will work in a court, *that* won't.

Let us go back now and look again at the first of the three principles that I said lie behind the moral attitude of the Kantian moral sophisticate. The first principle is: the moral value of what you do in the world turns on and only on that part of it which is entirely under your control. That seems to me to be false, and

for the reason I have pointed to. Admittedly the two faulty drivers, Lucky Fault Driver and Unlucky Fault Driver, both acted equally negligently, and the difference between them has its source in the fact that one had good luck, the other bad luck. All the same, the difference which has that source is a moral difference, and of a very grave order. For the one is *by* his negligence to blame for a death, and the other is not.

A similar point surely holds of failures to act. Edward and Frank both failed to throw the switch; Edward's (but not Frank's) negligence caused a crash, for which he is therefore to blame. That, I think, is why we think that what he did was worse than what Frank did.

It seems to me, however, that we should be more sympathetic to the third of the three principles I mentioned, which yields that Unlucky Fault Driver is no worse a person than Lucky Fault Driver is, and that Edward is no worse a person than Frank. Counterfactual truths about what people would have done and been to blame for if they had been in circumstances which they were lucky enough to have avoided really are important to us in assessing how good a person is—as important, I think, as truths about what they in fact did and in fact are to blame for.

This difference between our judgments of acts on the one hand and the people who perform them on the other hand may perhaps be due to the fact that different kinds of consequences flow from our arriving at these two different kinds of judgments. When we learn that someone is a bad person—untrustworthy, unreliable, prone to acting without thought for others—what flows from this judgment? Well, our attitude toward him changes, and in consequences we will behave differently toward him in many more or less delicate ways in the future. This reaction is appropriate whether the judgment is provoked by what he actually did *or* by what we have come to learn he would do if he were in circumstances he has not in fact been in. By contrast, some of the consequences of learning that a person has actually acted badly are backward looking. If we learn he is to blame for a dreadful outcome, we do not merely alter our behavior toward him in future, we may also lock him up for what he did, or exact compensation for it from him, or both.[13]

V

Candor, however, compels me to mention a difficulty for what I have been saying. Let us go back to Adam Smith. He said: "the actual consequences which happen to proceed from any action, have a great effect upon our sentiments concerning its merit or demerit, and *almost always* either enhance or diminish our sense of both."[14] I mentioned one class of exceptions. Unlucky No Fault Driver, for example, was merely unlucky. He caused a child's death, but because this was through no fault of his own, we do not think the worse of his actions. Where there is fault, however, I said that consequences do make a difference. We do think worse of Unlucky Fault Driver's actions than of Lucky Fault Driver's actions, and that is because the one is, and other is not, to blame for a bad outcome.

But there is yet another class of exceptions to Adam Smith's remarks, which makes trouble for any simple treatment of these issues. The simplest examples comes from a case I mentioned at the outset, namely *Summers v. Tice*.[15] (That is a wonderful case. If it had not occurred, we would have had to invent it.) The two defendants, Tice and Simonson, both fired negligently in Summers' direction, and one of them shot Summers, but we cannot tell which. Who should pay Summers' bills? Most people feel it right that Tice and Simonson should split the costs. The actual outcome in court was joint and several liability, but arguably that comes to roughly the same thing given the possibility of a suit for contribution, and in any case there are reasons to think that outcome fairer to Summers than a division of the costs. So far so good, nothing puzzling yet.

Now for the source of the puzzlement. Suppose that during the course of the trial evidence had come forward which made it as certain as empirical matters ever are that the pellet that caused Summers' injury came from Tice's gun, so that it is Tice who is to blame for Summers' injury. We do, I think, take it to be clear that Simonson should now be dismissed from the suit: no doubt he acted badly, but he is not to blame for the injury, and hence he is not appropriately held liable for its costs.[16] But our *moral* assessment of Tice and Simonson does not shift. We do not think the worse of Tice, or even of Tice's acts, because he, as it turns out, is to blame for the harm; and we do not think the better of Simonson, or of Simonson's acts, because *he*, as it turns out, is not to blame for the harm. Our moral attitude does not shift in any way by virtue of the discovery that it is Tice who actually caused the harm. So we really seem to have a second kind of exception to Adam Smith's remarks.

It could of course be said that it is just irrational on our part to fail to distinguish between Tice and Simonson in the way in which we do distinguish between Lucky and Unlucky Fault Drivers. But it does

not *feel* irrational. And the moral views of the man and woman in the street are deserving of great respect: they ought not be dismissed as irrational unless it really does turn out that there is no rationale for them.

What bubbles up in us men-and-women-in-the-street is, I think, this: "Simonson nearly caused the very same harm that Tice caused." It is not true of Lucky Fault Driver that he nearly caused the very same harm that Unlucky Fault Driver caused. Or at least you were not thinking of him as having done so. One driver goes out in one part of town, the other in another; they both have bad brakes; a child runs in front of one, no child runs in front of the other. So far so good. One is to blame for a death and the other is not, and we feel very differently about what they did.

But now let the two drivers set out from the same part of town, down the same street. A child runs in front of both. Both come to a long screeching halt. The child is hit by one truck and not by the other. If the child had been running *ever* so slightly slower, it would have been hit by the other truck. Now the drivers seem to us like Tice and Simonson: we think no worse of what the one did than of what the other did.

This suggests that something else is at work in these cases, possibly two things, in fact.

In the first place, Tice and Simonson did not merely act equally negligently; they each imposed roughly the same risk of harm on a person. Similarly for the two truck drivers who set out from the same part of town, and in front of both of whom one child runs. Not so for two truck drivers who set out from different parts of town. If they both set out with bad brakes, they acted equally negligently; but if a child runs in front of one, and no child so much as gets near the other, they do not in fact impose even roughly the same risk of harm on anyone.

This does make a difference to us. Suppose you back your car out of your driveway without looking, but no child was anywhere near you. Perhaps you will feel bad later on thinking the matter over: after all, it is negligent to back out without looking. But you will not *dwell* on what you did; it would be irrational to lie awake at night shuddering at the thought of what you *might* have caused. But suppose you back your car out of your driveway without looking, and there was a child in the vicinity; indeed, you nearly hit it, and would have hit it but for the child's having noticed a penny up ahead and run faster to get to it. Here the shudder is not out of place. We all know what that terrible, nagging thought is like: it is not merely of what you might have caused, but of what you nearly did cause. You do not feel as bad as you would if you had actually hit the child; but you do feel considerably worse than you would if there had been no child in the vicinity at all.

Adam Smith said that the bad consequences of an act affect our sense of its merit or demerit, and I agreed that this is so if the act was faulty: for the bad things an act causes are things that its agent is to blame for, if his act was faulty. What seems to come out here is that it is not merely the actual bad consequences of an act that affect our sense of its demerit: the higher the risk of bad consequences that the act actually imposes on others, the greater the demerit of the act.

It is puzzling that this should be so, however. Your negligence in backing out of your driveway without looking is no greater or worse if there is a child in the vicinity than if there is not; and since you did not actually hit the child, [you] cannot explain [your] feeling that what you did was worse by appeal to the fact that you are to blame for a harm to the child. *Nobody* was harmed. So there is a gap here, and I hope you will find it as interesting a question as I do just how it is to be filled.

I said it is possible that there are two further things at work in these cases. The second of them is this: Tice and Simonson did not merely act equally negligently, and they did not merely each impose roughly the same risk of harm on *a* person; they each imposed roughly the same risk of harm on one and the same person, namely Summers. Similarly for the two truck drivers who set out from the same part of town, and in front of both of whom one child runs. Does *that* matter to us? I do not find it clear that it does. Dickenson fired his shotgun negligently last Wednesday, and nearly hit someone. He feels awful about what he did, and we think it right that he feel awful about it. Do we think worse of what Simonson did, given he nearly hit someone on Thursday, *and* given also that the person Simonson nearly hit was in fact hit by Tice? Perhaps so. But it is even harder, I think, to see why that should be so—if it is.

VI

Let me now try to pull this material together just briefly. I began by drawing attention to two phenomena in law—more precisely, one in law itself, the other in legal theory—which seem to warrant saying that as far as tort law is concerned at any rate, there has been a decline of cause. Many people think that if cause declines in law, law to that extent departs from morality. It therefore seemed to me worth drawing attention to the fact that there has been a decline of cause in moral theory too. That decline in part explains why moral theorists who interest themselves in law have welcomed those developments in law and legal theory. But it is of interest for its own sake. As Adam Smith said, when you think about these matters in the abstract, the philosophers seem to be right; but when you come out of the study, they seem to be wrong. Moral theorists must of course ask themselves why that is, and whether there is a rationale for it; that is the job of the moral theorist. But I hope that lawyers will find these questions of interest too. The law certainly is not, and need not be, an exact reflection of the morality of those governed by it; but responsible government tries to be sure it has a sound rationale whenever it departs from that morality, and therefore does well to try to become clear about what that morality is.

Endnotes

[1] 26 Cal. 3d 88, 163 Cal. Rptr. 132, 607 P.2d 924, *cert. denied,* 449 U.S. 912 (1980).

[2] 33 Cal. 2d 80, 199 P.2d 1 (1948).

[3] For an interesting discussion of these and related matters, which brings out their bearing on a particular case, see P. Shuck, Agent Orange on Trial, Mass Toxic Disasters in the Courts (1986).

[4] Landes & Posner, *Causation in Tort Law: An Economic Approach,* 12 J. L. Stud. 109, 131 (1983).

[5] Calabresi, *Concerning Cause and the Law of Torts: An Essay for Harry Kalven, Jr.,* 43 U. Chi. L. Rev. 69, 106–07 (1975) (emphasis in original).

[6] *See, e.g.,* Kelman, *The Necessary Myth of Objective Causation Judgments in Liberal Political Theory,* 63 Chi-Kent L. Rev. 579 (1987).

[7] *See* S. Milgram, Obedience to Authority (1974)(summarizing results of Milgram's experiments).

[8] I. Kant, Foundations of the Metaphysics of Morals 12–13 (Bobbs-Merrill ed. 1969).

[9] *See, e.g.,* Fischer & Ennis, *Causation and Liability,* 15 Phil. & Pub. Affairs 33 (1986); Kagan, *Causation, Liability, and Internalism,* 15 Phil. & Pub. Affairs 41 (1986).

[10] A. Smith, The Theory of Moral Sentiments 134 (Arlington House ed. 1969).

[11] The emphasis is mine.

[12] T. Nagel, Mortal Question 28–29 (1979).

[13] As I wrote in part III, the moral sophisticate may say that while the law does well to mark a difference between Alfred and Bert (punishing Bert more severely than Alfred, exacting compensation for the injury from Bert), this is for reasons extraneous to the moral valuation proper to them and their acts. I think it is one thing to say the moral valuation proper to *them* does not warrant differential legal consequences: Bert is surely no worse a person than Alfred is. But it is another thing to say the moral valuation proper to *their* acts does not warrant differential legal consequences: Bert, after all, is to blame for a harm and Alfred is not, so there really is a moral difference between what Bert did and what Alfred did.

[14] A. Smith, *supra* note 10, at 134. The emphasis is mine.

[15] 33 Cal. 2d 80, 199 P.2d 1(1948).

[16] Why this should be so is discussed in Thomson, *Remarks on Causation and Liability,* 13 Phil. & Pub. Affairs 101 (1984). Criticism of that discussion may be found in Fischer & Ennis, *supra* note 9, and in Kagan, *supra* note 9.

Study Questions

1. The court in *Lynch* admits that the injury in the case arose in an unforeseeable manner. Why does the court find the defendant liable in spite of this fact? On what does the court rest its reasoning?

2. According to Cardozo, why was the railroad not negligent in regard to Mrs. Palsgraf? What does Cardozo mean by saying that "negligence in the air" is not enough to ground liability? Do you agree?

3. How does Andrews understand the idea of proximate cause? How does Andrews respond to Cardozo's claim about "negligence in the air"?

4. As noted in the text, the *Lynch* and *Palsgraf* cases represent two competing views of causation in tort law. *Lynch* stands for the first and somewhat older principle that my liability for events that would not have occurred except for my negligent conduct extends to any such consequences directly traceable to me, to my causal agency. Under *Lynch*, in other words, I am liable for any consequences of my conduct traceable through a series of events back to me, as long as that chain is unbroken by the causal contribution of an intervening actor. This principle is preserved in the maxim "You take your victim as you find him (or her)": *A* hits *B* with a force that would normally only bruise a person, but, unknown to *A*, *B* has a very thin skull or is a hemophiliac; *B* dies. Under the *Lynch* view,

A is liable for *B*'s death. The second, newer principle is represented by Cardozo's opinion in *Palsgraf:* My liability extends only to those whom I might foreseeably harm through my negligent conduct. A number of causation cases line up on either side. Which view seems to you to make more sense? Can these principles be reconciled?

5. According to Hart and Honoré, what distinguishes cases in which event *A* causes event *B* from cases in which *A* and *B* are coincidences?

6. According to Hart and Honoré, what differentiates a cause from a condition?

7. Hart and Honoré argue that human intervention in a causal sequence "breaks the chain" of causation. Why should this be so?

8. Elsewhere in their book, Hart and Honoré maintain that their analysis of causal attribution agrees with the law's position on the "thin-skull" cases (see question 4, above): They distinguish between a state of a person or thing *existing at the time* of a wrongful act and a later or *subsequent* event or state. Existing abnormal states (thin skulls, hemophilia, and so on) are "mere circumstances" or conditions on which the cause operates and do not "break" the chain of causation, so the defendant is liable for the entire harm produced. But, they add, subsequent abnormal events or conditions *do* break the chain. They put it this way: Suppose plaintiff is run over through defendant's negligence. If on the way to the hospital he is hit by a falling tree, that is a coincidence [for which defendant is not liable]. If, just previously to being run over, he had been hit by a [falling] tree and severely injured, that is a circumstance existing at the time of the running over and will not negate the causal connection between the running over and the victim's death [so the defendant is liable], even if the victim would not have died from the running down but for the previous blow from the tree (*Causation in the Law,* 2nd ed., p. 161). Does this argument make sense? Is it consistent with the basic outlines of Hart and Honore's analysis?

9. What result would Hart and Honoré's analysis of causal attribution yield in *Lynch*? Does that result seem to you to count for or against their view?

10. Why do the critics whom Thomson attacks think cause is unimportant?

11. According to Thomson, how are the positions of Kant and the "moral sophisticate" linked?

12. Do you agree with Thomson that the decline of cause is an undesirable trend? How would you recommend that the courts handle cases such as *Summers* and *Sindell*?

13. Negligence law takes the position that, with respect to certain qualities—general skill, intelligence, and judgment—everyone is presumed to be equal, and equally reasonable, and is held to that standard. If you fall below that standard, this will not excuse you. However, as Oliver Wendell Holmes notes, certain specific conditions—for example, blindness or other physical disabilities, are such that we adjust our expectations accordingly. Blind people are judged against what a "reasonable blind person" would have done in a given situation. Are there other conditions that should be included on this list? Children, for instance, have traditionally been judged on the standard of reasonable conduct for people of their actual age, intelligence, and experience. What about the elderly? The infirm? Do the fact of these excep-

tions to the objective test of reasonableness show that the standard is itself suspicious?

14. How would you decide these cases:

(a) Defendant, driving while intoxicated, strikes a woman on the side of the road. Severely injured, the victim is taken to the hospital, where a trauma team determines that both surgery and a blood transfusion are necessary to save her life. The victim, a Jehovah's Witness, declines the transfusion and subsequently dies. Did the defendant proximately cause the victim's death, or was her death the result of her own refusal of medical treatment?

(b) Plaintiff is severely injured by defendant's negligence. An ambulance is summoned. En route to the hospital, the ambulance driver suffers a heart attack and the ambulance swerves into a tree, killing the plaintiff. Is the defendant liable for plaintiff's death because the ambulance trip was necessitated by defendant's original carelessness? Or is the wreck of the ambulance a "freakish" intervening cause, which relieves the defendant of complete liability?

C. Acts, Omissions, and the Duty to Rescue

"I Didn't Do Anything"

In an incident that aroused widespread moral condemnation, a nineteen-year-old college freshman admitted in 1998 that he witnessed the beginning of what became a murder and did nothing to stop it. David Cash and a friend were at a Nevada casino in 1997. The friend took a seven-year-old girl into a bathroom stall, sexually assaulted her, and then strangled her. Cash admitted that he saw his friend in the stall with his hand over the girl's mouth but left the bathroom just before the attack began. The friend was convicted of murder and sentenced to life imprisonment.

Nevada authorities questioned and then released Cash, confessing that although they found Cash's conduct "morally reprehensible," it did not violate the law, since Cash neither encouraged nor aided the assailant. The decision not to pursue charges against Cash sparked numerous calls for changes in the law, ranging from a requirement that those who witness a crime must report it to bills that would require adults to come to the aid of a child under attack. Currently only three or four states have any such laws. Throughout the controversy, Cash continued to maintain his innocence: Speaking on a radio talkshow, Cash insisted, "I have done nothing wrong."

The Failure to Act

When we try to fit Cash's case into the categories of tort law, puzzles quickly emerge. Did Cash *cause* the girl's death? Did he breach a duty to her? In one sense, of course, Cash was not the cause the girl's death, his friend was. But Cash's failure to stop his companion allowed the companion to kill the girl. Is allowing someone to be killed the same thing as killing her? Did Cash help to bring about the death? In describing her death to others, would we say that she was strangled? That she was killed by the companion? That her death was the result of callous inaction? Would we say all of these things?

Certainly of significance here is whether we would say that Cash breached a duty to the decedent. We are all familiar with situations in which the law imposes upon as a duty to *refrain* from acting in ways harmful to other people or their property, with prohibitions on murder, theft, assault, and so on. But what of situations in which the *failure* to act constitutes a breach of duty? Are there such cases? It is true that the law recognizes certain instances in which *omitting* to do something *for* someone, as opposed to *doing* something *to* him, is a breach of duty: for example, when that person is your child or your spouse, or when you have entered into a contract to care for another—in other words, cases involving an otherwise legally recognized relationship.

As a general matter, the law's approach to the question of duty is governed by two principles: Everyone has a general duty of reasonable care for *misfeasance*, but no one (with few exceptions) has a duty of care for *nonfeasance*. What do these terms mean? *Misfeasance* refers to the infliction of harm, or acting in a way that inflicts harm. *Nonfeasance* refers to the failure to prevent harm. All of us are under a general legal duty not to inflict harm upon one another, but none of us (with few exceptions) is under a legal duty to prevent harm from befalling another.

Misfeasance and Nonfeasance

The concepts of misfeasance and nonfeasance are difficult ones. Part of the difficulty, as several of the readings in this section make clear, is that the distinction itself is problematic. The difference between misfeasance and nonfeasance is supposed to mark the difference between *acts* (or *commissions*) and *omissions*. But what makes something one rather than the other? Take this, for example: It is Monday morning, and my daughter has to be ready for school by 7:00 A.M. I wake her up early, even though she did not get much sleep the night before. Have I performed the *act* of "getting my daughter ready for school"? Or have I *omitted* to perform the act of "letting her sleep in"? (I know how she will see it!) Some who have thought about this question argue that the answer depends upon how the situation is described, and that how we describe it turns on our *evaluation* of the alternatives:

> Unless the defendant has a duty to act, an omission is not culpable. Of course, the line between omissions and commissions is blurry. There is considerable circularity in claiming that a defendant can be culpable only if he had committed an act, when we often describe an event in active conduct terms rather than passively if we have already (somehow) determined that the party is culpable. For instance, a parent who *does not feed* a child may readily be said to *starve* the child—to commit an act— while a stranger would be said to *fail to feed*—a passive nonact.[1]

You would be more inclined to say "Adams (selflessly) got his daughter ready for (a wonderful day at) school" than to say "Adams (inexcusably) forgot to let his daughter sleep in," the more you are inclined to view one positively and the other negatively. This is revealed by the (loaded) way in which each alternative is described.

Another suggestion, defended in our selection from Ernest Weinrib, distinguishes misfeasance from nonfeasance on the ground that the former always involves a situation in which the defendant has played some role in creating the risk to which the plaintiff has been exposed, whereas in situations of pure nonfeasance, this is not the case. Weinrib contrasts these cases:

1. Driver (defendant) fails to apply his brakes in time and Pedestrian (plaintiff) is hurt.

2. One person (defendant) sees another (plaintiff) drowning in a pool and fails to throw him an easily available rope.

Here our conviction that case 1 is an instance of misfeasance whereas case 2 is "mere" nonfeasance can be explained by seeing that Driver plays a role in creating the danger to which Pedestrian is exposed; presumably this is not true of the defendant in case 2.

---

[1] Mark Kelman, "Interpretive Construction in the Substantive Criminal Law," *Stanford Law Review*, 33 (1981), p. 637.

What significance does the misfeasance/nonfeasance distinction have for the question of which duties the law imposes upon us? The collective meaning of the two principles stated above is this: If you find a stranger in a position of peril, perhaps even of imminent death—a situation you did nothing to create—and you do nothing to help that person (even when this would pose no risk to you), your conduct is mere nonfeasance and you generally are *not* legally liable for that person's injuries or death. The law's position is starkly summarized by the language of an older case:

> Actionable negligence is the neglect of a legal duty. The defendants are not liable unless they owed to the plaintiff a legal duty which they neglected to perform. With purely moral obligations the law does not deal. For example, the priest and Levite who passed by on the other side were not, it is supposed, liable at law for the continued suffering of the man who fell among thieves, which they might and morally ought to have prevented or relieved. Suppose *A*, standing close by a railroad, sees a two-year-old babe on the track and a car approaching. He can easily rescue the child with entire safety to himself, and the instincts of humanity require him to do so. If he does not, he may, perhaps, justly be styled a ruthless savage and a moral monster; but he is not liable in damages for the child's injury, or indictable under the statute for its death. . . . There is a wide difference—a broad gulf—both in reason and in law, between causing and preventing an injury; between doing by negligence or otherwise a wrong to one's neighbor, and preventing him from injuring himself; between protecting him against injury by another and guarding him from injury that may accrue to him from the condition of the premises which he has unlawfully invaded. The duty to do no wrong is a legal duty. The duty to protect against wrong is, generally speaking and excepting certain intimate relations in the nature of a trust, a moral obligation only, not recognized or enforced by law.[2]

---

[2] *Buch v. Amory Mfg. Co.*, 44 A. 809 (1897).

McFall v. Shimp

The impact of the misfeasance/nonfeasance distinction as it bears on the scope and limits of the duty of care owed to others is dramatically illustrated in the tragic case of Robert McFall.

Thirty-nine-year-old McFall suffered from aplastic anemia, a disease in which the patient's bone marrow fails to manufacture certain necessary blood components. McFall's condition was diagnosed in July 1978, and a search was immediately undertaken to locate a bone marrow donor. Transfusions of bone marrow require that there be a high degree of genetic compatibility between patient and donor, so McFall's relatives were looked to first. Initial tests of McFall's immediate family failed to produce a donor, but eventually the medical team located McFall's first cousin, David Shimp. Preliminary tests indicated a high compatibility rating, and Shimp was scheduled for further testing during the third week of July. He failed to appear, stating in a later interview that his wife had asked him not to undergo the procedure. Running out of time and with no one else to turn to, McFall hired an attorney and filed a suit, asking the court for an *injunction* ordering Shimp to submit to the transfusion procedure.

Counsel for McFall could cite little in the way of prior authority dealing with this case, beyond an invocation of the court's equitable powers, and ended its arguments with a plea: "The time for study is over. The exigencies require action in order to save a human life. Our noblest traditions as a free people and our common sense of decency, society and morality all point to the proper result in this case. We respectfully suggest that it is time our law did likewise."

Judge Flaherty denied the injunction on two grounds. First, there is no legal duty to save another, he conceded, and this is perhaps as it should be; to force Shimp to submit to the procedure would be to usher in a new rule with no limitations. Second, the forcible intrusion into the body contemplated here is wholly impermissible. Flaherty's ruling was announced on July 26. Robert McFall died on August 10.

The Duty to Rescue

The essays by Thomas Macaulay and Ernest Weinrib review the legal and moral dimensions of the debate over the "no-duty-to-rescue" rule. Macaulay defends the traditional position of the law by invoking a fundamental distinction. On the one hand, duties to aid others are uncontested where the actor fails to fulfill a pre-existing responsibility (for example, the nurse who omits to care for her patient, or the parent who fails to feed his children). These situations are ones in which the omission would be "on other grounds illegal," as Macaulay says. On the other hand, the wealthy executive who walks past the homeless man, and the physician who stays at home rather than travel long distances to help the needy, though they may be "bad men," nonetheless cannot be held accountable legally without "disturbing the whole order of society." The homeless and needy, Macaulay confesses, have nothing more than a "claim of humanity" upon those who are in a position to help them. Most troubling to Macaulay is the problem of legal line-drawing: If the law requires "rescue" in these kinds of cases, just how much should the law compel on the part of a would-be rescuer?

Others who defend the law's stance toward rescue raise several points. To the degree that the law is correct in requiring that your liability for another's injuries depends upon whether you *caused* harm to that person, it must follow that there can be no duty to rescue in cases of pure nonfeasance; these are cases in which you have not caused the harm in question. Furthermore, regardless of which of several possible formulations of a general duty to rescue one selects, Macaulay's worry remains: there are no principled limits that could be placed on the invasion of individual liberty resulting from the imposition of such a duty. By encroaching upon individual liberties in this way, a general duty of rescue would require "forced exchanges" between people.

As Weinrib indicates, proponents of a legal duty to rescue commonly make the utilitarian argument that a general legal duty to aid those in peril is required by the goal of promoting the overall welfare. Critics of a legal duty to rescue have sought to build a moral case for their position by aligning themselves with the moral theory of Kant. Kant argued that the moral value of an act depends not upon the consequences or results it produces, but solely upon the motive or "will" from which it springs. The moral worth of an action turns exclusively on the moral acceptability of the principle on the basis of which one acts: doing the right thing because it is the right thing to do. This view seems to imply that to compel acts of rescue through the law would be to destroy their moral worth; my reason for coming to the aid of another would not simply be to "do my duty for duty's sake" but to avoid punishment. Thus the world would in a sense be made a morally worse place for having a legal duty to rescue. Those opposed to requiring rescue also raise a common complaint about utilitarianism: Because the sole concern of the utilitarian is with producing good results—maximizing the overall welfare—individuals are under a moral obligation to do whatever they can to achieve this maximization. But this, the critics allege, leaves no room in our moral life for "saints" or "heroes," for those who act "above and beyond the call of duty." For a utilitarian, any act that conduces to greater net good is already required; it is not something for which one can be lionized as a hero. The opponents of a duty to rescue regard this as a loss to our collective moral life.

The case for a general duty of rescue is made here by Weinrib. He endeavors to respond to the critics' fundamental objection that to impose upon all a general duty to rescue is to make all help obligatory and destroy individual moral freedom and choice. Why, Weinrib asks, is it more of a deprivation of liberty to be told that you have to call the police if you see a person in obvious danger than to be told that you must stop at a red light? The critics worry that a general duty to rescue might mean that a solvent person could be held civilly liable for refusing to supply the means of subsistence to someone who might otherwise starve. But what is the difference between this and our familiar system of social welfare programs?

More fundamentally, Weinrib tries to show that preoccupation with the infringement of liberty as an objection to a duty to rescue is misplaced. He maintains that the values supporting our deep concern with individual liberty operate most visibly in the law of contract. Contract law assumes that parties can reach agreements incurring only minimal transaction costs, that negotiations are possible and manageable, and that the parties occupy roughly equal bargaining positions. When these conditions hold and when the proposed arrangements are not otherwise illegal, the liberty of the parties to make such agreements as they see fit is accorded maximum scope. But, cautions Weinrib, there are situations—and rescue is one of them—in which these "contract" values are conspicuously absent, so a limited duty of "easy rescue," creating an affirmative obligation to aid another in an emergency when little or no inconvenience is posed for the rescuer, is consistent with liberty values. Weinrib tries to show that a duty of easy rescue could be explained and accounted for on either utilitarian or Kantian grounds.

McFall v. Shimp

Flaherty, [Judge].

The Plaintiff, Robert McFall, suffers from a rare bone marrow disease and the prognosis for his survival is very dim, unless he receives a bone marrow transplant from a compatible donor. Finding a compatible donor is a very difficult task, and limited to a selection among close relatives. After a search and certain tests, it has been determined that only the Defendant is suitable as a donor. The Defendant refuses to submit to the necessary transplant, and before the Court is a request for a preliminary injunction which seeks to compel the defendant to submit to further tests, and, eventually, the bone marrow transplant.

Although a diligent search has produced no authority, the Plaintiff cites the ancient statute of King Edward I, St. Westminster 2, 13 Ed., I, c 24, pointing out, as is the case, that this Court is a successor to the English courts of Chancery and derives power from this statute, almost 700 years old. The question posed by the Plaintiff is that, in order to save the life of one of its members by the only means available, may society infringe upon one's absolute right to his "bodily security"?

The common law has consistently held to a rule which provides that one human being is under no legal compulsion to give aid or to take action to save that human being or to rescue. A great deal has been written regarding this rule which, on the surface, appears to be revolting in a moral sense. Introspection, however, will demonstrate that the rule is founded upon the very essence of our free society. It is noteworthy that counsel for the Plaintiff has cited authority which has developed in other societies in support of the Plaintiff's request in this instance. Our society, contrary to many others, has as its first principle, the respect for the individual, and that society and government exist to protect the individual from being invaded and hurt by another. Many societies adopt a contrary view which has the individual existing to serve the society as a whole. In preserving such a society as we have it is bound to happen that great moral conflicts will arise and will appear harsh in a given instance. In this case, the chancellor is being asked to force one member of society to undergo a medical procedure which would provide that part of that individual's body would be removed from him and given to another so that the other could live. Morally, this decision rests with the Defendant, and, in the view of the Court, the refusal of the Defendant is morally indefensible. For our law to *compel* the Defendant to submit to an intrusion of his body would change the very concept and principle upon which our society is founded. To do so would defeat the sanctity of the individual, and would impose a rule which would know no limits, and one could not imagine where the line would be drawn. This request is not to be compared with an action at law for damages, but rather is an action in equity before a Chancellor, which, in the ultimate, if granted, would require the [forcible] submission to the medical procedure. For a society, which respects the rights of *one* individual, to sink its teeth into the jugular vein or neck of one of its members and suck from it sustenance for *another* member, is revolting to our hard-wrought concept of jurisprudence. [Forcible] extraction of living body tissue causes revulsion to the judicial mind. Such would raise the specter of the swastika and the inquisition, reminiscent of the horrors this portends.

The court makes no comment on the law regarding the Plaintiff's right in an action at law for damages, but has no alternative but to deny the requested equitable relief. An Order will be entered denying the request for a preliminary injunction.

No. 78-177711 (July 26, 1978), 10th Penn. District, Allegheny County.

Against a Legal Duty to Rescue

Thomas Babington Macaulay

Early in the progress of the Code it became necessary for us to consider the following question: When acts are made punishable on the ground that those acts produce, or are intended to produce, or are known to be likely to produce, certain evil effects, to what extent ought omissions which produce, which are intended to produce, or which are known to be likely to produce, the same evil effects to be made punishable?

Two things we take to be evident; first, that some of these omissions ought to be punished in exactly the same manner in which acts are punished; secondly, that not all these omissions ought to be punished. It will hardly be disputed that a jailer who voluntarily causes the death of a prisoner by omitting to supply that prisoner with food, or a nurse who voluntarily causes the death of an infant entrusted to her care by omitting to take it out of a tub of water into which it has fallen, ought to be treated as guilty of murder. On the other hand, it will hardly be maintained that a man should be punished as a murderer because he omitted to relieve a beggar, even though there might be the clearest proof that the death of the beggar was the effect of this omission, and that the man who omitted to give the alms knew that the death of the beggar was likely to be the effect of the omission. It will hardly be maintained that a surgeon ought to be treated as a murderer for refusing to go from Calcutta to Meerut to perform an operation, although it should be absolutely certain that this surgeon was the only person in India who could perform it, and that if it were not performed, the person who required it would die. It is difficult to say whether a penal code which should put no omissions on the same footing with acts, or a penal code which should put all omissions on the same footing with acts, would produce consequences more absurd and revolting. There is no country in which either of these principles is adopted. Indeed, it is hard to conceive how, if either were adopted, society could be held together.

It is plain, therefore, that a middle course must be taken; but it is not easy to determine what that middle course ought to be. The absurdity of the two extremes is obvious. But there are innumerable intermediate points; and wherever the line of demarcation may be drawn it will, we fear, include some cases which we might wish to exempt, and will exempt some which we might wish to include. . . .

What we propose is this, that where acts are made punishable on the ground that they have caused, or have been intended to cause, or have been known to be likely to cause, a certain evil effect, omissions which have caused, which have been intended to cause, or which have been known to be likely to cause the same effect, shall be punishable in the same manner, provided that such omissions were, on other grounds, illegal. An omission is illegal . . . if it be an offense, if it be a breach of some direction of law, or if it be such a wrong as would be a good ground for a civil action.

We cannot defend this rule better than by giving a few illustrations of the way in which it will operate. A omits to give Z food, and by that omission voluntarily causes Z's death. Is this murder? Under our rule it is murder if A was Z's gaoler, directed by the law to furnish Z with food. It is murder if Z was the infant child of and had, therefore, a legal right to sustenance, which right a Civil Court would enforce against A. It is murder if Z was a bedridden invalid, and A a nurse hired to feed Z. It is murder if A was detaining Z in unlawful confinement, and had thus contracted . . . a legal obligation to furnish during the continuance of the confinement, with necessaries. It is not murder if Z is a beggar, who has no other claim on A than that of humanity.

From Lady Trevelyan (ed.), *The Works of Lord Macaulay* (New York: D. Appleton & Co., 1866), Vol. 7, pp. 493–497.

A omits to tell *Z* that a river is swollen so high that *Z* cannot safely attempt to ford it, and by this omission voluntarily causes *Z*'s death. This is murder, if *A* is a peon stationed by authority to warn travelers from attempting to ford the river. It is a murder if *A* is a guide who had contracted to conduct *Z*. It is not murder if *A* is a person on whom *Z* has no other claim than that of humanity.

A savage dog fastens on *Z*. *A* omits to call off the dog, knowing that if the dog not be called off, it is likely that *Z* will be killed. *Z* is killed. This is murder in *A*, if the dog belonged to *A*, inasmuch as his omission to take proper order with the dog is illegal. But if *A* be a mere passerby, it is not murder.

We are sensible that in some of the cases which we have put, our rule may appear too lenient; but we do not think that it can be made more severe without disturbing the whole order of society. It is true that the man who, having abundance of wealth, suffers a fellow creature to die of hunger at his feet, is a bad man, a worse man, probably, than many of those whom we have provided very severe punishment. But we are unable to see where, if we make such a man legally punishable, we can draw the line. If the rich man who refuses to save a beggar's life at the cost of a little copper is a murderer, is the poor man just one degree above beggary also to be a murderer if he omits to invite the beggar to partake his hard-earned rice? Again, if the rich man is a murderer for refusing to save the beggar's life at the cost of a little copper, is he also to be a murderer if he refuses to save the beggar's life at the cost of a thousand rupees? Suppose *A* to be fully convinced that nothing can save *Z*'s life unless *Z* leave Bengal and reside a year at the Cape; is *A*, however wealthy he may be, to be punished as a murderer because he will not, at his own expense, send *Z* to the Cape? Surely not. Yet it will be difficult to say on what principle we can punish *A* for not spending an anna to save *Z*'s life, and leave him unpunished for not spending a thousand rupees to save *Z*'s life. The distinction between a legal and an illegal omission is perfectly plain and intelligible; but the distinction between a large and a small sum of money is very far from being so, not to say that a sum which is small to one man is large to another.

The same argument holds good in the case of the ford. It is true that none but a very depraved man would suffer another to be drowned when he might prevent it by a word. But if we punish such a man, where are we to stop? How much exertion are we to require? Is a person to be a murderer if he does not go fifty yards through the sun of Bengal at noon in May in order to caution a traveler against a swollen river? Is he to be a murderer if he does not go a hundred yards?—if he does not go a mile?—if he does not go ten? What is the precise amount of trouble and inconvenience which he is to endure? The distinction between the guide who is bound to conduct the traveler as safely as he can, and a mere stranger is a clear distinction. But the distinction between a stranger who will not give a halloo to save a man's life, and a stranger who will not run a mile to save a man's life, is very far from being equally clear.

It is, indeed, most highly desirable that men should not merely abstain from doing harm to their neighbours, but should render active services to their neighbours. In general, however, the penal law must content itself with keeping men from doing positive harm, and must leave to public opinion, and to the teachers of morality and religion, the office of furnishing men with motives for doing positive good. It is evident that to attempt to punish men by law for not rendering to others all the service which it is their duty to render to others would be preposterous. We must grant impunity to the vast majority of those omissions which a benevolent morality would pronounce reprehensible, and must content ourselves with punishing such omissions only when they are distinguished from the rest by some circumstance which marks them out as peculiarly fit objects of penal legislation. Now, no circumstance appears to us so well fitted to be the mark as the circumstance which we have selected. It will generally be found in the most atrocious cases of omission; it will scarcely ever by found in a venial case of omission; and it is more clear and certain than any other mark that has occurred to us. That there are objections to the line which we propose to draw, we have admitted. But there are objections to every line which can be drawn, and some lines must be drawn. . . .

The Case for a Duty to Rescue

Ernest Weinrib

No observer would have any difficulty outlining the current state of the law throughout the common-law world regarding the duty to rescue. Except when the person endangered and the potential rescuer are linked in a special relationship, there is no such duty. This general rule rests on the law's distinction between the infliction of harm and the failure to prevent it. The distinction between misfeasance and nonfeasance in turn reflects deeply rooted intuitions about causation, and it has played a critical role in the development of the common-law notions of contract and tort and of the boundary between them. In large part because this distinction is so fundamental to the common law, the courts have uniformly refused to enunciate a general duty to rescue, even in the face of repeated criticisms that the absence of such a duty is callous. Nonetheless, recent developments, both judicial and academic, justify a reconsideration of the common-law position.

On the judicial side, many of the outposts of the doctrine that there is no general duty to rescue have fallen. Recognizing the meritoriousness of rescue and the desirability of encouraging it, the courts have increasingly accorded favorable treatment to injured rescuers. When a rescuer sues for compensation for his injuries, voluntary assumption of risk cannot be interposed as a defense, contributory negligence comes into play only if the plaintiff has been reckless, and a broad range of rescue attempts are deemed reasonably foreseeable by the defendant. Moreover, the courts have increased the number of special relationships that require one person to aid another in peril. These developments have made the general absence of a duty to rescue seem more eccentric and isolated. They have also raised the possibility that the general rule is in the process of being consumed and supplanted by the widening ambit of the exceptions and that the rela-

tionship between the general rule and the exceptions may be fundamentally incoherent.

. . .

Consideration of the utilitarian approach towards rescue must begin with Jeremy Bentham's thought on the problem. "[I]n cases where the person is in danger," he asked, "why should it not be made the duty of every man to save another from mischief, when it can be done without prejudicing himself . . . ?"[1] Bentham supported the implicit answer to this question and several illustrations: using water at hand to quench a fire in a woman's headdress; moving a sleeping drunk whose face is in a puddle; warning a person about to carry a lighted candle into a room strewn with gunpowder. Bentham clearly had in mind a legal duty that would be triggered by the combination of the victim's emergency and the absence of inconvenience to the rescuer—that is, by the features of most of the proposed reforms requiring rescue. Unfortunately, the rhetorical question was the whole of Bentham's argument for his position. With this question, Bentham appealed directly to his reader's moral intuition; he did not show how his proposed duty can be derived through his distinctive felicific calculus.

Can one supply Benthamite justification that Bentham himself omitted? Because the avoidance of injury or death obviously contributes to the greatest happiness of the greatest number, the difficulties revolve not around the basic requirement of rescue but around the limitations placed upon that requirement by the notions of emergency and absence of inconvenience. Those limitations have no parallel with respect to participation in putting others at risk; they apply only in cases of nonfeasance. Indeed, Bentham's comments come in a section of his *Introduction to the Principles of Morals and Legislation* that distinguishes beneficence (increasing another's happiness) from probity (forbearing to diminish another's happiness). Yet Bentham had earlier contended that the distinction between acts of omission and acts of commission was of no significance.[2] The utilitarian's only concern is that an individual

From Ernest Weinrib, "The Case for a Duty to Rescue," *The Yale Law Journal*, Vol. 90 (1980): 247–293. Reprinted by permission of the Yale Law Journal and the author.

bring about a situation that results in a higher surplus of pleasure over pain than would any of the alternative situations that his actions could produce. Consequences are important; how they are reached is not. The distinction between nonfeasance and misfeasance has no place in this theory, and neither would the rescue duty's emergency or convenience limitations, which apply only after that distinction is made.

One solution to the apparent inconsistency between the rescue limitations and Benthamite theory's regard only for consequences is to drop the conditions of emergency and convenience as limitations on the duty to rescue. The position could be taken that there is an obligation to rescue whenever rescuing would result in greater net happiness than not rescuing. This principle, it is important to observe, cannot really be a principle about rescuing as that concept is generally understood. As a matter of common usage, a rescue presupposes the existence of an emergency, of a predicament that poses danger of greater magnitude and imminence than one ordinarily encounters. The proposed principle, however, requires no emergency to trigger a duty to act. The principle, in fact, is one of beneficence, not rescue, and should be formulated more generally to require providing aid whenever it will yield greater net happiness than not providing aid.

Eliminating the limitations regarding emergency and convenience might transform a requirement of rescue conceived along utilitarian lines into a requirement of perfect and general altruism. This demand of perfect altruism would be undesirable for several reasons. First, it would encourage the obnoxious character known to the law as the officious intermeddler. Also, its imposition of a duty of continual saintliness and heroism is unrealistic. Moreover, it would overwhelm the relationships founded on friendship and love as well as the distinction between the praiseworthy and the required; it would thereby obscure some efficient ways, in the utilitarian's eyes, of organizing and stimulating beneficence. Finally, the most fundamentally, it would be self-defeating. The requirement of aid assumes that there is some other person who has at least a minimal core of personhood as well as projects of his own that the altruist can further. In a society of perfect and general altruisms, however, any potential recipient of aid would himself be an altruist, who must, accordingly, subordinate the pursuit of his own projects to the rendering of aid to others. No one could claim for his own projects the priority that would provide others with a stable object of their altruistic ministrations. Each person would continually find himself obligated to attempt to embrace a phantom.

Although the utilitarian principle that requires the provision of aid whenever it will result in greater net happiness than failure to aid easily slips into the pure-altruism duty, it need not lead to so extreme a position. The obvious alternative interpretation of the principle is that aid is not obligatory whenever the costs to one's own projects outweigh the benefits to the recipient's. This interpretation avoids the embracing-of-phantoms objection to pure altruism, but it is subject to all the other criticisms of the purer theory. Because the cost-benefit calculus is so difficult to perform in particular instances, the duty would remain ill-defined. In many cases, therefore, it would encourage the officious intermeddler, seem unrealistically to require saintliness, overwhelm friendship and love, and obliterate the distinction between the praiseworthy and the required. Moreover, the vagueness of the duty would lead many individuals unhappily and inefficiently to drop their own projects in preference for those of others.

A different formulation of the rescue duty is needed to harness and temper the utilitarian impulses toward altruism and to direct them more precisely toward an intelligible goal. One important weakness of a too-generally beneficent utilitarianism is that it tempts one to consider only the immediate consequences of particular acts, and not the longer term consequences, the most important of which are the expectations generated that such acts will continue. If, as the classical utilitarians believed, the general happiness is advanced when people engage in productive activities that are of value to others, the harm done by a duty of general beneficence, in either version discussed above, would override its specific benefits. The deadening of industry resulting from both reliance on beneficence and devotion to beneficence would in the long run be an evil greater than the countenancing of individual instances of unfulfilled needs or wants. "In all cases of helping," wrote John Stuart Mill, in a passage concerned only with the reliance costs:

> there are two sets of consequences to be considered: the consequences of the assistance and the consequences of relying on the assistance. The former are generally beneficial, but the latter, for the most part, injurious. . . . There are few things for which it is more mischievous that people should rely on the habitual aid of others than for the means of subsistence, and unhappily there is no lesson which they more easily learn.[3]

Utilitarianism can use the notion of reliance to restrict the requirement of beneficence. If an act of beneficence would tend to induce reliance on similar acts, it should be avoided. If the act of beneficence does not have this tendency, it should be performed as long as the benefit produced is greater than the cost of performance. In the latter case, there are no harmful effects on industry flowing from excessive reliance to outweigh the specific benefits. This rule can account for Bentham's restriction of the duty to rescue to situations of emergency. People do not regularly expose themselves to extraordinary dangers in reliance on the relief that may be available if the emergency materializes, and only a fool would deliberately court a peril because he or others had previously been rescued from a similar one. As Sidgwick put it, an emergency rescue "will have no bad effect on the receiver, from the exceptional nature of the emergency."[4] Furthermore, an emergency is not only a desperate situation; it is also a situation that deviates from society's usual pattern. The relief of an emergency is therefore unlikely to induce reliance on the assistance of others in normal conditions. The abnormality of emergencies also means that rescuers can confidently pursue their own projects under normal circumstances. The motive for industry that Bentham located in each person's needs is not undermined by extraordinary and isolated events.

The role of emergency in the utilitarian obligation to rescue corresponds to, and illuminates, the definition of a legal duty to rescue by reference to the absence of contract values, as set out in the previous section. Utilitarian philosophy and the concept of the market are closely related. Both regard individuals as maximizers of their own happiness, and both see the use of contracts to acquire and to exchange property as conducive to the public good. Contract law's refusal to enforce certain transactions sets them apart from the usual structure of relationships, in which the satisfaction of the parties' needs and desires can legitimately serve as a stimulus to exchange. The person who sees a member of his own family in difficulty and the police officer who notices a hazard on the highway may not act as ordinary members of the market with respect to those endangered. Those pockets of contractual nonenforcement are sufficiently isolated that they are unlikely to be generalized: they will not generate a widespread reliance on assistance or sense of obligation to assist in settings where market exchanges are permitted and common.

An emergency is similar. Contract values are absent in such a situation because the assistance required is of such a kind that it cannot be purchased on ordinary commercial terms. Suspension of contract values in an emergency will not result in a general deadening of individual industry; the utilitarian can therefore confine his calculus to the specific consequences of the rescue. The denial of relief to the Southwark squatters[5] is a case in point. The desperate situation there was a consequence of poverty and not an extraordinary condition that deviated from the ordinary pattern of contemporary existence. The utilitarian must be concerned in that situation that judicially coercing individual assistance to the poor will generate a reliance whose harmful effects will, in the long run and across society as a whole, outweigh the benefits of the specific assistance.

Bentham's intuitive restriction of beneficence to situations of emergency can thus be supported on utilitarian grounds. Is the same true of the inconvenience limitation? As with the emergency restriction, finding utilitarian support requires looking behind the specific action to its social and legal context. For the utilitarian, the enforcement of a duty through legal sanctions is always an evil, which can be justified only to avoid a greater evil. If the sanction is applied, the offender suffers the pain of punishment. If the prospect of the sanction is sufficient to deter conduct, those deterred suffer the detriment of frustrated preferences. Moreover, the apparatus of enforcement siphons off social resources from other projects promoting the general happiness.

Accordingly, a utilitarian will be restrained and circumspect in the elaboration of legal duties. In particular, he will not pitch a standard of behavior at too high a level: the higher the standard, the more onerous it will be to the person subjected to it, the greater the pleasure that he must forego in adhering to it, and the greater his resistance to its demands. A high standard entails both more severe punishment and a more elaborate apparatus of detection and enforcement. Applied to the rescue situation, this reasoning implies that some convenience restriction should be adopted as part of the duty. Compelling the rescuer to place himself in physical danger, for instance, would be inefficacious, to use Bentham's terminology, because such coercion cannot influence the will: "the evil, which he sees himself about to undergo . . . is so great that the evil denounced by the penal clause . . . cannot appear greater."[6] Limiting the duty of rescue to emergency situations where the rescue will not inconvenience the rescuer—as judicial decisions would elaborate that limitation and thus give direction to individuals—minimizes both the interference with the rescuer's own preferences and the difficulties of enforcement that would result from recalcitrance. Bentham's second limitation can thus also be supported on a utilitarian basis.

The utilitarian arguments for the duty to rescue and for the limitations on that duty rest primarily on administrative considerations. The arguments focus not so much on the parties and their duties as persons as on the difficulties that might be created throughout the whole range of societal interactions. The elements of the duty are evaluated in terms of their likely consequences, no matter how remote. In the convenience limitation, for instance, whether the rescuer *ought* to feel aggrieved at the requirements of a high standard is of no concern. The likelihood that he *will* feel aggrieved is all that matters: for the Benthamite utilitarian, general happiness is the criterion of evaluation and not itself an object of evaluation. Moreover, recalcitrance necessitates more costly enforcement, and that consequence must also enter the calculus. The same is true for the emergency limitation. The argument for that limitation focused on the possibility that a particular instance of assistance would, by example, induce socially detrimental general reliance on beneficence. This use of example does not explore either the fairness of singling out particular persons for particular treatment or the consistency and scope of certain principles. Rather, the argument examines the cumulative consequences of repetition, and decides whether a particular person should perform a particular act on the basis of the act's implications for the entire society's market arrangements.

At least one philosopher has argued that administrative considerations of this sort are not moral ones at all, or that they are moral only in a derivative sense.[7] In this view, the administrative and enforcement considerations on which the utilitarian account of rescue rests are irrelevant to the individual's obligations as a moral agent. The individual should ask what he ought to do, not how others can compel him to fulfill his duty. The merit of this view is its observation that any utilitarian version of a duty to rescue has nuances that do not ring true to the moral contours of the situation. The person in need of rescue stands in danger of serious physical injury or loss of life, harms not quite comparable by any quantitative measure to other losses of happiness. Health and life are not merely components of the aggregate of goods that an individual enjoys. Rather, they are constitutive of the individual, who partakes of them in a unique and intimate way; they are the preconditions for the enjoyment of other goods. Moreover, there is something false in viewing an act of rescue as a contribution to the greatest happiness of the greatest number. If there

is an obligation to rescue, it is owed to particular persons rather than to the greatest number. Any such duty would require the rescuing not only of the eminent heart surgeon but also of the hermit bachelor; and even the duty to rescue the heart surgeon would be owed primarily to him, not to his present or prospective patients.

Because the utilitarian account of rescue thus appears to lack an important moral ingredient, and because utilitarianism is not the law's only important philosophical tradition, it is worth attempting to outline a non-utilitarian version of the obligation to rescue. Although the two approaches support the same conclusion, the arguments are different in texture. In particular, the non-utilitarian argument recognizes the distinctive importance of avoiding physical injury or death; it resists the assimilation of health and life to other goods. This attention to the centrality of the person avoids the utilitarian dilemma of either demanding excessive beneficence or having recourse to administrative considerations, which shifts the focus away from the rescuer's obligation to a particular endangered individual. In the non-utilitarian argument, or course, administrative considerations are not ignored; to do so would be impossible in elaborating an argument that attempts to provide an ethical foundation for a judicially enforced duty to rescue. Nonetheless, the non-utilitarian's use of administrative considerations differs from the utilitarian's. The utilitarian weaves the fabric of the duty to rescue out of administrative strands; the cost of administration and enforcement are relevant to the very existence of the duty. The non-utilitarian, by contrast, justifies a legal duty to rescue independently of the administrative costs; the mechanisms of enforcement are invoked only to structure and to coordinate the operation of the duty.

The deontological argument begins with the observation that the idea of an individual's being under a moral duty is intimately related to the notion that health and life are of distinctive importance. The concept of duty applies only to an individual endowed with the capacity to make choices and to set ends for himself. Further, the person, as a purposive and choosing entity, does not merely set physical integrity as one of his ends; he requires it as a precondition to the accomplishment of the purposes that his freedom gives him the power to set. As Kant put it, physical integrity is "the basic *stuff* (the matter) in man without which he could not realize his ends."[8]

A person contemplating the ethical exercise of his freedom of action must impose certain restrictions on that freedom. Because morality is something he shares with all humanity, he cannot claim a preferred moral position for himself. Any moral claim he makes must, by its very nature as a moral claim, be one to which he is subject when others can assert it. Acting on the basis of his own personhood therefore demands recognition of the personhood of others. This recognition, however, cannot be elaborated in the first instance in terms of the enjoyment of ordinary material goods. Because no conception of happiness is shared by everyone and is constant throughout any individual's life, the universal concept of personhood cannot be reflected in a system of moral duties directed at the satisfaction of unstable desires for such goods. Physical integrity, by contrast, is necessary for the accomplishment of any human aim, and so is an appropriate subject for a system of mutually restraining duties.

An individual contemplating his actions from a moral point of view must recognize that all others form their projects on a substratum of physical integrity. If he claims the freedom to pursue his projects as a moral right, he cannot as a rational and moral agent deny to others the same freedom. Because his claim to that freedom implies a right to the physical integrity that is necessary to its exercise, he must concede to others the right to physical integrity that he implicitly and inevitably claims for himself.

This conception of the right to life and health derives from the notion of personhood that is presupposed by the concept of moral action. So too do the right's natural limitations. The duty of beneficence exacted by this right need not collapse into a comprehensive and self-defeating altruism. Respect for another's physical security does not entail foregoing one's own.[9] The right to life and health, seen to give content to the universal concept of personhood, must be ascribed not only to others, but also to oneself. As Kant put it,

> since all *other* men with the exception of myself would not be *all* men, and the maxim would then not have the universality of a law, as it must have in order to be obligatory, the law prescribing the duty of benevolence will include myself, as the object of benevolence, in the command of practical reason.[10]

Moreover, the universalizing process radiates outward from the actor: it is only one's desire to act that makes necessary the exploration of the action's implicit claims and thus of the rights that he must rationally concede to others.[11] The priority of the actor is thus embedded in the structure of the argument and should be reflected in the concrete duties that the argument yields.

This outline of deontological analysis can be applied to examine the standard suggestion that the common law should recognize a duty to effect an easy rescue. Such a duty would be the judicial analogue of a moral obligation to respect the person of another and to safeguard his physical integrity, which is necessary for whatever aims he chooses to pursue. The emergency and convenience limitations also fit quite readily into the analysis. An emergency is a particularly imminent threat to physical security, and the convenience limitation reflects the rescuer's entitlement to the priority of his own physical security over that of the endangered person. Although the proposed legal duty fits comfortably within the deontological moral duty of beneficence, however, the two are not coextensive. Emergencies are not the only circumstances in which life and health are threatened; disease, starvation, and poverty can affect the physical substratum of personhood on a routine basis. If legal duties must reflect moral ones, should not a legal duty to rescue be supplemented by a legal duty to alleviate those less isolated abridgments of physical security?

The convenience limitation on the rescue duty might similarly be loosened in a deontological analysis. One tempting extension would be very far-reaching: if the physical substratum is the "basic *stuff* (the matter) in man without which he could not realize his ends," and if we are under a duty to safeguard that substratum in others as in ourselves, the priority that the rescuer can legitimately grant to himself can be only with respect to his physical integrity. Under this extension, a rescuer could—indeed would be obligated to—abstain from acting only if the act would place him in physical danger; if it would not put him in danger, he would be required to attempt a rescue, no matter what the disruption of his life. In Macaulay's famous example, the surgeon would have to travel from Calcutta to Meerut to perform an operation that only he could perform, because the journey, though inconvenient, would not be dangerous. Indeed, he would have to make the trip even if he were about to leave for Europe or to greet members of his family arriving on an incoming ship. The patient's right to physical security would rank ahead of the satisfaction of the surgeon's contingent desires.

The deontological approach to rescue does not compel such a drastic extension. Although every moral person must value physical integrity, its protection is not an end in itself. Rather, physical security is valued because it allows individuals to realize their own projects and purposes. Whatever the reach of the right to physical integrity, therefore, it must allow the rescuer to satisfy his purposes in a reasonably coherent way. Still, though the extension of the moral duty cannot be so drastic as to require the sacrifice of all of a person's projects, it can be substantial. It can require the rescuer to undergo considerable inconvenience short of fundamental changes in the fabric of his life. The deontological duty relaxes both the emergency and convenience limitations of the duty of easy rescue in emergencies: it applies not only in emergencies but whenever physical integrity is threatened, and it applies even when the rescuer might have to undergo considerable inconveniences. The duty might, after all, obligate Macaulay's surgeon to travel from Calcutta to Meerut. Would it also require the wealthy to use at least some of their resources to alleviate the plight of the starving and the afflicted? For those concerned about the possibility of setting principled limits to a duty of rescue, the question is critical.

The objection to an affirmative answer to the question rests on the premises that even the wealthy are under no obligation to be charitable and that the afflicted have no right to receive charity. Under the deontological theory, those premises are incorrect. The duty of beneficence derives from the concept of personhood; it is therefore not properly called charity, for the benefactor's performance of this duty is no reason for self-congratulation. Although the duty is an imperfect one—"since no determinate limits can be assigned to what should be done, the duty has in it a play-room for doing more or less,"[12] as Kant said—it is nonetheless a duty to the performance of which the recipient is entitled.

The extent of the duty of beneficence, of course, can still be troubling. It is the indeterminateness of the duty, the "play-room," that is particularly relevant to this problem. Kant meant by this expression that the form and the amount of the benefaction would vary, depending on the resources of the benefactor, the identity of the recipient, and the recipient's own conception of happiness. The indeterminateness, however, applies not only to the form of the benefaction but also to the linking of particular benefactors to particular beneficiaries. Why should any particular person be singled out of the whole group of potential benefactors, and why should the benefit be conferred on one rather than another person in need? If a duty "may be *exacted* from a person, as one exacts a debt," it is a debt that leaves unclear the precise terms of discharge as well as the identities of obligor and obligee.

The proper response to this indeterminacy is not to deny that there is a duty. What is required is to set up social institutions to perform the necessary tasks of coordination and determination. Those institutions would ensure that no person is singled out unfairly either for burdens or for benefits, and that the forms of benefaction correlate both with the resources of those who give and with the needs of those who receive. In fact, all Western democracies undertake to perform this task through programs for social assistance. The institutions they establish, however, are primarily legislative and administrative; precisely because a general duty of beneficence is imperfect, it cannot be judicially enforced. The traditional claim-settling function of courts does not permit the transfer of a resource from one person to another solely because the former has it and the latter needs it. Such judicial action would unfairly prefer one needy person over others and unfairly burden one resourceful person over others. Because the duty of beneficence is general and indeterminate, it does not, in the absence of legislative action that specifies and coordinates, yield judicially enforceable moral claims by individuals against others.

The significant characteristic of the emergency and convenience limitations is that, in combination, they eliminate the "play-room" inherent in the duty of beneficence, thus providing a principled response to Kant and to Epstein and rendering the narrower duty to rescue appropriate for judicial enforcement. An emergency marks a particular person as physically endangered in a way that is not general or routine throughout the society. An imminent peril cannot await assistance from the appropriate social institutions. The provision of aid to an emergency victim does not deplete the social resources committed to the alleviation of more routine threats to physical integrity. Moreover, aid in such circumstances presents no unfairness problems in singling out a particular person to receive the aid. Similarly, emergency aid does not unfairly single out one of a class of routinely advantaged persons; the rescuer just happens to find himself for a short period in a position, which few if any others share, to render a service to some specific person. In addition, when a rescue can be accomplished without a significant disruption of his own projects, the rescuer's freedom to realize his own ends is not abridged by the duty to preserve the physical security of another. In sum, when there is an emergency that the rescuer can alleviate with no inconvenience to himself, the general duty of beneficence that is suspended over society like a floating charge is temporarily revealed to identify a particular obligor and obligee, and to define obligations that are specific enough for judicial enforcement.

Conclusion

The problem of rescue is a central issue in the controversies about the relationships between law and morality, between contract and tort, and between utilitarian and deontological ethics. The argument of this article has been that tort law's adoption of a duty of easy rescue in emergencies would fit a common-law pattern, found principally in contract law, that gives expression to the law's understanding of liberty. This pattern reveals that the common-law is already instinct with the attitude of benevolence on which a duty to rescue is grounded. The attitude of benevolence is accepted by many legal commentators as a basic moral intuition, yet the particular duty proposed in this article can be systematically elaborated in both the utilitarian and deontological traditions. For those who believe that law should attempt to render concrete the notion of ethical dealing between persons, as well as for those concerned about the method of common-law evolution or about the social costs of legal rules, the article provides an argument for changing the common-law rule on rescue.

Endnotes

[1] *See* J. Bentham, An Introduction to the Principles of Morals and Legislation 74–83 (J. Burns & H. Hart eds. 1970); *see* J. Bentham, The Principles of Legislation 85–86 (R. Hildreth ed. 1840).

[2] *See* J. Bentham, *supra* note 1, at 74–83

[3] J. S. Mill, The Principles of Political Economy 967 (W. Ashley ed. 1923).

[4] H. Sidgwick, The Methods of Ethics 219 (7th ed. 1907) at 437.

[5] *London Borough of Southwark v. Williams*, [1971] 2 All E. R. 175 (C.A.).

[6] Bentham, *supra* note 1, at 162 (footnote omitted).

[7] *See* Fried, *Right and Wrong—Preliminary Considerations*, 5 J. Legal Studies 165, 181–182 (1976).

[8] I. Kant, *The Metaphysical Principles of Virtue* 49 (M. Gregor trans. 1964), at 112.

[9] [*Id.*] at 53, 122.

[10] *Id.* at 118.

[11] [*Id.*] at 112.

[12] *Id.* at 121.

Study Questions

1. Why did judge Flaherty refuse to order Shimp to undergo the bone marrow donation?

2. What two limitations or qualifications does Weinrib place on the duty to rescue?

3. According to Weinrib, how is the duty of easy rescue consistent with a deontological basis for a duty to rescue?

4. It is a widely followed rule that when you *begin* a rescue, by taking steps upon which the victim or other potential rescuers might rely, you may not legally stop or abort the rescue, saying that you are merely leaving the situation unaltered; the law says that after you have acted, any subsequent abandonment is no longer a mere failure to act. Why is it worse to begin treatment and then abandon the victim than never to have begun in the first place? Can you see how this rule might create perverse incentives for potential rescuers?

5. In *Depue v. Flateau* (111 N.W. 1[1907]), a traveling cattle buyer called upon a customer and asked to stay for dinner. During the meal, he was overcome by a "fainting spell" and fell seriously ill. He asked permission to stay the night (it being a cold winter evening in Minnesota) but was refused. Flateau led Depue to his cart, set him in it, handed him the reins (which Depue was too weak to hold), and started the horses on their way. Depue was found in a ditch the following morning, nearly frozen to death. Depue alleged that Flateau was negligent in not allowing him to stay the night. The court, ruling in favor of Depue, articulated the following principle: "Whenever a person is placed in such a position with regard to another that it is obvious that, if he does not use due care in his own conduct, he will cause injury to that person, the duty at once arises to exercise care commensurate with the situation in which he thus finds himself . . . to avoid such danger." Should the law incorporate this language as stating a general duty to rescue? If applied across the board, what consequences would this principle have?

6. Why was the "intrusion" into David Shimp's body requested by McFall an impermissible one? The donation procedure required the insertion of a curved needle into the donor's hip bone and the removal of 5 cc of marrow. Because 500 cc would

have been required by McFall, roughly 100 such taps would have been performed on Shimp. Consider that the law not only permits but actually requires some forms of "bodily intrusion," such as vaccinations. And a few courts have allowed blood transfusions to be performed upon patients who oppose them on religious grounds (*John F. Kennedy Memorial Hospital v. Heston*, 58 N.J. 576[1971]). Why are these cases different from Shimp's? What is an intrusion, anyway? Is simply breaking the skin enough? If so, how is a bone marrow transplant more of an intrusion than a blood transfusion? Would it make a difference had a scalpel been necessary for the marrow donation procedure?

7. Commentators Alan Meisel and Loren H. Roth argue that Judge Flaherty made the correct decision in *McFall*: "Despite the high potential benefits to the recipient [and] the relatively low risks . . . to the donor, . . . irreparable harm would be done to the values of individual autonomy, privacy, and bodily and psychic integrity from compelling a transplant of any kind. . . . No matter how idiosyncratic Shimp's reasons for refusal, his mere wish not to donate marrow should not be overridden. . . . [W]e must be willing to respect his decision even if he could articulate no reasons whatsoever for refusing" (Meisel and Roth, "Must a Man Be His Cousin's Keeper?" *Hastings Center Report* [October 1978]: 5–6.) Do you agree? Why or why not?

8. Why should so much weight be placed by the law upon the misfeasance/nonfeasance distinction? Imagine the following situation (this hypothetical scenario is taken from John Harris, "The Survival Lottery," *Philosophy,* Vol. 50 [1975]: 81–87): Two patients, Y and Z, will each die soon unless they obtain, respectively, a new heart and a new lung. No donor organs are available in the normal way, so Y and Z make a proposal. If just one healthy person, A, were killed, his or her organs could be removed and transplanted into Y and Z, saving two lives at the cost of one. Using this approach, many lives could be saved. To allay the inevitable insecurity that would attend such a proposal (Will I be the next to go?) and to quell the legitimate fear of abuse, Y and Z suggest a "survival lottery": Everyone is given a number; if and when your number is called, you are secretly taken into custody and painlessly killed so that your organs might "give life" to others. To the doctors' objec-

tion that killing the innocent A is morally impermissible, Y and Z respond that, should the doctors fail to kill one to save two, *they* (the doctors) will be responsible for the deaths of the two; and even if it is wrong to kill "innocent" persons, Y and Z are just as innocent as A. Is there some morally relevant difference between bringing about the death of A through misfeasance and bringing about the deaths of Y and Z through nonfeasance? Given the assumption that a world in which Y and Z both live is better overall than the one in which A lives, can it matter how that world comes about? Compare the reasoning of Y and Z to the case of Robert McFall. Can it be said that Judge Flaherty, by refusing to grant McFall's request, is responsible for McFall's death? Did McFall die as a result of the inaction by Judge Flaherty or by "natural causes"? Is there a difference?

9. Recent critics of negligence law argue that existing doctrine and its language of "standards of care" for the "safety of others" and "unreasonable" conduct focuses upon abstract categories and cost-benefit calculations in a way unresponsive to real human needs. Preoccupation with a reasoned and distanced analysis of cases such as *McFall v. Shimp* fails, they contend, to show respect for people and to acknowledge their sufferings, forcing out the caring, compassionate human response that the plight of people such as McFall tends to evoke. Rather than appeal to the duties of the "reasonable man," one critic has suggested that the law "measure the conduct of a tortfeasor [one who commits a tort] by the care that would be taken by a . . . responsible person with conscious care and concern for another's safety," the way one would act "out of care for a neighbor or friend"(Leslie Bender, "A Lawyer's Primer on Feminist Theory and Tort," *Journal of Legal Education*, Vol. 38 [1988]: 25). The duty to act with the conscious care and concern of a responsible neighbor would require an affirmative duty to rescue "under appropriate circumstances," measured by one's "ability to aid and one's proximity to the need" (*Ibid*, p. 36). Does this language state a workable standard? Does the proposed standard represent an improvement over the existing reasonable-man standard? Why or why not?

10. An early proposal for changing the legal doctrine concerning rescue is attributed to James Barr Ames,

"Law and Morals," 22 *Harvard Law Review* 97 (1908). Ames proposed that the rule should be as follows: One who fails to interfere to save another from impending death or great bodily harm, when he might do so with little or no inconvenience to himself, and the death or great bodily harm follows as a consequence of his inaction, shall be punished criminally and shall make compensation to the party injured or to his widow and children in case of death.

Is this an acceptable formulation of a duty to rescue? What implications might it have? Why should rescue be limited to situations in which there is "little or no inconvenience" to the would-be rescuer? Couldn't one make a utilitarian argument that even significant inconvenience is likely to be a lesser cost than the loss of life resulting from a failure to rescue?

11. Macaulay insists that we "must leave to public opinion, and to the teachers of morality and religion, the office of furnishing men with motives for doing positive good." Why can't the law shape people's motives and teach them that coming to the aid of others is something they ought to do?

12. Do your intuitions agree with Macaulay regarding the illustrative cases he outlines?

13. In *Dalton v. Marietta* [No. 2002A-94244-2 (Cobb Co. GA ; 2002)] a 16-year-old boy suffered a head injury while playing soccer. A neurosurgeon, shopping across town at a store owned by Marietta, was paged to the hospital on an emergency basis. Leaving the store quickly, the physician started backing out when he noticed an SUV blocking his exit. The driver of the SUV became irate, claiming that the physician had hit her car (a claim he denied), and contacted the police. Despite his urgent pleas, the police detained the doctor, and the boy died. Who caused the boy's death? Who should be held responsible for it?

14. Driver got drunk at a party and, despite pleas from his friends, left in his car. Driver careened down the road and struck Victim. Victim was rushed to the hospital with severe internal bleeding. A devout Jehovah's Witness, Victim adamantly and repeatedly refused a transfusion that physicians testified would almost certainly have saved her life. What was the cause of Victim's death? The refusal of a transfusion? The negligence of Driver? Should Driver be made to "take his victim as he found her"? Did Victim fail to "mitigate damages"? (See "Jury to Decide if Victim Was Murdered or Let Herself Die," *Los Angeles Times*, Sat., March 13, 1999, p. B5.)

Cases for Further Reflection
Quirke v. City of Harvey

The facts of this case are "quirky" indeed. Study the court's analysis, then consider these questions: Do you agree with the court's ruling that it was a "remote risk" that Cain and Miller would collide at night in a darkened intersection with the inoperative signals? How many drivers would actually come to a complete stop in such a situation? Would the "reasonable drive" expect that a traffic officer or a portable stop sign would have been stationed at the intersection? Are you convinced by the court's effort to distinguish the situation in this case from the precedent case, *Bentley v. Saunemin Township*? In that case, the city was held liable for allowing a stop sign to be obscured by tree branches. How is the situation in *Quirke* different? Would Hart and Honoré's way of distinguishing a "cause" from a "condition" lead to the same conclusion arrived at by the court here? Though the court does not discuss it here, do you think that Quirke would have a case in negligence against Lewis, the man who climbed the power pole?

OPINION: JUSTICE THIES delivered the opinion of the court:

We are called upon to determine whether the actions of City officials and an electric company in turning off the power line that supplied local traffic signals and street lighting created a condition or a proximate cause of an intersectional automobile collision. We conclude that these actions created a condition, and we affirm the grant of summary judgment in favor of the City and the electric company.

This bizarre sequence of events began at approximately 9:30 P.M. on August 21, 1990, when defendant James Lewis, who had recently been fired by Commonwealth Edison, climbed up a 34,000-volt power pole in the City of Harvey and threatened to electrocute himself. By 12:30 or 1.00 A.M., the crowd had grown to about 75 persons, including the chiefs of both the police and fire departments. Lewis eventually agreed to come down from the pole in a Commonwealth Edison lift truck that had been brought to the site.

During the time Lewis was atop the power pole, the Harvey police chief directed Commonwealth Edison to turn off the City's major power line. This power line supplied electricity to many traffic signals and street light systems in Harvey. As a result of the power shutdown, one area left without power to its traffic signals and overhead street lights was the intersection at 147th Street and Halsted, three or four blocks from the site where Lewis had climbed the electrical pole.

At approximately 1:00 A.M., Michael Cain, then 18, was driving a Jeep CJ-7 with passenger Brian Quirke after the two had attended a concert in Tinley Park. After stopping for pizza, they got lost while trying to return to Interstate 294. Not realizing that they were heading east on 147th Street in Harvey, Cain drove along looking for signs that would lead them back to the expressway. Cain recalled at his deposition that the street was poorly lit and that they drove through areas where the street lights had been "knocked out." Nevertheless, he testified that he could see the roadway in front of him "just fine."

After driving for some three or four miles from the pizza restaurant, Cain noticed that there was no

street lighting ahead of the car. As he approached within 100 yards of the intersection at 147th and Halsted, he saw that the traffic control light hanging over the intersection was out. He testified that as he came within 50 yards of the intersection, he slowed down from 25 or 30 miles per hour to 10 or 15 because of the inoperative traffic light.

Cain also testified that the lack of lighting obscured his view ahead on 147th and that the surrounding buildings obstructed his view down Halsted. He did not stop at the intersection because he saw another car proceed through it and because he "wasn't quite up on the rules of the road." At the time he proceeded into the intersection, Cain testified he was traveling 10 miles per hour. In his written answer to an interrogatory about the rate of speed he was driving at the time of the accident, however, Cain responded that he was driving 30 miles per hour.

Cain's jeep collided with a car driven by Denise Miller, who had entered the intersection heading northbound on Halsted. Cain stated that he did not see Miller's vehicle until a "split second" before his vehicle collided into hers. Cain was looking "probably straight ahead right before she hit me." According to Cain, Miller was driving 40 or 45 miles per hour. The impact from the collision caused passenger Brian Quirke to be thrown out the door, which had flown open. The jeep spun around three or four times. Cain was not injured.

Plaintiff Quirke testified that approximately five minutes before the accident, he noticed that their vehicle had moved from an area illuminated by street lighting to an area obscured in relative darkness. Quirke stated that their jeep was traveling 40 to 45 miles per hour at the time. He added that despite the darkened conditions, Cain never slowed down before entering the intersection at 147th and Halsted.

On march 5, 1991, Quirke brought a negligence action against the City of Harvey, Cain, Miller, Commonwealth Edison, and James Lewis for personal injuries sustained in the accident. Miller's insurer filed a subrogation claim against Cain, and that case was consolidated with this one on October 29, 1991. The City of Harvey subsequently counterclaimed for contribution against Cain and Commonwealth Edison, and Cain counterclaimed against the City of Harvey and Commonwealth Edition.

639 N.E.2d 1355 (1944), Appellate Court of Illinois, First District, Fourth Division.

On September 15, 1992, Commonwealth Edison moved for summary judgment with respect to Quirke's action and all counterclaims, and the City of Harvey joined the motion. On January 29, 1993, the trial court granted summary judgment in favor of both Commonwealth Edison and the City of Harvey against Quirke and against Cain on Cain's counterclaims. In announcing her ruling, the trial judge stated that the darkened street and inoperative traffic lights at the intersection constituted a condition and not a proximate cause of the accident.

Quirke subsequently moved for reconsideration and, for the first time, tendered to the trial court an unsworn statement of Denise Miller, dated September 13, 1990, who responded to oral interrogatories posed by an investigator hired by Quirke. In that statement, Miller asserted that on the night of the accident, she did not realize that there was an intersection until she had driven right into it. She also blamed the City of Harvey for failing to position someone at the intersection after the power outage to direct traffic. The defendants objected to admission of this testimony on the grounds that it was unsworn, untimely, and added little information to that which was already contained in the record. Cain adopted and joined in Quirke's motion for reconsideration.

The trial judge refused to alter her ruling. She explained that the Miller statement was not newly acquired evidence unavailable to Quirke at the time of the summary judgment ruling. She noted, additionally, that even if she did consider the contents of the statement, nothing in the statement would cause her to change her ruling. In denying the motion for reconsideration, the court again stated that the inoperative traffic controls constituted merely a condition:

> "It is my opinion and my interpretation of the law that the creation of the darkness at this particular intersection where the plaintiff sustained his injuries was a creation of a condition . . . , [and the] conduct [of the drivers of the motor vehicles] is something entirely different."

Quirke and Cain then filed this appeal.

Discussion

Summary judgment is appropriate where the pleadings, depositions, and affidavits show that there is no genuine issue of material fact, and the moving party is entitled to judgment as a matter of law. . . .

Quirke and Cain argue on appeal that the trial court erred in entering summary judgment in favor of Commonwealth Edison and the City of Harvey because the appellees' negligence furnished a proximate cause rather than a condition of the accident. Quirke and Cain also argue that Commonwealth Edison and the City of Harvey should have foreseen that an intersection collision would occur once the appellees shut off the power line supplying electricity to traffic and street lights.

Illinois case law distinguishes between the proximate cause of an injury and a condition which provides an opportunity for the causal agency to act. The supreme court has articulated this "cause vs. condition" analysis in the following terms: "If a defendant's negligence does nothing more than furnish a condition by which injury is made possible, that negligence is not the proximate cause of injury." (*Thompson v. County of Cook* [1993], 154 Ill. 2d 374, 383).

Proximate cause exists when the injury is the natural and probable result of the defendant's negligent act, and the injury is of the sort that an ordinary prudent person ought to have foreseen as likely to occur as a result of the negligence. A defendant's negligence is not a proximate cause of a plaintiff's injury if some intervening act supersedes defendant's negligence; however, if a defendant could reasonably foresee the intervening act, that act will not relieve the defendant of liability. Proximate cause is generally a question of fact; however, where the facts alleged suggest that a party would never be able to recover, proximate cause can become a question of law. Contrary to appellants' assertions, the distinction between causation and condition remains viable in Illinois.

The "cause vs. condition" doctrine was recently applied by this court in *Quintana v. City of Chicago* (1992), 230 Ill. App. 3d 1032, 596 N.E.2d 128, 172 Ill. Dec. 849. In that case, the pedestrian plaintiff brought a negligence action against the City of Chicago and four individual drivers after she was struck by an automobile that had collided with two other vehicles as she was crossing a Chicago street. At the time of the accident, the traffic lights at the intersection were inoperative. The appellate court affirmed the grant of summary judgment in favor of the City, concluding that the inoperative signal lights were not the proximate cause of the pedestrian's injuries. Any causal connection between the original wrong and the injury was broken by the conduct of the drivers in failing to comply with the statutory requirement that inoperative lights be treated as stop signs.

Appellants attempt to distinguish *Quintana* on the basis that the traffic signals in that case malfunctioned during daylight hours. Appellants argue that no such unforeseeable malfunctioning occurred here. Rather, they contend the City and the electric company made an affirmative decision to shut off the power line supplying electricity to traffic signals and street lights at night.

We are not persuaded by this distinction. The relevant inquiry here is not whether traffic lights are rendered inoperative through malfunctioning or affirmative actions, but rather whether the drivers' conduct was foreseeable.

Appellants argue that the intervening acts of Cain and Miller were a reasonably foreseeable result of the appellees' decision to turn off all the street lights and traffic signals at a busy intersection in the middle of the night. In support, appellants cite *Bentley v. Saunemin Township* (1980), 83 Ill. 2d 10, 413 N.E.2d 1242, 46 Ill. Dec. 129, an automobile collision case involving an intervening negligent act. In *Bentley*, the driver of a car in which the plaintiff's decedent was a passenger failed to see the sign and collided with another vehicle in the intersection of the highway. The Illinois Supreme Court held that the township was negligent as a matter of law for allowing the branches of a tree to obscure the visibility of a stop sign at the entrance to a State Highway. The township should have foreseen that a driver who lacked the benefit of a stop sign would fail to recognize the approaching hazardous intersection. Because more than one proximate cause of an injury can exist, the negligence of the driver was not a superseding cause that relieved the township of liability.

Appellant's reliance on *Bentley* is misplaced. In that case, the township's failure to remove the overhanging foliage prevented drivers from recognizing the approaching hazards. Here, by contrast, appellees' alleged negligence did not prevent the appellants from discerning that the traffic lights at the intersection of 147th and Halsted had been turned off. It is undisputed that Michael Cain saw the intersection when he was about 100 yards away, and that he noticed that the traffic control lights at the intersection were not operating. Furthermore, under the Illinois Vehicle Code, a driver approaching a traffic control signal on which no signal light is illuminated must stop before entering the intersection. Appellees here could not have reasonably foreseen that one or both of the drivers would violate their statutory duty to treat an inoperable traffic light as a stop sign and then proceed into the intersection. . . .

We also reject appellants' suggestion that the City of Harvey's counterclaim for contribution against Commonwealth Edison establishes that the City foresaw the prospect of an accident if the intersection were left unlit or unpatrolled. The counterclaim is neither at issue in this appeal nor relevant to the question of whether summary judgment on the issue of causation was properly granted. Similarly, the statement of Denise Miller attributing blame to the City of Harvey is only an opinion and does not establish any disputed issue of fact as to the question of whether appellees' acts created a condition or proximate cause of the accident.

The City of Harvey and Commonwealth Edison cannot be held legally responsible for the remote risk that someone, when encountering a major intersection that has been rendered dark due to an emergency power shutdown, will disregard the rules of the road and proceed through the intersection without stopping.

For the foregoing reasons, we affirm the judgment of the trial court.

Affirmed.

HOFFMAN, P. J., and JOHNSON, J., concur.

Derdiarian v. Felix Contracting Corp.

This case was discussed in the introduction to Section B of this chapter on Causation and Liability. As noted there, this case nicely raises a number of issues dealing with the concept of proximate cause in the law of tort. When reading this case, consider these questions: What is it that made the actions of Felix Contracting negligent? On what grounds did Felix argue that the accident was "freakish"? Even if it was freakish, why should that relieve Felix of liability? How would you assess the responsibility of the motorist, Dickens? Suppose Dickens had crashed because he was drunk? Would that change the way the causal analysis works out?

Plaintiff obtained a judgment after a jury verdict. The appellate division affirmed. The facts are set forth in the opinion.

Chief Judge Cooke.

. . .

The order of the Appellate Division should be affirmed. As a general rule, the question of proximate cause is to be decided by the finder of fact, aided by appropriate instructions. There is no basis on this record for concluding, as a matter of law, that a superseding cause or other factor intervened to break the nexus between defendant's negligence and plaintiff's injury.

During the fall of 1973 defendant Felix Contracting Corporation was performing a contract to install an underground gas main in the City of Mount Vernon for defendant Con Edison. Bayside Pipe Coaters, plaintiff Harold Derdiarian's employer, was engaged as a subcontractor to seal the gas main.

On the afternoon of November 21, 1973, defendant James Dickens suffered an epileptic seizure and lost consciousness, allowing his vehicle to careen into the work site and strike plaintiff with such force as to throw him into the air. When plaintiff landed, he was splattered over his face, head and body with 400 degree boiling hot liquid enamel from a kettle struck by the automobile. The enamel was used in connection with sealing the gas main. Although plaintiff's body ignited into a fire ball, he miraculously survived the incident.

At trial, plaintiff's theory was that defendant Felix had negligently failed to take adequate measure to insure the safety of workers on the excavation site. Plaintiff's evidence indicates that the accident occurred on Oak Street, a two-lane, east-west roadway. The excavation was located in the eastbound lane, and ran from approximately one foot south of the center line within 2 or 3 feet of the curb. When plaintiff arrived on the site, he was instructed by Felix' foreman to park his truck on the west side of the excavation, parallel to the curb. As a result, there was a gap of some 7½ feet between the side of the truck and the curb line. Derdiarian testified that he made a request to park his truck on the east side of the hole, so he could set up the kettle away from the oncoming eastbound traffic. The Felix foreman instructed him to

leave his truck where it was, and plaintiff then put the kettle near the curb, on the west side of the excavation.

James Dickens was driving eastbound on Oak Street when he suffered a seizure and lost consciousness. Dickens was under treatment for epilepsy and had neglected to take his medication at the proper time. His car crashed through a single wooden horse-type barricade that was set up on the west side of the excavation site. As it passed through the site, the vehicle struck the kettle containing the enamel, as well as the plaintiff, resulting in plaintiff's injuries.

To support his claim of an unsafe work site, plaintiff called as a witness Lawrence Lawton, an expert in traffic safety. According to Lawton, the usual and accepted method of safe-guarding the workers is to erect a barrier around the excavation. Such a barrier, consisting of a truck, a piece of heavy equipment or a pile of dirt, would keep a car out of the excavation and protect workers from oncoming traffic. The expert testified that the barrier should cover the entire width of the excavation. He also stated that there should have been two flagmen present, rather than one, and that warning signs should have been posted advising motorists that there was only one lane of traffic and that there was a flagman ahead.

. . . Defendant Felix now argues that plaintiff was injured in a freakish accident, brought about solely by defendant Dickens' negligence, and therefore there was no casual link, as a matter of law, between Felix' breach of duty and plaintiff's injuries.

The concept of proximate cause, or more appropriately legal cause, has proven to be an elusive one, incapable of being precisely defined to cover all situations. . . . This is, in part, because the concept stems from policy considerations that serve to place management limits upon the liability that flows from negligent conduct (e.g., *Ventricelli v. Kinney System Rent A Car*, 45 N.Y.2d 950, 952; *Palsgraf v. Long Is. R. R. Co.*, 248 N.Y.339, 352 [Andrews, J., dissenting]). Depending upon the nature of the case, a variety of factors may be relevant in assessing legal cause. Given the unique nature of the inquiry in each case, it is for the finder of fact to determine legal cause, once the court has been satisfied that a prima facie case has been established. . . . To carry the burden of proving a prima facie case, the plaintiff must generally show that the defendant's negligence was a substantial cause of the events which produced the injury. . . . Plaintiff need not demonstrate, however, that the precise manner in which the accident happened, or the extent of injuries, was foreseeable. . . .

Where the acts of a third person intervene between the defendant's conduct and the plaintiff's injury, the causal connection is not automatically. In such a case, liability turns upon whether the intervening act is a normal foreseeable consequence of the situation created by the defendant's negligence. . . . If the intervening act is extraordinary under the circumstances, not foreseeable in the normal course of events, or independent of or far removed from the defendant's conduct, it may will be a superseding act which breaks the causal nexus. . . . Because questions concerning what is foreseeable and what is normal may be the subject of varying inferences, as is the question of negligence itself, these issues generally are for the fact finder to resolve.

There are certain instances, to be sure, where only one conclusion may be drawn from the established facts and where the question of legal cause may be decided as a matter of law. Those cases generally involve independent intervening acts which operate upon but do not flow from the original negligence. Thus, for instance, we have held that where an automobile lessor negligently supplies a car with a defective trunk lid, it is not liable to the lessee who, while stopped to repair the trunk, was injured by the negligent driving of a third party. Although the renter's negligence undoubtedly served to place the injured party at the site of the accident, the intervening act was divorced from and not the foreseeable risk associated with the original negligence. And the injuries were different in kind than those which would have normally been expected from a defective trunk. In short, the negligence of the renter merely furnished the occasion for an unrelated act to cause injuries not ordinarily anticipated.

By contrast, in the present case, we cannot say as a matter of law that defendant Dickens' negligence was a superseding cause which interrupted the link between Felix' negligence and plaintiff's injuries. From the evidence in the record, the jury could have found that Felix negligently failed to safeguard the excavation site. A prime hazard associated with such dereliction is the possibility that a driver will negligently enter the work site and cause injury to a worker. That the driver was negligent, or even reckless, does not insulate Felix from liability. . . . Nor is it decisive that the driver lost control of the vehicle through a negligent failure to take medication, rather than a driving mistake. . . . The precise manner of the event need not be anticipated. The finder of fact could have concluded that the foreseeable, normal and natural result of the risk created by Felix was the injury of a worker by a car entering the improperly protected work area. An intervening act may not serev as a superseding cause, and relieve an actor of responsibility, where the risk of the intervening act occurring is the very same risk which renders the actor negligent.

In a similar vein, plaintiff's act of placing the kettle on the west side of the excavation does not, as a matter of law, absolve defendant Felix of responsibility.[1] Serious injury, or even death, was a foreseeable consequence of a vehicle crashing through the work area. The injury could have occurred in numerous ways, ranging from a worker being directly struck by the car to the car hitting an object that injures the worker. Placement of the kettle, or any object in the work area, could affect how the accident occurs and the extent of injuries. That defendant could not anticipate the precise manner of the accident or the exact extent of injuries, however, does not preclude liability as a matter of law where the general risk and character of injuries are foreseeable.

. . .

Endnote

[1] Plaintiff testified that a Felix foreman had directed him to park his truck on the west side of the excavation. From this, and other related testimony, the jury could have concluded that Felix effectively dictated the location of the kettle, obviating any question of plaintiff's own conduct breaking the causal nexus.

Summers v. Tice

A classic case in the annals of tort, *Summers* should be read in conjunction with a review of the essay by Judith Thomson. In this case, a sole reliance upon the idea of *sine qua non* or "factual" causation yields not only an indeterminate result but what seems to be precisely the wrong result: namely, that neither defendant caused the injury. Can you see why?

Actions by Charles A. Summers against Harold W. Tice and against Ernest Simonson for negligently shooting plaintiff while hunting. From judgments for plaintiff, defendants appeal. . . .

Carter, Justice.

Each of the two defendants appeals from a judgment against them in an action for personal injuries. Pursuant to stipulation the appeals have been consolidated.

Plaintiff's action was against both defendants for an injury to his right eye and face as the result of being struck by bird shot discharged from a shotgun. The case was tried by the court without a jury and the court found that on November 20, 1945, plaintiff and the two defendants were hunting quail on the open range. Each of the defendants was armed with a 12 gauge shotgun loaded with shells containing 7 ½ size shot. Prior to going hunting plaintiff discussed the hunting procedure with defendants, indicating that they were to exercise care when shooting and to "keep in line." In the course of hunting, plaintiff proceeded up a hill, thus placing the hunters at the points of a triangle. The view of defendants with reference to plaintiff was unobstructed and they knew his location. Defendant Tice flushed a quail which rose in flight to a ten foot elevation and flew between plaintiff and defendants. Both defendants shot at the quail, shooting in plaintiff's direction. At that time defendants were 75 yards from plaintiff. One shot struck plaintiff in his eye and another in his upper lip. Finally it was found by the court that as the direct result of the shooting by defendants the shots struck plaintiff as above mentioned and that defendants were negligent in so shooting and plaintiff was not contributorily negligent.

199 P. 2d 1 (1948), Supreme Court of California.

. . . First, on the subject of negligence, defendant Simonson contends that the evidence is insufficient to sustain the finding on that score, but he does not point out wherein it is lacking. There is evidence that both defendants, at about the same time or one immediately after the other, shot at a quail and in so doing shot toward plaintiff who was uphill from them, and that they knew his location. That is sufficient from which the trial court could conclude that they acted with respect to plaintiff other than as persons of ordinary prudence. . . .

Defendant Tice states in his opening brief, "we have decided not to argue that insufficiency of negligence on the part of defendant Tice." It is true he states in his answer to plaintiff's petition for a hearing in this court that he did not concede this point but he does not argue it. Nothing more need be said on the subject.

. . . Defendant Simonson urges that plaintiff was guilty of contributory negligence and assumed the risk as a matter of law. He cites no authority for the proposition that by going on a hunting party the various hunters assume the risk of negligence on the part of their companions. Such a tenet is not reasonable. It is true that plaintiff suggested that they all "stay in line," presumably abreast, while hunting, and he went uphill at somewhat of a right angle to the hunting line, but he also cautioned that they use care, and defendants knew plaintiff's position. We hold, therefore, that the trial court was justified in finding that he did not assume the risk or act other than as a person of ordinary prudence under the circumstances. . . .

The problem presented in this case is whether the judgment against both defendants may stand. It is argued by defendants that they are not joint tort feasors, and thus jointly and severally liable, as they were not acting in concert, and that there is not sufficient evidence to show which defendant was guilty of the negligence which caused the injuries—the shooting by Tice or that by Simonson. Tice argues that there is evidence to show that the shot which struck plaintiff came from Simonson's gun because of admissions allegedly made by him to third persons and no evidence that they came from his gun. Further in connection with the latter contention, the court failed to find on plaintiff's allegation in his complaint that he did not know which one was at fault—did not find which defendant was guilty of the negligence which caused the injuries to plaintiff.

. . . Considering the last argument first, we believe it is clear that the court sufficiently found on the issue that defendants were jointly liable and that thus the negligence of both was the cause of the injury or to that legal effect. It found that both defendants were negligent and "That as a direct and proximate result of the shots fired by *defendants, and each of them,* a birdshot pellet was caused to and did lodge in plaintiff's right eye and that another birdshot pellet was caused to and did lodge in plaintiff's upper lip." In so doing the court evidently did not give credence to the admissions of Simonson to third persons that he fired the shots, which it was justified in doing. It thus determined that the negligence of both defendants was the legal cause of the injury—or that both were responsible. Implicit in such finding is the assumption that the court was unable to ascertain whether the shots were from the gun of one defendant or the other or one shot from each of them. The one shot that entered plaintiff's eye was the major factor in assessing damages and that shot could not have come from the gun of both defendants. It was from one or the other only.

It has been held that where a group of persons are on a hunting party, or otherwise engaged in the use of firearms, and two of them are negligent in firing in the direction of a third person who is injured thereby, both of those so firing are liable for the injury suffered by the third person, although the negligence of only one of them could have caused the injury. . . . *Oliver v. Miles,* Miss., 110 So. 666, 50 A.L.R. 357. . . . The same rule has been applied in criminal cases . . . and both drivers have been held liable for the negligence of one where they engaged in a racing contest causing an injury to a third person. . . . These cases speak of the action of defendants as being in concert as the ground of decision, yet it would seem they are straining that concept and the more reasonable basis appears in *Oliver v. Miles,* supra. There two persons were hunting together. Both shot at some partridges and in so doing shot across the highway injuring plaintiff who was traveling on it. The court stated that they were acting in concert and thus both were liable. The court then

stated . . . : "We think that . . . each is liable for the resulting injury to the boy, although no one can say definitely who actually shot him. *To hold otherwise would be to exonerate both from liability, although each was negligent, and the injury resulted from such negligence.*"

. . .

. . . When we consider the relative position of the parties and the results that would flow if plaintiff was required to pin the injury on one of the defendants only, a requirement that the burden of proof on that subject be shifted to defendants becomes manifest. They are both wrongdoers—both negligent toward plaintiff. They brought about a situation where the negligence of one of them injured the plaintiff, hence it should rest with them each to absolve himself if he can. The injured party has been placed by defendants in the unfair position of pointing to which defendant caused the harm. If one can escape the other may also and plaintiff is remediless. Ordinarily defendants are in far better position to offer evidence to determine which one caused the injury. This reasoning has recently found favor in this Court. In a quite analogous situation this Court held that a patient injured while unconscious on an operating table in a hospital could hold all or any of the persons who had any connection with the operation even though he could not select the particular acts by the particular person which led to his disability. *Ybarra v. Spangard . . .* 154 P.2d 687. . . . There the Court was considering whether the patient could avail himself of res ipsa loquitur, rather than where the burden of proof lay, yet the effect of the decision is that plaintiff has made out a case when he has produced evidence which gives rise to an inference of negligence which was the proximate cause of the injury. It is up to defendants to explain the cause of the injury. It was there said: "If the doctrine is to continue to serve a useful purpose, we should not forget that 'the particular force and justice of the rule, regarded as a presumption throwing upon the party charged the duty of producing evidence, consists in the circumstance that the chief evidence of the true cause, whether culpable or innocent, is practically accessible to him but inaccessible to the injured person.'" . . . Similarly in the instant case plaintiff is not able to establish which of defendants caused his injury.

The foregoing discussion disposes of the authorities cited by defendants . . . , stating the general rule that one defendant is not liable for the independent tort of the other defendant, or that ordinarily the plaintiff must show a causal connection between the negligence and the injury. There was an entire lack of such connection in the Hernandez case and there were not several negligent defendants, one of whom must have caused the injury.

Defendants rely upon *Christensen v. Los Angeles Electrical Supply Co.,* 112 Cal.App. 629, 297 P. 614, holding that a defendant is not liable where he negligently knocked down with his car a pedestrian and a third person then ran over the prostrate person. That involves the question of intervening cause which we do not have here. Moreover it is out of harmony with the current rule on that subject and was properly questioned in *Hill v. Peres,* 136 Cal.App. 132, 28 P.2d 946 (hearing in this Court denied), and must be deemed disapproved.

Cases are cited for the proposition that where two or more tort feasors acting independently of each other cause an injury to plaintiff, they are not joint tort feasors and plaintiff must establish the portion of the damage caused by each, even though it is impossible to prove the portion of the injury caused by each. . . .

. . . In view of the foregoing discussion it is apparent that defendants in cases like the present one may be treated as liable on the same basis as joint tort feasors, and hence the last cited cases are distinguishable inasmuch as they involve independent tort feasors.

. . . In addition to that, however, it should be pointed out that the same reasons of policy and justice shift the burden to each of [the] defendants to absolve himself if he can—relieving the wronged person of the duty of apportioning the injury to a particular defendant, apply here where we are concerned with whether plaintiff is required to supply evidence for the apportionment of damages. If defendants are independent tort feasors and thus each liable for the damage caused by him alone, and, at least, where the matter of apportionment is incapable of proof, the innocent wronged party should not be deprived of his right to redress. The wrongdoers should be left to work out between themselves any apportionment. . . . Some of the cited cases refer to the difficulty of apportioning the burden of damages between the independent tort feasors, and say that where factually a correct division cannot be made, the trier of fact may make it the best it can, which would be more or less a guess, stressing the factor that the wrongdoers are not in a position to complain of uncertainty. . . .

. . . It is urged that plaintiff now has changed the theory of his case in claiming a concert of action; that he did not plead or prove such concert. From what has been said it is clear that there has been no change in theory. The joint liability, as well as the lack of knowledge as to which defendant was liable, was pleaded and the proof developed the case under either theory. We have seen that for the reasons of policy discussed herein, the case is based upon the legal proposition that, under the circumstances here presented, each defendant is liable for the whole damage whether they are deemed to be acting in concert or independently.

The judgment is affirmed.

Yania v. Bigan

Frequently cited as among the more egregious examples of the "no-duty-to-rescue" rule, this case should be read with these questions in mind: Did Bigan cause Yania's death? How would Hart and Honorés theory handle this case? Would it change the outcome of these theories if Bigan knew Yania to be especially suspectible to dares or to attacks upon his manliness and prowess? Why didn't Bigan have a legal duty to rescue Yania once the latter was in the water? Might the answer to this question turn on whether Bigan caused Yania to be in the water? Is Bigan's conduct misfeasance or nonfeasance, according to Weinrib's definition?

Benjamin R. Jones, Justice.

A bizarre and most unusual circumstance provides the background of this appeal.

155 A. 2d 343 (1959), Supreme Court of Pennsylvania.

On September 25, 1957 John E. Bigan was engaged in a coal strip-mining operation in Shade Township, Somerset County. On the property being stripped were large cuts or trenches created by Bigan when he removed the earthen overburden for the purpose of removing the coal underneath. One cut contained water 8 to 10 feet in depth with side walls or embankments 16 to 18 feet in height; at this cut Bigan had installed a pump to remove the water.

At approximately 4 p.m. on that date, Joseph F. Yania, the operator of another coal strip-mining operation, and one Boyd M. Ross went upon Bigan's property for the purpose of discussing a business matter with Bigan, and, while there, were asked by Bigan to aid him in starting the pump. Ross and Bigan entered the cut and stood at the point where the pump was located. Yania stood at the top of one of the cut's side walls and then jumped from the side wall—a height of 16 to 18 feet—into the water and was drowned.

Yania's widow, in her own right and on behalf of her three children, instituted wrongful death and survival actions against Bigan contending Bigan was responsible for Yania's death. Preliminary objections, in the nature of demurrers, to the complaint were filed on behalf of Bigan. The court below sustained the preliminary objections; from the entry of that order this appeal was taken.

. . . Since Bigan has chosen to file preliminary objections, in the nature of demurrers, every material and relevant fact well pleaded in the complaint and every inference fairly deducible therefrom are to be taken as true. . . .

The complaint avers negligence in the following manner: (1) "The death by drowning of . . . [Yania] was caused entirely by the acts of [Bigan] . . . in *urging, enticing, taunting and inveigling* [Yania] to jump into the water, which [Bigan] knew or ought to have known was of a depth of 8 to 10 feet and dangerous to the life of anyone who would jump therein" (emphasis supplied); (2) ". . . [Bigan] violated his obligations to a business invitee in not having his premises reasonably safe, and not warning his business invitee of a dangerous condition and to the contrary urged, induced and inveigled [Yania] into a dangerous position and a dangerous act, whereby [Yania] came to his death"; (3) "After [Yania] was in the water, a highly dangerous position, having been induced and inveigled therein by [Bigan], [Bigan] failed and neglected to take reasonable steps and action to protect or assist [Yania], or [extricate Yania] from the dangerous position in which [Bigan] had placed him." Summarized, Bigan stands charged with three-fold negligence: (1) by urging, enticing, taunting and inveigling Yania to jump into the water; (2) by failing to warn Yania of a dangerous condition on the land, i.e., the cut wherein lay 8 to 10 feet of water; (3) by failing to go to Yania's rescue after he had jumped into the water.[1]

. . . The Wrongful Death Act . . . and the Survival Act . . . really confer no more than rights to recover damages growing out of a single cause of action, namely, *the negligence of the defendant* which caused the damages suffered. . . . While the law presumes that Yania was not negligent, such presumption affords no basis for an inference that Bigan was negligent. . . . Our inquiry must be to ascertain whether the well-pleaded facts in the complaint, assumedly true, would, if shown, suffice to prove negligent conduct on the part of Bigan.

. . . Appellant initially contends that Yania's descent from the high embankment into the water and the resulting death were caused "entirely" by the spoken words and blandishments of Bigan delivered at a distance from Yania. The complaint does not allege that Yania slipped or that he was pushed or that Bigan made any *physical* impact upon Yania. On the contrary, the only inference deducible from the facts alleged in the complaint is that Bigan, by the employment of cajolery and inveiglement, caused such a *mental* impact on Yania that the latter was deprived of his volition and freedom of choice and placed under a compulsion to jump into the water. Had Yania been a child of tender years or a person mentally deficient then it is conceivable that taunting and enticement could constitute actionable negligence if it resulted in harm. However, to contend that such conduct directed to an adult in full possession of all his mental faculties constitutes actionable negligence is not only without precedent but completely without merit. . . .

. . . Appellant next urges that Bigan, as the possessor of the land, violated a duty owed to Yania in that his land contained a dangerous condition, i.e., the water-filled cut or trench, and he failed to warn Yania of such condition. Yania was a business invitee in that he entered upon the land for a common business purpose for the mutual benefit of Bigan and himself. . . . As possessor of the land, Bigan would become subject to liability to Yania for any physical harm caused by any artificial or natural condition upon the land (1) if, and only if, Bigan knew or could have discovered the condition which, if known to him he should have realized involved an unreasonable risk of harm to Yania, (2) if Bigan had no reason to believe Yania would discover the condition or realize the risk of harm and (3) if he invited or permitted Yania to enter upon the land without exercising reasonable care to make the condition reasonably safe or give adequate warning to enable him to avoid the harm. . . . The inapplicability of this rule of liability to the instant facts is readily apparent.

The *only* condition on Bigan's land which could possibly have contributed in any manner to Yania's death was the water-filled cut with its high embankment. Of this condition there was neither concealment nor failure to warn, but, on the contrary, the complaint specifically avers that Bigan not only requested Yania and Boyd to assist him in starting the pump to remove the water from the cut but "led" them to the cut itself. If this cut possessed any potentiality of danger, such a condition was as obvious and apparent to Yania as to Bigan, both coal strip-mine operators. Under the circumstances herein depicted Bigan could not be held liable in this respect.

. . . Lastly, it is urged that Bigan failed to take the necessary steps to rescue Yania from the water. The mere fact that Bigan saw Yania in a position of peril in the water imposed upon him no legal, although a moral, obligation or duty to go to his rescue unless Bigan was legally responsible, in whole or in part, for placing Yania in the perilous position. The language of this Court in *Brown v. French,* 104 Pa. 604, 607, 608, is apt: "If it appeared that the deceased, by his own carelessness, contributed in any degree to the accident which caused the loss of his life, the defendants ought not to have been held to answer for the consequences resulting from that accident. . . . He voluntarily placed himself in the way of danger, and his death was the result of his own act. . . . That his undertaking was an exceedingly reckless and dangerous one, the event proves, but here was no one to blame for it but himself. He had the right to try the experiment, obviously dangerous as it was, but then also upon him rested the consequences of that experiment, and upon no one else; he may have been, and probably was, ignorant of the risk which he was taking upon himself, or knowing it, and trusting to his own skill, he may have regarded it as easily superable. But in either case, the result of his ignorance, or of his mistake, must rest with himself—and cannot be charged to the defendants." The complaint does not aver any facts which impose upon Bigan legal responsibility for placing Yania in the dangerous position in the water and, absent such legal responsibility, the law imposes on Bigan no duty of rescue.

Recognizing that the deceased Yania is entitled to the benefit of the presumption that he was exercising due care and extending to appellant the benefit of every well pleaded fact in this complaint and the fair inferences arising therefrom, yet we can reach but one conclusion: that Yania, a reasonable and prudent adult in full possession of all his mental faculties, undertook to perform an act which he knew or should have known was attended with more or less peril and it was the performance of that act and not any conduct upon Bigan's part which caused his unfortunate death.

Order affirmed.

Endnote

[1] So far as the record is concerned we must treat the 33-year-old Yania as in full possession of his mental faculties at the time he jumped.

Appendix 1

Legal Citations and Law Reports

This appendix provides a brief explanation of the system currently in use for collecting, publishing, and citing judicial opinions and decisions. We'll begin with an example of a typical case citation, of the sort found throughout this text. Take the citation to the *Hudnut* case in Chapter Two:

American Bookseller's Association v. Hudnut
771 F.2d 323 (1985)
United States Court of Appeals, Seventh Circuit

The first line of the citation lists the last names of the parties involved. If the case is a civil rather than a criminal case, the first name appearing in the citation normally is that of the *plaintiff* in the case, the individual filing the complaint. If there is more than one plaintiff, the name of the first plaintiff (listed in alphabetical order) is given. In a criminal case, the complaining party is the state; hence a criminal case situation typically reads *State v. Bradbury* or *People v. Burroughs*. The second name appearing in the first line is that of the person responding to a suit or charged with a crime: the *defendant*.

Occasionally, a citation will refer to a case that is being heard on *appeal*. This means that the party who lost at the lower or trial court level, where evidence is presented and a judgment rendered, is requesting that a higher or appellate court review the record of the trial court proceedings to determine if an error occurred in the definition or application of the rules of law applicable to the case. If the citation refers to a case being heard on appeal, the order of the names— plaintiff/defendant—is the same if the plaintiff is the party instituting the appeal (called the *appellant*); a few states, however, reverse the names when the defendant is the appellant or "plaintiff in error."

The publication of court opinions is sanctioned by statute throughout the states and by the federal government. *United States Reports* (cited as *U.S.*), for example, is the official collection of opinions issued by the United States Supreme Court. Opinions and decisions are also collected and published by private firms: *The Supreme Court Reporter* (cited as *S. Ct.*) is the collection of the Supreme Court's decisions published by West Publishing Company.

Court reports are organized in several ways: by jurisdiction of the court issuing the opinion (for example, *California Reports* contains the opinions of the Supreme Court of California); by geography (for example, West's *Pacific Reporter* includes opinions by appellate courts in a number of Western states); and by subject matter (for example, the *Military Justice Reporter* reports the decisions of the Court of Military Appeals).

The second line of the citation for *Hudnut* reads:

771 F.2d 323 (1985)

This refers to volume 771 of the *Federal Reporter, Second Series*. The *Hudnut* case appears beginning on page 323. The case was decided in 1985. The *Federal Reporter*, published by West, collects opinions handed down by all the various "circuits" or divisions of the United States Court of Appeals. West's *Federal Supplement* (cited as *F. Supp.*) does the same for United States district courts (the trial courts of the federal system). (A diagram outlining the federal system and a typical state court system is provided.) The last line of the citation for *Hudnut* indicates that the case was heard by the Seventh Circuit of the United States Court of Appeals.

Many judicial opinions are easily obtained through West's National Reporter System, consisting of a set of volumes reporting both state and federal cases. The United States has seven regional reporters: Atlantic, North Eastern, North Western, Pacific, South Eastern, Southern, and South Western. (Abbreviations for many of the regional and federal reporters are given below.)

In addition to the regional reporters, West publishes special reporters for two states: the *California Reporter* and the *New York Supplement*.

Abbreviations for Selected State, Regional, and Federal Reporters

Cal., Cal. 2d, Cal. 3d	*California Reports*
Cal. Rptr.	*West's California Reporter*
Cal. App., Cal. App. 2d, Cal. App. 3d	*California Appellate Reports*
Ill., Ill. 2d	*Illinois Reports*
N.Y., N.Y. 2d	*New York Reports*
A.D., A.D. 2d	*Appellate Division Reports (N.Y.)*
N.Y. Sup. Ct.	*Supreme Court Reports (N.Y.)*
N.Y.S. 2d	*West's New York Supplement*
Atl.	*Atlantic Reporter*
A. 2d	*Atlantic Reporter, Second Series*
N.E.	*North Eastern Reporter*
N.W.	*North Western Reporter*
Pac.	*Pacific Reporter*
P. 2d	*Pacific Reporter, Second Series*
S.E.	*South Eastern Reporter*
So.	*Southern Reporter*
S.W.	*South Western Reporter*
U.S.	*United States Reports*
S. Ct.	*Supreme Court Reporter*

The U.S. Court System

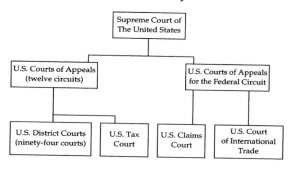

California State System

Amendments to the Constitution of the United States

Amendment I [1791]

Congress shall make no law respecting an establishment of religion, or prohibiting the free exercise thereof; or abridging the freedom of speech, or of the press; or the right of the people peaceably to assemble, and to petition the Government for a redress of grievances.

Amendment II [1791]

A well regulated Militia, being necessary to the security of a free State, the right of the people to keep and bear Arms, shall not be infringed.

Amendment III [1791]

No Soldier shall, in time of peace be quartered in any house, without the consent of the Owner, nor in time of war, but in a manner to be prescribed by law.

Amendment IV [1791]

The right of the people to be secure in their persons, houses, papers, and effects, against unreasonable searches and seizures, shall not be violated, and no Warrants shall issue, but upon probable cause, supported by Oath or affirmation, and particularly describing the place to be searched, and the persons or things to be seized.

Amendment V [1791]

No person shall be held to answer for a capital, or otherwise infamous crime, unless on a presentment or indictment of a Grand Jury, except in cases arising in the land or naval forces, or in the Militia, when in actual service in time of War or public danger; nor shall any person be subject for the same offense to be twice put in jeopardy of life or limb; nor shall be compelled in any criminal case to be a witness against himself, nor be deprived of life, liberty, or property, without due process of law; nor shall private property be taken for public use, without just compensation.

Amendment VI [1791]

In all criminal prosecutions, the accused shall enjoy the right to a speedy and public trial, by an impartial jury of the State and district wherein the crime shall have been committed, which district shall have been previously ascertained by law, and to be informed of the nature and cause of the accusation; to be confronted with the witnesses against him; to have compulsory process for obtaining witnesses in his favor, and to have the Assistance of Counsel for his defense.

Amendment VII [1791]

In Suits at common law, where the value in controversy shall exceed twenty dollars, the right of trial by jury shall be preserved, and no fact tried by a jury, shall be otherwise re-examined in any Court of the United States, than according to the rules of the common law.

Amendment VIII [1791]

Excessive bail shall not be required, nor excessive fines imposed, nor cruel and unusual punishments inflicted.

Amendment IX [1791]

The enumeration in the Constitution, of certain rights, shall not be construed to deny or disparage others retained by the people.

Amendment X [1791]

The powers not delegated to the United States by the Constitution, nor prohibited by it to the States, are reserved to the States respectively, or to the people.

Amendment XI [1798]

The Judicial power of the United States shall not be construed to extend to any suit in law or equity, commenced or prosecuted against one of the United States by Citizens of another State, or by Citizens or Subjects of any Foreign State.

Amendment XII [1804]

The Electors shall meet in their respective states and vote by ballot for President and Vice-President, one of whom, at least, shall not be an inhabitant of the same state with themselves; they shall name in their ballots the person voted for as President, and in distinct ballots the person voted for as Vice-President, and they shall make distinct lists of all persons voted for as President, and of all persons voted for as Vice-President, and of the number of votes for each, which lists they shall sign and certify, and transmit sealed to the seat of the government of the United States, directed to the President of the Senate;—The President of the Senate shall, in the presence of the Senate and House of Representatives, open all the certificates and the votes shall then be counted;—The person having the greatest number of votes for President, shall be the President, if such number be a majority of the whole number of Electors appointed; and if no person have such majority, then from the persons having the highest numbers not exceeding three on the list of those voted for as President, the House of Representatives shall choose immediately, by ballot, the President. But in choosing the President, the votes shall be taken by states, the representation from each state having one vote; a quorum for this purpose shall consist of a member or members from two thirds of the states, and a majority of all the states shall be necessary to a choice. And if the House of Representatives shall not choose a President whenever the right of choice shall devolve upon them, before the fourth day of March

next following, then the Vice-President shall act as President, as in the case of the death or other constitutional disability of the President.—The person having the greatest number of votes as Vice-President, shall be the Vice-President, if such number be a majority of the whole number of Electors appointed, and if no person have a majority, then from the two highest numbers on the list, the Senate shall choose the Vice-President; a quorum for the purpose shall consist of two-thirds of the whole number of Senators, and a majority of the whole number shall be necessary to a choice. But no person constitutionally ineligible to the office of President shall be eligible to that of Vice-President of the United States.[1]

Amendment XIII [1865]

Section 1. Neither slavery nor involuntary servitude, except as a punishment for crime whereof the party shall have been duly convicted, shall exist within the United States, or any place subject to their jurisdiction.

Section 2. Congress shall have power to enforce this article by appropriate legislation.

Amendment XIV [1868]

Section 1. All persons born or naturalized in the United States, and subject to the jurisdiction thereof, are citizens of the United States and of the State wherein they reside. No State shall make or enforce any law which shall abridge the privileges or immunities of citizens of the United States; nor shall any State deprive any person of life, liberty, or property, without due process of law, nor deny to any person within its jurisdiction the equal protection of the laws.

Section 2. Representatives shall be apportioned among the several States according to their respective numbers, counting the whole number of persons in each State, excluding Indians not taxed. But when the right to vote at any election for the choice of electors for President and Vice-President of the United States, Representatives in Congress, the Executive and Judicial officers of a State, or the members of the Legislature thereof, is denied to any of the male inhabitants of such State, being twenty-one years of age, and citizens of the United States, or in any way abridged, except for participation in rebellion, or other crime, the basis

---

[1] Superseded by section 3 of the Twentieth Amendment.

of representation therein shall be reduced in the proportion which the number of such male citizens shall bear to the whole number of male citizens twenty-one years of age in such State.

Section 3. No person shall be a Senator or Representative in Congress, or elector of President and Vice-President, or hold any office, civil or military, under the United States, or under any State, who, having previously taken an oath, as a member of Congress, or as an officer of the United States, or as a member of any State legislature or as an executive or judicial officer of any State, to support the Constitution of the United States, shall have engaged in insurrection or rebellion against the same, or given aid or comfort to the enemies thereof. But Congress may by a vote of two-thirds of each House, remove such disability.

Section 4. The validity of the public debt of the United States, authorized by law, including debts incurred for payment of pensions and bounties for services in suppressing insurrection or rebellion, shall not be questioned. But neither the United States nor any State shall assume or pay any debt or obligation incurred in aid of insurrection or rebellion against the United States, or any claim for the loss of emancipation of any slave; but all such debts, obligations and claims shall be held illegal and void.

Section 5. The Congress shall have power to enforce, by appropriate legislation, the provisions of this article.

Amendment XV [1870]

Section 1. The right of citizens of the United States to vote shall not be denied or abridged by the United States or by any State on account of race, color, or previous condition of servitude.

Section 2. The Congress shall have power to enforce this article by appropriate legislation.

Amendment XVI [1913]

The Congress shall have power to lay and collect taxes on incomes, from whatever source derived, without apportionment among the several states, and without regard to any census or enumeration.

Amendment XVII [1913]

[1] The Senate of the United States shall be composed of two Senators from each State, elected by the people thereof, for six years; and each Senator shall

have one vote. The electors in each State shall have the qualifications requisite for electors of the most numerous branch of the State legislatures.

[2] When vacancies happen in the representation of any State in the Senate, the executive authority of such State shall issue writs of election to fill such vacancies: *Provided*, That the legislature of any State may empower the executive thereof to make temporary appointments until the people fill the vacancies by election as the legislature may direct.

[3] This amendment shall not be so construed as to affect the election or term of any Senator chosen before it becomes valid as part of the Constitution.

Amendment XVIII [1919]

Section 1. After one year from the ratification of this article the manufacture, sale, or transportation of intoxicating liquors within, the importation thereof into, or the exportation thereof from the United States and all territory subject to the jurisdiction thereof for beverage purposes is hereby prohibited.

Section 2. The Congress and the several States shall have concurrent power to enforce this article by appropriate legislation.

Section 3. This article shall be inoperative unless it shall have been ratified as an amendment to the Constitution by the legislatures of the several States, as provided in the Constitution, within seven years from the date of the submission hereof to the States by the Congress.[2]

Amendment XIX [1920]

[1] The right of citizens of the United States to vote shall not be denied or abridged by the United States or by any State on account of sex.

[2] Congress shall have power to enforce this article by appropriate legislation.

Amendment XX [1933]

Section 1. The terms of the President and Vice President shall end at noon on the 20th day of January, and the terms of Senators and Representatives at noon on the 3d day of January, of the years in which such terms would have ended if this article had not

---

[2] Repealed by the Twenty-first Amendment.

been ratified; and the terms of their successors shall then begin.

Section 2. The Congress shall assemble at least once in every year, and such meeting shall begin at noon on the 3d day of January, unless they shall by law appoint a different day.

Section 3. If, at the time fixed for the beginning of the term of the President, the President elect shall have died, the Vice President elect shall become President. If a President shall not have been chosen before the time fixed for the beginning of his term, or if the President elect shall have failed to qualify, then the Vice President elect shall act as President until a President shall have qualified; and the Congress may by law provide for the case wherein neither a President elect nor a Vice President elect shall have qualified, declaring who shall then act as President, or the manner in which one who is to act shall be selected, and such person shall act accordingly until a President or Vice President shall have qualified.

Section 4. The Congress may by law provide for the case of the death of any of the persons from whom the House of Representatives may choose a President whenever the right of choice shall have devolved upon them, and for the case of the death of any of the persons from whom the Senate may choose a Vice President whenever the right of choice shall have devolved upon them.

Section 5. Sections 1 and 2 shall take effect on the 15th day of October following the ratification of this article.

Section 6. This article shall be inoperative unless it shall have been ratified as an amendment to the Constitution by the legislatures of three-fourths of the several States within seven years from the date of its submission.

Amendment XXI [1933]

Section 1. The eighteenth article of amendment to the Constitution of the United States is hereby repealed.

Section 2. The transportation or importation into any State, Territory, or possession of the United States for delivery or use therein of intoxicating liquors, in violation of the laws thereof, is hereby prohibited.

Section 3. This article shall be inoperative unless it shall have been ratified as an amendment to the Constitution by conventions in the several States, as provided in the Constitution, within seven years from the date of the submission hereof to the States by the Congress.

Amendment XXII [1951]

Section 1. No person shall be elected to the office of the President more than twice, and no person who has held the office of President, or acted as President, for more than two years of a term to which some other person was elected President shall be elected to the office of the President more than once. But this Article shall not apply to any person holding the office of President when this Article was proposed by the Congress, and shall not prevent any person who may be holding the office of President, or acting as President, during the term within which this Article becomes operative from holding the office of President or acting as President during the remainder of such term.

Section 2. This article shall be inoperative unless it shall have been ratified as an amendment to the Constitution by the legislatures of three-fourths of the several States within seven years from the date of its submission to the States by the Congress.

Amendment XXIII [1961]

Section 1. The District constituting the seat of Government of the United States shall appoint in such manner as the Congress may direct:

A number of electors of President and Vice President equal to the whole number of Senators and Representatives in Congress to which the District would be entitled if it were a State, but in no event more than the least populous State; they shall be in addition to those appointed by the States, but they shall be considered, for the purposes of the election of President and Vice President, to be electors appointed by a State; and they shall meet in the District and perform such duties as provided by the twelfth article of amendment.

Section 2. The Congress shall have power to enforce this article by appropriate legislation.

Amendment XXIV [1964]

Section 1. The right of citizens of the United States to vote in any primary or other election for President or Vice President, for electors for President or Vice President, or for Senator or Representative in Congress, shall not be denied or abridged by the United States or any State by reason of failure to pay any poll tax or other tax.

Section 2. The Congress shall have power to enforce this article by appropriate legislation.

Amendment XXV [1967]

Section 1. In case of the removal of the President from office or of his death or resignation, the Vice President shall become President.

Section 2. Whenever there is a vacancy in the office of the Vice President, the President shall nominate a Vice President who shall take office upon confirmation by a majority vote of both Houses of Congress.

Section 3. Whenever the President transmits to the President pro tempore of the Senate and the Speaker of the House of Representatives his written declaration that he is unable to discharge the powers and duties of his office, and until he transmits to them a written declaration to the contrary, such powers and duties shall be discharged by the Vice President as Acting President.

Section 4. Whenever the Vice President and a majority of either the principal officers of the executive departments or of such other body as Congress may by law provide, transmit to the President pro tempore of the Senate and the Speaker of the House of Representatives their written declaration that the President is unable to discharge the powers and duties of his office, the Vice President shall immediately assume the powers and duties of the office as Acting President.

Thereafter, when the President transmits to the President pro tempore of the Senate and the Speaker of the House of Representatives his written declaration that no inability exists, he shall resume the powers and duties of his office unless the Vice President and a majority of either the principal officers of the executive department or of such other body as Congress may by law provide, transmit within four days to the President pro tempore of the Senate and the Speaker of the House of Representatives their written declaration that the President is unable to discharge the powers and duties of his office. Thereupon Congress shall decide the issue, assembling within forty-eight hours for that purpose if not in session. If the Congress, within twenty-one days after receipt of the latter written declaration, or, if Congress is not in session, within twenty-one days after Congress is required to assemble, determines by two-thirds vote of both Houses that the President is unable to discharge the powers and duties of his office, the Vice President shall continue to discharge the same as Acting President; otherwise, the President shall resume the powers and duties of his office.

Amendment XXVI [1971]

Section 1. The right of citizens of the United States, who are eighteen years of age or older, to vote shall not be denied or abridged by the United States or by any State on account of age.

Section 2. The Congress shall have power to enforce this article by appropriate legislation.

Legal Resources on the Internet

Many of the legal issues explored in this text concern areas of constitutional, criminal, and civil law that develop and change constantly. One of the best ways to explore the latest developments in any part of the law is to use the legal research tools now available on the Internet and World Wide Web. The following list is a guide to some of the most useful sites available at the time of this edition. These sites can be used to search for a vast array of information: updates on cases covered in the text, appeals of rulings mentioned in the text and readings, new rulings on particular topics (e.g., hate speech or the death penalty), recent legislative activity (state and federal), and law journal and law review essays on all aspects of the law.

The Internet sites listed below can serve as useful starting points for those who wish to research topics of interest. The sites are grouped into several categories, beginning with general sites with links to numerous, more specific sites. Following are all-purpose search engines that can help users look up court rulings, legislative enactments, and other legal texts; federal government sites; university law school libraries; and a few single-focus sites. The list is not exhaustive, but it should provide enough information to get you started.

General Legal Information Sites

Online Catalogs

Following are a few of the best networks for links to legal sites on the Internet:

American Bar Association
http://www.abanet.org   Information on educational opportunities, legal forums and discussion groups, *ABA Journal*.

Hieros Gamos Internet Law Library
http://www.hg.org   Bar and legal associations, law schools, publishers, law firms, legal education, law library.

Global Legal Information Network
lcweb2.loc.gov/law/GLINv1   A database of laws, regulations, and other complementary legal sources. Full text available.

Government Printing Office
http://www.access.gpo.gov   Easy, one-step, no-fee access to legal information available from the federal government.

Internet Legal Resource Guide
http://www.ilrg.com   Categorized index of hundreds of Web sites throughout the world. Web pages and downloadable files.

The Legal List
http://www.lcp.com/The-Legal-List/index.html General assistance on searching for legal materials on the internet.

Lawlinks.com
http://lawlinks.com   Law library; areas of law; case law; commercial resources; constitutions, statutes, and codes; international resources; law journals and law reviews.

Library of Congress
http://www.loc.gov   Comprehensive collection of federal, state, and local government Web sites.

U.S. House of Representatives
Internet Law Library
http://law.house.gov   Member, Committee, and House organizational information; U.S. federal laws;

U.S. state and territorial laws; treaties and international law; law school law library catalogs.

World Wide Web Virtual Law Library
http://www.law.indiana.edu/law/lawindex.html
Federal and state government Web servers, law journals and law reviews, legal information by topic.

General Legal Search Engines

The best all-purpose legal search tools are listed below.

Lexis-Nexis
http://www.lexis-nexis.com   Comprehensive database with access to full text of over 2.5 billion documents online. Lexis-Nexis is *not* a free service; however, many universities subscribe to an academic version of the service, which allows access to most of the features available.

Cornell Legal Information Institute
http://www.law.cornell.edu   Comprehensive search capabilities for state and federal statutes, case law, administrative law, international law, and academic law journals and law reviews.

Findlaw
http://www.findlaw.com   Comprehensive search capabilities for state and federal statutes, case law, and academic law journals and law reviews.

Other Useful Engines:

LawCrawler
http://www.lawcrawler.com   Affiliated with Findlaw.

Lawguru
http://www.lawguru.com   Includes: Searchable resources for every state, cases, court opinions, codes, statutes, and bills. Links to many other search engines.

Lawlinks
http://www.lawlinks.com   Court decisions, state codes, courtroom and trial procedure, ethics and professional responsibility.

Fastsearch
http://www.fastsearch.com

Federal Legislation

U.S. Legislative Information at the Library of Congress (Thomas)
http://thomas.loc.gov

Code of Federal Regulations
http://www.access.gpo.gov/nara/cfr   Official site for searching the CFR.

Federal Court Locator
http://www.law.vill.edu/Fed-Ct/fedcourt.html
Useful portal site to federal courts.

Governmental Agencies

Equal Employment Opportunity Commission (EEOC)
http://gsa.gov/eeo

Federal Trade Commission (FTC)
http://www.gopher.ftc.gov

Environmental Protection Agency (EPA)
http://www.epa.gov

Occupational Safety and Health Administration (OSHA)
http://www.osha-slc.gov

Consumer Product Safety Commission
http://www.epsc.gov

Law School Libraries

Following are some of the most useful sites:

American Association of Law Libraries
http://www.aallnet.org   Offers links to a broad range of primary and secondary legal sources. Direct access to more than 90 law libraries, all law-related journals on the Internet, and more.

Jurist: University of Pittsburgh School of Law
http://www.jurist.law.pitt.edu

Chicago-Kent College of Law
http://www.kentlaw.edu

Emory University School of Law
http://www.law.emory.edu

Georgetown University Law Center
http://www.ll.georgetown.edu

Indiana University Law School
http://www.law.indiana.edu

New York University Law School
http://www.nyu.edu/law

University of Chicago Law School
http://www-law.lib.uchicago.edu

University of Southern California Law Center
http://www.use.edu/dept/law-lib/index.html

Washburn University Law School
http://lawlib.wuacc.edu

Internet Resources on Specific Areas of Law

Civil Rights/Human Rights

American Civil Liberties Union
http://www.aclu.org

Privacy International
http://www.privacy.org

Amnesty International
http://www.amnesty.org

Cato Institute
http://www.cato.org

Criminal Law

U.S. Department of Justice
http://www.usdoj.gov

Death Penalty Information Center
http://essential.org/dpic/dpic.html

Victims of Crime, National Criminal Justice Reference Service
http://www.ncjrs.org/victhome.htm

Employment Law

Equal Employment Opportunity Commission
http://www.eeoc.gov

First Amendment/Freedom of Expression

Cato Institute
http://www.cato.org

American Civil Liberties Union
http://www.aclu.org

Gender, Sexual Orientation, and the Law

Women's Rights and Resources
http://sunsite.unc.edu/cheryb/women/
wresources.html

National Organization for Women
http://www.now.org

National Right to Life
http://www.nrlc.org

Lambda Legal Defense and Education Fund
http://www.thebody.com/lambda/lambda.html

International Law

Statute of the International Court of Justice
http://www.us.org/overview/statute/
content.html

United Nations
http://www.un.org

Other Sites of Interest

Law News Network
http://www.lawnewsnetwork.com

Legal News
http://www.ljx.com

Glossary of Legal Terms

Accessory: One who aids or contributes in a secondary way or assists in the commission of a crime as a subordinate.

Accomplice: An individual who voluntarily engages with another in the commission or attempted commission of a crime.

Acquittal: The verdict in a criminal trial in which the **defendant** is found not guilty.

Action: A judicial proceeding whereby one party prosecutes another for a wrong done; in a civil action, a dispute or controversy brought before the court because of damage or injury. See **tort.**

Actus Reus: The "guilty act" or "deed of crime"; an act of wrongdoing that is forbidden by the law and that, when committed in conjunction with a specified state of mind (*mens rea*), constitutes a **crime.**

Adjourn: To postpone or delay a court proceeding.

Affirmed: In the practice of appellate courts, refers to the fact that the decree or order at issue is declared valid and will remain as rendered by the lower court.

Amici: *See amicus curiae.*

Amicus Curiae: "Friend of the court"; a person or group who files a brief with the court, supplying relevant information bearing on the case or urging a particular result. While not parties in a case, *amici* typically are third parties who will be indirectly affected by the court's decision.

Answer: The legal document by which a **defendant** responds to the allegations contained in the **complaint** of the **plaintiff.**

Appeal: The resort to a superior or appellate court to review the decision of an inferior or trial court.

Appellant: The party or person who appeals a decision (usually, but not always, the loser in the lower court).

Appellee: The party of person against whom an **appeal** is taken (usually, but not always, the winner in the lower court).

Bench Warrant: An order issued by a judge for the arrest of a person.

Brief: A written statement prepared by an attorney arguing a case in court; a summary of the facts of the case, relevant laws, and an argument of how the law applies to the facts in support of the attorney's position.

Burden of Proof: In a civil case, the common standard of proof is *preponderance of the evidence*, or the greater weight of the evidence. In a criminal case, the standard is *beyond a reasonable doubt*, which means that the evidence is such as to remove all reasonable doubt from the mind of the ordinary person.

Cause of Action: A claim in law based on facts sufficient to bring the case to court; the grounds of an action against another (e.g., a suit in **negligence**).

Certiorari: A writ issued by a superior court to an inferior court requiring the latter court to produce the records of a particular case heard before it. Most often used with regard to the U.S. Supreme Court, which uses "cert." as a means of deciding which cases it wishes to hear.

Chambers: A judge's private office. A hearing in chambers takes place in the judge's office, outside the presence of the jury.

Charge to the Jury: The judge's **instruction** to the jury concerning the law that applies to the facts of the case.

Citation: A reference to an authority used (e.g., a prior case, a statute) to substantiate the validity of one's argument or position.

Common Law: The origin of the Anglo-American legal systems; the system of law originally based on the customary and unwritten laws of England and developed by the doctrine of **precedent** as opposed to legislative enactments. In theory, common law is not created by the courts but rather discovered in the customs, habits, and basic principles of justice acknowledged by society.

Complaint: The legal document (also called a **petition**) that informs a **defendant** of the grounds on which he or she is being sued.

Concurring Opinion: An appellate court opinion by one or more judges that agrees with the result reached by the majority but not necessarily its reasoning.

Counsel: Attorney, lawyer.

Crime: A wrongful act against society as defined by law; a wrong that is prosecuted by a public official and punishable by fine, imprisonment, or death.

Damages: Monetary compensation awarded by a court for an injury caused by the act of another. Damages may be *actual* or *compensatory* (equal to the amount of loss proven) or *exemplary* or *punitive* (in excess of the actual damages given as a form of punishment to the wrongdoer).

Decedent: One who has ceased to live; in criminal law, the victim of a **homicide.**

Declaration: A solemn statement made by witnesses, not under oath, subjecting them to perjury for its violation.

Defendant: The person against whom a lawsuit (**cause of action**) or criminal action is brought.

Deposition: The **testimony** of a witness taken under oath in preparation for a trial.

Dictum: A statement or remark, not necessary for the decision of a case, made by the judge in the judge's opinion; a statement not binding as **precedent.**

Discovery: That set of procedures through which the parties to a suit obtain information about matters relevant to the case.

Dissent: An **opinion** given by a judge in a case which differs from that given by the majority of the court. A dissent typically points out the deficiencies of the majority position and states reasons for arriving at a different conclusion.

Equity: Justice administered according to fairness as opposed to the strictly formulated rules of the **common law;** a system of principles that originated in England as an alternative to the perceived harshness of rigidly applying the rules of the common law in every case.

Et Al.: Latin term meaning "and others."

Ex Parte: Done for, or on behalf of one party only.

Ex Post Facto: "After the fact"; a law that makes illegal an action that was done before the law was passed. Such laws violate Article I, Sections 9 and 10 of the United States Constitution.

Felony: Any of a group of "high" or "serious" crimes (as distinguished from minor offenses called **misdemeanors**) generally punishable either by death or imprisonment.

Felony-Murder: An unlawful **homicide** occurring during the commission of (or attempt to commit) a **felony** and which (under this doctrine) is considered first-degree **murder.**

Finding: A formal conclusion by a judge on issues of fact or law; also, a conclusion by a jury regarding a fact.

"Fighting Words": Words that, given their nature and the context in which they are uttered, are very likely to provoke their hearer to an immediate breach of the peace. Such words have been held not protected by the First Amendment to the U.S. Constitution.

First Impression: A case that presents a question of law never before considered by any court within the relevant **jurisdiction** and that is therefore not controlled by the doctrine of **precedent.**

Guilty: The condition of having been found to have committed the crime charged.

Habeas Corpus: The name given a variety of writs or orders, the object of which is to bring a **party** before a court or judge.

Holding: A declaration or statement of the law as it applies to the facts of a specific case and given by the court in its **opinion.**

Homicide: Any killing of a human being by another human being. Homicide does not necessarily constitute a **crime;** to be a crime, homicide must be an **unlawful** killing (e.g., **murder**).

Hung Jury: A jury whose members cannot reconcile their differences and reach a **verdict.**

Ignoratia Legis Non Excusat: "Ignorance of the law is no excuse"; the fact that the defendant did not think her or his act was against the law does not prevent the law from punishing the prohibited act.

In Camera **Hearing:** In **chambers,** or in private. A hearing "in camera" usually occurs in the judge's chambers, outside the presence of the jury and the public with only one side or the other present, but not both.

Indictment: An accusation by a grand jury charging a person with a **crime.**

Infancy: The state of being a minor; not yet having attained the age of majority.

Information: Accusatory document filed by the **prosecutor**, detailing the charges against the **defendant.**

Injunction: A judge's order that a person do, or more commonly, refrain from doing a certain act.

Injunction: A judge's order that a person do, or more commonly, refrain from doing a certain act. The court's power to issue an injunction is based in equity.

In Propria Persona: In one's own proper person. A party who conducts his or her own case instead of using an attorney.

Instruction: Directions the judge gives to the jury, informing them of the law that they are to apply to the facts of the case in order to reach a **verdict.**

Judgment: The final decision of the court in a case, resolving the dispute and determining the rights and obligations of the parties involved.

Jurisdiction: The power of a court to make legally binding decisions over certain persons or property; the geographical area in which a court's decisions or a legislature's enactments are binding.

Liability: The condition of being responsible for **damages** resulting from an injurious act, for discharging an obligation or debt, or for paying a penalty for wrongdoing.

Malum In Se: "That which is wrong in itself"; refers to an act that would be thought evil or wrong even without a specific criminal prohibition (e.g., **murder**).

Malum Prohibitum: "That which is wrong because prohibited"; refers to an act that is wrong only because it is made so by **statute** (e.g., failure to file for income tax).

Miranda Warning: Requirement that police tell a suspect in their custody of the suspect's constitutional rights before questioning.

Miscegenation: "The mixing of the races"; older statutes (now invalid) typically defined miscegenation as marriage between a Caucasian (white) and a member of another race.

Misdemeanor: That class of criminal offenses less serious than a **felony** and punished with lesser severity.

Misfeasance: The doing of a wrongful or injurious act.

Mistrial: A trial terminated and declared void prior to the return of the **verdict.**

Moot Case: A case that no longer presents an actual controversy, either because the issues involved have ceased to exist or they have been rendered "academic" by the circumstances.

Motion: A formal request made to a judge pertaining to any issue arising during a lawsuit.

Movant: The party who requests a **motion.**

Murder: The unlawful killing of a human being. Modern law distinguishes between several degrees of murder. *First-degree murder* is a deliberate and premeditated **homicide;** *second-degree murder* is a homicide committed with malice but without premeditation.

Negligence: The failure to exercise due care for the safety and welfare of others; failure to exercise that degree of care which, under the circumstances, a **reasonable person** would take.

Nonfeasance: Nonperformance of an act that one has a duty to perform; neglect of a duty; failure to act so as to prevent harm.

Nuisance: An unreasonable or unwarranted use by a person of his or her own property that produces such annoyance, inconvenience, or discomfort as to interfere with the rights of others to use and enjoy their property.

Obiter Dictum: See **dictum.**

Objection: The process by which one party asserts that a particular witness, line of questioning, etc., is improper and should not be continued. An objection is either sustained or overruled by the judge.

On the Merits: A decision or judgment based upon the essential facts of the case rather than upon a "technicality" such as improper **jurisdiction.**

Opening Statements: Statements made by the attorneys for each **party** outlining the evidence that each party intends to present in order to prove their theory of the case.

Opinion: A statement of the reasons why a certain decision or **judgment** was reached in a case. A *majority opinion* is usually written by one judge and represents the principles of law that a majority of the members of a court regard as central to the **holding** in the case. A *concurring opinion* agrees with the ultimate judgment of the majority but disagrees with the reasons leading to that result. A *plurality opinion* is agreed to by less than a majority so far as reasoning is concerned but is agreed to by a majority as stating the correct result. A *per curiam opinion* is an opinion expressing the decision of the court but whose author is not identified. *See also* **dissent.**

Ordinance: The equivalent of a municipal **statute** passed by a city council and dealing with matters not already covered by federal or state law.

Overbreadth: A situation in which a law not only prohibits that which may constitutionally be prohibited but also prohibits conduct that is constitutionally protected (e.g., freedom of speech under the First Amendment).

Overrule: To overturn or invalidate the **holding** of a prior case. A decision can be overruled only by the same court or by a higher court within the same **jurisdiction.**

Party: A litigant (**plaintiff** or **defendant**).

Pecuniary: Related to money and monetary affairs.

Penal Code: State code regarding the definition of **crime,** rules of criminal procedure, and criminal punishment.

Peremptory Challenge: In the selection of a jury, each side has the right to a fixed number of peremptory challenges to reject a certain number of prospective jurors without giving a reason.

Petition: A formal, written application to a court requesting judicial action on a particular matter.

Petitioner: The person presenting the petition to a court; one who starts an equity proceeding; one who takes an appeal from a **judgment.**

Plaintiff: The person who brings a lawsuit or *cause of action* against another.

Plea: In the law of procedure, an **answer** or response to a **complaint** or allegation of fact; in criminal procedure, the response of the **defendant** in answer to the charge made against him or her.

Pleadings: The **complaint** and the **answer** in a civil suit.

Precedent: The doctrine of Anglo-American law whereby once a court has formulated a principle of law as applied to a given set of facts, it will follow that principle and apply it in future cases where the facts are substantially similar. *See also **stare decisis.***

Preliminary Hearing: A **felony** proceeding in municipal court to test the evidence of the prosecution.

Preponderance of the Evidence: The general standard of proof in a civil case (i.e., one involving a lawsuit); to prevail, a party must show that the preponderance of the evidence (better than 50 percent) weighs in her or his favor.

Presumption: A rule of law that requires the assumption of a fact from another fact or set of facts.

Prima Facie Case: A case that, at first view or "on its face," is supported by enough evidence to entitle a **party** to have the case go to a jury.

Probation: A procedure whereby a **defendant** found guilty of a **crime** is released into society subject to conditions laid down by the court and under the supervision of a probation officer.

Proceeding: The form and manner of conducting legal business before a court or judicial officer; the series of events constituting the process through which judicial action takes place.

Prosecution: The act of pursuing a lawsuit or criminal trial; the party initiating a criminal suit, i.e., the state.

Prosecutor: A trial lawyer representing the government in a criminal case.

Proximate Cause: An event without which injury or damage would not have occurred and which is closely enough related to the occurrence of the injury to make it fair, reasonable, or just to hold the **defendant** liable for that injury.

Quash: To vacate or void a summons, subpoena, etc., by a judicial decision.

Ratio Decidendi: The point in a case that determines the result or **judgment;** the basis or reason for the decision.

Reasonable Doubt: The degree of certainty required of a juror before the juror may find a **defendant guilty;** innocence is to be presumed unless the guilt of the defendant is so clearly proven that the jury can see that no reasonable doubt remains as to the guilt of the defendant.

Reasonable Person: A phrase used to refer to that hypothetical person who exercises those qualities of attention, knowledge, intelligence, and judgment which society requires of its members of the protection of their own interest and the interests of others.

Recidivist: A "habitual criminal," often subjected to extended terms of imprisonment under habitual offender statutes.

Relief: That assistance, redress, or benefit sought by a person filing a **complaint** before a court.

Remand: To send back for further proceedings, as when a higher court sends a case back to a lower court.

Remedy: The means by which a right is enforced or the violation of a right is redressed or compensated. The most common remedy at law consists of money **damages.**

Respondent: The party who contends against an appeal; the party who makes an answer to a complaint in an **equity** proceeding.

Reversal: The invalidating or setting aside of the contrary decision of a lower court.

Reverse: Action of a higher court in setting aside or revoking a lower court decision.

Reversible Error: An error sufficiently prejudicial (harmful) to justify reversing the judgment of a lower court.

Sanctions: Penalty imposed by the court for willful disobedience or misuse of procedures.

Scienter: The **defendant's** "guilty knowledge"; refers to the defendant's alleged previous knowledge of the cause that led to the injury complained of.

Sentence: The punishment a court orders to be inflicted upon a person convicted of a crime.

Sine Qua Non: "That without which there is not"; in tort law, the act of the **defendant** without which there would not have been a **tortious** injury to the **plaintiff.**

Stare Decisis: "Let the decision stand"; refers to the doctrine that courts should follow **precedent,** the authority of earlier, analogous cases.

Statute: An act of a legislature, consistent with constitutional authority and in such proper form that it becomes the law governing the conduct to which it refers.

Statute of Limitations: Any law which fixes the time within which parties must take judicial action to enforce rights or else be thereafter barred from enforcing them.

Statute of Wills: Those statutory provisions of a particular **jurisdiction** stating the requirement for a valid will.

Stay: A court order halting a judicial proceeding.

Stipulation: Any agreement, oral or in writing, made by attorneys on both sides about some aspect of a lawsuit.

Strict Liability: Liability without proof of fault. In civil law, one who engages in activity that carries an inherent risk of injury or is ultra-hazardous (e.g., blasting) is often liable for all injuries proximately caused by that activity; in criminal law, strict liability offenses are those that do not require proof of *mens rea* (criminal intent).

Subpoena: A court order compelling a witness to appear and testify in a **proceeding.**

Suit: Any **proceeding** before a court in which a person pursues that **remedy** which the law affords as redress for the injury that person has suffered.

Summary Judgment: A judgment in a civil **suit,** granted on the basis of the **pleadings** and prior to trial, holding that there is no genuine factual dispute between the parties regarding the legal issues involved and that the case need not therefore go before a jury.

Suppress: Forbidding the use of evidence at a trial because it is improper or was improperly obtained.

Sustain: Court order allowing an **objection** or **motion** to prevail.

Testator: One who is disposing of property by **will.**

Testimony: Evidence given by a witness under oath; does not include evidence from documents and other physical evidence.

Tort: A civil wrong, other than a breach of contract, for which a court will provide a **remedy.**

Tortfeasor: One who commits a **tort.**

Tortious: Used to describe conduct that subjects a person to **tort liability.**

Trial: A judicial examination and determination of issues between parties to **action.**

Ultra Vires: An act beyond the scope of one's powers or authority, as, for example, by a corporation.

Vacate: To set aside.

Venue: The proper geographical area—county, city, or district—in which a court with **jurisdiction** over the subject matter may hear a case.

Verdict: The decision of a jury following the trial of a civil or criminal case.

Vicarious Liability: The imputation of **liability** upon one person for the actions of another person.

Void: That which is entirely null, having no legal force.

Volenti Non Fit Injuria: "To one who consents, no harm is done"; in **tort,** the doctrine that one generally cannot claim **damages** when one has consented to the activity which caused an injury.

Will: A document executed with specific legal formalities containing a person's instructions about the disposition of his or her property upon death.